1922	**The Newbery Medal First Awarded to an Outstanding Author of Children's Literature**
	Willem Van Loon's *The Story of Mankind*
	Honor Books:
	Charles Hawes' *The Great Quest*
	Bernard Marshall's *Cedric the Forester*
	William Bowen's *The Old Tobacco Shop*
	Padraic Colum's *The Golden Fleece and the Heroes Who Lived Before Achilles*
	Cornelia Meig's *Windy Hill*
1924	**The *Horn Book Magazine* First Published**
1938	**The first Caldecott Medal was presented to the illustrator of the most distinguished picture book published in the United States**
	Animals of the Bible by Helen Dean Fish, ill. by Dorothy P. Lathrop
	Honor Books:
	Seven Simeon: A Russian Tale by Boris Artzybasheff
	Four and Twenty Blackbirds: Nursery Rhymes of Yesterday Recalled for Children of Today by Helen Dean Fish, ill. by Robert Lawson
1940s	**A Time of Happy Family Stories**
	Elizabeth Enright's *Thimble Summer* (1938)
	Eleanor Estes's *The Moffats* (1941)
	Sydney Taylor's *All-of-a-Kind Family* (1951)
1957	**Soviet Union Launches Sputnik—An Abundance of Nonfictional Books Considered Necessary for a Better Education**
	Irving Adler's *Tools in Your Life* (1956)
	Isaac Asimov's *Building Blocks of the Universe* (1957) and *Words of Science: and the History Behind Them* (1959)
	Franklyn M. Branley's *Mickey's Magnet* (1956)
	Katherine Shippen's *Men, Microscopes, and Living Things* 1955)

1960s	**A Time of Popular High Fantasy**
	C. S. Lewis's *The Lion, the Witch, and the Wardrobe* (1961) First of the "Chronicles of Narnia"
	Lloyd Alexander's *The Book of Three* (1964) First of the "Prydain Books"
	Susan Cooper's *Over Sea, Under Stone* (1965)
	Lavish Full-Color Books Emphasize Excellence in Design. Many Gifted Illustrators Enter Field of Children's Books
	Leo Lionni's *Inch by Inch* (1960)
	Maurice Sendak's *Where the Wild Things Are* (1963)
	Ezra Jack Keat's *The Snowy Day* (1963)
	Blair Lent's *The Wave* (1964)
	Evaline Ness's *Sam, Bangs & Moonshine* (1967)
	Ed Emberley's *Drummer Hoff* (1967)
1965	**Beginning of an Increased Sensitivity to Racial Perspectives in Children's Books**
	Nancy Larrick's *Saturday Review* article "The All-White World of Children's Books"
1970s	**Authors and Illustrators Representing Ethnic Minorities Make Major Contributions to Children's Literature**
	Virginia Hamilton's *The Planet of Junior Brown* (1972) and *M. C. Higgins, the Great* (1974)
	Lawrence Yep's *Dragonwings* (1975)
	Jamake Highwater's *Anpao: An American Indian Odyssey* (1977)
	Illustrators—Leo and Diane Dillon's *Why Mosquitoes Buzz in People's Ears* (1975)
1982	**First Newbery Medal Awarded to a Book of Poetry**
	Nancy Willard's *A Visit to William Blake's Inn*

Through the Eyes of a Child

Illustration from the winner of the 1998 Caldecott medal: Rapunzel *by Paul O. Zelinsky.*
Copyright ©1997 by Paul O. Zelinsky. Used by permission of Dutton Children's Books, a division
of Penguin Putnam Inc.,

FIFTH EDITION

Through the Eyes of a Child

An Introduction to Children's Literature

Donna E. Norton
Texas A & M University
with
Saundra E. Norton

Merrill,
an imprint of Prentice Hall
Upper Saddle River, New Jersey   Columbus, Ohio

Library of Congress Cataloging-in-Publication Data

Norton, Donna E.
    Through the eyes of a child: an introduction to children's
literature / by Donna E. Norton. — 5th ed.
      p. cm.
    Includes bibliographical references and index.
    ISBN 0-13-667973-0
    1. Children—United States—Books and reading.
    2. Children's literature—History and criticism. I.
    Title.
Z1037.A1N68   1999
[PN1009.A1]
028.1'62—dc2
                    97-39057
                    CIP

Cover art: Trinka Hakes Noble
Editor: Bradley J. Potthoff
Developmental Editor: Linda McElhiney
Production Editor: Mary M. Irvin
Photo Researcher: Anthony Magnacca
Design Coordinator: Tracey B. Ward/Karrie M. Converse
Text Designer: Anne Flanagan
Art Development: Tracey B. Ward
Cover Designer: Tracey B. Ward
Production Manager: Pamela D. Bennett
Director of Marketing: Kevin Flanagan
Marketing Manager: Suzanne Stanton
Advertising/Marketing Coordinator: Krista Groshong

This book was set in Usherwood by Carlisle
Communications, Inc., and was printed and bound by
Von Hoffman Press, Inc. The cover was printed by
Phoenix Color Corp.

 © 1999, 1995 by Prentice-Hall, Inc.
Simon & Schuster/A Viacom Company
Upper Saddle River, New Jersey 07458

Printed in the United States of America

10 9 8 7 6 5 4 3 2 1

ISBN: 0-13-667973-0

Prentice-Hall International (UK) Limited, *London*
Prentice-Hall of Australia Pty. Limited, *Sydney*
Prentice-Hall of Canada, Inc., *Toronto*
Prentice-Hall Hispanoamericana, S. A., *Mexico*
Prentice-Hall of India Private Limited, *New Delhi*
Prentice-Hall of Japan, Inc., *Tokyo*
Simon & Schuster Asia Pte. Ltd., *Singapore*
Editora Prentice-Hall do Brasil, Ltda., *Rio de Janeiro*

Preface

If you are an adult who wants to share books with children, *Through the Eyes of a Child* is written for you. Whether the children's literature course is offered in the department of Education, English, or Library Science, the text's unique two-part chapter organization and special features will work for you. This book is intended to help adults discover ways to share their enchantment with books, our literary heritage, and an appreciation for literature that will last a lifetime.

 ## A SPECIAL THANKS TO TRINKA HAKES NOBLE FOR THE COVER ILLUSTRATION

The inspirational art especially designed for the cover of the fifth edition was rendered in watercolor by noted author and illustrator Trinka Hakes Noble. The spirit of the illustration is intended to highlight the newly recognized area of language arts known as visual literacy. Often, young readers' first responses are to the illustrations in books, and children often share their personal responses by drawing illustrations of their own. The cover illustration celebrates the connection between children, art, nature, and storytelling in the "one-room school days" of early rural America. Trinka Hakes Noble chose a palette of autumn colors representing the first days of the school year which the designer carried into the textbook. Children's books authored or authored and illustrated by Trinka Hakes Noble include: *The Day Jimmy's Boa Ate the Wash, Jimmy's Boa Bounces Back, Jimmy's Boa and the Big Splash Birthday Bash, Meanwhile Back at the Ranch,* and *Apple Tree Christmas.*

 ## CHAPTER OPENER ILLUSTRATIONS REINFORCE THE THEME OF VISUAL LITERACY

The full-color illustrations that appear as the frontispiece and at the beginning of each chapter represent carefully selected illustrations in a variety of media crafted by some of the most talented children's book illustrators. The use of large-sized illustrations continues to highlight the importance of visual literacy, a theme for the fifth edition of *Through the Eyes of a Child.* From cut paper to woodcuts, through watercolors and oil paintings, and through the camera's eye, the illustrators represented on the opening pages of each chapter give children special stimulation for their visual, interpretive skills.

In addition, you will find a comparison of three illustrated versions of "The Golem": the 1997 Caldecott Award winner by David Wisniewski, Trina Schart Hyman's illustrations for Barbara Rogasky's version (1996), and Uri Shulevitz's illustrations for Isaac Bashevis Singer's 1982 version of the story of the giant, Golem.

 ## UNIQUE TWO-PART CHAPTER ORGANIZATION

Beginning in Chapter 3 and extending through Chapter 12, each chapter contains two parts. The first discusses in depth the characteristics, history, and classic titles for each genre suitable for courses emphasizing Education, English, or Library Science. The second parts of Chapters 3 through 12 present field-tested strategies for involving children in literature. This section will be of special interest to teachers and librarians.

NEW TITLES FOR THE FIFTH EDITION

As in the past, there has been a careful selection of new books, which has resulted in the addition of over 800 new titles representing the best children's books published since 1995. The books discussed in this edition were chosen for their quality of literature and to create a balance between new books and those that have passed the test of time and are considered to be classics. In addition to the newest literature, the text includes numerous adult references that reflect the viewpoints, issues, and scholarly findings of professionals who write and work in the area of children's literature.

Whereas 800 new titles have been added, 500 titles were cut because the books are no longer in print. The exclusion of books that are out of print assists librarians, educators, and other professionals who may want to order the books that are discussed or mentioned in the text. A very limited number of out-of-print books are included when they are the best examples for a specific discussion or when they are just too good to be ignored. Most of these books are still available in libraries.

 ## PROFESSORS, DO YOU REQUIRE YOUR STUDENTS TO WRITE AN IN-DEPTH ANALYSIS OF ONE OR MORE CHILDREN'S BOOKS?

Many professors have indicated that their students would benefit from models of deep discussions related to the literary elements in children's literature, because this type of lengthy analysis is often an assignment in their courses. Consequently, the quality of literary criticism has been increased in the fifth edition by providing such model discussions. In Chapter 3, such elements as plot and conflict, characterization, setting, and theme are discussed. Chapter 10 contains an in-depth discussion comparing settings and conflicts, social levels, and themes in Medieval England as developed by Karen Cushman in her two Newbery Award winning books, *Catherine, Called Birdy* and *The Midwife's Apprentice*. In addition, Chapter 12 contains a model for applying evaluation criteria for informational literature using another Newbery winner, *The Great Fire* by Jim Murphy.

 ## BATCHELDER AWARDS, LISTED IN APPENDIX, AS STRONG MULTICULTURAL THEME CONTINUES IN FIFTH EDITION

The Batchelder Award is presented to books translated into English. Over fifty percent of the books receiving this award since 1968 are historical fiction. This important list will provide many useful sources for literature about other cultures. The strong multicultural theme of *Through the Eyes of a Child* continues, especially in Chapter 6, Traditional Literature, and Chapter 11, Multicultural Literature. A new issue is presented in Chapter 6 entitled, "Whose Cultural Values and Belief Systems Should be Reflected in Folklore?"

 ## FIFTEEN NEW ISSUES ADDED TO SPARK CLASS DISCUSSIONS

Fifteen new issues are included in the fifth edition. Researching for the issues included reading the major journals in literature, library science, and education. These issues reflect current concerns as well as highlight possible future concerns. The number of issues presented has been increased because professors who use the book indicate that the issues often spark lively class discussions and suggest areas for further study.

 ## YOUR STUDENTS WILL LOVE THE CD-ROM, WHICH CONTAINS A DATABASE OF OVER 3000 TITLES

A CD-ROM that will work with either Windows or Macintosh computer systems is included in each copy of the text. Each chapter contains special activities utilizing this wonderful resource. Each of the database activities is marked in the text with a special miniature CD icon. Not only will the activities allow students to discover the value of this technological tool, but students will be able to add titles to the database that they find their own students enjoy—a professional resource that will grow through the years.

SPECIAL FEATURES IN EACH CHAPTER

Each chapter builds a model for evaluating and selecting books based upon literary and artistic characteristics that readers can then use themselves. The importance of child development in this process is also stressed.

■ *Issues.* Each chapter identifies important issues that are related to the genre or content of the chapter and are designed to introduce teachers, librarians, and parents to current concerns. Most of these issue highlights are referenced to current periodicals and professional journals and are written to encourage readers' contemplation and further investigation. For this reason, they are presented as open-ended discussions.

■ *Through the Eyes of . . . .* Each chapter includes a personal statement by a well-known author, illustrator, publisher, or librarian, providing a special glimpse into that person's "view" of the creation of children's books. In this edition are two "Through the Eyes of a Child" features that emphasize children's responses to specific literature.

■ *Annotated Bibliographies of Children's Literature.* The extensive bibliographies of children's literature at the end of each chapter include readability by grade level and interest by age range. These bibliographies are also available on a CD-ROM packaged with this book.

■ *Text Teaching Aids.* Each part of the two-part chapters concludes with suggested activities designed to foster either adult understanding of or children's appreciation for the genre. Special web diagrams are used to highlight the interrelationships in literature, the many values of literature, and the multiple learning possibilities available. Webs are also used to illustrate the development of instructional activities and oral discussions about literature. The webbing process, according to my students, helps them clarify concepts, visualize relationships, and identify numerous values for sharing literature with children.

■ *Separate Chapter on Multicultural Literature.* The material on multicultural literature was organized as a separate chapter to make it more accessible to librarians, teachers, and students of children's literature. Information about the criteria for selection, the choice of literature, and the development of literature-related activities resulted from longitudinal research that was partially supported by Texas A&M Research Association and the Meadows Foundation of Dallas, Texas. Educators at national and state meetings have been especially emphatic when they recommended that this chapter remain as a strong content in this textbook.

 ## ACKNOWLEDGMENTS

A massive project such as writing and publishing a children's literature text would not be possible without the enthusiasm, critical evaluation, suggestions, and hard work of many people. My appreciation is extended to my student's in children's literature, teachers, and librarians who discussed books with me, created enthusiasm for books, and shared books with children. The multicultural literature chapter was enhanced by research supported by the Meadows Foundation; work by research associates Sue Mohrmann, Blanche Lawson, and Charmaine Bradley; field testing in the Bryan, Texas, schools; teachers and librarians across Texas who took part in the research; and support by curriculum coordinators Barbara Erwin and Dana Marable. The children's librarians at the Houston Public Library and the Houston Library archives deserve a special thank-you. They discussed reactions to books, searched for hard-to-locate literature, and allowed me to check out hundreds of books at one time. My consulting with school districts such as Wheeling, Willamette, Skokie, and Glenview, Illinois, allowed me to work with teachers, students, and administrators as these districts develop and improve their own literature-based curricula.

Special thanks to Brad Potthoff, Mary Irvin, Beth Dubberley, Linda Scharp McElhiney, and Jeff Johnston for the extra efforts they made to ensure that the fifth edition matched the high standards achieved in the previous editions.

My sincere appreciation is also extended to Ethel Ambrose, Ashley Bryan, Beverly Cleary, Suzanne Canavan, Tomie dePaola, Jean Fritz, Jamake Highwater, Hiram Howard, Madeleine L'Engle, and Jack Prelutsky for their contribution to this text. The insights, personal statements, and viewpoints of these publishers, librarians, authors, and illustrators are especially rewarding in a textbook about children's literature.

I wish to thank reviewers Susan A. Cooper, University of Kentucky; Alice Denham, Texas Tech University; Barbara Kupetz, Indiana University of Pennsylvania; Eleanor Lofquist, Western Carolina University; Rebecca Lukens, Miami University; Marilyn Ohlhausen, University of Nevada, Las Vegas; and Sam Sebesta, University of Washington. Their efforts have been invaluable in ensuring an accurate, timely, and lively text.

Finally, I wish to dedicate this book to my husband, Verland, and my children, Saundra and Bradley, for their constant support, immense understanding, and insightful viewpoints.

Donna E. Norton

Contents in Brief

Contents

1

2

3

Evaluating and Selecting Literature for Children 108

4

5

6

7

8

9

Contemporary Realistic Fiction 456

10

11

Multicultural Literature 570

12

$\mathcal{S}$pecial Features

▪ THROUGH THE EYES OF . . .

From *Alphabet City* by Stephen T. Johnson, copyright © 1995 by Stephen T. Johnson. Viking Penguin.

1 *The Child Responds to Literature*

- Values of Literature for Children
- Promoting Child Development Through Literature

- Children's Responses to Literature

children and suggests books that reflect children's needs during different stages of the maturing process. All of these developmental areas influence children's understanding and appreciation of literature and their responses to literature.

 ## VALUES OF LITERATURE FOR CHILDREN

Following a rabbit down a rabbit hole or walking through a wardrobe into a mythical kingdom sounds like fun. There is nothing wrong with admitting that one of the primary values of literature is pleasure, and there is nothing wrong with turning to a book to escape or to enjoy an adventure with new or old book friends. Time is enriched, not wasted, when children look at beautiful pictures and imagine themselves in new places. When children discover enjoyment in books, they develop favorable attitudes toward them that usually extend into a lifetime of appreciation.

Books are the major means of transmitting our literary heritage from one generation to the next. Each new generation can enjoy the words of Lewis Carroll, Louisa May Alcott, Robert Louis Stevenson, and Mark Twain. Through the work of storytellers such as the Brothers Grimm, each generation can also experience the folktales originally transmitted through the oral tradition.

Literature plays a strong role in helping us understand and value our cultural heritage as well. Developing positive attitudes toward our own culture and the cultures of others is necessary for both social and personal development. Carefully selected literature can illustrate the contributions and values of the many cultures. It is especially critical to foster an appreciation of the heritage of the ethnic minorities in American society. A positive self-concept is not possible unless we respect others as well as ourselves; literature can contribute considerably toward our understanding and thus our respect.

The vicarious experiences of literature result in personal development as well as pleasure. Without literature, most children could not relive the European colonists' experiences of crossing the ocean and shaping a new country in North America; they could not experience the loneliness and fear of a fight for survival on an isolated island; they could

*L*iterature entices, motivates, and instructs. It opens doors to discovery and provides endless hours of adventure and enjoyment. Children need not be tied to the whims of television programming nor wait in line at the theater to follow a rabbit down a hole into Wonderland, save a wild herd of mustangs from slaughter, fight in the Revolutionary War, learn about a new hobby that will provide many enjoyable hours, or model themselves after real-life people of accomplishment. These experiences are available at any time on the nearest bookshelf.

Adults have a responsibility to help children become aware of the enchantment in books. The extent to which books, however, play a significant role in the life of young children depends upon adults. Adults provide the books and, through sharing literature, adults transmit the literary heritage contained in nursery rhymes, picture storybooks, and traditional tales. As you read this book, you will gain knowledge about literature so that you can share stimulating books and book-related experiences with children. This chapter introduces various values of literature for children to help you search for books that can play significant roles in children's lives. It also looks at the importance of considering children's stages of language, cognitive, personality, and social development when selecting literature for not travel to distant places in the galaxy. Historical fiction provides children with opportunities to live in the past. Science fiction allows them to speculate about the future. Contemporary realistic fiction encourages them to experience relationships with the people and the environment of today. Because children can learn from literature how other people handle their problems, characters in books can help children deal with similar problems, as well as understand other people's feelings.

Another value of literature is illustrated by a television interview with a high school sophomore who was a promising young scientist. When asked how he had become so knowledgeable, the boy replied, "I read a lot." For him, books had opened doors to new knowledge and interests. Don't educators and parents want such doors opened for all children? Hazel Rochman (1989) maintains that children should read books set in many locations and times because if children read books that reflect their own views only, they miss the interesting diversity of the world.

Informational books relay new knowledge about virtually every topic imaginable, and they are available at all levels of difficulty. Biographies and autobiographies tell about the people who gained knowledge or made discoveries. Photographs and illustrations show the wonders of nature or depict the processes required to master new hobbies. Realistic stories from a specific time bring history to life. The use of concept books that illustrate colors, numbers, shapes, and sizes may stimulate the cognitive development of even very young children. On the flyleaf of his *A History of Reading,* Alberto Manguel (1996) summarizes the values gained through literature. He states:

At one magical instant in your early childhood, the page of a book—that string of confused, alien ciphers—shivered into meaning. Words spoke to you, gave up their secrets; at that moment, whole universes opened. You became, irrevocably, a reader.

Any discussion about the values of literature must stress the role that literature plays in nurturing and expanding the imagination. Books take children into worlds that stimulate additional imaginative experiences when children tell or write their own stories and interact with each other during creative drama inspired by what they have read. Both well-written literature and illustrations, such as those found in picture books and picture storybooks, can stimulate

aesthetic development. Children enjoy and evaluate illustrations and may explore artistic media by creating illustrations of their own.

The values gained from literature in childhood often have profound influences on adults. Children's author George Shannon (1988) describes vividly the importance to him of books and stories read in childhood. While most are forgotten,

a few, however, have always been with me and always are, functioning as a type of personalized amulet. They are the ones I returned to literally hundreds of times as I fed some unknown hunger and treasured the intimate pleasure they gave. They are the stories I remembered even after the books have been lost and I had left home. They are the books that I've sought out to own again and now keep on my shelf of special books. (p. 122)

 ## PROMOTING CHILD DEVELOPMENT THROUGH LITERATURE

Research in child development has identified stages in the language, cognitive, personality, and social development of children. Not all children progress through these stages at the same rate, but all children do pass through each stage as they mature. Researchers associate developmental stages with children of certain ages, but these connections are approximate, not absolute. Specific developmental characteristics apply to many, but not all, children in a particular age group. The general characteristics of children at each developmental stage provide clues for appropriate literature. Certain books can benefit children during a particular stage of development, helping the children progress to the next stage. Understanding the types and stages of child development is useful for anyone who works with children.

Language Development

Literature has profound influences on children's language development. Chart 1–1 lists characteristics, implications, and books that are appropriate for language development.

Preschool Children. During their first few years, children show dramatic changes in language ability. Most children learn language very rapidly. They speak their first words at about one year of age; at

CHART 1-1 (PP. 6-9) Language development

Characteristics	Implications	Literature Suggestions
Preschool: Ages Two–Three 1 Very rapid language growth occurs. By the end of this period, children have vocabularies of about nine hundred words.	1 Provide many activities to stimulate language growth, including picture books and Mother Goose rhymes.	Ginsburg, Mirra. *Asleep, Asleep.* Ho, Minfong. *Hush!: A Thai Lullaby.* Lobel, Arnold. *The Random House Book of Mother Goose.* Wells, Rosemary. *Max's Birthday.*
2 Children learn to identify and name actions in pictures.	2 Read books that contain clear, familiar action pictures; encourage children to identify actions.	Fleming, Denise. *In the Tall, Tall Grass.* Lillie, Patricia. *Everything Has a Place.* Steptoe, John. *Baby Says.* Wells, Rosemary. *Max's Breakfast.* Oxenbury, Helen. *Dressing.*
3 Children learn to identify large and small body parts.	3 Allow children to identify familiar body parts in picture books.	
Preschool: Ages Three–Four 1 Vocabularies have increased to about fifteen hundred words. Children enjoy playing with sound and rhythm in language.	1 Include opportunities to listen to and say rhymes, poetry, and riddles.	Aylesworth, Jim. *Old Black Fly.* Barton, Byron. *The Wee Little Woman.* Griego, Margot C., et al. *Tortillitas Para Mama.* Rosen, Michael. *We're Going on a Bear Hunt.* Wilson, Sarah. *Good Zap, Little Grog.* Yolen, Jane. *The Three Bears Rhyme Book.*
2 Children develop the ability to use past tense but may overgeneralize the *ed* and *s* markers.	2 Allow children to talk about what they did yesterday; discuss actions in books.	Hill, Eric. *Spot's First Walk.* _____. *Spot Goes to School.* Keats, Ezra Jack. *The Snowy Day.* Weiss, Nicki. *Where Does the Brown Bear Go?*
3 Children use language to help find out about the world.	3 Read picture storybooks to allow children to find out about and discuss pets, families, people, and the environment.	Brown, Ruth. *Toad.* Carle, Eric. *The Very Busy Spider.* Fleming, Denise. *In the Small, Small Pond.* Keller, Holly. *Geraldine's Big Snow.* Potter, Beatrix. *The Tale of Peter Rabbit.* Tafuri, Nancy. *Early Morning in the Barn.* Waddell, Martin. *Let's Go Home, Little Bear.*

CHART 1-1   *Continued*

Characteristics	Implications	Literature Suggestions
4 Speech becomes more complex, with more adjectives, adverbs, pronouns, and prepositions.	4 Expand the use of descriptive words through detailed picture books and picture storybooks. Allow children to tell stories and describe characters and their actions.	Barton, Byron. *Machines at Work.* Crews, Donald. *Freight Train.* _____. *Harbor.* Hill, Eric. *Spot Goes to the Beach.* Narahashi, Keiko. *I Have a Friend.*
Preschool: Ages Four–Five 1 Language is more abstract; children produce grammatically correct sentences. Their vocabularies include approximately twenty-five hundred words.	1 Children enjoy books with slightly more complex plots. Ask them to tell longer and more detailed stories. They enjoy retelling folktales and can tell stories using wordless books.	Brett, Jan. *Goldilocks and the Three Bears.* Haas, Irene. *A Summertime Song.* McCully, Emily Arnold. *School.* McPhail, David. *Pigs Aplenty, Pigs Galore!* Wiesner, David. *Free Fall.* _____. *Tuesday.* Zimmerman, H. Werner. *Henny Penny.*
2 Children understand the prepositions *over, under, in, out, in front of*, and *behind*.	2 Use concept books or other picture books in which prepositions can be reinforced.	Dodds, Dayle Ann. *Wheel Away!* Hoban, Tana. *All About Where.* Hutchins, Pat. *Rosie's Walk.* _____. *What Game Shall We Play?* Noll, Sally. *Watch Where You Go.*
3 Children enjoy asking many questions, especially those related to *why* and *how*.	3 Take advantage of natural curiosity and find books to help answer children's questions. Allow them to answer each other's questions.	Barton, Byron. *Airport.* Gammell, Stephen. *Is That You, Winter?* Oppenheim, Joanne. *Have You Seen Birds?* Showers, Paul. *Look at Your Eyes.* Sill, Cathryn. *About Birds: A Guide for Children.*
Preschool—Kindergarten: Ages Five–Six 1 Most children use complex sentences frequently and begin to use correct pronouns and verbs in present and past tense. They understand approximately six thousand words.	1 Give children many opportunities for oral language activities connected with literature.	Aardema, Verna. *Bringing the Rain to Kapiti Plain.* Gág, Wanda. *Millions of Cats.* Grimm, Brothers. *Hansel and Gretel.* Moss, Lloyd. *Zin! Zin! Zin! A Violin.* Opie, Iona. *My Very First Mother Goose.* Taback, Simms. *There Was An Old Lady Who Swallowed A Fly.*

CHART 1–1 *Continued*

Characteristics	Implications	Literature Suggestions
Preschool—Kindergarten: Ages Five–Six 2 Children enjoy taking part in dramatic play and producing dialogue about everyday activities such as those at home and the grocery store.	2 Read stories about the home and community. Allow children to act out their own stories.	Hurd, Edith Thacher. *I Dance in My Red Pajamas.* Lucht, Irmgard. *In This Night. . . .* Martin, Rafe. *Will's Mammoth.* Ryder, Joanne. *White Bear, Ice Bear.* Seuss, Dr. *And to Think That I Saw It on Mulberry Street.*
3 Children are curious about the written appearance of their own language.	3 Write chart stories using the children's own words. Have children dictate descriptions of pictures.	Baker, Jeannie. *Window.* McCully, Emily Arnold. *Picnic.* Wood, Audrey. *The Flying Dragon Room.* Willard, Nancy. *Night Story.*
Early Elementary: Ages Six–Eight 1 Language development continues. Children add many new words to their vocabularies.	1 Provide daily time for reading to children and allow for oral interaction.	Bryan, Ashley. *The Cat's Purr.* Cooper, Melrose. *I Got a Family.* Defelice, Cynthia. *Willy's Silly Grandma.* George, Kristine O'Connell. *The Great Frog Race: And Other Poems.* Johnston, Tony. *The Ghost of Nicholas Greebe.* Lewin, Hugh. *Jafta.* Silverstein, Shel. *A Light in the Attic.*
2 Most children use complex sentences with adjectival clauses and conditional clauses beginning with *if.* The average oral sentence length is seven and one-half words.	2 Read stories that provide models for children's expanding language structure.	Burton, Virginia Lee. *The Little House.* Hodges, Margaret. *Saint George and the Dragon.* McCloskey, Robert. *Make Way for Ducklings.*

about eighteen months, they begin to put words together in two-word combinations, called *telegraphic speech.* Speech during this stage of language development consists of nouns, verbs, and adjectives. It usually contains no prepositions, articles, auxiliary verbs, or pronouns. When children say "pretty flower" or "milk gone," they are using telegraphic speech. The number of different two-word combinations increases slowly. Then, it shows a sudden upsurge around age two. Martin Braine (1978) began recording the speech of three eighteen-month-old children. He reported that the cumulative number of different two-word combinations for one child in successive months was 14, 24, 54, 89, 350,

CHART 1–1 *Continued*

Characteristics	Implications	Literature Suggestions
Middle Elementary: Ages Eight–Ten 1 Children begin to relate concepts to general ideas. They use connectors such as *meanwhile* and *unless*.	1 Supply books as models. Let children use these terms during oral language activities.	Schotter, Roni. *Nothing Ever Happens on 90th Street.* Steptoe, John. *Mufaro's Beautiful Daughters: An African Tale.* Young, Ed. *Lon Po Po: A Red Riding Hood Story from China.*
2 The subordinating connector *although* is used correctly by 50 percent of children. Present participle active and perfect participle appear. The average number of words in sentence is nine.	2 Use written models and oral models to help children master their language skills. Literature discussions allow many opportunities for oral sentence expansion.	Brett, Jan. *Beauty and the Beast.* Levine, Arthur A. *The Boy Who Drew Cats: A Japanese Folktale.* Mayer, Marianna. *The Twelve Dancing Princesses.* Sandburg, Carl. *More Rootabagas.* Walter, Mildred Pitts. *Brother to the Wind.*
Upper Elementary: Ages Ten–Twelve 1 Children use complex sentences with subordinate clauses of concession introduced by *nevertheless* and *in spite of.* Auxiliary verbs *might, could,* and *should* appear frequently.	1 Encourage oral language and written activities that permit children to use more complex sentence structures.	L'Engle, Madeleine. *A Swiftly Tilting Planet.* Lisle, Janet Taylor. *The Gold Dust Letters.* Lunn, Janet. *Shadow in Hawthorn Bay.* McKinley, Robin. *The Hero and the Crown.* Paulsen, Gary. *Hatchet.* _____. *The Winter Room.* Pullman, Philip. *The Golden Compass.*

Sources: Bartel (1990); Braga and Braga (1975); Brown (1973); Gage and Berliner (1979); Hendrick (1992); and Loban (1976).

1,400, and 2,500+. This is a rapid expansion of speech in a very short time.

A longitudinal study conducted by Roger Brown (1973) demonstrated how widely the rate of language development can vary from child to child. For example, one child successfully used six grammatical morphemes (the smallest meaning-bearing units in a word) by the age of two years, three months; a second child did not master them until the age of three years, six months; and a third was four years old before reaching an equivalent stage in language development.

Speech usually becomes more complex by age three, when most children have added adverbs, pronouns, prepositions, and more adjectives to their vocabularies. Children also enjoy playing with the sounds of words at this stage of language development. By age four, they produce grammatically correct sentences. This stage is a questioning one, during which language is used to ask why and how.

Literature and literature-related experiences can encourage language development in preschool children. Joanne Hendrick (1992) recommends children's books and related activities to enhance language development. Steven Herb (1997) reviews research findings and concludes, "Children's early experiences with books directly relate to their success in learning to read in school" and "storybook reading is a more effective influence on literacy development when children have opportunities to engage in conversation about the story" (p. 23). Child development authority George Maxim (1993) states:

Stories, either told or read aloud, have an extremely important place in the language program of preschool classrooms. Storytelling is one of the most effective ways of exposing children to rich and varied language, and it is basic to the effective development of speaking vocabularies. (p. 330)

Book experiences in the home, at the library, and at nursery school can help children use language to discover the world, identify and name actions and objects, gain more complex speech, and enjoy the wonder of language. Many children first experience literature through picture books, which help children give meaning to their expanding vocabularies. For example, children who are just learning to identify their hands and other parts of their bodies may find these parts in drawings of children. Parents of very young children may share Helen Oxenbury's excellent baby board books. (Board books are toy books made of cardboard for young children.) *Dressing,* for example, includes a picture of a baby's clothing, followed by a picture of the child dressed in those items. The illustrations are sequentially developed to encourage talking about the steps in dressing. Nancy Tafuri's board book *One Wet Jacket* follows the opposite approach. In *One Wet Jacket,* each of the labeled pieces of clothing is taken off until the child is shown in the tub.

Young children also learn to identify actions in pictures, and enjoy recognizing and naming familiar actions, such as those in Eve Rice's *Oh, Lewis!* In this picture storybook, Lewis is going shopping with his mother, but first he must find his mittens and have his jacket zipped, his boots buckled, and his hood tied. Patricia Lillie's *Everything Has a Place* introduces young children to the concept that things have places where they belong. Children can name these places such as "a book on a shelf" as they listen to the story and observe the pictures. *Richard Scarry's The Best Word Book Ever* appeals to young children and provides practice in naming common objects.

Many excellent books allow children to listen to the sounds of language and experiment with these sounds. For example, Woody Guthrie's *Woody's 20 Grow Big Songs* includes songs that contain both repetition and actions that are enjoyed by younger children.

Mirra Ginsburg's *Asleep, Asleep* is a picture-book lullaby. The author uses a rhythmic, repetitive text as a mother tells her baby about the sleeping animals. Books with repetitive language are excellent for enticing listeners to join in during oral reading. Nancy Carlstrom's *Baby-O* is a cumulative story in which the members of a West Indian family gather produce for the market. Listeners enjoy joining in the repetitive refrain. They may even clap to the language. Jim Aylesworth's *Old Black Fly* is another rhythmic chant that encourages listeners to join in the story as they say, "Shoo fly! Shoo fly! Shooo." Children may respond in both Spanish and English when they interact with the rhymes in *Tortillitas Para Mama* by Margot C. Griego et al.

Books that encourage children to play with and appreciate language are also excellent for language development. The vivid language in Lloyd Moss's *Zin! Zin! Zin! A Violin* is especially appealing. Children can join in as the trombone plays mournful tones by "gliding, sliding" or the oboe plays "gleeful, bleating, sobbing, pleading." This book provides an excellent source for acting out the sounds and movements related to the instruments of the orchestra. The language in Jonathan London's *Fireflies, Fireflies, Light My Way* also encourages young children to join in as they become part of a nocturnal jaunt as various animals are asked to "lead me to the . . ." In the final refrain all the animals are joined together.

Unusual words and stories in rhyme encourage children to play with language. In *Good Zap, Little Grog,* Sarah Wilson uses unusual language to create a story in rhyme. As the fantasy story progresses, ooglets are tuzzling, parobbies are churling, and glipneeps are jumping. Rhymes and nonsensical words such as *shmuffle* and *smarge* highlight a humorous story in *Pigs in the Mud in the Middle of the Rud* by Lynn Plourde. The pigs refuse to move until Grandma finally solves the problem.

Repetitive language and a satisfying ending make Bryon Barton's *The Wee Little Woman* a good choice for reading aloud to preschool children who may join in by describing the wee little woman, the wee little stool, the wee little table, and even the wee lit-

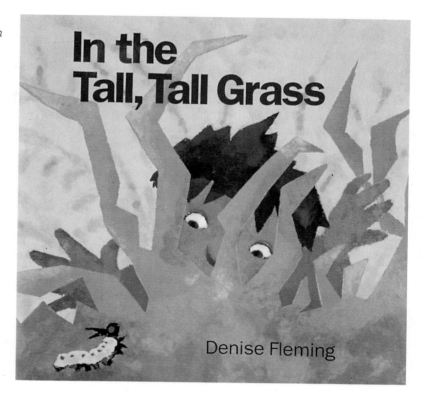

The language in In the Tall, Tall Grass *encourages both observation and play with words. From* In The Tall, Tall Grass *by Denise Fleming. Copyright © 1991 by Denise Fleming. Reprinted by permission of Henry Holt and Company, Inc.*

tle cat. Repetitive language and humor combine to create an enjoyable story in Gail Forgensen's *Gotcha!* as the text repeats the words "Wallop!," "Gotcha!," and "Missed!" in an effort to catch a beastly fly. Repetitive language and humor also provide the appeal in Simms Taback's *There Was An Old Lady Who Swallowed A Fly.*

The poems in Jane Dyer's collection *Animal Crackers: A Delectable Collection of Pictures, Poems, and Lullabies for the Very Young* include rhythm, rhyme, and sound patterns that appeal to young children. Iona Opie's *My Very First Mother Goose* is a collection of over 60 rhymes illustrated with Rosemary Wells's humorous illustrations.

Elementary-Age Children.

Language development of course continues as children enter school and progress through the grades. Walter Loban (1976) conducted the most extensive longitudinal study of language development in school-age children. Loban's study is so important that Marilyn Hanf Buckley (1992) states that Loban's work es-

tablished the firm relationship between oral language development and success at reading and writing and "provided the base upon which our present-day thinking about the integrated language arts curriculum rests" (p. 622). Loban examined the language development of the same group of over two hundred children from age five to age eighteen. He found that children's power over language increases through successive control over different forms of language, including pronouns, verb tenses, and connectors, such as *meanwhile* and *unless.*

Loban identified dramatic differences between children who ranked high in language proficiency and those who ranked low. The high group reached a level of oral proficiency in first grade that the low group did not attain until sixth grade and a level of written proficiency in fourth grade that the low group did not attain until tenth grade. Those who demonstrated high language proficiency excelled in the control of ideas expressed, showing unity and planning in both their speech and writing. These students spoke freely, fluently, and easily, using a rich vocabulary and adjusting the pace of their words to their listeners. They were attentive and creative listeners themselves, far outranking the low group in listening ability. The oral communication of those with low language proficiency was characterized by rambling and unpurposeful dialogue that demonstrated a meager vocabulary.

Children who were superior in oral language in kindergarten and first grade also excelled in reading and writing in sixth grade. They were more fluent in written language than were the low-ranked children, used more words per sentence, showed a richer written vocabulary, and were superior in using connectors and subordination to combine thoughts into complex forms of expression. Given the demonstrated connection between oral and written language skills, Loban concluded that teachers, librarians, and parents should give greater attention to developing children's oral language. Discussion should be a vital part of elementary school and library programs because it helps children organize ideas and make complex generalizations. Unfortunately, however, Marie Clay (1991) concludes, "[W]hile teachers see oral language as central to writing and reading acquisition, they often do not recognize the need to foster its further development" (p. 41).

Books with repetitive language are excellent for enticing listeners to join in during oral reading. Mem Fox's *Hattie and the Fox* includes both a cumulative plot and repetitive refrains. The illustrations are excellent for predicting language because they show various features of the approaching fox. John Ivimey's *The Complete Story of the Three Blind Mice* includes repetitive lines, rhyming language, and descriptive terms. This extended story, illustrated by Paul Galdone, allows readers to discover what caused the loss of the tails. This version even has a happy ending.

Wordless picture books are excellent stimulators for oral and written language. Emily Arnold McCully's *School* follows the exploits of the littlest mouse child, who discovers what happens during a real school day. Peter Collington's *The Angel and the Soldier Boy* provides an exciting adventure, in which an angel and a soldier rescue a coin from pirates and return it to a sleeping child.

David Wiesner's *Free Fall* shows the adventures that are possible within dreams. Wiesner's *Tuesday* is a story filled with surprising and unexpected elements. Readers enjoy extending the book into the next Tuesday. Wiesner's final illustration shows that now the pigs have their opportunity to fly, to explore the neighborhood, and to baffle the people. The book provides an interesting stimulus for oral stories, creative writing, and drawing illustrations and for children to create their own stories about "The Night the Pigs Could Fly."

Books with vivid language, similes, and metaphors stimulate language development and appreciation for literary style. The text for Jane Yolen's *Owl Moon* is filled with figurative language. It personifies trees, dogs, and shadows. For example, footprints in the snow "follow us," shadows "bumped after me," and cold places an "icy hand . . . palm-down on my back." Similes and metaphors produce vivid comparisons; voices in the night fade away "as quiet as a dream," snow is "whiter than milk in a cereal bowl," and an owl moves "like a shadow without a sound." The vivid language in Nancy Willard's *Pish, Posh, Said Hieronymus Bosch* presents a fantasy world in which the housekeeper wrestles with dragons "while the cats chase the cucumbers, slickity-slink." The language in Nancy Carlstrom's *Raven and River* sounds like the actions of various animals as they wake the sleeping river from its icy slumber.

Literature is a crucial resource, providing both a model for language and a stimulation for oral and written activities. This text suggests a wealth of literature for use in the elementary grades: literature to be read aloud to children; literature to provide models for expanding language proficiency; and literature to stimulate oral discussion, creative dramatics, creative writing, and listening enjoyment.

Literature provides stimulation for the dramatic play and creative dramatics that inspire children in the primary grades to express themselves verbally with much enjoyment. For example, in Maurice Sendak's *Where the Wild Things Are,* Max gets into so much mischief when he is wearing his wolf suit that his mother sends him to his room without any supper. His vivid imagination turns the room into a forest inhabited by wild things. Max stays in the forest and becomes its king, but finally, he gets lonely and wants to return to the land where someone loves him. Children can relate to Max's experience and use it to stimulate their own wild experiences. Children enjoy using their imaginations and turning common occurrences into creative experiences.

Books that encourage children to make up their own stories are also excellent for language develop-

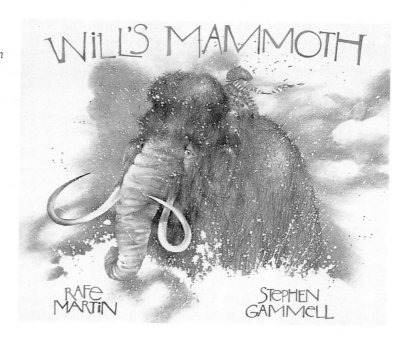

A boy turns a day in the snow into a very imaginative experience. Illustration by Stephen Gammell, reproduced with permission of G. P. Putnam's Sons from Will's Mammoth *by Rafe Martin, illustrations copyright © 1989 by Stephen Gammell.*

ment. Authors may develop their books on the premise of what would happen if a character from a book came to life. In Susan Cooper's *Matthew's Dragon,* the dragon from a boy's favorite book comes to life and the boy and the dragon share an adventure. In Else Holmelund Minarik's *The Little Girl and the Dragon,* a dragon from a book comes to life and causes much destruction, and a girl discovers how to make him return to the book. By reading and viewing *The Flying Dragon Room,* text by Audrey Wood and illustrations by Mark Teague, children can use their imaginations to create their own fantasy worlds inhabited by strange animals and unusual experiences, or they can pretend that they are riding the flying dragon or sailing on the Jolly Mermaid. In *Edward and the Pirates,* David McPhail uses a young boy's love for reading and his powerful imagination to create adventures. Any of these books can encourage children to create their own stories. For example, children can choose a figure from a fictional book and pretend that it comes to life. What would happen? What might the figure do for good or for bad? How would they control the figure?

"What if" stories may encourage children to explore vicariously new worlds and to tell about experiences if they could accompany the literary characters. Paul Fleischman's *Time Train* provides a marvelous opportunity for children to enter the Rocky Mountain Unlimited and to go back in time chronologically until they finally enter a tropical world inhabited by dinosaurs. Jon Scieszka's *Your Mother Was a Neanderthal* allows children to accompany a time warp trio back to the time of woolly mammoths and saber-toothed tigers. Alison Lester's *The Journey Home* encourages readers to accompany two children who dig a hole that takes them to the other side of the world. They have numerous adventures as they explore the earth in their endeavor to reach home. These books encourage children to create imaginative fantasies.

Cognitive Development

Factors related to helping children remember, anticipate, integrate perceptions, and develop concepts fill numerous textbooks and have been the subject of both research and conjecture. Jean Piaget and B. Inhelder (1969) maintained that the order in which children's thinking matures is the same for all children, although the pace varies from child to child. Stimulation is also necessary for cognitive development. Children who grow up without a variety of experiences may be three to five years behind other children in developing the mental strategies that aid recall. Chart 1–2 lists books that can promote cognitive development in children.

CHART 1–2 (PP. 14–18)   Cognitive development

Characteristics	Implications	Literature Suggestions
Preschool: Ages Two–Three 1 Children learn new ways to organize and classify their worlds by putting together things that they perceive to be alike. 2 Children begin to remember two or three items.	1 Provide opportunities for children to discuss and group things according to color, shape, size, or use. Use picture concept books with large, colorful pictures. 2 Exercise children's short-term memories by providing opportunities to recall information.	Cabrera, Jane. *Cat's Colors.* Hoban, Tana. *Look! Look! Look!* _____. *Of Colors and Things.* _____. *1, 2, 3.* _____. *What Is It?* Gunson, Christopher. *Over On the Farm: A Counting Picture Book Rhyme.*
Preschool: Ages Three–Four 1 Children develop an understanding of how things relate to each other: how parts go together to make a whole, and how they are arranged in space in relation to each other. 2 Children begin to understand relationships and classify things according to certain perceptual attributes that they share, such as color, size, shape, and what they are used for. 3 Children begin to understand how objects relate to each other in terms of number and amount. 4 Children begin to compare two things and tell which is bigger and which is smaller.	1 Give children opportunities to find the correct part of a picture to match another picture. Use simple picture puzzles. 2 Share concept books on color, size, shape, and use. Provide opportunities for children to group and classify objects and pictures. 3 Give picture counting books to children. Allow them to count. 4 Share and discuss books that allow comparisons in size, such as a giant and a boy, a big item and a small item, or a series of animals.	Emberley, Rebecca. *City Sounds.* Hoban, Tana. *Take Another Look.* Hutchins, Pat. *Changes, Changes.* Oxenbury, Helen. *I See.* Aylesworth, Jim. *One Crow: A Counting Rhyme.* Carle, Eric. *My Very First Book of Colors.* de Brunhoff, Laurent. *Babar's Book of Color.* Hoban, Tana. *Shapes, Shapes, Shapes.* Bang, Molly. *Ten, Nine, Eight.* Carle, Eric. *My Very First Book of Numbers.* Christelow, Eileen. *Five Little Monkeys Jumping on the Bed.* Fleming, Denise. *Count!* Tafuri, Nancy. *Who's Counting?* Walsh, Ellen Stoll. *Mouse Count.* Campbell, Rod. *Dear Zoo.* Hutchins, Pat. *Shrinking Mouse.* Voake, Charlotte. *Mrs. Goose's Baby.*
Preschool: Ages Four–Five 1 Children remember to do three things told to them or retell a short story if the material is presented in a meaningful sequence.	1 Tell short, meaningful stories and allow children to retell them. Use flannelboard and picture stories to help children organize the story. Give practice in following three-step directions.	Asbjøjornsen, Peter Christen. *Three Billy Goats Gruff.* Galdone, Paul. *The Gingerbread Boy.* _____. *What's in Fox's Sack? An Old English Tale.* Gray, Libba Moore. *Is There Room on the Feather Bed?*

CHART 1–2 *Continued*

Characteristics	Implications	Literature Suggestions
Preschool: Ages Four–Five		
2 Children increase their ability to group objects according to important characteristics but still base their rules on how things look to them.	2 Provide many opportunities to share concept books and activities designed to develop ideas of shape, color, size, feel, and use.	Carle, Eric. *My Very First Book of Shapes.* Emberley, Ed. *Go Away, Big Green Monster!* Hoban, Tana. *Circles, Triangles, and Squares.* _____. *Is It Red? Is It Yellow? Is It Blue?*
3 Children pretend to tell time but do not understand the concept. Things happen "now" or "before now."	3 Share books to help children understand sequence of time and when things happen, such as the seasons of the year and different times of the day or different days of the week.	Johnson, Angela. *Tell Me a Story, Mama.* Peters, Lisa Westberg. *October Smiled Back.* Rockwell, Anne. *First Comes Spring.*
Preschool—Kindergarten: Ages Five–Six		
1 Children learn to follow one type of classification (such as color or shape) through to completion without changing the main characteristic partway through the task.	1 Continue to share concept books and encourage activities that allow children to group and classify.	Giganti, Paul, Jr. *How Many Snails? A Counting Book.* Lobel, Arnold. *On Market Street.* Theodorou, Rod, and Telford, Carole. *Big and Small.*
2 Children count to ten and discriminate ten objects.	2 Reinforce counting skills with counting books and other counting activities.	Carle, Eric. *My Very First Book of Numbers.* Dubanevich, Arlene. *Pigs in Hiding.* Parker, Vic. *Bearobics: A Hip-Hop Counting Story.* Sierra, Judy. *Counting Crocodiles.*
3 Children identify primary colors.	3 Reinforce identification through the use of color concept books and colors found in other picture books.	Ehlert, Lois. *Color Zoo.* Hutchins, Pat. *Changes, Changes.*
4 Children learn to distinguish between "a lot of" something or "a little of" something.	4 Provide opportunities for children to identify and discuss the differences between concepts.	Gág, Wanda. *Millions of Cats.* Zemach, Margot. *It Could Always Be Worse.*
5 Children require trial and error before they can arrange things in order from smallest to biggest.	5 Share books that progress from smallest to largest. Have children retell stories using flannelboard characters drawn in appropriate sizes.	Galdone, Paul. *The Three Billy Goats Gruff.* Jenkins, Steve. *Big & Little.* Zemach, Margot. *It Could Always Be Worse.*
6 Children still have vague concepts of time.	6 Share books to help children understand time sequence.	Fowler, Susi. *When Summer Ends.*

CHART 1–2   *Continued*

Characteristics	Implications	Literature Suggestions
Early Elementary: Ages Six–Eight 1 Children are learning to read; they enjoy reading easy books and demonstrating their new abilities.	1 Provide easy-to-read books geared to children's developing reading skills.	Byars, Betsy. *My Brother, Ant.* Lobel, Arnold. *Frog and Toad All Year.* Rylant, Cynthia. *Henry and Mudge and the Long Weekend.* _____. *Mr. Putter and Tabby Pour the Tea.* Seuss, Dr. *The Cat in the Hat.* Van Leeuwen, Jean. *Oliver Pig at School.*
2 Children are learning to write and enjoy creating their own stories.	2 Allow children to write, illustrate, and share their own picture books. Use wordless books to suggest plot.	Van Allsburg, Chris. *The Mysteries of Harris Burdick.* Waber, Bernard. *The Snake: A Very Long Story.* Wiesner, David. *Free Fall.* _____. *Tuesday.*
3 Children enjoy longer stories than they did when they were five because their attention spans are increasing.	3 Read longer storybooks to children, such as books in which the chapters can be completed in a short time.	Alexander, Lloyd. *The Fortune Tellers.* Lester, Julius. *The Last Tales of Uncle Remus.* Milne, A. A. *The House at Pooh Corner.* San Souci, Robert. *The Talking Eggs: A Folktale from the American South.* Van Allsburg, Chris. *The Polar Express.*
4 Children under seven still base their rules on immediate perception and learn through real situations.	4 Provide experiences that allow children to see, discuss, and verify information and relationships.	Micklethwait, Lucy. *A Child's Book of Play in Art: Great Pictures. Great Fun.* Peters, Lisa Westberg. *The Sun, the Wind and the Rain.* Priceman, Marjorie, *How to Make an Apple Pie and See the World.* Reiss, John J. *Shapes.*

CHART 1–2   *Continued*

Characteristics	Implications	Literature Suggestions
Early Elementary: Ages Six–Eight 5 Sometime during this age, children pass into the stage that Piaget refers to as concrete operational. Children have developed a new set of rules, called groupings, so they don't have to see all objects to group; they can understand relationships among categories.	5 Provide opportunities for children to read and discuss concept books.	Anno, Mitsumasa. *Anno's Counting Book.* _____. *Anno's Math Games II.* Feelings, Muriel. *Moja Means One: Swahili Counting Book.* Grossman, Bill. *My Little Sister Ate One Hare.* Haskins, Jim. *Count Your Way Through Italy.* Hoban, Tana. *26 Letters and 99 Cents.* McMillan, Bruce. *Eating Fractions.* Murphy, Stuart J. *The Best Bug Parade.* Robbins, Ken. *Power Machines.*
Middle Elementary: Ages Eight–Ten 1 Children's reading skills improve rapidly, although there are wide variations in reading ability among children within the same age group.	1 For independent reading, provide books at appropriate reading levels. Allow children opportunities to share their book experiences with peers, parents, teachers, and other adults.	Blume, Judy. *Tales of a Fourth Grade Nothing.* Cleary, Beverly. *Ramona and Her Father.* Lowry, Lois. *Attaboy, Sam!* Nichol, Barbara. *Beethoven Lives Upstairs.* Wilder, Laura Ingalls. *Little House in the Big Woods.*
2 Children's level of interest in literature may still be above their reading levels.	2 Provide a daily time during which children can listen to a variety of books being read aloud.	Burnett, Frances Hodgson. *The Secret Garden.* Grahame, Kenneth. *The Wind in the Willows.* Konigsburg, E. L. *The View From Saturday.* Lewis, C. S. *The Lion, the Witch, and the Wardrobe.* White, E. B. *Charlotte's Web.*
3 Memory improves as children learn to attend to certain stimuli and ignore others.	3 Help children set purposes for listening or reading before the actual literature experience.	Freedman, Russell. *The Wright Brothers: How They Invented the Airplane.* Malnig, Anita. *Where the Waves Break: Life at the Edge of the Sea.* Viorst, Judith. *The Alphabet from Z to A (With Much Confusion on the Way).*

CHART 1–2 *Continued*

Characteristics	Implications	Literature Suggestions
Upper Elementary: Ages Ten–Twelve 1 Children develop an understanding of the chronological ordering of past events.	1 Encourage children to read historical fiction and books showing historic changes to help them understand differing viewpoints and historical perspectives.	Arnold, Caroline. *Stone Age Farmers Beside the Sea: Scotland's Prehistoric Village of Skara Brae.* Forbes, Esther. *Johnny Tremain.* McCurdy, Michael. *Escape from Slavery: The Boyhood of Frederick Douglass in His Own Words.* Meyer, Carolyn, and Charles Gallenkamp. *The Mystery of the Ancient Maya.* Speare, Elizabeth George. *The Sign of the Beaver.* Orlev, Uri. *The Man from the Other Side.*
2 Children apply logical rules, reasoning, and formal operations to abstract problems.	2 Use questioning and discussion strategies to develop higher level thought processes. Children enjoy more complex books.	Ash, Russell. *Incredible Comparisons.* Avi. *Nothing But the Truth: A Documentary Novel.* *Beowulf.* Blumberg, Rhoda. *The Incredible Journey of Lewis & Clark.* Freedman, Russell. *Lincoln: A Photobiography.* Greenberg, Jan, and Sandra Jordan. *The Sculptor's Eye: Looking at Contemporary American Art.*

Sources: Braga and Braga (1975); Maxim (1993); Mussen, Conger, and Kagan (1989); Piaget and Inhelder (1969); and Shaffer (1989).

According to child development authority David Shaffer (1989), cognitive development "refers to the changes that occur in children's mental skills and abilities over time" (p. 306). Shaffer states, "We are constantly attending to objects and events, interpreting them, comparing them with past experiences, placing them into categories, and encoding them into memory" (p. 306). Mussen, Conger, and Kagan (1989) define cognition as the process involved in

(1) perception—the detection, organization, and interpretation of information from both the outside world and the internal environment, (2) memory—the storage and retrieval of the perceived information, (3) reasoning—the use of knowledge to make inferences and draw conclusions, (4) reflection—the evaluation of the quality of ideas and solutions, and (5) insight—the recognition of new relationships between two or more segments of knowledge.

George Maxim (1993) emphasizes cognitive development that includes two major areas: physical knowledge and logicomathematical ability. Physical knowledge is gained through observing properties of objects within the child's experience. The child learns about the physical environment through observation and experimentation. Logicomathematical ability includes the ability to classify or group objects on some common criterion; to arrange objects according to size, quality, or quantity and then compare likenesses and differences among objects in the same category and order them according to relative differences; to understand spatial relations in terms of direction, distance, and perspective; to understand temporal relations that allow perception of time sequences; and to conceptualize properties of objects.

Scientist and author Chet Raymo (1992) highlights the role of children's books in developing a scientific imagination. He states, "Creative science depends crucially upon habits of mind that are most readily acquired by children: curiosity; voracious observation; sensitivity to rules and variations within the rules; and fantasy. Children's books that instill these habits of mind sustain science" (p. 561).

All of the preceding processes are essential for success in both school and adult life. Each is also closely related to understanding and enjoying literature. Without visual and auditory perception, literature could not be read or heard; without memory, there would be no way to see the relationships among literary works and to recognize new relationships as experiences are extended. Literature is also important in stimulating cognitive development by encouraging the oral exchange of ideas and the development of thought processes. Children's literature is especially effective for developing the basic operations associated with thinking: (1) observing, (2) comparing, (3) classifying, (4) hypothesizing, (5) organizing, (6) summarizing, (7) applying, and (8) criticizing.

Observing. Colorful picture books are excellent means of developing observational skills in both younger and older children. Young children discover how many animals they can locate in *Keep Looking!* by Millicent Selsam and Joyce Hunt. Suse MacDonald's *Alphabatics* encourages young children to observe how a letter changes within three or four drawings to a picture of an object that begins with that letter. Keith Baker's *Hide and Snake* encourages viewers to search through the illustra-

tions to find the snake that is mixed in with colored yarns, curled around hats, wrapped among presents, and napping with cats. The colors of the snake blend with the colors in the illustrations. Consequently, this book becomes a game of hide and seek. Using Stephen T. Johnson's *Alphabet City,* students may search for the various letters of the alphabet captured through paintings of various scenes. For example, the letter A is a construction sawhorse, the letter M is a bridge structure, and the letter Z is formed with fire escapes. The illustrations in Lucy Micklethwait's *A Child's Book of Play in Art: Great Pictures, Great Fun* encourage children to find details, imitate sounds, adapt patterns, and interpret costumes. In *Look Book* by Tana Hoban viewers first see a portion of an object before they turn the page to reveal the identity of the object. Careful observation is enhanced through the photographs.

Ten Flashing Fireflies by Philemon Sturges also stimulates observing and counting. The text begins by asking viewers what they see in the summer night and then shows two children trying to catch one of the fireflies. Viewers can observe and count their successes as the ten fireflies are finally reduced to zero fireflies. The fireflies are not observed and counted first in a jar and then released into the night. *Over On the Farm: A Counting Picture Book Rhyme* by Christopher Gunson also encourages viewers to observe and count the animals.

Older children enjoy searching for art objects, literary and historical characters, and present-day personalities in Mitsumasa Anno's detailed, wordless books, such as *Anno's U.S.A. Lentil,* by Robert McCloskey, contains excellent drawings of a midwestern town in the early 1900s: the town square, the houses on the streets, the interior of the schoolhouse, the train depot, and a parade. Single lines of text accompany each picture, but the pictures show the life-styles and the emotions of the characters in the story. Kathy Jakobsen's *My New York* encourages children to locate the narrator within each picture and to describe the detailed New York settings. Jean Marzollo's *I Spy: School Days: A Book of Picture Riddles* and *I Spy Spooky Night: A Book of Picture Riddles* encourage readers to locate specific objects in the photographs and illustrations.

The detailed illustrations in The Inside-Outside Book of Washington, D.C. *provide an excellent source for observing. (From* The Inside-Outside Book of Washington, D.C. *by Roxie Munro. Copyright © 1987 by Roxie Munro. Reproduced by permission of the publisher, Dutton Children's Books, a division of Penguin Books USA, Inc.)*

Comparing.   Picture books and other literature selections provide opportunities for comparing. For example, young children can compare the various attributes of the hats illustrated in Stan and Janice Berenstain's *Old Hat, New Hat.* The hats include ones that are heavy, light, loose, tight, flat, tall, big, small, shiny, frilly, fancy, silly, and lumpy. Children can compare these new hats with the old hat, still considered the best of all. The illustrations in Sandy Nightingale's *A Giraffe on the Moon* encourage children to compare reality and visions stimulated by the imagination. In Patrick Benson's *Little Penguin,* viewers compare the size of Pip, an Adélie penguin, with that of Emperor penguins. The illustrations also compare big and little fish. The illustrations in Jez Alborough's *Where's My Teddy?* encourage comparisons between a giant teddy and a large real bear and between a small teddy and a real boy. Comparisons in sizes are encouraged in Steve Jenkins's *Big & Little.*

Cut-paper collages highlight differences in sizes such as those found between a shark and a turtle.

Different artists' renditions of the same story provide opportunities for artistic comparisons. For example, there are several illustrated versions of Margery Williams's *The Velveteen Rabbit,* originally published in 1922, including those by Allen Atkinson, Michael Hague, and Ilse Plume. Versions of the popular folktale "Beauty and the Beast" include those illustrated in different styles by Warwick Hutton, Barry Moser, Jan Brett, and Michael Hague. Students can consider the impact of color, line, design, and media on the interpretation of the text, as well as evaluate the accuracy of the illustrations. In addition to comparing artists' renditions, children may compare traditional versions of the tales and those adapted by authors such as William J. Brooke in *Untold Tales,* Jon Scieszka in *The Stinky Cheese Man and Other Fairly Stupid Tales,* and Eugene Trivizas in *The Three Little Wolves and the Big Bad Pig.*

Two retellings of *Little Black Sambo* provide interesting comparisons. For example, Julius Lester's *Sam and the Tigers: A New Telling of Little Black Sambo* may be compared with a new version of Helen Bannerman's *The Story of Little Babaji*. The original story was ridiculed for offensive language and illustrations.

Upper-elementary children can compare the main characters, their struggles for survival, and their growing up in books such as Maia Wojciechowska's *Shadow of a Bull* and Elizabeth George Speare's *The Bronze Bow*. They can compare one author's depiction of characters and survival in Gary Paulsen's *Hatchet* and *The Voyage of the Frog*. They can compare themes, characterizations, and person-against-self conflicts in Marion Dane Bauer's *On My Honor* and Paula Fox's *One-Eyed Cat*. They can compare Russell Freedman's depiction of Lincoln in *Lincoln: A Photobiography* with the depiction of Lincoln by other biographers.

Older children and university students may compare Penny Pollock's heavily illustrated version of a Native American folktale, *The Turkey Girl: A Zuni Cinderella Story* with the original source of the tale, "The Poor Turkey Girl" found in Frank Hamilton Cushing's *Zuni Folktales* (University of Arizona Press, 1986).

Two other interesting comparisons may be accomplished using Lois Duncan's *The Magic of Spider Woman* and Shonto Begay's *Navajo: Visions and Voices Across the Mesa*. Students may compare the similarities in values, beliefs, and themes in Duncan's folklore with the values, beliefs, and themes expressed in three poems in Begay's text: "Echoes," "Creation," and "Mother's Lace."

Classifying.
Concept books provide excellent stimulation for classifying. Books such as Tana Hoban's *All About Where* foster classifying according to concepts such as above, between, and under. Children must also be able to classify objects or ideas before seeing or understanding the relationships among them. Various concept books use different levels of abstractness to introduce children to such concepts as color, shape, size, and usefulness. Eric Carle allows children to match blocks of color with the color shown in an illustration in his *My Very First Book of Colors* and illustrates the colorful story of a chameleon who wants to change his appearance in *The Mixed-up Chameleon*.

Shape concept books vary in level of difficulty. Carle's *My Very First Book of Shapes* encourages children to match black shapes with similar shapes in color. John Reiss's *Shapes* presents shapes, their names, and their three-dimensional forms. Photographs in Tana Hoban's *Shapes, Shapes, Shapes* encourage children to search for circles, rectangles, and ovals.

Many other types of books can be used to develop children's classification skills and responses to literature. For example, after listening to the folktale "The Three Bears," children may classify the bears, porridge bowls, chairs, and beds according to their size and then identify which bear could best use a particular bowl, bed, or chair. (Flannelgraph characters and objects make classification more concrete for young children.) Stories can be classified using a category for wild animals or pets; a boy or girl category for the main character; or a category for settings such as country or city. For example, country and city settings may be compared in Rebecca Emberley's *City Sounds* and Anne Hunter's *Possum's Harvest Moon*. Characteristics of a story can also be used for classification: realistic or unrealistic; likable or unlikable; happy or sad; and funny or serious. For example, children can compare the realistic and unrealistic qualities found in Patricia Lauber's *The News About Dinosaurs*, Henry Schwartz's *How I Captured a Dinosaur*, and Rafe Martin's *Will's Mammoth*.

Hypothesizing.
Several illustrated books encourage younger children to hypothesize about what they will find when they turn the page. In *Look! Look! Look!*, Tana Hoban uses cutout squares to reveal portions of pictures. The total picture appears on the page following the portions. At a more complex level, students must turn the page to determine the possible dialogue in Chris Van Allsburg's *The Z Was Zapped*.

Hypothesizing is stimulated as children search for clues in pictures and text to answer various questions. Books such as James Stevenson's *Which One Is Whitney?* encourage young readers to identify the correct dugong. In Mary Serfozo's *What's What?: A Guessing Game*, readers hypothesize about the answer to a question such as "What's light?" After they guess they can turn the page to discover the artist's answer. Finding objects may encourage both hypothesizing about the potential for the object and expanding the imagination. When a young girl finds a red ribbon on the ground in Carole Lexa Schaefer's *The Squiggle,* she twists and twirls the ribbon as she imagines it to be objects such as a thunder cloud and a dragon. In Edith Baer's *This Is the Way We Go to School: A Book About Children Around the World,* readers must locate clues in the illustrations and then identify where in the world the children attend school. A map with the correct answers appears in the back of the book.

Books that encourage hypothesizing include texts or illustrations in which children are asked to speculate about what may happen next. Adults who read Janet Stevens's *Tops & Bottoms* could stop after the second time in which Hare tricks Bear by getting the best part of the vegetable crop. Adults can ask students to speculate about how Hare will trick Bear during the third year when Bear states that he wants both the tops and bottoms. In a humorous ending, Hare plants corn so that Bear gets the roots (bottoms) and the tassels (tops), while Hare gets the ears of corn (middles). By reading or listening to Shirley Isherwood's *Something for James,* young children can hypothesize about what they believe is in the mysterious brown paper bag. They can decide if they agree with the stuffed elephant and the puppy who maintain that it will be a "fierce pouncer" or if they agree with the stuffed bear's verdict that it is a new toy that must be coaxed out of the bag.

Hypothesizing about the subject, plot, or characters in a story helps children develop their cognitive skills and interests. It also motivates them to read or listen to literature. For example, before reading Ian Strachan's *The Flawed Glass,* older children can speculate about the author's purposes for using a plot that parallels the struggles of a girl with a physical handicap that makes it difficult to walk and to speak and the struggles of a weak eagle that tries to survive on the island. Before reading Patricia Lauber's *The News About Dinosaurs,* children can speculate about the content of the text.

Descriptive chapter titles and titles to subsections of books are excellent stimuli for verbal or written speculations by older children. For example, before reading or listening to Kathryn Lasky's *Think Like an Eagle: At Work with a Wildlife Photographer,* children can discuss what information they believe will be in each of the following sections: "A Walk Through the Night," "A Key to the Forest," "Dreams of Birds," "Corkscrew Swamp," "Thinking Like a Beaver," "Another Wilderness," and "The Last Golden Days." After reading each section, they can review the accuracy of their predictions.

Organizing. Young children have difficulty understanding concepts and sequences of time. Illustrated books for young children, such as Helen Oxenbury's *Dressing,* show the sequential order related to familiar activities. Books that allow children to follow changes in seasons increase children's understandings about sequences of time. In *Sky Tree: Seeing Science through Art,* Thomas Locker follows the seasonal cycle of a tree beginning in summer and progressing through the seasons until the tree again experiences summer. Lisa Westberg Peters's *October Smiled Back* portrays each of the months in both text and illustrations. Longer sequences of time are also presented in many books. For example, the organizational structure in Donald Hall's *Old Home Day* follows the evolution of a pond in New Hampshire from the Ice Age to the late 1990s. For older children, Kathryn Lasky's *Sugaring Time* follows the sequential order in which maple syrup is collected and processed, and Russell Freedman's *The Wright Brothers: How They Invented the Airplane* traces the major events in the lives of these two inventors.

Plot development in literature encourages children to learn forms of logical organization. After listening to or reading a literature selection, children can improve their abilities to put ideas into order by retelling the story or developing a creative drama based on the story. With their strong sequential plots and repetition of sequence and detail, folktales are especially appropriate for developing organizational skills. "The Little Red Hen" uses chronological order. The story progresses from the seed, to the planting, to the tilling, to the harvesting, to the baking, and finally to the eating.

"Why" tales also frequently depict a series of events to explain something. For example, Verna Aardema's *Why Mosquitoes Buzz in People's Ears: A West African Tale* describes the sequence of events that prevented the owl from waking the sun and bringing in a new day. Such folktales make excellent selections for flannelboard stories. When children retell the stories using the flannelgraphs or use the stories as the basis for creative drama, they develop and reinforce their organizational skills.

Summarizing.
Summarizing skills can be developed with literature of any genre or level of difficulty. Children may summarize stories orally or in writing. Oral summaries may motivate other children to read the same book or story. After a recreational reading period in the classroom, library, or home, members of the group can retell a story, retell the part of the story they liked best, discuss the most important information that they learned, describe the funniest part of the story, discuss the most exciting part, and describe the actions of the character they admired the most or the least.

Summaries can be related to specific content. For example, children can summarize the most important historical information in Rhoda Blumberg's *The Incredible Journey of Lewis & Clark* and *Commodore Perry in the Land of the Shogun,* or the most important scientific information in Patricia Lauber's *Volcano: The Eruption and Healing of Mount St. Helens.* They may summarize the major contributions of Theodore Roosevelt after reading Jean Fritz's *Bully for You, Teddy Roosevelt!* or of Eleanor Roosevelt after reading Russell Freedman's *Eleanor Roosevelt: A Life of Discovery.*

Applying and Responding.
Young children need many opportunities to apply the skills, concepts, information, or ideas in books. When children read concept books, for example, they should see and manipulate concrete examples, not merely look at pictures. Children who read Tana Hoban's *26 Letters and 99 Cents* can count and group objects. Children also can apply their counting skills when reading Paul Giganti's *How Many Snails? A Counting Book.*

How-to books provide numerous opportunities for applying directions found in the books. *Ed Emberley's Picture Pie 2: A Drawing Book and Stencil* includes a group of stencils and directions for turning the stencil drawings into various animal forms such as birds, lions, and mice. The step-by-step instructions show which shape to use, its color, its size, and where to place it. Denis Roche's *Loo-Loo, Boo, And Art You Can Do,* includes step-by-step instructions for making eleven art projects such as face masks, potato prints, and papier-mâché. Diane Rhoades's *Garden Crafts for Kids: 50 Great Reasons to Get Your Hands Dirty* includes detailed directions for accomplishing various garden projects. Photographs and drawings help clarify the instructions for tasks such as designing a garden, testing soil, and caring for the garden. They can follow directions for making clay models and compare the models with the illustrations in Joanne Oppenheim's *Have You Seen Birds?* Children also can read a humorous story about following directions in Eileen Browne's *No Problem* and then follow the instructions for constructing a paper airplane.

Criticizing.
Neither adults nor children should be required or encouraged to accept everything that they hear or read without criticism. Children should be given many opportunities to evaluate critically what they read or hear. Children develop critical evaluation skills when they sense the appropriateness, reliability, value, and authenticity of literature selections. Historical fiction selections are excellent for investigating and discussing the authenticity of plots, characters, and settings. For older readers, evaluation might include assessing the authenticity of biographies, such as Gary Schwartz's *Rembrandt* or informational books such as Francine Jacobs's *The Tainos: The People Who Welcomed Columbus* and Mary Barrett Brown's *Wings Along the Waterway.* Research indicates that the levels and types of questioning strategies used with children affect their levels of thinking and their development of critical evaluative skills.

Books provide many opportunities for students to critically evaluate the effectiveness of the literature. For example, older students can summarize the development of themes in Sharon Creech's *Walk Two Moons* and critically evaluate the effectiveness of the messages in developing themes, conflict, and characterization. Using Lloyd Alexander's *The Arkadians,* students can search for and critically evaluate the effectiveness of Alexander's use of Greek mythology in this modern fantasy. Using Carol Fenner's *Yolanda's Genius,* students can critically evaluate the effectiveness of Fenner's use of music to develop themes and characterizations.

Personality Development
According to George Maxim (1993), personality characteristics are "the traits that give each person a unique style of reacting to other people, places,

things, and events" (p. 81). To gain these traits, children go through many stages of personality development. Children gradually learn to express emotions acceptably, experience empathy toward others, and develop feelings of self-esteem.

Child development authority Joanne Hendrick (1992) states that children "pass through a series of stages of emotional development wherein basic attitudes are formed. Early childhood encompasses three of these: the stages of trust versus mistrust, autonomy versus shame and doubt, and initiative versus guilt" (p. 112). Hendrick maintains that people who work with children must foster mental health in young children by providing many opportunities to develop healthy emotional attitudes. Slowly, with guidance, children learn to handle their emotions productively rather than disruptively. Expanded experiences, adult and sibling models, and personal success show positive ways of dealing with emotions.

Overcoming fears, developing trust, relinquishing the desire to have only one's own way, and learning acceptable forms of interaction with both peers and adults inevitably involve traumatic experiences. Progressing through the stages of personality development is part of the maturing process, and books can play a very important role in that process. Chart 1–3 lists books that can promote children's personality development.

Bibliotherapy is interaction between readers and literature. In bibliotherapy, the ideas inherent in the reading materials have a therapeutic effect. Experts in child development frequently suggest bibliotherapy to help children through various times of stress, such as hospitalization, loss of a friend, and parents' divorce. Although most of the emotional problems that young children experience are not so severe as coping with loss and separation, all children must face numerous smaller crises that require personal adjustment. Literature can help children understand their feelings, identify with characters who experience similar feelings, and gain new insights into how others have coped with the same problems. According to Masha Rudman and Anna Pearce (1988), "Books can serve as mirrors for children, reflecting their appearance, their relationships, their feelings and thoughts in their immediate environment" (p. 159). In addition, books can act as windows on the world, inviting children to look beyond themselves and to form bonds with characters and circumstances.

Joan Glazer (1991) identifies four ways in which literature contributes to the emotional growth of children. First, literature shows children that many of their feelings are common to other children and that those feelings are normal and natural. Second, literature explores a feeling from several viewpoints, giving a fuller picture and providing a basis for naming the feeling. Third, actions of various characters show options for ways of dealing with particular emotions. Fourth, literature makes clear that one person experiences many emotions and that these emotions sometimes conflict.

Jan Ross (1993) emphasizes that because children are small and are constantly dwarfed by their environment, they frequently suffer from lack of self-esteem. She states:

Books can help children understand that size is relative. Mary Norton's "Borrowers" books, which concern tiny creatures who live in people's houses and survive by "borrowing" from "Human Beans," are wonderful examples. After all, if Arriety, who is small enough to stand in a child's hand, can be stalwart, then surely a child can be, too. (p. 53)

Animal characters in books for young children frequently act very much like people. The problems that the characters face, especially their fears, can assist the personality development of young children. Books with animal characters are very satisfying for readers because the authors allow the animal characters to face and overcome common fears and emotions. For example, Martin Waddell's *Can't You Sleep, Little Bear?* focuses on a young bear's fear of the dark. In *Let's Go Home, Little Bear,* Waddell's characters focus on overcoming fears of sounds. In both books, Big Bear's compassion and understanding help the young bear overcome his fears. The bear in Sarah Hayes's *This Is the Bear and the Scary Night* is a teddy bear who has a series of misadventures when he is accidently left out in the park. Fortunately, he is rescued and finally reunited with the boy who loves him. The circus dog in Lisa Campbell Ernst's *Ginger Jumps* overcomes fear of jumping because of the companionship of an understanding girl. Searching for identity is a common theme in books with young animal characters. In Molly Bang's *Goose,* a goose egg falls out of the nest, and the baby is raised by a loving family of woodchucks. The baby goose, however, feels like an outsider until she discovers that she has her own

CHART 1-3 (P. 25–28)   Personality development

Characteristics	Implications	Literature Suggestions
Preschool: Ages Two–Three 1 Children begin to think that they have an identity separate from that of other members of the family. 2 Children feel the need for security.	1 Help children understand that they are people who have their own identity and their own worth. 2 Hold a child during lap reading to add to a sense of security and enjoyment of books.	Duke, Kate. *Clean-Up Day.* Henkes, Kevin. *Owen.* Holzenthaler, Jean. *My Hands Can.* Carlstrom, Nancy. *Jesse Bear, What Will You Wear?* Lindgren, Barbro. *The Wild Baby.* Murphy, Mary. *I Like It When . . .* Waddell, Martin. *Can't You Sleep, Little Bear?*
Preschool: Ages Three–Four 1 Children have developed a fairly steady self-concept; they identify themselves as "I" and have sets of feelings about themselves. 2 Children require warm and secure environments. 3 Children hide from unhappy situations by withdrawing, suggesting that problems don't exist, or blaming someone else. 4 Children begin to become aware of their cultural heritage.	1 Children's self-concepts are affected by attitudes and behavior of those around them, so make them feel that others care about them, accept them, and think they are worthy. 2 Share books with children in a warm atmosphere in classrooms, in libraries, or at home. 3 Give special guidance to help children accept mistakes without decreasing their feelings of self-worth. 4 Children need to be proud of who they are, so provide literature to stress cultural contributions and the contributions of the home and neighborhood.	Harris, Robie H. *Happy Birth Day!* Jonas, Ann. *When You Were a Baby.* Krauss, Ruth. *The Carrot Seed.* Pomerantz, Charlotte. *Flap Your Wings and Try.* Rylant, Cynthia. *Birthday Presents.* Wahl, Jan. *Humphrey's Bear.* Ashforth, Camilla. *Monkey Tricks.* Babbit, Natalie. *BUB: Or the Very Best Thing.* Dabcovich, Lydia. *Sleepy Bear.* Hill, Eric. *Spot's Birthday Party.* McPhail, David. *The Dream Child.* Rice, Eve. *Benny Bakes a Cake.* Cazet, Denys. *A Fish in His Pocket.* Sharmat, Marjorie. *A Big Fat Enormous Lie.* Adoff, Arnold. *Black Is Brown Is Tan.* Bunting, Eve. *The Wednesday Surprise.*
Preschool: Ages Four–Five 1 Children continue to be egocentric: they talk in first person and consider themselves the center of the world.	1 Present literature in which children can identify with the character and the story.	Cutler, Jane. *Darcy and Gran Don't Like Babies.* Engel, Diana. *Josephina Hates Her Name.* Henkes, Kevin. *Chrysanthemum.* Hest, Amy. *The Purple Coat.* Mark, Jan. *Fun.* Small, David. *Imogene's Antlers.* Vincent, Gabrielle. *Feel Better, Ernest!*

CHART 1–3 *Continued*

Characteristics	Implications	Literature Suggestions
Preschool: Ages Four–Five		
2 Children improve in their ability to handle their own emotions in productive ways.	2 Help children identify other ways to handle problems. Use literature to help them see how others handle their emotions.	Ernst, Lisa Campbell. *Ginger Jumps.* Keats, Ezra Jack. *Peter's Chair.* McCully, Emily Arnold. *New Baby.* Naylor, Phyllis Reynolds. *Keeping a Christmas Secret.* Steig, William. *Spinky Sulks.* Viorst, Judith. *Alexander and the Terrible, Horrible, No Good, Very Bad Day.* Wood, Audrey. *The Rude Giants.*
3 Fears of unknown situations cause children to lose confidence and to lose control of their emotions.	3 Help children understand what is new to them and help them feel comfortable with their ability to handle unknown situations. Read about and discuss new situations.	Carle, Eric. *Do You Want to Be My Friend?* Rockwell, Harlow. *My Dentist.* Rogers, Fred. *Going to Day Care.*
4 Children begin to respond to intrinsic motivation.	4 Children require good models for intrinsic motivation, so provide books as sources of models.	Bunting, Eve. *The Mother's Day Mice.* Vincent, Gabrielle. *Feel Better, Ernest!* dePaola, Tomie. *Christopher: The Holy Giant.* Wells, Rosemary. *McDuff Moves In.*
5 Children require warm and secure environments.	5 Continue reading to children in a loving atmosphere.	
Preschool—Kindergarten: Ages Five–Six		
1 Children are usually outgoing, sociable, and friendly.	1 Read stories showing outgoing, sociable, and friendly characteristics in the main characters.	Flournoy, Valerie. *The Patchwork Quilt.* Johnson, Angela. *Tell Me a Story, Mama.* Marshall, James. *George and Martha One Fine Day.* Rosenberg, Liz. *Monster Mama.* Bang, Molly. *Goose.* Day, Alexandra. *Frank and Ernest Play Ball.*
2 Children are quite stable and adjusted in their emotional life; they are developing self-assurance and confidence in others.	2 Encourage children to develop self-assurance and confidence in others. Provide opportunities for children to expand self-assurance—it is closely related to self-worth.	Howard, Arthur. *When I Was Five.* Ormerod, Jan. *Sunshine.* Purdy, Carol. *Least of All.* Rathmann, Peggy. *Ruby the Copycat.* Seuss, Dr. *Oh, the Places You'll Go!*

CHART 1–3   *Continued*

Characteristics	Implications	Literature Suggestions
Preschool—Kindergarten: Ages Five–Six 3 Children require warmth and security in adult relationships even though self-assurance increases.	3 Continue to provide warm relationships through a close association during story time.	Brown, Margaret Wise. *The Runaway Bunny.* Curtis, Jamie Lee. *Tell Me Again About the Night I Was Born.* Hest, Amy. *The Crack-of-Dawn Walkers.* Slate, Joseph. *Miss Bindergarten Gets Ready for Kindergarten.* Stewart, Sarah. *The Gardener.* Zolotow, Charlotte. *My Grandson Lew.*
Early Elementary: Ages Six–Eight 1 Children are not so emotionally stable as before; they show more tension and may strike out against a teacher or parent. 2 Children seek independence from adults but continue to require warmth and security from the adults in their lives.	1 Help children discover acceptable ways to handle their tensions. Read stories to illustrate how other children handle their tensions. 2 Provide opportunities for children to demonstrate independence; allow them to choose books and activities for sharing. Supply books in which characters develop independence.	Ehrlich, Amy. *Leo, Zack, and Emmie.* Hesse, Karen. *Lester's Dog.* Jukes, Mavis. *I'll See You in My Dreams.* ————. *Like Jake and Me.* Khalsa, Dayal Kaur. *I Want a Dog.* Preston, Edna Mitchell, and Rainey Bennett. *The Temper Tantrum Book.* Cleary, Beverly. *Ramona Quimby, Age 8.* Demi. *One Grain of Rice: A Mathematical Folktale.* Rankin, Joan. *Wow! It's Great Being a Duck.* Waddell, Martin. *What Use Is a Moose?* Williams, Vera B. *Something Special for Me.* Zamorano, Ana. *Let's Eat!*
Middle Elementary: Ages Eight–Ten 1 The personality characteristic of cooperation is highly valued by fourth graders but declines in later grades. 2 Children have fewer fears about immediate and possible dangers but may have strong fears about remote or impossible situations, such as ghosts, lions, and witches.	1 Encourage literature activities that allow for cooperation; provide books stressing cooperation as the theme. 2 Use literature selections describing children's fears for discussion and developing understanding of realistic fears.	Baylor, Byrd. *The Best Town in the World.* George, Jean Craighead. *The First Thanksgiving.* Brittain, Bill. *The Wish Giver.* McCully, Emily Arnold. *Mirette on the High Wire.*

CHART 1–3 *Continued*

Characteristics	Implications	Literature Suggestions
Upper Elementary: Ages Ten–Twelve 1 Many children have internalized their control; they believe that they are in control of what happens and assume personal responsibility for their successes and failures.	1 Reinforce responsibility, organizing, and making decisions. Provide books that illustrate the development of internalized control.	Cleary, Beverly. *Dear Mr. Henshaw.* Fox, Paula. *One-Eyed Cat.* Hesse, Karen. *The Music of Dolphins.* Kinsey-Warnock, Natalie. *As Long As There Are Mountains.* Lowry, Lois. *The Giver.* MacLachlan, Patricia. *The Facts and Fictions of Minna Pratt.* ————. *Sarah, Plain and Tall.* Macy, Sue. *Winning Ways: A Photohistory of American Women in Sports.*
2 Children value independence as a personality trait.	2 Supply literature to illustrate developing independence for both male and female characters.	Farmer, Nancy. *A Girl Named Disaster.* O'Dell, Scott. *Island of the Blue Dolphins.* Park, Ruth. *Playing Beatie Bow.* Radley, Gail. *The Golden Days.* Sperry, Armstrong. *Call It Courage.* Staples, Suzanne Fisher. *Shabanu: Daughter of the Wind.* Voigt, Cynthia. *Dicey's Song.* ————. *A Solitary Blue.*
3 Rapid changes in physical growth may cause some children to become self-conscious and self-critical; others may be preoccupied with their appearance.	3 Provide stories of other children who experience problems growing during this time.	Hughes, Dean. *Team Picture.* Kehret, Peg. *Small Steps: The Year I Got Polio.* Krull, Kathleen. *Wilma Unlimited: How Wilma Rudolph Became the World's Fastest Woman.* Paterson, Katherine. *Come Sing, Jimmy Jo.*

Sources: Hendrick (1992); Mussen, Conger, and Kagan (1989); and Sarafino and Armstrong (1986).

special abilities: She can fly. Now she is able to be herself and return to her adoptive family.

Many of these books are very satisfying for readers because the authors allow animal characters to face and overcome common emotions. For example, *In the Rain with Baby Duck,* by Amy Hest, allows Baby Duck to discover that when his mother was little she also disliked rain, puddles, mud, and getting her feet wet. Grampa Duck solves the problem by giving Baby Duck the umbrella and boots that his mother wore when she was young. This text shows that two generations had the same feelings about going out in the rain.

Jealousy is an emotion that is familiar to most children when they feel threatened by a new baby. Books about new babies can help children express their fears and realize that their parents still love them but that it is not unusual to feel fearful about a

In Can't You Sleep, Little Bear?, *a young bear experiences fears that are similar to those expressed by children. Illustration from* Can't You Sleep, Little Bear? *by Martin Waddell. Illustration © 1988 Barbara Firth. Used by permission of Candlewick Press, Cambridge, MA.*

new relationship. Ezra Jack Keats's *Peter's Chair* shows how one child handles fear and jealousy when he not only gets an unwanted baby sister but also sees his own furniture painted pink for the new arrival. The main character in Marisabina Russo's *Waiting for Hannah* questions her mother about preparations made for her birth.

In Jacqueline Martin's *Buzzy Bones and the Lost Quilt,* a mouse child experiences troubled dreams when he loses his security quilt. An understanding uncle and numerous friends help him search for the quilt. After the tattered quilt is found, the friends create a new quilt that includes pieces from the old one. Thus, books can help children anticipate and prepare themselves for situations that frighten them.

Many children fear going to school for the first time or moving into a new school or neighborhood. In *Miss Bindergarten Gets Ready for Kindergarten,* Joseph Slate creates two parallel stories as both the teacher, who is a black and white dog, and a group of animals prepare for the first day of school. All the animals except a reluctant iguana discover a

very satisfying experience. In Kathryn Lasky's *Lunch Bunnies,* Clyde worries about all the terrible things that might happen during lunch on his first day of school. Fortunately, the experience is more pleasant than he imagined. Eric Carle's *Do You Want to Be My Friend?,* Miriam Cohen's *Will I Have a Friend?,* and Rosemary Wells's *Timothy Goes to School* present heroes who successfully cope with this problem. The conflict between individuality and conformity provides the plot in Peggy Rathmann's *Ruby the Copycat.* Many children who are unsure of their capabilities relate to this story of a girl who feels so unsure of herself that she copies a classmate's actions. By the end of the story, the girl discovers that she has her own creative resources. In fact, she is so good at hopping that the class now copies her. In Kevin Henkes's *Chrysanthemum,* a mouse child experiences problems adjusting to other children in school who make fun of her name. An understanding adult helps her learn to appreciate her name. Harlow Rockwell has written and illustrated *My Doctor* and *My Dentist* to help answer young children's questions about the procedures and equipment used during physical and dental checkups.

The necessity of love is developed as an important theme in Martin Waddell's humorous book, *What Use Is a Moose?* The theme develops as Jack brings a moose home and tries to justify the animal's presence in his home. Jack fails miserably as he tries to show the usefulness of the animal only to have his mother banish the moose. When Jack becomes very unhappy, his mother realizes that being loved is a good use for a moose.

Literature provides children with many examples of how to cope with anger. Many children have days when absolutely nothing goes right. Books can act as stimuli for discussing how children handled or could have handled similar situations. Young children, for example, can certainly identify with Judith Viorst's Alexander in *Alexander and the Terrible, Horrible, No Good, Very Bad Day* or with Patricia Giff's Ronald in *Today Was a Terrible Day.* Edna Mitchell Preston and Rainey Bennett's *The Temper Tantrum Book* shows that even animals can have tantrums, and the animals explain what makes them angry. The book can prompt children to share what makes them angry and to explain how they deal with this problem. Betsy Everitt's *Mean Soup* shows that a child, with his mother's assistance, can release anger through proper channels rather than by locking it inside.

Literature can play a dramatic role in helping children develop positive and realistic self-concepts. Infants do not think of themselves as individuals. Between the ages of two and three, children slowly begin to realize that they have identities separate from those of other members of the family. By age three, with the assistance of warm, loving environments, most children have developed a set of feelings about themselves; they consider themselves "I."

Egocentric feelings continue for several years, and children consider themselves the center of the universe. If the development of self-esteem is to progress positively, children need to know that their families, friends, and the larger society value them. Valerie Flournoy's *The Patchwork Quilt,* Jane Yolen's *Owl Moon,* and Karen Ackerman's *Song and Dance Man* are books in which children are valued by family members.

Books also show children that it is all right to be different from their families. Jan Mark's *Fun* shows that a boy who prefers quiet, contemplative activities can be happy living with an active, boisterous mother and father.

Books that stress creative problem solving are especially valuable for the personal development of young children. Denys Cazet's *A Fish in His Pocket* follows a young bear who accidently causes the death of a fish, discovers a solution to the problem, and concludes a satisfactory ending to his dilemma. In Dayal Kaur Khalsa's *I Want a Dog,* a young girl finds a way to show her parents that she will be ready to take care of a dog when she is old enough to own a pet. Her solution, to practice taking care of a roller skate as if it were a dog, is both novel and humorous. In Amy Hest's *The Purple Coat,* a young girl finds a way to have the purple coat she wants and still have the navy blue coat preferred by her mother. The reversible coat results when Gabrielle and her grandfather work on the problem together.

Picture storybooks written for younger children may help children cope with the loss of a loved one, especially an older member of the family. In these books animals frequently face problems similar to those of young humans. Margaret Wild's *Old Pig* develops such a theme as Old Pig and Granddaughter share a last evening in which they take a walk together, taste the rain, and hold each other tight as Old Pig lovingly prepares Granddaughter for their final separation.

A young girl and her grandfather share many happy experiences in Rosemary Wells's *The Language of Doves.* Grandfather tells Julietta how he and his carrier pigeons (doves) sent messages during World War I. Now Grandfather continues to raise doves. After Grandfather dies, Julietta is heartbroken when the doves are sold. Her grief is lightened when a dove flies home with a final message from her grandfather.

In a book for slightly older readers, *When Dinosaurs Die: A Guide to Understanding Death,* Laurie Krasny Brown and Marc Brown provide a more detailed exploration of death by asking and answering questions such as "Why does someone die?" and "What does dead mean?" Various emotions and feelings about death are explored through the text. The book concludes with a positive section, "Ways to Remember Someone."

Divorce is another emotional and stressful experience faced by many children. Fred Rogers's *Let's Talk About It: Divorce* provides examples of ways that children can deal with their emotions. Through such statements as "Their divorce is not your fault," Rogers approaches one of the greatest concerns of young children and provides them with reassurance. Rogers recommends that adults use this book to discuss the topic with children. Photographs show three families whose members are experiencing divorce.

Adoption is another emotional experience. In *Tell Me Again About the Night I Was Born,* Jamie Lee Curtis tells a story that develops a loving relationship between the child and the adoptive parents. This book encourages children to overcome fear by celebrating adoption and suggesting that it is a very important decision for both parents and children.

Several excellent books for older children are based on the themes of overcoming problems. In Scott O'Dell's *Island of the Blue Dolphins,* a girl survives alone on an island off the coast of California. She is not rescued for eighteen years and must overcome loneliness, develop weapons that violate a taboo of her society, and create a life for herself. Gary Paulsen's *Hatchet* follows a boy as he learns about personal and physical survival in the Canadian wilderness. *Call It Courage,* by Armstrong Sperry, is another survival book. In this book, a boy must overcome his fear of the sea before he can return home. Survival during the Holocaust is devel-

In Wilma Unlimited: How Wilma Rudolph Became the World's Fastest Woman *by Kathleen Krull, readers learn about overcoming daunting obstacles and reaching for goals. (Illustration from* WILMA UNLIMITED: HOW WILMA RUDOLPH BECAME THE WORLD'S FASTEST WOMAN *by Kathleen Krull, Copyright ©1996 By David Diaz, reproduced by permission of Harcourt Brace & Company.)*

oped in Livia Bitton-Jackson's *I Have Lived A Thousand Years: Growing Up in the Holocaust* as the heroine survives the ghetto, labor camps, and Auschwitz. Her bravery and determination help her realize that she is happy to be Jewish.

All children must feel pride in their accomplishments and cultural heritage and must develop positive sex-role identifications. Those who develop positive feelings of self-worth will be able to assume responsibility for their own successes and failures. Literature can help young children discover the capabilities they have and realize that acquiring some skills takes considerable time. For example, in Ezra Jack Keats's *Whistle for Willie,* Peter tries and tries to whistle. After considerable practice, he finally learns this skill. Books such as Jean Holzenthaler's *My Hands Can* help children realize that they can do many things. The importance of feeling pride in one's accomplishments is developed in Florence Parry Heide and Judith Heide Gilliland's *The Day of Ahmed's Secret.* This story, set in Cairo, follows a boy through his day of work and encourages readers to empathize with his excitement as he shares his secret with his family: He can write his own name.

The importance of using talent and wisely maintaining one's dreams are important themes in Oliver Dunrea's *The Painter Who Loved Chickens.* In this story the painter discovers that it is possible to both live where he wants to live—on a farm—and paint the

subjects he wants to paint—chickens. Dunrea develops this important message when "The painter became famous. And he never again painted anything that he did not love to paint" (unnumbered). Helen Lester's *Author: A True Story* focuses on how the author overcame both learning disabilities as a child and rejection slips as an adult to become an author of children's books. Kathleen Krull's *Wilma Unlimited: How Wilma Rudolph Became the World's Fastest Woman* provides an excellent model for achievement through overcoming obstacles that would discourage many people. She overcame polio, competed in a male-dominated sport, and as an African American grew up in the segregated South of the 1940s. Another book that emphasizes the accomplishments of female sports stars is Sue Macy's *Winning Ways: A Photohistory of American Women in Sports.*

Positive attitudes toward one's heritage can be reinforced through reading about the contributions of the people who belong to that heritage. In addition, books can provide excellent role models and illustrate that both males and females can function successfully in many different roles.

Personality development in children is extremely important. If children do not understand themselves and believe that they are important, how can they value anyone else? Many literary selections and literature-related experiences reinforce positive personality development. Such experiences include

The Child Responds to Literature 31

A review of many series books suggests that terror is stalking children. This same conclusion may be reached by viewing current television programs and movies. Compilations of bestselling children's books such as those reported monthly in *Publishers Weekly*[1] suggest that children are buying and/or reading the books in record numbers. Two series by R. L. Stine, "Goosebumps" and "Fear Street," are bestsellers.

In an article in *The New York Times,* Doreen Carvajal[2] discusses this phenomena as books, movies, and television become "grittier, scarier, edgier, and more violent than ever before" (p. E. 5) and seem to appeal to younger and younger audiences. Carvajal reports both positive and negative responses to this increase in frightening content.

On the positive side, publishers report that they are trying to make books as interesting and exciting as television. In addition, publishers argue that the scary content entices reluctant readers to read books.

In contrast, Carvajal cites responses of experts on child behavior who are concerned with the increase in nightmares and other responses by young children. Carvajal states, "Some librarians worry about the impact on girls who are often featured as victims of violence. There are also female characters who can dish out violence as well as take it—the high-school heroine of Buffy the Vampire Slayer, for example. Are TV portrayals of feminine aptitudes for violence a good thing? A bad thing? Both?" (p. E. 5).

Ask yourself these same three questions as you read a book with particularly scary content. Also, what is your response to Carvajal's concluding paragraph? "Ms. Pipher (a psychologist and author) advises parents to form small co-ooperatives to share information about books, films and television programs appropriate for their children. 'My grandmother used to tell me to choose your books like your own friends,' she said. Grandma never had friends like these" (p. E. 5).

---

[1] "Publishers Weekly: Children's Bestsellers." *Publishers Weekly* 244 (July 21, 1997): 177.

[2] Carvajal, Doreen. "In Kids' Pop Culture, Fear Rules." *The New York Times.* Sunday, June 1, 1997, E. 5.

---

reading orally in a warm and secure environment, discussing and acting out various roles from literature, and simply enjoying a wide variety of literature.

Social Development

According to David Shaffer (1989), socialization "is the process by which children acquire the beliefs, values, and behaviors deemed significant and appropriate by the older members of their society" (p. 560). Shaffer identifies three ways in which socialization serves society: (1) as a means of regulating children's behavior and controlling their undesirable or antisocial impulses, (2) as a way to promote the personal growth of the individual, and (3) as a means to perpetuate the social order. George Maxim (1993) emphasizes the role of literature in influencing positive racial and cultural attitudes. He believes that we must start to integrate multicultural education into the curriculum of the very young by enhancing self-concepts and cultural identity, developing social skills and responsibility, broadening the cultural base of the curriculum, and studying particular groups. To meet this multicultural component, Maxim recommends reading or telling stories that describe the lives of people in other cultures, inviting guest speakers from other cultures, visiting museums, and playing with games and toys from various cultures. Chart 1–4 lists books that can promote the social development of children.

Socialization. Socialization is said to occur when children learn the ways of their groups so that they can function acceptably within those groups. Children must learn to exert control over aggressive and hostile behavior if they are to have acceptable relationships with family members, friends, and the larger community. Acceptable relationships require an understanding of the feelings and viewpoints of others. Quite obviously,

CHART 1–4 (PP. 33–38)   Social Development

Characteristics	Implications	Literature Suggestions
Preschool: Ages Two–Three 1 Children learn to organize and represent their world; they imitate actions and behaviors they have observed. 2 Children transform things into make-believe: a yardstick may be a horse.	1 Encourage children to role-play so they can begin to take others' points of view and learn about other behavior. 2 Provide objects and books that suggest creative interpretations.	Carle, Eric. *The Mixed-Up Chameleon.* Oxenbury, Helen. *Family.* Steptoe, John. *Baby Says.* Hutchins, Pat. *Changes, Changes.*
Preschool: Ages Three–Four 1 Children begin to realize that other people have feelings, just as they do. 2 Children enjoy playing together and develop strong attachments to other children. 3 Children begin to enjoy participating in group activities and group games. 4 Children begin to identify others' feelings by observing facial expressions.	1 Encourage children to talk about how they felt when something similar happened to them; provide books that show feelings. 2 Encourage the growing social skills of sharing, taking turns, and playing cooperatively. 3 Let children be both leaders and followers during group activities after reading a book. 4 Encourage children to become sensitive to their own and others' feelings by talking about the feelings that accompany different facial expressions in books.	Alexander, Martha. *Nobody Asked Me If I Wanted a Baby Sister.* Keats, Ezra Jack. *Peter's Chair.* McBratney, Sam. *Guess How Much I Love You.* Winthrop, Elizabeth. *Bear and Mrs. Duck.* Cohen, Miriam. *Best Friends.* Hoban, Russell. *Best Friends for Frances.* Lindgren, Barbro. *Sam's Ball.* Bulla, Clyde. *Keep Running, Allen!* Scott, Ann Herbert. *Sam.* Berger, Terry. *I Have Feelings.* Bonsall, Crosby. *It's Mine!—A Greedy Book.* Henkes, Kevin. *Jessica.* Hutchins, Pat. *Where's the Baby?* Wells, Rosemary. *Bunny Cakes.*
Preschool: Ages Four–Five 1 Children start to avoid aggression when angry and to look for compromises. They are, however, frequently bossy, assertive, and prone to using alibis. 2 Children begin to understand consequences of good and bad and may engage in unacceptable behavior to elicit reactions.	1 Praise children for talking out anger, help them to calm down and talk about the situation, direct them toward finding solutions. Choose books in which aggression is avoided. 2 Explain actions in terms that children understand. Let children discuss alternative actions.	Reiser, Lynn. *Best Friends Think Alike.* Vincent, Gabrielle. *Smile, Ernest and Celestine.* Viorst, Judith. *I'll Fix Anthony.* Zolotow, Charlotte. *The Quarreling Book.* Galdone, Paul. *The Little Red Hen.* Gross, Theodore Faro. *Everyone Asked About You.* Hadithi, Mwenye. *Crafty Chameleon.*

CHART 1–4 *Continued*

Characteristics	Implications	Literature Suggestions
Preschool: Ages Four–Five		
3 Children seldom play alone, but they begin to work by themselves.	3 Encourage persistence; let children work at something until it is completed to their satisfaction. This is crucial for problem solving and self-directed learning.	Burton, Virginia Lee. *Mike Mulligan and His Steam Shovel.* Carle, Eric. *The Very Busy Spider.* Morozumi, Atsuko. *My Friend Gorilla.*
4 Children increase their awareness of the different roles people play—nurse, police officer, grocery clerk, man, woman, etc.	4 Provide opportunities to meet different kinds of people through real life and books: encourage dramatic play around different roles.	Barton, Byron. *I Want to Be an Astronaut.* Rockwell, Harlow. *My Doctor.*
5 Children exhibit unreasonable fears, such as fear of the dark, thunder, and animals.	5 Help children overcome fears by sharing experiences of others who had fears but overcame them.	Bunting, Eve. *Ghost's Hour, Spook's Hour.* Ernst, Lisa Campbell. *Ginger Jumps.*
Preschool—Kindergarten: Ages Five–Six		
1 Children like to help parents around the house; they are developing dependable behavior.	1 Allow children to be responsible for jobs that they can realistically complete. Read stories about children helping.	Rice, Eve. *Benny Bakes a Cake.* Rylant, Cynthia. *When I Was Young in the Mountains.* Williams, Vera B. *A Chair for My Mother.*
2 Children protect younger brothers and sisters and other children.	2 Let children help and read to younger children, encourage them to become aware that they are growing into independent people. Share reasons why all people need security.	Howe, James. *There's a Monster Under My Bed.* Hughes, Shirley. *Dogger.* Schwartz, Amy. *Annabelle Swift, Kindergartner.* Waggoner, Karen. *The Lemonade Babysitter.*
3 Children are proud of their accomplishments; they take pride in going to school and in their possessions.	3 Encourage a feeling of self-worth: praise accomplishments, encourage children to share school and home experiences, and allow them to talk about their possessions.	Fassler, Joan. *Howie Helps Himself.* Miller, Margaret. *Now I'm Big.* Schwartz, Amy. *Annabelle Swift, Kindergartner.* Udry, Janice May. *What Mary Jo Shared.*
4 Children continue to show anxiety and unreasonable fear.	4 Help children overcome their fears and anxieties; stress that these are normal.	James, Betsy. *Mary Ann.* Waber, Bernard. *Ira Sleeps Over.* Wells, Rosemary. *Timothy Goes to School.*

CHART 1-4 *Continued*

Characteristics	Implications	Literature Suggestions
Preschool—Kindergarten: Ages Five–Six 5 Children enjoy playing outside on their favorite toys, such as tricycles and sleds.	5 Provide opportunities for play, discussions about play, reading and drawing about outside play, and dictating stories about outside play.	Keats, Ezra Jack. *The Snowy Day.* McLeod, Emilie Warren. *The Bear's Bicycle.* Martin, Rafe. *Will's Mammoth.* Smalls-Hector, Irene. *Jonathan and His Mommy.*
6 Children enjoy excursions to new places and familiar ones.	6 Plan trips to zoos, fire stations, historic sites, and such. Read about these places, encourage children to tell about family trips.	Asch, Frank. *Moonbear's Pet.* Coy, John. *Night Driving.* Griffith, Helen V. *Grandaddy's Place.*
7 Children enjoy dressing up, role playing, and creative play.	7 Provide opportunities for children to dress up and play different roles. Read stories that can be used for creative play.	Aardema, Verna. *Who's in Rabbit's House?* Cauley, Lorinda Bryan. *Goldilocks and the Three Bears.* Ichikawa, Satomi. *Nora's Castle.* Wells, Rosemary. *Max and Ruby's First Greek Myth: Pandora's Box.*
Early Elementary: Ages Six–Eight 1 Children may defy parents when they are under pressure; they have difficulty getting along with younger siblings.	1 Encourage children to become more sensitive to family needs and to talk and read stories about similar situations. Direct children toward finding solutions.	Blume, Judy. *The One in the Middle Is the Green Kangaroo.* Flournoy, Valerie. *The Patchwork Quilt.* Hartmann, Wendy, and Niki Daly, *The Dinosaurs Are Back and It's All Your Fault Edward!* Hoberman, Mary Ann. *Mr. and Mrs. Muddle.* Ness, Evaline. *Sam, Bangs, and Moonshine.* Nomura, Takaaki. *Grandpa's Town.* Sendak, Maurice. *Where the Wild Things Are.*
2 Children want to play with other children but frequently insist on being first.	2 Encourage children both to lead and follow, read books in which children overcome similar problems.	Kellogg, Steven. *Best Friends.* Udry, Janice May. *Let's Be Enemies.*

CHART 1–4 *Continued*

Characteristics	Implications	Literature Suggestions
Early Elementary: Ages Six–Eight 3 Children respond to teachers' help or praise. They try to conform and please teachers.	3 Allow children to share work and receive praise. Show and tell is especially enjoyable for six- and seven-year-olds. Praise their reading and sharing of books.	Henkes, Kevin. *Lilly's Purple Plastic Purse.* Lobel, Arnold. *Frog and Toad All Year.* Van Leeuwen, Jean. *More Tales of Oliver Pig.*
4 Children enjoy sitting still and listening to stories read at school, at home, or in the library.	4 Provide frequent storytelling and story-reading times.	Fleischman, Sid. *The Scarebird.* Godden, Rumer. *Premlata and the Festival of Lights.* Hutton, Warwick. *Persephone.* Melmed, Laura Krauss. *Little Oh.* Say, Allen. *Grandfather's Journey.*
5 Children have definite inflexible ideas of right and wrong.	5 Discuss attitudes and standards of conduct in books.	Barbour, Karen. *Mr. Bow Tie.* Friedman, Ina R. *How My Parents Learned to Eat.* Hanson, Regina. *The Face At the Window.* Schotter, Roni. *Captain Snap and the Children of Vinegar Lane.* Wild, Margaret. *Mr. Nick's Knitting.*
6 Children are curious about differences between boys and girls.	6 Ask children questions about differences between boys and girls and where babies come from. Provide books that help answer such questions.	Andry, Andrew, and Steven Schepp. *How Babies Are Made.*
Middle Elementary: Ages Eight–Ten 1 Concepts of right and wrong become more flexible; the situation in which the wrong action occurred is taken into consideration.	1 Provide experiences and books to help children relate to different points of view; they begin to realize there are attitudes, values, and standards different from those their parents stress.	Bradley, Kimberly. *Ruthie's Gift.* Callen, Larry. *Who Kidnapped the Sheriff? Tales from Tickfaw.* Goble, Paul. *The Girl Who Loved Wild Horses.*
2 Children begin to be influenced by their peer groups.	2 Read and discuss books in which peer groups become more important; these groups can influence attitudes, values, and interests.	Allard, Harry. *Miss Nelson Is Missing.* Soto, Gary. *Taking Sides.*

CHART 1–4 *Continued*

Characteristics	Implications	Literature Suggestions
Middle Elementary: Ages Eight–Ten 3 Children's thinking is becoming socialized; children can understand other people's points of view. They feel that their reasoning and solutions to problems should agree with others.	3 Provide many opportunities for children to investigate differing points of view. Literature is an excellent source.	Byars, Betsy. *The Animal, the Vegetable, and John D. Jones.* Lacapa, Kathleen, and Michael Lacapa. *Less Than Half, More Than Whole.* Monjo, F. N. *The Drinking Gourd.* Peet, Bill. *Bill Peet: An Autobiography.* Sandin, Joan. *The Long Way to a New Land.*
Upper Elementary: Ages Ten–Twelve 1 Children have developed racial attitudes; low-prejudiced children increase in perception of nonracial characteristics; high-prejudiced children increase in perception of racial characteristics.	1 Provide literature and instructional activities to develop multiethnic values and stress contributions of ethnic minorities.	Adoff, Arnold. *All the Colors of the Race.* ———. *Malcolm X.* Freedman, Russell. *An Indian Winter.* Highwater, Jamake. *Anpao—An American Indian Odyssey.* McKissack, Patricia, and Fredrick McKissack. *The Civil Rights Movement in America from 1865 to the Present.* Paulsen, Gary. *Dogsong.* Soto, Gary. *Neighborhood Odes.* Cobb, Vicki, and Kathy Darling. *Bet You Can't! Science Impossibilities to Fool You.*
2 Children want to do jobs well instead of starting and exploring them; feelings of inferiority and inadequacy may result if children feel that they cannot measure up to their own personal standards. 3 Children have a sense of justice and resist imperfections in the world.	2 Encourage expansion of knowledge in high-interest areas; provide books in these areas; provide assistance and encouragement to allow children to finish jobs to meet their expectations. 3 Read and discuss stories where people overcome injustice, improve some aspect of life, or raise questions about life.	Arnold, Caroline. *Saving the Peregrine Falcon.* Carr, Terry. *Spill: The Story of the Exxon Valdez.* Kuklin, Susan. *Irrepressible Spirit.* Lasky, Kathryn. *The Night Journey.* Lowry, Lois. *Number the Stars.* Riskind, Mary. *Apple Is My Sign.* Severance, John B. *Gandhi, Great Soul.* Yates, Elizabeth. *Amos Fortune, Free Man.*

CHART 1-4 *Continued*

Characteristics	Implications	Literature Suggestions
Upper Elementary: Ages Ten–Twelve 4 Peer groups exert strong influences on children; conformity to parents decreases and conformity to peers increases in social situations. Children may challenge their parents.	4 If differences between peer and family values are too great, children may experience conflicts. Provide literature selections and discussions to help.	Brooks, Bruce. *The Moves Make the Man.* Byars, Betsy. *The Cybil War.* Fine, Anne. *The Book of the Banshee.* Greenberg, Jan. *The Iceberg and Its Shadow.* Hahn, Mary Downing. *Stepping on the Cracks.* Lisle, Janet Taylor. *Afternoon of the Elves.* Slepian, Jan. *Risk N' Roses.*
5 Children have developed strong associations with gender-typed expectations: Girls may fail in "masculine" tasks; boys in "feminine" tasks.	5 Provide books and discussions that avoid sex-stereotyped roles; emphasize that both sexes can succeed in many roles.	Cleary, Beverly. *A Girl from Yamhill: A Memoir.* Cummings, Pat. *Talking with Artists.* Freedman, Russell. *Eleanor Roosevelt: A Life of Discovery.* Johnson, Rebecca L. *Braving the Frozen Frontier: Women Working in Antarctica.* Macy, Sue. *Winning Ways: A Photohistory of American Women in Sports.* Paige, David. *A Day in the Life of a Marine Biologist.*
6 Boys and girls accept the identity of the opposite sex. Girls more than boys begin to feel that marriage would be desirable.	6 Provide books that develop relationships with the opposite sex; such books interest girls especially.	Cole, Brock. *The Goats.* Cooper, Susan. *Seaward.* L'Engle, Madeleine. *A Ring of Endless Light.* Lunn, Janet. *The Root Cellar.* MacLachlan, Patricia. *The Facts and Fictions of Minna Pratt.*

Sources: Braga and Braga (1975); Mussen, Conger, and Kagan (1989); Piaget and Inhelder (1969); and Shaffer (1989).

socialization is a very important part of child development. Understanding the processes that influence social development is essential for anyone who works with children. Researchers have identified three processes influential in the socialization of children.

First, reward or punishment by parents and other adults reinforces socially acceptable attitudes and behaviors and discourages socially unacceptable ones. For example, a child who refuses to share a toy with another child may be deprived of the toy, while appropriate sharing may be rewarded with a hug and a favorable comment.

Second, observation of others teaches children the responses, behaviors, and beliefs considered appropriate within their culture. Children learn how to act and what to believe by imitating adults and peers. For example, a girl may learn about gender distinctions in our culture by observing and trying to copy her mother's role in the family. Children also

Grandpa's Town

By Takaaki Nomura

observe what other members of the family fear and how members of their group react to people who belong to different racial or cultural groups.

The third process, identification, may be the most important for socialization. It requires emotional ties with models. Children's thoughts, feelings, and actions become similar to those of people they believe are like them.

Children's first relationships usually occur within the immediate family, then extend to a few friends in the neighborhood, to school, and finally to the broader world. Literature and literature-related activities can aid in the development of these relationships by encouraging children to become sensitive to the feelings of others. For example, Ann Herbert Scott's *Sam* is very unhappy when the members of his family are too busy to play with him. When they realize what is wrong, they remember to include Sam in their activities. The four-year-old in Eve Rice's *Benny Bakes a Cake* helps his mother in the kitchen but faces disappointment when his dog eats the cake.

Books for younger children frequently deal with such problems as developing satisfactory relationships with family, friends, and neighbors. In Martin Waddell's *You and Me, Little Bear,* the author develops the importance of loving parent and child relationships as Little Bear wants to play, but Big Bear has work to do. Both the text and Barbara Firth's illustrations reflect the warm relationships between the two animals and the possibilities of resolving these types of family conflicts. In *Guess How Much I Love You,* Sam McBratney creates a loving bond between two rabbits as the father and son try to explain the measure of their love for each other.

In Leah Komaiko's *Just My Dad & Me,* a young girl wishes she could spend the day alone with her father only to find many extended family members joining them on the water. After a fanciful dive alone in the ocean, she discovers that she needs her family, especially her father. Aliki's *Those Summers* details the carefree times at the beach and the interactions with children and adults. This book could be used to motivate discussions about special times during the summer.

Relations with a neighbor are explored in a very generous way in Elaine Greenstein's *Mrs. Rose's Garden.* When Matilda Rose discovers that her special fertilizer produces huge vegetables certain to win all the blue ribbons at the county fair, she also discovers that it is no longer fun competing with her neighbor. To balance the outcome she places some of her vegetables in her neighbor's garden. Mrs. Rose becomes a double winner as her pumpkin wins a blue ribbon and her husband gives her a special award for "having the biggest heart" (unnumbered).

Kathleen and Michael Lacapa in *Less Than Half, More Than Whole* explore the questions asked by a boy who is part Native American and part Anglo. The authors use the symbol of the Creator's gift of corn to show the boy that like the corn of many colors he is also special. Consequently, like the corn, he is more than whole.

Overcoming problems related to sibling rivalry is a frequent theme in children's books and is one that children can understand. In *Stevie*, by John Steptoe, Robert is upset when his mother takes care of a child from another family, but he discovers that he actually misses Stevie when Stevie leaves.

Many books for preschool and early-primary children deal with various emotions related to friendship. Best friends may have strong attachments with each other, as shown in Miriam Cohen's *Best Friends* and Russell Hoban's *Best Friends for Frances*. In contrast, children may experience problems, as Crosby Bonsall demonstrates in *It's Mine!—A Greedy Book*. In this book, best friends quarrel when one of them wants to play with the other's toys. Developing friendships and the positive role of friends are major themes in Theodore Faro Gross's *Everyone Asked About You*. In this imaginative story, Charlie convinces his friend Nora to come out of her room by telling her about all of the people who inquired about her. These individuals include neighbors and friends, as well as more uncommon creatures such as sea horses, yellow butterflies, and even the man in the moon and a Martian platoon. The importance of friendship is also the theme in Karen Barbour's *Mr. Bow Tie*. A boy and his family befriend a homeless man and help him locate his own family.

Social development includes becoming aware of and understanding the different social roles that people play. One of the greatest contributions made by literature and literature-related discussions is the realization that both boys and girls can succeed in a wide range of roles. Books that emphasize non-stereotyped sex roles and achievement are excellent models that can stimulate discussion. Biographies about women leaders and women authors show that women have made many important contributions, even during historical time periods when women did not usually have leadership roles. For example, Diane Stanley and Peter Vennema's *Good Queen Bess: The Story of Elizabeth I of England* presents a strong female who overcame many obstacles to rule her people. Biographies such as Norma Johnston's *Louisa May: The World and Works of Louisa May Alcott* and Angelica Shirley Carpenter and Jean Shirley's *Frances Hodgson Burnett: Beyond the Secret Garden* show that there were important female authors even during a time that writing was dominated by male authors.

Becoming aware of different views of the world is important in socialization, and literature can help accomplish this. Children may sympathize with the Native American girl who loves her family but longs for a free life among the wild horses in *The Girl Who Loved Wild Horses* by Paul Goble. They may view a cross-cultural Christmas as they read Allen Say's *Tree of Cranes* and become involved in a Christmas celebration that includes elements from both the Japanese and American cultures. They may understand the slave's viewpoint and the consequences of prejudice when they read F. N. Monjo's *The Drinking Gourd*. Older children discover the consequences of prejudice when they read Mildred Taylor's *Let the Circle Be Unbroken*, Belinda Hurmence's *A Girl Called Boy*, or Virginia Hamilton's *Many Thousand Gone: African Americans from Slavery to Freedom*. When children read Ellen Levine's *Freedom's Children: Young Civil Rights Activists Tell Their Own Stories*, they may empathize with young people who worked for civil rights in the 1950s and 1960s.

Contemporary realistic fiction, historical fiction, and information books present many different viewpoints on issues familiar to children today. These issues include divorce (Judy Blume's *It's Not the End of the World*) and homelessness and runaways (Theresa Nelson's *The Beggars' Ride*). Issues in historical fiction include persecution of the Jewish people (Nelly S. Toll's *Behind the Secret Window: A Memoir of a Hidden Childhood During World War Two* and Karen Hesse's *Letters from Rifka*) and persecution of Chinese Americans (Laurence Yep's *The Star Fisher*). Issues in information books include environmental protection (Molly Cone's *Come Back, Salmon*) and solving social problems (Barbara A. Lewis's *The Kid's Guide to Social Action*).

Moral Development.   Acquiring moral standards is an important part of each child's social development. Preschool children start to develop concepts of right and wrong when they identify with their parents and with parental values, attitudes, and standards of conduct. The two-year-old knows that certain acts are wrong. According to Piaget and Inhelder (1969), children younger than seven or eight have rigid and inflexible ideas of right and wrong, which they have learned from their parents. Piaget and Inhelder suggest that between the ages of eight and eleven, many changes occur in the moral development of children. At this time, children start to develop a sense of equality and to take into account the situation in which a wrong action occurs. Children become more flexible and realize that there are exceptions to their original strict rules of behavior; at this time, peer groups begin to influence conduct.

Lawrence Kohlberg (1981) defines the stages of moral judgment of adults and children according to the choices made when two or more values conflict. Kohlberg considers the moral decisions made, as well as the reasons for the decisions, when he identifies the stages in moral development. At Stages 1 and 2, Kohlberg's "preconventional" level, a child responds to external, concrete consequences. During Stage 1, a child chooses to be good, or to obey rules, in order to escape physical punishment. During Stage 2, a child obeys or conforms in order to obtain rewards. Kohlberg's stages and children's ages cannot be equated because some people progress more rapidly through the sequence. However, Stages 1 and 2 apparently dominate the behavior of most children during the primary years.

At Stages 3 and 4, Kohlberg's "conventional" level, a child is concerned with meeting the external social expectations of family, group, or nation. During Stage 3, a child desires social approval and consequently makes decisions according to the expectations of the people who are important to the child. Stage 4 has a law-and-order orientation; a child conforms because of a high regard for social order and for patriotic duty. Although one stage builds on another, the transition between stages is gradual. Stage 3 behaviors usually begin in the upper-elementary grades, and Stage 4 behaviors usually emerge in adolescence.

Stages 5 and 6 (which may be incorporated into a single stage) are at the "postconventional," au-

tonomous, or principled level. At this level, a person establishes his or her own moral values. At Stage 5, a person responds to equal rights and consequently avoids violating the rights of others. At Stage 6, an individual conforms to his or her inner beliefs in order to avoid self-condemnation. Kohlberg estimates that only 25 percent of the population moves on in late adolescence or adulthood to a morality of equal rights, justice, and internal commitment to the principles of conscience.

Kohlberg suggested that a Stage 7 in moral development is the highest level of ethical and religious thinking. He refers to this stage as one of qualitatively new insight and perspective, in which a person experiences wholeness—a union with nature, a deity, and the cosmos. Although Kohlberg recognizes Stage 7 as an aspiration rather than as a complete possibility, he maintains that Stage 7 behaviors support individuals through experiences of suffering, injustice, and death.

Children's literature contains numerous moments of crisis, when characters make moral decisions and contemplate the reasons for their decisions. Although Kohlberg does not apply his stages of moral development to children's literature, both Donna Norton (1986) and Cheryl Gosa (1977) have developed such applications. Norton uses Kohlberg's stages of moral development for evaluating the moral decisions of characters in biographical literature. Gosa maintains that Kohlberg's stages are appropriate as guidelines for categorizing and evaluating the moral decisions of characters in realistic fiction. If adults expect children to understand the decision-making process of characters in a story, Gosa asserts, they should be aware of the level of the decisions that the characters are making and consider whether or not the children are at a stage when they can appreciate those decisions. Otherwise, she contends, "fiction containing . . . high level decisions [will be] meaningless for early character development . . . and beyond the level of their readers" (p. 530).

Students of children's literature may find it valuable to consider the stages of moral decisions represented by the characters in children's books when selecting literature for use with children. Chart 1–5 identifies Kohlberg's stages of moral development and lists decisions made by characters in books written for children from approximately age four through age twelve. As can be seen from the chart,

CHART 1-5 Decision making in realistic fiction

Kohlberg's Stages of Moral Development	Ages 4–7 Send Wendell by Genevieve Gray	Ages 6–8 Benjie on His Own by Joan M. Lexau	Ages 8–10 Tales of a Fourth Grade Nothing by Judy Blume	Ages 10 + Jacob Have I Loved by Katherine Paterson
1 Premoral Level. *Stage 1:* A punishment and obedience orientation. Rules are obeyed to avoid punishment.		Benjie obeys the big boys; he turns his pockets out to show them he has no money; he is very frightened.	Three-year-old Fudge eats to avoid punishment. Nine-year-old Peter believes Fudge would behave if he were punished. Father allows Fudge in commercial to keep his firm's account.	
Stage 2: Naive instrumental hedonism. A child conforms in order to obtain rewards.			Peter obeys his mother and tricks Fudge so they can go to lunch. Fudge stops complaining when he gets popcorn. Peter's puppy is a reward for his good behavior.	
2 Level of Morality of Conventional Role Conformity. *Stage 3:* A good-boy morality of maintaining good relations. A child conforms to avoid disapproval.	Six-year-old Wendell happily goes on errands because he loves Mama and likes to help her.	Benjie does not want his grandmother to walk him home after school but he puts up with it. Benjie promises to be good while his grandmother is in the hospital.	Peter does not want to share his room but knows there is no point in arguing with his mother. Peter says thank you for a gift he does not like.	Louise takes off her dirty overalls rather than argue with her grandmother.

Stage 4: An authority maintaining morality. A child conforms to avoid censure by authorities and resulting guilt.	Wendell's self-esteem increases as his uncle recognizes his worth. He now says he is busy and suggests they send someone else.	Louise expects her teacher to defend and explain her position. She is surprised and hurt when he does not. Louise does not talk back to her grandmother because such behavior is disrespectful to those who are older.
3 Level of Morality of Self-Accepted Principles. *Stage 5*: A morality of contract. A duty is defined in terms of contract and general avoidance of violation of the rights of others.	Benjie wants to ask his grandmother to wait for him but does not because he knows it would worry her. Benjie laughs because he knows his grandmother is trying to cheer him up.	
Stage 6: A morality of individual principles of conscience. A child conforms to avoid self-condemnation.		Louise suggests that Christmas be cancelled because people are suffering and dying in World War II. Her classmates object; they do not understand her principles.

the only book in this group that relies on Stage 6 decision-making processes is *Jacob Have I Loved,* which was written for older readers. Stage 7 decisions are not found in the books. Decision-making processes may be used for discussions in which children consider the options open to the characters and ways that the children might have responded in similar circumstances.

CHILDREN'S RESPONSES TO LITERATURE

Encouraging children to respond to the literature that they read is one of the most important tasks for adults who interact with children and literature. Lee Galda (1988) states, however:

Responding to literature is a complex process involving readers, texts, and contexts. Responding to literature has to do with what we make of a text as we read, how it becomes alive and personal for us, the pleasure and satisfaction we feel, and the way in which we display these feelings. Our responses to the books we read are influenced by many factors and come in many forms. (p. 92)

This section discusses each of the preceding factors and relates the factors to specific literature.

Factors Within Readers

Readers bring past experiences, present interests, and expectations of stories with them when they read a selection. Consequently, different readers often read, interpret, and respond to the same piece of literature in different ways. Arthur Applebee (1979) emphasizes that the stories children hear lead the children to expectations about what a story should be and about what new stories will be like. Consequently, early and continual reading to children is extremely important.

In addition, children's responses to literature are influenced by the developmental factors discussed in this chapter. Children's language, cognitive, personality, social, and moral development affect the ways in which children interpret and respond to a story. In a review of response research, Miriam Martinez and Nancy Roser (1991) state, "Researchers have identified numerous reader characteristics that influence response, including reader beliefs and expectations, reading ability, socioeco-

nomic status, cultural background, cognitive development, sex, and personal style" (p. 644). Robert Probst (1991) adds that insights gained from Piaget's work on cognitive development and Kohlberg's research on the development of moral reasoning are important for understanding and examining children's responses to literature.

As children bring their developmental, emotional, cultural, and scholastic backgrounds to their reading of literature, they approach the reading with their previous knowledge of the subject, their purposes for reading that literature, and their various strategies for gaining meaning from text. Rewarding interpretations of literature require personal responses that allow readers to connect experiences, emotions, and text; to understand and appreciate the unique requirements of different literary elements and genres; and to use various types of responses to expand their reactions to the literature. Consequently, the descriptions of various types of development and knowledge gained from the age and stage charts in this chapter will add to your knowledge of factors that influence readers and the examples of literature that you may use at different stages of development to enhance children's responses to literature.

Factors Within Texts

Literature texts vary from fairly simple narrative structures in folktales to elaborate novel-length plots with interwoven themes, detailed characterizations, and vivid, complex styles and language. In addition, each of the genres of literature has unique requirements: poetry has a form different from that of biography; expository texts have reading requirements and purposes for reading different from those of realistic fiction; and mythology has a fundamental belief system different from that of fantasy. Even within expository writing, texts vary from simple, literal descriptions to structures that develop complex ideas such as cause and effect.

Galda (1988) states that factors in texts are important because, "The text guides the response of the reader in that it presents content in a specific style and form which generate and modify expectations as a reader reads" (p. 98). Galda then identifies specific characteristics that influence response. The characteristics that influence readers' emotional involvement include aspects of style

Is there a gender issue in studies related to children's moral development? Is there a gender issue in studies related to children's language and communication development and to children's visual-spatial development? Was Piaget incorrect when he stated that children under the age of seven or eight do not have a grasp of cause-and-effect relationships? These are a few of the developmental issues discussed in both the scientific press and the popular press.

Several researchers are questioning Kohlberg's and Piaget's assertions about the social and moral development of children. Carol Gilligan contends that the developmental models of Kohlberg and Piaget "equate male development with child development"[1] and thereby ignore female development. Kohlberg, for example, based his hierarchy of moral development on a twenty-year study of eighty-four males. Gilligan's research, which involved both female and male subjects, indicated that females and males develop different value systems due to the traditional gender role that assigns females the primary responsibility for taking care of others' needs. Females develop a "morality of responsibility," which stresses the importance of maintaining relationships and considering other people's feelings and points of view (roughly equivalent to Kohlberg's Stage 3). Males learn to place more value on competitive self-assertion and to develop a "morality of rights," which consid-

ers rules more important than relationships (roughly equivalent to Kohlberg's Stages 5 and 6).

The implications of the gender differences between the Kohlberg and the Gilligan theories of moral development are highlighted by John West and Davele Bursor.[2] These educators argue that counselors or anyone else who works with children should understand gender differences in moral development and should be able to use these differences when counseling either girls or boys during the decision-making process.

Studies reported by Jo Durden-Smith and Diane Desimone[3] also question theories of language and cognitive development that are based primarily on male subjects. These authors report results from brain research suggesting sex-related differences between males and females. They outline brain research studies demonstrating female superiority in verbal skills, fine-motor coordination, and response to emotional content. These studies suggest that the left hemisphere and its abilities develop faster in girls than in boys. In contrast, males demonstrate superiority in visual–spatial skills and in mathematical and mechanical tasks. Consequently, some researchers conclude that the right hemisphere and its abilities develop faster in boys than in girls.

The ages of children in Piaget's pre-causal level are also being chal-

lenged. Maya Pines[4] reports on research by psychologists such as Rochel Gelman and Thomas Shultz, which shows that children as young as three or four have an understanding of cause and effect.

As might be expected, these studies, the interpretations of these studies, and the implications of these studies are highly controversial. Both Janet Shibley Hyde[5] and Mary Roth Walsh[6] identify these earlier studies as controversial in their discussions of issues related to the psychology of women. Students of children's literature and child development may read the conflicting theories and discuss the implications.

---

[1]Gilligan, Carol. *In a Different Voice: Psychological Theory and Women's Development*. Cambridge, Mass.: Harvard University Press, 1982.

[2]West, John D., and Davele E. Bursor. "Gilligan and Kohlberg: Gender Issue in Moral Development." *Humanistic Education and Development* 22 (June 1984): 134–142.

[3]Durden-Smith, Jo, and Diane Desimone. *Sex and the Brain*. New York: Arbor House, 1983.

[4]Pines, Maya. "Can a Rock Walk?" *Psychology Today* 17 (November 1983): 46–52.

[5]Hyde, Janet Shibley. *Half the Human Experience: The Psychology of Women*. Lexington, Mass.: D. C. Heath Co., 1985.

[6]Walsh, Mary Roth, ed. *The Psychology of Women: Ongoing Debates*. New Haven, Conn.: Yale University Press, 1987.

and characterization, the point of view of the story, the level of abstraction, and the complexity of the syntax. The age and maturation level of the main character frequently influence interest in the story and the type of response generated. The

genre of the literature also influences types of responses. For example, fantasy frequently elicits a type of response different from that to realistic fiction. Likewise, readers may respond to poetry in different ways than they respond to biography.

Factors Within Contexts

The literature environment influences children's responses to literature. When adults support and encourage growth in children's responses and provide numerous experiences with many types of literature, they create an environment that stimulates children's responses. Martinez and Roser (1991) summarize some of the context factors that influence children's responses within home and school settings. They found that adults who positively influence children's responses make books accessible to children, select titles that emphasize quality and that allow children to make connections among literature selections, read to children daily, discuss books using critical terminology, suggest literature-related activities and share the results of those activities with peers, plan numerous experiences with literature, provide repeated opportunities for children to interact with the same books, and model personal responses to literature for the children.

Responses

When literary critics and authorities discuss responses related to literature, they frequently emphasize at least two major types of responses: efferent and aesthetic. Rosenblatt (1985) distinguishes between the two when she states that efferent reading focuses attention on "actions to be performed, information to be retained, conclusions to be drawn, solutions to be arrived at, analytic concepts to be applied, propositions to be tested" (p. 70). Aesthetic reading, according to Rosenblatt, focuses on "what we are seeing and feeling and thinking, on what is aroused within us by the sound of the words, and by what they point to in the human and natural world" (p. 70). A worthy literature program should include both efferent and aesthetic responses to literature.

Robert Ruddell (1992) states:

A critical issue in this process is for the teacher to recognize the instructional stance taken toward literature in the classroom. One stance focuses attention on aesthetic-type reading, leading to identification with story characters, personal interpretation, and transaction with the text as the child steps through the "magic curtain" into the book with the character. A different stance, however, may focus attention on efferent-type reading, emphasizing content and information to be "taken away" from the book. Both aesthetic and efferent stances are needed in the instruc-

tional setting but serve very different purposes. Our overall literacy program must have balance across these two stances. (p. 615)

Purves and Monson (1984) also emphasize the importance of encouraging both efferent and aesthetic responses within a literature program. They emphasize the relationships between texts and readers as the readers draw meaning. They describe two important functions in any literature program that prepares readers through a transactional approach. First, the program provides a broad background of literary genres and allows the students to talk about books using words like *plot, metaphor, characterization, theme, style,* and *tone.* This function encourages students to understand the reasons for deciding that one book is better than another book (efferent responses). The program also exposes students to a variety of approaches and critical questions that allow the students to consider, "How does the literature or character affect me? What does it mean? How good is it?" Such responses allow aesthetic involvement and individual transactions.

Notice how Purves and Monson stress both the efferent and the aesthetic responses to literature when they state:

It would seem therefore that students should be exposed to a variety of critical questions, including those which are personal and affective, those which are analytical, those which are interpretive, and those which are evaluative. Each of these questions can be answered intelligently and answering each can help a student learn to read and think and feel. And you can teach your students how to answer them. (p. 189)

Analyzing Responses

Use of realistic fiction and other types of books for role playing and bibliotherapy is more effective when there is a general understanding of children's responses to literature. Louise Rosenblatt (1978) states that literature selection "should not be thought of as an object, an entity, but rather as an active process lived through during the relationship between a reader and a text" (p. 12). Readers bring past experiences, present interests, and expectations that influence their responses to texts.

Studies of children's oral and written responses to literature analyze the types of comments that children make when they retell a selection or talk about a story. In a review of children's responses to literature, Alan C. Purves and Dianne L. Monson (1984) identify characteristic responses of children in different grades. For example, children up to the third grade tend to respond to and retell literal aspects of a story. In addition to literal responses, fourth- and fifth-grade students tend to elaborate on their responses by placing themselves in the roles of the characters, comparing themselves to the characters, and talking about their personal reactions. By sixth grade, students begin to emphasize and interpret characters. In seventh and eighth grades, students increase their interpretations and frequently emphasize meaning and understanding in their evaluations. Eighth-grade students begin to look for deeper or hidden meanings in stories.

Working with children and literature, you can learn a great deal about children's responses to literature by analyzing what children choose to say or write about when they discuss literature. Purves and Monson recommend a classification system to use when analyzing children's comments about literature (see Chart 1–6).

The Role of Motivation

Ruddell (1992) emphasizes the importance of the aesthetic stance in encouraging readers to "step into the story, experience, and live through the story" (p. 616). Ruddell identifies the following six internal motivators that foster aesthetic responses in readers and build personal connections with literature: problem resolution, prestige, aesthetic motivation, escape, intellectual curiosity, and understanding of self. Numerous examples of literature may be associated with each of these internal motivators and consequently may encourage aesthetic responses from children.

Problem resolution books encourage readers to see themselves as successful problem solvers. In this response, readers relate to characters who are able to solve or resolve problems and vicariously associate with successful characters. Young children can become successful problem solvers as they respond to the boy who uses his wits to encourage the king to leave the bathtub in Audrey Wood's *King Bidgood's in the Bathtub.*

Older children can see themselves as successful problem solvers by responding to Marty in Phyllis Reynolds Naylor's *Shiloh* when Marty resolves to

CHART 1–6 Classifying children's responses to books

Type of Response	Examples
Descriptive	Retelling the story, naming the characters, listing the media used in illustration.
Analytic	Pointing to the uses of language, structure, point-of-view in the work.
Classificatory	Placing the work in its literary historical context.
Personal	Describing the reader's reactions to the work and the emotions and memories that have been evoked.
Interpretive	Making inferences about the work and its parts, relating the work to some way of viewing phenomena (e.g., psychology).
Evaluative	Judging the work's merit on personal, formal, or moral criteria.

Source: From Alan C. Purves and Dianne L. Monson. *Experiencing Children's Literature.* Glenview, Ill.: Scott, Foresman, 1984, p. 143.

save the dog from being mistreated by its owner and then uses much initiative to solve his problem by bargaining successfully for the dog. With Molly Cone's *Come Back, Salmon,* children can associate with the members of a fifth-grade class who cleaned up a salmon stream in Washington. With Susan Cooper's *The Boggart,* children can accompany three Canadian children as they figure out how to send a mischievous spirit back to his castle. With E. B. White's *Charlotte's Web,* children can respond to Charlotte, certainly one of the most successful problem solvers in children's fantasy.

The internal motivation of prestige enables a child to vicariously become a person of significance, who receives attention and exerts influence and control. Through picture *storybooks,* children can visualize themselves as heroines or heroes. Young children can associate themselves with a girl who bravely helps save her farm during an 1839 rebellion in Candace Christiansen's *Calico and Tin Horns* or a boy who proves himself a hero when he encounters a ghost in Patricia Polacco's *Picnic at Mudsock Meadow.* Older children can visualize themselves in the prestigious heroic role in Dean Harvey's *The Secret Elephant of Harlan Kooter.* In this story, a boy befriends an escaped circus elephant and they become heroes during a hurricane.

Highly illustrated biographies allow children to respond to characters who have had prestige in history, such as those in Diane Stanley and Peter Vennema's *Good Queen Bess: The Story of Elizabeth I of England, Bard of Avon: The Story of William Shakespeare,* and *Shaka: King of the Zulus.* The prestige of an artist may appeal to readers who can associate themselves with the successful career of an animator for Disney Studios and an illustrator of children's books in Bill Peet's *Bill Peet: An Autobiography.* Pat Cummings' *Talking with Artists* presents interviews with fourteen illustrators of children's books and shows examples of their works.

Aesthetic motivation involves the elevation of an aesthetic sense and ranges from appreciation of beauty in nature to the enjoyment of family harmony and interaction. Children are motivated to respond to both the aesthetic beauty in nature and to the beauty of language when they read Jane Yolen's *Owl Moon.* In Monro Leaf's *The Story of Ferdinand,* children can respond to a bull who favors the aesthetic response to nature to the glory of the bull ring. Aesthetic responses to beautiful language are heightened through poetry books such as Nancy Willard's *Pish, Posh, Said Hieronymus Bosch* and Stephen Dunning, Edward Lueders, and Hugh Smith's *Reflections on a Gift of Watermelon Pickle . . . and Other Modern Verse.* Enjoyment of family harmony and interactions are found in Pat Mora's *A Birthday Basket for Tia.* This book develops loving relationships between a Hispanic girl and her aunt. Laura Ingalls Wilder's *Little House in the Big Woods* develops strong family relationships in pioneer times.

Escape literature enables readers to vicariously accompany literary characters to unfamiliar or even fantasy places. Readers can escape to Africa with a carpenter who discovers how to tell fortunes in Lloyd Alexander's *The Fortune Tellers.* Africa is also the escape location for an African American girl who imagines what it would be like to live in East Africa in Virginia Kroll's *Masai and I.* The illustrations in David Wiesner's *Free Fall* allow readers to escape through a character's dreams. Anne Lindbergh's *Travel Far, Pay No Fare* follows children as they travel through the pages of several books. Books such as A. A. Milne's *Winnie-the-Pooh* allow readers to escape to the Hundred Acre Wood of personified toys. J. R. R. Tolkien's *The Hobbit* takes children into Middle Earth and allows them to become heroes as they accomplish their quest and regain the realm of the dwarfs. Lloyd Alexander's *The Remarkable Journey of Prince Jen* allows children to accompany a hero on a quest through a mythical land that has oriental characteristics.

Fiction and nonfiction set in other time periods encourage children to vicariously escape into those times. Avi's *Who Was That Masked Man, Anyway?* takes children back to World War II and allows them to interact with a boy who is infatuated with the radio shows of that time. Rhoda Blumberg's *Commodore Perry in the Land of the Shogun* encourages readers to accompany Commodore Perry to Japan in 1853. Classics such as Robert Louis Stevenson's *Treasure Island* have encouraged generations to escape into the adventures that are possible with treasure maps, mysterious islands, and questionable characters.

The motivator of intellectual curiosity encourages curious minds to explore and learn about new words and new ideas. Some picture books, such as Arthur Geisert's *Pigs from 1–10,* challenge readers to find animals that are hiding within the illustrations. Numerous nonfiction books also encourage intellectual curiosity. Lois Ehlert's *Red Leaf, Yellow Leaf* follows a child's curiosity as she plants a sugar maple tree and discovers how the seedling arrived at the nursery. Joanna Cole's *The Magic School Bus on the Ocean Floor* presents science facts through an amusing excursion through the ocean. Anne Baird's *Space Camp: The Great Adventure for NASA Hopefuls* includes numerous photographs and descriptions that will motivate and excite future astronauts. Kathryn Lasky's *Think Like an Eagle: At Work with a Wildlife Photographer* challenges readers to think like animals in order to acquire the best photographs.

Understanding of self is a powerful motivator. Books allow children to understand and respond to personal motivations and motivations that influence others. Many of the books listed under personal

THROUGH THE EYES OF A JOURNAL PUBLISHER

Tapping Professional Resources

SUSANNE F. CANAVAN and HIRAM HOWARD own Christopher-Gordon Publishers, Inc., publishers of the children's literature journal *The New Advocate* as well as professional books for educators.

FOR MANY EDUCATORS, journals represent important professional resources. These diverse publications keep them in touch with many different parts of their fields. Journals offer educators the opportunities to examine the in-progress work of researchers; to take one-on-one tours of colleagues' classrooms thousands of miles or whole cultures away; and to consider differing viewpoints on various "hot topics." They may also inspire, frustrate, or motivate. Journals invite involvement, either emotionally or intellectually.

If journals have a mission, or focus (and most do have at least a general editorial policy), it is the vision of the editor, within the framework of parameters established jointly with the publisher, and not that of the publisher, that should be the driving force. *The New Advocate* is fortunate to have Joel Taxel as its editor. His integrity and vision have been primary forces in establishing and maintaining the journal's quality. Since the journal exists in a changing world, readership needs evolve. We all need to be constantly aware of change—not for itself, but as a reflection of the dynamic nature of education in general and children's literature in particular. This is not always easy, but it is something that has to be dealt with in any publishing endeavor.

The New Advocate intentionally does not examine research; rather it focuses on enrichment in experience and practice and on using children's books effectively and with enjoyment in the classroom. Our readers particularly like articles by and about children's writers and illustrators (so do we), particularly pieces that offer some insights into the creative process, some glimpses behind the scenes as it were. Readers also respond to concept and theme pieces, in which issues such as censorship, the role of reading tests, or cultural literacy are discussed. *The New Advocate* welcomes thoughtful teachers' insights and experiences in practical reflections.

With journals, it is possible to have a much closer relationship with readers than with books. If we were to try to characterize reader response to *The New Advocate,* the words that come immediately to mind are *personal* and *stimulating.* On the one hand, it's lovely to hear how much people enjoy certain articles or issues, but we'll also find out as quickly if something is not to their liking. What's good about this, though, is that the journal can be responsive to these likes and dislikes. And, we want to hear from people because it helps us do our jobs better.

In all our years of publishing, we have never experienced such immediate or enthusiastic feedback. We have talked to people who read each issue cover to cover, making copious notes in the margin. Some school districts personnel have told us that they regularly Xerox copies of articles to hand out to teachers, while others purchase single copies or subscriptions for their school libraries. It's very gratifying to know that the journal is being used and to be told how helpful it is.

Publishing a journal is nothing like publishing a book. It is always immediate, ongoing, and persistent. It is never *not* a part of our thinking. Since we are likely to be working on more than one issue at a time, juggling multiple (sometimes conflicting) priorities is part of everyday life. Most readers rarely are aware of this behind-the-scenes activity. *The New Advocate* has enabled us to feel much closer to educators, to be more closely involved, which is not such a bad thing. And as a couple of English literature majors, [we have found that] the journal has been fun too. We're proud to be the publishers.

Cynthia Rylant

MISSING MAY

In Missing May, *a girl makes discoveries about herself when she faces her aunt's death. Illustration from* Missing May *by Cynthia Rylant. Copyright © 1992 by Cynthia Rylant. Used by permission of Orchard Books.*

development may be used to elicit and increase personal responses to literature because they are closely related to emotions faced by children. In Cynthia Rylant's *Missing May,* a girl faces her aunt's death and makes discoveries about herself and those whom she loves. In Nina Bawden's *Humbug,* the heroine learns about deceit and honesty. Anne Fine's *The Book of the Banshee* allows readers to respond to the various emotional reactions in a family when one of the family members is a teenager. Avi's *Nothing But the Truth: A Documentary Novel* elicits very personal responses and insights into the motives of older students. Memos, letters, diary pages, phone and personal conversations, speeches and telegrams encourage readers to develop and defend their own point of view about which character is telling the truth.

Throughout, this book contains many literature recommendations and literature-related activities that entice and enhance children's responses to literature. These recommendations encourage both efferent and aesthetic responses to literature. For example, through oral responses such as drama, discussions, role playing, and storytelling, children can respond to and critically evaluate development of the literary elements such as plot, conflict, characterization, and theme (efferent responses) and can provide personal reactions to those literary elements (aesthetic responses). Likewise, readers can evaluate the effectiveness of the setting and mood as created by the author or illustrator (efferent responses) and provide personal responses that emphasize emotional reactions through their own drawings (aesthetic responses).

 SUGGESTED ACTIVITIES

for The Child Responds to Literature

- Listen to the language of several children who are the same age. Do you notice any differences in their language development? Are these differences similar to those identified by Walter Loban (1976, p. 7)?
- Select several books, such as Eve Rice's *Oh, Lewis!* to encourage young children to identify familiar actions in books. Share these books with a few preschool children and let the children interact orally with the text.
- Ask several children how school and reading literature could be made more enjoyable. Compare the responses of students in different grades.
- Select several books that you believe would stimulate children's language development. Present the books and your rationales for choosing them.
- With a group of your peers, compile a list of picture books that would be useful when developing one of the following cognitive skills: observing, comparing, hypothesizing, organizing, summarizing, applying, or criticizing. Share your findings with your class.
- Read several books in which young children must overcome such problems as jealousy, fear, or anger. Compare the ways in which the authors have allowed the children to handle their problems. Do the feelings seem normal and natural? Is more than one aspect of a feeling developed? Are options shown for handling each emotion?

[Note: If you are unfamiliar with using database software, please select the "read me" file icon on the CD for specific directions. The methodology for conducting a simple search is included in the first activity.]

■ Use the database to select books that will demonstrate how the subject of "birth" is treated for very young children versus for children in upper elementary grades. Using passages from each book, compare and contrast the treatment of birth. Give two examples that demonstrate how the author treats the topic in appropriate ways for children at each age (developmental) level.

Begin a KEY WORD SEARCH for "birth."

Select the RETAIN option to show the results of the search.

Next, set up a GENERAL LAYOUT.

Choose the fields INTEREST LEVEL, TITLE, and DESCRIPTION to select books.

Eliminate the books that do not fit the category (or your criteria).

■ The parent of a preschool child asks for help in finding books of rhyme. Use the database to select books that will improve language development of young children by increasing their vocabulary and developing a sense of sound and rhythm in speech patterns.

■ Use the database to locate books with either "ghost" or "monster" characters. Now add at least three new books to the database by selecting ADD USER RECORD from the EDIT menu. Print the new, updated list.

CHILDREN'S LITERATURE*

Aardema, Verna. *Bringing the Rain to Kapiti Plain.* Illustrated by Beatriz Vidal. Dial, 1981.
_____. *Who's in Rabbit's House?* Illustrated by Leo and Diane Dillon. Dial, 1977.
_____. *Why Mosquitoes Buzz in People's Ears: A West African Tale.* Illustrated by Leo and Diane Dillon. Dial, 1975.
Ackerman, Karen. *Song and Dance Man.* Illustrated by Stephen Gammell. Knopf, 1988.
Adoff, Arnold. *All of the Colors of the Race.* Illustrated by John Steptoe. Lothrop, Lee & Shepard, 1982.
_____. *Black Is Brown Is Tan.* Harper & Row, 1973.
_____. *Malcolm X.* Crowell, 1970.
Alborough, Jez. *Where's My Teddy?* Candlewick, 1992.
Alexander, Lloyd. *The Arkadians.* Dutton, 1995.
_____. *The Fortune Tellers.* Illustrated by Trina Schart Hyman. Dutton, 1992.
_____. *The Remarkable Journey of Prince Jen.* Dutton, 1991.
_____. *Westmark.* Dutton, 1981.
Alexander, Martha. *Nobody Asked Me If I Wanted a Baby Sister.* Dial, 1971.
Aliki. *Those Summers.* HarperCollins, 1996.
Allard, Harry. *Miss Nelson Is Missing.* Illustrated by James Marshall. Houghton Mifflin, 1977, 1985.
Andry, Andrew, and Steven Schepp. *How Babies Are Made.* Time-Life, 1968.
Anno, Mitsumasa. *Anno's Counting Book.* Crowell, 1977.
_____. *Anno's Math Games II.* Philomel, 1989.
_____. *Anno's U.S.A.* Philomel, 1983.
Arnold, Caroline. *Saving the Peregrine Falcon.* Photographed by Richard R. Hewett. Carolrhoda, 1985.
_____. *Stone Age Farmers Beside the Sea: Scotland's Prehistoric Village of Skara Brae.* Photographs by Arthur P. Arnold. Clarion, 1997.
Arnosky, Jim. *Flies in the Water, Fish in the Air.* Lothrop, Lee & Shepard, 1986.
_____. *Freshwater Fish and Fishing.* Four Winds, 1982.
Asbornsen, Peter Christen. *Three Billy Goats Gruff.* Retold and illustrated by Glen Rounds, Holiday House, 1993.
Asch, Frank. *Moonbear's Pet.* Simon & Schuster, 1997.
Ash, Russell. *Incredible Comparisons.* Kindersley, 1996.
Ashforth, Camilla. *Monkey Tricks.* Candlewick, 1993.
Asian Cultural Centre for UNESCO. *Folktales from Asia for Children Everywhere.* 1977, 1978, 1979.
Avi. *Nothing But the Truth: A Documentary Novel.* Orchard, 1991.
_____. *Who Was That Masked Man, Anyway?* Orchard, 1992.
Aylesworth, Jim. *Old Black Fly.* Illustrated by Stephen Gammell. Holt, 1992.
_____. *One Crow: A Counting Rhyme.* Illustrated by Ruth Young. Lippincott, 1988.
Babbit, Natalie. *BUB: Or the Very Best Thing.* HarperCollins, 1994.
_____. *Baby's Boat.* Illustrated by Jeanne Titherington. Greenwillow, 1992.
Baer, Edith. *This Is the Way We Go to School: A Book About Children Around the World.* Illustrated by Steven Bjorkman. Scholastic, 1990.
Baird, Anne. *Space Camp: The Great Adventure for NASA Hopefuls.* Photographs by Robert Kropp. Morrow, 1992.
Baker, Jeannie. *Window.* Greenwillow, 1991.
Baker, Keith. *Hide and Snake.* Harcourt Brace Jovanovich, 1991.
Bang, Molly. *Goose.* Scholastic, 1996.
_____. *Ten, Nine, Eight.* Greenwillow, 1983.
Bannerman, Helen. *The Story of Little Babaji.* Illustrated by Fred Marcellino. HarperCollins, 1996.
Barbour, Karen. *Mr. Bow Tie.* Harcourt Brace Jovanovich, 1991.
Barton, Byron. *Airport.* Crowell, 1982.
_____. *I Want to Be an Astronaut.* Crowell, 1988.
_____. *Machines at Work.* Crowell, 1987.

*Most of these titles are annotated and discussed in depth in later chapters. The references cited in the chapter are in a special reference section at the back of the book.

The Child Responds to Literature **51**

_____. *The Wee Little Woman*. HarperCollins, 1995.

Bauer, Marion Dane. *On My Honor*. Houghton Mifflin, 1986.

Bawden, Nina. *Humbug*. Clarion, 1992.

Baylor, Byrd. *The Best Town in the World*. Scribner's, 1983.

Begay, Shonto. *Navajo: Visions and Voices Across the Mesa*. Scholastic, 1995.

Bellville, Cheryl Walsh. *Rodeo*. Carolrhoda, 1985.

Benjamin, Carol Lea. *The Wicked Stepdog*. Crowell, 1982.

Benson, Patrick. *Little Penguin*. Philomel, 1990.

Beowulf. Translated by Kevin Crossley-Holland. Illustrated by Charles Keeping. Oxford University Press, 1984.

Berenstain, Stan, and Janice Berenstain. *Old Hat, New Hat*. Random House, 1970.

Berenzy, Alix. *A Frog Prince*. Holt, 1989.

Berger, Terry. *I Have Feelings*. Human Science, 1971.

Bitton-Jackson, Livia. *I Have Lived A Thousand Years: Growing Up in the Holocaust*. Simon & Schuster, 1997.

Blumberg, Rhoda. *Commodore Perry in the Land of the Shogun*. Lothrop, Lee & Shepard, 1985.

_____. *The Incredible Journey of Lewis & Clark*. Lothrop, Lee & Shepard, 1987.

Blume, Judy. *It's Not the End of the World*. Bradbury, 1972.

_____. *The One in the Middle Is the Green Kangaroo*. Bradbury, 1981.

_____. *Tales of a Fourth Grade Nothing*. Dutton, 1972.

Bonsall, Crosby. *It's Mine!—A Greedy Book*. Harper & Row, 1964.

Bradley, Kimberly. *Ruthie's Gift*. Delacorte, 1998.

Brett, Jan. *Beauty and the Beast*. Clarion, 1989.

_____. *Goldilocks and the Three Bears*. Dodd, Mead, 1987.

Briggs, Raymond. *The Snowman*. Random House, 1978.

British Museum of Natural History. *Man's Place in Evolution*. Cambridge, 1981.

Brittain, Bill. *The Wish Giver*. Illustrated by Andrew Glass. Harper & Row, 1983.

Brooke, William J. *Untold Tales*. HarperCollins, 1992.

Brooks, Bruce. *The Moves Make the Man*. Harper & Row, 1984.

Brown, Laurie Krasny, and Brown, Marc. *When Dinosaurs Die: A Guide to Understanding Death*. Little, Brown, 1996.

Brown, Marc. *Arthur's Baby*. Little, Brown, 1987.

Brown, Margaret Wise. *The Runaway Bunny*. Harper & Row, 1972, 1991.

Brown, Mary Barrett. *Wings Along the Waterway*. Orchard, 1992.

Brown, Ruth. *The Tale of Monstrous Toad*. Andersen, 1996.

Browne, Eileen. *No Problem*. Illustrated by David Parkins. Candlewick, 1993.

Bryan, Ashley. *The Cat's Purr*. Atheneum, 1985.

Bulla, Clyde. *Keep Running, Allen!* Crowell, 1978.

Bunting, Eve. *Ghost's Hour, Spook's Hour*. Illustrated by Donald Carrick. Houghton Mifflin, 1987.

_____. *The Mother's Day Mice*. Illustrated by Jan Brett. Clarion, 1986.

_____. *The Wednesday Surprise*. Illustrated by Donald Carrick. Clarion, 1989.

Burnett, Frances Hodgson. *The Secret Garden*. Illustrated by Tasha Tudor, Lippincott, 1909, 1962.

Burton, Virginia Lee. *Mike Mulligan and His Steam Shovel*. Houghton Mifflin, 1939.

_____. *The Little House*. Houghton Mifflin, 1942.

Busch, Phyllis. *Cactus in the Desert*. Crowell, 1979.

Byars, Betsy. *The Animal, the Vegetable, and John D. Jones*. Illustrated by Ruth Sanderson. Delacorte, 1982.

_____. *My Brother, Ant*. Illustrated by Marc Simont. Viking, 1996.

Cabrera, Jane. *Cat's Colors*. Dial, 1997.

_____. *The Cybil War*. Viking, 1981.

Calhoun, Mary. *High-Wire Henry*. Illustrated by Erick Ingraham. Morrow, 1991.

Callen, Larry. *Who Kidnapped the Sheriff? Tales from Tickfaw*. Illustrated by Stephen Gammell. Little, Brown, 1985.

Calmenson, Stephanie and Cole, Joanna. *Rockin' Reptiles*. Illustrated by Lynn Munsinger. Morrow, 1997.

Campbell, Rod. *Dear Zoo*. Four Winds, 1982.

Carle, Eric. *Do You Want to Be My Friend?* Crowell, 1971.

_____. *The Mixed-Up Chameleon*. Crowell, 1975, 1984.

_____. *The Very Busy Spider*. Putnam, 1985.

_____. *My Very First Book of Colors*. Crowell, 1974, 1985.

_____. *My Very First Book of Numbers*. Crowell, 1974, 1985.

_____. *My Very First Book of Shapes*. Crowell, 1974, 1985.

Carlstrom, Nancy. *Baby-O*. Illustrated by Erick Ingraham. Morrow, 1991.

_____. *Jesse Bear, What Will You Wear?* Illustrated by Bruce Degen. Macmillan, 1986.

_____. *Raven and River*. Illustrated by Jon Van Zyle. Little, Brown, 1997.

Carpenter, Angelica Shirley, and Jean Shirley. *Frances Hodgson Burnett: Beyond the Secret Garden*. Lerner, 1990.

Carr, Terry. *Spill: The Story of the Exxon Valdez*. Watts, 1991.

Carson, Jo. *You Hold Me and I'll Hold You*. Illustrated by Annie Cannon. Orchard, 1992.

Cauley, Lorinda Bryan. *Goldilocks and the Three Bears*. Putnam, 1981.

Cazet, Denys. *A Fish in His Pocket*. Watts, 1987.

_____. *I'm Not Sleepy*. Orchard, 1992.

Christelow, Eileen. *Five Little Monkeys Jumping on the Bed*. Clarion, 1989.

Christiansen, Candace. *Calico and Tin Horns*. Illustrated by Thomas Locker. Dial, 1992.

Cleary, Beverly. *Dear Mr. Henshaw*. Illustrated by Paul O. Zelinsky. Morrow, 1983.

_____. *A Girl from Yamhill: A Memoir*. Morrow, 1988.

_____. *Ramona and Her Father*. Illustrated by Alan Tiegreen. Morrow, 1977.

_____. *Ramona Quimby, Age 8*. Morrow, 1981.

Cobb, Vicki, and Kathy Darling. *Bet You Can't! Science Impossibilities to Fool You*. Illustrated by Martha Weston. Lothrop, Lee & Shepard, 1980.

Cohen, Miriam. *Best Friends*. Macmillan, 1971.

_____. *Will I Have a Friend?* Macmillan, 1971, 1989.

Cole, Brock. *The Goats*. Farrar, Straus & Giroux, 1987.

Cole, Joanna. *The Magic School Bus on the Ocean Floor*. Illustrated by Bruce Degen. Scholastic, 1992.

Collington, Peter. *The Angel and the Soldier Boy*. Knopf, 1987.

Cone, Molly. *Come Back, Salmon*. Photographs by Sidnee Wheelwright. Sierra Club, 1992.

Conly, Jane Leslie. *Racso and the Rats of NIMH*. Harper & Row, 1986.

Cooper, Melrose. *I Got a Family*. Illustrated by Dale Gottlieb. Holt, 1993.

Cooper, Susan. *The Boggart*. Macmillan, 1993.

_____. *Matthew's Dragon*. Illustrated by Jos. A. Smith. Macmillan, 1991.

_____. *Seaward*. Atheneum, 1983.

Coy, John. *Night Driving*. Holt, 1996.

Creech, Sharon. *Walk Two Moons*. HarperCollins, 1994.

Crews, Donald. *Freight Train*. Greenwillow, 1978.

_____. *Harbor*. Greenwillow, 1982.

Cummings, Pat. *Talking with Artists*. Bradbury, 1992.

Curtis, Jamie Lee. *Tell Me Again About the Night I Was Born*. Illustrated by Laura Cornell. HarperCollins, 1996.

Cutler, Jane. *Darcy and Gran Don't Like Babies*. Illustrated by Susannah Ryan. Scholastic, 1993.

Dabcovich, Lydia. *Sleepy Bear*. Dutton, 1982.

Day, Alexandra. *Frank and Ernest Play Ball*. Scholastic, 1990.

_____. *Frank and Ernest on the Road*. Scholastic, 1994.

de Brunhoff, Laurent. *Babar's Book of Color*. Random House, 1984.

Defelice, Cynthia. *Willy's Silly Grandma*. Illustrated by Shelley Jackson. Orchard, 1997.

Demi. *One Grain of Rice: A Mathematical Folktale*. Scholastic, 1997.

dePaola, Tomie. *Christopher: The Holy Giant*. Holiday, 1994.

_____. *The Clown of God*. Harcourt Brace Jovanovich, 1978.

_____. *Fin M'Coul: The Giant of Knockmany Hill*. Holiday House, 1981.

_____. *The Legend of the Bluebonnet*. Putnam, 1983.

_____. *The Quicksand Book*. Holiday House, 1977.

Dodds, Dayle Ann. *Wheel Away!* Illustrated by Thatcher Hurd. Harper & Row, 1989.

Dubanevich, Arlene. *Pigs in Hiding*. Four Winds, 1983.

Duke, Kate. *Clean-Up Day*. Dutton, 1986.

Duncan, Lois. *The Magic of Spider Woman*. Illustrated by Shonto Begay. Scholastic, 1995.

Dunning, Stephen, Edward Lueders, and Hugh Smith, compilers. *Reflections on a Gift of Watermelon Pickle . . . and Other Modern Verse*. Lothrop, Lee & Shepard, 1967.

Dunrea, Oliver. *The Painter Who Loved Chickens*. Farrar Straus & Giroux, 1995.

Dyer, Jane. *Animal Crackers: A Delectable Collection of Pictures, Poems, and Lullabies for the Very Young*. Little, Brown, 1996.

Ehlert, Lois, *Color Zoo*. Lippincott, 1989.

_____. *Hands*. Harcourt Brace 1997.

_____. *Red Leaf, Yellow Leaf*. Harcourt Brace Jovanovich, 1991.

Ehrlich, Amy. *Leo, Zack, and Emmie*. Dial, 1981.

Emberley, Ed. *Ed Emberley's Picture Pie 2: A Drawing Book and Stencil*. Little, Brown, 1996.

_____. *Go Away, Big Green Monster!* Little, Brown, 1992.

Emberley, Rebecca. *City Sounds*. Little, Brown, 1989.

Engel, Diana. *Josephina Hates Her Name*. Morrow, 1989.

Ernst, Lisa Campbell. *Ginger Jumps*. Bradbury, 1990.

_____. *When Bluebell Sang*. Bradbury, 1989.

Everitt, Betsy. *Mean Soup*. Harcourt Brace Jovanovich, 1992.

Farmer, Nancy. *A Girl Named Disaster*. Jackson, 1996.

Fassler, Joan. *Howie Helps Himself*. Illustrated by Joe Lasker. Whitman, 1975.

Feelings, Muriel. *Moja Means One: Swahili Counting Book*. Illustrated by Tom Feelings. Dial, 1971.

Fenner, Carol. *Yolonda's Genius*. McElderry, 1995.

Fine, Anne. *The Book of the Banshee*. Little, Brown, 1992.

Fleischman, Paul. *Time Train*. Illustrated by Claire Ewart. HarperCollins, 1991.

Fleischman, Sid. *The Scarebird*. Greenwillow, 1988.

Fleming, Denise. *Count!* Holt, Rinehart & Winston, 1992.

_____. *In the Small, Small Pond*. Holt, 1993.

_____. *In the Tall, Tall Grass*. Holt, 1991.

Flournoy, Valerie. *The Patchwork Quilt*. Illustrated by Jerry Pinkney. Dial, 1985.

Forbes, Esther. *Johnny Tremain*. Illustrated by Lynd Ward. Houghton Mifflin, 1943.

Fowler, Susi. *When Summer Ends*. Illustrated by Marisabina Russo. Greenwillow, 1989.

Fox, Mem. *Hattie and the Fox*. Illustrated by Patricia Mullins. Bradbury, 1987.

Fox, Paula. *One-Eyed Cat*. Bradbury, 1984.

Frasier, Debra. *On the Day You Were Born*. Harcourt Brace Jovanovich, 1991.

Freedman, Russell. *Eleanor Roosevelt: A Life of Discovery*. Clarion, 1993.

_____. *An Indian Winter*. Illustrated by Karl Bodmer. Holiday House, 1992.

_____. *Lincoln: A Photobiography*. Houghton Mifflin, 1987.

_____. *The Wright Brothers: How They Invented the Airplane*. Holiday House, 1991.

Friedman, Ina R. *How My Parents Learned to Eat*. Illustrated by Allen Say. Houghton Mifflin, 1987.

Fritz, Jean. *Bully for You, Teddy Roosevelt!* Illustrated by Mike Wimmer. Putnam, 1991.

_____. *Make Way for Sam Houston*. Illustrated by Elise Primavera. Putnam, 1986.

Gág, Wanda. *Millions of Cats*. Coward-McCann, 1928.

Galdone, Paul. *The Gingerbread Boy*. Seabury, 1975.

_____. *The Little Red Hen*. Houghton Mifflin, 1973.

_____. *The Three Billy Goats Gruff*. Houghton Mifflin 1973.

_____. *What's in Fox's Sack? An Old English Tale*. Clarion, 1982.

Gammell, Stephen. *Is That You, Winter?* Harcourt Brace, 1997.

_____. *Wake Up, Bear . . . It's Christmas!* Lothrop, Lee & Shepard, 1981.

Gauch, Patricia Lee. *Christina Katerina and the Time She Quit the Family*. Illustrated by Elise Primavera. Putnam, 1987.

Geisert, Arthur. *Pigs from 1–10*. Houghton Mifflin, 1992.

George, Jean Craighead. *The First Thanksgiving*. Illustrated by Thomas Locker. Philomel, 1993.

_____. *My Side of the Mountain*. Dutton, 1975.

George, Kristine O'Connell. *The Great Frog Race: And Other Poems*. Illustrated by Kate Kiesler. Clarion, 1997.

Giff, Patricia. *Today Was a Terrible Day*. Viking, 1980.

Giganti, Paul, Jr. *How Many Snails? A Counting Book*. Illustrated by Donald Crews. Greenwillow, 1988.

Ginsburg, Mirra. *Asleep, Asleep*. Illustrated by Nancy Tafuri. Greenwillow, 1992.

_____. *Clay Boy*. Greenwillow, 1997.

Goble, Paul. *The Girl Who Loved Wild Horses*. Bradbury, 1978.

_____. *Iktomi and the Berries*. Watts, 1989.

Godden, Rumer. *Premlata and the Festival of Lights*. Illustrated by Ian Andrew. Greenwillow, 1997.

Goodall, John S. *The Story of a Main Street*. Macmillan, 1987.

Grahame, Kenneth. *The Wind in the Willows*. Illustrated by E. H. Shepard. Scribner's, 1908, 1940.

Gray, Genevieve. *Send Wendell*. New York: McGraw-Hill, 1974.

Gray, Libba Moore. *Is There Room on the Feather Bed?* Illustrated by Nadine Bernard. Orchard, 1997.

Greenberg, Jan. *The Iceberg and Its Shadow*. Farrar, Straus & Giroux, 1980.

_____. and Sandra Jordan. *The Sculptor's Eye: Looking at Contemporary American Art*. Delacorte, 1993.

Greenstein, Elaine. *Mrs. Rose's Garden*. Simon & Schuster, 1996.

Griego, Margot C., Betsy L. Bucks, Sharon S. Gilbert, and Laurel H. Kimball. *Tortillitas Para Mama*. Illustrated by Barbara Cooney. Holt, Rinehart & Winston, 1981.

Griffith, Helen V. *Grandaddy's Place*. Illustrated by James Stevenson. Greenwillow, 1987.

Grimm, Brothers. *Hansel and Gretel*. Retold by Rika Lesser. Illustrated by Paul O. Zelinsky. Dodd, Mead, 1984.

Gross, Theodore Faro. *Everyone Asked About You*. Illustrated by Sheila White Samton. Philomel, 1990.

Grossman, Bill. *My Little Sister Ate One Hare*. Illustrated by Kevin Hawkes. Crown, 1996.

Gunson, Christopher. *Over On the Farm: A Counting Picture Book Rhyme*. Scholastic, 1997.

Guthrie, Woody. *Woody's 20 Grow Big Songs*. HarperCollins, 1992.

Haas, Irene. *A Summertime Song*. McElderry, 1997.

Hadithi, Mwenye. *Crafty Chameleon*. Illustrated by Adrienne Kennaway. Little, Brown, 1987.

Hague, Michael. *Beauty and the Beast*. Holt, 1983.

Hahn, Mary Downing. *Stepping on the Cracks*. Clarion, 1991.

Hale, Sarah Josepha. *Mary Had a Little Lamb*. Illustrated by Tomie de Paola. Holiday House, 1984.

Hall, Donald. *Old Home Day*. Illustrated by Emily Arnold McCully. Harcourt, 1996.

Hamilton, Virginia. *Many Thousand Gone: African Americans from Slavery to Freedom*. Illustrated by Leo and Diane Dillon. Knopf, 1993.

Hanson, Regina. *The Face At the Window*. Illustrated by Linda Saport. Clarion, 1997.

Harris, Robie H. *Happy Birth Day!* Illustrated by Michael Emberley. Candlewick, 1996.

Hartmann, Wendy, and Niki Daly. *The Dinosaurs Are Back and It's All Your Fault Edward!* Illustrated by Niki Daly. McElderry, 1997.

Harvey, Dean. *The Secret Elephant of Harlan Kooter*. Illustrated by Mark Richardson. Houghton Mifflin, 1992.

Haskins, Jim. *Count Your Way Through Italy*. Illustrated by Beth Wright. Carolrhoda, 1990.

Hayes, Sarah. *This Is the Bear and the Scary Night*. Illustrated by Helen Craig. Little, Brown, 1992.

Heide, Florence Parry, and Judith Heide Gilliland. *The Day of Ahmed's Secret*. Illustrated by Ted Lewin. Lothrop, Lee & Shepard, 1990.

Henkes, Kevin. *Chrysanthemum*. Greenwillow, 1991.

_____. *Jessica*. Greenwillow, 1989.

_____. *Lilly's Purple Plastic Purse*. Greenwillow, 1996.

_____. *Owen*. Greenwillow, 1993.

Heo, Yumi. *The Green Frogs*. Houghton, 1996.

Hesse, Karen. *Lester's Dog*. Illustrated by Nancy Carpenter. Crown, 1993.

_____. *Letters from Rifka*. Holt, 1992.

_____. *The Music of Dolphins*. Scholastic, 1996.

Hest, Amy. *The Crack-of-Dawn Walkers*. Illustrated by Amy Schwartz. Macmillan, 1984.

_____. *In the Rain with Baby Duck*. Illustrated by Jill Barton. Candlewick, 1995.

_____. *The Purple Coat*. Illustrated by Amy Schwartz. Four Winds, 1986.

Highwater, Jamake. *Anpao—An American Indian Odyssey*. Harper & Row, 1980.

Hill, Eric. *Spot's Birthday Party*. Putnam, 1981.

_____. *Spot's First Walk*. Putnam, 1981.

_____. *Spot Goes to the Beach*. Putnam, 1985.

_____. *Spot Goes to School*. Putnam, 1984.

Hirschi, Ron. *Who Lives on . . . the Prairie?* Photographs by Galen Burrell. Putnam, 1989.

Ho, Minfong, *Hush!: A Thai Lullaby*. Orchard, 1996.

Hoban, Russell. *Best Friends for Frances*. Harper & Row, 1976.

Hoban, Tana. *All About Where*. Greenwillow, 1991.

_____. *Circles, Triangles, and Squares*. Macmillan, 1974.

_____. *Is It Red? Is It Yellow? Is It Blue?* Greenwillow, 1978.

_____. *Look Again!* Macmillan, 1971.

_____. *Look Book*. Greenwillow, 1997.

_____. *Look! Look! Look!* Greenwillow, 1988.

_____. *Of Colors and Things*. Greenwillow, 1989.

_____. *1, 2, 3*. Greenwillow, 1984.

_____. *Round & Round & Round*. Greenwillow, 1983.

_____. *Shapes, Shapes, Shapes*. Greenwillow, 1986.

_____. *Take Another Look*. Greenwillow, 1981.

_____. *26 Letters and 99 Cents*. Greenwillow, 1987.

_____. *What Is It?* Greenwillow, 1984.

Hoberman, Mary Ann. *Mr. and Mrs. Muddle*. Illustrated by Catharine O'Neill. Little, Brown, 1988.

Hodges, Margaret. *Saint George and the Dragon*. Illustrated by Trina Schart Hyman. Little, Brown, 1984.

Holzenthaler, Jean. *My Hands Can*. Dutton, 1978.

Houston, Gloria. *My Great-Aunt Arizona*. Illustrated by Susan Condie Lamb. HarperCollins, 1992.

Howard, Arthur. *When I Was Five*. Harcourt Brace, 1996.

Howe, James. *There's a Monster Under My Bed*. Atheneum, 1986.

Hughes, Dean. *Family Pose*. Atheneum, 1989.

_____. *Team Picture*. Atheneum, 1996.

Hughes, Shirley. *Dogger*. Bodley Head, 1977.

Hunter, Anne. *Possum's Harvest Moon*. Houghton Mifflin, 1996.

Hurd, Edith Thacher. *I Dance in My Red Pajamas*. Illustrated by Emily Arnold McCully. Harper & Row, 1982.

Hurmence, Belinda. *A Girl Called Boy*. Clarion, 1982.

Hutchins, Pat. *Changes, Changes*. Macmillan, 1971.

_____. *Rosie's Walk*. Macmillan, 1968.

_____. *Shrinking Mouse*. Greenwillow, 1997.

_____. *The Very Worst Monster*. Greenwillow, 1985.

_____. *What Game Shall We Play?* Greenwillow, 1990.

_____. *Where's the Baby?* Greenwillow, 1988.

_____. *Which Witch Is Which?* Greenwillow, 1989.

Hutton, Warwick. *Beauty and the Beast*. Atheneum, 1985.

_____. *Persephone*. Macmillan, 1994.

Ichikawa, Satomi. *Nora's Castle*. Putnam, 1986.

Isherwood, Shirley. *Something for James*. Illustrated by Neil Reed. Dial, 1996.

Ivimey, John. *The Complete Story of the Three Blind Mice*. Illustrated by Paul Galdone. Clarion, 1987.

Jacobs, Francine. *The Tainos: The People Who Welcomed Columbus*. Illustrated by Patrick Collins. Putnam, 1992.

Jakobsen, Kathy. *My New York*. Little, Brown, 1993.

James, Betsy. *Mary Ann*. Dutton, 1994.

Jenkins, Steve. *Big & Little.* Houghton, 1996.

Johnson, Angela. *Tell Me a Story, Mama.* Illustrated by David Soman. Watts, 1989.

Johnson, Rebecca L. *Braving the Frozen Frontier: Women Working in Antarctica.* Lerner, 1997.

Johnson, Stephen T. *Alphabet City.* Viking, 1995.

Johnston, Norma. *Louisa May: The World and Works of Louisa May Alcott.* Four Winds, 1991.

Johnston, Tony. *The Ghost of Nicholas Greebe.* Illustrated by S. D. Schindler. Dial, 1996.

Jonas, Ann. *When You Were a Baby.* Greenwillow, 1982.

Jorgensen, Gail. *Gotcha!* Illustrated by Kerry Argent. Scholastic, 1997.

Joyce, William. *Bentley & Egg.* HarperCollins, 1992.

_____. *Santa Calls.* HarperCollins, 1993.

Jukes, Mavis. *I'll See You in My Dreams.* Illustrated by Stacey Schuett. Knopf, 1993.

_____. *Like Jake and Me.* Illustrated by Lloyd Bloom. Knopf, 1984.

Keats, Ezra Jack. *Peter's Chair.* Harper & Row, 1967.

_____. *The Snowy Day.* Viking, 1962.

_____. *Whistle for Willie.* Viking, 1964.

Kehret, Peg. *Small Steps: The Year I Got Polio.* Whitman, 1996.

Keller, Holly. *Geraldine's Big Snow.* Greenwillow, 1988.

Kellogg, Steven. *Best Friends.* Dial, 1986.

_____. *A Rose for Pinkerton.* Dial, 1981.

Khalsa, Dayal Kaur. *I Want a Dog.* Clarkson, 1987.

_____. *The Snow Cat.* Clarkson Potter, 1992.

Kinsey-Warnock, Natalie. *As Long As There Are Mountains.* Cobblehill, 1997.

Kipling, Rudyard. *Rikki-Tikki-Tavi.* Adapted and illustrated by Jerry Pinkney. Morrow, 1997.

Knight, Hilary. *Hilary Knight's The Twelve Days of Christmas.* Macmillan, 1981.

Komaiko, Leah. *Just My Dad & Me.* Illustrated by Jeffrey Greene. HarperCollins, 1995.

Konigsburg, E. L. *Journey to an 800 Number.* Atheneum, 1982.

_____. *The View From Saturday.* Atheneum, 1996.

Kraus, Robert. *Leo the Late Bloomer.* Illustrated by Jose Aruego. Windmill, 1971.

Krauss, Ruth. *The Carrot Seed.* Harper & Row, 1945.

Kroll, Virginia. *Masai and I.* Illustrated by Nancy Carpenter. Four Winds, 1992.

Krull, Kathleen. *Wilma Unlimited; How Wilma Rudolph Became the World's Fastest Woman.* Illustrated by David Diaz. Harcourt Brace, 1996.

Kuklin, Susan. *Irrepressible Spirit.* Putnam, 1996.

Lacapa, Kathleen, and Lacapa, Michael. *Less Than Half, More Than Whole.* Northland, 1994.

Lasky, Kathryn. *Lunch Bunnies.* Illustrated by Marylin Hafner. Little, Brown, 1996.

_____. *The Night Journey.* Warne, 1981.

_____. *Sugaring Time.* Photographs by Christopher G. Knight. Macmillan, 1983.

_____. *Think Like an Eagle: At Work with a Wildlife Photographer.* Photographs by Christopher G. Knight and Jack Swedberg. Little, Brown, 1992.

Lauber, Patricia. *The News About Dinosaurs.* Bradbury, 1989.

_____. *Volcano: The Eruption and Healing of Mount St. Helens.* Bradbury, 1986.

Leaf, Munro. *The Story of Ferdinand.* Illustrated by Robert Lawson. Viking, 1936, 1964.

L'Engle, Madeleine. *A Ring of Endless Light.* Farrar, Straus & Giroux, 1980.

_____. *A Swiftly Tilting Planet.* Farrar, Straus & Giroux, 1978.

Lester, Alison. *The Journey Home.* Houghton Mifflin, 1991.

Lester, Helen. *Author: A True Story.* Houghton Mifflin, 1997.

Lester, Julius, edited by. *The Last Tales of Uncle Remus.* Illustrated by Jerry Pinkney. Dial, 1994.

_____. *Sam and the Tigers: A New Telling of Little Black Sambo.* Illustrated by Jerry Pinkney. Dial, 1996.

Levine, Arthur A., adapted by. *The Boy Who Drew Cats: A Japanese Folktale.* Illustrated by Frédéric Clément. Dial, 1994.

Levine, Ellen. *Freedom's Children: Young Civil Rights Activists Tell Their Own Stories.* Putnam's, 1993.

Lewin, Hugh. *Jafta.* Illustrated by Lisa Kopper. Carolrhoda, 1983.

Lewis, Barbara A. *The Kid's Guide to Social Action.* Free Spirit, 1991.

Lewis, C. S. *The Lion, the Witch, and the Wardrobe.* Macmillan, 1951.

Lexau, Joan M. *Benjie on His Own.* New York: Dial Press, 1970.

Lillie, Patricia. *Everything Has a Place.* Illustrated by Nancy Tafuri. Greenwillow, 1993.

Lindbergh, Anne. *Travel Far, Pay No Fare.* HarperCollins, 1992.

Lindgren, Barbro. *Sam's Ball.* Illustrated by Eva Eriksson. Morrow, 1983.

_____. *Sam's Bath.* Illustrated by Eva Eriksson. Morrow, 1983.

_____. *The Wild Baby.* Illustrated by Eva Eriksson. Greenwillow, 1981.

Lisle, Janet Taylor. *Afternoon of the Elves.* Watts, 1989.

_____. *The Gold Dust Letters.* Orchard, 1994.

Lobel, Arnold. *Frog and Toad All Year.* Harper & Row, 1976.

_____. *Grasshopper on the Road.* Harper & Row, 1978.

_____. *On Market Street.* Illustrated by Anita Lobel. Greenwillow, 1981.

_____. ed. *The Random House Book of Mother Goose.* Random House, 1986.

_____. *Uncle Elephant.* Harper & Row, 1981.

Locker, Thomas. *Sky Tree: Seeing Science Through Art.* HarperCollins, 1995.

London, Jonathan. *Fireflies, Fireflies, Light My Way.* Illustrated by Linda Messier. Viking, 1996.

_____. *Like Butter On Pancakes.* Illustrated by G. Brian Karas. Viking, 1996.

Lowry, Lois. *Attaboy, Sam!* Houghton Mifflin, 1992.

_____. *The Giver.* Houghton Mifflin, 1993.

_____. *Number the Stars.* Houghton Mifflin, 1989.

Lucht, Irmgard. *In this Night. . . .* Hyperion, 1993.

Lunn, Janet. *The Root Cellar.* Scribner's Sons, 1983.

_____. *Shadow in Hawthorn Bay.* Scribner's, 1986.

McBratney, Sam. *Guess How Much I Love You.* Illustrated by Anita Jeram. Candlewick, 1995.

McCloskey, Robert. *Lentil.* Viking, 1940.

_____. *Make Way for Ducklings.* Viking, 1941.

McCully, Emily Arnold. *Mirette on the High Wire.* Putnam's, 1992.

_____. *Picnic.* Harper & Row, 1984.

_____. *School.* Harper & Row, 1987.

McCurdy, Michael, edited by. *Escape from Slavery: The Boyhood of Frederick Douglass in His Own Words.* Knopf, 1994.

McDermott, Gerald. *Tim O'Toole and the Wee Folk*. Viking, 1990.

MacDonald, Suse. *Alphabatics*. Bradbury, 1986.

_____. *Zomo the Rabbit: A Trickster Tale from West Africa*. Hacourt Brace Jovanovich, 1992.

McKinley, Robin. *The Hero and the Crown*. Greenwillow, 1984.

McKissack, Patricia, and Fredrick McKissack. *The Civil Rights Movement in America from 1865 to the Present*. Children's Press, 1991.

MacLachlan, Patricia. *The Facts and Fictions of Minna Pratt*. Harper & Row, 1988.

_____. *Mama One, Mama Two*. Illustrated by Ruth Lercher Bornstein. Harper & Row, 1982.

_____. *Sarah, Plain and Tall*. Harper & Row, 1985.

McLeod, Emilie Warren. *The Bear's Bicycle*. Little, Brown, 1975.

McMillan, Bruce. *Eating Fractions*. Scholastic, 1991.

McMullan, Kate and McMullan, Jim. *Hey, Pipsqueak!* HarperCollins, 1995.

McPhail, David. *The Dream Child*. Dutton, 1985.

_____. *Edward and the Pirates*. Little, Brown, 1997.

_____. *Pigs Aplenty, Pigs Galore!* Dutton, 1993.

Macy, Sue. *Winning Ways: A Photohistory of American Women in Sports*. Holt, 1996.

Mahy, Margaret. *17 Kings and 42 Elephants*. Illustrated by Patricia MacCarthy. Dial, 1987.

Malnig, Anita. *Where the Waves Break: Life at the Edge of the Sea*. Photographed by Jeff Rotman. Carolrhoda, 1985.

Marshall, Edward. *Four on the Shore*. Illustrated by James Marshall. Dial, 1985.

Marshall, James. *George and Martha One Fine Day*. Houghton Mifflin, 1978.

Martin, Eva, ed. *Canadian Fairy Tales*. Illustrated by Laszlo Gal. Douglas & McIntyre, 1984.

Martin, Jacqueline. *Buzzy Bones and the Lost Quilt*. Illustrated by Stella Ormai. Lothrop, Lee & Shepard, 1988.

_____. *Good Times on Grandfather Mountain*. Illustrated by Susan Gaber. Orchard, 1992.

Martin, Rafe. *Will's Mammoth*. Illustrated by Stephen Gammell. Putnam, 1989.

Marzollo, Jean. *I Am Water*. Illustrated by Judith Moffatt. Scholastic, 1996.

_____. *I Spy: School Days: A Book of Picture Riddles*. Photographs by Walter Wick, Scholastic, 1995.

_____. *I Spy Spooky Night: A Book of Picture Riddles*. Photographs by Walter Wick. Scholastic, 1996.

Mayer, Marianna, ed. *The Twelve Dancing Princesses*. Illustrated by K. Y. Craft. Morrow, 1989.

Melmed, Laura Krauss. *Little Oh*. Lothrop, Lee, & Shepard,1997.

Meyer, Carolyn, and Charles Gallenkamp. *The Mystery of the Ancient Maya*. Atheneum, 1985.

Micklethwait, Lucy, selected by. *A Child's Book of Play in Art: Great Pictures, Great Fun*. Kindersley, 1996.

Miller, Margaret. *Now I'm Big*. Greenwillow, 1996.

Milne, A. A. *The House at Pooh Corner*. Illustrated by E. H. Shepard, Dutton, 1928, 1956.

_____. *Winnie-the-Pooh*. Illustrated by Ernest H. Shepard. Dutton, 1926, 1954.

Minarik, Else Holmelund. *The Little Girl and the Dragon*. Illustrated by Martine Gourbault. Greenwillow, 1991.

Monjo, F. N. *The Drinking Gourd*. Harper & Row, 1969.

Mora, Pat. *A Birthday Basket for Tia*. Illustrated by Cecily Lang. Macmillan, 1992.

Morozumi, Atsuko. *My Friend Gorilla*. Farrar, Strauss & Giroux, 1998.

Moss, Lloyd. *Zin! Zin! Zin! A Violin*. Illustrated by Marjorie Priceman. Simon & Schuster, 1995.

Munro, Roxie. *The Inside-Outside Book of Washington, D.C.* Dutton, 1987.

Murphy, Jill. *Peace at Last*. Dial, 1980.

Murphy, Mary. *I Like It When . . .* Harcourt Brace, 1997.

Murphy, Stuart J. *The Best Bug Parade*. Illustrated by Holly Keller: HarperCollins, 1996.

Nance, John. *Lobo of the Tasaday*. Pantheon, 1982.

Narahashi, Keiko. *I Have a Friend*. Macmillan, 1987.

Naylor, Phyllis Reynolds. *Keeping a Christmas Secret*. Illustrated by Lena Shiffman. Atheneum, 1989.

_____. *Shiloh*. Atheneum, 1991.

Nelson, Theresa. *The Beggars' Ride*. Orchard, 1992.

Ness, Evaline. *Sam, Bangs, and Moonshine*. Holt, Rinehart & Winston, 1966.

Nichol, Barbara. *Beethoven Lives Upstairs*. Illustrated by Scott Cameron, Orchard, 1994.

Nightingale, Sandy. *A Giraffe on the Moon*. Harcourt Brace Jovanovich, 1991.

Noll, Sally. *Watch Where You Go*. Greenwillow, 1990.

Nomura, Takaaki. *Grandpa's Town*. Translated by Amanda Mayer Stinchecum. Kane/Miller, 1991.

O'Dell, Scott. *Island of the Blue Dolphins*. Houghton Mifflin, 1960.

Opie, Iona, ed. *My Very First Mother Goose*. Illustrated by Rosemary Wells. Candlewick, 1996.

Opie, Iona, and Peter Opie. *I Saw Esau: The Schoolchild's Pocket Book*. Illustrated by Maurice Sandak. Candlewick, 1992.

Oppenheim, Joanne. *Have You Seen Birds?* Illustrated by Barbara Reid. Scholastic, 1986.

_____. *Have You Seen Trees?* Illustrated by Jean and Mou-sien Tseng. Scholastic, 1995.

Ormerod, Jan. *Sunshine*. Lothrop, Lee & Shepard, 1981.

Oxenbury, Helen. *The Checkup*. Dial, 1983.

_____. *Dressing*. Simon & Schuster, 1981.

_____. *Family*. Simon & Schuster, 1981.

_____. *Friends*. Simon & Schuster, 1981.

_____. *I See*. Random House, 1986.

_____. *Playing*. Simon & Schuster, 1981.

_____. *Working*. Simon & Schuster, 1981.

Paige, David. *A Day in the Life of a Marine Biologist*. Photographed by Roger Ruhlin. Troll Associates, 1981.

Paraskevas, Betty. *The Tangerine Bear*. Illustrated by Michael Paraskevas. HarperCollins, 1997.

Park, Ruth. *Playing Beatie Bow*. Atheneum, 1982.

Parker, Vic. *Bearobics: A Hip-Hop Counting Story*. Illustrated by Emily Bolam. Viking, 1997.

Paterson, Katherine. *Come Sing, Jimmy Jo*. Lodestar, 1985.

_____. *Jacob Have I Loved*. Crowell, 1980.

Paulsen, Gary. *Dogsong*. Bradbury, 1985.

_____. *Hatchet*. Bradbury, 1987.

_____. *The Winter Room*. Orchard, 1989.

_____. *The Voyage of the Frog*. Orchard, 1989.

Peet, Bill. *Bill Peet: An Autobiography*. Houghton Mifflin, 1989.

Peters, Lisa Westberg. *October Smiled Back*. Illustrated by Ed Young. Holt, 1996.

———. *The Sun, the Wind and the Rain*. Illustrated by Ted Rand. Holt, 1988.

Plourde, Lynn. *Pigs in the Mud in the Middle of the Rud*. Illustrated by John Schoenherr. Scholastic, 1997.

Polacco, Patricia. *Picnic at Mudsock Meadow*. Putnam, 1992.

Pollock, Penny. *The Turkey Girl: A Zuni Cinderella Story*. Illustrated by Ed Young. Little, Brown, 1996.

Pomerantz, Charlotte. *Flap Your Wings and Try*. Illustrated by Nancy Tafuri. Greenwillow, 1989.

Porte, Barbara. *Harry in Trouble*. Illustrated by Yossi Abolafin. Greenwillow, 1989.

Potter, Beatrix. *The Tale of Peter Rabbit*. Warne, 1902, 1986.

Preston, Edna Mitchell, and Rainey Bennett. *The Temper Tantrum Book*. Penguin, 1976.

Priceman, Marjorie. *How to Make an Apple Pie and See the World*. Knopf, 1994.

Pullman, Philip. *The Golden Compass*. Knopf, 1996.

Purdy, Carol. *Least of All*. Illustrated by Tim Arnold. Macmillan, 1987.

Radley, Gail. *The Golden Days*. Macmillan, 1991.

Rankin, Joan. *Wow! It's Great Being a Duck*. Simon & Schuster, 1998.

Raskin, Ellen. *The Westing Game*. Dutton, 1978.

Rathmann, Peggy. *Ruby the Copycat*. Scholastic, 1991.

Reiser, Lynn. *Best Friends Think Alike*. Greenwillow, 1997.

Reiss, John J. *Numbers*. Bradbury, 1971.

———. *Shapes*. Bradbury, 1974.

Rhoades, Diane. *Garden Crafts for Kids: 50 Great Reasons to Get Your Hands Dirty*. Sterling, 1995.

Rice, Eve. *Benny Bakes a Cake*. Greenwillow, 1981.

———. *Oh, Lewis!* Macmillan, 1974.

Riskind, Mary. *Apple Is My Sign*. Houghton Mifflin, 1981.

Robbins, Ken. *Power Machines*. Holt, 1993.

Roche, Denis. *Loo-Loo, Book, And Art You Can Do*. Houghton Mifflin, 1996.

Rockwell, Anne. *First Comes Spring*. Harper & Row, 1985.

Rockwell, Harlow. *My Dentist*. Greenwillow, 1975.

———. *My Doctor*. Macmillan, 1973.

Rogers, Fred. *Going to Day Care*. Photographed by Jim Judkis. Putnam, 1986.

———. *Let's Talk About It: Divorce*. Photographs by Jim Judkis. Putnam, 1996.

Rosen, Michael, ed. *We're Going on a Bear Hunt*. Illustrated by Helen Oxenbury. Macmillan, 1989.

Rosenberg, Liz. *Eli and Uncle Dawn*. Illustrated by Susan Gaber. Harcourt Brace, 1997.

———. *Monster Mama*. Illustrated by Stephen Gammell. Putnam, 1993.

Russo, Marisabina. *Waiting for Hannah*. Greenwillow, 1989.

Ryder, Joanne. *White Bear, Ice Bear*. Illustrated by Michael Rothman. Morrow, 1989.

Rylant, Cynthia. *Birthday Presents*. Illustrated by Sucie Stevenson. Orchard, 1987.

———. *A Blue-Eyed Daisy*. Bradbury, 1985.

———. *Henry and Mudge and the Long Weekend*. Illustrated by Sucie Stevenson. Bradbury, 1992.

———. *Missing May*. Orchard, 1992.

———. *Mr. Putter and Tabby Pour the Tea*. Illustrated by Arthur Howard. Harcourt, 1994.

———. *When I Was Young in the Mountains*. Illustrated by Diane Goode. Dutton, 1982.

Sandburg, Carl. *More Rootabagas*. Illustrated by Paul O. Zelinsky. Knopf, 1993.

Sandin, Joan. *The Long Way to a New Land*. Harper & Row, 1981.

San Souci, Robert. *The Hobyahs*. Illustrated by Alexi Natchev. Doubleday, 1994.

———. retold by. *The Talking Eggs: A Folktale from the American South*. Illustrated by Jerry Pinkney. Dial, 1989.

Sattler, Helen Roney. *Hominids: A Look Back at Our Ancestors*. Lothrop, Lee & Shepard, 1988.

Say, Allen. *Allison*. Houghton Mifflin, 1997.

———. *Grandfather's Journey*. Houghton Mifflin, 1993.

———. *Tree of Cranes*. Houghton Mifflin, 1991.

Scarry, Richard. *Richard Scarry's The Best Word Book Ever*. Western, 1963.

Schaefer, Carole Lexa. *The Squiggle*. Illustrated by Pierre Morgan. Crown, 1996.

Schotter, Roni. *Captain Snap and the Children of Vinegar Lane*. Illustrated by Marcia Sewall. Watts, 1989.

———. *Nothing Ever Happens on 90th Street*. Illustrated by Kyrsten Brooker. Orchard, 1997.

Schwartz, Alvin. *There Is a Carrot in My Ear and Other Noodle Tales*. Illustrated by Karen Ann Weinhaus. Harper & Row, 1982.

Schwartz, Amy. *Annabelle Swift, Kindergartner*. Orchard, 1988.

Schwartz, Gary. *Rembrandt*. Abrams, 1992.

Schwartz, Henry. *How I Captured a Dinosaur*. Illustrated by Amy Schwartz. Watts, 1989.

Scieszka, Jon. *The Stinky Cheese Man and Other Fairly Stupid Tales*. Illustrated by Lane Smith. Viking, 1992.

———. *Your Mother Was a Neanderthal*. Illustrated by Lane Smith. Viking, 1993.

Scott, Ann Herbert. *Sam*. Illustrated by Symeon Shimin. McGraw-Hill, 1967.

Selsam, Millicent. *Mushrooms*. Photographed by Jerome Wexler. Morrow, 1986.

Selsam, Millicent, and Joyce Hunt. *Keep Looking!* Illustrated by Normand Chartier. Macmillan, 1989.

Sendak, Maurice. *Where the Wild Things Are*. Harper & Row, 1963.

Serfozo, Mary. *What's What?: A Guessing Game*. Illustrated by Keiko Narahashi. McElderry, 1996.

Seuss, Dr. *And to Think That I Saw It on Mulberry Street*. Vanguard, 1937.

———. *The Cat in the Hat*. Beginner, 1957.

———. *Oh, the Places You'll Go!* Random House. 1990.

Severance, John B. *Gandhi, Great Soul*. Clarion, 1997.

Sharmat, Marjorie. *The Best Valentine in the World*. Illustrated by Lilian Obligado. Holiday House, 1982.

———. *A Big Fat Enormous Lie*. Dutton, 1978.

Shaw, Nancy. *Sheep Out to Eat*. Illustrated by Margot Apple. Houghton Mifflin, 1992.

Showers, Paul. *Look at Your Eyes*. Crowell, 1962.

Shura, Mary Francis. *The Search for Grissi*. Illustrated by Ted Lewin. Dodd, Mead, 1985.

Sierra, Judy. *Counting Crocodiles*. Illustrated by Will Hillenbrand. Harcourt Brace, 1997.

The Child Responds to Literature

Sill, Cathryn. *About Birds: A Guide for Children.* Illustrated by John Sill. Peachtree, 1991.

Silverstein, Shel. *A Light in the Attic.* Harper & Row, 1981.

Simon, Seymour. *Storms.* Morrow, 1989.

Slate, Joseph. *Miss Bindergarten Gets Ready for Kindergarten.* Illustrated by Ashley Wolff. Dutton, 1996.

Slepian, Jan. *Risk N' Roses.* Philomel, 1990.

Small, David. *Imogene's Antlers.* Crown, 1985.

Smalls-Hector, Irene. *Jonathan and His Mommy.* Little, Brown, 1992.

Soto, Gary. *Neighborhood Odes.* Harcourt Brace Jovanovich, 1992.

_____. *Taking Sides.* Harcourt Brace Jovanovich, 1991.

Speare, Elizabeth George. *The Bronze Bow.* Houghton Mifflin, 1961.

_____. *The Sign of the Beaver.* Houghton Mifflin, 1982.

Sperry, Armstrong. *Call It Courage.* Macmillan, 1940.

Stanek, Muriel. *All Alone After School.* Illustrated by Ruth Rosner. Whitman, 1985.

Stanley, Diane, and Peter Vennema. *Bard of Avon: The Story of William Shakespeare.* Illustrated by Diane Stanley. Morrow, 1992.

_____. *Good Queen Bess: The Story of Elizabeth I of England.* Illustrated by Diane Stanley. Four Winds, 1990.

_____. *Shaka: King of the Zulus.* Illustrated by Diane Stanley. Morrow, 1988.

Staples, Suzanne Fisher. *Shabanu: Daughter of the Wind.* Knopf, 1989.

Steig, William. *Spinky Sulks.* Farrar, Straus & Giroux, 1988.

Steptoe, John. *Baby Says.* Lothrop, Lee & Shepard, 1988.

_____. *Mufaro's Beautiful Daughters: An African Tale.* Lothrop, Lee & Shepard, 1987.

_____. *Stevie.* Harper & Row, 1969.

_____. *The Story of Jumping Mouse.* Lothrop, Lee & Shepard, 1984.

Stevens, Janet. *Tops & Bottoms.* Harcourt Brace, 1995.

Stevenson, James. *Which One Is Whitney?* Greenwillow, 1990.

Stevenson, Robert Louis. *Treasure Island.* Scribner's, 1911.

Stewart, Sarah. *The Gardener.* Illustrated by David Small. Farrar Straus & Giroux, 1997.

Strachan, Ian. *The Flawed Glass.* Little, Brown, 1990.

Sturges, Philemon. *Ten Flashing Fireflies.* Illustrated by Anna Vojtech. North-South, 1995.

Taback, Simms. *There Was An Old Lady Who Swallowed A Fly.* Viking, 1997.

Tafuri, Nancy. *Early Morning in the Barn.* Greenwillow, 1983.

_____. *One Wet Jacket.* Greenwillow, 1988.

_____. *Who's Counting?* Greenwillow, 1986.

Taylor, Mildred. *Let the Circle Be Unbroken.* Dial, 1981.

_____. *Roll of Thunder, Hear My Cry.* Dial, 1976.

Tejima. *Fox's Dream.* Philomel, 1987.

Theodorou, Rod, and Telford, Carole. *Big and Small.* Illustrated by Gwen Tourret and Trevor Dunton. Rigby, 1996.

Thompson, Colin. *How to Live Forever.* Knopf, 1996.

Tolkien, J. R. R. *The Hobbit.* Random House, 1937, 1977.

Trivizas, Eugene. *The Three Little Wolves and the Big Bad Pig.* Macmillan, 1993.

Troll, Nelly S. *Behind the Secret Window: A Memoir of a Hidden Childhood During World War Two.* Dial, 1993.

Turkle, Brinton. *Do Not Open.* Dutton, 1981.

Udry, Janice May. *Let's Be Enemies.* Harper & Row, 1961.

_____. *What Mary Jo Shared.* Whitman, 1966.

Urlev, Uri. *The Man from the Other Side.* Houghton Mifflin, 1991.

Van Allsburg, Chris. *The Mysteries of Harris Burdick.* Houghton Mifflin, 1984.

_____. *The Polar Express.* Houghton Mifflin, 1985.

_____. *The Wretched Stone.* Houghton Mifflin, 1991.

_____. *The Z Was Zapped.* Houghton Mifflin, 1987.

Van Leeuwen, Jean. *More Tales of Oliver Pig.* Dial, 1981.

_____. *Oliver Pig at School.* Illustrated by Ann Schweninger. Dial, 1990.

Vincent, Gabrielle. *Feel Better, Ernest!* Greenwillow, 1988.

_____. *Smile, Ernest and Celestine.* Greenwillow, 1982.

Viorst, Judith. *Alexander and the Terrible, Horrible, No Good, Very Bad Day.* Illustrated by Ray Cruz. Atheneum, 1972.

_____. *The Alphabet from Z to A (With Much Confusion on the Way).* Illustrated by Richard Hull. Atheneum, 1994.

_____. *I'll Fix Anthony.* Harper & Row, 1969.

Voake, Charlotte. *Mrs. Goose's Baby.* Little, Brown, 1989.

Voigt, Cynthia. *Dicey's Song.* Atheneum, 1982.

_____. *A Solitary Blue.* Atheneum, 1983.

Waber, Bernard. *Ira Sleeps Over.* Houghton Mifflin, 1972.

_____. *The Snake: A Very Long Story.* Houghton Mifflin, 1978.

Waddell, Martin. *Can't You Sleep, Little Bear?* Illustrated by Barbara Firth. Candlewick, 1992.

_____. *Farmer Duck.* Illustrated by Helen Oxenbury. Candlewick, 1992.

_____. *Let's Go Home, Little Bear.* Illustrated by Barbara Firth. Candlewick, 1993.

_____. *What Use Is a Moose?* Illustrated by Arthur Robins. Candlewick, 1996.

_____. *You and Me, Little Bear.* Illustrated by Barbara Firth. Candlewick, 1996.

Waggoner, Karen. *The Lemonade Babysitter.* Little, Brown, 1992.

Wahl, Jan. *Humphrey's Bear.* Illustrated by William Joyce. Holt, 1987.

Walsh, Ellen Stoll. *Mouse Count.* Harcourt, 1991.

Walter, Mildred Pitts. *Brother to the Wind.* Illustrated by Diane and Leo Dillon. Lothrop, Lee & Shepard, 1985.

Weiss, Nicki. *Where Does the Brown Bear Go?* Greenwillow, 1989.

Wells, Rosemary. *Bunny Cakes.* Dial, 1997.

_____. *The Language of Doves.* Illustrated by Greg Shed. Dial, 1996.

_____. *Max and Ruby's First Greek Myth: Pandora's Box.* Dial, 1993.

_____. *Max's Birthday.* Dial, 1985.

_____. *Max's Breakfast.* Dial, 1985.

_____. *McDuff Moves In.* Illustrated by Susan Jeffers. Little, Brown, 1997.

_____. *Timothy Goes to School.* Dial, 1981.

White, E. B. *Charlotte's Web.* Harper & Row, 1952.

Wiesner, David. *Free Fall.* Lothrop, Lee & Shepard, 1988.

_____. *Tuesday.* Clarion, 1991.

Wild, Margaret. *Mr. Nick's Knitting.* Illustrated by Dee Huxley. Harcourt Brace Jovanovich, 1988.

_____. *Old Pig.* Illustrated by Ron Brooks. Dial, 1996.

Wilder, Laura Ingalls, *The First Four Years.* Illustrated by Garth Williams. Harper & Row, 1971.

_____. *Little House in the Big Woods.* Harper & Row, 1932.

_____. *These Happy Golden Years.* Harper & Row, 1943.

Wilkes, Angela. *My First Nature Book.* Knopf, 1990.

Willard, Nancy. *Beauty and the Beast*. Illustrated by Barry Moser. Harcourt Brace Jovanovich, 1992.

_____. *Cracked Corn and Snow Ice Cream: A Family Almanac*. Illustrated by Jane Dyer. Harcourt Brace, 1997.

_____. *Night Story*. Illustrated by Ilse Plume. Harcourt Brace Jovanovich, 1986.

_____. *Pish, Posh, Said Hieronymus Bosch*. Illustrated by Leo and Diane Dillon. Harcourt Brace Jovanovich, 1991.

_____. *The Velveteen Rabbit*. Illustrated by Ilse Plume. Godine, 1982.

_____. *The Velveteen Rabbit*. Illustrated by Michael Hague. Holt, Rinehart & Winston, 1983.

_____. *The Velveteen Rabbit*. Illustrated by Allen Atkinson. Knopf, 1984.

Williams, Margery. *The Velveteen Rabbit: Or How Toys Become Real*. Doubleday, 1922, 1958.

Williams, Vera B. *A Chair for My Mother*. Greenwillow, 1982.

_____. *Lucky Song*. Greenwillow, 1997.

_____. *Something Special for Me*. Greenwillow, 1983.

Wilson, Sarah. *Good Zap, Little Grog*. Illustrated by Susan Meddaugh. Candlewick, 1995.

Winthrop, Elizabeth. *Bear and Mrs. Duck*. Illustrated by Patience Brewster. Holiday House, 1988.

Wise, William. *Ten Sly Piranhas: A Counting Story in Reverse*. Illustrated by Victoria Chess. Dial, 1993.

Wojciechowska, Maia. *Shadow of a Bull*. Illustrated by Alvin Smith. Atheneum, 1964.

Wood, Audrey. *The Flying Dragon Room*. Illustrated by Mark Teague. Scholastic, 1996.

_____. *King Bidgood's in the Bathtub*. Illustrated by Don Wood. Harcourt Brace Jovanovich, 1985.

_____. *The Rude Giants*. Harcourt Brace Jovanovich, 1993.

Yates, Elizabeth. *Amos Fortune, Free Man*. Aladdin, 1950.

Yep, Laurence. *The Star Fisher*. Morrow, 1991.

Yolen, Jane. *The Devil's Arithmetic*. Viking Kestrel, 1988.

_____. *Owl Moon*. Illustrated by John Schoenherr. Philomel, 1987.

_____. *The Three Bears Rhyme Book*. Illustrated by Jane Dyer. Harcourt Brace Jovanovich, 1987.

Young, Ed, trans. *Lon Po Po: A Red Riding Hood Story from China*. Philomel, 1989.

Zamorano, Ana. *Let's Eat!* Illustrated by Julie Vivas. Scholastic, 1997.

Zemach, Margot. *It Could Always Be Worse*. Farrar, Straus & Giroux, 1977.

Zimmerman, H. Werner. *Henny Penny*. Scholastic, 1989.

Zolotow, Charlotte. *My Grandson Lew*. Illustrated by William Pène du Bois. Harper & Row, 1974.

_____. *The Quarreling Book*. Illustrated by Arnold Lobel. Harper & Row, 1963.

Zolotow, Charlotte. *Who Is Ben?* Illustrated by Kathryn Jacobi. HarperCollins, 1997.

_____. *William's Doll*. Illustrated by William Pène du Bois. Harper & Row, 1972.

2 *The History of Children's Literature*

- Milestones in the History of Children's Literature
- The History of Censorship
- Children and the Family in Children's Literature

any people are surprised to discover that childhood has not always been considered an important time of life. When students of children's literature look at the beautiful books published to meet children's needs, interests, and reading levels, many are amazed to learn that not long ago books were not written specifically for children. Changes in printing technology provided affordable books, but more important were changes in social attitudes toward children. When society looked upon children as little adults who must rapidly step into the roles of their parents, children had little time or need to read books. When childhood began to be viewed as a special part of the human life cycle, literature written specifically for children became very important.

Within the context of human history as a whole, the history of children's literature is very short. Neither early tales told through the oral tradition nor early books were created specifically for children. When eventually written, children's books usually mirrored the dominant cultural values of their place and time. Thus, a study of children's literature in Western Europe and North America from the fifteenth century through contemporary times reflects both changes in society as a whole and changes in social expectations of children and the family.

Literature researchers view children's literature as a vehicle for studying social values and changing attitudes. Karen J. Winkler (1981) maintains that the 1970s and 1980s have been characterized by an ever-increasing interest in the scholarly study of children's literature as an index to the social attitudes of a particular time. Robert Gordon Kelly's (1970) "Mother Was a Lady: Self and Society in Selected American Children's Periodicals, 1865–1890," Mary Lystad's (1980) *From Dr. Mather to Dr. Seuss: Two Hundred Years of American Books for Children,* and Ruth M. Phelps's (1985) "A Comparison of Newbery Award Winners in the First and Last Decade of the Award (1922–31 and 1976–85)" are examples of such research. The increasing number of doctoral dissertations that critically evaluate certain aspects of children's literature also suggest the current importance of children's literature as a research subject. For example, from the 1930s until 1970, approximately two hundred dissertations covered topics related to children's literature. In contrast, the 1970s alone produced nearly eight hundred such dissertations. Several of these studies suggest the interrelatedness of social, cultural, and economic factors and the story themes and values presented in children's literature of a certain period.

MILESTONES IN THE HISTORY OF CHILDREN'S LITERATURE

This chapter first considers some milestones in the development of children's literature. Then, it looks at changing views of children and the family as reflected in early books for children and in more contemporary stories. Chart 2–1 provides a brief overview of the historical milestones.

The Oral Tradition

Long before recorded history, family units and tribes shared their group traditions and values through stories told around the campfire. On every continent around the globe, ancient peoples developed folktales and mythologies that speculated about human beginnings, attempted to explain the origins of the universe and other natural phenomena, emphasized ethical truths, and transmitted history from one generation to the next. When hunters returned

CHART 2-1 Historic milestones in children's literature

—	The Oral Tradition "Beowulf" "Jack the Giant Killer"	1800s	The Romantic Movement in Europe The Brothers Grimm Hans Christian Andersen
1400s	Early Books Hornbooks Caxton's Printing Press—1476		The Impact of Illustrators on Children's Books Walter Crane
1500s	The Introduction of Chapbooks "Jack the Giant Killer"		Randolph Caldecott Kate Greenaway
1600s	The Puritan Influence *Spiritual Milk for Boston Babes in Either England, Drawn from the Breasts of Both Testaments for Their Souls' Nourishment* *Pilgrim's Progress*	1860s	The Victorian Influence Charlotte Yonge's *The Daisy Chain* and *The Clever Woman of the Family*
1693	A View of Childhood Changes John Locke's *Some Thoughts Concerning Education*	1840–1900	Childhood Seen as an Adventure, Not a Training Ground for Adulthood Fantasy
1697	First Fairy Tales Written for Children Charles Perrault's *Tales of Mother Goose*		Lewis Carroll's *Alice's Adventures in Wonderland* Edward Lear's *A Book of Nonsense*
1719	Great Adventure Stories Daniel Defoe's *Robinson Crusoe* Jonathan Swift's *Gulliver's Travels*		Adventure Robert Louis Stevenson's *Treasure Island* Howard Pyle's *The Merry Adventures of Robin Hood*
1744	Children's Literature: A True Beginning John Newbery's *A Little Pretty Pocket Book* and *History of Little Goody Two- Shoes* (1745)		Jules Verne's *Twenty Thousand Leagues Under the Sea* Real People
1762	Guidance of Children in Their Search for Knowledge Jean Jacques Rousseau's *Emile*		Margaret Sidney's *The Five Little Peppers and How They Grew* Louisa May Alcott's *Little Women*
1789	Poetry About Children William Blake's *Songs of Innocence*		Johanna Spyri's *Heidi*

from their adventures, they probably told about the perils of the hunt and hostile encounters with other tribes. Heroic deeds were certainly told and retold until they became a part of a group's heritage. This tradition has existed since the first oral communication among human beings and goes back to the very roots of every civilization on earth. These tales were not told specifically to children, but children were surely present—listening, watching, learning, and remembering.

The various native peoples of North America developed mythologies expressing their reverence for the rolling prairies, lush forests, ice floes, deserts, and blue lakes of their continent. In Latin and South America, storytellers of the Yucatán Peninsula and the Andes chronicled the rise of Maya, Aztec, and Inca empires, wars of expansion, and, eventually, the Spanish conquest of their homelands. Across Africa, highly respected storytellers developed a style that encouraged audiences to interact with storytellers in relating tales of dramatic heroes, personified animals, and witty tricksters. In the extremely ancient cultures of Asia, from Mesopotamia to Japan, early myths and folktales were eventually incorporated into the complex mythologies and philosophical tenets of Taoism, Confucianism, Hinduism, and Buddhism. In Europe, the earliest oral traditions of the Celts, Franks, Saxons, Goths, Danes, and many other groups eventually influenced one another as a result of migration, trade, and warfare;

and the mythologies of ancient Greece and Rome became widely influential as the Roman Empire expanded over much of the continent.

The European oral tradition, according to Robert Leeson (1977), reached its climax in the feudal era of the Middle Ages. What are often called *castle tales* and *cottage tales* provided people with literature long before those tales were widely accessible in writing or print. The ruling classes favored poetic epics about the reputed deeds of the lord of the manor or his ancestors. In the great halls of castles, minstrels or bards accompanied themselves on lyres or harps while singing tales about noble warriors, such as Beowulf and King Arthur, or ballads of chivalrous love in regal surroundings, such as those found in the French version of *Cinderella*.

Around cottage fires or at country fairs, humbler people had different heroes. Storytellers shared folktales about people much like the peasants themselves, people who daily confronted servitude, inscrutable natural phenomena, and unknown spiritual forces. In these tales, even the youngest or poorest person had the potential to use resourcefulness or kindness to go from rags to riches and to live "happily ever after." Often, such achievement required outwitting or slaying wolves, dragons, malevolent supernatural beings, or great lords.

By whatever name they were known—bards, minstrels, or devisers of tales—the storytellers of medieval Europe were entertainers: If they did not entertain, they lost their audiences or even their meals and lodging. Consequently, they learned to tell stories that had rapid plot development and easily identifiable characters. These storytellers also possessed considerable power. Sir Philip Sidney (1595), a sixteenth-century English poet, described storytellers as able to keep children away from their play and old people away from their chimney corners. Whether woven from imagination or retold from legends and stories of old, the tales of storytellers could influence the people who heard them. Thus, if a minstrel's story offended or discredited a lord, the minstrel could be punished. By the end of the fourteenth century, feudal authority sought to control the tales being told and often jailed storytellers who angered either a ruler or the church.

German scholar August Nitschke (1988) describes the role of fairy tales in earlier times. He states:

In the fifteenth and sixteenth centuries fairy tales were told to children, but grown men took fairy tales so seriously that they would interpret them symbolically. Geiler of Kaiserberg, for instance, and Martin Luther were able to interpret the Cinderella story in such a way. They foretold a good future for those persons working in the kitchen as humbly and shyly as Cinderella did. Others such as Cardinal Giovanni Dominici opposed fairy tales because he thought they could foster vanity such as toys might—like the wooden horses or the pretty trumpets or the artificial birds or the golden drums—or because they might frighten children. (p. 164)

Today, many early European folktales, myths, and legends are considered ideal for sharing with children, but this was not the attitude of feudal Europe. Storytellers addressed audiences of all ages. A child was considered a small adult who should enter into adult life as quickly as possible, and stories primarily for young people were considered unnecessary. Consequently, the stories about giants, heroes, and simpletons that relieved the strain of adult life also entertained children. These favorite tales, which had been told and retold for hundreds of years, were eventually chosen for some of the first printed books in Europe.

Early Printed Books

Prior to the mid-1400s, the literary heritage of Europe consisted of the oral tradition and parchment manuscripts laboriously handwritten by monks and scribes. Manuscript books were rare and costly, prized possessions of the nobles and priests, who were among the few Europeans able to read and write. To the extent that these books were meant for the young, they were usually designed to provide instruction in rhetoric, grammar, and music for the children privileged enough to attend monastery schools. Children were rarely trusted with the books themselves and usually wrote on slates as monks dictated their lessons.

A significant event occurred in the 1450s, when the German Johannes Gutenberg discovered a practical method for using movable metal type, which made possible the mass production of books. After learning the printing process in Germany, William Caxton established England's first printing press in 1476. The use of printing presses led to the creation of hornbooks, which were printed sheets of text mounted on wood and covered with translucent animal horn. Hornbooks were used to teach reading and numbers. The books were in the shape of a paddle. Gillian Avery (1995) states that "This convenient and relatively indestructible form of presenting the alphabet (followed by a syllabary, invocation to the Trinity, and the Lord's Prayer) was in common use from the sixteenth century until well on in the eighteenth" (p. 3).

Hornbooks remained popular into the 1700s, when the battledore, a lesson book made of folded paper or cardboard, became more prevalent. Like hornbooks, battledores usually contained an alphabet, numerals, and proverbs or prayers.

When William Caxton opened his printing business in 1476, most of the books used with children were not written for their interest. Instead, books for children adhered to the sentiment that young readers should read only what would improve their manners or instruct their minds. *Caxton's Book of Curtesye,* first printed in 1477 (Furnivall, 1868), contained directions for drawing readers away from vice and turning them toward virtue. Verses guided readers toward personal cleanliness (comb your hair, clean your ears, clean your nose but don't pick

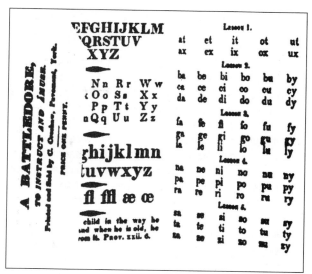

This lesson book, or battledore, was made from folded paper or cardboard. (Courtesy of The Horn Book, Inc.)

The hornbook, which was used for instruction, usually contained the alphabet, numerals, and the Lord's Prayer. (Photo courtesy of The Horn Book, Inc.)

it), polite social interactions (look people straight in the face when speaking, don't quarrel with dogs), suitable reverence in church (kneel before the cross, don't chatter), and correct table manners (don't blow on your food or undo your girdle at the table).

The majority of books that Caxton published were not meant to be read by children, but three of his publications are now considered classics in children's literature. In 1481, Caxton published the beast fable *Reynart the Foxe* (*The History of Reynard the Fox*), a satire of oppression and tyranny. This tale of a clever fox who could outwit all his adversaries became popular with both adults and children.

Caxton's most important publication may be *The Book of the Subtyle Historyes and Fables of Esope* (*The Fables of Aesop*), which Caxton translated from a manuscript by the French monk Machault in 1484. These fables about the weaknesses of people and animals were popular with readers of various ages and are still enjoyed by children. F. J. Harvey Darton (1966) maintains that Caxton's version of Aesop, "with infinitely little modernization, is the best text for children today" (p. 10). Caxton's publication in 1485 of Sir Thomas Malory's *Le Morte d'Arthur* (*The Death of Arthur*) preserved the legendary story of King Arthur and his knights, which has been published since in many versions suitable for young readers.

Caxton's translations, standardization of English, and literary style had a major impact upon English literature, according to Jane Bingham and Grayce Scholt (1980). At least eight of Caxton's books are mentioned in the "Famous Prefaces" volume of *The Harvard Classics* (Lenaghan, 1967). Cornelia Meigs et al. (1969) also stress Caxton's importance in creating the first printed books in the English language. In outward form, these books were of a standard not easily equaled. The ample pages, the broad margins, and the black-letter type that suggested manuscript contributed to their beauty, dignity, and worthiness to be England's first widespread realization of her own literature.

Caxton's books were beautiful, but they were too expensive for the common people. Soon, however, peddlers (or chapmen) were selling crudely printed chapbooks for pennies at markets and fairs, along with ribbons, patent medicines, and other wares. Customers could also go directly to a printer and select from large uncut sheets of as many as sixteen pages of text, which then were bound into a hardcover book.

Some of the first chapbooks were based on ballads, such as "The Two Children in the Wood," and traditional tales, such as "Jack the Giant Killer." According to Lou J. McCulloch (1979), the content of chapbooks fell into the following categories: religious instruction, interpretations of the supernatural, romantic legends, ballad tales, and historic narratives. John Ashton's (1882) *Chap-Books of the Eighteenth Century* includes religious titles, such as "The History of Joseph and His Brethren" and "The Unhappy Birth, Wicked Life, and Miserable Death of the Vile Traytor and Apostle Judas Iscariot"; traditional tales, such as "Tom Thumb" and "A True Tale of Robin Hood"; and supernatural tales, such as "The Portsmouth Ghost."

Chapbooks were extremely popular in both England and the United States during the 1700s, but their popularity rapidly declined during the early 1800s. McCulloch (1979) maintains that they were especially important as forerunners to many modern literary forms: children's books, western tales, and even comic books.

The Puritan Influence

According to Jane Bingham and Grayce Scholt (1980), political upheaval, religious dissent, and censorship affected English literature in the 1600s. As printing increased and literacy spread, the British monarchy realized the power of the press. In 1637, it decreed that only London, Oxford, Cambridge, and York could have printing establishments.

According to Anne Scott MacLeod (1995), "The story of children's reading in America begins with the Puritans. . . . From the beginning, Puritans thought about the children and provided for their schooling, at home and in the tiny communities they called towns. By the 1640s, Massachusetts law required heads of families to teach their children and apprentices to read" (p. 102).

The beliefs of the Puritans, dissenters from the established Church of England who were growing in strength and numbers in England and North America, also influenced literature of the period. Puritans considered the traditional tales about giants, fairies, and witches found in chapbooks to be impious and corrupting. They urged that children not be allowed to read such materials and instead be provided with literature to instruct them and reinforce their moral de-

From the sixteenth to the nineteenth century, peddlers sold inexpensive chapbooks in Europe and North America.
(From Chap-Books of the Eighteenth Century *by John Ashton. Published by Chatto and Windus, 1882. From the John G. White Collection, Cleveland Public Library.)*

velopment. Puritans expected their offspring to be children of God first and foremost. Bernard J. Lonsdale and Helen K. Macintosh (1973) describe:

Family worship, admonitions from elders, home instruction, strict attendance at school, and close attention to lessons all were aimed at perpetuating those ideals and values for which the parents themselves had sacrificed so much. To the elders, the important part of education was learning to read, write, and figure. Only literature that would instruct and warn was tolerated. (p. 161)

Awesome titles for books that stressed the importance of instructing children in moral concerns were common in Puritan times. In 1649, the grandfather of Cotton Mather (a Puritan who was influential during the Salem witch-hunts in New England) wrote a book called *Spiritual Milk for Boston Babes in Either England, Drawn from the Breasts of Both Testaments for Their Souls' Nourishment*. In 1671, the leading Puritan writer, James Janeway, published a series of stories about children who had led saintly lives until their deaths at an early age. His *A Token for Children, Being an Exact Account of the Conversion, Holy and Exemplary Lives, and Joyful Deaths of Several Young Children* was meant not for enjoyment, but to instruct Puritan children in moral development.

The most influential piece of literature written during this period was John Bunyan's *The Pilgrim's Progress from this world, to that which is to come. Delivered under the similitude of a Dream. Wherein is discovered, the manner of his setting out, his dangerous journey and safe arrival at the Desired Country*, or *Pilgrim's Progress*, published in England in 1678. While moral improvement was the primary purpose of this book, *Pilgrim's Progress* also contained bold action that appealed to both children and older readers, some of whom adopted it for its entertainment, as well as religious, value. Bunyan's hero, Christian, experiences many perilous adventures as he journeys alone through the Slough of Despond and the Valley of Humiliation in his search for salvation. Characters such as Mr. Valiant-for-Truth and Ignorance appear in such settings as the Valley of the Shadow of Death, the Delectable Mountains, and the Celestial City. Christian acquires a companion, Faithful, who is executed in the town of Vanity Fair. Then another companion, Hopeful, helps him fight the giant Despair and finally reach his goal.

Pilgrim's Progress and the *Spiritual Milk for Boston Babes in Either England* were required read-

The New England Primer *taught both Puritan ideals and the alphabet. (From* The New England Primer, Enlarged, Boston, 1727 edition. *From the Rare Books and Manuscript Division, The New York Public Library, Astor, Lenox, and Tilden Foundations.)*

ing for colonial children in North America. Another important book in colonial homes was *The New England Primer*, a combination alphabet and catechism designed to teach Puritan ideals. The primer was written in such a way that spiritual instruction was the main theme. The primer appeared around 1690 and was printed in hundreds of editions until 1830. According to Cornelia Meigs et al. (1969), the influence of the primer lasted so long because in that era "the chance of life for young children was cruelly small" (p. 114), and spiritual preparation for an early death was thus imperative.

John Locke's Influence on Views of Childhood

In a social environment that viewed children as small adults and expected them to behave accordingly, few considered that children might have interests and educational needs of their own. The Puritans and other Calvinist Christians believed that everyone was born predestined to achieve either salvation or damnation. Thus, all must spend their lives attempting to prove predestined worthiness to be saved.

The English philosopher John Locke, however, envisioned the child's mind at birth as a *tabula rasa,* a blank page on which ideas were to be imprinted. In *Some Thoughts Concerning Education* (1910), published in 1693, Locke stressed the interrelatedness of healthy physical development and healthy mental development, and he advocated milder ways of teaching and bringing up children than had been recommended previously. According to John Rowe Townsend (1975), Locke believed that children who could read should be provided with easy, pleasant books suited to their capacities—books that encouraged them to read and rewarded them for their reading efforts but that did not fill their heads with useless "trumpery" or encourage vice.

Locke found a grave shortage of books that could provide children with pleasure or reward, but he did recommend *Aesop's Fables* and *Reynard the Fox* for the delight that they offered children and the useful reflections that they offered the adults in children's lives. Locke's attitude was quite enlightened for his time. It provided a glimmer of hope that children might be permitted to go through a period of childhood rather than immediately assume the same roles as their parents. While seventeenth-century European and North American culture contained few books appropriate for children, a realization dawned that children might benefit from books written to encourage their reading.

Charles Perrault's Tales of Mother Goose

An exciting development in children's literature occurred in seventeenth-century France. Charles Perrault, a gifted member of the Academie Française, published a book called *Contes de ma Mère l'Oye* (*Tales of Mother Goose*). The stories in this collection were not those normally referred to as Mother Goose rhymes today. Instead, they were well-known fairy tales, such as "Cinderella," "Sleeping Beauty," "Puss in Boots," "Little Red Riding Hood," and "Blue Beard." Perrault did not create these tales; he retold stories from the French oral tradition that had entranced children and provided entertainment in the elegant salons of the Parisian aristocracy for generations.

Perrault was one of the first writers to recognize that fairy tales have a special place in the world of

A Nursery Companion *is a collection of Mother Goose rhymes that were originally published in the early 1800s. (From* A Nursery Companion *by Iona and Peter Opie, Oxford University Press, 1980.)*

children. Readers can thank Perrault or, as many scholars (Muir, 1954) now believe, his son Pierre Perrault d'Armancour, for collecting these tales, which have been translated and retold by many different contemporary writers and illustrators of children's books. At last, entertainment was written for children rather than adopted by them because nothing else was available.

The Adventure Stories of Defoe and Swift

Two adventure books that appeared in the early eighteenth century were, like virtually all literature of the time, written for adults, but these two were quickly embraced by children. A political climate that punished dissenters by placing them into prison molded the author of the first great adventure story, *Robinson Crusoe,* which was published in 1719. Daniel Defoe was condemned to Newgate Prison after he wrote a fiery pamphlet responding to the political and religious controversies of his time. However, Defoe wrote constantly, even while in jail.

Defoe was motivated to write *Robinson Crusoe* when he read the personal accounts of a Scottish sailor, Alexander Selkirk, who had been marooned on one of the Juan Fernandez Islands, located off the coast of Chile. This Scottish sailor had deserted ship after a disagreement with the captain and had lived alone on the island for four years before he was discovered by another ship and brought back to England. Defoe was so captivated by Selkirk's experience that he wrote an adventure story to answer his questions about how a person might acquire food, clothing, and shelter if shipwrecked on an island.

The resulting tale appeared first in serial publication and then in a book. Children and adults enjoyed the exciting and suspenseful story. The book was so influential that thirty-one years after Defoe's death, French philosopher Jean Jacques Rousseau, the founder of modern education, said that *Robinson Crusoe* would be the first book read by his son, Emile.

According to Brian W. Alderson (1959) *Robinson Crusoe* reflects an era in Western history when people had begun to believe in the natural goodness of human beings uninfluenced by corruption in the world around them. *Robinson Crusoe* became and remained so popular that it stimulated a whole group of books written about similar subjects, which came to be known as Robinsonades. The most popular Robinsonade was Johann Wyss's *The Swiss Family Robinson*. Susan Naramore Maher (1988) states:

> Robinsonades commanded an eager juvenile readership ready to devour the latest fiction about castaways, no matter how didactic or improbable the tale. In the nineteenth century, *Robinson Crusoe* itself became a prized nursery book, favored by children for its detail and adventure, by parents for its religious sentiment and work ethic. (p. 169)

The second major adventure story written during the early eighteenth century also dealt with the subject of shipwreck. Jonathan Swift's *Gulliver's Travels*, published in 1726, described Gulliver's realistic adventures with strange beings encountered in mysterious lands: tiny Lilliputians, giant Brobdingnagians, talking horses, and flying islands. Swift wrote *Gulliver's Travels* as a satire for adults. Children,

however, thought of the story as an enjoyable adventure and adopted Gulliver as a hero.

These adventure stories must have seemed truly remarkable to children otherwise surrounded by literature written only to instruct or to moralize. The impact of these eighteenth-century writers is still felt today, as twentieth-century children enjoy versions of the first adventure stories.

Newbery's Books for Children

The 1740s are commonly regarded as the time when the idea of children's books began in Europe and North America. New ways of thought emerged as the middle class became larger and strengthened its social position. Because more people had the time, money, and education necessary for reading, books became more important. Middle-class life also began to center on the home and family rather than on the marketplace or the great houses of nobility. With the growing emphasis on family life, a realization began that children should be children rather than small adults.

Into this social climate came John Newbery, an admirer of John Locke and an advocate of a milder way of educating children. Newbery was also a writer and publisher, who began publishing a line of books for children in 1744 with *A Little Pretty Pocket Book*. "Although his work reflected the didactic tone of the time," say Jane Bingham and Grayce Scholt (1980), "his books were not intended to be textbooks. Their gilt-paper covers, attractive pages, engaging stories and verses—and sometimes toys which were offered with the books—provided 'diversion' for children of the English-speaking world" (p. 86). *A Little Pretty Pocket Book* included a letter from Jack the Giant Killer written to both instruct and entertain children. Modern readers would not consider this early book for children very entertaining compared with books written to amuse today's children, but it must have been revolutionary for its time. In 1765, Newbery published a more famous book, *History of Little Goody Two-Shoes,* a fictitious story by Oliver Goldsmith. Sylvia Patterson Iskander (1988) identifies several features that characterized this book: like its predecessors, it had a lengthy title page, a dedication, an introduction, descriptive chapter headings, and stories and poems interrelated within the text.

THE

LIFE

AND

STRANGE SURPRIZING

ADVENTURES

OF

ROBINSON CRUSOE,

Of *YORK,* MARINER:

Who lived Eight and Twenty Years,
all alone in an un-inhabited Island on the
Coaft of AMERICA, near the Mouth of
the Great River of OROONOQUE;

Having been caft on Shore by Shipwreck, wherein all the Men perifhed but himfelf.

WITH

An Account how he was at laft as ftrangely deliver'd by PYRATES.

Written by Himfelf.

LONDON:
Printed for W. TAYLOR at the *Ship* in *Pater-Nofter-Row.* MDCCXIX.

Although not written for children, Daniel Defoe's adventure story became popular with eighteenth-century children. (Courtesy of Lilly Library, Indiana University, Bloomington, Indiana.)

Newbery's company, set up in London, became a success. His accomplishments are often attributed to his bustling energy, his interest in literature and writers, his love for children, and his taking note of children's tastes as measured by the popularity of their favorite chapbooks. Newbery's publications included *Nurse Truelove's New Year's Gift, Mother Goose, Tom Thumb's Folio,* and old favorites, such as *Aesop's Fables, Robinson Crusoe,* and *Gulliver's Travels.* Because of Newbery's success, publishers realized that there was indeed a market for books written specifically for children. It is fitting that the coveted award given annually to the outstanding author of a children's literature selection bears Newbery's name.

Rousseau's Philosophy of Natural Development

While John Locke had advocated a milder and more rational approach to educating children, Jean Jacques Rousseau recommended a totally new approach. Locke believed that children should be led in their search for knowledge, but Rousseau believed that they should merely be accompanied. Rousseau maintained that children could and should develop naturally, with gentle guidance from wise adults who could supply necessary information. Margaret C. Gillespie (1970) maintains:

At a time when the major emphasis was on sharpening the muscles of the mind and filling it to the brim with all the knowledge in the world it could absorb, Jean Jacques

Rousseau's exhortations to "retournez à la nature" had a strong impact on the complacency of educators. (p. 21)

In his *Emile,* published in 1762, Rousseau described stages of children's growth, stressing the importance of experiences in harmony with children's natural development physically and mentally. Rousseau's stages progressed from early sensory motor development, through a concrete learning period, into a period where intellectual conceptualization was possible. As mentioned, Rousseau believed that Daniel Defoe's *Robinson Crusoe* was the most important piece of literature because it emphasized the necessity of using one's own ideas to cope with one's environment. Rousseau's impact on parents' attitudes toward children was "forceful and unmistakable," says Gillespie. "Now children were looked upon as 'little angels' who could do no wrong. They were permitted to be children rather than 'little adults.' They became the center of the educational scene rather than satellites around the curriculum" (p. 23).

William Blake's Poetry About Children

The English poet William Blake, who is credited with writing verses as if a child had written them, published his *Songs of Innocence* in 1789 and his *Songs of Experience* in 1794. F. J. Harvey Darton (1932, 1966) characterizes Blake in the spiritual sense as "a child happy on a cloud, singing and desiring such songs as few but he could write" (p. 179). Blake's often quoted poem that introduces *Songs of Innocence* provides readers an opportunity to visualize this happy child (the punctuation and spelling are from the engraved first edition cited in Darton, 1932):

Introduction

Piping down the valleys wild
Piping songs of pleasant glee
On a cloud I saw a child.
And he laughing said to me.

Pipe a song about a Lamb:
So I piped with merry chear,
Piper pipe that song again—
So I piped, he wept to hear.

Drop thy pipe thy happy pipe
Sing thy songs of happy chear.
So I sung the same again
While he wept with joy to hear.

Piper sit thee down and write
In a book that all may read—
So he vanish'd from my sight.
And I pluck'd a hollow reed

And I made a rural pen,
And I stain'd the water clear,
And I wrote my happy songs,
Every child may joy to hear.

The Fairy Tales of Andersen and the Brothers Grimm

Sir Walter Scott's novels about the Middle Ages, enthusiasm for Gothic architecture, lyrical ballads, and Rousseau's philosophy of a return to nature typified the Romantic Movement in late-eighteenth-century Europe. This atmosphere encouraged an interest in folk literature.

In the early 1800s, two German scholars, Jacob and Wilhelm Grimm, became interested in collecting folktales that reflected the ancient German language and tradition. In researching their subject, the brothers listened to tales told by Dortchen and Gretchen Wild; the Wilds' maid, Marie; a farmer's wife called Frau Viehmännin; and other storytellers from throughout Germany. Although scholars disagree about how exactly the Brothers Grimm transcribed the tales they heard, Bettina Hürlimann (1980) maintains that the brothers

did not just write down what they heard. Even for the first edition they did a lot of revising, comparing with other sources, and trying to find a simple language which was at the same time full of character. With time and with later editions it became clear that Jacob, the more scholarly, tried to keep the tales in the most simple, original form, more or less as they had heard them, and that Wilhelm, more of a poet, was for retelling them in a new form with regard to the children. (p. 71)

The Grimms' first edition of tales, published in 1812, contained eighty-five stories, including "Cinderella," "Hansel and Gretel," "Little Red Riding Hood," and "The Frog Prince." According to Hürlimann, the second edition, published in 1815, was designed more specifically for children, with illustrations and a minimum of scholarly comment on the tales it contained.

In 1823, the tales collected by the Brothers Grimm were translated into English and published under the title *German Popular Stories.* Since that time, artists in many countries have illustrated such tales as "Snow

German Popular Stories, *such as this 1826 edition, introduced the Grimms' folktales to English-speaking children. (Courtesy of Lilly Library, Indiana University, Bloomington, Indiana.)*

White and the Seven Dwarfs," "Rumpelstiltskin," and "The Elves and the Shoemaker," which have become part of our literary heritage.

Most of the published folktales and fairy tales discussed thus far were written down by either Charles Perrault or the Brothers Grimm. The stories had been told in castles and cottages for many generations. Hans Christian Andersen, however, is generally credited with being the first to create and publish an original fairy tale. Andersen used his own experiences to stimulate his writing. "The Ugly Duckling," "The Little Mermaid," and "The Red Shoes" are among Andersen's famous stories.

Andersen was born to a poor but happy family in Odense, Denmark. His cobbler father shared stories with him and even built a puppet theater for Andersen. Even when his father died and it seemed that Andersen would have to learn a trade, Andersen retained his dream of becoming an actor. During these poverty-stricken years, he tried to forget his troubles by putting on puppet shows and telling stories to children.

Because Andersen wanted to write stories and plays, he returned to school to improve his writing skills. While there, he suffered from cruel jokes about his looks; he was thin and had large feet and a large nose. (Doesn't this sound like a theme for one of his fairy tales?)

In 1828, when Andersen was twenty-three, he began to write stories and poems. Five years later, he was recognized as a promising writer by the Danish government, whose financial support allowed him to travel and write about his experiences. When his *Life in Italy,* a rather scholarly work, was published, Andersen at last started to make money. His next book was far different; it was the first of his famous fairy tale books, and it was written in the same colloquial language used to tell stories.

When *Fairy Tales Told for Children* was published, a friend told Andersen that his *Life in Italy* would make him famous but his fairy tales would make people remember him forever. Although Andersen did not believe his fairy tales were as good as his other books, he enjoyed writing them and produced a new fairy tale book each Christmas as a gift to children of all ages. When Andersen was sixty-two, he was invited back to Odense, the town in which he had known happiness, poverty, and sadness. This time, however, he was the honored guest at a celebration that lasted for an entire week.

Andersen's fairy stories are still popular; newly illustrated versions are published every year. These colorful picture-book versions, as well as tales in anthologies, are still enjoyed by children of many ages.

A typical woodcut from Orbis Pictus, *the first picture book for children. (A reprint of the* Orbis Pictus *has been published by Singing Tree Press, Gale Research Company, Detroit, Michigan.)*

Early Illustrators of Children's Books

The identity of the first picture book for children is debated. Eric Quayle (1971) identifies *Kunst und Lehrbüchlein (Book of Art and Instruction for Young People),* published in 1580 by the German publisher Sigmund Feyerabend, as the "first book aimed at the unexplored juvenile market" (p. 11). The detailed, full-page woodcuts showing European life were the work of Jost Amman. Of particular interest are the pictures of a young scholar reading a hornbook and of a child holding a doll.

Johann Amos Comenius, a Moravian teacher and former bishop of the Bohemian Brethren, is usually credited with writing the first nonalphabet picture book that strove to educate children. Bettina Hürlimann (1980) describes Comenius as a great humanist, who wanted children to observe God's creations—plants, stars, clouds, rain, sun, and geography—rather than to memorize abstract knowledge.

In order to achieve this goal, Comenius took children out of the conventional classrooms and into the natural world. He then wrote down their experiences in simple sentences, using both Latin and the children's own language. He published these simple sentences and accompanying woodcuts in 1658 as *Orbis Pictus (Painted World).* Educational historian Ayers Bagley (1985) identifies allegorical meanings in the illustrations and text. According to Bagley, Comenius saw true understanding, right action, and correct speech as important contributors to the attainment of wisdom.

Scholars disagree about whether Comenius drew the illustrations for *Orbis Pictus* himself or whether he instructed artists in their execution. Jane Bingham

and Grayce Scholt (1980) credit the woodcuts in the 1658 edition to Paul Kreutzberger and the wood engravings in the 1810 American edition to Alexander Anderson. Whoever the artist was, Hürlimann emphasizes that "the pictures are in wonderful harmony with the text, and the book was to become for more than a century the most popular book with children of all classes" (p. 67).

Most book illustrations before the 1800s, especially those in the inexpensive chapbooks, were crude woodcuts. If color was used, it was usually hand applied by amateurs who filled in the colors according to a guide. Thomas Bewick is credited with being one of the earliest artists to illustrate books for children. His skillfully executed woodcuts graced *The New Lottery Book of Birds and Beasts,* published in 1771, and *A Pretty Book of Pictures for Little Masters and Misses; or Tommy Trip's History of Beasts and Birds,* published in 1779.

Three nineteenth-century English artists had enormous impact on illustrations for children's books. According to Ruth Hill Viguers in the introduction to Edward Ernest's (1967) *The Kate Greenaway Treasury,* the work of these artists "represents the best to be found in picture books for children in any era: the strength of design and richness of color and detail of Walter Crane's pictures; the eloquence, humor, vitality, and movement of Randolph Caldecott's art; and the tenderness, dignity, and grace of the very personal interpretation of Kate Greenaway's enchanted land of childhood" (p. 13).

Walter Crane's *The House That Jack Built,* published in 1865, was the first of his series of toy books,

Walter Crane's illustrated texts, characterized by subdued colors, strong design, and rich detail, are credited with marking the beginning of the modern era in color illustrations. (From The Baby's Own Aesop. *Reproduced by permission of the Department of Special Collections, Research Library, University of California, Los Angeles.)*

Randolph Caldecott's illustrations suggest action and vitality. (From The Hey Diddle Diddle Picture Book *by Randolph Caldecott. Reproduced by permission of Frederick Warne & Co., Inc., Publishers.)*

the name used for picture books published for young children. These books, engraved by Edmund Evans, are credited with marking the beginning of the modern era in color illustrations. From 1865 through 1898, Crane illustrated over forty books, including folktales, such as *The Three Bears* and *Cinderella,* and alphabet books, such as *The Farmyard Alphabet* and *The Absurd ABC.*

Many of Crane's illustrations reflect his appreciation of Japanese color prints. Crane (1984) specified this appreciation in lectures that he gave before the Society of Arts in 1889, when he stated that Japanese art was "a living art, an art of the people, in which traditions and craftsmanship were unbroken, and the results full of attractive variety, quickness, and naturalistic force" (p. 133).

Kate Greenaway was one of the early influential illustrators. Her name is now attached to the Kate Greenaway Medal for outstanding illustrators in Great Britain. (From Almanack for 1884 *by Kate Greenaway.)*

Randolph Caldecott's talent was discovered by Edmund Evans, the printer. Caldecott's illustrations for *The Diverting History of John Gilpin,* printed by Evans in 1878, demonstrated his ability to depict robust characters, action, and humor. (The Caldecott Medal for children's book illustration, named for the artist, is embossed with the picture of Gilpin galloping through an English village.) Caldecott's lively and humorous figures jump fences, dance to the fiddler, and flirt with milkmaids in such picture books as *The Fox Jumps over the Parson's Gate, Come Lasses and Lads,* and *The Milkmaid.*

Caldecott's picture books are now reissued by Frederick Warne. Brian Alderson's (1986) *Sing a Song of Sixpence* provides a pictorial history of English picture books and Randolph Caldecott's art.

Printer and engraver Edmund Evans also encouraged and supported the work of Kate Greenaway. Delighted by Greenaway's drawings and verses, Evans printed her first book, *Under the Window,* in 1878. It was so successful that 70,000 English editions and over 30,000 French and German editions were sold.

Greenaway continued illustrating books that reflected happy days of childhood and the blossoming apple trees and primroses that dotted the English countryside of her youth. In a letter to her friend John Ruskin, Greenaway described her view of the world:

I go on liking things more and more, seeing them more and more beautiful. Don't you think it is a great possession to be able to get so much joy out of things that are always there to give it, and do not change? What a great pity my hands are not clever enough to do what my mind and eyes see, but there it is! (Ernest, 1967, p. 19)

Other picture books illustrated by Greenaway include *Kate Greenaway's Birthday Book* (1880), *Mother Goose* (1881), *The Language of Flowers* (1884), and Robert Browning's *Pied Piper of Hamelin* (1880). Greenaway's name, like Caldecott's, has been given to an award honoring distinguished artistic accomplishment in the field of children's books. The Kate Greenaway Medal is given annually to the most distinguished British illustrator of children's books.

By the late 1800s, when Crane, Caldecott, and Greenaway began drawing for children, European and North American attitudes toward children were also changing. According to Frederick Laws (1980), these three artists were under no public compulsion to be morally edifying or factually informative. Children were no longer supposed to be "young persons" whose taste would be much the same whether they were five or fifteen. So long as they pleased children, artists were free; indeed, Crane wrote that "in a sober and matter-of-fact age Toybooks afford perhaps the only outlet for unrestricted flights of fancy open to the modern illustrator who likes to revolt against the despotism of facts." (p. 318)

This brief discussion of illustrators does not mention all of the artists who made contributions in the nineteenth century, but it does outline the relatively short history of children's book illustration. Chart 2–2 summarizes some milestones in the illustration of children's books from the fifteenth century into the early twentieth century.

Students of children's literature who are interested in or investigating the history of illustrations will enjoy *Landmarks in Print Collecting,* edited by Antony Griffiths (1996). This highly illustrated book published by the British Museum provides a history of print collecting beginning with Sir Hans Sloane in the 1600s and extending to collections in the twentieth century.

The Victorian Influence

English-speaking people identify the reign of Great Britain's Queen Victoria, from 1837 to 1901, with a distinct social epoch, the Victorian Age, although so-called Victorian social influences certainly preceded and followed the queen's life. The rise of a highly competitive industrial technology, the growth of large cities and the decline of rural traditions, an emphasis on strictly controlled social behavior and Christian piety, and a romantic focus on home and family are factors usually associated with the Victorian Age in Europe, North America, and elsewhere. Alan Rauch (1989) describes this period as one of "scientific didacticism," a time when authors used scientific subjects for moral and religious instruction of children. In addition, the increasingly prosperous middle and upper classes began to view childhood sentimentally, as an even more special stage in the human life cycle, while children of the working poor labored many hours a day in mines and factories.

Juliana Horatia Ewing was one of the most prolific authors of the Victorian period. Many of her popular tales for children first appeared in such English periodicals as *The Monthly Packet* and *Aunt Judy's Magazine for Young People.* Her first book, *Melchior's*

From Mrs. Ewing's Stories *by Mrs. Ewing, Roberts Brothers, Publishers, Boston.*

Dream and Other Stories, was published by the Society for the Promotion of Christian Knowledge in 1862. Among her other books were *Mrs. Overtheway's Remembrances* (1869), *Jan of the Windmill* (1876), *Brothers of Pity, and Other Tales* (1882), *Jackanapes* (1884), and *Daddy Darwin's Dovecot* (1884). The last two books were illustrated by Randolph Caldecott.

Literary critics considered Mrs. Ewing's writing to be among the best of the time. Their comments also reflected typically Victorian concerns and values. For example, a critic for the *Worcester Spy* described Mrs. Ewing as a genius whose writing touched the heart, excited tender and noble emotion, encouraged religious feeling, and deepened the scorn for the mean and the cowardly. This same critic recommended that children read Mrs. Ewing's stories because they nourished everything that was lovely in children's characters. Mrs. Ewing's "refining" and "ennobling" stories were popular for many years, remaining in print until the 1930s.

CHART 2–2 Milestones in the history of children's illustration

1484	William Caxton, *Aesop's Fables*, contained over one hundred woodcuts.	1878	Randolph Caldecott, *The Diverting History of John Gilpin*, the first of sixteen picture books.
1658	Johann Amos Comenius, *Orbis Pictus* (Painted World), considered by many to be the first picture book for children.	1878	Kate Greenaway, *Under the Window*.
1771	Thomas Bewick, *The New Lottery Book of Birds and Beasts*.	1883	Howard Pyle, *The Merry Adventures of Robin Hood*.
1784	Thomas and John Bewick, *The Select Fables of Aesop and Others*.	1900	Arthur Rackham, illustrations for Grimms' *Fairy Tales*.
1789	William Blake, *Songs of Innocence*.	1901	Beatrix Potter, *The Tale of Peter Rabbit*.
1823	George Cruikshank, translation of Grimms' *Fairy Tales*.	1924	E. H. Shepard, illustrations for A. A. Milne's *When We Were Very Young*.
1853	George Cruikshank, *Fairy Library*.	1933	Kurt Wiese, illustrations for Marjorie Flack's *The Story of Ping*.
1865	John Tenniel, illustrations for Lewis Carroll's *Alice's Adventures in Wonderland*.	1933	E. H. Shepard, illustrations for Kenneth Grahame's *The Wind in the Willows*.
1865	Walter Crane, *The House That Jack Built*, the first of the toy books engraved by Evans.	1937	Dr. Seuss, *And to Think That I Saw It on Mulberry Street*.

Fred Raymond Erisman (1966) has concluded that American children's literature of the late nineteenth and early twentieth centuries chiefly reflected upper-middle-class values, although it fell into two main categories: fiction and nonfiction. Nonfiction was realistic, dealing with the social, technological, and biographical concerns of an urban society. Fiction presented the ideal values of the well-to-do, implying that these were the typical American values.

Robert Gordon Kelly's (1978) research also reveals that American children's literature in the nineteenth century presented children with an ideal concept of selfhood for emulation. As well, it indicated unresolved tensions about America's growing cities, a beginning emphasis on the responsibilities of a cultural elite, and changing ideas about childhood. According to Kelly, the "gentleman and lady" in children's literature "offered models for negotiating the difficult and precarious passage from childhood to adulthood as well as for moderating the economic competition . . . that was the most important social fact of American life" (p. 42). Children's literature encouraged the young to confront a dog-eat-dog world with courage, temperance, prudence, courtesy, self-reliance, and presence of mind. "So great was the emphasis on self-control," says Kelly, "that one author warned that carelessness is worse than stealing" (p. 41).

Kelly identifies two typical story patterns in children's literature of the period. In the *ordeal*, a child loses the protection and influence of parents or other adults for a short time. Circumstances force the child to act decisively; the situations described often seem contrived to emphasize sound character rather than sound reasoning. The child demonstrates the expected behaviors and then returns to the safety of the family and is justly rewarded.

The heroine of "Nellie in the Light House," published in an 1877 edition of *St. Nicholas* magazine, is the seven-year-old daughter of a lighthouse keeper. When her father goes to the mainland for supplies, the housekeeper is called away to nurse a neighbor, the housekeeper's husband collapses from a stroke, a storm causes high winds, and the beacon light is extinguished. Alone, Nellie must overcome her fear and find a way to rekindle the beacon. She remembers a hymn her mother sang to her and rekindles the light, which then saves her father, who is caught in the storm.

In the second type of story, *change of heart*, a child who has not yet reached the ideal of self-discipline and sound moral character realizes the need for improvement. In "Charlie Balch's Metamorphosis," which appeared in an 1867 edition of the *Riverside Magazine for Young People*, the hero is a sullen and lazy boy who has withdrawn into himself after his mother's death. His father sends him to a boarding school, where he joins a rough crowd of boys. Charlie realizes the errors of his ways during a sermon, and the rest of the story places him in situations that test his resolution for a change of heart. By the end of the story, Charlie has a cheerful disposition and better manners.

Charlotte Yonge was a prolific author of children's literature. She wrote about the large families so common in Victorian times; her own childhood involved close ties with her brother and many cousins. Conversations among the people in her extended family later provided her with realistic settings and dialogue for her fiction. Yonge's stories also reflect the pronounced Christian ethic of the Victorian period.

In Yonge's *The Daisy Chain,* for example, a husband and wife become missionaries in the Loyalty Islands. In typical Victorian fashion, Yonge's fiction portrays females as inferior to males. In *The Daisy Chain,* the hero's sister is advised not to compete with her brother at the university because a woman cannot equal a man scholastically. In *The Clever Woman of the Family,* published in 1865, the heroine thinks for herself, but whenever there is a disagreement between her ideas and those of a man, she must adhere to the superior wisdom of a brother, father, or husband.

Myra Stark (1979) maintains that the Victorian Age was in the grip of an ideology that viewed women as either wives and mothers or failed wives or mothers. Stark declares:

Woman was the center of the age's cult of the family, "the angel in the house," tending to the domestic altar. She was viewed as man's inferior—less rational, weaker, needing his protection; but at the same time, she was exalted for her spirituality, her moral influence. Man was the active one, the doer; woman was the inspirer and the nurturer. The spheres of work in the world and in the home were rigidly divided between the sexes. (p. 4)

Consequently, most Victorian literature for children directed middle- and upper-class girls and boys into the rigidly distinct roles expected of them as adults.

Robert MacDonald's analysis of illustrations in the boys' magazine *Chums* defines the masculine role model found in Victorian illustrations. MacDonald (1988) states that by

repetition and emphasis, a vocabulary of patriotic images was developed and exploited, which for a generation of British males dramatized the myth of Empire. The pri-

mary motifs of these illustrations defined manhood, race, and individual action: manhood shown in the heroics of courageous soldiers or brave frontiersmen; lessons of race demonstrated by the examples of barbarous natives or uncivilized Dutchmen; and the complicated relationship between choice and duty set forth as an insistent expectation that the wars of school led to the games of war. A close relationship was established between the world of boys and the world of men. (p. 33)

Some Victorian authors were sensitive to the realities of life for poor children. In 1862, the English poet Elizabeth Barrett Browning wrote of the woes of these children in her poem, "The Cry of the Children," describing the weeping of children in mines and factories while other children played. Another famous English author of the period, Charles Dickens, aroused the Victorian conscience to the plight of unfortunate children, such as the fictional orphan in *Oliver Twist.*

The "Ragged Dick" series, published in 1868, told of the sad plight of children who tried to survive in a city without family or friends. They often worked long hours in factories or on farms. Many died. Horatio Alger, Jr., wrote the series in the hope that readers would be sympathetic to the cause of poor children

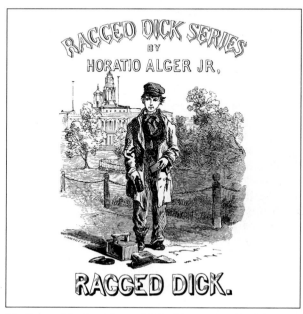

The Ragged Dick *series, published in 1868, told of the sad plight of children who tried to survive in a city without family or friends.*

and the Children's Aid Society. Since 1854, the society has been finding homes for abandoned children.

Horatio Alger's *Frank's Campaign* (1864) was the first of a series of books in which poor American youths went from rags to riches. Other books by Alger that have a similar theme include *Fame and Fortune* (1868), *Sink or Swim* (1870), *Strong and Steady* (1871), *Brave and Bold* (1874), *Risen from the Ranks* (1874), and *From Farm Boy to Senator: Being the History of the Boyhood and Manhood of Daniel Webster* (1882).

Reissues of lesser-known books and stories published during the Victorian period provide opportunities for further study. For example, *What I Cannot Tell My Mother Is Not Fit for Me to Know* is a collection of stories, poems, and songs selected by Gwladys and Brian Rees-Williams (1981) from texts published in the nineteenth century. Andrew Tuer's *Stories from Forgotten Children's Books* (1986) is a facsimile edition of a book published in 1898.

Fantasy, Adventure, and Real People

As the world was changing, views of childhood were changing, too. Emphases in children's literature mirrored the new attitudes and world developments. Childhood was becoming, at least for middle- and upper-class children, a more carefree and enjoyable period of life, and this change was reflected in the increase in fantasy stories for children. As adventurers explored unknown areas of the world, their experiences inspired new adventure stories. Also, the characters of specific families and localities were captured in the growing popularity of literature about ordinary people, places, and events in sometimes extraordinary circumstances.

Fantasy. By the mid-1800s, the puritanical resistance to fantasy in children's literature was on its way toward extinction in most segments of European and North American society. Children had been reading and enjoying the folktales of Perrault and the Brothers Grimm, and Andersen's stories had been translated into English. More and more educators and parents believed that literature should entertain children rather than merely instruct them.

According to Raymond Chapman (1968), fantasy created a world where fears could be projected onto impossible creatures of the imagination while a child remained safe. Although growing to maturity seemed dangerous, the happiest people acquired new knowledge while retaining childlike qualities. Brian W. Alderson (1959) describes the creation of one of the landmarks in fantasy and nonsense:

One summer's day on the river at Oxford [England] a thirty-year-old lecturer in mathematics at Christ Church was taking the three daughters of his Dean, Edith, Lorina, and Alice, out for a row. His name was Charles Lutwidge Dodgson. The day was hot and the children wanted to have a story told them, a thing they had come to expect from Mr. Dodgson. So the young lecturer complied, his mind relaxing in the drowsy heat and his thoughts, which did not tire so easily, following paths of their own making. (p. 64)

The paths led directly down the rabbit hole and into adventures in Wonderland with the Cheshire Cat, the Queen of Hearts, and the Mad Hatter. The

The illustrations and text for Alice's Adventures in Wonderland *were designed to give pleasure, not to teach a lesson. (Illustration by John Tenniel. From* Alice's Adventures in Wonderland *by Lewis Carroll. Published by Macmillan and Co., 1865. Courtesy of Lilly Library, Indiana University, Bloomington, Indiana.)*

story told that afternoon in 1862 made such an impression on Alice that she pestered Dodgson to write it down. He wrote it for her, gave it to her as a gift, and, after it had been thoroughly enjoyed by many people, published it for others under the pseudonym Lewis Carroll.

According to Cornelia Meigs et al. (1969), the revolutionary nature of Lewis Carroll's *Alice's Adventures in Wonderland* and *Through the Looking Glass* when compared with earlier books written for children is due to "the fact that they were written purely to give pleasure to children. . . . Here . . . for the first time we find a story designed for children without a trace of a lesson or moral" (p. 194).

Edward Lear, the other great writer of fantasy for children in the nineteenth century, created absurd and delightful characters in nonsense verses. Lear's *A Book of Nonsense* appeared in 1846, his *More Nonsense* in 1872. *Nonsense Songs, Botany and Alphabets,* published in 1871, contained Lear's "Nonsense Stories," "Nonsense Geography," "Natural History," and "Nonsense Alphabets." *Laughable Lyrics* (1877) included the nonsense verses "The Quangle-Wangle's Hat," "The Dong with the Luminous Nose," and "The Youghy-Bonghy-Bo."

There was an Old Person of Pinner,
As thin as a lath, if not thinner ;
They dressed him in white,
And roll'd him up tight,
That elastic Old Person of Pinner.

Edward Lear's illustrations heightened the humor of his limericks. (From A Book of Nonsense *by Edward Lear. Published by Heinrich Hoffman, 1846. Courtesy of Lilly Library, Indiana University, Bloomington, Indiana.)*

Lear's work, like Carroll's, was popular with both young and adult readers. Today, both writers are often quoted and enjoyed as much as they were when their works were created.

Adventure. Europeans and North Americans were having many real-life adventures in the nineteenth century. Explorers were seeking the North Pole, Florence Nightingale was pioneering for female independence as a director of nursing in the Crimean War, and a railroad was being constructed across the United States. If a person could not go to a remote region and overcome the perils lurking there, the next best adventure was the vicarious one offered through books.

Robert Louis Stevenson was the master of the adventure stories written during this time. When *Treasure Island* was published, it was considered the greatest adventure story for children since *Robinson Crusoe.* Brian W. Alderson (1959) agrees that Stevenson had the greatest influence on children's literature after Daniel Defoe.

Stevenson was born in Edinburgh, Scotland, the son of a lighthouse engineer. When he was a young boy, his father told him bedtime tales filled with "blood and thunder," and his nurse told him stories of body snatchers, ghosts, and martyrs. As an adult, Stevenson traveled to many lands, but he still loved the lochs, islands, and misty forests of his home. Stevenson's early experiences are evident in his two most famous adventure stories, *Treasure Island* and *Kidnapped.*

Treasure Island had an interesting beginning. While trying to entertain his stepson, Stevenson drew a watercolor map of an island, then followed his drawing with the now famous story of pirates, buried treasure, and a young boy's adventures.

Both *Treasure Island* and *Kidnapped* have the ingredients of outstanding adventure literature: action, mystery, and pursuit and evasion in authentic historical settings. Stevenson believed that an adventure story should have a specific effect on its readers: It should absorb and delight them, fill their minds with a kaleidoscope of images, and satisfy their nameless longings. According to Bernard J. Lonsdale and Helen K. Macintosh (1973), Stevenson believed that Robinson Crusoe's discovering a footprint on his lonely beach, Achilles's shouting against the Trojans, and Ulysses's bending over his great bow were culminating moments that have been printed in the mind's eye forever. In addition, according to Brian W. Alderson (1959), Stevenson believed that children and adults should demand such moments in their literature, and Stevenson achieved that quality in tales of "treasure and treachery . . . the comings and goings of . . . pirates, the ominous hints of the fearful events which are to come" (p. 257).

While Robert Louis Stevenson wrote of pirates and buried treasure in the not-so-distant past, Howard Pyle took readers back to the Middle Ages to fight evil, overcome Prince John's injustice, and have a rollicking good time in the green depths of Sherwood Forest. Pyle's *The Merry Adventures of Robin Hood,* published in 1883, retold the old English ballad about Robin Hood, Little John, Friar Tuck, and the other merry men who robbed the rich to give to the poor and constantly thwarted the evil plans of the Sheriff of Nottingham. Here was swashbuckling entertainment that also provided children with a glimpse of an early period in European history.

The historical novel became popular in the 1800s with the publication of stories by Sir Walter Scott. Scott's story of medieval English life, *Ivanhoe: A Romance* (1820), was often used as a school assignment for older children. Other popular books by Scott included *The Lady of the Lake* (1810), *Waverly: Or, 'Tis Sixty Years Since* (1814), *Rob Roy* (1818), and *Tales of the Crusaders* (1825).

The Industrial Revolution, the invention of the steam engine, and the prevalent feeling of new possibilities always just around the corner laid the groundwork for a new kind of adventure story in the last half of the nineteenth century. Jules Verne's science fiction adventure stories can certainly be classified as another benchmark in children's literature. Verne envisioned submarines, guided missiles, and dirigibles long before such things were possible. His first science fiction book, *Five Weeks in a Balloon,* was published in France in 1863. His two most famous books, *Twenty Thousand Leagues Under the Sea,* published in 1869, and *Around the World in Eighty Days,* published in 1872, have also been immortalized on film. Consequently, the heroes of these books, Captain Nemo and Phileas Fogg, are well known to both readers and movie fans.

Verne admired the work of an earlier author, Daniel Defoe, and Verne's *The Mysterious Island,* published in 1875, was written because of Verne's

The historical novel became popular in the 1800s with the publication of stories by Sir Walter Scott and Charlotte Yonge.

interest in *Robinson Crusoe.* Verne's genius can be seen in the popularity of his works even today, after his glorious inventions have become reality. Verne's detailed descriptions are so believable they seem as modern now as they did when they were published in the 1800s. The popularity of Verne's literature also caused other authors to write science fiction and to expand the new genre.

Real People. During the later nineteenth and early twentieth centuries, the local-color story came into its own. Realistic situations and people are the settings and subjects of such stories, in which place, plot, and characters are tightly integrated. According to James H. Fraser (1978), "This integration, which reveals the complex involvement of human, cultural, and geographical influences, produces a rich literature—peculiarly rich for the student of American culture, and extraordinarily rich for the young persons fortunate enough to read it" (p. 55). The diversity of American geography and people are found in books like Edward Eggleston's *The Hoosier School Boy* (rural Indiana), Thomas Bailey Aldrich's *The Story of a Bad Boy* (a

Mark Twain wrote adventures about life in the Mississippi River environment in which he himself had grown up. (From The Adventures of Huckleberry Finn by Mark Twain. Published by Charles L. Webster and Co., 1885. Courtesy of Lilly Library, Indiana University, Bloomington, Indiana.)

New England seafaring town), Kate Douglas Wiggins's *Rebecca of Sunnybrook Farm* (rural Maine), Mark Twain's *The Adventures of Huckleberry Finn* (Mississippi River towns), and Frances Courtenay Baylor's *Juan and Juanita* (the Southwest). Fraser maintains that these local-color stories also transmit a conservative, traditional view of American life to the next generation. Their characters are "carryovers from an earlier age, an agrarian, preindustrial age, which the stories sentimentalize for their modern readers" (p. 59).

The greatest American writer of realistic adventure in this period was Mark Twain (Samuel Clemens). While Robert Louis Stevenson was writing about adventures on far-off islands, Twain was immortalizing life on the Mississippi River before the Civil War. Twain captured the human, cultural, and geographical influences that affected a boy's life in this era of American history. Twain grew up in the river town of Hannibal, Missouri, where he lived many of the adventures about which he later wrote. He explored the river, raided melon patches, and used a cave as a rendezvous to plan further adventures and mischief with his friends. These adventures made Tom Sawyer and Huckleberry Finn come alive for many adventure-loving children. Twain's heroes did not leave the continent, but they did have exciting adventures on a nearby island, return in time to hear plans for their own funerals, and then attend those momentous occasions. Characters such as Injun Joe, Aunt Polly, Tom Sawyer, Becky Thatcher, and Huckleberry Finn still provide reading pleasure for children and adults. Donald A. Barclay (1992) concludes that Mark Twain's *The Adventures of Huckleberry Finn* is also one of the most frequently illustrated novels in history. Barclay estimates that there are approximately eight hundred editions of the novel, most of which are illustrated.

Many American books in the Victorian era took the family as their subject, and series stories dealing with the everyday lives of large families became popular. Margaret Sidney, for example, wrote a series of books about the five little Peppers. The first book, *The Five Little Peppers and How They Grew,* published in 1881, was followed by *The Five Little Peppers Midway* and *The Five Little Peppers Grown Up.*

Louisa May Alcott's account of family life in *Little Women,* published in 1868, is so real that readers feel they know each member of the March family intimately. This book showing the warm relationships and everyday struggles in a family of meager means is actually about Alcott's own family.

In many ways, Alcott's life was quite different from the usual Victorian model, which accounts for the ways in which *Little Women* was ahead of its time. Alcott's father believed in educating his daughters. Consequently, Alcott was first educated at home by her father and then sent to the district school.

In 1867, a publisher asked Alcott to write a book for girls, and she decided to write about her own family. The resulting book, *Little Women,* was an overwhelming success. Readers enjoyed the intimate details of a warm, loving, and very human family. The most popular character, Jo, shares many characteristics with Alcott herself. Jo is courageous, warm, and honest, but she has a quick temper that often gets her into difficulty. She

The writings of Mark Twain (Samuel Clemens), especially *The Adventures of Huckleberry Finn,* were under protest in the 1980s because of Twain's depictions of black people. Those who suggest that *The Adventures of Huckleberry Finn* should be banned or rewritten point to the numerous uses of the word *nigger* and instances in which African Americans are stereotyped rather than presented as individual, well-rounded characters.

Twain might find this 1980s protest ironic; in the 1880s, he was accused of going too far in advancing the cause of human equality and justice. Robert Scott Kellner,[1] a recognized Twain scholar, believes, however, that "a close examination of Twain's writing reveals an element of satire in his seemingly racist language, a satire directed at the reader who would choose to agree with the stereotyped image. Twain's language and imagery about the blacks in his stories work together as a mirror in which bigoted readers ultimately see themselves."

Kellner stresses that in the relationship between Huckleberry Finn and Jim, Twain makes clear that a black man is capable of earning a trust that withstands the pressures of an anti-black heritage—that he can give love and loyalty, strive for physical emancipation, and be a wise father figure for a misinformed boy. As you read Twain's work, consider whether it reflects a belief in the inequality of human beings or whether it suggests that people of all races share a common humanity.

[1]Kellner, Robert Scott. "Defending Mark Twain." *The Eagle.* Bryan-College Station, Texas (April 11, 1982): 1D.

also leaves home to earn a living as a writer and to help support her family. *Little Women* was so popular that in 1869 Alcott wrote a sequel, *Little Women, Part II.* She also wrote other favorites, such as *An Old-Fashioned Girl, Little Men,* and *Eight Cousins.*

One very popular realistic story published in the nineteenth century had a setting foreign to most readers of its English translation. Mountains that climb into the sky, sheepherders, tinkling bells, rushing streams, flower-strewn meadows, a hut with a bed of fresh hay, and the freedom to wander in delightful Swiss surroundings were found in Johanna Spyri's *Heidi,* published in Switzerland in 1880 and translated into English in 1884. Spyri based her book on her own childhood experiences in the Swiss Alps, which may help explain its realistic appeal.

Actual experience in a foreign land was not the only basis that an author had for providing a believable setting. Mary Mapes Dodge used research and imagination to provide credible background and characters in *Hans Brinker, or the Silver Skates, a Story of Life in Holland.* Readers in the Netherlands accepted this story as authentic in 1865, even though Dodge had never visited their country.

Space does not allow a complete discussion of all the books written for children or written for adults and read by children in earlier eras of our history. Chart 2–3 lists some previously discussed literature that brings the world of children's books into the twentieth century. As you read this chart, however, remember that book publishing for children is a fairly recent activity. As Betsy Hearne (1988) points out, the first children's book department to be established in a publishing house in the United States was Macmillan's children's book department, established in 1918. Although children's books were published prior to this date, this is certainly a milestone in the publication of children's literature.

 ## THE HISTORY OF CENSORSHIP

According to *Webster's Dictionary: The New Lexicon of the English Language,* 1988 edition, a censor is "a person empowered to suppress publications or excise any matter in them thought to be immoral, seditious, or otherwise undesirable" (p. 158). What is considered immoral, seditious, or undesirable changes, however, with various time periods and with political and social attitudes.

CHART 2–3   Notable authors of children's literature

1477	William Caxton, *Caxton's Book of Curtesye*
1484	William Caxton, *The Fables of Aesop*
1485	William Caxton, *Le Morte d'Arthur*
1678	John Bunyan, *Pilgrim's Progress*
1698	Charles Perrault or Pierre Perrault d'Armancour, *Tales of Mother Goose*
1719	Daniel Defoe, *Robinson Crusoe*
1726	Jonathan Swift, *Gulliver's Travels*
1744	John Newbery, *A Little Pretty Pocket Book*
1789	William Blake, *Songs of Innocence*
1812	First volume of Grimm Brothers' fairy tales, *Kinder-und Hausmärchen*
	Johann Wyss, *Swiss Family Robinson*
1820	Sir Walter Scott, *Ivanhoe: A Romance*
1823	Clement G. Moore, *A Visit from St. Nicholas*
1826	James Fenimore Cooper, *The Last of the Mohicans*
1843	Charles Dickens, *A Christmas Carol*
1846	Edward Lear, *A Book of Nonsense*
	Hans Christian Andersen's fairy tales in English translations
1851	John Ruskin, *King of the Golden River*
1856	Charlotte Yonge, *The Daisy Chain*
1862	Christina Georgina Rossetti, *Goblin Market*
1863	Charles Kingsley, *The Water Babies*
1865	Lewis Carroll, *Alice's Adventures in Wonderland*
	Mary Elizabeth Mapes Dodge, *Hans Brinker, or the Silver Skates, a Story of Life in Holland*
1868	Louisa May Alcott, *Little Women*
1870	Thomas Bailey Aldrich, *The Story of a Bad Boy*
1871	George MacDonald, *At the Back of the North Wind*
1872	Jules Verne, *Around the World in Eighty Days*
1873	*St. Nicholas: Scribner's Illustrated Magazine for Girls and Boys,* edited by Mary Mapes Dodge
1876	Mark Twain, *The Adventures of Tom Sawyer*
1877	Anna Sewell, *Black Beauty*
1881	Margaret Sidney, *The Five Little Peppers and How They Grew*
	Joel Chandler Harris, *Uncle Remus; His Songs and Sayings: The Folklore of the Old Plantation*
1883	Howard Pyle, *Merry Adventures of Robin Hood of Great Renown, in Nottinghamshire*
	Robert Louis Stevenson, *Treasure Island*

1884	Johanna Spyri, *Heidi; Her Years of Wandering and Learning*
1885	Robert Louis Stevenson, *A Child's Garden of Verses*
1886	Frances Hodgson Burnett, *Little Lord Fauntleroy*
1889	Andrew Lang, *The Blue Fairy Book*
1892	Carlo Collodi, *The Adventures of Pinocchio*
	Arthur Conan Doyle, *The Adventures of Sherlock Holmes*
1894	Rudyard Kipling, *The Jungle Book*
1901	Beatrix Potter, *The Tale of Peter Rabbit*
1903	L. Leslie Brooke, *Johnny Crow's Garden*
	Kate Douglas Wiggins, *Rebecca of Sunnybrook Farm*
	J. M. Barrie, *Peter Pan; or The Boy Who Would Not Grow Up*
1904	Howard Garis, *The Bobbsey Twins; or Merry Days Indoors and Out* (There are over seventy books in the series.)
1908	Kenneth Grahame, *The Wind in the Willows*
1911	Frances Hodgson Burnett, *The Secret Garden*
1913	Eleanor H. Porter, *Pollyanna*
1918	O. Henry, *The Ransom of Red Chief*
1921	Hendrik Willem Van Loon, *The Story of Mankind* (One of the first informational books attempting to make learning exciting; first Newbery Medal, 1922)
1922	Margery Williams Bianco, *The Velveteen Rabbit*
1924	A. A. Milne, *When We Were Very Young*
1926	A. A. Milne, *Winnie-the-Pooh*
1928	Wanda Gág, *Millions of Cats*
	Carl Sandburg, *Abe Lincoln Grows Up*
1929	Rachel Field, *Hitty, Her First Hundred Years*
1932	Laura Ingalls Wilder, *Little House in the Big Woods*
	Laura E. Richards, *Tirra Lirra: Rhymes Old and New*
1933	Jean de Brunhoff, *The Story of Babar*
1937	Dr. Seuss, *And to Think That I Saw It on Mulberry Street*
	John Ronald Reuel Tolkien, *The Hobbit*
1939	James Daugherty, *Daniel Boone*
1940	Armstrong Sperry, *Call It Courage*
	Doris Gates, *Blue Willow*
1941	Lois Lenski, *Indian Captive, The Story of Mary Jemison*
	Robert McCloskey, *Make Way for Ducklings*
1942	Virginia Lee Burton, *The Little House*

CHART 2–3   *Continued*

1944	Robert Lawson, *Rabbit Hill*	1971	Arnold Lobel, *Frog and Toad Are Friends*
1946	Esther Forbes, *Johnny Tremain*		Muriel Feelings, *Moja Means One: Swahili Counting Book*
1947	Marcia Brown, *Stone Soup*		Robert Kraus, *Leo, the Late Bloomer*
1950	Beverly Cleary, *Henry Huggins*	1972	Judith Viorst, *Alexander and the Terrible, Horrible, No Good, Very Bad Day*
1951	Olivia Coolidge, *Legends of the North*		
1952	Lynd Ward, *The Biggest Bear*	1973	Doris Smith, *A Taste of Blackberries*
	E. B. White, *Charlotte's Web*	1974	Janet Hickman, *The Valley of the Shadow*
	David McCord, *Far and Few*	1975	Lawrence Yep, *Dragonwings*
1953	Mary Norton, *The Borrowers*	1976	Mildred Taylor, *Roll of Thunder, Hear My Cry*
1954	Rosemary Sutcliff, *The Eagle of the Ninth*	1977	Jamake Highwater, *Anpao: An Indian Odyssey*
1955	L. M. Boston, *The Children of Green Knowe*		
1957	Else Holmelund Minarik, *Little Bear*		Patricia Clapp, *I'm Deborah Sampson: A Soldier in the War of the Revolution*
1958	Jean Fritz, *The Cabin Faced West*		
	Elizabeth George Speare, *The Witch of Blackbird Pond*		Katherine Paterson, *Bridge to Terabithia*
			Margaret Musgrove, *Ashanti to Zulu: African Traditions*
1959	Leo Lionni, *Little Blue and Little Yellow*		
	Jean George, *My Side of the Mountain*	1978	Tomie de Paola, *The Clown of God*
1960	Michael Bond, *A Bear Called Paddington*	1979	José Aruego and Ariane Dewey, *We Hide, You Seek*
	Scott O'Dell, *Island of the Blue Dolphins*		
1961	C. S. Lewis, *The Lion, the Witch, and the Wardrobe*	1981	Nancy Willard, *Visit to William Blake's Inn*
		1982	Nina Bawden, *Kept in the Dark*
1962	Ronald Syme, *African Traveler, The Story of Mary Kingsley*		Laurence Pringle, *Water: The Next Great Resource Battle*
	Madeleine L'Engle, *A Wrinkle in Time*		Cynthia Rylant, *When I Was Young in the Mountains*
	Ezra Jack Keats, *The Snowy Day*		
1964	Louise Fitzhugh, *Harriet the Spy*	1984	Paula Fox, *One-Eyed Cat*
	Irene Hunt, *Across Five Aprils*	1985	Rhoda Blumberg, *Commodore Perry in the Land of the Shogun*
	Lloyd Alexander, *The Book of Three*		
1967	John Christopher, *The White Mountains*	1986	Jean Fritz, *Make Way for Sam Houston*
	E. L. Konigsburg, *Jennifer, Hecate, MacBeth, William McKinley and Me, Elizabeth*	1987	Russell Freedman, *Lincoln: A Photobiography*
	Virginia Hamilton, *Zeely*	1988	Paul Fleishman, *Joyful Noise: Poems for Two Voices*
1969	John Steptoe, *Stevie*		
	William H. Armstrong, *Sounder*	1989	Janet Taylor Lisle, *Afternoon of the Elves*
	Theodore Taylor, *The Cay*	1990	Dr. Seuss, *Oh, the Places You'll Go!*
	Vera and Bill Cleaver, *Where the Lilies Bloom*	1991	Avi, *Nothing But the Truth: A Documentary Novel*
	William Steig, *Sylvester and the Magic Pebble*		
		1993	Lois Lowry, *The Giver*
1970	Betsy Byars, *Summer of the Swans*	1997	E. L. Konigsburg receives her Second Newbery Medal for *The View from Saturday*
	Judy Blume, *Are You There God? It's Me, Margaret*		

According to Kirk Polking (1990), although "censorship has always existed to some degree, the criteria for proposing that books be banned seem to shift with social trends. In the late 1960s and early 1970s, racism, sexism, and other forms of discrimination were considered objectionable; in the 1980s, it was material alleged to be anti-American, anti-family, or obscene that was challenged. While educators traditionally have chosen books for use by school children for their literary value and for their handling of controversial topics in what they consider to be a tasteful manner, some conservative lobbying groups emerged in the early 1980s as opponents of certain works of literature" (p. 67).

The History of Children's Literature **85**

CHART 2–4 Milestones in the history of censorship

411 B.C.	Works of Protagoras were burned in Athens.
387 B.C.	Plato suggested expurgating Homer's *The Odyssey* for immature readers.
213 B.C.	Chinese Emperor Shih Huang-ti tried to burn all the books in his realm because he disapproved of the traditional Chinese culture.
168 B.C.	Jewish library in Jerusalem was destroyed during the Maccabean uprising.
1st century	Augustus exiled poets and banned their works. Emperor Caligula ordered books by Homer and Virgil burned.
A.D. 303	Diocletian condemned and burned all Christian books.
1497	Works of Ovid and Dante were burned in Florence.
1559	The Sacred Congregation of the Roman Inquisition published the first *Index of Forbidden Books*— books considered dangerous to the faith and morals of Roman Catholics (abandoned in 1996).
1624	The Bible, translated by Martin Luther in 1534, was burned in Germany.
1660	Charles II of England decreed that the Council for Foreign Plantations instruct natives, servants, and slaves of the British colonies in the precepts of Christianity by teaching them to read. But British slave owners feared literate blacks might find dangerous revolutionary ideas in books.
1683	John Locke escaped from England to Holland because his theory of civil, religious, and philosophical liberty was considered too radical.
1713	Daniel Defoe was prosecuted and imprisoned by the Whigs for writing treasonable anti-Jacobite pamphlets. In 1720, his *Robinson Crusoe* was placed on the *Index of Forbidden Books*.
1726	*Gulliver's Travels* by Jonathan Swift was denounced as wicked and obscene because of its satire on courts, political parties, and statesmen.
1760	South Carolina passed strict laws forbidding all blacks from being taught to read.
1762	Jean-Jacques Rousseau's *Emile* was condemned and burned by Parliament of Paris.
1872	Anthony Comstock founded in New York the Society for the Suppression of Vice. This was the first effective censorship board in the United States.
1925	John Scopes found guilty of teaching evolution based on *The Origin of Species*.
1933	In Berlin, propaganda minister Paul Goebbels spoke during the burning of over 20,000 books while a crowd of more than 100,000 cheered.
	Rudolf Frank was arrested in Germany for writing *No Hero for the Kaiser,* a juvenile literature book with an anti-war theme.

In his recent book, *A History of Reading,* Alberto Manguel (1996) identifies some of the milestones in the history of censorship beginning in 411 B.C. and relates censorship with power. He states, "Censorship, therefore, in some form or another, is the corollary of all power, and the history of reading is lit by a seemingly endless line of censors' bonfires, from the earliest papyrus scrolls to the books of our time" (p. 283).

In Chart 2–4, the milestones in the history of censorship include some of the landmarks identified by Manguel in his chapter, "Forbidden Reading," and listings in Anne Lyon Haight's *Banned Books: 387 B.C. to 1978 A.D.* (1978), and in William Noble's *Bookbanning in America: Who Bans Books?—and Why* (1990). Additional milestones in censorship that specifically influenced children's literature have also been added

to the list. As you read the list of books in the chart, try to identify the social, religious, or political attitudes that might have been behind these actions.

 ## CHILDREN AND THE FAMILY IN CHILDREN'S LITERATURE

Attitudes toward the place for children in the family have changed considerably over time. Before the Middle Ages, children were not greatly valued, and infanticide was a regular practice. During the Middle Ages, poor children shared the poverty and hard work of their parents, while children from the upper class and nobility spent most of their childhood separated from their families, receiving instruction and training in the roles that they would assume as

CHART 2–4 *Continued*

1942	In Athens, performances of classic Greek plays were banned by Nazi occupation authorities.
1955	In Connecticut, African Americans protested against a dramatized version of Harriet Beecher Stowe's *Uncle Tom's Cabin, or Life Among the Lowly.*
1957	New York City dropped works of Mark Twain from lists of approved books for junior and senior high schools because of racial language.
1980	Parents took Hawkins County Tennessee Public Schools to court because an elementary school series was believed to violate their fundamentalist religious beliefs.
1984	*The Adventures of Huckleberry Finn* was removed from the high school reading list in Waukegan, Illinois.
1989	A survey of schools showed that Mark Twain's *The Adventures of Huckleberry Finn* was one of the most read books in high schools.
1994–95	List compiled by People for the American Way of the ten leading books that various groups tried to ban during the year and the reasons for the banning:
	Alvin Schwartz. *More Scary Stories to Tell in the Dark* (supernatural tales).
	Alvin Schwartz. *Scary Stories to Tell in the Dark* (supernatural tales).
	Maya Angelou. *I Know Why the Caged Bird Sings* (sexual content).
	Lois Lowry. *The Giver* (profanity, violence, depressing story).
	Eve Merriam. *Halloween ABC* (supernatural theme).
	Alvin Schwartz. *Scary Stories 3: More Tales to Chill Your Bones* (supernatural tales).
	Katherine Paterson. *Bridge to Terabithia* (sexual content, profanity, "satanic" material).
	Robert Cormier. *The Chocolate War* (profanity, violence, sexual content).
	John Steinbeck. *Of Mice and Men* (profanity, sexual content).
	Christopher and James Lincoln Collier. *My Brother Sam Is Dead* (profanity, violence, challenge to patriotism, challenge to parental authority).
1997	February 17 issue of *Publishers Weekly* lists *The Giver* as number four in "Children's Bestsellers" (one of the books groups sought to ban in 1995).

adults. Not until relatively recently has childhood become the time for the close family interaction that we are familiar with today.

Books written for children or adopted by children over the last few centuries have usually reflected views of childhood and the family typical of their time. Researchers are increasingly viewing children's literature as an important source of information about these changing attitudes. In *Fifteen Centuries of Children's Literature: An Annotated Chronology of British and American Works in Historical Context,* Jane Bingham and Grayce Scholt (1980) consider the historical background of children's books, including attitudes toward and treatment of children, discuss the development of children's books, and provide an annotated chronology of children's books. Robert Gordon Kelly (1970), in *Mother Was a Lady: Self and Society in Selected American Children's Periodicals, 1865–1890,* considers the social values reflected in children's stories of the late nineteenth century. Mary Lystad (1980) considers the sociology of children's books over two

centuries in *From Dr. Mather to Dr. Seuss: Two Hundred Years of American Books for Children.*

Other researchers have analyzed children's literature over time: Mary Cadogan and Patricia Craig (1976) have looked at the changing role of females in *You're a Brick, Angela! A New Look at Girls' Fiction from 1839 to 1975;* Alma Cross Homze (1963) has analyzed the changing interpersonal relationships depicted in realistic fiction published between 1920 and 1960; and Jean Duncan Shaw (1966) has studied themes in children's books published between 1850 and 1964. Lynne Vallone (1988) analyzed the role of females in eighteenth-century adolescent fiction. Studies of more recent historical periods include Carolyn Wilson Carmichael's (1971) analysis of social values reflected in contemporary realistic fiction, John Rowe Townsend's (1975) analysis of the relationships between generations depicted in the literature of the 1950s and the 1960s, and Beverly Young's (1985) analysis of female protagonists in literature of the 1930s, the 1950s, and the 1970s.

Unsurprisingly, a prominent theme in children's literature has been the relationships of children within the family. Changing views about children and the family over time necessarily reflect other social attitudes as well. The following time periods reflect the publication dates of a few popular American children's books in eras otherwise not easily demarcated by precise years. All of these books are available today. The older books have been published in reproductions by Garland Publishing Company of New York and London.

The Child and the Family, 1856–1903

An emphatic sense of duty to God and parents, the rise of the public school and Sunday School movements, and the beginning of a belief that children are individuals in their own right are among the characteristics of the Victorian era identifiable in children's literature of the time. According to Karen I. Adams (1989), "In the latter half of the nineteenth century and early decades of the twentieth century, religion was most often represented by the moralizing of Louisa May Alcott in *Little Women*" (p. 5). Much Victorian children's literature stresses the development of conscience, the merit of striving for perfection, and the male and female roles exemplified by family members. Illuminating examples of the social attitudes of this period may be drawn from Charlotte Yonge's *The Daisy Chain* (1856), Louisa May Alcott's *Little Women* (1868), Thomas Bailey Aldrich's *The Story of a Bad Boy* (1870), Margaret Sidney's *The Five Little Peppers and How They Grew* (1880), and Kate Douglas Wiggins's *Rebecca of Sunnybrook Farm* (1903) (see also Chart 2–5).

While these books have their differences, all of them stress the importance of accepting responsibility, whether for one's family, the poor and unfortunate, or self-improvement. For example, the older children in *The Daisy Chain* assume the task of raising the younger children when their mother dies; their greatest concerns are instilling Christian goodness in their siblings and living up to their father's wishes. Likewise, the children in *Little Women* and *The Five Little Peppers and How They Grew* feel responsible for their siblings and their mothers. Rebecca, in *Rebecca of Sunnybrook Farm,* feels this responsibility to such an extent that she completes four years of work at the academy in three years so that she can earn a living and help educate her siblings.

May Alcott's illustrations for her sister Louisa May Alcott's Little Women *reinforce the vision of a warm, loving Victorian family. (Illustration by May Alcott. From* Little Women or, Meg, Jo, Beth and Amy *by Louisa M. Alcott. Published by Roberts Brothers, 1868. Courtesy of Lilly Library, Indiana University, Bloomington, Indiana.)*

The characters in these books respect adult authority. Children strive to live up to their parents' ideals or want the acceptance and respect of their parents. The protagonist in *The Story of a Bad Boy* may not always ask or follow his grandfather's advice, but he admits that he deserves the terrible things that usually happen to him when he disobeys.

Respect for authority is underscored by the characteristic religious emphasis in these books. In *The Daisy Chain,* family members read the Bible together, discuss the meaning of the minister's sermons, debate the relative importance of the temptations in their lives, and organize a church and school for the poor. In *Little Women,* the family members receive strength from prayer and Bible

Twentieth-century American publishers of children's books, like publishers in all historical periods, must respond to the issues of the times. Ann Durell identifies some of these changing issues in two articles published in *The Horn Book*.[1,2]

According to Durell, the 1950s was a time when publishing was fun because the rules were clear-cut. The taboos of the early 1900s were still in place: no lying or stealing unless suitably punished, no drinking, and no bad language. Racial prejudice was evidenced by the controversy that greeted Garth William's black and white couple in *The Rabbits' Wedding*.

In the late 1950s, the library market took on new significance, as Russia launched Sputnik and our educational system came under attack. Books were considered means of improving education. Durell categorizes the 1960s as a time of rapidly expanding school libraries in the United States. Title II of the Elementary and Secondary School Act mandated funds for the purchase of nontextbooks for schools. The sales of both nonfiction and easy-to-read book titles increased rapidly and school libraries expanded rapidly.

New issues affected the publishing trade, however, as the country was polarized by the Vietnam War and the new demands of the Great Society. The all-white world of children's books was challenged; editors started searching for African American authors. For the most part, however, children's books did not reflect the social upheavals of the time.

The 1970s introduced literature that reflected the social upheavals. Reactions to two children's books in the early 1970s exemplify the changing times. When a white author won the Newbery Medal for writing about a black family (*Sounder*), protests intensified editors' searches for authors and illustrators who represented ethnic minorities. Mickey's nudity in Maurice Sendak's *In the Night Kitchen* resulted in actions ranging from covering the nudity before the book was placed on the shelf to actual banning of the book.

As the 1970s continued, concern about the sex roles portrayed in children's books increased; lists of taboos in children's books were reduced; and books reflected ethnic minorities more positively. Durell emphasizes the paradox created by these changes and the new pressures exerted on publishers. On the one hand, the only criterion for allowing books to be published was positive portrayal of females, minority groups, senior citizens, and individuals with disabilities. On the other hand, groups demanding conservative standards insisted on returning to the 1950s taboos. Consequently, censorship, but for different reasons, became an issue on both sides.

Interestingly, one of the issues affecting book publishing in the 1990s is related to the growing financial success of children's trade book publishing. Eden Ross Lipson[3] discusses the impact of giant corporations, which buy out publishing houses and then try to make the publishing companies as profitable as possible. Consequently, there are concerns that mass market favorites may overshadow quality children's books.

[1] Durell, Ann. "There Is No Happy Ending: Children's Book Publishing—Past, Present, and Future," Part 1. *The Horn Book* 58 (February 1982): 23–30.

[2] _____. "There Is No Happy Ending: Children's Book Publishing—Past, Present, and Future," Part 2. *The Horn Book* 58 (April 1982): 145–50.

[3] Lipson, Eden Ross. "The Little Industry That Could," Part 2. *The New York Times Magazine*. (December 3, 1989): 20–21, 50, 52.

reading. In *The Story of a Bad Boy,* Sundays are solemn days in which the family attends church, reads the scriptures, and eats food prepared the day before. The five little Peppers voice admiration for the clergy and want to become "good." Rebecca of Sunnybrook Farm's aunt, like her father before her, is an influential member of her church.

Family life in these books reiterates the definite social roles assigned to males and females in the Victorian era. Females usually run the household and make decisions related to everyday life, but the husband and father is usually the undisputed head of the family. The author may even state this fact point-blank, so there is no misunderstanding on the part of readers—as Louisa May Alcott does in *Little Women:*

To outsiders, the five energetic women seemed to rule the house, and so they did in many things; but the quiet scholar, sitting among his books, was still the head of the family, the household conscience, anchor, and comforter: to him the busy, anxious women always turned in troublous times, finding him, in the truest sense of those sacred words, husband and father. (p. 294)

CHART 2–5 (PP. 90–94) Social values, family life, and personal relationships, 1856–1903

	Author, Book, Date, Setting				
	Charlotte Yonge, *The Daisy Chain*, 1856, 1868. Rural England, Middle class.	Louisa May Alcott, *Little Women*, 1868. New England city suburb; large gardens, quiet streets.	Thomas Bailey Aldrich, *The Story of a Bad Boy*, 1870. New Orleans then to small New Hampshire town.	Margaret Sidney, *The Five Little Peppers and How They Grew*, 1881. Poverty level. United States.	Kate Douglas Wiggins, *Rebecca of Sunnybrook Farm*, 1903. Small New England town.
SOCIAL VALUES					
Dignity of Human Beings	Concern for family members. Some poor described as uncivilized. Wanted to improve role of poor by building church.	More important to have personal dignity, self-respect, and peace than wealth. Concern for the ill and the poor.	In New Orleans, Tom kicked a "negro boy" who was in his way. Tom believed Indians scalp children. In New Hampshire household, aunt and servant were friends. No social criticism mentioned.	Peppers were proud and believed they had a good life, although they were poor.	Prejudice stated by neighbor against being "dark complected." Aunt Miranda disowned her sister when she married against her wishes. Rebecca respected many people.
Acceptance of Responsibility	Duty to tend to poor. Founded and taught in school for poor. Each member accepted responsibility to younger siblings after mother's death.	Duty to poor; gave their Christmas breakfast to a poor family. Strong duty to family.	Main character did not dwell on unhappy events in story but believed in accepting reality.	Each member expressed responsibility for siblings and mother. Polly almost ruined her eyes sewing for mother when Polly had measles.	Rebecca worked hard to complete the academy in three years instead of four.
Belief in Equality of Opportunity	Boys had advanced education. Girls not expected to understand mathematical concepts. Girls trained to guide family. Poor children worked at early ages.	Girls were educated but not at the university. Males attended university.	Stressed Puritan ethic of diligence and common sense. Veneer of well-being. Main character thought all adults had money when they wanted it.	Family said their ship would come in and hard times would be over.	Rebecca thought boys could do more exciting things than girls. Teacher stressed that girls could have a profession. Brother hoped to become a doctor.

Ambition	Charity, humility, devotion to good works. Development of Christian goodness.	Heroine, Jo, wanted to write. Other sisters: drawing, music. Work ethic stressed by son-in-law.	Males should learn "manly arts" and become self-reliant. Tom did not want to be lowest in his class. No single drive expressed by the main character.	Members wanted to help mother. Polly wanted to play the piano. Ann wanted their ship to come in. To be "good."	Rebecca wanted an education to help her family. To become a writer.
Obedience to Law, Patriotism	Respect stated for military profession.	Mother encouraged her husband to serve in the Union army. Mother devoted time to Soldiers Aid Society.	Boys escaped from jail so father would not learn about their prank. Military experience held in high esteem.	No disrespect stated.	No disrespect stated.
Importance of Education and Knowledge	Both sexes read many books. Read Bible in Greek and English. Males attended university. Asked not to use slang.	Jo loved Aunt March's large library. They all read. Felt humiliated when punished at school. Father described as scholar. Jo asked not to use slang.	Gained enjoyment and escaped by reading. Attended boys' academy. Wanted to be promoted to higher position in class.	Polly wanted to learn. Wealthy cousins had tutor. Wealthy old gentleman promised to educate Polly.	Reading gave pleasure. Education could make it possible to improve one's position in life. Rebecca respected intelligence.
Respect for Adult Authority	Children wanted to live up to their father's wishes and ideals. Asked mother's permission at home.	Children wanted their parents' acceptance. Looked up to a "noble" mother and turned to the "quiet scholar" who helped them during "troublesome times."	Respected adults but did not always ask permission. Tom did not mention something when he knew that his grandfather would disapprove.	Children always respected their widowed mother. Jasper wanted his father's respect.	Rebecca respected knowledge of English teacher and sought her advice.

CHART 2–5 *Continued*

Author, Book, Date, Setting

	Charlotte Yonge, *The Daisy Chain*, 1856, 1868. Rural England, Middle class.	Louisa May Alcott, *Little Women*, 1868. New England suburb; large gardens, quiet streets.	Thomas Bailey Aldrich, *The Story of a Bad Boy*, 1870. New Orleans then to small New Hampshire town.	Margaret Sidney, *The Five Little Peppers and How They Grew*, 1881. Poverty level. United States.	Kate Douglas Wiggins, *Rebecca of Sunnybrook Farm*. 1903. Small New England town.
FAMILY LIFE Description	Warm, close, and self-sufficient. Family center of heroine's existence. Cleanliness of home considered a virtue.	Warm, filled with laughter and singing. Children made their own fun; played "Pilgrim's Progress" and acted out plays. At 9:00. stopped work and sang before going to bed.	Family and main character generally cheerful and affectionate. "Old Puritan austerity cropped up but once a week." Main character interacted more with friends as they put on plays. formed a club, attended school, and played pranks.	Close, happy family who told stories and expressed love and concern for each other. Boys argued with new cousins.	Rebecca had a happy-go-lucky family led by father who had difficulty making money. Two aunts led a very conservative life.
Religion, Stability	Stressed responsibility for raising good and holy children. Family read Bible and discussed meaning of Sunday services.	Father asked his wife to pray for the girls each evening. They turned to God to help them overcome troubles and temptations.	Nutter house had been in the family nearly one hundred years. Attic with its treasures was symbolic of the long residence of one family. Sundays were solemn. Attended church, read Bible, and ate cold meals.	Stable because of closeness but grew up under considerable pressure. Expressed great respect for minister.	Contrasts drawn between the two families. Rebecca's parents moved often. Aunts lived in the same home as their father.

Numbers in Family	Eleven children. Father. Mother (died early in story).	Four girls. Mother. Father (away in Army in Part 1).	One child living with grandfather in the north. Parents living in New Orleans.	Five children, widowed mother.	One of seven children. Father died, mother had difficulties.
Extended Family	Prim, middle-aged governess. Nurse. Servants.	Housekeeper.	Grandfather. Maiden aunt. Servant.	Wealthy old gentleman, his son, his daughter, and her children.	Two spinster sisters. Rebecca lived with them.
Relationships Within Family	Definite male and female roles. Children relied upon mother in the home. Father was head of household. Children respected each other.	Mother guided the heart. Father guided the soul. Father was head of family. Strong ties among sisters. Oldest sister's gentle advice influenced her sisters.	Grandfather understood boy; he had once run away to sea. Grandfather showed pride when Tom won fight with a bully who harassed smaller boys.	Everyone pampered Phronsie, the pretty baby in the family. Phronsie and Polly brought changes in others' lives because of the influence of their personalities.	Aunt Jane was warmer and more understanding. Aunt Miranda was strict, head of household and respected traditional values.

PERSONAL RELATIONSHIPS AND FEELINGS

Independent Male or Female	Mother: at home, gentle power, strong authority. Father: skillful, clever, sensitive but showed vexation and sarcasm. Ethel: secretly kept up with brother's classical studies.	Jo: didn't want to grow up to be a lady. Jo: wanted to do something extraordinary. Jo: said her quick temper and restless spirit got her in trouble. Mother: managed household while husband was away.	Grandfather lived at ease on money invested in shipping. A maiden sister managed the household with her brother and servant. Tom had freedom to explore the countryside. Tom stressed male need to "learn to box, to ride, to pull an oar, and to swim."	Mother made family decisions but often had no idea about how they would manage. Boys got into more trouble than girls.	Rebecca was "plucky," "dauntless," and "intelligent." Aunt Miranda was strong-willed, managed their lives. Rebecca usually self-reliant.

CHART 2–5 *Continued*

Author, Book, Date, Setting

	Charlotte Yonge, *The Daisy Chain.* 1856, 1868. Rural England, Middle class.	Louisa May Alcott, *Little Women.* 1868. New England city suburb; large gardens, quiet streets.	Thomas Bailey Aldrich, *The Story of a Bad Boy.* 1870. New Orleans then to small New Hampshire town.	Margaret Sidney, *The Five Little Peppers and How They Grew,* 1881. Poverty level. United States.	Kate Douglas Wiggins, *Rebecca of Sunnybrook Farm.* 1903. Small New England town.
PERSONAL RELATIONSHIPS AND FEELINGS (cont.)					
Dependent Male or Female	Mother: reserved and shrinking from society. Males made major decisions. Girls clung to males.	Mother worried about guiding children to meet husband's ideals. Children turned to parents for guidance. Beth: too bashful to attend school.	Girls attended separate school and were graduated by "a dragon of watchfulness." Pony's vanities compared to female "weaknesses."	Mother eventually accepted help from a wealthy gentleman who brought the family out of poverty. Polly, although plucky, often fainted.	Aunt Jane infrequently spoke out against Miranda. Aunts wanted dependent, obedient child.
Problems	Concerned with not living up to parents' expectations and God's desire. Love of glory considered a temptation.	Overcoming problems that led to "sweetness of self-denial and self-control."	Problems allowed main character to consider his moral code. When he disobeyed something usually went wrong.	Concerned with being good. Problems connected with survival in poverty.	Tried to live up to the traditional behavioral ideals of a strict aunt and Rebecca's desire to be "respectably, decently good."
Friendships	Mainly with family members or people in own class.	Greatest among sisters. Neighbor boy.	A group of boys at the academy. The Centipede Club—all boys. Tom and older seaman. Aunt and female servant were friends.	Mainly each other in the family. A wealthy boy who rescued Phronsie and was impressed with the warm family. Phronsie and the wealthy gentleman whom she changed.	Rebecca was friendly. Liked many adults and children.

Males and females attend separate schools in *The Story of a Bad Boy,* and only male characters attend the university in *The Daisy Chain* and *Little Women.* Education may also stress different objectives for males and females. Yonge's heroine in *The Daisy Chain* completes her brother's school assignments but is not expected to understand mathematical concepts. Aldrich's hero wants training in manly arts, such as boxing, riding, and rowing. In contrast, drawing, writing, and music are desired accomplishments for the females in *Little Women,* piano lessons are sought by the oldest female Pepper, and writing is Rebecca's desire.

Insights about the children and families in these books are gained by viewing the problems that the heroes and heroines experience. Many of these problems involve attempts to abide by the period's standards of moral rectitude. Yonge's heroine strives to raise her family and help the poor. She works to keep the youngest baby an "unstained jewel" until the baby returns to her mother. She and her brother also face the problems associated with providing spiritual guidance to the poor. Many of Jo's problems in *Little Women* are related to controlling her "unfeminine" high energy and self-assertiveness. Jo looks to her pious mother for guidance in how to be "good":

Jo's only answer was to hold her mother close, and, in the silence which followed, the sincerest prayer she had ever prayed left her heart without words; for in that sad, yet happy hour, she had learned not only the bitterness of remorse and despair, but the sweetness of self-denial and self-control; and, led by her mother's hand, she had drawn nearer to the Friend who welcomes every child with a love stronger than that of any father, tenderer than that of any mother. (p. 103)

Rebecca of Sunnybrook Farm also confronts problems caused by the conflicts between her own high-spirited nature and adults' strict expectations about a young girl's behavior. She, too, experiences personal misgivings when her actions do not live up to her desire to be good. The advantages of these conflicts, however, are stated by Rebecca's English teacher at the academy: "Luckily she attends to her own development. . . . In a sense she is independent of everything and everybody; she follows her saint without being conscious of it."

The problems that Thomas Bailey Aldrich creates for his protagonist allow the "bad" boy to consider and strengthen his own moral code. Although he has several unhappy and even disastrous experiences, the boy does not dwell upon them, believing that they have caused him to become more manly and self-reliant.

Overcoming problems related to poverty and growing up without a father are major concerns of the Pepper children, but Margaret Sidney has their mother encourage them in this way: "You keep on a-tryin', and the Lord'll send some way; don't you go to botherin' your head about it now . . . it'll come when it's time." The family's financial problems are finally solved when a wealthy old gentleman invites them to share his home.

The Child and the Family, 1938–1960

The 1900s brought much change to the lives of American children. Many states passed child labor laws, John Dewey's influential theories encouraged a more child-centered educational philosophy, the quality and extent of public education improved, and religious training placed less emphasis on sinfulness and more emphasis on moral development and responsibility toward others. Children's literature reflected these changes, and children's book publishing expanded to meet the needs of an increasingly literate youthful population. Optimism was a keynote in the twentieth-century "Age of Progress," and, especially after World War II, "children's book editors saw a bright future for the children of this country and the world" (McElderry, 1974, p. 89).

This optimism is reflected in the views of the children and families depicted in American children's books of the late 1930s through the beginning of the 1960s. John Rowe Townsend's (1975) conclusions about depictions of family life in children's literature of the 1950s apply to earlier literature as well: Children live in stable communities, where most children are happy and secure, the older generations are wise and respected, and the generations follow one another into traditional social roles in an orderly way.

The following books, written by award-winning authors, characterize the social values, the stability of family life, and the types of personal relationships depicted in children's literature of this period: Elizabeth Enright's *Thimble Summer* (1938), Eleanor Estes's *The Moffats* (1941), Sydney Taylor's *All-of-a-Kind Family* (1951), and Madeleine L'Engle's *Meet the Austins* (1960) (see also Chart 2–6). The families in these books live in different locations around the

CHART 2–6 (PP. 96–98) Social values, family life, and personal relationships, 1938–1960

	Author, Book, Date, Setting			
	Elizabeth Enright, *Thimble Summer*, 1938. Rural Wisconsin farm.	Eleanor Estes, *The Moffats*, 1941. Middle-sized New England city. Poor family.	Sydney Taylor, *All-of-a-Kind Family*, 1951. New York, East Side (1912). Jewish family.	Madeleine L'Engle, *Meet the Austins*, 1960. Country home. Father M.D.
SOCIAL VALUES **Dignity of Human Beings**	An orphan boy was given love and respect of the family.	They trusted each other and strangers. They expected strangers to give them help when they were lost.	You accept people. "You don't ask them about their personal lives."	Family felt empathy toward others' problems. Children included in serious discussions.
Acceptance of Responsibility	Children accepted farm chores without complaining.	Older members responsible for younger brothers and sisters. Joe felt terrible when he lost coal money, and his mother would need to work late. He searched until he found it.	Child felt responsible for lost library book; her sisters offered their few pennies. They tried to avoid household chores. A promise was considered important.	Consideration for others was essential. One child could not disrupt the family.
Belief in Equality of Opportunity	Father believed his daughter could be the farmer in the family.	Family worked together. Males and females did many things together. Positive mood.	Father believed his work and savings would make it possible to have a better life.	Aunt Elena was a well-known concert pianist.
Ambition	Strong work ethic: Children talk about saving money to buy a farm.	Mother worked hard to keep the family. Took in sewing. Traded sewing for free dancing lessons.	Father wanted more for his family than he could give them. Worked and saved for the day he could make their lives better.	Scientific experiments were considered important. Education was important.
Obedience to Law, Patriotism	No conflicts mentioned.	Nine-year-old always walked cautiously by police chief's house; never stood on his lawn.	Father did not want the U.S. flag placed on the floor.	Family rules were stressed.

Importance of Education and Knowledge	Reading important to the girls as a means of escape.	Five-year-old Rufus looked forward to school. "Go to school or be a dunce." All children had dancing lessons.	Great excitement because Friday was library day. Books were treasured.	Homework was to be finished before playing. Grandfather collected books.
Respect for Adult Authority	Children respected parents. Enjoyed listening to friends, great-grandmother tells stories about her life.	Girl worried about mimicking new superintendent of schools. Mother: "Do as the teacher says." Mother was voice of authority; they went to her to ask questions.	Children obediently followed parents. Called themselves "Mama's children."	"When daddy speaks that way we hop." Children did not want their parents to come home and find work not finished.
FAMILY LIFE Description	Very happy and secure family. Garnet had a nice mother and a nice family. Considerable trust of others.	Family was happy and secure in their relationships, although their rented house had a "for sale" sign on it. Mother didn't really share children's experiences but listened to them.	Happy, secure family: a "gentle, soft" father; a loving but strong mother. After five girls, father cried with happiness when boy was born.	Spontaneous family love. Mutual respect and understanding. Warmth and humor. Strong father who made them accept the consequences when they didn't do their homework.
Religion, Stability	Families had lived in the valley for generations. No strong religious emphasis.	Worked together for good of the family, even when Rufus had scarlet fever and they were quarantined. Went to Sunday school.	Very stable; could not imagine what it would be like not to have a family. Law of the Sabbath carefully observed.	Strong family ties. Sunday school and church important. Family prayed before meals and at other times in their day.
Numbers in Family	Three children. Mother. Father.	Four children. Widowed mother.	Six children. Father. Mother.	Four children. Father. Mother.
Extended Family	Brought an orphaned boy to work on farm without checking I.D.		Mother's brother was a frequent visitor.	Orphaned ten-year-old daughter of a friend.
Relationships Within Family	Strong, trusting. Slight brother and sister friction.	Had fun together. Humorous experiences. Mother was supportive and loving. Not critical except about getting clothes dirty.	Mother planned games for children to make them enjoy dusting. Children were proud of their mother; wanted to introduce her to new librarian.	Children disagreed with each other but always made up. Father and mother talked over family problems with children.

CHART 2–6 *Continued*

Author, Book, Date, Setting

	Elizabeth Enright, *Thimble Summer*, 1938. Rural Wisconsin farm.	Eleanor Estes, *The Moffats*. 1941. Middle-sized New England city. Poor family.	Sydney Taylor, *All-of-a-Kind Family*, 1951. New York, East Side (1912). Jewish family.	Madeleine L'Engle, *Meet the Austins*. 1960. Country home. Father M.D.
PERSONAL RELATIONSHIPS AND FEELINGS				
Independent Male or Female	Independent female who loved her family. Hitch-hiked to town without fear. Angry when brother suggested she do women's work.	Children could travel around town. Always found their way back.	Strong mother who took care of the family. Father owned his own business: a "junk shop." Children hid their candy from their mother.	Children were individual thinkers.
Dependent Male or Female		They relied upon each other and upon their mother to answer questions.	Children gave in to firm mother.	Vicky believed her older brother always knew what to say and could get her out of difficulties. Family depended on each other.
Types of Problems	No real problems.	Their house was for sale, and they accepted the possibility of moving. Some problems because of family illness or need for money. Problems overcome in humorous ways.	No major problems. Saved for lost library book, hid candy.	Maggy, an orphaned girl, was disturbed because she had never known love. Problems centered around helping her make adjustments.
Friendships	Next-door girl whose family had lived there for generations.	Family members. Neighbors. They made friends with strangers around town.	Very close to each other; no other children mentioned. Neighborhood peddlers and librarian were friends.	Children close friends. Uncle Douglas always understood them and knew how to make them feel good about themselves.

United States and range from lower-middle class to upper-middle class, but the values that they support are similar. The characters admire and emulate the traditional family model of breadwinning father, housewife mother, and their children, living together in one place for a number of years.

Family members have happy and secure relationships with one another, complemented by mutual respect, warmth, and humor. The actions of the Moffats express confidence and trust in the family unit. The children in *All-of-a-Kind Family* cannot imagine what it would be like not to have a family. In *Meet the Austins,* Vicky is pleased because her mother looks just the way that she believes a mother should look.

Religious values are suggested in these stories by Sunday school attendance, preparation for the sabbath, or prayers before meals. Dignity is stressed. The family in *Thimble Summer* brings an orphaned boy into its home on trust without checking his background. The parents in *All-of-a-Kind Family* tell their children to accept people and to not ask them about their personal lives. The Austin family feels empathy for others' problems, and the parents include their children in serious discussions.

Patriotism is strong in all of the books, and the law is respected. Education is considered important; children enjoy reading, go to school with the expectation that it will increase their understanding, and finish their homework before playing. Families prize even small collections of books. The work ethic is a powerful force in the lives of these families. Children talk about saving their money to buy a farm, a mother takes in sewing to keep the family together, and a father works long hours, saving for the day when he can make life better for his family. Children respect adult wisdom and authority; they obey rules, minding their teachers and complying with parental desires. Children also enjoy listening to their elders tell about their own experiences.

Unsurprisingly, given their secure lives and confident adherence to established social standards, the children in these books have few emotional problems. They usually feel good about themselves and other family members. Their actions suggest dependence upon the family for emotional stability, but independence in their daily experiences, as they move without fear around the neighborhood, city, or countryside.

The Child and the Family, 1969–1990s

Researchers who have analyzed children's literature over time have identified the 1960s, 1970s, and 1980s as decades in which traditional social, family, and personal values appeared to be changing. Alma Cross Homze (1963) found that in the late 1950s, adult characters in children's books were becoming less authoritarian and critical in their relationships with children, while children were becoming more outspoken, independent, and critical of adults. John Rowe Townsend (1975) later concluded that children's literature of the 1960s suggested an erosion of adult authority and a widening of the generation gap. When Beverly Young (1985) compared female protagonists of the 1930s, the 1950s, and the 1970s, she concluded that the characters became increasingly protest-oriented. Craig Werner and Frank Riga (1989) used religious questions developed by authors in the late 1900s to analyze changes in questions pertaining to religious matters in literature written in the 1800s. They found that nineteenth-century authors such as George MacDonald addressed questions such as "What must I do to enter the kingdom of God?" or "How should I pray?" In contrast, contemporary authors such as Cynthia Rylant and M. E. Kerr address questions such as "Is there a Kingdom of God?" or "Does it do any good to pray?" Werner and Riga conclude that the questions have shifted radically from the searchable to the searching because modern authors present partial answers, "not the full-blown declarations of faith that characterized earlier religious writings for children" (p. 2).

Binnie Tate Wilkin (1978) connects these trends in the children's literature of the 1960s and 1970s with changing "educational, social and political, and economic concerns" (p. 21), citing as examples the civil rights movements, protest marches, and assassinations of the period. Wilkin says:

Almost all levels of society were challenged to respond to the activism. Book publishers responded with new materials reflecting dominant concerns. Distress about children's reading problems, federal responses to urban unrest, the youth movements, new openness about sexuality, religious protest, etc. were reflected in children's books. (p. 21)

In 1981, polls quoted by John F. Stacks (1981) showed that about 20 percent of Americans still expressed belief in most of the traditional values of hard work, family loyalty, and sacrifice, while the majority of respondents embraced only some of those values, doubted that self-denial and moral rectitude were their own rewards, and held tolerant views about abortion, premarital sex, remaining single, and not having children. Still, Stacks concluded that people who believed in traditional values were becoming an increasingly vocal group that "could set to a significant degree the moral tone for the 1980s" (p. 18). Other research indicates that the American family has experienced far more continuity than change over the last fifty years. Norman Lobsenz (1981) reports findings from the study *Middletown Families: 50 Years of Change and Continuity* showing that marriage is still viewed as important, although divorce is widely accepted; many wives and mothers have jobs, but they still do most of the housework and child care; and many married couples see more of their relatives than they do of their friends.

Comparison of children's literature written between the 1930s and the early 1960s with children's literature written in the 1970s through the 1990s reveals both similarities and differences between the American families in the two periods. Many books still portray strong family ties and stress the importance of personal responsibility and human dignity, but the happy, stable unit of the earlier literature is often replaced by a family in turmoil as it adjusts to a new culture, faces the prospects of surviving without one or both parents, handles the disruption resulting from divorce, or deals with an extended family, exemplified by grandparents or a foster home. Later literature also suggests that many acceptable family units do not conform to the traditional American model.

While many children's books could be selected for this discussion, the following books contain some of the diverse attitudes toward family and children in the period from 1969 into the 1990s: Vera and Bill Cleaver's *Where the Lilies Bloom* (1969), Norma Klein's *Mom, the Wolf Man, and Me* (1972), Paula Fox's *The Moonlight Man* (1986), Theresa Nelson's *The Beggars' Ride* (1992), and Ruth White's *Belle Prater's Boy* (1996) (see also Chart 2–7). While children in the literature of the 1940s and 1950s had few personal and emotional problems, children between 1969 and the 1990s may have much responsibility and may experience emotional problems as they try to survive. The strongest character in *Where the Lilies Bloom* attempts to hold the family together, but she discovers that she needs people outside her immediate family. The heroine of *Mom, the Wolf Man, and Me* fears that her life will change if her mother marries. The main character in *The Moonlight Man* must accept her father and his behavior as well as her parents' divorce. The heroine of *The Beggars' Ride* runs away because her mother's boyfriend is abusing her. She tries to survive in a city with a group of homeless children. The main characters in *Belle Prater's Boy* learn how to overcome the inner hurt caused by the suicide of a parent and the disappearance of another parent.

Characters in the literature of this period may express concern about equal opportunities and question respect for the law, education, and adult authority. In *Mom, the Wolf Man, and Me,* the mother is a successful photographer and allows the daughter to accompany her on women's rights and peace marches. The main character in *The Beggars' Ride* is afraid to tell authorities about her abuse. None of the homeless children in the gang trust social workers because all have had difficulties when they trusted adults in authority.

The strongest story related to the dignity of human beings and acceptance of responsibility is Vera and Bill Cleaver's *Where the Lilies Bloom,* which is about the proud, independent mountain people who earn their livings through wildcrafting (the gathering of wild plants for human use). Before the father dies, he asks his daughter to keep the family together without accepting charity and to instill in the children pride in having the name Luther. *Belle Prater's Boy* is also a strong story about the dignity of human beings as the children discover the truth in Grandpa's belief that it is what is in the heart that counts.

An opposite condition is found as the father in *The Moonlight Man* is an alcoholic, and when his daughter says, "See you," as she leaves him, he whispers, "Not if I see you first" (p. 179). The mother in *The Beggars' Ride* is irresponsible and does not know how to help her daughter. There is finally a happy ending in the story. The heroine is helped by an understanding older man and is finally reunited with her mother. Clearly, children's literature now presents a greater range and more realistic representations of family diversity.

In an article edited by Diane Roback and Shannon Maughan,[1] several publishers and editors speculate about the future of children's book publishing. Many of these speculations provide issues that can be analyzed, researched, and discussed in children's literature courses. For example, the following quotes and concerns provide interesting discussion topics:

Stephen Roxburgh, President and Publisher, Front Street Books, provides two issues that are of interest. First, he maintains that we are currently dealing with an industry that has changed from privately held businesses to publicly held businesses whose investors demand return on their money. He states, "The potential for profit and growth is enormous, hence, the headlong rush and ruthless tactics" (p. 152). Second, he believes that the old publishing model based on serving libraries has been replaced by the media industry model that sells entertainment to the masses. He states, "Those who publish books supported primarily by the institutions (hardcover fiction, nonfiction, poetry, 'high-end' picture books) will find themselves under siege to justify their existence" (p. 152).

Tracy Tang, Vice President and Publisher, Puffin Books, discusses the results of the market-driven type of publishing that may cause publishers to lose sight of more traditional, book-based publishing. She states, "I'm speaking optimistically when I say I hope that there will be a return to publishing books for the strength of their story and their illustrations" (p. 153). Tang's second issue focuses on the quality of the huge numbers of paperbacks for middle-grade and young adult series. She states, "A lot of people are trying to clone Goosebumps and the Baby-sitters Club. I think it's safe to say that most of these series aren't working as well as publishers hoped. I'm not sure that there will ever be fewer new series being published, but hopefully we'll see more high-quality, author-based series" (p. 153).

Jasan Higgins, Vice President and Director of Marketing Children's Books, William Morrow, discusses the impact on purchasing power for both public and school libraries. She emphasizes the controversy between book and technology purchases as the libraries try to stretch dollars to meet both demands.

David Ahlender, Vice President and Editorial Director, Children's Book-of-the-Month Club, argues for the future of books and literacy. He believes that "It really does come down to a book and a child. Parents today cannot take literacy for granted the way they used to; they need to provide books in the home if they want their children to be literate. Our industry has a tremendous cultural relevance and a bright future. I hope that publishers will take that as a cause and a mission, because that's what really matters" (p. 153).

There are differences of opinion provided among these comments by publishers. Their comments, however, provide interesting topics for discussion and debate. You may consider questions such as the following: What is the impact on children's literature for each of these positions? How does the newer impact of a market-driven economy influence the types of books that will be published? How can the public ensure that there will be high quality books for children? What will happen to children's literacy if there is a reduction in higher quality books? What do you believe will be the future outcome of the debate between book purchases and technology?

[1] Roback, Diane, and Shannon Maughan, eds. "Fall 1996 Children's Books: The Road Ahead." *Publishers Weekly* 243 (July 22, 1996): 151–153.

CHART 2–7 (PP. 102–105)   Social values, family life, and personal relationships, 1969–1997

	Author, Book, Date, Setting				
	Vera and Bill Cleaver, *Where the Lilies Bloom*, 1969. Smoky Mountains. Poor wildcrafters.	Norma Klein, *Mom, the Wolf Man, and Me*, 1972. Middle class.	Paula Fox, *The Moonlight Man*, 1986. Nova Scotia.	Theresa Nelson, *The Beggars' Ride*. 1992. City.	Ruth White, *Belle Prater's Boy*. 1996. Small town.
SOCIAL VALUES **Dignity of Human Beings**	Father took pride in family name of Luther; wanted to instill pride in family. Wanted to keep family together and not accept charity.	Daughter sometimes bragged about her illegitimacy to see people's reactions. A best friend did not ask about her father.	Father does not believe in himself; he is also an alcoholic.	Mother does not believe in herself.	Woodrow tries to protect others from being hurt. Gypsy and Woodrow respect each other.
Acceptance of Responsibility	Fourteen-year-old promised her father that she would keep the family together. Kept her older sister from marrying their neighbor.	Mother had a non-traditional schedule. They were not constrained by time and other more conventional family living styles. Mother responsible for care of daughter.	Father does not get Catherine to school when he promises. Daughter lies to cover her father's actions.	Mother does not accept responsibility. Daughter (Clare) runs away from an abusive situation.	Gypsy finally accepts her father's suicide. Woodrow accepts his mother's disappearance.
Belief in Equality of Opportunity	Father stressed that you don't thank people who put you in bondage. You hate them or get out.	Mother was a professional photographer. Took her daughter on marches for women's rights and peace.	Father believed that it is the battle within yourself that causes the problems with opportunity.	Children believe that they must make their own way.	Miner's daughters were not invited to be debutantes.
Ambition	Daughter wanted to overcome her ignorance and keep the family together.	Profession important to the mother.	Daughter attends private school but is overcome by her father's problems.	Children want to survive as a gang of children.	To be a pianist. To cure eyes.

Obedience to Law, Patriotism	Father disliked people in authority who might place him in bondage.	Strong feelings against war.	Father seems to attract less desirable friends. Mother says that he always had a "streak of lawlessness."	Children fear the law and social workers.	Not mentioned.
Importance of Education and Knowledge	Daughter knew that books would give her answers that she wanted.	Not stressed.	Father has much knowledge. Mother is excited about visiting the Lake Country, the home of Wordsworth.	Not stressed.	Gypsy always had good books to read. Both Gypsy and Woodrow want to learn. Gypsy's mother is a teacher.
Respect for Adult Authority	Children respected their father. Tried to do his wishes.	Eleven-year-old had frank discussions with her mother. Some disagreement.	Daughter discovers that her father's promises are not to be taken seriously. She gains new respect for her mother. Father likes to "go against things."	Mother's ex-boyfriend is not reliable.	Gypsy at first does not respect her stepfather.
FAMILY LIFE Description	A proud independent family who learned to gather medicinal plants on slopes of Smoky Mountains.	Mother and daughter had enjoyable relationship; they had fun together.	Father and mother are divorced. Father is an alcoholic. Daughter takes care of her father.	Daughter lives with single mother. She runs away because of her mother's abusive boyfriend.	Gypsy lives with mother and stepfather. Woodrow lives with grandparents because of his father's actions.
Religion, Stability	Long-time mountain resident.	Mother did not set household schedule. They enjoyed this freedom. They were Jewish but never talked about it.	Daughter is at boarding school. Father is unreliable. Mother lived in same apartment, mother remarried.	Daughter questions her religion. Stability results from a gang of homeless children.	Families attend church and Sunday school.
Numbers in Family	Four children. Father died early in the story.	One child. Mother.	One child.	One child.	One child in each family.

CHART 2–7 *Continued*

	Vera and Bill Cleaver, *Where the Lilies Bloom.* 1969. Smoky Mountains. Poor wildcrafters.	Norma Klein, *Mom, the Wolf Man, and Me.* 1972. Middle class.	Paula Fox, *The Moonlight Man.* 1986. Nova Scotia.	Theresa Nelson, *The Beggars' Ride,* 1992. City.	Ruth White, *Belle Prater's Boy,* 1996. Small town.
			Author, Book, Date, Setting		
FAMILY LIFE (cont.) Relationships Within Family	Strong family ties.	Daughter loved her unconventional life with her unmarried mother. Mother, daughter had frank discussions.	Father cannot rely on himself, so others cannot rely on him. Daughter discovers mother's strength and the meaning of love.	Daughter cannot rely on her mother.	Children rely on their grandparents. Gypsy relies on her family.
Extended Family		Mother's boyfriend lived with them on weekends.	Both father and mother have remarried.	Homeless gang acts as family.	Grandparents take boy into their home when his father starts drinking.
PERSONAL RELATIONSHIPS AND FEELINGS Independent Male or Female	Mary Call was very resourceful. Found a way to earn money wildcrafting.	Mother had strong character. Daughter self-assured but worried about possible changes in their lives.	Catherine was very resourceful.	Daughter is resourceful.	Woodrow uses humor and stories to overcome his problems. Gypsy uses her wits to solve problems.
Dependent Male or Female	The children were dependent upon fourteen-year-old Mary who tried to hold family together.		Catherine wanted to understand her parents and to have a father who resembled her hopes for a father.	Clare must rely on members of the gang.	Many women in the town believe in traditional roles.

Types of Problems	After father died, they tried to survive as a family. Mary discovered that she needed other people.	Daughter feared how her life might change if her mother married.	Catherine spends her vacation with her alcoholic father. She must grow to understand and accept him for himself.	Child abuse. Runaways. Homelessness.	Gypsy's nightmares because of her father's suicide. Woodrow's mother leaving him.
Friendships	People could not trust friends when they had secrets.	Daughter's best friend was a boy whose father was a rabbi. He never asked her questions about her father.	Father/daughter relationships are stressed.	Relationships within the gang are stressed. An older man helps them.	Woodrow and Gypsy become best friends. Belle and her sister were not friends. Woodrow and Gypsy help each other overcome their inner hurts.

for Understanding the History of Children's Literature

- Investigate the life and contributions of William Caxton. What circumstances led to his opening a printing business in 1476? Why were *Reynart the Foxe, The Book of the Subtyle Historyes and Fables of Aesop,* and *Le Morte d'Arthur* considered such important contributions to children's literature?

- Compare the literary quality of William Caxton's books with the literary quality of a reproduced chapbook. Why have chapbooks been identified as forerunners of children's books, western tales, and comic books?

- Trace the development of the hornbook from its introduction in the 1400s until it was superseded by the battledores in the 1700s. Consider any changes in these two types of lesson books and how they have influenced the development of children's literature.

- Read John Bunyan's *Pilgrim's Progress.* Identify the characteristics that would make it acceptable Puritan reading. Compare these characteristics with the characteristics of books that would appeal to children.

- Choose a tale published by Charles Perrault in his *Tales of Mother Goose,* such as "Cinderella," "Sleeping Beauty," "Puss in Boots," "Little Red Riding Hood," "Blue Beard," or "Little Thumb." Compare the language and style of Perrault's early edition with the language and style in a twentieth-century version of the same tale. What differences did you find? Why do you believe that the changes were made?

- Select one of the Robinsonades published after Daniel Defoe's *Robinson Crusoe* became successful. Compare the plot development, characterization, and setting with those of Defoe's text.

- Investigate the impact of John Newbery's publications on the history of children's literature.

- Choose one of the following great nineteenth-century English artists who had an impact on children's illustrations: Kate Greenaway, Walter Crane, or Randolph Caldecott. Read biographical information and look at examples of their illustrations. Share your information and reactions with your literature class.

- Read a Victorian novel such as Charlotte Yonge's *The Daisy Chain.* Identify how the book reflects Victorian values, such as fortitude, temperance, prudence, justice, self-reliance, and strong family ties.

- Read Mark Twain's *The Adventures of Tom Sawyer* or *The Adventures of Huckleberry Finn.* Consider the controversy about racism in Twain's work. Compare Mark Twain's writing for the nineteenth century with writing for the twentieth century.

- Using a book such as Peter Hunt's *Children's Literature: An Illustrated History* (1995), compare the history of children's literature in Australia, Canada, or New Zealand with the history of children's literature in the United States or England.

- Use the database to select books from a specific historical time period for a specific interest or reading level. For example, select "early 1800s" illustrated books for primary age children. Print the list and describe how you might use these books in your classroom.

- Use the database to select books from three different cultures. Refine your list to include only those books suitable for the grade level you plan to teach. Print the list. Describe two ways you could share this list with parents.

- Pretend you are preparing a unit or a display on the contemporary family for either primary or middle-school students. Use the database to select appropriate books. Print the list. How many genres are represented in your list?

- The media specialist has asked your help in locating a list of the Newbery and Caldecott award winning books. Use the database to make a list of each. Describe your decision-making process for sorting the list to make it as useful as possible for the specialist.

Illustration from *Golem* by David Wisniewski. Copyright © 1996 by David Wisniewski.
Reprinted permission of Clarion Books/Houghton Mifflin Company. All rights reserved.

3

*E*valuating and Selecting Literature for Children

 Standards, Literary Elements, and Book Selection

- Standards for Evaluating Books
- Literary Elements
- The Right Book for Each Child
- The Child as Critic

 Involving Children in Literary Elements

- Involving Children in Plot
- Involving Children in Characterization
- Involving Children in Setting
- Involving Children in Theme
- Involving Children in Style
- Webbing the Literary Elements
- Questioning to Encourage Aesthetic Responses

Standards, Literary Elements, and Book Selection

ecause thousands of books have been published for children, selecting books appropriate to the needs of children can be difficult. Teachers and librarians, who share books with groups of children as well as with individual children, should select books that provide balance in a school or public library. The objectives of literature programs also affect educators' selections of children's books.

A literature program should have five objectives. First, a literature program should help students realize that literature is for entertainment and can be enjoyed throughout their lives. Literature should cater to children's interests as well as create interests in new topics. Consequently, educators must know these interests and understand ways to stimulate new ones.

Second, a literature program should acquaint children with their literary heritage. To accomplish this, literature should foster the preservation of knowledge and allow its transmission to future generations. Therefore, educators must be familiar with fine literature from the past and must share it with children.

Third, a literature program should help students understand the formal elements of literature and lead them to prefer the best that our literature has to offer. Children need to hear and read fine literature and to appreciate authors who not only have some-

thing to say but also say it extremely well. Educators must be able to identify the best books in literature and share these books with children.

Fourth, a literature program should help children grow up understanding themselves and the rest of humanity. Children who identify with literary characters confronting and overcoming problems like their own learn ways to cope with their own problems. Educators should provide literature that introduces children to people from other times and nations and that encourages children to see both themselves and their world in a new perspective.

Fifth, a literature program should help children evaluate what they read. Literature programs should extend children's appreciation of literature and their imaginations. Therefore, educators should help students learn how to compare, question, and evaluate the books that they read.

Rosenblatt (1991) adds an important sixth objective, encouraging "readers to pay attention to their own literary experiences as the basis for self-understanding or for comparison with others' evocations. This implies a new, collaborative relationship between teacher and student. Emphasis on the reader need not exclude application of various approaches, literary and social, to the process of critical interpretation and evaluation" (p. 61). Children need many opportunities to respond to literature.

If children are to gain enjoyment, knowledge of their heritage, recognition and appreciation of good literature, and understanding of themselves and others, they must explore balanced selections of literature. A literature program should include classics and contemporary stories, fanciful stories as well as realistic ones, prose as well as poetry, biographies, and books containing factual information. In order to provide this balance, educators must know about many kinds of literature. Alan Purves (1991) identifies basic groups of items usually found in literature programs: literary works, background information, literary terminology and theory, and cultural information. He states that some curricula also include the responses of the readers themselves.

This text provides information about numerous types of books written for children. This chapter looks at standards for evaluating books written for children. It presents and discusses the literary elements of plot, characterization, setting, theme, style, and point of view. It also discusses children's literature interests, characteristics of literature found in books chosen by children, and procedures to help children evaluate literature.

 ## STANDARDS FOR EVALUATING BOOKS AND LITERARY CRITICISM

According to Jean Karl (1987), in true literature, "there are ideas that go beyond the plot of a novel or picture-book story or the basic theme of a nonfiction book, but they are presented subtly and gently; good books do not preach; their ideas are wound into the substance of the book and are clearly a part of the life of the book itself" (p. 507). In contrast, Karl maintains that mediocre books overemphasize their messages or they oversimplify or distort life; mediocre books contain visions that are too obvious and can be put aside too easily. If literature is to help develop children's potentials, merit rather than mediocrity must be part of children's experiences with literature. Both children and adults need opportunities to evaluate literature. They also need supporting context to help them make accurate judgments about quality.

Literary criticism provides guidelines for evaluating children's literature. Paul Heins maintains that critics must be acquainted with the best children's literature of the past and present. In fact, he says, no real criticism can occur unless "judgments are being made in a context of literary knowledge and of literary standards" (1978b, p. 76). Concern with the place of a book in a larger historical context or an aesthetic context and with its structure, technical subtlety, and overall literary integrity is not just dry analysis; it is part of "the joy of discovering the skill of the author" (1978a, p. 82).

Mary Kingsbury (1984) builds a strong rationale for high-quality criticism that describes, compares, and judges literary texts. According to Kingsbury, critics must interpret a text accurately by understanding what the author is doing with language, contrast and compare a book with other books and with various book reviews, and then make their own judgments as objectively as possible. Kingsbury emphasizes the importance of both reading and writing literary criticism.

Northrop Frye, Sheridan Baker, and George Perkins (1985) identify five focuses of all literary criticism, two or more of which are usually emphasized in an evaluation of a literary text:

(1) The work in isolation, with primary focus on its form, as opposed to its content; (2) its relationship to its own time and place, including the writer; the social, economic, and intellectual milieu surrounding it; the method of its printing or other dissemination; and the assumptions of the audience that first received it; (3) its relationship to literary and social history before its time, as it repeats, extends, or departs from the traditions that preceded it; (4) its relationship to the future, as represented by those works and events that come after it, as it forms a part of the large body of literature, influencing the reading, writing, and thinking of later generations; (5) its relationship to some eternal concept of being, absolute standards of art, or immutable truths of existence. (p. 130)

The relative importance of each of the preceding areas to a particular critic depends on the critic's degree of concern with the work itself, the author, the subject matter, and the audience.

Book reviews and longer critical analyses of books in the major literature journals are valuable sources for librarians, teachers, parents, and other students of children's literature. As might be expected from the five focuses of Frye, Baker, and Perkins, reviews emphasize different aspects of evaluation and criticism. Phyllis K. Kennemer (1984) identified three categories of book reviews and longer book analyses: (1) descriptive, (2) analytical, and (3) sociological. Descriptive reviews report factual information about the story and illustrations of a book. Analytical reviews discuss, compare, and evaluate literary elements (plot, characterization, setting, theme, style, and point of view), the illustrations, and relationships with other books. Sociological reviews emphasize the social context of a book, concerning themselves with characterizations of particular social groups, distinguishable ethnic characteristics, moral values, possible controversy, and potential popularity.

Although a review may contain all three types of information, Kennemer concludes that the major sources of information on children's literature emphasize one type of evaluation. For example, reviews in the *Bulletin of the Center for Children's Books* tend to be descriptive, but they also mention literary elements. Reviews in *Booklist, The Horn Book, Kirkus Reviews,* and *The School Library Journal* chiefly analyze literary elements. *The School Library Journal* places the greatest emphasis on sociological analysis of any source Kennemer studied.

Selection criteria and reviews in specific journals also emphasize the particular content and viewpoints of the group that publishes the journal. For example, each year the Book Review Subcommittee of the National Council for the Social Studies—Children's Book Council Joint Committee publishes in *Social Education* their recommended list of Notable Children's Trade Books in the Field of Social Studies (1992). The criteria for books selected in this bibliography, for children in grades K–8, "emphasize human relations; represent a diversity of groups and are sensitive to a broad range of cultural experiences; present an original theme or a fresh slant on a traditional topic; are easily readable and of high literary quality; and have a pleasing format and, when appropriate, illustrations that enrich the text" (p. 253).

The reviews accompanying the books in *Social Education* (1992) emphasize human relationships and social studies issues. For example, the review for Milton Meltzer's *Thomas Jefferson: The Revolutionary Aristocrat* states:

This biography details the complex and productive life of the third U.S. president and considers the contradictions between his words and actions on issues such as slavery, freedom of the press, and the limits of presidential power. The author explains his own efforts to weigh evidence, shape information, and interpret Jefferson's life. (p. 254)

Likewise, standards for evaluating science trade books have specific evaluation criteria as recommended by science professionals. Kathleen S. Johnston (1991) states that accuracy in facts presented and in depictions of scientific methods is of primary consideration. In addition, the criteria in-

---

$\mathcal{I}$SSUE   The Core Collection: What Is In and What Is Out?

An interesting but frequently unanswerable question arises when teachers, college professors, librarians, and students of children's literature debate which books should be considered in a core collection of recommended books. The question may be easier to answer in literature for younger readers. Articles such as Peggy J. Miller's "Peter Rabbit and Mr. McGregor Reconciled, Charlotte Lives: Preschoolers Re-Create the Classics"[1] extol the use of books that most people consider classics in children's literature. In addition, highly recommended lists of books for children usually include Caldecott and Newbery winners as well as classics such as *Peter Rabbit, Winnie-the-Pooh, Charlotte's Web,* and *The Hobbit*.

More debate seems to surround the recommendations for the canon of books for students in the upper grades and literature that is frequently labeled for young adults. Hazel Rochman[2] discusses the issues associated with the selection of recommended titles for the fifteenth edition

of H. W. Wilson's *Senior High School Library Catalog.* How would you respond to Rochman's answer to which classics should be kept? "We kept a lot of Charles Dickens, Jane Austen, Mark Twain, and Willa Cather, and I vehemently supported keeping those. But there are some old books that no longer speak to kids" (p. 114).

Rochman then provides a list of some of the new titles that have been nominated to appear in the list for the first time and some that have been excluded from the current listing.

Many of the books that are listed in "What's In" and "What's Out" are also considered children's literature. As you read the following examples of titles, do you agree that the books should either be included or excluded? What is your argument for your decision?

"What's In:" Avi's *Nothing But the Truth* and *The True Confessions of Charlotte Doyle;* Sandra Cisneros's *House on Mango Street;* Brock Cole's *The Goats;* Chris Crutcher's *Athletic Shorts;* Russell Freedman's *The Life*

and *Death of Crazy Horse* and *Lincoln;* Virginia Hamilton's *Her Stories, The People Could Fly,* and *The Planet of Junior Brown;* Walter Dean Myers's *Somewhere in the Darkness;* and Suzanne Staples's *Shabanu*.

"What's Out:" Avi's *Wolf Rider,* James Fenimore Cooper's *The Deerslayer,* Lois Duncan's *Summer of Fear,* Jamake Highwater's *Legend Days,* Anne McCaffrey's *Crystal Singer,* and Gary Paulsen's *Hatchet* and *The Island*.

After you have considered if you agree or disagree with these listings, select an age level for children and develop a core list of books that you would highly recommend for them. What is your criteria for selection?

---

[1]Miller, Peggy J. "Peter Rabbit and Mr. McGregor Reconciled, Charlotte Lives: Preschoolers Re-Create the Classics." *The Horn Book Magazine* LXXIII (May/June 1997): 282–283.

[2]Rochman, Hazel. "Loose Canon." *Booklist* 92 (September 1, 1996): 114–115.

clude clarity of purpose, organization, and accuracy in presenting the process of science; scope and completeness of the subject; quality of the illustrations and graphic design; and instructional value.

Reading and discussing excellent books as well as analyzing book reviews and literary criticism can increase one's ability to recognize and recommend excellent literature for children. Those of us who work with students of children's literature are rewarded when for the first time people see literature with a new awareness, discover the techniques that an author uses to create a believable plot or memorable characters, and discover that they can provide rationales for why a book is excellent, mediocre, or poor. Ideally, reading and discussing excellent literature can help each student of children's literature become a worthy critic, what Mary Kingsbury (1984) defines as one "who offers us new perspectives on a text, who sees more in it than we saw, who motivates us to return to it for another reading" (p. 17).

New perspectives may be of special concern when evaluating books written by authors from other countries. Jeffrey Garrett (1992/1993), a member of the Hans Christian Andersen Award Committee, makes a strong case for including the works of the best international authors and illustrators. Garrett states, "We have much to gain by reading and sharing the works of international authors and illustrators. Let's begin by learning who other cultures regard as their great writers, and then approach them with the respect they deserve. The experience may be eye-opening" (p. 314).

 ## LITERARY ELEMENTS

The focus of this chapter is literary elements. This section looks at the ways in which authors of children's books use plot, characterization, setting, theme, style, and point of view to create memorable stories.

Plot

Plot is important in stories, whether the stories reflect the oral storytelling style of Chaucer's *The Canterbury Tales* or the complex interactions in a mystery. When asked to tell about a favorite story, children usually recount the plot, or plan of action. Children want a book to have a good plot: enough action, excitement, suspense, and conflict to develop

interest. A good plot also allows children to become involved in the action, feel the conflict developing, recognize the climax when it occurs, and respond to a satisfactory ending. Children's expectations and enjoyment of conflict vary according to their ages. Young children are satisfied with simple plots that deal with everyday happenings, but as children mature, they expect and enjoy more complex plots.

Following the plot of a story is like following a path winding through it; the action develops naturally. If the plot is well developed, a book will be difficult to put down unfinished; if the plot is not well developed, the book will not sustain interest or will be so prematurely predictable that the story ends long before it should. The author's development of action should help children enjoy the story.

Developing the Order of Events.   Readers expect a story to have a good beginning, one that introduces the action and characters in an enticing way; a good middle section, one that develops the conflict; a recognizable climax; and an appropriate ending. If any element is missing, children consider a book unsatisfactory and a waste of time. Authors have several approaches for presenting the events in a credible plot. In children's literature, events usually happen in chronological order. The author reveals the plot by presenting the first happening, followed by the second happening, and so forth, until the story is completed. Illustrations reinforce the chronological order in picture storybooks for younger children.

Very strong and obvious chronological order is found in cumulative folktales. Actions and characters are related to each other in sequential order, and each is mentioned again when new action or a new character is introduced. Children who enjoy the cumulative style of the nursery rhyme "The House That Jack Built" also enjoy a similar cumulative rhythm in Verna Aardema's *Bringing the Rain to Kapiti Plain: A Nandi Tale.* Cumulative, sequential action may also be developed in reverse, from last event to first, as in Verna Aardema's *Why Mosquitoes Buzz in People's Ears.*

Authors of biographies frequently use chronological life events to develop plot. Jean Fritz, for example, traces the life of a famous president and constitutional leader in *The Great Little Madison.* In *Lincoln: A Photobiography,* Russell Freedman begins with Lincoln's childhood and continues through his life as president. In *The Wright Brothers: How They Invented*

The plot structure of The Canterbury Tales *follows the oral tradition. (The Franklin from* The Canterbury Tales *by Geoffrey Chaucer, selected, translated, and adapted by Barbara Cohen, illustrated by Trina Schart Hyman. Text © 1988 by Barbara Cohen. Illustration © 1988 by Trina Schart Hyman. Reprinted by Lothrop, Lee & Shepard Books [a division of William Morrow & Company].)*

the Airplane, Freedman follows the lives of the Wright brothers and emphasizes major changes in aeronautics, and in *Eleanor Roosevelt: A Life of Discovery,* Freedman follows the life of one of the great women in American history. Dates in these texts help readers follow the chronological order.

The events in a story also may follow the maturing process of the main character. In *The Borning Room,* Paul Fleischman begins with the birth of the heroine in a borning room on a farm in Ohio in 1851. The plot then develops according to major events that occurred in the borning room as the family uses the special room at times of births and deaths. The book concludes as the heroine, after years of a rewarding life, is herself waiting in the borning room for her probable death.

Books written for older readers sometimes use flashbacks in addition to chronological order. At the point when readers have many questions about a character's background or wonder why a character is acting in a certain way, the author interrupts the order of the story and reveals information about a previous time or experience. For example, memories of a beloved aunt allow readers to understand the character and the conflict in Cynthia Rylant's *Missing May.* The memories of twelve-year-old Summer allow readers to understand the grief following the aunt's death and to follow Summer and her uncle as they try to overcome the grief and begin a new life for themselves. Without the memories, readers would not understand May's character.

Developing Conflict. Excitement in a story occurs when the main characters experience a struggle or overcome conflict. Conflict is the usual source of plots in literature. According to Rebecca J. Lukens (1990), children's literature contains four kinds of conflict: (1) person-against-person, (2) person-against-society, (3) person-against-nature, and (4) person-against-self. Plots written for younger children usually develop only one kind of conflict, but many of the stories for older children use several conflicting situations.

Person Against Person. One person-against-person conflict that young children enjoy is the tale of that famous bunny, Peter Rabbit, by Beatrix Potter. In this story, Peter's disobedience and greed quickly bring him into conflict with the owner of the garden, Mr. McGregor, who has sworn to put Peter into a pie. Excitement and suspense develop as Peter and Mr. McGregor proceed through a series of life-and-death encounters. Mr. McGregor chases Peter with a rake, Peter becomes tangled in a gooseberry net, and Mr. McGregor tries to trap Peter inside a sieve. Knowledge of Peter's possible fate increases the suspense of these adventures. The excitement intensifies each time Peter narrowly misses being caught, and young readers' relief is great when Peter escapes for good. Children also sympathize with Peter when his disobedience results in a stomachache and a dose of chamomile tea.

Conflicts between animals and humans, or animals and animals, or humans and humans are common in children's literature, including many popular folktales. Both Little Red Riding Hood and the three little pigs confront a wicked wolf. Cinderella and Sleeping Beauty are among the fairytale heroines mistreated by stepmothers, and Hansel and Gretel are imprisoned by a witch. Josepha Sherman's

Vassilisa the Wise: A Tale of Medieval Russia develops conflict between a clever and courageous female and an arrogant prince. The heroine saves her husband's life by proving that she is wiser than the prince.

A humorous person-against-person conflict provides the story line in Beverly Cleary's *Ramona and Her Father*. Seven-year-old Ramona's life changes drastically when her father loses his job and her mother must work full-time. Ramona's new time with her father is not so enjoyable as she had hoped that it would be, however. Her father becomes tense and irritable as his period of unemployment lengthens. Ramona and her father survive their experience, and by the end of the story, they have returned to their normal, warm relationship.

Katherine Paterson develops a more complex person-against-person conflict for older children in *Jacob Have I Loved*. In this story, one twin believes that she is like the despised Esau in the Old Testament, while her sister is the adored favorite of the family. The unhappy heroine's descriptions of her early experiences with her sister, her growing independence as she works with her father, and her final discovery that she, not her sister, is the strong twin create an engrossing plot and memorable characters.

Person Against Society. Conflicts also develop when the main character's actions, desires, or values differ from those of the surrounding society. This society may consist of groups of children who cannot tolerate

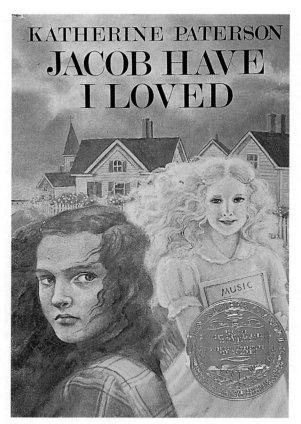

Complex person-against-person conflict develops between twin sisters in Jacob Have I Loved *by Katherine Paterson. (Jacket by Kinoko Craft, Thomas Y. Crowell Co. Copyright © 1980 by Katherine Paterson.)*

Children's books often portray person-against-society conflicts that result from being different from the majority in terms of race, religion, or physical characteristics. Gary Paulsen's *Nightjohn* develops the brutality of a society that mistreats slaves. Life for twelve-year-old Sarney becomes even more miserable when Nightjohn secretly teaches her how to read and both of them are punished for this action. Judy Blume's *Blubber* shows the cruelty to which a fat child is subjected by her peers. For the conflict between person and society in such books to be believable, the social setting and its values must be presented in accurate detail.

Numerous survival stories set in wartime develop person-against-society conflicts. In Uri Orlev's *The Island on Bird Street,* the conflict is between a Jewish boy and the society that forces him to live in loneliness and starvation rather than surrender. Throughout the story, Orlev describes the boy's fear and the society that causes him to feel and respond in this way. For example, in the following quote, notice how Orlev describes the actions of the society and the boy's responses to that society when a group of Jewish people are found living in a hidden bunker:

Its inhabitants began to come out. It took a long while for the last of them to emerge. The Germans and the policemen kept shouting and footsteps kept crossing the ruins from the cellar to the front gate. Now and then someone stumbled. . . . Somebody fell once or maybe twice. A shot rang out. Nobody screamed, though. Even the children had stopped crying. The last footsteps left the building. I heard voices in the street and an order to line up in threes. The same as had been given us. Then they were marched away. A few more shots. Finally, the car started up and drove away. . . . It was strange to think that all those people had been hiding with me in one house without us even knowing about each other. . . . They'd never take me away like that. (p. 81)

Person Against Nature. Nature—not society or another person—is the antagonist in many memorable books for older children. When the author thoroughly describes the natural environment, readers vicariously travel into a world ruled by nature's harsh laws of survival. This is the case in Jean Craighead George's *Julie of the Wolves.* Miyax, a thirteen-year-old Eskimo girl also called by the English name Julie, is lost and without food on the North Slope of Alaska. She is introduced lying on her stomach, peering at a pack of wolves. The wolves are not her enemy, however. Her adversary is the vast cold tundra that

children who are different from themselves. In Brock Cole's *The Goats,* a boy and a girl who are considered social outcasts by their peers at camp are stripped of their clothing and marooned on a deserted island. The author reveals the social attitudes of this camp when girls are classified as queens, princesses, dogs, and real dogs. The girl on the island is considered a real dog. Cole reveals the feelings of the children through their ordeal when he uses terms such as *they* and *them* to identify the society. When the girl wants the boy to leave her, his actions, thoughts, and dialogue reveal the strength of his dislike for the society that placed him in this isolation: "'I'm afraid. Maybe you'd better go without me.' 'No,' he said. He didn't try to explain. He knew he was afraid to leave her alone, but even more important, it wouldn't be good enough. He wanted them both to disappear. To disappear completely" (p. 16).

stretches for hundreds of miles without human presence, a land so harsh that no berry bushes point to the south, no birds fly overhead so that she can follow, and continuous summer daylight blots out the North Star that might guide her home:

No roads cross it; ponds and lakes freckle its immensity. Winds scream across it, and the view in every direction is exactly the same. Somewhere in this cosmos was Miyax; and the very life in her body, its spark and warmth, depended upon these wolves for survival. And she was not so sure they would help. (p. 6)

The constant wind; the empty sky; and the cold, deserted earth are ever present as Miyax crosses the Arctic searching for food, protecting herself from the elements, and making friends with the wolves, who bring her food. The author encourages readers to visualize the power and beauty of this harsh landscape and to share the girl's sorrow over human destruction of this land, its animals, and the Eskimo way of life.

Another book that pits a young person against the elements of nature is Armstrong Sperry's *Call It Courage*. The hero's conflict with nature begins when the crashing, stormy sea—"a monster livid and hungry"—capsizes Mafatu's canoe during a hurricane:

Higher and higher it rose, until it seemed that it must scrape at the low-hanging clouds. Its crest heaved over with a vast sigh. The boy saw it coming. He tried to cry out. No sound issued from his throat. Suddenly the wave was upon him. Down it crashed. Chaos! Mafatu felt the paddle torn from his hands. Thunder in his ears. Water strangled him. Terror in his soul. (p. 24)

The preceding quote makes clear that there are two adversaries in the story: The hero is in conflict with nature and also in conflict with himself. The two adversaries are interwoven in the plot as Mafatu sails away from his island in order to prove that he is not a coward. Each time that the boy wins a victory over nature, he also comes closer to his main goal, victory over his own fear. Without victory over fear, the boy cannot be called by his rightful name Mafatu, "Stout Heart," nor can he have the respect of his father, his Polynesian people, and himself. In *A Girl Named Disaster*, Nancy Farmer develops a survival story set in Mozambique and Zimbabwe. As the heroine struggles to escape starvation on her lonely journey, she discovers that the spirits of her ancestors help both her physical and emotional survival.

Authors who write strong person-against-nature conflicts use many of the techniques shown in the quotes by George and Sperry. Personification gives human actions to nature, vivid descriptions show that characters are in a life-and-death struggle, sentences become shorter to show increasing danger, and actions reveal that characters know that they are in serious conflict with nature.

Person Against Self. In *Hatchet,* Gary Paulsen creates person-against-self and person-against-nature conflicts for his major character, thirteen-year-old Brian. These two major conflicts are intertwined throughout the book. For example, Paulsen creates an excellent transition between unconsciousness at the end of chapter three and consciousness at the beginning of chapter four. In the following quote, notice how Paulsen ties together the two most destructive experiences in Brian's life: the plane crash that could have killed him and the secret about his mother that caused his parents' divorce.

Without knowing anything. Pulling until his hands caught at weeds and muck, pulling and screaming until his hands caught at last in grass and brush and he felt his chest on land, felt his face in the coarse blades of grass and he stopped; everything stopped. A color came that he had never seen before, a color that exploded in his mind with the pain and he was gone, gone from it all, spiraling out into the world, spiraling out into nothing. Nothing. (p. 30, end of chapter 3)

The Memory was like a knife cutting into him. Slicing deep into him with hate. The Secret. (p. 31, beginning of chapter 4)

Symbolically, the secret is the first thing that Brian remembers after waking from unconsciousness. Paulsen reveals the destructive nature of the secret through flashbacks, as Brian's memory returns, and through comparisons between the hate that cut him like a knife and the sharp pain caused by the crash. As Brian gains confidence and ability to survive in the Canadian wilderness, he gains understanding about his parents' conflict and ability to face his own person-against-self conflict.

While few children face the extreme personal challenges described in *Hatchet, Call It Courage,* and *Julie of the Wolves,* all children must overcome fears and personal problems while growing up. Person-against-self conflict is a popular plot device in children's literature. Authors of contemporary realistic fiction often develop plots around children who face and overcome problems related to family

disturbances. For example, the cause of the person-against-self conflict in Jerry Spinelli's *Wringer* is a boy's realization that if he does not accept the violence associated with killing pigeons, he must find the courage to oppose the actions and attitudes expressed by both his friends and the town. In Ruth White's *Belle Prater's Boy,* the characters struggle to understand the suicide of the girl's father and desertion by the boy's mother.

Good plots do not rely on contrivance or coincidence. They are credible to young readers because many of the same conflicts occur in the children's own lives. Credibility is an important consideration in evaluating plot in children's books. Although authors of adult books often rely on sensational con-

flict to create interest, writers of children's books like to focus on the characters and the ways in which they overcome problems.

An In-Depth Analysis of the Plot and Conflict in One Book

Christopher Paul Curtis's *The Watsons Go to Birmingham—1963,* a 1996 Newbery Honor book, provides an excellent source for both literary analysis and historical authenticity. It is a book that changes mood at about the half-way point in the story. At the beginning of the book, the author develops a typical African American family need to be developed differently—adults are set in their reading habits; children are still in the process of becoming readers.

In responding to the needs of children, it is important to remember that children's choices for the most part are made based on the books adults make available to them. Therefore, while I consider lists that have been voted on by children, I try to keep in mind that they can vote only for books that are available to them.

However, the true measure of success of a collection is circulation. How do you get the books into the hands of children and their parents? I think it is important to have a mindset that escapes the four walls of the library building itself.

Librarians have to develop a realistic profile of the community to aid in book selection. I encourage my branch librarians to take neighborhood walks. How many laundromats are there? Medical facilities? Child care sites? Census information and statistics kept by health care providers can help round out this profile.

Our library system continues a program that began with federal funding in the '60s, and our bookmobiles visit seventy-five child care centers on an every-other-week schedule. That exemplifies our efforts to connect children and books!

Another specific program that our library system sponsors in conjunction with the community support of the Junior League of Little Rock is the *Reading Aloud Renaissance.* This ongoing program is designed to help prevent illiteracy by having adults (Junior League committee members) read aloud to school children in grades K–6 in four local elementary schools on a regular schedule—two-and-one–half hours per week at each school. We coordinate with principals and teachers on selection of materials so that classroom teachers can provide follow-up discussions. We have compiled a reading list for use by both parents and teachers.

Reading: The Key to the Dream was another read-aloud project co-sponsored by the library, schools, and churches. Any group could receive a "Read-In" packet by calling the library. The packet contained

suggestions for preparing to read aloud, a book list focused on Black History Month, a name tag, and background information on the program's theme. The theme was based on Dr. Martin Luther King, Jr.'s, belief that a better world is achievable through education, and that literacy is the key to the dream.

A local art center sponsored a program of readings by authors whose art was represented in a traveling art exhibit. They did not schedule regular classes, but provided this activity on a walk-in basis. Thousands of children participated in this read-aloud program.

You cannot be bashful. It is important to seek out someone in the local media who is interested in children and cultivate publicity for your library programs fifty-two weeks a year.

Finally, let me say that well-honed management skills, creative programming, and garnering publicity cannot substitute for being a reader yourself. Read. Then share your enthusiasm for reading by connecting children and their families to books!

---

that lives and works in Flint, Michigan. The problems of the various characters are typical for many families. The main character, ten-year-old Kenny, is a bright boy who reads very well. Kenny's scholastic achievements frequently place him in conflict with his older brother, Bryon, whose escapades vary from the humorous to the more serious. At the point in which the parents decide that Bryon is heading for a life of delinquency, they decide that he should spend time with his strict grandmother in Birmingham.

When they decide to travel to Alabama, the tone of the book changes. In this time of racial tension, person-against-society conflict is the most prominent. The racial conflict is developed early in the story when the mother wants to go from Flint to Birmingham because life is slower in Alabama and the people are friendlier. Dad responds, " 'Oh yeah, they're a laugh a minute down there.

Let's see, where was that 'Coloreds Only' bathroom downtown?' " (p. 5). The culmination of this person-against-society conflict results toward the end of the book when a church is bombed and several African American children are killed.

Curtis develops parallels between the person-against-society and person-against-self conflicts. As Kenny tries to understand the hatred that could cause such deaths he also, with the help of his older brother, reaches a point where he releases his personal feelings and begins to cry. The author shows the impact of this release in the following quote: "he knew that was some real embarrassing stuff so he closed the bathroom door and sat on the tub and waited for me to stop, but I couldn't. I felt like someone had pulled a plug on me and every tear inside was rushing out" (p. 199).

At the moment of complete self-understanding Kenny admits to his brother that he was no longer afraid of the bombing incident; instead, he was ashamed of himself because he ran from the church rather than try to find his sister, who he believed was inside the church. His older brother helps him clarify the situation and makes him realize that he has no reason for embarrassment.

The themes and language in the book also relate to the person-against-society and person-against-self conflicts. Through the actions of various characters we learn that prejudice and hatred are harmful and destructive forces. To increase understanding of these conflicts, Curtis effectively uses comparative language and symbolism. For example, he compares the steering of a big car to being grown up when the father tells Kenny that both are scary at first, but with a lot of practice the car and life are under control. The symbolism of the Wool Pooh (Winnie-the-Pooh's evil twin brother) is of particular interest. When Kenny swims in dangerous waters he almost drowns. He believes it is the Wool Pooh who is trying to kill him. Later in the bombed church he believes he sees this same faceless monster. Students of literature may find interesting comparisons for discussion as they analyze the possible significance of this evil symbolism as it relates to both the conflicts and themes developed in the book.

When using this book with older students, adults may ask them to trace the parallels between person-against-society and person-against-self conflicts, conduct historical studies to analyze the 1963 setting and conflicts for authenticity and to relate them to the church bombings in 1996, and trace the emergence of the themes. Curtis's text provides an interesting discussion to show the relationships among conflict, theme, and author's style.

WHAT·ANGEL·WAKES·ME·FROM·MY·FLOWERY·BED

Strong characterization from Shakespeare's plays are available in a version for children. (From Tales from Shakespeare *by Charles and Mary Lamb with sundry pictures and illuminations both in color and in line by Elizabeth Shippen Green Elliott. Reproduced by permission of Children's Classics. Crown Publishers.)*

Characterization

A believable, enjoyable story needs main characters who seem lifelike and who develop throughout the story. Characterization is one of the most powerful of the literary elements, whether the story is a contemporary tale in which characters face realistic problems or an adaptation of classic literature.

The characters whom we remember fondly from our childhood reading usually have several sides; like real people, they are not all good or all bad, and they change as they confront and overcome their problems. Laura, from the various "Little House" books by Laura Ingalls Wilder, typifies a rounded character in literature. She is honest, trustworthy, and courageous, but she can also be jealous, frightened, or angry. Her character not only is fully developed in the story but also changes during its course.

One child who enjoyed Wilder's books described Laura this way: "I would like Laura for my best friend. She would be fun to play with but she would also understand when I was hurt or angry. I could tell Laura my secrets without being afraid she would laugh at me or tell them to someone else." Any writer who can create such a friend for children is very skilled at characterization.

How does an author develop such a memorable character? How can an author show the many sides of the character as well as demonstrate believable change as this character matures? The credibility of a character depends upon the writer's ability to reveal the full nature of the character, including strengths

Yolonda's positive attitudes create strong characterization in a story about sister and brother relationships. The author uses the symbolism of music to show characterization. (From Yolonda's Genius *by Carol Fenner. Jacket illustration copyright © 1995 by Stephen Marchesi, Margaret K. McElderry Books. Reprinted by permission of Simon & Schuster, Inc.)*

and weaknesses. An author can achieve such a three-dimensional character by describing the character's physical appearance, recording the conversations of the character, revealing the character's thoughts, revealing the perceptions of other characters, and showing the character in action.

In *Call It Courage,* Armstrong Sperry uses all of these methods to reveal Mafatu's character and the changes that occur in him as he overcomes his fears. Sperry first tells readers that Mafatu fears the sea. Then, through narration, Sperry shows the young child clinging to his mother's back as a stormy sea and sharks almost end their lives. Mafatu's memories of this experience, revealed in his thoughts and actions, make him useless in the eyes of his Polynesian

tribe, as Sperry reveals through the dialogue of other characters: "That is woman's work. Mafatu is afraid of the sea. He will never be a warrior" (p. 12).

The laughter of the tribe follows, and Sperry then describes Mafatu's inner feelings:

Suddenly a fierce resentment stormed through him. He knew in that instant what he must do: he must prove his courage to himself, and to the others, or he could no longer live in their midst. He must face Moana, the Sea God—face him and conquer him. (p. 13)

Sperry portrays Mafatu's battle for courage through a combination of actions and thoughts: terror and elation follow each other repeatedly, as Mafatu lands on a forbidden island used for human sacrifice, dares to take a ceremonial spear even though doing so may mean death, confronts a hammerhead shark that circles his raft, and then overcomes his fear and attacks the shark to save his dog. Mafatu celebrates a final victory when he kills a wild boar, whose teeth symbolize courage. Mafatu's tremendous victory over fear is signified by his father's statement of pride: "Here is my son come home from the sea. Mafatu, Stout Heart. A brave name for a brave boy" (p. 115).

In *The Moves Make the Man,* Bruce Brooks develops character through basketball terminology. Brooks uses the words of Jerome Foxworthy, a talented black student, to express these thoughts about his own character:

Moves were all I cared about last summer. I got them down, and I liked not just the fun of doing them, but having them too, like a little definition of Jerome. Reverse spin, triple jump, reverse dribble. . . . These are me. The moves make the man, the moves make me, I thought, until Mama noticed they were making me something else. (p. 44)

Brooks uses contrasting attitudes toward fake moves in basketball to reveal important differences between Jerome and Bix Rivers, a talented but disturbed white athlete.

This textbook discusses many memorable characters in children's literature. Some of these characters—such as the faithful spider Charlotte and a terrific pig named Wilbur, in E. B. White's *Charlotte's Web*—are old favorites who have been capturing children's imaginations for decades. Others—such as Max in Maurice Sendak's *Where the Wild Things Are* and Karana in Scott O'Dell's *Island of the Blue Dolphins*—are more recent arrivals in the world of children's books. Authors of picture storybooks, historical fiction, science fiction, fantasy, and contemporary realistic fiction have created characters who are likely to be remembered long after the details of their stories have been forgotten.

An In-Depth Analysis of Characterization in One Book

Carol Fenner, the author of one of the 1996 Newbery Honor books, *Yolonda's Genius,* uses several techniques to develop the characteristics of two African American children, bright fifth-grade Yolonda and her slower younger brother Andrew. For example, the author reveals both Yolonda's intelligence and her retaliation ability after she is teased about her size through an incident in which Yolonda responds to being called a whale: Yolonda tells her fellow bus rider that he knows nothing about whales because, "Whales are the most remarkable mammals in the ocean—all five oceans" (p. 16). She then provides information about whales, such as, "The whales sank, lifting their tails high above the water like a signal. Deep in the ocean, their voices sent out a high swelling cry, sharing their message of victory for a hundred miles" (p. 17). We learn later that Yolonda goes to the library each week to learn new facts.

Yolonda's positive attitudes and Andrew's possible musical genius are developed as Yolonda shares Andrew's abilities. She reviews what Andrew can do and not what he cannot do when she thinks, "If there was music on the TV or the blaster, he could keep it company by beating out a rhythm on anything—his knees, a table, a wall. Or he could play a sweet line of sound on his harmonica just underneath the music, like water under a bridge. He played people's voices—an argument, cries of surprise, hushed conversation. The harmonica lived in his pocket. He fell asleep with it in his hand" (p. 38).

Later, Yolonda's actions show both her respect for Andrew's talents and her dislike for those who torment her younger brother because he is a slower learner in school and gains his enjoyment from playing his harmonica. Yolonda takes vengeance on the three boys who destroy Andrew's harmonica. She does this while Andrew is watching because she wants it to be Andrew's vengeance as well as her own.

The author continues to show characterization through the symbolism of music. Andrew makes discoveries about people through sounds, he learns the alphabet after a teacher relates the alphabet to the instruments, and Andrew eventually plays his harmonica to reveal the character of Yolonda. As you read the following quote, analyze how the author describes Yolonda through Andrew's music: "Yolonda walking, a steady, strong beat—great big moves, slow, making waves of air pass by. Yolonda eating a chocolate eclair—full mouth—soft and happy. Yolonda reading to him, voice purring around the big words, Yolonda dancing. This is the sound of Yolonda's body—large, gobbling, space, powerful and protecting—great like a queen, frightening everyone with a scowl and a swelling of her shoulders" (p. 203).

Notice in this example how the author uses several different techniques to develop the characterizations of

Yolonda and her brother. After reading the book, readers understand that both characters have well-rounded personalities.

Setting

The setting of a story—its location in time and place—helps readers share what the characters see, smell, hear, and touch, as well as makes the characters' values, actions, and conflicts more understandable. Whether a story takes place in the past, present, or future, its overall credibility may depend on how well the plot, characterizations, and setting support one another. Different types of literature—picture storybooks, fantasy, historical fiction, and contemporary realistic fiction—have their own requirements as far as setting is concerned. When a story is set in an identifiable historical period or geographical location, details should be accurate. Plot and characters also should be consistent with what actually occurred or could have occurred at that time and place.

Jean Craighead George (1991), author of numerous survival stories, emphasizes the setting for the book. To do this, George walks through the setting, smells the environment, looks at the world to see careful details, and searches for protagonists. During her final writing, she closes her eyes and recreates in her imagination the land, the people, and the animals. George states:

I strive to put the reader on the scene. I want to make each child feel that he is under a hemlock tree with Sam Gribley in *My Side of the Mountain* or on his hands and knees talking to the tundra wolves in *Julie of the Wolves*. I want my reader to hear and see the ice on the Arctic Ocean in *Water Sky*. (p. 70)

In some books, setting is such an important part of the story that the characters and plot cannot be developed without understanding the time and place. In other stories, however, the setting provides only a background. In fact, some settings are so well known that just a few words place readers immediately into the expected location. "Once upon a time," for example, is a mythical time in days of yore when it was possible for magical spells to transform princes into beasts or to change pumpkins into glittering carriages. Thirty of the thirty-seven traditional fairy tales in Andrew Lang's *The Red Fairy Book* begin with "Once upon a time." Magical spells cannot happen everywhere; they usually occur in "a certain kingdom," "deep in the forest," in "the humble hut of a wise and good peasant," or "far, far away, in a warm and pleasant land." Children become so familiar with such phrases—and the visualizations of setting that such phrases trigger—that additional details and descriptions are not necessary.

Even a setting that is described briefly may serve several different purposes. It may create a mood, provide an antagonist, establish historical background, or supply symbolic meanings.

Setting as Mood. Authors of children's literature and adult literature alike use settings to create moods that add credibility to characters and plot. Readers would probably be a bit skeptical if a vampire appeared in a sunny American kitchen on a weekday morning while a family was preparing to leave for school and work. The same vampire would seem more believable in a moldy castle in Transylvania at midnight. The illustrations and text can create the mood of a location. Readers can infer the author's and illustrator's feelings about the setting. For example, Cynthia Rylant's text and Barry Moser's illustrations for *Appalachia: The Voices of Sleeping Birds* provide a setting that radiates warm feelings about the varied people, their strengths, and their way of life.

The epic story of Attila the Hun, a famous invader of Eastern Europe in the fifth century A.D., can be told as historical fiction, with a setting that emphasizes accuracy of geographical and biographical detail. In *The White Stag,* Kate Seredy takes a mythical approach to telling how a migratory Asiatic people reached their new homeland in what became Hungary. Gods, moonmaidens, and a supernatural animal are among the characters in this story, and Seredy uses setting to create a mood in which such beings seem natural. The leader of the tribe stands before a sacrificial altar in a cold, rocky, and barren territory, waiting to hear the voice of the god Hadur, who will lead his starving people to the promised land.

At this time, the white stag miraculously appears to guide the Huns in their travels—through "ghost hours" onto grassy hills covered with white birch trees, where they hear a brook tinkling like silver bells and a breeze that sounds like the flutes of minstrels. Readers expect magic in such a place, and they are not disappointed to see:

Moonmaidens, those strange changeling fairies who lived in white birch trees and were never seen in the daylight; Moonmaidens who, if caught by the gray-hour of dawn, could never go back to fairyland again; Moonmaidens who brought good luck. . . . (p. 34)

The setting becomes less magically gentle when Attila is born. Attila's father has just challenged his god, and the result is terrifying:

Suddenly, without warning it [the storm] was upon them with lightning and thunder that roared and howled like an army of furious demons. Trees groaned and crashed to the ground to be picked up again and sucked into the spinning dark funnel of the whirlwind. (p. 64)

This setting introduces Attila, the "Scourge of God," who in the future will lead his people home, with the help of the white stag.

In the preceding quotes, notice how Seredy uses descriptive words that create the mood. Through word choice and ability to paint pictures with words, authors of excellent literature create moods that range from happy and nostalgic to frightening and forbidding.

In *The Thief*, Megan Whalen Turner also goes back to a time of the old legends in a country that resem-

The illustrations create a nostalgic look at childhood in In Coal Country. *(From* In Coal Country *by Judith Hendershot, illustrated by Thomas B. Allen. Illustration copyright © 1987 by Thomas B. Allen. Reprinted by permission of Alfred A. Knopf.)*

bles Greece. As the thief searches for an ancient treasure, readers are introduced to a setting complete with ancient temples, gods and goddesses, and objects of power that set the mythical mood.

Setting as Antagonist. Setting can be an antagonist in plots based on person-against-society or person-against-nature conflict. The descriptions of the Arctic in Jean Craighead George's *Julie of the Wolves* are essential. Without them, readers would have difficulty understanding the life-and-death peril facing Miyax. These descriptions make it possible to comprehend Miyax's love for the Arctic, her admiration of and dependence on the wolves, and her preference for the old Eskimo ways.

In *The Witch of Blackbird Pond,* by Elizabeth George Speare, a Puritan colony in New England is the setting as well as the antagonist of newcomer Kit Tyler, whose colorful clothing and carefree ways immediately conflict with the standards of an austere society. Careful depiction of the colony's strict standards of dress and behavior helps readers understand why the Puritans accuse Kit of being a witch.

The setting in Ida Vos's *Hide and Seek* provides the antagonist, the Netherlands during German occupation. In the foreword to the text, Vos introduces the setting for the story and helps readers understand that the setting is the antagonist. For example, she states,

Come with me to a small country in Western Europe. To the Netherlands, a land also known as Holland. Come with me, back to the year 1940. I am eight years old. German soldiers are parading through the Dutch streets. They have helmets on their heads and they are wearing black boots. They are marching and singing songs that have words I don't understand. "They're going to kill all the Jews!" shouts my mother. I am afraid, I have a stomachache. I am Jewish. (p. vii)

The reactions of the characters and the descriptions of the occupation in the remainder of the book leave no doubt that this setting is an antagonist. Vos based *Hide and Seek* on her family's life during World War II.

Setting as Historical Background. Accuracy in setting is extremely important in historical fiction and in biography. Conflict in the story and the actions of the characters may be influenced by the time period and the geographical location. Unless authors describe settings carefully, children cannot comprehend unfamiliar historical periods or the stories that unfold in them. *A Gathering of Days,* by Joan W. Blos, is an example of historical fiction that carefully depicts setting—in this case, a small New Hampshire farm in the 1830s. Blos brings rural nineteenth-century America to life through descriptions of little things, such as home remedies, country pleasures, and country hardships.

Blos describes in detail the preparation of a cold remedy. The character goes to the pump for water, blows up the fire, heats a kettle of water over the flames, wrings out a flannel in hot water, sprinkles the flannel with turpentine, and places it on the patient's chest. Blos describes discipline and school life in the 1830s. Disobedience can result in a thrashing. Because of their sex, girls are excused from all but the simplest arithmetic. Readers vicariously join the characters in breaking out of the snow

Lois Lowry develops a setting that is historically accurate for World War II Denmark. (From Number the Stars *by Lois Lowry, copyright © 1989. Reproduced with permission of Houghton Mifflin Co.)*

with a team of oxen, tapping the maple sugar trees, and collecting nuts. Of this last experience, the narrator says, "O, I do think, as has been said, that if getting in the corn and potatoes are the prose of a farm child's life, then nutting's the poetry" (p. 131).

In *Number the Stars,* set in Copenhagen during the 1940s, Lois Lowry develops a fictional story around the actions of the Danish Resistance. Actions of King Christian add to the historical accuracy of the time period. In addition to developing historically accurate backgrounds, Lowry develops the attitudes of the Danish people. Consequently, readers understand why many Danes risked their lives to relocate the Jewish residents of Denmark.

Both the illustrations and the text develop the World War II background in Michael Foreman's *War Boy: A Country Childhood.* Detailed illustrations show life in England as characters build shelters, put on gas masks, watch bombs falling, work, and relax. The illustrations add much information and help readers understand the time period.

The settings in Graham Salisbury's *Under the Blood-Red Sun* develop the historical time period associated with the bombing of Pearl Harbor on December 7, 1941. The author describes the sights and sounds of the bombing.

The authors of historical fiction and biography must not only depict the time and location but also be aware of values, vocabulary, and other speech patterns consistent with the time and location. To do this, the authors must be immersed in the past and do extensive research. Joan Blos researched her subject at the New York Public Library, libraries on the University of Michigan campus, and the town library of Holderness, New Hampshire. She also consulted town and county records in New Hampshire and discussed the story with professional historians. Lois Lowry visited Copenhagen and researched documents about the leaders of the Danish Resistance.

Setting as Symbolism.   Settings often have symbolic meanings that underscore what is happening in the story. Symbolism is common in traditional folktales, where frightening adventures and magical transformations occur in the deep, dark woods, and splendid castles are the sites of "happily ever after." Modern authors of fantasy and science fiction for children often borrow symbolic settings from old folktales in order to establish moods of strangeness and enchantment, but authors of realistic fiction also use subtly symbolic settings to accentuate plot or help develop characters.

In one children's classic, *The Secret Garden,* by Frances Hodgson Burnett, a garden that has been locked behind a wall for ten years symbolizes a father's grief after the death of his wife, his son's illness, and the emotional estrangement of the father and son from each other. The first positive change in the life of a lonely, unhappy girl occurs when she discovers the buried key to the garden and opens the vine-covered door: "It was the sweetest, most mysterious-looking place anyone could imagine. The high walls which shut it in were covered with the leafless stems of climbing roses which were so thick that they were matted together." (p. 76)

Finding the garden, working in it, and watching its beauty return bring happiness to the girl, restore health to the sick boy, and reunite the father and son. The good magic that causes emotional and physical healing in this secret kingdom is symbolized by tiny new shoots emerging from the soil and the rosy color that the garden's fresh air brings to the cheeks of two pale children.

In a more recent book, Katherine Paterson's *Bridge to Terabithia,* a secret kingdom in the woods is the "other world" shared by two young people who do not conform to the values of rural Virginia. The boy, Jess, would rather be an artist than follow the more masculine aspirations of his father, who accuses him of being a sissy. Schoolmates taunt the girl, Leslie, because she loves books and has no television. Jess and Leslie find that they have much in common, so they create a domain of their own, in which a beautiful setting symbolizes their growing sense of comradeship, belongingness, and self-love.

Even the entrance to their secret country is symbolic: "It could be a magic country like Narnia, and the only way you can get in is by swinging across on this enchanted rope" (p. 39). They grab the old rope, swing across the creek, and enter their stronghold, where streams of light dance through the leaves of dogwood, oak, and evergreen, fears and enemies do not exist, and anything they want is possible. Paterson develops credible settings as Jess and Leslie go from the world of school and home to the world that they make for themselves in Terabithia.

A dilapidated house, with its uncared-for backyard, becomes a symbolic setting in Janet Taylor

A boy and girl create a secret kingdom in which they can escape the problems of the real world. (Illustration by Donna Diamond from Bridge to Terabithia *by Katherine Paterson. Copyright* © *1977 by Katherine Paterson. A Newbery Medal winner. By permission of Thomas Y. Crowell, Publishers.)*

Lisle's *Afternoon of the Elves.* In this setting, two girls, Hillary and Sara-Kate, make discoveries about each other and the importance of accepting people who are different. The girls work together in a miniature village that Sara-Kate maintains was built by elves. Like Paterson, Lisle creates two credible settings: (1) Hillary's normal world of school and home and (2) the almost otherworld existence of a yard that is entered through a thick hedge. Like many other authors of books that have symbolic settings, Lisle relates the settings to the theme.

An In-Depth Analysis of Setting in One Book

The settings in Philip Pullman's award-winning fantasy from England, *The Golden Compass,* reveal several purposes for setting that may be found in the same book. For example, in the beginning of the book notice how the author creates a suspenseful setting through the following quote showing the characters' actions: " 'Behind the chair—quick!' whispered Pantalaimon, and in a flash Lyra was out of the armchair and crouching behind it. It wasn't the best one for hiding behind: she'd chose one in the very center of the room, and unless she kept very quiet . . ." (p. 4).

On the following pages readers discover how dangerous this setting might be for Lyra: "What she saw next, however, changed things completely. The Master took from his pocket a folded paper and laid it on the table beside the wine. He took the stopper out of the mouth of a decanter containing a rich golden wine, unfolded the paper, and poured a thin stream of white powder into the decanter before crumpling the paper and throwing it into the fire. Then he took a pencil from his pocket, stirred the wine until the powder had dissolved, and replaced the stopper" (p. 6).

As the story moves from England to the far north, the setting frequently becomes an antagonist as Lyra faces both the cold and the fear found in the wilderness. Pullman creates both of these moods in quotes such as the following: "The other girls went on talking, but Lyra and Pantalaimon nestled down deep in the bed and tried to get warm, knowing that for hundreds of miles all around her little bed there was nothing but fear" (p. 246).

Pullman's settings create both a realistic background and suggest the fantasy settings of other worlds. For example, the following quote provides realistic background for a small town in the far north. It also allows readers to visualize, hear, and even smell the setting: "Directly ahead of the ship a mountain rose, green flanked and snow-capped, and a little town and harbor lay below it: wooden houses with steep roofs, an oratory spire, cranes in the harbor, and clouds of gulls wheeling and crying. The smell was of fish, but mixed with it came land smells too: pine resin and earth and something animal and musky, and something else that was cold and blank and wild: it might have been snow. It was the smell of the North" (p. 168).

Many of Pullman's settings also reflect a universe inhabited by witches, supernatural beings, and parallel worlds. Pullman describes this parallel world in this way: "The city hanging there so empty and silent looked new-made, waiting to be occupied; or asleep, waiting to be woken. The sun of that world was shining into this, making Lyra's hands golden, melting the ice on Roger's wolf-skin hood, making his pale cheeks transparent, glistening in his open sightless eyes" (p. 397).

Pullman concludes his fantasy in a way that prepares readers for the next book in the series by summarizing some of the moods found in the previous settings and foreshadowing the fantasy to come: "She turned away. Behind them lay pain and death and fear; ahead of them lay doubt, and danger, and fathomless mysteries. But they weren't alone. So Lyra and her deamon turned away from the world they were born in, and looked toward the sun, and walked into the sky" (p. 399). To continue analyzing Pullman's fantasy setting, read *The Subtle Knife,* the sequel to *The Golden Compass.*

Theme

The theme of a story is the underlying idea that ties the plot, characters, and setting together into a meaningful whole. When evaluating themes in children's books, consider what the author wanted to convey about life or society and whether that theme is worthwhile for children. A memorable book has a theme—or several themes—that children can understand because of their own needs. Laurence Perrine (1983) states:

There is no prescribed method for discovering theme. Sometimes we can best get at it by asking in what way the main character has changed in the course of a story and what, if anything, the character has learned before its end. Sometimes the best approach is to explore the nature of the central conflict and its outcome. Sometimes the title will provide an important clue. (p. 110)

Authors of children's books often directly state the theme of a book, rather than imply it, as authors commonly do in books for adults. Theme may be stated by characters or through the author's narrative. The characters' actions and the outcome of the story usually develop and support the theme in children's literature. Picture storybooks, with their shorter texts and fewer themes, allow readers to analyze, trace, and discuss evidence of theme in a briefer, whole story. For example, many readers identify the theme in Patricia Polacco's *Appelemando's Dreams* as "It is important to dream." The following evidence from the book supports this theme:

1. The boy who does not have anything to do in a drab village makes his life interesting by dreaming about magic chariots pulled by galloping hues of color.
2. Appelemando shares his beautiful colored dreams with his friends and makes them happy.
3. The friends try to capture Appelemando's dreams on paper so that they can keep the dreams forever.
4. The children fear that they will lose Appelemando's dreams after the villagers angrily make them wash the dreams off the village walls.
5. The dreams allow the children to be found after they lose their way in the forest.
6. The villagers weep for joy after they follow Appelemando's vision and find the children.
7. The villagers conclude, "Never again would they question the importance of dreams" (p. 28, unnumbered).
8. The village becomes a colorful and dreamy place that people enjoy visiting.

Theme Revealed by Changes in Characters.

In *The Whipping Boy,* Sid Fleischman develops the theme that friendship is important. Fleischman shows how the main characters change in their attitudes toward each other. For example, the names that the main characters call each other progress from hostility to comradeship. At the beginning of the story, Jemmy thinks of the prince as "Your Royal Awfulness." Likewise, the prince refers to Jemmy as "Jemmy-from-the-Street" and "contrary rascal." As the story develops and the two characters learn to respect and admire each other, Jemmy refers to the prince as "friend" and the Prince calls himself "Friend-o-Jemmy's."

In *Darkness and the Butterfly,* Ann Grifalconi develops the theme that we can, and must, overcome our fears. Grifalconi reveals the theme by describing Osa's actions as she moves from fearing the dark to seeing beauty in the night. In this book for younger children, the theme is stated by Osa when she excitedly exclaims, "I can be as brave as the butterfly. . . . SEE? I'm not afraid of the dark anymore" (unnumbered).

Theme and the Nature of Conflict.

Stories set in other time periods frequently develop themes by revealing how the main characters respond to conflicts caused by society. For example, Rudolf Frank's *No Hero for the Kaiser,* set in World War I, develops several antiwar themes. Frank develops the harsh nature of war by exploring the actions and responses of a boy who is unwittingly drawn into battle. Through the viewpoint of the boy, Frank reveals that it takes more courage not to fight than to fight, that it is important to respect oneself, and that "guns never go off by themselves" (p. 13). Frank reinforces these themes through symbolism, similes, and contrasts. The contrasts are especially effective as Frank compares the same soldiers at home and on the battlefield and contrasts peacetime and wartime meanings for terms such as *bull's-eye, shot,* and *field.*

Janet Lunn's main character in *Shadow in Hawthorn Bay,* a historical novel set in 1800s Canada, discovers that prejudice is a harmful force and that respecting one's own beliefs is important. The impact of prejudice is explored when the main character, a girl with second sight, leaves Scotland and arrives in a community where her abilities are feared, not honored. Prejudice is a harmful force in other historical fiction, such as Elizabeth George Speare's *The Witch of Blackbird Pond,* Paula Fox's *The Slave Dancer,* Mary Stolz's *Cezanne Pinto: A Memoir,* Uri Orlev's *The Island on Bird Street,* and Mildred D. Taylor's *Roll of Thunder, Hear My Cry.*

The Theme of Personal Development.

Literature offers children opportunities to identify with other people's experiences and thus better understand their own growing up. Consequently, the themes of many children's books deal with developing self-understanding. In an earlier study, Gretchen Purtell Hayden (1969) concluded that the following themes related to personal development are predominant in children's books that have received the Newbery Medal: difficulties in establishing good relationships between adults and children, the need for morality to guide one's actions, the importance of support from other people, an acceptance of oneself and others, a respect for authority, the ability to handle problems, and the necessity of cooperation. As you read more current books, search to see if these themes are still found in the literature.

Superior rats consider the morality of their actions in a complex plot. (Illustration by Zena Bernstein from Mrs. Frisby and the Rats of NIMH *by Robert C. O'Brien. Copyright © 1971 by Robert C. O'Brien. [New York: Charles Scribner's Sons, 1971]. Reprinted with the permission of Atheneum Publishers.)*

In Robert O'Brien's *Mrs. Frisby and the Rats of NIMH,* a group of intellectually superior rats search for a moral code to guide their actions. They have studied the human race and do not wish to make the same mistakes, but they soon realize how easy it is to slip into dishonest behavior. Some equipment that they find allows them to steal electricity, food, and water from human society, which then makes their lives seem too easy and pointless. Eventually, the rats choose a more difficult course of action, moving into an isolated valley and working to develop their own civilization. In Lois Lowry's *The Giver,* a boy discovers that his ideal world has dark secrets and that the people may be better off if they have memories of their history and are responsible for their actions.

One book that develops the importance of support from another human being is Theodore Taylor's *The Cay.* When Phillip and his mother leave Curaçao in order to find safety in the United States, their boat is torpedoed by a German submarine. Phillip, a white boy, and Timothy, a black West Indian, become isolated first on a life raft and then on a tiny Caribbean island. Their need for each other is increased when Phillip becomes blind after a blow to the head and must, in spite of his racial prejudice, rely on Timothy for his survival. Phillip's superior attitudes gradually vanish, as he becomes totally dependent on another

person. When Phillip is finally rescued, Phillip treasures the way in which a wonderful friend has helped change his life for the better.

The Cay also stresses the theme of accepting oneself and others, as does Joan W. Blos's *A Gathering of Days,* in which Catherine experiences injustice for the first time when she and her friends secretly help a runaway slave. Catherine learns to respect authority as well when after years of responsibility for her widowed father and little sister, she must trust and obey her new stepmother.

Many children's books deal in some way with the necessity of overcoming problems. Characters may overcome problems within themselves or in their relationships with others, or problems caused by society or nature. Memorable characters face their adversaries, and through a maturing process, they learn to handle their difficulties. Handling problems may be as dramatic and planned as Mafatu's search for courage in Armstrong Sperry's *Call It Courage* or may result from accident, as in Theodore Taylor's *The Cay.* In Phyllis Reynolds Naylor's *Shiloh,* Marty solves the problem of animal abuse and finds a way to keep a dog. In Cynthia Rylant's *Missing May,* Summer overcomes her grief and gains the strength to have a full life with her uncle after the death of her beloved aunt. In Cynthia Rylant's *The Islander,* Daniel must overcome his feelings of being a loner before he recognizes the love of his family. Katherine Paterson has Jess and Leslie cross *The Bridge to Terabithia* in order to overcome the difficulties of being nonconformists in the rest of their everyday lives.

Cooperation, the importance of personal growth, and the need for kindness and sharing are all themes in E. L. Konigsburg's *The View from Saturday.* These themes are developed as a group of sixth graders form a winning team for the Academic Bowl.

An In-Depth Analysis of Theme in One Book

Sharon Creech's 1995 Newbery Medal Winner, *Walk Two Moons,* allows readers to analyze the effectiveness of the author's use of theme and to consider how it relates to thirteen-year-old Sal, her grandparents, her friend, her father, and her mother, who has left home. The themes in Creech's book tie the plot, characters, and setting together into a meaningful whole. For example, Creech uses mysterious messages left by a stranger to tie together the plot, characters' actions, and motivation. The messages are also written in the form of themes.

The first message is, "Don't judge a man until you have walked two moons in his moccasins" (p. 51). Father then interprets the meaning of the message on page 61. The second message is, "Everyone has his own agenda" (p. 60). This message is tied to Gramps's interpretation of the message (p. 60), Prudence's and Sal's actions (p. 104), and Phoebe's thoughts about her agenda (p. 140). The third message is, "In the course of a lifetime what does it matter" (p. 105). This message is related to Sal's thoughts about the meaning of the message (p. 106). The fourth message is, "You can't keep the birds of sadness from flying over your head, but you can keep them from nesting in your hair" (p. 154). This message is related to Phoebe's story (p. 155), Phoebe's father's response (p. 162), Phoebe's crying and Sal's response (p. 169), hope related to the story of Pandora's box (pp. 174–175), the birds of sadness around Phoebe's family (p. 189), and the birds of sadness around Mrs. Cadaver (p. 220). The fifth message is, "We never know the worth of water until the well runs dry" (p. 198). This message is related to the discussion about Mrs. Cadaver's and Sal's realization that the messages have changed the way they look at life.

The final and sixth message is the same as the first, "Don't judge a man until you have walked two moons in his moccasins" (p. 252). The importance of this message is developed when Gramps and Sal play the moccasin game in which they take turns pretending they are walking in someone else's moccasins (p. 275) and when Gramps's gift to Sal is to let her walk in her mother's moccasins. This book provides an interesting source for tracing the emergence of themes and the relation of those themes to various characters and conflicts developed in the text.

Style

Authors have a wide choice of words to select from and numerous ways to arrange words in order to create plots, characters, and settings and to express themes. Many authors use words and sentences in creative ways. To evaluate style, read a piece of literature aloud. The sound of a story should appeal to your senses and be appropriate to the content of the story. The language should help develop the plot, bring the characters to life, and create a mood.

The Girl Who Loved Wild Horses, by Paul Goble, was a Children's Choice selection. The most frequent reason that children give for choosing this book is the author's use of language. Goble uses precise similes to evoke a landscape of cliffs and canyons, beautiful wild horses, and the high-spirited Indian girl who loves them. One stallion's eyes are "cold stars," while his floating mane and tail are "wispy clouds." During a storm, the horses gallop "faster and faster, pursued by thunder and lightning . . . like a brown flood across hills and through valleys" (p. 12, unnumbered).

Sid Fleischman uses many metaphors and similes to create the setting in *The Midnight Horse,* such as "It was raining bullfrogs. The coach lurched and swayed along the river road like a ship in rough seas. Inside clung three passengers like unlashed cargo. One was a blacksmith, another was a thief, and the third was an orphan boy named Touch." (p. 1)

Fleischman also uses similes to develop characters. For example, Touch, the orphan, is described as "skinny and bareheaded, with hair as curly as wood shavings" (p. 1), and "he chose to bring himself up, free as a sail to catch any chance wind that came along" (p. 29). Compare these similes with those for Otis Cratt, the thief, who is described as a long-armed man who looked "like a loosely wrapped mummy" (p. 3), was drawn to the blacksmith's billfold "like a compass needle to true north" (p. 4), and ran "like a wolf returning to its den" (p. 29). Fleischman uses similes that relate to the actions of each character within the story.

Figurative language also helps develop characters, plot, and setting in Jan Hudson's *Sweetgrass,* a historical novel about the Blackfoot, set on the Canadian prairies. Early in the story, for example, sweet berries symbolize a young girl's happiness and hopes: "Promises hung shimmering in the future like glowing berries above sandy soil as we gathered our bags for the walk home" (p. 12). Later, the same girl's acceptance of a disillusioning reality is symbolized again by berries, which are then bitter.

Frank's figurative language in *No Hero for the Kaiser* reinforces the antiwar themes developed within the story. In the following quote, Frank first uses contrasts to show the changing nature of terms previously understood and to reveal the destructiveness of cannons:

Jan could not help remembering that among those invisible men called enemies there was his own father. His own father was in the field and his father's son was in the field. Why could they not tend the field together as before? Because this field that the soldiers were taking was not a field at all. A real field does not kill, a field lies at peace under God's sun, rain, and wind, a field is where things grow. He had caught the military in a lie. The soldiers were sent into a field of deceit. Like huge wolves the four cannon of the Seventh Battery went "into the field," across Polish fields, deeper and deeper into Russia, and behind them walked the gunners. (p. 46)

Authors also may select words and sentence structures with rhythms evoking different moods. Armstrong Sperry creates two different moods for Mafatu in *Call It Courage*. As Mafatu goes through the jungle, he is preoccupied and moves leisurely. Sperry uses long sentences to set this mood: "His mind was not in this business at all: he was thinking about the rigging of his canoe, planning how he could strengthen it here, tighten it there" (p. 77). This dreamy preoccupation changes rapidly as Mafatu senses danger. Sperry's verbs become harsh and his sentences short and choppy as Mafatu's tension builds: "The boar charged. Over the ground it tore. Foam flew back from its tusks. The boy braced himself" (p. 78).

The language and style in Lloyd Alexander's *The Arkadias* seems appropriate for a fantasy formulated on Greek mythology. There are numerous words reflecting Greek terminology and poetry such as "rosy-fingered dawn," "your life-threads are spun," and "wine-dark seas."

Many of the enjoyable stories contain repetition of words, phrases, or sentences. Repetition is appealing because it encourages children to join in. It provides a pleasing rhythm in *When I Was Young in the Mountains,* by Cynthia Rylant. The author introduces her memories of Grandfather's kisses, Grandmother's cooking, and listening to frogs singing at dusk with "When I was young in the mountains," a phrase that adds an appropriate aura of loving nostalgia to the experiences that she describes.

Point of View

Several people may describe an incident in different terms. The feelings they experience, the details they choose to describe, and their judgments about what occurred may vary because of their backgrounds, values, and perspectives. Consequently, the same story may change drastically when told from another point of view. How would Peter Rabbit's story be different if Beatrix Potter had told it from the viewpoint of the mother rabbit? How would Armstrong Sperry's *Call It Courage* differ if told from the viewpoint of a Polynesian tribesman who loves the sea rather than from the viewpoint of a boy who fears it? Author Patricia Lauber (1991) emphasizes the importance of point of view when she states, "The best stories have a point of view. They involve readers by making them care—care about the characters, whether people or animals, care about a town, care about an idea, and most of all, care about how it all comes out" (p. 46).

Avi's *Nothing but the Truth: A Documentary Novel* stimulates interesting discussions about point of view and fosters responses to literature. The book, a fictional novel written in documentary format, allows readers to interpret each incident, draw their own conclusions about the truthfulness of the documents, and decide which characters are changed the most. As a consequence, readers gain insights into how emotions can define and distort the truth.

As children read this novel, they can analyze how Avi documents various reactions to and points of view on the same incident through the use of memos, letters, diary pages, discussions, phone and personal conversations, speeches, and telegrams. Avi also develops characters, conflicts, and various emotional responses through these same documents. Consequently, the book may be used to stimulate personal responses among readers.

Authors may retell familiar tales by changing the point of view of the original story. For example, Michael Cadnum retells the Robin Hood story by telling *In a Dark Wood* from the viewpoint of the Sheriff of Nottingham.

Paul Fleischman's *Bull Run* is a story of the first battle of the Civil War. It is unique because Fleischman develops the story around the points of view of sixteen different people involved in the battle. Eight characters tell their story from the perspective of the Union and eight characters reflect the perspective of the Confederacy. Fleischman's characters range from generals to foot soldiers. Some of the characters tell their stories while waiting for men to return from battle, while others are artists, photographers, and doctors who observe or play important parts in the battle. By the end of the book, all of the characters reflect the disillusionment and horror associated with this first battle.

Michael Dorris's *Morning Girl* is the story of a twelve-year-old Taino girl and her younger brother, Star Boy, who lived on a Bahamian island in 1492. Dorris's chapters alternate between the point of view of Morning Girl and that of Star Boy. The story concludes with the arrival of the Spaniards.

An author has several options when selecting point of view. A first-person point of view speaks through the "I" of one of the characters. An author who wishes to use a first-person narrative must decide which character's actions and feelings should influence the story. An objective point of view lets actions speak for themselves. The author describes only the characters' actions, and readers must infer the characters' thoughts and feelings.

An omniscient point of view tells the story in the third person ("they," "he," or "she"). The author is not restricted to the knowledge, experiences, and feelings of one person. The feelings and thoughts of all characters can be revealed. A limited omniscient point of view, however, concentrates on the experiences of one character but has the option to be all-knowing about other characters. A limited omniscient point of view may clarify conflicts and actions that would be less understandable in a first-person narrative.

Although no point of view is preferred for all children's literature, an author's choice can affect how much children of certain ages believe and enjoy a story. Contemporary realistic fiction for children age eight and older often uses a first-person point of view or a limited omniscient point of view that focuses on one child's experiences. Older children often empathize with one character if they have had similar experiences.

Consistency of point of view encourages readers to believe in a story. Such belief is especially crucial in modern fantasy, where readers are introduced to imaginary worlds, unusual characters, and magical incidents. A writer may describe a setting as if it were being viewed by a character only a few inches tall. To be believable, however, the story cannot stray from the viewpoint of the tiny character. The character's actions, the responses of others toward the character, and the setting must be consistent.

Stereotypes

Consider stereotypes when evaluating literature for young children. Educators and other concerned adults strongly criticize stereotypical views of both race and sex. Of particular concern are literary selections that inadequately represent minority groups and females or that represent them in insensitive or demeaning ways.

Teachers, librarians, and parents may confront a shortage of high-quality stories about members of racial and ethnic minority groups, of works by authors who write from a minority perspective, and of materials that depict the literary, cultural, and historical influences of minorities. However, children's literature should present honest, authentic pictures of different people and their cultural and historical contributions.

When evaluating literature about minorities, for example, keep the following questions in mind: Are African American, Native American, Hispanic, and other minority characters portrayed as distinct individuals, or are they grouped in one category under depersonalizing clichés? Does the author recognize and accurately portray the internal diversity of minority cultures? Are minority cultures respected or treated as inferior? Does the author accurately describe the values, behavior, and environment of characters who are members of minority groups? Are illustrations realistic and authentic? Research indicates that if stereotypical attitudes are to change, reading of positive multicultural literature must be followed by discussions or other activities that allow interactions between children and adults.

Sexism in children's literature also requires adults to evaluate children's books with care. Masha Kabakow Rudman (1984) states:

Books for children have reflected societal attitudes in limiting choices and maintaining discrimination. Most traditional books show females dressed in skirts or dresses even when they are engaged in activities inappropriate for this sort of costume. Illustrations also have conventionally placed females in passive observer roles, while males have been pictured as active. Studies have demonstrated time and time again that illustrations confirm the subordinate, less valued role for the female, while stressing the active, adventuresome, admirable role of the male. . . . When a female is permitted to retain her active qualities, it is usually made clear to the reader that she is the notable exception and that all the other girls in the story are "normal." (p. 105)

Some children's books also stereotype males in ways that limit the options of boys to express a wide range of feelings and interests. Books should treat all characters as individuals. A book that groups all males or all females together and makes insulting remarks about either sex as a whole is sexist. However, you must read an entire book before you reach this decision, because you should not judge isolated quotes out of context.

 ## THE RIGHT BOOK FOR EACH CHILD

Because of developmental stages, children have different personal and literary needs at different ages. Children in the same age group or at the same stage of development also have diverse interests and reading abilities that you must consider. Understanding why and what children read is necessary in order to help them select materials that stimulate their interests and enjoyment. Jeanne S. Chall and Emily W. Marston (1976) found that the most powerful determinants of adult reading are accessibility, readability, and interest. These factors also influence children's reading. If developing enjoyment through literature is a major objective of your reading program for children, you must make available many excellent books, consider children's reading levels, and know how to gain and use information about children's reading interests.

Accessibility

Literature must be readily accessible if children are to read at all. In order to know what books interest them, gain knowledge of their heritage, recognize and appreciate good literature, and understand themselves and others through literature, children must have opportunities to read and listen to many books. As suggested, a literature program for children should include a wide variety of high-quality literature, both old and new. Unfortunately, studies show that children do not have enough opportunities to read literature in school. Roger Poole (1986) surveyed schools in England and reported, "Findings of the research show that teachers do not make much use of quality narrative" (p. 179). Rebecca Barr and Marilyn Sadow (1989) analyzed American schools and found "little reading of literary selections other than those available in the basal program" (p. 69).

Accessibility in the home is also important for developing interest in books. In a review of studies of children who read early and who do voluntary reading, Lesley Mandel Morrow (1991) discusses environments that foster children's early interest in books. She concludes that the environments must have a large supply of accessible books, plus parents who read to children regularly and who are responsive to their children's questions about books. In addition, these parents must serve as models by reading a great deal themselves.

A survey by Susan Swanton (1984) showed that gifted students owned more books and used public libraries more than did other students. Fifty-five percent of the gifted students whom Swanton surveyed identified the public library as their major source of reading materials, as opposed to only 33 percent of the other students, most of whom identified the school library as their major source for books. Thirty-five percent of the gifted children owned more than one hundred books. Only 19 percent of other students owned an equal number of books. Swanton made the following recommendations for cooperation between public libraries and schools:

1. Promote students' participation in summer reading programs that are sponsored by public libraries.
2. Inform parents about the value of reading aloud to children, of giving children their own books, and of parents as role models for developing readers.
3. Encourage school librarians to do book talks designed to entice children into reading.
4. Provide field trips to public libraries.
5. Advertise public library programs and services.
6. Make obtaining the first library card a special event.

The physical environment in the classroom library is also important for increasing children's reading of books. Library centers provide one of the best ways to provide accessibility for books. Research summarized by Morrow (1991) identified characteristics of classroom library centers that promote children's reading. These library centers are accessible and visually attractive. They have comfortable seating and attractive bulletin boards and posters to stimulate children's interests in books. They include books from all genres and varied reading levels. They categorize the books for easy selection and include new books

Children's literature is evaluated by not only children but also literary critics, teachers, librarians, parents, and publishers. Jean Karl[1] maintains, "The informed bookstore and the informed bookstore purchaser of children's books have always been in a minority" (p. 506). Questions related to literary quality, social philosophy, and suitability of content are debated along with the potential and proven ability of a book to attract children's interest.

The evaluation criteria used for book awards, criticism, and recommendations for book purchases frequently reflect the standards of diverse groups. The adult-selected award winners—exemplified by the Newbery Medal, Caledecott Medal, Notable Children's Books, and Boston Globe-Horn Book Award—suggest that literary value should be the primary consideration when choosing books for children. In contrast, the various readers' choice awards, which are compiled from the preferences of young readers, imply that the popularity of the books among children should be the essential consideration. A third position, represented by groups such as the Council of Interracial Books for Children, suggests that books should be evaluated according to values that stem from child development and psychology, cultural pluralism, and aesthetic standards.

The selection standards reflected by these three positions may or may not identify the same books as literature worthy of sharing with children. The merits of each type of evaluation are debated in professional literature, in college classrooms, and during professional conferences. Reviewers of children's books may emphasize one or more of these positions when they evaluate new books or compile lists of recommended books. It is helpful to identify any particular bias of a reviewer so that you can interpret and use recommendations to meet your own needs.

Carolyn Bauer and LaVonne Sanborn[2] maintain that both literary quality and popularity are important. They suggest that books having won both types of awards deserve emphasis. Children do enjoy some books with literary value. From a list of 193 books that won readers' choice awards, Bauer and Sanborn identified 39 that were also literary merit award winners. Of these, *Mrs. Frisby and the Rats of NIMH, The Mouse and the Motorcycle, Old Yeller, Rascal,* and *The Trumpet of the Swan* have each won four readers' choice awards. Authors Beverly Cleary, George Selden, and E. B. White each have written two titles that have won awards for literary value and popularity.

Current lists of bestsellers also suggest possible differences between literary merit and popularity. For example, the July 22, 1996, issue of *Publishers Weekly*[3] lists books such as Lois Lowry's *The Giver* and Karen Cushman's *Catherine, Called Birdy* and *The Midwife's Apprentice* as among the top bestsellers of hardback books. In contrast, the top bestsellers in paperback series include R.L. Stine's "Goosebumps" and "Fear Street."

Increased sensitivity to the values expressed in books may result in debates about the merit of previously acclaimed literature. For example, Walter Edmond's *The Matchlock Gun* won the Newbery Medal in 1942, but it was criticized in the 1970s because of insensitive descriptions of Native Americans.

When evaluating literature and reading literature critiques, you should consider each selection standard. Does the book have literary merit? Is it popular? Is it socially significant?

---

[1] Karl, Jean E. "What Sells—What's Good?" *The Horn Book* 63 (July/August 1987): 505–508.

[2] Bauer, Carolyn J., and LaVonne H. Sanborn. "The Best of Both Worlds: Children's Books Acclaimed by Adults and Young Readers." *Top of the News* 38 (Fall 1981): 53–56.

[3] "Publishers Weekly: Children's Bestsellers." *Publishers Weekly* (July 22, 1996).

regularly. Library centers also include story props, such as feltboards and puppets for storytelling, as well as taped stories with headsets. Consequently, it is important for books and library centers to be accessible to children, to be attractive, and to encourage interaction with various types of story props.

Readability

Readability is another major consideration in choosing literature for children. A book must conform to a child's reading level in order for the child to read independently. Children become frustrated when books contain too many words that they don't know. A child is able to read independently when able to pronounce about 98–100 percent of the words in a book and to answer 90–100 percent of the comprehension questions asked about it. Reading abilities in any one age group or grade level range widely, so adults working with children must provide and be familiar with an equally wide range of literature. Many children have reading levels lower than their interest levels. Thus, they need many opportunities to listen to, and otherwise interact with, fine literature.

Books listed in the annotated bibliographies at the end of chapters in this book are identified by grade-level and readability, although a book will not be applicable to every child in the grade indicated.

Interest and Reader Response

Interests are also extremely important when developing literature programs. Margaret Early (1992/1993) states, "Decades of experience have shown that children are more likely to develop as thoughtful readers when they are pursuing content that interests them" (307). You can learn about children's interests from studies of children's interests and from interest inventories. You should consider information gained from each source.

For many years, researchers have investigated factors related to the leisure reading habits and interests of children at different age levels. Vincent Greaney (1980) identified some of these factors. First, American and British studies indicate that the time and amount of leisure reading varies with age. Children at the end of primary school read the most, after which a decline in leisure reading occurs among all but high-ability readers. Second, girls read more books than boys do, although boys read more nonfiction. Third, children from working-class homes do not read as much as do those from higher socioeconomic backgrounds. Finally, the amount of leisure reading and the level of student achievement are directly related; good students read more and read higher-quality materials.

Dianne Monson and Sam Sebesta (1991) reviewed the research on children's interests and reading preferences. They conclude, "The results of a good number of studies reveal agreement of types of subject matter that appeal to students of a particular age level and support the notion that interests change with age" (p. 667). Monson and Sebesta found that children in the first and second grades prefer stories about animals, nature, fantasy, and child characters. Children in

the third and fourth grades continue to be interested in nature and animals and begin to develop interest in adventure and familiar experiences. Boys in the fifth and sixth grades are interested in war, travel, and mystery, while girls are interested in animal stories, westerns, and fairy tales. Children in the intermediate grades show an increasing interest in history and science as well as continuing interest in mystery and adventure. By the seventh and eighth grades, girls prefer mysteries; romances; stories about animals, religion, and careers; humorous stories; and biographies. Boys prefer science fiction, mysteries, adventure stories, biographies, histories, and stories about animals and sports. Both boys and girls have an increased interest in nonfiction, romantic fiction, historical fiction, and books dealing with adolescence. All children like books that contain humor and adventure.

Research indicates that children's reading interests are also influenced by their reading ability. Susan Swanton's (1984) survey comparing gifted students with students of average ability reports that gifted children prefer mysteries (43 percent), fiction (41 percent), science fiction (29 percent), and fantasy (18 percent). In contrast, the top four choices for students of average ability were mysteries (47 percent), comedy/humor (27 percent), realistic fiction (23 percent), and adventure (18 percent). Gifted students indicated that they liked "science fiction and fantasy because of the challenge it presented, as well as its relationship to Dungeons and Dragons" (p. 100). Gifted students listed Judy Blume, Lloyd Alexander, J. R. R. Tolkien, and C. S. Lewis as favorite authors. Average students listed Judy Blume, Beverly Cleary, and Jack London.

While this information can provide some general ideas about what subjects and authors that children of certain ages, sexes, and reading abilities prefer, do not develop stereotyped views about children's preferences. Without asking questions about interests, for example, there is no way to learn that a fourth-grade boy is a Shakespeare buff, since research into children's interests does not indicate that a fourth-grader should like Shakespeare's plays. A first-grade girl's favorite subject was dinosaurs, which she could identify by name. Discovering this would have been impossible without an interview; research does not indicate that first-grade girls are interested in factual, scientific subjects. These two cases point to the need to discover children's interests before helping children select books. Informal conversation is one of the simplest ways to uncover

CHART 3–1   An Informal Interest Inventory

1. Do you have a hobby? _____
   If you do, what is your hobby? _____
2. Do you have a pet? _____
   What kind of pet do you have? _____
3. What is your favorite book that someone has read to you? _____
4. What kinds of books do you like to have read to you?

real animals _____	picture books _____
real children _____	information books _____
science fiction _____	mysteries _____
funny stories _____	fairy tales _____
sports stories _____	poetry _____
true stories _____	historical fiction _____
fantasy animals _____	science books _____
family stories _____	adventures _____

5. What is your favorite book that you have read by yourself? _____
6. What kinds of books do you like to read by yourself? (Similar to 4) _____
7. What sports do you like? _____
8. Who are your favorite sports stars? _____
9. What do you do when you get home from school? _____
10. What do you like to do on Saturday? _____
11. Do you like to collect things? _____
    What do you like to collect? _____
12. What are your favorite subjects in school? _____
13. Would you rather read a book by yourself or have someone read it to you? _____
14. Name a book you read this week _____
15. Where would you like to go on vacation? _____
16. Do you go to the library? _____
    If you do, how often do you go? _____
    Do you have a library card? _____
17. Do you watch television? _____
18. If you do, what kinds of programs do you like?

comedies _____	cartoons _____
sports _____	westerns _____
animal programs _____	music _____
family stories _____	game shows _____
educational TV _____	mysteries _____
true stories _____	detective shows _____
specials _____	science fiction _____
news _____	other _____

19. Name your favorite television programs _____
20. Who are your favorite characters on TV? _____
21. Name several subjects that you would like to know more about _____

children's interests. Ask a child to describe what he or she likes to do and read about. Usually, you should record the information when working with a number of children.

For interest inventories in which students answer questions about their favorite hobbies, books, sports, television shows, and other interests, write down the answers of young children, but let older children read questionnaires themselves and write their own responses. Interest inventories may include some of the questions asked in Chart 3–1. Make changes according to the age levels of the chil-

"Read This, It's Good for You" is the title of a critical evaluation of books. Children's author Natalie Babbitt[1] discusses books that have messages about instructing children in the values of reading. She asks, "What's the use of writing a story for children about the value of reading when it will be read only by those children who are already readers?" (p. 23) She argues that in many books there is no story. Instead, there is a message about the way life is supposed to be. In place of books whose main purpose is delivering a message, Babbitt wants children to learn to love reading by reading books such as *Millions of Cats, Make Way for Ducklings,* and *Where the Wild Things Are.*

Babbitt concludes, "Good stories are always a pleasure to read, and we like pleasure, regardless of our ages. The risk with message books, and message attitudes, is that children's books will get classed with broccoli and end up shoved under the mashed potatoes of television" (p. 24).

Author John Neufeld[2] provides a contrasting view for evaluating books in an article titled, "Preaching to the Unconverted." He states, "I have often been criticized for being didactic. Sometimes that criticism has been warranted. At other times, I have felt that reviewers were unable to distinguish between information offered—valuable information for young people—and what they perceive as a Message. . . . I may direct a reader's attention to, or help focus it on, an idea or problem, but I can only induce readers to decide whether that story applies to their lives" (p. 36).

Neufeld believes that the stories that last are the ones that encourage readers to think about what they would do in similar circumstances. Neufeld concludes, "Stories about young people, for young people, are feasts authors serve their youthful readers. I like to think that some of what we offer sticks to their bones" (p. 36).

As you read and evaluate children's literature, consider the impact of the content to bring pleasure and increase joy in reading versus the importance of the message. Which is more important, pleasure or message? Which type of book do you remember from your own childhood? What was the impact of the book on you?

---

[1]Babbitt, Natalie. "Read This, It's Good for You." *The New York Times Book Review.* May 18, 1997, pp. 23–24.
[2]Neufeld, John. "Preaching to the Unconverted." *School Library Journal* 42 (July 1996): 36.

---

dren involved. You may discover additional information if you ask children why they like certain books. The findings of an interest inventory can help you help children select books and extend children's enjoyment of literature.

When considering interests and selecting literature, remember that children of different ages may be interested in the same books but for different reasons. Michael Tunnell (1987) analyzes why readers from age eight through adulthood enjoy Natalie Babbitt's *Tuck Everlasting.* Tunnell says that eight-year-olds enjoy the carefully foreshadowed plot, twelve-year-olds identify with Winnie's rites of passage, fifteen-year-olds empathize with Winnie's final decision, and adults appreciate Babbitt's craft as a writer.

Educators should remember that many children need to be led into reading and enjoying books that are beyond their normal interests. Perry Nodelman (1987) warns:

Children who experience nothing but conventional books do quickly learn to be intolerant of the unconventional. That's a pity, because being able to respond to more unusual or more complicated books makes one's life more interesting, one's knowledge of the world deeper and subtler, one's tolerance and humility greater. Being capable of enjoying just about anything is certainly a good place to start; but children deserve better than beginnings so that they will become more than just beginners, in reading, in understanding literature, and in understanding the subtle complexities of life. (p. 38)

 ## THE CHILD AS CRITIC

Children are the ultimate critics of what they read, and you should consider their preferences when evaluating and selecting books to share with them. For the last few years, a joint project of the International

Reading Association and the Children's Book Council has allowed approximately 10,000 children from around the United States to evaluate children's books published during a given year. Each year, their reactions are recorded, and a research team uses this information to compile a list called "Children's Choices" in the following categories: beginning independent reading, younger children, middle grades, older readers, informational books, and poetry. This very useful annotated bibliography is published each year in the October issue of *The Reading Teacher,* and it may be obtained from the Children's Book Council, 67 Irving Place, New York, NY 10003.

A look at these lists of children's favorites also gives an understanding of the characteristics of books that appeal to children. In order to identify characteristic elements found in the Children's Choices, Sam Leaton Sebesta (1979) evaluated the books listed and tried to discover if their characteristics were different from those of books not chosen by children. His evaluation produced the following conclusions:

1. Plots of the Children's Choices are faster paced than those found in books not chosen as favorites.
2. Young children enjoy reading about nearly any topic if the information is presented in detail. The topic itself may be less important than interest studies have indicated; specifics rather than topics seem to underlie children's preferences.
3. Children like detailed descriptions of settings; they want to know exactly how a place looks and feels before the main action occurs.
4. One type of plot structure does not dominate Children's Choices. Some stories have a central focus with a carefully arranged cause-and-effect plot; others have plots that meander with unconnected episodes.
5. Children do not like sad books.
6. Children seem to like some books that explicitly teach a lesson, even though critics usually frown on didactic literature.
7. Warmth was the most outstanding quality of the books that children preferred. Children enjoy books in which the characters like each other, express their feelings in things that they say and do, and sometimes act selflessly.

Sebesta believes that this information should be used to help children select books and to stimulate reading and discussions. For example, you can draw children's attention to the warmth, pace, or descriptions in a story in order to encourage involvement with the story.

The various Children's Choices lists also suggest particular types of stories that appeal to young readers. For example, a review of the "Children's Choices for 1992" (1992) reveals the importance of humor in children's books. Ten of the twenty-three books that are categorized as being appropriate for all ages have annotations using terms such as *humorous, mischievous, comical, laughter,* and *hilarious.* These twenty-three books include fantasy, realistic fiction, nonfiction, folktales, riddles, haiku poetry, mysteries, and biographies.

The beginning independent reading category again includes books that emphasize humor. Repetitive language and rhyming words are important, and animal fantasies are popular subjects at this level.

The younger reader category includes many realistic stories that explore children's problems and solutions to those problems, such as Peggy Rathmann's *Ruby the Copycat,* in which a young girl searches for acceptance and then discovers her own worth. There are also numerous animal fantasies and other types of fantasies, nonfiction information books, and biographies.

Stories chosen by children in the middle grades include realistic stories about sibling rivalry, peer acceptance, and high adventure; fantasies; folktales and legends; biographies; and information books. Information books are especially prominent in this list and include information about cars, aquatic animals, earthquakes, land animals and birds, time zones, science experiments, tidal pools, Pearl Harbor, projects with shadow characters, volcanoes, forms of water, and wonders of science. Several of the science-related books have projects that invite reader participation.

Books chosen by older readers include realistic stories about problems facing older children, mystery and suspense stories, fantasies, biographies, and informational books. The biographies range from biographies about Christopher Columbus to Jean Fritz's *Bully for You, Teddy Roosevelt!* As in the books chosen by students in the middle grades, the information books cover a wide range of topics, such as sea creatures, exploring the *Bismark,* dinosaurs, Vesuvius, weather, and disasters caused by the Exxon *Valdez.*

Children choose books from a wide variety of genres. Some are on lists of highly recommended children's books; others are not. Many educators and authorities on children's literature are concerned about the quality of books that children read. To improve their ability to make valid judgments about literature, children must experience good books and investigate and discuss the elements that make books memorable. Young children usually just enjoy and talk about books, but older ones can start to evaluate what they do and do not like about literature.

One sixth-grade teacher encouraged her students to make literary judgments and to develop a list of criteria for selecting good literature (Norton, 1993). The motivation for this literature study began when the students wondered what favorite books their parents might have read when they were in the same grade. To answer this question, the children interviewed their parents and other adults, asking them which books and characters were their favorites. The children listed the books, characters, and number of people who recommended each book on a large chart.

Each student then read a book that a parent or another respected adult had enjoyed. (Many adults also reread these books.) Following their reading, the children discussed the book with the adult, considering what made or did not make the book memorable for them. At this time, the teacher introduced the concepts of plot, characterization, setting, theme, and style. The children searched the books that they had read for examples of each element. Finally, they listed questions to ask themselves when evaluating a book (see the evaluative criteria box to the right).

A review of the fourteen evaluative questions shows how closely they correspond to the criteria that should be used in evaluating plot, characterization, setting, theme, and style.

Research shows that children have preferences in the books that they choose. Other research indicates that children also have preferences about how and when books should be read to them. Alicia Mendoza (1985) reports the results of a survey of five hundred twenty elementary school children ranging in age from five to thirteen. The following recommendations, taken from Mendoza's longer report, highlight the importance of reading books to children and the preferences of children during those listening experi-

ℰVALUATION CRITERIA

Literary Criticism: Questions to Ask Myself When I Judge a Book

1. Is this a good story?
2. Is the story about something I think could really happen? Is the plot believable?
3. Did the main character overcome the problem, but not too easily?
4. Did the climax seem natural?
5. Did the characters seem real? Did I understand the characters' personalities and the reasons for their actions?
6. Did the characters in the story grow?
7. Did I find out about more than one side of the characters? Did the characters have both strengths and weaknesses?
8. Did the setting present what is actually known about that time or place?
9. Did the characters fit into the setting?
10. Did I feel that I was really in that time or place?
11. What did the author want to tell me in the story?
12. Was the theme worthwhile?
13. When I read the book aloud, did the characters sound like real people actually talking?
14. Did the rest of the language sound natural? (Norton, 1993)

ences. First, children throughout elementary grades enjoy having books read to them. Consequently, parents and teachers should read to children frequently. Second, during conferences with parents, teachers should emphasize the importance of reading to children at home. Third, role models are important, so both parents should read to children. Fourth, because children enjoy listening to stories in groups, teachers should encourage parents to make reading at home a group activity. Fifth, parents and teachers should provide opportunities for children to read to other children. Sixth, children should have opportunities to select the books read to them or read by them to others. Seventh, children like information about a book before it is read to them. They should be told who the author is and be given a brief summary of the plot, characters, and setting. Finally, children like and should be given an opportunity to discuss books and to read books after the books are read aloud.

When children are encouraged to share, discuss, and evaluate books and are given opportunities to do so, they are able to expand their reading enjoyment and to select worthwhile stories and characters. Sharing and discussion can take place in the library, in the classroom, or at home.

SUGGESTED ACTIVITIES

for Adult Understanding of Evaluating and Selecting Literature for Children

- Compare the plots of several books written for younger children with the plots in books written for older children. Compare the ways in which events are ordered, the ways in which the conflicts are developed, the amounts of suspense or tension, and the climaxes of the stories.

- Find examples of person-against-person, person-against-society, person-against-nature, and person-against-self conflicts in children's literature. Do some books develop more than one type of conflict? What makes the conflict believable? Share these examples with your class.

- Read one of Laura Ingalls Wilder's "Little House" books. Do you agree with the child who said that she would like the character Laura for her best friend? How has the author developed Laura into a believable character? Give examples of techniques that Wilder uses to reveal Laura's nature.

- Compare the main character in a fairy tale such as "Cinderella" or "Snow White" with the main character in a book such as Scott O'Dell's *Island of the Blue Dolphins*, Armstrong Sperry's *Call It Courage,* or Gail Carson Levine's *Ella Enchanted*. Describe each character. Does the character change in the course of the story? How does the author show that change?

- Find descriptions of settings that (1) are used to create a mood, (2) develop conflict, (3) are symbolic, and (4) describe a historical period. What is the importance of each setting? Close your eyes and try to picture the setting. If it is realistic, what did the author do to make it so? If it does not seem realistic, what is wrong? How would you improve it?

- Investigate themes found in children's literature published during the 1960s, 1970s, 1980s, and 1990s. Which ones are most common? Can you draw any conclusions about the social, cultural, and economic influences of the times? Make a time line to summarize the results.

- Review the books in the most recent list of Children's Choices. What are some characteristics of books chosen by younger, middle elementary, and older readers?

- The following five authors or illustrators from the United States have won the Hans Christian Andersen Award: Virginia Hamilton, Paula Fox, Meindert DeJong, Maurice Sendak, and Scott O'Dell. Pretend that you are a member of the worldwide committee. What qualities encourage you to select books of these authors and illustrators?

- Read a current list of the top best sellers in children's literature such as the monthly report listed in *Publishers Weekly.* The categories are usually picture books, fiction, nonfiction, and paperback series. Analyze the list. Do you think the books reflect literary merit, popularity, or social significance? Support your viewpoint.

- The Hans Christian Andersen International Award for Children's Literature is presented every two years to an author and an illustrator (both contemporary) whose body of work has been exceptional. Select an author or illustrator who has won this award. Add that fact under USER COMMENTS to update the database. If possible, obtain at least two examples of books by the same author or illustrator. Using the appropriate evaluative criteria from this chapter to analyze the books, cite three ways the books meet those criteria.

- You are a fourth-grade teacher planning a reading and writing unit for which the culminating activity will be writing a story emphasizing plot development. Use the database to locate at least 12 books that you will want to have your students read that will match their interests and reading level as well as demonstrating plot development. Print your list and write three reasons that explain the reasons for your choices.

Involving Children in Literary Elements

hether developing a literature program, developing literature-based reading instruction, or sharing literature on a one-to-one basis, remember the dual roles of literature: providing enjoyment and developing understanding. If you want children to respond to, love, and appreciate literature, provide them with a varied selection of fine literature and give them many opportunities to read, listen to, share, discuss, and respond to literature.

Throughout this children's literature text, children are encouraged to respond to various genres of literature in exciting ways. Chapter 5 involves children in picture books through sharing nursery rhymes and wordless books, reading books aloud, and developing appreciation for illustrations. Chapter 6 involves children in traditional literature through storytelling, comparing folktales from different countries, investigating folktales from a single country, and developing creative dramatizations through folklore. Chapter 7 involves children in modern fantasy through identifying traditional elements in fantasy, developing artistic interpretations, and interacting with science fiction. Chapter 8 involves children in poetry through movement, choral speaking, music, and writing. Chapter 9 involves children in contemporary realistic fiction through interacting with survival literature. Chapter 10 in-

volves children in historical fiction through simulating time periods and developing creative dramatizations. Chapter 11 involves children in multicultural literature by developing activities that enhance children's appreciation for African American, Native American, Hispanic American, and Asian American literature. Chapter 12 involves children in biographies and informational books by using biographies in creative dramatizations, evaluating different versions of biographies, and evaluating scientific materials. Through these activities, children learn to both appreciate and understand various genres of literature. This section of Chapter 3 focuses on developing children's appreciation of and understanding for the literary elements of plot, characterization, setting, theme, and style.

INVOLVING CHILDREN IN PLOT

According to David Booth (1985) and Kaile Kukla (1987), creative drama interpretations based on story texts help children expand their imaginations, stimulate their feelings, enhance their language, and clarify their concepts. Through the playmaking process, children discover that plot provides a framework, that there is a beginning in which the conflict is introduced, that there is a middle that moves the action toward a climax, and that there is an ending with a resolution to the conflict.

Geraldine Siks (1983) believes that nursery rhymes are excellent for introducing both younger and older children to the concept that a story has several parts—a beginning, a middle, and an end. The simple plots in many nursery rhymes make them ideal for this purpose. "Humpty Dumpty" contains three definite actions that cannot be interchanged and still retain a logical sequence: (1) a beginning—"Humpty Dumpty sat on a wall," (2) a middle—"Humpty Dumpty had a great fall," and (3) an end—"All the king's horses and all the king's men couldn't put Humpty Dumpty together again." Children can listen to the rhyme, identify the actions, discuss the reasons for the order, and finally act out each part. Encourage them to extend their parts by adding dialogue or characters to beginning, middle, or ending incidents. Other nursery rhymes illustrating sequential plots include "Jack and Jill,"

The rhyme "Humpty Dumpty" contains three definite actions that cannot be interchanged and still retain a logical sequence. (From Humpty Dumpty.*)*

"Pat-a-Cake, Pat-a-Cake, Baker's Man," and "Rock-a-Bye Baby."

After children understand the importance of plot structure in nursery rhymes, proceed to folktales, such as "Three Billy Goats Gruff," in which there is also a definite and logical sequence of events. Divide the children according to the beginning incidents, middle incidents, and ending incidents. After each group practices its part, put the groups together into a logical whole. To help children learn the importance of order, have them rearrange the incidents. They will discover that if the ending incidents are enacted first, the story is over and there is no rising action or increasing conflict.

Diagramming plot structures is another activity that helps children appreciate and understand that many stories follow a structure in which the characters and the problems are introduced at the beginning of the story, the conflict increases until a climax or turning point is reached, and the conflict ends.

Have children listen to or read stories and then discuss and identify the important incidents. For example, the important incidents in Dianne Snyder's *The Boy of the Three-Year Nap* are placed on the plot diagram in Figure 3–1.

With their easily identified plot incidents, many folktales are excellent for plot diagramming. Additional stories that have this characteristic include John Steptoe's *Mufaro's Beautiful Daughters: An African Tale,* Paul Zelinsky's retelling of the Grimms' *Rumpelstiltskin,* and Selina Hastings's *Sir Gawain and the Loathly Lady.* Most of the conflicts in these stories result because the characters are in conflict with outside forces, such as another person. Children also enjoy comparing and responding to the differences in plot between the traditional versions of folktales and Jon Scieszka's adaptions in *The Stinky Cheese Man and Other Fairly Stupid Tales.*

Stories in which the conflict results because characters must overcome problems within themselves

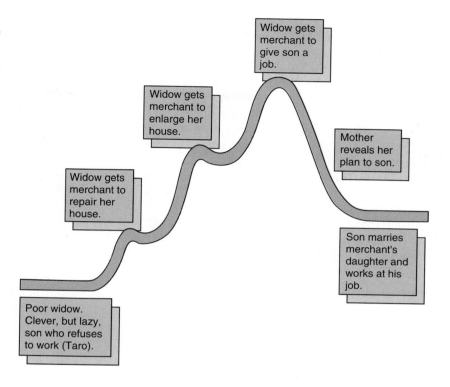

FIGURE 3–1 *Plot diagram for Dianne Snyder's* The Boy of the Three-Year Nap

Widow gets merchant to give son a job.

Widow gets merchant to enlarge her house.

Mother reveals her plan to son.

Widow gets merchant to repair her house.

Son marries merchant's daughter and works at his job.

Poor widow. Clever, but lazy, son who refuses to work (Taro).

may also be placed on plot diagrams. Caron Lee Cohen (1985) identifies four major components in the development of person-against-self conflicts: (1) problem, (2) struggle, (3) self-realization, and (4) achievement of peace or truth. Cohen states, "The point at which the struggle wanes and the inner strength emerges seems to be the point of self-realization. The point leads immediately to the final sense of peace or truth that is the resolution of the quest" (p. 28). Literature selections such as Marion Dane Bauer's *On My Honor,* in which the author develops struggles within the main characters, are good for this type of discussion and plot diagramming. In this plot structure, identify (1) the problem and the characters, (2) the incidents that reflect increasing struggle with self, (3) the point of self-realization, and (4) the point at which the main character attains peace or truth. Because person-against-self conflicts are frequently complex, lead students in the identification of significant incidents and ask them to provide support for these major struggles.

For example, in *On My Honor,* the problem results for Bauer's character, Joel, because he betrays his parents' trust and swims with his friend in a treacherous river. The struggle continues as Joel feels in-

creasing guilt, tries not to accept his friend's disappearance and probable death, and blames his father for allowing the two boys to go on a bike ride in the first place. Self-realization begins when Joel admits that Tony drowned and realizes that his father is not the cause of his problem: "But even as he slammed through the door and ran up the stairs to his room, he knew. It wasn't his father he hated. It wasn't his father at all. He was the one. . . . Tony died because of him" (p. 81).

Peace and truth begin, although the seriousness of the problem does not allow complete resolution. After Joel sobbingly tells his father the whole truth, he feels "tired, exhausted, but tinglingly aware" (p. 89). Even though there cannot be a total resolution of the conflict, because Joel's father cannot give him the reassurance that he desires or take away his pain, Joel forgives his father and asks him to stay in the room until he (Joel) falls asleep.

Students may compare Bauer's person-against-self conflict with that in Paula Fox's *One-Eyed Cat* (see Chapter 9). Additional person-against-self conflicts for older students include Cynthia Rylant's *A Fine White Dust,* a traumatic conflict in which a thirteen-year-old boy becomes involved with an unscrupulous

Involving Children In Literary Elements 🍃 143

traveling evangelist and struggles to understand his own beliefs, Karen Hesse's *Out of the Dust,* a story in which the protagonist blames herself and her father for her mother's accidental death, and Janet Lunn's *Shadow in Hawthorn Bay,* a historical novel in which the protagonist must overcome her fears and gain the insight that she needs to believe in herself.

Although many of the books with person-against-self conflicts are written for older students, several books may be used with younger students. For example, Arthur Yorinks's *Hey, Al* is a picture story-book in which Al and his dog Eddie overcome dissatisfaction and decide that "Paradise lost is sometimes Heaven found" (p. 27, unnumbered). Evaline Ness's *Sam, Bangs & Moonshine* is a picture storybook in which the main character faces the consequences of her lies.

INVOLVING CHILDREN IN CHARACTERIZATION

Authors of books with notable characters develop three-dimensional personalities that allow readers to gain insights into the strengths, weaknesses, pasts, hopes, and fears of the characters. You can help students understand how authors develop characters by discussing books in which the authors use several techniques for developing characters. You may also help students understand the often complex nature of inferencing about characters by modeling activities in which you show the students how to analyze evidence from the text and to speculate about the characters.

Characterization Techniques

Have students search for examples in which an author reveals a character through such techniques as narration, thoughts, actions, and dialogue. Have the students list examples in which each of these techniques is used and identify what each example reveals. Have the students summarize what they know about a specific character and discuss whether the characterization is flat or rounded.

A group of students led by Diana Vrooman (1989) used this approach to identify and discuss the characterization of Sarah in Patricia MacLachlan's *Sarah, Plain and Tall.* First, Vrooman introduced the story and reviewed the techniques that authors may use

to develop characters. Second, she listed on the board the techniques that MacLachlan uses to reveal Sarah's character in *Sarah, Plain and Tall.* Third, she read the first chapter to the students and asked them to identify the examples in the chapter and to stipulate what they learned about Sarah from those examples. Fourth, she asked the students to complete the search for other examples of Sarah's characterization in the remaining chapters. Finally, she asked the students to summarize Sarah's characterization and to defend whether or not they believed that Sarah was a rounded character.

Chart 3–2 shows a few of the characterizations and proofs for Sarah. Through the narration, the students discovered that Sarah was independent, plain, tall, loved by animals, kind, homesick, intelligent, educated, and that she loved animals. Through the thoughts of others, they discovered that Sarah was dependable, hardworking, and homesick and that she loved the sea. Through Sarah's actions, they learned that she was understanding, adventurous, homesick, hardworking, foresighted, playful, and independent and that she had a sense of humor. Through the character's conversations, they learned that Sarah was particular, educated, proficient, poetic, versatile, strong, independent, and confident.

The students concluded that Sarah was a fully developed, three-dimensional character. In addition, they discovered the techniques that authors use to develop such well-rounded characters. The same book may be used to analyze the characterization of the young boy, Caleb, or the young girl, Anna.

Modeling Inferencing

Some of MacLachlan's characterizations in *Sarah, Plain and Tall* are stated, while others are implied. Students frequently need much assistance in analyzing implied characterizations. Researchers such as Laura Roehler and Gerald Duffy (1984) and Christine Gordon (1985) have developed modeling approaches that place an adult in an active role with students and that show the adult's thought processing to the students. Modeling is one of the most effective ways to improve comprehension (Dole, Duffy, Roehler, and Pearson, 1991) and is an effective way to help students understand characterization (Norton, 1992). The following activity shows the modeling process with Patricia MacLachlan's *Sarah, Plain and Tall.*

CHART 3–2 Revealing Characterization

Author's Technique	Characterization	Evidence
Narration	Plain and tall	"She was plain and tall." (p. 19)
	Loved by animals	"The dogs loved Sarah first." (p. 22)
	Loved animals	"The sheep made Sarah smile. . . . She talked to them." (p. 28)
	Intelligent	"Sarah was quick to learn." (p. 52)
Thoughts about the character	Loved the sea	Anna thought: "Sarah loved the sea, I could tell." (p. 12)
	Homesick	Anna thought: "Sarah was not smiling. Sarah was already lonely." (p. 20)
The character's actions	Adventurous	Sarah answers an advertisement asking for a wife. (p. 9)
	Sense of humor	When Sarah finished describing seals, she barked like one. (p. 27)
Dialogue	Hardworking	Sarah learned how to plow the fields. (p. 33)
	Strong	"I am strong and I work hard." (p. 9)
	Independent	Papa tells Sarah that the cat will be good in the barn. Sarah tells Papa that the cat will be good in the house. (p. 19)
	Confident	"I am fast and I am good." (p. 46)

Requirements for Effective Reasoning. Effective inferencing requires readers to go beyond the information that an author provides in a text. Readers must use clues from the text to hypothesize about a character's emotions, beliefs, actions, hopes, and fears. Readers must also be aware that authors develop characters by narration, a character's thoughts or the thoughts of others about the character, the character's actions, and the dialogue between the characters.

An Introduction to Inferencing. Review characterization by asking students to identify how authors develop three-dimensional, believable characters. Share examples of each technique of characterization as part of this review. Also explain that students will listen to you ask a question, answer the question, provide evidence from the story that supports the answer, and share the reasoning process used to reach the answer. Tell the students that after they have listened to you proceed through the sequence, they will use the same process to answer questions, identify evidence, and explore their own reasoning

processes. As part of this introduction, discuss the meanings of *evidence* and *reasoning*. Encourage the students to identify evidence about a character in the literature and to share how to use this evidence.

The Importance of Inferencing. Ask students to explain why it is important to be able to make inferences about characters. Encourage the students to discuss how inferencing characterizations makes a story more exciting, enjoyable, and believable.

An Introduction to the Story. There are two important settings in *Sarah, Plain and Tall:* (1) the pioneer setting in one of the prairie states and (2) the pioneer setting in Maine. To identify students' understandings of these locations and time periods, ask the students to pretend that they are sitting on the front porch of a cabin in one of the prairie states in the 1800s, to look away from the cabin, and to describe what they see. Make sure that they describe prairie grass, wheat fields, few trees, a dirt road, and flat or gently rolling land. Ask them to tell which colors they see. Then, ask them to turn around and describe what they see through the open door of the cabin. Make sure that they describe a small space, a fireplace, and characteristic furnishings, such as wooden chairs and a wooden table.

The Maine setting is also important to this story because Sarah's conflict results from love of a very different setting. Ask the students to pretend that they are sitting on the coast of Maine, to look out at the ocean, and to describe what they see. Ask them to turn toward the land and describe the setting. Ask them to discuss the differences between the prairie and the Maine coast and to consider whether the differences in these settings could cause conflicts for a character.

The First Modeling Example. Read orally from the beginning of the book through the line, "That was the worst thing about Caleb," on page 5. Ask, "What was Anna's attitude toward her brother Caleb when he was a baby?" Answer, "Anna disliked her brother a great deal. We might even say she hated him." Provide the evidence. Say, "Anna thinks that Caleb is homely, plain, and horrid smelling. Anna associates Caleb with her mother's death." Provide the reasoning that you used to reach the answer. For example, "The words Anna uses, especially *horrid,* are often associated with things that we do not like. I know from the reference to the happy home that Anna loved her mother. When she says that her mother's death was the worst thing about Caleb, I believe that she blamed him for the death."

The Second Modeling Example. At this point, verify that the students understand the procedure. If they do not, continue by completely modeling another example. If the students understand the process, let them join the discussion by providing an answer, the evidence, and the reasoning. It is advisable to have the students jot down brief answers to the questions, evidence, and reasoning; these notes will increase the quality of the discussion that follows each question.

The next logical discussion point occurs at the bottom of page 5. Read through the line, "And Papa didn't sing." Ask the question, "What is Anna really telling us about her inner feelings?" Ask the students to answer the question. They should provide answers similar to this one: "She believes that nothing can replace her lost mother and that the home will not be happy again." Ask the students to provide evidence, such as, "The author tells us that the relatives could not fill the house. The days are compared to long, dark winter days. The author states that Papa did not sing." Ask the students to provide reasoning, such as, "The author created a very sad mood. We see a house filled with relatives that do not matter to Anna. I know what long, dark, winter days are like. I can visualize a house without singing. I think Anna is very unhappy and it may take her a long time to get over her loss."

Continue this process, having the students discuss the many instances of implied characterization in the book. The letters written by Sarah to Mr. Wheaton (p. 9), to Anna (pp. 9–10), and to Caleb (p. 11) are especially good for inferencing about the characters because students need to infer what was in the letters written by Anna and Caleb. To help the students infer the contents of the letters, ask the students to write the letters themselves.

Longer stories, such as *Sarah, Plain and Tall,* lend themselves to discussions according to chapters. Students may read and discuss several chapters each day. After each session, however, ask the students to summarize what they know about Sarah, Anna, Caleb, and Papa. Ask them, "What do you want to know about these characters?"

 ## INVOLVING CHILDREN IN SETTING

Believable settings place readers in geographic locations and time periods that they can see, hear, and even feel. In literature, authors use settings for four purposes: (1) creating appropriate moods, (2) developing antagonists, (3) developing historical and geographical backgrounds, and (4) suggesting symbolic interpretations.

Settings That Create Moods

Authors use settings to create moods. Through word choices and the visual pictures created by words, authors create moods that range from humorous and happy to frightening and foreboding. Asking students to tell their reactions to words and illustrations and comparing words and illustrations in a text helps students understand and evaluate the appropriateness of a mood. For example, students can respond to the frightening, eerie mood created by Marcia Brown's illustrations for Blaise Cendrars's *Shadow* and examine the influence of words, such as *prowler*, and descriptions, such as "teeming like snakes," in Cendrars's poem. Likewise, they can respond to and compare the equally frightening moods created by Charles Keeping's stark, black lines and Alfred Noyes's sinister and disastrous text in the narrative poem "The Highwayman." When a house sits precariously under a wave, as in Shelley Jackson's *The Old Woman and the Wave*, readers can respond to the frightening mood or the more symbolic fear of the unkown.

Teachers may use illustrated texts, such as *Song and Dance Man*, to show students very different moods. Stephen Gammell's illustrations create a warm, happy mood as children watch their beloved grandfather re-create the joyful days of his youth. The transition from a common, dreary, crowded attic to an uncommon experience is enhanced by the artist's drawing of a brightly colored, shadowy shape. From this point on, both the children and their grandfather seem to be transported to the joyful dazzling days when Grandfather was a vaudeville entertainer. Karen Ackerman's text supports the mood as Grandfather's voice "is as round and strong as a canyon echo, and his cheeks get rosy as he sings" (p. 14, unnumbered), as he tells jokes and "slaps his knee and laughs until his eyes water" (p. 19, unnumbered), and as the children "laugh so hard, the hiccups start" (p. 21, unnumbered).

Additional literature selections that develop warm, happy moods through both illustrations and text are Cynthia Rylant's *When I Was Young in the Mountains*, Kate Banks's *And if the Moon Could Talk*, Margaret Wild's *Our Granny*, Alexandra Day's *Frank and Ernest Play Ball*, and Valerie Flournoy's *The Patchwork Quilt*. Funny, even absurd, moods are created in both the text and illustrations of Simms Taback's *There Was an Old Lady Who Swallowed a Fly*, Mary Ann Hoberman's *Mr. and Mrs. Muddle*, Patricia Polacco's *Meteor!*, Jacqueline Briggs Martin's *Good Times on Grandfather Mountain*, Susan Meddaugh's *Martha Speaks*, Kevin Henkes's *Owen*, and Angela Johnson's *Julius*.

Authors of fantasy frequently prepare their readers for the fantastical experiences to come by creating settings and moods in which fantasy seems possible. Sharing and discussing introductions to fantasies allows students to appreciate and understand the techniques that authors use to prepare

them for both fantasy and conflict. For example, read and discuss the following introduction to Natalie Babbitt's *Tuck Everlasting*:

The road that led to Treegap had been trod out long before by a herd of cows who were, to say the least, relaxed. It wandered along in curves and easy angles, swayed off and up in a pleasant tangent to the top of a small hill, ambled down again between fringes of bee-hung clover, and then cut sidewise across a meadow. Here its edges blurred. It widened and seemed to pause, suggesting tranquil bovine picnics: slow chewing and thoughtful contemplation of the infinite. And then it went on again and came at last to the wood. But on reaching the shadows of the first trees, it veered sharply, swung out in a wide arc as if, for the first time, it had reason to think where it was going, and passed around.

On the other side of the wood, the sense of easiness dissolved. The road no longer belonged to the cows. It became, instead, and rather abruptly, the property of people. And all at once the sun was uncomfortably hot, the dust oppressive, and the meager grass along its edges somewhat ragged and forlorn. On the left stood the first house, a square and solid cottage with a touch-me-not appearance, surrounded by grass cut painfully to the quick and enclosed by a capable iron fence some four feet high which clearly said, "Move on—we don't want you here." So the road went humbly by and made its way, past cottages more and more frequent but less and less forbidding, into the village. But the village doesn't matter, except for the jailhouse and the gallows. The first house only is important; the first house, the road, and the wood. (pp. 5–6)

After you read this introduction, to enhance personal response have the students consider the effect of the contrasts used by Babbitt, the influence of personification, and the impact of such wordings as "tranquil bovine picnics," "veered sharply," "touch-me-not," and "grass cut painfully to the quick." Have the students speculate about the changing mood in the introduction and the type of story that might follow. Of course, have them read the story to verify their predictions.

Settings That Develop Antagonists

Authors of both historical fiction and contemporary adventure stories frequently develop plots in which nature or society is the antagonist. Vivid descriptions of either nature or society are essential if readers are to understand why and how the setting has created conflicts or even life-and-death perils.

Sharing and discussing quotations will help students respond to, identify, and appreciate vivid descriptions. Kevin Crossley-Holland's *Storm* is written for young readers. The author, however, vividly describes a fearful storm and a girl who fears the storm and faces her fears of a ghostly creature who supposedly roams the English marshlands. Crossley-Holland uses personification and metaphor to develop believable settings. For example, Crossley-Holland says that the storm "whistled between its salty lips and gnashed its sharp teeth" (p. 14) and "gave a shriek" (p. 27). Other elements in nature respond. The moon "seemed to be speeding behind grey lumpy clouds, running away from something that was chasing it" (p. 23). The young girl responds in ways that suggest fear: "Annie felt a cold finger slowly moving from the base of her spine up to her neck, and then spreading out across her shoulders" (p. 12) and she swayed in the saddle as she "thought she could bear it no longer—the furious gallop, the gallop of the storm, the storm of her own fears" (p. 35). By the end of the story, Annie has faced her fears of both the storm and the ghost.

In *Call It Courage,* Armstrong Sperry uses personification to give human actions to the sea and decreasing sentence lengths to show increasing danger. Have your students search for vivid descriptions throughout the book. After students discuss such examples, encourage them to find additional quotations in which nature is depicted through vivid descriptions, to share the quotations, and to tell why they believe that nature is the antagonist. Vivid descriptions of nature as an antagonist also are found in Gary Paulsen's *Hatchet,* Farley Mowat's *Lost in the Barrens,* Scott O'Dell's *Island of the Blue Dolphins,* and Jean Craighead George's *Julie of the Wolves.*

It is more difficult for students to understand the setting if society, and not nature, causes the conflict because the students must understand both the larger societal attitudes and the reasons that the characters are in conflict with those attitudes. Thematic studies that allow students to read from several genres are usually best for developing understanding about complex subjects, such as anti-Semitism or slavery. In thematic studies, have students use nonfictional sources to authenticate the settings in historical fiction. For example, a series of books about the Holocaust might include nonfiction, biography, historical fiction, and even time-warp

fantasy. Beginning with Barbara Rogasky's nonfictional *Smoke and Ashes: The Story of the Holocaust,* students can discover the historical background of the time period, the roots of anti-Semitism, the development of ghettos and concentration camps, and the tragic consequences. Have the students read Milton Meltzer's nonfictional *Rescue: The Story of How Gentiles Saved Jews in the Holocaust* to provide historical background about heroic people who risked their own lives to save the lives of other people. Next, have the students read Albert Marrin's biographical text, *Hitler.* Pages 17–20 are especially revealing. Within these pages, Marrin discusses the roots of Hitler's anti-Semitism and his developing hatred. For example:

Once Adolph began to hate, it became harder and harder to stop hating. From the age of nineteen, his hatred deepened, grew stronger, until it passed the bounds of sanity. He had only to hear Jews mentioned, to see them or think he saw them, to lose self-control. . . . One day, he vowed, he'd get even with them. They'd pay, every last one of them, for the humiliation they'd caused him. (p. 20)

Have the students read Uri Orlev's historical fiction, *The Island on Bird Street* and *The Man from the Other Side,* Lois Lowry's historical fiction about the Danish resistance, *Number the Stars,* and Jane Yolen's time-warp story, *The Devil's Arithmetic.* Then, have the students use the background information from the first three books to evaluate the authenticity of the settings that cause so much conflict in the fictional books.

You may use a similar approach to develop understandings of settings that reflect slavery and racism. This study might include nonfictional texts such as Milton Meltzer's *The Black Americans: A History in Their Own Words, 1619–1983,* Virginia Hamilton's *Many Thousand Gone: African Americans from Slavery to Freedom,* Walter Dean Myers's *Now Is Your Time!: The African-American Struggle for Freedom,* Michael McCurdy's *Escape from Slavery: The Boyhood of Frederick Douglass in His Own Words,* and Ellen Levine's *Freedom's Children: Young Civil Rights Activists Tell Their Own Stories;* Belinda Hurmence's time-warp fantasy, *A Girl Called Boy;* Gary Paulsen's historical fiction story about a slave girl, *Nightjohn;* Joyce Hansen's *I Thought my Soul Would Rise and Fly: The Diary of Patsy, A Freed Girl;* and Mildred D. Taylor's historical fiction story set in the Depression, *Roll of Thunder, Hear My Cry.* Again, use the nonfictional texts to authenticate the conflicts in the historical fiction.

Settings That Develop Historical and Geographical Backgrounds

Settings in historical fiction and biography should be so integral to the story and so carefully developed that readers are encouraged to imagine the sights, sounds, and even smells of the environment. For example, have groups of students choose one of the settings developed in Elizabeth George Speare's *The Sign of the Beaver,* such as the log cabin, the wilderness, or the Penobscot village. Lead them to discover as much information as possible about the sights, sounds, and even tastes associated with that environment. Have them identify and analyze quotations that describe the setting.

A group analyzing the log cabin will discover that the cabin is located in a clearing with wilderness all around it (p. 1); is one room constructed from spruce logs, cedar splints, and pine boughs (pp. 1, 3); is without windows (p. 3); was built with an axe but without any nails (p. 38); is sparsely furnished with shelves, two stools, a puncheon table, and a pine bed (p. 122); and is heated and lighted by a temporary and dangerous log chimney (pp. 3, 124). The only reading materials in the cabin are the Bible and *Robinson Crusoe* (pp. 29–30). By identifying luxuries that Matt longs for, students discover that he is without candles and lamplight (p. 124). By identifying objects that he makes for himself and for his mother, they discover the ruggedness and isolation of this 1700s wilderness.

Students enjoy creating maps and illustrations depicting well-defined settings. Have students use details from historical fiction or fantasy to draw maps, homes, or other settings. Carefully crafted fantasy worlds provide evidence for map locations and show the importance of settings in creating believable worlds. For example, after students read J. R. R. Tolkien's *The Hobbit,* ask them to draw maps of Middle Earth. C. S. Lewis's *The Lion, the Witch and the Wardrobe* includes detailed information about Narnia. Likewise, Lewis Carroll's *Alice's Adventures in Wonderland* provides descriptions of Wonderland.

After students have read literature with well-developed settings, divide the class into groups and ask each group to draw a map so that visitors to the land would be able to travel. Ask the students to defend their map locations by providing evidence from the literature. After the maps are completed, ask each group to share its map with the larger group and to defend why it placed landmarks in specific places.

Two sources provide interesting stimulation for these drawing tasks. Alberto Manguel and Gianni Guadalupi's *The Dictionary of Imaginary Places* (1980) includes maps and descriptions of numerous fantasy worlds. Rosalind Ashe and Lisa Tuttle's *Children's Literary Houses: Famous Dwellings in Children's Fiction* (1984) includes interpretations of the homes found in Frances Hodgson Burnett's *The Secret Garden,* T. H. White's *The Sword in the Stone,* Esther Forbes's *Johnny Tremain,* and Louisa May Alcott's *Little Women.*

Settings That Are Symbolic

According to Laurence Perrine (1983), a literary symbol "is something that means more than what it is. It is an object, a person, a situation, or some other item that has a literal meaning in the story but suggests or represents other meanings as well" (p. 196). Perrine maintains that to understand and interpret symbolism, readers must be aware of the following four requirements: (1) The story must furnish clues that details are to be taken symbolically, (2) the symbolic meaning must be established and supported by the context of the story, (3) an item must suggest a meaning that is different from its literal meaning, and (4) a symbol may have more than one meaning.

Settings in literature frequently meet these requirements for symbolism. For example, the easiest symbolic setting for students to understand is probably the once-upon-a-time setting found in folktales. Readers know that "once upon a time" means much more than long ago. When readers close their eyes, they often visualize deep woods or majestic castles, where enchantment, magic, and heroic adventures are expected. Folktale settings are excellent introductions to symbolic settings.

Authors of other types of literature also use symbolic settings to develop understandings of plots, characters, and themes. Frances Hodgson Burnett's *The Secret Garden* is one of the best literature selections for showing symbolic settings. Students can trace parallel changes that take place in the garden and in the people living in Misselthwaite Manor. For example, the story begins in a cold, dreary mansion surrounded by gardens that are dormant from winter. The characters are equally unresponsive. Mary is "the most disagreeable-looking child ever seen. . . . She had a little thin face and a little thin body, thin light hair and a sour expression" (p. 1). Colin is a disagreeable invalid, Mr. Craven is still in mourning for his dead wife, and Colin and his father are estranged. The setting and the people begin to change after Mary finds the door to the secret garden. Finding the key to the garden is the symbolic turning point, after which the characters and the garden are slowly nurtured back to both physical and emotional health.

As students trace the parallel changes in the garden and the people, they may ask themselves the following questions: Why does the author focus attention on a garden that has been locked and mostly uncared for for ten years? What is the significance of a key that opens a door? How do the people change and what happens to the garden? Why does the author draw parallels between nurturing a garden and healing people both physically and emotionally? Does the garden meet Perrine's requirements for symbolism in literature? Is the garden a good symbolic setting for both characterization and plot development? Why or why not?

Students may explore the symbolism of gardens in other books. For example, in Philippa Pearce's *Tom's Midnight Garden,* Tom receives both personal understanding and healing from the garden. Even when he is ill, he steals downstairs into the garden, and "there the feverishness of his chill always left him, as though the very greenness of trees and plants and grass cooled his blood" (p. 101).

 INVOLVING CHILDREN IN THEME

Students need many opportunities to read and discuss literature in order to identify controlling ideas or central concepts in stories. Themes are difficult because they are frequently implied rather than directly stated. Students learn about themes, however, by studying the actions of characters, analyzing the central conflict, and considering the outcome of a story. When looking for theme, it is important to consider how the main character changes in the story, what conflicts are found in the story, what actions are rewarded or punished, and what the main character has learned as a result. Even the title may provide clues to the theme.

The following sequence of events develops an understanding of theme in Ann Grifalconi's *Darkness and the Butterfly.* First, explain to the students that theme is the controlling idea or central concept in a story. Themes often reveal important beliefs about life, and a story may contain more than one theme. When searching for theme, ask, "What is the author trying to tell us that would make a difference in our lives?" Review some of the ways in which authors reveal themes, such as through conflict, the characters' actions, the characters' thoughts, the outcome of the story, the actions that are rewarded or punished, and narrative. In addition, the title and illustrations may provide clues.

Next, read orally *Darkness and the Butterfly.* Ask the students, "What is the author trying to tell us that would make a difference in our lives?" They will probably identify two important themes: (1) It is all right to have fears—we all may have fears that cause us problems—and (2) we can and must overcome our fears.

After the students have identified the themes, ask them to listen to the story a second time. This time, ask them to search for proof that the author is developing these themes. Their discussion and evidence probably will include some of the following examples:

1. It is all right to have fears; we all may have fears that cause us problems.
   a. The illustrations show contrasts between the beauty of the world in the day, which is without fear, and the monsters that surface in Osa's mind at night.
   b. The actions of the mother show that she is understanding. She even gives beads to help Osa feel less fearful.
   c. The actions of Osa show that she is a normal child during the day but a fearful child at night.
   d. The wise woman tells Osa that she was once afraid, "'specially at night!"
2. We can and must overcome our fears.
   a. The author tells the story of the yellow butterfly, the smallest of the small, as it flies into the darkness.
   b. The butterfly story is based on an important African proverb, "Darkness pursues the butterfly."
   c. The wise woman tells Osa, "You will find your own way."
   d. The wise woman compares finding your way to the wings of the butterfly.

e. The dream sequence reveals the beauties of the night.
f. The actions of the butterfly show that it is not afraid.
g. Osa reveals her self-realization: "I can go by myself. I'm not afraid anymore."
h. The author states that Osa, the smallest of the small, "found the way to carry her own light through the darkness."
i. The butterfly symbolizes that the smallest, most fragile being in nature can light up the darkness, trust the night, and not be afraid.
j. The title of the book is *Darkness and the Butterfly.*

Folktales, with their easily identifiable conflicts and characterizations, are excellent for developing understanding of theme. For example, when searching for themes in John Steptoe's *Mufaro's Beautiful Daughters,* students discover that greed and selfishness are harmful and that kindness and generosity are beneficial. Much evidence in the story reflects these themes. This is especially true at the conclusion of the conflict. The kind and generous daughter becomes queen, and the greedy and selfish daughter becomes a servant to the queen.

 ## INVOLVING CHILDREN IN STYLE

Many of the discussions and activities related to plot, characterization, setting, and theme emphasize an author's style. By selecting words that create visual images and arranging the words to create moods or to increase tension, authors show the power of carefully chosen words and sentence structures. When reading carefully crafted stories, you may not even notice the techniques that authors use. When you read aloud a carefully crafted story and one that is not so well developed, however, the differences become obvious. This section looks at developing students' appreciation for personification through narrative stories and for pleasing style.

Personification

Many of the most enjoyable books read to and by younger children develop characterizations through personification. This is probably so believable be-

cause children tend to give human characteristics to their pets and toys. Personification is an excellent introduction to style for younger children because the texts that include personification of objects and animals often are reinforced through illustrations that also personify the subjects.

Virginia Lee Burton's *The Little House* provides an enjoyable introduction to personification. As you read appropriate pages to the students, ask them: What pronoun is used when the author talks about the house? What actions can the house do that are similar to your actions? What feelings does the house express that are similar to your feelings? What causes the house to have each of these feelings? When have you had similar feelings? How do the illustrations help you understand the house's feelings and character? After the students have discussed the answers to these questions, share with them that the author is giving the house human feelings and behaviors through both the text and the illustrations.

Extend this understanding of personification in *The Little House* by asking the students to use pantomime or creative drama to enact the feelings expressed in the book. For example, have them listen to the text being read and pantomime the feelings expressed by the house. Have them create conversations that might occur between the house and her country or city neighbors. Have them tell the story from the point of view of one of the other objects found in the story.

Use similar discussions with books in which toys are personified, such as Anthony Browne's *Gorilla* and Margery Williams's *The Velveteen Rabbit.* Books in which animals are personified include Alexandra Day's *Frank and Ernest on the Road,* Diana Engel's *Josephina Hates Her Name,* Rosemary Wells's *Bunny Cakes,* and Lillian Hoban's *Arthur's Great Big Valentine.*

Pleasing Style

Jette Morache (1987) recommends having older students collect and share quotations from literature that they find pleasing or that support other literary elements, such as characterization, setting, and theme. Morache recommends having students work in groups to find quotes that illustrate a certain technique, to compare and discuss the quotes chosen by their group and other groups, to compile a page of quotes that they find particularly appealing, and to develop a list of qualities that make a "quotable quote." This type of activity is appropriate for developing appreciation for any of the literary elements discussed in this chapter. Have students find quotes to support characterization, setting, and theme.

Quotes also can emphasize specific literary techniques, such as personification, symbolism, simile, or metaphor. Older students might read Henry Wadsworth Longfellow's "Hiawatha" and Jamake Highwater's *Moonsong Lullaby* and *Anpao: An American Indian Odyssey* to find examples of personification in nature. Jan Hudson's *Sweetgrass* is filled with symbolism, similes, and metaphors. Cynthia Voigt's *Dicey's Song* has many references to music, a sailboat, and a tree as symbols.

WEBBING THE LITERARY ELEMENTS

Webbing is an excellent way to help children understand important characteristics of a story (Norton, 1992). Webbing also helps students increase their appreciation of literature and improve their reading and writing competencies. In addition, webbing helps students understand the interrelationships among the literary elements. Prior to the webbing experience, introduce the literary elements of setting, characterization, conflicts (plot), and themes by including many of the activities previously discussed in this chapter. To introduce the idea of webbing literary elements, read and discuss folktales with the children. Then, draw simple webs with the title of the book in the center and the elements of setting, characterization, conflicts, and themes on spokes that extend from the center. Lead discussions that help students identify the important characteristics being placed on the web.

The complex web presented in Figure 3–2 was completed with Karen Cushman's *Catherine, Called Birdy*. This historical fiction novel is set in medieval England. Notice on the web that the story takes place in an English manor. It also has strong characterizations, conflicts, and themes. An interesting comparison may be made by webbing Cushman's *The Midwife's Apprentice,* a tale set in the same time period but with a heroine from the lowest level of society.

QUESTIONING TO ENCOURAGE AESTHETIC RESPONSES

Many literature authorities stress that students' first responses to any literary work should be personal ones. For example, Patricia Cianciolo (1990) recommends that adults encourage personal responses during the sharing of a picture storybook before introducing any other activities related to the literature. These responses can take many forms. Children may discuss their reactions, write their responses, create responses through art, or even create or select music that depicts their responses to the moods or content of the literature.

Robert Probst (1989) states that adults who direct students' reading must encourage students "to attend not only to the text, but to their own experience with it as well—the emotions, associations, memories, and thoughts that are evoked during the reading of the work" (p. 180). Probst recommends the following types of questions to encourage students to provide aesthetic responses to literature:

1. Questions that encourage students' immediate emotional and intellectual responses to literature:
   a. What is your first response or reaction to the literature?
   b. What emotions did you feel as you read the literature?
   c. What ideas or thoughts were suggested by the literature?
   d. How did you respond emotionally or intellectually to the literature? Did you feel involved with the literature or did you feel distance from the text?
2. Questions that encourage students to pay attention to the text, without ignoring their roles while reading the literature:
   a. What did you focus on within the text? What word, phrase, image, or idea caused this focus?
   b. If you were to write about your reading, upon what would you focus? Would you choose an association or memory, an aspect of the text, something about the author, or something else about the literature?
   c. Describe an image that was called to your mind by the text.

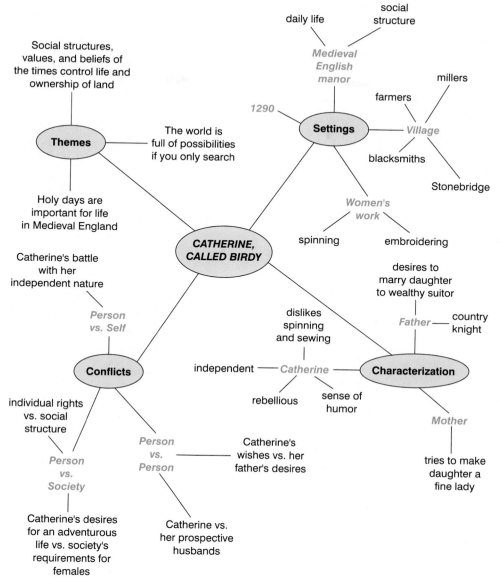

FIGURE 3–2 Semantic web of *Catherine, Called Birdy*. Source: Donna E. Norton's *The Effective Teaching of Language Arts,* 5th edition. Merrill, 1997.

d. What in the text or in your reading of the literature caused you the most trouble?

e. Do you think that this is a good piece of literature? Why or why not?

3. Questions that direct attention to the context in which students encounter the literature, a context of other readers, other texts, and personal history:

a. What memories do you have after reading the literature: memories of people, places, sights, events, smells, feelings, or attitudes?

b. What sort of person do you think the author is?

c. How did your reading of the literature differ from that of your classmates? How was your reading similar?

d. What did you observe about others as they read or discussed the literature?

e. Does this text remind you of any other literary work, such as a poem, a play, a film, a story, or another genre? If it does, what is the literature and what connection do you see between the two works?

Throughout this text are many examples of literature that develops understanding of the various literary elements and that encourages various types of responses to that literature.

 ## SUGGESTED ACTIVITIES

for Children's Understanding of Literary Elements

- Choose a book and develop a plot diagram that shows a person-against-person or a person-against-self conflict.

- Choose a story that reveals character through a variety of techniques. Identify the techniques, the characterization, and the evidence for the character traits revealed. Share your findings with your class.

- Develop an activity that models inferencing of characterization. Share the modeling activity with a group of children or your class.

- Choose settings that create moods, antagonists, historical backgrounds, or symbolism. Develop a list of books and references to help students understand these important purposes for setting.

- Choose a book and trace the author's development of theme. Share your book and activity with a child or your class.

- Develop a literary web that shows the various literary elements developed in a book.

- Share a book with a child and encourage the child to provide an aesthetic response to that literature.

 ## CHILDREN'S LITERATURE

Aardema, Verna. *Bringing the Rain to Kapiti Plain: A Nandi Tale*. Illustrated by Beatriz Vidal. Dial, 1981 (I:5–8 R:6). A cumulative tale from Kenya tells how a herdsman brings rain to the parched land.

———. *Why Mosquitoes Buzz in People's Ears*. Illustrated by Leo and Diane Dillon. Dial, 1975 (I:5–9 R:6). A cumulative African folktale tells the humorous reason for mosquitoes' buzzing.

Ackerman, Karen. *Song and Dance Man*. Illustrated by Stephen Gammell. Knopf, 1988 (I:3–8 R:4). Grandfather recreates the magic of vaudeville for his grandchildren.

Alcott, Louisa May. *Little Women*. Little, Brown, 1868 (I:10+ R:7). This classic story tells about a loving family.

Alexander, Lloyd. *The Arkadians*. Dutton, 1995 (I:10+ R:6). This epic adventure is based on elements from Greek mythology.

Avi. *Nothing but the Truth: A Documentary Novel*. Orchard, 1991 (I:12+). The conflict between a boy and an English teacher is developed through various documents that show differing points of view.

———. *The True Confessions of Charlotte Doyle*. Orchard, 1990 (I:10+ R:6). All of the literary elements are developed in this historical fiction novel.

Babbitt, Natalie. *Tuck Everlasting*. Farrar, Straus & Giroux, 1975 (I:8–12 R:6). A fantasy story about everlasting life.

Banks, Kate. *And If the Moon Could Talk*. Illustrated by Georg Hallensleben. Farrar Straus Giroux, 1998 (I:3–6 R:4). A peaceful bedtime mood is developed.

Barber, Antonia. *The Enchanter's Daughter*. Illustrated by Errol Le Cain. Farrar, Straus & Giroux, 1987 (I:6–9 R:5). A young woman outwits an enchanter to regain her past life.

Barton, Byron. *I Want to Be an Astronaut*. Crowell, 1988 (I:2–6). Very large pictures show the work of astronauts.

Bauer, Marion Dane. *On My Honor*. Clarion, 1986 (I:10+ R:4). A boy faces guilt when his friend drowns.

Ben-Ezer, Ehud. *Hosni the Dreamer*. Illustrated by Uri Shulevitz. Farrar Straus Giroux, 1997 (I:5–9 R:5). This Arabian tale stresses the importance of wisdom.

Benjamin, Carol Lea. *The Wicked Stepdog*. Crowell, 1982 (I:9–12 R:4). A twelve-year-old girl believes she has lost her father when he remarries.

Berenzy, Alix. *A Frog Prince*. H. Holt, 1989 (I:6–10 R:6). In a twist on a folktale, a frog searches for a suitable mate.

Blos, Joan W. *A Gathering of Days*. Scribner, 1979 (I:8–14 R:6). The fictional journal is about a thirteen-year-old girl's life on a farm in New Hampshire in 1830.

Blume, Judy. *Blubber*. Bradbury, 1974 (I:10+ R:4). A girl becomes the victim in peer conflict.

Brooks, Bruce. *The Moves Make the Man*. Harper & Row, 1984 (I:10+ R:7). Basketball develops understanding between a black boy and a white boy.

———. *What Hearts*. HarperCollins, 1992 (I:10+ R:6). Asa's story is revealed through four stories that tell about his life during different time periods.

Browne, Anthony. *Gorilla*. Watts, 1983 (I:3–8 R:4). A toy gorilla comes to life for a young girl.

Bunting, Eve. *The Wednesday Surprise*. Illustrated by Donald Carrick. Clarion, 1989 (I:3–9 R:5). A girl teaches her grandmother to read.

Burnett, Frances Hodgson. *The Secret Garden*. Illustrated by Tasha Tudor. Lippincott, 1911, 1938, 1962 (I:8–12 R:7). A garden that hasn't been seen by anybody for ten years

---

I = Interest by age range.

R = Readability by grade level.

works its magic spell on a lonely girl, a sick boy, and an unhappy father.

Burton, Virginia Lee. *The Little House.* Houghton Mifflin, 1942 (I:3–7 R:3). A house is strong but needs love as it becomes dilapidated and lonely over the years.

Cadnum, Michael. *In a Dark Wood.* Orchard, 1998 (I:10+ R:6). The story of Robin Hood is told through the viewpoint of the sheriff.

Carrick, Carol. *Stay Away from Simon!* Illustrated by Donald Carrick. Clarion, 1985 (I:7–10 R:3). A mentally retarded boy helps two children realize his worth.

Carroll, Lewis. *Alice's Adventures in Wonderland.* Illustrated by John Tenniel. Macmillan, 1866; Knopf, 1984 (I:8+ R:6). A classic is presented in a facsimile edition.

Cendrars, Blaise. *Shadow.* Illustrated by Marcia Brown. Scribner, 1982 (I:all). A highly illustrated version of an African poem is about the world of spirits.

Chaucer, Geoffrey. *The Canterbury Tales.* Retold by Barbara Cohen. Illustrated by Trina Schart Hyman. Lothrop, Lee, & Shepard, 1988 (I:8+ R:5). Chaucer's tales are adapted for young readers.

Cleary, Beverly. *The Mouse and the Motorcycle.* Illustrated by Louis Darling. Morrow, 1965 (I:7–11 R:3) Ralph makes friends with a boy who owns a toy motorcycle.

_____. *Ramona and Her Father.* Illustrated by Alan Tiegreen. Morrow, 1977 (I:7–12 R:6). A warm and humorous story about Ramona, a second-grader, who tries to help her father through a trying period after he loses his job.

_____. *Ramona Quimby, Age 8.* Illustrated by Alan Tiegreen. Morrow, 1981 (I:7–12 R:6). A humorous story is about how a third-grader helps her family when her father returns to college.

Cole, Brock. *The Goats.* Farrar, Straus & Giroux, 1987 (I:8+ R:5). Two children are marooned on an island by their peers at camp.

Creech, Sharon. *Walk Two Moons.* HarperCollins, 1994 (I:12+ R:6). Secret messages are used to develop the theme.

Crossley-Holland, Kevin. *Storm.* Illustrated by Alan Marks. Heinemann, 1985 (I:6–12 R:5). A girl faces her fear and gets a doctor for her sister.

Curtis, Christopher Paul. *The Watsons Go to Birmingham—1963.* Delacorte, 1995 (I:10+ R:6). The text follows the experiences of an African American family when they visit Alabama.

Cushman, Karen. *Catherine, Called Birdy.* Clarion, 1994 (I:12+ R:9). Set in medieval England, the story centers around the life of the thirteen-year-old daughter of a knight.

_____. *The Midwife's Apprentice.* Clarion, 1995. Set in medieval England, the story centers around a young girl who overcomes homelessness.

Dabcovich, Lydia. *Sleepy Bear.* Dutton, 1982 (I:3–6 R:1). Illustrations and text follow a bear as he hibernates and wakes up in the spring.

Day, Alexandra. *Frank and Ernest Play Ball.* Scholastic, 1990 (I:5–8 R:5). The two characters provide a humorous look at baseball.

_____. *Frank and Ernest on the Road.* Scholastic, 1994 (I:5–8 R:5). The bear and elephant learn CB language.

Dorris, Michael. *Morning Girl.* Hyperion, 1992 (I:8+ R:4). The story tells the life of a Taino Indian girl and boy prior to the encounter with the Spaniards in 1492.

Edmonds, Walter D. *The Matchlock Gun.* Dodd, Mead, 1941 (I:8+ R:5). A boy and his family live on the frontier.

Engel, Diana. *Josephina Hates Her Name.* Morrow, 1989 (I:5–8 R:4). An alligator child discovers pride in her name.

Farmer, Nancy. *A Girl Named Disaster.* Orchard, 1996 (I:10+ R:6). An eleven-year-old girl experiences a survival story in Zimbabwe.

Fenner, Carol. *Yolanda's Genius.* McElderry, 1995 (I:10+ R:3). Music symbolism is used to suggest characteristics.

Fleischman, Paul. *The Borning Room.* HarperCollins, 1991 (I:10+ R:5). The story traces events in a home on the Ohio frontier beginning in 1851.

_____. *Bull Run.* Illustrated by David Frampton. HarperCollins, 1993 (I:10+ R:5). Sixteen people tell about the first battle of the Civil War.

_____. *Dateline: Troy.* Illustrated by Gwen Frankfeldt and Glenn Morrow. Candlewick, 1996 (I:12+ R:7). The Trojan War story is illustrated with clippings from modern news stories.

Fleischman, Sid. *The Midnight Horse.* Illustrated by Peter Sis. Greenwillow, 1990 (I:8–12 R:5). Numerous similes are used to develop characterization in this historical novel.

_____. *The Whipping Boy.* Illustrated by Peter Sis. Greenwillow, 1986 (I:8+ R:5). A prince and his whipping boy exchange places.

Flournoy, Valerie. *The Patchwork Quilt.* Illustrated by Jerry Pinkney. Dial, 1985 (I:5–8 R:4). Constructing a quilt brings a family together.

Forbes, Esther. *Johnny Tremain.* Illustrated by Lynd Ward. Houghton Mifflin, 1943 (I:10+ R:6). A silversmith's apprentice survives early Revolutionary wartime in Boston.

Foreman, Michael. *War Boy: A Country Childhood.* Little, Brown, 1990 (I:all R:6). The illustrations and text provide background for World War II England.

Fox, Paula. *Monkey Island.* Orchard, 1991 (I:10+ R:6). Strong characterizations are developed as a homeless boy survives in New York City.

_____. *One-Eyed Cat.* Bradbury, 1984 (I:10+ R:5). An eleven-year-old boy shoots a cat and then must face his guilt.

_____. *The Slave Dancer.* Illustrated by Eros Keith. Bradbury, 1973 (I:12+ R:7). In 1849, a fife player experiences the misery of the slave trade.

Frank, Rudolf. *No Hero for the Kaiser.* Translated from German by Patricia Crampton. Illustrated by Klaus Steffens. Lothrop, Lee & Shepard, 1986 (I:10+ R:7). A historical fiction is set in World War I.

Freedman, Russell. *Eleanor Roosevelt: A Life of Discovery.* Clarion, 1993 (I:10+ R:6). A biography of the political leader.

_____. *Lincoln: A Photobiography.* Clarion, 1987 (I:8+ R:6). Abraham Lincoln's life is carefully documented.

_____. *The Wright Brothers: How They Invented the Airplane.* Holiday, 1991 (I:8+ R:5). This biography traces the development of the airplane.

Fritz, Jean. *Bully for You, Teddy Roosevelt!* Illustrated by Mike Wimmer. Putnam, 1991 (I:8+ R:5). A biography of the president who lived between 1858 and 1919.

_____. *The Cabin Faced West.* Illustrated by Feodor Rojankousky. Coward, McCann, 1958 (I:7–10 R:5). A young girl whose family has moved West dreams of going back home until she begins to see the frontier with new eyes.

_____. *The Great Little Madison.* Putnam, 1989 (I:10+ R:6). The life of the fourth president is presented in a biography.

_____. *Make Way for Sam Houston*. Illustrated by Elise Primavera. Putnam, 1986 (I:9+ R:6). The biography is of a nineteenth-century hero.

_____. *Traitor: The Case of Benedict Arnold*. Putnam, 1981 (I:8+ R:5). The book tells the life of a man who chose the British cause in the Revolutionary War.

George, Jean Craighead. *Julie of the Wolves*. Illustrated by John Schoenherr. Harper & Row, 1972 (I:10–13 R:7). An Eskimo girl lost on the North Slope of Alaska survives with the help of wolves.

_____. *My Side of the Mountain*. Dutton, 1959 (I:10+ R:6). Sam Gribley creates a home inside a rotted-out tree.

_____. *Water Sky*. Harper & Row, 1987 (I:10+ R:6). A boy discovers his Eskimo heritage.

Gipson, Fred. *Old Yeller*. Illustrated by Carl Burger. Harper & Row, 1956 (I:10+ R:6). Old yeller is bitten by a rabid wolf as he saves the lives of those he loves.

Goble, Paul. *The Girl Who Loved Wild Horses*. Bradbury, 1978 (I:6–10 R:5). An American Indian girl loves wild horses, joins them in a flight during a storm, and finally goes to live with them.

Grahame, Kenneth. *Wind in the Willows*. Illustrated by E. H. Shepard. Scribner's, 1908 (I:7–12 R:7). Mole, Water-Rat, and Toad have a series of adventures.

Grifalconi, Ann. *Darkness and the Butterfly*. Little, Brown, 1987 (I:4–8 R:4). A young African girl learns not to fear the darkness.

Grimm, Brothers. *Rumpelstiltskin*. Retold and illustrated by Paul O. Zelinsky. Dutton, 1986 (I:all R:5). A miller's daughter is helped to spin gold by a little man who demands her first-born child.

Hamilton, Virginia. *Anthony Burns: The Defeat and Triumph of a Fugitive Slave*. Knopf, 1988 (I:9+ R:6). The biography of a slave from 1839–1854.

_____. *Many Thousand Gone: African Americans from Slavery to Freedom*. Illustrated by Leo and Diane Dillon. Knopf, 1993 (I:8+ R:5). The text includes short stories about many people who were involved in the struggle for freedom.

Hansen, Joyce. *I Thought My Soul Would Rise and Fly: The Diary of Patsy, A Freed Girl*. Scholastic, 1997 (I:10+ R:4). The story of Reconstruction is told through the viewpoint of a twelve-year-old girl.

Hastings, Selina, retold by, *Sir Gawain and the Loathly Lady*. Illustrated by Juan Wijngaard. Lothrop, Lee & Shepard, 1985 (I:9–12 R:6). A legend tells about one of King Arthur's knights.

Hendershot, Judith. *In Coal Country*. Illustrated by Thomas B. Allen. Knopf, 1987 (I:5–9 R:3). The artist and author depict growing up in an Ohio coal town.

Henkes, Kevin. *Owen*. Greenwillow, 1993 (I:3–7 R:4) A resourceful mouse and his parents face a humorous problem about a blanket.

Hesse, Karen. *Out of the Dust*. Scholastic, 1997 (I:10+ R:6). A girl must overcome feelings of guilt.

Highwater, Jamake. *Anpao: An American Indian Odyssey*. Illustrated by Fritz Scholder. Lippincott, 1977 (I:12+ R:5). Anpao journeys across the history of Native American traditional tales.

_____. *Moonsong Lullaby*. Photographs by Marcia Keegan. Lothrop, Lee & Shepard, 1981 (I:all). A personified nature poem was inspired by ancient Native American stories.

Hoban, Lillian. *Arthur's Great Big Valentine*. Harper & Row, 1989 (I:5–7 R:2). An "I Can Read Book" tells about a monkey and his sister.

Hoberman, Mary Ann. *Mr. and Mrs. Muddle*. Illustrated by Catharine O'Neill. Little, Brown, 1988 (I:3–8 R:4). A humorous story tells about two animals who disagree.

Hudson, Jan. *Sweetgrass*. Tree Frog, Philomel, 1984, 1989 (I:10+ R:4). A young Blackfoot girl grows up during the winter of the smallpox epidemic in 1837.

Hurmence, Belinda. *A Girl Called Boy*. Houghton Mifflin, 1982 (I:10+ R:6). An African American girl goes back in time to 1853 and experiences slavery.

Jackson, Shelley. *The Old Woman and the Wave*. DK, 1998 (I:4–7 R:4). Collage illustrations create the enviroment.

Johnson, Angela. *Julius*. Illustrated by Dav Pilkey. Orchard, 1993 (I:3–7 R:4). A pet pig adds to the fun.

_____. *Tell Me a Story, Mama*. Illustrated by David Soman. Watts, 1989 (I:3–7 R:4). A mother tells her daughter stories about when she was young.

Konigsburg, E. L. *Journey to an 800 Number*. Atheneum, 1982 (I:10+ R:6). A boy's life-style and ideas change drastically when he accompanies his father and a camel act.

_____. *The View from Saturday*. Atheneum, 1996 (I:10+ R:6). A group of sixth-grade children work together to win the Academic Bowl.

Lamb, Charles, and Mary Lamb, retold by *Tales from Shakespeare*. Illustrated by Elizabeth Shippen Green Elliott. Crown, 1988 (I:8+). Shakespeare's plays are retold for younger readers.

Lang, Andrew. *The Red Fairy Book*. Illustrated by H. J. Ford and Lancelot Speed. McGraw-Hill, 1967 (I:all R:6). This is a recent edition of the classic fairy tale book first published in 1890.

Levine, Ellen. *Freedom's Children: Young Civil Rights Activists Tell Their Own Stories*. Putnam's, 1993 (I:all) First-person narratives written by children who experienced the 1950s & 1960s.

Levine, Gail Carson. *Ella Enchanted*. HarperCollins, 1997 (I:10+ R:6). The novel expands the Cinderella story.

Levitin, Sonia. *Nine for California*. Illustrated by Cat Bowman Smith. Orchard, 1996 (I:5–8 R:4). The setting is the late 1800s.

Lewis, C. S. *The Lion, the Witch and the Wardrobe*. Illustrated by Pauline Baynes. Macmillan, 1950 (I:9+ R:7). Four children enter Narnia through a wardrobe.

Lisle, Janet Taylor. *Afternoon of the Elves*. Watts, 1989 (I:10+ R:5). Two children gain understanding as they work on a miniature village.

Lowry, Lois. *The Giver*. Houghton Mifflin, 1993 (I:10+ R:5). A boy learns the truth about his society.

_____. *Number the Stars*. Houghton Mifflin, 1989 (I:8–12 R:5). A ten-year-old girl helps the Danish Resistance.

Lunn, Janet. *Shadow in Hawthorn Bay*. Scribner's Sons, 1986 (I:10+ R:5). A girl with second sight experiences prejudice in 1800s Canada.

McCully, Emily Arnold. *The Ballot Box Battle*. Knopf, 1996 (I:7–9 R:4). The setting is in the 1880s.

McCurdy, Michael, ed. *Escape from Slavery: The Boyhood of Frederick Douglass in His Own Words*. Knopf, 1994 (I:9+ R:6). This text preserves Douglass's original vocabulary and spelling.

McKinley, Robin. *The Hero and the Crown*. Greenwillow, 1984 (I:10+ R:7). Aerin faces the forces of evil during a quest.

McKissack, Patricia C. *The Dark-Thirty: Southern Tales of the Supernatural*. Illustrated by Brian Pinkney. Knopf, 1992 (I:all R:5). This is a collection of ghost stories that are rooted in African American history.

MacLachlan, Patricia. *The Facts and Fictions of Minna Pratt*. Harper & Row, 1988 (I:7–12 R:4). A girl learns to appreciate herself and her family.

———. *Mama One, Mama Two*. Illustrated by Ruth Lercher Bornstein. Harper & Row, 1982 (I:5–7 R:2). A foster mother shares a story about a girl's real mother.

———. *Sarah, Plain and Tall*. Harper & Row, 1985 (I:7–10 R:3). A frontier family longs for a mother.

Marrin, Albert. *Hitler*. Viking Kestrel, 1987 (I:10+ R:7). A biographer emphasizes Hitler's rise to power, his victories, and his final defeat.

Martin, Jacqueline Briggs. *Good Times on Grandfather Mountain*. Illustrated by Susan Gaber. Orchard, 1992 (I:4–8 R:5). A mountain man's good natured optimism helps him see the best in all situations.

Maruki, Toshi. *Hiroshima No Pika*. Lothrop, Lee, & Shepard, 1982 (I:8–12 R:4). The consequences of the Hiroshima bombing are shown in an illustrated text.

Meddaugh, Susan. *Martha Speaks*. Houghton Mifflin, 1992 (I:4–8 R:4). After eating alphabet soup, the family dog learns to speak.

Meltzer, Milton. *Rescue: The Story of How Gentiles Saved Jews in the Holocaust*. Harper & Row, 1988 (I:10+ R:6). A nonfictional source describes heroism.

———. *Thomas Jefferson: The Revolutionary Aristocrat*. Watts, 1991 (I:10+ R:6). A biography of the early president.

———, ed. *The Black Americans: A History in Their Own Words 1619–1983*. Crowell, 1984 (I:10+). Short excerpts written by people in history.

Merriam, Eve. *Halloween ABC*. Illustrated by Lane Smith. Macmillan, 1987 (I:all). Illustrations and poems about Halloween.

Mowat, Farley. *Lost in the Barrens*. Illustrated by Charles Geer. McClelland & Stewart, 1956, 1984 (I:9+ R:6). A Cree Indian boy and his friend are lost in Northern Canada.

Myers, Walter Dean. *Now Is Your Time! The African-American Struggle for Freedom*. HarperCollins, 1991 (I:10+ R:6). This is a history of the African American struggle for freedom.

Naylor, Phyllis Reynolds. *Shiloh*. Atheneum, 1991 (I:8+ R:5). A boy overcomes problems associated with animal abuse.

Ness, Evaline. *Sam, Bangs & Moonshine*. Holt, Rinehart & Winston, 1966 (I:5–9 R:3). Sam's imagination almost costs a friend his life.

North, Sterling. *Rascal*. Dutton, 1963 (I:10+ R:6). A boy makes a pet of a wild animal.

Noyes, Alfred. *The Highwayman*. Illustrated by Charles Keeping. Oxford, 1981 (I:10+). Strong black-and-white drawings complement the mood of the poem.

O'Brien, Robert C. *Mrs. Frisby and the Rats of NIMH*. Illustrated by Zena Bernstein. Atheneum, 1971 (I:8–12 R:4). Mrs. Frisby, a mouse, asks for help from a superior group of rats who are able to read.

O'Dell, Scott. *Island of the Blue Dolphins*. Houghton Mifflin, 1960 (I:10+ R:6). A girl survives alone on an island for eighteen years.

O'Neill, Catharine. *Mrs. Dunphy's Dog*. Viking, 1987 (I:3–8 R:4). A humorous text results from misinterpretations.

Orlev, Uri. *The Island on Bird Street*. Translated by Hillel Halkin. Houghton Mifflin, 1984 (I:10+ R:6). A twelve-year-old Jewish boy survives World War II in Warsaw.

———. *The Man from the Other Side*. Translated by Hillel Halkin. Houghton Mifflin, 1991 (I:10+ R:6). The book is based on a true story of a Polish journalist who helped the Jewish people during the Holocaust.

Paterson, Katherine. *Bridge to Terabithia*. Illustrated by Donna Diamond. Crowell, 1977 (I:10–14 R:6). Terabithia is the special kingdom of a boy who wishes to be an artist and a girl different from the rest of her classmates.

———. *Jacob Have I Loved*. Crowell, 1980. (I:10 R:6). A girl overcomes the belief that her younger twin sister has stolen her birthright.

Paulsen, Gary. *Hatchet*. Bradbury, 1987 (I:10+ R:6). A thirteen-year-old boy learns personal and physical survival in the Canadian wilderness.

———. *Nightjohn*. Delacorte, 1993 (I:12+ R:6). A twelve-year-old slave girl receives brutal treatment when she is taught to read.

Pearce, Philippa. *Tom's Midnight Garden*. Illustrated by Susan Einzig. Lippincott, 1958 (I:8+ R:6). In a time-warp story, a boy goes back to a garden in an earlier time.

Pienkowski, Jan. *Haunted House*. Dutton, 1979 (I:all). Movable pictures show the ghostly inhabitants.

Polacco, Patricia. *Appelemando's Dreams*. Philomel, 1991 (I:6–9 R:5). In a picture storybook, the author develops the importance of dreams.

———. *Meteor!* Dodd, Mead, 1987 (I:6–10 R:7). A humorous fictional account tells of the reactions of a town when a meteor falls to earth.

Potter, Beatrix. *A Treasury of Peter Rabbit and Other Stories*. Avenel, 1979 (I:2–7 R:5). Peter has an unhappy experience in Mr. McGregor's garden.

Pullman, Philip. *The Golden Compass*. Knopf, 1996 (I:10+ R:7). A girl solves the mystery of kidnapped children in this fantasy.

———. *The Subtle Knife*. Knopf, 1997 (I:10+ R:7). This is a sequel to *The Golden Compass*.

Raskin, Ellen. *The Westing Game*. Dutton, 1978 (I:10–14 R:5). Sixteen heirs are invited to solve the riddle surrounding the death of an eccentric millionaire.

Rathmann, Peggy. *Ruby the Copycat*. Scholastic, 1991 (I:5–8 R:3). A young girl discovers her own identity.

Rodowsky, Colby. *Sydney Herself*. Farrar, Straus & Giroux, 1989 (I:11+ R:6). A journal helps a girl make discoveries about herself.

Rogasky, Barbara. *Smoke and Ashes: The Story of the Holocaust*. Holiday House, 1988 (I:10+ R:6). A history tells of the Holocaust.

Rylant, Cynthia. *Appalachia: The Voices of Sleeping Birds*. Illustrated by Barry Moser. Harcourt Brace Jovanovich, 1991 (I:all R:5). A warm mood is created through the illustrations and descriptions of the people and the setting.

———. *A Fine White Dust*. Bradbury, 1986 (I:10+ R:6). A thirteen-year-old boy faces challenges to his religious beliefs.

———. *The Islander*. DK, 1998 (I:10+ R:6). Set in British Columbia, a boy overcomes feelings of being a loner.

———. *Missing May*. Orchard, 1992 (I:10+ R:6). Set in West Virginia, a girl and her uncle try to overcome the grief associated with the death of her beloved aunt.

_____. *When I Was Young in the Mountains*. Illustrated by Diane Goode. Dutton, 1982 (I:4–7 R:3). A young girl remembers special childhood experiences such as her grandmother's corn bread and going to the swimming hole.

Salisbury, Graham. *Under the Blood-Red Sun*. Doubleday, 1995 (I:10+ R:5). This historical fiction is set in Hawaii in 1941.

Scieszka, Jon. *The Stinky Cheese Man and Other Fairly Stupid Tales*. Illustrated by Lane Smith. Viking, 1992 (I:all R:4). Through adaptations of traditional folktales, the author creates stories such as "The Other Frog Prince," "Little Red Running Shorts," and "Jack's Bean Problem."

Sendak, Maurice. *Where the Wild Things Are*. Harper & Row, 1963 (I:4–8 R:6). A room turns into an imaginative world.

Seredy, Kate. *The White Stag*. Viking, 1937; Puffin, 1979 (I:10–14 R:7). An epic story tells of the Huns and Magyars as they migrate from Asia to Europe.

Sherman, Josepha, retold by *Vassilisa the Wise: A Tale of Medieval Russia*. Illustrated by Daniel San Souci. Harcourt Brace Jovanovich, 1988 (I:6–10 R:5). A clever and courageous female outwits the prince.

Snyder, Dianne. *The Boy of the Three-Year Nap*. Illustrated by Allen Say. Houghton Mifflin, 1988 (I:4–9 R:4). A Japanese tale tells about a lazy son and his resourceful mother.

Speare, Elizabeth George. *The Sign of the Beaver*. Houghton Mifflin, 1983 (I:8–12 R:5). A boy survives in a frontier cabin after an Indian friend teaches him survival techniques.

_____. *The Witch of Blackbird Pond*. Houghton Mifflin, 1958 (I:9–14 R:4). Kit Tyler leaves her island home and rapidly comes into conflict with the Puritan way of life in colonial New England.

Sperry, Armstrong. *Call It Courage*. Macmillan, 1940 (I:9–13 R:6). A Polynesian boy travels alone in an outrigger canoe to overcome his fear of the sea.

Spinelli, Jerry. *Wringer*. HarperCollins, 1997 (I:9+ R:4). A boy develops courage when he goes against the actions of his friends.

Steptoe, John. *Mufaro's Beautiful Daughters: An African Tale*. Lothrop, Lee & Shepard, 1987 (I:all R:4). An African folktale has some Cinderella elements.

Stolz, Mary. *Cezanne Pinto: A Memoir*. Knopf, 1994 (I:10+ R:6). A boy and a woman travel the Underground Railroad to freedom.

Strachan, Ian. *Flawed Glass*. Little, Brown, 1990 (I:10+ R:6). A physically handicapped girl learns to appreciate her true worth and overcomes her person-against-self conflict.

Taback, Simms. *There Was An Old Lady Who Swallowed A Fly*. Viking, 1997 (I:all). The humorous illustrations reinforce the ridiculous situation.

Taylor, Mildred D. *Roll of Thunder, Hear My Cry*. Dial, 1976 (I:10+ R:6). A black Mississippi family in 1933 experiences humiliating and frightening situations but retains its pride and independence.

Taylor, Theodore. *The Cay*. Doubleday, 1969 (I:8–12 R:6). A prejudiced young white boy and a black West Indian are shipwrecked on a barren Caribbean island.

Tolkien, J. R. R. *The Hobbit*. Houghton Mifflin, 1938 (I:9–12 R:6). Bilbo Baggins, a hobbit, joins forces with dwarfs in a quest to overthrow the evil dragon.

Treece, Henry. *The Magic Wood*. Illustrated by Barry Moser. HarperCollins, 1992 (I:8+). The illustrations enhance the frightening mood of the poem.

Trivizas, Eugene. *The Three Little Wolves and the Big Bad Pig*. Illustrated by Helen Oxenbury. Macmillan, 1993. (I:4–8 R:5). In a twist on the folktale, the pig is the villain.

Turner, Megan Whalen. *The Thief*. Greenwillow, 1996 (I:11+ R:6). In a country similar to ancient Greece, a thief searches for an important object in a hidden temple.

Voigt, Cynthia. *Bad Girls*. Scholastic, 1996 (I:9+ R:7). Two fifth-grade girls get into trouble.

_____. *Dicey's Song*. Atheneum, 1982 (I:10+ R:5). Dicey learns about her own possibilities as she takes care of her brothers and sister.

Vos, Ida. *Hide and Seek*. Translated by Terese Edelstein and Inez Smidt. Houghton Mifflin, 1991 (I:8–12 R:5). The setting is the antagonist in this person-against-society conflict set in World War II.

Wells, Rosemary. *Max's Chocolate Chicken*. Dial, 1989 (I:2–6). Two rabbits share an Easter experience.

_____. *BunnyCakes*. Dial, 1997 (I:2–6). The bunnies make cakes for Grandma's birthday.

White, E. B. *Charlotte's Web*. Illustrated by Garth Williams. Harper & Row, 1952 (I:7–11 R:3). Charlotte saves Wilbur's life.

_____. *Trumpet of the Swan*. Puffin, 1970 (I:7–11 R:5). This is another of White's enjoyable animal fantasies.

White, Ruth. *Belle Prater's Boy*. Farrar, Straus & Giroux, 1996 (I:10+ R:6). Two children discover how to face the truth in their lives.

White, T. H. *The Sword in the Stone*. Collins, 1938 (I:10+ R:7). This is the story of Arthur before he became king.

Wild, Margaret. *Our Granny*. Illustrated by Julie Vivas. Ticknor & Fields, 1994 (I:3–6 R:5) Text and illustrations present many types of grandmothers.

Wilder, Laura Ingalls. *Little House in the Big Woods*. Harper & Row, 1932 (I:8–12 R:6). The first book in a series is about family life on the American frontier, told from a girl's viewpoint.

Williams, Margery. *The Velveteen Rabbit*. Illustrated by William Nicholson. Doubleday, 1958 (I:6–9 R:5). A toy rabbit is given life after he faithfully serves a child.

Williams, Vera B. *Stringbean's Trip to the Shining Sea*. Illustrated by Vera B. Williams and Jennifer Williams. Greenwillow, 1988 (I:5–10). Postcards and illustrations show a summer vacation.

Yolen, Jane. *The Devil's Arithmetic*. Viking Kestrel, 1988 (I:8+ R:5). In a time-warp story, a Jewish girl finds herself in World War II.

Yorinks, Arthur. *Hey, Al*. Illustrated by Richard Egielski. Farrar, Straus & Giroux, 1986 (I:all). A janitor discovers that his home is better than he thinks.

Reprinted with the permission of Simon & Schuster Books for Young Readers, an imprint of Simon & Schuster's Children's Publishing Division from *Zin! Zin! Zin! A Violin* by Lloyd Moss, illustrated by Marjorie Priceman. Illustrations copyright © 1995 Marjorie Priceman.

4 *Artists and Their Illustrations*

 Understanding Artists and Their Illustrations

- Visual Elements: The Grammar of Artists
- Design: Organizing the Visual Elements
- Artistic Media
- Artistic Style
- Evaluating the Illustrations in Children's Books
- Outstanding Illustrators of Children's Books

 Involving Children with Artists and Their Illustrations

- Aesthetic Scanning
- Visual Literacy
- Studying Historic Books and Illustrations
- Studying Inspirations for Art
- Investigating the Works of Great Artists

Understanding Artists and Their Illustrations

Writers create compelling stories by arranging words; artists arrange visual elements to create pictures that complement stories. A visual grammar consists of the elements of line, color, shape, and texture. Artists who organize these elements into unified wholes create visual designs that convey meaning.

Line

Artists use line to suggest direction, motion, energy, and mood. Lines can be thin or wide, light or heavy, feathery or jagged, straight or curved. H. W. Janson and Anthony F. Janson (1995) maintain that line is the most basic visual element. They state, "A majority of art is initially conceived in terms of contour line. Its presence is often implied even when it is not actually used to describe form" (p. 17). According to these authorities in art and art history, drawings represent line in its purest form and artists commonly treat drawing as a form of note taking. Artists such as Michelangelo based their finished art on carefully developed drawings, but line is also extremely important in children's book illustration. According to Edmund Burke Feldman (1972), line is the most crucial visual element for several reasons:

1. Line is familiar to virtually everyone because of experience with drawing and writing.
2. Line is definite, assertive, intelligible (although its windings and patternings may be infinitely complex); it is precise and unambiguous; it commits artists to specific statements.
3. Line conveys meaning through its identification with natural phenomena.
4. Line leads the eye and involves viewers in the line's "destiny."
5. Line permits eyes to do as children do when getting to know the world: handle objects and feel their contours. The outlines of things eventually become more important than their color, size, or texture as means of identifying them.

Feldman's discussion of the relationship between line and natural phenomena is especially interesting to people involved with children and the illustrations

Many young children mention the illustrations when asked what attracted them to a book. The bright colors of an East African setting may entice children into searching for camouflaged animals. Jagged lines and dark colors may excite children with the prospect of dangerous adventures, while delicate lines and pastel colors may set children to dreaming about fairyland. The textures in illustrations may invite children to "feel" a bear's fur or an eagle's feathers. In these and many other ways, illustrations are integral to picture books for young children. Outstanding artists illustrate books for older children—such as Laura Ingalls Wilder's "Little House" series—but in such books, the text can stand on its own. In picture books, however, the illustrations join the text in telling the stories.

This chapter discusses the visual elements, media, and styles used by illustrators of all books for children, but it focuses on the special requirements of picture books. It suggests criteria for evaluating illustrations in picture books, provides examples of high-quality books, and looks at some outstanding illustrators to see how they create memorable picture books.

found in literature for them. Experiences with common natural phenomena may help children relate meaningfully to works of art. Vertical lines, for example, look like trees in a windless landscape or like people who stand rather than move. Consequently, they suggest lack of movement.

Horizontal lines, such as the surface of a placid lake or a flat horizon, suggest calm, sleep, stability, and an absence of strife. Most young children use a horizontal baseline in their drawings to convey the idea of the firm ground upon which they walk.

Vertical lines and horizontal lines joined at right angles depict artificial elements that differ considerably from the natural world of irregular and approximate shapes. Two vertical lines connected by a horizontal line at the top give the feeling of a solid, safe place: a doorway, house, or building.

In contrast, diagonal lines suggest loss of balance and uncontrolled motion—unless they form a triangle that rests on a horizontal base, which suggests safety. In both human design and nature, jagged lines have connotations of breakdown and destruction. Consequently, jagged lines suggest danger.

People see curved lines as fluid because of their resemblance to the eddies, whirlpools, and concentric ripples in water. Because of this, circles and curved lines seem less definite and predictable than do straight lines.

In *The Girl Who Loved Wild Horses,* Paul Goble uses line effectively to depict the natural setting of a Native American folktale. Goble introduces readers to the main character as she goes down to the river at sunrise to watch the wild horses. The illustration shows a calm, nonthreatening scene. The lines of the horses' legs are vertical, since the horses are quietly drinking from the river. The calm mood is supplemented by the reflections in the water; not even a ripple breaks the tranquillity.

On the next page, the girl rests in a meadow close to home. Goble illustrates the triangular shapes of teepees sitting securely on the ground. The text relates, however, a rumble while the girl sleeps. The outlines of the clouds suggest this break in a peaceful afternoon: they are still rounded, but they are also heavy, with protrusions jutting into the sky.

Movement in the story and the illustrations becomes more pronounced as lightning flashes and as the horses rear and snort in terror. Sharp lines of lightning extend from black, rolling clouds to the ground.

Even the lines of the plants are diagonal, suggesting dangerous wind as the horses gallop away in front of the storm. When night falls and the storm is over, the tired girl and horses stop to rest. Goble illustrates the hills with vertical lines connected by horizontal lines, suggesting the new feeling of safety and shelter under the moon and the stars.

In contrast to Paul Goble's depiction of familiar natural phenomena, the soft, delicate lines of Marcia Brown's illustrations for Charles Perrault's *Cinderella* create a mythical kingdom that could exist only "once upon a time." The drawing of Cinderella's fairy godmother transforming her into a beautiful princess has an ethereal quality, as if the scene were floating on air. Because these illustrations seem to be almost as diaphanous and changeable as clouds, viewers are not surprised when a pumpkin turns into a coach and a rat becomes the driver of the coach. Even the architecture has a magical quality. Delicately curved windows, softly flowing draperies, and graceful pillars provide fitting backgrounds for a favorite fairy tale.

Marjorie Priceman's illustrations for Lloyd Moss's *Zin! Zin! Zin! A Violin* create a flowing movement and a feeling that matches the text. For example, on the page in which the text reads, "And soaring high and moving in, With Zin! Zin! Zin! A Violin" (unnumbered), the violinist seems to float across the pages. Even the cats illustrated in the top of the illustration create a similar flowing movement as they chase a mouse across the page.

Both Mary Barrett Brown and Ruth Sanderson use contrasting lighter and heavier lines in illustrations. In *Tiger with Wings: The Great Horned Owl* by Barbara Juster Esbensen, Brown supports Esbensen's text, which compares the horned owl and a tiger as fierce hunters. The accompanying illustration shows a tiger, drawn in almost transparent lines, following the horned owl, drawn with heavier dark lines. In *The Nativity: From the Gospels of Matthew and Luke,* Sanderson illustrates almost transparent angels appearing above the shepherds, who are depicted on the solid ground. By using contrasting lines, both illustrators suggest a mystical connection.

In *The Highwayman,* Charles Keeping's illustrations for Alfred Noyes's ghost poem create quite a different mood. Stark black lines create ghostly, terrifying subjects and suggest sinister and disastrous consequences. Several of Roberto Innocenti's

Line and color combine to create a feeling of impending danger and terror. Notice the heavy black clouds with circular lines and jagged lightning. The diagonal lines of the horses' legs and manes complement the mood. (From the book The Girl Who Loved Wild Horses *by Paul Goble. Reprinted with permission of Bradbury Press, Inc., an affiliate of Macmillan. Copyright © 1978 by Paul Gobel.)*

illustrations for Charles Dickens's *Christmas Carol* use thin white lines against a darker background to depict the ghostly apparitions that visit Mr. Scrooge.

In *Michael Foreman's Mother Goose,* Michael Foreman uses line to suggest movement and to take viewers into the next picture. Soldiers or animals move from one page to the next, lines continue on the next illustration, and hills or houses introduced on one page become the source for the action on the next page. Many of Errol Le Cain's illustrations for T. S. Eliot's *Mr. Mistoffelees with Mungojerrie and Rumpelteazer* suggest the movement and vitality associated with the eccentric cats.

Even invisible lines, or suggestions of lines, have impact in illustrations. Lyn Ellen Lacy (1986) emphasizes the role of invisible vertical and horizontal lines as directional influences. For example, when analyzing pages 43 and 44 in Robert McCloskey's *Make Way for Ducklings,* Lacy states:

Tethered to a top coat button, the whistle manages to fly behind Michael like a free pixie spirit. It points in the direction opposite Michael's intended hasty path. Literally, it points toward the townscape; figuratively, it points our way back into the picture in case we missed something. We do not then turn the page too soon, but instead we follow the whistle's path of gesture along an invisible line, back into the maze of buildings whose vertical lines have a downward thrust to the sidewalk. This underlying structure in the picture is a gentle reminder that there are minute spots on the sidewalk. McCloskey did not want us to miss them. (p. 47)

The minute spots prove to be mother duck and her ducklings.

Color

Color plays an extremely important role in illustration. Janson and Janson (1995) contrast the role of line and color when they state, "The role of color in art rests primarily on its sensuous and emotive appeal, in contrast to the more cerebral quality generally associated with line" (p. 19).

Combining line and color is perhaps the most common way in which artists convey mood and emotion in picture books. Describing picture books of the 1990s, Dilys Evans (1992) emphasizes the roles of line and color in the illustrations of David Wiesner, Lane Smith, and David Wisniewski. Evans states, "Now the world of children's book illustration is witnessing bold new visual voices as they surface upon the page with bright vibrating color, strong black containing lines, and a new reverence for black as color" (p. 760).

Many colors are associated with natural phenomena. Reds, yellows, and oranges are most associated with fire, sun, and blood, and they usually have warm or hot connotations: friendliness, high energy, or anger. Blues, greens, and some violets are most associated with air, water, and plant life, and their coolness or coldness can suggest moods and emotions ranging from tranquillity to melancholy.

To evaluate an illustrator's use of color, consider how well the color language of the artist conveys or complements the mood, characters, setting, and theme that the writer develops in words. Marcia Brown complements the delicate lines in her illustrations for Charles Perrault's *Cinderella* by using soft pastels, bringing a shimmering radiance to the pictures. In contrast, Paul Goble uses bright colors and black, in addition to strong line, to illustrate a desert setting and the tension and movement of animals and forces of nature in *The Girl Who Loved Wild Horses*.

Color can reflect the mood of a story. In *Ox-Cart Man*, Barbara Cooney uses pastels and muted hues of darker colors to translate Donald Hall's gentle story about a quieter time in American history. Cooney portrays the hills of rural New England in the early 1800s as gentle curves of green, gray, and blue. The deep rusts, blues, and greens of the clothing look authentic for the time period.

Cooney's color choices also show the passing of time. When the farmer begins his journey over hills and past villages, the countryside is aflame with the rusts and oranges of fall. When he reaches Portsmouth, the trees have only a few brown leaves. As he returns home, a soft, brown land awaits the first snowfall. The scene turns white in winter. Then, soft greens cover the hills before the trees explode with white and pink apple blossoms. One child said that the pictures made her feel homesick because she had lived in an area that had hills, valleys, quiet farms, and distinct seasons. In Michael Bedard's *Emily* and Jane Yolen's *Letting Swift River Go,* Cooney also uses colors that reflect the settings and times. Many readers of *Ox-Cart Man* mention its feeling of tranquillity. Cooney creates tranquillity in her illustrations for *Island Boy,* which she also wrote.

Blues and greens emphasize the cold setting in Michael Rothman's illustrations for Joanne Ryder's *White Bear, Ice Bear* and in Jon Van Zyle's illustrations for Debbie S. Miller's *A Polar Bear Journey*. Frosty whites and shades of blue and green are equally effective in Dan Guravich's photographs for Downs Matthews's *Polar Bear Cubs*. The colors in these texts reinforce the cold winds, ice, and blizzards.

Bright primary colors highlight the illustrations in Jessica Souhami's *The Leopard's Drum: An Asante Tale from West Africa*. In this retelling of an African folktale, Souhami uses bright primary colors and shapes that are very similar to paper puppets placed on sticks. According to the artist, the illustrations are adapted from the shadow puppets she uses in her oral performances of folktales. To bring a unity to the text, the various geometric designs in primary colors also illustrate the endpapers.

Rich, vivid colors attract attention and reinforce the happy mood of exploration in Denise Fleming's *In the Small, Small Pond*. Printed in deep black, the text stands out against the colorful illustrations.

Artists may use changes in color to contrast moods within a book. For example, Donald Carrick's illustrations for Eve Bunting's *Ghost's Hour, Spook's Hour* use color to create moods. The dark shades used in the early illustrations develop and reinforce the scary environment and the young boy's fear of the dark. When the father rescues his frightened son, the father is shown in an open doorway that has a warm yellow background. The warm yellows are retained as the boy is comforted by his parents and joins them in the big couch bed.

The colors in Thomas Allen's illustrations for Judith Hendershot's *In Coal Country* are appropriate for a story about growing up in a 1930s Ohio coal mining town. The impressionistic pastel and charcoal illustrations create a landscape observed through a combination of coal dust and nostalgia.

The Children of Lir *presents motifs from Irish folklore completed in watercolors. (From* The Children of Lir, *by Sheila MacGill-Callahan, illustrated by Gennady Spirin. Copyright © 1993 by Gennady Spirin, pictures. Used by permission of Dial Books for Young Readers, a division of Penguin Books USA Inc.)*

Artists may also use contrasts in illustrations to create drama and complement plot. Helen Oxenbury's illustrations for Michael Rosen's *We're Going on a Bear Hunt* alternate between black and white and color. On the pages with black-and-white illustrations, the characters chant the portion of the bear hunt that they are about to experience. The color illustrations show the family swishing through long grass, splashing across a river, squishing in mud, and stumbling through a dark forest.

A totally different mood may be created by black-and-white paintings. For example, in a book for older readers, *The Middle Passage: White Ships/Black Cargo,* Tom Feelings uses white tempera paint, black ink, and wet tissue paper to create the emotions and characteristics of the people associated with a slave ship and the human cargo. By studying these illustrations, viewers proceed from the mystical and idyllic homeland of the Africans to their cruel experiences on the ship to the final landing of the ship in America. All of the moods and emotions associated with the passage are reflected in the illustrator's black-and-white illustrations.

Shape

Lines join and intersect to suggest shapes, and areas of color meet to produce shapes. Organic shapes, irregular and curving, are common in nature and in handmade objects. Geometric shapes—exact, rigid, and often rectangular—usually have mechanical origins. As discussed in relation to line, different shapes have different connotations. Illustrators may use organic, free-form shapes to convey anything from receptivity and imagination to frightening unpredictability. They may use geometric shapes to connote complexity, stability, assertion, or severity.

Gerald McDermott, illustrator and author of *Arrow to the Sun,* uses traditional Native American patterns of line and color to create shapes that draw readers into a desert world where humans, nature, and spiritual forces intertwine. Rich yellow, orange, and brown rectangles depict the pueblo home of the people. This building constructed by humans from natural materials is separated by a black void from the circular orange and yellow sun, which is the people's god. The people worship this god in the kiva, a circular ceremonial chamber. A rectangular ray from the sun to the pueblo represents the spark of life that becomes the sun god's earthly son. He is illustrated as a black and yellow rectangle, while his mother's form is more circular. Black and yellow rectangles predominate in the illustrations until the son decides to search for his father and takes on the sun's power as well as the rainbow of colors available to the sun. He returns to earth as an arrow, and his people, now illustrated in all of the colors that he has brought with him, celebrate with the dance of life.

Shape and color are also important in the illustrations for Paul Owen Lewis's *Storm Boy*. The bold paintings and shapes reflect the cultures and the graphic art of the Haida, Tlingit, and other native peoples from the Pacific Northwest.

A person's shape says much about self-image. In *Crow Boy*, Taro Yashima uses line and color to create shapes that emphasize a small boy's growth from fright and alienation to self-confidence. Yashima first draws the boy as a small, huddled shape isolated from his classmates in white space. As an understanding teacher helps Crow Boy become more self-assured, his shape on the page becomes larger, more outreaching, and closer to the shapes of other characters. Yashima also stresses Crow Boy's transformation by outlining his new form with shades of white that suggest shimmering light.

Shape provides the most important element in alphabet books such as David Pelletier's *The Graphic Alphabet* and Stephen T. Johnson's *Alphabet City*. In *The Graphic Alphabet*, Pelletier relates the shape of the letters to meaning. For example, the letter *f* reflects the meaning of *fire* by showing red flames emerging from the top of the letter. There is no text in *Alphabet City*. Consequently, all of the paintings reflect the shapes of various letters of the alphabet.

Shape is another way to emphasize the mood of a picture and story. According to illustrator Uri Shulevitz (1985), two areas are related to shape and mood: (1) the overall form of an illustration if viewed as a silhouette (with no interior details) and (2) the edges of the picture, which can be hard, soft, jagged, or straight. Shulevitz states that symmetrical picture shapes, such as rectangles, squares, circles, and

Geometric shapes and sunny colors give a powerful feeling to a Native American tale from the southwestern United States. (From Arrow to the Sun *by Gerald McDermott. Copyright © 1974 by Gerald McDermott. Used by permission of Viking Penguin, a division of Penguin Books USA Inc.)*

ovals, are calm and solid, while asymmetrical picture shapes are unbalanced, irregular, and dynamic.

To evaluate the impact of shape on mood in illustrated books, analyze several recent award-winning books and books on the Children's Literature Association's touchstone list. Consider David Wisniewski's illustrations for *Golem*, David Diaz's illustrations for Eve Bunting's *Smoky Night*, Stephen Gammell's illustrations for Karen Ackerman's *Song and Dance Man*, John Schoenherr's illustrations for Jane Yolen's *Owl Moon*, Richard Egielski's illustrations for Arthur Yorinks's *Hey,*

For one minute,
three minutes,
maybe even a hundred minutes,
we stared at one another.

Lines and color re-create the texture of an owl. (From Owl Moon *by Jane Yolen. Illustrated by John Schoenherr, text copyright 1987, by Jane Yolen, illustrations © 1987 by John Schoenherr. Reprinted by permission of Philomel books.)*

Al, Emily Arnold McCully's illustrations for *Mirette on the High Wire,* Paul O. Zelinsky's illustrations for Grimm's *Rapunzel,* David Small's illustrations for Sarah Stewart's *The Gardener,* and Simms Taback's illustrations for *There Was An Old Lady Who Swallowed A Fly.* Earlier illustrated books on the touchstone list include Robert McCloskey's *Make Way for Ducklings,* Dr. Seuss's *The 500 Hats of Bartholomew Cubbins,* L. Leslie Brooke's *Johnny Crow's Garden,* Kate Greenaway's *A: Apple Pie,* Walter Crane's *The Baby's Opera,* and Wanda Gág's *Millions of Cats.* Do the shapes reinforce the moods of these texts?

Texture

Looking at an object for the first time, a child usually wants to touch it to know how it feels. Experience in touching rough bark, smooth skin, sharp thorns,

and soft fur enables children later to imagine how something feels without actually touching it. Illustrators use such visual elements as line, color, and shape to create textural imagery.

Frequently, illustrators who depict the wonders of nature use line to show texture in their illustrations. In Jane Yolen's *Owl Moon,* John Schoenherr (1988) re-creates the texture of the woods outside his studio windows. Viewers can almost feel the tree trunks, the snow-covered landscapes, the small animals peeking from behind trees, and the ultimate owl.

In *Bear,* Schoenherr reproduces the hide of an angry moose and the fur on the hungry bear. In contrast, his stream imparts the impression of cool, smooth water. Animal fur, corn husks, and corn silks are important textures that bring to life Janet Stevens's *Tops & Bottoms.* Viewers can describe the feel of the lazy bear's fur, the corn husks, and the silk protruding from each ear of corn. Raven's feathers, bear's fur, and tree bark are all vicariously felt in Jon Van Zyle's illustrations for Nancy White Carlstrom's *Raven and River.*

The bird paintings in *Roger Tory Peterson's ABC of Birds: A Book for Little Birdwatchers,* written by Linda Westervelt, create the feeling of feathers. The texture is particularly noticeable in the paintings of the owls and the meadowlark. The textures in the painting of the roadrunner include the feathers on the bird, the needles on the cacti, and the smooth, silky flowers blooming on the plants.

In *The Story of Jumping Mouse,* Steptoe uses line and shades of black and white to create textures ranging from sharp spikes on cacti to delicate petals on flowers. In Nancy Willard's *A Starlit Somersault Downhill,* Jerry Pinkney creates the winter world of bears with heavy fur, of rabbits with soft coats, of foxes with hair that stands on end, and of owls that peer from branches as they search for food.

A child's response to Kenneth Lilly's illustrations in Joyce Pope's *Kenneth Lilly's Animals: A Portfolio of Paintings* shows how effective texture can be in an informational book. The child did not want to put the book away because, "I was there with the animals. I kept touching the Koala bears to see if they were real."

 ## DESIGN: ORGANIZING THE VISUAL ELEMENTS

Design, or composition, is the way in which artists combine the visual elements of line, color, shape, and texture into a unified whole. When an illustration has an overall unity, balance, and sense of rhythm, viewers experience aesthetic pleasure; when the design is weak, viewers often feel that they are looking at an incomplete, incoherent, or boring picture.

Illustrators of children's books emphasize certain characters, develop main ideas, and provide background information. They also organize their illustrations so that viewers can identify the most important element in a picture and follow a visual sequence within the picture. Artists show dominance in their work by emphasizing size (the largest form is seen first), contrasting intense colors (an intense area of warm color dominates an intense area of cool color of the same size), placing the most important item in the center, using strong lines to provide visual pathways, and emphasizing nonconfor-

mity (viewers' eyes travel to an item that is different). When evaluating illustrations in children's books, consider whether or not the dominant images are consistent with those of the story.

Tomie dePaola achieves balance through symmetry in his illustrations for Clement Moore's *The Night Before Christmas.* The strong vertical lines of the central fireplace are reinforced by stockings hanging beneath the mantle, candles on the mantle, rows of trees in a picture over the mantle, and the legs of a chair and a table in the room. To the left and the right of the fireplace, portraits face the center of the illustration, where Santa stands on the hearth. For further emphasis, Santa's beard and the fur on his jacket are strikingly white against the rich reds and greens of the room.

Both authors and illustrators of children's books use repetition for emphasis. In illustrations, repetition can create rhythms and provide visual pathways. Virginia Lee Burton's illustrations are excellent examples of this technique. Burton's background in ballet and interest in the spatial concepts of dance may help account for her success in capturing rhythm and movement on paper. In *The Little House,* for example, Burton shows the house sitting on a hill and trees on either side. A row of trees follows the curve of several hills behind the house. On each hill are progressively smaller trees, houses, people, and animals. Beyond the last curving line of trees, the text tells us, lies the city that will soon spread out and surround the little house with traffic and skyscrapers.

Page design can provide a unifying quality. Several artists develop visual continuity by framing text pages or illustrations. Trina Schart Hyman frames each text page in Margaret Hodges's *Saint George and the Dragon* with drawings of plants that are indigenous to the British Isles. In Barbara Cohen's adaptation of Chaucer's *Canterbury Tales,* Hyman borders the illustrations with rich gold designs. Laszlo Gal borders each illustration in Eva Martin's *Canadian Fairy Tales* with lightly penciled sketches of objects chosen from the appropriate story. In *Hiawatha's Childhood,* derived from Henry Wadsworth Longfellow's famous poems, artist Errol LeCain borders each page with the tall birch trees shown in the cover illustration. Helen Davie uses Native American designs to add authenticity to the borders in Barbara Esbensen's *The Star Maiden.*

Kathy Jakobsen's borders for Reeve Lindbergh's *Johnny Appleseed* use details associated with the early American setting of the poem. Isabelle Brent's

DePaola achieves balance through symmetry. Notice the lines of the trees in the painting over the fireplace, the pictures on each side of the fireplace, and the fireplace decorations. (Copyright © 1980 by Tomie dePaola. Reprinted from The Night Before Christmas *by permission of Holiday House, Inc.)*

Repetition and line provide a visual pathway and suggest movement. (Illustration by Virginia Lee Burton from The Little House. *Copyright 1942 by Virginia Lee Demetrios. Copyright renewed 1969 by George Demetrios. Reprinted by permission of Houghton Mifflin Co.)*

illustrations for Neil Philip's retelling of *The Golden Bird* by the Brothers Grimm include gold-leaf borders that frame each text and illustration. This framing provides a unifying quality and develops a feeling of formality to this tale of a magical quest.

Jan Brett uses page design and borders to help develop the action in her stories. For example, the borders in *Berlioz the Bear* disclose what is happening in the village, while the text and the main illustrations focus on the bear and the other animals on the road.

Page and book design are especially effective when the design matches and adds to the content of the book. For example, the page design in Janet Stevens's *Tops & Bottoms* provides an interesting topic for discussion as readers consider the impact of the book's design, which is illustrated and printed from top to bottom, with the book bound at the top instead of the normal side-to-side page turning.

In addition to providing unifying qualities, page design should reflect the level of formality of the text. Lyn Ellen Lacy (1986) emphasizes choosing levels of formality or informality that are in harmony with the text. Lacy identifies five levels of formality in book and page design. As you look at total book design, analyze the impact and the appropriateness of each of the levels of formality. First, text placed opposite illustrations on adjacent pages is considered the most formal arrangement. *Saint George and the Dragon,* by Margaret Hodges, has such an arrangement. Each text page is blocked in black type and surrounded by a formal border. To add to this formal feeling, each illustrated page is also bounded by a consistent border. The resulting text provides the formal feeling of a traditional legend. Likewise, in *Fables,* Arnold Lobel carefully balances the text and illustrations on facing pages and places them within a border.

Second, text positioned above or beneath illustrations is considered formal. The text for Sid Fleischman's *The Scarebird* is consistently placed under Peter Sis's illustrations. Notice how texts such as *The Scarebird* and Donald Hall's *Ox-Cart Man* still appear formal but not so formal as *Saint George and the Dragon* and *Fables.*

Third, text shaped with irregular boundaries to fit inside, between, around, or to the side of illustrations is considered informal. For example, notice how the text is shaped in Virginia Lee Burton's *The Little House* or in Wanda Gág's *Millions of Cats.*

Fourth, text combined with two or more arrangements is very informal. Julian Scheer's *Rain Makes Applesauce* is a good example of a very informal arrangement. The text is printed in different forms, colors, and sizes, and it appears to be part of Marvin Bileck's illustrations. This level of informality seems appropriate for a nonsense poem.

Finally, lack of text, such as in wordless books and almost-wordless books, is considered the most informal. *Will's Mammoth,* with Rafe Martin's text and Stephen Gammell's illustrations, has such a level of informality. The words that introduce an imaginary experience are printed in different sizes and colors. The illustrations then continue the story wordlessly. Words again written in different sizes and colors conclude the story. This combination is appropriate for a text that encourages imaginative play. As you look at page design, consider the different responses that are possible.

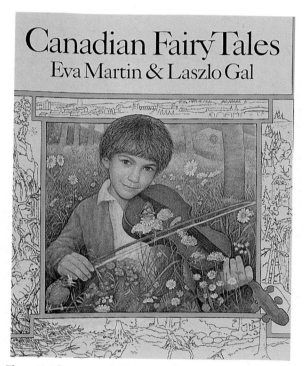

The artist frames each illustration with sketches of objects found in the fairy tale. (From Canadian Fairy Tales, published as Tales from the Far North, by Eva Martin and Laszlo Gal. Illustrated by Laszlo Gal. Copyright © 1984 by Laszlo Gal. Reprinted by permission of Farrar, Straus & Giroux.)

The elements of line, color, shape, and texture are expressed through the materials and techniques that artists use in illustrating. Ink, wood, paper, paint, and other media can create a wide variety of visual effects. Artist Harry Borgman (1979) indicates a few of the possibilities in stating his own preferences:

If I want a bright, translucent wash tone, I would either use watercolor or dyes. For an opaque paint that is water resistant, I would use acrylics. If I want to draw a line that will dissolve a bit when water is washed over it, I would use a Pentel Sign pen. (p. 113)

Borgman's remarks suggest the importance of choosing the media and artistic techniques most appropriate for conveying characterization, setting, and mood in a particular story.

Lines and Washes

Many illustrations discussed in this chapter rely on lines drawn in ink to convey meaning and develop the mood. For example, the crisp lines and repetition in Wanda Gág's pen-and-ink drawings help readers visualize and believe in a world inhabited by *Millions of Cats,* each of which has special qualities appealing to an old man.

Ink is a versatile medium. It may be applied with brush, sponge, cloth, or even fingers, as well as with pen. According to Norman Laliberté and Alex Mogelon (1976), what often emerges is "a terribly direct, strong, and uncompromising statement of the nature of our time and the talent of the artist. The very character of ink is challenging, demanding and a spur to experimentation and creativity. It is a bold form of expression, sparkling clean because it is so definite and positive" (p. 43).

In most cases, an author's words inspire the illustrator, but Tom Feelings's sensitive drawings of children inspired the accompanying poetry written by Nikki Grimes in *Something on My Mind.* Feelings's black-and-white drawings portray the loneliness, fear, sorrow, and hope that children experience while growing up. The backgrounds in the illustrations are also superb. Heavy black wrought-iron gates, lighter picket fences, an old Victorian house, and apartment-house steps provide believable settings and atmospheres for children's wishful thinking.

Artists also use varying qualities of pen-and-ink line to convey emotions corresponding to characterizations in books. Ray Cruz's drawings for Judith Viorst's *Alexander and the Terrible, Horrible, No Good, Very Bad Day* communicate the essence of a boy who experiences unhappy and frustrating emotions. The scowling expressions and hair on end convey the spirit of a boy who has lost his best friend and doesn't have any dessert in his lunch box.

Shades of water-thinned ink, sparely drawn figures, and textured paper suggest a traditional Japanese setting in Sumiko Yagawa's *The Crane Wife.* Illustrator Suekichi Akaba's traditional Japanese painting techniques complement the story of a transformed crane who rewards a poor farmer for his care but returns to animal form when the young man becomes greedy and breaks his promise.

Watercolors, Acrylics, Pastels, and Oils

Watercolor is one of the most common artistic media chosen by illustrators of children's books. According to art director Lucy Bitzer (1992), "The opportunities offered by the luminous and transparent hues of the watercolor medium make this form a pliant choice to evoke mood, mystery, and timelessness. Specifically, it allows the structure of descriptive drawing to hold its own against a color style" (p. 227). Bitzer identifies Arthur Rackham, who illustrated books in the late 1800s and early 1900s, as one of the first illustrators to recognize the transparent qualities obtainable with watercolors. Edmund Dulac was another early artist who used watercolors, especially when illustrating folktales.

Watercolor can be applied in various ways—from thin, transparent washes to thick pigments. The choice depends on the effect that the artist wishes to create. A mythical setting is provided by Cheng-Khee Chee's watercolors for Douglas Wood's *Old Turtle.* The soft colors seem to promote a close relationship between the earth and the beings who inhabit it.

David Wiesner's *Tuesday* is an excellent example of watercolors in illustration. The paintings go from the transparency of a curtain to the heavy leaves and trees of the outdoors setting. Likewise, the lighting changes from dark shadows to brilliant moonlight. In Sheila MacGill-Callahan's *The Children of Lir,* Gennady Spirin also creates different effects with watercolors, ranging from the rich textures of sheaves of grain to the transparent feeling of ocean foam. A similar feeling is de-

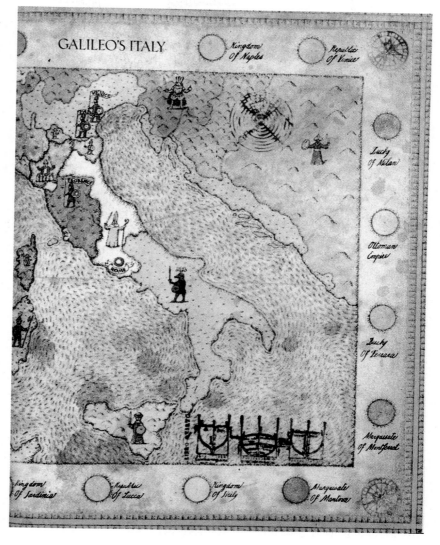

Watercolors, pen, and rubberstamp provide detailed illustrations for Peter Sis's Starry Messenger: Galileo Galilei. *(From Starry Messenger, text and illustrations by Peter Sis, copyright © 1996. Reprinted by permission of Farrar, Straus & Giroux, Inc.)*

veloped in Spirin's illustrations for Aaron Shepard's *The Sea King's Daughter: A Russian Legend.* In Frances Ward Weller's *I Wonder If I'll See a Whale,* Ted Lewin's illustrations contrast the colors of life above the sea and the blues and greens of life below the sea. Several pictures create a feeling of looking through the water with its levels of color and changes in current. Michael Foreman uses watercolors to depict the moods of the sea in *Seal Surfer.* A very different setting is created by Uri Shulevitz's use of watercolors in Ehud Ben-Ezer's *Hosni the Dreamer: An Arabian Tale.* Now watercolors create the hues of the desert. Watercolors seem appropriate for creating these settings.

The effects of three color media—watercolors, pastels, and acrylics—are seen in Leo and Diane Dillon's illustrations for Margaret Musgrove's *Ashanti to Zulu: African Traditions.* Vibrantly colored jewelry and designs on artifacts contrast with the soft shades of the flowing garments. The river in the illustration that depicts the Lozi people is so transparent that the bottom of the boat shimmers through the water. In other pictures, the sky vibrates with heat from the sun and jewel-like tones express the breathtaking beauty of exotic birds and plants.

According to an interview with Marisa Bulzone (1993), illustrator Gary Kelley is inspired by oil

Strong line and repetition in pencil-and-ink drawings complement a story. (Illustration by Wanda Gág from Millions of Cats. *Copyright 1928; renewed 1956, by Wanda Gág. Reprinted by permission of Coward McCann & Geoghegan, Inc.)*

paintings, but he creates his works in pastels. Kelley used pastels in the illustrations for Washington Irving's *The Legend of Sleepy Hollow* because he was influenced by the paintings of John Singleton Copley, Charles Wilson Peale, and the Hudson River and Naive schools of painting. He states, "I wanted my illustrations to reflect their color palettes and the way these painters handled similar subject matter" (p. 96). As you look at illustrations by Gary Kelley, try to analyze how he was influenced by oil paintings.

Paul O. Zelinsky's full-page oil paintings create a somber mood for *Hansel and Gretel,* as told by the Brothers Grimm. Zelinsky's woods are menacing, where evil is likely to exist. The rich highlights that are possible with oil are shown in Zelinsky's illustrations for Brothers Grimm's *Rumpelstiltskin* and *Rapunzel.* Likewise, Thomas Locker's full-page oil paintings for Jean Craighead George's *The First Thanksgiving* show the shadings, highlights, colors, and textures possible with oils. Lane Smith (1993), the illustrator of Jon Scieszka's *The True Story of the 3 Little Pigs!* and *The Stinky Cheese Man and Other Fairly Stupid Tales,* describes how he uses oil paint on illustrated board to acquire the desired effects:

Everything I do is oil paint on board. I get texture from a variety of means. Usually it involves some sort of acrylic paints or sprays to cause a reaction. . . . Sometimes, if the painting gets really thick, I'll sand down areas to another layer. I've always been attracted to texture. (p. 70)

Woodcuts

Woodcuts are among the oldest and most influential artistic media in both Western and Eastern cultures. In the fifteenth century, the black-and-white woodcuts of the German artist Albrecht Dürer brought this medium to a new level of sophistication in Europe. These early woodcuts, which were often drawings of animals, influenced the ways in which people saw nature and thought about it (Quammen, 1993). The first printed books, including the earliest books for children, were illustrated with black-and-white woodcuts. Later, Japanese artists pioneered in the creation of full-color woodcuts, inspiring other artists in Europe and North America, such as the famous French artist Paul Gauguin.

To create a woodcut, an artist draws an image on a block of wood and cuts away the areas around the design. After rolling ink onto this raised surface, the artist presses the woodblock against paper, transferring the image from the block to the paper. Color prints require a different woodblock for each color in the picture. Woodcuts can be printed in colors with varying degrees of transparency, and the grain and texture of the wood can add to the effect of the composition.

The strong lines and bold colors of woodcuts create a simplicity often desired by illustrators of folktales. Gail Haley used woodcuts to illustrate her version of an African folktale *A Story, a Story.* The grain

Oil paints on board create the desired textures. (From The Stinky Cheese Man and Other Fairly Stupid Tales *by Jon Scieszka and Lane Smith. Copyright © 1992 by Jon Scieszka. Reprinted by permission of Viking Penguin, a division of Penguin Books USA Inc.)*

Dark, somber tones in full-page oil paintings create an appropriately menacing setting for a dramatic folktale. (From Hansel and Gretel. *Illustrated by Paul O. Zelinsky and retold by Rika Lesser. Illustrations copyright © 1984 by Paul O. Zelinsky, Dodd Mead. Reprinted by permission.)*

of the wood replicates the texture of native huts and communicates the earthy nature of a traditional setting. The strong lines possible with woodcuts are found in Michael McCurdy's illustrations for his adaptation of the Russian folktale, *The Devils Who Learned to Be Good.* (See chapter 6 for an example of this woodcut illustration.)

Betsy Bowen's woodcuts for *Antler, Bear, Canoe: A Northwoods Alphabet Year* re-create the rough interiors of simple cabins and produce textures in woodland pictures. Helen Siegl's woodcuts illustrate Barbara K. Walker's *The Dancing Palm Tree: And Other Nigerian Folktales.* Again, the rough texture of the woodcuts seems appropriate for a collection of traditional tales.

In *Bayberry Bluff,* Blair Lent uses cardboard cuts. Cardboard cuts are similar to woodcuts or linoleum cuts, except that the designs are cut into thick cardboard with single-edged razor blades.

Collage

Collage—a word derived from the French word *coller,* meaning "to paste" or "to stick"—is a recent addition to the world of book illustration. Pasting and sticking are exactly what artists do when using this technique. Any object or substance that can be attached to a surface can be used to develop a design. Artists may use cardboard, paper, cloth, glass, leather, metal, wood, leaves, flowers, or even butterflies. They may cut up and rearrange their own paintings or use paint and other media to add background. When photographically reproduced, collages still communicate texture. In an analysis of current illustration in picture storybooks, Dilys Evans (1992) emphasizes the increased use of cut paper and collage, fabrics, plasticine, and embroidery in illustrations.

Corporal Farrell
brought the barrel,
Private Parriage
brought the carriage,
but Drummer Hoff
fired it off.

Strong lines of the woodcuts and bold colors enhance the traditional quality of this cumulative tale. (From the book Drummer Hoff *by Barbara Emberley. Illustrated by Ed Emberley. Copyright © 1967 by Edward R. Emberley and Barbara Emberley. Used by permission of the publisher, Prentice-Hall, Inc., Upper Saddle River, N.J. 07458.)*

Eric Carle, a popular artist of picture books for children, is known for his striking, colorful storybooks. *The Very Hungry Caterpillar* won the American Institute of Graphic Art's award for 1970. Carle develops his collages through a three-step process. He begins by applying acrylic paints to tissue paper. Then, he uses rubber cement to paste the paper into the desired designs. Finally, he applies colored crayon to provide accents. In *Eric Carle's Animals Animals,* tissue-paper collage creates a dazzling array of animals. In Laura Whipple's *Eric Carle's Dragons Dragons & Other Creatures That Never Were,* Carle painted onto thin tissue papers and then cut or tore the tissue papers into shapes and glued them onto the illustration boards. The painted tissue papers create smooth and silky illustrations. Carle's collages for *From Head to Toe* compare movements among animals and children. Carle's books often also include pop-ups and other features that encourage children to interact. *The Honeybee and the Robber: A Moving/Picture Book* has tabs to move a honeybee's wings, stinger, and tongue.

Another artist who illustrates with collage is Ezra Jack Keats. In *Peter's Chair,* lace looks realistic as it cascades from the inside of a bassinet. On the same page, pink wallpaper with large flowers provides the background for the baby sister's room. Keats also combines paints and collage in his illustrations,

which he used effectively in *The Trip,* where the illustrations have a three-dimensional quality appropriate for a story about a boy who builds his old neighborhood within a box and then visits it in his imagination. Photographs used in the collage illustrations in Keats's *Regards to the Man in the Moon* suggest the diversity found in one medium.

Marcia Brown uses collage and paint to match the mood of the text in Blaise Cendrars's *Shadow.* Brown's strong, dark images of the nighttime forest and her wispy ghosts strongly reinforce the spell cast by the storyteller. Drama results from Shelley Jackson's use of collage in *The Old Woman and the Wave.*

Lois Ehlert's illustrations in *Red Leaf, Yellow Leaf* show that many objects may be used in collage illustrations. In this nature book about trees, Ehlert creates a heavily textured look by using real seeds, roots, leaves, wood, grasses, shells, and fur, as well as artificial materials, in collage illustrations. In *Where the Forest Meets the Sea,* Jeannie Baker combines many natural and artificial substances to create a glorious rain forest and forest animals in North Queensland, Australia. Baker's collages in *Window* also have the heavy texture of the outdoor setting.

Illustrators use numerous materials to acquire three-dimensional pictures. In the illustrations for Eve Bunting's *Smoky Night,* David Diaz uses cut frag-

Go home,
build a fire.
Behold once more,
Shadow!
What is Shadow?
In the crackling coals,
is it the spark?
Light up!
The spark has no shadow.
The eye has no shadow,
but Shadow is in the eye.
It is the pupil!
Every breath stirs it to life.
It is a game.
A dance.

Collage and paint combine to create a shadowy, supernatural setting. (Illustration from Shadow *by Marcia Brown. Illustrations © 1982 Marcia Brown. Reprinted with the permission of Charles Scribner's Sons.)*

ments of glass, scattered cereals, burned matches, and jagged paper to create a feeling of confusion and terror associated with the Los Angeles riots.

Molly Bang uses natural and painted objects to create her illustrations for Sylvia Cassedy and Kunihiro Suetake's book of haiku, *Red Dragonfly on My Shoulder.* In the illustrator's note, Bang lists such objects as yams, potato chips, crab legs, and seeds because, "I wanted the pictures to have the same ease and playfulness as haiku, and the same spareness. Using pieces of ordinary life to make something special seemed appropriate" (illustrator's note). Numerous objects are also found in Javaka Steptoe's collages for *In Daddy's Arms I am Tall: African Americans Celebrating Fathers.*

David Wisniewski uses cut paper illustrations very effectively in *Rain Player,* a Mayan tale. In the author's note, Wisniewski describes his technique:

The pictures were first drawn on layout paper in pencil, then drawn more tightly with a technical pen on tracing paper. . . . Each portion was transferred to the back of col-

ored papers with carbon paper, then cut out with a #11 X-Acto blade. The pieces were assembled with double-stick photo mountings and foam tape. The finished artwork was then photographed, with each piece lit to provide the most dramatic shadows. (author's note)

You may compare Wisniewski's cut paper illustrations in *Rain Player* with those he created for *Golem,* a Jewish tale.

ARTISTIC STYLE

Every artist has a style that distinguishes his or her artistic vision from that of other artists, serving as a signature of the distinct individual. Numerous individuals, however, gravitate toward similar ways of making visual statements through the use of line, color, shape, and texture. The many different styles of visual art identified by art critics and historians are too complex for this text to discuss in detail. This section, however, considers two very general categories of artistic style, the *representational* and the *abstract.*

Representational Art

Representational art, sometimes also called realistic art, depicts subjects as they are seen in everyday life. Representational artists do not necessarily attempt to create photographically exact images of their subjects. Instead, they create compositions that clearly refer to people, objects, or natural phenomena in realistic ways. Many of the paintings and sculptures most familiar to us, such as Leonardo da Vinci's *Mona Lisa* and Auguste Rodin's *The Thinker,* are representational in style.

Since the first books for children were illustrated, the pictures in most children's books have been representational, as examples show throughout this text. Realistic imagery helps children identify with and learn more about things in their environments, giving them familiar bases from which to expand their understandings of the world. In Susan Jeffers's line-and-wash illustrations for *Three Jovial Huntsmen,* for example, children can easily identify a leaf on the tip of a dog's tongue and two humans walking through the woods. At the same time, Jeffers's use of line encourages children to discover three deer hidden among the trees.

Lynd Ward's illustrations for *The Biggest Bear* are excellent examples of the use of representational art to create the details of a realistic story. Readers can almost feel the rough shingles and unpainted siding on the buildings, and the wheat looks ripe enough to harvest. When the bear cub runs in to claim the mash prepared for the chickens, several frightened chickens look as if they will fly off the page.

Author-illustrator Holling Clancy Holling combines imaginative fiction with factual information in beautifully illustrated books that take their themes from North American history and geography. Holling's detailed realistic illustrations draw older children into both new adventure and new learning. In *Paddle-to-the-Sea,* a Native American boy in the Canadian wilderness carves a wooden canoe and "paddle person," which he launches on a journey from Lake Superior to the Atlantic Ocean. *Seabird* is an ivory gull carved by a young sailor on a whaling vessel. The gull accompanies several generations of one American family on their ocean voyages around the world. In each book, full-page realistic paintings in color encourage readers to enter the different settings of the story, while detailed black-and-white drawings on the text pages show, for example, how a sawmill turns logs into boards and how volcanoes in an ocean create islands.

Modern book illustrators, like most twentieth-century artists, have been profoundly influenced by stylistic innovations that have occurred over the last hundred years. Nineteenth-century French artist Claude Monet was among those who initiated a new approach to representational art, known as impressionism (originally a derogatory term applied by a disapproving contemporary critic). Impressionists departed from the tradition of representing the world in complex detail. Instead, they focused on the play of light over objects in the natural environment. Usually working from outdoor subjects, they experimented with breaking up colors and shapes to create an *impression* of the scintillating, changeable quality of light (Preble, 1978).

Thomas Locker's oil paintings for *Where the River Begins* reveal impressionist influences on this modern artist. Locker's magnificent landscapes shimmer with sunlight emerging through mist, the moon illuminating rushing water, and the reflection of sunset on billowing clouds.

Expressionism, a later stylistic development in representational art, uses visual elements to express artists' deepest inner feelings. Expressionist paintings by such artists as Vincent van Gogh and Edvard Munch reverberate with the rhythm of intense emotion expressed through emphatic color, texture, and

Cut paper illustrations provide color and dimension for a Mayan tale. (From Rain Player *by David Wisniewski. Copyright © 1991 by David Wisniewski. Used by permission of Clarion Books/Houghton Mifflin Co. All rights reserved.)*

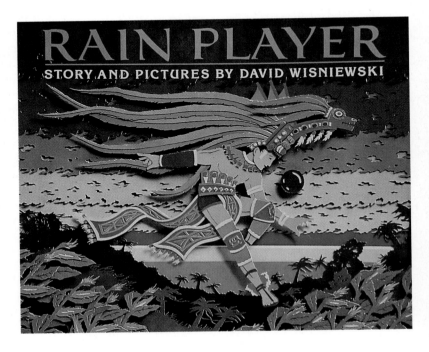

movement of line. Such art begins to move away from the representational into the more abstractly symbolic. (Later, twentieth-century artists such as Jackson Pollock developed a style known as abstract expressionism.)

Expressionistic influences are vividly evident in Toshi Maruki's illustrations for her book *Hiroshima No Pika* (*The Flash of Hiroshima*). Maruki's uses of color and shape reinforce the emotional impact of horrific devastation, as a mother and child experience the aftereffects of the atomic bomb. Swirling red flames pass over the forms of fleeing people and animals. Black clouds cover the forms of huddling masses and destroyed buildings. A more realistic rendering of this holocaust would probably be far less powerful.

Leonard Fisher's expressionistic paintings complement the mood of Myra Livingston's poems in *A Circle of Seasons*. Whites and pinks suggest apple blossoms and dogtooth violets. Greens and yellows symbolize the warming sun, the rain, and awaken-

ing earth in spring. Hot sun reds, watery blues, and corn-ripened yellows seem appropriate for paintings accompanying summer poems, while the oranges, reds, and shimmering frost against a dark blue sky suggest changing moods of autumn. In winter paintings, white squares against shades of blue and purple suggest ice crystals and snowflakes converging on a bleak winter world. The wintery mood is supplemented by hoarfrost, icicles, and frosted windowpanes that gleam in silvery needle shapes against a dark blue background.

Abstract Art

Some abstract art takes ordinary things as subjects but emphasizes certain characteristics by changing or distorting the usual images. Pablo Picasso's abstract paintings, for example, reduce people and familiar objects to angular forms and shifting planes. The work of other modern artists has become so abstract—focusing on pure form and representing no actual person, place, or thing—that art experts describe it as nonrepresentational. For example, Piet Mondrian's famous geometrical compositions in oil show the artist's attempts at visual statements that are "objective, impersonal, and universal" in their implications (Preble, 1978, p. 39).

The elimination of representational images characteristic of abstract art is evident in Beverly Brodsky McDermott's illustrations for *The Golem*, a Jewish legend about a rabbi who uses a magic spell to create a man out of clay. McDermott (1976) says:

As I explored the mysteries of the Golem, an evolution took place. At first, he resembled something human. Then he was transformed. His textured body became a powerful presence lurking in dark corners, spilling out of my paintings. In the end he shatters into pieces of clay-color and returns to the earth. All that remains is the symbol of silence. (foreword)

Both expressionist and abstract influences are apparent in Leo Lionni's illustrations. Lionni uses watercolors, textured collages, and thickly painted surfaces to recreate the feeling of a watery world in *Swimmy*. This is not a realistic world of easily discernible water plants and animals. Seaweed has the texture of painted doilies, and fish are only suggestive outlines. Vivid colors and strong shapes predominate in Lionni's *Pezzettino*, the story of a

An oil painting reflecting impressionist style depicts a sunset landscape and a tranquil mood. (From Sailing with the Wind *by Thomas Locker, copyright © 1986 by Thomas Locker. Reprinted by permission of Dial Books for Young Readers.)*

small orange shape who is convinced that he is a piece of someone else. Pezzettino's search takes him to larger shapes composed of many smaller squares of solid color.

Janice Hartwick Dressel (1984) presents arguments for and against using abstract art in children's books. She concludes that exposing children to such sophisticated, symbolical art may encourage higher levels of thinking and may enhance aesthetic response to all art.

EVALUATING THE ILLUSTRATIONS IN CHILDREN'S BOOKS

The collaborative process of creating picture books for children makes special demands on artists. Even when illustrator and author are the same person, the artist is a partner to the writer and must place his or her talents in the service of a certain story. Lee Galda (1991) emphasizes that when evaluating books, it is crucial to consider how the story is expressed through visual elements as well as through words. Galda maintains that you should consider artists' personal style, choice of pictorial content, the elements of design chosen to convey the story or theme, and the ways in which illustrations convey the visual meaning.

Lucy Bitzer (1992), an art designer for a major publisher, states her own evaluation criteria and describes the books that she enjoys:

The illustrations will be eminently appropriate in interpreting the text and bring an extended dimension to the subject matter. The soul of the text should permeate the visual images, expressing the right mood and feeling. Essentially this begins with the right juxtaposition of medium, technique, and style in the illustrations. (p. 227)

Another viewpoint that you may consider when evaluating illustrations in children's books is the one presented by Maurice Sendak in an interview with Hazel Rochman (1992b). When Sendak was asked "What makes a good illustrated book?", he responded:

The illustrations don't simply, prosaically echo the verse. . . . The only thing you can do is to use the verse as a springboard for personal interpretation, so that what you offer is a surprise, at best as surprising and amusing or serious as the verse, but at the very least a counterpoint, an interpretation, a variation of the verse. (p. 1848)

Consider the criteria shown in the box on this page when evaluating the illustrations in picture books for children.

Artistic Criticism and Personal Response

Comparing illustrations of the same or similar story and evaluating your personal responses to the different illustrations is an excellent way to compare the impact of illustrations and artists' techniques. As you look at three illustrations from various interpretations of "The Golem," consider the impact of the artist's use of line, color, shape, texture, design, and artistic media. How did you respond to each illustration? What do you believe is the cause of your response?

ℰVALUATION CRITERIA

Illustrations

1. The illustrator's use of visual elements—line, color, shape, texture— and of certain artistic media should complement or even extend the development of plot, characterization, setting, and theme in the text.

2. The design of the illustrations—individually and throughout an entire book—should reinforce the text and convey a sense of unity that stimulates aesthetic appreciation.

3. The artistic style chosen by the illustrator should enhance the author's literary style.

4. The illustrations should help the readers anticipate the unfolding of a story's action and its climax.

5. The illustrations should convincingly delineate and develop the characters.

6. The illustrations should be accurate in historical, cultural, and geographical detail, and they should be consistent with the text.

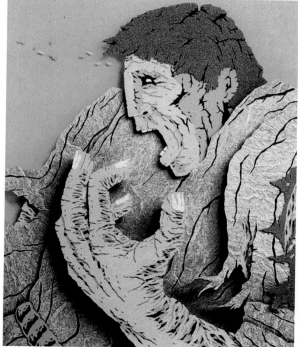

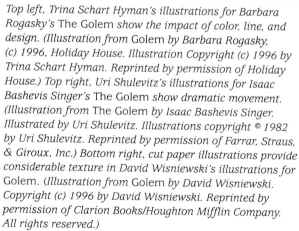

Top left, Trina Schart Hyman's illustrations for Barbara Rogasky's The Golem *show the impact of color, line, and design. (Illustration from* Golem *by Barbara Rogasky, (c) 1996, Holiday House. Illustration Copyright (c) 1996 by Trina Schart Hyman. Reprinted by permission of Holiday House.) Top right, Uri Shulevitz's illustrations for Isaac Bashevis Singer's* The Golem *show dramatic movement. (Illustration from* The Golem *by Isaac Bashevis Singer. Illustrated by Uri Shulevitz. Illustrations copyright © 1982 by Uri Shulevitz. Reprinted by permission of Farrar, Straus, & Giroux, Inc.) Bottom right, cut paper illustrations provide considerable texture in David Wisniewski's illustrations for* Golem. *(Illustration from* Golem *by David Wisniewski. Copyright (c) 1996 by David Wisniewski. Reprinted by permission of Clarion Books/Houghton Mifflin Company. All rights reserved.)*

A close look at several artists reveals the wide range of excellence in children's book illustration and the ways in which individuals fluent in artistic grammar create visual narratives that appeal to young children. The artists discussed in this chapter use the elements of line, color, shape, and texture to create memorable illustrations that highlight the moods of the texts. These illustrations provide numerous opportunities for both children and adults to interact with visual elements and to improve their appreciation of art.

Barbara Cooney

Barbara Cooney's illustrations for Donald Hall's *Ox-Cart Man* use gentle colors and rounded shapes to evoke the peaceful countryside of early nineteenth-century New England. Cooney creates the same mood in *Island Boy*. Soft colors and curved landscapes add to the feeling of an unhurried way of life in which a young boy can explore the joys of his New England home. In Cooney's illustrations for *Chanticleer and the Fox*, however, bold, black lines create a strutting, vain rooster in the earlier portion of the book and a frightened, humble one as the story reaches its climax in the life-and-death struggle between Chanticleer and his enemy, the fox.

Cooney is skilled in using artistic techniques that best complement a particular text. Her illustrations for Margot Griego et al.'s *Tortillitas Para Mama and Other Spanish Nursery Rhymes* re-create the varied settings associated with Spanish nursery rhymes. Warm browns depict the interior of a Mexican home, cool blues warmed by the shining moon suggest a village by the water, and warm fuchsia pinks reflect the warmth of a mother and father sharing a quiet time with their baby.

Cooney uses Aztec colors to capture the settings in her illustrations for John Bierhorst's *Spirit Child: A Story of the Nativity*. The colors range from the strong reds and yellows used to create volcanic eruptions and the dead land to the softer greens used to create a gentler setting for Mary and Jesus. In Delmore Schwartz's *"I Am Cherry Alive," The Little Girl Sang*, Cooney uses shades of gold to depict the pleasure and well-being of a little girl who is observing a tree covered with autumn leaves and uses blue to depict a mist-covered valley seen by the light of a pale moon.

Cooney's illustrations for Jane Yolen's *Letting Swift River Go* take viewers back to the rural life in western Massachusetts and to the memories of a town that was submerged when the Quabbin Reservoir was formed. Before illustrating Michael Bedard's *Emily*, Cooney conducted research at Emily Dickinson's home in Amherst, Massachusetts. Cooney painted the illustrations for *Emily* on China silk mounted on illustration board, using liquitex acrylic paints, prismacolor, and Derwent colored pencils and pastels.

Tomie dePaola

Tomie dePaola has illustrated, or written and illustrated, over one hundred books, including traditional folktales from Italy, Scandinavia, and Mexico; informational books; realistic fiction; and Bible stories. DePaola's illustrations for *The Clown of God* reveal the influence of two pre-Renaissance artists, Giotto and Fra Angelico, whose simplicity and strength of line dePaola admires: "I almost reduce

Three-dimensional paper constructions provide depth for the illustrations. (From Sing a Song of People *by Lois Lenski, and illustrated by Giles Laroche. Illustrations copyright 1987 by Giles Laroche. Reproduced with permission from Little, Brown and Company.)*

ERIC A. KIMMEL[1] CONTENDS that a noticeable trend in children's literature is "the appearance of a growing number of exotically illustrated, high-priced picture books that appear to be far too unusual or sophisticated to attract many children" (p. 41). In this category of picture books, he identifies Wayne Anderson's *Ratsmagic,* Chris Van Allsburg's *The Garden of Abdul Gasazi* and *Jumanji,* Molly Bang's *The Grey Lady and the Strawberry Snatcher,* Graham Oakley's *Magical Changes,* David Macauley's *Unbuilding,* most of Harlin Guin's books, and Maurice Sendak's *Outside over There.*

Kimmel argues that books such as these are being written and illustrated to appeal to adult critics rather than to children. He speculates that children will ignore these books in favor of books by Ezra Jack Keats, Leo Lionni, and Tomie dePaola and books such as Virginia Lee Burton's *Mike Mulligan and His Steam Shovel,* Robert McCloskey's *Blueberries for Sal,* and Maurice Sendak's *Where the Wild Things Are.*

Michael Cart[2] is concerned, however, that too many people are "dumbing down" art and text to appeal to recent lower expectations of children's ability to understand children's literature. He states:

Yet today, here's the irony, after several generations of elevating our expectations of children's literature, a growing chorus of voices seems to be calling instead for its degradation, for what might be crankily described as its "dumbing down," for its demotion from the penthouse of aesthetic and intellectual experience to the bargain basement of mere passive pleasure, by decreeing that the kind of artistry that we used to look for is suddenly too arcane to be apprehended by young readers of the MTV generation. And therefore, instead of being a hallmark of excellence, art is now considered an impediment to readers' appreciation. (p. 160)

Although Cart is discussing both text and illustrations, he does refer to several picture books that he believes are excellent because the illustrations present artistic challenges to their readers. For example, Cart further states:

Indeed, a book as short as a picture book can be a marvel of artistic challenge and opportunity. David Macaulay's *Black and White* is a classic example of what literature should do: provide an interactive opportunity for readers (something that MTV cannot do), stimulate their imaginations, and invite them to think. It is an artistic antidote to the likes of the cretinous Markie Mark who, strutting about in his Calvins, bellowing, enjoins the MTV generation, "Yo, move your body." More civilly, Macaulay invites readers, "Yo, move your mind!" (p. 161)

Look at the preceding books, talk to librarians about children's preferences, and share the books with children. How do children of different ages respond to the pictures and the text? Do the ways in which adults share illustrated books with children affect how children respond to them? What do children like about the pictures and the text? What do you like about the pictures and the text? Do the illustrations encourage readers to "move their minds"?

[1]Kimmel, Eric A. "Children's Literature Without Children." *Children's Literature in Education* 13 (Spring 1982): 38–43.

[2]Cart, Michael. "What Literature?" *School Library Journal* 39 (September 1993): 160–161.

features to a symbol. And yet I think of my faces as good and warm. I try to show expression in very few lines" (Hepler, 1979, p. 299). For *The Clown of God,* dePaola first penciled in the lines and then went over the sketches with raw sienna waterproof ink, a second brown pencil line, and brown ink. He completed the artwork with watercolors.

DePaola emphasizes that his great love of folk art is a strong element in his work. Consequently, according to Masha Rudman (1993), he was inspired by the early works of Alice and Martin Provensen. Strong feelings for Americana are found in dePaola's *An Early American Christmas.* Many of dePaola's illustrations and texts such as *Christopher: The Holy Giant* reflect his belief that children and adults should be exposed to the rich heritage of ethnic folklore. In his illustrations for *The Legend of the Bluebonnet, The Legend of the Indian Paintbrush,* and numerous folktales from various European countries, dePaola combines folk art and folktale.

DePaola also values his theater experience and makes use of it in his illustrations: "There are so many ways picture books are like theater-scenes, settings, characterization. A double page spread can be like a stage" (Hepler, 1979, p. 300). DePaola's illustrations often have the symmetry of stage settings, with actions that appear to take place in front of a backdrop. *Giorgio's Village,* for example, a pop-up book that re-creates an Italian Renaissance village, is itself a stage-like setting in which windows open and tabs allow movement. Some of the illustrations in *Tomie dePaola's Mother Goose* also have the appearance of stage settings.

Other books show the influence of films. In *Watch Out for the Chicken Feet in Your Soup,* the action in the story and illustrations starts before the title page, which becomes part of both the narrative and the action. In these and other ways, dePaola's large body of work demonstrates his belief that children should be exposed to many types of visual imagery.

Leo and Diane Dillon

Leo and Diane Dillon's strong interest in the folklore of traditional peoples is evident in their award-winning books. Their work reflects careful research into the decorative motifs of many cultures and helps re-create and preserve traditional ways of life.

The text for Mildred Pitts Walter's *Brother to the Wind* is rich in folklore, symbols, and dreams. The Dillons use light and dark, pastels and deep colors, to contrast a boy's mythical quest to fly and the earth-bound unbelievers who are sure that he will fail. In one illustration, the wind, which makes it possible for the boy to fly, is a transparent woman whose color and shape blend into the pale cloudy sky. Viewers are given the impression that only they and the boy, not the doubting villagers, can see the wind.

The Dillons also use shades of black and white to contrast myth and reality in the illustrations for Virginia Hamilton's *The People Could Fly: American Black Folktales.* Their illustrations for Verna Aardema's *Why Mosquitoes Buzz in People's Ears* re-create the setting of a traditional African folktale. In Virginia Hamilton's *Her Stories: African American Folktales, Fairy Tales, and True Tales* the artists painted with acrylics on illustration board. Acrylics are also used to illustrate Howard Norman's *The Girl Who Dreamed Only Geese and Other Tales of the Far North.* In every case, careful research preceded the Dillons' illustrations.

Susan Jeffers

Susan Jeffers uses texture and line to convey differences between reality and fantasy in her realistic but magical illustrations. Her skilled use of line is especially apparent in her illustrations for Hans Christian Andersen's *The Wild Swans.* Strong lines depict forest, hillside, and stormy sea. More delicate, cross-hatched lines depict the sunshine and plants within the fragrant cedar grove. When a beautiful fairy enters the girl's dreams to guide her in freeing her brothers, Jeffers contrasts the reality of the characters sleeping on the ground and the fairyland of the palace in the clouds. The girl herself is in warm greens and browns, while the fairy and the fairy castle are almost transparent blues and grays.

Jeffers uses variety of line to depict similar distinctions of nature and the mythical spirit world in her illustrations for Henry Wadsworth Longfellow's *Hiawatha.* Other books in which Jeffers develops mood and setting through detailed line drawings include Robert Frost's *Stopping by Woods on a Snowy Evening,* the Grimms' *Hansel and Gretel,* Eugene Field's *Wynken, Blynken and Nod,* Charles Perrault's *Cinderella,* adapted by Amy Ehrlich, and Jeffers's own *Brother Eagle, Sister Sky.*

Ezra Jack Keats

Ezra Jack Keats combines collage, paint, and empathy for children's needs and emotions in compositions that portray inner-city life. Sometimes, the environment is peaceful, as in *The Snowy Day,* where Keats uses brilliantly white torn paper to convey the snow covering chimneys and rooftops as Peter looks out on a fresh, white world. Later, shadowy blue footprints bring the text and the illustrations together, asking readers to look at Peter's footprints in the snow. Snowbanks are rounded shapes, and buildings are rectangles of color in the background. Peter's simple, red-clad figure stands out against the snowy background.

Keats evokes quite a different mood with collage and paint in *Goggles!* Here, two children confront harsher realities, as they try to escape from bigger boys who want their possessions. The colors are dark, and the collages include thrown-away items that one might find in back alleys. Keats shows the frightening big boys as almost featureless. In one picture, a hole in a piece of wood frames the scene as the two small boys look through it and plan how to get home. In other books—such as *Louie, The Trip,* and *Peter's Chair*—illustrations by Keats complement the loneliness, daydreams, or jealousy described in the text.

THROUGH THE EYES OF AN ILLUSTRATOR

Illustrating and Books

TOMIE DEPAOLA, illustrator of over one hundred books and winner of the Caldecott honor award, discusses early art experiences and the importance of doodling.

I AM A DOODLER. IN FACT, I *love* to doodle. I always have. I keep pads of scratch paper and black and red fine-line markers by the telephones, at my drawing table, on my desk, in my carry-on bag when I fly; and when I was teaching, I never went to a meeting (faculty, committee, etc.) without my handy pad and markers.

Growing up, coloring books were absent from our house . . . at least, in my room. My tools were plain paper, pencils, and my trusty Crayolas. After all, I was going to be an artist when I grew up. And besides, my own drawings and doodles seemed to be far more interesting to me, and those around me, than the simple coloring book images. (My mother also admitted recently that plain paper was lots cheaper.)

I learned at an early age that there was a definite difference between out-and-out drawing and serious doodling. A drawing had more structure, more direction. A definite idea was usually the beginning of a drawing. For example, I might say, "I think I will do a drawing of a girl ice skating, wearing a fancy Ice Follies-type costume." (Yes, the Ice Follies were around way back then.) Then the problem would be to try to do a drawing that coincided with my original idea or vision.

Doodles were (and are) totally different. I would just put pencil to paper and see what happened. All sorts of interesting images would result. I might start out not really concentrating on my doodle but on what else I was doing at the time. Talking on the phone was a very good activity for doodling. Late at night under the covers with a flashlight and listening to the radio was another activity that produced more terrific doodles—some actually on sheets rather than on paper. The "state of the art" doodles of this early period, though, appeared as if by magic on my arithmetic papers. There would be columns of figures copied from the blackboard and before I knew it, the paper would be covered with pictures with no room for the answers. My teachers—well, at least, a few of them—were *not* amused. They warned me. I'd never learn to add, subtract, multiply, etc. They were right, but for me as an artist, the doodling proved to be a far more important activity. I was able to buy a calculator with a royalty check, and now, I have an accountant.

"Meeting doodles," especially faculty meeting doodles, proved to be among the most valuable for me. It was during a college faculty meeting that was about the same issues the previous dozen meetings had been about, that "Strega Nona" appeared on my pad. I didn't know who she was at that moment, but a few months on my studio wall, and she soon let me know all about herself.

I've just opened a drawer and found some doodles that were done several years ago. (I stash doodles in different drawers so they can show up later and surprise me. My assistant saves all the phone-call doodles for me. My mother and an old friend both have doodles of mine in special drawers, waiting for the day they can cash in on them.)

The newfound doodles are on the wall of my studio. There is a rather fetching sheep and two classy cats, dressed to kill. Who knows . . . someday. . . . But remember! You read about them here first!

Watercolors present a vision of a mythical Alaskan setting. (Illustration by Leo and Diane Dillon. Reprinted by permission of Philomel Books from Northern Lullaby *by Nancy White Carlstrom, illustrations copyright © 1992 by Leo and Diane Dillon.)*

Joseph Schwarcz (1982) believes that children respond to books by Keats, such as *Apt. 3,* because

the illustrations dramatize the lyrical mood, probably also making it more easily accessible for the younger reader. The gestures and postures of the people in the story are down to earth, outspoken. The important visual motifs are the ones we know well. The apartment building is muddy and ugly. The large shapes of the boys, painted from a close angle, evoke intimacy. From the beginning there is visual metaphor. (p. 188)

W. Nikola-Lisa (1991) analyzes the art of Ezra Jack Keats and discusses Keats's use of lines to direct the viewers' attention to a portion of his illustrations.

Robert McCloskey

Robert McCloskey's illustrations present the real world of boys, girls, families, and animals. Detailed black-and-white drawings depict the settings in most of his books, although McCloskey also uses color to evoke the essence of an island susceptible to forces of nature in *Time of Wonder.* In that book, McCloskey's watercolors first depict a serene world. When gentle rain approaches, the painting is so transparent that the first thing seen is a thin mist descending. Later, diagonal lines of raindrops break the surface of the peaceful water, and light fog surrounds two children, who experience the whispering sound of growing ferns. The island is not always serene, however. A hurricane bends the lines of the trees, as the illustrations themselves almost move on the page. McCloskey's use of line is so compelling that Lyn Ellen Lacy (1986) uses page-by-page discussion of *Make Way for Ducklings* and *Time of Wonder* to analyze line in McCloskey's Caldecott Award-winning books.

Black-and-white drawings illustrate McCloskey's delightful *Blueberries for Sal.* The child, whether stealing berries from a pail or mistakenly following a mother bear instead of her own mother, looks as if she could walk right off the page.

Alice and Martin Provensen

Color, symmetry, and effective use of space are noteworthy elements in the work of Alice and Martin Provensen. Many illustrations by the Provensens, whose collaborative efforts include more than fifty books, reflect the world in earlier times or worlds of fantasy. The Provensens create a feeling of flying through space in their book about the first flight across the English Channel, *The Glorious Flight Across the Channel with Louis Bleriot, July 25, 1909.* Consecutive illustrations proceed from a close-up of the plane before it soars to a wide-angle view of the small plane surrounded by clouds and sky. The corresponding text reveals that Louis Bleriot is alone, lost in a world of swirling fog. The illustrators' use of space and color reinforces this mood of danger and exhilaration.

The impact of symmetry in design is felt in several of the Provensens' illustrations for Nancy Willard's *A Visit to William Blake's Inn: Poems for Innocent and Experienced Travelers.* In one illustration, for example, the Wonderful Car hovers over buildings that provide a visual center for the car; the steps of the flying vehicle lead viewers toward the passengers; and the two smaller sets of propeller blades balance the larger center blade.

Other books demonstrating the Provensens' skill in re-creating historical periods include *A Peaceable Kingdom: The Shaker Abecedarius, Shaker Lane,* and *Leonardo da Vinci.*

Maurice Sendak

Time magazine has called Maurice Sendak "the Picasso of children's books." Sendak's artistic versatility in using color, line, and balance is evident in the many books that Sendak has illustrated or written and illustrated, including Janice Udry's *The Moon Jumpers.* One of Sendak's primary aims in illustrating a text is to make "the pictures so organically akin to the text, so reflective of its atmosphere, that they look as if they could have been done in no other way. They should help create the special world of the story . . . creating the air for a writer" (Moritz, 1968, p. 352).

Sendak's special relationship between text and illustrations may be most apparent in *Outside over There* and *Where the Wild Things Are.* Sendak (Davis, 1981) described the steps that he took in creating the illustrations for *Outside over There,* which he considers his best and most significant children's book. One of his first concerns was drawing ten-year-old Ida holding a baby. In order to reproduce realistic body postures, Sendak made photographs of a child holding a baby. The baby kept slipping out of the child's arms, so that the clothes on both children drooped and became disheveled. Sendak referred to watercolors by the British poet and artist William Blake for inspiration in choosing colors that communicate the setting, characterization, and mood:

The colors belong to Ida. She is rural, of the time in the country when winter sunsets have that certain yellow you never see in other seasons. There's a description of women's clothing, watered silk, and that's what those skies are like—moist, sensuous, silken, almost transparent—the color I copied in the cape Ida wears and in other things showing up against soft mauve, blue, green, tan—all part of the story's feeling. (p. 46)

The illustrations for *Where the Wild Things Are* are totally integrated with the text and play a crucial role in the plot and characterization, as well as the setting. When Max is banished to his room for bad behavior, the room gradually becomes the kingdom of the wild things, with trees growing naturally out of the bedposts and the shag rug turning into grass. As the story progresses, the illustrations cover more and more of the page; when Max becomes king of the wild things, six pages of illustrations are uninterrupted by text. Sendak creates a believably mischievous boy and humorous but forceful wild things with terrible rolling eyes and horrible gnashing teeth.

Brian Alderson (1993b) maintains that with the illustration of *Where the Wild Things Are,* Sendak shifted the load-bearing responsibility in his books from words to pictures. As you look at books illustrated by Maurice Sendak, notice how much of the story is extended, or even totally told, through the illustrations. The illustrations are especially important in Sendak's *We Are All in the Dumps with Jack and Guy,* where Sendak uses two nursery rhymes to provide minimal text. The illustrations, however, develop a contemporary story about the

Maurice Sendak was inspired by the watercolors in William Blake's paintings in creating his illustrations for this book. (Illustrations from Outside Over There *by Maurice Sendak. Copyright © 1981 by Maurice Sendak. By permission of Harper & Row, Publishers, Inc.)*

harsh reality of homelessness and poverty. Even the newspapers used as protection emphasize the contemporary social conflict between wealth and poverty.

Selma Lanes's *The Art of Maurice Sendak* (1980) provides biographical information as well as examples from Sendak's numerous books. Sendak's *Posters by Maurice Sendak* (1986) provides examples from many occasions. The posters also show how important wild things are in Sendak's art.

Chris Van Allsburg

Chris Van Allsburg's *The Garden of Abdul Gasazi, Jumanji, The Mysteries of Harris Burdick,* and *The Widow's Broom* demonstrate the effectiveness of black-and-white illustrations. Both line and subtle shading focus attention along a visual pathway in the illustrations for *The Garden of Abdul Gasazi.* In one picture, the main character is framed by a central doorway. On either side of the doorway, a bright statue against dark leaves points down a black tunnel toward a circle of white. This circle represents the garden in which the story line develops. (Symmetry is one way that artists create balance in their designs.)

In *The Wreck of the Zephyr,* Van Allsburg uses line to create movement and color to convey mood. As the story begins, rolling waves and billowing dark clouds suggest movement and the ominous forces of angry sea and sky. Later, the mood changes to fantasy, and Van Allsburg uses color to create a calm sea sparkling with light, a fantasy harbor town seen through shadows, soft clouds tinged with sunset, and a star-studded sky.

Compare Van Allsburg's use of line and shading in his black-and-white illustrations with his use of line and color in *The Wreck of the Zephyr, The Polar Express, Swan Lake* (retold by Mark Helprin), *The Wretched Stone,* and *The Sweetest Fig.* In *The Polar Express,* Van Allsburg uses line to create the furry textures of lean wolves roaming the dark forests and the feathery texture of newly fallen snow. Even Santa Claus's beard and mittens seem to have texture. Van Allsburg also uses contrasting light and dark colors and shadings effectively. Moonlight focuses attention on the boy in his darkened bedroom, train windows glow with warmth as the train winds through cold forests and up snow-covered mountains, and city lights stream from windows to pierce the darkness.

Symmetry of design directs viewers toward the distant garden. (Illustration by Chris Van Allsburg from The Garden of Abdul Gasazi. *Copyright 1979 by Chris Van Allsburg. Reprinted by permission of Houghton Mifflin Company.)*

The glowing colors and contrasts between light and dark are appropriate for a children's fantasy. (Illustrations from The Polar Express *by Chris Van Allsburg, copyright © 1985 by Chris Van Allsberg. Reproduced with permission from Houghton Mifflin Co.)*

David Wiesner

David Wiesner is best known for his wordless books, Caldecott Medal winner *Tuesday* and Caldecott Honor book *Free Fall*. In an interview conducted by Susan Caroff and Elizabeth Moje (1992/1993), Wiesner states:

Wordless books have been my passion for a long time. It's something that goes way back. I've always liked telling stories with pictures, more than just painting a single painting. If I came up with an image that I liked—

I would always be interested in seeing what had happened before or after the particular image I had painted. (p. 284)

Wiesner is pleased when his wordless books are used to stimulate creativity. He maintains that his books need readers because the author's voice is not there in the form of text. Words do not anchor the stories to reality. Instead, readers must interpret the illustrations themselves and create their own interpretations.

Watercolors allow the artist to create illustrations that appear to vary from transparent to heavy. (From Tuesday *by David Wiesner. Copyright © 1991 by David Wiesner. Reprinted by permission of Clarion Books/Houghton Mifflin Co. All rights reserved.)*

In *Free Fall,* Wiesner's illustrations seem to move into the next page. As you look at these illustrations, notice how the squares in the boy's blanket become the fields in a countryside divided into geometric shapes and then become a lifelike chess board. When the boy returns from his fantasy experience, the squares return to the bed covering. Flying shapes are important in creating the fantasy in both Wiesner's *Tuesday* and *June 29, 1999.*

Wiesner uses color to create moods appropriate for the settings. In *Tuesday,* blues and greens create the coolness of the night and provide an appropriate background for a story in which frogs explore their environment at night.

 ## SUGGESTED ACTIVITIES

for Adult Understanding of Artists and Their Illustrations

■ With some of your peers, select one of the following criteria for evaluating the illustrations and narrative portions of a picture book, find books that clearly exemplify the criteria, and share them with the class:

    a. The illustrations help readers anticipate both the action of the story and the climax (for example,

Richard Egielski's illustrations for Arthur Yorinks's *Hey, Al* or Maurice Sendak's illustrations for *Where the Wild Things Are*).

    b. The pictures help create the basic mood of the story (for example, Paul Goble's *The Girl Who Loved Wild Horses* or Marcia Brown's illustrations for *Cinderella,* by Charles Perrault.

    c. The illustrations portray convincing characters (for example, Taro Yashima's *Crow Boy*).

    d. All pictures are accurate and consistent with text (for example, Barbara Cooney's illustrations for Donald Hall's *Ox-Cart Man*).

■ Consider the ways in which lines are related to natural phenomena. Look carefully at the illustrations in several books. Are there examples in which vertical lines suggest lack of movement, horizontal lines suggest calmness or an absence of strife, vertical and horizontal lines connected at the top suggest stability and safety, diagonal lines suggest motion, and jagged lines symbolize danger?

■ Select a fairy tale, such as "Cinderella" or "Snow White," that has been illustrated by several artists. Compare the artists' use of line, color, and shape to create mood and setting.

■ Read the narrative portion of several picture storybooks. Evaluate whether or not the dominant images in the illustrations complement the emphasis in the texts. Choose an example that complements the text and one that does not. Share the examples and your rationales for choosing them with the class.

- With a group of your peers, select one medium available to artists, such as woodcuts, collage, inks, watercolors, acrylics, or pastels. Investigate how different artists use the medium in picture-book illustrations. Share your findings with the class.

- With some of your peers, investigate how artists use representational and abstract artistic styles. Consider the styles used by the illustrators of several picture books. In each case, does the style complement the intended mood of the text? Share your findings with the class.

- Choose an outstanding illustrator of children's books. Find as many of the illustrator's works as you can. Analyze the artist's use of the elements of art—line, color, shape, and texture—and the various media and styles used by the artist. Compare the books. Does the artist use a similar style in all works, or does the style change with the subject matter of the text? Compare earlier works with later ones. Are there any changes in the use of artistic elements, style, or media?

- Read a book about an illustrator, such as the San Diego Museum of Art's *Dr. Seuss from Then to Now* (1986), Selma Lanes's *The Art of Maurice Sendak* (1980), or Bill Peet's *Bill Peet: An Autobiography.* How has the work of the illustrator changed? What motivated the illustrator to work in children's book illustration? What impact has the illustrator had on young readers? If possible, discover how the illustrator's background influenced his or her work.

- Read an article such as Nathalie OpDeBeeck's "David Wisniewski: Crafting Serious Entertainment" from *Publisher's Weekly* February 16, 1998, pp 189–190. What is this Caldecott winner's approach to art? What is his attitude about illustrating books? How did he develop his abilities? What influenced his work?

- Choose your favorite illustrator mentioned in this chapter. Use the database to create a list of books illustrated by that person. Locate as many of the books as you can and determine the artistic medium or media used to create the illustrations.

    a. Add this information to your database under USER COMMENTS. Print your updated list and share your information with your classmates.

    b. Use the information provided by your classmates' lists and add it to your database.

- Each chapter of this book opens with an illustration and caption. Locate each of the twelve books in the database and add the information included in the caption under USER COMMENTS for each book.

Involving Children with Artists and Their Illustrations

A growing trend is helping children appreciate, respond to, and understand art. Hallowell Judson (1989), Supervisor of Children's Programs at the Carnegie Museum of Art in Pittsburgh, states:

The case for the need to learn how to read, or decode, visual images is currently being made in many quarters, including psychology, museum education, and art education, and in reports such as the Getty Trust's *Beyond Creating* and the National Endowment for the Arts' *Toward Civilization*. That children's literature specialists are now joining the ranks of those advocating visual literacy comes as no surprise, especially when one considers the plethora of children's picture books on the market and their popularity. (p. 59)

Children's librarian and author Sylvia S. Marantz (1992) argues that to awaken their visual perceptions, children need experiences designed to help them learn. She states:

Unfortunately most of their experience comes to them through a barrage of photographed images from a television screen. The children have no opportunity to examine what they see, to question its form or validity, to compare or contrast it critically with other pictures their eyes are receiving or with those their imaginations might provide if given the chance. (p. v)

Marantz uses her experience with children and books to recommend a program in which children, with the aid of adults, examine, discuss, question, and compare the illustrations in books and accomplish art activities that relate to the specific illustrations. Marantz progresses through a series of activities that focus on the book jacket; the front end papers; the title page; and each illustration, leading children to understand and appreciate such elements as color, movement, page design, and format. She recommends viewing and discussing additional books by the same illustrator and books to use for comparisons.

Susan Boulanger (1996) emphasizes using art education books that provide "opportunities for sharing the experience of looking at, thinking about, and discussing art" (p. 298). Such books allow children living in all locations to develop an appreciation for and an understanding of art, even if museum collections are not available.

Children's literature authority Perry Nodelman (1984a) also emphasizes helping children develop art appreciation. He states:

In fact, children with nothing to operate on but instinct inevitably like bad art, and for good reason: it's the only kind they've seen, so it's the only kind they've learned to understand. Children who haven't been taught the subtleties of visual communication have as much chance of responding to skilled art as people who speak only English have of enjoying a novel in Chinese. (p. 40)

Nodelman then discusses the many conventions that are peculiar to pictures and to understanding illustrations, analyzing Virginia Lee Burton's illustrations in *Mike Mulligan and His Steam Shovel*. Nodelman concludes, "Librarians, educators, and parents should enrich the experience of children by making them, too, conscious of the breathtaking, ingenious aspects of pictures that we all take too much for granted" (p. 41).

This section of the chapter presents a few of the ways that you can help children experience "breathtaking, ingenious aspects of pictures." The techniques include aesthetic scanning, visual literacy, studying historic books and illustrations, studying inspirations for art, and investigating the works of great artists.

AESTHETIC SCANNING

Art educators who are involved with developing programs that encourage informed aesthetic responses in children recommend a technique called aesthetic scanning. Hallowell Judson (1989) states:

Aesthetic scanning consists of locating and identifying the aesthetic properties of an artwork while looking at it. It is a pedagogical version of what artists do when they are making art and what connoisseurs do when contemplating it. The aesthetic properties involved in aesthetic scanning include the sensory, the formal, the expressive, and the technical. (p. 62)

The sensory properties include the visual elements of art, such as line, color, shape, and texture. The formal properties include the principles of art used to organize or compose art, such as balance, repetition, variety, and contrast. Expressive qualities are visual characteristics used to express feelings or ideas, such as mood, conflict, energy, and meaning. The technical properties are the media, such as watercolor and chalk, and techniques used by artists.

Judson recommends using the aesthetic scanning approach developed by H. S. Broudy (1981) and described by Gloria J. Hewett and Jean C. Rush (1987) when encouraging students to respond to the illustrations in children's literature. Hewett and Rush maintain:

Teaching children to make informed aesthetic responses by means of aesthetic scanning has all the excitement of a treasure hunt. The hunters are the children and their teacher. Their tools are a pair of sharp eyes. The treasures they seek to discover are the sensory, formal, expressive, and technical properties of works of art. (p. 41)

Hewett and Rush also identify two rules for this type of treasure hunt: (1) the aesthetic property must be in the artwork and observable by others and (2) the viewer must be able to identify and describe the property. Chart 4–1 presents examples of questions that adults may ask to encourage children to examine a work of art carefully and to volunteer information based on their own perceptions. Hewett and Rush recommend that adults build confidence by beginning with easier questions. Notice that the questions are presented in the order of difficulty. The questions toward the end of the chart require higher levels of artistic knowledge and lead to better informed aesthetic responses. As children become experienced at looking at art and talking about aesthetic properties, expect longer, more detailed descriptions of the properties and ask more open-ended questions.

Hewett and Rush also recommend encouraging students to expand their responses by asking questions that clarify and elaborate the responses. Hewett and Rush warn, however, that the questions in the table are merely examples to be modified, amended, changed, or rearranged to meet the goals of instruction. They state that if the questions are followed mechanically or methodically and are used with every lesson, discussions may be limited rather than enhanced. Remember that questions should expand children's responses to art.

Gladys S. Blizzard used her experience as an art teacher and a curator of education at an art museum to create a series of books that use similar techniques. For example, *Come Look with Me: World of Play* is an interactive art appreciation book that encourages children to look at a painting, to read information about the painting and the artist, and to locate or discuss characteristics found in the art. Following a painting by Diego Rivera (*Piñata*, 1953), Blizzard asks readers to respond to the following observations and questions:

The children are reacting in different ways to what is happening in this painting. Find a happy child, a sad child, and a frightened child.
Which child looks the most eager to gather the falling fruits and candies? How did the artist show that?
How does the artist show movement in this painting? Describe the different ways.
Where do you think the children are playing? Explain how you decided that. (p. 27)

Then, Blizzard provides information about Diego Rivera, his use of earth colors, and some of the Mexican symbols in the painting. Additional books in this "Come Look with Me" series include *Enjoying Art with Children, Exploring Landscape Art with Children,* and *Animals in Art.*

In *The Painter's Eye: Learning to Look at Contemporary American Art,* a book for older students, Jan Greenberg and Sandra Jordan also use many similar techniques. Greenberg and Jordan state that the book introduces a way of seeing and experiencing art. Students should consider and discuss such questions as What makes a painting work? What is the artist trying to communicate? What is the feeling expressed? Greenberg and Jordan maintain that answering these questions is not easy, because "At first, whether we find a particular painting beautiful or interesting or disturbing may be subjective, a matter of personal preference. It has to do with the memories, feelings, and ideas we bring to a work of art. But there is a common vocabulary of art that we can explore together" (p. 8). This common vocabulary includes the elements of color, line, shape, and texture and the principles of organization. These elements remain constant whether the art is in ancient cave dwellings or contemporary paintings. Greenberg and Jordan believe, "By learning something about these constants, the most basic vocabulary of art, we come to all paintings with greater understanding" (p. 8).

You may use Greenberg and Jordan's text to provide guidance for developing discussions about art. The text begins with a discussion of contemporary American art, including steps in which viewers describe what they see by using sensory

CHART 4–1   Aesthetic scanning: Initiating questions

Kind of Question*	Properties	Sample Questions
Leading (Agreement, disagreement)	Sensory	This painting has a lot of red, doesn't it?
	Formal	The balance in this fabric pattern is symmetrical, isn't it?
	Expressive	Don't you agree that the smooth shapes in this sculpture convey a feeling of peace?
	Technical	You can feel how rough the surface texture of this pot is, can't you?
Selective (Choice)	Sensory	Do you see more red or blue in this painting?
	Formal	Is this balance symmetrical or asymmetrical?
	Expressive	Do the shapes make you feel peaceful or upset?
	Technical	Is the surface texture rough or smooth?
Parallel (Additional information)	Sensory	What other colors are there in this painting besides red?
	Formal	Is there any kind of balance here other than symmetrical?
	Expressive	What else might these smooth shapes suggest?
	Technical	Are there more surfaces on this clay piece than the rough ones?
Constructive (Specific new information)	Sensory	What colors can you find in this painting?
	Formal	What kinds of balance do you see here?
	Expressive	What kinds of shapes can you find in this sculpture, and what mood do they evoke?
	Technical	How has the artist treated the surface of this clay pot?
Productive (General new information)	Sensory	How would you describe one of the painting's sensory properties?
	Formal	Can you describe one of the formal properties in this fabric pattern?
	Expressive	What does this sculpture express?
	Technical	What medium and techniques did the artist use in constructing this pot?

*Initiating questions are presented in order of how difficult they are to answer.
Reprinted from Gloria J. Hewett and Jean C. Rush, "Finding Buried Treasures: Aesthetic Scanning with Children," *Art Education* 40 (January 1987).

words that remind them of things that they touch, taste, see, hear, or smell. Next, it considers how artists use the elements of painting, including line, shape, texture, and color, and different styles, media, and methods. Other sections emphasize the meaning of various paintings; putting all of the elements together; and visual effects, including balance, visual rhythms that form patterns, emphasis, and space. The text is written to encourage interactions among readers and text. Thus, you may use it to develop aesthetic discussions with your students. Greenberg and Jordan use a similar approach in *The Sculptor's Eye: Looking at Contemporary American Art.*

A series of four books by Colleen Carroll develops art appreciation for numerous artists and their works. Each of the following illustrated texts focuses on different artistic subjects: *How Artists See Animals: Mammal Fish Bird Reptile; How Artists See People: Boy Girl Man Woman; How Artists See the Elements: Earth Air Fire Water;* and *How Artists See*

the Weather: Sun Rain Wind Snow. Each of the books includes discussions related to the artistic works and reproductions of paintings. To provide additional information for readers, each text includes bibliographies, biographies, and locations for artists' works.

Use the discussion of various artistic elements, design, artistic media, artistic styles, and outstanding illustrators of children's books presented earlier in this chapter to help you select interesting artwork from children's illustrators and to develop your own treasure hunt. Lyn Ellen Lacy's *Art and Design in Children's Picture Books* (1986) provides in-depth suggestions for analyzing the visual elements in several Caldecott Medal-winning illustrations. Use Chart 4–1 to help you include questions related to sensory, formal, expressive, and technical aspects of the artistic work. After discussing Blizzard's books, many children enjoy developing their own observations and formulating questions that allow them to interact with art.

Readers are asked to respond to Diego Rivera's painting, Piñata. *(From* Come Look with Me: World of Play *by Gladys S. Blizzard. Published by Thomasson-Grant, 1993. Diego Rivera Piñata 1953. Tempera on canvas 97" × 171½" Hospital Infantil de Mexico "Federico Gomez," Mexico City. Reproduced by permission of the hospital.)*

Involving Children with Artists and Their Illustrations

You may use many books for finding insights into visual art. According to museum curator Daniel Rice (1988):

It is only when these elements are considered in the context of the subject matter and the emotional effect that they communicate that they are truly related to visual literacy. If diagonal lines communicate motion in a painting, it is important to know why, and also how that dynamism relates to the particular subject that is being depicted, the personal style of the artist as well as the style of the period or location. It is not enough to merely identify and notice them. (p. 16)

Many books provide opportunities for developing aesthetic scanning and cultural understanding. Paul Goble's *The Girl Who Loved Wild Horses* includes excellent examples of visual elements and illustrations that develop understanding of the Native American culture, specifically that of the Plains Indians. (Although the pages in the book are unnumbered, page numbers here refer to pages as if the title page were page 1.)

Information about the artist. Paul Goble grew up in England, where he listened to his mother read him stories that interested him in the culture of the Plains Indians. Later, he visited Montana and South Dakota, where he studied the Native American culture. He lives in the Black Hills of South Dakota, writing and illustrating many stories about Native American peoples. His special area of interest is traditional literature of the Plains Indians. He has been adopted into the Yakima and Sioux tribes. Additional books that you may use for aesthetic scanning and comparisons include *Beyond the Ridge, Buffalo Woman, Death of the Iron Horse, The Gift of the Sacred Dog, Iktomi and the Berries, Iktomi and the Boulder: A Plains Indian Story,* and *Star Boy.* Many of Goble's books include helpful notes about the stories and the illustrations.

Endpapers, both front and back. The color red develops a feeling of warmth and provides a harmonious introduction to the title page, in which red also dominates. Consider the possible mood for a book that is introduced by red.

Page 1, the title page. The title here is written in the same form as it is on the cover of the book. The color red develops a feeling of warmth and high energy. The sun in this illustration shines on a Native American girl on her Appaloosa stallion. According to Goble (1978), the geometric sun design comes from the Plains Indians. Women painted this geometric sun design on buffalo robes that men wore. The circle surrounded by white space creates a sense of balance. The plants in the foreground increase this sense of balance.

Pages 2 and 3. The horizontal lines suggest calm, sleep, and stability. The vertical lines in the plants and horses' necks suggest lack of movement and reinforce the feeling of calm. The sleeping girl adds to this total, nonthreatening scene.

Pages 6 and 7. The running buffalo herd creates the sense of movement and direction. According to Goble, the buffalo hunters approach the sacred buffalo on the right side so that they may use the bow and arrow to the best effect. Several hunters are trying to help the hunter who has had a mishap.

Pages 8 and 9. This two-page spread uses horizontal and vertical lines to create a peaceful, nonthreatening scene. Notice that the horizontal lines of the horses are reflected in the surface of the lake. Not a ripple mars the tranquility. Also notice that the vertical lines of the cattails and the horses' manes mirror the peaceful setting described in the text. Because the horses are not frightened by the girl, we can infer a close relationship. The gold colors in the aspens show that it is autumn. According to Goble, reflection, as seen through the water, is a theme found in Indian painting. The quill and beadwork designs frequently have reflections (or up and down motifs), which symbolize sky and earth.

Pages 10 and 11. The teepees sitting securely on the ground suggest a safe place. Changes in color and movement are found, however, in the far left. The black, circular clouds suggest changes. The jagged lines protruding from the clouds even indicate the direction that the storm is moving. These changes of color and line foreshadow danger.

Pages 12 and 13. Diagonal lines suggest loss of balance and uncontrolled motion. Notice the jagged diagonal line of the lightning. Feelings of fear explode in this picture because lightning is one of nature's most fearsome elements. The danger is imminent because the black clouds cover almost half of the two-page spread. Notice that the lines of the birds, the horses' legs, and the horses' manes suggest movement and danger.

Pages 14 and 15. Notice that Goble develops movement and direction through the horses, other animals, and even the plants leaning away from the wind. The jagged yellow lines and the black clouds approach and cover portions of the sun that earlier provided warmth.

Pages 16 and 17. Horizontal lines on the mountain tops and the horses' backs show that the danger is over and that peace and tranquility exist once again. The high canyon walls have a special awe and quietness at night. The stars and the sky are important in this illustration. According to Goble, much Native American mythology concerns the Sky World. When a person dies, his spirit walks along the Milky Way to the world above. A sense of peace in the dark is provided by knowing that one has relatives in the sky and by remembering that the moon is the sun's wife.

Pages 20 and 21. According to Goble, pairs of scouts were sent out to find the buffalo herds so that when returning to camp each scout could vouch for the truth of the other's report. The stallion takes a position of defense in the rear of his mares, whom he drives in front of him.

Pages 24, 25, 26, and 27. According to Goble, this is a Blackfoot camp. Looking at all four pages at the same time, one sees half of the camp circle. Each teepee design is divinely revealed. The top portion represents the sky, and the cross at the very top symbolizes the morning star and a wish for wisdom and good dreams, while the discs represent stars. The middle portion of the teepee contains the animals, who have their feet on earth and their heads in heaven. These designs display vital tracts, kidneys, and leg joints because they are sources of the animals' power. The bottom border of the teepee represents the earth, and the projecting triangles or rounded shapes represent mountains or hills. Such lodges are still held sacred by the Blackfoot Indians.

Pages 30 and 31. According to Goble, these pages parallel page 1. The girl, however, may have become a horse. The figures share the warmth of each other

and the sun. The crocuses and the bluebirds show that winter is over and springtime is here.

After discussing the illustrations in this book, ask students to respond to and compare the illustrations in other books by Paul Goble.

STUDYING HISTORIC BOOKS AND ILLUSTRATIONS

Rita Lipkis (1993) describes a project conducted by the Friends of the Beverly Hills (California) Public Library, who introduced children to book collecting. In addition, the project introduced children to the history of books by examining and discussing the art in early books and the illustrations in Aesop's fables. Lipkis states, "*Fascinated* is the word most frequently used by observers in regard to children's responses" (p. 115).

Other public libraries and schools may easily develop similar projects. The following suggestions for such projects include procedures recommended by Lipkis, as well as some additional techniques and materials.

First, introduce the subject of book collecting. During this introduction, discuss the meaning of rare books, the reasons for collecting and saving books, and the benefits gained from reading or owning rare books. Also include the reasons for any type of book collecting. Students may suggest the kinds of books that they would like to collect or the types of books collected by people whom they know. For example, maybe someone has a collection of Mother Goose rhymes, folktales, the illustrated books by a specific artist, or science fiction.

Next, provide a capsule history of books and illustrations by showing and discussing pictures of early cave paintings. Discuss how stories of the hunt were illustrated long before they were written down. Photographs of early cave paintings are found in such adult sources as Andre Leroi-Gourhan's *Treasures of Prehistoric Art*. Show and discuss a facsimile of an early scroll or a facsimile of a page of medieval manuscript. Blanche Cirker's (1982) *The Book of Kells: Selected Plates in Full Color* contains reproductions of illuminated books and manuscripts from about A.D. 800. Be sure that children realize that before the invention of printing presses, people spent many hours hand copying books. These books were very valuable and were owned by few people.

As part of the history of books, show the students pictures of early printing presses and discuss the impact of printing presses on book production. Show pieces of lead type and wood blocks to demonstrate the art of early printing and illustration. Show reproductions of hornbooks or battledores used to provide instruction for children in colonial times. (See chapter 2 to obtain information on the printing press and early books.)

Introduce and discuss additional facsimiles, or even first editions of illustrated books if available. For example, *Favourite Fairy Tales*, edited by Jennifer Mulherin, is an excellent source for a comparative study of illustrations. The reproductions in this text include the title page and other woodcuts from the 1742 edition Charles Perrault's *Histoires ou Contes du Tems Passe*, as well as Walter Crane's illustrations from the 1876 edition of *The Blue Beard Picture Book* and the 1879 *The Children's Musical Cinderella*. Edmund Dulac's illustrations for traditional tales are reproduced in B. Mitchell's *Edmund Dulac's Fairy Book: Fairy Tales of the World*, which first appeared in 1916. Dulac's illustrations are also found in a facsimile edition of the 1910 *The Sleeping Beauty and Other Fairy Tales*, retold by Sir Arthur Quiller-Couch.

Many of the famous picture books illustrated in the nineteenth century by Randolph Caldecott, Kate Greenaway, and Walter Crane are available in facsimiles. (See chapter 2.) Randolph Caldecott's *Come Lasses and Lads, The Fox Jumps over the Parson's Gate, A Frog He Would A-Wooing Go, Hey Diddle Diddle and Baby Bunting*, and *Ride a Cock Horse to Banbury X & a Farmer Went Trotting upon His Grey Mare* have been reproduced as New Orchard Classics. *A: Apple Pie* and *Kate Greenaway* are sources for viewing Kate Greenaway's early illustrations. Illustrations of Walter Crane are in *The Baby's Opera*, and Walter Crane's own analysis of illustrations are in a facsimile, *The Decorative Illustration of Books Old and New* by Walter Crane, which was first published in 1896 and reissued in 1984. Have students use the aesthetic scanning approach to view and discuss the illustrations.

Also, be sure that students are aware that the Caldecott Medal for outstanding illustration in the United States is named after Randolph Caldecott and that the Greenaway Medal for outstanding illustration in England is named after Kate Greenaway. Have students speculate about why these two illustrators have been so honored. Have students compare the early works of Caldecott and Greenaway with later winners of the Caldecott and Greenaway medals.

Many students are fascinated by movable books. Facsimile editions of these books are other excellent sources for early illustrations. Facsimile editions include Lothar Meggendorfer's *The City Park*, published around 1890; J. F. Schreiber's *The Great Menagerie*, originally published in 1884; and Ernest Nister's *Revolving Pictures*, first published in 1892, and *Animal Tales*, first published in 1894 under the title *Happy Families and Their Tales*. Additional background information on movable books appears in John Gross's "Pop-Up Books: The Magical Art of Making Movable Pictures over the Years," (1988) and Peter Haining's *Movable Books: An Illustrated History* (1979).

Finally, Lipkis recommends dividing the class into small groups to compare and discuss the illustrations in as many different editions of Aesop's fables as are available. Have students focus on various aspects of the books, such as the physical properties revealed by the endpapers, bindings, styles, and decorative elements; the impact of color and other elements in the illustrations; the media and styles used by the artists; the moods created by the illustrations; and illustration of storyline that is not developed in the text.

 ## STUDYING INSPIRATIONS FOR ART

After children have had many opportunities to look at and to discuss the art in picture books, make connections between artists' illustrations and the artists' inspirations. It is interesting to discover what artists, artistic time periods, artistic styles, or works have inspired contemporary artists and to compare the picture-book illustrations.

For example, for *Outside over There*, Maurice Sendak was inspired by the watercolors of British poet and artist William Blake in his choice of colors. H. W. Janson and Anthony F. Janson (1995) describe Blake, who lived from 1757 to 1827, as a painter of the Romantic movement who was inspired by literature to develop new ranges of subjects, emotions, and attitudes. Encourage children to discuss Sendak's illustrations in *Outside over There* and to compare them with illustrations by William Blake in art texts.

Help children make connections between the art of Maurice Sendak and the art of Randolph Caldecott, who lived from 1846 to 1886. In a review of Sendak's *We Are All in the Dumps with Jack and Guy*, Brian Alderson (1993a), the children's book editor of *The Times of London*, states: "Put it all down to Randolph Caldecott. As you may know, Maurice Sendak is a devotee of that Victorian picture-book artist, and indeed he designated an early book, *Hector Protector*, 'an intentionally contrived homage to this beloved teacher' " (p. 17). Like Caldecott, Sendak transforms rhymes into epics by introducing a pictorial narrative inspired by the slender texts of the rhymes. Alderson compares Sendak and Caldecott because "Caldecott loved to play with such visual counterpointing (the tragic demise of the dish eloping with the spoon; the decrepit beggar man fiddling while bonny lasses and lads dance around the maypole). The exercise probably helped to keep up his interest in his rudimentary copy" (p. 17). Many reissues of Caldecott's books, as discussed earlier, are available.

Make other connections using Caldecott's illustrations. Caldecott's style of creating movement in illustration strongly influenced artists such as Vincent Van Gogh and Paul Gauguin, as well as illustrators such as Beatrix Potter. Locate the paintings of Van Gogh and Gauguin in art books, including Carol Strickland's *The Annotated Mona Lisa: A Crash Course in Art History from Prehistoric to Post-Modern*, which includes a discussion of artists and their identifying characteristics. The illustrations of Beatrix Potter are readily available in her books, such as *The Tale of Peter Rabbit*. Enid and Leslie Linder's *The Art of Beatrix Potter* (1980) includes a large collection of Potter's drawings and paintings along with discussions about the works.

There are interesting connections between Clement Hurd's illustrations for Margaret Wise Brown's *Goodnight Moon* and a painting by Goya. Leonard S. Marcus (1991) describes how Hurd created the illustrations:

All March and for the rest of the spring, the artist worked on the illustrations for *Goodnight Moon*. Margaret had not given him many suggestions for the art, as she sometimes did. She simply scribbled a few brief notes and, along with them, offered inspiration in the form of a small color reproduction of Goya's dashing *Boy in Red*, which she pasted onto the notebook's front cover. (p. 20)

Ask students to look carefully at Hurd's illustrations for *Goodnight Moon* and respond to the mood created by colors, lines, shapes, and light. Ask the students to aesthetically scan Goya's painting and discuss the sensory and expressive qualities found in that art (see Ann Waldron's *Francisco Goya*). Are there any similarities between Goya's and Hurd's works? Was Hurd motivated by the *Boy in Red*? Why do you believe that Margaret Wise Brown sent Hurd the photo?

Leo Lionni identified the inspirational connections for his illustrations in an interview with Amanda Smith (1991). When Smith asked him about the artists whom he admired and who were his role models, Lionni said, "I think it's impossible today not to have Picasso as a hero, a role model. . . . I love Bonnard because of his way of handling his brush and color. For each [aspect] you have a different role model. My heroes are here" (p. 118). Hanging in his studio, Lionni has works of Giacometti, Calder, Klee, and Moore. Encourage children to view a number of Lionni's picture books and to compare his works with those of his heroes and role models. (Many of Picasso's works are found in Juliet Heslewood's *Introducing Picasso*.)

In an interview with David Wiesner, Susan Caroff and Elizabeth Moje (1992/1993) report that the greatest impact on Wiesner's work and the ways in which he tells stories is a book illustrated by Lynd Ward, *Mad Man's Drum*. Ward developed this novel for adults completely in woodcuts, without words. Wiesner states that he was very impressed with Ward's ability to develop a complex story dealing with complicated themes and imagery in a 250-page book with no words. Wiesner states:

I saw *Mad Man's Drum* in my sophomore year. Ward just amazed me—the process from page to page and the way he conveyed information and paced images. His ideas fit in with things I had begun to think about. . . . When I got to the point where I was ready to write my own books, I decided on the wordless book. My first attempt was *Free Fall*. (p. 284)

Encourage students to either compare Ward's and Wiesner's illustrations or to analyze Wiesner's ability to convey themes and imagery through wordless books.

In an interview with Gary Kelley, Marisa Bulzone (1993) explores Kelley's inspiration for illustrating Washington Irving's *The Legend of Sleepy Hollow*. Kelley states:

The story takes place sometime before 1790, so I did a lot of research into the painting of John Singleton Copley,

Is moralizing an appropriate role for picture books, or should the main role be the development of art and storytelling? In "The New Didacticism," Anita Silvey[1] states that creating messages in books for children is "an issue which has long been a cause for concern for those of us connected with children's books" (p. 5). Silvey points out:

Children's books have always alternated between periods when art for art's sake prevailed and times when using books to impart values prevailed. And until recently I believed that we were fortunate to be working with books in a period when the art of the book for children was of prime importance—what it taught, less so. But there seems to be a growing trend toward a new didacticism by the best of our authors and creators. The picture book these days seems particularly prone to moralizing. . . . But once we accept that moralizing is the appropriate role of a picture book, we begin to throw art and storytelling aside and invite the preachers and teachers into our books for children. (p. 5)

Silvey identifies books such as Chris Van Allsburg's *The Wretched Stone* and Susan Jeffers's *Brother Eagle, Sister Sky* as recent books that exemplify the new didacticism.

In the same issue of *The Horn Book*, Robert Hale[2] discusses the role of messages in books such as *Brother Eagle, Sister Sky* and Roald Dahl's *The Minpins*. He states:

Regardless of author's intent—whether there was meant to be a message or merely a very good story—what comes across to the child can depend upon the slant given by whoever is doing the reading. However, I can remember times when my children were little when they seemed to understand better than I the meaning of a book I was reading to them. Perhaps they would have seen through the truth of the story no matter how I slanted it. That's hopeful, isn't it? It confirms my faith in the young. They will get the message if we just make sure they get the books. (p. 113)

Authors of articles in the popular press are also questioning the role of didacticism in children's literature. Writing in *Newsweek*, Malcolm Jones[3] states:

In the current crop of children's literature, linguistic anarchy—any kind of anarchy—is largely passé. The emphasis is all on being good—respecting others, respecting yourself, allowing for cultural differences. It's tough stuff to knock, but you have to wonder whatever happened to old-fashioned fun like gluing your sister's hair to the bedpost. You wonder even harder if the people who create these "good" books ever had childhoods themselves. (p. 54)

After reading these three brief articles, debate the following issues:

1 What is the major role of a picture storybook written and illustrated for children?
2 If moralizing is appropriate in picture storybooks, what type of moralizing should be found in books for young children?
3 What should be the role of adults when sharing books with children?

Analyze recent illustrated picture books to decide if you believe that there is a new didacticism in the illustrations and stories. Find examples of books in which you believe that what is taught is of prime importance in the illustrations and in the text and find examples of books in which you think that the art and the storytelling are of prime importance.

---

[1]Silvey, Anita. "The New Didacticism." *The Horn Book* 68 (January/February 1992): 5.

[2]Hale, Robert. "Musings." *The Horn Book* 68 (January/February 1992): 112–113.

[3]Jones, Malcolm, Jr. "Kid Lit's Growing Pains: Books: Multiculturalists and Postmodern Ironists Invade the Nursery." *Newsweek* (November 22, 1993): 54–57.

Charles Wilson Peale, the Hudson River, and the Naive schools of painting because these were styles contemporary to the period in which the story took place. I wanted my illustrations to reflect their color palettes and the way these painters handled similar subject matter. You can see this especially in the illustrations with horses; the horse gallops in an unnatural way because that's the way horses were painted then. There was no photographic reference for painters. (p. 96)

Encourage children to compare Kelley's paintings and those that he used to conduct his research.

Quite different art works influenced artist Lane Smith (1993). Smith states that he was influenced by Monty Python, *Mad* magazine, and comic books. Smith says:

I think my palette, my sensibilities, and my composition were greatly influenced by films I saw as a child, especially the old Disney films like *Snow White* and *The Jungle Book.* Some of my work in *The Stinky Cheese Man*—the ugly duckling sequence in particular—is directly influenced by Tex Avery. He was an animation director from the forties—the one who always had his cartoon characters' eyeballs popping right out of their heads. All his work was very exaggerated. (p. 68)

Encourage students to compare Lane Smith's illustrations with those that inspired his art.

You may use many additional illustrators for similar activities. For example, Peter Sis (1992) states that he has always admired medieval artists like Bosch and Breughel and artists from the German Gothic school. Henrik Drescher's illustrations have been compared to those of Paul Klee and the German expressionists. John Steptoe, who illustrated *Stevie,* has been compared to the French painter Georges Rouault. According to Herbert R. Lottman (1993), illustrator Satomi Ichikawa was motivated to illustrate books after she discovered the art of Maurice Boutet de Monvel. In an interview with Masha Kabakow Rudman (1993), Ashley Bryan says that he was inspired by early religious books printed by hand using woodcuts when he illustrated texts based on African American spirituals, such as *I'm Going to Sing: Black American Spirituals.*

Two contemporary children are included in the artworks of specific periods. (Illustration by Bob Knox from The Great Art Adventure. *Copyright © 1993 by Bob Knox and Rizzoli International Publications. Reprinted by permission of Rizzoli International Publications.)*

INVESTIGATING THE WORKS OF GREAT ARTISTS

Many books currently published for children encourage the children to make discoveries about the history of art, to learn about elements and style in art, and to explore the art of renowned artists. Art history is introduced in a unique way in books by Bob Knox and by Laurene Krasny Brown and Marc Brown. In Knox's *The Great Art Adventure,* two children tour an art gallery, the Museum of World Art, beginning in the Hall of Ancient Egypt and continuing historically through such areas as Ancient Greece, Scandinavia, China, Oceania, North American Indian, and Mexico. You may use this book in several ways. Have students follow the trail through the museum and discuss the art. In addition to great art of the areas and periods, Knox illustrates Dave and Jane, the two picture-book characters, within the paintings. Consequently, you may use this book as a model for students to create their own tour of a museum in art. Have them place themselves in the

settings. Have them focus on the details of an artistic period in order to draw themselves into appropriate settings. *Visiting the Art Museum,* by Brown and Brown, follows a family through an art museum. Endnotes provide identification and interpretations for the art seen in the various galleries.

Two books for older readers introduce students to the history of art. H. W. Janson and Anthony F. Janson's *History of Art for Young People,* fifth edition, is a comprehensive text that proceeds from prehistoric art through twentieth-century art. It includes both color and black-and-white photographs of great paintings. A chronological chart lists milestones in political history, religion and literature, science, architecture, sculpture, painting, and photography from 1750 through 1980. Use this source to stimulate various research projects into time periods, artists, or connections among great contributions and events in history. Carol Strickland's *The Annotated Mona Lisa: A Crash Course in Art History from Prehistoric to Post-Modern* is another source for research projects. You may make interesting comparisons between the two books.

The artist introduces readers to the artistic elements. (From Picture This: Perception & Composition *by Molly Bang. Copyright © 1991 by Molly Bang. By permission of Little, Brown and Company.)*

Use books by Molly Bang and Kathleen Westray to introduce students to artistic elements. Bang's *Picture This: Perception & Composition* is especially good for learning about and experimenting with line, color, and shape. As Bang makes decisions about lines, colors, and shapes for a picture storybook version of "Little Red Riding Hood," she discusses the emotional impact of each choice. Use this book to stimulate students to experiment, make choices within these elements, and develop their own pictures.

To help students learn more about painting, use Bang's preface, which includes information about how she searched for structure in her own paintings and for ways to improve her painting. Bang states that she took a painting course, read books on art and psychology of art, looked at pictures, decided what she was feeling as she looked at each painting, determined how those feelings related to the structure of the picture, and defined what she was accomplishing by teaching children concepts about illustrating. She concludes:

The principles in *Picture This* are tools, but like any tools, they can't be truly understood until they are used. Once you begin to cut and play with pieces of construction paper on your own, you will understand how the principles work. As you make pictures that are increasingly clear and meaningful, you will also see the artist in you begin to come alive. (p. xi)

This excellent advice can help people of all ages gain insights into perception and composition.

Use Kathleen Westray's *A Color Sampler* to encourage students to experiment with color. In addition to discussing and illustrating primary, secondary, intermediate, and complementary colors, Westray develops color concepts, such as the influences of darker and lighter backgrounds, placement of colors, and optical illusions created by colors. Creating optical illusions is of special interest to many students.

Have students investigate specific artistic styles, using books by Jude Welton and by Jan Greenberg and Sandra Jordan. Welton's *Impressionism* interweaves biographical information about the artists with color reproductions of their paintings. Use this book as introductory research for artistic style or to stimulate students to conduct further research into the lives and works of specific artists. Greenberg and Jordan's *The Painter's Eye: Learning to Look at Contemporary American Art* provides an in-depth discussion of modern art.

You may use numerous highly illustrated books for research projects in which students investigate the works of one artist. One of the most interesting books for all children is Christina Bjork's *Linnea in Monet's Garden.* According to Roni Natov (1989), this

The author used William Johnson's paintings to illustrate a fictional story. (From Li'l Sis and Uncle Willie: A Story Based on the Life and Paintings of William H. Johnson by Gwen Everett, illustrations by William H. Johnson. Published by Rizzoli International Publications, Inc., 1991. Illustration reprinted by permission of the National Museum of American Art, the Smithsonian Institution, Washington, D.C.)

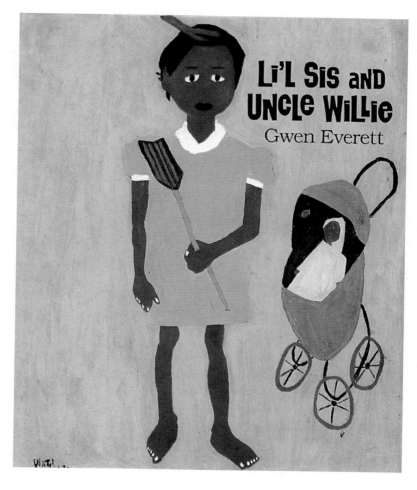

book is exciting because "it recreates, with the excitement and wonder of the most fantastic fictional journeys, the external journey of the informational narrative as it is internalized into a child's consciousness. Linnea's perceptions are noted all along the way and serve to guide us into the world of 19th century Paris, Impressionism, and Monet's famous paintings of water lilies" (p. 96). Along with Linnea, readers can learn about Monet and discover the excitement of visualizing nature and paintings in new ways. After children read *Linnea in Monet's Garden,* have them conduct their own research into the work and life of Monet. Jude Welton's *Monet* is a source for numerous reproductions of paintings, discussions about the paintings, and biographical information about Monet. Patricia Wright's *Manet* is another source for researching French artists and impressionism.

Use *Linnea in Monet's Garden* as a model to stimulate students to create stories in which they make discoveries about great artists. Leonardo da Vinci is an excellent subject for such a visual journey. For this task, have students use Richard McLanathan's *Leonardo da Vinci,* Diane Stanley's *Leonardo da Vinci,* or Rosabianca Skira-Venturi's *A Weekend with Leonardo da Vinci.* For a study of Rembrandt, have students use Gary Schwartz's *Rembrandt.* Use Ann Waldron's *Francisco Goya* for a study of Goya. Likewise, introduce a study of Picasso, his life, and his art with Juliet Heslewood's *Introducing Picasso* or introduce a study of Andrew Wyeth with Richard Meryman's *Andrew Wyeth.* For a study of Grant Wood use John Duggleby's *Artist In Overalls: The Life of Grant Wood.*

Use the paintings of one artist to stimulate students to write a story to accompany existing art. For this task, use Gwen Everett's *Li'l Sis and Uncle Willie:*

A Story Based on the Life and Paintings of William H. Johnson as a model. Everett uses paintings and events in the life of African American painter William Johnson to create a fictional story. The artist's paintings appear to be the illustrations for the story. In addition, you may use many of the previously discussed art texts as sources for such activities.

Robyn Montana Turner's books focusing on "Portraits of Women Artists for Children" are interesting sources for a study of female artists. These books include *Frida Kahlo, Mary Cassatt, Faith Ringgold, Georgia O'Keeffe,* and *Rosa Bonheur. The American Eye: Eleven Artists of the Twentieth Century* by Jan Greenberg and Sandra Jordan provides short biographies of artists.

For a focus on illustrators of children's books, have students begin their study with Pat Cummings's *Talking with Artists.* This book provides information on fourteen artists, including Leo and Diane Dillon, Steven Kellogg, Jerry Pinkney, Lane Smith, Chris Van Allsburg, and David Wiesner. Throughout this text are suggestions for motivating children to respond to literature through artistic interpretations of books or to create their own illustrations using specific art media.

SUGGESTED ACTIVITIES

for Involving Children with Artists and Their Illustrations

- Lead a discussion group and encourage aesthetic responses to illustrations.

- Using a specific book, show how you would apply aesthetic scanning and visual literacy to the book.

- Using Gladys S. Blizzard's *Come Look with Me: World of Play* as a model, develop a series of questions that focus on aesthetic elements in an illustration.

- Choose a folktale and locate as many illustrated versions as you can that are published during different time periods. Compare the illustrations in the texts.

- Compare the illustrated works of Maurice Sendak and Randolph Caldecott, or choose another artist and investigate the inspirations for that artist.

- Choose an artist and develop a bibliography of the artist's works.

- Using Rosemary Davidson's *Take a Look: An Introduction to the Experience of Art* as a resource, discuss the varied purposes for art such as storytelling and recording events and images.

CHILDREN'S LITERATURE

Aardema, Verna. *How the Ostrich Got Its Long Neck: A Tale from the Akamba of Kenya.* Illustrated by Marcia Brown. Scholastic, 1995 (I:4–7 R:5). The illustrator has won several awards.

_____. *Why Mosquitoes Buzz in People's Ears.* Illustrated by Leo and Diane Dillon. Dial, 1975 (I:5–9 R:6) An African cumulative tale tells the humorous reason for mosquitoes' buzzing.

Ackerman, Karen. *Song and Dance Man.* Illustrated by Stephen Gammell. Knopf, 1988 (I:3–8 R:4). Grandpa re-creates the magic of vaudeville for his grandchildren.

Andersen, Hans Christian. *The Nightingale.* Retold by Eva LeGalliene. Illustrated by Nancy Ekholm Burkert. Harper & Row, 1968 (I:6–12 R:8). The fairy tale is beautifully illustrated.

_____. *The Wild Swans.* Retold by Amy Ehrlich. Illustrated by Susan Jeffers. Dial, 1981 (I:7–12 R:7). Finely detailed illustrations develop a fantasy setting.

Aylesworth, Jim. *Country Crossing.* Illustrated by Ted Rand. Atheneum, 1991 (I:3–7). The artist's use of color creates moods reflecting warmth and danger.

Baker, Jeannie. *Where the Forest Meets the Sea.* Greenwillow, 1988 (I:4–10). An Australian forest comes to life through the collage technique.

_____. *Window.* Greenwillow, 1991 (I:all). Heavy collage illustrations create the feelings of outdoor settings.

Baker, Olaf. *Where the Buffaloes Begin.* Illustrated by Stephen Gammell. Warne, 1981 (I:8+ R:7). Illustrations with soft, irregular shapes add power to a Native American legend.

Bang, Molly. *Picture This: Perception & Composition.* Little, Brown, 1991 (I:10+). Bang uses various shapes to illustrate perception concepts.

Banks, Kate. *And If the Moon Could Talk.* Illustrated by Georg Hallensleben. Farrar Straus Giroux, 1998 (I:3–6 R:4). Oil paintings illustrate the text.

Beckett, Sister Wendy. *A Child's Book of Prayer in Art.* Dorling Kindersley, 1995 (I:all). Paintings from great artists are reproduced to show spiritual values.

Bedard, Michael. *Emily.* Illustrated by Barbara Cooney. Doubleday, 1992 (I:all). Acrylic paints and pastels create the world of Emily Dickinson.

Bemelmans, Ludwig. *Madeline.* Viking, 1939, 1977 (I:4–9 R:5). Madeline lives in Paris with eleven other little girls and has an appendectomy.

_____. *Madeline in London.* Viking, 1961, 1977 (I:4–9 R:3). Madeline and eleven little girls visit London.

Ben-Ezer, Ehud. *Hosni the Dreamer: An Arabian Tale.* Illustrated by Uri Shulevitz. Farrar, Straus, and Giroux, 1997 (I:4–8 R:4). Watercolors depict the hues of the desert.

Bierhorst, John, trans. *Spirit Child: A Story of the Nativity.* Illustrated by Barbara Cooney. Morrow, 1984 (I:8–10 R:6). Pre-Columbian style illustrations accompany an Aztec story.

Bjork, Christina. *Linnea in Monet's Garden.* Illustrated by Lena Anderson. Farrar, Straus & Giroux, 1987 (I:all R:6). Photographs show Monet's paintings and garden.

_____

I = Interest by age range

R = Readability by grade level

Blizzard, Gladys S. *Come Look with Me: World of Play.* Thomasson-Grant, 1993 (I:all). Art appreciation is developed through works of art and accompanying questions that stimulate discussion.

Bowen, Betsy. *Antler, Bear, Canoe: A Northwoods Alphabet Year.* Little, Brown, 1991 (I:all). The illustrations are woodcuts.

Brett, Jan. *Berlioz the Bear.* Putnam, 1991 (I:5–8 R:6). Two complementary stories are developed through the illustrations and the borders.

Brooke, L. Leslie. *Johnny Crow's Garden.* Warne, 1903, 1986 (I:all). A personified animal tale is considered a classic in children's book illustration.

Brown, Laurene Krasny, and Marc Brown. *Visiting the Art Museum.* Dutton, 1986 (I:6+). A family tours an art museum.

Brown, Marcia. *Once a Mouse.* Scribner's Sons, 1961 (I:3–7 R:6). Woodcuts provide powerful illustrations for a fable from India.

Brown, Margaret Wise. *Goodnight Moon.* Illustrated by Clement Hurd. Harper, 1947 (I:2–7). A book for young children that creates a calm atmosphere at bedtime.

Bryan, Ashley. *I'm Going to Sing: Black American Spirituals*, Vol. 2. Atheneum, 1982 (I:all). Words, music, and illustrations present a black experience.

Bunting, Eve. *Ghost's Hour, Spook's Hour.* Illustrated by Donald Carrick. Clarion, 1987 (I:2–7 R:2). The colors express fear and later security.

_____ . *Smoky Night.* Illustrated by David Diaz. Harcourt Brace, 1994 (I:all). Collage illustrations depict this story of the Los Angeles riots.

Burkert, Nancy Ekholm. *Valentine & Orson.* Farrar, Straus and Giroux, 1989 (I:10+). The illustrations depict a setting in the Middle Ages.

Burton, Virginia Lee. *The Little House.* Houghton Mifflin, 1942 (I:3–7 R:3). Repetition creates a sense of rhythm in illustrations.

_____ . *Mike Mulligan and His Steam Shovel.* Houghton Mifflin, 1939 (I:3–7 R:3). Mike Mulligan and his steam shovel work together.

Caldecott, Randolph. *Come Lasses and Lads.* New Orchard, 1988. This is a reissue of a book published in the 1800s.

_____ . *The Fox Jumps over the Parson's Gate.* New Orchard, 1988. This is a reissue of a book published in the 1800s.

_____ . *A Frog He Would A-Wooing Go.* New Orchard, 1988. This is a reissue of a book published in the 1800s.

_____ . *Hey Diddle Diddle and Baby Bunting.* New Orchard, 1988. This is a reissue of a book published in the 1800s.

_____ . *Ride a Cock Horse to Banbury X & a Farmer Went Trotting upon His Grey Mare.* New Orchard, 1988. This is a reissue of a book published in the 1800s.

Carle, Eric. *Catch the Ball.* Philomel, 1982 (I:3–6). A string attached to a ball encourages vocabulary development in children.

_____ . *Eric Carle's Animals Animals.* Philomel, 1989 (I:3–9). Collage illustrations accompany an anthology of poetry.

_____ . *From Head to Toe.* HarperCollins, 1997 (I:3–7). Brightly colored collages of animals and children illustrate body movements.

_____ . *The Honeybee and the Robber: A Moving/Picture Book.* Philomel, 1981 (I:3–6). A brightly colored pop-up allows children to move the wings of a bee and a butterfly.

_____ . *Let's Paint a Rainbow.* Philomel, 1982 (I:3–6). Rainbow colors help children learn eight basic colors.

_____ . *The Very Hungry Caterpillar.* Crowell, 1971 (I:2–7). A colorful collage picture book presents the life cycle of a caterpillar, who eats his way through the pages.

Carlstrom, Nancy White. *Northern Lullaby.* Illustrated by Leo and Diane Dillon. Philomel, 1992 (I:4–7). The illustrations depict Alaskan native peoples.

_____ . *Raven and River.* Illustrated by Jon Van Zyle. Little, Brown, 1997 (I:4–8). Considerable texture accompanies the poetic text.

Carroll, Colleen. *How Artists See Animals: Mammal Fish Bird Reptile.* Abbeville, 1996 (I:8–12). Paintings of animals are discussed.

_____ . *How Artists See the Elements: Earth Air Fire Water.* Abbeville, 1996 (I:8–12). Paintings of the elements are discussed.

_____ . *How Artists See People: Boy Girl Man Woman.* Abbeville, 1996 (I:8–12). Paintings of people are discussed.

_____ . *How Artists See the Weather: Sun Rain Wind Snow.* Abbeville, 1996 (I:8–12). Paintings of weather are discussed.

Cassedy, Sylvia, and Kunihiro Suetake, translated by. *Red Dragonfly on My Shoulder.* Illustrated by Molly Bang. HarperCollins, 1992 (I:7+). Collage illustrations are created out of materials such as cookies and foil.

Cendrars, Blaise. *Shadow.* Illustrated by Marcia Brown. Scribner's Sons, 1982 (I:all). Collage and dark colors create the world of the spirits.

Chaucer, Geoffrey. *Canterbury Tales.* Adapted by Barbara Cohen. Illustrated by Trina Schart Hyman. Lothrop, Lee & Shepard, 1988 (I:8+). Illustrations are framed in a formal manner.

Cooney, Barbara. *Chanticleer and the Fox.* Adapted from Geoffrey Chaucer. Crowell, 1958 (I:5–10 R:4). Chanticleer the rooster and a sly fox trick each other.

_____ . *Eleanor.* Viking, 1996 (I:6–8 R:4). The illustrations emphasize Eleanor Roosevelt's isolation and loneliness as a child.

_____ . *Island Boy.* Viking Kestrel, 1988 (I:3–8 R:3). Text and illustrations show an earlier time on a New England island.

Crane, Walter. *The Baby's Opera.* Simon & Schuster, 1981 (I:all). This is a reprint of a classic in illustration.

Croll, Carolyn. *Redoute: The Man Who Painted Flowers.* Putnam's, 1996 (I:8+). The author presents the life of the French artist who lived in the 1800s.

Crossley-Holland, Kevin. *Beowulf.* Illustrated by Charles Keeping. Oxford, 1982 (I:10+ R:6). Strong lines depict the power of a heroic character.

Cummings, Pat, ed. *Talking with Artists.* Bradbury, 1992 (I:8+). The text includes conversations with many well-known children's artists.

Davidson, Rosemary. *Take a Look: An Introduction to the Experience of Art.* Viking, 1994 (I:10+ R:6). This is an introduction to art appreciation.

Day, Nancy Raine. *The Lion's Whiskers: An Ethiopian Folktale.* Illustrated by Ann Grifalconi. Scholastic, 1995 (I:5–8 R:5). A woman discovers how to solve her problems.

dePaola, Tomie. *Big Anthony and the Magic Ring.* Harcourt Brace Jovanovich, 1979 (I:5–9 R:3). Big Anthony uses Strega Nona's magic ring to turn himself into a handsome young man.

_____ . *Charlie Needs a Cloak.* Prentice-Hall, 1973 (I:3–6 R:4). A simple information book tells in a humorous way how a shepherd shears sheep, cards and spins wool, weaves and dyes the cloth, and then sews a cloak.

_____ . *Christopher: The Holy Giant.* Holiday, 1994 (I:4–8 R:4). The story of the man who carries the child Jesus across the water.

_____ . *The Clown of God.* Harcourt Brace Jovanovich, 1978 (I:all R:4). A legend tells about a juggler and a miracle.

_____ . *An Early American Christmas.* Holiday House, 1987 (I:4–7 R:6). A text and illustrations depict Christmas with a New England family living in the early 1800s.

_____ . *Giorgio's Village.* Putnam, 1982 (I:all). A pop-up book illustrates an Italian Renaissance village.

_____ . *Helga's Dowry: A Troll Love Story.* Harcourt Brace Jovanovich, 1977 (I:5–9 R:4). Helga leaves the world of trolls to earn a dowry.

_____ . *The Legend of the Bluebonnet.* Putnam, 1983 (I:all R:6). In a Comanche tale, unselfish actions are rewarded.

_____ . *The Legend of the Indian Paintbrush.* Putnam, 1987 (I:all R:6). A Native American tale tells about the beginning of a wildflower.

_____ . *Tomie dePaola's Mother Goose.* Putnam, 1985 (I:2–6). Folk art makes this an appealing edition.

_____ . *Watch Out for the Chicken Feet in Your Soup.* Prentice-Hall, 1974 (I:3–7 R:2). Joey is embarrassed by his grandmother's old-fashioned ways until his friend shows great admiration for her.

Dickens, Charles. *Christmas Carol.* Illustrated by Roberto Innocenti. Stewart, Tabori & Chang, 1990 (I:10+ R:6). Full-page watercolors enhance the setting.

Duggleby, John. *Artist In Overalls: The Life of Grant Wood.* Chronicle, 1995 (I:8+ R:8). Reproductions of paintings and a selection of drawings should interest art students.

Dunrea, Olivier. *The Trow-Wife's Treasure.* Farrar Straus Giroux, 1998 (I:4–8). Gouache paintings develop the setting.

Ehlert, Lois. *Cuckoo/Cucu.* Harcourt Brace, 1997 (I:4–7). The paper-collage illustrations were inspired by Mexican folk art.

_____ . *Red Leaf, Yellow Leaf.* Harcourt Brace Jovanovich, 1991 (I:3–7). Collage illustrations follow the life of a maple tree.

Eliot, T. S. *Mr. Mistoffelees with Mungojerrie and Rumpelteazer.* Illustrated by Errol Le Cain. Harcourt Brace Jovanovich, 1991 (I:6+). Considerable movement is created in the illustrations.

Emberley, Barbara. *Drummer Hoff.* Illustrated by Ed Emberley. Prentice-Hall, 1967 (I:3–7 R:6). A cumulative rhyme depicts in woodcuts all the people associated with firing a cannon.

Emberley, Ed. *Ed Emberley's Picture Pie 2: A Drawing Book and Stencil.* Little, Brown, 1996 (I:all). Stencils and directions encourage children to create their own drawings.

Esbensen, Barbara. *The Star Maiden.* Illustrated by Helen Davie. Little, Brown, 1988 (I:all). Illustrations reinforce the Ojibway origins of the tale.

_____ . *Tiger with Wings: The Great Horned Owl.* Illustrated by Mary Barrett Brown. Orchard, 1991 (I:6–10). Lines create the textures of the animals.

Everett, Gwen. *Li'l Sis and Uncle Willie: A Story Based on the Life and Paintings of William H. Johnson.* Illustrated by William H. Johnson. Rizzoli, 1992 (I:5–8 R:5). The author tells a story using the paintings of a famous African American painter.

Fain, Moira. *Snow Day.* Walker, 1996 (I:6–10 R:4). Oil illustrations provide the setting.

Feelings, Tom. *The Middle Passage: White Ships/Black Cargo.* Dial, 1995 (I:10+). The illustrations in this wordless book are in pen, ink, and tempera.

Field, Eugene. *Wynken, Blynken and Nod.* Illustrated by Susan Jeffers. Dutton, 1982. The classic poem appears in a newly illustrated edition.

Fleischman, Sid. *The Scarebird.* Illustrated by Peter Sis. Greenwillow, 1988 (I:7+ R:4). An old man's loneliness is changed by friendship.

Fleming, Denise. *In the Small, Small Pond.* Holt, 1993 (I:3–6). Rich colors enhance the pond setting.

Foreman, Michael. *Michael Foreman's Mother Goose.* Harcourt Brace Jovanovich, 1991 (I:6+). The illustrator suggests movement by relating one illustration to the following illustration.

_____ . *Seal Surfer.* Harcourt Brace, 1997 (I:5–9). Watercolors depict the many moods of the sea.

Frost, Robert. *Stopping by Woods on a Snowy Evening.* Illustrated by Susan Jeffers. Dutton, 1978 (I:all). This is a highly illustrated version of the poem.

Gaffney, Timothy R. *Grandpa Takes Me to the Moon.* Illustrated by Barry Root. Morrow, 1996 (I:4–8 R:4). Watercolors and gouache paintings illustrate the book.

Gág, Wanda. *Millions of Cats.* Coward, McCann, 1928 (I:3–7 R:3). An old woman's desire for a pretty cat results in a fight among trillions of cats.

Geisert, Arthur. *The Etcher's Studio.* Houghton Mifflin, 1997 (I:all). The artist uses full-color etchings to illustrate a book about an etcher's studio.

George, Jean Craighead. *The First Thanksgiving.* Illustrated by Thomas Locker. Philomel, 1993 (I:all). Oil paintings provide a rich setting for the story of the Pilgrims.

Goble, Paul. *Beyond the Ridge.* Bradbury, 1989 (I:all R:5). An elderly Indian woman from the Great Plains experiences death and goes to the afterlife.

_____ . *Buffalo Woman.* Bradbury, 1984 (I:all R:6). A bond between animals and humans is developed in a tale from the Great Plains.

_____ . *Death of the Iron Horse.* Bradbury, 1987 (I:8+ R:5). This story is based on an incident in 1867 when a Union Pacific freight train was derailed by Cheyenne Indians.

_____ . *The Gift of the Sacred Dog.* Bradbury, 1980 (I:all R:6). The Sioux tale tells how the horse was given to the people.

_____ . *The Girl Who Loved Wild Horses.* Bradbury, 1978 (I:6–10 R:5). Colors and line are especially important in this story about a Native American girl.

_____ . *Iktomi and the Berries.* Watts, 1989 (I:4–10 R:4). Iktomi is a trickster character from the Lakota Sioux.

_____ . *Iktomi and the Boulder: A Plains Indian Story.* Orchard, 1988 (I:4–10 R:4). Another trickster tale from the Lakota Sioux.

_____ . *Star Boy.* Bradbury, 1983 (I:6–10 R:5). This is a tale from the Blackfoot Indians.

Greenaway, Kate. *A: Apple Pie.* Castle, 1979 (I:all). This is a reissue of a classic in illustration.

_____ . *Kate Greenaway.* Rizzoli, 1977 (I:all). This is a collection of many of Kate Greenaway's illustrations.

Greenberg, Jan, and Sandra Jordan. *The American Eye: Eleven Artists of the Twentieth Century.* Delacorte, 1995 (I:10+ R:7). The text includes short biographies of artists.

_____ . *The Painter's Eye: Learning to Look at Contemporary American Art.* Delacorte, 1991 (I:10+ R:6). The text and illustrations help explain contemporary art.

_____ . *The Sculptor's Eye: Looking at Contemporary American Art.* Delacorte, 1993 (I:10+ R:6). The text and illustrations help explain sculpture.

Griego, Margot C., Betsy L. Bucks, Sharon S. Gilbert, and Laurel H. Kimball. *Tortillitas Para Mama and Other Spanish Nursery Rhymes.* Illustrated by Barbara Cooney. Holt, Rinehart & Winston, 1981 (I:3–7). Nursery rhymes appear in Spanish and English.

Grimes, Nikki. *Something on My Mind.* Illustrated by Tom Feelings. Dial, 1978 (I:all). Beautifully illustrated poems tell about the joys, fears, hopes, and sorrows of growing up.

Grimm, Brothers. *The Golden Bird,* retold by Neil Philip. Illustrated by Isabelle Brent. Little, Brown, 1995 (I:all). The illustrations and text pages are framed with gold-leaf designs.

_____ . *Hansel and Gretel.* Illustrated by Susan Jeffers. Dial, 1980 (I:5–9 R:6). Illustrations convey the dark mood of this classic folk tale.

_____ . *Hansel and Gretel.* Retold by Rika Lesser. Illustrated by Paul O. Zelinsky. Dodd, Mead, 1984 (I:all R:6). The folktale appears in another beautifully illustrated version.

_____ . *Little Red Riding Hood.* Illustrated by Trina Schart Hyman. Holiday House, 1983 (I:6–9 R:7). Richly bordered text pages add to the visual effect.

_____ . *Rapunzel.* Retold and illustrated by Paul O. Zelinsky. Dutton, 1997 (I:all). Oil paintings provide dramatic settings.

_____ . *Rumpelstiltskin.* Retold and illustrated by Paul O. Zelinsky. Dutton, 1986 (I:all). Oil paintings add a glowing mood to the tale.

_____ . *Snow White and the Seven Dwarfs.* Illustrated by Nancy Ekholm Burkert. Farrar, Straus & Giroux, 1972 (I:7–12 R:6). Carefully researched illustrations complement this fairy tale.

Grimm, Wilhelm. *Dear Mili.* Translated by Ralph Manheim. Illustrated by Maurice Sendak. Farrar, Straus & Giroux, 1988 (I:all R:6). This story was found in a letter written in 1816.

Haley, Gail E. *A Story, a Story.* Atheneum, 1970 (I:6–10 R:6). An African tale tells about a spider man's bargain with Sky God.

Hall, Donald. *Ox-Cart Man.* Illustrations by Barbara Cooney. Viking, 1979 (I:3–8 R:5). Subtle illustrations complement a tale about a New England farmer in the early 1800s.

Hamilton, Virginia. *Her Stories: African American Folktales, Fairy Tales, and True Tales.* Scholastic, 1995 (I:all). The illustrations are painted in acrylics.

_____ . *The People Could Fly: American Black Folktales.* Illustrated by Leo and Diane Dillon. Knopf, 1985 (I:9+ R:6). Black-and-white illustrations reinforce the folktale quality of the book.

Helprin, Mark. *Swan Lake.* Illustrated by Chris Van Allsburg. Houghton Mifflin, 1989 (I:all R:8). The text is a retelling of the classic ballet.

Hendershot, Judith. *In Coal Country.* Illustrated by Thomas Allen. Knopf, 1987 (I:5–9 R:3). The artist and author depict growing up in an Ohio coal town.

Heslewood, Juliet. *Introducing Picasso.* Little, Brown, 1993 (I:9+). Numerous colored reproductions highlight Picasso's art.

Ho, Minfong. *Hush! A Thai Lullaby.* Illustrated by Holly Meade. Orchard, 1996 (I:3–8). The illustrations were inspired by Thai art forms.

Hoban, Tana. *Shadows and Reflections.* Greenwillow, 1990 (I:all). Photographs show the power of lines as shown in reflections.

Hodges, Margaret. *Saint George and the Dragon.* Illustrated by Trina Schart Hyman. Little, Brown, 1984 (I:9+ R:7). The classic tale is beautifully illustrated.

Holling, Holling Clancy. *Paddle-to-the-Sea.* Houghton Mifflin, 1941 (I:7–12 R:4). A Native American boy carves a canoe and places it where it will flow into Lake Superior.

_____ . *Seabird.* Houghton Mifflin, 1948 (I:7–12 R:4). A carved gull travels with several generations of one family.

Hughes, Langston. *The Sweet and Sour Animal Book.* Illustrated by students from the Harlem School of Arts. Oxford University Press, 1994 (I:all). Sculptures made from paper, cardboard, and clay illustrate the poems.

Innocenti, Roberto. *Rose Blanche.* Stewart, Tabori & Shang, 1990 (I:8+ R:4). Somber tones create the setting for a Holocaust story.

Irving, Washington. *The Legend of Sleepy Hollow.* Illustrated by Gary Kelley. Creative Education, 1990 (I:9+). A newly illustrated version of the classic.

_____ . *The Legend of Sleepy Hollow.* Illustrated by Will Moses. Philomel, 1995 (I:all). The illustrator is the great grandson of the folk artist Grandma Moses.

Isaacs, Anne. *Swamp Angel.* Illustrated by Paul O. Zelinsky. Dutton, 1994 (I:all). Paintings create a folk-art dimension.

Jackson, Shelley. *The Old Woman and the Wave.* DK, 1998 (I: 4–7 R:4). Collage illustrations create the environment.

Janson, H. W., and Anthony F. Janson. *History of Art for Young People,* 5th Ed. Abrams, 1997 (I:10+). This text provides an extensive survey of art.

Jeffers, Susan. *Brother Eagle, Sister Sky.* Dial, 1991 (I:all). The illustrations accompany an adaptation of a letter written by Chief Seattle.

_____ . *Three Jovial Huntsmen.* Bradbury, 1973 (I:4–8). The nursery rhyme is highly illustrated.

Johnson, James Weldon. *The Creation.* Illustrated by Carla Golembe. Little, Brown, 1993 (I:all). Striking colors accompany the poem by an African American poet.

Johnson, Stephen T. *Alphabet City.* Viking, 1995 (I:all). Urban settings illustrate each letter of the alphabet.

Keats, Ezra Jack. *Apt. 3.* Macmillan, 1974 (I:3–8 R:3). A young boy and a blind man interact in a rundown apartment building.

_____ . *Dreams.* Macmillan, 1974 (I:3–8 R:3). Everyone dreams about Robert's handmade mouse.

_____ . *Goggles!* Macmillan, 1969 (I:5–9 R:3). Two boys escape from bullies.

_____ . *Louie.* Greenwillow, 1975 (I:3–8 R:2). Other children surprise Louie with a puppet.

_____ . *Peter's Chair.* Harper & Row, 1967 (I:3–8 R:2). Peter overcomes jealousy about a new baby sister.

_____ . *Regards to the Man in the Moon.* Four Winds, 1981 (I:4–8 R:3). Two children build a spaceship out of junk and take an imaginary ride.

_____ . *The Snowy Day.* Viking, 1962 (I:2–6 R:2). Peter experiences a great snowfall.

_____ . *The Trip.* Greenwillow, 1978 (I:3–8 R:2). Louie is lonesome in a new neighborhood.

Kleven, Elisa. *Hooray, A Pinata!* Dutton, 1996 (I:4–7). Collages illustrate the book.

_____ . *The Puddle Pail.* Dutton, 1997 (I:5–8). Collage illustrations use paper and fabric.

Knox, Bob. *The Great Art Adventure*. Rizzoli, 1992 (I:all). Two children visit an art museum where the paintings come to life.

Krauss, Ruth. *A Hole Is to Dig*. Illustrated by Maurice Sendak. Harper & Row, 1952 (I:2–6 R:2). Illustrations of children depict children's definitions for such things as brothers, mud, and mountains.

Krensky, Stephen. *Breaking Into Print: Before and After the Invention of the Printing Press*. Illustrated by Bonnie Christensen. Little, Brown, 1996 (I:7–10 R:4). Colored wood engravings illustrate the book.

Lawson, Robert. *Ben and Me*. Little, Brown, 1939 (I:7–11 R:6). Amos Mouse tells the story of his friend Benjamin Franklin.

_____. *Rabbit Hill*. Viking, 1944 (I:7–11 R:7). Will the new humans on the hill be friends or enemies to the animals that live there?

Leaf, Munro. *The Story of Ferdinand*. Illustrated by Robert Lawson. Viking, 1936 (I:4–10 R:6). Ferdinand proves that he'd rather smell the flowers than fight the matador.

LeGalliene, Eva. *The Nightingale*. A retelling of Hans Christian Andersen's tale. Illustrated by Nancy Ekholm Burkert. Harper & Row, 1965 (I:6–12 R:8). An emperor learns that a live nightingale is preferable to a jeweled mechanical bird.

Lenski, Lois. *Sing a Song of People*. Illustrated by Giles Laroche. Little, Brown, 1987. (I:all). Cut-paper illustrations depict the poem.

Lent, Blair. *Bayberry Bluff*. Houghton Mifflin, 1987 (I:3–8 R:6). A town evolves from a tenting community to elaborately decorated houses.

Lewis, Paul Owen. *Storm Boy*. Beyond Words, 1995 (I:7+ R:6). The illustrations follow the mythic traditions of native peoples.

Lindbergh, Reeve. *Johnny Appleseed*. Illustrated by Kathy Jakobsen. Little, Brown, 1990 (I:all). The illustrations create the early American setting for the poem.

Lionni, Leo. *Alexander and the Wind-up Mouse*. Pantheon, 1969 (I:3–6 R:3). A real mouse envies a lovable windup mouse.

_____. *A Color of His Own*. Random House, 1975 (I:2–7 R:5). In an animal fable, the chameleon looks for his own color.

_____. *Pezzettino*. Pantheon, 1975 (I:2–6 R:3). Pezzettino, or Little Piece, is so small that he believes he must be a piece of someone else.

_____. *Swimmy*. Pantheon, 1963 (I:2–6 R:3). A little fish learns about the marvels of the sea.

Livingston, Myra Cohn. *A Circle of Seasons*. Illustrated by Leonard Everett Fisher. Holiday House, 1982 (I:all). Poems look at the four seasons.

Lobel, Arnold. *Fables*. Jonathon Cape, 1980 (I:all). Literary fables are created by the author.

Locker, Thomas. *Sailing with the Wind*. Dial, 1986. (I:all). Oil paintings complement the mood of the story.

_____. *Where the River Begins*. Dial, 1984 (I:all). Full-page paintings complement a search for the source of a river.

Longfellow, Henry Wadsworth. *Hiawatha*. Illustrated by Susan Jeffers. Dial, 1983 (I:all). The poem is beautifully illustrated.

_____. *Hiawatha's Childhood*. Illustrated by Errol LeCain. Farrar, Straus & Giroux, 1984 (I:all). Excerpts appear from Longfellow's longer poem.

McCloskey, Robert. *Blueberries for Sal*. Viking, 1948 (I:4–8 R:6). A little girl mistakes a bear for her mother.

_____. *Lentil*. Viking, 1940 (I:4–9 R:7). Lentil saves a homecoming celebration.

_____. *Make Way for Ducklings*. Viking, 1941 (I:4–8 R:4). A city park provides a safe home for the ducklings.

_____. *One Morning in Maine*. Viking, 1952 (I:4–8 R:3). Sal and her family live on an island.

_____. *Time of Wonder*. Viking, 1957 (I:5–8 R:4). A family confronts a hurricane on its island.

McCully, Emily Arnold. *The Ballot Box Battle*. Knopf, 1996 (I:4–8 R:5). The illustrations depict an 1880s setting.

_____. *The Bobbin Girl*. Dial, 1996 (I:6–9 R:5). The picture storybook is set in New England in the 1830s.

_____. *Mirette on the High Wire*. Putnam, 1992 (I:all). The illustrations are completed in watercolors.

McCurdy, Michael. *The Devils Who Learned to Be Good*. Little, Brown, 1987 (I:6–9 R:6). Wood engravings illustrate a Russian tale.

McDermott, Beverly Brodsky. *The Golem*. Lippincott, 1976 (I:9–14 R:5). Illustrations capture the magic spell that creates the Golem from a lump of clay.

McDermott, Gerald. *Arrow to the Sun*. Viking, 1974 (I:3–9 R:2). Strong shapes and colors complement a Native American tale.

_____. *Sun Flight*. Four Winds, 1980 (I:all R:6). Daedalus the master craftsman and his son construct wings and escape from Crete.

MacGill-Callahan, Sheila. *The Children of Lir*. Illustrated by Gennady Spirin. Dial, 1993 (I:6+ R:5). Watercolors enhance this Celtic tale.

MacLachlan, Patricia. *What You Know First*. Illustrated by Barry Moser. HarperCollins, 1995 (I:all). The illustrations are engraved in Resingrave, a synthetic wood engraving medium.

McLanathan, Richard. *Leonardo da Vinci*. Abrams, 1990 (I:10+). The text and reproductions introduce the works of this famous artist.

Mallat, Kathy, and Bruce McMillan. *The Picture That Mom Drew*. Walker, 1997 (I:8+). The text introduces and illustrates terms such as shape, line, and form.

Martin, Eva. *Canadian Fairy Tales*. Illustrated by Laszlo Gal. Douglas & McIntyre, 1984 (I:7–16 R:4). Fairy tales are illustrated in realistic detail.

Martin, Rafe. *Will's Mammoth*. Illustrated by Stephen Gammell. Putnam, 1989 (I:2–7). A child has a make-believe ride on a mammoth.

Maruki, Toshi. *Hiroshima No Pika*. Lothrop, Lee & Shepard, 1982 (I:8–12 R:4). A powerfully illustrated story reveals the horror of the atomic bomb.

Matthews, Downs. *Polar Bear Cubs*. Photographs by Dan Guravich. Simon & Schuster, 1989 (I:4–10 R:4). The photographs and text follow two bear cubs and their mother.

Meggendorfer, Lothar. *The City Park*. Collins, 1982. This is a reproduction of a movable book first published around 1890.

Meryman, Richard. *Andrew Wyeth*. Abrams, 1991 (I:10+). Colored reproductions and text introduce readers to this artist.

Miller, Debbie S. *A Polar Bear Journey*. Illustrated by Jon Van Zyle. Little, Brown, 1997 (I:6–9 R:5). Colors reinforce the tundra.

Mitchell, B. *Edmund Dulac's Fairy Book: Fairy Tales of the World*. Omega, 1984. This is a reissue of a book first published in 1916.

Moore, Clement. *The Night Before Christmas*. Illustrated by Tomie dePaola. Holiday House, 1980 (I:all). The popular poem is brightly illustrated.

Mosel, Arlene. *Tikki Tikki Tembo*. Illustrated by Blair Lent. Holt, Rinehart & Winston, 1968 (I:5–9 R:7). A Chinese folktale explains why Chinese children now have shorter names.

Moss, Lloyd. *Zin! Zin! Zin! A Violin.* Illustrated by Marjorie Priceman. Simon & Schuster, 1995 (I:all). The illustrations match the movement of the poetic text.

Mulherin, Jennifer, ed. *Favourite Fairy Tales.* Granada, 1982. (I:8+). This text includes many reproductions of early illustrations.

Musgrove, Margaret. *Ashanti to Zulu: African Traditions.* Illustrated by Leo and Diane Dillon. Dial, 1976 (I:7–12). Traditions of twenty-six African peoples are presented in alphabetical order.

Myers, Walter Dean. *Toussaint L'Ouverture: The Fight for Haiti's Freedom.* Illustrated by Jacob Lawrence. Simon & Schuster, 1996 (I:8+ R:5). The paintings document the problems of the Haitian people.

Newberry, Clare Turlay. *Marshmallow.* Harper & Row, 1942 (I:2–7 R:7). Oliver the cat has a new rabbit roommate.

Nister, Ernest. *Animal Tales.* London: Benn, 1981. This is a reproduction of a movable book first published in 1894.

———. *Revolving Pictures.* Putnam, 1979. This is a reproduction of a movable book first published in 1892.

Norman, Howard, retold by. *The Girl Who Dreamed Only Geese and Other Tales of the Far North.* Illustrated by Leo and Diane Dillon. Harcourt Brace, 1997 (I:9+ R:6). Acrylics illustrate Inuit folklore.

Noyes, Alfred. *The Highwayman.* Illustrated by Charles Keeping. Oxford, 1981 (I:10+). Strong black-and-white drawings complement the mood of the poem.

Oppenheim, Joanne. *Have You Seen Trees?* Illustrated by Jean and Mou-sien Tseng. Scholastic, 1995 (I:all). Watercolors illuminate the qualities of different trees.

Peet, Bill. *Bill Peet's Autobiography.* Houghton Mifflin, 1989 (I:all R:5). This text is highlighted with numerous drawings by Peet.

Pelletier, David. *The Graphic Alphabet.* Orchard, 1996 (I:all). Shape is an important element in an almost wordless book.

Perrault, Charles. *Cinderella.* Adapted by Amy Ehrlich. Illustrated by Susan Jeffers. Dial, 1985 (I:5–8 R:4). Large, detailed illustrations accompany a simplified version of the fairy tale.

———. *Cinderella.* Illustrated by Marcia Brown. Harper & Row, 1954 (I:5–8 R:5). Fine lines suggest the mood of the fairy tale.

Pope, Joyce. *Kenneth Lilly's Animals: A Portfolio of Paintings.* Illustrated by Kenneth Lilly. Lothrop, Lee & Shepard, 1988 (I:all). Textured paintings add to the appeal of an informational book.

Potter, Beatrix. *The Tale of Peter Rabbit.* Warne, 1902, 1986 (I:all). This text includes Potter's original illustrations.

Provensen, Alice, and Martin Provensen. *The Glorious Flight Across the Channel with Louis Bleriot, July 25, 1909.* Viking, 1983 (I:all R:4). An account of the first flight across the English Channel is highly illustrated.

———. *Leonardo da Vinci.* Viking, 1984 (I:all R:8). A pop-up book describes Leonardo da Vinci's accomplishments.

———. *A Peaceable Kingdom: The Shaker Abecedarius.* Viking, 1978 (I:all). A Shaker ABC is newly illustrated.

———. *Shaker Lane.* Viking, 1987 (I:5–9 R:3). Illustrations show changing society along a street.

Pyle, Howard. *Bearskin.* Illustrated by Trina Schart Hyman. Morrow, 1997 (I:6–9 R:5). India ink and acrylics illustrate this folklore.

Quiller-Couch, Sir Arthur, retold by. *The Sleeping Beauty and Other Fairy Tales.* Illustrated by Edmund Dulac. London: Hodder and Stoughton, 1981. This is a reissue of a book first published in 1910.

Ransome, Arthur. *The Fool of the World and the Flying Ship.* Illustrated by Uri Shulevitz. Farrar, Straus & Giroux, 1968 (I:6–10 R:6). Lines and warm colors focus attention in a Russian tale.

Richardson, Judith Benét. *Come to My Party.* Illustrated by Salley Mavor. Macmillan, 1993 (I:3–7). The illustrations are three-dimensional fabric relief.

———. *The Way Home.* Illustrated by Salley Mavor. Macmillan, 1991 (I:3–7). The illustrations are three-dimensional fabric relief.

Rogasky, Barbara. *The Golem.* Illustrated by Trina Schart Hyman. Holiday, 1996 (I:9+ R:5). The setting is sixteenth-century Prague.

Rosen, Michael, retold by. *Crow and Hawk: A Traditional Pueblo Indian Story.* Illustrated by John Clementson. Harcourt Brace, 1995 (I:4–8 R:6). Cut-paper collage illustrates the book.

———. *We're Going on a Bear Hunt.* Illustrated by Helen Oxenbury. Macmillan, 1989 (I:2–6). Large illustrations accompany a favorite story.

Ryder, Joanne. *White Bear, Ice Bear.* Illustrated by Michael Rothman. Morrow, 1989 (I:3–8 R:4). In an imaginative story, a young boy changes into a polar bear.

Sanderson, Ruth. *The Nativity: From the Gospels of Matthew and Luke.* Little, Brown, 1993 (I:all). Oil paintings and rich borders highlight the text.

Say, Allen. *Allison.* Houghton Mifflin, 1997 (I:4–8 R:4). The illustrations are watercolors.

Scheer, Julian. *Rain Makes Applesauce.* Illustrated by Marvin Bileck. Holiday House, 1964 (I:3–8). The illustrations combine with a poetic text.

Schoenherr, John. *Bear.* Philomel, 1991 (I:5–8 R:4). The textures of the northwoods are created in animals and setting.

Schreiber, J. F. *The Great Menagerie.* Viking, 1979. (I:all). This is an adaptation of a book originally published in 1884.

Schwartz, Delmore. *"I Am Cherry Alive," The Little Girl Sang.* Illustrated by Barbara Cooney. Harper & Row, 1979. An illustrated poem is about a little girl who is celebrating being alive.

Schwartz, Gary. *Rembrandt.* Abrams, 1992 (I:10+ R:7). Photographs and reproductions provide considerable artistic interest.

Scieszka, Jon. *The Stinky Cheese Man and Other Fairly Stupid Tales.* Illustrated by Lane Smith. Viking, 1992 (I:all). Full-page humorous illustrations and text printed in different sizes creates a unique book.

———. *The True Story of the 3 Little Pigs!* Illustrated by Lane Smith. Viking, 1989 (I:all). Humorous illustrations accompany a new version of the tale.

Sendak, Maurice. *In the Night Kitchen.* Harper & Row, 1970 (I:5–7). A young child dreams himself into a night world.

———. *Outside over There.* Harper & Row, 1981 (I:5–8 R:5). Goblins steal a baby sister.

———. *We Are All in the Dumps with Jack and Guy.* HarperCollins, 1993 (I:all). The story is developed through the illustrations.

———. *Where the Wild Things Are.* Harper & Row, 1963 (I:4–8 R:6). Max is very mischievous and very imaginative.

Seuss, Dr. *The 500 Hats of Bartholomew Cubbins.* Vanguard, 1938 (I:4–9 R:4). A bewitched hat keeps reappearing.

Shannon, George. *Dance Away.* Illustrated by Jose Aruego and Ariane Dewey. Greenwillow, 1982 (I:2–6). Line and color complement the repetitive language as a rabbit outwits a hungry fox.

Involving Children with Artists and Their Illustrations 209

Shepard, Aaron, retold by. *The Sea King's Daughter: A Russian Legend*. Illustrated by Gennady Spirin. Atheneum, 1997 (I:7+R:5). Watercolors illustrate an underwater world.

Simon, Seymour. *Jupiter*. Morrow, 1985 (I:all R:7). Photographs enhance this informational book.

Simont, Marc. *The Goose That Almost Got Cooked*. Scholastic, 1997 (I:3–7 R:4). Watercolors and charcoal lines illustrate the book.

Singer, Isaac Bashevis. *The Golem*. Illustrated by Uri Shulevitz. Farrar, Straus & Giroux, 1982. (I:8+ R:5). This is a longer version of the Jewish tale.

_____. *Zlateh the Goat*. Illustrated by Maurice Sendak. Harper & Row, 1966 (I:6–10 R:6). This is a collection of Jewish folktales.

Sis, Peter. *Starry Messenger: Galileo Galilei*. Farrar, Straus & Giroux, 1996 (I:all). The illustrations are watercolor, pen, and rubberstamp.

Skira-Venturi, Rosabianca. *A Weekend with Leonardo da Vinci*. Translated by Ann Keay Beneduce. Rizzoli, 1992 (I:10+). Many reproductions highlight the text.

Souhami, Jessica. *The Leopard's Drum: An Asante Tale from West Africa*. Little, Brown, 1995 (I:4–8 R:6). Bright colors and shapes illustrate a folktale.

Spier, Peter. *The Fox Went Out on a Chilly Night*. Doubleday, 1961 (I:all). The folk song is highly illustrated.

_____. *London Bridge Is Falling Down!* Doubleday, 1967 (I:5–12). The nursery rhyme is illustrated in detail.

_____. *Noah's Ark*. Doubleday, 1977 (I:3–9). This is a detailed, almost wordless book.

_____. *The Star-Spangled Banner*. Doubleday, 1973. (I:8+). Our national anthem is illustrated.

_____. *The Toy Shop*. Doubleday, 1981 (I:3–7). Drawings detail a toy store.

Stanley, Diane. *Leonardo da Vinci*. Morrow, 1996 (I:8+ R:6). The illustrations include miniature reproductions.

_____. *Saving Sweetness*. Illustrated by G. Brian Karas. Putnam, 1996 (I:5–8 R:5). The illustrations combine gouache, acrylic, and pencil.

Steig, William. *The Amazing Bone*. Farrar, Straus & Giroux, 1976 (I:6–9 R:5). A pig and a talking bone escape from robbers and a hungry fox.

Steptoe, Javaka. *In Daddy's Arms I Am Tall: African Americans Celebrating Fathers*. Lee & Low, 1997 (I:all). Collage illustrations highlight poetry.

Steptoe, John. *The Story of Jumping Mouse*. Lothrop, Lee & Shepard, 1984 (I:all R:4). Steptoe's illustrations convey the softness of a butterfly's wing and the sharpness of bristling cacti.

Stevens, Janet. *Tops & Bottoms*. Harcourt Brace, 1995 (I:4–7). The page design matches the title of the book.

Stevenson, Robert Louis. *My Shadow*. Illustrated by Ted Rand. Putnam, 1990 (I:all). A feeling of motion is created through the shadows and the actions of the children.

Stewart, Sarah. *The Gardener*. Illustrated by David Small. Farrar Straus Giroux, 1997 (I:5–8 R:4). The illustrations depict a 1930s setting.

Strickland, Carol. *The Annotated Mona Lisa: A Crash Course in Art History from Prehistoric to Post-Modern*. Andrews and McMeel, 1992 (I:10+). Illustrations and text present the history of art.

Sykes, Julie. *This and That*. Illustrated by Tanya Linch. Farrar, Straus & Giroux, 1996 (I:4–7). Torn-paper collages illustrate the story.

Taback, Simms. *There Was An Old Lady Who Swallowed A Fly*. Viking, 1997 (I:all). The humorous illustrations reinforce the ridiculous situation.

Turner, Robyn Montana. *Faith Ringgold*. Little, Brown, 1993 (I:9+ R:5). This is one of a series of books on women artists.

_____. *Frida Kahlo*. Little, Brown, 1993 (I:9+ R:5). Introduces the works of this Mexican painter.

_____. *Georgia O'Keeffe*. Little, Brown, 1991 (I:9+ R:5). The biography includes numerous reproductions of O'Keeffe's paintings.

_____. *Mary Cassatt*. Little, Brown, 1992 (I:9+ R:5). Develops understanding of the artist who lived from 1844–1926.

_____. *Rosa Bonheur*. Little, Brown, 1991 (I:9+ R:5). The biography includes numerous reproductions of Bonheur's paintings.

Udry, Janice May. *The Moon Jumpers*. Illustrated by Maurice Sendak. Harper & Row, 1959 (I:3–9 R:2). Colors create a mood as children go out to play in the moonlight.

Van Allsburg, Chris. *The Garden of Abdul Gasazi*. Houghton Mifflin, 1979 (I:5–8 R:5). A boy has a magical experience in a magician's garden.

_____. *Jumanji*. Houghton Mifflin, 1981 (I:5–8 R:6). An unusual game creates a jungle environment.

_____. *The Mysteries of Harris Burdick*. Houghton Mifflin, 1984. (I:all). Pictures encourage children to solve mysteries.

_____. *The Polar Express*. Houghton Mifflin, 1985 (I:5–8 R:6). Glowing illustrations accompany an original Christmas story.

_____. *The Sweetest Fig*. Houghton Mifflin, 1993 (I:all R:6). This is a story filled with irony and unexpected situations.

_____. *The Widow's Broom*. Houghton Mifflin, 1992 (I:5–8 R:6). A witch's broom helps a widow.

_____. *The Wreck of the Zephyr*. Houghton Mifflin, 1983 (I:5–8 R:6). A boy tries to become the greatest sailor in the world.

_____. *The Wretched Stone*. Houghton Mifflin, 1991 (I:5–8 R:6). A glowing stone has a terrible effect on a ship's crew.

Viorst, Judith. *Alexander and the Terrible, Horrible, No Good, Very Bad Day*. Illustrated by Ray Cruz. Atheneum, 1972 (I:3–8 R:6). Nothing goes right for Alexander.

Waber, Bernard. *The Lion Named Shirley Williamson*. Houghton Mifflin, 1996 (I:5–8 R:5). Watercolor and ink cartoons illustrate the text.

Waddell, Martin. *Farmer Duck*. Illustrated by Helen Oxenbury. Candlewick, 1992 (I:4–7). Watercolors create a humorous text.

Waldron, Ann. *Francisco Goya*. Abrams, 1992 (I:10+). This is an introduction to the Spanish painter who was a forerunner of the impressionist movement.

Walker, Barbara K., retold by. *The Dancing Palm Tree: And Other Nigerian Folktales*. Illustrated by Helen Siegl. Texas Tech University Press, 1990 (I:all R:4). Woodcuts are used for the illustrations.

Walter, Mildred Pitts. *Brother to the Wind*. Illustrated by Diane and Leo Dillon. Lothrop, Lee & Shepard, 1985 (I:all R:3). An original story set in Africa tells about a young boy who wishes to fly.

Ward, Lynd. *The Biggest Bear*. Houghton Mifflin, 1952 (I:5–8 R:4). A boy wants a bearskin to hang on his barn.

Weller, Frances Ward. *I Wonder If I'll See a Whale*. Illustrated by Ted Lewin. Philomel, 1991 (I:6–10 R:4). Watercolors create the feeling of the ocean.

Welton, Jude. *Impressionism*. Kindersley/The Art Institute of Chicago, 1993 (I:10+). Numerous colored reproductions provide an introduction to impressionism.

_____ . *Monet*. Kindersley/The Musee Marmottan, Paris, 1992 (I:10+). Numerous colored reproductions provide an introduction to the artworks of Monet.

Westervelt, Linda. *Roger Tory Peterson's ABC of Birds: A Book for Little Birdwatchers*. Illustrated by Roger Tory Peterson. Photographs by Seymour Levin. Rizzoli, 1995 (I:all). The illustrations create a feeling of texture.

Westray, Kathleen. *A Color Sampler*. Ticknor & Fields, 1993 (I:all). The text introduces primary, secondary, intermediate, and complementary colors.

Whipple, Laura, compiled by. *Eric Carle's Dragons Dragons & Other Creatures That Never Were*. Illustrated by Eric Carle. Philomel, 1991 (I:all). The illustrations are collages formed from painted tissue paper.

Wiesner, David. *Free Fall*. Lothrop, Lee & Shepard, 1988. (I:all). Watercolors provide a fantasy trip in a wordless book.

_____ . *June 29, 1999*. Clarion, 1992 (I:all). A science experiment produces an unusual story.

_____ . *Tuesday*. Clarion, 1991 (I:all). Watercolors are used in this wordless book.

Wild, Margaret. *Let the Celebrations BEGIN!* Illustrated by Julie Vivas. Orchard, 1991 (I:all). Lighter colors create a less somber mood for a Holocaust story.

Willard, Nancy. *Pish, Posh, Said Hieronymus Bosch*. Illustrated by Leo and Diane Dillon. Harcourt Brace Jovanovich, 1991 (I:all). The illustrations are painted in acrylics and overpainted with oils.

_____ . *A Starlit Somersault Downhill*. Illustrated by Jerry Pinkney. Little, Brown, 1993 (I:all). Watercolors create a wintery scene for this poetic text.

_____ . *A Visit to William Blake's Inn: Poems for Innocent and Experienced Travelers*. Illustrated by Alice and Martin Provensen. Harcourt Brace Jovanovich, 1981 (I:all). Poems describe a menagerie of guests.

Winter, Jonah. *Diego*. Translated by Amy Prince. Illustrated by Jeanette Winter. Knopf, 1991 (I:6–10 R:5). The text and illustrations present the life and work of Diego Rivera.

Wisniewski, David. *Golem*. Clarion,1996 (I:all). Cut-paper illustrations create a three-dimensional appearance.

_____ . *Rain Player*. Clarion, 1991 (I:5–8 R:5). Paper constructions enhance this Mayan tale.

Wood, Audrey. *King Bidgood's in the Bathtub*. Illustrated by Don Wood. Harcourt Brace Jovanovich, 1985 (I:6–9 R:1). The story tells of a humorous predicament.

Wood, Douglas. *Old Turtle*. Illustrated by Cheng-Khee Chee. Pfeifer-Hamilton, 1992 (I:all). Watercolors enhance this environmental tale.

Wright, Patricia. *Manet*. Kindersley/National Gallery, London, 1993 (I:10+). Numerous colored reproductions introduce readers to the art of Manet.

Yagawa, Sumiko. *The Crane Wife*. Translated by Katherine Paterson. Illustrated by Suekichi Akaba. Morrow, 1981 (I:all R:6). A traditional Japanese tale expresses the dangers of greed.

Yashima, Taro. *Crow Boy*. Viking, 1955 (I:4–8 R:4). A lonely outcast at school gains respect and self-confidence.

_____ . *Umbrella*. Viking, 1958 (I:3–7 R:7). Momo receives an umbrella for her third birthday and then waits impatiently for the rain to come.

Yolen, Jane. *Letting Swift River Go*. Illustrated by Barbara Cooney. Little, Brown, 1992 (I:all). The illustrations depict the changes in a town following the construction of the Quabbin Reservoir.

_____ . *Owl Moon*. Illustrated by John Schoenherr. Philomel, 1987 (I:all). A poetic story follows father and son as they search for owls in the winter woods.

Yorinks, Arthur. *Hey, Al*. Illustrated by Richard Egielski. Farrar, Straus & Giroux, 1986 (I:all). A janitor discovers that his home is better than he thinks.

_____ . *The Miami Giant*. Illustrated by Maurice Sendak. HarperCollins, 1995 (I:all). The illustrations could be compared with other Sendak illustrations.

Young, Ed, translated by. *Lon Po Po: A Red-Riding Hood Story from China*. Philomel, 1989 (I:all R:5). The girls outwit the wolf in this version.

_____ . *Seven Blind Mice*. Philomel, 1992 (I:all). Collage illustrations tell the fable.

Zheng, Zhensun, and Alice Low. *Young Painter: The Life and Paintings of Wang Yani—China's Extraordinary Young Artist*. Scholastic, 1991 (I:all R:5). A nonfictional book presents life of a young Chinese painter.

Zolotow, Charlotte. *Mr. Rabbit and the Lovely Present*. Illustrated by Maurice Sendak. Harper & Row, 1962 (I:3–8 R:2). With the help of a rabbit, a little girl searches for a gift for her mother's birthday.

_____ . *When the Wind Stops*. Illustrated by Stefano Vitale. HarperCollins, 1995 (I:4–8). The illustrations are painted on wood.

Illustration from *Storm Boy,* written and illustrated by Paul Owen Lewis, copyright © 1995 by Paul Owen Lewis. Beyond Words Publishing, Inc., 1-800-284-9673.

5 | *Picture Books*

 A Book Is More Than Words

- What a Picture Book Is
- Literary Criticism: Evaluating Picture Books
- Mother Goose
- Toy Books
- Alphabet Books
- Counting Books
- Concept Books
- Wordless Books
- Easy-to-Read Books
- Picture Storybooks

 Involving Children in Picture Books

- Sharing Mother Goose
- Encouraging Interaction Between Children and Texts
- Sharing Wordless Books
- Reading to Children
- Stimulating Development
- Developing Aesthetic Sensitivity
- Motivating Writing with Picture Storybooks
- Other Activities Possible

A Book Is More Than Words

 he thought of a child, a lap, and a picture book arouses warm feelings and recollections in many adults. When a loving adult provides opportunities for a child to experience the enchantment found in picture books, both the child and the adult benefit.

The books included in the genre of picture books have many values in addition to pleasure. The rhythm, rhyme, and repetition in nursery rhymes stimulate language development as well as auditory discrimination and attentive listening skills in young children. Alphabet books reinforce ability to identify letter/sound relationships and help expand vocabularies. Concept books enhance intellectual development by fostering understanding of abstract ideas. Wordless books encourage children to develop their observational skills, descriptive vocabularies, and abilities to create stories characterized by logical sequence. Illustrations found in picture books stimulate sensitivity to art and beauty. Well-written picture storybooks encourage children to appreciate literary style. Thus, picture books have important roles in children's development.

WHAT A PICTURE BOOK IS

Most children's books are illustrated, but not all illustrated children's books are picture books. As Perry Nodelman (1988) points out, picture books "communicate information or tell stories through a series of many pictures combined with relatively slight texts or no texts at all" (p. VII, preface).

Zena Sutherland and Betsy Hearne (1984) stress that in picture books, the illustrations are as important as the text or even more important than the text. Because children respond to stories told visually as well as verbally, some picture books are quite effective with no words at all. Many picture books, however, maintain a balance between the illustrations and the text, so that neither is completely effective without the other.

Thus the term *picture books* covers a wide variety of children's books, ranging from Mother Goose books and toy books for very young children to picture storybooks with plots that satisfy more experienced, older children. Many of the picture books discussed in this chapter rely heavily upon illustrations to present content. In some, each scene or rhyme is illustrated. Other books, with more complex verbal story lines, are not so dependent upon pictures to develop their plots.

Many picture books have a characteristic not often shared by other children's books: The writer and the illustrator may be the same person. Well-known artists often create picture books. This chapter emphasizes authors, author-illustrators, and their literature.

LITERARY CRITICISM: EVALUATING PICTURE BOOKS

Because the text and the illustrations in picture books should complement each other, consider the relationships between the words and pictures when evaluating a picture book. Betsy Hearne (1983) recommends that evaluators also "think complexity versus clutter, originality versus banality, loving versus cute, strong versus ponderous, and deepened versus decorated. Think of what you'd like to hang on the wall of your mind" (p. 577). Zena Sutherland (1997) makes further recommendations for evaluating picture books if the books are written for young children. She states:

A story should be brief and straightforward if it is for young children; it should contain few concepts and none that are beyond comprehension if they are not familiar concepts; it should be written in a direct and simple style; and it should have illustrations that complement the text and are not in conflict with it. (p. 64)

The questions in the Evaluation Criteria box above can help you select high-quality picture books for children.

Educators, researchers, and authorities in children's literature are increasingly interested in children's responses to picture books and in the characteristics of picture books that appeal to children. You should consider children's own evaluations when selecting picture books to share with children.

Peggy Whalen-Levitt (1984) emphasizes the roles that age and experience play in a child's response to a picture book. The first interactions of a very young child with a picture book are largely physical, as the child investigates the size, shape, texture, and moving parts of the unfamiliar object. The child may stick the book into his or her mouth to become acquainted with it or turn the pages even if the book is upside down. With adult guidance, the child soon learns the specific purposes and pleasures associated with books and responds to the symbolic nature of books, focusing on the content of the pictures and connecting illustrated objects and concepts with the sounds and names given to them. The child quickly begins to assume that books will contain stories.

As a sense of time develops, a child begins to see connections among past, present, and future in pictures and text and to expect that a story will have a beginning, a middle, and an end. Finally, after time and experience with both books and everyday living, a child evaluates book text and illustrations in terms of his or her own view of reality and his or her own feelings and desires. Thus, different types of books and book-related experiences are appropriate for children at different ages and stages of development.

Patricia Cianciolo (1983) identified four major factors that influence how a child perceives and evaluates the illustrations in picture books: (1) the child's age and stage of cognitive and social development, (2) the way in which an adult has (or has not) prepared the child for the experience with a picture book, (3) the child's emotional state of readiness, and (4) the number of times the child looks at the illustrations. Cianciolo's analysis of picture books listed in the Children's Choices also reveals that children prefer illustrations that depict here-and-now situations, fantasies of all kinds, and humorous exaggerations and slapstick; illustrations that are colorful and add more detail to the descriptions of characters, action, and setting in the text; and illustrations that are drawn in either a realistic or a cartoon-like style. Such preferences may help adults select picture books for children, but Cianciolo stresses that adults can and should also use books and book-related activities to teach children "how to be more evaluative and discriminating in their selections" (p. 28).

Additional insights into evaluating picture books are gained by analyzing picture books that are highly rated in journals that review books written for children. For example, twice a year, *The Horn Book* publishes *The Horn Book Guide to Children's and Young Adult Books*. This publication uses a rating system from 1 to 6. Books receiving a 1 rating are considered noteworthy according to style, content, or illustration. In contrast, books receiving a 6 rating are considered unacceptable according to style, content, or illustration (1993, p. 10).

The reviews in this publication include both a brief outline of the story and several sentences that focus on the literary qualities and the illustrations in the book. Here, we consider the portions of several reviews that emphasize qualities related to style and illustration. For example, when reviewing Lloyd

Alexander's *The Fortune-Tellers,* a picture storybook set in Africa and illustrated by Trina Schart Hyman, the reviewer emphasizes a combination of effective illustrations and author's style: "Hyman's rendering of scenes in the central-Africa country of Cameroon delights the eye. A book that pulses with life and good humor" (p. 18). For *Emily,* the reviewer also emphasizes the integration of Barbara Cooney's illustrations and the author's style: "In a perfect convergence of text and art, Cooney's illustrations reflect the spirit of Bedard's prose, which resonates with the mystical wonder and terse rhythms of Dickinson's poetry. An afterword on Dickinson's life and poetry is appended" (p. 21). For *Shortcut,* the reviewer emphasizes the pacing of the text: "In perhaps his finest achievement to date, Crews blends motifs from earlier books to create a suspense thriller for picture-book readers. . . . The pacing of text and illustration is perfect; a superb example of the picture book as theater" (p. 26). For *June 29, 1999,* the reviewer emphasizes both the language and the illustrations: "Playful, alliterative language catalogs the sightings; the understated text is a perfect foil for the outrageous scenes of vegetables run amok. Fans of Wiesner's offbeat sense of humor will be delighted" (p. 50).

As noted, most of the reviews for outstanding picture books emphasize a close integration between the illustrations and text as well as author style that excites readers. As you read these picture books, decide if you do or do not agree with *The Horn Book* reviewers.

MOTHER GOOSE

Mother Goose rhymes are the earliest literature enjoyed by many young children; the rhymes, rhythms, and pleasing sounds of these jingles appeal to young children, who are experimenting with their own language patterns, and aid children's language development. Betsy Hearne (1992) emphasizes the appeal of Mother Goose when she states, "Nursery rhymes are only a step away from song in their changing cadence and compressed story elements" (p. 22). A brief review of the basic characteristics of nursery rhymes indicates why children enjoy them, as well as why nursery rhymes encourage language development in children.

Appealing Characteristics

The rhythm in many nursery rhymes almost forces children to react. For example, children may clap their hands or jump up and down to the rhythm of this jingle:

> Handy dandy, Jack-a-Dandy
> Loves plum cake and sugar candy;
> He bought some at a grocer's shop
> And out he came, hop, hop, hop.

Rhyme is another aspect of many nursery verses that children enjoy. Rhyming words, such as *dandy* and *candy,* and *shop* and *hop,* invite children to join in and add the rhyming word or to make up their own rhymes. Rhymes enhance the adventures of many favorite characters: "Little Miss Muffet sat on a tuffet"; "Jack and Jill went up the hill"; "Bobby Shafto's gone to sea, Silver buckles on his knee." Many verses rhyme at the end of each line, but some verses also use internal rhyming elements: "Hickory, dickory, dock, the mouse ran up the clock" and "Rub, a dub, dub, three men in a tub." To test the influence of these rhyming verses, ask older children to share one of their favorite Mother Goose rhymes. They can probably say several although they may not have heard or recited them for years.

Children also respond to the repetition of sounds in a phrase or line of a nursery rhyme. Alliteration, the repetition of an initial consonant in consecutive words, creates phrases that children enjoy repeating just to experience the marvelous feelings that result from the repetition of beginning sounds: "One misty, moisty, morning"; "Sing a song of sixpence"; and "Diddle, diddle, dumpling." Sentences that contain a great deal of alliteration become tongue twisters. Children love the challenge of this jingle:

Peter Piper picked a peck of pickled peppers.
A peck of pickled peppers Peter Piper picked.
If Peter Piper picked a peck of pickled peppers,
Where's the peck of pickled peppers Peter Piper picked?

Humor is another great appeal of Mother Goose verses for children:

> Hey, diddle, diddle!
> The cat and the fiddle,
> The cow jumped over the moon;
> The little dog laughed
> To see such sport,
> And the dish ran away with the spoon.

Mother Goose rhymes, which contained maxims or morals, were popular in both Great Britain and North America. (The Original Mother Goose's Melody printed in London by John Newbery, 1760.)

This verse is also an example of hyperbole, the use of exaggeration for effect, which is common in Mother Goose rhymes. Children appreciate exaggerated, ridiculous situations, such as an old woman's living in a shoe with so many children she doesn't know what to do, a barber's trying to shave a pig, or Simple Simon's going for water with a sieve:

> He went for water with a sieve,
> But soon it ran all through:
> And now poor Simple Simon
> Bids you all adieu.

Rhyme, repetition of sounds, humor, and exaggeration combine to create appealing subjects for young children.

Collections

The many different collections of Mother Goose rhymes contain more or less the same verses, but their formats, sizes, and illustrations are quite different. Some editions contain several hundred verses in large-book format, while others have fewer verses and are small enough for a young child to hold. Some editions have illustrations reminiscent of eighteenth-century England, while others have modern illustrations. Many adult students in American university classes prefer the Mother Goose editions with settings in the England of the 1600s and 1700s—either reissues of the original early editions or editions first published in the twentieth century.

Two popular early editions, John Newbery's *The Original Mother Goose's Melody* and Kate Greenaway's *Mother Goose: Or, the Old Nursery Rhymes,* continue to be reissued. Newbery's edition may be of greater interest to adults than to children (the text contains a history of Mother Goose), although many older children enjoy looking at the early orthography in Newbery's edition and comparing the verses and illustrations with twentieth-century editions, which do not share Newbery's tendency to add a moral to the close of each nursery rhyme. In Newbery's edition, for example, "Ding, dong, bell, the cat is in the well," is followed by this maxim: "He that injures one threatens a Hundred" (p. 25).

The edition illustrated by the well-known author-illustrator Kate Greenaway was first published in 1881. Greenaway's book is a small text suitable for sharing with one child. She illustrates the nursery rhymes with pictures of delicate children that appeal to the sentiments of most readers.

Collections assembled by Iona and Peter Opie provide older children and adults with an opportunity to examine early illustrated versions of Mother Goose. *A Nursery Companion* is a large, highly illustrated collection of nursery rhymes originally published in the early 1800s. The *Oxford Nursery Rhyme Book* contains eight hundred rhymes categorized

Kate Greenaway was an influential illustrator of children's books in the nineteenth century. (From Kate Greenaway's Mother Goose, *copyright © 1988. Reprinted by permission of Dial Books for Young Readers.)*

according to contents. Black-and-white woodcuts, from both earlier editions and newly created works, illustrate this large volume. An informative preface and a list of sources for the illustrations increase the usefulness for those who wish to study early editions of nursery rhymes. *Tail Feathers from Mother Goose: The Opie Rhyme Book* is a collection of lesser-known rhymes, many of which are previously unpublished. The rhymes are illustrated by contemporary artists. Iona Opie's *My First Mother Goose* is an anthology of sixty rhymes. Rosemary Wells's illustrations enhance the verses and are very appealing to children. *The Glorious Mother Goose,* a collection of Mother Goose rhymes by Cooper Edens, is another source for analyzing earlier illustrations. The text is illustrated with works by such artists as Randolph Caldecott, Walter Crane, and Kate Greenaway.

In *I Saw Esau: The Schoolchild's Pocket Book,* the Opies assemble a collection of rhymes, chants, and riddles that are appropriate for various ages. The illustrations by Maurice Sendak and the rhymes appeal to younger children. Older children and adults benefit from the notes section, which explains the origins of the rhymes.

Arnold Lobel's *Gregory Griggs and Other Nursery Rhyme People* contains rhymes about lesser-known characters, such as Theophilus Thistle, the successful thistle sifter; Gregory Griggs, who had twenty-seven different wigs; Charley, Charley, who stole the barley; Michael Finnegan, who grew a long beard right on his chinnigan; and Terence McDiddler, the three-stringed fiddler. The language and strong rhyming patterns in these verses make the book appropriate for reading aloud. The humorous, nonsensical rhymes are enriched by Lobel's pastel illustrations. Each rhyme is illustrated with a large picture, making it especially good for sharing with a group of children. Lobel's *The Random House Book of Mother Goose* is a collection of three hundred and six rhymes. The illustrations emphasize Lobel's ability to create humorous situations in pictures.

The placement of illustrations next to the matching nursery rhyme, the large-page format, and the humorous folk-art illustrations make *Tomie dePaola's Mother Goose* especially appealing to younger children. The pictures that accompany multiple verses illustrate the sequential development in longer rhymes, such as "Simple Simon." The plots of some of the rhymes are extended through the illustrations. For example, the illustrations accompanying "Jack and Jill" show the actions on a marionette stage.

Michael Foreman's Mother Goose, selected and illustrated by Michael Foreman, is another large collection of nursery rhymes. Because of the visual links, the illustrations provide interesting opportunities to increase observational abilities and interactions. For example, the illustration on page 23 shows someone falling off the wall in front of the Pretty Maid, who is gathering roses in her garden. When readers turn the page, they find that the legs belong to Humpty Dumpty, who now cannot be put back together again.

Mother Goose collections illustrated by Tedd Arnold and Lucy Cousins show the impact of different types of illustrations. Use these books for comparative purposes and responses. Arnold's *Mother Goose's Words of Wit and Wisdom: A Book of Months* includes cross-stitched illustrations and samplers

Hey diddle, diddle,
The cat and the fiddle,
The cow jumped over the moon;
The little dog laughed
To see such sport,
And the dish ran away with the spoon.

Humorous illustrations and large-book format provide an appealing volume for young children. (Illustration by Tomie dePaola reprinted by permission of G. P. Putnam's Sons from Tomie dePaola's Mother Goose. *Copyright © 1985 by Tomie dePaola.)*

that were created from Arnold's original designs. The rhymes are categorized by the months of the year. The illustrations give the book an early American mood. Notes at the end of the book provide additional information about the samplers. Compare these illustrations with those in Cousins's *Little Dog Laughed.* Cousins's bold, bright, and childlike illustrations develop humor. To compare the impact of photographs with these other types of illustrations, analyze the influence of color photographs by Bruce McMillan in Sarah Josepha Hale's *Mary Had a Little Lamb.*

In *We Are All in the Dumps with Jack and Guy,* a potentially controversial Mother Goose, Maurice Sendak provides social commentary in illustrations showing newspaper headlines on papers worn by homeless children. Sendak's images, which reflect poverty, crime, AIDS, and unemployment, should encourage much discussion.

Books That Illustrate One Rhyme or Tale

Children often want to know more about their favorite nursery rhyme characters. The humor and simple plots found in nursery rhymes lend themselves to expansion into picture storybook format. Each verse of Sarah Josepha Hale's *Mary Had a Little Lamb* has several full-page color illustrations of nineteenth-century farm and school settings by Tomie dePaola.

Picture storybook versions of Mother Goose rhymes may stimulate creative interpretations if children think about what might happen, expanding and illustrating the plots in other nursery rhymes. John Ivimey's text and Paul Galdone's illustrations for *The Complete Story of the Three Blind Mice* reveal how the mice lost their sight as well as tails. This version has a happy ending, as the mice regain their sight and tails and become "three wise mice." Texts that extend the story line beyond that found in the Mother Goose rhyme provide motivation for children to create their own expanded story lines of other favorite Mother Goose rhymes.

Susan Ramsay Hoguet's *Solomon Grundy* extends the nursery rhyme through historical illustrations. The illustrations allow readers and viewers to visualize what life was like in the United States at an earlier time. This Solomon Grundy is born in 1836 and is buried in 1910 near the church in which he was christened.

"Old MacDonald Had a Farm" provides the foundations for Jan Ormerod's *Ms. MacDonald Has a Class.* In this variant of the rhyme, Ms. MacDonald's class takes a field trip to a farm and then prepares a show that depicts their adventures. Young children enjoy joining in with a "Here a hop, there a waddle, everywhere a quack quack" (unnumbered). This variant may also be compared with the original rhyme.

Nursery Rhymes in Other Lands

Traditional nursery rhymes and jingles for children are found in many different lands. The language and style may differ from the English Mother Goose, but the content is amazingly alike. Nursery rhymes everywhere tell about good and bad children, wise and foolish people, animals, and nature. The multicultural nature of nursery rhymes is emphasized with a collection of Chinese nursery rhymes that were adapted and illustrated by Demi. The rhymes in *Dragon Kites and Dragonflies* are illustrated with drawings that depict an ancient culture. Illustrations show kites, emperors, dragons, boats, dancers, weavers, acrobats, and pagodas.

Robert Wyndham has translated Chinese nursery rhymes into English versions that are designed to appeal to English-speaking readers and listeners. *Chinese Mother Goose Rhymes* are about dragons, Buddhas, carriage chairs, the Milky Way, and ladybugs, which seem to fascinate children of many nationalities. Each of the sprightly rhymes is shown in both English and Chinese, with a simple, colorful drawing to illustrate it. Turning games and nonsense words are well represented, as they are in English nursery rhymes.

> Gee lee, gu lu, turn the cake,
> Add some oil, the better to bake.
> Gee lee, gu lu, now it's done;
> Give a piece to everyone. (p. 40, unnumbered)

N. M. Bodecker has translated and illustrated Danish nursery rhymes in *It's Raining, Said John Twaining*. Wooden shoes and royalty are common characters in the Danish verses. Like English verses, Danish nursery rhymes use rhyming elements, tongue-twisting nonsense words, and riddles. The names of some characters in the rhymes, such as Skat Skratterat Skrat Skrirumskrat, appeal to young children, who love nonsense and alliterative sounds. Each rhyme in this book is illustrated with a colorful, full-page picture.

Margot C. Griego et al. have collected nursery rhymes and lullabies from Mexico and Spanish-speaking communities in the United States. *Tortillitas Para Mama and Other Spanish Nursery Rhymes* contains finger plays, counting rhymes, and clapping rhymes written in both Spanish and English.

Nursery rhymes from many nations are important contributions to our cultural heritage. They foster the self-esteem and language skills of the children who are members of ethnic minorities in the United States and help all American children appreciate the values and contributions of cultures other than their own.

The illustrations reinforce the Chinese settings for the nursery rhymes. (Jacket cover from Dragon Kites and Dragonflies *copyright © 1986 by Demi. Reprinted by permission of Harcourt Brace & Company.)*

An increasing number of toy books, including board books, pop-up books, flap books, cloth books, and plastic books, entice children into interacting with stories, developing their vocabularies, counting, identifying colors, and discussing book content with adults. These books are valuable additions to children's literature because they stimulate the language, cognitive, personal, and social development of preschool children. They also provide happy experiences with books that, ideally, extend into later childhood and adulthood. Board books range from identifying a baby's clothing to describing experiences at school or in a doctor's office.

Some of Helen Oxenbury's board books are especially appropriate for younger children. In five appealing books in a series, *Dressing, Family, Friends, Playing,* and *Working,* each page contains an easily identifiable picture of a baby's actions as he or she gets dressed, interacts with family members, or accomplishes a new skill. Another book by Oxenbury, *I Hear,* identifies sounds within the environment.

Board books help children understand their expanding experiences and environments. Nancy Tafuri uses familiar items in *One Wet Jacket* and *Two New Sneakers* to encourage reader involvement. Lucy Cousins's *Maisy's Colors* and *Count With Maisy* encourage counting and identifying familiar objects.

Two "Sam" board books, *Sam's Ball* and *Sam's Bath,* written by Barbro Lindgren and illustrated by Eva Eriksson, encourage language development through identification of objects and discussion of actions. A humanized rabbit provides similar subjects for discussion and enjoyment in *Max's Bath, Max's Bedtime, Max's Birthday,* and *Max's Breakfast,* by Rosemary Wells.

Five board books written and illustrated by Cynthia Rylant introduce everyday experiences. Colorful collages in *Everyday Children, Everyday Garden, Everyday House, Everyday Pets,* and *Everyday Town* encourage children to describe what they find in each illustration.

Four board books by Sophie Fatus develop concepts in *Spots, Stripes, Holes,* and *Squares.* Concepts are also developed in Patrick Yee's *Rosie Rabbit's Colors, Rosie Rabbit's Numbers, Rosie Rabbit's Opposites,* and *Rosie Rabbit's Shapes.*

Pop-up books, flap books, and other mechanical books encourage children to interact with text. Pop-up books also may introduce children to beloved storybook characters, tell simple stories, or create fascinating three-dimensional settings. *The Peter Rabbit Pop-Up Book* is based on Beatrix Potter's classic story. Margaret Wise Brown's *The Goodnight Moon Room: A Pop-Up Book* and Richard and Florence Atwater's *Mr. Popper's Penguins* introduce settings from popular fiction.

Jan Pienkowski's *Haunted House* uses pop-up and flap techniques to create the detailed setting of a house inhabited by ghostly characters. Lucy Cousins's *Maisy Goes to the Playground* and *Maisy Goes to School* use flaps and pull tabs to tell the simple story of a mouse's adventures. Shen Roddie's *Chicken Pox!* in which a baby chick tries to overcome the itching caused by chicken pox adds a sense of touch to many of the flaps and tabs.

Eric Hill has written and illustrated an excellent series of flap books for preschool children. *Where's Spot?,* for example, revolves around a dog's full dinner bowl and discovering where the dog could be. Children join Spot's mother as they open a door or lift a covering in search of Spot. Each opening reveals a different animal. The lettering of Hill's books is large and clear against a white background, and the illustrations are both colorful and humorous. Young children return many times to rediscover what is behind each flap.

Tana Hoban's *Look! Look! Look!* uses square openings on black pages to reveal small portions of the colored photograph on the next page. A child can guess what the object is and then turn the page to see if he or she is correct. Harriet Ziefert's *Night Knight* and *Baby Buggy* uses flaps to help readers explore homonyms. Lionel's *Peekaboo Babies: A Counting Book* uses tabs and flaps to encourage counting.

Toy books may be created for older readers. For example, pulling the tabs in Robert Crowther's *Pop-Up Olympics: Amazing Facts and Record Breakers* allows readers to both move the athletes in their respective sports and to discover information about records or the people who have been active in the sport. Some of the paper-engineered movements allow readers to visualize the actions of the athletes participating in the sport.

The numerous toy books discussed here and listed in the children's literature at the end of the

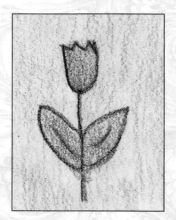
chapter indicate a trend toward publishing more books for very young children. A visit to a bookstore or a search through publishers' catalogues will show even more texts. *Booklist,* the journal for the American Library Association, regularly reviews toy books as part of its coverage of children's books.

ALPHABET BOOKS

Alphabet books have long been used to help young children identify familiar objects, as well as letters and sounds. The objects pictured in alphabet books should be easy for children to identify and should

not have more than one commonly used name. For example, since young children often call a rabbit a bunny, *rabbit* might not be the best choice for illustrating the letter *r* in an alphabet book for very young children. If letter/sound identification is a major concern, the letters and corresponding illustrations should be easily identifiable. If young children use the book independently, the pages should not be cluttered with numerous objects that can confuse letter/sound identification.

When adults share alphabet books with older children, however, pages rich with detail and numerous objects may help children develop their observational and discussion skills. A child's age and the educational objectives are basic considerations when evaluating any alphabet book. Some were appropriate because the story also used a recycling rhyme. She said, "Recycled paper, recycled rhymes, give a modern story that tells about hunger and homelessness. I think it is important."

On the dedication page, the children discussed the possible significance of the stars in the sky and the rope that several thought looked like the Star of Bethlehem. They speculated about why the star was either broken or being used to hang clothes for the homeless.

All of the children responded to the child calling for help and the other children in the dump. They thought that it was important that the child calling for help was black because "there is a great deal of hunger in Africa." They noticed the boy identifying his own private property while living in the crowded conditions of the dump. The children thought that it is important for everyone to identify what is "mine," even if it is only a box or a sack.

The children all commented on the moon's changing expressions: It seemed to show sadness, anger, and tears. They thought that the moon was sad because "he sees these kids,

their hunger, and their homelessness and no one seems to be doing anything to help them." They also noted that as life became more difficult for the children, the moon became angrier, until he finally changed into a cat and came to earth to rescue the children.

The rats caused much speculation. Several children thought that the rats were probably in disguise because they had hands. They worried about what the rats would do to the kittens and to the boy. The fact that they seemed to be gambling over the fate of their captives caused concern.

These fifth graders were interested in every detail in the book. They found "Trumped Tower" and discussed the significance of placing the homeless children below this setting. They were particularly interested in reading the newspaper headlines that formed both the clothes of and shelter for many of the children. They discussed the importance of the changing headlines that went from the availability of expensive housing to chaos in shelters, job layoffs, and AIDS. Several of the children concluded that one cannot create a strong shelter with newspa-

pers. They discussed the possible connections between a bakery and an orphanage and noticed how the black smoke from the building partially covered the face of the moon. At the end of the story, they were pleased that the boy and the kittens were saved (one child referred to the moon, the kittens, and the boy "as the moon's family"), but they were not pleased that the final setting in the book was again the dump.

When asked if there is a message in this book, the children provided several important messages. One child stated, "We must remember to give money to the poor and to try to change their lives." Another child said, "The moon is watching over all of us." Still another felt that rats should not be able to take kids away. When asked what age children they thought should read the book, most of them responded with age ten. They thought that children much younger than ten would not understand the message in the book or recognize the symbolism. As you read *We Are All in the Dumps with Jack and Guy,* compare your responses with those of these fifth-grade children.

alphabet books are most appropriate for young children, while others contain enough detail or historical insight to interest even older children. Julie Cummins (1996) maintains that alphabet books convey information and challenge imaginations. Leslie Cafakum (1993) contrasts the changes in alphabet books from those for young children only to a wide variety of books for older readers when she states:

A, once nearly synonymous with apple, today may be just as easily the standard bearer for Alfa Romeo, aigrette, alchemist, or agouti. Although the importance of ABC books for young children shouldn't be minimized, the content, background detail, artwork, and design elements found in these books offer older children interesting connections to a variety of curricular areas. (p. 41)

Early Alphabet Books

Like Mother Goose rhymes, alphabet books were among the first books published for children. Some early alphabet books have been reissued, and some new books are reminiscent of earlier texts. One very early ABC rhyme, "History of an Apple Pie," tells how "*B* bit it," "*C* cut it," and so forth, until the end of the alphabet and the pie. In 1886, Kate Greenaway illustrated the pie's alphabetical history in *A— Apple Pie,* and her original wood-block designs have been used in a reissue of this charming text.

Ruth Baldwin's *One Hundred Nineteenth-Century Rhyming Alphabets in English* contains a version of "History of an Apple Pie," as well as other early alphabets. The two hundred ninety-six pages of this large book are filled with colorful reproductions of

E LEPHANT,   Badger,   Pelican,   Ox,

Shaker costumes and occupations influence these illustrations. (From A Peaceable Kingdom, *illustrated by Alice and Martin Provensen. Copyright © 1978 by Alice and Martin Provensen. Reprinted by permission of Viking/Penguin Inc.)*

nineteenth-century pictures and verses. Each rhyme is identified according to title, illustrator, publisher, and date of publication.

Alice and Martin Provensen have illustrated another early ABC, *A Peaceable Kingdom: The Shaker Abecedarius.* The Shaker alphabet book was first published in the Shaker Manifesto of July 1882 under the title "Animal Rhymes." According to Richard Barsam (1978), it was written to teach reading. While Shaker teachers were strict disciplinarians, singing and dancing were part of children's school life. The rhyme and rhythm of these verses must have appealed to Shaker children, as they appeal to children today. The Provensens' charming illustrations show people engaged in typical Shaker occupations, wearing the dress of an earlier time in American history. Such historical alphabet books give contemporary children a sense of what life was like in the past because they share a reading and learning experience that children in earlier eras also enjoyed.

Animal Themes

The animal theme in the Shaker alphabet book is still very popular. Contemporary animal alphabet books range in complexity. Some show one letter and a single animal for each entry; some have a single letter, a single animal, and a rhyming phrase; some have very descriptive phrases with each letter; and some develop an integrated story in alphabetical order.

Bert Kitchen's *Animal Alphabet* is a book that at first glance seems simple. Each page in this large,

handsome text contains a crisp black capital letter and an animal that climbs, hangs onto, sits upon, or peeks out from behind the letter. Even older readers may have difficulty guessing the identities of the animals. Answers in the back of the book reveal jerboas, newts, and umbrella birds in addition to frogs, lions, and elephants.

Roger Tory Peterson's ABC of Birds: A Book for Little Birdwatchers includes text by Linda Westervelt, paintings by Roger Tory Peterson, and photographs by Seymour Levin. The text for each bird includes a large upper case letter, a short description, and either a painting or a photograph. For example, the text on the O page states: "O is for Owl. In the night, sharp eyes and ears watch and listen. 'Whoo, whoo, whoo' " (unnumbered).

Interaction with text is also encouraged in Arthur Geisert's *Pigs from A to Z*. In this detailed text, each letter is introduced by one or two sentences. Full-page illustrations depict pigs performing the accompanying actions. Within each illustration are hidden several examples of the specific letter as well as the letter that precedes the applicable letter and the letter that follows it. The book concludes with a key so that readers may verify the locations of the letters within the picture puzzle.

Mary Beth Owens's *A Caribou Alphabet* is unusual because the illustrations and alphabetical order reveal information about one of the large wild animals. The text begins "A caribou's antlers can grow mighty large/Bulls spar in the autumn to see who's in charge" (unnumbered). Each page continues with a letter, an illustration, and a rhyming text that highlights a word beginning with that letter.

The letters of the alphabet are shown in animals. (From Animal Alphabet *by Bert Kitchen. Copyright © 1984 by Bert Kitchen. Reprinted by permission of Dial Books.)*

F l a m b o y a n t

The alphabetical order is based on words containing ant. *("Flamboy*ant*" from* Antics! *by Cathi Hepworth, copyright © 1992 by Catherine Hepworth. Reprinted by permission of G. P. Putnam's Sons.)*

Ann Jonas's *Aardvarks, Disembark!* focuses on endangered and now-extinct animals as they leave the ark. Jonas pictures the animals in reverse alphabetical order, proceeding from zebus to aoudads. A glossary in the back of the book defines the animals and indicates whether the animals are endangered or are extinct.

Cathi Hepworth's *Antics!* is another unusual animal ABC for older children. Each of the words illustrated from *A* to *Z* has the word *ant* somewhere within the word. For example, a wizard ant illustrates an ench*ant*er for the letter *E*. Adults who work with older children indicate that this book provides an interesting motivation for writing ABC books that use a similar approach.

Other Alphabet Books

Anno's Alphabet: An Adventure in Imagination is a beautifully illustrated book by Mitsumasa Anno. The title is an excellent introduction to what is in store for observant readers. Large, simple objects suggest the beginning sound of each large letter, but Anno has also cleverly entangled numerous objects into the black-and-white borders circling the pages. For example, the *B* pages are bordered with beanstalks in which are entwined buttons, bees, bells, and birds. Children enjoy discovering these picture puzzles and searching for the hidden objects.

In *Alison's Zinnia,* Anita Lobel uses flowers as the central theme. The alphabetic theme is continued when the flowers are associated with verbs and girls' names. For example, "Alison acquired an Amaryllis for Beryl" and "Beryl bought a Begonia for Crystal" (pages 1–2, unnumbered). The large format of the book and the watercolor and gouache illustrations are visual treats for anyone interested in flowers.

Two recently published award-winning alphabet books provide opportunities for careful observation and comparisons. For example, Stephen T. Johnson's *Alphabet City* presents the letters through paintings of city scenes. Viewers look carefully to discover letters such as *p* as part of a handrail or *v* as part of the structure on an electric transmission pole. David Pelletier's *The Graphic Alphabet* presents each of the letters through the interpretations of a graphic designer. In the illustrator's note, Pelletier states that the book grew out of his interest in letterforms: "Expanding on a traditional form for children, the alphabet book, he decided that the illustration of the letterform had to retain the natural shape of the letter as well as represent the meaning of the word" (unnumbered). Viewers will observe this relationship through examples such as a *y* that is yawning and an *f* that is burning with a fire.

A buying excursion in an old-fashioned market provides an enjoyable trip through the alphabet in Arnold Lobel's *On Market Street,* illustrated by Anita Lobel. The child buys gifts from the shopkeepers: apples, books, clocks, doughnuts, . . . and finally zippers. The colorful illustrations help children develop concepts as they see and discuss the goods offered for sale. Lois Ehlert's *Eating the Alphabet: Fruits and Vegetables from A to Z* is another theme approach to introducing the alphabet to young children.

Suse MacDonald's *Alphabatics* is an extremely creative alphabet book. The illustrator uses a series of pictures that proceed from the original letter to an object that represents the letter. For example, the *A* proceeds from a drawing of a capital *A,* to an *A* tilted on blue waves, to an *A* upside down on the waves, to an *A* turned into an ark, and finally to an ark filled with animals. This book can be used to motivate children's drawings of similar examples.

Alphabet books by Betsy Bowen, Jim Aylesworth, Oscar de Mejo, and Cynthia Chin-Lee are organized around specific locations. Bowen's *Antler, Bear, Canoe: A Northwoods Alphabet Year* follows the seasons in the Northwoods of Minnesota, beginning in January and proceeding into the following winter. The wood-block prints depict activities such as kayaking in spring, watching northern lights in summer, and taking part in potluck dinners of grouse and wild rice in the autumn. Aylesworth's *The Folks in the Valley: A Pennsylvania Dutch ABC* is illustrated with pictures depicting the Pennsylvania Dutch heritage. De Mejo's *Oscar de Mejo's ABC* depicts an earlier time in United States history. Chin-Lee's *A Is for Asia* presents information about Asia.

The Z Was Zapped by Chris Van Allsburg also encourages interaction between the text and readers. Van Allsburg presents the alphabet in the form of a

quilts,

Detailed illustrations may assist understanding of concepts and development of oral discussion skills. (From On Market Street, *by Arnold Lobel. Illustrated by Anita Lobel. Text copyright © 1981 by Arnold Lobel. Illus. copyright © 1981 by Anita Lobel. By permission of Greenwillow Books [a division of William Morrow & Co., Inc.].)*

twenty-six-act play. Each act is a letter being treated to some action that begins with that sound. For example, the play is introduced with the letter *A* as it is bombarded with falling rocks. Readers become involved because they must turn the page to discover that Act 1 is "The A was in an Avalanche." Teachers may encourage writing by asking students to create their own descriptions of each act.

Eve Merriam's *Halloween ABC,* an alphabet poetry book for older students, uses the ABC format to introduce poems about Halloween topics. For example, the *K* page has an illustration of the letter *K* and a key. The accompanying poem is about a key that opens a mysterious gate that in turn leads to adventure. This poem is another selection that may stimulate writing. Students may write a second verse to the key poem to reveal what happens when they find the key that spells "Follow me." Rhythmic verse also provides the focus for Bill Martin, Jr., and John Archambault's ABC, *Chicka Chicka Boom Boom.*

Several alphabet books are designed to provide information to older students rather than to teach letter/sound relationships to younger ones. Two award-winning books present information about African life. Margaret Musgrove's *Ashanti to Zulu: African Traditions,* vividly illustrated by Leo and Diane Dillon, depicts the customs of twenty-six African peoples. *Jambo Means Hello: Swahili Alphabet Book,* by Muriel Feelings, introduces Swahili words and customs. These beautiful books can encourage children of all cultural backgrounds to learn more about African people. Jonathan Hunt's *Illuminations* focuses on the people and events of the Middle Ages, alphabetically presenting terms such as *Excalibur, falconry,* and *Grail.* The book makes an interesting accompaniment for English legends such as those about King Arthur.

Bruce Whatley and Rosie Smith's *Whatley's Quest* includes illustrations of numerous objects that begin with the sound. A secret scroll on the inside of the dust jacket provides a guide through this colorful alphabet. For example, the guide for the *Q* page: "Sitting on the quay is a Queen. The Queen wants to join the treasure hunt, and she is using a quill to chart her course. She is in a quandary about where to look for the treasure, though, so one of the Quintuplets is telling the other four to be quiet so the Queen can think" (inside dust jacket).

Historical content and subject-related topics are popular subjects for alphabet books. Wes Hardin's *Henry Ford Museum: An ABC of American Innovation* uses illustrations of objects from the museum to depict the letters. The captions provide dates and additional information about the various objects. Diana Pomeroy's *Wildflower ABC: An Alphabet of Potato Prints* presents various wildflowers using alphabetical order. This is another example of an alphabet book that may appeal to older readers.

 ## COUNTING BOOKS

Counting books, like alphabet books, are often used for specific educational purposes. To develop one-to-one correspondence and ability to count sequentially from one through ten, a counting book should contain easily identifiable numbers and corresponding objects. Effective number books for young children usually show one large number, the word for the number, and the appropriate number of objects—all on one page or on facing pages. The actual number represented should be clear. For example, one star showing five points may be a poor choice for depicting the number five, since children may not understand that five, not one, is being depicted.

Books that stimulate the manipulation of concrete objects are especially useful. For example, a counting book showing the number two and two blocks might encourage a young child to count two real blocks. One very simple counting book for young children, Eric Carle's wordless *My Very First Book of Numbers,* is designed so that children can easily match numbered squares with their corresponding illustrations.

Counting books for children may stimulate language development and interaction with the text. In *Roll Over!* Mordicai Gerstein uses a nursery rhyme, fold-out flaps, and humorous illustrations to involve children in counting the number of people in a bed. In Molly Bang's *Ten, Nine, Eight,* an African American father and child observe objects and then say a rhythmic counting lullaby that proceeds backward from ten to one until the drowsy child is ready for bed. Eileen Christelow also uses the text of a nursery rhyme in *Five Little Monkeys Jumping on the Bed* to develop a counting book that proceeds backward from five to zero. In Nancy Tafuri's *Who's Counting?* children are encouraged to develop concepts related to the numbers one through nine. Caron Lee Cohen's *How Many Fish?* encourages counting of fish under the water.

Merle Peek's *The Balancing Act: A Counting Song* appeals to children. The illustrations and text proceed from one elephant to ten. The lines "They thought it was such an amusing stunt/that they called in another elephant" are repeated each time another elephant balances on the piece of string. With the count of ten, the elephants drop into a safety net. Christopher Gunson's *Over On the Farm: A Counting Picture Book Rhyme,* another book for young children, uses farm animals and rhyming text to develop numbers from one through ten. Language is also a strength in Vic Parker's *Bearobics: A Hip-Hop Counting Story.* The text uses a hip-hop beat, alliteration, and onomatopoeia. Olivier Dunrea's *Deep Down Under* encourages counting from one to ten and identifying various creatures that dig under the ground.

One Hole in the Road, by W. Nikola-Lisa and illustrated by Dan Yaccarino, uses the idea of a tremendous hole that requires such counting concepts as four flashing stoplights, five sirens, and six engineers to try to control the situation. Young children enjoy the action in this setting with its vivid colors.

Ellen Stoll Walsh's *Mouse Count,* William Wise's *Ten Sly Piranhas: A Counting Story in Reverse (A Tale of Wickedness—and Worse!),* and Denise Fleming's *Count!* introduce counting concepts for young children. *Mouse Count* follows the adventures of ten hapless mice who are captured by a hungry snake and then outsmart the snake. The counting proceeds as the snake drops each of them individually into a glass jar. The greed of the snake for just one more mouse allows the mice to escape from the jar and lets the illustrator count backward from ten to one. The numbers in this text are presented as written words. *Ten Sly Piranhas: A Counting Story in Reverse (A Tale of Wickedness—and Worse!)* also develops counting backward as the "Ten sly piranhas were swimming in the river" and find "Ten hungry fishes, hoping very much to dine." The rest is history, as one by one the fish disappear. The piranhas also disappear one by one until the last one is seen in the jaws of a crocodile. *Count!* encourages readers to count various animals from one to ten. The two-page spreads also present the number concepts twenty, thirty, forty, and fifty. The large, colorful format appeals to young children. The subtraction concepts beginning with ten to one are developed as two children go out in the night and try to catch ten fireflies in Philemon Sturges's *Ten Flashing Fireflies.* As each firefly is captured and placed in a jar, the text and illustrations show what happens as the fireflies are either subtracted by one or added by one in a jar. The counting backwards and subtraction continues as the ten fireflies are released into the night.

Some books develop both observational skills and counting abilities. Arthur Geisert's *Pigs from 1 to 10* encourages children to find the numbers and count the pigs that are hidden within the illustrations. This counting book includes a story line in which the ten pigs go on a quest to find a lost land. There is a key to the location of the numbers in the back of the book.

Counting books for older children may develop the concept of numbers, addition, or subtraction, or they may encourage children to search for many groups of the same number on a single page. You should consider children's abilities so that you select books of appropriate difficulty.

Mitsumasa Anno presents the numbers one through ten and the concepts of addition and subtraction in *Anno's Counting House.* On alternating double pages, Anno shows the interiors and exteriors of two houses. In the old house, ten people are preparing to move. Then, only nine people are in the old house and one is in the new house. The process continues until the new house is furnished. *Anno's Math Games II* includes numerous picture puzzles and mathematical concepts. *Anno's Math Games, No. III* provides opportunities for readers to interact with the text and try their own experiments with triangles, rectangles, and mazes.

Count and See and *26 Letters and 99 Cents,* by Tana Hoban, are simple counting books with easy-to-identify number concepts that also extend to sets and higher numbers. In *Count and See,* each number, its corresponding written word, and a circle or circles illustrating the number appear in white on a black background. On the opposite page, a photograph illustrates the number with things found in the environments of many children: one fire hydrant, two children, . . . twenty watermelon seeds, . . . forty peanuts shown in groups of ten, . . . and one hundred peas shown in pods of ten each. The book may also be used for counting and grouping concrete items. (Counting and grouping aid cognitive development.) This book may be used as either a counting book or an alphabet book. In one direction, the illustrations and text emphasize counting, and in the other direction it is an alphabet book.

Handtalk Birthday: A Number & Story Book in Sign Language, by Remy Charlip, Mary Beth Miller, and George Ancona, presents an unusual story. It is about a surprise party for a deaf woman. Photographs show the characters using sign language as the woman guesses the contents of her presents and the guests question her about her age.

Muriel Feelings's *Moja Means One: Swahili Counting Book* is the counting-book partner to her Swahili alphabet book. Each two-page spread provides a numeral from one to ten, the Swahili word for the number, a detailed illustration (by Tom Feelings) that depicts animal or village life in Africa, and a sentence describing the contents of the illustration. This book may be more appropriate for stimulating interest in an African culture or providing information for older

6 sita
(see-tah)

The clothing East Africans wear includes the kanga, busuti, lapa, kanzu, and dashiki.

This unusual counting book depicts East African culture. (From Moja Means One, *by Muriel Feelings. Illustrated by Tom Feelings. Illustrations copyright © 1971 by Tom Feelings. Used by permission of Dial Press.)*

children than for presenting number concepts to younger children.

Counting concepts in English and Spanish are reinforced in Ginger Foglesong Guy's *!Fiesta!* The text develops counting and vocabulary concepts as children go through a village gathering items for a fiesta. The items eventually become the objects in a piñata, which is broken during the party.

Jim Haskins's *Count Your Way Through Italy* is part of the "Count Your Way Through" series of counting books. Haskins develops counting concepts from one through ten in Italian. He then provides background information about Italian culture and geography. Beth Wright's illustrations depict the numbers and the text for such things as Mount Etna (one), the products for which Italy is known (nine), and the horses that are chosen to race in the Corsa del Palio (ten). Additional books in this series provide counting opportunities through Africa, the Arab world, Canada, China, Germany, Japan, Korea, Mexico, and Russia.

 CONCEPT BOOKS

Many of the books recommended for use in stimulating the cognitive development of children are concept books. These books rely on well-chosen illustrations to help children grasp both relatively easy concepts, such as red and circle, and more abstract concepts (which may be difficult for children to comprehend), such as prepositions (*through,* for example) and antonyms (*fast* and *slow,* for example). Like counting books, concept books come in various degrees of difficulty, so teachers should consider a child's level of understanding when selecting concept books.

Numerous books have been designed to help young children learn basic concepts, such as colors and shapes. Eric Carle's *My Very First Book of Colors* is a simple, wordless book that asks a child to match a block of color with the picture of an object illustrated in that color. In *Of Colors and Things,* Tana Hoban uses both colors and photographs of objects to invite children to search for matching colors. In *Circles, Triangles, and Squares,* Hoban uses large black-and-white photographs to show common shapes in everyday objects. In *Shapes, Shapes, Shapes,* she uses photographs to depict such shapes as circles, rectangles, and ovals. Photographs also depict shapes in Hoban's *Spirals, Curves, Fanshapes and Lines.* These books also encourage readers to look for similar shapes in their own environments. In *Over, Under and Through and Other Spatial Concepts,* Tana Hoban uses photographs that show children jumping *over* fire hydrants, walking *under* outstretched arms, and crawling *through* large pipes.

Comparisons can be made among three books in which spatial concepts such as above, behind, and under are explored. For example, Tana Hoban's *All About Where* presents the concept words on the sides of the photographs. Children are then encouraged to find the concepts in the illustrations. Pat Hutchins's *What Game Shall We Play?* presents the concepts in a game format. Readers follow the various animals across the fields, among the grass, over the wall, and into the hole. Sally Noll's *Watch Where You Go* follows a gray mouse through the grass, up a tree, along branches, down vines, between rocks, into marsh grass, and into a hole that is home. This trip is not as easy as it might appear, however. The journey includes going through, along, and down many areas that are dangerous for the mouse.

Authors have tackled the challenge of explaining opposites, too. Hoban uses photographs in other excellent concept books, such as *Push-Pull, Empty-Full: A Book of Opposites*. Hoban uses photographs to develop the meanings of such antonyms as *wet* (a puddle in the street) and *dry* (leaves on the street). Peter Spier's *Fast-Slow, High-Low: A Book of Opposites* is more detailed and complex. It shows, for example, many empty and full things, such as bal-loons, toothpaste tubes, flower vases, buses, and refrigerators. In *Big & Little,* Steve Jenkins uses pairs of animals to show relationships related to size.

Bruce McMillan's *Super Super Superwords* uses photographs to illustrate comparative words, such as *long, longer,* and *longest.* In the photographs, kindergarten children effectively demonstrate the meanings.

Donald Crews familiarizes children with various concepts in *Freight Train.* The cars of the train are different colors, and the movement of the train *across* trestles, *through* cities, and *into* tunnels encourages understanding of spatial concepts and of opposites, such as *darkness* and *daylight.* Trains fascinate many young children, and children eagerly learn concepts while enjoying the colors, movements, and sounds developed in this book.

Susi Gregg Fowler's text and Marisabina Russo's illustrations in *When Summer Ends* encourage children to identify happenings that are appropriate for each season. Anne Rockwell helps children understand seasonal changes and appropriate activities for each season in *First Comes Spring,* while Lisa Westberg Peters in *October Smiled Back* uses the twelve months of the year to help readers understand concepts related to changes in nature. In *City*

ISSUE   Picture Books and Controversy

SEVERAL BOOKS DISCUSSED in this chapter have stirred controversy and subsequently have been removed from library shelves. Other books have had illustrations altered to meet specific standards.

In the 1960s, Garth Williams's *The Rabbit's Wedding* was criticized because the illustrations showed the marriage of a black rabbit and a white rabbit. In 1969, William Steig's *Sylvester and the Magic Pebble* was criticized because some parents objected to his portrayal of police officers as pigs and others objected to his having the mother do housework while Sylvester and his father relaxed.

When Maurice Sendak's *In the Night Kitchen* was published in 1970, some parents, teachers, and librarians deplored the child's nudity. In several incidents, the nudity was covered with a drawn-on washcloth or the book was removed from the shelf. In the 1970s, too, some people criticized *Changes, Changes,* by Pat Hutchins, because the man has a more active role than does the woman. He drives and decides what to make from the blocks, while the woman pulls the train whistle and hands him the blocks.

One book not discussed in this chapter illustrates the changing sensitivities of Americans toward certain social issues. Helen Bannerman's *Little Black Sambo* (1899) was popular for many years. Eventually, however, many people considered the crudely drawn features of the characters and the story line to be offensive, and the book was taken off many library shelves.

As you evaluate picture books, consider which books might be controversial and the reasons for the controversy. Does controversy change with the times? What subjects might have caused controversy in picture books published in the 1950s, 1960s, 1970s, or 1980s? Are those subjects still controversial? Are any new areas of controversy developing today?

Sounds, Rebecca Emberley encourages children to listen for and to make appropriate sounds. Nancy Tafuri encourages concept and language development with large illustrations of animals in her almost wordless book *Early Morning in the Barn.* These concept books and others offer children pleasure as well as important learning experiences.

 ## WORDLESS BOOKS

In a newer type of picture book, the illustrations tell the whole story, without words. Children enjoy the opportunity to provide the missing text for wordless books—an excellent way of developing their oral and written language skills. Dorothy Strickland (1977) maintains, "Experiences with books that are thoughtfully planned to promote active verbal exchanges of ideas will have lasting positive effects upon both the communicative mode and the cognitive structure of the child" (p. 53). Wordless books stimulate creative thinking and enhance visual literacy abilities, as children must watch the pages for clues to the action. Wordless books are especially valuable because they allow children of different backgrounds and reading levels to enjoy the same book.

Wordless books have various degrees of detail and plot complexity. Some contain much detail, while others do not. Some develop easily identifiable plots, while others can be interpreted in many different ways. Some are large, making them appropriate for sharing with a group, while others are small, easily held by one child or one adult with a child in the lap. You should consider all of these characteristics when choosing wordless books for children of different ages, reading levels, and interests.

Henrik Drescher's *The Yellow Umbrella* is a small-format book designed for individual viewing or lap sharing. The detailed illustrations follow a mother and baby monkey as they retrieve a yellow umbrella in a zoo, sail away to the ocean, float along a river into their homeland, find the father monkey, and use the umbrella to shield their obviously happy home in the top of a palm tree. The two-tone illustrations encourage the eye to focus on the bright yellow umbrella.

Pat Hutchins's *Changes, Changes* is a simple wordless book that appeals to children in preschool and kindergarten who enjoy building with blocks. The illustrations show two wooden dolls building a house of blocks, coping with a fire by turning the house into a fire truck, solving the problem of too much water by building a boat, reaching land by constructing a truck, and eventually rebuilding their home. The large and colorful pictures make actions easily identifiable. The book stimulates oral language, as well as problem solving and manipulation of children's own blocks.

Realistic humor is a popular theme of wordless books for young children. A series of wordless books by Mercer Mayer shows the humorous adventures of a boy, a dog, and a frog. *Frog Goes to Dinner*—the most detailed book in the series and, to many children, the funniest—illustrates the humorous disruptions that can occur if a frog hides in a boy's pocket and accompanies a family to a fancy restaurant. Each of Mayer's books is small, just the right size for individual enjoyment or for sharing with an adult. The illustrations are expressive and contain sufficient detail to stimulate language development and enjoyment.

Several wordless books develop plots involving the antics of animals from the world of fantasy. John S. Goodall's *Paddy Under Water* follows Paddy Pork as he dives underwater and discovers a sunken ship. Emily Arnold McCully's *Picnic* follows a family of mice as they jubilantly go on a picnic, unhappily discover that a small mouse is missing, and joyfully reunite the whole family. McCully's *School* follows the same family as they experience common occurrences. The illustrations depict enough plot to stimulate the creation of narrative even by older children.

Peter Collington's *The Angel and the Soldier Boy* is a large-format book that can be viewed and discussed by groups of students. The wordless plot follows the actions in a young girl's dream. Her toy soldier and angel come to life and challenge the pirates who rob the girl's piggy bank, capture the soldier, and return to their ship on top of the piano. The illustrations include enough detail to stimulate storytelling.

Another dream sequence forms the plot in David Wiesner's *Free Fall.* This beautifully illustrated, wordless book takes the dreamer on a fantasy in which he explores uncharted lands. Interestingly, many of the objects that seem so real in his dream are by his bed when he awakes. Plots in wordless books frequently take characters on magical excursions. In Lisa Maizlish's *The Ring,* a boy finds the

The sequential organization and detail of the illustrations provide a story line that stimulates language development. (Illustration on unnumbered page 11 from Picnic *by Emily Arnold McCully. Copyright © 1984 by Emily Arnold McCully. Reprinted by permission of Harper & Row Publishers, Inc.)*

magical object in a New York City park, puts it on, and flies through the air. Photographs follow the boy and reveal his adventures. Ask students to compare the influence of the illustrator's use of black-and-white and color photographs. In *Tuesday,* Wiesner uses the wordless format and glowing watercolors to create a book filled with surprising and unexpected elements. Readers enjoy not only creating their own story to accompany the illustrations but also extending the book into the next Tuesday. Wiesner's final illustration shows the following Tuesday, when the pigs have their opportunity to fly, to explore the neighborhood, and to baffle the people. The book provides interesting stimuli for creative writing and illustrating, allowing students to create their own stories about "The Night the Pigs Could Fly."

Some wordless books are exceptional because of their detail. John Goodall's *Story of a Main Street* encourages historical comparisons and analysis by allowing older students to trace the evolution of an English town from medieval to contemporary times. When developing observational skills, have students focus on differences in architecture, clothing, and transportation. Goodall shows that the market square location is the same even though the times change. The times include medieval, Elizabethan, Restoration, Georgian, Regency, Victorian, Edwardian, and modern. In *The Story of the Seashore,* Goodall traces the history of seaside holidays through different time periods.

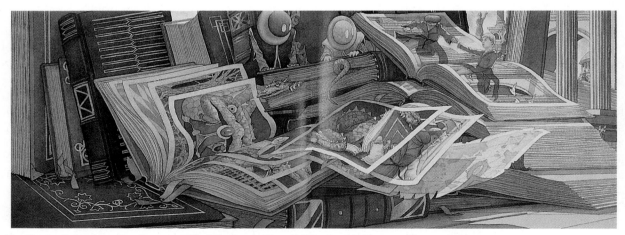

The illustrations show the dream world of the boy in Free Fall *by David Wiesner. (Illustration by David Weisner from* Free Fall *by David Wiesner. Copyright © 1988 by David Wiesner. Reprinted by permission of Lothrop, Lee and Shepard Books, a division of William Morrow & Co., Inc.)*

Peter Spier's *Noah's Ark* is another excellent picture book. The only words occur at the beginning of the book. The pictures show the building of the ark, the boarding of the animals, the long wait, and the starting of life again on the land, which is plowed and cultivated. The pictures contain so much detail that children can discover something new each time they read the book.

Jeannie Baker's *Window* is an exceptional example of collage illustrations that explore textures found in various settings. The illustrations use a window to show the changes that occur in an Australian neighborhood. These changes, which are shown through the growth of a child and the changing view from the window, also develop a strong environmental theme: People affect the environment. By tracing the changes, the artist shows how rapidly a community can change from rural to urban and investigates the possible consequences of moving to a rural area again. The artist reinforces the theme through her endnotes when she states, "By understanding and changing the way we personally affect the environment, we can make a difference."

Several beautifully illustrated wordless books by Mitsumasa Anno also encourage oral discussion and storytelling by older children. The detailed drawings in *Anno's Journey,* for example, are the result of the artist's travels through the countryside, villages, and larger towns of Europe. Anno adds to the enjoyment by suggesting that readers look for certain details in the pictures, such as paintings and characters from children's literature. The pictures are detailed enough to keep even adults occupied.

One enticing, almost wordless book is Chris Van Allsburg's *The Mysteries of Harris Burdick.* A title and a one-line caption precede each picture. In the introduction to the book, Van Allsburg asks readers to provide the missing stories. Teachers and librarians report that the illustrations contain enough elements of mystery and fantasy to motivate excellent oral and written stories.

Many wordless books are ideal for promoting oral language development. Others, however, are so obscure in story line that children may be frustrated when asked to tell the story. When choosing wordless books, consider the questions posed in the Evaluation Criteria box on this page.

The varied levels of complexity found in wordless books indicate that wordless books are appropriate

for young children as well as older ones. This same complexity, however, means that adults must select the materials carefully. As an example of the differences in wordless books and relationships with age, compare wordless books for young readers such as those by Mercer Mayer with Tom Feelings's *The Middle Passage: White Ships/Black Cargo,* a wordless book about the slave trade.

 EASY-TO-READ BOOKS

Easy-to-read books are designed to be read by children with beginning reading skills. These beginner books serve as transitions between basal readers and library trade books. Like picture storybooks, these books contain many pictures designed to suggest the story line. Unlike picture storybooks, however, the vocabulary is controlled so that young readers can manage independently. Controlling the vocabulary to fit the needs of beginning readers may result in contrived language, however, because it is difficult to write stories that sound natural if all of the words must be selected from the easiest level of readability.

Authors, teachers, and librarians use several different readability formulas to determine the approximate level of reading skill required to read a book. The Fry Readability Formula (Fry, 1977), for example, measures the reading level by finding the average number of sentences and syllables per hundred words. These averages are plotted on a graph that identifies the corresponding grade level for the book. Readability experts assume that easier books have shorter sentences and more monosyllabic words. As the reading level becomes higher, the sentences become longer and multisyllabic words become more numerous.

Compare the readability of an easy-to-read book and another picture storybook. A one hundred-word selection from one popular easy-to-read book, Dr. Seuss's *The Cat in the Hat,* shows sixteen sentences and one hundred syllables for those one hundred words. The sentences are very short and all words are of one syllable. Plotting these two findings on the Fry graph indicates a first-grade reading level. In contrast, a picture storybook also written for first-grade interests by Dr. Seuss, *And to Think That I Saw It on Mulberry Street,* has seven and one-half sentences and one hundred twenty-six syllables in a one hundred-word selection. The reading level for this book is fifth grade. While both books appeal to children of about the same age, children themselves usually read the first book, and adults usually read the second to children.

Even though easy-to-read books may not meet all standards for literary quality, they may meet the needs of beginning readers. Because children need experiences with books that allow them to reinforce their reading skills independently and to develop pride in their accomplishments, you should include easy-to-read books in every book collection for primary-age children. Easy-to-read books are also helpful to students who need successful experiences in remedial reading classes. Because of controlled use of language and sentence structure, easy-to-read books are less appropriate for adults to read aloud to children, although children may enjoy reading them aloud to appreciative adults.

Animal antics appeal to young children, and many favorite easy-to-read books have animals as the main characters. In Dr. Seuss's *The Cat in the Hat,* a cat amazes and entertains two children when he

Humorous illustrations enhance an unexpected experience in a favorite easy-to-read book. *(From* The Cat in the Hat, *by Dr. Seuss. TM and copyright © 1957 and renewed 1989 by Dr. Seuss Enterprises, L.P. Reprinted by permission of Random House, Inc.)*

balances a fish bowl, a carton of milk, and a cake simultaneously. Dr. Seuss's humorous illustrations and rhyming dialogue appeal to children. The cat emphasizes this enjoyment:

> Look at me!
> Look at me!
> Look at me Now!
> It is fun to have fun
> But you have to know how. (p. 8)

Arnold Lobel has written and illustrated several enchanting easy-to-read books. The soft brown and green illustrations in Lobel's stories about Frog and Toad re-create the atmosphere of a woodland setting and show the friendship felt by these two characters. In *Frog and Toad Are Friends,* Frog tries to entice Toad out of his home in order to enjoy the new spring season. Children enjoy Toad's reactions when Frog knocks on the door:

> "Toad, Toad," shouted Frog,
> "wake up. It is spring!"
> "Blah," said a voice
> from inside the house.

In Lobel's *Grasshopper on the Road,* a curious insect decides to follow a winding country lane just to discover where it leads. Lobel's characterization is fuller than that found in many other easy-to-read books. Lobel has the grasshopper encounter the rural inhabitants and then try to change their behaviors.

Easy-to-read books may be series books such as those written by Cynthia Rylant. Rylant includes several books in her Henry and Mudge series. *Henry and Mudge and the Happy Cat* develops the new relationship between the dog Mudge and a stray cat. *Henry and Mudge and the Bedtime Thumps* is set in Grandmother's house in the country. A strange noise shows Henry and Mudge that it is better to be together during scary times. In *Henry and Mudge and the Long Weekend,* Rylant tells a warm story in which boredom and "February cranks" are overcome by creating a castle out of large boxes. An elderly man and an old yellow-and-white cat develop a strong companionship in *Mr. Putter and Tabby Pour the Tea* and *Mr. Putter and Tabby Walk the Dog. Poppleton* includes stories about a pig. Rylant's easy-to-read books are unique because of their interesting stories and their descriptive language.

Charlotte Pomerantz's "I Can Read Book" *Outside Dog* takes place in a Puerto Rican neighborhood. Pomerantz has incorporated Spanish words and phrases into the text. Short, scary stories are found in both Edward Marshall's *Four on the Shore* and Alvin Schwartz's *In a Dark, Dark Room.*

Ready. . .Set. . .Read! is an anthology of easy-to-read stories, poems, and games compiled by Joanna Cole and Stephanie Calmenson. The stories are written by such well-known authors as Dr. Seuss, Else Minarik, Arnold Lobel, Joanna Cole, and Bernard Wiseman. This anthology lets students of children's literature analyze and compare several sources of this type of literature.

Soft woodland colors and animals with human characteristics combine in a memorable easy-to-read book. (From Grasshopper on the Road, *written and illustrated by Arnold Lobel. Copyright © 1978 by Arnold Lobel. By permission of Harper & Row Publishers, Inc.)*

PICTURE STORYBOOKS

A characteristic common to many picture books discussed thus far is the use of illustrations to present all or most of the content of a book. Reliance on pictures is especially crucial in concept books, counting books, a majority of the alphabet books, and all wordless picture books. Many of these books do not have continuous story lines; instead, the illustrations are grouped according to common themes or are presented in numerical or alphabetical sequence.

Although picture storybooks contain many illustrations, they also develop strong story lines in text. In a well-written picture storybook, the text and narrative complement each other, so children cannot deduce the whole story merely by viewing the pictures. The illustrations are integral to the story line, enhancing the actions, settings, and characterizations (Norton, 1993).

Elements in Picture Storybooks

When adults think about enjoyable book experiences shared by adults and children during story hour or at bedtime, they usually remember picture storybooks. Childhood would be less exciting without friends like Mike Mulligan, Frances the badger, and Ferdinand the bull. What makes some books so memorable for both children and adults? Originality and imagination are crucial in outstanding picture books, but so are strong plot, characterization, setting, theme, style, and humor.

Originality and Imagination. A man and his dog discover that "Paradise lost is sometimes Heaven found"; a young man goes to a fortune teller and discovers that the predictions about his future can come true; and a child's bedroom becomes the kingdom of wild things. Some adults never lose touch with the dreams, fears, and fantasies of childhood and, as authors of picture storybooks for children, they create imaginative new worlds in which the impossible becomes both real and believable.

In *Hey, Al,* Arthur Yorinks's plot helps a janitor and his dog find a more satisfying way of life. Through experience in a beautiful location, where they do not need to work, they discover that beautiful places can have dangerous secrets.

In *The Fortune-Tellers,* Lloyd Alexander develops the story of a young carpenter who is unhappy with his life. When he seeks a fortune teller to reveal what will happen in his life, he discovers that his life will change in unexpected ways. In humorous dialogue, the fortune teller gives the carpenter his wishes. For example, when the carpenter asks, "Do you see me rich, then?" the fortune teller answers, "Rich you will surely be. . . . On one condition: that you earn large sums of money" (p. 5, unnumbered). After the seer mysteriously disappears, the carpenter discovers an unexpected way for the prophesies to come true. Older readers will also enjoy the irony in the conclusion.

A child's imagination structures the delightful story in Maurice Sendak's *Where the Wild Things Are.* Only in such fantasy can young children who have been disciplined turn their rooms into kingdoms inhabited by other wild things like themselves and then return home in safety before their suppers get cold.

Picture storybooks and their accompanying illustrations are filled with many imaginative episodes. They provide hours of enjoyment and are excellent for stimulating children's imaginations during creative play, storytelling, and creative writing.

Plot. The short attention spans of children who read or hear picture storybooks place special demands on plot development. The plots of picture

The original plot suggests that beautiful places may be dangerous. (Illustrations from Hey, Al *by Arthur Yorinks. Illustrated by Richard Egielski. Illustrations copyright © 1986 by Richard Egielski. Reprinted by permission of Farrar, Straus & Giroux, Inc.)*

storybooks are usually simple, clearly developed, and brief. They involve few subplots or secondary characters. Such plots usually allow young children to become involved with the action, identify the problem, and solve it rapidly.

For example, in the first three pages of Maurice Sendak's *Where the Wild Things Are,* children know that Max is in so much trouble that he has been sent to bed without supper. Even though the thirty-seven words used thus far do not reveal what Max has done, the pictures explain his problems. Children see him standing on books, hammering nails into the wall, and chasing the dog with a fork. The plot is swiftly paced, and children rapidly join Max in his imaginary world, as the room becomes wilder and wilder.

Sendak introduces additional conflict and excitement when Max encounters the wild things and overcomes them with a magic trick. Children empathize with Max when he has played long enough, sends his new subjects off to bed, and returns home to his mother's love and his supper. The author uses only thirty-eight words to tell what happens between the time Max leaves the wild things and returns home. This book is an excellent example of the important relationship between illustrations and plot development; the illustrations become larger and larger as the drama increases and then become smaller again as Max returns to his everyday life.

It is interesting to compare Sendak's illustrations and Richard Egielski's illustrations for *Hey, Al.* Both illustrators increase the sizes of their illustrations as conflict develops, use two-page spreads at the height of interest, and include much information about characters and settings within the illustrations.

Other picture books deal with children's problems in more realistic plots. In *Like Jake and Me,* Mavis Jukes portrays the strained relationship between Alex and his big, powerful stepfather Jake, who refuses to allow Alex to help with various chores. When a large, hairy spider crawls into Jake's clothes, Alex discovers that even a powerful, ex-rodeo cowboy can be afraid, and Jake discovers that even a small boy can provide assistance. In Ana Zamorano's *Let's Eat!* a boy experiences grown-up responsibilies when Mama is expecting a baby.

Whether a plot is based on fantasy or realism, it usually involves a rapid introduction to the action, a fast pace, and a strong, emotionally satisfying climax. In *The Patchwork Quilt,* Valerie Flournoy devel-

ops a warm, emotionally satisfying plot that follows the construction of a family quilt. The quilt gradually draws the members of the family together, as they remember past experiences associated with scraps of material, help Grandma sew, and marvel over the completed masterpiece, which reveals the family's life story. In Patricia Polacco's *Thunder Cake,* a grandmother and her granddaughter assemble a special cake as a thunderstorm grows nearer. These actions help the girl realize that she is brave enough to face the storm. In *Yo! Yes?,* Chris Raschka uses only thirty-four words to show the beginning of friendship when an African American boy and a white boy meet on the street. Their brief exchanges, accompanied by cartoonlike illustrations, show many universal feelings and emotions as the two boys become acquainted.

Characterization. The characters in picture storybooks must have specific traits that make them appealing to young children and that meet the demands of the short format. Since a short story does not allow for the fully developed characters that older children and adults prefer, the characters in picture storybooks must experience situations and emotions immediately familiar and credible to the children.

Maurice Sendak, for example, did not need to describe Max, the wild things, or the rumpus that takes place between them. His illustrations show these effectively. Likewise, Stephen Gammell's illustrations for Karen Ackerman's *Song and Dance Man* re-create the magic of vaudeville and express the love between grandchildren and their grandfather.

Any child can understand the feelings of Judith Viorst's hero in *Alexander and the Terrible, Horrible, No Good, Very Bad Day.* Alexander wakes up with gum in his hair, does not get a prize in his cereal when everyone else does, receives reprimands from his teacher, loses his best friend, has a cavity filled by the dentist, gets into trouble for making a mess in his dad's office, has to eat lima beans for dinner, and is ignored by the cat, who goes to sleep with his brother. In this book, as in most picture storybooks, the illustrations supplement the characterizations in the text by showing the characters' actions and reactions.

Children can understand stories about loneliness and friendship. In *The Scarebird,* Sid Fleischman develops a story of friendship between a lonely older farmer and his creation of a lifelike scarecrow and then between the farmer and an equally lonely and homeless young farm worker. As the human friendship increases, the farmer takes needed objects from the scarecrow and gives them to the boy. In *Captain Snap and the Children of Vinegar Lane*, Roni Schotter's characters use friendship and thoughtfulness to change the life of a lonely older man. In *The Gardener*, both Sarah Stewart's text and David Small's illustrations show changes that may be brought to a city landscape and a scowling man through flowers.

Children frequently have close attachments with older people and want to hear more about their lives. Such a character is developed in Gloria Houston's *My Great-Aunt Arizona*. The tone of Houston's text and Susan Condie Lamb's illustrations develop the loving character of a woman who gave her life to teaching. Houston tells readers that although she never traveled from the Blue Ridge Mountains, she educated generations of children and touched their lives wherever they traveled. This book stimulates a strong response in adults. When using this book for the first time with adults (college students), the adults decided it would be a good book to give as a present to their favorite teacher.

Many storybooks contain animal characters that act and speak like humans. Margaret Wise Brown's *The Runaway Bunny* uses a credible little bunny to demonstrate a child's need for independence and love. The dialogue between the mother rabbit and the bunny stresses the bunny's desire to experience freedom by running away. Each time that he suggests ways to run away, however, the mother rabbit counters with actions that she would take to get him back. The love between the two animals is visible in the dialogue and pictures, and the bunny decides to stay with the mother who loves him.

Setting.   In picture storybooks, as in all literature, setting is used to establish the location of a story in time and place, create a mood, clarify historical

Children and an old man develop a warm relationship. (From Captain Snap and the Children of Vinegar Lane *by Roni Schotter, illustrated by Marcia Sewall. Copyright © 1989 by Roni Schotter, illustrations copyright © 1989 by Marcia Sewall. Reprinted by permission of Orchard Books.)*

background if necessary, provide an antagonist, and emphasize symbolic meaning. Picture storybooks, however, strongly rely on illustrations to serve these functions. Many books, such as Judith Viorst's *Alexander and the Terrible, Horrible, No Good, Very Bad Day,* Valerie Flournoy's *The Patchwork Quilt,* and Vera Williams's *Something Special for Me,* take place in the familiar contemporary world of television sets, blue jeans, and shopping centers. Other books take place in locations or times unfamiliar to the readers.

The illustrations in Catherine Stock's *Armien's Fishing Trip* show an African coastal village. Carole Byard's illustrations for Sherley Anne Williams's *Working Cotton* create the world of an African American child as she labors in the migrant farming fields of central California. Holly Meade's illustrations for Minfong Ho's *Hush! A Thai Lullaby* create the environment of rural Thailand.

Ronald Himler's illustrations for Byrd Baylor's *The Best Town in the World* show how important illustrations are for illuminating time in picture storybooks. The brief poetic text alone cannot describe the details of a turn-of-the-century general store, the warmth created by a kerosene lamp, and the many activities associated with a picnic celebration in the days when a picnic was a major social event. Rachel Isadora's illustrations for *Young Mozart* take readers back to the historical setting of the composer's youth.

Toshi Maruki's dramatically expressive illustrations for *Hiroshima No Pika (The Flash of Hiroshima)* clarify the horrifying nature of the story's antagonist and the mood as seven-year-old Mii confronts the consequences of atomic warfare on August 6, 1945. The colors are especially dramatic. Swirling red flames pass over fleeing people and animals. Black clouds cover huddling masses and destroyed buildings. The illustrations suggest both the setting as antagonist and a destructive, frightening mood.

In *The Wreck of the Zephyr,* Chris Van Allsburg's illustrations create a light mood, subtly mixing reality and make-believe. A boy who dreams of becoming the best sailor in the world experiences a calm sea sparkling with light and a star-studded night disturbed by only a magical ship flying through the sky. The illustrations in all such worthy picture storybooks enhance the times, places, conflicts, and moods of the stories.

Theme. The themes in picture storybooks for young children are closely related to children's needs and understandings. The importance of adjusting to new siblings and the need for security are popular themes in books. In *Darcy and Gran Don't Like Babies,* Jane Cutler uses a unique approach to help Darcy accept the new baby. When Gran arrives for a visit, Gran agrees with Darcy as they discuss what they do not like about babies. After they have a fun-filled day together, however, Gran gently helps Darcy understand that she will eventually like the baby.

In *Owen,* Kevin Henkes explores the need for security. The mouse child outmaneuvers his parents in their efforts to take away his security blanket, but in a very satisfying ending, the mother mouse cuts the blanket into handkerchiefs so that Owen can take his security with him wherever he goes. The need for love is a related theme developed in books such as Natalie Babbitt's *BUB: Or the Very Best Thing.* A young child lets his parents know that love is the best. A similar theme is developed in Mary Murphy's *I Like It When . . .* as a young penguin tells about happy shared experiences such as holding hands.

An understanding grandparent figure plays a key role in Patricia Polacco's *Babushka Baba Yaga.* Instead of the fearsome Russian witch, Polacco develops a kinder, gentler Baba Yaga, who learns to love Victor, a small boy in her care. Victor's devotion to her and Baba Yaga's actions when she saves Victor develop the themes that loving relationships between generations and tolerance when judging others are important.

Authors who develop conflicts usually develop the theme that overcoming fear is important. In *Lester's Dog,* Karen Hesse develops the theme as she introduces the fearful boy who was bitten by a neighbor's dog. With the help of a deaf friend, the boy bravely overcomes his fear and saves a homeless kitten. In *Mirette on the High Wire,* Emily Arnold McCully shows how debilitating fear can be. The heroine helps the Great Bellini, a former master wire walker, face and overcome his fear.

Themes related to friendship are also very important in picture storybooks. In *Santa Calls,* William Joyce develops a unique story set in Abilene, Texas, in 1908. Art Atchinson Aimesworth, his sister Esther, and his friend Spaulding discover a mysterious box left by Santa Claus. The directions accompanying the flying machine invite the children to join

Santa at the North Pole. While at the North Pole, they not only meet Santa but also combat dark elves and an evil queen. Readers do not know why the children are asked by Santa to come to the North Pole until they read two letters that are folded and attached to the final two pages. The first letter, from Esther, is addressed to Santa: "You can send me toys if you like, but what I *really* wish for is for my brother Art to be my friend." The final letter, from Santa, states, "Such a rare and wonderful request could not be refused. I am glad our little adventure did the trick."

The importance of friendships, the need to respect others, and the necessity for conducting wise negotiations are all important themes found in picture books. Peggy Rathmann's *Officer Buckle and Gloria* develops a theme about the importance of friendship as the story concludes with the safety tip, "Always Stick With Your Buddy!" (unnumbered). Both Lynn Reiser's *Best Friends Think Alike* and A. M. Monson's *Wanted: Best Friend* stress friendship, the obligations of friendship, and the often difficult tasks of sharing. The importance of getting along with one's neighbors and developing respect for and understanding of others is an important theme in Eve Bunting's *Smoky Night*. The importance of conducting wise negotiations, using one's wits, and doing one's share of the work are developed in Janet Stevens's *Tops & Bottoms*.

Style. Because a picture storybook contains so few words, its author must select those words very carefully. In an interview with Carolyn Phelan (1993), author Mem Fox emphasizes the importance of and the need for rhythm when writing for children. She states, "I think rhythm is important in all writing, but I think it's of particular importance in a picture book because of the deep-seated, collective unconscious need for rhythm" (p. 29). The rhythm in many of the Mother Goose rhymes, discussed earlier, indicates just how important this rhythm is in books for young children. A storybook also must be designed to catch children's attention and to stimulate their interest when adults read the story aloud. Adults can evaluate the effectiveness of style by reading a storybook orally to themselves or to a child.

Authors of picture storybooks frequently use repetition of single words or phrases to create stronger impressions when the books are read aloud. African folktales, for example, sometimes repeat words several times. In Gail E. Haley's *A Story, a Story,* the Sky God describes Ananse, the tiny spider man, as "so small, so small, so small." Similar use of repetition conveys the impression of a dancing fairy and rain on a hornet's nest. Verna Aardema uses this form of repetition to make a strong statement stronger in *Why Mosquitoes Buzz in People's Ears.* When a mother owl finds her dead baby, she is "so sad, so sad, so sad." The night that doesn't end is described as "long, long, long."

Young children enjoy listening to words that create vivid images. In the preface to *A Story, a Story,* Gail Haley says that many African words are found in the book and asks readers to listen carefully to the sounds so they can tell what the words mean. Haley uses many unknown words to describe the movements of animals. A python slithers "wasawusu, wasawusu, wasawusu" down a rabbit hole; a rabbit bounds "krik, krik, krik" across an open space; and sticks go "purup, purup" as they are pulled out of the iguana's ears. Minfong Ho uses a similar style in *Hush! A Thai Lullaby* as the various animals are introduced with the sounds they might create. For example, a monkey goes "Jiak-jiak! Jiak-jiak!" and a water buffalo goes "MAAAU, MAAAU."

Careful word choice also creates evocative moods in well-written picture storybooks. In *The Seeing Stick,* Jane Yolen creates a mood of wonder as Hwei Ming, the unhappy, blind daughter of a Chinese emperor, "sees" her father for the first time:

She reached out and her fingers ran eagerly through his hair and down his nose and cheek and rested curiously on a tear they found there. And that was strange, indeed, for had not the emperor given up crying over such things when he ascended the throne? (p. 19, unnumbered)

Carefully chosen words allow readers or listeners to place themselves in the setting and to feel the mood, as in Michael Bedard's *Emily,* in which a young girl sits in Emily Dickinson's parlor and listens to her mother play the piano: "I sat upon the parlor chair. Still the music played—but now I felt it breathe. My hand felt in my pocket. I thought of sunlight dancing on the sun-room floor, of Father plucking petals, and of poetry" (p. 25, unnumbered).

Humor. Selecting and sharing books that contribute to merriment is a major goal of any literature program. Research shows that humorous literature is particularly effective in attracting children to the pleasures of reading and writing. In a study of children's reading preferences, Dianne Monson and Sam Sebesta (1991) identified humor as a very important element in books preferred by children. They state:

Some forms of humor seem to have greatest appeal and perhaps are better understood by children in elementary and junior high school than others. The totally ridiculous situation and humorous characters are well liked, as is the humor associated with exaggeration, a surprising event, and play on words. (p. 668)

Many elements in picture storybooks can cause children to laugh out loud. An investigation by Sue Anne Martin (1969) concluded that humor in books awarded the Caldecott Medal had five general sources: (1) word play and nonsense, (2) surprise and the unexpected, (3) exaggeration, (4) the ridiculous and caricatures, and (5) superiority.

Word Play and Nonsense. Theodor Geisel, better known as Dr. Seuss, was one of the most popular authors of books for children and was an undisputed authority on word play and nonsense. Dr. Seuss often made up totally new words and names to describe the animals found in his imagination. In *Good Zap, Little Grog* Sarah Wilson uses a style similar to that of Dr. Seuss. Wilson creates new words for her story in rhyme. Here little Grog must "zoodle opp," the "ooglets are tuzzling," and "smibblets are giggling." A "Grog Guide" at the end of the book reveals the identity of the various animals in this fantasy world.

In Seuss's *If I Ran the Zoo,* Gerald McGrew's imaginary zoological garden contains an elephant-cat, a bird known as a Bustard, a beast called Flustard, and bugs identified as thwerlls and chugs. Of course, no one could find such animals in the usual jungles, so Gerald must search for them in Motta-fa-Potta-fa-Pell, in the wilds of Nantasket, and on the Desert of Zind. Children enjoy not only the nonsense found in the rhyming text but also the nonsensical illustrations of these strange animals.

Bill Peet's nonsense rhymes and nonsensical illustrations in *No Such Things* appeal to children. Peet uses both internal and end-of-line rhyming to create text such as the following:

The blue-snouted Twumps feed entirely on weeds,
And along with the weeds they swallow the seeds.

Eating seeds causes weeds to sprout on their backs,
Till they look very much like walking haystacks. (p. 5)

Margaret Mahy creates equally enjoyable nonsense in *17 Kings and 42 Elephants,* as "Tinkling tunesters, twangling trillicans,/Butterflied and fluttered by the great green trees" (unnumbered). Patricia MacCarthy's illustrations support these nonsense words.

Surprise and the Unexpected. Both Audrey Wood's text and Mark Teague's illustrations in *The Flying Dragon Room* create surprise and the unexpected. In this fantasy world created by a bored child are rooms in which people slide down a snake, fly through the air in the jumping room, sail into a world inhabited by friendly alligators, and give carrots to Tyrannosaurus Rex. The illustrations in Peggy Rathmann's *Officer Buckle and Gloria* add considerable humor and unexpected situations when the police dog performs behind Officer Buckle's back as he gives safety tips to school children. The dog's actions, unknown by Officer Buckle, change a presentation from dull to exciting.

Wilson Gage also uses irony to create the unexpected. In *Cully, Cully and the Bear,* a hunter discovers that the bear he's after is chasing him. The hunter decides that he does not need a bearskin and that, in fact, the ground is softer than any bearskin rug. Irony provides an unexpected conclusion in Frank Asch and Vladimir Vagin's *Here Comes the Cat!* The text and illustrations lead readers to believe that the cat will harm the mice, but instead, the cat brings cheese and the mice repay this friendship with combing and milk. Irony also creates surprise and the unexpected in Amy Hest's *In the Rain With Baby Duck.* Hest tells the story of a duck who dislikes to get wet feet, hop in puddles, or waddle through the water. Instead of loving rainy weather, he dawdles, dallies, pouts, and drags behind his parents who are thoroughly enjoying the setting. In a satisfying conclusion, Grampa gives Baby Duck a red umbrella and matching boots that once belonged to Baby Duck's mother, who also did not like the rain. Now Grampa and Baby Duck enjoy the weather together.

Surprise occurs in Jon Agee's *The Incredible Painting of Felix Clousseau* when the paintings come to life. Chaos takes place and imprisonment of the artist results until a dog in one of the paintings captures a jewel thief. The unexpected also occurs in

Mem Fox's *Night Noises*—the frightening night noises are caused by family members who are coming to give a surprise birthday party for the grandmother.

The humor in *The Chanukkah Guest* by Eric A. Kimmel emerges through the unexpected when an old woman mistakes a bear for the rabbi and serves the bear the delicious latkes that she has prepared for her special guest. In *Appelemando's Dreams,* Patricia Polacco calls upon the unexpected when children are able to show disbelieving villagers how important dreams can be.

Exaggeration. Children's imaginations are often filled with exaggerated tales about what they can do or would like to do. In James Stevenson's *Could Be Worse!,* however, the grandfather is the one who exaggerates. Grandpa does and says the same things day after day. Whenever anyone complains, Grandpa responds, "Could be worse." When he overhears his grandchildren commenting on his dull existence, he tells them what happened to him the previous evening: He was captured by a large bird and dropped in the mountains, where he encountered an abominable snowman. Then, he crossed a burning desert, escaped from a giant animal, landed in the ocean, and finally returned home on a paper airplane. After the grandchildren hear his story, they respond with his favorite expression, "Could be worse!" Stevenson uses similar exaggeration in *There's Nothing to Do.*

Patricia Polacco uses exaggeration to develop her humorous *Meteor!* After a meteor lands on a farm, the whole town exaggerates the power of the meteor. Individuals claim that it gives the ability to play a trumpet, create a marvelous recipe, and even see extraordinary distances. The book is humorous because readers know that such an incident might really happen.

Exaggeration is the source of humor in both Anne Isaacs's text and Paul O. Zelinsky's illustrations for *Swamp Angel.* This tall-tale story set in the American frontier develops a female character with unusual powers such as the ability to wrestle a bear. The exaggeration begins on the day of her birth when, "The newborn was scarcely taller than her mother and couldn't climb a tree without help" (unnumbered). The story concludes when Swamp Angel turns Thundering Tarnations (the bear) into a rug.

Unfortunately, the bear skin is too big for Tennessee so she moves to Montana where she can spread the rug on the ground in front of her cabin. "Nowadays, folks call it the Shortgrass Prairie" (unnumbered).

In *I Was Born About 10,000 Years Ago,* Steven Kellogg also uses the exaggeration of a tall tale as the narrator romps through history and reports being part of momentous occasions such as eating the core of the apple (Adam and Eve) and building the pyramids. The exaggeration of a tall tale is important in Debbie Dadey's *Shooting Star: Annie Oakley, the Legend* as Dadey creates a heroine whose skills include being able to shoot the points off a star and hit the moon.

The Ridiculous and Caricatures. The consequences of having antlers suddenly appear on a young girl's head provides the humor in *Imogene's Antlers,* in which author David Small caricatures the ridiculousness of the fears of some people. To extend the humor, the story concludes with another what-if: The antlers disappear, but an even more beautiful appendage replaces the antlers.

Foolishness and ridiculous situations may change to wisdom, as shown in Eric Kimmel's *The Chanukkah Tree.* In this Jewish tale, the people of Chelm believe a peddler when he sells them a Christmas tree as "a Chanukkah tree. From America. Over there Chanukkah trees are the latest thing" (unnumbered). The townspeople decorate the tree with potato latkes and candles. The only star that they can find for the top is on a door, so they place the whole door on top of the tree. When they discover that they have been duped by the peddler, they are unhappy at first. Later, birds take sanctuary on the tree during a snowstorm, and the people discover that their tree is not so ridiculous: The potato latkes feed the birds, the candles warm them, and the door protects them.

The humor in Janet Stevens's *Tops & Bottoms* results from the ridiculous situation and foolish actions of rich, lazy Bear when he is tricked out of the garden produce by Hare, who uses his wits to secure the best portions of the crop. The illustrations of Bear are particularly interesting as they epitomize this humorous and ridiculous situation.

Numerous ridiculous situations occur in Martin Waddell's *What Use Is A Moose?* when Jack brings a moose home and tries to convince his mother that the moose would be helpful around the house. The ridiculous situations increase as Jack tries to use the moose in such roles as a clothesline, a gardener, and a chauffeur. The cartoon-style illustrations add to the humorous situations.

Superiority. Some humorous picture storybooks gratify the desire of young children to be superior to everyone else for a change or to easily overcome their problems. When a town simpleton surpasses not only his clever brothers but also the czar of the land, the result is an unusual tale of humorous superiority. Arthur Ransome's *The Fool of the World and the Flying Ship* is a Russian tale. In it, the good deeds performed by a simple lad allow him to obtain a flying ship, discover companions who have marvelous powers, overcome obstacles placed in his path by the czar, win the hand of the czar's daughter, and live happily ever after.

A singing cow solves her problems by using superiority against a greedy human in Lisa Campbell Ernst's *When Bluebell Sang.* When the cow and the farmer become tired of being taken advantage of by a talent agent, the cow hides herself among a herd of cows, where the agent cannot identify her without her dress, hat, and shoes.

Typical Characters and Situations

Children's picture storybooks include stories about people disguised as animals, talking animals with human emotions, personified objects, humans in realistic situations, and humorous and inventive fantasies. This section discusses stories by some outstanding writers of books on these subjects.

People Disguised as Animals.
Many children's stories with animal characters are so closely associated with human life-styles, behavior patterns, and emotions that it is difficult to separate them from stories with human characters. If these stories were read without reference to the illustrations or to a specific type of animal, children might assume that the stories are about children and adults like themselves. These stories may be popular with children because the children can easily identify with the characters' emotions and the actions.

Russell Hoban's Frances the badger, for example, lives in a nice house with her two parents, loves bread and jam, and feels jealous when she gets a new baby sister. Children identify with Frances when, in *Bread and Jam for Frances,* she refuses to eat anything but her two favorite foods. Hoban has her parents, like good human parents, carefully guide Frances into her decision that eating only bread and jam is boring and that trying different foods is pleasant.

In *A Baby Sister for Frances,* the young badger decides to run away from home when her mother becomes busy with the new baby. She packs a lunch to take with her on her journey, but she goes only as far as the next room, from which she looks longingly at her parents and her sister. In this warm story, Hoban shows how Frances's need for her family helps her overcome her jealousy and decides to accept the new arrival. The warmth is expressed in Hoban's choice of language:

> Big sisters really have to stay
> At home, not travel far away,
> Because everybody misses them
> And wants to hug-and-kisses them. (p. 26, unnumbered)

In *Leo the Late Bloomer,* Robert Kraus develops a credible character through experiences shared by many children: Leo, a young tiger, cannot read, write, draw, talk, or even eat neatly. One of Leo's parents worries, while the other suggests that Leo is merely a late bloomer. Kraus uses repetition to emphasize Leo's problem as the seasons go by: "But Leo still wasn't blooming." A satisfactory ending results in both the text and illustrations when Leo finally discovers that he can do everything that he couldn't do before, and a happy father and mother hear their happy child declare, "I made it!"

Fears and experiences that result in temporary unhappiness are popular causes of conflict in stories about animals disguised as people. In *Rockin' Reptiles* by Stephanie Calmenson and Joanna Cole, two alligator friends must work out a fair solution to a conflict that at first threatens their friendship. David McPhail uses a temporarily unhappy experience to create a happy ending in *Fix-It.* A bear, Emma, who could easily be a young child, cries when the television does not work. After successive disappointments, her mother reads a book to try to calm the unhappy Emma. Emma discovers that reading is so much fun that she stays with the book rather than returning to the television. In *Owen,* Kevin Henkes uses a mouse child's fear of losing his security blanket to create a story that could be about any young child.

In Marc Brown's *Arthur's Family Vacation,* the mouse family plans and goes on a vacation to the seashore. Like many human vacations, their vacation at first looks like a disaster because it rains every day, the motel room is too small, the pool is not as large as a bathtub, and the children complain that their friends are not with them. The disaster is averted when Arthur decides to plan field trips for the family. Trips to a cow festival, Gatorville, Flo's Fudge Factory, and Jimmy's Jungle Cruise provide entertainment until the last day, when the sun shines and the family spends a glorious day at the beach. Children respond to the experiences and the problem solving by the oldest mouse child. If the book were read without pictures, however, the story could be about any family. A common dispute also forms the conflict in Rosemary Wells's *Bunny Cakes* as Max and Ruby develop a sibling rivalry over baking Grandma's birthday cake.

Talking Animals with Human Emotions. In other animal stories, the animals live in traditional animal settings, such as meadows, barnyards, jungles, and zoos. The animals in these stories display some animal traits, but they still talk like humans and have many human feelings and problems.

Although the main characters in Martin Waddell's *Can't You Sleep, Little Bear?* live in a cave in the woods, the cave has furnishings, the bears talk, and they express emotions that are very human. The universal fear of darkness and the need to be comforted by a caring adult provide the story line in this warm, loving story. The father, who continually leaves his book to soothe the child and provide security, develops a good response among children. In a totally satisfying ending, "Big Bear carried Little Bear back into the Bear Cave, fast asleep, and he settled down with Little Bear on one arm and the Bear Book on the other, cozy in the Bear Chair by the fire" (p. 25, unnumbered). In *Let's Go Home, Little Bear,* Waddell continues the loving relationship between the two bears, and Little Bear is helped to overcome his fears of the sounds that he hears in the woods. In *You and Me, Little Bear,* the bear tries to get mother bear's attention.

The main character in Munro Leaf's *The Story of Ferdinand* lives in a meadow with his mother and other cattle. Leaf develops contrasts between Ferdinand, who sits under his favorite cork tree smelling the flowers, and the bulls who run, jump, and butt their heads together practicing for the bullring. The theme of the story is relevant to any human child: All individuals should be themselves, and being different is not wrong. Leaf allows Ferdinand to remain true to his individual nature. When Ferdinand is taken to the bullring, he merely sits and smells the flowers.

Jean de Brunhoff uses a variety of emotional experiences in the various Babar books. Emotionally, Babar grows up; grieves when his mother dies; runs away to the city; returns to the jungle, where he is crowned king; and raises a family.

In Roger Duvoisin's *Petunia,* a goose becomes conceited when she finds a book and believes that merely carrying it around gives her wisdom. Petunia's advice creates an uproar in the barnyard when she maintains that firecrackers discovered in the meadow are candy and thus good to eat. Her true wisdom begins when she discovers that books have words and that she will need to learn to read if she really wants to be wise.

A farm setting is also the location for Martin Waddell's *Farmer Duck.* In the beginning, the duck does all the work while the lazy human farmer lies in bed, eats chocolates, and reads the paper. In a satisfying ending, the animals work together, chase the farmer away, and retrieve the farm for the duck and the other animals.

Many young children like a combination of fast, slapstick adventure and an animal with easily identifiable human characteristics, such as Hans Rey's *Curious George.* Readers are introduced to this comedic monkey as he observes a large yellow hat lying on the jungle floor. His curiosity gets the better of him, he is captured by the man with the yellow hat, and his adventures begin. The text and illustrations develop one mishap after another. George tries to fly but falls into the ocean, grabs a bunch of balloons and is whisked away by the wind, and is finally rescued again by the man with the yellow hat. The rapid verbal and visual adventures bring delight to young children, who are curious about the world around them and would like to try some of the same activities.

Other picture storybooks with animal characters satisfy children's desires for absurd situations, flights of fancy, and magical transformations. In William

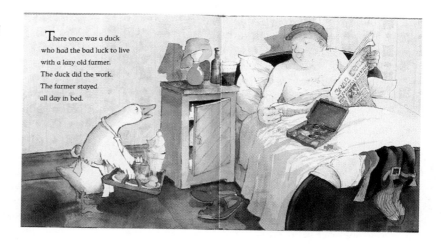

The animals in Farmer Duck *display human emotions and traits. (Reproduced from* Farmer Duck *by Martin Waddell with permission from Candlewick Press, Cambridge, MA. Illustration copyright © by Helen Oxenbury.)*

There once was a duck who had the bad luck to live with a lazy old farmer. The duck did the work. The farmer stayed all day in bed.

Steig's *Sylvester and the Magic Pebble,* for example, a young donkey accidentally changes himself into a rock and must figure out how to communicate with his grieving parents and return to his donkey form.

Personified Objects. The technique of giving human characteristics to inanimate objects is called personification. Children usually see nothing wrong with a house that thinks, a doll that feels, or a steam shovel that responds to emotions. Virginia Lee Burton, a favorite writer for small children, is the highly skilled creator of things that have appealing personalities and believable emotions. In Burton's *Katy and the Big Snow,* an extraordinary red tractor named Katy responds to calls for help from the chief of police, the postmaster, the telephone company, the water department, the hospital, the fire chief, and the airport. "Sure," she says, and digs the town of Geopolis out from a big snow that is two stories deep. When city departments believe in Katy, it is easy for the readers to believe in her also.

In *Mike Mulligan and His Steam Shovel,* also by Burton, Mike's best friend is a large piece of machinery named Mary Anne. A suspenseful story unfolds as the two friends try to dig the basement of Popperville's town hall in only one day. *The Little House* is a heroine who is strong and also needs love. In this story, a growing city encroaches upon the house and she becomes dilapidated and lonely. The house proceeds, like a real person, through a series of emotions until she is moved away from the city and settles down happily on a new foundation,

where "once again she was lived in and taken care of" (p. 39).

Humans in Realistic Situations. Young children enjoy stories about other children who share their concerns, problems, and pleasures. The numerous books written and illustrated by Ezra Jack Keats, for example, easily draw young children into the private worlds of other children. One of Keats's realistic heroes is *Louie,* a shy boy who usually does not talk to anyone. He responds to a puppet when the neighborhood children present a show, however, and a warm feeling results when the children give the puppet to him. In another book, Louie is very lonely when his family moves to a new neighborhood. He solves his problems in *The Trip* by building a model of his old neighborhood and going on an imaginative adventure with his old friends. In *Regards to the Man in the Moon,* other children tease Louie because his father is a junk dealer. His father's advice—that Louie build a spacecraft from junk—and his own imagination allow Louie and a friend to experience flight into outer space. When the other children hear of these adventures, they want to take part in them also.

While Keats's books usually have inner-city settings, the settings created by another well-known children's author are usually the country or the coast of Maine. Robert McCloskey stresses warm family relationships in books such as *Blueberries for Sal.* This delightful story allows readers to share the berry-picking expeditions of a human mother and daughter and an adult bear and her cub. McCloskey develops drama when the youngsters get mixed up and start following the wrong parents. He provides a satisfying ending as both children are reunited with their mothers.

Stories about relationships between grandparents and grandchildren are also popular in current picture storybooks. In *The Day Gogo Went to Vote: South Africa, April 1994,* Elinor Batezat Sisulu tells the story of how Thembi's great-grandmother who has not left the house in years casts her vote for the first time. This story told through Thembi's viewpoint shows the importance of this milestone in South African history. In *The Language of Doves,* Rosemary Wells develops a close relationship between a girl and her grandfather as he tells her about his experiences during World War II as part of the Italian army. When her grandfather dies, Julietta loses both her special friend and the carrier pigeons who were part of their lives. In an emotional ending one of the pigeons returns with a special message from her grandfather.

Vera Williams's *A Chair for My Mother* shows that even a young child can help her mother fulfill a dream. After a fire destroys the family's furniture, Williams's heroine earns money to help fill the large coin jar that represents her mother's and grandmother's desire: a new, soft, comfortable chair. This goal is not easily reached, however; both mother and daughter must work together.

Emily Arnold McCully's heroine in *Mirette on the High Wire* is an independent female protagonist. When Mirette meets a retired high-wire walker, the Great Bellini, she wants to learn the art. Despite his refusal, Mirette practices and teaches herself. Later, Mirette rescues her friend from the high wire by helping him overcome his fear. In the sequel, *Starring Mirette & Bellini,* McCully develops the theme about the importance of freedom.

In Sharon Bell Mathis's *The Hundred Penny Box* a young boy develops an important relationship with his Great-great-aunt Dew, who moves into his home with an old box containing a penny for every year of her long life. This is one of many picture storybooks, such as those of Ezra Jack Keats, that share with children of all backgrounds the warm relationships in nonwhite families. Arnold Adoff's *Black Is Brown Is Tan* tells the story of two children, their black mother and white father, and their loving grandmothers from both sides of the family.

Of course, young children also confront problems in their families, including sex-role biases. In Char-lotte Zolotow's *William's Doll,* a young boy wants a doll to hug, cradle, and play with. His brother calls him a creep, and his neighbor calls him a sissy. His father tries to interest him in "masculine" toys and brings him a basketball and an electric train. William enjoys both toys but still wants a doll. When his grandmother visits, he explains his wish to her, shows her that he can shoot baskets, and tells her that his father does not want him to play with a doll. Grandmother understands William's need, buys him a baby doll, and then explains to William's upset father that William wants and needs a doll so that he can practice being a father just like his own father. Tomie dePaola deals with a similar situation in *Oliver Button Is a Sissy.* Such books can reassure children that there is nothing wrong with non-stereotypical behavior.

Some picture storybooks that deal with realistic situations show protagonists trying to solve their problems. In *Letting Swift River Go,* Jane Yolen creates a happy childhood for Sally in rural Massachusetts. It is a life filled with walking through the countryside, sleeping under the stars, catching and releasing fireflies, and gathering sap from maple trees. This life changes when the river is dammed and the people are moved. The author develops the theme that "You have to let go" as Sally and her father row across the new lake and she hears her mother reminding her years ago that you have to let the fireflies go. Then, Sally realizes that she must let the past go, too.

Two picture storybooks about the Holocaust show that the realistic situations in picture books may sometimes be about very serious subjects. These books also make interesting comparisons for both content and illustrations. In *Rose Blanche,* Roberto Innocenti develops a strong protagonist who discovers the concentration camp near her home in Germany during World War II. As a consequence, she hides food and takes it to the Jewish prisoners. Unfortunately, Rose Blanche is killed by stray bullets as she stands in the woods. The somber colors in the illustrations reflect the sadness of both the concentration camps and Rose Blanche's death. In *Let the Celebrations Begin!,* Margaret Wild focuses on the same time in history. In Wild's book, however, the Jewish prisoners are preparing for soldiers to liberate the camp. Compared with Innocenti's somber shades, Julie Vivas's illustrations for *Let the Celebrations Begin!* are colorful pastels. As you read these two books, compare the illustrations and the contents. Both books have received some criticisms. Is *Rose Blanche* too depressing for children? Do the pastel illustrations and the party preparations found in *Let the Celebrations Begin!* trivialize a very serious subject? You decide as you read the two books.

The fiftieth anniversary of the end of World War II produced numerous books about the time period. Topics in current picture storybooks include war experiences in both Europe and Japan. For example, Jo Hoestlandt's *Star of Fear, Star of Hope* is set in Nazi-occupied France on the eve of Helen's ninth birthday. Her best friend, Lydia, is Jewish and leaves Helen's celebration to go home to warn her family that the Nazis are forcibly collecting the Jewish residents of the city. Helen feels abandoned by her friend and lets her know that she is no longer her friend. Unfortunately, Helen never sees Lydia again. Now, years later, Helen hopes that her best friend will see the message in the book and call her. The story ends with an important message that is also one of the themes of the book: "I'll always have hope . . ." (unnumbered). In Tatsuharu Kodama's *Shin's Tricycle,* a young atomic bomb victim in Hiroshima is remembered through his tricycle, which is now on display at the Peace Museum. Both of these books about different World War II experiences are reminders about the tragedy of war.

Humorous and Inventive Fantasies. Dr. Seuss is one of the most popular authors of books for children. In his many outlandish stories, he develops characters who are original and humorous and who talk in a style that children enjoy. In *The 500 Hats of Bartholomew Cubbins,* both conflict and humor result when the king orders a peasant to remove his magical hat. Every time that Bartholomew tries to remove one hat, another hat appears. When the number reaches one hundred fifty-seven hats, the magicians cast a spell:

> Dig a hole five furlongs deep,
> Down to where the night snakes creep,
> Mix and mold the mystic mud,
> Malber, Balber, Tidder, Tudd. (p. 31, unnumbered)

As the hats begin to number in the hundreds, the king threatens Bartholomew with execution. Then, hat number five hundred is so beautiful that the king offers to buy it for five hundred gold pieces. With that offer, the spell is broken and a rich Bartholomew returns home.

Several of Dr. Seuss's characters face moral issues. In *Horton Hatches the Egg,* Horton the elephant remains 100 percent faithful to his promise to hatch a lazy bird's egg in spite of leering bystanders and other unpleasant experiences. He gains his reward when the egg hatches and is an elephant-bird.

Chris Van Allsburg's *Jumanji* begins with a realistic scene involving two children who are asked to keep the house neat until their parents return with guests. Bored, the children make a mess with their toys and then go to the park, where they find instructions for a jungle adventure game that cannot be ended until one player reaches the golden city. When the children take the game home, they realize the consequences of the rules. A lion appears on the piano and chases one of them around the house. Other jungle animals and jungle-related actions enter the scene each time that the children frantically throw the dice. Van Allsburg ends the story on a note of suspense and speculation. The children return the game, but two other children, who are notorious for never reading directions, pick up the game and run through the park.

The plot in Van Allsburg's fantasy *The Widow's Broom* develops after a witch leaves her broom with a widow, Minna Shaw. As in all fantasies with witches, the broom has special powers and does Minna's work for her. Complications arise when suspicious neighbors express fear of the broom and then burn it. In a happy ending, the broom arises, rejoins the widow, and plays music for their pleasure. The positive power of books versus the negative hypnotic power of a strange glowing stone provides the conflict in Van Allsburg's fantasy *The Wretched Stone.* Children understand the message when they discover that the people who know how to read books recover more rapidly than do others from the debilitating power of the glowing stone.

SUGGESTED ACTIVITIES

for Adult Understanding of Picture Books

■ Read a journal that evaluates children's literature such as *The Horn Book Guide to Children's and Young Adult Books.* Select two picture books that are highly rated and two books that are not. Compare the literary elements and the illustrations in the books. Do you agree with the evaluation of the journal? Why or why not?

- Choose several different editions of Mother Goose that contain the same nursery rhymes. Compare the artists' interpretations of these characters—for example, the illustrations of Jack Sprat found in *Marguerite De Angeli's Book of Nursery and Mother Goose Rhymes*, Cooper Eden's *The Glorious Mother Goose*, Kate Greenaway's *Mother Goose*, and Wallace Tripp's *Granfa' Grig Had a Pig*.

- Select a common animal or object that often appears in books for children. Find several picture books that develop a story about that animal or object. Compare the ways in which the different artists depict the animal or object through the illustrations and the ways in which the writers describe the animal or object and develop the plots.

- Select several alphabet books appropriate for young children and for older children. Evaluate each group of books. Share the books, your rationales, and your evaluations with the class.

- Find examples of rhythm, rhyme, repetition of sounds, and hyperbole in Mother Goose.

- Select several wordless books appropriate for stimulating oral language development in young children and several that are more appropriate for use with older children. Compare the details and plots.

- Begin a collection of nursery rhymes from other lands to illustrate the universal nature of children and the unique characteristics of the people living in these countries.

- Find examples of humor in picture storybooks. Look for word play and nonsense, the unexpected, exaggeration, the ridiculous, and superiority.

- Choose a picture storybook that develops characters through the illustrations. Try this same characterization through narration. Compare the lengths of the two stories.

- This text includes various responses to Maurice Sendak's *We Are All in the Dumps with Jack and Guy*. Respond to the illustrations and text in *The Miami Giant*, written by Arthur Yorinks and illustrated by Maurice Sendak. This latest book has also received mixed reviews. As you read the book, analyze the effectiveness of the satire.

- Use the database to prepare a list of at least 30 wordless books. Plan a writing activity that will be appropriate for either a primary, upper elementary, or middle school class based on a wordless book. If possible, use the activity in a learning center or try it out with a group of elementary or middle school students.

- The art teacher has asked for at least ten alphabet books to use as examples for a primary grade activity in which each student will be asked to create one illustrated "letter" to contribute to a class alphabet book. Use the database to locate appropriate books. Print your list. If possible, you may want to try this activity with a primary class.

- Write directions suitable for fourth graders so that they could use the database to prepare a list of books that contain Mother Goose rhymes. Use the directions to prepare and print a list. Give your directions to someone else and compare their search results to yours. Modify your directions if necessary.

Involving Children in Picture Books

To truly share picture books, you must care enough to select books and prepare book-related activities that children find stimulating and enjoyable. Picture-book experiences involve sharing nursery rhymes to stimulate oral language development and dramatization; wordless books that encourage children to find objects in pictures, tell their own stories, or write creatively; picture storybooks ideal for reading aloud; illustrations that encourage aesthetic sensitivity; and picture books of all sorts that encourage children to join in with songs and movement. Picture books are important for developing experiences with song and story because, according to Betsy Hearne (1992): "Meaning emerges from experience patterned by artistry, an artistry in association with the senses. Song and story are sensuous. . . . Children's books are the continuation of speech, song, and story" (p. 31).

Patricia Cianciolo (1990) develops a strong argument for using picture books with students at all grade levels, from three-year-old children who cannot yet read to sophisticated young adults who can analyze the illustrations and grasp new meaning and significance. Cianciolo states:

In these picture books the illustrations are superbly accomplished works of visual and graphic art, and the texts are written in beautifully expressive language. . . . In addition to bringing out and emphasizing the text, they con-

vey other meanings and impressions that readers would not have envisioned from the verbal information on its own. They encourage higher-level thinking and imaginative thinking. Readers can and do grasp their meaning and significance and can go well beyond what the illustrator and author suggested. (p. 2)

Whatever the book, if it is worth sharing, the sharing experience is worth thoughtful preparation. This section discusses a few of the many ways in which you can use picture books to enhance personal development in children and to increase children's responses to literature.

SHARING MOTHER GOOSE

Mother Goose rhymes are natural means of stimulating language development and listening appreciation in very young children. Linda Gibson Geller (1985), who strongly endorses the use of nursery rhymes with young children, maintains that nursery rhymes popular with preschool children have one or more of the following characteristics: a simple story line that encourages finger play, a story or song with a repeated chorus, a verse with nonsense words, a description of daily actions, and a choral reading in which children join in with the rhyming words.

Even two- and three-year-olds thoroughly enjoy and respond to the rhyme, rhythm, and nonsense found in nursery rhymes. Because passive listening may not encourage language development, adults must create experiences that motivate children to interact with the verses in enjoyable ways. Once children have heard the simpler Mother Goose rhymes several times, they usually can help you finish the verses by filling in missing words or rhyming elements: "Jack and Jill, went up the _____ to fetch a pail of water. Jack fell down, and broke his _____, and Jill came tumbling after." In addition to providing enjoyment during shared experience, this activity encourages auditory discrimination and attentive listening, skills necessary for later successes in reading and language arts.

You may also insert an incorrect word into a rhyme familiar to children and have the children correct the error. Children especially enjoy this exercise when the nursery rhyme book has large, colorful illustrations in which the children can point out what is wrong with your version. For example, say, "Jack be nimble, Jack be quick, Jack jump over a pumpkin," or "Little Boy Blue come blow your horn. The pig's in the meadow, the chick's in the corn." Many children also enjoy making up their own incorrect versions.

Books such as Joanna Cole and Stephanie Calmenson's *Miss Mary Mac: And Other Children's Street Rhymes* help children become involved in the rhythmic elements of rhyme. This collection includes hand-clapping, ball-bouncing, and counting rhymes.

Young children enjoy creative play and spontaneously dramatize many of their favorite rhymes. Dramatization allows children to explore body movements, develop their senses, expand their imaginations and language, and experiment with characterization (Siks, 1983). One of the first adult-led creative drama activities recommended for beginning school-age children encourages development of a sense of movement and interpretation of a situation without the use of words. Read or tell various nursery rhymes while children pretend to be each character in the rhyme and perform the actions expressed in the verses. Following each line, allow enough time for the children to act out each part. Children especially enjoy acting out such action rhymes as "Little Miss Muffet," "Jack Be Nimble," and "Hey Diddle Diddle."

After children have experiences with a number of roles in nursery rhymes, lead them in the development of cooperative pantomimes. For example, "Little Miss Muffet" has two characters, a girl and a spider, while "Hey Diddle Diddle" has four. Have the children form small groups and informally interact with others as they pantomime the actions. A child or a group of children can also pantomime the actions of a nursery rhyme character while another child or group guesses the identity of the character.

Nursery rhymes that children have memorized can be used for choral-speaking arrangements, even though the children may not have developed reading skills. Chapter 8 suggests ways to stimulate oral language and appreciation through choral speaking.

You can also use nursery rhymes with five- through eight-year-olds to stimulate creative dramatic skills in pantomime and role playing, to introduce the concept of plot, to expand children's interpretive skills through choral speaking, and to encourage children's own storytelling.

You can encourage children to expand upon one of their favorite nursery rhymes, as do several delightful picture books devoted to one rhyme—such as John Ivimey's *The Complete Story of the Three Blind Mice*. You may use Susan Ramsay Hoguet's *Solomon Grundy* to encourage children to extend the nursery rhyme through historical illustrations. Children may select a time period for any Mother Goose rhyme, conduct research to make discoveries about the time period, and illustrate the rhyme accordingly. Other Mother Goose rhymes that lend themselves to extended oral, written, or artistic versions are "Old Mother Hubbard," "Old King Cole," and "Simple Simon." After sharing one of these books or rhymes with children, ask the children if they would like to know more about any other Mother Goose characters.

A discussion with first graders, for example, revealed that several children wanted to know what it would be like to live in a pumpkin. They talked about how they might decorate its interior, what they could do inside a pumpkin, and how neighbors might react to a pumpkin in the neighborhood. They dictated their story to the teacher and then divided it into separate sentences, each written and illustrated on tagboard by one child and then placed in the classroom library. This book was read by many children and became one of the most popular picture storybooks in the classroom. When more children created their own books, the children's librarian developed a library display of both commercially published Mother Goose books and books printed and illustrated by the children. Some illustrated stories are take-offs on earlier nursery rhymes. After reading Jan Ormerod's *Ms. MacDonald Has a Class,* have students compare the story to "Old MacDonald Had a Farm." Then have them write interpretations of other nursery rhymes.

Even sixth graders can benefit from activities related to Mother Goose rhymes. In one sixth-grade class, students were discussing their favorite early childhood stories and wondered whether or not Mother Goose had been a real person. This question led to library research and debate. The search led to conflicting answers. Some sources indicated that the original Mother Goose was Dame Goose of Boston. Another resource said that she was goose-footed Bertha, wife of Robert II of France. Still others referred to Charles Perrault's *Tales of Mother Goose,* published in 1697. Many others stated that there never was a Mother Goose. Following this research, members of the class chose the version that they favored and debated the issue with one another.

Several of the children's sources indicated that some Mother Goose rhymes are based upon the lives of real people. The children found this idea fascinating, and they wondered who or what incident might have been the basis of "Little Miss Muffet," "Little Jack Horner," or "Humpty Dumpty." A search for possible personages and situations resulted in the information shown in Chart 5–1 on pp. 251–252. (Please note

CHART 5–1   Mother Goose Personages (pp. 251–252)

Mother Goose Rhyme	Personages	Situations
There was an old woman who lived in a shoe.	Parliament James VI of Scotland and I of England	Geographic location of Parliament. England had many people. This disliked monarch was not English, but Parliament told the people to get along as well as they could.
Old King Cole was a merry old soul.	Third century—King Cole	He was a brave and popular monarch.
Humpty Dumpty sat on a wall.	Richard III—1483	The "usurper" when he lay slain upon Bosworth Field.
I love sixpence, pretty little six-pence.	Henry VII—1493 Charles of France	Miserliness of Henry resulted in public jest. French ruler pacified Henry with £149,000 when Henry signed the treaty of Etaples.
Little Jack Horner sat in a corner eating his Christmas pie.	Jack Horner, an emissary of the Bishop of Glastonbury	Jack lived at Horner Hall and was taking twelve deeds to church-owned estates to Henry VIII. The deeds were hidden in a pie. On his way, he pulled out the deed to Mells Park estate and kept it.
Sing a song of sixpence, a pocket full of rye.	Henry VIII	Henry's humming over the confiscated revenues from the friars' rich grain-fields.
Four and twenty blackbirds baked in a pie	The friars and monks	The title deeds to twenty-four estates owned by the church were put into a pie and delivered to Henry VIII.
When the pie was opened, The birds began to sing:	The friars and monks	The monks put their choicest treasures in chests and hid them in a lake.
Wasn't that a dainty dish To set before a king?	Henry VIII	Henry picked the deeds he wanted and bestowed others as payment.
The King was in the counting house Counting out his money	Henry VIII	Henry was counting his revenues.
The Queen was in the pantry Eating bread and honey;	Catherine of Aragon	She was eating the bread of England, spread with Spain's assurances that the King could not divorce her.
The maid was in the garden, Hanging out the clothes.	Anne Boleyn	Anne had dainty frocks from France and was smiling at the King in the garden of Whitehall Palace.

CHART 5–1   *Continued*

Mother Goose Rhyme	Personages	Situations
When down flew a blackbird, And snipped off her nose.	Anne Boleyn, Cardinal Wolsey, and the royal headsman.	Cardinal Wolsey broke Anne's engagement to Lord Percy. After Anne married Henry VIII, the royal headsman executed Anne—1563.
To market, to market to buy a fat pig.	Henry VIII	Henry VIII declared himself head of the Church of England to obtain a divorce from Catherine of Aragon.
Needles and pins, needles and pins, When a man marries his trouble begins.	Catherine Howard and Henry VIII	After her marriage to Henry, she introduced pins from France to the English court. Ladies had to begin a separate allowance for this luxury.
Punch and Judy fought for a pie; Punch gave Judy a sad blow in the eye.	Punch—England Judy—France	England and France fought over Italy.
Little Boy Blue	Cardinal Wolsey	The cardinal was too busy with pleasant dreams about his fame to be aware of danger.
Hey diddle, diddle, The cat and the fiddle.	The cat—Queen Elizabeth I—1561	Queen Elizabeth played with her ministers as if they were mice. She liked to dance.
A frog he would a-wooing go.	Duke of Anjou and Queen Elizabeth I—1577	A satire about the wooing of forty-nine-year-old Elizabeth by the twenty-three-year-old French prince.
I saw a ship a sailing, A sailing on the sea,	Sir Francis Drake	Drake brought back potatoes and other foods that were introduced to England.
Mistress Mary, quite contrary. How does your garden grow?	Mary Queen of Scots and her royal maids	She wore flashing jewels and gowns from Paris.
Little Miss Muffet sat on a tuffet Eating her curds and whey;	Mary Queen of Scots	At eighteen (1560), Mary was made monarch of Scotland. She laughed with her maids.
When along came a spider, and sat down beside her,	John Knox	John Knox denounced the frivolous Mary from the pulpit of St. Giles.
Little Bo-Peep has lost her sheep.	Mary Queen of Scots	Tells about Mary's problems as the clans rose and prepared for battle.
Jack Sprat could eat no fat, His wife could eat no lean.	Charles I Henrietta Maria of France	After their marriage, they each went their heedless ways and plundered England.
Yankee Doodle came to town, Riding on a pony; He stuck a feather in his hat, and called it macaroni.	Prince Rupert of the Palatinate, Royalist General of the Civil Wars—1653	Prince Rupert had a large following; he could lead men and showed great endurance. The feather signified that the wearer was one of his soldiers. Rupert could steal into an enemy's camp and take the horses.

that the authenticity of these connections between Mother Goose personages and real situations is not verifiable. The activity, however, proved fascinating to the students involved and increased their literary and historical awareness.) Finally, the children wrote their own rhymes about people and situations in the news or in history, which acquainted them with unfamiliar ideas, beliefs, and customs of the past and present.

University students in children's literature classes have developed other stimulating ways of using Mother Goose with older children. For example, they have had children compare the illustrations in different editions of Mother Goose, discuss their personal responses to the illustrations, discover more information about art media used by illustrators, demonstrate certain techniques to a group, and illustrate their own picture books to be shared with younger children.

ENCOURAGING INTERACTION BETWEEN CHILDREN AND TEXTS

Several books for young children encourage them to find hidden objects or to predict what is going to happen next. Young children love to play "I spy" and look for hidden objects in pictures. Active involvement in story experiences stimulates the language development, cognitive development, and enjoyment of children.

Familiar folktale and nursery rhyme characters are hiding in the illustrations of Janet and Allan Ahlberg's *Each Peach Pear Plum: An I-Spy Story.* The two lines that precede each picture tell who is in the picture; the text also suggests a hidden figure. Children enjoy searching the pastel watercolor drawings for such favorites as Tom Thumb, Mother Hubbard, Cinderella, the three bears, Jack and Jill, and Robin Hood. Children, not adults, should locate the hidden characters.

Counting books often encourage interaction and discovery. For example, Lionel's *Peekaboo Babies: A Counting Book* encourages counting as readers pull the tabs and open the flaps. Arthur Geisert's *Pigs from 1 to 10* encourages readers to search for the pigs and for the numerals 0 through 9 that are hiding in each picture.

Tana Hoban's *Take Another Look* and *Look! Look! Look!* encourage children to make predictions.

These fascinating books allow the readers to peek through a hole and see a portion of the photograph on the following page. Ask children to tell what they think a picture is, and why, before turning the page to see if their prediction is correct. Denise Fleming's *Lunch* encourages viewers to predict what the mouse will eat next. The effectiveness of such books depends in part on your ability to stimulate children's participation, whether they are reading or listening, sitting in your lap, or sitting in a small group.

SHARING WORDLESS BOOKS

Wordless books are ideal for encouraging language growth, stimulating intellectual development, motivating creative writing, developing text for reading, and evaluating language skills. Consider children's ages and the complexity of plot or details when choosing wordless books. Some wordless books have much detail, which stimulates observational skills and descriptive vocabularies. Other wordless books are more appropriate for encouraging understanding and interpretation of sequential plot.

Stimulating Cognitive and Language Development

Shelley L. Knudsen Lindauer (1988) states that perhaps one of the most important roles of wordless books is promoting and refining language skills through creative expression. Wordless books lend themselves to a creative approach to storytelling by children. Masha Rudman (1993) believes, "Wordless books can help children use books to foster their storytelling skills" (p. 191). Rudman maintains that this goal is reached by helping children write stories to accompany the pictures. In addition, teachers may use wordless books to write stories that children may then read. This final use for wordless books is especially important during literature-based reading instruction.

Literature is valuable in promoting cognitive development in children. Several skills associated with the thinking process—observing, comparing, and organizing—can be developed through the use of wordless books. Children can describe what is happening in each picture and the details that they observe, compare pictures or changes that occur, and organize their thoughts into sequentially well-organized stories. Describing, comparing, and storytelling also help children expand their vocabularies.

Children can describe the action in each detailed picture in Peter Spier's *Noah's Ark,* for example, as they follow the building of the ark; the loading of food, utensils, and animals; the problems that develop inside the ark; and the final landing and starting of life anew. One group of seven-year-olds did the following:

1. Identified the animals they recognized in a two-page spread showing animals boarding the ark.
2. Described the color, size, mode of travel, and natural habitat of the animals.
3. Identified humorous details in the illustrations.
4. Identified Noah's problems and suggested possible causes and solutions.
5. Speculated about Noah's feelings as he tried to rid the roof of too many birds, dealt with a reluctant donkey, and finally closed the doors of the ark.
6. Thought of descriptive words for the animals, such as *slithering* for snakes, *leaping* for frogs, and *lazy, brown* for monkeys.
7. Compared the positions of the snails in the illustrations at the beginning of the book and at the end.
8. Chose one picture each and told or wrote a detailed description of the picture.

Spier's wordless book can be compared with Lisbeth Zwerger's illlustrations in Heinz Janisch's *Noah's Ark*. Mercer Mayer's funny wordless book *Frog Goes to Dinner* encourages before-and-after comparisons. People enjoy a leisurely meal in one picture, for example, and in the next experience the disruptions caused by Frog. A first grader made this comparison when he discussed two pictures of the band:

The band was playing beautifully. They had their eyes closed and were enjoying the music. All of a sudden the frog jumped in the saxophone. Now the saxophone player tried to play but couldn't. His face puffed out and he looked funny. The other players jumped. The frog made the drum player fall into his drum. The horn player thought it was funny.

The detailed illustrations in Jeannie Baker's *Window* are excellent for encouraging comparisons of the same setting across time. Children can observe, describe, and compare the illustrations that show changes in the Australian environment and ecology over a period of twenty-four years.

Stephen Gammell's illustrations in the wordless portion of Rafe Martin's *Will's Mammoth* encourage children to describe Will's imaginary experiences while playing in the snow. You also may use the book to stimulate children to describe their own imaginary lives.

Mitsumasa Anno's wordless books help develop observational skills in older children. *Anno's Journey* contains fascinating details that can be discovered during a visual trip through Europe. David Wiesner's *Free Fall* encourages readers to locate objects by the boy's bed that become part of his dream and to consider the literature that may have stimulated his dream response.

Motivating Writing and Reading

Educators in reading and language arts frequently recommend the use of language experiences that stimulate children's oral language and writing by exploring ideas and expressing feelings. These experiences in turn provide the content for group and individual stories composed by children and recorded by adults, who then use these stories for reading instruction.

Many teachers introduce students to the language experience approach to literature through group chart stories. These activities are appropriate for all age groups, but they are used most as reading-readiness or early reading activities in kindergarten or first grade. Usually, an entire group (guided by the teacher) writes a chart story after a shared motivational experience, such as a field trip, an art project, a film, music, or a story. Many of the wordless books discussed in this text are excellent sources for motivational activities.

If you use a wordless book to motivate the writing of a chart story, first share the book with the group. Following oral discussion, have the children dictate the story, as you record it on posterboard, the chalkboard, or large sheets of newsprint, repeating each word aloud. (Some teachers identify each child's contribution to the chart story by placing the child's name after the contribution.) It is essential that children be able to see each word as it is written. As you write the chart story, children will see that sentences flow from the top to the bottom on a page, follow a left-to-right sequence, begin with capital letters, and end with periods. Following completion of the chart story, read the whole story. Then, ask the children to reread the story with you. Following this experience, some individual children may choose to read the whole story aloud while others may choose to read only their own contributions.

Place wordless books and their accompanying chart stories in areas easily accessible to children, so that the children can enjoy reading the stories by themselves. Some teachers tape-record the children's reading of the chart stories and then place the recordings, the chart stories, and the wordless books in a listening center. The stories may also be read to children in other classes or added to the library.

Picnic and *School* by Emily Arnold McCully provide opportunities for children to write dialogue, describe settings, develop conflicts and characterizations, and discuss themes. David Wiesner's *Free Fall* encourages children to write interpretations of a fanciful dream. University students report that Chris Van Allsburg's *The Mysteries of Harris Burdick* is one of the most enticing nearly wordless books for older elementary students. Children can speculate about each fantasy in Van Allsburg's book, write their own stories, and share the stories with other children who have different interpretations. Because there is no correct answer, children may choose to write more than one story about a picture.

 ## READING TO CHILDREN

An adult who reads to children accepts an opportunity and a responsibility for sharing a marvelous experience. Author and illustrator Leo Lionni (quoted by Smith, 1991) states this very well when he describes the role of children's books in children's lives:

When a child is four or five, he has lived four or five years in a totally chaotic verbal environment. The picture book is the first thing that gets into his head where he is confronted with a verbal structure. If it's a good book, it has a beginning, a middle and an end. It's the first time that he will say "more, again" after the reading is over. Now he knows what the end and the beginning is—just think of what a complicated notion that is. Which means that he also has a notion of what's in between, so that he has a sense of whole. He's not conscious of it, but for the first time, he's faced with structure. That I think is an enormously convincing consideration on the importance of the picture book. (p. 119)

There is probably no better way to interest children in the world of books than to read to them. A study conducted by Walmsley and Walp (1989) found that reading aloud is the activity that teachers use the most to involve students in literature. Listening to books read aloud is a way for children to learn that literature is a form of pleasure. Without parents, librarians, or other adults, a very young child would not experience nursery rhymes or such stories as Beatrix Potter's *Peter Rabbit,* and younger elementary children would not experience the marvelous verses and stories of A. A. Milne or enter the joyous world of Dr. Seuss. For children just struggling to learn to read, a book may not be a source of happiness. In fact, books actually arouse negative feelings in many children. Being read to helps beginning readers develop an appreciation for literature that they could not manage with their own reading abilities.

The pleasure of the listening experience usually motivates children to ask for a book again or to read it themselves. Very young children may ask for a book to be reread so many times that they memorize it and then feel proud of being able to "read" it. When a teacher reads a particularly enjoyable selection to children in an elementary classroom, the children tend to check out all copies of that book in the class or school library. Michael Tunnell and James Jacobs (1989) report in a research review of literature-based programs that "daily reading aloud from enjoyable trade books has been the key that unlocked literacy growth" for many students (p. 475).

Another value of reading aloud is the improvement that it often brings to related areas, such as reading achievement, language development, and vocabulary development. A study by Feitelson, Kita, and Goldstein (1986) found that first graders who were read to for twenty minutes each day outscored comparable groups in decoding, reading comprehension, and active use of language. They attribute the success of their research to enriching children's information base, introducing them to unfamiliar language, increasing children's knowledge about various story structures, exposing children to literary devices such as the metaphor, and extending children's attention spans. Thus, reading aloud is important for parents, teachers, librarians, and other adults who interact with children.

Choosing the Books

An appropriate book for reading aloud depends, of course, upon the ages of the children, their interests, the need to balance the types of literature presented, the number of children who will share the listening experience, and the quality of the literature. A book selected for reading aloud should be worthy of the time spent by the readers and the listeners. It should not be something picked up hurriedly to fill in time.

The style and the illustrations are both considerations when choosing books to read aloud. The language in A. A. Milne's *Winnie-the-Pooh* and Dr. Seuss's *The 500 Hats of Bartholomew Cubbins* appeals to young listeners. The rhyming text in Linnea Riley's *Mouse Mess* is fun to listen to and read aloud. Likewise, young children enjoy illustrations that are integral to the story. For example, illustrations in Robert McCloskey's *Lentil* help children visualize a midwestern town in the early 1900s, and the illustrations in Maurice Sendak's *Where the Wild Things Are* bring Max's exceptional adventure to life. Other books, such as Arthur Yorinks's *Hey, Al* and Jane Yolen's *Owl Moon,* have such beautiful illustrations that they should be chosen to encourage aesthetic appreciation. Books such as Martin Waddell's *Can't You Sleep, Little Bear?,* Minfong Ho's *Hush! A Thai Lullaby,* and Eve Bunting's *Flower Garden* provide warm, satisfying moments to be shared with children.

Children's ages, attention spans, and reading ability are also important when selecting stories to be read aloud. The books chosen should challenge children to improve their reading skills and to increase their appreciation of outstanding literature. The numerous easy-to-read books should usually be left for children to read independently. Young children respond to short stories; in fact, four- or five-

year-olds may benefit from several short story times a day rather than a twenty- or thirty-minute period. Books such as Michael Rosen's *We're Going on a Bear Hunt,* Lloyd Moss's *Zin! Zin! Zin! A Violin,* Robert Kraus's *Leo the Late Bloomer,* and Margaret Mahy's *17 Kings and 42 Elephants* are short and have colorful pictures. *We're Going on a Bear Hunt* uses repetitive language to encourage children to join in during reading. *Zin! Zin! Zin! A Violin* uses rhyming words and sounds of instruments. *Leo the Late Bloomer* relates the problems of a young tiger who cannot talk, eat, or read correctly until all at once, when he finally blooms. *17 Kings and 42 Elephants* includes both delightful nonsense text and humorous illustrations.

As children enter kindergarten and advance into first grade, they begin to enjoy longer picture storybooks with more elaborate plots. Robert McCloskey's *Make Way for Ducklings* and the various Dr. Seuss books are favorites with beginning elementary school children. Books such as William Steig's *Caleb & Kate,* Eugene Trivizas's *The Three Little Wolves and the Big Bad Pig,* Peggy Rathmann's *Officer Buckle and Gloria,* and Robert San Souci's *The Hobyahs* have enough plot to appeal to second-grade children.

By the time children reach the third grade, they are ready for stories read a chapter at a time. (A reading period should not end in the middle of a chapter.) Third graders usually enjoy E. B. White's *The Trumpet of the Swan, Charlotte's Web,* and *Stuart Little.* Fourth and fifth graders often respond to books like Madeleine L'Engle's *A Wrinkle in Time* and C. S. Lewis's *The Lion, the Witch and the Wardrobe.* Armstrong Sperry's *Call It Courage* and Esther Forbes's *Johnny Tremain* often appeal to sixth- and seventh-grade students. (These books are discussed in later chapters.)

Reading to children should not end in the elementary grades. Without enjoyable oral listening experiences, many older children are not exposed to good literature because they cannot read it independently. Mary Kimmel and Elizabeth Segel (1983) have compiled an annotated list of books that are appropriate for reading aloud to older children. There are several additional excellent sources for choosing books to read aloud. For example, Jim Trelease's *The New Read-Aloud Handbook* (1989) is a guide to help parents introduce a love of books to children. It includes an annotated bibliography.

Masha Kabakow Rudman and Anna Markus Pearce's *For Love of Reading* (1988) describes numerous books that are appropriate for young children.

Preparing to Read Aloud

Many adults mistakenly believe that children's stories are so simple that there is no need for an adult to read a selection before reading it to children. Ramon R. Ross (1980) states his view to the contrary with considerable force: "If I were to lay down for you one single cardinal rule that must never be broken, it would be that you never, *never* read a story aloud to an audience unless you have first read it aloud to yourself" (p. 207). Many embarrassing situations, such as being unable to pronounce a word or selecting an inappropriate book, can be avoided if you first read the story silently—in order to understand it, identify the sequence of events, recognize the mood, and identify any problems with vocabulary or concepts—and then read it aloud in order to practice pronunciation, pacing, and voice characterization. Adults with little or no experience in reading to children can listen to themselves on tape recorders. You should also decide how to introduce the story and what type of discussion or other activity, if any, to use following the reading.

The Reading Itself

What makes the story hour a time of magic or an insignificant part of the day? Research conducted by Linda Lamme (1976) concludes that in addition to an enthusiastic reader and a carefully selected story, the following factors contribute to the quality of a reading performance:

1. *Child involvement.* Child involvement, including reading parts of a selection with an adult, predicting what will happen next, and filling in missing words, is the most influential factor during oral reading.
2. *Eye contact.* Eye contact between the reader and the audience is essential.
3. *Expression.* Adults who read with expression are more effective than those who read monotonously. Good oral readers try to put variety into their voices, but pitch should be neither too high nor too low, and volume should be neither too loud nor too soft.

4. *Pointing.* Readers who point to meaningful words or pictures in a book as they read are better oral readers than are those who merely read the story and show the pictures.
5. *Knowledge of the story.* Adults who know the story and do not need to read the text verbatim are more effective during a presentation.
6. *Large and appealing books.* Readers who select picture books large enough for the children to see and appealing enough to hold their interest or elicit their comments are most effective.
7. *Grouping.* Grouping children so that all can see the pictures and hear the story is important.
8. *Highlighting.* Adults who highlight the words and language of a story by making the rhymes apparent, discussing unusual vocabulary words, and emphasizing repetition are better readers.

You should consider all of these factors when preparing for an oral presentation and when actually reading a story to an audience of children. Properly prepared, you can take children on a much-appreciated literary journey.

Let us consider an example of a reading aloud experience that accompanies a book for early elementary students developed by Donna Norton (1992):

While reading Michael Rosen's *We're Going on a Bear Hunt* to kindergarten or first-grade students, emphasize the repetitive language and the descriptive words. Show the students that the illustrator, Helen Oxenbury, places the repetitive verses on black-and-white backgrounds and the descriptive action words on colored backgrounds. Ask the students: "Why would an illustrator choose both black-and-white and colored backgrounds in the same book? How should we read this story to show the differences between black-and-white and colored backgrounds?" After orally reading the first series of repetitive text, encourage the students to join in the reading. On the colored action pages ask them to predict the sounds that the family will make as they go through each obstacle. Ask them to notice that each action is repeated three times and that each line increases in size. Ask the students: "Why would an author increase the size of the letters? How could we use our voices and actions to show this increasing size?" Then have the students read and act out the lines such as:

Splash splosh!
Splash splosh!
Splash splosh!

Students enjoy acting out this whole rhyme as they start the bear hunt, swishy swashy through the grass, splash splosh through the river, squelch squerch through the mud, stumble trip through the forest, hoooo wooooo through the snowstorm, tiptoe through the cave, discover the bear and then go back through each obstacle until they reach the safety of home and bed. This book encourages students to become involved in the text and their own vocabulary development as they join in the repetitive language, act out the action words, and discover how an author and an illustrator might show how words should be spoken by changing the size of the text or by alternating the backgrounds. (p. 63)

 ### STIMULATING DEVELOPMENT

Child development authority Barbara Borusch (1980) maintains that adults can use picture storybooks to stimulate language, cognitive, moral, and social development in children, as well as to motivate interest in other books. Robert McCloskey's *Time of Wonder,* for example, describes a family's experiences on an island in Maine. The natural setting of the story can encourage children to expand their vocabularies and can help them to understand such concepts as porpoise, gull, barnacle, bay, island, and driftwood. McCloskey's vivid language and figures of speech can acquaint children with new ways of experiencing and describing what they see and hear in the world around them: rustling leaves, heavy stillness, slamming rain, and gentle wind, as soft as a lullaby. As choppy waves indicate the approaching storm, McCloskey gives children many opportunities to observe the sharp contrasts in nature. Sharing the book with children can help them apply observational powers to their own everyday lives.

Members of the family in *Time of Wonder* prepare for the hurricane and endure it together. Discussing the similarities and differences between the island before the hurricane and after it, between islands in different parts of the world, and between the island in the book and the children's own environment also can help children develop cognitively. Encourage children to observe storms in their own environment and to describe the changes that result, using vocabulary that best conveys the color, sound, size, and time of such experiences. Also, have chil-

dren evaluate the responsibilities and the possible feelings of each family member and consider what they or their families might feel and do under similar circumstances.

One of the most valuable things about picture storybooks such as *Time of Wonder* is the potential to motivate children to seek out other reading experiences. In this case, children may want to read or listen to other fictional or informational books about the Maine coast, storms, weather, coastal regions, water recreation, treasures from the sea, and water birds and other wildlife.

 ### DEVELOPING AESTHETIC SENSITIVITY

If the word *aesthetic* denotes sensitivity to art and beauty, then looking at the beautiful illustrations in children's books must be aesthetic. Aesthetic sensitivity is important, according to H. S. Broudy (1977), because "it is a primary source of experience on which all cognition, judgment, and action depend. It furnishes the raw material for concepts and ideals, for creating a world of possibility" (p. 636). Broudy believes that aesthetic experiences are so vital that they should be considered basic in children's education. He further believes that the best way to improve aesthetic sensitivity in children is to have them experiment with various artistic media themselves.

Children learn to appreciate the artistic media used in book illustrations when they are given the stimulation and time to become actively involved in making their own illustrations. Some artistic media are too complex for very young children, of course, but Lamme and Kane (1976) believe that collage is an ideal medium for stimulating creative interpretations of literature and for developing fine-motor skills. In the process of making their own collages and reacting to the collages in book illustrations, children can also improve their vocabularies and oral discussion skills. Ezra Jack Keats, Leo Lionni, and Jeannie Baker are among the well-known illustrators of children's books who use collage. Adults can use works of such artists first to enlighten themselves and then as sources of material for children to discuss and compare. (Jeannie Baker's collage illustrations for *Where the Forest Meets the Sea* and *Win-*

dow are fine sources of inspiration for both adults and children because Baker uses many different textures to create large, colorful pictures.)

Based on their work with young children, Lamme and Kane recommend use of the following sequence when introducing children to collage:

1. Encourage children to experiment with the collage technique by having them tear and cut shapes and pictures from plain paper or magazines and then to paste the shapes onto another piece of paper.

2. Provide opportunities for children to experience different textures in the world around them and then to use those textures in collages. Have the children take a texture exploration walk, for example, during which they feel and describe the textures of tree bark, leaves, grass, flowers, sidewalks, building materials, fabrics, paper, foods, and so forth. After they have experienced and discussed various textures, have them collect items with different textural qualities and then use the items in charts and texture collages. Encourage the children to touch their collage experiments, look at the textures carefully, and discuss their reactions to different texture combinations.

3. Have the children create their own collages or series of collages using as many different textures as they wish. Then, ask the children to share these illustrations with one another, along with accompanying stories or descriptions.

4. Share with the children a picture book illustrated with collage. While reading the story and showing the children the pictures, ask the children to recognize the collage technique, discuss the feelings produced by each collage object, tell why they think the illustrator chose a certain material to represent it, and describe the texture they would feel if they could touch the original collage. Let them decide whether or not the collage illustrations make the story better.

Some illustrations combine other artistic media with collage. Ezra Jack Keats's illustrations for *Maggie and the Pirate* are brightly colored combinations of collage and painting. Keats's *The Trip* even illustrates a young boy working with various colors and shapes of paper as he creates his own neighborhood within a box. This book can stimulate experimentation with both collage and painting. David Diaz, in his illustrations for Eve Bunting's *Smoky Night,* uses photographs, broken glass, and materials such as pieces of plastic bags to recreate a feeling of the Los Angeles riots. Christopher Myers's collage illustrations for Walter Myer's *Harlem* developed feelings for an inner-city setting.

Experimenting with simple cartoon techniques is another way that children can begin to develop their artistic skills and aesthetic sensitivities. Cartoons are very popular with children, who greatly enjoy watching Charles Schultz's "Peanuts" characters on television or reading about them when Schultz's cartoon books are available in the library.

After experimenting with their cartoons, children can look with new understanding and appreciation at picture storybooks illustrated by well-known cartoonists, such as Syd Hoff's book *Sammy the Seal,* James Stevenson's *Could Be Worse!,* Helen V. Griffith's *Grandaddy's Place,* and William Steig's *Caleb & Kate* and *Spinky Sulks.* Have the children discuss how well the cartoons complement the text and compare the effectiveness of cartoons and that of other types of book illustration. Also, have the children write stories and illustrate them with cartoons. Children enjoy creating their own cartoon books or creating a newspaper format that combines cartoons drawn by all of the children in a group.

 ## MOTIVATING WRITING WITH PICTURE STORYBOOKS

Picture storybooks provide many sources for expressive and imaginative writing. For example, writing letters to friends, relatives, teachers, librarians, authors, or even imaginary people is an excellent way to encourage expressive writing in children (Norton, 1997). Use stories that include situations in which characters write letters to motivate children to write letters of their own. Introduce younger children to letters through Janet and Allan Ahlberg's *The Jolly Postman.* In this book, the postman delivers letters to fairy-tale characters, such as Cinderella and the three bears.

Several books use trips or moving as reasons for letter writing. For example, in Pat Brisson's *Your Best Friend, Kate,* Kate writes letters to her best friend that describe her experiences as Kate takes a car trip with her family. In Vera Williams's *Stringbean's Trip* to the *Shining Sea*, a boy writes a series of postcards during a camping trip across the western United States.

Use picture storybooks that have mysterious endings or that develop speculations to encourage children's imaginative writing. David Wiesner's *June 29, 1999* is an excellent book for stimulating children's speculations about the mysterious vegetables and to motivate children to write and illustrate their own science fiction stories. Have children speculate about the mystery of the silver pear and write their own responses to Benjamin Darling's *Valerie and the Silver Pear*. Have children create a story about the finding of the silver pear in the fruit jar or imagine what it would be like if the grandfather and his granddaughter find the silver apple when they harvest the apple crop. Use books such as Paul Fleischman's *Time Train* to motivate children to select other times and locations and to write stories about their adventures on their own time train.

Stimulate imaginative writing by asking children to write a story in a point of view that is different from the one developed by the author. For example, read Reeve Lindbergh's humorous *The Day the Goose Got Loose* to children. Allow them to respond to the humorous situations and illustrations. After the children have discussed their responses to the book, ask them, "Who is telling the story about the goose—a human or the goose? How can you tell?" Reread the page on which grandmother asks, "I wonder what thoughts went through her head?" (p. 21, unnumbered). Ask the children why the grandmother is asking this question about the goose. Ask them, "How could we write this story if we were to tell the story through the goose's point of view? Why did she do these actions? What was she thinking about as she _____? How did she see each of the people and animals who chased her? How did she feel when she _____?" Finally, encourage the children to write their own stories about *The Day the Goose Got Loose* but to tell the incidents through the goose's point of view. (Notice that this writing also emphasizes personification because the children must retell the story through the point of view of the goose.)

For a similar activity, use Eric Kimmel's *The Chanukkah Guest*. After sharing and discussing the book, ask the children to imagine what the bear must have been thinking as the old woman, Bubba Brayna, mistakes him for the rabbi, feeds him potato latkes, and gives him a warm woolen scarf. Have the children rewrite or retell the story from the time that the bear approaches the house or have them tell the story through the dreams that the bear has after he returns to his den in the deep forest and falls asleep with his stomach full of potato latkes and his neck wrapped in the warm woolen scarf.

OTHER ACTIVITIES POSSIBLE

The recommendations in this chapter for ways to share picture books with children are only a few of the possible ways of creating stimulating and enjoyable experiences with books. The following list (Norton and Norton, 1999) shows the varied activities that teachers, librarians, and other adults have developed around Maurice Sendak's *Where the Wild Things Are*.

1. *Appreciative listening.* Read the story to children. Share the pictures and your enthusiasm.
2. *Oral language.* After reading the book, discuss with the children how they might also daydream like Max and make themselves heroes or heroines in a story. What activities would they dream about? Where would they go? What would they do? Ask the children to pantomime their dreams.
3. *Oral language and art interpretation.* Have the children create masks depicting the wild things and perform a creative drama of the story and other adventures that Max might have during another visit to the fantasy land.
4. *Oral language and art interpretation.* Have the children create puppets of the wild things and depict their adventures through a puppet production.
5. *Art interpretation.* At one time in his career, Maurice Sendak constructed papier-mâché models of storybook characters. Have the children select a favorite Sendak character and make a papier-mâché model.
6. *Art interpretation.* Maurice Sendak once designed window displays for new books. Have a group of children design a bulletin board as if it were a window display advertising *Where the Wild Things Are*.

Where did you purchase your latest children's book? How much help could the bookstore personnel provide if you had a question about a topic, a book, or an author? The answers to these questions may reflect changes in the selling of children's books as large superstores replace some of the independently owned children's bookstores.

Diane Roback and Cindi Di Marzo[1] report the findings of a children's bookselling survey in which they compared responses by bookstores that were classified as children's only, general independents, superstores, national chains, regional chains, or college/university. The survey covers many topics such as the proportion of backlist and frontlist titles in stock, the proportion of books and nonbook titles, and book sales.

Even though superstores are taking over in some areas, the children's-only stores still have a unique advantage: "According to the survey, children's only stores and regional chains are capitalizing on the fact that specialized service is their forte. . . . Handselling is extremely important for both categories (48% of children's only stores said they make over 50% of their sales that way . . .). For national chain and superstores, the picture is very different, with the majority reporting that, at most, 10% of their children's book sales are made through handselling" (p. 28).

How might these differences in handselling books (a direct and more personal selling technique) reflect the knowledge of booksellers or their ability to select books and provide advice for buyers? Why do you believe that the survey found that teachers account for 31 percent of the business in children's stories and 11 percent in superstores?

Changes in booksellers may have a definite influence on you as the buyer of children's books. Evaluate the types of bookstores you have in your community. How knowledgeable are the booksellers when you ask them questions? How complete is the stock of books? Can you find old favorites as well as current best sellers? Is the children's division attractive? What do the customers say about the quality of service and books? Who are the book buyers? (The survey reports the following: mothers 34 percent, teachers 13 percent, children 11 percent, fathers 9 percent, unknown 6 percent, other relatives 5 percent, and friends 4 percent.) If you have several types of booksellers, what do you believe are the strengths and weaknesses of each type?

[1] Roback, Diane, and Cindi Di Marzo. "Children's Book Survey: Consumer Awareness." *Publishers Weekly* 244 (June 16, 1997): 28–31.

7. *Art interpretation and oral language.* Ask the children to design a colorful poster to convince other people to buy and read Sendak's book.

8. *Art interpretation and oral language.* Have the children create a travel poster or travel brochure that advertises Max's fantasy land or that illustrates a new fantasy land of their own. The poster should be designed to convince others that they would enjoy visiting the fantasy land.

9. *Appreciative listening and creative writing.* Maurice Sendak enjoys listening to the music of Mozart, Beethoven, and Wagner while he works. Have the children listen to a recording of one of these composers, describe what they visualize as they listen, and draw a series of pictures stimulated by the listening experience. Have them write stories to accompany the pictures.

10. *Picture/mood interpretation.* Older children may also discover the relationship between the illustrations and text achieved by Sendak's book. Encourage older children to look carefully at the illustrations while reading or listening to the text. Discuss the enlargement of illustrations as the plot advances. Use the following quote from an interview with Sendak to stimulate the discussion:

One of the reasons why the picture book is so fascinating is that there are devices to make the form itself more interesting. In *Where the Wild Things Are* the device is really a matching of shapes. I used it to describe Max's moods pictorially: his anger, which is more or less normal in the beginning; its expansion into rage; then the explosion of fantasy as a release from that particular anger; and finally the collapse of that, when the fantasy goes and it's all over. The smell of food brings Max back to reality and he's a little boy again. A book is inert. What

I try to do is animate it, and make it move emotionally. (Wintle and Fisher, 1974, p. 23)

After children have discussed the pictorial devices that Sendak uses to animate the text, encourage them to use illustrations to animate their own writing.

11. *Motivation and enjoyment.* Create a Maurice Sendak reading center in the classroom or school library. In the center, place books written and illustrated by Sendak, books written by other authors and illustrated by Sendak, and any Sendak-motivated stories written and illustrated by children. Decorate the center with posters, papier-mâché characters, puppets, and other artwork created by children. Encourage the children to use the center.

While the preceding activities are related to one book, they suggest multiple experiences that may accompany many picture storybooks. Another source for developing activities around a single book or single illustrator is John Stewig's series, *Reading Pictures: Exploring Illustrations with Children* (1988). This series includes activities to accompany illustrated texts by Marcia Brown, Nonny Hogrogian, Ezra Jack Keats, and Gerald McDermott. Remember, however, that children's enjoyment of books and reading is the major goal. Books can be shared and savored without accompanying activities.

SUGGESTED ACTIVITIES

for Involving Children in Picture Books

- Choose a book of nursery rhymes appropriate for sharing with young children. Share the book with a child and encourage the child to interact with the rhymes by supplying missing words, making up rhyming games, or role-playing the characters found in the nursery rhymes.
- Choose several nursery rhymes that have a definite beginning, middle, and end. Use these rhymes with children to help them develop an understanding of plot development.
- Select several alphabet books that are appropriate for encouraging visual and verbal literacy. Develop a series of questions to encourage children to describe the pictures, compare the pictures, and evaluate their personal preferences for the pictures. Share the alphabet books and questions with a group of children.

- Select a wordless book appropriate for use with young children and another wordless book with enough detail for use with older children. Carefully plan an activity that encourages children to interact with each book. Share the books with the two different age groups, and compare the responses received from each group.
- Select a picture storybook appropriate for reading aloud to children. Prepare the story for reading, and share the book with a group of children or a peer group.
- Compile a list of picture storybooks appropriate for sharing with five-, six-, seven-, and eight-year-old children.
- Choose an art medium used to illustrate children's books. Research the methods used by illustrators who use that medium. Develop a series of activities that allow children to experience and experiment with the medium, create their own illustrations, and discuss literature illustrations that use the medium.
- Compile a list of picture-book illustrators and their illustrations to stimulate an understanding of collage, cartoons, and other artistic media.
- Choose a picture book that illustrates a nursery song, animal song, or holiday song. Plan an activity that encourages children to sing, accompany the song with rhythm instruments, play a singing game, or play a counting game. Share the activity with a group of children or a peer group.
- Choose a children's picture storybook, other than Maurice Sendak's *Where the Wild Things Are,* and list various activities based on the book.

CHILDREN'S LITERATURE

MOTHER GOOSE

Arnold, Tedd. *Mother Goose's Words of Wit and Wisdom: A Book of Months.* Dial, 1990 (I:4–8). The Mother Goose rhymes are categorized according to appropriate months of the year.

Bodecker, N. M. *It's Raining, Said John Twaining.* Antheneum, 1973 (I:4–7). Fourteen Danish nursery rhymes are translated and illustrated.

Cole, Joanna, and Stephanie Calmenson. Compiled by. *Miss Mary Mac: And Other Children's Street Rhymes.* Illustrated by Alan

I = Interest by age range.

R = Readability by grade level.

Tiegreen. Morrow, 1990 (I:4–8). This text is a collection of one hundred traditional rhymes.

Cousins, Lucy. *Little Dog Laughed.* Dutton, 1990 (I:3–9). This collection of Mother Goose rhymes is illustrated with humorous illustrations.

De Angeli, Marguerite. *Marguerite De Angeli's Book of Nursery and Mother Goose Rhymes.* Doubleday, 1954 (I:4–7). This large book contains 376 nursery rhymes and illustrations with early English settings.

De Forest, Charlotte B. *The Prancing Pony: Nursery Rhymes from Japan.* Illustrated by Keiko Hida. Walker/Weatherhill, 1968 (I:5–10). Translations of traditional Japanese nursery rhymes were collected by Tasuku Harada.

Demi. *Dragon Kites and Dragonflies.* Harcourt Brace Jovanovich, 1986 (I:all). Twenty-two Chinese nursery rhymes are illustrated with Chinese drawings.

dePaola, Tomie. *Tomie dePaola's Mother Goose.* Putnam, 1985 (I:2–6). The large format and folk art make this a very appealing edition.

Edens, Cooper, ed. *The Glorious Mother Goose.* Atheneum, 1988 (I:all). This is a collection of rhymes illustrated by artists from the past.

Foreman, Michael. *Michael Foreman's Mother Goose.* Harcourt Brace Jovanovich, 1991 (I:6+). This is a large collection of Mother Goose rhymes.

Greenaway, Kate. *Mother Goose: Or, the Old Nursery Rhymes.* Warne, 1881 (I:3–7). A small Mother Goose is illustrated with charming Greenaway children.

Griego, Margot C., Betsy L. Bucks, Sharon S. Gilbert, and Laurel H. Kimball. *Tortillitas Para Mama and Other Spanish Nursery Rhymes.* Illustrated by Barbara Cooney. Holt, Rinehart & Winston, 1981 (I:3–7). Nursery rhymes appear in Spanish and English.

Hale, Sarah Josepha. *Mary Had a Little Lamb.* Illustrated by Tomie dePaola. Holiday House, 1984 (I:3–7). The nursery rhyme is highly illustrated.

_____. *Mary Had a Little Lamb.* Photographs by Bruce McMillan. Scholastic, 1990 (I:3–8). The popular rhyme is illustrated through photographs.

Hoguet, Susan Ramsay. *Solomon Grundy.* Dutton, 1986 (I:3–7). Illustrations depict Solomon Grundy's life in early American history.

Ivimey, John. *The Complete Story of the Three Blind Mice.* Illustrated by Paul Galdone. Clarion, 1987 (I:2–8). A rhyming story extends information about the song.

Lobel, Arnold. *Gregory Griggs and Other Nursery Rhyme People.* Greenwillow, 1978 (I:4–7). Thirty-four lesser-known nursery rhymes tell about humorous predicaments.

_____. *The Random House Book of Mother Goose.* Random House, 1986 (I:2–6). A collection of three hundred and six nursery rhymes is highly illustrated.

Newbery, John. *The Original Mother Goose's Melody.* Reissue. Gale, 1969 (I:all). This is one of the early Mother Goose collections.

Opie, Iona, and Peter Opie. *I Saw Esau: The Schoolchild's Pocket Book.* Illustrated by Maurice Sendak. Candlewick, 1992 (I:all). The text includes notes that explain the origins of some of the rhymes.

_____. *My First Mother Goose.* Illustrated by Rosemary Wells. Candlewick, 1996 (I:2–8). Sixty rhymes are included in this anthology.

_____. *A Nursery Companion.* Oxford University Press, 1980 (I:all). A collection of twenty-seven early British nursery rhymes appears with the original colored illustrations.

_____. *The Oxford Nursery Rhyme Book.* Illustrated by Joan Hassall. Oxford University Press, 1955, 1984 (I:all). A collection of eight hundred rhymes and songs is illustrated with black-and-white woodcuts.

_____. *Tail Feathers from Mother Goose: The Opie Rhyme Book.* Little, Brown, 1988 (I:all). A collection of mostly previously unpublished rhymes is illustrated by many artists.

Ormerod, Jan. *Ms. MacDonald Has a Class.* Clarion, 1996 (I:5–8). This is a take-off on "Old MacDonald Had a Farm."

Rounds, Glen. *Old MacDonald Had a Farm.* Holiday House, 1989 (I:3–6). Bold pictures accompany the musical rhyme.

Sendak, Maurice. *We Are All in the Dumps with Jack and Guy.* Harper Collins, 1993 (I:all). Sendak develops a social commentary in the illustrations that accompany the rhymes.

Tripp, Wallace. *Granfa' Grig Had a Pig and Other Rhymes Without Reason from Mother Goose.* Little, Brown, 1976 (I:4–8). Humorous animal drawings illustrate 121 nursery rhymes in a large-book format.

Wyndham, Robert. *Chinese Mother Goose Rhymes.* Illustrated by Ed Young. World, 1968; Philomel, 1982 (paperback) (I:4–7). Traditional Chinese rhymes are translated into English.

TOY BOOKS

Atwater, Richard, and Florence Atwater. *Mr. Popper's Penguins.* Designed by Dick Dudley. Illustrated by Karin Williams. Little, Brown, 1993 (I:4–8). Pop-ups, pull-tabs, and flaps provide an introduction to the story.

Breeze, Lynn. *This Little Baby Goes Out.* Orchard, 1990 (I:2–4). In this board book, the baby does various activities while playing in the park.

_____. *This Little Baby's Playtime.* Orchard, 1990 (I:2–4). In this board book, the baby does such activities as blows a trumpet, plays with a telephone, and rides a tricycle.

Brown, Marc. *Kiss Hello, Kiss Good-bye.* Random, 1997 (I: 2–5). Part of the "Arthur Mini Play Book" series.

_____. *Say the Magic Word.* Random, 1997 (I:2–5). Flaps and press-out figures increase the interaction.

Brown, Margaret Wise. *The Goodnight Moon Room: A Pop-Up Book.* Illustrated by Clement Hurd. Harper & Row, 1984 (I:2–4). A combination of flaps and pop-ups encourages children to interact with the text.

Campbell, Rod. *Dear Zoo.* Four Winds, 1982 (I:2–4). Illustrations encourage children to hypothesize about the contents of a crate.

Carle, Eric. *The Very Quiet Cricket.* Philomel, 1997 (I:1–5). Readers hear the chirp of the cricket on the last page.

Cousins, Lucy. *Count With Maisy.* Candlewick, 1997 (I:2–4). Numbers from one through ten are presented.

_____. *Maisy Goes to the Playground.* Candlewick, 1992 (I:2–4). Flaps and tabs allow a mouse to accomplish various activities in the park.

_____. *Maisy Goes to School.* Candlewick, 1992 (I:2–4). Flaps and tabs allow a mouse to do activities such as paint pictures.

_____. *Maisy's Colors.* Candlewick, 1997 (I:2–4). Maisy identifies the colors in the pictures.

Crowther, Robert. *The Most Amazing Hide-and-Seek Alphabet Book.* Viking, 1978 (I:3–6). Each letter conceals an object that begins with that letter.

Involving Children in Picture Books   263

_____. *Pop-Up Olympics: Amazing Facts and Record Breakers*. Candlewick, 1996 (I:all). This paper-engineered text presents movable actions related to Olympic games.

Emberley, Barbara. *Drummer Hoff*. Illustrated by Edward Emberley. Simon & Schuster, 1997 (I:2–5). The folktale is now in boardbook format.

Fatus, Sophie. *Holes*. Abbeville, 1997 (I:2–6). This is one of the "Silly Shapes," board book series.

_____. *Spots*. Abbeville, 1997 (I:2–6). This is another "Silly Shape."

_____. *Squares*. Abbeville, 1997 (I:2–6). A "Silly Shape" board book.

_____. *Stripes*. Abbeville, 1997 (I:2–6). A "Silly Shape" board book.

Hill, Eric. *Spot Goes to School*. Putnam, 1984 (I:2–4). A flap-book encourages readers to discover a dog's activities at school.

_____. *Spot's Birthday Party*. Putnam, 1982 (I:2–4). In a "lift the flap" book, a dog plays hide-and-seek with the guests at his party.

_____. *Where's Spot?* Putnam, 1980 (I:2–4). Children search for a missing dog under the flaps.

Hoban, Tana. *Look! Look! Look!* Greenwillow, 1988 (I:3–6). Readers look through square cut-out spaces and hypothesize about what is in photographs.

Lindgren, Barbro. *Sam's Ball*. Illustrated by Eva Eriksson. Morrow, 1983 (I:2–4). A boy and a cat learn to play together.

_____. *Sam's Bath*. Illustrated by Eva Eriksson. Morrow, 1983 (I:2–4). A boy puts many toys and his dog into the bathtub.

Lionel. *Peekaboo Babies: A Counting Book*. Orchard, 1997 (I:2–6). Pull-tabs and flaps encourage counting.

Mackinnon, Debbie. *Daniel's Duck*. Photographs by Anthea Sieveking. Dial, 1997 (I:2–4). Readers search for items under flaps.

_____. *Pippa's Puppy*. Photographs by Anthea Sieveking. Dial, 1997 (I:2–4). The text uses flaps.

_____. *Sarah's Shovel*. Photographs by Anthea Sieveking. Dial, 1997 (I:2–4). The text uses flaps.

_____. *Tom's Train*. Photographs by Anthea Sieveking. Dial, 1997 (I:2–4). The text uses flaps.

Oxenbury, Helen. *The Car Trip*. Dial/Dutton, 1983 (I:2–4). A young boy enjoys a car ride even though he gets sick from eating too much.

_____. *Dressing*. Wanderer Books, 1981 (I:1–3). A board book shows step-by-step dressing.

_____. *Family*. Wanderer Books, 1981 (I:1–3). A board book shows a baby with a family.

_____. *Friends*. Wanderer Books, 1981 (I:1–3). A board book illustrates a baby and friends.

_____. *I Hear*. Random House, 1986 (I:1–3). This board book illustrates sounds in the environment.

_____. *I See*. Random House, 1986 (I:1–3). A child interacts with objects in the environment.

_____. *Playing*. Wanderer Books, 1981 (I:1–3). A board book shows a baby playing.

_____. *Working*. Wanderer Books, 1981 (I:1–3). A board book shows familiar work.

Pienkowski, Jan. *Haunted House*. Dutton, 1979 (I:all). A spooky house comes to life behind flaps and in pop-ups.

Potter, Beatrix. *The Peter Rabbit Pop-Up Book*. Warne, 1983 (I:3–8). This pop-up version creates a detailed setting for young children.

Roddie, Shen. *Chicken Pox!* Illustrated by Frances Cony. Little, Brown, 1993 (I:2–4). Flaps and tabs allow readers to experience the discomfort of chicken pox.

Rylant, Cynthia. *Everyday Children*. Bradbury, 1993 (I:2–4). This board book illustrates some common things that children do.

_____. *Everyday Garden*. Bradbury, 1993 (I:2–4). This board book introduces garden produce.

_____. *Everyday House*. Bradbury, 1993 (I:2–4). This board book shows common elements, such as a door and a porch.

Tafuri, Nancy. *One Wet Jacket*. Greenwillow, 1988 (I:1–3). Items are taken off a child before she takes a bath.

_____. *Two New Sneakers*. Greenwillow, 1988 (I:1–3). This book highlights items that a child puts on.

Wells, Rosemary. *Max's Bath*. Dial, 1985 (I:1–3). A young rabbit becomes stained when he takes juice and sherbet into the tub.

_____. *Max's Birthday*. Dial, 1985 (I:1–3). A young rabbit enjoys his birthday.

Yee, Patrick. *Rosie Rabbit's Colors*. Simon & Schuster, 1998 (I:1–4). A rabbit introduces colors.

_____. *Rosie Rabbit's Numbers*. Simon & Schuster, 1998 (I:1–4). A rabbit introduces numbers.

_____. *Rosie Rabbit's Opposites*. Simon & Schuster, 1998 (I:1–4). A rabbit introduces opposites.

_____. *Rosie Rabbit's Shapes*. Simon & Schuster, 1998 (I:1–4). A rabbit introduces shapes.

Ziefert, Harriet. *Baby Buggy*. Illustrated by Richard Brown. Houghton Mifflin, 1997 (I:2–6). This is a "Word Play Flap Book."

_____. *Night Knight*. Illustrated by Richard Brown. Houghton Mifflin, 1997 (I:2–6). Flaps allows readers to explore the idea of homonyms.

ALPHABET BOOKS

Anno, Mitsumasa. *Anno's Alphabet: An Adventure in Imagination*. Crowell, 1975 (I:5–7). A wordless alphabet book shows a single letter on one page and a single object beginning with that letter on the opposite page.

Aylesworth, Jim. *The Folks in the Valley: A Pennsylvania Dutch ABC*. Illustrated by Stefano Vitale. HarperCollins, 1992 (I:3–7). The ABC format uses Dutch motifs.

Baldwin, Ruth M. *One Hundred Nineteenth-Century Rhyming Alphabets in English*. Southern Illinois University, 1972 (I:all). A collection of older alphabets.

Bowen, Betsy. *Antler, Bear, Canoe: A Northwoods Alphabet Year*. Little, Brown, 1991 (I:all). A specialized alphabet book illustrates words associated with Minnesota.

Brent, Isabelle. *An Alphabet of Animals*. Little, Brown, 1993 (I:all). This is an alphabet of exotic animals.

Chin-Lee, Cynthia. *A Is for Asia*. Illustrated by Yumi Heo. Orchard, 1997 (I:5–10). This alphabet book about Asia presents information through both text and illustrations.

Cook, Lyn. *A Canadian ABC*. Penumbra, 1990 (I:all). Poetry and illustrations introduce readers to various aspects of Canada.

de Mejo, Oscar. *Oscar de Mejo's ABC*. HarperCollins, 1992 (I:all). Each of the entries develops an early American setting.

Doubilet, Anne. *Under the Sea from A to Z*. Photographs by David Doubilet. Crown, 1991 (I:all). Photographs of the animals accompany information about the animal.

Ehlert, Lois. *Eating the Alphabet: Fruits and Vegetables from A to Z*. Harcourt Brace Jovanovich, 1989 (I:3–6). An ABC book develops around food.

Feelings, Muriel. *Jambo Means Hello: Swahili Alphabet Book*. Dial, 1974 (I:all). A beautiful book uses the Swahili alphabet and drawings depicting the Swahili culture.

Geisert, Arthur. *Pigs from A to Z*. Houghton Mifflin, 1986 (I:all). Letters are hidden in the illustrations.

Greenaway, Kate. *A—Apple Pie*. Warne, 1886 (I:3–8). The old rhyme was first referenced in 1671.

Hague, Kathleen. *Alphabears: An ABC Book*. Illustrated by Michael Hague. Holt, Rinehart, & Winston, 1984 (I:3–7). Illustrations of teddy bears depict letters.

Hardin, Wes. *Henry Ford Museum: An ABC of American Innovation*. Abrams, 1997 (I:all). Objects from the museum illustrate each of the letters of the alphabet.

Hepworth, Cathi. *Antics!* Putnam's, 1992 (I:all). Each of the A to Z entries have the ant someplace in the word.

Hoban, Tana. *A, B, See!* Greenwillow, 1982 (I:4–6). Photographs illustrate objects that begin with the uppercase letters.

Hunt, Jonathan. *Illuminations*. Bradbury, 1989 (I:6–12). A specialized alphabet that includes pictures of words that are characteristic of the Middle Ages.

Johnson, Jean. *Postal Workers A to Z*. Walker, 1987 (I:all). Photographs show activities associated with postal workers.

Johnson, Stephen T. *Alphabet City*. Viking, 1995 (I:all). Urban settings illustrate each letter of the alphabet.

Jonas, Ann. *Aardvarks, Disembark!*. Greenwillow, 1990 (I:all). An alphabet book shows extinct and endangered animals.

Kitchen, Bert. *Animal Alphabet*. Dial, 1984 (I:all). Unusual animals accompany each letter of the alphabet.

Lear, Edward. *An Edward Lear Alphabet*. Illustrated by Carol Newsom. Lothrop, Lee & Shepard, 1983 (I:3–7). This text is a newly illustrated version of Lear's nonsense rhyme.

Lobel, Anita. *Alison's Zinnia*. Greenwillow, 1990 (I:5–8). This alphabet book shows flowers that begin with each letter.

Lobel, Arnold. *On Market Street*. Illustrated by Anita Lobel. Greenwillow, 1981 (I:4–7). Tradespeople show their wares from A to Z.

Lowe, Warren, and Sylvia Lowe. *Leroy's Zoo*. Illustrations by Leroy Ramon Archuleta. Black Belt, 1997 (I:all). Photographs of carved animals depict the animals.

MacDonald, Suse. *Alphabatics*. Bradbury, 1986 (I:all). A series of pictures change a letter into an object.

Magee, Doug, and Robert Newman. *Let's Fly from A to Z*. Cobblehill, 1992 (I:all). Photographs show different aspects of flying.

Martin, Bill, Jr., and John Archambault. *Chicka Chicka Boom Boom*. Simon & Schuster, 1989 (I:4–8). The ABC's are presented through rhythmic verse.

Martin, Cyd. *A Yellowstone ABC*. Rinehart, 1992 (I:all). The ABC format focuses on various animals, plants, and natural phenomena of the national park.

Merriam, Eve. *Halloween ABC*. Illustrated by Lane Smith. Macmillan, 1987 (I:6–12). Poems about Halloween are sequenced according to the alphabet.

Musgrove, Margaret. *Ashanti to Zulu: African Traditions*. Illustrated by Leo and Diane Dillon. Dial, 1976 (I:7–12). Traditions and customs from twenty-six African tribes are presented in alphabetical order.

Nicholson, William. *An Alphabet*. Wofsy, 1975 (I:all). A copy of an alphabet first published in 1897 is illustrated with different occupations.

Owens, Mary Beth. *A Caribou Alphabet*. Dog Ear, 1988 (I:all). Letters show actions and characteristics of caribou.

Pelletier, David. *The Graphic Alphabet*. Orchard, 1996 (I:all). The illustrations develop relationships between image and meaning.

Pomeroy, Diana. *Wildflower ABC: An Alphabet of Potato Prints*. Harcourt Brace, 1997 (I:all). Flowers provide the subjects for the book.

Pratt, Kristin Joy. *A Walk in the Rainforest*. Dawn, 1992 (I:all). An ant travels through the rain forest in this ABC.

Provensen, Alice, and Martin Provensen. *A Peaceable Kingdom: The Shaker Abecedarius*. Viking, 1978 (I:all). This book is a newly illustrated edition of alphabet animal rhymes first published in the Shaker Manifesto of July 1882.

Rosen, Michael. *Michael Rosen's ABC*. Illustrated by Bee Willey. Millbrook, 1997 (I:3–6). The text includes a poem for each letter.

Sloat, Teri. *From Letter to Letter*. Dutton, 1989 (I:all). Each page is decorated with large letters that have drawings of objects within the upper-case and lower-case forms.

Thornhill, Jan. *The Wildlife ABC: A Nature Alphabet Book*. Simon & Schuster, 1990 (I:all). North American animals are featured in this ABC.

Van Allsburg, Chris. *The Z Was Zapped*. Houghton Mifflin, 1987 (I:all). Letters form a twenty-six-act play.

Viorst, Judith. *The Alphabet from Z to A (With Much Confusion On the Way)*. Illustrated by Richard Hull. Atheneum, 1994 (I:7–10). Focuses on language curiosities and inconsistencies.

Westervelt, Linda. *Roger Tory Peterson's ABC of Birds: A Book for Little Birdwatchers*. Illustrated by Roger Tory Peterson, Photographs by Seymour Levin. Rizzoli, 1995 (I:all). Paintings and photographs introduce birds using an alphabetical order.

Whatley, Bruce, and Rosie Smith. *Whatley's Quest*. Illustrated by Bruce Whatley. HarperCollins, 1995 (I:all). Detailed illustrations show items beginning with each letter.

COUNTING BOOKS

Anno, Mitsumasa. *Anno's Counting Book*. Crowell, 1977 (I:3–7). Large, detailed drawings of landscapes illustrate each number.

———. *Anno's Counting House*. Philomel, 1982 (I:3–7). Cut-out windows show ten little people who demonstrate counting, adding, and subtracting.

———. *Anno's Math Games II*. Philomel, 1989 (I:5–10). The illustrations and text show picture puzzles and mathematical recreations.

———. *Anno's Math Games, No. III*. Philomel, 1991 (I:6–10). This book contains pictures, puzzles, and games that cover concepts such as triangles and mazes.

Aylesworth, Jim. *One Crow: A Counting Rhyme*. Illustrated by Ruth Young. Harper, 1988 (I:2–5). Groupings of animals represent the numbers.

Bang, Molly. *Ten, Nine, Eight*. Greenwillow, 1983 (I:3–6). A charming number game counts objects backward.

Bohdal, Susi. *1, 2, 3 What Do You See?* North-South, 1997 (I:3–6). The numbers are depicted through animal illustrations.

Carle, Eric. *My Very First Book of Numbers*. Crowell, 1974 (I:3–6). In this simple matching book, the child matches black squares with appropriate illustrations.

———. *The Very Hungry Caterpillar*. Crowell, 1971 (I:2–7). A colorful collage book shows the life cycle of a caterpillar.

Charlip, Remy, Mary Beth Miller, and George Ancona. *Handtalk Birthday: A Number & Story Book in Sign Language.* Four Winds, 1987 (I:all). Vocabulary and numbers are shown through photographs of people using sign language.

Christelow, Eileen. *Five Little Monkeys Jumping on the Bed.* Clarion, 1989 (I:2–6). An illustrated text accompanies a counting rhyme.

Cohen, Caron Lee. *How Many Fish?* Illustrated by S. D. Schindler, HarperCollins, 1998 (I:3–6). The text is set at the beach.

Dunrea, Olivier. *Deep Down Under.* Macmillan, 1989 (I:3–7). Creatures that dig under the ground show numbers from one to ten.

Feelings, Muriel. *Moja Means One: Swahili Counting Book.* Illustrations by Tom Feelings. Dial, 1971 (I:all). Numbers from one through ten are shown in numbers, written in Swahili, and illustrated with scenes of Africa.

Fleming, Denise. *Count!* Holt, Rinehart & Winston, 1992 (I:2–7). A counting book that includes numbers from one through ten as well as twenty, thirty, forty, and fifty.

Geisert, Arthur. *Pigs from 1 to 10.* Houghton, 1992 (I:2–7). Readers are encouraged to locate and count the pigs.

Gerstein, Mordicai. *Roll Over!* Crown, 1984 (I:3–6). A counting nursery rhyme uses various animals.

Giganti, Paul. Jr. *Each Orange Had Eight Slices: A Counting Book.* Illustrated by Donald Crews. Greenwillow, 1992 (I:5–9). Various number concepts are developed through the illustrations.

_____. *How Many Snails? A Counting Book.* Illustrated by Donald Crews. Greenwillow, 1988 (I:3–6). This is a combination counting and concept book.

Grossman, Bill. *My Little Sister Ate One Hare.* Illustrated by Kevin Hawkes. Crown, 1996 (I:5–8). A humorous cumulative rhyme that presents numbers through such actions as eating slimy creatures.

Gunson, Christopher. *Over On the Farm: A Counting Picture Book Rhyme.* Scholastic, 1997 (I:2–5). The text develops concepts from one through ten.

Guy, Ginger Foglesong. *¡Fiesta!* Illustrated by Rene King Moreno. Greenwillow, 1996 (I:5–8). This counting book is in English and Spanish.

Haskins, Jim. *Count Your Way Through Italy.* Illustrated by Beth Wright. Carolrhoda, 1990 (I:all). This counting book combines counting in Italian with information about the culture.

Hoban, Tana. *Count and See.* Macmillan, 1972 (I:4–7). Photographs illustrate numbers.

_____. *26 Letters and 99 Cents.* Greenwillow, 1987 (I:4–7). This is a combination alphabet and number book.

Kitchen, Bert. *Animal Numbers.* Dial, 1987 (I:all). This book is similar to the earlier *Animal Alphabet.*

Knight, Hilary. *Hilary Knight's The Twelve Days of Christmas.* Macmillan, 1981 (I:all). A bear gives his friend the gifts listed in the English folk song.

Lavis, Steve. *Cock-A-Doodle-DOO.* Lodestar, 1997 (I:2–6). Readers count animals.

McMillan, Bruce. *Eating Fractions.* Scholastic, 1991 (I:5–8). The photographs show how various foods can be cut into halves, thirds, and fourths.

Nikola-Lisa, W. *One Hole in the Road.* Illustrated by Dan Yaccarino. Holt, 1996 (I:4–7). Colorful illustrations of construction subjects present counting concepts.

Parker, Vic. *Bearobics: A Hip-Hop Counting Story.* Illustrated by Emily Bolam. Viking, 1997 (I:2–6). Counting is developed through a rhythmical text.

Peck, Merle. *The Balancing Act: A Counting Song.* Clarion, 1987 (I:3–6). A counting song proceeds from one to ten.

Roth, Susan L. *My Love for You.* Dial, 1997 (I:2–6). This counting book also has a theme of love.

Sierra, Lucy. *Counting Crocodiles.* Illustrated by Will Hillenbrand. Harcourt Brace, 1997 (I:3–7). The setting for this counting book is a tropical island.

Sturges, Philemon. *Ten Flashing Fireflies.* Illustrated by Anna Vojtech. North-South, 1995 (I:3–7). Develops subtraction concepts.

Tafuri, Nancy. *Who's Counting?* Greenwillow, 1986 (I:3–6). Viewers follow a dog through the development of the concepts one through nine.

Walsh, Ellen Stoll. *Mouse Count.* Harcourt Brace Jovanovich, 1991 (I:3–6). The illustrations and the text proceed from one through ten and then count backward from ten to one.

Wise, William. *Ten Sly Piranhas: A Counting Story in Reverse (A Tale of Wickedness—and Worse!).* Illustrated by Victoria Chess. Dial, 1993 (I:4–8). Readers count backward along with the disappearing fish.

CONCEPT BOOKS

Ahlberg, Janet, and Allan Ahlberg. *The Baby's Catalogue.* Little, Brown, 1982 (I:2–6). Pictures and labels are categorized according to daily events and common objects.

Barton, Byron. *Machines at Work.* Crowell, 1987 (I:2–6). Very large and colorful illustrations show construction equipment.

Carle, Eric. *The Grouchy Ladybug.* Crowell, 1971 (I:4–7). A ladybug progresses through the day from six in the morning to six at night.

_____. *The Mixed-Up Chameleon.* Crowell, 1975 (I:2–6). A chameleon that wishes to be other animals takes on different colors.

_____. *My Very First Book of Colors.* Crowell, 1974 (I:3–6). Nine colors shown in half-page blocks are matched with illustrations.

_____. *My Very First Book of Shapes.* Crowell, 1974 (I:4–7). Children match black shapes with similar shapes represented in color illustrations.

Crews, Donald. *Carousel.* Greenwillow, 1982 (I:4–8). Illustrations take readers on a carousel ride.

_____. *Freight Train.* Greenwillow, 1978 (I:3–7). Colors, cars on a freight train, and concepts such as *daylight* and *darkness* are developed.

_____. *Harbor.* Greenwillow, 1982 (I:3–7). Children name the harbor ships as they go in and out of the harbor.

Dubanevich, Arlene. *Pigs in Hiding.* Four Winds, 1983 (I:3–6). An almost wordless book encourages children to search for the pigs.

Emberley, Rebecca. *City Sounds.* Little, Brown, 1989 (I:2–7). This book includes urban sounds.

Falwell, Cathryn. *Shape Space.* Clarion, 1992 (I:4–7). Author uses graphic elements to introduce shapes.

Fowler, Susi Gregg. *When Summer Ends.* Illustrated by Marisabina Russo. Greenwillow, 1989 (I:3–7). A young girl and her mother discuss the seasons.

Gibbons, Gail. *Trains.* Holiday House, 1987 (I:4–7). Illustrations are labeled to show different types of cars and railroad functions.

Hoban, Tana. *All About Where.* Greenwillow, 1991 (I:3–7). Photographs illustrate words such as *under* and *between.*

_____. *Circles, Triangles, and Squares.* Macmillan, 1974 (I:4–8). Shapes are found in everyday objects.

_____. *Dig, Drill, Dump, Fill.* Greenwillow, 1975 (I:5–10). Photographs present the world of heavy machinery.

_____. *Look! Look! Look!.* Greenwillow, 1988 (I:3–6). Readers look through square cut-out spaces and hypothesize about what is in photographs.

_____. *Of Colors and Things.* Greenwillow, 1989 (I:3–6). The illustrations encourage children to match colors.

_____. *Over, Under and Through and Other Spatial Concepts.* Macmillan, 1973 (I:3–7). Photographs illustrate spatial concepts.

_____. *Push-Pull, Empty-Full: A Book of Opposites.* Macmillan, 1972 (I:3–7). Photographs illustrate antonyms.

_____. *Round & Round & Round.* Greenwillow, 1983 (I:2–7). Color photographs illustrate round objects found in the environment.

_____. *Shapes, Shapes, Shapes.* Greenwillow, 1986 (I:3–8). Photographs illustrate various shapes in the environment.

_____. *Spirals, Curves, Fanshapes and Lines.* Greenwillow, 1992 (I:3–8). Photographs illustrate various shapes.

_____. *Take Another Look.* Greenwillow, 1981 (I:4–8). Viewers look at an object through a circular cutout, guess what it is, and turn the page to see if they are correct.

Hutchins, Pat. *What Game Shall We Play?* Greenwillow, 1990 (I:3–7). The illustrations develop concept words.

Jenkins, Steve. *Big & Little.* Houghton Mifflin, 1996 (I:3–6). The illustrations depict pairs of animals that develop the concepts of big and little.

Kalan, Robert. *Blue Sea.* Illustrated by Donald Crews. Greenwillow, 1979 (I:3–7). Large illustrations of fish show size concepts.

McMillan, Bruce. *Super Super Superwords.* Lothrop, Lee & Shepard, 1989 (I:3–7). Concepts are related to adjectives.

Noll, Sally. *Watch Where You Go.* Greenwillow, 1990 (I:3–7). The illustrations show concepts.

Peters, Lisa Westberg. *October Smiled Back.* Illustrated by Ed Young. Holt, 1996 (I:5–8). Each of the 12 months are presented in verse and illustrations.

Rockwell, Anne. *First Comes Spring.* Crowell, 1985 (I:3–6). Seasonal changes, activities, and appropriate clothing are shown through the life of a young bear.

Serfozo, Mary. *What's What? A Guessing Game.* Illustrated by Keiko Narahashi. Simon & Schuster, 1996 (I:2–5). This concept book presents sensations associated with opposites.

Spier, Peter. *Fast-Slow, High-Low: A Book of Opposites.* Doubleday, 1972 (I:5–10). Numerous detailed pictures illustrate opposites.

Tafuri, Nancy. *Early Morning in the Barn.* Greenwillow, 1983 (I:2–5). An almost wordless book illustrates the journey of three chicks as they explore the barnyard.

WORDLESS BOOKS

Anno, Mitsumasa. *Anno's Journey.* Philomel, 1978 (I:6–12). Illustrations take the viewer through small towns and cities of Europe.

Baker, Jeannie. *Window.* Greenwillow, 1991 (I:all). Through collage illustrations, the artist chronicles changes in the environment.

Carle, Eric. *Do You Want to Be My Friend?* Crowell, 1971 (I:3–7). A mouse searches for a friend.

Collington, Peter. *The Angel and the Soldier Boy.* Knopf, 1987 (I:3–7). A wordless book adventure has a boy angel and a soldier as protagonists and pirates as antagonists.

dePaola, Tomie. *The Hunter and the Animals: A Wordless Picture Book.* Holiday House, 1981 (I:5–9). Forest animals convince the hunter to break his gun.

_____. *Pancakes for Breakfast.* Harcourt Brace Jovanovich, 1978 (I:3–7). The procedures for making pancakes are shown in this humorous, wordless book.

Drescher, Henrik. *The Yellow Umbrella.* Bradbury, 1987 (I:all). A small wordless book follows the adventures of two monkeys and one yellow umbrella.

Feelings, Tom. *The Middle Passage: White Ships/Black Cargo.* Dial, 1995 (I:10+). The wordless book depicts the slave trade.

Goodall, John. *Paddy Under Water.* Atheneum, 1984 (I:5–9). Paddy discovers a treasure chest.

_____. *Story of a Main Street.* Macmillan, 1987 (I:all). This wordless book traces the same street from medieval through contemporary times.

_____. *The Story of the Seashore.* Macmillan, 1990 (I:all). The illustrations provide a historical review.

Hutchins, Pat. *Changes, Changes.* Macmillan, 1971 (I:2–6). Two doll figures create different things out of blocks.

McCully, Emily Arnold. *Picnic.* Harper & Row, 1984 (I:3–7). A young mouse is lost on the day of the family picnic.

_____. *School.* Harper & Row, 1987 (I:3–8). This wordless book tells about the mouse family introduced in *Picnic*.

Maizlish, Lisa. *The Ring.* Greenwillow, 1996 (I:all). The photographs accompany a boy who finds a magical ring in the park.

_____. *A Boy, a Dog and a Frog.* Dial, 1967 (I:5–9). A boy and a dog try unsuccessfully to catch a frog.

Mayer, Mercer. *A Boy, a Dog, a Frog, and a Friend.* Dial, 1971 (I:5–9). The frog's son accompanies the boy and the dog when they find a turtle.

_____. *Frog Goes to Dinner.* Dial, 1974 (I:6–9). Boy secretly puts Frog into his pocket and takes him along when the family goes to a fancy restaurant.

_____. *Frog, Where Are You?* Dial, 1969 (I:5–9). Boy and Dog search for the missing Frog.

_____, and Marianna Mayer. *One Frog Too Many.* Dial, 1975 (I:5–9). Frog becomes jealous when Boy receives a new frog for his birthday.

Spier, Peter. *Noah's Ark.* Doubleday, 1977 (I:3–9). Detailed illustrations accompany Jacobris Revius's poem "The Flood."

Van Allsburg, Chris. *The Mysteries of Harris Burdick.* Houghton Mifflin, 1984 (I:all). Mystery and fantasy pictures encourage readers to plot their own stories.

Wiesner, David. *Free Fall.* Lothrop, Lee & Shepard, 1988 (I:all). A boy has a fantasy dream.

_____. *Tuesday.* Clarion, 1991 (I:all). Through a wordless format, the artist depicts what happens on Tuesday night when frogs float through the air.

EASY-TO-READ BOOKS

Allen, Laura Jean. *Rollo and Tweedy and the Ghost at Dougal Castle.* HarperCollins, 1992 (I:5–9). A detective tries to find the ghost.

Benchley, Nathaniel. *Oscar Otter.* Illustrated by Arnold Lobel. Harper & Row, 1966 (I:5–9 R:2). Oscar gets lost and is chased by a fox, a wolf, and a moose.

_____. *Small Wolf.* Illustrated by Joan Sandin. Harper & Row, 1972 (I:6–10 R:3). A Native American family moves west from Manhattan Island in order to avoid conflict with European colonists.

Bonsall, Crosby. *The Case of the Hungry Stranger*. HarperCollins, 1992 (new edition of 1963 publication) (I:5–9). Who stole the blueberry pie?

Brenner, Barbara. *Wagon Wheels*. Illustrated by Don Bolognese. Harper & Row, 1978 (I:6–9 R:1). The true story of Ed Muldie and his family as they move from Kentucky to Kansas in 1878.

Bulla, Clyde Robert. *Daniel's Duck*. Illustrated by Joan Sandin. Harper & Row, 1979 (I:6–9 R:2). Daniel lives in the mountains of Tennessee and admires his neighbor's talent for carving.

Byars, Betsy. *My Brother, Ant*. Illustrated by Marc Simont. Viking, 1996 (I:6–8 R:2). In a chapter book, Anthony is afraid of the monster under his bed.

Cole, Joanna, and Stephanie Calmenson. *Ready . . . Set . . . Read!* Doubleday, 1990 (I:5–8). This is an anthology of easy-to-read stories.

Ehrlich, Amy. *Leo, Zack and Emmie*. Dial, 1981 (I:5–8 R:2). A girl affects the friendship of two boys.

Griffith, Helen V. *Alex and the Cat*. Illustrated by Joseph Low. Greenwillow, 1982 (I:5–8 R:1). A dog tries to realize his great dreams, but discovers that he is better off as a house pet.

Hoff, Syd. *Chester*. Harper & Row, 1961 (I:5–8 R:1). Chester is a wild horse who wants to belong to someone.

_____. *Sammy the Seal*. Harper & Row, 1959 (I:5–8 R:1). Sammy lives in a zoo, but wants to see what it would be like on the outside.

Hopkins, Lee Bennett (ed.). *Surprises*. Illustrated by Megan Lloyd. Harper & Row, 1984 (I:5–9). This is a collection of short poems for beginning readers.

Kessler, Leonard. *Kick, Pass, and Run*. Harper & Row, 1966 (I:5–8 R:1). Football is explained in simple terms.

Levinson, Nancy Smiler. *Snowshoe Thompson*. Illustrated by Joan Sandin. HarperCollins, 1992 (I:5–8). In mid-19th century California, a boy helps a man make a pair of skis so that the man may deliver a letter across the mountains to the boy's father.

Lobel, Arnold. *Frog and Toad All Year*. Harper & Row, 1976 (I:5–8 R:1). Frog and Toad have some funny adventures throughout the various seasons of the year.

_____. *Frog and Toad Are Friends*. Harper & Row, 1970 (I:5–8 R:1). Frog and Toad are seen in five short stories.

_____. *Frog and Toad Together*. Harper & Row, 1972 (I:5–8 R:1). These five short stories are about the adventures of Frog and Toad.

_____. *Grasshopper on the Road*. Harper & Row, 1978 (I:5–8 R:2). Grasshopper sets out on a trip and meets some insects who don't like to do something different every day.

_____. *Owl at Home*. Harper & Row, 1975 (I:5–8 R:2). Five stories explore Owl's adventures.

_____. *Uncle Elephant*. Harper & Row, 1981 (I:5–8 R:2). Uncle Elephant takes care of his nephew when the parents are lost at sea.

Marshall, Edward. *Four on the Shore*. Illustrated by James Marshall. Dial, 1985 (I:5–9 R:1). Four boys tell ghost stories.

Pomerantz, Charlotte. *Outside Dog*. Illustrated by Jennifer Plecas. HarperCollins, 1993 (I:5–8 R:2). The text includes several Spanish words.

Porte, Barbara Ann. *Harry Gets an Uncle*. Illustrated by Yossi Abolafia. Greenwillow, 1991 (I:5–8). The story tells about a boy's experiences at his aunt's wedding.

Rylant, Cynthia. *Henry and Mudge and the Bedtime Thumps*. Illustrated by Sucie Stevenson. Bradbury, 1991 (I:5–8). In an easy-to-read book, Henry and Mudge experience scary sounds.

_____. *Henry and Mudge and the Happy Cat*. Illustrated by Sucie Stevenson. Bradbury, 1990 (I:5–8). Henry and Mudge discover a stray cat.

_____. *Henry and Mudge and the Long Weekend*. Illustrated by Sucie Stevenson. Bradbury, 1992 (I:5–8). The children build a castle from large boxes and create an exciting weekend.

_____. *Mr. Putter and Tabby Pour the Tea*. Illustrated by Arthur Howard. Harcourt Brace Jovanovich, 1994 (I:6–9). An elderly man gets a cat at the animal shelter.

_____. *Mr. Putter and Tabby Walk the Dog*. Illustrated by Arthur Howard. Harcourt Brace Jovanovich, 1994 (I:6–9). Another story about a man and his cat.

_____. *Poppleton*. Illustrated by Mark Teague. Scholastic, 1997 (I:4–7). This easy-to-read book includes three short stories about the pig, Poppleton.

Schwartz, Alvin. *In a Dark, Dark Room*. Illustrated by Dirk Zimmer. Harper & Row, 1984 (I:6–9 R:2). This book contains seven scary stories.

Seuss, Dr. *The Cat in the Hat*. Random House, 1957 (I:4–7 R:1). A very unusual cat causes both amusement and mischief when he entertains two bored children on a rainy day.

_____. *The Cat in the Hat Comes Back*. Random House, 1958 (I:4–7 R:1). The cat returns and brings little cats A through Z with him .

Van Leeuwen, Jean. *More Tales of Oliver Pig*. Dial, 1981 (I:5–7 R:2). Oliver has further adventures.

_____. *Oliver and Amanda's Halloween*. Illustrated by Ann Schweninger. Dial, 1992 (I:5–8). Oliver tries to show that he is brave on Halloween.

_____. *Oliver Pig at School*. Illustrated by Ann Schweninger. Dial, 1990 (I:5–8). Oliver attends school.

_____. *Tales of Oliver Pig*. Illustrated by Arnold Lobel. Dial, 1979 (I:5–7 R:2). Oliver the pig has five short adventures.

Wiseman, Bernard. *Morris Goes to School*. Harper & Row, 1970 (I:5–8 R:1). Morris Moose cannot count so he decides to go to school.

PICTURE STORYBOOKS

Aardema, Verna. *Why Mosquitoes Buzz in People's Ears*. Illustrated by Leo and Diane Dillon. Dial, 1975 (I:5–9 R:6). This is a cumulative African folk tale.

Ackerman, Karen. *Song and Dance Man*. Illustrated by Stephen Gammell. Knopf, 1988 (I:3–8 R:4). Grandpa re-creates the magic of vaudeville.

Ada, Alma Flor. *Jordi's Star*. Putnam, 1996 (I:4–8 R:4). A young goat herder believes he has captured a star in a pool.

Adoff, Arnold. *Black Is Brown Is Tan*. Illustrated by Emily Arnold McCully. Harper & Row, 1973 (I:3–7). A happy family with a black mother and a white father share experiences.

Agee, Jon. *The Incredible Painting of Felix Clousseau*. Farrar, Straus & Giroux, 1988 (I:5–8 R:4). Paintings come to life in an early Paris setting.

_____. *The Return of Freddy LeGrand*. Farrar, Straus & Giroux, 1992 (I:5–8 R:4). An aviator has many misfortunes when he tries to fly around the world.

Ahlberg, Janet, and Allan Ahlberg. *Each Peach Pear Plum: An I-Spy Story*. Viking, 1978 (I:3–7). Two short lines on each page suggest what the reader should find in a picture.

_____. *The Jolly Postman*. Little, Brown, 1986 (I:3–8). The postman delivers letters to fairy-tale characters.

Alexander, Lloyd. *The Fortune-Tellers*. Illustrated by Trina Schart Hyman. Dutton, 1992 (I:all). A carpenter in central Africa seeks the advice of a fortune teller.

Asch, Frank. *Moonbear's Pet*. Simon & Schuster, 1997 (I:4–6). The theme of this picture storybook is friendship.

_____, and Vladimir Vagin. *Here Comes the Cat!* Scholastic, 1989 (I:all). A bilingual story, written in Russian and English, shows what happens when a cat visits mice.

Ashforth, Camilla. *Monkey Tricks*. Candlewick, 1992 (I:3–6 R:4). A mischievous toy monkey causes problems in the nursery.

Auch, Mary Jane. *The Easter Egg Farm*. Holiday, 1992 (I:3–7 R:4). Pauline, the hen, lays eggs in which the shells reflect her location.

_____. *Peeping Beauty*. Holiday, 1993 (I:4–8 R:4). A fox tries to trick a hen who has dreams of becoming a ballerina.

Babbitt, Natalie. *BUB: Or the Very Best Thing*. HarperCollins, 1994 (I:all). A young prince teaches his parents about the importance of love.

Ballard, Robin. *My Father Is Far Away*. Greenwillow, 1992 (I:4–7 R:4). A child fantasizes about an absent parent.

Baker, Jeannie. *Where the Forest Meets the Sea*. Greenwillow, 1988 (I:4–10 R:5). An Australian forest comes to life through the collage technique.

Bang, Molly. *Goose*. Scholastic, 1996 (I:4–7). A goose discovers that it is all right to be different.

Bannerman, Helen. *The Story of Little Babaji*. Illustrated by Fred Marcellino. HarperCollins, 1996 (I:all). This retelling can be compared with Lester's version.

Baylor, Byrd. *The Best Town in the World*. Illustrated by Ronald Himler. Scribner's Sons, 1983 (I:all). The poetic text presents a nostalgic view of a small town.

Bedard, Michael. *Emily*. Illustrated by Barbara Cooney. Doubleday, 1992 (I:all). A girl visits Emily Dickinson when her mother is invited to play the piano for the author.

Blake, Quentin. *Cockatoos*. Little, Brown, 1992 (I:3–7 R:4). Observant readers can join the search for the professor's missing birds.

Bogacki, Tomek. *Cat and Mouse*. Farrar, Straus & Giroux, 1996 (I:3–5). A friendship develops between a cat and a mouse.

Brisson, Pat. *Your Best Friend, Kate*. Illustrated by Rick Brown. Bradbury, 1989 (I:4–7 R:4). A girl writes letters about her experiences during a car trip.

Brown, Marc. *Arthur's Baby*. Little, Brown, 1987 (I:3–6 R:3). Arthur adjusts to a new baby.

_____. *Arthur Goes to Camp*. Little, Brown, 1982 (I:3–6 R:3). Arthur has adventures at camp.

_____. *Arthur's Family Vacation*. Little, Brown, 1993 (I:3–6 R:3). The family must make other plans when it rains during their beach holiday.

Brown, Margaret Wise. *On Christmas Eve*. Illustrated by Nancy Edwards. Calder, 1996 (I:5–8). Three children experience Christmas Eve.

_____. *The Runaway Bunny*. Rev. ed. Illustrated by Clement Hurd. Harper & Row, 1972 (I:2–7 R:6). A beautiful children's story emphasizes the need for both independence and love.

Brown, Ruth. *The Picnic*. Dutton, 1993 (I:2–5 R:4). A family picnic almost turns into a disastrous situation for the animals that live near the picnic site.

Buehner, Carolun. *Fanny's Dream*. Illustrated by Mark Buehner. Dial, 1996 (I:5–8 R:5). A farm girl dreams about meeting Prince Charming.

Bunting, Eve. *Flower Garden*. Illustrated by Kathryn Hewitt. Harcourt Brace Jovanovich, 1994 (I:3–6). A rhymed verse presents a girl and her father creating a flower garden for mother.

_____. *Ghost's Hour, Spook's Hour*. Illustrated by Donald Carrick. Clarion, 1987 (I:2–7 R:2). A boy experiences fear when the lights go out and he cannot find his parents.

_____. *The Mother's Day Mice*. Illustrated by Jan Brett. Clarion, 1986 (I:3–6). Mice search the woods for perfect gifts.

_____. *My Backpack*. Illustrated by Maryann Cocca-Leffler. Boyds Mills, 1997 (I:4–8). A rhyming text tells about a child who fills a backpack with many items.

_____. *Smoky Night*. Illustrated by David Diaz. Harcourt Brace Jovanovich, 1994 (I:all). The story and the collage illustrations were inspired by the Los Angeles riots.

_____. *The Wednesday Surprise*. Illustrated by Donald Carrick. Clarion, 1989 (I:3–9 R:5). A seven-year-old girl teaches her grandmother to read.

Burton, Virginia Lee. *Katy and the Big Snow*. Houghton Mifflin, 1943, 1971 (I:2–6 R:4). Katy the strongest crawler tractor saves a town after a heavy snowfall.

_____. *The Little House*. Houghton Mifflin, 1942 (I:3–7 R:3). A house is strong but needs love as she becomes dilapidated and lonely over the years.

_____. *Mike Mulligan and His Steam Shovel*. Houghton Mifflin, 1939 (I:2–6 R:4). Mary Anne the steam shovel proves that she can dig in one day more than one hundred men can dig in a week.

Calmenson, Stephanie, and Joanna Cole. *Rockin' Reptiles*. Illustrated by Lynn Munsinger. Morrow, 1997 (I:7–9 R:4). This is a story about friendship.

Cannon, Janell. *Verdi*. Harcourt Brace, 1997 (I:4–10 R:5). A young python learns about life.

Carlstrom, Nancy White. *Jesse Bear, What Will You Wear?* Illustrated by Bruce Degen. Macmillan, 1986 (I:3–6). A rhyming text follows a young bear's activities.

Cazet, Denys. *A Fish in His Pocket*. Watts, 1987 (I:3–6 R:4). A young bear resolves the problem of a dead fish.

Cendrars, Blaise. *Shadow*. Illustrated by Marcia Brown. Scribner's Sons, 1982 (I:all). This is a highly illustrated version of an African poem.

Chetwin, Grace. *Box and Cox*. Illustrated by David Small. Bradbury, 1990 (I:6–9). This is a humorous story about a landlady who tries to rent a room to two boarders without the boarders knowing about each other.

Conrad, Pam. *Call Me Ahnighito*. Illustrated by Richard Egielski. HarperCollins, 1995 (I:7+ R:5). The author tells the story through the point of view of a meteorite.

_____. *The Lost Sailor*. Illustrated by Richard Egielski. HarperCollins, 1992 (I:4–8 R:4). A stranded sailor is finally rescued when his hut catches fire.

Cooper, Helen. *The Boy Who Would Not Go to Bed*. Dial, 1997 (I:3–6). A boy finds himself alone when even his toys go to sleep.

Coy, John. *Night Driving*. Illustrated by Peter McCarty. Holt, 1996 (I:5–8 R:4). A father and son take a trip across the prairie on their way to a camping trip.

Crews, Donald. *Night At the Fair*. Greenwillow, 1998. (I:4–7). A minimal text accompanies a trip to the fair.

_____. *Shortcut*. Greenwillow, 1992 (I:4–8 R:4). Children take a shortcut along the railroad tracks and experience an approaching train.

Curtis, Jamie Lee. *Tell Me Again About the Night I Was Born*. Illustrated by Laura Cornell. HarperCollins, 1996 (I:4–7 R:4). This is a warm story about adoptive parents.

Cutler, Jane. *Darcy and Gran Don't Like Babies*. Illustrated by Susannah Ryan. Scholastic, 1993 (I:3–7 R:3). A young girl adjusts to a new sibling.

Dadey, Debbie. *Shooting Star: Annie Oakley, the Legend*. Illustrated by Scott Goto. Walker, 1997 (I:5–9 R:5). The author uses exaggeration to create a heroine.

Darling, Benjamin. *Valerie and the Silver Pear*. Illustrated by Dan Lane. Four Winds, 1992 (I:5–8). A grandfather and his granddaughter share havesting pears.

de Brunhoff, Jean. *The Story of Babar*. Random House, 1933, 1961 (I:3–9 R:4). In this original story, Babar eventually becomes the king of the elephants.

_____, and Laurent de Brunhoff. *Babar's Anniversary Album: 6 Favorite Stories*. Random House, 1981 (I:3–9 R:4). This album contains *The Story of Babar, The Travels of Babar, Babar the King, Babar's Birthday Surprise, Babar's Mystery,* and *Babar and the Wully-Wully.*

Defelice, Cynthia. *Willy's Silly Grandma*. Illustrated by Shelley Jackson. Orchard, 1997 (I:5–8 R:4). The text uses repetitive language.

dePaola, Tomie. *The Clown of God*. Harcourt Brace Jovanovich, 1978 (I:all R:4). A legend about a juggler and a miracle.

_____. *An Early American Christmas*. Holiday House, 1987 (I:4–7 R:6). The book shows a Christmas with a New England family living in the early 1800s.

_____. *Nana Upstairs & Nana Downstairs*. Putnam, 1973 (I:3–7 R:6). Tommy has two beloved grandmothers: a great-grandmother upstairs and a grandmother downstairs.

_____. *Oliver Button Is a Sissy*. Harcourt Brace Jovanovich, 1979 (I:5–8 R:2). Other boys call Oliver a sissy because he likes to dance, read books, and dress in costumes.

Duvoisin, Roger. *Petunia*. Knopf, 1950 (I:3–6 R:6). Petunia, the silly goose, learns that she has to do more than carry a book to gain wisdom.

Ehlert, Lois. *Mole's Hill*. Harcourt Brace Jovanovich, 1994 (I:3–8). A mole uses ingenuity to keep a fox from destroying her kill.

Emberley, Barbara. *Drummer Hoff*. Illustrated by Ed Emberley. Prentice-Hall, 1967 (I:3–7 R:6). A cumulative rhyme depicts all of the people associated with firing a cannon.

Engel, Diana. *Josephina Hates Her Name*. Morrow, 1989 (I:5–8 R:4). An alligator child discovers pride in her name.

Ericsson, Jennifer A. *No Milk!* Illustrated by Ora Eitan. Tambourine, 1993 (I:3–8). In a repetitive text, a boy tries to milk a cow.

Ernst, Lisa Campbell. *Miss Penny and Mr. Grubbs*. Bradbury, 1991 (I:5–8 R:4). Irony develops in a humorous ending when revenge does not work.

_____. *Walter's Tail*. Bradbury, 1992 (I:4–8 R:4). When a pet dog grows up, his tail causes difficulties.

_____. *When Bluebell Sang*. Bradbury, 1989 (I:4–8 R:5). A singing cow overcomes her problems by reverting to animal behavior.

Fleischman, Paul. *Time Train*. Illustrated by Claire Ewart. HarperCollins, 1991 (I:4–8 R:4). Children enter a train that takes them back in time to the days of dinosaurs.

Fleischman, Sid. *The Scarebird*. Illustrated by Peter Sis. Greenwillow, 1988 (I:5–9 R:5). A lonesome farmer creates a scarecrow for a friend until he makes friends with a homeless boy.

Fleming, Candace. *The Hatmaker's Sign: A Story by Benjamin Franklin*. Illustrated by Robert Andrew Parker. Orchard, 1998 (I:5–9 R:5). The book retells a parable told by Franklin.

Fleming, Denise. *Lunch*. Holt, 1992 (I:2–7). This book helps children make predictions.

Flournoy, Valerie. *The Patchwork Quilt*. Illustrated by Jerry Pinkney. Dial, 1985 (I:5–8 R:4). The sewing of a family quilt develops close family memories.

Forward, Toby. *Ben's Christmas Carol*. Illustrated by Ruth Brown. Dutton, 1996 (I:5–8). A story of two mice is inspired by "A Christmas Carol."

Fox, Mem. *Hattie and the Fox*. Illustrated by Patricia Mullins. Bradbury, 1987 (I:3–7). In a cumulative tale, a hen tries to convince farm animals about approaching danger.

_____. *Night Noises*. Illustrated by Terry Denton. Harcourt Brace Jovanovich, 1989 (I:3–8 R:5). Night noises turn out to be pleasant rather than scary.

_____. *Wombat Divine*. Illustrated by Kerry Argent. Harcourt Brace, 1996 (I:4–7). Australian animals provide a story of the Nativity.

Gág, Wanda. *Millions of Cats*. Coward, McCann, 1929 (I:3–7 R:3). A little old woman's desire for a pretty cat results in a fight between trillions of cats.

Gage, Wilson. *Cully, Cully and the Bear*. Illustrated by James Stevenson. Greenwillow, 1983 (I:4–6 R:2). In a humorous tale, a hunter goes after a bearskin to make his house more comfortable.

Galbraith, Kathryn O. *Laura Charlotte*. Illustrated by Floyd Cooper. Putnam's 1990 (I:4–6 R:4). A mother tells her daughter about her own childhood experiences.

Gammell, Stephen. *Wake Up Bear . . . It's Christmas!* Lothrop, Lee & Shepard, 1981 (I:5–8 R:4). A Christmas story is accompanied by humorous illustrations.

Gantos, Jack. *Rotten Ralph's Rotten Romance*. Houghton Mifflin, 1997 (I:4–8 R:4). This is a humorous tale about a cat.

Gauch, Patricia Lee. *Christina Katerina and the Time She Quit the Family*. Illustrated by Elise Primavera. Putnam, 1987 (I:4–8 R:6). A young girl discovers that there are more important things than doing only what pleases her.

Gliori, Debi. *The Snow Lambs*. Scholastic, 1996 (I:4–8 R:4). A sheepdog saves a missing animal.

Griffith, Helen V. *Grandaddy and Janetta*. Illustrated by James Stevenson. Greenwillow, 1993 (I:6–10 R:5). Janetta visits her grandfather's farm and listens to his stories.

_____. *Grandaddy's Place*. Illustrated by James Stevenson. Greenwillow, 1987 (I:4–8 R:4). A young girl learns to appreciate her grandfather and her grandfather's rural home.

Haas, Irene. *A Summer Song*. Simon & Schuster, 1997 (I:4–8 R:4). Lucy attends a fantasy birthday party.

Hadithi, Mwenye. *Crafty Chameleon*. Illustrated by Adrienne Kennaway. Little, Brown, 1987 (I:4–8 R:5). An original story tells why the crocodile and the leopard do not bother the chameleon.

Haley, Gail E. *A Story, a Story.* Atheneum, 1970 (I:6–10 R:6). In an African tale, Ananse the spider man bargains with the Sky God.

Hanson, Regina. *The Face At the Window.* Illustrated by Linda Saport. Clarion, 1997 (I:5–8 R:4). The text emphasizes the importance of learning about a neighbor.

Hartmann, Wendy, and Daly, Niki. *The Dinosaurs Are Back and It's All Your Fault Edward!* McElderry, 1997 (I:5–8 R:4). This story stresses sibling relationships.

Henkes, Kevin. *Jessica.* Greenwillow, 1989 (I:3–6 R:5). A girl has an imaginary friend.

_____. *Lilly's Purple Plastic Purse.* Greenwillow, 1996 (I:4–8 R:4). This humorous story presents the consequences of bringing treasures to school in a purse.

_____. *Owen.* Greenwillow, 1993 (I:2–5 R:4). A mouse child does not want to give up his security blanket.

Herriot, James. *Moses the Kitten.* Illustrated by Peter Barrett. St. Martin's, 1984 (I:all R:5). A young kitten finds a home on a Yorkshire farm.

Hesse, Karen. *Lester's Dog.* Illustrated by Nancy Carpenter Crown, 1993 (I:6–9 R:5). A kitten helps a boy overcome his fear of a large dog.

Hest, Amy. *Baby Duck and the Bad Eyeglasses.* Illustrated by Jill Barton. Candlewick, 1996 (I:3–8 R:5). Grandpa helps baby duck accept her glasses.

_____. *The Crack-of-Dawn Walkers.* Illustrated by Amy Schwartz. Macmillan, 1984 (I:5–8 R:3). A young girl develops a close relationship with her grandfather.

_____. Hest, Amy. *In the Rain With Baby Duck.* Illustrated by Jill Barton. Candlewick, 1995 (I:3–8 R:5). Humor results through the irony of a baby duck who does not like to get wet.

Ho, Minfong. *Hush! A Thai Lullaby.* Illustrated by Holly Meade. Orchard, 1996 (I:3–8). A mother sings a lullaby to her child.

Hoban, Russell. *A Baby Sister for Frances.* Illustrated by Lillian Hoban. Harper & Row, 1964 (I:5–8 R:4). Frances the badger has a new baby sister, and things just aren't the same.

_____. *A Bargain for Frances.* Illustrated by Lillian Hoban. Harper & Row, 1970 (I:4–8 R:2). This easy-to-read book tells the story of Frances and her friend Thelma.

_____. *Best Friends for Frances.* Illustrated by Lillian Hoban. Harper & Row, 1969 (I:4–8 R:4). Frances discovers that her little sister is a lot of fun and a best friend.

_____. *Bread and Jam for Frances.* Illustrated by Lillian Hoban. Harper & Row, 1964 (I:4–8 R:4). Frances wants bread and jam, not eggs or anything else that is new.

Hoberman, Mary Ann. *Mr. and Mrs. Muddle.* Illustrated by Catharine O'Neill. Little, Brown, 1988 (I:3–8 R:4). In a humorous story, two animals disagree.

Hoestlandt, Jo. *Star of Fear, Star of Hope.* Illustrated by Johanna Kang. Walker, 1995 (I:all). A girl remembers the disappearance of her Jewish friend in occupied Paris during World War II.

Houston, Gloria. *My Great-Aunt Arizona.* Illustrated by Susan Condie Lamb. HarperCollins, 1992 (I:5–9 R:5). A girl in the Blue Ridge Mountains grows up to teach generations of children.

Hughes, Shirley. *Alfie Gives a Hand.* Lothrop, Lee & Shepard, 1983 (I:3–6 R:4). When he helps a friend, Alfie discovers that he no longer needs his security blanket.

Hunter, Anne. *Possum's Harvest Moon.* Houghton, Mifflin, 1996 (I:3–6). The animals prepare for winter.

Hurd, Edith Thacher. *I Dance in My Red Pajamas.* Illustrated by Emily Arnold McCully. Harper & Row, 1982 (I:3–7 R:3). A girl and her visiting grandparents form a warm relationship.

Hutchins, Pat. *Happy Birthday, Sam.* Greenwillow, 1978 (I:3–6 R:4). Grandpa's birthday present allows Sam to reach various items.

_____. *Where's the Baby?* Greenwillow, 1988 (I:3–6 R:4). A monster baby leaves tracks.

_____. *The Wind Blew.* Macmillan, 1974 (I:3–6 R:4). A short, rhyming story tells with colorful pictures what happened when the wind blew objects away from people.

Innocenti, Roberto. *Rose Blanche.* Stewart, Tabori & Chang, 1985 (I:all). A young German girl discovers concentration camps in Germany.

Isaacs, Anne. *Swamp Angel.* Illustrated by Paul O. Zelinsky. Dutton, 1994 (I:all). In a tall-tale format, a Tennessee girl is born with exceptional size and strength.

Isadora, Rachel. *Young Mozart.* Viking, 1997 (I:4–8 R:5). This is a highly illustrated biography of the young composer.

James, Simon. *Dear Mr. Blueberry.* Macmillan, 1991 (I:4–7 R:4). A girl writes letters about the whale that she thinks lives in the pool in her yard.

Janisch, Heinz. *Noah's Ark.* Illustrated by Lisbeth Zwerger. North-South, 1997 (I: all). An illustrated version of the Flood story.

Jennings, Dana Andrew. *Me, Dad & Number 6.* Illustrated by Goro Sasaki. Harcourt Brace, 1997 (I:4–8 R:5). This story about a race car is set in the 1940s.

Johnson, Angela. *Julius.* Illustrated by Dav Pilkey. Orchard, 1993 (I:3–8 R:4). Maya's granddaddy brings home an Alaskan pig named Julius, who provides Maya with exciting adventures.

_____. *The Rolling Store.* Illustrated by Peter Catalanotto. Orchard, 1997 (I:4–8 R:4). The story is based on the idea of a peddler's cart.

Johnson, Paul Brett. *The Cow Who Wouldn't Come Down.* Orchard, 1993 (I:5–8 R:5). In a humorous story, an elderly lady tries to keep her cow from flying.

Johnston, Tony. *The Ghost of Nicholas Greebe.* Illustrated by S. D. Schindler. Dial, 1996 (I:5–8 R:4). The ghost vows to haunt his farm until he finds his missing bone.

Jorgensen, Gail. *Gotcha!* Illustrated by Kerry Argent. Scholastic, 1997 (I:3–7). A fly causes the humor in a repetitive text.

Joyce, William. *Dinosaur Bob and His Adventures with the Family Lazardo.* Harper & Row, 1988 (I:5–9 R:5). A friendly dinosaur accompanies a family home from Africa.

_____. *Santa Calls.* HarperCollins, 1993 (I:4–9 R:6). Santa Claus increases the friendship between a brother and sister.

Jukes, Mavis. *Like Jake and Me.* Illustrated by Lloyd Bloom. Knopf, 1984 (I:6–9 R:4). An incident with a spider brings a boy and his stepfather closer together.

Keats, Ezra Jack. *Dreams.* Macmillan, 1974 (I:3–8 R:3). Robert makes a mouse at school, and everyone else dreams his mouse saves Archie's cat from a dog.

_____. *Goggles!* Macmillan, 1969 (I:5–9 R:3). Archie and Willie outwit bullies and reach home safely.

_____. *A Letter to Amy.* Harper & Row, 1968 (I:3–8 R:3). Peter writes a birthday party invitation to his friend Amy.

_____. *Louie.* Greenwillow, 1975 (I:3–8 R:2). Louie responds to a puppet in a play and later is given the puppet by the children who put on the show.

_____. *Maggie and the Pirate*. Four Winds, 1979 (I:4–8 R:3). A "pirate" steals Maggie's pet cricket.

_____. *Peter's Chair*. Harper & Row, 1967 (I:3–8 R:2). Peter overcomes jealousy when his furniture is painted for his new baby sister.

_____. *Regards to the Man in the Moon*. Four Winds, 1981 (I:4–8 R:3). Two children build a spaceship from junk and fuel it with their imaginations.

_____. *The Trip*. Greenwillow, 1978 (I:3–8 R:2). Louie constructs a shoe box scene so he can visit his friends.

Keller, Holly. *Island Baby*. Greenwillow, 1992 (I:4–8 R:4). A young boy helps an injured bird.

Kellogg, Steven. *I Was Born About 10,000 Years Ago*. Morrow, 1996 (I:all). This is a humorous tall tale.

_____. *A Rose for Pinkerton*. Dial, 1981 (I:4–8 R:3). In a humorous story, a girl chooses a kitten as a friend for her Great Dane.

_____. *Tallyho, Pinkerton!* Dial, 1982 (I:4–8 R:3). Rose the Great Dane and her owner go on a hilarious trip to the woods.

Khalsa, Dayal Kaur. *I Want a Dog*. Clarkson, 1987 (I:4–7 R:5). A girl pretends a roller skate is a dog to practice caring for a pet.

Kimmel, Eric A. *The Chanukkah Guest*. Illustrated by Giora Carmi. Holiday House, 1990 (I:5–9 R:5). In a humorous story, Bubba Brayna mistakes an old bear for the rabbi and gives him the latkes.

_____. *The Chanukkah Tree*. Illustrated by Giora Carmi. Holiday House, 1988 (I:5–9 R:5). A peddler convinces the people of a town that they need a special tree.

Kleven, Elisa. *The Puddle Pail*. Dutton, 1997 (I:4–8). Two brother crocodiles learn to live with their differences.

Kodama, Tatsuharu. *Shin's Tricycle*. Illustrated by Noriyuki Ando. Walker, 1995 (I:all). A young atomic bomb victim is remembered through his tricycle.

Kraus, Robert. *Leo the Late Bloomer*. Illustrated by Jose and Ariane Aruego. Windmill, 1971 (I:2–6 R:4). A large, colorful picture book tells the story of a young tiger who can't do anything right.

Leaf, Munro. *The Story of Ferdinand*. Illustrated by Robert Lawson. Viking, 1936 (I:4–10 R:6). A mild-mannered bull intended for the bullring manages instead to "be himself."

Lent, Blair. *Bayberry Bluff*. Houghton Mifflin, 1987 (I:3–8 R:6). A town evolves from a tenting community to elaborately decorated houses.

Lester, Julius. *Sam and the Tigers: A New Tale of Little Black Sambo*. Illustrated by Jerry Pinkney. Dial, 1996 (I:all). Compare this with the Bannerman version.

Lindbergh, Reeve. *The Day the Goose Got Loose*. Illustrated by Steven Kellogg. Dial, 1990 (I:5–9 R:4). Havoc reigns when the pet goose gets loose on the farm.

Lindenbaum, Pija. *Boodil My Dog*. Henry Holt, 1992 (I:5–9 R:5). In an ironic story, the illustrations do not show what the owner thinks of the dog.

Lindgren, Barbro. *The Wild Baby Goes to Sea*. Adapted from the Swedish by Jack Prelutsky. Illustrated by Eva Eriksson. Greenwillow, 1983 (I:2–6). A story in rhyme tells about an imaginative child and a box.

Lionni, Leo. *Alexander and the Wind-up Mouse*. Pantheon, 1969 (I:3–6 R:3). A real mouse learns it's better to be real than to be a toy.

_____. *Tillie and the Wall*. Knopf, 1989 (I:2–7 R:4). A mouse discovers what is on the other side of the wall.

Littlesugar, Amy. *Marie in Fourth Position: The Story of Degas' "The Little Dancer."* Illustrated by Ian Schoenherr. Philomel, 1996 (I:6–8). This is a fictional story about the dancer.

London, Jonathan. *The Owl Who Became the Moon*. Illustrated by Ted Rand. Dutton, 1993 (I:4–8). A lyrical text takes readers into the night of the owl and other animals.

Lyon, George Ella. *Come a Tide*. Illustrated by Stephen Gammell. Orchard, 1990 (I:5–8 R:5). High water causes a family to work together.

_____. *Dreamplace*. Illustrated by Peter Catalanotto. Orchard, 1993 (I:all). The text and illustrations take readers into the time of the Anasazi.

Macaulay, David. *Why the Chicken Crossed the Road*. Houghton Mifflin, 1987 (I:5–9 R:6). A chicken causes a series of fantastic events.

McCloskey, Robert. *Blueberries for Sal*. Viking, 1948 (I:4–8 R:6). A bear cub and a young girl get mixed up and start following the wrong mothers.

_____. *Lentil*. Viking, 1940 (I:4–9 R:7). Lentil saves the homecoming when Old Sneep tries to wreck the welcome.

_____. *Make Way for Ducklings*. Viking, 1941 (I:4–8 R:4). A city park provides a safe home for the ducklings.

_____. *One Morning in Maine*. Viking, 1952 (I:4–8 R:3). Sal and her family experience the joys of living on an island.

_____. *Time of Wonder*. Viking, 1957 (I:5–8 R:4). A family explores an island in the spring, during a hurricane, and after the storm has passed.

McCully, Emily Arnold. *Mirette on the High Wire*. Putnam, 1992 (I:5–9 R:5). A girl helps a wire-walker overcome his fear.

_____. *Starring Mirette & Bellini*. Putnam, 1997 (I:all). This sequel to *Mirette on the High Wire* includes political intrigue.

McDonald, Megan. *The Great Pumpkin Switch*. Illustrated by Ted Lewin. Orchard, 1992 (I:5–8 R:4). The setting is small town America in the early 1900s.

McKissack, Patricia C. *Nettie Jo's Friends*. Illustrated by Scott Cook. Knopf, 1989 (I:5–9 R:5). A girl faces a dilemma when she cannot take her doll to a wedding.

McPhail, David. *Edward and the Pirates*. Little, Brown, 1997 (I:5–8 R:4). The books Edward reads seem to become real.

_____. *Fix-It*. Dutton, 1984 (I:3–R:2). An emergency develops when the television does not function.

Mahy, Margaret. *17 Kings and 42 Elephants*. Illustrated by Patricia MacCarthy. Dial, 1987 (I:3–8). A nonsense poem is illustrated with cardboard cuts.

Marshall, James. *George and Martha One Fine Day*. Houghton Mifflin, 1978 (I:3–8). Two hippos have a thoroughly delightful day as they walk on a tightrope and visit an amusement park.

Martin, Bill, and John Archambault. *Up and Down on the Merry-Go-Round*. Illustrated by Ted Rand. Holt, Rinehart & Winston, 1988 (I:3–8). This is a rhyming story.

Martin, Jacqueline Briggs. *Buzzy Bones and the Lost Quilt*. Illustrated by Stella Ormai. Lothrop, Lee & Shepard, 1988 (I:4–8 R:6). A mouse child is distraught after losing his quilt.

_____. *Good Times on Grandfather Mountain*. Illustrated by Susan Gaber. Orchard, 1992 (I:4–8 R:4). A mountain man shows optimism even when disasters befall him.

Martin, Rafe. *Will's Mammoth.* Illustrated by Stephen Gammell. Putnam, 1989 (I:2–8). In an almost wordless book, a young boy has an imaginary experience while playing in the snow.

Maruki, Toshi. *Hiroshima No Pika.* Lothrop, Lee & Shepard, 1982 (I:10+ R:4). A family experiences the atomic bomb on August 6, 1945.

Mathis, Sharon Bell. *The Hundred Penny Box.* Illustrated by Leo and Diane Dillon. Viking, 1975 (I:6–9 R:3). Young Michael becomes friends with his Great-great-aunt Dew and learns about the old box in which she keeps a penny for every year of her life.

Mayer, Mercer. *There's a Nightmare in My Closet.* Dial, 1969 (I:3–7 R:3). A young boy decides to get rid of his nightmare by confronting the monster.

Meddaugh, Susan. *Martha Speaks.* Houghton Mifflin, 1992 (I:4–8 R:4). A dog speaks after eating alphabet soup.

Melmed, Laura Krass. *The First Song Ever Sung.* Illustrated by Ed Young. Lothrop, 1993 (I:3–6). This Japanese story is written in prose.

Milne, A. A. *Winnie-the-Pooh.* Illustrated by Ernest H. Shepard. Dutton, 1926, 1954 (I:6–10 R:5). Pooh has adventures with his nursery friends and Christopher Robin.

Monson, A. M. *Wanted: Best Friend.* Illustrated by Lynn Munsinger. Dial, 1997 (I:4–8 R:4). This story emphasizes friendship.

Moss, Lloyd. *Zin! Zin! Zin! A Violin.* Illustrated by Marjorie Priceman. Simon & Schuster, 1995 (I:all). The author's style depicts the instruments of a chamber orchestra.

Murphy, Mary. *I Like It When . . .* Harcourt Brace, 1997 (I:3–5). A little penguin describes favorite experiences.

Myers, Walter Dean. *Harlem.* Illustrated by Christopher Myers. Scholastic, 1997 (I: all). Collage illustrations reinforce a poetic text.

Narahashi, Keiko. *I Have a Friend.* Macmillan, 1987 (I:2–6+ R:3). A small boy has a shadow for a friend.

Naylor, Phyllis Reynolds. *Keeping a Christmas Secret.* Illustrated by Lena Shiffman. Atheneum, 1989 (I:3–7 R:3). A four-year-old boy reveals a secret and then redeems his action.

Ness, Evaline. *Sam, Bangs & Moonshine.* Holt, Rinehart & Winston, 1966 (I:5–9 R:3). Sam almost costs a friend his life.

Nivola, Claire. *Elisabeth.* Farrar, Straus, & Giroux, 1997 (I:4–8 R:4). Based on a true story, the narrator tells about her earlier life in Germany and how she eventually finds her doll, Elisabeth, in the United States.

Numeroff, Laura. *The Chicken Sisters.* Illustrated by Sharleen Collicott. HarperCollins, 1997 (I:4–7). Chickens outwit the wolf.

Oakley, Graham. *Hetty and Harriet.* Atheneum, 1982 (I:5–10 R:6). A discontented hen and her meek friend leave the security of their barnyard for a series of adventures.

Opkinson, Deborah. *Birdie's Lighthouse.* Illustrated by Kimberly Bulcken Root. Simon & Schuster, 1997 (I:5–9 R:5). The story is set in Maine in the 1800s.

Paz, Octavio. Translated by Catherine Cowan. *My Life With the Wave.* Illustrated by Mark Buehner. Lothrop, Lee & Shepard, 1997 (I:4–8). A boy tries to bring a wave home from the beach.

Peet, Bill. *Cyrus the Unsinkable Sea Serpent.* Houghton Mifflin, 1975 (I:5–9 R:7). A not-so-fierce sea serpent rescues a sailing ship from squalls and pirates.

_____. *The Gnats of Knotty Pine.* Houghton Mifflin, 1975 (I:5–9 R:6). Gnats save the forest animals during hunting season.

_____. *No Such Things.* Houghton Mifflin, 1983 (I:4–8 R:6). Nonsense words and creatures make humorous reading.

Plourde, Lynn. *Pigs in the Mud in the Middle of the Rud.* Illustrated by John Schoenherr. Scholastic, 1997 (I:3–7). Rhythmical text presents a humorous story.

Polacco, Patricia. *Appelemando's Dreams.* Philomel, 1991 (I:6–9 R:5). Villagers discover the importance of dreams.

_____. *Babushka Baba Yaga.* Philomel, 1993 (I:5–8 R:5). The Russian Baba Yaga takes on the role of a loving grandmother.

_____. *The Bee Tree.* Philomel, 1993 (I:5–8 R:5). A girl and her grandfather go in search of a bee tree.

_____. *Meteor!* Dodd, Mead, 1987 (I:6–10 R:7). Humorous fiction tells the reactions of a town when a meteor falls to earth.

_____. *Thunder Cake.* Philomel, 1990 (I:5–8 R:5). A grandmother helps her granddaughter overcome fear of storms.

Porte, Barbara Ann. *Harry in Trouble.* Illustrated by Yossi Abolafia. Greenwillow, 1989 (I:3–7 R:2). A boy learns that other people also lose possessions.

Provensen, Alice, and Martin Provensen. *Shaker Lane.* Viking, 1987 (I:5–9 R:3). Illustrations show changing society along Shaker Lane.

Purdy, Carol. *Least of All.* Illustrated by Tim Arnold. Macmillan, 1987 (I:5–8 R:5). The youngest girl in the family proves that she can be important when she learns to read.

Ransome, Arthur. *The Fool of the World and the Flying Ship.* Illustrated by Uri Shulevitz. Farrar, Straus & Giroux, 1968 (I:6–10 R:6). A humble Russian lad manages to marry the czar's daughter.

Raschka, Chris. *Yo! Yes?* Orchard, 1993 (I:3–7). The text shows the beginning of friendship.

Rathmann, Peggy. *Officer Buckle and Gloria.* Putnam's, 1995 (I:all). A police dog adds humorous displays to safety tips.

Reiser, Lynn. *Best Friends Think Alike.* Greenwillow, 1997 (I:3–6). This is a story about friendship.

Rey, Hans. *Curious George.* Houghton Mifflin, 1941, 1969 (I:2–7 R:2). George begins his slapstick adventures when he leaves the jungle with the man who has a yellow hat.

Riley, Linnea. *Mouse Mess.* Scholastic, 1997 (I:4–7). A rhyming text reinforces a humorous story.

Root, Phyllis. *Mrs. Potter's Pig.* Illustrated by Russell Ayto. Candlewick, 1996 (I:4–8). This is a humorous tale.

Rosen, Michael. *We're Going on a Bear Hunt.* Illustrated by Helen Oxenbury. Macmillan, 1989 (I:2–7). Repetitive language appeals to children.

Rosenberg, Liz. *Eli and Uncle Dawn.* Illustrated by Susan Gaber. Harcourt Brace, 1997 (I:3–8). A boy leaves his stuffed elephant behind when he goes on a picnic.

_____. *Moonbathing.* Illustrated by Stephen Lambert. Harcourt, Brace, 1996 (I:3–8). A family sees a beach by moonlight.

Rylant, Cynthia. *Mr. Griggs' Work.* Illustrated by Julie Downing. Watts, 1989 (I:4–8 R:5). A post office worker is reminded of his work when he is not in the office.

_____. *The Old Woman Who Named Things.* Illustrated by Kathryn Brown. Harcourt Brace, 1996 (I:4–8). An old woman outsmarts loneliness by naming objects.

Sanfield, Steve. *The Great Turtle Drive.* Illustrated by Dirk Zimmer. Knopf, 1996 (I:7–10). The humor is developed through an absurd situation.

San Souci, Robert. *The Hobyahs*. Illustrated by Alexi Natchev. Doubleday, 1994 (I:4–7 R:5). Faithful dogs rescue a girl from the goblins.

Schotter, Roni. *Captain Snap and the Children of Vinegar Lane*. Illustrated by Marcia Sewall. Orchard, 1989 (I:5–9 R:5). Children help a hermit who is ill.

_____. *Nothing Ever Happens on 90th Street*. Illustrated by Kyrsten Brooker. Orchard, 1997 (I:6–9 R:4). A girl tries to write about her street.

Schwartz, Amy. *Annabelle Swift, Kindergartner*. Orchard, 1988 (I:4–7 R:4). A girl faces kindergarten.

Schwartz, Henry. *How I Captured a Dinosaur*. Illustrated by Amy Schwartz. Orchard, 1989 (I:5–8 R:5). An eight-year-old girl finds a dinosaur while on a camping trip.

Sendak, Maurice. *In the Night Kitchen*. Harper & Row, 1970 (I:5–7). A young child dreams that he is in the world of the night kitchen.

_____. *Seven Little Monsters*. Harper & Row, 1977 (I:5–8). This is an illustrated account of the actions of Sendak's monsters.

_____. *The Sign on Rosie's Door*. Harper & Row, 1960 (I:5–9 R:2). Rosie pretends she's a singer and stages a show.

_____. *Where the Wild Things Are*. Harper & Row, 1963 (I:4–8 R:6). Max's vivid imagination turns his room into a forest inhabited by wild things.

Seuss, Dr. *And to Think That I Saw It on Mulberry Street*. Vanguard, 1937 (I:3–9 R:5). A young boy imagines all the fantastic things that could be on his street.

_____. *The 500 Hats of Bartholomew Cubbins*. Vanguard, 1938 (I:4–9 R:4). Bartholomew has a bewitched hat that keeps reappearing as he tries to take off his hat before the King.

_____. *Horton Hatches the Egg*. Random House, 1940, 1968 (I:3–9 R:4). Horton replaces lazy Mayzie on her nest and finally hatches an elephant-bird.

_____. *Hunches in Bunches*. Random House, 1982 (I:6–10 R:4). A young boy has problems deciding on his hunches.

_____. *If I Ran the Zoo*. Random House, 1950 (I:4–10 R:3). A boy searches in odd places for some unusual animals.

Sharmat, Marjorie Weinman. *The Best Valentine in the World*. Illustrated by Lilian Obligado. Holiday House, 1982 (I:3–7 R:4). A fox believes his friend has forgotten to make him a valentine.

Sis, Peter. *Starry Messenger*. Farrar, Straus & Giroux, 1996 (I:all). This heavily illustrated biography presents the life of Galileo.

Sisulu, Elinor Batezalt. *The Day Gogo Went to Vote: South Africa, April 1994*. Illustrated by Sharon Wilson. Little, Brown, 1996 (I:4–8 R:5). A great-grandmother votes for the first time.

Small, David. *Imogene's Antlers*. Crown, 1985 (I:5–8 R:6). A young girl wakes up wearing antlers.

Spier, Peter. *The Star-Spangled Banner*. Doubleday, 1973 (I:8+). The words of the national anthem are illustrated in accurate detail from history.

Standiford, Natalie. *Astronauts Are Sleeping*. Illustrated by Allen Garns. Knopf, 1997 (I:4–8). The text explores the possible dreams of astronauts.

Steig, William. *The Amazing Bone*. Farrar, Straus & Giroux, 1976 (I:6–9 R:3). A pig and a talking bone escape from robbers and a hungry fox.

_____. *Caleb & Kate*. Farrar, Straus & Giroux, 1977 (I:6–9 R:3). Caleb the carpenter goes to sleep in the woods and is changed into a dog by Yedida the witch.

_____. *Spinky Sulks*. Farrar, Straus & Giroux, 1988 (I:3–7 R:5). A sulky boy discovers that his family is really trying to help him.

_____. *Sylvester and the Magic Pebble*. Simon & Schuster, 1969 (I:6–9 R:5). A magical pebble causes a donkey to turn into a rock.

_____. *Toby Where Are You?* Illustrated by Teryl Euvremer. Harcourt Brace, 1997 (I:3–6). An animal's parents try to find him.

Stevens, Janet. *Tops & Bottoms*. Harcourt Brace, 1995 (I:4–7). A ridiculous situation provides the humor.

Stevenson, James. *Could Be Worse!* Greenwillow, 1977 (I:5–9 R:3). Grandpa tells his grandchildren a whopper.

_____. *Don't You Know There's a War On?* Greenwillow, 1992 (I:all). This text presents the author's memories of World War II.

_____. *July*. Greenwillow, 1990 (I:5–8 R:4). A book of memories takes readers back to summer visits at grandparents' home.

_____. *There's Nothing to Do*. Greenwillow, 1986 (I:5–9 R:3). Humor and exaggeration characterize this story.

_____. *The Wish Card Ran Out!* Greenwillow, 1981 (I:6–10 R:4). Cartoon illustrations enhance a spoof on credit cards.

Stock, Catherine. *Armien's Fishing Trip*. Morrow, 1990 (I:5–8 R:4). A boy sounds the alarm when a fisherman is swept overboard.

Stewart, Sarah. *The Gardener*. Illustrated by David Small. Farrar Straus Giroux, 1997 (I:5–8 R: 4). A girl's flowers bring joy.

Sutcliff, Rosemary. *The Minstrel and the Dragon Pup*. Illustrated by Emma Chichester Clark. Candlewick, 1993 (I:6–10 R:5). A minstrel's song awakens a dragon's abandoned egg.

Sykes, Julie. *Dora's Eggs*. Illustrated by Jane Chapman. Little Tiger, 1997 (I:3–7 R:4). A chicken shows off her egg and then is frightened when it breaks during the hatching.

Trivizas, Eugene. *The Three Little Wolves and the Big Bad Pig*. Illustrated by Helen Oxenbury. Macmillan, 1993 (I:4–9 R:4). This is a twist on the folktale.

Turner, Ann. *Shaker Hearts*. Illustrated by Wendell Minor. HarperCollins, 1997 (I:all). The text focuses on a Shaker village.

Ungerer, Tomi. *The Beast of Monsieur Racine*. Farrar, Straus & Giroux, 1971 (I:5–9 R:5). A strange beast steals prized pears and becomes a friend of Monsieur Racine.

Van Allsburg, Chris. *Jumanji*. Houghton Mifflin, 1981 (I:5–8 R:6). An unusual game creates a jungle environment.

_____. *The Polar Express*. Houghton Mifflin, 1985 (I:5–8 R:6). A boy has an unusual adventure when he meets Santa Claus.

_____. *The Sweetest Fig*. Houghton Mifflin, 1993 (I:all R:6). A dentist discovers an important lesson when he is given two magic figs.

_____. *The Widow's Broom*. Houghton Mifflin, 1992 (I:5–8 R:5). A broom has special powers.

_____. *The Wreck of the Zephyr*. Houghton Mifflin 1983 (I:5–8 R:6). A boy tries to become the greatest sailor in the world.

_____. *The Wretched Stone*. Houghton Mifflin, 1991 (I:5–8 R:5). A glowing stone changes the lives of the sailors who watch it.

Vincent, Gabrielle. *Ernest and Celestine's Picnic*. Greenwillow, 1982 (I:3–5 R:4). Ernest and Celestine have a picnic even though it is raining.

_____. *Feel Better, Ernest!* Greenwillow, 1988 (I:3–5 R:4). Celestine helps when Ernest becomes ill.

_____. *Smile, Ernest and Celestine*. Greenwillow, 1982 (I:3–5 R:4). Celestine experiences jealousy when she finds Ernest's pictures.

Viorst, Judith. *Alexander and the Terrible, Horrible, No Good, Very Bad Day*. Illustrated by Ray Cruz. Atheneum, 1972 (I:3–8 R:6). A boy experiences a series of bad incidents.

Voake, Charlotte. *Mrs. Goose's Baby*. Little, Brown, 1989 (I:2–6). The baby is really a chicken.

Waber, Bernard. *A Lion Named Shirley Williamson*. Houghton Mifflin, 1996 (I:4–7 R:4). In a humorous story, a lion tries to leave the zoo.

Waddell, Martin. *Can't You Sleep, Little Bear?* Illustrated by Barbara Firth. Candlewick, 1992 (I:2–4 R:4). Big Bear helps Little Bear overcome fears of darkness.

_____. *Farmer Duck*. Illustrated by Helen Oxenbury. Candlewick, 1992 (I:4–7 R:3). A lazy farmer takes advantage of a duck.

_____. *Let's Go Home, Little Bear*. Illustrated by Barbara Firth. Candlewick, 1993 (I:2–4 E:4). Little Bear is afraid of sounds.

_____. *What Use Is A Moose?* Illustrated by Arthur Robins. Candlewick, 1996 (I:5–8 R:4). Humor develops when a boy tries to convince his mother that a moose could be a pet.

_____. *You and Me, Little Bear*. Illustrated by Barbara Firth. Candlewick, 1996 (I:3–6 R:4). A little bear tries to get mother bear's attention.

Ward, Lynd. *The Biggest Bear*. Houghton Mifflin, 1952 (I:5–8 R:4). A boy searches for a bear because he wants a bearskin for the outside of his barn.

Wayland, April Halprin. *To Rabbittown*. Illustrated by Robin Spowart. Scholastic, 1989 (I:3–8 R:5). A young child interacts with rabbits in a fantasy world.

Wegman, William. *William Wegman's Farm*. Hyperion, 1997 (I:all). The author illustrates the book using dog models.

Wells, Rosemary. *Bunny Cakes*. Dial, 1997 (I:2–6). Max and Ruby bake a cake for Grandma's birthday.

_____. *The Language of Doves*. Illustrated by Greg Shed. Dial, 1996 (I:5–8 R:4). A grandfather shares his memories of World War II with his granddaughter.

_____. *A Lion for Lewis*. Dial, 1982 (I:3–7 R:4). Lewis, the youngest child, discovers a way to gain his big brother's and sister's attention.

_____. *Max and Ruby's First Greek Myth: Pandora's Box*. Dial, 1993 (I:3–8 R:3). A young rabbit learns the meaning of no.

_____. *McDuff Moves In*. Illustrated by Susan Jeffers. Hyperion, 1997 (I:2–5). A homeless dog is adopted by kindhearted people.

_____. *Timothy Goes to School*. Dial, 1981 (I:4–7 R:4). Timothy Raccoon goes through many trials during his first week in school.

Wiesner, David. *June 29, 1999*. Clarion, 1992 (I:all). This is a fantasy experience with huge vegetables.

Wild, Margaret. *Let the Celebrations Begin!* Illustrated by Julie Vivas. Orchard, 1991 (I:all). People at the concentration camp prepare for liberation.

_____. *Mr. Nick's Knitting*. Illustrated by Dee Huxley. Harcourt Brace Jovanovich, 1989 (I:4–8 R:4). This book develops the theme of friendship.

Williams, Jay. *Everyone Knows What a Dragon Looks Like*. Illustrated by Mercer Mayer. Four Winds, 1976 (I:5–10). The Great Cloud Dragon saves a town.

Williams, Sherley Anne. *Working Cotton*. Illustrated by Carole Byard. Harcourt Brace Jovanovich, 1992 (I:all). A migrant farm family works in the cotton fields.

Williams, Vera. *A Chair for My Mother*. Greenwillow, 1982 (I:3–7 R:6). A young girl helps save money for a new chair.

_____. *Something Special for Me*. Greenwillow, 1983 (I:3–7 R:6). Rosa uses coins in a jar to buy a birthday present.

_____. *Stringbean's Trip to the Shining Sea*. Greenwillow, 1988 (I:all). The text is written in the form of postcards from different locations.

Wilson, Sarah. *Good Zap, Little Grog*. Illustrated by Susan Meddaugh. Candlewick, 1995 (I:3–8). Humor is created through word play.

Winthrop, Elizabeth. *Bear and Mrs. Duck*. Illustrated by Patience Brewster. Holiday House, 1988 (I:3–6 R:2). A bear at first experiences fear when he has a babysitter.

Wood, Audrey. *The Flying Dragon Room*. Illustrated by Mark Teague. Scholastic, 1996 (I:4–8 R:6). A fantasy world is created.

_____. *The Red Racer*. Simon & Schuster, 1996 (I:4–8 R:5). Nona wants a shiny new bicycle to replace her old one.

Wood, Don. *Piggies*. Harcourt Brace Jovanovich, 1991 (I:2–7). Ten piggies dance on a young child's fingers.

Yolen, Jane. *Letting Swift River Go*. Illustrated by Barbara Cooney. Little, Brown, 1992 (I:5–8 R:5). Rural life changes after the valley is flooded.

_____. *Owl Moon*. Illustrated by John Schoenherr. Philomel, 1987 (I:all). A boy and his father search for owls in the woods.

_____. *The Seeing Stick*. Illustrated by Remy Charlip and Demetra Maraslis. Crowell, 1977 (I:5–8 R:6). In ancient China, an old man helps a blind girl by carving pictures on a stick.

Yorinks, Arthur. *Hey, Al*. Illustrated by Richard Egielski. Farrar, Straus & Giroux, 1986 (I:all R:5). A janitor discovers that his home is better than he thinks.

_____. *The Miami Giant*. Illustrated by Maurice Sendak. HarperCollins, 1995 (I:all). This story is filled with satire.

Zamorano, Ana. *Let's Eat!* Illustrated by Julie Vivas. Scholastic, 1997 (I:4–7 R:4). This story set in Spain develops a happy family who are also preparing for a new baby.

Zemach, Margot. *It Could Always Be Worse: A Yiddish Folktale*. Farrar, Straus & Giroux, 1976 (I:5–9 R:2). A rabbi advises a man who lives in a crowded hut.

Zolotow, Charlotte. *William's Doll*. Illustrated by William Péne du Bois. Harper & Row, 1972 (I:4–8 R:4). William's desire for a doll results in various responses from his family.

Illustration from *Papa Gatto, An Italian Fairy Tale,* retold and illustrated by Ruth Sanderson, copyright © 1995 by Ruth Sanderson. Used by permission of Little, Brown & Company.

6 *Traditional Literature*

 Of Castle and Cottage

- Our Traditional Literary Heritage
- Types of Traditional Literature
- Values of Traditional Literature for Children
- Folktales
- Fables
- Myths
- Legends

 Involving Children in Traditional Literature

- Telling Stories
- Comparing Folktales from Different Countries
- Investigating Folktales from a Single Country
- Initiating Creative Dramatizations
- Motivating Writing Through Traditional Tales

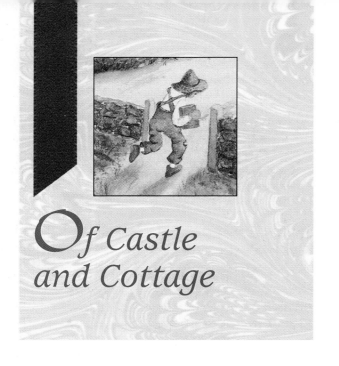

Of Castle and Cottage

$\mathcal{E}$nchanted swans who regain human form because of a sister's devotion, a brave boy who climbs into the unknown world at the top of a beanstalk, witches, warriors, supernatural animals, royal personages, and humans are brought to life in traditional literature. Such literature contains something that appeals to all interests: humorous stories, magical stories, and adventure stories. The settings of the stories are as varied as the enchanted places in the human imagination and as the geography of our world, from scorching deserts to polar icecaps. Regardless of location or subject, such tales include some of the most beloved and memorable stories of everyone's childhood. This chapter discusses the nature of our traditional literary heritage—its basic forms and themes and what it has to offer children.

OUR TRADITIONAL LITERARY HERITAGE

The quest for traditional literary heritage takes students of children's literature to times before recorded history and to all parts of the world. Tales of religious significance allowed ancient people to speculate about their beginnings. Mythical heroes and heroines from all cultures overcame supernatural adversaries to gain their rewards. Stories of real people who performed brave deeds probably gratified the rulers of ancient tribes. According to folklorist Stith Thompson (1977), similarities in the types of tales and in the narrative motifs and content of traditional stories from peoples throughout the world constitute tangible evidence that traditional tales are both universal and ancient.

Traditionally, young and old alike heard the same tales, but each social class cultivated the art of storytelling, reflecting the culture, natural environment, and social contacts of the storyteller and the audience. For example, storytellers who earned their livings in medieval European castles related great deeds of nobility. The English court heard about King Arthur, Queen Guinevere, and the Knights of the Round Table, and the French court heard stories of princely valor, such as "The Song of Roland." In ancient China, stories for the ruling classes often portrayed benevolent dragons, symbols of imperial authority.

Commoners in medieval Europe lived lives quite different from those of the nobility, and the traditional stories of the commoners differed accordingly. The stories that peasants told one another reflected the harsh, unjust, and often cruel circumstances of their existence as virtual slaves to the nobles. A common theme in their folktales is overcoming social inequality to attain a better way of life. In many tales, a poor lad outwits a nobleman, wins his daughter in marriage, and gains lifelong wealth. This theme is found in "The Flying Ship," a Russian tale; "The Golden Goose," a German tale; and "The Princess and the Glass Hill," a Norwegian tale.

Other traditional stories, such as the English "Jack the Giant Killer," tell of overcoming horrible adversaries with cunning and bravery. The peasants in these stories are not always clever. The consequences of stupidity are emphasized, for example, in the Norwegian tale "The Husband Who Has to Mind the House" and in the Russian tale "The Falcon Under the Hat." In place of the benevolent imperial dragon, the tales of early China's common people often involved cruel and evil dragons, whose power the heroines or heros overcame.

In the seventeenth century, the Puritans of England and its colonies considered folktales about giants, witches, and enchantment to be immoral for every-one. They maintained that children in particular should hear and read only what instructed them and reinforced their moral development. Other social groups in Europe and North America felt differently, however. In 1697, the Frenchman Charles Perrault published a collection of folktales called *Tales of Mother Goose,* which included "Cinderella" and "Sleeping Beauty."

Over one hundred years later, the Romantic movement in Europe generated enthusiasm for exploring folklore to discover more about the roots of European languages and traditional cultures. In Germany, the Brothers Grimm carefully collected and transcribed oral tales from the storytellers themselves. These tales have been retold or adapted by many contemporary writers. Perrault and the Brothers Grimm thus brought new respect to traditional tales and ensured their availability for all time. Their work influenced collectors in other countries, as well as writers of literature.

By the end of the nineteenth century, European and North American societies generally considered childhood a distinct, necessary, and valuable stage in the human life cycle. Improved technology created more leisure hours for the middle and upper classes and a need for literature to entertain children. Traditional literature became a valuable part of the childhood experience.

According to Betsy Hearne (1988), a significant happening in children's book publishing in the early 1900s also influenced the availability of traditional literature: numerous children's book departments were established. The editors were drawn from librarians who had knowledge of storytelling and the tales from the oral tradition. At the same time, illustrators with close cultural ties to their folklore and art immigrated from Europe. Consequently, newly illustrated folktales became an important part of the children's literature market.

Today, folk literature is considered an important part of every child's cultural heritage. It is difficult to imagine the early childhood and elementary school years of American children without "The Little Red Hen," "The Three Bears," and "Snow White and the Seven Dwarfs." The literary experiences of older children would not be complete without tales of Greek and Norse mythology.

TYPES OF TRADITIONAL LITERATURE

Traditional tales have been handed down from generation to generation by word of mouth. In contrast to a modern story, a traditional tale has no identifiable author. Instead, storytellers tell what they have received from previous tellers of tales. Folklorists and others interested in collecting and analyzing traditional literature do not always agree about how to categorize and define different types of traditional tales. This text discusses four types of traditional tales—folktales, fables, myths, and legends—drawing on definitions recommended by folklorist William Bascom (1965). Chart 6–1 summarizes and clarifies the differences among folktales, fables, myths, and legends, providing examples of each type of traditional literature.

Folktales

According to Bascom, folktales are "prose narratives which are regarded as fiction. They are not considered as dogma or history, they may or may not have happened, and they are not taken seriously" (p. 4). Because the tales are set in any time or place, they seem almost timeless and placeless. Folktales usually tell the adventures of animal or human characters. They contain common narrative motifs—such as supernatural adversaries (ogres, witches, and giants), supernatural helpers, magic and marvels, tasks and quests—and common themes—such as reward of good and punishment of evil. (Not all themes and motifs are found within one tale.) Subcategories of folktales include cumulative tales, humorous tales, beast tales, magic and wonder tales, *pourquoi* tales, and realistic tales.

Cumulative Tales. Tales that sequentially repeat actions, characters, or speeches until a climax is reached are found among all cultures. Most cumulative tales give their main characters—whether animal, vegetable, human, or inanimate object—intelligence and reasoning ability. Adults often share these stories with very young children because the structure of cumulative tales allows children to join in as each new happening occurs. A runaway baked food is a popular, culturally diverse subject for cumulative

CHART 6–1 Characteristics of folktales, fables, myths, and legends

Form and Examples	Belief	Time	Place	Attitude	Principal Characters
Folktale	*Fiction*	*Anytime*	*Anyplace*	*Secular*	*Human or Nonhuman*
1. "Snow White and Seven Dwarfs" (European)	Fiction	"Once upon a time"	"In the great forest"	Secular	Human girl and dwarfs
2. "The Crane Wife" (Asian)	Fiction	Long ago	"In a faraway mountain village"	Secular	Human man, supernatural wife
3. "Why Mosquitoes Buzz in People's Ears" (African)	Fiction	"One morning"	In a forest	Secular	Animals
Fable	*Fiction*	*Anytime*	*Anyplace*	*Secular/Allegorical*	*Animal or Human*
1. "The Hare and the Frog" (Aesop)	Fiction	"Once upon a time"	On the shore of a lake	Allegorical	Animals
2. "The Tyrant Who Became a Just Ruler" (Panchatantra—India)	Fiction	"In olden times"	In a kingdom	Allegorical	Human king
Myth	*Considered Fact*	*Remote Past*	*Other World or Earlier World*	*Sacred*	*Nonhuman*
1. "The Warrior Goddess: Athena" (European)	Considered fact	Remote past	Olympus	Deities	Greek goddess
2. "Zuñi Creation Myth" (Native American)	Considered fact	Before and during creation	Sky, earth, and lower world	Deities	Creator Awonawilona, Sun Father, Earth Mother
Legend	*Considered Fact*	*Recent Past*	*World of Today*	*Secular or Sacred*	*Human*
1. "King Arthur Tales" (European)	Considered fact	Recent past	Britain	Secular	King
2. "The White Archer" (Native American)	Considered fact	Recent past	Land of Eskimos	Secular	Indian who wanted to avenge parents' death

tales. It is found in not only the German "Gingerbread Boy" but also a Norwegian version, "The Pancake"; an English version, "Johnny Cake"; and a Russian version, "The Bun." In each of these tales, the repetition builds until the climax. Other familiar cumulative tales include the English "Henny Penny"; "The Fat Cat," a Danish tale; and "Why Mosquitoes Buzz in People's Ears," an African tale.

Humorous Tales. Folktales allow people to laugh at themselves as well as at others, an apparently universal pleasure. In tales such as the Russian "The Peasant's Pea Patch," the humor results from absurd situations or the stupidity of the characters. Human foolishness resulting from unwise decisions provides the humor and a moral in the English folktale "Mr. and Mrs. Vinegar" and in the Norwegian tale "The Husband Who Has to Mind the House."

Beast Tales. Beast tales are among the most universal folktales, being found in all cultures. For example, the coyote is a popular animal in Native American tales, while the fox and wolf are found in many European tales. The rabbit and the bear are popular characters in the folktales of African American culture in the United States. Beasts in folktales often talk and act quite like people. In some stories, such as "The Bremen Town Musicians," animal characters use their wits to frighten away robbers and claim wealth. In other tales, such as "The Three Billy Goats Gruff," animals use first their wits and then their strength to overcome an enemy. Still other animals win through industrious actions, such as those in "The Little Red Hen." Tales about talking animals may show the cleverness of one animal and the stupidity of another.

Magic and Wonder Tales. The majority of magic and wonder tales contain some element of magic. The fairy godmother transforms the kind, lovely, mistreated girl into a beautiful princess ("Cinderella"), the good peasant boy earns a cloth that provides food ("The Lad Who Went to the North Wind"), a kindhearted simpleton attains a magical ship ("The Fool of the World and the Flying Ship"), or the evil witch transforms the handsome prince into a beast ("Beauty and the Beast"). Transformations from humans to animals and animals to hu-

mans are also common in folktales. Mingshui Cai (1993) describes the relationships between humans and animals in both Eastern and Western folktales. He describes several tales in which magical animals become brides for humans. Cai categorizes these bride stories as brides from the sky, as in the Japanese story "The Crane Wife"; brides from the earth, as in the Native American folktale "The Serpent of the Sea"; and brides from the water, as in the Japanese story "Urashima Taro." Magic in wonder tales can be good or bad. When it is good, the person who benefits has usually had misfortune or is considered inferior by a parent or society. When it is bad, love and diligence usually overcome the magic—as in the German tale "The Six Swans" and the Norwegian tale "East of the Sun and West of the Moon."

Pourquoi Tales. *Pourquoi* tales—or "why" tales, in an English translation of the French word—answer a question or explain how animals, plants, or humans were created and why they have certain characteristics. For example, why does an animal or a human act in a certain way? Children enjoy *pourquoi* tales and like to make up their own stories about why animals or humans have certain characteristics.

Realistic Tales. The majority of folktales include supernatural characters, magic, or other exaggerated incidents. A few tales, however, have realistic plots and involve people who could have existed. One such tale, "Dick Whittington," tells about a boy who comes to London looking for streets paved with gold. He doesn't find golden streets, but he does find work with an honest merchant, and eventually, he wins his fortune. Some versions of this story suggest that at least parts of it are true. A Dick Whittington was lord mayor of London.

Fables

Fables are brief tales in which animal characters that talk and act like humans indicate a moral lesson or satirize human conduct. For example, in the familiar "The Hare and the Tortoise," the hare taunts the tortoise about her slow movements and boasts about his own speed. The tortoise then challenges the hare to a race. The hare starts rapidly and is soon far ahead, but he becomes tired and, in his confidence, decides to nap. Meanwhile, the tortoise, keeping at her slow and steady pace, plods across the finish line. When the hare awakens, he discovers that the tortoise has reached the goal. The moral of this fable is that perseverance and determination may compensate for lack of other attributes.

Myths

According to Bascom, myths are

prose narratives which, in the society in which they are told, are considered to be truthful accounts of what happened in the remote past. They are accepted on faith; they are taught to be believed; and they can be cited as authority in answer to ignorance, doubt, or disbelief. Myths are the embodiment of dogma; they are usually sacred; and they are often associated with theology and ritual. (p. 4)

Myths account for the origin of the world and humans; for everyday natural phenomena, such as thunder and lightning; and for human emotions and experiences, such as love and death. The main characters in myths may be animals, deities, or humans. The actions take place in an earlier world or another world, such as the underworld or the sky. Many ancient Greek myths, for example, explain the creation of the world, the creation of the gods and goddesses who ruled from Mount Olympus, and the reasons for natural phenomena. The myth about Demeter and Persephone, for example, explains seasonal changes.

Legends

Legends, Bascom says, are

prose narratives which, like myths, are regarded as true by the narrator and his audience, but they are set in a period considered less remote, when the world was much as it is today. Legends are more often secular than sacred, and their principal characters are human. (p. 4)

Many legends embroider the historical facts of human wars and migrations, brave deeds, and royalty. Legends from the British Isles tell about Robin Hood, the protector of the poor in the Middle Ages, who may have been an actual person. Legends from France tell about the miraculous visions of Joan of Arc, who led French armies into battle against the English. Legends from Africa describe how the prophet Amakosa saved the Juba people from extinction.

 ## VALUES OF TRADITIONAL LITERATURE FOR CHILDREN

Traditional literature helps children understand the world and identify with universal human struggles. It also provides pleasure.

Understanding the World

Traditional tales help children improve their understanding of the world. Storyteller Diane Wolkstein (1992) declares, "Every story is rooted in a culture, and the world of culture is limitless" (p. 704). (See the Evaluation Criteria on this page.) Ruth Kearney Carlson (1972) also emphasizes that a study of folklore increases world understanding. She outlines eight respects in which world understanding is increased. First, according to Carlson, traditional tales help children better understand the nonscientific cultural traditions of early humanity. Greek and Roman myths, for example, tell how early Europeans explained the mysteries of creation, human nature, and natural phenomena through the powers of gods, giants, and demons. These myths were taken so seriously that religions grew up around them. In addition to providing lively entertainment, traditional tales fill readers with admiration for the people who developed such answers for unanswerable questions.

Second, traditional tales show the interrelatedness of various types of stories and narrative motifs. For example, the tale of a girl who loses her mother, acquires a jealous or evil stepmother, is mistreated (but remains gentle and kind), and finally receives rewards for her goodness is found in folk literature everywhere. Scholars have identified more than one thousand versions of the Cinderella tale worldwide. While these stories have different characters, settings, and types of enchantment, their underlying themes are the same.

Third, children learn about cultural diffusion as they observe how different versions of a tale are dispersed. Anyone who has tried to categorize traditional literature according to country of origin is amazed at the similarity found among tales from different countries. Classifying the geographic location of a tale can be difficult if the author retelling it does not specify the source. Betsy Hearne (1993a) considers the identification of cultural sources in folktales so important that she makes the following proposals: "that the producers of picture-book folktales provide source notes that set these stories in their cultural context; that those of us who select these materials for children judge them, at least in part, on how well their authors and publishers meet this responsibility" (p. 22). Without cultural knowledge, readers cannot speculate about cultural diffusion. The similarities among tales indicate movement of people through migration and conquests. They also emphasize that humans throughout the world have had similar needs and problems. Some folktales from different countries are almost identical. For example, the German tale "The Table, the Donkey, and the Stick" is very similar to both the Norwegian tale "The Lad Who Went to the North Wind" and the English folktale "The Donkey, the Table, and the Stick." Also, almost every country has its traditional trickster, such as the fox in Palestine and the mouse-deer in Malaysia; its stupid, easily fooled creature, such as the bear in Lapland and the giraffe in West Africa; and its benevolent, good-natured animal, such as the kangaroo in Australia. The tales are very

similar, although the animals and the settings are characteristic of the countries in which they are told.

Fourth, traditional tales help children develop an appreciation for the culture and art of different countries. If the author who retells a tale retains authentic cultural detail and the illustrator carefully researches the culture before picturing its natural environment and customs, children gain appreciation for the social realities and cultural contributions of a country. Nancy Ekholm Burkert's illustrations for Randall Jarrell's version of the Grimms' *Snow White and Seven Dwarfs* reflect research into German history and culture. Paul O. Zelinsky studied seventeenth-century Dutch paintings before illustrating Rika Lesser's version of *Hansel and Gretel*. Suekichi Akaba used a traditional Japanese painting technique when illustrating Sumiko Yagawa's retelling of *The Crane Wife*.

Fifth, traditional tales provide factual information about different countries—information about geography, government, family patterns, food, celebrations, likes, and dislikes. For example, far from being an endangered species, wolves were numerous in medieval Europe and greatly feared by a largely rural population—as the German tale "Little Red Riding Hood" and the Hungarian tale "One Little Pig and Ten Wolves" demonstrate. In *Where the Buffaloes Begin,* Olaf Baker shows the economic and spiritual importance of the buffaloes to the traditional Native Americans of the Great Plains. Contrasts in weather and geography are evident when children compare the warm lands of Arabian folktales with the icy settings of Norse mythology.

Sixth, traditional tales familiarize children with the many languages and dialects of cultures around the world. The names in traditional tales from different countries fascinate children, who enjoy hearing stories about Russian Maria Morevna, the beautiful tsarevna; Vietnamese Tam, the girl who lived in the Land of Small Dragon; and Mazel and Shlimazel, who have a wager in the Yiddish folktale. Many tales include language or dialects characteristic of a country or time period. Howard Pyle's *The Story of King Arthur and His Knights* contains dialogue suggesting early English: "Sir Knight, I demand of thee why thou didst smite that shield. Now let me tell thee, because of thy boldness, I shall take away from thee thine own shield, and shall hang it upon yonder appletree, where thou beholdest all those other shields to be hanging" (p. 44). Reading this prose may be difficult even for older elementary children, but children enjoy hearing it when an adult reads it to them.

Seventh, traditional tales provide marvelous stimulation for creative drama, writing, and other forms of artistic expression. When children listen to traditional tales and then interact with their own imaginations, they gain respect for the people who created such tales.

Finally, traditional tales encourage children to realize that people from all over the world have inherent goodness, mercy, courage, and industry. In a Chinese tale, a loving brother rescues his sister from a dragon; in a German tale, a sister suffers six years of ordeals in order to bring her brothers back to human form. A Jewish folk character works hard to cultivate fig trees that may benefit his descendants but not himself, while the Norse Beowulf's strength of character defeats evil monsters.

Identifying with Universal Human Struggles

In *The Uses of Enchantment: The Meaning and Importance of Fairy Tales,* Bruno Bettelheim (1976) provides strong rationales for using traditional tales with children. In his psychoanalytic approach to traditional tales, Bettelheim claims that nothing is so enriching as traditional literature. To reinforce this claim, he argues that traditional tales allow children to learn about human progress and possible solutions to problems. Because tales state problems briefly, children can understand them. In addition, traditional tales subtly convey the advantages of moral behavior. Children learn that struggling against difficulties is unavoidable, but they can emerge victorious if they directly confront hardships.

Traditional tales present characters who are both good and bad. According to Bettelheim, children gain the conviction that crime does not pay. The simple, straightforward characters in traditional tales allow children to identify with the good and to reject the bad. Children empathize with honorable characters and their struggles, learning that while they may experience difficulty or rejection, they, too, will be given help and guidance when needed. Author and folklorist Gail E. Haley (1986) emphasizes the importance of reading about heroes in folklore because

heroes of the past teach us solutions for coping with today and tomorrow. They were synthesized out of the dreams and wishes of the people who created and consumed them. Those that survive are those whose faces, forms, and stature have fulfilled the nature and needs of succeeding generations. We still need heroes. (p. 118)

Joyce Thomas (1987) also emphatically supports the use of traditional tales with children. She states, "To deny fairy tales to children or to allow only those with 'acceptable' morals and innocuous fantasy is to retard their psychological and imaginative growth and expression" (p. 111).

Pleasure

Traditional literature is extremely popular with children. In particular, folktales—with their fast-paced, dramatic plots and easily identifiable good and bad characters—are among the types of literature most appealing to young audiences. Although folktales may appeal primarily to young children, children of various ages and interests find them enjoyable. Animal tales, such as "The Three Little Pigs," "The Little Red Hen," and "The Three Bears," have been illustrated in picture-book format for young children, while fairy tales, such as "Beauty and the Beast," are of interest to upper-elementary school children.

F. André Favat (1977) reviewed the relevant research and reached the following conclusions about interest in folktales among children of different ages:

1. Children between the ages of five and ten—or roughly from kindergarten through the fifth grade—are highly interested in folktales, whether they select books or are presented with books and asked for their opinions.
2. This interest follows a curve of reading preference—that is, children's interest in folktales emerges at a prereading age and gradually rises to a peak between the approximate ages of six and eight. It then gradually declines.
3. Concurrent with the decline in interest in folktales emerges an interest in realistic stories.

Favat maintains that the characteristics of folktales correspond with the characteristics that Jean Piaget ascribed to children. First, children believe that objects, actions, thoughts, and words can exercise magical influence over events in their own lives. Folktales are filled with such occurrences, as spells turn humans into animals, or vice versa, and humble pumpkins become gilded coaches.

One of the issues we face as we read and evaluate folklore from around the world is whose cultural values and belief systems should the tales reflect. Should the stories be rewritten to reflect current American beliefs? Or should the tales reflect their original cultures in both text and illustrations? Comments in articles by Nina Jaffe[1] and David Sacks[2] provide interesting points for discussion.

Jaffe evaluates the work of Harold Courlander as he collected and retold tales that preserved the values of the cultures. Jaffe highlights Courlander's difficulties in his desire to retain authenticity. She quotes his difficulties with editors who frequently wanted him to change style or content. Courlander states, "In one collection, there was a Hottentot tale. It was about how people die and don't live again. That was the theme of it—how that came about. It was a kind of how it began story. An editor I was dealing with said, 'A lot of people don't be-lieve that, they believe you do live again.' And I have to be adamant about it and say, 'This is the story!' They didn't think it was suitable for children. Well too bad, they have to learn other people don't think the same way as we do—that's what it's all about' " (p. 133). Jaffe believes that retellers can have creative integrity "as long as values of respect, sensitivity, and self-knowledge are present in the interpretation, research, and retelling" (p. 133).

Sacks provides an equally strong argument for using myths and other literature reflecting ancient Greece and Rome. He believes in retaining the authenticity even in highly illustrated books. He states, "In a collection of myths for elementary-aged audiences, it could mean using illustrations that convey immortal grandeur, not a trivializing goofiness" (p. 38). He then presents an annotated list of myths, history, and historical fiction that he recommends.

As you consider Jaffe and Courlander's concerns for cultural authenticity in the tales and Sacks's concern for cultural authenticity in the illustrations, ask yourself: What do you believe is the value in reading tales from another culture? Should the tales reflect the values and beliefs of the original culture or should they be rewritten to reflect the values and beliefs of contemporary American audiences? What happens to our understandings of earlier and frequently different cultures if the stories are changed? How does authenticity in illustrations add to or detract from folktales?

[1]Jaffe, Nina. "Reflections on the Work of Harold Courlander." *School Library Journal* 42 (September 1996): 132–133.

[2]Sacks, David. "Breathing New Life Into Ancient Greece and Rome." *School Library Journal* 42 (November 1996): 38–39.

Second, children believe that inanimate objects and animals have consciousness much like that of humans. In folktales, the objects and animals that speak or act like people are consistent with children's beliefs.

Third, young children believe in punishment for wrongdoing and reward for good behavior. Folktales satisfy children's sense of justice. The good Goose Girl, for example, is rewarded by marrying the prince, and her deceitful maid is punished harshly.

Fourth, the relationship between heroes and heroines and their environments is much the same as the relationship between children and their own environments. Children are the center of their universes, while heroes and heroines are the centers of their folktale worlds. For example, when Sleeping Beauty sleeps for a hundred years, so does the whole castle.

 FOLKTALES

Many folktales have similar characteristics and motifs. The folktales discussed in this section have many similar characteristics. They also reflect cultural differences. Chart 6–2 summarizes some of these similarities and differences by comparing tales from several cultures. This section looks at British, French, German, Norwegian, Russian, Jewish, Asian, African, and North American tales. You may analyze other tales from each culture to identify common characteristics.

Characteristics

Because folktales differ from other types of literature, they have characteristics related to plot,

CHART 6–2 Comparisons of folktales from different cultures

Culture and Examples	Protagonist—Main Character	Portrayal of Hero or Heroine	Portrayal of Other Characters	Setting
British "Jack the Giant Killer"	Simple peasant lad	The lad is brave and is clever enough to outwit the villain.	The giants are evil. The king is weak.	Mountain cave
French "Sleeping Beauty"	Adolescent princess (about fifteen)	The prince is "pursued by love and honor" and is valiant.	The fairy is wicked. The father cannot protect his daughter.	Castle with a series of rooms similar to Versailles
German "Hansel and Gretel"	Boy and girl (a woodcutter's children)	Hansel is caring, but Gretel is clever enough to outwit the witch.	The stepmother is uncaring. The father is weak. The witch is wicked.	Forest
Norwegian "The Lad Who Went to the North Wind"	Simple peasant lad	The lad is simple but honest.	The north wind is powerful. The mother is scolding. The innkeeper is dishonest and greedy.	Rural Far North
Russian "The Fool of the World and the Flying Ship"	Simple, young peasant	The young peasant is foolish but kindhearted.	The czar is dishonorable. The four companions have great powers.	Rural countryside and the czar's palace
Jewish "Mazel and Schlimazel"	Poor peasant	The bungler does poorly until good luck intercedes.	The spirit of good luck is happy and attractive. The spirit of bad luck is slumped and angry.	King's court and the countryside
Chinese "The Golden Sheng"	Poor adolescent girl	The boy grows up very rapidly.	The girl is helpless. The dragon is evil and cruel.	Rural
African "How Spider Got a Thin Waist"	Tricky and greedy spider	The greedy spider does not work; instead, he plays in the sun.	The villagers are hard-working.	Forest and village
Native American "The Fire Bringer"	Young Paiute Indian boy	The boy is concerned about his people.	The coyote is intelligent. The runners are swift.	Mesa and mountain
British "Jack the Giant Killer"	Common people	The hero is sent to rid the kingdom of giants.	Intelligence and bravery	Happy ending. The hero is rewarded with knighthood when the villains are slain.

Tale	Characters	Plot	Values	Ending
French "Sleeping Beauty"	Nobility	A threatened girl is rescued by a prince.	Beauty, wit, grace, dancing, and singing	Happy ending. The prince and princess are married.
German "Hansel and Gretel"	Common people	Abandoned children outwit a wicked witch.	Caring and cleverness	Happy ending. The children are rewarded with jewels after the witch is burned to death.
Norwegian "The Lad Who Went to the North Wind"	Common people	The hero sets out to retrieve a lost object.	Honesty and kindness	Happy ending. The boy beats the innkeeper and is rewarded with magical objects.
Russian "The Fool of the World and the Flying Ship"	Common people	A simple boy sets out on a quest. He is aided by a magical ship and companions.	Kindness and honesty	Happy ending. The peasant marries royalty.
Jewish "Mazel and Schlimazel"	Common people	A simple boy is accompanied by good luck and then bad luck on a series of quests.	Diligence, honesty, sincerity, and helpfulness	Happy ending. The hero marries the princess and eventually becomes the wisest of prince consorts.
Chinese "The Golden Sheng"	Common people	A young boy goes on a quest to save his sister from a dragon.	Helpfulness, diligence, and loyalty	Happy ending. After the dragon whirls himself to death, the brother and sister return to their mother.
African "How Spider Got a Thin Waist"	Common people	The spider tries to get food without working.	Industriousness	Unhappy ending. The greedy spider gets a thin waist.
Native American "The Fire Bringer"	Common people	A boy and a coyote set out to get fire for the Paiutes.	Intelligence, swiftness, and bravery	Happy ending. The boy and the coyote are honored.

characterization, setting, theme, and style that may differ from other types of children's stories.

Plot.   Conflict and action abound in folktales. The nature of the oral tradition made it imperative that listeners be brought quickly into the action. Consequently, even in written versions, folktales immerse readers into the major conflict within the first few sentences. For example, the conflict in Paul Galdone's *The Little Red Hen* is between laziness and industriousness. The first sentence introduces the animals who live together in a little house. The second sentence introduces the lazy cat, dog, and mouse. The third sentence introduces the industrious hen and the conflict. The remainder of the story develops the conflict between the lazy animals and the industrious fowl. The conflict is resolved when the hen eats her own baking and doesn't share it with her lazy friends.

Conflict between characters representing good and characters representing evil is typical of folktales. Even though the odds are uneven, the hero overcomes the giant in "Jack the Giant Killer," the girl and boy outsmart the witch in "Hansel and Gretel," the intelligent animal outwits the ogre in "Puss in Boots," and a brother saves his sister from a dragon in "The Golden Sheng."

Actions that recur in folktales have been the focus of several researchers. Vladimir Propp (1968) analyzed one hundred Russian folktales and identified thirty-one recurring actions that account for the uniformity and repetitiveness of folktales. While not all tales included all actions, actions occurred in the same sequence in most tales. More importantly, Propp discovered that similar patterns were apparent in non-Russian tales. Propp concluded that consistency of action in folktales does not result from the country of origin. Instead, consistency results from the fact that tales remain true to the folk tradition.

F. André Favat (1977) summarized Propp's findings and analyzed French and German tales according to their actions. The following list of recurring sequential actions that may be found in various combinations is adapted from Favat. In some tales, females are the primary actors, but most folktales, reflecting the values and social realities of their times and places of origin, assign actions primarily to male characters.

1. One family member leaves home.
2. The hero or heroine is forbidden to do some action.
3. The hero or heroine violates a forbidden order.
4. The villain surveys the situation.
5. The villain receives information about the victim.
6. The villain attempts to trick or deceive the victim in order to possess the victim or the victim's belongings.
7. The victim submits to deception and unwittingly helps the enemy.
8. The villain causes harm or injury to a member of a family.
9. One family member either lacks something or desires to have something.
10. A misfortune or lack is made known; the hero or heroine is approached with a request or command; and he or she is allowed to go or is sent on a mission.
11. The seeker agrees to, or decides upon, a counteraction.
12. The hero or heroine leaves home.
13. The hero or heroine is tested, interrogated, or attacked, which prepares the way for him or her to receive a magical agent or a helper.
14. The hero or heroine reacts to the actions of the future donor.
15. The hero or heroine acquires a magical agent.
16. The hero or heroine is transferred, delivered, or led to the whereabouts of an object.
17. The hero or heroine and the villain join in direct combat.
18. The hero or heroine is marked.
19. The villain is defeated.
20. The initial misfortune or lack is eliminated.
21. The hero or heroine returns.
22. The hero or heroine is pursued.
23. The hero or heroine is rescued from pursuit.
24. The hero or heroine, unrecognized, arrives home or in another country.
25. A false hero or heroine presents unfounded claims.
26. A difficult task is proposed to the hero or heroine.
27. The task is resolved.
28. The hero or heroine is recognized.
29. The false hero/heroine or the villain is exposed.
30. The hero or heroine is given a new appearance.

31. The villain is punished.
32. The hero or heroine is married and ascends to the throne.

Many of the folktales discussed in this chapter contain various combinations of these actions. All folktales have similar endings, just as they have similar beginnings and plot development, and most tales end with some version of "and they lived happily ever after."

Characterization. Folktale characters are less completely developed than are characters in other types of stories. Oral storytellers lacked the time to develop fully rounded characters. Thus, characters in folktales are essentially symbolic and flat—that is, they have a limited range of personal characteristics and do not change in the course of the story. A witch is always wicked, whether she is the builder of gingerbread houses in the German tale "Hansel and Gretel" or the fearsome Baba Yaga in the Russian "Maria Morevna." Other unchangeably evil characters include giants, ogres, trolls, and stepmothers.

Characters easily typed as bad are accompanied by those who are always good. The young heroine is fair, kind, and loving. The youngest son is honorable, kind, and unselfish even if he is considered foolish. Isaac Bashevis Singer's *Mazel and Shlimazel, or the Milk of the Lioness* demonstrates characteristic differences between good and bad characters: Mazel, the spirit of good luck, is young, tall, and slim, with pink cheeks and a jaunty stride; Shlimazel, the spirit of bad luck, is old, pale-faced, and angry-eyed, with a crooked red nose, a beard as gray as a spider's web, and a slumping stride.

Folktales usually establish the main characters' natures early on, as Charles Perrault does in the first paragraph of "Cinderella: or The Little Glass Slipper":

There was once upon a time, a gentleman who married for his second wife the proudest and most haughty woman that ever was known. She had been a widow, and had by her former husband two daughters of her own humor, who were exactly like her in all things. He had also by a former wife a young daughter, but of an unparalleled goodness and sweetness of temper, which she took from her mother, who was the best creature in the world. (*Histories or Tales of Past Times,* p. 73)

The characteristics of two female characters in an Italian folktale reveal honored and disrespected human characteristics in folktales. The actions of Sophia, who is beautiful, greedy, and lazy, and Beatrice, who is plainer but generous, loving, and hard working, provide the plot and develop the theme in Ruth Sanderson's *Papa Gatto: An Italian Fairy Tale.* The two girls either prove their worthlessness or their worth when they each take care of Papa Gatto's family of kittens. Even though Sophia tries to trick both her stepsister and a handsome prince, it is Beatrice's kind and generous nature that wins the prince, because "he knew he would do all in his power to win the one whose beauty shone from within" (unnumbered). Both Beatrice's lazy stepsister and stepmother earn their just rewards: "As for Sophia and the widow, they were left behind in the cottage, with no one to cook and clean and tend the garden but themselves" (unnumbered).

Children easily identify the good and bad characters in folktales. This easy identification of heroes and heroines, as well as lively action, may account for the popularity of folktales with young children.

Setting. Setting in literature includes both time and place. The time in folktales is always the far-distant past, usually introduced by some version of "once upon a time." The first line of a folktale usually places listeners into a time when anything might happen. A Russian tale, "The Firebird," begins "Long ago, in a distant kingdom, in a distant land, lived Tsar Vyslar Andronovich." Native American folktales may begin with some version of "When all was new, and the gods dwelt in the ancient places, long, long before the time of our ancients." A French tale is placed "on a day of days in the time of our fathers," while a German tale begins "In the olden days when wishing still helped one." These introductions inform listeners that enchantment and overcoming obstacles are possible in the tales about to unfold.

The symbolic settings found in many folktales are not carefully described because there is no need for description. One knows immediately that magic can happen in the great forest of the Grimms' "Snow White and the Seven Dwarfs" or in the great castle of Madame de Beaumont's version of "Beauty and the Beast." The title of a Romanian tale, "The Land Where Time Stood Still," establishes a setting where the imagination will accept and expect unusual occurrences.

The introduction that places the folktale in the far-distant past may also briefly sketch the location. A Chinese tale, "The Cinnamon Tree in the Moon," suggests a nature setting, "where not even a soft breeze stirs the heavens and one can see the shadows in the moon." After introducing such settings, folktales immediately identify the characters and develop the conflict.

Theme. Folktales contain universal truths and reflect the values of the times and societies in which they originated, many of which are still honored today. The characters, their actions, and their rewards develop themes related to moral and material achievement. Good overcomes evil; justice triumphs; unselfish love conquers; intelligence wins out over physical strength; kindness, diligence, and hard work bring rewards. The tales also show what happens to those who do not meet the traditional standards. The jealous queen is punished, the wicked stepsisters are blinded by birds, the foolish king loses part of his fortune or his daughter, and the greedy man loses the source of his success or his well-being.

The universality of these themes suggests that people everywhere have responded to similar ideals and beliefs. Consider, for example, the universality of the theme that intelligence is superior to physical strength. The hero in the English "Jack the Giant Killer" outwits the much larger and less intelligent giant. In the African tale "A Story, a Story," Spider outwits a series of animals and wins his wager with the being who controls stories. The hero in the Jewish "The Fable of the Fig Tree" is rewarded because he considers the long-range consequences of his actions. The heroine in the Chinese "The Clever Wife" uses her wits to bring the family power.

In contrast, another universal theme is that foolishness causes the loss of possessions. In an English tale, "Mr. and Mrs. Vinegar" lose their possessions because of foolish actions. In a German tale, "The Fisherman and His Wife," the couple returns to a humble position because of foolish choices and greed. The Russian characters in "The Falcon Under the Hat" lose their possessions because of foolish actions. These themes are found in traditional literature around the world.

Style. Charles Perrault, the famed collector of French fairy tales in the seventeenth century, believed "that the best stories are those that imitate best the style and the simplicity of children's verses" (Hearn, 1977, p. viii). Such style permits few distracting details or unnecessary descriptions. Simplicity is especially apparent in the thoughts and dialogues of characters in folktales: They think and talk like people. For example, the dialogue in the Grimms' "The Golden Goose" sounds as if the listener were overhearing a conversation. The little old gray man welcomes the first son with "Good morning. Do give me a piece of that cake you have got in your pocket, and let me have a draught of your wine—I am so hungry and thirsty."

The clever, selfish son immediately answers, "If I give you my cake and wine I shall have none left for myself; you just go your own way." Disaster rapidly follows this exchange.

When Dullhead, the youngest, simplest son, begs to go into the woods, his father's response reflects his opinion of his son's ability: "Both your brothers have injured themselves. You had better leave it alone; you know nothing about it." Dullhead begs hard, and his father replies, "Very well, then—go. Perhaps when you have hurt yourself, you may learn to know better." This German folktale is filled with rapid exchanges as Dullhead is rewarded with the golden goose and moves humorously on toward his destiny with the king and the beautiful princess.

The language of folktales is often enriched with simple rhymes and verses. In "Jack and the Beanstalk," the giant chants:

> Fee, fi-fo-fum,
> I smell the blood of an Englishman,
> Be he alive, or be he dead,
> I'll have his bones to grind my bread.

The enchanted frog from the Grimms' "The Frog King" approaches the door of the princess with these words:

> Princess! Youngest princess!
> Open the door for me!
> Dost thou not know what thou saidst to me
> Yesterday by the cool waters of the fountain?
> Princess, youngest princess!
> Open the door for me!

Likewise, the witch asks Hansel and Gretel:

> Nibble, nibble, gnaw,
> Who is nibbling at my little house?

As the story nears its end, another rhyme asks the duck for help:

> Little duck, little duck, dost thou see
> Hansel and Gretel are waiting for thee?
> There's never a plank or bridge in sight,
> Take us across on thy back so white.

The simple style, easily identifiable characters, and rapid plot development make folktales appropriate for sharing orally with children.

Motifs

Kind or cruel supernatural beings, magical transformations of reality, and enchanted young people who must wait for true love to break spells that confine them are elements that take folktales out of the ordinary and encourage people to remember and repeat the tales. Folklorists have identified hundreds of such elements, or motifs, found in folktales.

Although a folktale may be remembered for one dramatic story element, most tales have multiple elements. Consider the following motifs in "Jack and the Beanstalk": (1) the hero makes a foolish bargain, (2) the hero acquires a magical object, (3) a plant has extraordinary powers, (4) the ogre repeats "fee-fi-fo-fum," (5) the ogre's wife hides the hero, (6) the hero steals a magical object from the ogre, (7) the magical object possesses the power of speech, and (8) the hero summons the ogre.

Researchers use motifs to analyze and identify the similarities in tales from various cultures. Some motifs are practically universal, suggesting similar thought processes in people living in different parts of the world. Other motifs help trace diffusion from one culture to another or identify a common source. Chart 6–3 summarizes the discussion of motifs and demonstrates that folktales from many parts of the world contain the same motifs. The search for common motifs is enlightening and rewarding for children as well as adults. Some of the most common of the many motifs in folktales are supernatural beings; extraordinary animals; and magical objects, powers, and transformations.

Supernatural Adversaries and Helpers.
Supernatural beings in folktales are usually either adversaries or helpers. The wicked supernatural beings, such as ogres and witches, may find heroines or heroes, entice them into their cottages or castles, and make preparations to feast upon them. The main character may deliberately seek out the adversary, as in the Chinese tale "Li Chi Slays the Serpent," or the encounter with the evil being may be the result of an unlucky chance meeting, as in "Hansel and Gretel." Luckily, the intended victims usually outwit the adversaries. In addition to being evil, supernatural adversaries are usually stupid; consequently, they are overcome by characters who use wit and trickery.

Supernatural helpers support many folklore heroes and heroines in their quests. Seven dwarfs help Snow White in her battle against her evil stepmother. A supernatural old man causes hardships to the selfish older brothers and rewards the generous younger brother in the Russian tale "The Fool of the World and the Flying Ship." The same motif is found in tales from western Asia, eastern Europe, and India.

Extraordinary Animals.
Whether cunning or stupid, deceitful or upstanding, extraordinary animals are popular characters in the folktales of all cultures. In the English and German versions of "Little Red Riding Hood," the wolf plays the role of ogre, deceives a child, and is eliminated. In Japanese folklore, the fox has a malicious nature. It can assume human shape, and it has the power to bewitch humans. Tricky foxes and coyotes are important characters in African American and Native American folktales as well.

Some extraordinary animals are loyal companions and helpers to deserving human characters. The cat in the French "Puss in Boots" outwits an ogre and provides riches for his human master. The German version of "Cinderella" collected by the Brothers Grimm contains no fairy godmother; instead, white doves and other birds help Cinderella complete the impossible tasks that her wicked stepmother requires. The variety of extraordinary animals is apparent in texts such as Margaret Mayo's *Mythical Birds & Beasts from Many Lands*. Mayo includes folktales and mythology as well as notes on the stories.

Magical Objects, Powers, and Transformations.
The possession of a magical object or power is crucial in many folktales. When all seems lost, the hero may don the cloak of invisibility and follow "The Twelve Dancing Princesses" to solve a mystery and win his fortune, or the heroine's loving tears may fall into her true love's eyes and save him from blindness, as in "Rapunzel."

CHART 6-3   Common motifs in folktales from different cultures

Common Motif	Culture	Folktale
Supernatural Adversaries		
Ogre	England	"Jack the Giant Killer"
Ogress	Italy	"Petrosinella"
Troll	Norway	"Three Billy Goats Gruff"
Giant	Germany	"The Valiant Little Tailor"
Dragon	China	"The Golden Sheng"
Witch	Africa	"Marandenboni"
Supernatural Helpers		
Fairies	France and Germany	"The Sleeping Beauty"
Fairy godmother	Vietnam	"The Land of Small Dragon"
Jinni	Arabia	"The Woman of the Well"
Cat (fairy in disguise)	Italy	"The Cunning Cat"
Deceitful or Ferocious Beasts		
Wolf	Germany	"The Wolf and the Seven Little Kids"
Wolf	France	"Little Red Riding Hood"
Wolf	England	"The Three Little Pigs"
Wild hog, unicorn, and lion	United States	"Jack and the Varmints"
Magical Objects		
Cloak of invisibility	Germany	"The Twelve Dancing Princesses"
Magical cloth	Norway	"The Lad Who Went to the North Wind"
Magical lamp	Arabia	"Aladdin and the Magic Lamp"
Magical mill	Norway	"Why the Sea Is Salt"
Magical Powers		
Granted wishes	Germany	"The Fisherman and His Wife"
Wish for a child	Russia	"The Snow Maiden"
Humans with extraordinary powers	Mexico	"The Riddle of the Drum"
Humans with extraordinary powers	Russia	"The Fool of the World and the Flying Ship"
Magical Transformations		
Prince to bear	Norway	"East of the Sun and West of the Moon"
Prince to beast	France	"Beauty and the Beast"
Bird to human	Japan	"The Crane Wife"
Human to animal	United States (Native American)	"The Ring in the Prairie"

Folktale characters often obtain magical objects in extraordinary manners, lose them or have them stolen, and eventually recover them. This sequence occurs in the Norwegian "The Lad Who Went to the North Wind," in which a boy goes to the North Wind demanding the return of his meal, is given a magical object, loses it to a dishonest innkeeper, and must retrieve it. The dishonest innkeeper is eventually punished. In folktales, stealing a magical object often results in problems for the thief.

Magical spells and transformations are also common in folktales around the world. The spell of a fairy godmother turns a pumpkin into a golden coach, and the spell of a witch puts a princess to sleep for a hundred years. One of the most common transformation motifs is the transformation of a prince into an animal ("The Frog Prince") or a beast-like monster ("Beauty and the Beast"). A gentle, unselfish youngest daughter usually breaks the enchantment when she falls in love with the animal or beast. In a Basque tale, the beast is a huge serpent; a Magyar Hungarian tale has the prince transformed into a pig; and a Lithuanian tale tells of a prince who becomes a white wolf. "The Crane Wife," a Japanese folktale, contains another example of the transformation from animal to human, as a poor farmer gains a wife when a wounded crane he cares for transforms herself into a lovely woman.

Many Native American tales include humans who are transformed into animals. "The Ring in the Prairie," a Shawnee Indian tale, includes transformations of humans and sky dwellers: A human hunter transforms himself into a mouse to capture a girl who descends from the sky, and the sky dwellers secure part of an animal and are transformed into that specific animal. Many of the Native American transformation stories suggest close relationships between humans and animals.

Folktales from the British Isles

British folktales about ogres, giants, and clever humans were among the first stories published as inexpensive chapbooks in the 1500s. Joseph Jacobs collected the tales, and in 1890, he published over eighty of them as *English Fairy Tales*. In 1892, Jacobs published a collection of Celtic fairy tales. These books, in reissue or modern editions, are still available today. The number of possible folktales from the British Isles is further emphasized when we read Katharine Briggs's *Dictionary of British Folk-Tales* (1970–1971), which was originally published in four volumes and 2,558 pages. The fast plots and unpromising heroes of British tales are popular with children. For example, the various "Jack tales"—including "Jack the Giant Killer" and "Jack and the Beanstalk"—develop plots around villainous ogres or giants who terrorize a kingdom and the heroes who overcome their adversaries with trickery and cleverness rather than magical powers.

Steven Kellogg retells "Jack and the Beanstalk," which was first collected by Jacobs. Kellogg's *Jack and the Beanstalk* retains the familiar language: "Fee-fi-fo-fum! I smell the blood of an Englishman. Be he alive or be he dead, I'll grind his bones to make my bread" (p. 14, unnumbered). Kellogg's illustrations

reinforce the gentle mood of the cow, Milky-White, and the contrasting villainous mood of the ogre, whose food preferences include young boys. The story clearly defines good and bad characters and shows that a person with physical strength does not always succeed.

Other villains in British folktales play adversarial roles similar to those of giants and ogres. For example, "Three Little Pigs" must outwit a wolf, and a young girl is frightened by "The Three Bears." Glen Rounds's *Three Little Pigs and the Big Bad Wolf* includes a huffing, puffing wolf who tries unsuccessfully to lure the wittier third pig out of his home. Steven Kellogg's *The Three Little Pigs* includes a strong and industrious mother and a wolf that is not as bad as that portrayed in usual versions. In *What's in Fox's Sack? An Old English Tale*, retold and illustrated by Paul Galdone, the villain is a sly fox who manages to get a boy into his sack. A clever woman outsmarts the fox by placing a large bulldog inside the sack. The mother goat in "Grey Goat," retold in Alan Garner's *A Bag of Moonshine*, saves her three kids by killing the fox. In *Whuppity Stoorie: A Scottish Folktale*, retold by Carolyn White, the heroine must outwit a fairy.

In addition to clearly defined good and bad characters, repetitive language in many British folktales appeals to storytellers and listeners. In "The Three Little Pigs," the wolf threatens, "I'll huff and I'll puff and I'll blow your house in," and the pig replies, "Not by the hair on my chinny chin chin." "Goldilocks and the Three Bears" repeats chairs, bowls of porridge, and beds, and the three bears' questions: Who has been sitting in my chair? Who has been eating my porridge? Who has been sleeping in my bed? Several versions of this folktale appeal to young children. Lorinda Bryan Cauley's *Goldilocks and the Three Bears* has compelling illustrations. Paul Galdone's *The Three Bears*, which may be used to develop size concepts, has pictures that differentiate the sizes of bears, bowls, beds, and chairs. James Marshall's *Goldilocks and the Three Bears* frolic in humorous illustrations. Jan Brett's *Goldilocks and the Three Bears* includes large, detailed illustrations on pages bordered with objects and characters from the story.

Arnica Esterl's *The Fine Round Cake* is adapted from Jacob's 1889 story called "Johnny-Cake." Esterl retains the cumulative nature of the story and many of the original characters, except that the two ditch

diggers who chase the cake are now two girls who are gathering berries. The characters are clearly peasants, and the cake demonstrates foolish actions and is eaten by the witty fox.

British folk literature is filled with tales that stress foolishness, making a point about human foibles. Vivian French's retelling of *Lazy Jack* provides a humorous version of this tale about a boy who is so lazy that "He got out of bed in the afternoon and he yawned and he stretched and he ate and he burped. Then he went back to bed without ever doing anything for anybody" (unnumbered). After his mother insists that he go to work, a series of misunderstandings cause him to take his mother's previous advice. Consequently, he puts milk in his pocket, places cheese on his head, and drags fish home with a rope. The series related to each of these actions is developed in a sequence of humorous illustrations.

The consequences of greed, a universal motif in folktales from many countries, are found in Susan Cooper's *The Silver Cow: A Welsh Tale*. In this tale, the magic people, the Tylwyth Teg, send a marvelous cow out of Bearded Lake as a reward for a young boy's music. The greed of the boy's father causes the cow and her offspring to return to the lake, where they are turned into water lilies.

An impossible task created by foolish boasting is a motif in Harve Zemach's *Duffy and the Devil*, a Cornish tale resembling "Rumpelstiltskin." An inefficient maid named Duffy misleads her employer about her spinning ability and makes an agreement with the devil, who promises to do the knitting for three years. At the end of that time, she must produce his name or go with him. When the time arrives, the squire goes hunting and overhears the festivities of the witches and the devil as the little man with the long tail sings this song:

Tomorrow! Tomorrow! Tomorrow's the day!
I'll take her! I'll take her! I'll take her away!
Let her weep, let her cry, let her beg, let her
  pray—
She'll never guess my name is . . . Tarraway!
  (p. 30, unnumbered)

Thus, Duffy learns the magic name and cheats the devil from claiming her soul. The importance of a secret name is reflected in folktales from many cultures. In the English version of "Rumpelstiltskin," the name is Tim Tit Tot; a Scottish secret name is Whuppity Stoories; a tale from Nigeria is "The Hippopotamus Called Isantim."

A Cinderella-type story is found in several British folktales. In "Tattercoats," recorded by Joseph Jacobs in *More English Fairy Tales*, the heroine is mistreated by her grandfather, who mourns his daughter's death in childbirth and rejects the child who survived, and by the grandfather's cruel servants. In this British version, the prince invites her to attend the ball even though she is dressed in her rags. Only after she is at the ball does the gooseherd transform her into a beautifully dressed lady. Kevin Crossley-Holland's "Mossycoat," found in his *British Folk Tales*, is also mistreated by servants before she marries the young master.

In *Princess Furball*, retold by Charlotte Huck, the Cinderella-type heroine is at first ignored by her father, the king, and then promised in marriage to an ogre. Unlike many of the Cinderella tales, this heroine does not rely on magic to overcome obstacles. Instead, she relies on her own ingenuity. She demands and receives three gowns and a coat made from one thousand kinds of fur as a bridal gift from her father, but in order to escape the marriage, she runs away. Later, she is captured by a young king from a neighboring kingdom. At the castle, she becomes a servant to the servants. In this role she sweeps ashes, washes dishes, and fetches wood. When the king gives a ball, Furball wears one of her gowns, attends the ball, and dazzles the king. These actions continue through three balls, until a ring she is wearing shows the king that she is the girl that he loves.

One of the shortest British Cinderella-type stories is "Ashey Pelt," found in Katharine Briggs's *British Folktales*. In this variant, a black ewe provides the dress and horses for the girl to attend a party. It is also the black ewe who warns the prince that the stepsisters have been trimming their feet to fit into the silk slipper:

Nippet foot and clippet foot
Behind the king's son rides
But bonny foot and pretty foot
Is with the cathering hides.

The tale ends, "So he rode back and found her among the cows, and he married her, and if they live happy, so may you and me" (p. 21).

Folktales from Ireland are filled with fairies, leprechauns, and other little people. Jacob's "Guleesh," found in *Celtic Fairy Tales*, shows that the fairies do not always outwit people. A young man races with the "sheehogues," tricks those fairy hosts out of a captured princess, and breaks a spell so that the princess can speak. This tale has an ending characteristic of Irish folk literature: "But I heard it from a birdeen that there was neither cark nor care, sickness nor sorrow, mishap nor misfortune on them till the hour of their death, and may the same be with me, and with us all!" (p. 25).

Colorful language is a style of many Irish folktales. For example, Brendan Behan introduces *The King of Ireland's Son* in this way: "Once upon a time houses were whitewashed with buttermilk and the pigs ran around with knives and forks in their snouts shouting, 'Eat me, eat me!' " (unnumbered).

The Children of Lir, by Sheila MacGill-Callahan, is based on Irish folklore. In this tale, an evil stepmother transforms four children into swans; however, with the help of animals, the children finally break the evil spell. Some folklorists believe the Irish folktale to be the basis for Shakespeare's *King Lear*.

Peasants rather than royalty are usually the heroes and heroines in folktales of the British Isles. Consequently, readers or listeners can learn much about the problems, beliefs, values, and humor of common people in early British history. Themes in British folktales suggest that intelligence wins over physical strength, that hard work and diligence are rewarded, and that love and loyalty are basic values for everyone.

French Folktales

The majority of French folktales portray splendid royal castles rather than humble peasant cottages. Charles Perrault, a member of the Académie Française, collected and transcribed many of these tales. In 1697, he published a collection of folktales called *Tales of Mother Goose*, which included "Cinderilla" (original spelling), "Sleeping Beauty," "Puss in Boots," "Little Red Riding Hood," "Blue Beard," "Little Thumb," and "Diamond and the Toads." These stories had entertained children and adults of the Parisian aristocracy and, consequently, are quite different from tales that stress wicked, dishonest kings being outwitted by simple peasants. These folktales collected by Perrault provide the foundation for most of the French folktales published today.

Many illustrators and translators of French fairy tales depict royal settings. For example, Marcia Brown's *Cinderella* (based on Charles Perrault's version) is quite different from the German version. Cinderella has a fairy godmother who grants her wishes. A pumpkin is transformed into a gilded carriage, six mice become beautiful horses, a rat becomes a coachman with an elegant mustache, and lizards turn into footmen who are complete with fancy livery and lace. Cinderella is dressed in a beautiful gown, which is embroidered with rubies, pearls,

and diamonds. This version also has the magical hour of midnight, when everything returns to normal. Perrault's *Cinderella* contains stepsisters who are rude and haughty, but they are not as cruel as they are in the German version. Cinderella even finds it possible to forgive them:

Now her stepsisters recognized her. Cinderella was the beautiful personage they had seen at the ball! They threw themselves at her feet and begged forgiveness for all their bad treatment of her. Cinderella asked them to rise, embraced them and told them she forgave them with all her heart. She begged them to love her always. (p. 27)

Cinderella not only forgives them but also provides them with a home at the palace and marries them to the lords of the court. Brown's illustrations, drawn with fine lines and colored with pastels, depict a kingdom where life in the royal court is marvelous. Compare the influence of illustrations in

*I*SSUE   Are "Cinderella" and Similar Traditional Tales Sexist?

Puritans in England and the United States considered many of the traditional tales too violent to be shared with children. Today, the tales are being attacked by groups who consider the actions of the beautiful, often helpless females and the clever, handsome princes who rescue them to be sexist. Ethel Johnston Phelps believes the image of the good, obedient, meek, and submissive heroine is harmful and should be altered. She has published two books that depict brave and clever heroines: *Tatterhood and Other Tales*[1] and *The Maid of the North*.[2] *Time* magazine's review of these books concludes, "Though Phelps celebrates females who have brains and energy, her feminist lens at times distorts the drama beneath the surface of the folk tales."[3]

In defense of this criticism, the *Time* writer provides two examples. In "The Twelve Huntsmen," Phelps has the prince collapse at the appro-

priate moment; in the original story, the girl demonstrates this behavior. In "The Maid of the North," Phelps changes the dialogue from the original, in which the maid fends off a suitor by describing the disadvantages of leaving home to join a stranger's household. In Phelps's version, the maid expresses this viewpoint against marriage: "A wife is like a house dog tied with a rope. Why should I be a servant and wait upon a husband?"

Should these stories be rewritten to reflect changing attitudes of the times, or will rewriting distort the value of traditional tales? Are children harmed by the male and female stereotypes developed in traditional literature? If stories are tampered with, will children lose their identification with characters like themselves, who are often bewildered and feel like underdogs in traditional tales?

Writing on a related subject of the advisability of reshaping folktales, Susan Hepler[4] states, "New twists and role reversals delight children familiar with the original versions of folktales." She also declares, however, "authors, illustrators, and publishers owe it to their audiences to make it absolutely clear when they alter the original content and/or tamper with the spirit of a tale" (p. 154).

[1]Phelps, Ethel Johnston. *Tatterhood and Other Tales*. New York: Feminist Press, 1978.

[2]Phelps, Ethel Johnston. *The Maid of the North*. New York: Holt, Rinehart & Winston, 1981.

[3]"Sexes: Feminist Folk and Fairy Tales." *Time* (July 20, 1981): 60.

[4]Hepler, Susan. "Fooling with Folktales: Updates, Spin-offs, and Roundups." *School Library Journal* 36 (March 1990): 153–154.

William Wegman's *Cinderella,* in which Wegman photographs dogs in costumes.

The French version of "Sleeping Beauty" suggests traditional French values. Seven good fairies bestow the virtues of intelligence, beauty, kindness, generosity, gaiety, and grace on the infant princess. David Walker's version, *The Sleeping Beauty,* shows his background in theatrical set and costume design. His illustrations create the feeling of a stage setting, especially as his fairies dance lightly across the great hall of the castle. The collaboration between Lincoln Kirstein's retelling and Alain Vaes's illustrations for *Puss in Boots* also show the influence of backgrounds that come from the New York City Ballet. The text includes fast-paced storytelling, and the illustrations develop a world of baroque splendor that could provide stage settings for ballet. In addition, the common French motifs of enchantment and animals who help their masters attain high goals are developed through both the text and the illustrations. Readers will also enjoy searching the illustrations to find examples of seventeenth-century architecture and figures from art history.

Diane Goode has translated and illustrated an edition of Madame de Beaumont's *Beauty and the Beast.* Meant originally for the wealthy classes in French society, de Beaumont's tale begins with the traditional "Once upon a time," but it provides descriptions tailored for an aristocratic audience. For example, Beauty enjoys reading, playing the harpsichord, and singing while she spins. When she enters the beast's castle, he provides her with a library, a harpsichord, and music books. Goode's illustrations create the magical settings in which Beauty eventually loves the beast for his virtue, although he lacks good looks and wit. Beauty's moral discrimination permits the beast's transformation back into a handsome prince.

Jan Brett's *Beauty and the Beast* includes illustrations that Brett modeled after the work of Walter Crane. The tapestries in the illustrations include messages and show the people in the castle before they were enchanted.

Nancy Willard's *Beauty and the Beast* has an American setting, but the locations are just as grand and magical as those in France. In this retelling, the wealthy merchant leaves his home, a splendid townhouse in New York overlooking Central Park, and eventually seeks shelter from the storm in a rural

The illustrations in this version of Puss in Boots *feature seventeenth-century architecture. (From* Puss in Boots *by Lincoln Kirstein. Text copyright © 1992 by Lincoln Kirstein. Illustrations copyright © 1992 by Alain Vais. Reprinted by permission of Little, Brown and Company.)*

mansion that is magically untouched by the storm. Willard's descriptions allow readers to visualize and sense the grandeur of the occasion:

As he passed through room after room, his amazement grew. Each room seemed charged with the invisible presence of some loving soul who had lit candles in the sconces and fires in the fireplaces and moved on, leaving behind a fragrance of cloves and roses. In all his travels, the merchant had never seen rarities to compare with what the rooms contained. In one he found a cabinet of ivory centaurs that danced in a circle when he bent to admire them. Another held a chair carved like a merman from a single chunk of apricot jade. In a third he discovered a chess set with diamond and ruby pieces facing each other invitingly, ready for a game. On the walls were portraits of handsome men and women, elegantly dressed in the cloaks and ruffles of a hundred years ago. (p. 24)

Barry Moser's wood engravings add to the dramatic feeling of the tale.

Warwick Hutton's shorter *Beauty and the Beast* is not aimed at the wealthy classes. His Beauty is the youngest daughter of a merchant who has had bad luck. Unlike her ill-tempered and resentful older sisters, she looks on the bright side of their situation and tries to keep her family happy.

French folktales contain more enchantment than do tales from other countries. The motifs in these tales include fairy godmothers, other fairies, remarkable beasts who help their young masters, unselfish girls who break enchantments, and deceitful beasts.

German Folktales

The following words bring to mind one of the most popular childhood tales:

> Mirror, mirror on the wall.
> Who is the fairest of them all?

German folktales—whether they are about enchanted princesses and friendly dwarfs, clever animals, or poor but honest peasants—are among the most enjoyed folktales in the world. German scholar August Nitschke (1988) emphasizes the role of the German folktales historically. He states that by telling folktales, German "mothers allowed their children to come to an understanding of the world in which familiar and discomforting aspects were clearly separated, thus reaffirming that these two states of community existed" (p. 173). According to Nitschke, the storytelling and the stories allowed both mother and child to gain courage.

The accessibility of German folktales to modern audiences is owed to the work of Wilhelm and Jacob Grimm, German professors who researched the roots of the German language through the traditional tales, which had been told orally for generations. The Grimms asked village storytellers throughout Germany to tell them tales. Then, they wrote down the stories and published them as *Kinder-und Hausmärchen*. The stories ultimately were translated into many languages and became popular in Europe, North America, and elsewhere.

A wolf is the villain in several German folktales that young children enjoy. Wolves in these tales are cunning and dangerous, and they receive just punishments. Trina Schart Hyman's version of *Little Red Riding Hood* is involved and more appropriate for older children. In addition to the story, Hyman stresses the importance of a moral in the Grimms' folktales. The incident with the dangerous wolf teaches Red Riding Hood a lesson: "I will never wander off the forest path again, as long as I live. I should have kept my promise to my mother."

Quite a different mood is created by James Marshall's humorous text and cartoon-type illustrations in his *Red Riding Hood*. The last page even includes a crocodile. Little Red Riding Hood has learned her lesson, however, and refuses to speak to him. For another mood, see William Wegman's *Little Red Riding Hood,* which contains photographs of dogs in the various roles.

Not all animals in German folklore are as fearsome as the wolf. For example, "The Bremen Town Musicians," old animals about to be destroyed by their owners, have humorously appealing human qualities. P. K. Page gives *The Traveling Musicians of Bremen* a contemporary feeling through modern language, conversations, and situations. Kady MacDonald Denton's illustrations show the robbers as teenagers with punk hair styles whose loot includes television sets. Ilse Plume's softly colored illustrations for another version of this tale suggest the gentle nature of the animals and the setting, a sunlit forest.

Poor peasants and penniless soldiers are common heroes in German folklore. The peasant may not be cunning, but he is usually good. In "The Golden Goose," for example, the youngest son is even called Simpleton. When his selfish brothers leave home, their parents give each one a fine, rich cake and a bottle of wine, which they refuse to share with anyone. The despised Simpleton, however, is generous with the cinder cake and sour beer that his parents give him. His kind heart is rewarded when he acquires a golden goose with magical powers that allow him to marry a princess. In Neil Philip's retelling of *The Golden Bird,* the youngest son accomplishes his quest for three objects through honesty and dedication.

In Barbara Rogasky's *The Water of Life,* two prideful and treacherous older brothers are punished, while the kind and generous youngest brother is rewarded. This tale, as well as "The Golden Goose," contains many of the actions that are recurrent in folktales. Walter de la Mare's *The Turnip* includes both a poor but generous farmer and a wealthy but miserly merchant brother. With typical consequences, the poor farmer is rewarded for his generosity, while the merchant receives only a slice of his brother's huge turnip.

"Hansel and Gretel" is the classic tale of an evil witch, a discontented and selfish mother, an ineffectual father, and two resourceful children. Rika Lesser's *Hansel and Gretel* with Paul O. Zelinsky's illustrations provides a rich retelling of this favorite tale. James Marshall adds humorous text and cartoon-type illustrations to his *Hansel and Gretel*. In comparing these two books, consider the impact of illustrations on the mood of the tales.

Many of the best-loved German folktales are stories of princesses who sleep for a hundred years, have wicked stepmothers, and are enchanted by witches. One lovely version of the Grimms' "Snow White" is translated by Randall Jarrell and illustrated by Nancy Ekholm Burkert. Burkert undertook research in German museums and visited the Black Forest before creating her drawings for *Snow White and the Seven Dwarfs,* which portrays every aspect of the mystical forest, the dwarfs' cottage, and the wicked stepmother's secret tower room. Samuel Denis Fohr (1991) argues that "Snow White" is filled with spiritual symbolism. He states: "The changed mother in 'Snow White' not only represents the world but also worldliness. Similarly, Snow White not only symbolizes human beings but also the innocence or non-worldliness of youth" (p. 85). Consequently, he argues that the story is of value for adults as well as for children.

The German version of "Cinderella" in *The Complete Brothers Grimm Fairy Tales* differs from the French rendering of this tale in both detail and mood. A bird in the hazel tree growing by her mother's grave, not a fairy godmother, gives Cinderella a dress made of gold and silver and satin slippers for the ball. When Cinderella is united with the prince, no softness of heart leads her to forgive her cruel stepsisters. On her wedding day, the sisters join the bridal procession, but doves perched on Cinderella's shoulders peck out the sisters' eyes.

The elegance of the Italian renaissance is reflected in Paul O. Zelinsky's illustrations for *Rapunzel.* The elegance of courtly life is also reflected in tales such as *The Twelve Dancing Princesses.* Kinuko Craft's paintings re-create beautiful costumes, gardens, and magical settings in Marianna Mayer's retelling of this magical tale. Ruth Sanderson's *The Twelve Dancing Princesses* includes both enchantment and a supernatural helper who assists the poor but honest peasant break the spell, marry the princess, and inherit the kingdom.

Breaking enchantments through unselfish love is another common theme in German folklore. In the Grimms' "The Six Swans," the heroine can restore her brothers to human form only by sewing six shirts out of starwort. She cannot speak during the six years required for her task and suffers many ordeals before she is successful.

Jan Ormerod and David Lloyd's *The Frog Prince* is the classic tale of enchantment complete with rhythmical language, such as

> Let me eat from your plate,
>   my honey, my heart.
> Let me eat from your plate,
>   my own darling.
> Remember the promise
>   you made in the woods.
> Remember your promise
>   to love me. (p. 12, unnumbered)

Nonny Hogrogian's version of the Grimms' *The Devil with the Three Golden Hairs* contains many of the characteristics of German folktales. A poor, brave boy is rewarded; a wicked, greedy king is punished; a kind miller cares for the boy; a beautiful princess is rewarded; the devil's grandmother uses enchantment to help the boy; and the devil is outwitted. Common folktale motifs in this tale include a physical sign of luck, a quest, the importance of threes (three hairs, three questions), and magical transformations. The text concludes with a characteristic moral: "The youth, together with his bride, lived well and reigned well, for he who is not afraid can even take the hairs from the devil's head and conquer the kingdom" (unnumbered).

After reading a number of German folktales first recorded by Jacob and Wilhelm Grimm, you may approach the challenge of Wilhelm Grimm's *Dear Mili,* illustrated by Maurice Sendak. What is the origin of the tale recently found in a letter written to a young girl in 1816? Is it part of the oral tradition collected by this famous recorder of German folktales, or did Grimm use characteristics of traditional tales to write his own literary folktale?

German folktales are ideal candidates for storytelling. Their speedy openings, fast-paced plots, and drama keep listeners entertained for story after story. In these tales, adversaries include devils, witches, and wolves. The good-hearted youngest child is often rewarded, but selfishness, greed, and discontent are punished. The noble character frequently wins as a result of intervention by supernatural helpers, and magical objects and spells are recurring motifs.

Four illustrations of a familiar tale show the impact of the pictures on the moods of the story. A, *The formal border and illustrations create a traditional mood in the illustrations from* Little Red Riding Hood. *(Illustrations from* Little Red Riding Hood *by Trina Schart Hyman, copyright © 1983 by Trina Schart Hyman. Reprinted by permission of Holiday House.)* B, *The black and white photographs suggest a frightening mood in Rita Marshall's illustrations for* Little Red Riding Hood. *(From* Little Red Riding Hood *by Charles Perrault, edited by Ann Redpath and Etienne Delessert, illustrations by Rita Marshall. Copyright © 1983. Reprinted by permission of Creative Education, Inc.)* C, *James Marshall's cartoon illustrations add a humorous context to* Little Red Riding Hood. *(From* Little Red Riding Hood *by James Marshall. Illustrated by James Marshall, Dial Books for Young Readers. Copyright © 1987.)* D (p. 301), *Dark colors and frightened girls suggest the dangerous nature of the tale. (From* Lon Po Po: A Red-Riding Hood Story from China, *translated and illustrated by Ed Young, copyright © 1989 by Ed Young. Reprinted by permission of Philomel Books.)*

A

B

C

Shang listened through the door. "Po Po," she said, "why is your voice so low?"

"Your grandmother has caught a cold, good children, and it is dark and windy out here. Quickly open up, and let your Po Po come in," the cunning wolf said.

Tao and Paotze could not wait. One unlatched the door and the other opened it. They shouted, "Po Po, Po Po, come in!"

At the moment he entered the door, the wolf blew out the candle.

"Po Po," Shang asked, "why did you blow out the candle? The room is now dark."

The wolf did not answer.

D

Norwegian Folktales

Norwegian scholars Peter Christian Asbjörnsen and Jörgen Moe's interest in collecting the traditional tales of the Norwegian people was stimulated by reading the Grimms' *Kinder-und Hausmärchen*. They were also inspired by the national renaissance that was then sweeping Europe. Asbjörnsen and Moe's collection of traditional tales was published under the title *Norwegian Folk Tales* in 1845.

The first translation of the tales into English was by Sir George Webbe Dasent in 1859. According to Naomi Lewis (1991),

It was not surprising that Dasent was so captivated by Scandinavia. The plots of fairy tales everywhere have many likenesses; what changes them is the place where they are told—the country and the people. Wherever the landscape is wild, the winters long and bitter, and the villages small and isolated, magic and mystery thrive. Why should the folk there doubt that trolls live in the forest, as well as wolves and bears; or that animals, who share the same scene and hardships, can speak if they will, and even change into humans and back again? (Introduction)

Claire Booss (1984), a collector of the folktales of northern peoples, believes that climatic and geographic extremes created hardy, courageous, and independent people and that the folktales of these people reflect a strong sense of wonder, a fierce loyalty to ideals, and a great sense of humor. Booss also maintains that extremes inspire stories with the power to delight, haunt, and terrify.

It is interesting to compare Norwegian story elements with those of other European cultures. Consider, for example, Mercer Mayer's *East of the Sun and West of the Moon*. The story in this tale is similar to those in the French "Beauty and the Beast" and other tales of human enchantment and lost loves: An enchanted human demands a promise in return for a favor; the promise is at first honored; the maiden disenchants the human; he must leave because she does not honor her promise; she searches

The tale of enchanted princesses emphasizes a regal setting. (From Twelve Dancing Princesses *retold by Marianna Mayer. Illustrated by K. Y. Craft. Text © 1989 by Marianna Mayer. Illustrations © 1989 by K. Y. Craft. Reprinted by permission of Morrow Junior Books, a division of William Morrow & Co.)*

for him; and she saves him finally. The adversaries and helpers in this tale reflect a northern climate and culture. The human is enchanted by a troll princess who lives in a distant, icy kingdom. The loving maiden receives help from, among others, Father Forest, who understands the body of earth and stone; Great Fish, who knows the blood of salt and water; and North Wind, who understands the mind of the earth, the moon, and the sun. The gifts that each helper gives to the maiden allow her to overcome the trolls and free the prince. A tinderbox makes it possible to melt the ice encasing the youth, a shot from the bow and arrow causes the troll princess to turn to wood, and reflections in the fish scale cause the remaining trolls to turn to stone. Mayer's illustrations of snowy winters, creatures frozen in ice, icy mountains, and tree-covered landscapes also evoke northern settings.

Claire Booss's version of the tale in *Scandinavian Folk & Fairy Tales* differs from Mayer's version. In *East O' the Sun and West O' the Moon,* translated by George Webbe Dasent and illustrated by P. J. Lynch, a white bear offers a family riches if its youngest daughter is allowed to live in his castle. In *East of the Sun & West of the Moon: A Play,* Nancy Willard develops a style that is appropriate for oral presenta-

tions, as shown in the song that the woodcutter's daughter sings as she goes to the bear's palace:

> When you go through the forest at midnight,
> and your friends and relations are few,
> just remember the crow and the cricket
> are twice as nervous as you. (p. 17)

Norwegian folktale collections provide many excellent stories for retelling. Several favorites are found in Virginia Haviland's *Favorite Fairy Tales Told in Norway.* Young children love to listen to and dramatize "Three Billy Goats Gruff." Glen Rounds's *Three Billy Goats Gruff* is an excellent source for creative drama. Children can re-create the world of the hairy troll and the goats who finally are victorious.

Another favorite for storytelling and creative drama is "Taper Tom," found in Asbjörnsen and Mae's *Norwegian Folk Tales,* whose hero is the characteristic youngest son. Tom sits in a chimney corner amusing himself by grubbing in the ashes and splitting tapers for lights. His family laughs at his belief that he can win the hand of the princess in marriage and half of the kingdom by making the princess laugh. With the assistance of a magical golden goose who does not relinquish anyone who touches her, Tom forms a parade of unwilling fol-

The northern climate is found throughout the illustrations for this Norwegian tale. (Illustration from East O' the Sun and West O' the Moon *with an introduction by Naomi Lewis. Illustration © 1991 P. J. Lynch. Used by permission of Candlewick Press, Cambridge, MA.)*

lowers: an old woman, an angry man who kicks at the woman, a smithy who waves a pair of tongs, and a cook who runs after them waving a ladle of porridge. At the sight of this ridiculous situation, the sad princess bursts into laughter. Tom wins the princess and half of the kingdom. Compare this tale with the Grimms's "The Golden Goose."

The humor in Asbjörnsen and Moe's *The Man Who Kept House,* illustrated by Otto S. Svend, results from another ridiculous situation. A man who claims that keeping house is easy exchanges his field work for his wife's housework. Hilarious situations result when the man faces such common household chores as washing clothes.

Norwegian folktales help children appreciate Norwegian traditions as well as provide children with pleasure and excitement. Themes suggest the rewarding of unselfish love and the punishment of greed. The sharp humor, the trolls, and the poor boys who overcome adversity are excellent elements for storytelling.

Russian Folktales

Heroes and heroines who may be royalty or peasants, settings that reflect deep snows in winter, dark forests, the wooden huts of peasants, the gilded towers of palaces, and villains such as the witch Baba Yaga and dishonest nobility or commoners are found in Russian folktales. Talent, beauty, and kindness are usually appreciated and rewarded. In contrast, foolish actions, greed, broken promises, and jealousy are usually condemned. Peasants sometimes outwit tsars (or *czars*), and females are often strong and resourceful. Lenny Hort's retelling of Alexander Nikolayevich Afanasyév's *The Fool and the Fish: A Tale from Russia* shows that even a peasant can be accepted by the tsar and marry his daughter. The humor of the fool's actions expresses the universal need to laugh at oneself and others. The illustrations by Russian artist Gennady Spirin depict a prerevolutionary Russia. Compare Spirin's illustrations in this book with his illustrations in Aaron Shepard's retelling of *The Sea King's Daughter*.

Many Russian folktales are complex stories of quests, longing, and greed. Arthur Ransome's *Old Peter's Russian Tales* includes such quest tales as "The Fire-bird, the Horse of Power and the Princess Vasilissa." In many of the quests, generosity and kindness are rewarded and greed and foolishness are punished. Michael McCurdy's *The Devils Who Learned to Be Good,* a good-versus-evil tale, includes common Russian motifs: a generous old soldier and supernatural objects given to reward generosity and used to gain riches and outwit evil spirits.

Universal folktale themes found in Russian folktales include a desire for children, developed in a story about a childless couple who create "The Snow Maiden," and hatred of a beautiful child by her stepmother and stepsisters, developed in "Vassilissa the Fair," a Russian version of the Cinderella story. The latter tale and six others are collected in Alexander Nikolayevich Afanasyév's *Russian Folk Tales,* with illustrations by Ivan Bilibin, the late-nineteenth-century Russian illustrator, who depicts traditional costumes and early Russian settings. John Cech's retelling of *First Snow, Magic Snow* also presents the story of parents who wish for a child and find themselves parents of a snow child.

Alexander Pushkin was one of the first Russian writers to transcribe the orally transmitted folktales of his country. Four of Pushkin's tales are found in

THE DEVILS WHO LEARNED TO BE GOOD

MICHAEL McCURDY

The woodcuts enhance the traditional story line in The Devils Who Learned to Be Good. *(From* The Devils Who Learned to Be Good *by Michael McCurdy, copyright © 1987 by Michael McCurdy. Reprinted by permission of Little, Brown and Company.)*

The Golden Cockerel and Other Fairy Tales, originally published in French in 1925. This translation includes "The Dead Princess and the Seven Heroes," a tale similar to the German "Snow White."

Patricia Tracy Lowe has translated and retold *The Tale of Czar Saltan, or the Prince and the Swan Princess.* This tale reflects the importance of keeping promises and the consequences of jealously and greed. The consequences of greed are also developed in Elizabeth Winthrop's adaptation, *The Little Humpbacked Horse: A Russian Tale.* In this tale wisdom and friendship overcome greed.

The familiar theme of kindness rewarded and the motifs of magical powers and foolish but kind-hearted peasants are found in Arthur Ransome's *The Fool of the World and the Flying Ship.* The czar has offered his daughter's hand in marriage to anyone who can build a flying ship. Kindness to an old man provides an aspiring peasant with a magical ship.

Companions with extraordinary powers also aid the peasant in his quest. This tale implies that the czar does not want a peasant to marry his daughter.

Diane Wolkstein's *Oom Razoom: Or Go I Know Not Where, Bring Back I Know Not What: A Russian Tale* features a kind peasant who is the king's archer, a beautiful female who is wise and resourceful, and a deceitful king. The story includes motifs of enchantment and supernatural helpers who assist the archer as he eventually outwits the king. The story line repeats a Russian saying: "The morning is wiser than the evening." The story also suggests that even unreasonable requests from a king can be overcome.

Russian protagonists may be strong and resourceful females. Josepha Sherman's *Vassilisa the Wise: A Tale of Medieval Russia* shows that a clever and courageous female is able to outwit the prince and save her unwise husband from the prince's dark dungeon.

These and many other Russian folktales reflect a vast country containing numerous cultures. Talent, beauty, and kindness are appreciated and rewarded. People must pay the consequences for foolish actions, greed, broken promises, and jealousy. Humor suggests the universal need to laugh at oneself and others.

Jewish Folktales

Folktales, according to Rahel Musleah (1992), may be identified as Jewish if they contain any one of the following elements:

The components are a Jewish place (under a wedding canopy; in a synagogue); a Jewish character (King Solomon instead of a nameless judge); Jewish time (a holiday or life-cycle event); and most importantly, a Jewish message (faith, learning, remembrance, hospitality, family). (p. 42)

Jewish folktales are filled with stories in which sincerity, unselfishness, and true wisdom are rewarded. The stories also contain bunglers, ironic humor, and human foibles. According to Charlotte Huck, Susan Hepler, and Janet Hickman (1997), Jewish folktales "have a poignancy, wit, and ironic humor that is not matched by any other folklore" (p. 289). Wit and humor are found in Margot Zemach's *It Could Always Be Worse.* This Yiddish folktale relates the story of nine unhappy people who share a small one-room hut. The father desperately seeks the advice of the rabbi, who suggests that he bring a barnyard animal inside. A pattern of complaint and advice continues until most of the family's livestock is in the house. When the rabbi tells the father to clear the animals out of the hut, the whole family appreciates its large, peaceful home.

Advice from a rabbi is a frequent story plot technique that develops both the ridiculous situation and the moral of the story in Jewish folktales. Joan Rothenberg's *Yettele's Feathers* is a cautionary tale against spreading rumors and gossip. When the situation becomes extreme and no one will speak to Yettele Babbelonski, she asks the rabbi for advice. When Yettele declares that words are like feathers and not like rocks because words and feathers cannot hurt anyone, the rabbi tells her to cut off the top of her largest goose feather pillow and bring it to him. When the wind snatches the pillow from her arms, she is lost in a blizzard of feathers. Now the rabbi tells her he will help her after she retrieves all of the feathers. After Yettele becomes extremely fatigued trying to gather the feathers she concludes that in a lifetime she could never put all the feathers back into the pillow. Now the rabbi uses her own words to teach the moral of the story: "And so it is with those stories of yours, my dear Yettele. Once the words leave your lips, they are as impossible to put back as those feathers" (p. 31).

In *While Standing on One Foot: Puzzle Stories and Wisdom Tales from the Jewish Tradition,* Nina Jaffe and Steve Zeitlin retell the stories in two parts. They develop the problem in the first part and resolve it in the second, separating the two parts with a question that reinforces the role of wisdom in Jewish folklore.

Isaac Bashevis Singer's *Mazel and Shlimazel, or the Milk of the Lioness* is longer and more complex. It pits Mazel, the spirit of good luck, against Shlimazel, the spirit of bad luck. To test the strength of good luck versus bad, the two spirits decide that each of them will spend a year manipulating the life of Tam, a bungler who lives in the poorest hut in the village. As soon as Mazel stands behind Tam, he succeeds at everything he tries. He fixes the king's carriage wheel and is invited to court, where he accomplishes impossible tasks. Even Princess Nesika is in love with him.

Just as Tam is about to complete his greatest challenge successfully, Mazel's year is over, and an old, bent man with spiders in his beard stands beside Tam. With one horrible slip of the tongue encouraged by Shlimazel, Tam is in disfavor and condemned to death. Shlimazel has won. But wait! Mazel presents Shlimazel with the wine of forgetfulness, which causes Shlimazel to forget poor Tam. Mazel rescues Tam from hanging and helps Tam redeem himself

with the king and marry the princess. Tam's success is more than good luck, however: "Tam had learned that good luck follows those who are diligent, honest, sincere and helpful to others. The man who has these qualities is indeed lucky forever" (p. 42).

Singer's *When Shlemiel Went to Warsaw & Other Stories* contains several folktales that reflect both human foibles and folklore themes. For example, "Shrewd Todie & Lyzer the Miser" pits foolish, greedy actions against cunning and trickery. To his discomfort, the miser learns, "If you accept nonsense when it brings you profit, you must also accept nonsense when it brings you loss" (p. 12).

The Feather Merchants & Other Tales of the Fools of Chelm, retold by Steve Sanfield, is made up of thirteen traditional Eastern European Jewish tales about the good and decent people of Chelm, who can also be silly and foolish. Sanfield states that no one knows how Chelm came to be known as the town of fools. He declares:

Our Chelm is the Chelm of the spirit and imagination that has existed, generation after generation, in the minds and hearts of those who've told and listened to these tales. Our Chelm is a magical place filled with honest and righteous men and women for whom the idea of defeat passes as quickly as a gaggle of geese flying south. Our Chelm has a soul which yearns for beauty, which is full of mercy, which possesses faith, which seeks justice. Chelm is where hopes and dreams and laughter go on living—and will go on living as long as you and I go on telling these stories. (p. 97)

As you read Jewish folktales, notice how this spirit of Chelm emerges from the tales. Additional stories of Chelm are found in Francine Prose's *The Angel's Mistake: Stories of Chelm.*

The fools of Chelm as well as stories about witches, goblins, and King Solomon are found in Howard Schwartz and Barbara Rush's collection of stories, *The Diamond Tree: Jewish Tales from Around the World.* These fifteen tales originated in many countries, including Palestine, Iraq, Turkey, Babylon, and Poland. The text concludes with sources and commentary that are extremely useful to scholars and others who are interested in evaluating the sources of the stories. In addition, each tale is classified according to the Aarne-Thompson (AT) system. (Aarne-Thompson is a folklorist who identified tales according to specific characteristics.) For example, notice the useful information found in the notations for "The Bear and the Children" (Eastern Europe):

From *Yiddisher Folklor* (Yiddish), edited by Yehuda L. Cahan (Vilna: 1931). AT 123.

This is probably the best-known Jewish nursery tale of Eastern Europe—with the exception of the song "Had Gadya" ("One Kid"), sung at the end of the Passover seder. The story offers young children the assurance that if there is danger, their parents will do everything possible to save them. It is a variant of "The Wolf and the Seven Kids" from *Grimms' Fairy Tales*. (p. 119)

Asian Folktales

Asian folktales, like other folktales, portray the feelings, struggles, and aspirations of common people; depict the lives of the well-to-do; and reflect the moral values, superstitions, social customs, and humor of the times and societies in which they originated. Like medieval Europe, ancient Asia contained societies in which royalty and nobles led lives quite different from those of peasants. Females had less freedom and social influence than did males. Asian tales tell about the rich and the poor, the wise and the foolish, mythical quests, lovers, animals, and supernatural beings and powers, motifs common to all folklore, but they also reflect the customs and beliefs of specific cultures.

These Jewish tales collected from many countries reflect many of the values of the Jewish people. (From The Diamond Tree: Jewish Tales from Around the World *selected and retold by Howard Schwartz and Barbara Rush. Copyright © 1991 by Uri Shulevitz. Used by permission of HarperCollins Publishers.)*

Chinese Folktales. Traditional Chinese sayings (Wyndham, 1971) suggest Chinese values and philosophical viewpoints expressed in Chinese folktales over the centuries, for example: "A teacher can open the door, but the pupil must go through it alone," and "The home that includes an old grandparent contains a precious jewel."

According to Louise and Yuan-hsi Kuo (1976), Chinese tales often develop universal themes and contain roguish humor. Respect for ancestors, ethical standards, and conflict between nobility and commoners are popular topics in Chinese tales.

A dislike for imperial authority is evident in several Chinese equivalents to the cottage tales of medieval European peasants. The defeat of an evil ruler is the main conflict in Rosalind C. Wang's *The Treasure Chest: A Chinese Tale*. The hero in this tale is a poor widow's son who rescues a fish and earns the gratitude of the Ocean King. The gift from the King of three bamboo sticks helps the young man save the woman he loves from Funtong, the evil ruler who desires the young woman.

A benevolent dragon is found in "Green Dragon Pond" in Neil Philip's *The Spring of Butterflies and Other Folktales of China's Minority Peoples*. According to the tale, "From the very beginning to the end, this dragon did no harm, but only good deeds. For this reason, the villagers around Malong peak lived a happy life" (p. 119). In this tale of transformation, the dragon changes himself into a man and plays chess with an old monk who lives in the temple by the pond. The story has an unhappy ending because of the carelessness of the dragon and the monk, not because the dragon is cruel.

Marilee Heyer's *The Weaving of a Dream: A Chinese Folktale* reveals rewarded behavior: bravery, unselfish love, understanding, respect for one's mother, faithfulness, and kindness. In contrast, disrespect for one's mother and selfishness are punished. This tale also shows the power of a dream and the perseverance that may be required to gain the dream. Ed Young's *Lon Po Po: A Red-Riding Hood*

Story from China shows that the cleverness of the eldest daughter and the cooperation of the three sisters are powerful enough to outwit the intentions of the evil wolf.

In *Tiger Woman*, Laurence Yep uses a rhyming format to retell a Shantung folktale in which selfishness is punished and sharing is rewarded. When a beggar approaches a selfish woman and asks for some of her bean curd, she replies that she will not give up any of her food because she is a tiger when she is famished. The beggar then casts a spell so that whatever the selfish woman says she becomes. Consequently, she becomes an ox, a bird, an elephant, and a sow. At that point when she almost becomes a pork roast, she repents and turns back into a human. Now she realizes the importance of sharing her food. Steve Sanfield's *Just Rewards: Or Who Is That Man in the Moon & What's He Doing Up There Anyway?* is another Chinese folktale in which good deeds are rewarded and greed is punished.

Two tales from China show the importance of respecting nature and the need for overcoming injustices. Caryn Yacowitz's *The Jade Stone: A Chinese Folktale* reveals the importance of inspiration and adhering to the soul that is within jade. The importance of dreams is emphasized as the Great Emperor of all China allows his dreams to decide the stone carver's fate. The extraordinary qualities of the brothers in Margaret Mahy's *The Seven Chinese Brothers* allow justice to be served and the tyrannical Celestial Emperor to be defeated.

In *Two of Everything*, Lily Toy Hong develops the importance of both humor and wisdom. A poor farmer and his wife discover the unusual characteristics of a brass pot that the farmer unearths in his garden. If one item is placed in the pot, two identical items appear. This happy situation continues until the wife falls head first into the pot, but the woman uses her wits and solves the problem.

Numerous tales in *The Spring of Butterflies and Other Chinese Folktales* reveal the consequences of kindness, humor, and greed. Moss Roberts's large collection, *Chinese Fairy Tales and Fantasies,* is divided into tales about enchantment and magic, folly and greed, animals, women and wives, ghosts and souls, and judges and diplomats. Laurence Yep's *The Rainbow People* is a collection of twenty Chinese folktales from Chinese Americans in the United States. The text is divided according to tales about tricksters, fools, virtues and vices, Chinese America,

and love. Yep has included introductory comments for each of the sections.

Japanese Folktales. Ellen S. Shapiro in her introduction to Grace James's *Green Willow and Other Japanese Fairy Tales* (1987) summarizes some of the characteristics of Japanese folktales. According to Shapiro, the stories include appreciation for the beauty and mystery of life, belief in the power of the spirit to accomplish its will, and ridicule for pretensions. Shapiro states that within Japanese folktales, "Anything is possible; magic abounds, as long as it is faithful to the truths of the heart. Some stories are lighthearted, others disturbing, but all reveal the deep human values underlying the apparent transience of the physical world" (p. viii). In her discussion of style associated with Japanese folktales, Shapiro emphasizes that short phrases and repetitive sentences have great emotional impact, as in this quote from "The Wind in the Pine Tree": "the heavenly deity descended. Lightly, lightly he came by way of the Floating Bridge, bearing the tree in his right hand. Lightly, lightly his feet touched the earth" (p. x).

Chinese culture influenced Japanese culture, and many Japanese tales are similar to Chinese tales. Dragons, for example, are common in tales from both countries. The tiger, usually considered a symbol of power, is a creature often found in Japanese tales. The cat is important in *The Boy Who Drew Cats: A Japanese Folktale,* retold by Arthur Levine. When a boy paints cats on screens after he is trapped in an abandoned temple, the cats come alive to save him from a giant rat. "The Boy Who Drew Cats" is also included in Rafe Martin's *Mysterious Tales of Japan.* This is a collection of ten traditional tales such as "Urashima Taro," "Green Willow," and "The Crane Maiden." The book includes story notes that either provide additional information about the context of the story or about the source. For example, the source note for "The Snow Woman" includes: "My version is based on Lafcadio Hearn's 'Yuki-Onna,' a retelling of a story a Japanese farmer told him, which can be found in Hearn's *Kwaidan, Stories and Studies of Strange Things* (Kwaidan means 'weird tales')" (p. 71).

Japanese folktales reflecting respected values and disliked human qualities include Katherine Paterson's *The Tale of the Mandarin Ducks.* Paterson develops strong messages, such as kindness will be rewarded,

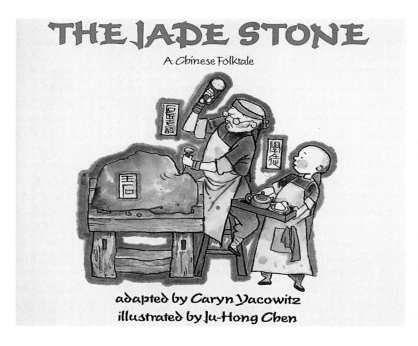

This tale develops the importance of respecting the jade during the carving. (From The Jade Stone: A Chinese Folktale, *adapted by Caryn Yacowitz, illustrated by Ju-Hong Chen. Holiday House, copyright © 1992.)*

THE JADE STONE

A Chinese Folktale

adapted by Caryn Yacowitz

illustrated by Ju-Hong Chen

creatures cannot survive when held captive, honor is important, and sharing helps people through trouble. These respected values are developed when two servants help a coveted mandarin duck, who has been captured by a greedy lord. When the kitchen maid releases the duck against the lord's command, she and another servant are sentenced to death. The grateful drake and his mate, however, outwit the lord and reward the kindness of the servants.

Cranes, like sparrows, are frequently important in Japanese folktales. Anne Laurin's *The Perfect Crane* suggests the desirability of friendship between humans and supernatural creatures. In this story, a lonely magician develops a strong friendship with a crane that he creates from rice paper. Molly Bang's *The Paper Crane* has a similar theme. A hungry man rewards a restaurant owner with a paper crane that can be brought to life by clapping hands, and this attraction creates many customers for the business.

Dianne Snyder's *The Boy of the Three-Year Nap* has a strong female protagonist who outwits her lazy son. The tale is a humorous match of wits. The lazy son tries to trick a wealthy merchant into letting him marry the merchant's daughter. The mother, however, shows that she is the equal of the son. She not only convinces the merchant to repair and enlarge her house but also tricks her son into getting a job. Other strong female protagonists are found in

Three Strong Women, retold by Claus Stamm. This is a humorous story about a powerful wrestler who learns about strength from three women who are even more powerful than he is. Another strong female protagonist is developed in Robert D. San Souci's *The Samurai's Daughter: A Japanese Legend.* In this tale, the beautiful daughter slays a sea monster and restores the sanity of the ruler who had banished her father into exile.

Strong associations with nature and ecology are developed in Sheila Hamanaka's *Screen of Frogs.* A landowner responds favorably when a large frog appears in a dream and begs the man not to sell his home. Through the dream, the frog stresses the disasters that will occur if the frogs do not retain their land. As a reward for not selling the land, a tattered white screen belonging to the man is transformed into a beautifully painted screen of frogs.

Other Asian Folktales. The Asian Cultural Centre for UNESCO has published a series of five books called *Folk Tales from Asia for Children Everywhere.* The series contains stories from many Asian countries. For example, a story from Burma, "The Four Puppets," stresses the harm that wealth and power can bring if they are not tempered with wisdom and love. "The Carpenter's Son," a tale from Afghanistan, is similar to the Arabian story of Aladdin and his magic lamp.

Many folktales from India are included in a series of animal stories traditionally known as the *Panchatantra*. The original tales were moralistic and included reincarnations of the Buddha. English translations, however, usually delete the morals and the references to Buddha. Consequently, the stories have characteristics of folktales. In Judith Ernst's retelling of *The Golden Goose King: A Tale Told by the Buddha,* the storyteller uses a tale told by the Buddha to reveal how a golden goose instructs the king and queen how to rule wisely. In *The Golden Carp and Other Tales from Vietnam,* a collection of six folktales, Lynette Dyer Vuong includes sources for the tales, interpretive notes, and pronunciation guides.

Mirra Ginsburg's *The Chinese Mirror* is a Korean folktale about humorous consequences when a group of people see themselves in a mirror for the first time. They cannot convince each other that each one sees something else in the mirror until the mirror is broken into a hundred shiny splinters. Then, "that was the end of the stranger who looked at the traveler, the young beauty from China, the wrinkled old crone, the neighbor's grandpa, the nasty brat who stole pebbles, and the big fat bully who hurt little boys" (unnumbered).

Nami Rhee's *Magic Spring: A Korean Folktale* develops both humorous irony and the consequences of greed. When a poor, older couple discover a magic spring in the forest, they learn that a drink returns them to their youth. When their rich, greedy neighbor learns about their secret, he goes in search of the spring. Unfortunately, his greed causes him to drink too much water and he becomes an infant. The renewed couple find him in the forest and raise him as their own child.

The theme in Nina Jaffe's *Older Brother, Younger Brother: A Korean Folktale* shows that greed will be punished and kindness will be rewarded. An author's note places this story in the mid-eighteenth century "when it was sung as part of the classic repertoire called pahn-SOH-ree. These epic poems were performed in the courtyards of rural aristocrats and are still preserved by Korean musicians and singers today. The story reflects the strong influence of Confucianism, the ancient Chinese philosophy of life and code of ethics, which was brought to Korea as early as the first century. Different versions of the tale also exist in the folklore of China and Japan, but

the core story probably originated in Northeast Asia from Mongol sources" (author's note).

Laurence Yep's *The Khan's Daughter: A Mongolian Folktale* develops both a quest motif and a change in character as Mongke, a shepherd boy, accomplishes three trials in order to win the Khan's daughter. Two of the trials are imposed by the girl's mother: he must demonstrate proof of strength and proof of bravery. The third trial is formulated by the Khan's daughter. It is this third trial that shows both the character of the girl in determining her own destiny and the changes in Mongke as he goes from a rather foolish and boastful character to one who is both contrite and filled with considerable wisdom.

Errol LeCain has illustrated *Alladin and the Wonderful Lamp,* one of Andrew Lang's versions of the Aladdin tale, one of several Arabian tales collected in the original *The Thousand Nights and a Night,* supposedly told by Scheherazade to King Shahryar of Baghdad in her effort to keep from being beheaded.

Eastern folktales contain such universal motifs as reward for unselfishness, assistance from magical objects, cruel adversaries, and punishment for dishonesty. The tales also emphasize the traditional values of the specific people: homage is paid to ancestors, knowledge and cleverness are rewarded, and greed and miserly behavior are punished.

African Folktales

African folktales are characterized by a highly developed oral tradition. Repetitive language and styles that encourage interaction with the storyteller make them excellent choices for sharing with children. Many of the stories are "why" tales. Such tales explain animal and human characteristics. Verna Aardema's *Why Mosquitoes Buzz in People's Ears* uses cumulative language to explain the buzz. Personified animals, often tricksters, are popular subjects. The hare, the tortoise, and Ananse the spider use wit and trickery to gain their objectives. Chapter 11, "Multicultural Literature," discusses other tales that reflect traditional values of African peoples.

North American Folktales

Many North American folktales have roots in the cultures of other parts of the world or have been influenced by written literature and characters created by professional writers. Consequently, identifying tales that began in a specifically North American oral tradition is often difficult or impossible.

Folklorists identify four types of folktales found in North America: (1) Native American (and Native Canadian) tales that were handed down over centuries of tribal storytelling; (2) folktales of African Americans that reflect African and European themes but that were changed as slaves faced difficulties in a new land; (3) variants of European folktales containing traditional themes, motifs, and characters that were changed to meet the needs of a robust, rural North America; and (4) boisterous, boastful tall tales that originated on this continent. Some collections of folktales, such as Amy L. Cohn's *From Sea to Shining Sea: A Treasury of American Folklore and Folk Songs,* include all of these types of tales. Other sources contain only one type of tale.

Native American Folktales.

Native American tales are usually considered the only traditional tales truly indigenous to the United States. Any study of the traditional literature of native peoples in North America reveals not one group of folktales, but tales different from region to region and tribe to tribe, although most Native American folklore has motifs in common.

Many of the traditional tales reveal why or how animals obtained specific characteristics. For example, Susan L. Roth's *The Story of Light* reveals how light was brought into the world and also why the opossum shuns the sun and has a tail with no fur, a buzzard has a head with no feathers, and a spider's web looks like the sun's rays.

Animal trickster tales are popular in Native American culture, as elsewhere. The tricksters are often ravens, rabbits, or coyotes that have powers of magical transformation. In Gerald McDermott's *Raven: A Trickster Tale from the Pacific Northwest,* the trickster character brings light to the people. Heroes and heroines may also use transformation in undertaking their quests. In McDermott's *Arrow to the Sun: A Pueblo Indian Tale,* for example, a boy becomes an arrow as he searches for his father, the sun-god.

The importance of folklore for passing on tribal beliefs is revealed in Olaf Baker's *Where the Buffaloes Begin.* A young Native American of the Great Plains learns from a tribal storyteller about a sacred spot where the buffaloes rise out of a lake. After he finds the lake, he waits quietly in the night. As he waits, he hears the words of the storyteller singing in his mind:

> Do you hear the noise that never ceases?
> It is the Buffaloes fighting far below.
> They are fighting to get out upon the prairie.
> They are born below the Water but are fighting
>   for the Air.
> In the great lake in the Southland where the
>   Buffaloes begin! (p. 20)

The diversity of Native American cultures, customs and folklore is illustrated in Jamake Highwater's *Anpao: An Indian Odyssey.* Highwater's book emphasizes the importance of traditional tales in transmitting Native American culture. Chapter 11, "Multicultural Literature," discusses these tales and others.

African American Folktales.

Many African American folktales reflect both an African origin and an adaptation to a new environment and the harsh reality of slavery. For example, a rabbit trickster who triumphs over more powerful animals is popular in African folklore. He is also one of the most popular characters in tales collected from black people on southern plantations. This character's popularity with African Americans was probably related to the experience of slavery. Cunning, wit, and deception were often the only weapons available against oppression. (The tortoise and Ananse the spider play similar trickster roles.) The trickster Brer Rabbit is famous in the African American folktales collected by Joel Chandler Harris in nineteenth-century Georgia and published as *Uncle Remus and His Friends* (1892) and *Told by Uncle Remus* (1905).

In 1981, Priscilla Jaquith published similar tales collected from African American people living on the Sea Islands off the coasts of Georgia and South Carolina. The tales in *Bo Rabbit Smart for True: Folktales from the Gullah* are excellent examples of the infusion of later culture, language, and environment into tales from other places and earlier times. African words, such as *cooter* for tortoise, combine with Elizabethan English and dialect from the provinces of Great Britain, such as *bittles* for victuals. In the African tradition, the stories repeat key words to increase their significance: "Alligator, Miz Alligator and all the little alligators slither into the field, KAPUK, kapuk, kapuk, kapuk, kapuk, kapuk, kapuk." These stories about a small, clever rabbit

THROUGH THE EYES OF AN AUTHOR

Traditional Native American Tales

Expert in traditional Native American literature and culture and a collector of traditional tales, JAMAKE HIGHWATER, author of *Anpao: An American Indian Odyssey*, discusses his feelings and beliefs.

In a very real sense, I am the brother of the fox. My whole life revolves around my kinship with four-legged things. I am rooted in the natural world. I'm two people joined into one body. The contradiction doesn't bother me. But people always assume the one they're talking to is the only one there is. That bothers me. There is a little of the legendary Anpao in me, but also a little of John Gardner. I stand in both those worlds, not between them. I'm very much a twentieth-century person, and yet I'm traditional Northern Plains Indian.

I've always had an enormous regard for the intellect. Still, I like to go home to my people, who are in touch with the beginning of things. At home, people are carpenters; some are poets, painters, and teachers; some work on construction jobs. They are people who perceive the importance of small things that are easily missed by those of us who move much too quickly.

I came to terms with the solemn aspects of life very early. I was always among Indians, for we traveled the powwow circuit. I was always listening to some older person telling stories. They are nameless to me now, and countless, because there were so many. I was introduced to the Indian world as children in my tribe were in the 1870s, when we were a nomadic people. I was rootless yet connected to a vital tradition. The elders talked to me and gave me a sense of the meaning of my existence.

I talk and think as a poet, but I don't want to perpetuate the romantic notion of the Indian as watching chipmunks his entire life [and] waiting to see which side of the tree the moss grows on.

For the Indian, art is not reserved for a leisure class, as it is in Anglo society. It is part of our fundamental way of thinking. We are an aesthetic people. Most primal people are. We represent a constant chord that's been resounding ever since man began. While those Cro-Magnon people in the caves of southern France (at least according to Western mentality) should have been out worrying about the great likelihood that they wouldn't survive, they were building scaffolds fifty or sixty feet high and with tiny oil lamps were painting the ceilings of their caves with marvelous magical images. These images were an implicit and important part of their lives. For us, this aesthetic reality is a continuous process. The kiva murals of the Hopi and the Mimbres pottery rival the finest accomplishments of Western art. This idea of life as art is part of being Indian. It's not quaint or curious or charming. It's fundamental, like plowing a field. There's great beauty in plowing a field.

I think Indians have become a metaphor for a larger idea. We are building bridges toward cultures. Some people in white society are also building bridges toward us, and they sometimes join together. That means that it's possible for everyone to find the Indian in himself. It's a kind of sensibility that I'm talking about.

Drawn from an interview with Jane B. Katz, 1980.

---

who outsmarts other animals, such as whales and elephants, are exciting to young children. The stories in Jaquith's and Harris's collections have motifs in common.

Other African American tales about a trickster rabbit are found in West Virginia. Though not as powerful as his adversaries, the rabbit is more intelligent, and he manages to outwit them. Some of these stories, such as Jaquith's version of "Alligator's Sunday Suit," contain a serious moral: "Don't go looking for trouble, else you might find it." Such morals are often found in African American folklore.

William H. Hooks's *The Ballad of Belle Dorcas* is a tale set in the tidewater section of the Carolinas during the time of slavery. The protagonists are a free issue woman and a slave who fall in love, but they are threatened with separation when the master wishes to sell the slave. In addition to revealing the consequences of social injustice, the tale reveals the power of love and the belief in the magical ability of the spells created by conjurers. These tales and other tales are discussed in Chapter 11, "Multicultural Literature."

Variants of European Tales.

The traditional literatures of the United States and Canada contain many variants of traditional European folktales. European settlers from England, France, and elsewhere brought their oral traditions with them. Then, they adapted the stories to reflect a new environment. Consequently, many North American folktales involve familiar European themes, motifs, and characters in settings that portray the unknown wilderness and harsh winters confronted by the early colonizers of North America. The only indigenous Canadian traditional literature comes from the Native Canadian and Inuit peoples.

Eva Martin's *Canadian Fairy Tales* contains twelve French-Canadian and English-Canadian variations of traditional European tales. Ti-Jean tales contain several familiar story elements. The lazy fellow kills one thousand flies with one blow, uses his wits to capture a unicorn and steal a giant's seven-league boots, and eventually marries the princess. In the Canadian variant of "Beauty and the Beast," the enchanted beast is female and the prince stays in her castle. William Hooks's *Moss Gown* is an adaptation of the English Cinderella tale. It also contains elements of King Lear and the plantation South.

The best-known North American variants of European tales belong to the Jack cycle. In these tales, a seemingly nonheroic person overcomes severe obstacles and outwits adversaries. The American "Jack and the Varmits," for example, is similar to the English "The Brave Little Tailor." In keeping with the European tradition, the American Jack is rewarded by a king. Instead of a giant, Jack must overcome a wild hog, a unicorn, and a lion. The influences of rural America are found in both the setting and language. The lion, who was killing cattle,

horses, and humans, came over the mountains from Tennessee. Both the king and Jack speak in frontier dialect. Gail E. Haley's *Jack and the Bean Tree* is an Appalachian variant of "Jack and the Beanstalk." Haley's *Mountain Jack Tales,* a collection of stories from the Jack cycle, has foundations in the mountain regions of America.

Tall Tales.

Boastful frontier humor is found in North American tall tales. These tales reflect the hardships of settlers, who faced severe climatic changes, unknown lands, and people whose lives reflected strange cultures. Exaggerated claims in tall tales—such as those found in Walter Blair's *Tall Tale America: A Legendary History of Our Humorous Heroes*—declare that the American soil is so rich that fast-growing vines damage pumpkins by dragging them on the ground; that frontier people are so powerful that they can lasso and subdue cyclones; and that the leader of the river boaters can outshoot, outfight, outrun, and outbrag everyone in the world.

The North American heroes and heroines who faced extremes in weather, conquered humans and beasts, and subdued the wilderness are not the godlike heroes and heroines of European mythology. Instead, their lives reflect the primitive virtues of brute force, animal cunning, and courage. The characters and situations in tall tales reflect frontier idealism. People are free to travel. They live self-sufficient lives and are extremely resourceful.

American tall tales contain fictional heroes and heroes based on real people. Hard-working, persevering characters—such as Johnny Appleseed, who considered it his mission to plant apple trees across the country—demonstrate duty and endurance. Boisterous, bragging roughnecks—such as Davy Crockett, Calamity Jane, and Paul Bunyan—perform otherwise impossible feats, outshooting a thousand enemies or conquering mighty rivers and immense forests. Other characters—such as the steel-driving man, John Henry—reflect a country that was changing from a rural and agricultural way of life to an urban and mechanized one. *John Tabor's Ride,* by Edward C. Day, reflects the whaling industry and the yarns told by whalers in New England. *Mike Fink: A Tall Tale,* retold by Stephen Kellogg, is another story that emphasizes numerous fantastic feats.

The characters of a supernatural man and an old whaler combine to make a tall tale about whaling. (From John Tabor's Ride *by Edward C. Day, illustrated by Dirk Zimmer. Copyright © 1989 by Edward C. Day, illustrations copyright 1989 by Dirk Zimmer. Reprinted by permission of Alfred A. Knopf, Inc.)*

You may find additional information about the folklore associated with Davy Crockett by reading *The Tall Tales of Davy Crockett: The Second Nashville Series of Crockett Almanacs 1839–1841,* which is published by the University of Tennessee Press. In the introduction to the text, Michael Lofaro (1987) states that Crockett's heroic death increased his image as a boasting, brawling backwoodsman. Lofaro continues:

The "wretched caricatures" soon became fantastic tall tales in the popular comic almanacs that bore Crockett's name. In these works Davy once again "assumed the character drawn for him by others"; it was, however, a character no longer bounded by the achievements of a mortal man, but only by the imagination. (p. x)

Robert D. San Souci's *Cut from the Same Cloth: American Women of Myth, Legend, and Tall Tale* is an excellent tall-tale collection about women in heroic conflicts. San Souci presents tales from different regions and ethnic groups. He also includes source notes and a bibliography.

FABLES

Legend credits the origin of the fable in Western culture to a Greek slave named Aesop, who lived in the sixth century B.C. Aesop's nimble wit supposedly got Aesop's master out of numerous difficulties. Aesop may not have been one person, however. Several experts attribute the early European fables to various sources. Fables are found worldwide; the traditional literatures of China and India, for example, contain fables similar to Aesop's. Whatever their origins, fables are excellent examples of stories handed down over centuries of oral and written literary tradition.

Characteristics

According to R. T. Lenaghan (1967) in his introduction to *Caxton's Aesop,* fables have the following characteristics: (1) they are fiction in the sense that they did not really happen, (2) they are meant to entertain, (3) they are poetic, with double or allegorical significance, and (4) they are moral tales, usually with animal characters. In fables, animals usually talk and behave like humans and possess other human traits. Fables are short, and they usually have not more than two or three characters. These characters perform simple, straightforward actions that result in a single climax. Fables also contain human lessons expressed through the foibles of personified animals.

The characteristics of fables apparently appealed to traditional storytellers around the world. In fifteenth-century England, fables were among the first texts that William Caxton printed on his newly created printing press. Lenaghan credits the popularity of fables to their generic ambiguity. They could be used as entertaining stories, teaching devices, or sermons. They could also reach people of various degrees of intelligence, be bluntly assertive or cleverly ironic, and be didactic or skeptical. Storytellers could emphasize whatever functions they chose.

The continuing popularity of fables led Randolph Caldecott to create his own edition of Aesop in the nineteenth century. *The Caldecott Aesop,* first

The Book of the subtyl historyes and Fables of Esope *published in the fifteenth century, is considered one of William Caxton's most important contributions to European literature.* (The Book of the Subtyl Historyes and Fables of Esope *by William Caxton, published in the fifteenth century.)*

¶ Here begynneth the book of the subtyl historyes and Fables of Esope whiche were translated out of Frensshe in to Englysshe by william Caxton

At Westmynstre In the yere of oure Lorde .m. cccc.lxxxiij

AESOPVS

HRYLAND

published in 1883 and reissued in 1978, provides modern readers with an opportunity to enjoy fables accompanied by hand-colored drawings of a great illustrator of children's books. Caldecott's illustrations show first the animals in a fable, then the people replacing the animals. Sir Roger L'Estrange's seventeenth-century translation of *Aesop's Fables* is also available in a reissued text.

Contemporary Editions

Fables are popular subjects for modern storytellers and illustrators. In his introduction to *Feathers and Tails: Animal Fables from Around the World,* David Kherdian (1992) states his reasons for believing that fables are popular:

These stories speak to our limitations as well as our possibilities, since one without the other is meaningless. We are confused by our potential, our possibilities. Each of us is born knowing there is more—but more of what? As we grow and begin to define what the more is for ourselves, we see that it is nothing more or less than our own wholeness. We need guidance, but we are uncertain how to seek it, or how to apply it once it has been found. In all of this the ancient teaching story can be our guide, for it speaks to us with humor, laughter, and enjoyment, from a source that we can all recognize because it is as old as mankind, as universal as the sun and stars. (p. 8)

Young children like the talking animals and the often humorous climaxes. Authors and illustrators of fables for young children sometimes expand fables into longer, more detailed narrative stories. In *The Tortoise and the Hare,* Janet Stevens expands the storyline of the fable by including the exercises Tortoise undertakes to prepare for the race and the actions of Tortoise's friends as they try to deter Hare. Stevens uses a similar approach in her picture storybook version of Aesop's *The Town Mouse & the Country Mouse.* Another heavily illustrated version of this fable is Helen Craig's *The Town Mouse and the Country Mouse.* Compare the impact of the illustrations and the retellings by each author.

Numerous collections of Aesop's fables have been compiled and illustrated for slightly older children, too. It is interesting to compare the various editions to see how the fables have been interpreted and illustrated. For example, a version of Aesop first published in 1919, *The Aesop for Children,* is in simple narrative form and dialogue. The capture of the mouse in "The Lion and the Mouse" is described in this way:

A Lion lay asleep in the forest, his great head resting on his paws. A timid little Mouse came upon him unexpectedly, and in her fright and haste to get away, ran across the Lion's nose. Roused from his nap, the Lion laid his huge paw angrily on the tiny creature to kill her.

"Spare me!" begged the poor Mouse. "Please let me go and some day I will surely repay you."

The Lion was much amused to think that a Mouse could ever help him. But he was generous and finally let the Mouse go. (p. 19)

The moral is simply stated in this version: "A kindness is never wasted."

The TOWN MOUSE & the COUNTRY MOUSE

AN AESOP FABLE
ADAPTED AND ILLUSTRATED BY
JANET STEVENS

The author has expanded on a fable to create a picture storybook in The Town Mouse & the Country Mouse. *(From* The Town Mouse & the Country Mouse, *adapted and illustrated by Janet Stevens. Copyright © 1987 by Janet Stevens. Reprinted by permission of Holiday House. All rights reserved.)*

Tom Paxton retells fables in verse in his *Aesop's Fables*. Paxton describes the incident in which the mouse is captured in "The Lion and the Mouse":

> He ran over the lion, who awoke with a roar:
> "Who's treating my back like the jungle floor?"
> He grabbed the poor mouse by his poor little tail.
> "Oh, please, Mister Lion, I swear without fail,
> If you'll please just release me, I promise someday
> The debt will be one that I'll gladly repay."
> The proud lion laughed and let the mouse go.
> (unnumbered)

The moral of this fable is presented in verse form in the last two lines:

> Yes, sometimes the weak and sometimes the
> strong
> Must help each other to save right from wrong.
> (unnumbered)

Jane Yolen's *A Sip of Aesop* provides an interesting version for comparison with more traditional versions of the fables. Yolen retells the fables in poetic form, including the moral at the end of the fable. For example, "The Dog and the Bone" ends with the moral:

> You may not have time
> For a final correction.
> Don't open your mouth
> Without proper reflection. (unnumbered)

Contemporary versions of fables differ in the illustrator's style as well as the author's style. Heidi Holder's *Aesop's Fables* contains detailed, elegant paintings surrounded by equally detailed borders. Michael Hague's *Aesop's Fables* is illustrated with full-page paintings in somber, earthy tones. Fulvio Testa's *Aesop's Fables* also follows each fable with a full-page illustration. Each illustration is framed with a colorful design.

An interesting cross-cultural comparison of both texts and illustrations may be made with John Bierhorst's *Doctor Coyote: A Native American Aesop's Fables*. Bierhorst identifies both Spanish-Aztec and ancient Latin connections. Bierhorst states:

The Aztec Aesop's was adapted in the 1500s by one or more Indian retellers, using a now-lost Spanish collection of the standard fables. All of these, however, can be traced to Latin and Greek manuscripts of late classical and medieval times. Compared with the originals, the Aztec variants differ mainly in the cast of characters, which includes Coyote and Puma, two of the best-known animal tricksters in Native American folklore. (author's note, unnumbered)

Wendy Watson's illustrations reflect settings in New Mexico.

Another text that may be used for cross-cultural comparisons of fables is David Kherdian's *Feathers and Tails: Animal Fables from Around the World*. This collection includes fables collected from many lands, including Russia, West Africa, Armenia, North America, India, and China. A list of sources identifies the origins of the fables.

Other interesting comparisons can be made between contemporary versions of Aesop and versions published in earlier centuries. The language, spellings, and illustrations in these various editions differ widely. Some were intended for adults; others were specifically for children. Older children can learn more about their literary heritage by comparing and discussing various versions of these ancient stories.

With a castle in the background, a detailed drawing creates an elegant setting for a fable. (From Aesop's Fables, *by Heidi Holder. Copyright © 1981 by Heidi Holder. Reproduced by permission of Viking Penguin Inc.)*

 MYTHS

Every ancient culture made up stories that answered questions about the creation of the earth, the origins of people, and the reasons for natural phenomena. The Greeks called these explanations *mythos,* which means tales or stories. Today, people sometimes use the word *myth* to describe any story they consider to be untrue. However, in literary terms, a myth is a story containing fanciful or supernatural incidents intended to explain nature or tell about the gods and demons of early peoples. In the distant past, as in some traditional cultures today, the stories were taken as fact made sacred by religious belief. The supernatural characters in the myths were considered divine. They controlled the forces of nature on earth and ruled the sun, moon, stars, and planets. Many of them had their own temples, where people worshipped them with prayer and sacrifice to win their favor.

Myths live on in contemporary literature and provide an understanding of the rich cultural heritage that we have acquired from ancient civilizations all over the world. Greek, Roman, and Norse mythology have been most influential in Western culture. Many terms used in those mythologies are also found in modern language, such as our names for the planets and for the days of the week. Children find these stories exciting and become interested in this rich literary heritage.

Joseph Campbell (1988) argues that myths are powerful literature and should be read and understood by everyone. He believes that four functions related to myths are as important today as they were in earlier times. The functions are (1) a mystical one that allows people to experience the awe of the universe, (2) a cosmological one that shows the shape and mystery of the universe, (3) a sociological one that supports and validates a certain social order, and (4) a pedagogical one that teaches people how to live.

James Houston (1990), a reteller of Inuit myths and legends, stresses the importance of preserving the ancient stories of any culture. He states:

Inuit songs and stories, like their carvings, often reveal an enormous freshness and ingenuity. But there is one enormous difference. A carving may be lost in the permafrost near some ancient campsite only to be excavated thousands of years later to tell us much about its maker. An unrecorded story or a song will disappear forever with the last breath of its teller and has no way to return. (p. 106)

Myths provide children with knowledge about ancestral cultures and allow the children to look at other cultures from the inside out. Myths are models for belief; they are serious statements about existence. They provide a framework for understanding the things that other people did or thought. Myths are tools for understanding and expanded expression. They offer new dimensions for imagination and suggest ways for children to gain insights from their daydreams. Myths also provide means of introducing children to literary allusions: An author describing something as being "as swift as Diana" or "as mighty as Zeus" is alluding to characteristics of gods.

Greek and Roman Mythology

Probably, the best-known myths in Western culture originated in ancient Greece. When the Romans conquered Greece, they adopted many Greek myths, applying them to their own equivalent deities. In order to understand these stories, Helen Sewell states in the introduction to *A Book of Myths, Selections from Bulfinch's Age of Fable* (1942, 1964) that one must be acquainted with ancient Greek ideas about the structure of the universe. The Greeks believed that the universe had been created out of unorganized matter called *chaos,* swirling and transparent vapor. Form and shape resulted in *order* and *cosmos.* The Greeks believed that the first things formed out of chaos were the gods: *Gaia* (meaning earth; *terra* is the Roman name) and *Ouranos* (meaning sky; *Uranus* is the Roman name). From the offspring of the female Gaia and the male Ouranos emerged the remaining Greek gods and goddesses, who lived on Mount Olympus (an actual mountain in Greece) and frequently came into the human world.

The Greeks believed that the earth was flat and circular and that their own country was the center. Around the earth flowed the river Ocean. The dawn, the sun, and the moon were supposed to rise out of the eastern Ocean, driven by gods and giving light to gods and mortals. The majority of the stars also rose out of and sank into this river.

The Greeks believed that the northern part of the earth beyond the mountains was inhabited by a race of people called Hyperboreans. In these mountains were the caverns from which came the piercing north winds that sometimes chilled Greece. To the south lived the Ethiopians, whom the gods favored; on the west lay the Elysian Plain, where mortals favored by the gods were transported to enjoy immortality. Roman myths drew essentially the same picture.

Although mythology and folktales contain similar motifs and themes, myths include Bascom's requirements for setting, time, attitude, and principal characters. Chart 6–4 compares points in Edna Barth's version of the myth *Cupid and Psyche* and the Norse folktale "East of the Sun and West of the Moon."

The plot in the two tales is similar: A young girl breaks a promise, her loved one leaves, she searches for him, and she overcomes obstacles or performs tasks before they are reunited. The principal characters differ in important characteristics, however. Psyche, a beautiful mortal princess, is the object of a goddess's anger and jealousy. She later falls in love

CHART 6–4   A comparison of a myth and a folktale

Cupid and Psyche	"East of the Sun and West of the Moon"
Setting Mount Olympus, Greece	Any kingdom
Time In a remote past, when gods and goddesses dwelt on the earth	Once upon a time
Attitude Sacred—worship of the deity was required or punishment resulted	Secular
Principal Characters Venus (the goddess of love) Cupid (the son of Venus) Psyche (a mortal girl who becomes immortal)	Transformed human boy Human girl Troll princess

with a god, performs tasks stipulated by the goddess, and requires intervention from the most divine ruler, Jupiter.

Barth sees strong religious significance in the Cupid and Psyche myth. The myth, she reminds us, originally represented the progress of the human soul as it travels toward perfection. Symbolized by Psyche, the soul originated in heaven, where all is love, which is symbolized by Cupid. The soul is then condemned for a period of time to wander the earth and undergo hardship and misery. If the soul proves worthy, it is returned to heaven and reunited with love.

Circumstances surrounding the creation of the gods and goddesses, their places within the Olympian family, the consequences of their varied personality traits, and their accomplishments create exciting tales and enjoyable reading for children. Chart 6–5 lists Greek and Roman gods and goddesses, their accomplishments, their powers, and texts that include myths about these deities.

CHART 6–5   Greek and Roman gods and goddesses*

Name	Accomplishments	Powers	Examples of Texts
Zeus (Jupiter)	Ruler of Mount Olympus King of deities and humans	Used lightning to gain control of the universe	Gates's *Lord of the Sky: Zeus*
Hera (Juno)	Queen of deities and humans Goddess of marriage and childbirth	Protected married women	Bulfinch's *A Book of Myths*
Athena (Minerva)	Goddess of wisdom, war, and handicrafts	Established rule of law Gave olive tree to mankind Protected cities	Gates's *The Warrior Goddess: Athena*
Apollo (Apollo)	God of Sun Patron of truth, music, medicine, and archery	Established the oracle (prophets who gave advice)	Gates's *The Golden God: Apollo* Bulfinch's *A Book of Myths*
Artemis (Diana)	Goddess of moon and the hunt Mighty archer and hunter	Guarded animals, nature, and women	Bulfinch's *A Book of Myths*
Aphrodite (Venus)	Goddess of love and beauty: Flowers sprang up where she walked	Had power to beguile gods Gave birth to Fear and Terror	Gates's *Two Queens of Heaven: Aphrodite and Demeter*
Demeter (Ceres)	Goddess of crops	Gave grain and fruit Caused famine when Hades took her daughter to the underworld	Coolidge's *Greek Myths* Gates's *Two Queens of Heaven: Aphrodite and Demeter*

Contemporary versions of Greek and Roman myths vary widely in terms of author's style, complexity of text, and illustration. Consider these factors when choosing myths to share with children of various ages and interests. Eight- or nine-year-olds, for example, enjoy Edna Barth's *Cupid and Psyche*. Barth's rendition of this myth is appropriate for children who enjoy such folktales as "Beauty and the Beast" and "East of the Sun and West of the Moon."

Children also enjoy Warwick Hutton's *The Trojan Horse*. This story recounts how the Greeks used a wooden horse to conquer the city of Troy. The two-page illustrations provide detail from the period and encourage younger readers to visualize the setting.

Leonard Everett Fisher's *Theseus and the Minotaur* has bold, full-page illustrations to accompany his version of the story of a brave youth who slays an evil monster. Warwick Hutton's *Theseus and the Minotaur* is illustrated with watercolor paintings that are especially effective in the depiction of the tragic return of the hero.

Fisher's *The Olympians: Great Gods and Goddesses of Ancient Greece* provides a brief introduction to the characters in mythology. Gerald McDermott's *Daughter of Earth: A Roman Myth* is a highly illustrated version of the Ceres and Proserpina story. These two highly illustrated books are appropriate for all ages.

Many older children enjoy longer, more developed versions of the myths. Doris Gates develops stories with fast-paced plots and language that suggests word pictures. Her style reads well and her

CHART 6–5 Continued

Name	Accomplishments	Powers	Examples of Texts
Hermes (Mercury)	Divine messenger of the gods Trickster who was named god of commerce, orators, and writers	Protected flocks, cattle, and mischief makers	Gates's *The Golden God: Apollo*
Poseidon (Neptune)	God of the sea and earthquakes	Gave horses to humans Answered voyagers' prayers	*D'Aulaires' Book of Greek Myths*
Dionysus (Bacchus)	God of wine, fertility, the joyous life, and hospitality	Gave Greece the gift of wine	Bulfinch's *A Book of Myths* Coolidge's *Greek Myths*
Ares (Mars)	God of war	Caused the evils and sufferings of war	*D'Aulaires' Book of Greek Myths*
Hephaestus (Vulcan)	God of fire and artisans	From his forges, he produced Pandora, the first mortal woman Created mechanical objects	*D'Aulaires' Book of Greek Myths*
Eros (Cupid)	God of love (son of Venus)	Shot arrows at people to make them fall in love	Barth's *Cupid and Psyche*

*Roman names in parentheses.

books are excellent for sharing orally. For example, her description of the creation of Athena in *The Warrior Goddess: Athena* seems appropriate:

She sprang from the head of Zeus, father of gods. Born without a mother, she was fully grown and fully armed. Her right hand gripped a spear, while her left steadied a shield on her forearm. The awful aegis, a breast ornament bordered with serpents, hung from her neck, and from her helmeted head to her sandaled feet she was cloaked in radiance, like the flash of weaponry. So the great goddess Athena came to join the family of gods on high Olympus, and, of all Zeus's children, she was his favorite. (p. 11)

Older children can contrast this description by Gates with her description of the creation of the goddess of love and beauty in *Two Queens of Heaven: Aphrodite and Demeter:*

There appeared a gathering of foam on the water. It resembled the white spindrift that trails behind a great wave as it breaks. But this form did not trail. It formed itself into

a raft rising and falling with the sea. Suddenly a woman's figure appeared atop the raft balancing on slender feet. She was young and beautiful beyond anything in human form the sun had ever shone on. (pp. 9–10)

Geraldine McCaughrean's *Greek Myths* is a collection of sixteen epic tales about heroes, gods, and warriors. Bernard Evslin's *The Nemean Lion* is the story of the Nemean Lion, which according to Greek mythology was created so that Zeus could destroy Heraclea. The various art galleries and museums that are the sources of the illustrations are acknowledged at the back of the text. Versions of myths told by Olivia Coolidge, Charles Kingsley, and Padraic Colum are also good choices for older children.

In *Dateline: Troy*, Paul Fleischman retells the Greek myth about the Trojan War and places the war into a contemporary context by placing appropriate, actual contemporary newspaper articles on pages facing similar content. In his introduction, Fleischman

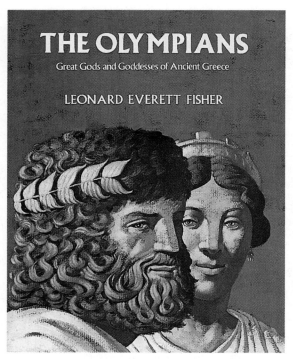

Fisher's illustrations and text provide an introduction to the Greek gods and goddesses. (From The Olympians: Great Gods and Goddesses of Ancient Greece *by Leonard Everett Fisher. Copyright © 1984 by Leonard Everett Fisher. Reprinted by permission of Holiday House.)*

makes readers feel that they are reading about conflicts and people that are still found in the world today: "Listeners and readers had always found real human nature in what had transpired there. Envy-maddened Ajax, lovestruck Paris, crafty Odysseus, and all the others have walked the earth in every age and place. They come from the distant Bronze Age, it's as current as this morning's headlines. The Trojan War is still being fought. Simply open a newspaper . . . ." (p. 9).

Norse Mythology

A far different group of gods and heroes existed in the Norse universe of ice, glaciers, and cold mountains. The harsh conditions of the far North helped form the Norse people and their legends. According to Kevin Crossley-Holland (1983), recurring strains in Norse mythology include a strong sense of fate that governs the lives of both gods and humans; a heroic bond between characters that is character-ized by physical and moral courage, loyalty, and a willingness to take vengeance; a belief in omens; an ironic wit; a restless spirit of adventure; and a keen sense of wonder in the natural world and a close identification with nature. Unsurprisingly, Norse mythology tells that a frost giant was the first being created on earth.

Norse mythology influenced subsequent oral and written literature in northern Europe. Shakespeare was influenced by an old Norse tale when he wrote *Hamlet;* J. R. R. Tolkien, a professor of Anglo-Saxon literature at Oxford University, relied on his knowledge of the northern sagas when he wrote *The Hobbit* and *The Lord of the Rings.*

The tales of the northern gods and goddesses were collected during the twelfth and thirteenth centuries from the earlier oral tradition. These original tales formed two volumes, the *Elder Edda* and the *Younger Edda.* These texts are now the sources for most of our knowledge about Norse mythology. According to Olivia Coolidge (1951), Norse mythology maintains that the earth began when a frost giant, Ymir, came out of swirling mists. The shifting particles formed a great cow, whose milk nourished Ymir. As time went by, sons and daughters were also created out of the mists. Gods took form when the cow began to lick the great ice blocks that filled the mists. As she licked, a huge god appeared. When he stood up, his descendants were formed from his warm breath.

The frost giants were evil, so the gods vowed to destroy them. A mighty battle resulted between the gods and the frost giants, with the gods finally overpowering the giants. Ymir was destroyed, and the remaining giants fled into the outer regions and created a land of mists and mountains. The mightiest of the gods, Odin, looked at the dead frost giant, Ymir, and suggested that the gods use his body to make a land where they could live. They formed Ymir's body into the round, flat earth, and on its center, they built mountains to contain their home, Asgard. Ymir's skull was used to form the great arch of heaven; his blood was the ocean, a barrier between the earth and giantland. The gods stole sparks from the fiery regions to light the stars, and they built chariots in which they placed sun and moon spirits to ride over the earth.

The Norse world of tales filled with heroism, humor, and wisdom and peopled with gods, goddesses, giants, and dwarfs comes alive in Mary Pope

Osborne's *Favorite Norse Myths.* These tales retold from the *Elder Edda* and the *Younger Edda* are introduced with quotes from the *Poetic Edda,* written down in the tenth century. For example, the first myth, "Creation: The Nine Worlds," begins with the following quote:

Twas the earliest of times
When Ymir lived:
There was no sand nor sea
Nor cooling wave.
Earth had not been,
Nor heaven on high,
There was a yawning void
And grass no where (p. 1)

Osborne then begins the tale in a similar manner that places readers into this far distant time: "In the morning of time there was no sand, no sea, and no clouds. There was no heaven, no earth, and no grass. There was only a region of icy mist called Niflheim, a region of fire called Muspell, and a great yawning empty void between them called Ginnuga-gap" (p. 1). The author provides an introduction that places the Norse myths into their historic time and setting. In addition, sections contain pronunciation guides and identifications of the gods, goddesses, giants, and other creatures; meanings of symbols and runes; a bibliography; and an index.

Padraic Colum portrays the strong moral code of Odin in his version of "The Building of the Wall," found in *The Children of Odin: The Book of Northern Myths.* Even though a protective wall is built around Asgard, Odin grieves:

But Odin, the Father of the Gods, as he sat upon his throne was sad in his heart, sad that the Gods had got their wall built by a trick, that oaths had been broken, and that a blow had been struck in injustice in Asgard. (p. 12)

Olivia E. Coolidge's *Legends of the North* is an excellent source of stories about the Norse gods and goddesses who lived on earth in the mighty citadel of Asgard and the heroes and heroines who lived under their power. In "The Apples of Idun," the divine beings often walked on earth because the mighty Odin believed they should know their realm intimately, in stone, flower, and leaf.

In Coolidge's text, Thor, the god of war, strides around with red hair bristling and fierce eyes ablaze. Sometimes, he rides in his chariot drawn by red-eyed goats, which are as shaggy and fierce as their master.

"The Hammer of Thor" is an excellent choice for storytelling. (From Legends of the North, *by Olivia Coolidge. Copyright © 1951 and renewed 1979 by Olivia E. Coolidge. Reprinted by permission of Houghton Mifflin Co.)*

One humorous selection from this book is "The Hammer of Thor." In this story, Thor searches loudly for his missing hammer. Children probably feel close to Thor as he responds in exasperation when Freyja, the goddess of beauty, asks him where he put it. He shouts, "If I knew where I put it, I should not be looking for it now" (p. 35).

Thor discovers that the giant Thyrm has stolen the hammer and wants Freyja as ransom. When the goddess vehemently refuses to become the giant's bride, the suggestion is made that Thor dress up as a bride and go to giantland to retrieve his own hammer. After considerable argument, the huge god dresses in gown and veil to cover his fierce eyes and bristling beard, and accompanied by the impish Loki, he leaves for giantland.

Mighty Thor remains quiet as the wedding feast progresses, and fast-witted Loki answers the giant's questions and calms his suspicions. Finally, Thor is able to touch his hammer as the wedding ceremony begins. This is what he has been waiting for; he regains his hammer, overpowers the giant, removes his skirts, and leaves for home.

Thor's courage, loyalty, and willingness to take vengeance are recurring strains found in this mythology. The humor and action in this tale make it excellent for storytelling. Other enjoyable Norse tales suitable for sharing with children include Ingri and Edgar Parin D'Aulaire's *Norse Gods and Giants* and Kevin Crossley-Holland's *The Faber Book of Northern Legends.*

Myths from Other Cultures

All cultures include mythology that allows their peoples to experience and to explain the awe of the universe. As do the Greek and Norse myths, these myths reflect the cultures and the settings from which they originated. For example, Kiri Te Kanawa's *Land of the Long White Cloud: Maori Myths, Tales, and Legends* is a collection of ancient folklore told by the Polynesian sailors who discovered New Zealand—The Land of the Long White Cloud. Here are creation stories, trickster tales, and legends of various Maori tribes. The first tale, "The Birth of Maui," describes the birth of this trickster character and explains why he grew up to be a maker of mischief. The setting is appropriate for a culture that is so influenced by the ocean:

Out in the middle of the wide, wide ocean, where the sky rests on the edges and there is no land to be seen, a little bundle of seaweed rose and fell in the swell. Seabirds wheeled around overhead, their lonely cries echoing across the water. The sun beat down and a breeze stirred the surface, pushing the seaweed for miles and miles. (p. 12)

Michael Foreman's predominantly blue and green illustrations create a mood of a land surrounded by water.

Virginia Hamilton's *In the Beginning: Creation Stories from Around the World* includes twenty-five myths from various cultures. Each myth includes a comment in which Hamilton provides information about the source of the myth and some interpretative information. For example, the myth "Apsu and Tiamat the Creators" includes the following comment:

This myth is taken from the stunning Babylonian creation verse narrative, *Enuma elish*, perhaps the most famous of the Near Eastern texts. It symbolizes unity from which all life begins, and it also represents a World-Parent myth type. Apsu and Tiamat are not only ancestors of the gods, they also symbolize the living, unformed matter of the world.

One of the purposes of the *Enuma elish* was to praise Marduk, who was the main god of Babylon—to establish him as supreme, and to honor Babylon as the highest city.

The *Enuma elish* was discovered in the ruins of King Ashurbanipal's library at Nineveh dating back to 668–626 B.C., but it has been traced back to the First Babylonian Dynasty, 2050–1750 B.C., and the age of King Hammurabi, 1900 B.C., and even further back to the Sumerians who lived in the region before the Babylonians. The narrative takes its name from the first line: "Enuma elish la nabu shamanu . . . ," meaning "When on high the heaven had not been named. . . ." (p. 85)

Barry Moser's illustrations add to the feelings of wonder that are reflected in these myths.

Some of the folklore from the Middle East reflects the common ground between Islam and Christianity. Shulamith Levy Oppenheim's *Ibis,* thought to date back to the ninth century B.C., is both a creation story explaining the beginnings of humankind and our troubles and a cautionary tale showing the dangers of disobeying God's orders. The author tells us that this version of the Adam and Eve story "can be found in the work of Jarir at-Tabari, a famous Islamic scholar who was a religious authority and historian. Born about 839 A.D. in Amul, a city near the southern shore of the Caspian Sea, he traveled throughout the Islamic world as a young man and finally settled in Baghdad, in what is now Iraq. He acquired material for his history of the world from oral storytelling and literary sources, as well as from the Koran" (author's note, unnumbered). You may compare this variant of the Adam and Eve story with the Christian version.

 LEGENDS

According to Richard Cavendish in his Introduction to *Legends of the World* (1982):

Legends stand the test of time, better than genuine history does. . . . The territory of legend has history on one of its borders, myth on another and folk-tale on a third. The frontier zones are vague and shifting, and perhaps no two people will ever agree about precisely where the boundary lines fall. . . . Everywhere in the world, legendary stories of what happened in the past have been handed down from generation to generation. They are part of the inherited conglomerate of accepted beliefs, values and attitudes which give a people its identity. These stories consequently provide invaluable evidence about the societies that give birth to them, and insights into human nature in general. (p. 9)

The great legends in traditional literature are closely related to mythology. Many of these legends have been transmitted over the centuries in the form of epics. Epics are long narrative poems about the deeds of traditional or historical human heroes and heroines of high station. Two of the better-known Greek epics are *The Iliad* and *The Odyssey*. *The Iliad* is an account of the Trojan War. *The Odyssey* reports the journey of Odysseus (Ulysses in Latin) as he defeats the Cyclops, overcomes the song of the sirens, and manages to survive ten long years of hazardous adventures. Gods, goddesses, and other supernatural beings play important roles in such epics, but the focus is human characters.

"Beowulf," the story of a human warrior, is usually considered the outstanding example of Norse epic poetry. Beowulf's struggle against evil has three main episodes. First, Beowulf fights and kills the monster Grendel. Second, Beowulf dives to the depths of a pool and attacks Grendel's mother, She. Third, Beowulf fights the dragon Firedrake and is mortally wounded.

Versions of this epic are available in both narrative and poetic form. One version, which the author Robert Nye calls a new telling, is written in narrative form for young readers. In this version, Beowulf is strong, but he is also good—loyal, courageous, and willing to take vengeance. His character epitomizes the heroic code found in Norse myths. A combination of heroic deeds and honorable characteristics make it possible for his good name to live after him. For example, Nye describes the hero as having real strength. It "lay in the balance of his person—which is perhaps another way of saying that he was strong because he was good, and good because he had the strength to accept things in him which were bad" (p. 25). His good is so powerful that it is felt by the evil monsters and is instrumental in their defeat.

Fate, a strong code of honor, and a willingness to avenge wrong are emphasized in Kevin Crossley-Holland's *Beowulf*. Crossley-Holland develops the importance of fate as Beowulf ponders the outcome of his forthcoming struggle with the monster Grendel: "Who knows? Fate goes always as it must" (p. 11) and "If a man is brave enough and not doomed to die, fate often spares him to fight another day" (p. 13). The importance of fate is reem-

phasized after Beowulf's victory, as King Hrothgar declares: "Beowulf, bravest of men, fate's darling! Your friends are fortunate, your enemies not to be envied" (p. 34).

Crossley-Holland develops a strong code of honor when Beowulf refuses to use a sword or a shield because the monster fights without weapons. Crossley-Holland combines honor and vengeance as Beowulf cries that he will avenge the Danes, the people who gave refuge to his father. Honor and vengeance are also part of the monster's code, and Beowulf is pleased when he discovers: "There is honor amongst monsters as there is honor amongst men. Grendel's mother came to the hall to avenge the death of her son" (p. 25). The conclusion emphasizes Beowulf's heroic characteristics: "They said that of all kings on earth, he was the kindest, the most gentle, the most just to his people, the most eager for fame" (p. 46).

Many of the heroes and heroines in epic legends reflect a strong sense of goodness as they overcome various worldly evils. The line between legend and myth is often vague, however. The early legends usually enlarged upon the lives of religious figures, such as martyrs and saints. In more recent times, legends developed around royal figures and folk heroes and heroines. Chart 6–6 shows similarities and differences between myth and legend.

We consider the tales of King Arthur to be legends rather than myths because they are stories primarily about humans rather than supernatural beings and because historical tradition maintains that King Arthur actually existed in fairly recent times. Tales of this legendary British king were so popular in early England that Sir Thomas Malory's *Morte d'Arthur* was one of the first books published in England.

Another early version of the tale is Howard Pyle's *The Story of King Arthur and His Knights*. The first section of Pyle's version, "The Book of King Arthur," reveals how Arthur removed the sacred sword Excalibur from a stone and signified that he was the rightful king of England, claimed his birthright, wed Guinevere, and established the Round Table. The second section, "The Book of Three Worthies," tells about Merlin the magician, Sir Pellias, and Sir Gawaine. The original version of this book, with Pyle's illustrations, has been reissued. Other editions of Arthurian legends include Rosemary Sutcliff's *The Sword and the Circle: King Arthur and the Knights of the Round Table, The Light*

CHART 6–6 Similarities and differences between myth and legend

Myth: "The Birth of Athena"	Legend: "Tales of King Arthur"
Belief Told as factual—the birth of a goddess	Told as factual—the life of a British chieftain of the fifth–sixth century
Setting Mount Olympus, Greece	British Isles
Time In a remote past, when gods and goddesses dwelt on the earth	In the time of kings and knights, within a recognizable world
Attitude Sacred—Athena (a goddess) sprang from the head of Zeus (father of the gods)	Sacred—a quest for the Holy Grail Secular—King Arthur established the Round Table and was the leader of the knights
Principal Characters Nonhuman—the goddess assists heroes and heroines in quests	Human—the king does not have supernatural powers

Beyond the Forest, and *The Road to Camlann: The Death of King Arthur.* In *Parzival: The Quest of the Grail Knight,* Katherine Paterson retells a legendary tale about another knight from Arthur's court.

Selina Hastings's *Sir Gawain and the Loathly Lady* retells one of the Arthurian legends in a picture-book format. Characteristically, the tale includes a challenge, a quest, enchantment, and a promise demanded by the code of chivalry. Juan Wijngaard's illustrations capture both the evil menace of the black knight and the ancient splendor of Arthur's court.

Another legendary figure in English culture is Robin Hood, the hero of Sherwood Forest. Stories about Robin Hood were told orally for centuries and were mentioned in manuscripts as early as 1360. Legend suggests that he was born Robert Fitzooth, Earl of Huntingdon, in Nottinghamshire, England, in 1160. According to the tales, he was a great archer. He and his band of outlaws poached the king's deer, robbed the rich, and gave to the poor.

Stories of Robin Hood are popular with children. Movies and television plays have been produced about his adventures. Howard Pyle's *The Merry Adventures of Robin Hood* provides visions of what it would be like to live "in merry England in the time of old" and to interact with Little John, Maid Marian, Friar Tuck, the Sheriff of Nottingham, and King Richard of the Lion's Heart. Margaret Early's *Robin Hood* is a highly illustrated version of the legend. Children enjoy comparing the various editions and describing the strengths and weaknesses of each. For this purpose, even the Walt Disney movie that presents Robin Hood as a fox, Little John as a bear, and Prince John as a lion adds to a lively discussion, especially about characterization.

The Outlaws of Sherwood is Robin McKinley's interpretation of the Robin Hood legend. McKinley has created a vivid and readable story that includes both a castle-versus-cottage conflict and romanticism of the original time. For example, through the words of Alan-a-Dale, she shows the conflict between the outlaws and their wealthier antagonists:

Indeed, perhaps I have heard of this band for enough of time that I have written a ballad or two about them; a ballad or two received well enough at market day among the yeoman farmers and goodwives, but not so well among those who live in great castles and feel the need to have an eye to their own wealth. (p. 71)

This text is good for reading and for making comparisons among Robin Hood legends. You may also compare Michael Cadnum's *In a Dark Wood,* which is told from the point of view of the sheriff.

Page design is enhanced by plain-colored borders on illustrated pages and drawings of plants and scenes bordering text pages. (From Saint George and the Dragon. *Retold by Margaret Hodges and illustrated by Trina Schart Hyman. Illustration copyright © 1984 by Trina Schart Hyman. Used by permission of Holiday House.)*

The hero in Margaret Hodges's adaptation of the English legend *Saint George and the Dragon* exemplifies the characteristics found in legendary heroes. He is noble, courageous, and willing to avenge a wrong. A legendary fight for freedom and independence is retold by Margaret Early in *William Tell.* This beautifully illustrated text captures the mood of the historic period as well as the life of the Swiss hero, William Tell. Another highly illustrated version of the legend is Leonard Everett Fisher's *William Tell.* Kate Seredy's *The White Stag* tells how the Hun-Magyar tribes migrated into Eastern Europe and created Hungary. Selma Lagerlof's *The Legend of the Christmas Rose,* retold by Ellin Greene, is the Swedish tale about the creation of the beautiful flower that blooms every Christmas Eve in remembrance of the birth of the Christ Child.

The Hawaiian Islands provide the setting for Marcia Brown's *Backbone of the King: The Story of Pakáa and His Son Ku.* The characters display the qualities of other legendary heroes. Bravery, honor, and willingness to avenge a wrong characterize the chief, a trusted adviser to the king, who is unjustly wronged and then brought back to honor through the brave actions of his son.

Jewish legends with Biblical sidelights are important for understanding the Jewish culture. Sandy Eisenberg Sasso's *But God Remembered: Stories of Women from Creation to the Promised Land* includes legends about Lilith, who tradition tells us was Adam's first wife, and other little-known female figures such as Serach, the Granddaughter of Jacob, and the five daughters of Zelophehad, who come to Moses after their father dies and ask to inherit their father's land. The characteristics of these women reflect many of the important values found in Jewish folklore. For example, in "The Psalm of Serach," Serach has the characteristics of grace and wisdom. She feels honored because her father taught her the wisdom of the ancestors. Through her beautiful singing voice and the Psalm she writes, the storyteller shows the importance of music and of Psalms to impact knowledge and understanding. Through the Psalm, readers discover the importance of hope, forgiveness, and God's role in Jewish history.

Three versions of the legend about the Golem provide opportunities for comparisons of both illustrations and text. For example, David Wisniewski's *Golem* is a highly illustrated tale about a rabbi who brings to life a clay giant to help the people during a very dangerous time in sixteenth-century Prague. The cut-paper illustrations give a three-dimensional appearance to both the architecture and the characters. They also stress the power that is found in the form of the Golem. Within the illustrations are numerous examples of Jewish culture such as Hebrew letters, the rabbi, the holy texts, the yellow circles worn on the left shoulders or sleeves of many of the characters, and the synagogue.

Wisniewski's version may be compared with Barbara Rogasky's *The Golem,* illustrated by Trina Schart Hyman, and Isaac Bashevis Singer's *The Golem,* illustrated by Uri Shulevitz. Both of these books present longer versions of the Golem story and include fewer illustrations. As you read these three texts, compare the power of the writing, consider the information provided in the author's or illustrator's notes, and view the impact of the illustrations.

Legends help children understand the conditions of times that created a need for brave and honorable men and women. These tales of adventure stress the noblest actions of humans. In legends, justice reigns over injustice. Children can feel the magnitude of the oral tradition as they listen to these tales, so reading legends aloud is the best way to introduce them to children.

 ## SUGGESTED ACTIVITIES

for Adult Understanding of Traditional Literature

- Choose a folktale that is found in more than one media. Compare the different interpretations and versions.

- Read the stories included in Charles Perrault's *Tales of Mother Goose* and some tales collected by the Brothers Grimm. Note similarities and differences in the characterizations, settings, and actions. Describe the people for whom you believe the stories were originally told.

- Choose a professional group that has been interested in researching and interpreting traditional literature (such as early Christian scholars, folklorists, psychologists, or anthropologists). Investigate this group's interpretations of several folktales.

- Read a cumulative tale, a humorous tale, a beast tale, a magic and wonder tale, a *pourquoi* tale, and a realistic tale. Compare the characterizations, settings, themes, and styles.

- Choose a common theme found in folktales, such as that in Cinderella or in trickster stories. Find examples of similar stories in folktales from several countries. What are the similarities and differences? How do the stories reflect cultural characteristics?

- Select a country and several traditional tales from that country. Choose stories for which illustrators conducted extensive research before completing the drawings. Share your discoveries about the fine arts of the country with the class.

- Choose three folktales from different countries. Compare the actions developed in the three tales.

- Choose several folktales that are not compared in Chart 6–2. Following a similar format, analyze the tales.

- Read a fable in *Caxton's Aesop* and in *The Caldecott Aesop.* Compare these versions of the fables with a modern version. Are there differences in writing style, language, spelling, and illustrations between the earlier and later versions? If there are, what do you believe are the reasons for the differences? Share the versions with a child. How does the child respond to each version?

- Select numerous folktales from one country. Investigate the culture, people, and country with your peers. Share your findings with the class.

- Compare the versions of creation and the characteristics of gods and goddesses in Greek and Norse mythology. Why do you believe differences exist?

- Choose a folktale, fable, myth, and legend. Develop a chart similar to Chart 6–1 to compare the four types of stories.

- Write a step-by-step set of directions for using the database that will result in a list of books that contain Russian folktales. Try out your directions and print your list.

- You are planning a unit for middle school students that will require them to compare legends from different geographic regions. Use the database to prepare a list of resources for this unit.

- Use the database to create a list of books to use as part of a display entitled, "Folktales from Africa." Print your list.

Involving Children in Traditional Literature

 TELLING STORIES

*T*raditional tales are among the most memorable that children experience in literature. With their well-defined plots, easily identifiable characters, rapid action, and satisfactory endings, the tales lend themselves to enjoyable experiences. This section explores ways to recapture the oral tradition through telling stories, comparing folktales from different countries, investigating folktales from a single country, initiating creative dramatizations, and motivating writing.

Learning the ancient art of oral storytelling is well worth the effort in the pleasure that it affords both the teller and the audience. This is true whether the storyteller is an adult or a child. Lesley Mandel Morrow (1991) found that encouraging children to tell stories promotes children's voluntary reading. According to Jack Maguire (1988), "storytelling encompasses so much that it defies an easy label. The telling part of the term touches on its most manifest aspect; but it also includes listening, imagining, caring, judging, reading, adapting, creating, observing, remembering, and planning" (p. 6). Maguire main-

tains that storytelling has three important values. First, it encourages a social exchange because it is alive, intimate, and personally responsible. Second, storytelling stretches the imagination of both tellers and listeners by encouraging the formation of mental images and visualization. Third, storytelling has a homespun quality that makes it accessible and encourages spur-of-the-moment changes and exclamatory bursts.

In addition, storytelling helps children understand the oral tradition of literature and encourages them to develop an understanding of the past. Storytelling allows adults to bring children into the literary experience. Free from dependence on a book, storytellers can use gestures and actions to involve children in the story. When adults tell stories, children understand that storytelling is a worthy activity and are stimulated to try telling stories themselves.

Choosing a Story

The most important factor in choosing a story is selecting one that is really enjoyable. Narrators should enjoy spending time preparing stories and should retell them with conviction and enthusiasm.

Storytelling demands an appreciative audience. Storytellers must be aware of the interests, ages, and experience of the listeners involved. Young children have short attention spans, so story length must be considered when selecting a tale. Children's ages also should influence the subject matter of a tale. Young children like stories about familiar subjects, such as animals, children, or home life. They respond to the repetitive language in cumulative tales and enjoy joining in when stories such as "Henny Penny" reach their climax. Simple folktales, such as "The Three Bears," "The Three Little Pigs," and "The Three Billy Goats Gruff," are excellent to share with young children. Children from roughly ages seven through ten enjoy folktales with longer plots, such as those collected by the Brothers Grimm. "Rapunzel" and "Rumpelstiltskin" are favorites. Other favorites include such Jewish folktales as "It Could Always Be Worse." Older children enjoy adventure tales, myths, and legends. Anne Pellowski's *Hidden Stories in Plants* (1990), *The Family Story-Telling Handbook* (1987), and Sue McCord's *The Storybook Journey: Pathways to Literacy Through Story and Play* (1995), include recommended stories and suggestions for how to use them.

Folktales have several characteristics that make them appropriate for storytelling: strong beginnings that bring listeners rapidly into the fast-paced action; several characters with whom listeners easily identify; climaxes that are familiar to children; and satisfactory endings. These characteristics suggest worthwhile criteria for selecting tales.

Storytellers should also consider the mood that they wish to create, whether it be humorous and lighthearted or serious and scary. If, for example, you want to choose a story appropriate for Halloween, then mood is important. Even the site for storytelling may affect the mood and story selection. Assume, for example, that a group of people is sitting on high rocks overlooking Lake Superior. The wind is causing the waves to crash with a mighty roar onto the rocks below. When the people look out over the lake, they can see only a wide stretch of water. No one else is in sight. The view to the north is one of thick forests, ferns, and distant waterfalls. The Norse myth, "The Hammer of Thor," from Olivia E. Coolidge's *Legends of the North* seems ideal for this setting.

Preparing the Story for Telling

Storytelling does not require memorization, but it does require preparation. Certain steps will help you prepare for an enjoyable experience. An experienced storyteller, Patti Hubert (Norton, 1997), recommends the following sequence of steps:

1. Read the story completely through about three times.
2. List mentally the sequence of events. You are giving yourself a mental outline of the important happenings.
3. Reread the story, noting the events you did not remember.
4. Go over the main events again and add the details that you remember. Think about the meaning of the events and ways to express that meaning, rather than memorize the words in the story.
5. When you believe that you know the story, tell the story to a mirror. (You will be surprised at how horrible the story sounds the first time.)
6. After you have practiced two or three more times, the wording will improve, and you can change vocal pitch to differentiate characters.
7. Change your posture or hand gestures to represent different characters.

8. Do not be afraid to use pauses to separate scenes.
9. Identify background information, share information about hearing the story for the first time, or share an object related to the story.

Sharing the Story with an Audience

Because you have spent considerable time in preparation, you should present the story effectively. However, you can enhance your presentation by creating an interest in the story, setting a mood, creating an environment where children can see and hear you, and presenting the story with effective eye contact and voice control. You may use book jackets, giant books, miniature books, travel posters, art objects and everyday objects, puppets, or music to stimulate children's interest in the story. A librarian or teacher who regularly tells stories to large groups of children can use any of these methods so that children will look forward to the story hour.

Colorful book jackets from folktales or myths not only entice children but also help set a mood for storytelling. For example, you might develop a display around the book jacket for Steven Kellogg's *Jack and the Beanstalk*. In addition to the book jacket, you could display a picture of a beanstalk (or even a real beanstalk), a toy chicken, an egg, and a picture of a castle. To show comparative sizes, you might include a picture of a giant and a picture of a boy. Your accompanying questions might include the following: How could a beanstalk make it possible for a boy to reach a castle that is up in the sky? How could a chicken and eggs cause a boy and his mother to obtain great wealth?

Stories about giants also lend themselves to displays of large books. One librarian drew huge figures of giants and beanstalks on large sheets of tagboard and then placed the sheets together to form a gigantic book that stimulated interest in "Jack and the Beanstalk." The giant book worked well in this case. The children speculated about the size or strength of anyone who could read such a large book. Drawings of a huge hammer stimulated interest about Thor when another librarian prepared the Norse myth for telling. Miniature books stimulated children's interest before another story hour when "Tom Thumb" was the story. The storyteller used other tiny objects, many formed out of clay, that would be appropriate for a little person.

Identifying sources for folklore is important according to George Shannon (1986). He stresses that we must acknowledge the sources for the folktales because "sources are a part of the folk process—the chain of human sharing—both oral and written" (p. 117). Consequently, information about the sources for the folklore should be included in the introduction.

Travel posters can stimulate interest and provide background information. They are especially appealing when used with folktales from other countries. Travel posters showing ancient English sites might introduce an oral telling of Barbara Cohen's adaptation of Geoffrey Chaucer's *Canterbury Tales.* You may use travel posters about Greece and Italy with Greek and Roman mythology. Travel posters showing Norwegian fjords and mountains can accompany Norse myths, while posters showing the Black Forest and old European castles are appropriate for "Snow White and the Seven Dwarfs" and "Sleeping Beauty."

Objects from the story or from the country that is the setting of the story can also increase children's interest. Dolls, plates, figurines, stuffed animals, and numerous other everyday objects and curios can add to the story hour.

After interest is high, concentrate on setting the mood for story time. Many storytellers use story-hour symbols. For example, if a small lamp is the symbol for story hour, children know that when the lamp is lit, it is time to listen. Music can also be a symbol; a certain record, music box tune, piano introduction, or guitar selection can introduce story hour. These techniques are usually effective, since children learn to associate them with enjoyable listening experiences. Donna E. Norton (1997, p. 84) has the following suggestions for telling the story:

1. Find a place in the room where all of the children can see and hear the presentation.
2. Either stand in front of the children or sit with them.
3. Select an appropriate introduction. Use a prop, tell something about the author, discuss a related event, or ask a question.
4. Maintain eye contact with the children. This engages them more fully in the story.
5. Use an appropriate voice rate and appropriate volume for effect.

6. While telling the story, use a short step or shift in footing to indicate a change in scene or character or to heighten the suspense. If seated, lean forward or away from the children.
7. After telling the story, pause to give the audience a chance to soak in everything you said.

Mary Ann Paulin (1985) includes sample story-telling programs in her *Creative Uses of Children's Literature.* These programs include story introductions, texts, and follow-up suggestions.

Observing Children's Responses to Storytelling

Children may have emotional responses to the story, to the interpretation of the story, or to various literary elements within the story. The responses may be as subtle as facial expressions or as expressive as vocal interactions with the story and the storyteller. Zena Sutherland (1997) recommends that you ask yourself the following questions after telling a story to a group of children:

1. Which children showed response during the story period?
2. What parts of the story evoked the most response?
3. How did the children show their reactions?
4. Did the reactions influence, in any way, your telling of the story?
5. Did any child comment about the story at some time after the story hour? If so, did the comment indicate emotional response? interpretation of the story? attention to literary characteristics such as style?
6. Do their reactions give you ideas for future story choices for this group? (p. 552)

Encouraging Children to Be Storytellers

Storytelling by children is frequently a natural continuation of storytelling by adults because children learn to tell and appreciate oral storytelling by imitating adults. Storytellers Martha Hamilton and Mitch Weiss (1993) believe that when children tell stories, they gain confidence, improve verbal skills, learn how to think inventively, and develop a love of language and stories.

Hamilton and Weiss provide valuable guidelines for helping children choose their stories, learn their stories, and tell their stories. These storytellers stress that when helping children choose their stories, adults should select a pool of appropriate stories from which the children can select so that the children choose stories appropriate to the age and interests of their audience. A sign-up sheet will help children avoid duplicating stories that they are preparing for telling.

The techniques for helping students learn the story are similar to those identified for adults. You should ask children to read their stories a number of times. Use pictorial outlines to help children understand and visualize the sequence of the story rather than memorize the story. It is also helpful to have the children practice their stories by tape recording them, telling the stories in front of a mirror, telling the stories to only one person, and then telling the stories to a larger audience.

Encourage children to use their voices to bring expression and life to the story. Have them practice varying their speed of speaking to convey various moods. Facial expressions, gestures, and movements should be natural and be appropriate for the story. Additional guidelines for helping children learn to tell stories are found in Hamilton and Weiss's *Children Tell Stories: A Teaching Guide* (1990).

Using Feltboards to Share Folktales

Storytelling does not require any props. In fact, some of the best storytellers use nothing except their voices and gestures to recapture the plots and characters found in traditional tales. Most storytellers, however, enjoy adding variety to their repertoire. Children also enjoy experimenting with different approaches to storytelling; the flannelboard or feltboard lends itself to storytelling by both adults and children.

A feltboard is a rectangular, lightweight board covered with felt, flannel cloth, or lightweight indoor-outdoor carpeting. This board acts as the backdrop for figures cut from felt, pellon, or another material. Felt or pellon figures will cling directly to a feltboard, while any object, even leather, wood, or foam rubber, will adhere to the felt if backed with a small square or strip of Velcro. Other materials, such as yarn or cotton balls, will also cling to a feltboard and may be used to add interest and texture to a story.

Stories that lend themselves to feltboard interpretations have only a few major characters, plots that depend upon oral telling rather than physical action, and settings that do not demand exceptional detail. These characteristics are similar to those already stipulated for the simple folktales that young children enjoy. Pleasing stories to retell on the feltboard include the folktales "Three Billy Goats Gruff," "The Three Bears," "The Gingerbread Boy," and "Henny Penny." Stories should include actions that can be shown on the board. In addition, the number of figures should not overwhelm the board (see Figure 6–1).

Consider the Norwegian folktale "The Three Billy Goats Gruff." First, use simple cutouts or objects to represent the characters. The three goats range in size from a small goat to a great big goat with curved horns. The ugly old troll has big eyes and a long, long nose. You can show the setting easily: a bridge crossing a stream and green grass on the other side of the bridge. You can illustrate the action effectively: each goat can go "Trip, trap! Trip, trap!" over the bridge. The troll can challenge each goat with "Who's that tripping over my bridge?" You can also illustrate the climax easily: The big billy goat knocks the troll off the bridge and continues to cross to the other side. The plot develops sequentially from a small billy goat, to a medium-sized billy goat, and finally to a great big billy goat.

The English folktale "The Donkey, the Table, and the Stick" is another story that is effective for feltboard production. Children enjoy seeing the magic donkey produce gold coins when his ear is pulled, and they laugh over the poor lad's exasperation as nothing happens when he pulls and pulls the common donkey's ear. They are enthusiastic about the table that can produce turkey, sausages, and other good things. They laugh when the storyteller tries to get the ordinary table to produce food. Finally, they are overjoyed when the magic stick beats the evil innkeeper. You can use feltboard characters to show these actions effectively.

Cumulative tales are excellent for feltboard presentations. As you introduce each new character, place it on the feltboard. Have the children join the dialogue as "The Fat Cat," for example, encounters first the gruel, then the pot, the old woman, Skahottentot, Skilinkenlot, five birds, seven dancing girls, the lady with the pink parasol, the parson, and the woodsman.

Through such presentations, children learn about sequential order and improve their language skills. Using feltboard stories with children, you will often find that the children either ask if they can retell the

FIGURE 6–1 *Stories that lend themselves to feltboard interpretations have only a few major characters, plots that depend on oral telling rather than physical action, and settings that do not demand exceptional detail.*

stories or make up their own feltboard stories to share. If you provide feltboards and materials, children naturally enjoy telling stories in this manner. Whether you tell a story to one child or to a group, storytelling is well worth the effort of preparation and presentation. Watching children as they respond to a magical environment and then make their own efforts as storytellers will prove to you that storytelling should be included in every child's experience.

 ## COMPARING FOLKTALES FROM DIFFERENT COUNTRIES

Understanding how various types of traditional stories are related, becoming aware of cultural diffusion, and learning about different countries are benefits of traditional literature. One way to help children gain these benefits is to compare folktales from different countries.

Comparing Different Versions of the Same Tale

Many older children are fascinated to discover that some tales appear in almost every culture. The names vary, magical objects differ, and settings change, but the basic elements of the story remain the same. Folklorist Alan Dundes (1988) claims that

over one thousand versions of the Cinderella story have been found throughout the world. Jane M. Bingham and Grayce Scholt (1974) and Elinor P. Ross (1979) suggest that older children should investigate the motifs in these tales. Compile questions such as the following with the children's assistance to guide their search and discovery:

1. What caused Cinderella to have a lowly position in the family?
2. What shows that Cinderella has a lowly position in the household?
3. How is Cinderella related to other household members?
4. What happens to keep Cinderella away from the ball?
5. How does Cinderella receive her wishes or transformation?
6. Where does Cinderella meet the prince?
7. What is the test signifying the rightful Cinderella?
8. What happens to the stepsisters?

Sources for comparisons include Mary Ann Nelson's (1972) anthology, Bingham and Scholt's (1974) synopses of twelve variants of the Cinderella story, Sutherland and Livingston's anthology (1984), and folklore collections from around the world. Chart 6–7 represents some key variants found in Cinderella tales from different countries.

Involving Children in Traditional Literature **331**

Hundreds of versions of the Cinderella story from around the world have been found. The illustrations are just as varied. Top left, from a Chinese varient. (Illustration by Ed Young reprinted by permission of Philomel Books from Yeh Shin: A Cinderella Story from China retold by Ai-Ling Louie, illustrations © 1982 by Ed Young.) Top right, Native American. (Illustration by David Shannon reprinted by permission of G.P. Putnam's Sons from The Rough Face Girl by Rafe Martin, illustrations © 1992 by David Shannon.) Bottom, Cinderella as a dog. (From Cinderella by William Wegman. Text and photos © 1993 by William Wegman. Reprinted by persmission of Hyperion Books for Children, a Walt Disney Company. All rights reserved.)

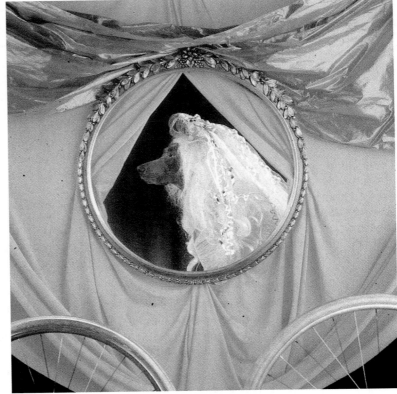

CHART 6–7 Variations found in Cinderella stories from different countries

Origin	Cause of Lowly Position	Outward Signs of Lowly Position	Cinderella's Relationship to Household	How She Receives Wishes	What Keeps Her from Social Occasion	Where She Meets the Prince	Test of Rightful Cinderella	What Happens to Stepsisters
French Perrault's "Cinderilla"	Mother died. Father remarried.	Sitting in ashes. Vilest household tasks.	Stepdaughter to cruel woman. Unkind stepsisters.	Wishes to fairy godmother.	(Ball) No gown. Family won't let her go.	Castle ball. Beautifully dressed.	Glass slipper.	Forgiven. Live in palace. Marry lords.
German Grimm's "Cinderella"	Mother died. Father remarried.	Wears clogs, old dress. Sleeps in cinders. Heavy work.	Stepdaughter to cruel woman. Cruel stepsisters.	Wishes to bird on tree on mother's grave.	(Ball) Must separate lentils.	Castle ball. Beautifully dressed.	Glass slipper.	Blinded by birds.
English "Tatercoats"	Mother died at her birth. Grandfather blames her.	Ragbag clothes. Scraps for food.	Despised granddaughter. Hated by servants.	Gooseherd plays pipe.	(Ball) Grandfather refuses.	In forest. Dressed in rags.	None.	Grandfather weeps. Hair grows into stones.
Vietnamese "In the Land of Small Dragon"	Mother died. Father's number two wife hates her.	Collects wood. Cares for rice paddies.	Stepdaughter to hateful woman. Hated by half-sisters.	Fairy. Bones of fish.	(Festival) Must separate rice from husks.	Festival. Beautifully dressed.	Jeweled slipper (hai).	Not told.
Chinese "Beauty and Pock Face"	Mother turned into cow.	Straightens hemp. Hard work.	Stepdaughter to cruel woman. Cruel stepsister.	From bones of mother in earthenware pot.	(Theater) Straighten hemp. Separate sesame seeds.	Theater. Scholar picks up shoe from road.	Walks on eggs. Climbs ladder of knives. Jumps into oil.	Roasted in oil.
Micmac— Native American "Little Burnt Face"	Mother died.	Burned face. Ragged garments.	Despised by two jealous sisters.	The Great Chief's sister changes her.	She must make her own dress.	Wigwam by the lake.	Describe the Great Chief.	Sent back to wigwam in disgrace.

After children have read, listened to, and discussed many Cinderella tales, their investigations may agree with conclusions found in Bingham and Scholt's research. These investigators (1974) compared twelve Cinderella tales and concluded the following:

1. The menial position of the heroine is usually shown by describing the impossible tasks that she is asked to do. These tasks reflect the culture of the story.
2. Supernatural powers aid the heroine. Many powers relate to the dead mother: She returns in the form of an animal, or a tree appears over her grave.
3. The magical clothes of the transformed heroine are usually elegant and appropriate for the culture: gold and silver, or Native American dress of leather and beads.
4. The hero and heroine usually meet in places that are important to the culture: a ball, a theater, a church, or a wigwam.
5. The male figure has an elevated position in society. He is of noble birth in the majority of the tales, but the Chinese tale describes him as a scholar.
6. Seven of the twelve tales include cruel stepmothers. The heroine also has to contend with cruel stepsisters or sisters.
7. Eight tales have some form of shoe test for identifying Cinderella. A Japanese version requires the heroine to compose a song; a Native American version asks the heroine to identify what the chief's sledstrings and bowstrings are made of.
8. In five of the twelve tales, the wicked stepmother or stepsisters meet violent ends.
9. All of the tales reflect the societies that produced them. Native American tales refer to wigwams, moccasins, and bowstrings; Japanese stories refer to kimonos, rice, and oni.

In addition to these comparisons of "Cinderella" stories, M. Joe Worthy and Janet W. Bloodgood (1992/1993) suggest sources and activities that can accompany the study of three categories of "Cinderella" stories: the heroine is mistreated by stepmother or stepsisters, sibling rivalry, and the daughter flees an unnatural or misunderstanding father.

Other tales are also suitable for comparisons. P. T. Travers (1975) has included five versions of the "Sleeping Beauty" tale and one of her own translations in *About the Sleeping Beauty*. This collection contains her own version, which has Arabian roots; "Dornroschen or Briar-Rose," from the Grimms' *Household Tales;* "La Belle au Bois Dormant, or The Sleeping Beauty in the Wood," from Charles Perrault; "Sole, Luna, e Talia or Sun, Moon, and Talia," from the Italian *The Pentamerone of Giambattista Basile;* "The Queen of Tubber Tintye," from *Myths and Folklore of Ireland;* and "The Petrified Mansion," from *Bengal Fairy Tales.* In addition, "Little Red Riding Hood" (Norton, 1987a) and "The Lad Who Went to the North Wind" have many variants. The "Snow White" tale may be compared with Eric A. Kimmel's Egyptian version, *Rimonah of the Flashing Sword: A North African Tale.* Linda Western's "A Comparative Study of Literature Through Folk Tale Variants" (1980) is another source of different versions of tales. Betsy Hearne's *Beauty and the Beast: Visions and Revisions of an Old Tale* (1989) provides a scholarly analysis of this folktale across time and place.

A search for variant versions of a tale encourages children to develop an understanding of the impact of cultural diffusion on literature. Children also realize that each culture has placed the tale in a context that reflects the society of the storyteller and the audience.

Analyzing Variants

Variants of folktales, especially those that changed as the original audiences moved to new lands, are especially interesting for developing the understanding that folktales frequently change as storytellers adjust to their new environments. In addition, if tales still retain the original motifs and themes, use the variants to help students analyze possible sources of the original tales. As a logical extension of a comparative study of Cinderella tales for upper-elementary and middle-school students, use William H. Hooks's *Moss Gown* to analyze variations on themes and motifs, to search for references to time and place, and to speculate about the country of origin.

To begin, provide some background knowledge gained from other sources of literature and from geography. First, furnish a knowledge of Cinderella-type elements by having the children read many variants of the Cinderella story. This activity can help children understand that most Cinderella-type stories have such characteristics as a girl who is given the hardest tasks, a helper with supernatural powers, and an occasion that the girl wants to attend. Supply a knowledge of the English versions of Cinderella through "Tattercoats" and "Mossycoat" to help the children understand how the English Cinderella stories differ from those in other countries. Also, give the children at least a brief introduction to Shakespeare's *King Lear* to help them identify these elements in the story. A King Lear story written for children is included in E. Nesbit's *Beautiful Stories from Shakespeare* (1907) and Charles and Mary Lamb's *Tales from Shakespeare* (1986). William H. Hooks's *Moss Gown* is a variant collected from the tidewater section of North Carolina. Consequently, there are references to the environment and to the southern plantations of an earlier time.

After providing these background understandings, ask the children to listen to or to read Hooks's *Moss Gown*. Ask them to search for (1) Cinderella elements, (2) King Lear elements, (3) references to time and place, and (4) evidence of the European country the early storytellers came from. From this activity, the children will discover evidence that is similar to the information in Chart 6–8.

After the children complete this task, ask them to speculate about why *Moss Gown* has a happy ending and not the tragic ending of *King Lear*. The children will probably decide that the Cinderella theme requires a happy ending. Consequently, the storytellers needed to find a way for the heroine and her father to live happily. Compare the themes in both *King Lear* and *Moss Gown* for an interesting and lively discussion. Additional variants for this type of activity include Gail E. Haley's *Jack and the Bean Tree,* an Appalachian variant of "Jack and the Beanstalk"; John Bierhorst's *Doctor Coyote: A Native American Aesop's Fables,* a Spanish-Aztec variant; and Eva Martin's *Canadian Fairy Tales,* a collection that includes Canadian variants from French, German, and English sources.

CHART 6–8   An analysis of William H. Hooks's *Moss Gown*

Cinderella elements found in Moss Gown:
A helper with supernatural powers.
A gown that changes to rags.
A girl who is given the hardest kitchen work.
An heir who holds a dance.
A heroine who cannot attend the dance because she lacks a dress.
A supernatural being who casts a spell and provides a dress.
An order that must be obeyed.
A handsome heir who dances with the heroine only.
An heir who searches for the heroine.
An heir and a heroine who marry.
King Lear elements found in Moss Gown:
A question asked to prove love.
A father who rejects youngest and most loving daughter's declaration.
A father who wanders after cruel treatment by elder daughters.
A youngest daughter who eventually proves her love for her father.
References to time and place found in Moss Gown:
A great plantation.
A "snow-white house, pillared with eight marble columns on every side" (p. 5).
A reference to fine fields.
A reference to riding and hunting in the murky, mysterious swamp.
A reference to black-green cypress treetops.
A reference to gray Spanish moss.
French words used in the Carolinas to cast a powerful, magical spell.
A party that is called a frolic.
Evidence that the original storytellers came from English backgrounds:
King Lear elements show knowledge of Shakespeare, an English author.
There are similarities to the British Cinderella. For example, in "Tattercoats," servants mistreat a girl, and a man of wealthy position loves the girl even though she is dressed in rags.

INVESTIGATING FOLKTALES FROM A SINGLE COUNTRY

Collectors of tales from various cultures support the strong relationships between traditional folklore and the culture. For example, Laurence Yep (1989) suggests that folktales offer strategies for living that are accepted by the culture. He states, "A culture defines its virtues and vices within its folktales. . . . Defining vices is as important as defining virtues" (p. 69). Yep argues that studying folktales provides an excellent way to understand the Chinese-American culture.

Educators also provide strong reasons for using folk-lore units to develop cultural understanding.

J. Diakiw (1990) maintains that children's literature units help develop global education and understanding. One of the units that he recommends focuses on African folktales and then compares the tales with traditional tales from other cultures. B. Barnes (1991) recommends using traditional tales to make discoveries about cultural understandings and anthropological concepts. He maintains that even young students learn about the cultures of Native Americans, Asians, and Hispanics from the traditional literature.

Children can learn a great deal about a country and its people by investigating a number of traditional tales from that country. Such an investigation also increases understanding of the multicultural heritage of this country and develops understanding of, and positive attitudes toward, cultures other than one's own.

This fact was made clear when a group of fifth-grade children was studying folktales to learn more about the people of other countries. They were reading and discussing Russian folktales at a time when relationships between the Soviet Union and the United States were strained. As they read the tales, especially the merry ones, with their rapid, humorous dialogues and absurd plots, the children decided that people who could invent and enjoy those stories must be similar to themselves. They realized that they were laughing at the same stories that brought humor to children in the Soviet Union.

During the sharing of folktales, the children commented, for example, that Jewish folktales often stress the unselfish desire for a better world or reward sincerity and wisdom. They were also impressed by the fact that the Chinese "Cinderella" married a scholar and not a nobleman. Through the folktales, they learned to respect the values of the people who created them.

The web in Figure 6–2 uses traditional tales from China to analyze personal values, important symbols, and disliked human qualities in the Chinese culture. It also looks at supernatural beings. Finally, it lists stimulating activities and motivating introductions for the study of the traditional tales. Another fifth-grade class conducted a successful study of folktales from China. Objects displayed throughout the room stimulated interest. A large red paper dragon met the children as they entered the room.

Other objects included joss sticks (incense), lanterns, Chinese flutes, a tea service, fans, statues of mythical beasts, lacquered boxes and plates, silk, samples of Chinese writing, a blue willow plate, jade, and pictures of artwork, temples, pagodas, people, and animals. Many Chinese folktales were displayed on the library table. In the background, a recording of Chinese music played. The chalkboard contained a message, written in Chinese figures, welcoming the children to China.

The students looked at the displays, listened to the music, tried to decipher the message, and discussed what they saw and heard. They located China on a map and on a globe. Then, they listed questions about China—questions about the people, country, values, art, music, food, houses, animals, and climate.

The teacher read aloud some of the foreword to Louise and Yuan-hsi Kuo's *Chinese Folk Tales* (1976). She asked the students to close their eyes and imagine the scene, to listen carefully, and then to tell whether the following scene took place in modern times or many centuries ago.

But suddenly the room echoes with an ear-splitting clash of cymbals and the sonorous boom of a drum and in the street below our window prances a splendid lion. The sound of cymbals and the beat of drums have been heard incessantly since early morning and are merely a prelude to a major part to come: a procession with gay silk banners flying, votive offerings of barbecued pigs . . . golden brown and saffron, cartloads heaped with fruit, red-colored eggs and other delicacies, giant joss sticks, candles and lanterns. A magnificent dragon, gyrating and performing with vigor and intensity to the rapid beat of a drum, will bring the procession to a climax. Throngs crowd the doorways, line the path, as excited onlookers join the ranks to mingle with those on their way to the temple . . . journey's end. This is the day of days . . . the grand finale of five days of celebration in homage to T'ien Ho, the Heavenly Goddess of the Sea . . . she who will bestow blessings on all who worship her, and protect them for the entire year. (p. 7)

After listening to the selection, the children speculated about the time period and gave their reasons for choosing either ancient or modern times. Many children were quite surprised to hear that the festival was held in modern Hong Kong. This discussion led to reading Chinese folktales in order to learn more about the Chinese people and a heritage that still influences people.

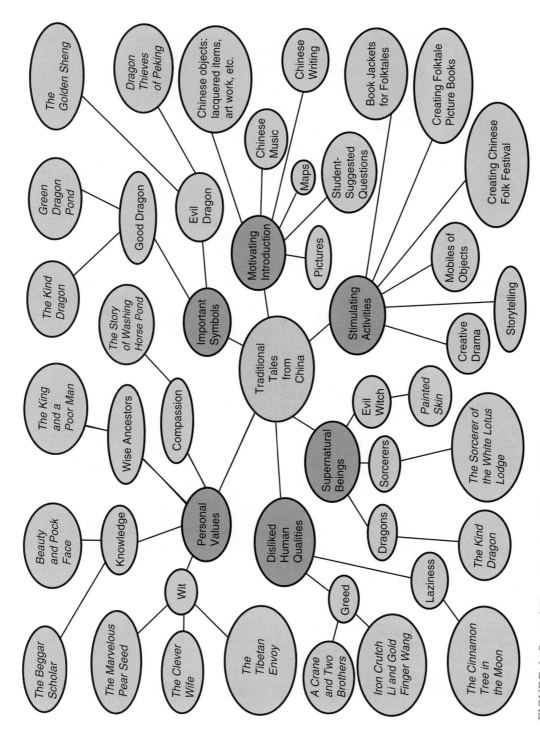

FIGURE 6–2 *A fifth-grade study of Chinese folktales*

Next, the teacher shared several of her favorite Chinese folktales with the children. They included Marilee Heyer's *The Weaving of a Dream: A Chinese Folktale,* Margaret Mahy's *The Seven Chinese Brothers,* Demi's *The Empty Pot,* and several tales from Neil Philip's *The Spring of Butterflies and Other Chinese Folktales.* The selections included "The Tibetan Envoy," which shows the importance of wit and intelligence; "The Story of Washing Horse Pond," which shows the importance of compassion for others; "The King and a Poor Man," which shows the importance of wise ancestors; and "A Crane and Two Brothers," which shows dislike for greed. The teacher also provided brief introductions to other tales to stimulate the children's interest in reading the tales. The children then chose tales to read independently. As they read, they considered their questions about China. Consequently, when they discovered information about the culture and the people, they jotted the information down so that they could share it with the class.

After collecting their information, the children discussed ways of verifying whether or not the information was accurate. They compared the information with library reference materials and magazines, such as *National Geographic.* They also invited to the classroom several visitors who were either Chinese or had visited China.

The students used their knowledge about the people, culture, and literature of China in their own art, creative drama, and writing. They drew travel posters as well as book jackets and illustrations for folktales. They also made mobiles of folk-literature objects.

One artistic activity was to create picture storybooks from single folktales. The children chose a favorite tale not already in picture-book format, illustrated it with drawings, and bound the pages together. Because many of the published picture books contained information about the origins of their tales, the children included similar information inside their own front covers. Because published book jackets often tell about the illustrator and the research to provide authentic pictures, the students' books contained this information. The children told about themselves and the ways in which they prepared for their drawing assignments. They described the mediums they used for their illustrations. Then, they shared their books with one another and other classes and proudly displayed the books in the library.

The class also chose some stories for creative drama. The teacher divided the class into groups according to favorite folktales. Each group then chose a method for sharing the story with the rest of the class. Some groups re-created the stories as plays, others chose puppetry, and one group used pantomime with a narrator who read the lines.

The children invited their parents to attend a Chinese folktale festival. The children shared their art projects, picture storybooks, new information, and creative dramas with an appreciative audience.

This unit about one country led to an interest in folktales from other countries. The children next read folktales from Japan and other Asian countries. They discovered the similarities among many of these tales, especially in the symbolic animals found in both Chinese and Japanese tales. The children went on to detect Chinese influence on non-Asian writers when they read the beautiful version of Hans Christian Andersen's *The Nightingale,* illustrated by Nancy Ekholm Burkert.

The discovery of similar mythical animals led to another interesting search through folklore. The teacher read Winifred Miller's article "Dragons—Fact or Fantasy?" (1975) and the children discovered that both Chinese and Japanese folktales had good and evil dragons; good dragons, a representation of Han nobility, were found in folktales told to ruling classes, but folktales about the common people referred to dragons as evil. With the teacher's guidance, the students accomplished many of the activities suggested by Miller's article.

Folktales lend themselves well to many activities. Teachers and librarians will find many ways to increase world understanding through literature.

 ### INITIATING CREATIVE DRAMATIZATIONS

Folklore is a natural source of materials for storytelling. It also stimulates creative drama. Elizabeth Cook (1976) maintains that the most exciting way of retelling traditional tales is drama, either in movement alone or in movement accompanied by words. Children can mime many sequences as you read to them. They can act out individual parts, or groups of children can re-create their own versions of the tales.

Pantomime

Pantomime is creative drama in which an actor plays a part with gestures and actions without using words. According to Geraldine Siks (1983), pantomime should be part of a planned drama curriculum. In such a curriculum, children learn to experiment with body movement, use their senses, stimulate their imaginations, develop language and speech, and understand and use characterization. The first pantomime experiences of children usually include activities in which they learn to relax and to experiment with different ways to move their bodies. After children have ideas about what their bodies can express, pantomiming folktales can help them interpret various actions and emotions.

Familiar folktales young children enjoy are excellent for pantomime. For example, children can pretend to be each character in Paul Galdone's *The Three Bears* as you read the story aloud. The experience allows children to develop believable characterizations through body movements. Other folktales that young children like to pantomime are "The Three Little Pigs," "The Three Billy Goats Gruff," and "The Little Red Hen."

When children start to enjoy longer folktales, use these many tales as sources of materials for pantomime. Children can put on their cloaks of invisibility and tiptoe behind "The Twelve Dancing Princesses" as the princesses descend the winding stairs. They can stop in fright as they accidentally step on the long dress of a princess. They can walk in wonderment through the silver forest, gold forest, and diamond forest. As princes or princesses, they can dance gracefully through the night and then sleepily climb the winding stairs.

Because many magical tales show vivid contrasts between good and evil characters, children can form pairs and play opposing or complementary roles. "Cinderella" has scenes between good and evil characters: Cinderella and her stepmother, or Cinderella and her stepsisters. There are also scenes between evil characters and evil forces: the stepmother and stepsisters plot to leave Cinderella at home, force her to work, or try to fit their feet inside the slipper. Also, children can pantomime the opposing characters of good and bad luck in Isaac Bashevis Singer's Jewish tale *Mazel and Shlimazel, or the Milk of the Lioness.*

Scenes from Greek and Norse mythology are excellent for older children to pantomime. Children can enact Psyche's search for Cupid; Jason's search for the golden fleece; Persephone's descending into the underground world of Hades; Apollo's trailing across the sky in his sun chariot; and Thor's frantically searching for his missing hammer, dressing as a bride, and retrieving his hammer from the giant Thrym. Quite different movements and expressions are necessary to depict gods, goddesses, heroes, and heroines found in Greek and Norse mythology. Acting out scenes through pantomime helps children understand the qualities of these traditional folklore characters and appreciate the language found in the myths.

Creative Interpretations

As children pantomime stories such as "The Three Bears" or "Mazel and Shlimazel," they usually want to add words and create their own plays. It is a natural extension of pantomime to add "Somebody has been sitting in my chair" or to create a dialogue in which the hero tries to convince the baroness that she should lend him her pig. Pantomiming provides a foundation for other creative activities; it allows children to experience the movement and emotion of the story and characters before they try to work with dialogue.

Stories used to stimulate pantomime can also be used for creative interpretations requiring words. Folklore meets Barbara M. McIntyre's (1974) criteria for stories that are appropriate for dramatization. They should (1) have ideas worth sharing, (2) involve conflict, (3) include action in the development of the plot, (4) contain characters who seem real, and (5) have situations in which interesting dialogue can be developed. The folktales discussed in this chapter qualify in all of these areas.

Folklore can be used to stimulate creative dramatizations in two ways. The stories themselves can be re-created, or the stories can serve as stimulators to help children create new interpretations. Usually, children begin by acting out stories and closely following the original in plot and characterization. As they become more secure, they enjoy making up new stories or creating additional ones about a character. Whatever the purpose for using the folktales, however, you must guide children's dramatizations in a sequence of steps:

1. *Stimulate children's interest in the story.* For example, for "The Golden Goose," a third-grade teacher placed a yellow toy goose, a dry crust of bread, and a bottle of sour liquid in front of the class. She then asked the children if they thought they could acquire a fortune and a beautiful princess if they had those objects. She let them try to think of ways they might accomplish this miracle. The children decided that a little magic might help.

2. *Present the story so that the children will have a foundation to draw upon in creating their dramatization.* The teacher next told the story of "The Golden Goose," using the toy goose, the stale bread, and the sour liquid to assist her. This time, however, as the stale bread was transformed, she had a pastry to take its place, and as the sour liquid was changed, she had a jug of sweet grape juice to exchange.

3. *Guide the children's planning and presentation of their creative dramatization.* The teacher encouraged the class to talk about their favorite characters in the story. She then asked them to improvise the actions of each character in various scenes in the story—the despised and mistreated Dummling (or Simpleton, depending upon the version used), his parents, and his brothers: for example, Dummling's sharing his food with the old man, cutting down the trees, and discovering the golden goose. The children discussed which actions they would like to include in the play and what sequence of events they would use. They decided to use the goose, the bread, the liquid, the pastry, and the grape juice as props. After the children were satisfied with the sequence and who should play each role (at least for the first time), they acted out the story with encouragement from the teacher when necessary. They did not try to memorize lines. Instead, they improvised the general mood. They put on their production several times so that they could play various roles and take turns being the audience.

4. *Help the children evaluate their presentation.* The teacher encouraged the children to discuss the good things about their play: Why did they feel sorry for Dummling? How did the older brothers show that they thought they were brighter than Dummling? What did they do so that the children did not feel sorry for their bad luck? What did the old man do to let them know he was very old? Why did they laugh at Dummling? The children made many positive comments about their play. Then, they talked about how they could improve the presentation.

 ## MOTIVATING WRITING THROUGH TRADITIONAL TALES

Reading and studying traditional tales encourages numerous written activities. For example, after completing a study of "Cinderella" variants and a study of specific cultures, groups of fifth-grade students wrote their own "Cinderella" story that might have been told to audiences in various other cultures. One group wrote and performed a Jewish "Cinderella" including the values and beliefs that they discovered following the reading of many Jewish folktales. Another group created an African "Cinderella," while another group wrote a Native American "Cinderella." After each group performed its story, the class responded to the presentation and the cultural information found in the story.

The current examples of adaptations of folktales by Jon Scieszka and William J. Brooke provide exciting motivation for children to write their own versions of folktales. For example, read a traditional version of the folktale, "The Three Little Pigs." Discuss the characters and the plot of the story. Ask the children to identify whose point of view the story reflects. Next, read Scieszka's *The True Story of the 3 Little Pigs!* to the children. Allow the children to give individual responses to this story. Ask them to identify the point of view in this adaptation and to discuss how they know that the point of view is that of the wolf rather than of the pigs. Encourage the children to compare the characterizations, plots, and point of view in the two versions. Then, have them write their responses to the two versions.

Use a similar activity to accompany Scieszka's *The Stinky Cheese Man and Other Fairly Stupid Tales.* Have the children read traditional versions of these tales and compare them with Scieszka's adaptations of "Chicken Licken," "The Tortoise and the Hair," "Cinderumpelstiltskin," "Little Red Running Shorts," and "Jack's Bean Problem." After students respond to and discuss Scieszka's text and Lane Smith's illustrations, have them choose other folktales and rewrite the stories to reflect another point of view. Place these new writings in the library along with the more traditional tales.

In *A Telling of the Tales: Five Stories,* William J. Brooke tells readers, "The telling of a tale links you with everyone who has told it before. There are no new tales, only new tellers, telling in their own way, and if you listen closely you can hear the voice of everyone who ever told the tale" (introduction). This book tells traditional tales with a new twist. The stories answer such questions as, What if Cinderella did not want to try on the glass slipper? What if Sleeping Beauty did not believe she had been asleep? What if Paul Bunyan, the greatest tree chopper of them all, met Johnny Appleseed, the fastest tree grower? Encourage children to brainstorm other questions to ask characters from folktales, myths, and legends. Then, have them use these questions to write their own adaptations of the stories that answer the concerns. Another book that may stimulate writing is Diane Stanley's *Rumpelstiltskin's Daughter.* In this version the daughter not only outwits the king but she also makes him better the lives of the poor farmers.

SUGGESTED ACTIVITIES

for Involving Children in Traditional Literature

- Choose a folktale of interest, prepare the story for telling, and share the story with one child or a group of children.

- Select a cumulative tale, such as "The Gingerbread Boy," or a simple folktale, such as "The Three Bears," and prepare it as a feltboard story. Share the story with one child or a group.

- Select a folktale that has many versions from diverse cultures. For example, "Sleeping Beauty" is found in many cultures. What questions should you ask children when they investigate the tales? Develop a chart similar to Chart 6–7, the one on the text for Cinderella. What are the key similarities and differences? How do the tales reflect the culture? List the conclusions that you and the children made from the folktales.

- With a peer group, select a country to investigate. Develop a list of appropriate traditional tales and a list of

related examples of art, music, and so forth. Design some activities to help children develop an understanding of the country.

- Choose a folktale that has rapid action appropriate for pantomiming. Lead a peer group or a group of children through the pantomime.

- Lead a peer group or a group of children through the four steps described in this chapter for developing creative interpretations: (1) stimulating interest, (2) presenting the story, (3) guiding the planning and presentation of the creative dramatization, and (4) helping the group evaluate the presentation.

- Compile a file of creative writing ideas motivated by traditional literature.

- Compile a file of folktales that contain vivid word pictures. Discuss ways to use these tales to help children interpret the moods through art.

CHILDREN'S LITERATURE

FOLKTALES

African—African American
See Chapter 11.

American—Native American
See Chapter 11.

Asian
Asian Cultural Centre for UNESCO. *Folk Tales from Asia for Children Everywhere.* Book Three. Weatherhill, 1976 (I:8–12 R:6). Stories are from Afghanistan, Burma, Indonesia, Iran, Japan, Pakistan, Singapore, Sri Lanka, and Vietnam.

———. *Folk Tales from Asia for Children Everywhere.* Book Five. Weatherhill, 1977 (I:8–12 R:6). Stories are from India, Philippines, Pakistan, Japan, Malaysia, Burma, and Iran.

Bang, Molly. *The Paper Crane.* Mulberry Books, 1987 (I:8+ R:5). A paper crane brings success.

Clark, Ann Nolan. *In the Land of Small Dragon.* Illustrated by Tony Chen. Viking, 1979 (I:7–12 R:7). This is a Vietnamese variation of Cinderella.

Conger, David. *Many Lands, Many Stories: Asian Folktales for Children.* Illustrated by Ruth Ra. Tuttle, 1987 (I:8+ R:5). Fifteen folktales are identified by their countries of origin.

Day, Noreha Yussof. *Kancil and the Crocodiles: A Tale from Malaysia.* Illustrated by Britta Teckentrup. Simon & Schuster, 1996 (I:4–7 R:4). This is a trickster tale in which animals outwit the crocodiles.

Demi. *The Empty Pot.* Henry Holt, 1990 (I:5–9 R:4). This tale develops the importance of honesty.

Ernst, Judith. *The Golden Goose King: A Tale Told by the Buddha.* Parvardigar, 1995 (I:10+ R:5). A goose's wisdom helps a king learn to rule wisely.

Fang, Linda. *The Ch'i-lin Purse: A Collection of Ancient Chinese Stories.* Illustrated by Jeanne M. Lee. Farrar, Straus & Giroux, 1995 (I:10+ R:5). This is a collection of nine stories.

Ginsburg, Mirra, ed. *The Chinese Mirror.* Illustrated by Margot Zemach. Harcourt Brace Jovanovich, 1988 (I:5–8 R:4). A mirror causes confusion in a Korean folktale.

Hamanaka, Sheila. Retold by. *Screen of Frogs.* Orchard, 1993 (I:5–10 R:5). A Japanese folktale in which a man is rewarded for saving the land for the frogs.

Hearn, Lafcadio. *The Voice of the Great Bell.* Retold by Margaret Hodges. Illustrated by Ed Young. Little, Brown, 1989 (I:7+ R:6). A girl gives her life for her father in a Chinese tale.

Heyer, Marilee. *The Weaving of a Dream: A Chinese Folktale.* Viking, 1986 (I:8+ R:5). This is a retelling of "The Chuang Brocade."

Hong, Lily Toy. Retold by. *Two of Everything.* Whitman, 1993 (I:5–8 R:4). A Chinese folktale in which a magical pot duplicates everything that it contains.

Hyun, Peter, ed. *Korea's Favorite Tales and Lyrics.* Illustrated by Dong-il Park. Tuttle/Seoul International, 1986 (I:5–10 R:6). This is a collection of folktales, poems, and stories.

Ishii, Momoko. *The Tongue-Cut Sparrow.* Translated by Katherine Paterson. Illustrated by Suekichi Akaba. Dutton, 1987 (I:7–10 R:6). A kind man and a greedy wife receive quite different rewards.

Jaffe, Nina. Retold by. *Older Brother, Younger Brother: A Korean Folktale.* Illustrated by Wenhai Ma. Viking, 1995 (I:5–8 R:5). A younger brother's kindness is rewarded.

James, Grace. *Green Willow and Other Japanese Fairy Tales.* Illustrated by Warwick Goble. Avenel, 1987 (I:10+ R:6). This is a large collection of Japanese folktales.

Kuo, Louise, and Yuan-hsi Kuo. *Chinese Folktales.* Celestial Arts, 1976 (I:8+ R:6). This is a collection of tales.

Lang, Andrew. *Aladdin and the Wonderful Lamp.* Illustrated by Errol LeCain. Viking, 1981 (I:7–9 R:6). Deep color and ornamentation appropriately illustrate a tale from *The Arabian Nights.*

Laurin, Anne. *The Perfect Crane.* Illustrated by Charles Mikolaycak. Harper & Row, 1981 (I:5–9 R:6). A Japanese tale tells about the friendship between a magician and the crane he creates from rice paper.

Lee, Jeanne M. *Legend of the Milky Way.* Holt, Rinehart & Winston, 1982 (I:6–9 R:5). A heavenly princess and her earthly husband are transformed into stars.

Levine, Arthur. Retold by. *The Boy Who Drew Cats: A Japanese Folktale.* Illustrated by Frédéric Clément. Dial, 1994 (I:5–9 R:6). The cats come to life to defeat a giant rat.

Louie, Ai-Lang. *Yeh Shen: A Cinderella Story from China.* Illustrated by Ed Young. Philomel, 1982 (I:7–9 R:6). This ancient Chinese tale has many similarities with versions from other cultures.

Mahy, Margaret. Retold by. *The Seven Chinese Brothers.* Illustrated by Jean and Mou-Sien Tseng. Scholastic, 1990 (I:5–8 R:4). Watercolors complement the traditional tale.

Martin, Rafe. *Mysterious Tales of Japan.* Illustrated by Tatsuro Kiuchi. Putnam, 1996 (I:8+ R:5). This is a collection of ten tales.

Mosel, Arlene. *The Funny Little Woman.* Illustrated by Blair Lent. Dutton, 1972 (I:5–8 R:5). A little woman pursues a rice dumpling and is captured by wicked people.

Paterson, Katherine. *The Tale of the Mandarin Ducks.* Illustrated by Leo and Diane Dillon. Lodestar, 1990 (I:5–10 R:6). A couple is rewarded for their kindness to a pair of ducks.

Philip, Neil, ed. *The Spring of Butterflies and Other Folktales of China's Minority Peoples.* Translated by He Liyi. Illustrated by Pan Aiqing and Li Zhao. Lothrop, Lee & Shepard, 1986 (I:9+ R:6). These tales are from northwestern China.

Pratt, Davis, and Elsa Kula. *Magic Animals of Japan.* Parnassus, 1967 (I:8–12 R:7). These are tales of the fabled creatures of Japan.

Rhee, Nami. Retold by. *Magic Spring: A Korean Folktale.* Putnam, 1993 (I:7–10 R:5). A magic spring changes the lives of an elderly couple.

Roberts, Moss. *Chinese Fairy Tales and Fantasies.* Pantheon, 1979 (I:10 R:6). A collection of tales tells about enchantment, greed, animals, women, ghosts, and judges.

Sanfield, Steve. *Just Reward: Or Who Is That Man in the Moon & What's He Doing Up There Anyway?* Illustrated by Emily Lisker. Orchard, 1996 (I:5–8 R:5). The theme shows that good deeds receive just rewards.

San Souci, Robert D. *The Samurai's Daughter: A Japanese Legend.* Illustrated by Stephen T. Johnson. Dial, 1992 (I:5–8 R:6). The heroine slays a sea monster.

Snyder, Dianne. *The Boy of the Three-Year Nap.* Illustrated by Allen Say. Houghton Mifflin, 1988 (I:all R:6). A Japanese woman tricks her lazy son into working.

Stamm, Claus. *Three Strong Women.* Illustrated by Jean and Mou-sien Tseng. Viking, 1990 (I:5–9 R:4). Three women teach a wrestler lessons about strength.

Vuong, Lynette Dyer. *The Golden Carp and Other Tales from Vietnam.* Illustrated by Manabu Saito. Lothrop, Lee & Shepard, 1993 (I:8+ R:5). This book includes six folktales.

Wang, Rosalind C., retold by. *The Treasure Chest: A Chinese Tale.* Illustrated by Will Hillenbrand. Holiday, 1995 (I:8–12 R:5). A widow's son earns the gratitude of the Ocean King.

Yacowitz, Caryn. Adapted by. *The Jade Stone: A Chinese Folktale.* Illustrated by Ju-Hong Chen. Holiday, 1992 (I:4–8 R:4). A stone carver goes against the wishes of the Emperor in this Chinese folktale.

Yagawa, Sumiko, ed. *The Crane Wife.* Translated by Katherine Paterson. Illustrated by Suekichi Akaba. Morrow, 1981 (I:7–10 R:6). A husband loses his wife when he breaks his promise.

Yep, Laurence. *The Khan's Daughter: A Mongolian Folktale.* Illustrated by Jean and Mou-sien Tseng. Scholastic, 1997 (I:5–8 R:4). A shepard must complete three trials to win the Khan's daughter in marriage.

_____ . *The Rainbow People.* Illustrated by David Wiesner. Harper & Row, 1989 (I:9+ R:6). Twenty Chinese folktales were collected from Chinese Americans.

_____ . *Tiger Woman.* Illustrated by Robert Roth. Bridge Water, 1995 (I:5–8 R:5). In this Chinese tale a woman is transformed into different forms.

Young, Ed. Translated by. *Lon Po Po: A Red-Riding Hood Story from China.* Philomel, 1989 (I:all R:5). The girls outwit the wolf in this version of the tale.

British (United Kingdom)

Behan, Brendan. *The King of Ireland's Son.* Illustrated by P. J. Lynch. Orchard, 1997 (I:all). The king offers half his kingdom to the son who discovers the source of music.

Brett, Jan. *Goldilocks and the Three Bears.* Dodd, Mead, 1987 (I:3–7 R:6). This is a highly illustrated version of the folktale.

Briggs, Katharine. *British Folktales*. Pantheon, 1977, Dorset, 1989 (I:all). An adult anthology also provides many sources for children.

Buchan, David, ed. *Scottish Tradition: A Collection of Scottish Folk Literature*. Routledge & Kegan Paul, 1984 (I:9+ R:5). A large adult collection provides selections for oral sharing.

Cauley, Lorinda Bryan. *The Cock, the Mouse, and the Little Red Hen*. Putnam, 1982 (I:3–6 R:4). The repetitive language appeals to young children.

_____. *Goldilocks and the Three Bears*. Putnam, 1981 (I:3–7 R:4). Large, colorful illustrations appeal to children.

Chaucer, Geoffrey. *Canterbury Tales*. Adapted by Barbara Cohen. Illustrated by Trina Schart Hyman. Lothrop, Lee & Shepard, 1988 (I:8+ R:6). Four tales include the prologue and an introduction.

Cooper, Susan. Retold by. *The Silver Cow: A Welsh Tale*. Illustrated by Warwick Hutton. Atheneum, 1983 (I:5–8 R:5). A cow and her offspring return to the lake because of a farmer's greed.

Crossley-Holland, Kevin. *British Folk Tales*. Watts, 1988 (I:8+ R:5). A large collection of tales includes sources and notes.

dePaola, Tomie. *The Friendly Beasts: An Old English Christmas Carol*. Putnam, 1981 (I:3–9). The Bethlehem setting is depicted in this folk song.

Esterl, Arnica. Adapted by. *The Fine Round Cake*. Translated by Pauline Hejl. Illustrated by Andrej Dugin and Olga Dugina. Four Winds, 1991 (I:3–7 R:4). This folktale is adapted from "Johnny-Cake," collected by Joseph Jacobs.

French, Vivian. Retold by. *Lazy Jack*. Illustrated by Russell Ayto. Candlewick, 1995 (I:4–8 R:5). A retelling of the English tale.

Galdone, Paul. *The Little Red Hen*. Clarion, 1985 (I:3–7 R:3). The industrious hen won't share her cake with her lazy friends.

_____. *The Three Bears*. Clarion, 1985 (I:3–7 R:5). The traditional tale is illustrated with large, humorous pictures.

_____. *What's in Fox's Sack? An Old English Tale*. Clarion, 1982 (I:3–7 R:2). A fox is outsmarted by a woman who puts a bulldog in his bag.

Garner, Alan. *A Bag of Moonshine*. Illustrated by Patrick James Lynch. Collins, 1986 (I:5–9 R:4). A collection contains twenty-two folktales.

Glassie, Henry, ed. *Irish Folktales*. Viking, 1987 (I:all). An adult source has many tales that may be shared with children.

Hodges, Margaret. Retold by. *Buried Moon*. Illustrated by Jamichael Henterly. Little, Brown, 1990 (I:6–9 R:5). This English folktale has a classic battle between good and evil.

Huck, Charlotte. Retold by. *Princess Furball*. Illustrated by Anita Lobel. Greenwillow, 1989 (I:6–10 R:6). The Cinderella-type character in this tale does not rely on magic.

Jacobs, Joseph. *Celtic Fairy Tales*. Illustrated by John D. Batten. David Nutt, 1890; reissued 1968 (I:9+ R:6). This is a selection of Celtic, Irish, and Gaelic tales.

_____. *More English Fairy Tales*. David Nutt, 1894 (I:all R:6). The English collector includes more tales.

Jones, Gwyn. *Welsh Legends and Folktales*. Oxford, 1955, Puffin, 1982 (I:9+ R:7). This is a collection of over thirty Welsh tales.

Kellogg, Steven. *Chicken Little*. Morrow, 1985 (I:5–8 R:5). This is a humorous modern version of the tale, with cars, trucks, and helicopters.

_____. *Jack and the Beanstalk*. Morrow, 1991 (I:4–9 R:5). This folktale is adapted from "Jack and the Beanstalk," collected by Joseph Jacobs.

_____. *The Three Little Pigs*. Morrow, 1997 (I:5–8 R:4). This humorous adaptation of the tale has an industrious mother who sends her pigs to Hog Hollow Academy before they meet the wolf.

Kimmel, Eric. Retold by. *The Gingerbread Man*. Illustrated by Megan Lloyd. Holiday, 1993 (I:3–6). This is the cumulative tale of the runaway cookie.

MacGill-Callahan, Sheila. *The Children of Lir*. Illustrated by Gennady Spirin. Dial, 1993 (I:6+ R:5). An evil stepmother changes children into swans in this Irish tale.

Marshall, James. *Goldilocks and the Three Bears*. Dial, 1988 (I:3–8 R:5). Humorous illustrations add to the folktale.

Rounds, Glen. Retold and illustrated by. *Three Little Pigs and the Big Bad Wolf*. Holiday, 1992 (I:3–8 R:5). The illustrations in the folktale focus on the antics of the wolf.

White, Carolyn. *Whuppity Stoorie: A Scottish Folktale*. Illustrated by S. D. Schindler. Putnam, 1997 (I:4–8 R:4). A girl must guess a fairy's name within three days.

Zemach, Harve. *Duffy and the Devil*. Illustrated by Margot Zemach. Farrar, Straus & Giroux, 1973 (I:8–12 R:6). A Cornish tale resembles "Rumplestiltskin," but the maid makes an agreement with the devil.

French

Aylesworth, Jim. *The Gingerbread Man*. Illustrated by Barbara McClintock. Scholastic. 1998 (I:2–6). Rhythmic Language accompanies the tale.

Brett, Jan. Retold by. *Beauty and the Beast*. Clarion, 1989 (I:8–12 R:6). Tapestries show the real characters.

de Beaumont, Madame. *Beauty and the Beast*. Translated and illustrated by Diane Goode. Bradbury, 1978 (I:8–14 R:7). Lovely illustrations accompany the tale of a girl who is willing to sacrifice her own life for the love of her father.

Hutton, Warwick. Retold by. *Beauty and the Beast*. Atheneum, 1985 (I:9 R:6). Love breaks an evil spell.

Perrault, Charles. *Cinderella*. Illustrated by Marcia Brown. Scribner's Sons, 1954 (I:5–8 R:5). Fine lines suggest the mood of the fairy tale.

_____. *The Glass Slipper: Charles Perrault's Tales of Time Past*. Translated by John Bierhorst. Illustrated by Mitchell Miller. Four Winds, 1981 (I:9–12 R:6). This is a new translation of *Histoires ou contes du temps passé*.

_____. *Histories or Tales of Past Times*. Garland, 1977 (I:10+ R:6). This is a reprint of the 1729 London edition.

_____. *Puss in Boots*. Retold by Lincoln Kirstein. Illustrated by Alain Vais. Little, Brown, 1992 (I:6–10 R:5). This is a beautifully illustrated retelling of the French folktale.

_____. *Puss in Boots*. Translated by Malcolm Arthur. Illustrated by Fred Marcellino. Farrar Straus Giroux, 1990 (I:6–10 R:6). This is the tale of the cat who wins a kingdom for his master.

_____. *The Sleeping Beauty*. Translated and illustrated by David Walker. Crowell, 1976 (I:8–14 R:6). A beautifully illustrated book resembles the stage setting for an opera or ballet.

Wegman, William. Retold by. *Cinderella*. Hyperion (I:5–8 R:5). Photographs of dogs dressed as the characters accompany the story.

Willard, Nancy. Retold by. *Beauty and the Beast*. Illustrated by Barry Moser. Harcourt Brace Jovanovich, 1992 (I:8+ R:6). This version of the tale is set in New York state in the early 1900s.

German

Galdone, Paul. *Hansel and Gretel.* McGraw-Hill, 1982 (I:5–7 R:3). The folktale is appropriate for younger children.

———. *Little Red Riding Hood.* McGraw-Hill, 1974 (I:4–8 R:4). Large, colorful pictures retell the Grimms' folktale.

Grimm, Brothers. *The Brave Little Tailor.* Translated by Anthea Bell. Illustrated by Sergei Goloshapov. North-South, 1997 (I:5–8 R:5). This is the tale about a tailor who swats seven flies at one blow.

———. *The Bremen Town Musicians.* Retold and illustrated by Ilse Plume. Doubleday, 1980 (I:5–8 R:5). Soft color illustrations show animals going through the forest.

———. *The Bremen Town Musicians.* Translated by Anthea Bell. Illustrated by Bernadette Watts. North-South, 1997 (I:5–8 R:5). The artwork presents a rustic environment.

———. *The Complete Brothers Grimm Fairy Tales.* Edited by Lily Owens. Avenel, 1981 (I:all R:7). The tales were previously published in *Grimms' Household Tales.*

———. *The Devil with the Three Golden Hairs.* Retold and illustrated by Nonny Hogrogian. Knopf, 1983 (I:5–9 R:7). A boy completes a quest to earn the king's daughter for his bride.

———. *The Frog Prince.* Retold by Jan Ormerod and David Lloyd. Illustrated by Jan Ormerod. Lothrop, Lee & Shepard, 1990 (I:6–9 R:5). A princess breaks an enchantment in this German tale.

———. *The Golden Bird.* Retold by Neil Philip. Illustrated by Isabelle Brent. Little, Brown, 1995 (I:all). A tale about an enchanted prince and a quest for a golden bird.

———. *The Golden Goose.* Illustrated by Diane Paterson. Troll, 1981. A younger son's generosity wins him a princess.

———. *Hansel and Gretel.* Illustrated by Susan Jeffers. Dial, 1980 (I:5–9 R:6). The illustrations with strong lines and a magnificent gingerbread house should appeal to readers.

———. *Hansel and Gretel.* Retold by Rika Lesser. Illustrated by Paul O. Zelinsky. Dodd, Mead, 1984 (I:all R:6). Full-page illustrations depict a dark forest of an earlier time.

———. *Little Red Cap.* Translated by Elizabeth Crawford. Illustrated by Lisbeth Zwerger. Morrow, 1983 (I:4–7 R:4). The folktale tells about a deceitful wolf.

———. *Little Red Riding Hood.* Retold and illustrated by Trina Schart Hyman. Holiday House, 1983 (I:6–9 R:7). Richly detailed page borders add to this attractive version.

———. *Rapunzel: From the Brothers Grimm.* Retold by Barbara Rogasky. Illustrated by Trina Schart Hyman. Holiday House, 1982 (I:6–9 R:6). The forest setting seems right for a girl imprisoned in a high tower.

———. *Rapunzel.* Retold and illustrated by Paul O. Zelinsky. Dutton, 1997 (I:all). Settings reflect the Italian Renaissance.

———. *Rose Red and Snow White.* Retold by Ruth Sanderson. Little, Brown, 1997 (I:4–8 R:4). The family shelters a bear who is revealed as a prince.

———. *Rumpelstiltskin.* Retold and illustrated by Paul O. Zelinsky. Dutton, 1986 (I:all R:6). A miller's daughter spins gold with the help of a supernatural being.

———. *The Sleeping Beauty.* Illustrated by Warwick Hutton. Atheneum, 1979 (I:7–12 R:6). Watercolors illustrate a story of magic and enchantment.

———. *Snow White and the Seven Dwarfs.* Translated by Randall Jarrell. Illustrated by Nancy Ekholm Burkert. Farrar, Straus & Giroux, 1972 (I:7–12 R:6). The illustrations were carefully researched by the artist to show the Black Forest and German heritage.

———. *The Traveling Musicians of Bremen.* Retold by P. K. Page. Illustrated by Kady MacDonald Denton. Little, Brown, 1992 (I:3–9 R:5). The author and artist give this German folktale some contemporary twists.

———. *The Twelve Dancing Princesses.* Illustrated by Errol LeCain. Viking, 1978 (I:7–12 R:7). Twelve princesses mysteriously dance holes in their shoes every night.

———. *The Twelve Dancing Princesses.* Retold by Marianna Mayer. Illustrated by Kinuko Craft. Morrow, 1989 (I:8+ R:5). Beautiful paintings accompany the tale.

———. *The Twelve Dancing Princesses.* Retold by Jane Ray. Dutton, 1996 (I:5–8 R:5). The princesses are both bold and clever.

———. *The Twelve Dancing Princesses.* Retold by Ruth Sanderson. Little, Brown, 1990 (I:7–10 R:5). The gardener breaks the enchantment and marries the princess in this German tale.

———. *The Twelve Dancing Princesses and Other Tales from Grimm.* Illustrated by Lidia Postma. Dial, 1986 (I:9–12 R:5). This is an anthology of German tales.

———. *The Turnip.* Retold by Walter de la Mare. Illustrated by Kevin Hawkes. Godine, 1992 (I:5–8 R:4). A generous farmer is rewarded while his miserly brother does not gain the reward he thinks he deserves.

———. *The Water of Life.* Retold by Barbara Rogasky. Illustrated by Trina Schart Hyman. Holiday House, 1986 (I:4–9 R:3). A quest leads the youngest son to a princess.

———. *The Wolf and the Seven Little Kids.* Translated by Anne Rogers. Illustrated by Otto S. Svend. Larousse, 1977 (I:4–8 R:4). Seven little goats have a conflict with a wolf when their mother leaves the house.

Grimm, Wilhelm. *Dear Mili.* Translated by Ralph Manheim. Illustrated by Maurice Sendak. Farrar, Straus & Giroux, 1988 (I:all R:6). The story was found in a letter written in 1816.

Marshall, James. *Hansel and Gretel.* Dial, 1990 (I:3–8 R:4). Marshall's illustrations and text provide a comical version of this German folktale.

———. *Red Riding Hood.* Dial, 1987 (I:3–8 R:5). Cartoonlike illustrations develop a humorous text.

Wegman, William. Retold by. *Little Red Riding Hood.* Hyperion, 1993 (I:5–8 R:5). The story is accompanied by photographs of dogs playing the characters.

Hispanic

See Chapter 11.

Jewish

Geras, Adele. *My Grandmother's Stories: A Collection of Jewish Folk Tales.* Illustrated by Jael Jordan. Knopf, 1990 (I:8+ R:4). These stories are based on a Russian Jewish heritage.

Jaffe, Nina, and Steve Zeitlin. *While Standing on One Foot: Puzzle Stories and Wisdom Tales from the Jewish Tradition.* Illustrated by John Segal. Holt, 1993 (I:8+ R:5). Seventeen tales and questions challenge readers.

Prose, Francine. *The Angel's Mistake: Stories of Chelm.* Illustrated by Mark Podwal. Greenwillow, 1997 (I:all). This is a collection of Yiddish folktales about the foolish people of Chelm.

Rothenberg, Joan. *Yettele's Feathers.* Hyperion, 1995 (I:5–8 R:6). A widow learns a lesson about gossiping.

Sanfield, Steve. *The Feather Merchants & Other Tales of the Fools of Chelm.* Illustrated by Mikhail Magaril. Orchard, 1991

(I:7–12 R:5). These thirteen folktales are from traditional Jewish culture.

Schwartz, Howard, and Barbara Rush. Selected and retold by. *The Diamond Tree: Jewish Tales from Around the World.* Illustrated by Uri Shulevitz. HarperCollins, 1991 (I:8+ R:5). This is a collection of fifteen tales from different countries.

Singer, Isaac Bashevis. *The Golem.* Illustrated by Uri Shulevitz. Farrar, Straus & Giroux, 1982 (I:8+ R:5). This is another version of a Jewish folktale.

———. *Mazel and Shlimazel, or the Milk of the Lioness.* Illustrated by Margot Zemach. Farrar, Straus & Giroux, 1967 (I:8–12 R:4). Mazel, the spirit of good luck, and Shlimazel, the spirit of bad luck, have a contest.

———. *When Shlemiel Went to Warsaw & Other Stories.* Illustrated by Margot Zemach. Farrar, Straus & Giroux, 1968 (I:8–12 R:4). This is a collection of both folktales and original stories.

Zemach, Margot. *It Could Always Be Worse.* Farrar, Straus & Giroux, 1977 (I:5–9 R:2). A small hut seems larger when all the animals are removed.

Norwegian

Asbjörnsen, Peter Christian, and Jörgen E. Moe. *East O' the Sun and West O' the Moon.* Translated by George Webbe Dasent. Illustrated by P. J. Lynch. Candlewick, 1992 (I:6–10 R:6). The Norwegian landscape is re-created in the beautiful illustrations that accompany a tale of enchantment.

———. *The Man Who Kept House.* Illustrated by Otto S. Svend. Macmillan, 1992 (I:5–9 R:5). In this humorous tale, a man discovers that keeping house is not as easy as he believes.

———. *Norwegian Folk Tales.* Illustrated by Erik Werenskiold and Theodor Kittelsen. Viking, 1960 (I:6–10 R:3). This is a collection of thirty-five Norwegian folktales.

———. *The Three Billy Goats Gruff.* Illustrated by Marcia Brown. Harcourt Brace Jovanovich, 1957 (I:3–7 R:5). Goats prance across the pages of this favorite tale for telling.

———. *Three Billy Goats Gruff.* Retold and illustrated by Glen Rounds. Holiday, 1993 (I:3–7 R:5). The illustrations depict the classic battle between the goats and the troll.

Booss, Claire, ed. *Scandinavian Folk & Fairy Tales.* Avenel, 1984 (I:10+). A large adult collection of tales from Norway, Sweden, Denmark, Finland, and Iceland will provide sources for storytelling.

Galdone, Paul. *The Three Billy Goats Gruff.* Seabury, 1973 (I:5–8 R:5). A picture storybook tells about three billy goats who defeat the troll who lives under the bridge.

Hague, Kathleen, and Michael Hague. *East of the Sun and West of the Moon.* Harcourt Brace Jovanovich, 1980 (I:7–9 R:5). A maiden lives in the castle of an enchanted white bear.

Haviland, Virginia. *Favorite Fairy Tales Told in Norway.* Illustrated by Leonard Weisgard. Little, Brown, 1961 (I:6–10 R:4). This collection includes "The Princess on the Glass Hill," "Why the Sea Is Salt," "The Three Billy Goats Gruff," "Taper Tom," "Why the Bear Is Stumpy-Tailed," "The Lad and the North Wind," and "Boots and the Troll."

Mayer, Mercer. *East of the Sun and West of the Moon.* Four Winds, 1980 (I:8–10 R:4). This is a beautifully illustrated version of the Asbjörnsen and Moe tale.

Willard, Nancy. *East of the Sun & West of the Moon: A Play.* Illustrated by Barry Moser. Harcourt Brace Jovanovich, 1989 (I:all). This retelling uses both narrative and poetry.

Russian

Afanasyév, Alexander Nikolayevich. *The Fool and the Fish: A Tale from Russia.* Retold by Lenny Hort. Illustrated by Gennady Spirin. Dial, 1990 (I:5–8 R:4). Enchantment helps a peasant win the tsar's daughter.

———. *Russian Folk Tales.* Translated by Robert Chandler. Illustrated by Ivan I. Bilibin. Random House, 1980 (I:8–12 R:7). Seven memorable tales were collected by the nineteenth-century folklorist.

Cech, John. *First Snow, Magic Snow.* Illustrated by Sharon McGinley-Nally. Four Winds, 1992 (I:5–9 R:5). A woodsman and his wife wish for a child and become parents of a snow child.

Fonteyn, Margot. *Swan Lake.* Illustrated by Trina Schart Hyman. Harcourt Brace Jovanovich, 1989 (I:all R:6). This is a retelling of the ballet.

Helprin, Mark. *Swan Lake.* Illustrated by Chris Van Allsburg. Houghton Mifflin, 1989 (I:all R:6). This is a retelling of the ballet.

Kimmel, Eric A. *One Eye, Two Eyes, Three Eyes.* Illustrated by Dirk Zimmer. Holiday, 1996 (I:5–8 R:4). This Ukrainian tale tells about a girl who becomes the slave of a three-eyed witch.

Kismaric, Carole. *The Rumor of Pavel and Paali: A Ukrainian Folktale.* Illustrated by Charles Mikolaycak. Harper & Row, 1988 (I:6–9 R:6). In the battle between good and evil, evil wins first but good finally overcomes.

McCurdy, Michael. *The Devils Who Learned to Be Good.* Little, Brown, 1987 (I:6–9 R:6). An old soldier outwits several devils in this Russian folktale.

Mikolaycak, Charles. Retold by. *Babushka.* Holiday House, 1984 (I:6–9 R:7). An old woman leaves gifts as she searches for the Christ Child.

Pushkin, Alexander. *The Golden Cockerel and Other Fairy Tales.* Illustrated by Boris Zvorykin. Doubleday, 1990 (I:8–12 R:6). This book was originally published in France in 1925.

———. *The Tale of Czar Saltan, or the Prince and the Swan Princess.* Translated by Patricia Tracy Lowe. Illustrated by I. Bilibin. Crowell, 1975 (I:8–12 R:6). The czar marries the youngest daughter, but her sisters trick her into exile.

———. *The Tale of Tsar Saltan.* Illustrated by Gennady Spirin. Dial, 1996 (I:7+ R:6). Good wins out over jealousy.

Ransome, Arthur. *The Fool of the World and the Flying Ship.* Illustrated by Uri Shulevitz. Farrar, Straus & Giroux, 1968 (I:6–10 R:6). A simple lad overcomes obstacles to wed the czar's daughter.

———. *Old Peter's Russian Tales.* Jonathan Cape, 1916, 1985 (I:7+ R:6). This is a collection of tales.

Shepard, Aaron, Retold by. *The Sea King's Daughter.* Illustrated by Gennady Spirin. Atheneum, 1997 (I:7+ R:5). A musician's music is heard by the Sea King.

Sherman, Josepha. *Vassilisa the Wise: A Tale of Medieval Russia.* Illustrated by Daniel San Souci. Harcourt Brace Jovanovich, 1988 (I:8+ R:6). A clever woman outwits a prince and saves her husband.

Winthrop, Elizabeth, adapted by. *The Little Humpbacked Horse: A Russian Tale.* Illustrated by Alexander Koshkin. Clarion, 1997 (I:5–8 R:4). The theme of this tale focuses on wisdom and friendship.

Wolkstein, Diane. Retold by. *Oom Razoom: Or Go I Know Not Where, Bring Back I Know Not What: A Russian Tale.* Illustrated by Dennis McDermott. Morrow, 1991 (I:5–9 R:5). A resourceful woman and her husband outwit the king.

Involving Children in Traditional Literature **345**

Other Folktales

Aardema, Verna. *Why Mosquitoes Buzz in People's Ears: A West African Tale.* Illustrated by Leo and Diane Dillon. Dial, 1975 (I:5–9 R:6). A cumulative African folktale tells the humorous reason for mosquitoes' buzzing.

Baker, Olaf. *Where the Buffaloes Begin.* Illustrated by Stephen Gammell. Warne, 1981 (I:8 R:7). Illustrations with soft, irregular shapes add power to a Native American legend.

Ben-Ezer, Ehud. *Hosni the Dreamer: An Arabian Tale.* Illustrated by Uri Shulevitz. Farrar, Straus & Giroux, 1997 (I:4–8 R:4). A shepherd boy longs for adventure.

Blair, Walter. *Tall Tale America: A Legendary History of Our Humorous Heroes.* Illustrated by Glen Rounds. Coward, McCann, 1944 (I:8–12 R:5). This is a collection of exaggerated tales.

Brooke, William J. *A Telling of the Tales: Five Stories.* Harper & Row, 1990 (I:8+ R:4). The text includes the author's adaptations of "Sleeping Beauty," "Paul Bunyan," "Cinderella," "John Henry," and "Jack and the Beanstalk."

Chase, Richard. Retold by. *The Jack Tales.* Illustrated by Berkeley Williams, Jr. Houghton Mifflin, 1943 (I:all R:5). This collection of tales is from the southern Appalachians.

Cohn, Amy L. complied by. *From Sea to Shining Sea: A Treasury of American Folklore and Folk Songs.* Illustrated by Caldecott Award Artists. Scholastic, 1993 (I:all). This is a large collection of folklore.

Day, Edward C. *John Tabor's Ride.* Illustrated by Dirk Zimmer. Knopf, 1989 (I:8+ R:5). This text is a retelling of a tall tale.

Demi. *Buddha Stories.* Holt, 1997 (I:all). The text includes ten moral tales.

_____ . *One Grain of Rice: A Mathematical Folktale.* Scholastic, 1997 (I:5–8 R:4). This is a traditional tale from India about a raja who hoards rice.

dePaola, Tomie. *Days of the Blackbird: A Tale of Northern Italy.* Putnam, 1997 (I:5–9 R:5). The story is based on a tale from northern Italy.

Goode, Diane. *Diane Goode's Book of Silly Stories and Songs.* Dutton, 1992 (I: 5–8 R:4). The collection includes seventeen folktales from around the world.

Haley, Gail E. *Jack and the Bean Tree.* Crown, 1986 (I:4–10 R:5). This is an Appalachian variant of "Jack and the Beanstalk."

_____ . *Mountain Jack Tales.* Dutton, 1992 (I:8+ R:5). These tales are from the mountain regions of the United States.

Harris, Joel Chandler. *Told by Uncle Remus.* McClure, Philips & Co., 1905 (I:all R:4). More adventures of Brer Rabbit are told.

_____ . *Uncle Remus and His Friends.* Houghton Mifflin, 1892 (I:all R:4). Tales are told of Brer Rabbit's adventures.

Hickox, Rebecca. *The Golden Sandal: A Middle Eastern Cinderella Story.* Illustrated by Will Hillenbrand. Holiday, 1998 (I:5–8 R:4). This is an Iraqi variant of the tale.

Highwater, Jamake. *Anpao: An American Indian Odyssey.* Illustrated by Fritz Scholder. Lippincott, 1977 (I:12+ R:6). Anpao journeys across the history of Native American traditional tales in order to search for his destiny.

Ho, Minfong, and Saphan Ros. *Brother Rabbit: A Cambodian Tale.* Illustrated by Jennifer Hewiston. Lothrop, Lee & Shepard, 1997 (I:5–8 R:4). This tale may be compared with Brer Rabbit.

Hooks, William H. *The Ballad of Belle Dorcas.* Illustrated by Brian Pinkney. Knopf, 1990 (I:8+ R:5). An African American tale is about the love between a freeborn woman and a slave.

_____ . *Moss Gown.* Illustrated by Donald Carrick. Clarion, 1987 (I:8+ R:5). This Cinderella-type folktale is from eastern North Carolina.

Jaquith, Priscilla. *Bo Rabbit Smart for True: Folktales from the Gullah.* Illustrated by Ed Young. Philomel, 1981 (I:all R:6). These four tales are from islands off the Georgia coast.

Kellogg, Stephen. Retold by. *Johnny Appleseed.* Illustrated by Stephen Kellogg. Morrow, 1988 (I:6–9 R:6). This version of the tall tale is highly illustrated.

_____ . Retold by. *Mike Fink: A Tall Tale.* Morrow, 1992 (I:5–8 R:6). This is a humorous tale of an American tall-tale hero.

_____ . *Paul Bunyan.* Retold by. Morrow, 1984 (I:6–9 R:7). This version of the tall tale is highly illustrated.

Kimmel, Eric A. *Billy Lazroe and the King of the Sea: A Tale of the Northwest.* Illustrated by Michael Steirnagle. Harcourt Brace, 1996 (I:5–8 R:4). This sea tale is a northwestern version of an old Russian tale.

_____ . Adapted by. *Rimonah of the Flashing Sword: A North African Tale.* Illustrated by Omar Rayyan. Holiday, 1995 (I:5–9 R:5). This is an Egyptian version of the "Snow White" tale.

_____ . *The Three Princes.* Illustrated by Leonard Everett Fisher. Holiday, 1994 (I:4–8 R:5). In an Arabian setting, three princes try to prove themselves the most worthy.

Manna, Anthony L., and Mitakidou. *Mr. Semolina-Semolinus: A Greek Folktale.* Simon & Schuster, 1997 (I:5–8 R:4). The folktale emphasizes the power of love.

Martin, Eva. Retold by. *Canadian Fairy Tales.* Illustrated by Laszlo Gal. Douglas & McIntyre, 1984 (I:7–10 R:4). Twelve traditional tales reflect the Canadian influence on the French, Irish, and British oral traditions.

Mayo, Margaret. *Mythical Birds & Beasts from Many Lands.* Illustrated by Jane Ray. Dutton, 1997 (I:all). The collection includes both folktales and myths.

McDermott, Gerald. *Arrow to the Sun: A Pueblo Indian Tale.* Viking, 1974 (I:3–9 R:2). Strong shapes and colors complement a Native American tale.

_____ . *Raven: A Trickster Tale from the Pacific Northwest.* Harcourt Brace Jovanovich, 1993 (I:all). Raven brings light to the people.

Roth, Susan L. *The Story of Light.* Morrow, 1990 (I:6–10). This is a Cherokee tale about the bringing of light.

Sanderson, Ruth. *Papa Gatto: An Italian Fairy Tale.* Little, Brown, 1995 (I:8+ R:7). A generous and loving heart is more important than the beautiful face of a greedy girl.

San Souci, Robert D. *Cut from the Same Cloth: American Women of Myth, Legend, and Tall Tale.* Illustrated by Brian Pinkney. Philomel, 1993 (I:8+ R:5). This is a collection of tall-tale heroines from various ethnic backgrounds.

_____ . *A Weave of Words.* Illustrated by Raul Colon. Orchard, 1998 (I:5–9 R:5). Education is important in an Armenian tale.

Schroeder, Alan. *Smoky Mountain Rose: An Appalachian Cinderella.* Illustrated by Brad Sneed. Dial, 1997 (I:5–9 R:4). This adaptation of Perrault's tale is set in the Smoky Mountains.

Scieszka, Jon. *The Stinky Cheese Man and Other Fairly Stupid Tales.* Illustrated by Lane Smith. Viking, 1992 (I:all). These are adaptations of folktales.

_____ . *The True Story of the 3 Little Pigs!* Illustrated by Lane Smith. Viking, 1989 (I:all) Humorous illustrations accompany a new version of the tale.

Sierra, Judy. *Multicultural Folktales for the Feltboard and Readers' Theater.* Oryx, 1996. This collection of tales for children in the elementary grades provides sources and directions for teachers and librarians.

Stanley, Diane. *Rumpelstiltskin's Daughter.* Morrow, 1997 (I:5–9 R:5). Stanley uses the traditional tale to develop a sequel to the story.

Yep, Laurence. *The Khan's Daughter: A Mongolian Folktale.* Illustrated by Jean and Mou-sien Tseng. Scholastic, 1997 (I:5–8 R:4). A shepard must complete three trials to win the Khan's daughter in marriage.

FABLES

Aesop. *Aesop's Fables.* Illustrated by Heidi Holder. Viking, 1981 (I:9–12 R:7). Nine fables are illustrated with full-color paintings.

_____ . *Aesop's Fables.* Illustrated by Fulvio Testa. Barron's, 1989 (I:all R:5). Twenty fables are in this collection.

_____ . *Aesop's Fables.* Retold by Tom Paxton. Illustrated by Robert Rayevsky. Morrow, 1988 (I:all). The fables are retold in verse form.

_____ . *Aesop's Fables.* Selected and illustrated by Michael Hague. Holt, Rinehart & Winston, 1985 (I:9–12 R:7). Thirteen fables are illustrated with full-page paintings.

_____ . *Aesop's Fables.* Translated by Sir Roger L'Estrange. Illustrated by Percy J. Billinghurst. Gallery, 1984 (I:9+). This is a reissue of the seventeenth-century translation.

Bierhorst, John. *Doctor Coyote: A Native American Aesop's Fables.* Illustrated by Wendy Watson. Macmillan, 1987 (I:all R:5). This is a fable from the Indians of Mexico.

Caldecott, Randolph. *The Caldecott Aesop: A Facsimile of the 1883 Edition.* Doubleday, 1978 (I:all R:7). This is a reproduction of the earlier Aesop's fables retold and illustrated by Caldecott.

Craig, Helen. *The Town Mouse and the Country Mouse.* Candlewick, 1992 (I:6–8 R:5). This is an extended story about the mice.

Kherdian, David. *Feathers and Tails: Animal Fables from Around the World.* Illustrated by Nonny Hogrogian. Philomel, 1992 (I:8+ R:5). This is a collection of twenty-one fables from different cultures.

Stevens, Janet. Retold by. *The Tortoise and the Hare.* Holiday House, 1984 (I:6–8 R:3). This is a picture storybook version of the Aesop fable.

_____ . *The Town Mouse & the Country Mouse.* Holiday House, 1987 (I:6–8). This is a highly illustrated version of the Aesop fable.

Te Kanawa, Kiri. Retold by. *Land of the Long White Cloud: Maori Myths, Tales, and Legends.* Illustrated by Michael Foreman. Arcade, 1989 (I:8–12 R:5). This is a collection of Polynesian tales.

Yolen, Jane. Retold by. *A Sip of Aesop.* Illustrated by Karen Barbour. Scholastic, 1995 (I:5–10). The fables are retold in verse form.

MYTHOLOGY

Greek and Roman Myths

Barth, Edna. *Cupid and Psyche.* Illustrated by Ati Forberg. Seabury, 1976 (I:7–12 R:6). Princess Psyche is loved by Cupid but hated by Venus, the goddess of love.

Bulfinch, Thomas. *A Book of Myths.* Illustrated by Helen Sewell. Macmillan, 1942, 1964 (I:10+ R:6). A collection of Greek myths is written in short-story format.

_____ . *Myths of Greece & Rome.* Penguin, 1981 (paperback) (I:10 R:8). This is a good source for the myths.

Colum, Padraic. *The Golden Fleece and the Heroes Who Lived Before Achilles.* Illustrated by Willy Pogany. Macmillan, 1921, 1949, 1962 (I:9+ R:6). Jason and the Greek heroes search for the Golden Fleece.

Coolidge, Olivia. *Greek Myths.* Illustrated by Edouard Sandoz. Houghton Mifflin, 1949 (I:10+ R:7). This is an excellent collection of myths.

D'Aulaire, Ingri, and Edgar Parin D'Aulaire. *D'Aulaires' Book of Greek Myths.* Doubleday, 1962 (paperback, 1980) (I:8+ R:6). This collection of tales is about gods, goddesses, and heroes.

Evslin, Bernard. *Hercules.* Illustrated by Jos A. Smith. Morrow, 1984 (I:9 R:6). These are tales of a great hero.

_____ . *The Nemean Lion.* Chelsea House, 1990 (I:10+ R:6). The Greek myth about the monster created so that Zeus could destroy Heraclea.

Fisher, Leonard Everett. *The Olympians: Great Gods and Goddesses of Ancient Greece.* Holiday, 1984 (I:8 R:3). Brief biographies accompany large illustrations.

_____ . *Theseus and the Minotaur.* Holiday House, 1988 (I:8–12 R:6). Theseus defeats the monster in this heroic tale.

Fleischman, Paul. *Dateline: Troy.* Illustrated by Gwen Frankfeldt and Glenn Morrow. Candlewick, 1996 (I:12+ R:7). This is a retelling of the Trojan War with contemporary news articles.

Gates, Doris. *The Golden God: Apollo.* Illustrated by Constantinos CoConis. Viking, 1973 (I:9+ R:6). This is a story of Apollo and his associations with other gods and goddesses.

_____ . *Lord of the Sky: Zeus.* Illustrated by Robert Handville. Viking, 1972 (I:10+ R:7). The myths center on Zeus.

_____ . *Two Queens of Heaven: Aphrodite and Demeter.* Illustrated by Trina Schart Hyman. Viking, 1974 (I:9+ R:5). A group of myths tells the exploits of Aphrodite and Demeter.

_____ . *The Warrior Goddess: Athena.* Illustrated by Don Bolognese. Viking, 1972 (I:9+ R:6). This book tells the exploits of the goddess Athena, Zeus's daughter.

Hamilton, Virginia. *In the Beginning: Creation Stories from Around the World.* Illustrated by Barry Moser. Harcourt Brace Jovanovich, 1988 (I:all R:6). Creation stories come from many cultures.

Hutton, Warwick. Retold by. *Persephone.* Macmillan, 1994 (I:7–12 R:5). This is the myth about the abduction to the underworld.

_____ . Retold by. *Theseus and the Minotaur.* Macmillan, 1989 (I:7–12 R:6). This is the Greek myth in which the hero kills the Minotaur.

_____ . *The Trojan Horse.* Macmillan, 1992 (I:8+ R:5). This is the Greek story of the capture of Troy.

Kingsley, Charles. *The Heroes.* Mayflower, 1980 (I:8+ R:6). These tales are of Greek heroes.

McCaughrean, Geraldine. *Greek Myths.* Illustrated by Emma Chichester Clark. Macmillan, 1993 (I:8+ R:6). A collection of sixteen tales.

Philip, Neil. Retold by. *The Adventures of Odysseus.* Illustrated by Peter Malone. Orchard, 1997 (I:8+ R:5). This is a new retelling of Homer's Odyssey.

Richardson, I. M. *The Adventures of Hercules*. Illustrated by Robert Baxter. Troll, 1983 (I:9 R:6). The Roman hero performs twelve labors.

_____. *Demeter and Persephone, The Seasons of Time*. Illustrated by Robert Baxter. Troll, 1983 (I:9 R:6). The Greek myth tells about Hades, Persephone, and Demeter.

_____. *Prometheus and the Story of Fire*. Illustrated by Robert Baxter, Troll, 1983 (I:9 R:6). A Greek myth tells how Prometheus gave mortals fire.

Norse Myths and Epics

Colum, Padraic. *The Children of Odin: The Book of Northern Myths*. Illustrated by Willy Pogany. Macmillan, 1920, 1984 (I:9+ R:6). This book contains thirty-five tales.

Coolidge, Olivia E. *Legends of the North*. Illustrated by Edouard Sandoz. Houghton Mifflin, 1951 (I:9–14 R:6). This book contains the northern legends and the tales from the sagas.

Crossley-Holland, Kevin. *The Faber Book of Northern Legends*. Illustrated by Alan Howard. Faber & Faber, 1983 (I:9+ R:6). This is a collection of Norse myths, Germanic heroic legends, and Icelandic sagas.

D'Aulaire, Ingri, and Edgar Parin D'Aulaire. *Norse Gods and Giants*. Doubleday, 1967 (I:8–12 R:6). A collection of Norse tales includes explanations about creation and tales of Thor, Odin, and Loki.

Harrison, Michael. *The Curse of the Ring*. Illustrated by Tudor Humphries. Oxford University Press, 1987 (I:9+ R:6). This book contains a retelling of the Norse Ring saga.

Osborne, Mary Pope. Retold by. *Favorite Norse Myths*. Illustrated by Troy Howell. Scholastic, 1996 (I:8+ R:9). This collection of fourteen myths is based on the *Elder Edda* and the *Younger Edda*.

Philip, Neil. Retold by. *Odin's Family: Myths of the Vikings*. Illustrated by Maryclare Foa. Orchard, 1996 (I:8+ R:5). The fifteen myths are based on the "Prose Edda."

OTHER MYTHS

McCaughrean, Geraldine. *The Silver Treasure: Myths and Legends of the World*. Illustrated by Bee Willey. Simon & Schuster, 1997 (I:9+ R:5). Tales include a story of the Hawaiian pig-faced god.

Oppenheim, Shulamith Levy. Retold by. *Iblis*. Illustrated by Ed Young. Harcourt Brace, 1994 (I:all R:5). This is an Islamic version of Adam and Eve and their fall from Paradise.

Rattigan, Jama Kim. *The Woman in the Moon: A Story from Hawai'i*. Illustrated by Carla Golembe. Little, Brown, 1996 (I:4–8 R:4). This is a Polynesian myth.

LEGENDS

Brown, Marcia. *Backbone of the King: Story of Pakáa and His Son Ku*. University of Hawaii Press, 1966 (I:10+ R:5). A boy helps his father regain his noble position.

Cadnum, Michael. *In A Dark Wood*. Orchard, 1998 (I:10+ R:6). The Robin Hood legend is told from the viewpoint of the Sheriff.

Crossley-Holland, Kevin. Retold by. *Beowulf*. Illustrated by Charles Keeping. Oxford, 1982 (I:9+ R:4). This is a highly illustrated narrative version of the epic.

Early, Margaret. Retold by. *Robin Hood*. Abrahams, 1996 (I:8+ R:6). This is a highly illustrated version of the legend.

_____. Retold by. *William Tell*. Abrams, 1991 (I:7–10 R:6). This is the legend of a Swiss hero.

Fisher, Leonard Everett. *William Tell*. Farrar, Straus & Giroux, 1996 (I:5–8 R:5). The legend of the Swiss marksman.

Hastings, Selina. *Sir Gawain and the Green Knight*. Illustrated by Juan Wijngaard. Lothrop, Lee & Shepard, 1981 (I:9–12 R:4). One of King Arthur's knights is challenged by a giant adversary.

_____. *Sir Gawain and the Loathly Lady*. Illustrated by Juan Wijngaard. Lothrop, Lee & Shepard, 1985 (I:10+ R:6). This is an elaborately illustrated version of one of the Arthurian tales.

Hodges, Margaret. *Saint George and the Dragon*. Illustrated by Trina Schart Hyman. Little, Brown, 1984 (I:all R:7). An English legend is adapted from Edmund Spenser's *The Faerie Queene*.

Jaffe, Nina. *The Mysterious Visitor: Stories of the Prophet Elijah*. Illustrated by Elivia Savadier. Scholastic, 1997 (I:5–9 R:4). The text includes eight stories from Jewish traditional tales.

Lagerlof, Selma. *The Legend of the Christmas Rose*. Retold by Ellin Greene. Illustrated by Charles Mikolaycak. Holiday, 1990 (I:8+ R:5). The story tells about the origin of the Christmas Rose.

McCully, Emily Arnold. *Beautiful Warrior: The Legend of the Nun's Kung Fu*. Scholastic, 1998 (I:6–10 R:5). The story of two female kung fu masters.

McKinley, Robin. *The Outlaws of Sherwood*. Greenwillow, 1988 (I:10+ R:7). The author interprets the Robin Hood legend.

Middleton, Haydn. *Island of the Mighty: Stories of Old Britain*. Illustrated by Anthea Toorchen. Oxford University Press, 1987 (I:9+ R:6). This is a collection of Celtic tales.

Miles, Bernard. *Robin Hood: His Life and Legend*. Illustrated by Victor G. Ambrus. Hamlyn, 1979 (I:8–12 R:7). This is a highly illustrated version of the English legend.

Morpurgo, Michael. *Robin of Sherwood*. Illustrated by Michael Foreman. Harcourt Brace, 1996 (I:9+ R:6). The author combines a modern-day tale with the legend.

Nye, Robert. *Beowulf, A New Telling*. Illustrated by Allan E. Cober. Hill, 1968 (I:10+ R:5). The epic is written in narrative form.

Paterson, Katherine, retold by. *Parzival: The Quest of the Grail Knight*. Lodestar, 1998 (I:10+ R:7). The legend includes background notes.

Pyle, Howard. *The Merry Adventures of Robin Hood*. 1883. Reprint by Scribner's Sons, 1946 (I:10–14 R:8). This is Pyle's original, longer version of Robin Hood's adventures.

_____. *The Story of the Champions of the Round Table*. Scribner's Sons, 1905; reissued 1968 (I:12+ R:8). Four books include "Story of Lancelot" and "Book of Sir Tristram."

_____. *The Story of King Arthur and His Knights*. Scribner's Sons, 1903; reissued 1978 (I:12+ R:8). This is a reissue of the classic.

Riordan, James. *Tales of King Arthur*. Illustrated by Victor G. Ambrus. Rand McNally, 1982 (I:9–12 R:6). New illustrations accompany a classic legend about the English hero.

Rogasky, Barbara. *The Golem*. Illustrated by Trina Schart Hyman. Holiday, 1996 (I:all). The illustrations depict sixteenth-century Prague.

San Souci, Robert D. *Young Guinevere*. Illustrated by Jamichael Henterly, Dell, 1996 (I:all). This is the story of the girl who will become King Arthur's queen.

_____. *Young Lancelot*. Illustrated by Jamichael Henterly. Doubleday, 1996 (I:all). The illustrations present a romantic setting.

Sasso, Sandy Eisenberg. *But God Remembered: Stories of Women from Creation to the Promised Land*. Illustrated by Bethanne Andersen. Jewish Lights, 1995 (I:8+ R:7). Legends about four women who lived during Biblical times.

Seredy, Kate. *The White Stag*. Viking, 1937, 1965 (I:10–14 R:7). This is the story of the Hun-Magyar migration into what became Hungary.

Singer, Isaac Bashevis. *The Golem*. Illustrated by Uri Shulevitz. Farrar, Straus & Giroux, 1982, 1996 (I:all). A story of persecution and the Golem who came to the rescue.

Sutcliff, Rosemary. *The Light Beyond the Forest*. Dutton, 1981 (I:10+ R:7). This book tells of the quest for the Holy Grail.

_____ . *The Road to Camlann: The Death of King Arthur*. Illustrated by Shirley Felts. Dutton, 1982 (I:10+ R:7). Mordred attempts to destroy the kingdom by exposing Queen Guinevere and Sir Lancelot.

_____ . *The Sword and the Circle: King Arthur and the Knights of the Round Table*. Dutton, 1981 (I:10+ R:7). Thirteen stories are associated with King Arthur.

Williams, Marcia. Retold by. *King Arthur and the Knights of the Round Table*. Candlewick, 1996 (I:5–9 R:5). Cartoons illustrate the legend.

Wisniewski, David. *Golem*. Clarion, 1996 (I:all). The legend about the rabbi who brings to life a clay giant.

Illustration from *The Tinderbox* by Hans Christian Andersen, adapted, illustrated and designed by Barry Moser, copyright © 1990 by Pennyroyal Press, Inc. Used by permission of Little, Brown & Co.

7 *Modern Fantasy*

Time, Space, and Place

W hen children escape into Beatrix Potter's world, they enter the intriguing sphere of fantasy. With the following rhythmical words from *The Tailor of Gloucester,* one of the most popular authors of modern fantasy takes her readers into a time and setting where the impossible becomes convincingly possible:

In the time of swords and periwigs and full-skirted coats with flowered lappets—when gentlemen wore ruffles, and gold-laced waistcoats of paduasoy and taffeta—there lived a tailor in Gloucester. (p. 11)

Authors create modern fantasy by altering one or more characteristics of everyday reality. They may create entirely new worlds, as J. R. R. Tolkien does Middle Earth in *The Hobbit,* or they may give their characters extraordinary experiences in the real world, as Margaret J. Anderson does in *In the Keep of Time.* A realistic character may go down a rabbit hole and enter another domain, as in Lewis Carroll's *Alice's Adventures in Wonderland,* or nonrealistic characters, such as Mary Norton's little people in *The Borrowers,* may exist in an otherwise realistic setting. In one way or another, however, authors of fantasy permit readers to enter imaginative realms of possibility. More than one-fourth of the sixty-three books listed by the Children's Literature Association

in *Touchstones: A List of Distinguished Children's Books* (1985) are modern fantasy.

Modern fantasy is considered by many adults to be among the most valuable literature selections for children. For example, Chet Raymo (1992), a scientist and author, maintains that fantasy writing helps children expand their curiosity, become observers of life, learn to be sensitive to rules and variations within the rules, and open their minds to new possibilities. Some of Raymo's favorite fantasy books include C. S. Lewis's "Narnia" series, J. R. R. Tolkien's books set in Middle Earth, Dr. Seuss's various fantasies, and Kenneth Grahame's *The Wind in the Willows.* Raymo recommends these fantasies because in such children's books, "we are at the roots of science—pure, childlike curiosity, eyes open with wonder to the fresh and new, and powers of invention still unfettered by convention and expectation" (p. 567). Another science educator, Lazer Goldberg (1991), concludes, "My study of literature persuaded me that reading fantasy can serve children well. Their suspension of belief for the duration of the reading will, among other things, help children deal more effectively with the real world" (p. 38).

This chapter suggests criteria for evaluating modern fantasy. It stresses the ways in which modern authors of fantasy literature follow in the footsteps of the anonymous storytellers who created and transmitted the traditional fantasies of oral literature. It also discusses various types of modern fantasy and recommends numerous outstanding fantasy stories.

 ## EVALUATING MODERN FANTASY

Like all authors of fiction, authors of high-quality modern fantasy use basic literary elements to create stories that are interesting, engrossing, and believable. In evaluating modern fantasy for children, you should use the criteria recommended in chapter 3, while considering the special uses of literary elements that the fantasy genre requires. Consider the questions in the Evaluation Criteria box on page 353 when selecting modern fantasy to share with children.

Many books of modern fantasy admirably satisfy these criteria and provide great enjoyment to children and adults alike.

Suspending Disbelief: Plot

The author's ability to make readers suspend disbelief and to accept the possibility that the story could have happened is one of the greatest requirements for modern fantasy. Fantasy writer Patricia Wrightson (1990) states this very well:

Fantasy is story, and no story has any business to begin by asking you weakly to suspend disbelief. It is the business of story to require and work for your belief. It may be more difficult in fantasy, but that is the writer's affair; no one is forcing him to try. If he invites you to go flying with him, the very least he can do is to build a strong pair of wings. The freedom of fantasy is not license: if it abandons the laws and logic of reality, it must provide other laws and logic to govern itself. It may invent circumstances to suit its purpose, but the purpose must be the story's obligation to explore life and humanity. It has great strengths: the power of the extraordinary, the broad definition of symbol, the evocative voice of poetry; having them, it mustn't also ask for your weak and complaisant credulity. If fantasy is not strong, it is nothing (p. 75).

ℰVALUATION CRITERIA

Selecting Modern Fantasy

1. Is every action consistent with the framework developed by the author?

2. How does the author's characterization allow children to suspend disbelief? Do characters begin in a real world before they travel to the world of fantasy? Does a believable character accept a fanciful world, characters, or happenings? Does the author use an appropriate language or create a believable language consistent with the story?

3. Does the author pay careful attention to the details in the setting? If the author develops several time periods, are the settings authentic and integral to the story?

4. Is the theme worthwhile for children?

5. Does the author encourage readers to suspend disbelief by developing a point of view that is consistent in every detail, including sights, feelings, and physical reactions?

A story may seem believable if it begins in a realistic context and then moves into the realm of fantasy. In "The Chronicles of Narnia," C. S. Lewis develops normal human characters who visit a realistic English home and enter into childhood games familiar to most children. When these realistic characters confront the fantastic and believe it, readers believe it too. Likewise, Margaret Anderson's characters in *In the Keep of Time* have a strong foundation in reality before they enter their time-warp fantasies, encouraging readers' belief.

When an author develops a logical framework and develops characters' actions consistently within this framework, there is an internal consistency in the story. This consistency is important. If, for example, animals supposedly live and behave like animals, they should do so *consistently* unless the author carefully develops when they change, why they change, and how they change.

Suspending Disbelief: Characterization

Of course, the character from whose point of view a story is told must be believable for readers to suspend disbelief. Whether an author humanizes animals and inanimate objects, gives supernatural beings human traits, or places realistic human characters into fantastic situations, the characters in a fantasy story must be internally coherent as well as accessible to the readers.

Language is one way that authors of fantasy can make characters believable. In *The Hobbit* and *The Lord of the Rings,* for example, J. R. R. Tolkien creates distinct languages for different groups of characters. Ruth Noel (1977), in her evaluation of Tolkien's use of language, concludes that the musical flow of Elfish words and names implies that the Elves are noble people and that they love beauty and music. In contrast, the guttural Dwarfish, which sounds less familiar to English-speaking readers, indicates that the Dwarfs themselves are different from humans and Elves. Likewise, the croaked curses of the Orcs establish them as coarse, cruel, and unimaginative, and the prolonged chants of the Ents demonstrate their peaceful life in the forest. David Rees (1988) states that Joan Aiken has a similar talent for characterization through language because in such fantasies as *The Wolves of Willoughby Chase,* she is able to create "the dialects, vocabulary, and speech rhythms of various periods in history" (p. 42).

Creating a World: Setting

The magical settings of traditional tales let children know that anything is possible in those environments. Writers of modern fantasy may also create worlds in which unusual circumstances are believable, or they may combine reality and fantasy as characters or stories go back and forth between two worlds. In either case, if the story is to be credible, the author must develop the setting so completely that readers can see, hear, and feel it.

The settings for Mary Norton's "Borrowers" books, described through the eyes of little people, are integral to each story. The inside of a cottage drain becomes both an escape route and an antagonist in *The Borrowers Afloat*. Readers experience a new world as they vicariously join the Borrowers inside the drain:

There were other openings as they went along, drains that branched into darkness and ran away uphill. Where these joined the main drain, a curious collection of flotsam and jetsam piled up over which they had to drag the soap lid . . . the air from that point onwards, smelled far less strongly of tea leaves. (p. 105)

The setting in the drain changes from a fairly calm escape route to one filled with drumming noises and fright as a bath drain opens. Norton describes an antagonistic setting:

A millrace of hot scented water swilled through her clothes, piling against her at one moment, falling away the next. Sometimes it bounced above her shoulders, drenching her face and hair; at others it swirled steadily about her waist and tugged at her legs and feet. (p. 110)

Norton provides so much detail in her description of this setting that readers can see the contents of the inside of the drain as if they too were only six inches tall, can smell the soap and tea leaves deposited in the drain, and can hear the changing sounds of water echoing through the drainage system or gushing down in thundering torrents.

Other authors create convincing new worlds as characters go from realistic to fantasy settings. In *Al-*

ice's Adventures in Wonderland, by Lewis Carroll, Alice begins her adventures on a realistically peaceful river bank in nineteenth-century England and then travels down a rabbit hole into a unique world quite different from her normal one, which Carroll describes in great detail from her viewpoint.

In Janet Lunn's *The Root Cellar,* twelve-year-old Rose goes down into a root cellar on an old dilapidated farm in twentieth-century Canada. When she leaves the root cellar, she enters a nineteenth-century world in which the farm is prosperous. The people in that earlier time are engrossed by the approaching American Civil War. Believable descriptions of the same setting in two different centuries are important

Detailed descriptions of a parallel universe create a believable setting. (From The Golden Compass *by Philip Pullman, jacket illustration copyright © 1996 by Eric Rohmann, Alfred A. Knopf, Inc. Used by permission of Random House, Inc.)*

to the story. Lunn develops an authentic Civil War setting by describing the sights, sounds, feelings, and concerns that the main character experiences as she travels throughout the northeastern United States to find a boy who has not returned from the war. Authors whose characters travel in time warps must create believable, authentic settings for two time periods.

Jane Yolen uses a similar approach in *The Devil's Arithmetic*. After a contemporary girl steps through a door and finds herself in a Jewish village in the 1940s, the sights, sounds, conflicts, and concerns become those of people living in a death camp during the Holocaust.

Universality: Themes

Memorable modern fantasies develop themes related to universal struggles, values, and emotions. The constant battle between good and evil, faith and perseverance in the face of obstacles, personal and social responsibility, love, and friendship are important themes in works of modern fantasy ranging from George MacDonald's Victorian story *At the Back of the North Wind* to Madeleine L'Engle's contemporary books of science fiction. Children easily identify with such themes, especially when an author develops them within the framework of consistently believable plots, characterizations, settings, and points of view.

Suspending Disbelief: Point of View

Rebecca J. Lukens (1986) says:

If fantasy is to be successful, we must willingly suspend disbelief. If the story's characters, conflict, and theme seem believable to us, we find it plausible and even natural to know the thoughts and feelings of animal characters or tiny people. In fact, the story may be so good that we wish it were true. . . . This persuasion that the writer wishes to bring about—persuasion that "what if" is really "it's true"—is most successful when the writer is consistent about point of view. (p. 108)

The point of view of a story is determined by the author's choice of the person telling it. A story could be told quite differently from the perspective of a child, a mother, a wicked witch, an animal or a supernatural beast, or an objective observer. Authors of fantasy must decide which point of view best facilitates a believable telling of a story and then sustain that point

of view in order to persuade readers to keep suspending disbelief in the fantastic elements of the story.

The Borrowers, by Mary Norton, seems believable because most of this story about "little people" is told from the viewpoint of Arrietty, who is only six inches tall. The little people's family sitting room seems authentic because readers see, through Arrietty's eyes, the postage-stamp-sized portraits on the walls, a work of art created by a pillbox that is supporting a chess piece, and a couch made from a human's padded trinket box. Even the reaction to a miniature book that is Arrietty's diary is dealt with through the physical capabilities of a miniature person: "Arrietty braced her muscles and heaved the book off her knees, and stood upright on the floor" (p. 20). Readers are ready to believe the story because Norton describes sights, feelings, and physical reactions as if a six-inch-tall person were actually living through the experience.

In *The Tale of Peter Rabbit,* Beatrix Potter creates believable situations by telling the story from both Peter Rabbit's point of view and the first-person point of view of the storyteller, who occasionally interjects comments such as "I am sorry to say that Peter was not very well during the evening." In this case, the authoritative, realistic voice of the storyteller reassures readers that the fantastic events being described are normal and understandable.

Perry Nodelman (1984b) emphasizes the need for an author to consider both the storyteller and the audience when creating a credible fantasy. Nodelman says:

Only by ignoring the fact that it is fantastic, by pretending to be a true story about a real world shared by characters in the story, the storyteller, and the people who hear the story, can a fantasy establish its credibility and work its magic on those who actually hear it. (p. 16)

Jane Yolen (1986) emphasizes the importance of these elements in making a real world for children. She states that the fantasy world seems real to children because

the world of fantasy has three very persuasive parts to it. First, it has identifiable laws that always work. Second, it has a hero or heroine who is often lost, unlikely, powerless at first glance, or unrecognized, which makes him or her easy for the child reader (who feels lost, unlikely, unrecognized or powerless) to identify with. And third, in a fantasy world things end justly though not always happily. (p. 89)

BRIDGES BETWEEN TRADITIONAL AND MODERN FANTASY

In many ways, modern fantasy stories are direct descendants of the folktales, fables, myths, and legends of the oral tradition. Tales about talking animals, wise and foolish humans, supernatural beings, heroic adventurers, and magical realms are as popular with children and adults today as they were hundreds of years ago. Many authors of modern fantasy have drawn upon themes, motifs, settings, and characterizations common in traditional literature. Of course, in the distant past, people believed that the content of some fairy tales, myths, and legends had basis in fact, while most readers of modern fantasy only suspend their disbelief in extraordinary beings and events. Still, to entice their readers into out-of-the-ordinary experiences, authors of modern fantasy play roles similar to those of storytellers of old, who enchanted live audiences with tales that had been orally transmitted over generations. The bridges between traditional fantasy and modern fantasy are evident in many contemporary tales of wonder, but they are especially strong in literary folktales, allegories, and tales about mythical quests and conflicts.

Literary Folktales

In the past hundred years or so, some authors of fantasy have deliberately attempted to replicate the "Once upon a time" of traditional folktales, with their dark forests, castles, princesses and princes, humble people of noble worth, and "happily ever afters." The traditional theme that goodness is rewarded and evil is punished is common in literary folktales, as are motifs involving magic. Betsy Hearne (1992) states that many folklore elements are found in William Steig's *The Amazing Bone,* and archetypal characters from folktales abound in the fantasies of James Marshall.

Ursula K. LeGuin's *A Ride on the Red Mare's Back* is a literary folktale that contains many elements from folklore. First, the setting is similar to that in a folktale: "A long time ago, when the world was wild, a family lived in the forests of the North, far from any other house" (p. 11). Second, the heroine is a young girl who bravely sets out to rescue her brother, who has been stolen by trolls. The plot is advanced by a magical object, a small toy horse that turns into a real horse during a time of need. This magical object

The battle between good and evil is found in literature that bridges traditional and modern fantasy. (From Hershel and the Hanukkah Goblins *by Eric A. Kimmel, illustrated by Trina Schart Hyman. Reprinted by permission of Holiday House. Text copyright 1989 by Eric A. Kimmel. Illustrations copyright 1989 by Trina Schart Hyman. All rights reserved.)*

then gives aid and advice to the heroine. The importance of threes is revealed when the girl takes three objects with her and these objects allow her to successfully rescue her brother: (1) bread baked by her mother is given to the troll under the bridge, (2) knitting needles made by her father and a ball of yarn are given to the old troll who guards the children, and (3) a scarf she knitted for her little brother makes him aware that he wants to come home.

Likewise, Walter Dean Myers's literary folktale, *The Story of Three Kingdoms,* begins in a folkloric style: "Long ago, when the earth had not settled in its turning and the stars had not found their places in the night sky, there were three kingdoms" (unnumbered). In addition, the fantasy has elements that are similar to those found in folktales including types of conflict, characteristics of characters, and theme. Notice in the following ending how Myers has used a folkloric style: "From that day on the People held their heads high, never forgetting to sit by the fire and tell their stories.

Never forgetting that in the stories could be found wisdom and in wisdom, strength" (unnumbered).

Fantasies by Jennifer Armstrong and Shulamith Levy Oppenheim also have folkloric elements. Armstrong's *Wan Hu Is in the Stars* ends in a folkloric tradition as a new star formation appears in the sky: "And some believe Wan Hu achieved his hope and one desire. The gardener is sure that he did" (unnumbered). The setting for Oppenheim's *The Hundredth Name* is similar to a folktale because it is set "far back in time" in Muslim Egypt. This literary folktale has an emphasis on Allah as the young hero tries to discover through his camel the hundredth name for Allah.

Hans Christian Andersen.

Charles Perrault is usually credited with publishing the first children's book of fairy tales, but Hans Christian Andersen is credited with writing, a century later, the first fairy tale for children. While Perrault wrote down stories from the oral tradition, Andersen created new stories for theater audiences and readers.

Zena Sutherland (1997) points out that although Andersen's first stories for children were

elaborations of familiar folk and fairy tales, . . . he soon began to allow his imagination full rein in the invention of plot, the shaping of character, and the illumination of human condition. These later creations, solely from Andersen's fertile imagination, are called literary fairy tales, to distinguish them from the fairy tales of unknown origin, those created by common folk. Andersen's work served as inspiration for other writers. (p. 230)

Andersen's "The Wild Swans" is a literary fairy tale quite similar to the Grimms's traditional tale "The Six Swans." Both stories involve enchantment by an evil stepmother and the courage and endurance of a young girl who is willing to suffer in order to free her brothers.

Experts in children's literature believe that some of Andersen's other literary fairy tales are based on his own life. For example, Andersen's unpleasant experiences in school, where the teacher poked fun at the poor boy's lack of knowledge, large size, and looks, may have inspired his story "The Ugly Duckling." Lorinda Bryan Cauley's illustrations for a book-length version of this story show the transformation of the ugly duckling into the most beautiful swan in the garden lake. Cauley's realistic and humorous pictures portray the duckling's agony in the barnyard, where every animal seems to show contempt for him. Chil-

Hans Christian Andersen was the earliest author of modern fantasy. (From The Emperor's New Clothes *by Hans Christian Andersen, text copyright © 1997 by Naomi Lewis, illustrations copyright © 1997 by Angela Barrett. Reprinted by permission of Candlewick Press.)*

dren can follow, in pictures and text, the sorrow felt by the duckling and then his realization that he is not something to be pitied. They can observe his head emerging from under his wing, not in conceit, but in wonder, as he senses his transformation.

Andersen's *The Tinderbox*, adapted and illustrated by Barry Moser, includes many of the motifs found in folklore: A poor tattered soldier who eventually wins riches and the beautiful girl; challenges in the form of three doors, each guarded by a huge dog; a magical object; and a leader who tries to prevent the soldier from marrying his daughter. This book can also be used to analyze the change in setting from the original story. Moser places his adaptation in the Tennessee mountains at the end of the Civil War. His characters include a Confederate soldier and the people who live in a mountain village.

Nancy Ekholm Burkert has beautifully illustrated one of Andersen's stories that reflects the beauty of natural life versus the heartbreak associated with longing for mechanical perfection or metallic glitter. *The Nightingale* tells of a Chinese emperor who turned from the voice of a faithful nightingale to a jeweled, mechanical bird. He learns, however, that only the real, unjeweled bird's song can bring comfort and truth. Compare Alison Claire Darke's illustrations for *The Nightingale* with Burkert's illustrations. Both illustrators emphasize the beauty of the Chinese setting.

Illustrator Susan Jeffers and author Amy Ehrlich have combined their talents to create three beautiful versions of Andersen's tales. Jeffers's finely detailed drawings suggest fantasy settings in *Thumbelina* and *The Wild Swans*. Contrast her illustrations for and Amy Ehrlich's retelling in *The Snow Queen* with two other versions of the same tale, one retold by Naomi Lewis and illustrated by Errol LeCain and the other retold by Naomi Lewis and illustrated by Angela Barrett.

Three adapters and illustrators have chosen to retell Andersen's *The Steadfast Tin Soldier*. The version translated by Naomi Lewis and illustrated by P. J. Lynch includes illustrations drawn as if they were from

Finely detailed lines enhance the dreamlike quality of the fairy tale setting. (From The Wild Swans, *retold by Amy Ehrlich, illustrated by Susan Jeffers. Illustrations copyright ©1981 by Susan Jeffers. Used by permission of the publisher Dial Books for Young Readers.)*

a toy's-eye view. The version retold by Tor Seidler and illustrated by Fred Marcellino is illustrated with a Christmas setting, because according to the illustrator, the story was first published during the Christmas of 1838. Rachel Isadora's illustrations for her version reflect her background in theater and dance.

Michael Hague, Kay Nielson, and Edward Ardizzone are among those who have illustrated collections of Andersen's tales for adults to read aloud to children or for children to read independently. *Michael Hague's Favorite Hans Christian Andersen Fairy Tales* includes nine stories in large print. More extensive collections include *Hans Andersen: His Classic Fairy Tales*, illustrated by Michael Foreman.

Religious and Ethical Allegory

Religious themes provide strong links between traditional and modern fantasy. According to Bruno Bettelheim (1976), "Most fairy tales originated in periods when religion was a most important part of life; thus, they deal, directly or by inference, with religious themes" (p. 13). Traditional tales from around the world reflect the religions prominent in their times and places of origins, including Islam, Buddhism, and Judaism, to name but a few.

Some European folktales, such as the German "Our Lady's Child," directly refer to the Roman Catholic beliefs of the Middle Ages. In this tale recorded by the Brothers Grimm, a young girl becomes mute when she disobeys the Virgin Mary and then lies about what she has done. After suffering severe ordeals, she desires only to confess her sin, and the Virgin Mary rewards her confession by renewing her power of speech and granting her happiness. Other European folktales and legends develop less explicit religious themes by using allegory, or prolonged metaphors. Characters representing goodness or wisdom must confront and overcome characters representing evil or foolishness.

Many authors writing in the 1800s created strong stories with ethical and religious themes. John C. Hawley (1989) contends that Charles Kingsley's *The Water-Babies* is a classic example of children's literature employed to disarm and to teach. He states:

As unusual and even quirky as the water world of Kingsley's novel may be, however, this priest/novelist somehow succeeds in showing readers young and old something

Censoring Classic Texts: Should Classic Literature Be Protected from Censorship?

Mandates for literature-based language arts curricula are increasing in states and communities across the nation. States such as California[1] have not only mandated the use of literature in language arts and reading classes but also provided recommended readings for kindergarten through grade eight. These recommended readings include many literary classics. According to Robert Rothman,[2] this use of primary sources of literature rather than texts with "laundered" and "sanitized" vocabularies and plots has resulted in school materials that some people want to censor. To clarify this issue, Rothman quotes the director of the California State Education Office of Curriculum Framework and Textbook Development, Glen Thomas:

Unlike the past, when publishers might have kept such material out of textbooks for fear of offending a potential customer, the new literature policy encourages the use of classic texts. Moreover, such literature is exempt from California regulations governing the social content of classroom materials. . . . In our view, classic literature has to be viewed differently. Content that twentieth-century Americans may regard as offensive may reflect the historical context of the time. (p. 5)

Many of the selections discussed in this chapter are classics. As you read this literature, consider the advantages and disadvantages of using classic literature with children. Should classic literature be protected from censorship? Also, consider the impact of fantasy on adult literature. Robert K. J. Killheffer[3] attributes much of the adult interest in fantasy to children's exposure to mythic quests and the battle between good and evil. What is it in the classical fantasy that continues to hook readers to the genre?

---

[1] California State Department of Education. *Recommended Readings in Literature: Kindergarten through Grade Eight.* Sacramento, Calif.: State Department of Education, 1986.

[2] Rothman, Robert. "Experts Warn of Attempts to Censor Classic Texts." *Education Week* (February 21, 1990): 5.

[3] Killheffer, Robert K. J. "Fantasy Charts New Realms." *Publishers Weekly* 244 (June 16, 1997), pp. 34–40.

---

very familiar and even comforting in the strange and mysterious, sugaring a pill he considers necessary medicine for his generation. (p. 19)

In our more secular age, as Bettelheim (1976) points out, "these religious themes no longer arouse universal and personally meaningful associations" in the majority of people, as they once did. However, modern authors of fantasy still create religious and ethical allegories. Some authors actually replicate the heroic humans, witches, personified animals, and magical settings of traditional literature. Others use characters and settings consistent with their own times. Readers may respond to these stories on different levels, since they are both allegories and tales of enchantment and high adventure.

George MacDonald. The strongly moralistic atmosphere of Victorian England and training as a Congregational minister influenced a writer who used allegorical fantasy to portray and condemn the flaws in his society. Cynthia Marshall (1988) states that George MacDonald's concern for distinguishing good from evil leads to "moralizing interventions" (p. 61) in books, such as *At the Back of the North Wind.* First published in 1871 and reissued in 1966, is the story of Diamond, the son of a poor coach driver. Diamond lives two lives: the harsh existence of impoverished working-class Londoners, and a dreamlike existence in which he travels with the North Wind, who takes him to a land of perpetual flowers and gentle breezes, where no one is cold or sick or hungry.

MacDonald uses the North Wind, a beautiful woman with long flowing hair, to express much of his own philosophy. "Good people see good things; bad people, bad things" (p. 37), she tells Diamond, whom MacDonald describes as a good boy, "God's baby." When Diamond questions her reality, she says, "I think . . . that if I were only a dream, you would not have been able to love me so. You love me when you are not with me, don't you?" (p. 363). Diamond clings to the back of the North Wind. With her streaming hair enfolding him, they fly to a land where it is always May. Diamond returns home from

The flowing lines of the North Wind seem to enfold little Diamond. (Illustration by E. H. Shepard from At the Back of the North Wind, *by George MacDonald. Copyright © 1956, 1994. J. M. Dent, Children's Classics Series. Reprinted with permission of J. M. Dent & Sons, Ltd.)*

that visit, but the end of the story has further allegorical implications:

> I walked up the winding stair, and entered his room. A lovely figure, as white and almost as clear as alabaster, was lying on the bed. I saw at once how it was. They thought he was dead. I knew that he had gone to the back of the North Wind. (p. 378)

C. S. Lewis. A professor of medieval and Renaissance literature at Cambridge University, C. S. Lewis used his interest in theology and his knowledge about medieval allegory, classical legend, and Norse mythology to create a highly acclaimed and popular fantasy saga. "The Chronicles of Narnia" (winner of the Carnegie Medal for best children's books), beginning with *The Lion, the Witch and the Wardrobe* and ending seven books later with *The Last Battle,* develop marvelous adventure stories interwoven with Christian allegory. Children can enjoy the series

for its high drama alone, or they can read it for its allegorical significance.

While *The Lion, the Witch and the Wardrobe* is the first book in the series, *The Magician's Nephew* explains how the saga began and how the passage between the magical world of Narnia and earth was made possible. The tree grown from the magical Narnia apple has blown over, and its wood is used to build a large wardrobe. This is the same wardrobe through which the daughters of Eve and the sons of Adam enter into the kingdom, meet the wicked White Witch, and help the great lord-lion Aslan defeat the powers of evil.

In *The Lion, the Witch and the Wardrobe,* Aslan gives his life to save Edmund, who has betrayed them all. Aslan, however, rises from the dead and tells the startled, bereaved children that the deeper magic before the dawn of time has won:

> It means that though the witch knew the Deep Magic, there is a magic deeper still which she did not know. Her knowledge goes back only to the dawn of Time. But if she could have looked a little further back, into the stillness and the darkness before Time dawned, she would have read there a different incantation. She would have known that when a willing victim who has committed no treachery was killed in a traitor's stead, the Table would crack and Death itself would start working backward. (pp. 132–33)

From Aslan, the children learn that after they have once been crowned, they will remain kings and queens of Narnia forever.

The remaining books in the chronicle tell other fantastic tales of adventure in which the characters overcome evil. The final Christian allegory is contained in the last book of the series, *The Last Battle.* Here, the children are reunited with Aslan after their death on earth and discover:

> for them it was only the beginning of the real story. All their life in this world and all their adventures in Narnia had only been the cover and the title page: now at last they were beginning Chapter One of the Great Story which no one on earth has read: in which every chapter is better than the one before. (p. 184)

The stories in the chronicles of Narnia are filled with adventures and characters that appeal to children. There are magical spells, centaurs, dwarfs, unicorns, ogres, witches, and minotaurs. Throughout the stories, characters strive to meet high ideals and recognize the importance of faith.

Brian Sibley's *The Land of Narnia* (1989) provides additional information about C. S. Lewis and Narnia. The book includes photographs of Lewis and his environment as well as an overview of the various Narnia books. The book includes "C. S. Lewis's Outline of Narnian History."

Mythical Quests and Conflicts

Quests for lost or stolen objects of power, descents into darkness to overcome evil, and settings where lightning splinters the world and sets the stage for battle between two opposing forces are found in traditional myths, legends, and modern fantasy. Some authors of modern fantasy borrow magical settings and characters from traditional tales of heroism, while others create new worlds of enchantment. Modern stories may contain some threads of the allegory that characterizes many traditional tales—such as the English legends about King Arthur, his knights of the Round Table, and the quest for the Holy Grail. Most modern fantasies about mythical quests and conflicts, however, emphasize adventure. Their characters acquire new knowledge and learn honorable uses of personal power.

Mythical elements are found in Megan Whalen Turner's *The Thief*, set in the time of a belief in gods and legends. Turner develops the mythical setting by describing the statues of the gods and goddesses and then encouraging the hero to hear them speak. Turner's themes are closely related to those found in mythology and legend: fate rules our lives, dreams are important as a way to predict what will happen, and the old stories about gods are very important for people's lives.

Naomi Lewis's translation of *Proud Knight, Fair Lady: The Twelve Lais of Marie de France* includes heroic characters who usually have unfailing valor. There are also objects of power, tests of faith, and high purposes. Josepha Sherman's *Child of Faerie, Child of Earth* is a fantasy set in twelfth-century France. The fantasy includes an evil sorceress, the Faerie queen, the Faerie prince, and a human girl who has repressed magical talents but is finally able to use her talents to save the Faerie prince.

Philip Pullman's *The Golden Compass* is a high fantasy that has numerous fantasy elements that may be identified and analyzed. Characters with supernatural powers include humans with their daemons (spirits, souls in animal form), witches who fly, and talking bears wearing armor. Objects of power include an ancient gold and crystal disk or alethiometer that always tells the truth. The symbols on this alethiometer also reveal both themes and possible conflict. For example, the various meanings for the anchor symbol are revealed to be hope, because hope holds you fast like an anchor; steadfastness; snag or prevention; and the sea. The importance of this object of power is revealed through quotes such as the following: "She knew one thing: she was not pleased or proud to be able to read the alethiometer—she was afraid. Whatever power was making that needle swing and stop, it knew things like an intelligent being" (p. 147). Pullman's sequel to *The Golden Compass, The Subtle Knife*, provides another source for identifying and analyzing fantasy elements.

Sheila Egoff (1988) states that epic, or heroic, fantasies, especially those related to "the Arthurian legends and the Welsh tales of the Mabinogion form the largest cauldron of story into which modern fantasists have dipped" (p. 6). Other popular sources include *Beowulf, Child Roland of the Dark Tower*, and Scandinavian myths and legends. According to Egoff, the fantasies of authors such as J. R. R. Tolkien, Lloyd Alexander, and Susan Cooper are not retellings of the original. Instead, the authors "use both the matter and structure of legend to infuse their works with the epic quality of the original—its emotional impact and grand design" (p. 7).

J. R. R Tolkien.   Destiny, supernatural immortals, evil dragons, and rings of power are found in J. R. R. Tolkien's popular stories. According to Ruth S. Noel (1977), Tolkien's writings "form a continuation of the mythic tradition into modern literature. . . . In no other literary work has such careful balance of mythic tradition and individual imagination been maintained" (pp. 6–7). This balance between myth and imagination is not accidental in Tolkien's writing. Tolkien studied mythology for most of his life; he was a linguistic scholar and professor of Anglo-Saxon literature at Oxford University. His chief interest was the literary and linguistic tradition of the English West Midlands, especially as revealed in *Beowulf* and *Sir Gawain and the Green Knight*. Tolkien respected the quality in myths that allows evil to be unexpectedly averted and good to succeed. He masterfully develops this battle between good and

Several articles in a 1993 issue of *The Lion and the Unicorn* focus on the writing and rewriting of some children's literature in a process that some authors call "dumbing down" and other authors refer to as "manufacturing kiddie lit(e)." This issue is concerned with not only the process of writing simpler stories for children but also the forces that caused this phenomenon.

In the editor's note, Jan Susina first emphasizes the devaluing of children's literature through such terms as *kiddie lit*.[1] Susina states, "For those concerned with children's literature, the term 'kiddie lit,' with its wholesale dismissal of children's literature as a significant and important aspect of literary studies, is disturbing and short-sighted" (p. vi). Susina also traces some of the history of, and the consequences of, "dumbing down" and worries that the increased emphasis on selling more books to broader audiences will have negative results on the quality of the literature. She continues, "So while the dumbing down of children's literature has always been an aspect of the children's book industry, it appears in recent years to have become more pronounced" (p. viii).

The articles in this issue consider the implications of the process of watering down literature for children. For example, "The Dynamics of Dumbing: The Case of Merlin," by Judith Kellogg, traces the watering down of Arthurian legends in contemporary children's books.[2]

As publishers and booksellers try to reach broader audiences and, consequently, generate larger sales, there is a trend toward rewriting other classics into simpler language that supposedly appeals to larger audiences. In a Knight-Ridder article, "Publishers Take Hatchet to Potter's Classic 'Peter Rabbit'," Peter Slevin reports changes in a new series of Beatrix Potter's works, including *Peter Rabbit, The Tale of Squirrel Nutkin, Tom Kitten,* and *Jemima Puddle-Duck*.[3] Slevin compares both the illustrations (Potter's illustrations were replaced with photographs of stuffed animals) and the text. For example, the first paragraph for *The Tale of Squirrel Nutkin* as originally written by Potter reads: "This is a Tale about a tail—a tail that belonged to a little red squirrel, and his name was Nutkin." In the updated version, this paragraph reads: "This is the story of a red squirrel called Nutkin, and what happened to his tail." Slevin quotes Pat Roth, a spokesman for Ladybird Books, as stating the reasons for the changes, "We're looking to the market. It's broadening of the audience. . . . That's what business is all about" (p. 24A).

As you compare original classic versions of tales and various updated versions, decide which version is more appealing in style, characterizations, plot, and illustrations.

---

[1] Susina, Jan. "Editor's Note: Kiddie Lit(e): The Dumbing Down of Children's Literature." *The Lion and the Unicorn* 17 (1993): v–viii.

[2] Kellogg, Judith L. "The Dynamics of Dumbing: The Case of Merlin." *The Lion and the Unicorn* 17 (1993): 57–72.

[3] Slevin, Peter. "Publishers Take Hatchet to Potter's Classic 'Peter Rabbit'." Knight-Ridder Newspapers. *The Dallas Morning News* (September 20, 1987): 24A.

---

evil in *The Hobbit* and in *The Lord of the Rings,* its more complex sequel. According to Tolkien (1965), these stories were at first a philological game in which he invented languages: "The stories were made rather to provide a world for the languages than the reverse. I should have preferred to write in 'Elvish' " (p. 242). These languages with their own alphabets and rules help make Tolkien's characters believable.

Careful attention to detail and vivid descriptions of setting in Middle Earth also add credibility to Tolkien's stories. For example, he introduces the reluctant hobbit, Bilbo Baggins, to the challenge of a quest to regain the dwarfs' treasures by using a dwarfs' chant:

Far over the misty mountains cold
To dungeons deep and caverns old
We must away ere break of day
To find our long-forgotten gold. (*The Hobbit,*
p. 37)

As Bilbo, the wizard Gandalf, and the thirteen dwarfs proceed over the mountains toward the lair of the evil dragon Smaug, Tolkien describes a lightning that splinters the peaks and rocks that shiver. When Bilbo descends into the mountain dungeons to confront Smaug, Tolkien's setting befits the climax of a heroic quest: Red light, wisps of vapor, and rumbling noises gradually replace the subterranean darkness and quiet. Ahead, in the bottom-most cellar, lies a huge red-golden dragon surrounded by precious gold

The mythological text and illustrations are strongly interrelated in this edition of J. R. R. Tolkien's books, illustrated by Michael Hague. (From The Hobbit by J. R. R. Tolkien, illustrated by Michael Hague. Illustrations copyright © 1984 by Oak, Ash & Thorn, Ltd. Reprinted by permission of Houghton Mifflin Company.)

and jewels. As in traditional tales, the quest is successful, the dragon is slain, and the goblins are overthrown. The hero retains his decency, his honor, and his pledge always to help his friends.

The ring found during the hobbit's quest becomes the basis of the plot in the ring trilogy: *The Fellowship of the Ring, The Two Towers,* and *The Return of the King.* In his foreword to *Fellowship of the Ring,* Tolkien says that he had no intention of writing a story with an inner meaning or message. The story is not meant to be allegorical:

As the story grew it put down roots (into the past) and threw out unexpected branches; but its main theme was settled from the outset by the inevitable choice of the Ring as the link between it and *The Hobbit.* (*The Fellowship of the Ring,* p. 6)

Many junior-high and high-school students, college students, and other adults have been brought back into the world of mythology through Tolkien's books.

Lloyd Alexander.   The stories that unfold in Lloyd Alexander's mythical land of Prydain reflect Alexander's vivid recollections of Wales, favorite childhood stories, and knowledge of Welsh legends. When Alexander researched the Mabinogion, a collection of traditional Welsh legends, he discovered the characters of Gwydion Son of Don, Arawn Death-Lord of Annuvin, Dallben the enchanter, and Hen Wen the oracular pig (Tunnell and Jacobs, 1988). In Alexander's outstanding Prydain chronicles, these characters become involved in exciting adventures of good versus evil.

Alexander's books take place in a time when fairy folk lived with humans, a time of enchanters and enchantments, a time before the passages between the world of enchantment and the world of humans were closed. In the first Prydain chronicle, *The Book of Three,* Alexander introduces the forces of good and evil and an assistant pig-keeper, Taran, who dreams of discovering his parentage and becoming a hero. (Alexander tells readers that all people are assistant pig-keepers at heart because their capabilities seldom match their aspirations and they are often unprepared for what is to happen.)

The forces of good include the enchanter Dallben, who reads the prophecy written in *The Book of Three;* the sons of Don and their leader Prince Gwydion, who in ancient times voyaged from the Summer Country to stand as guardians against the evil Annuvin; and the Princess Eilonwy, descendant of enchanters. They are aided by Hen Wen, a pig who can foretell the future by pointing out ancient symbols carved on letter sticks. The forces of evil are led by a warlord who wants to capture Hen Wen because she knows his secret name. This name is powerful because "once you have the courage to look upon evil, seeing it for what it is and naming it by its true nature, it is powerless against you, and you can destroy it" (p. 209).

Throughout his Prydain series—*The Black Cauldron, The Castle of Llyr, Taran Wanderer,* and *The High King*—Alexander develops strong, believable characters with whom upper-elementary and older children can identify. The world of fantasy becomes relevant to the world of reality. The characters gain credibility through Alexander's history of the people and their long struggle against the forces of evil. Alexander encourages readers to believe in the tangible objects of power because the characters place so much faith in the legend of the sword, the

Time, Space, and Place   **363**

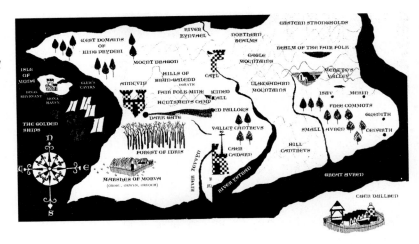

A detailed map helps make the land of Prydain more credible to readers. (From The High King, by Lloyd Alexander. Map by Evaline Ness. Copyright © 1968 by Lloyd Alexander. Copyright © 1968 by Holt, Rinehart and Winston. Reproduced by permission of Holt, Rinehart and Winston.)

prophecies written in *The Book of Three,* and the fearsome black cauldron.

Alexander's literary style also strengthens the credibility of the fantasy, the plot, and the characterization in his other fantasy adventure stories, such as *Westmark, The Iron Ring,* and *The Beggar Queen.* In *The Beggar Queen,* Alexander carefully builds a foundation for the action that follows. He develops strong person-against-person, person-against-self, and person-against-society conflicts. He uses ghosts from the past to introduce the various conflicts and factions; he uses animal symbolism to describe characters; and he concludes each chapter at a point of tension and excitement, foreshadowing the conflict to come.

Quests, battles of good versus evil, and carefully built foundations are also found in Alexander's *The Remarkable Journey of Prince Jen.* In this book, Alexander creates the oriental Kingdom of T'ien-Kuo, complete with a map at the beginning of the book. The story follows Prince Jen's quest to find a legendary court and his learning to govern from his experiences. As part of the quest, the prince takes six gifts of homage: a saddle, a sword, a paint box, a bowl, a kite, and a flute. Along the way, these common objects unexpectedly become objects of power and reveal different characteristics of the people who handle the objects. Alexander highlights tension and excitement, foreshadowing the conflict to come. At the conclusion of each chapter, Alexander poses questions or provides comments that take readers into the next chapter.

In *The Arkadians,* Alexander develops a high fantasy with foundations in Greek mythology. Alexander encourages readers to suspend disbelief in the mystical setting by introducing the setting through a map showing Arkadia. Mystical places and magical substances include the Water of Forgetting and the Water of Remembering; groves of trees, rings of stones, and fountains; and amulets that protect heroes. Alexander's fantasy includes many similarities with Greek mythology such as a wooden animal with a hollow stomach, men with special abilities, winged horses, prophecies that come true, and voyages that include fantastic adventures. In *The Iron Ring* Alexander develops a high fantasy with foundations in mythology from India.

Ursula K. LeGuin. Somewhere in the land of fantasy lies Earthsea, an archipelago of imaginary islands where wizards cast their spells and people live in fear of fire-blowing winged dragons. Responsible wizards attempt to retain a balance between the forces of good and the forces of evil that seek dominance. LeGuin helps her readers suspend disbelief through detailed descriptions of Earthsea, its inhabitants, and a culture permeated with magic. LeGuin's series of Earthsea books develops the theme that responsibility is attached to great power by tracing the life of Sparrowhawk from when he is an apprentice wizard until he is finally the most powerful wizard in the land.

In the first book of the series, *A Wizard of Earthsea,* the young boy has powers strong enough to save his village, but pride and impatience place him in grave danger. A master wizard cautions Spar-

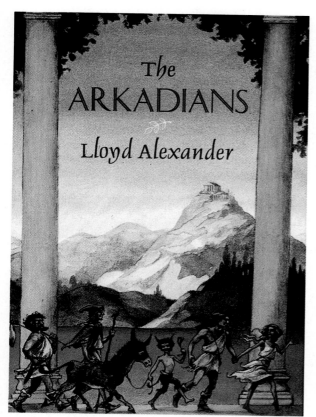

From The Arkadians *by Lloyd Alexander. Jacket art by Trina Schart Hyman. Copyright© 1995 by Trina Schart Hyman. Used by permission of Dutton Children's Books, a division of Penguin Putnam, Inc.*

rowhawk about wanting to learn and use powers of enchantment that he is not yet mature enough to understand:

Have you never thought how danger must surround power as shadow does light? This sorcery is not a game we play for pleasure or for praise. Think of this: that every act of our Art is said and is done either for good, or for evil. Before you speak or do you must know the price that is to pay! (p. 35)

Sparrowhawk, renamed Ged, does not understand the warning. Conflict with another apprentice leads to a duel of sorcery skills, in which Ged calls up a dead spirit and accidentally unleashes an evil being onto the world. LeGuin's descriptions of the rent in the darkness, the blazing brightness, the hideous black shadow, and Ged's reaction to the beast convince

readers that evil really is released, important because the remainder of the book follows Ged as he hunts the shadow-beast across the islands to the farthest waters of Earthsea and develops an understanding that he is responsible for his own actions. The series ends with *Tehanu: The Last Book of Earthsea.*

Alan Garner. According to John Rowe Townsend (1975), Alan Garner was the most influential writer of fantasy in Great Britain of the 1960s. Garner's books are full of magic: the old magic of sun, moon, and blood that survives from crueler times, as well as the high magic of thoughts and spells that checks the old magic and serves as a potent but uncertain weapon against the old evil. Garner's stories transcend time barriers by allowing children from the present to discover objects that contain ancient spells influential in old legends. The ancient masters of good and evil then emerge either to pursue or to safeguard the children.

Garner creates a believable fantasy in *The Weirdstone of Brisingamen* by first placing two realistic characters into a realistic English country setting. He achieves credibility through the reactions of these children as they discover the powers in a tangible object, a tear-shaped piece of crystal that has been handed down over many generations. The plot then revolves around this "weirdstone." It is sought by both the forces of good and the forces of evil. The children, aided by two dwarfs, set out to return the stone to the good wizard who is its guardian. Along the way, however, they encounter evil characters—a shape-changing witch, giant troll women, and a wolf who chases them through underground tunnels and across the countryside. The final confrontation reveals the power of the weirdstone.

Robin McKinley. Magical objects are the focus of quests in Robin McKinley's *The Blue Sword* and *The Hero and the Crown.* McKinley makes *The Blue Sword* believable by depicting a realistic colony called Daria and realistic characters—colonial officials of Her Majesty's government, career army officers—who are unlikely to be influenced by the extraordinary. Fantasy elements enter the story when Harry is kidnapped by the leader of the Hillfolk and taken to the kingdom of Damar. From Harry's point of view, McKinley reveals a people who have the ability to speak in the old tongue, the language of the gods.

In *The Hero and the Crown*, which McKinley describes as a "prequel" to *The Blue Sword*, the power of a magical object is revealed through the sword that brings power from its original owner, Lady Aerin, who was the savior of her people. There is a strong feeling of destiny as the heroine sets forth to regain the objects of power and restore the power to her kingdom. As in many traditional epics, Aerin's quest results in increasingly difficult tests. She proceeds from slaying small dragons to finally overcoming an evil magician. McKinley strongly emphasizes responsibility, as Aerin discovers that even though the price is high, her destiny and her responsibility to her people require this quest.

Susan Cooper. Students of children's literature may identify the influence of English, Celtic, and Welsh legends and myths in Susan Cooper's series of modern fantasies. Her books about the guardians of light combating the forces of darkness contain references to the legend in which King Arthur does not die but lies resting in a place from which he will arise when the need is greatest. According to Celtic tradition, the words on Arthur's tomb mean "Here lies Arthur, King once and King to be."

Richard Cavendish (1982) reports that the Welsh version of the legend places Arthur's resting place in a cave in Snowdonia. A similar cave is important in Cooper's *The Grey King,* and Arthur and his knights rise again in *Silver on the Tree* to assist in the final battle against evil. The wizard Merlin, Arthur's legendary confidant, plays a crucial role throughout Cooper's series. Introduced as Merriman Lyon, Merlin has the ability to suspend the laws of nature and to travel into the past as well as the future. Throughout the series, Merriman retains Merlin's profound wisdom from an ancient past that leads the powers of good against the powers of evil.

Legendary objects, places, and occurrences are found throughout the series. For example, the power of a seventh son of a seventh son dominates the characters on heroic quests. Arthur's sword, his ship, and even his dog's name are important in Cooper's books. Quests for the objects of power form a thread of continuity in Cooper's stories. In *Over Sea, Under Stone,* three children visit Cornwall and find an old map that discloses a hidden trea-

sure. This treasure, the grail, could hinder the forces of darkness. With the help of the good Old Ones, the children find the grail, but they lose the manuscript that is the key to its inscriptions.

In *The Dark Is Rising,* the responsibility for continuing the quest falls upon eleven-year-old Will Stanton. While born in twentieth-century England, Will has a special responsibility as the seventh son of a seventh son and the last born of the Old Ones, whose powers can be used against the powers of darkness. Early in Will's quest, his impatience and ignorance cause him to help the forces of darkness. He swears that he will never again use his powers unless he knows the consequences. His knowledge increases until he finally understands the magnitude of his powers and is able to use them successfully:

Will realized once more, helplessly, that to be an Old One was to be old before the proper time, for the fear he began to feel now was worse than the blind terror he had known in his attic bed, worse than the fear the Dark had put into him in the great hall. This time, his fear was adult, made of experience and imagination and care for others, and it was the worst of all. (p. 127)

Greenwitch, the third book of the series, continues the quest for the grail and the missing manuscript. *The Grey King* and *Silver on the Tree* complete the series.

Cooper encourages readers to suspend disbelief in her fantasies by developing a strong foundation in the reality of the twentieth century. When her realistic contemporary characters travel into earlier centuries and mythical worlds, her readers follow them willingly and share their quests for greater knowledge. There is a tie, however, between the past and present. For example, in *The Dark Is Rising,* Will goes back into the past to recover the Sign of Fire. When he has fulfilled his quest, there are a great crashing roar, a rumbling, and a growling. Back in the present, thunder is creating earsplitting sounds. The action is believable, and readers feel that the old ways are actually awakening and that the powers live again.

 ## CATEGORIES OF MODERN FANTASY

Modern fantasies cover a wide range of topics. These topics include articulate animals, toys that come alive, preposterous characters and situations, strange and curious worlds, little people, friendly and frightening spirits, time warps, and science fiction.

Articulate Animals

Concerned rabbit parents worry about what will happen to their family when new folks move into the house on the hill, a mongoose saves his young owner from a deadly cobra, and a mole and a water rat spend an idyllic season floating down an enchanting river. Animals who talk like people but still retain some animal qualities are among the most popular modern fantasy characters. Authors such as Beatrix Potter and Kenneth Grahame have been able to create animal characters who display a balance between animal and human characteristics. This balance is not accidental; many successful authors write from close observations of animal life.

Young children are drawn to the strong feelings of loyalty that the animals in modern fantasies express as they help each other out of dangerous predicaments, stay with friends when they might choose other actions, or protect their human owners while risking their own lives. The memorable animal characters, like all memorable characters in literature, show a wide range of recognizable traits. Children often see themselves in the actions of their animal friends.

Retaining a consistent point of view is very important in believable modern fantasy. This may be particularly important in articulate animal stories. In Mary James's *Shoebag*, a cockroach changes into a boy. In this humorous story, James's protagonist retains his cockroach point of view.

Robert O'Brien's *Mrs. Frisby and the Rats of NIMH* is an excellent example of an author's use of believable plot, characters, and setting; interesting theme; and consistent point of view in modern fantasy. This consistency continues in Jane Leslie Conly's sequel, *Racso and the Rats of NIMH*, in which the author, who is the daughter of O'Brien, extends the story. In this sequel, the intelligent rat colony must save their Thorn Valley home from the threat of a dam and the accompanying tourism.

Beverly Cleary develops humorous animal stories for young children through imaginative and unusual plots. *The Mouse and the Motorcycle* and Cleary's other books about a mouse named Ralph are good introductions to modern fantasy.

Ursula K. LeGuin's *Catwings* and *Catwings Return* are also good introductions to fantasy for young chil-

dren. LeGuin's *Catwings* introduces a family of kittens whose mother wishes a better life for them than her own city slums. As a result of her dreams, the kittens are born with wings and are able to fly to a safe home in the country. In *Catwings Return,* two of the cats return to the city because they miss their mother. In a satisfying conclusion, they discover and save their sister, who also has wings. In addition, children lovingly protect and care for the cat family in the end. Dick King-Smith's *Martin's Mice* is another fantasy that develops the need for protection and understanding. In this book, a cat protects the farm mice from his own predatory family. Through his experiences, Martin also discovers the importance of freedom.

The characterization in Brian Jacques's *Redwall* is effective. For example, Jacques introduces Matthias,

These articulate animals talk like humans but have the additional power of flight. (From Catwings Return *by Ursula K. LeGuin, illustrated by S. D. Schindler. Copyright © 1989 by Ursula K. LeGuin, illustrations copyright © 1989 by S. D. Schindler. Reprinted by permission of Orchard Books, a division of Franklin Watts, Inc.)*

an unlikely and frequently clumsy mouse protagonist, with a description that reveals a great deal about the character's physical and emotional characteristics:

Matthias cut a comical little figure as he wobbled his way along the cloisters, with his large sandals flip-flopping and his tail peeping from beneath the baggy folds of an oversized novice's habit. He paused to gaze upwards at the cloudless blue sky and tripped over the enormous sandals. Hazelnuts scattered out upon the grass from the rush basket he was carrying. Unable to stop, he went tumbling cowl over tail. (p. 13)

After Matthias lands at the feet of Abbot Mortimer, the language reinforces the bumbling nature of the apologetic mouse: "Er, sorry, Father Abbot, I tripped, y'see. Trod on my Abbot, Father Habit. Oh dear, I mean . . ." (p. 13).

Compare the description of Matthias and the description of Cluny, the vicious antagonist:

Cluny was a bilge rat; the biggest, most savage rodent that ever jumped from ship to shore. He was black, with grey and pink scars all over his heavy vermin-ridden back to the enormous whiplike tail which had earned him his title: Cluny the Scourge! (p. 17)

Thus, Jacques sets the tone for a contest between two opposite characters.

Readers who enjoy Jacques's *Redwall* will enjoy additional books in the series. In *Mossflower,* a prequel to *Redwall,* Jacques goes back in time to reveal the story of Martin the Warrior, the original hero of Redwall Abbey and the savior of the land of Mossflower. *Mattimeo,* a sequel to *Redwall,* is about the exploits of Matthias's son, Mattimeo. In *Mariel of Redwall,* a mousemaid leads a battle at sea and saves Redwall animals from a savage pirate rat. As in his other books, Jacques stresses prophecies and provides readers with clues in a poem and a dream. In *Martin the Warrior* an epic tale is told about the time Martin leads his forces against Badrang, the ruthless stoat who enslaves peaceful forest animals. In *Pearls of Leitra* the Abbot is kidnapped and the animals of Redwall must save him. All of Jacques's books have strong characters who reveal the best or the worst of animalkind.

Beatrix Potter. Children of all ages can identify the following sentence as the beginning of an enjoyable story, *The Tale of Peter Rabbit:* "Once upon a time there were four little Rabbits, and their names were—Flopsy, Mopsy, Cotton-tail, and Peter" (p. 3). Beatrix Potter, who wrote so knowledgeably about small animals, spent many holidays in the country observing nature, collecting natural objects, and making detailed drawings. Potter had small pets, including a rabbit, a hedgehog, and mice, who later became very real in her illustrated books for children. As an adult, Potter purchased a farm that offered further stimulation for her stories about articulate animals.

Potter's first book, *The Tale of Peter Rabbit,* began as a letter sent to a sick child. When she later submitted the story to a publisher, it was rejected. She did not let this rejection dissuade her; she had the book printed independently. When young readers accepted Peter Rabbit with great enthusiasm, the publisher asked if he might print the book.

Potter's characters may seem real to children because they show many characteristics that children themselves demonstrate. Peter Rabbit, for example, wants to go to the garden so badly that he disobeys his mother. In a vast store of vegetables, happiness changes rapidly to fright when Peter encounters the enemy, Mr. McGregor. Children can sympathize with Peter's fright as he tries unsuccessfully to flee. They also can respond to a satisfying ending, as Peter narrowly escapes and reaches the security of his mother. Children know that such behavior cannot go unpunished. Peter must take a dose of chamomile tea for a stomachache, while his sisters feast on milk and blackberries.

Potter's illustrations, drawn in careful detail, complement the story and suggest the many moods of the main character. Peter stealthily approaches and squeezes under the garden gate. He appears ecstatic as he munches carrots. When Peter discovers that he is too fat to squeeze under the gate, his ears hang dejectedly, a tear trickles down his cheek, one front paw is clenched in fright against his mouth, and his back paws are huddled together. The illustrated moods are so realistic that children feel a close relationship with Peter. *The Tale of Peter Rabbit* is found in a reissue of the 1902 Warne publication, as well as collections such as *A Treasury of Peter Rabbit and Other Stories* and *Tales of Peter Rabbit and His Friends.*

Michael Bond. Paddington Bear is another animal character whose warmth and appeal are related to the author's ability to encourage children to see themselves in the actions of an animal. Unlike Beatrix Potter's Peter Rabbit, who lives in an animal world, Michael Bond's Paddington lives with an English family after the family discovers the homeless bear in Paddington Station. Acceptance of the bear by the family and neighborhood creates a credible and humorous series of stories beginning with *A Bear Called Paddington*.

Bond's Paddington may seem real to children because Paddington displays many childlike characteristics. He gets himself into trouble, and he tries to hide his errors from people who would be disappointed in or disapprove of his actions. Paddington is hard to communicate with when he is in one of his difficult moods, and like a human child, he often is torn between excitement and perplexity. The excitement of preparing the itinerary for a trip in *Paddington Abroad* is balanced by Paddington's trouble in spelling hard words, his difficulty understanding why the bank does not return the same money that he put into his savings account, and his inability to read his prepared map. Children in the early elementary grades greatly enjoy these humorous episodes.

Rudyard Kipling. While the majority of articulate animal stories familiar to Americans occur in the woods and farmlands of the United States and Europe, one series uses the jungles of India. Rudyard Kipling spent his early years in Bombay, India, and this time had a great influence on his later writing. He spent much time in the company of Indian *ayahs* (nurses) who told him native tales about the jungle animals. His own young children were the first to hear his most famous stories about the man-cub Mowgli and his brothers, Akela the wolf, Baloo the bear, and Bagheera the panther, published in *The Jungle Book* in 1894.

The story "Mowgli's Brothers" is one of Kipling's most popular. Kipling develops animal characters as diverse as the man-eating tiger Shere Khan, who claims the young Mowgli as his own, and Mother Wolf, who demonstrates her maternal instincts as she protects the man-cub and encourages him to join her own cubs. The law of the jungle is a strong element in the story, as the animals sit in council to decide Mowgli's fate. This story has the flavor of a traditional tale. The suspense rises until old Baloo the bear finally speaks for the man-cub. As in traditional tales about articulate animals, powerful feelings of loyalty grow as Mowgli saves the life of his old friend Akela, the wolf.

The characters, plot, and language of "Rikki-Tikki-Tavi" make it an excellent choice for oral storytelling. The wicked cobras Nag and Nagaina live in the garden of a small boy and his parents. They plan a battle against the humans and the heroic mongoose, Rikki-Tikki-Tavi, a hunter with eyeballs of flame and the sworn enemy of all snakes. In keeping with the oral tradition, the action develops rapidly. The boy's loyal mongoose kills Nag. Then, he faces his most deadly peril, a female cobra avenging her mate and protecting her unborn babies. Kipling's language is excellent for oral recitation. As the tension mounts, Rikki-Tikki-Tavi asks:

What price for a snake's egg? For a young cobra? For a young king-cobra? For the last—the very last of the brood? The ants are eating all the others down by the melon-bed. (p. 117)

Kipling's young children were the first to hear his stories of articulate animals and a boy raised by the jungle animals. Illustration by W. H. Drake. (From The Jungle Book *by Rudyard Kipling. Illustrated by W. H. Drake, copyright © 1894. Macmillan and Co.)*

A happy-ever-after ending has Rikki-Tikki-Tavi defeating his enemy and remaining on guard so there will not be another threat in the garden.

Humorous incidents and language that is most effective when shared orally are characteristics of Kipling's *Just So Stories*. Young children enjoy the language in such favorite tales as "The Elephant's Child," the story of an adventurous young animal who lives near the banks of the "great, gray-green, greasy Limpopo River."

Kenneth Grahame. Kenneth Grahame first told his stories to his young children; however, scholarly analysis reveals that *The Wind in the Willows* may be read at several levels. For example, Michael Mendelson (1988) analyzed the contrast between the values of the dusty road and the riverbank. Peter Hunt (1988) analyzed the language and class structure. Richard Gillin (1988) searched for evidence of romanticism.

The animals in *The Wind in the Willows* are much more human than are Mowgli's friends in Kipling's jungle (Townsend, 1975). Grahame creates characters who prefer the idyllic life and consider work a bore, who long for wild adventures, who demonstrate human frailties through their actions, and who are loyal to friends. The idyllic life is exemplified in the experiences of Mole and Water-Rat as they explore their river world. Grahame introduces his readers to Mole as the scent of spring is penetrating Mole's dark home with a spirit of longing and discontent. Lured out of his hole, Mole observes the busy animals around him and muses that the best part of a holiday is not resting. Instead, it is seeing other animals busy at work. Through detailed description, Grahame communicates this perpetual vacationer's delight and carefree joy to readers:

He thought his happiness was complete when, as he meandered aimlessly along, suddenly he stood by the edge of a full-fed river. Never in his life had he seen a river before—this sleek, sinuous, full-bodied animal, chasing and chuckling, gripping things with a gurgle and leaving them with a laugh, to fling itself on fresh playmates that shook themselves free, and were caught and held again. All was a-shake and a-shiver—glints and gleams and sparks, rustle and swirl, chatter and bubble. The Mole was bewitched, entranced, fascinated. (p. 6)

Grahame creates credibility for the adventures of his most eccentric character, Toad of Toad Hall, by taking him away from the peaceful surroundings of his ancestral home. In the Wide World, where presumably such adventures could happen, he wrecks cars, is imprisoned, and escapes in a washerwoman's clothing basket. While he is gone, the less desirable animals who live in the Wild Wood, the stoats and the weasels, take over his home. When he returns, Toad's friends—brave Badger, gallant Water-Rat, and loyal Mole—help Toad recapture Toad Hall and tame the Wild Wood. Grahame suggests that a subdued and altered Toad, accompanied by his friends, recaptures his life of contentment along the river, at the edge of the Wild Wood, far away from the Wide World beyond.

Grahame's writing creates strong characters and visual images of the settings. Many children find the text difficult to read, however, so it may be preferable for adults to read this story to children. Many adults find Grahame's writing to be very enjoyable. As illustrator Fritz Eichenberg (1990) states in his Arbuthnot Lecture address, "At my age I can still read with pleasure and profit *The Wind in the Willows*. That should prove a pleasant platform on which we all can meet, peacefully, or better still let's meet at Toad Hall!" (p. 53).

Robert Lawson. This winner of the Newbery Award, the Caldecott Medal, and the Lewis Carroll Shelf Award has created a believable world in which animals retain their individualized characters. Unlike the river world of Mole in *The Wind in the Willows*, Robert Lawson's animal kingdom is influenced by humans. Like other distinguished authors of articulate animal stories, Lawson spent time closely observing animals (Weston, 1970). In 1936, Lawson built a house called Rabbit Hill in Connecticut. He says that he had wanted to write a story about the animals who ate everything he planted, the deer who trampled his garden, the skunks who upset his garbage pail, and the foxes who killed his chickens. Instead, when he started to write, he found himself growing fond of Little Georgie, a young rabbit, and the other animals on the hill.

The resulting book, *Rabbit Hill,* presents the impact of humans on the animals from the point of view of the animals. Lawson maintains this point of view to create believable characters. The animals on the hill wait expectantly after they learn that new folks are coming. They wonder if this change will bring about a renewal of older and pleasanter days when the fields were planted, a garden cultivated, and the lawns manicured. However, Mother Rabbit fears that the folks will be lovers of shotguns, traps, and poison gases, or worst of all, boys.

Lawson centers his book on the exploits of the exuberant Little Georgie, a rabbit who retains his curiosity and love for a good chase even when his father warns him that misbehavior and parental indulgence can have swift and fatal consequences. The animals believe that all will be well when the new owners put up a sign saying "Please drive carefully on account of small animals." Then, Little Georgie has a dreadful experience with a car on the black road, and the folks from the hill take the limp rabbit into the house. Gloom settles over the animals. Is Georgie alive, and, if so, why does he not appear? What terrible experiences are the folks planning for Little Georgie? The animals learn that the new folks are considerate and caring. The story has a satisfactory ending, and the animals pay tribute to their new folks on the hill.

George Selden.

Like Robert Lawson, George Selden loves the Connecticut countryside and creates animals with strong and believable personalities. His *The Cricket in Times Square,* however, has an urban setting, the subway station at Times Square. Two animal characters, Tucker Mouse and Harry Cat, are city dwellers. The other animal, Chester Cricket, arrives accidentally, having jumped into a picnic basket in Connecticut and been trapped until he arrived in New York.

Selden tells their story from the point of view of the animals and develops additional credibility by retaining some of each animal's natural characteristics: The city-wise Tucker Mouse lives in a cluttered drainpipe because he enjoys scrounging and does not consider neatness important. Chester Cricket is a natural musician and prefers to play when the spirit moves him rather than when people want to hear him. The plot develops around Chester's remarkable ability to play any music he hears and his need for returning kindness to the poor owner of the newsstand in the subway. Selden concludes his story with a longing that might be felt by anyone taken from his native environment. Chester becomes homesick for autumn in Connecticut and leaves the city to return home. When Tucker asks him how he'll

know that he has reached home, Chester reassures him, "Oh, I'll know! . . . I'll smell the trees and I'll feel the air and I'll know" (p. 154).

This is a touching story of friendship, of longing for one's home, and of the love and understanding that can be felt between even a child and a tiny insect. Additional stories about these animals are found in Selden's *Tucker's Countryside, Harry Cat's Pet Puppy,* and *Chester Cricket's Pigeon Ride. Chester Cricket's Pigeon Ride* has a large format and illustrations designed to appeal to young children.

E. B. White.

Roger Sale (1978) has identified *Charlotte's Web* as "the classic American children's book of the last thirty years" (p. 258), while Rebecca Lukens (1986) uses the book as a touchstone, the story around which she develops her critical standards for literature. Therefore, this book is a fitting example for an extended illustration of the techniques an author of fantasy may use to encourage readers to suspend disbelief.

E. B. White introduces his characters within the reality of an authentically described working farm. His human characters have no unusual powers. They do not treat animals like people, and White does not give his animals human characteristics. The harsh reality is that the farmer must keep only animals that can produce a profit. In this setting, Mr. Arable moves toward the hoghouse with an ax in his hand to kill the runt in a newly born litter of six pigs. His daughter, Fern, pleads with him to let her raise the pig. As Wilbur grows, the profitability of the farm again influences Wilbur's fate. Mr. Arable is not willing to provide for Wilbur's growing appetite. Fern again saves Wilbur, but without a hint of fantasy: She sells him to Uncle Homer Zuckerman, who lives within easy visiting distance.

Wilbur's new home also begins on a firm foundation of reality. White describes the barn in which Wilbur will live and the afternoons when Fern visits Wilbur. On an afternoon when Fern does not arrive, White changes the story from reality to fantasy. Wilbur discovers that he can talk. As he realizes this, his barnyard neighbors begin to talk to him. From this point on, White develops the animal characters into distinct individuals, consistent in speech, actions, and appearance.

Wilbur feels lonely, friendless, and dejected. He often complains. He is a character who must be helped by others. When he discovers that he is being fattened to become smoked bacon and ham, he acts nonheroically: He bursts into tears, screams that he wants to live, and cries for someone to save him. Fern does not rescue him this time. Instead, White answers Wilbur's needs by giving him a barnyard friend, Charlotte A. Cavatica, a beautiful gray spider. Charlotte has quiet manners, and she is intelligent and loyal. She reassures Wilbur during their quiet talks, spins the webs that save Wilbur's life, and accompanies him on his trip to the fair.

The character of Templeton, the barnyard rat, is revealed through his convincing actions. He creeps furtively in his search for garbage, talks sneeringly to the barnyard animals, and eats until he gorges himself. White underscores this characterization by describing Templeton as having no morals or decency.

Through the reactions of the farm families, White allows readers to suspend disbelief about the possibility of a spider's spinning a web containing words. When the local residents react in "joyful admiration" and notify their local newspaper (the *Weekly Chronicle*), White's readers tend to believe this could really have happened. Readers can accept even the final, natural death of Charlotte, because life and friendship continue through Charlotte's offspring. Wilbur understands this as he welcomes three of Charlotte's daughters to his home:

Welcome to the barn cellar. You have chosen a hallowed doorway from which to string your webs. I think it is only fair to tell you that I was devoted to your mother. I owe my very life to her. She was brilliant, beautiful, and loyal to the end. I shall always treasure her memory. To you, her daughters, I pledge my friendship, forever and ever. (p. 182)

You may wish to compare E. B. White's *Charlotte's Web* with Dick King-Smith's believable characters and plot in *Pigs Might Fly*. Like Wilbur, Daggie Dogfoot is the runt of the litter. Unlike Wilbur, Daggie Dogfoot is physically disabled.

Toys

When children play with dolls or have conversations with their stuffed animals and other toys, they demonstrate belief in the human characteristics that they give their playthings. An author who tells a story from the point of view of a toy encourages young readers to draw upon their imaginative experiences with toys and to suspend disbelief.

Rumer Godden. Every child who loves dolls knows that a doll is only a thing unless a child loves it. This is also Rumer Godden's philosophy. She writes books about the dolls who live in her own observatory house, and she has her dolls carry on a correspondence with another old family of dolls (Commire, 1971).

Telling *The Dolls' House* from the viewpoint of a doll, Godden creates a believable story about a group of small dolls who long to leave a shoebox and live in their own house. Godden tells her readers:

It is an anxious, sometimes a dangerous thing to be a doll. Dolls cannot choose; they can only be chosen; they cannot "do"; they can only be done by; children who do not understand this often do wrong things, and then the dolls are hurt and abused and lost; and when this happens, dolls cannot speak, nor do anything except be hurt and abused and lost. If you have any dolls, you should remember that. (p. 13)

Godden creates dolls who have a range of human characteristics. For example, Mr. and Mrs. Plantagenet are quite ordinary dolls with extraordinary hearts; Tottie is an antique Dutch doll with a warm, friendly character; and Marchpane is an elegant nineteenth-century china doll with a vile disposition. These characteristics play important roles as the dolls express the desire for a new home. When an elegant dollhouse arrives, Marchpane declares that the house is rightfully hers and that the rest of the dolls are her servants. Godden describes the dolls' increasing unhappiness until a tragedy opens the eyes of the two children and the story ends on a note suggesting that justice is related to one's conduct.

Margery Williams. *The Velveteen Rabbit* is told from the viewpoint of a stuffed toy that lives in a nursery and learns to know his owner. Conversations between the stuffed rabbit and an old toy horse are especially effective. They allow Margery Williams to share her feelings about the reality of toys. When the rabbit asks the wise, old Skin Horse what it means to be real, the Skin Horse informs him, "Real isn't how you are made. . . . It's a thing that happens to you. When a child loves you for a long, long time, not just to play with, but REALLY loves you, then you become Real" (p. 17). The horse tells the rabbit that becoming real usually happens after a toy's hair has been loved off, its eyes have

Companionship and love between a boy and a toy seem believable in this fantasy. (From The Velveteen Rabbit, *by Margery Williams. Illustrated by Michael Hague. Illustrations copyright © 1983 by Michael Hague. Reprinted by permission of Henry Holt and Company, Inc.)*

A. A. Milne.   According to his creator A. A. Milne (1966), Winnie-the-Pooh does not like to be called a teddy bear because a teddy bear is just a toy, whereas Pooh is alive. The original Pooh was a present to Milne's son, Christopher Robin, on his first birthday. The boy and Pooh became inseparable, playing together on the nursery floor, hunting wild animals among the chairs that became African jungles, and having lengthy conversations over tea. Christopher Robin's nursery contained other "real" animals, including Piglet, Eeyore, Kanga, and Roo. When Milne wrote his stories about Christopher Robin's adventures with these animals, he was not only thinking about his own son but also remembering himself as a boy.

Winnie-the-Pooh and *The House at Pooh Corner* are filled with stories about Pooh because Pooh likes to hear stories about himself. Milne develops credibility for the actions in his stories by taking Pooh and the others out of the nursery and into the hundred-acre wood, where an inquisitive bear can have many adventures. Several stories suggest Pooh's reality: He climbs trees looking for honey and eats Rabbit's honey when he pays a visit. The text and illustrations leave no doubt that Pooh is a toy, however. No real bear would be so clumsy as to fall from branch to branch or to become stuck in Rabbit's doorway. Children may feel a close relationship with Christopher Robin because every time that Pooh gets into difficulty, the human child must rescue the "silly old bear."

Carlo Collodi.   The adventures of a wooden marionette who is disobedient, prefers the joys of playtime to the rigors of school, and finally learns his lesson and wins an opportunity to become a real boy are similar to the experiences of Carlo Collodi, his creator. The Italian author of *The Adventures of Pinocchio* described himself as "the most irresponsible, the most disobedient and impudent boy in the whole school" (De Wit, 1979, p. 74). His story reflects a lesson that Collodi learned in school:

I persuaded myself that if one is impudent and disobedient in school he loses the good will of the teachers and the friendship of the scholars. I too became a good boy. I began to respect the others and they in turn respected me. (p. 76)

Pinocchio's insistence on doing only what he wants leads to a series of adventures: He sells his

dropped out, and its joints have loosened. Then, even if the toy is shabby, it does not mind because it has become real to the child who loves it.

The story develops around the growing companionship between a boy and the boy rabbit. Children's reactions to this story suggest how meaningful the toy–child relationship is. Teachers and librarians describe the concern of young children when the rabbit is placed on the rubbish pile because the rabbit spent many hours in bed with the boy when he had scarlet fever. When the nursery fairy appears and turns the toy into a real rabbit, however, children often say that this is the right reward for a toy who has given so much love. These reactions suggest the credibility of a story written from the point of view of a toy. You may wish to compare the versions of this book illustrated by William Nicholson (the original edition), Michael Green, Ilse Plume, Allen Atkinson, and Michael Hague.

spelling book instead of attending school, he becomes involved with a devious fox and cat, he goes to a land of perpetual playtime, and he is transformed into a donkey. After Pinocchio learns some bitter lessons, he searches for his creator, Geppetto, who works to restore his health. Pinocchio begins to practice his reading and writing, and eventually becomes a real person. Through the words of the blue fairy, Collodi explains why Pinocchio is rewarded:

Because of your kind heart I forgive you for all your misdeeds. Boys who help other people so willingly and lovingly deserve praise, even if they are not models in other ways. Always listen to good counsel and you will be happy. (p. 193)

The influence of traditional folktales and fables is evident in Collodi's use of animals with human traits to teach lessons. Magical transformations punish and reward Pinocchio on his path to self-improvement (Heins, 1982).

Preposterous Characters and Situations

Children love exaggeration, ridiculous situations, and tongue-twisting language. Stories that appeal to a sense of humor usually include repetition, plays on words, and clever and original figures of speech. The characters in this section are developed through vivid descriptions of dress, features, or actions.

Floating through the air inside a huge peach propelled by five hundred and two seagulls provides a getaway for an unhappy child in Roald Dahl's *James and the Giant Peach*. Children thoroughly enjoy the freshness and originality of this story. Other enjoyably preposterous journeys occur when a housepainter is granted an unusual wish in *Mr. Popper's Penguins,* by Richard and Florence Atwater; when an eccentric inventor restores an old car in Ian Fleming's *Chitty Chitty Bang Bang;* and when a bed takes flight in Mary Norton's *Bed-Knob and Broomstick.* Pamela L. Travers's preposterous nanny, Mary Poppins, goes on many adventures.

Carl Sandburg. Readers might expect some unusual characters to be the residents of Rootabaga Country, where the largest city is a village called Liver and Onions. They are usually not disappointed when they hear Carl Sandburg's *Rootabaga Stories.* Told originally to the author's own children, these stories lose part of their humor if they are read rather than heard. The alliteration and nonsensical names are hard for children to read themselves, but they are fun to listen to.

Sandburg begins his ridiculous situation by describing how to get to Rootabaga Country by train: Riders must sell everything that they own, put "spot-cash money" into a ragbag, and then go to the railroad station and ask for a ticket to the place where the railroad tracks run into the sky and never come back. They will know that they have arrived when the train begins running on zigzag tracks; when they have traveled through the country of Over and Under, where no one gets out of the way of anyone else; and when they look out the train windows and see pigs wearing bibs.

The residents of Rootabaga Country have tongue-twisting names, such as Ax Me No Questions, Rags Habakuk, Miney Mo, and Henry Hagglyhoagly, and they become involved in tongue-twisting situations. For example, when Blixie Bimber puts a charm around her neck, she falls in love with the first man that she meets with one *x* in his name (Silas Baxby), then with a man with two *x*'s (Fritz Axanbax), and finally with a man with three *x*'s (James Sixbixdix).

Sandburg's characters often talk in alliteration, repeating an initial sound in consecutive words. When the neighbors see a family selling their possessions, for example, they speculate that the family might be going "to Kansas, to Kokomo, to Canada, to Kankakee, to Kamchatka, to the Chattahoochee" (p. 6). The stories are brief enough to share with children during a short story time, but the uncommon names and the language require preparation by a storyteller or an oral reader. *More Rootabagas* is a new collection of previously unpublished stories.

Astrid Lindgren. In *Pippi Longstocking,* Swedish author Astrid Lindgren creates an unusual and vivacious character, who wears pigtails and stockings of different colors. Lindgren relies on exaggeration to develop a character who is supposedly the strongest girl in the world. Pippi demonstrates her ability when she lifts her horse onto the porch of her house.

Pippi's unconventional behavior and carefree existence appeal to many children. Pippi is a child who lives in a home all by herself. She sleeps on a bed with her feet where her head should be and decides to attend school because she doesn't want to miss Christmas and Easter vacation. Pippi's adventures continue in *Pippi in the South Seas,* in which Pippi saves her friend Tommy from a shark attack.

Strange and Curious Worlds

While on their way to Carl Sandburg's Rootabaga Country, young readers may find themselves falling down rabbit holes or flying off into even stranger and more curious worlds of modern fantasy.

Lewis Carroll.   A remarkable realm unfolds when one falls down a rabbit hole, follows an underground passage, and enters a tiny door into a land of cool fountains, bright flowers, and unusual inhabitants. The guide into this world is also unusual: an articulate white rabbit who wears a waistcoat complete with a pocket watch.

Perhaps even more remarkable is the fact that this world of fantasy was created by a man who was dreadfully shy with adults, had a tendency to stammer, and displayed prim and precise habits. Charles Lutwidge Dodgson, better known as Lewis Carroll, was a mathematics lecturer at Oxford University during the sedate Victorian period of English history. Warren Weaver (1964) describes the life of this Victorian don:

Dodgson's adult life symbolized—indeed, really caricatured—the restraints of Victorian society. But he was essentially a wild and free spirit, and he had to burst out of these bonds. The chief outlet was fantasy—the fantasy which children accept with such simplicity, with such intelligence and charm. (p. 16)

Dodgson may have been shy with adults, but he showed a very different personality with children. He kept himself supplied with games to amuse them, made friends with them easily, and enjoyed telling them stories. A story told on a warm July afternoon to three young daughters of the dean of Dodgson's college at Oxford made Lewis Carroll almost immortal. As the children—Alice, Edith, and Lorina Liddell—rested on the riverbank, they asked Dodgson for a story. The result was the remarkable tale that later became *Alice's Adventures in Wonderland.* Even the first line of the story is reminiscent of a warm, leisurely afternoon:

Alice was beginning to get very tired of sitting by her sister on the bank and having nothing to do: Once or twice she had peeped into the book her sister was reading, but it had no pictures or conversations in it, "And what is the use of a book" thought Alice, "without pictures or conversations?" (p. 9)

From that point on, however, the day enters another realm of experience. Alice sees a strange white rabbit muttering to himself and follows him down, down, down into Wonderland, where the unusual is the ordinary way of life. Drinking mysterious substances changes one's size; strange animals conduct a race with no beginning and no finish that everyone wins; a hookah-smoking caterpillar gives advice; Dormouse, March Hare, and Mad Hatter have a very odd tea party; Cheshire Cat fades in and out of sight; and the King and Queen of Hearts conduct a ridiculous trial. According to Weaver, the strange adventures have a broad appeal to children everywhere because:

Something of the essence of childhood is contained in this remarkable book—the innocent fun, the natural acceptance of marvels, combined with a healthy and at times slightly saucy curiosity about them, the element of confusion concerning the strange way in which the adult world behaves, the complete and natural companionship with animals, and an intertwined mixture of the rational and the irrational. For all of these, whatever the accidents of geography, are part and parcel of childhood. (p. 6)

Throughout the book, Alice expresses a natural acceptance of the unusual. When she finds a bottle labeled "Drink Me," she does so without hesitation. When the White Rabbit sends her to look for his missing gloves, she thinks to herself that it is queer to be a messenger for a rabbit, but she goes without question. During her adventures in this strange land she does, however, question her own identity. When the caterpillar opens their conversation by asking, "Who are you?" Alice replies:

I—I hardly know, Sir, just at present—at least I know who I was when I got up this morning, but I think I must have been changed several times since then. . . . I can't explain myself. I'm afraid, Sir, because I'm not myself, you see. (p. 23)

Lewis Carroll's language is appealing to children, especially if an adult reads the story to them, but children have difficulty reading the story for themselves, and some of the word plays are difficult for them to understand. Carroll's version of the story for young children, *The Nursery "Alice,"* is written as though the author were telling the tale directly to children:

This is a little bit of the beautiful garden I told you about. You see Alice had managed at last to get quite small, so that she could go through the little door. I suppose she was

A tea party with unusual guests adds to Alice-in-Wonderland's confusion. (From The Nursery "Alice," *by Lewis Carroll. Illustrated by John Tenniel. Published by Macmillan Publishing Co., 1890, 1979.)*

about as tall as a mouse, if it stood on its hind legs; so of course this was a very tiny rose-tree: and these are very tiny gardeners. (p. 41)

Carroll is noted for his nonsense words as well as for his nonsensical situations. He claimed that even he could not explain the meanings of some words. Myra Cohn Livingston (1973) quotes a letter in which Carroll explains at least some words in his popular poem "Jabberwocky":

I am afraid I can't explain "vorpal blade" for you—nor yet "tulgey wood:" but I did make an explanation once for "uffish thought"—It seems to suggest a state of mind when the voice is gruffish, the manner roughish, and the temper huffish. Then again, as to "burble"; if you take the three verbs, "<u>b</u>leat," "<u>mur</u>mur" and "war<u>ble</u>," and select the bits I have underlined, it certainly makes "burble": though I am afraid I can't distinctly remember having made it that way.

The appeal of Carroll's nonsensical characters and fantasy, both to himself and to children, may be explained in a quote from a letter that he wrote in 1891:

In some ways, you know, people that don't exist are much nicer than people that do. For instance, people that don't exist are never cross: and they never contradict you: and they never tread on your toes! Oh, they're ever so much nicer than people that do exist!

James Barrie.   *Peter Pan,* the classic flight of James Barrie's imagination into Never Land, was first presented as a play in 1904. Barrie begins his fantasy

in the realm of reality, describing the children of Mr. and Mrs. Darling in their nursery as their parents prepare to leave for a party. When the parents leave the house, the world of fantasy immediately enters it in the form of Peter Pan and Tinker Bell, who are looking for Peter's lost shadow. Thus begins an adventure in which the Darling children fly, with the help of fairy dust, to Never Land, the kingdom that is "second to the right and then straight on till morning" (p. 31).

In Never Land, they meet the lost boys, children who have fallen out of their baby carriages when adults were not looking, and discover that there are no girls in Never Land because girls are too clever to fall out of their baby carriages. Along with Peter Pan, who ran away from home because he didn't want to grow up, the children have a series of adventures in Mermaids' Lagoon with the fairy Tinker Bell and against their archenemy, Captain Hook, and his pirates. The children finally decide to return home and to accept the responsibility of growing up.

Barrie's description of Mermaids' Lagoon encourages readers to visualize this fantasy land:

If you shut your eyes and are a lucky one, you may see at times a shapeless pool of lovely pale colours suspended in the darkness; then if you squeeze your eyes tighter, the pool begins to take shape, and the colours become so vivid that with another squeeze they must go on fire. But just before they go on fire you see the lagoon. This is the nearest you ever get to it on the mainland, just one heavenly moment; if there could be two moments you might see the surf and hear the mermaids singing. (p. 111)

Barrie's settings and characters seem real. They may seem especially real to children who do not wish to grow up. Readers who do not want to take on the responsibility of adulthood may sympathize with the adult Wendy, who longs to accompany Peter Pan but cannot. The book closes on a touch of nostalgia, as Peter Pan returns to claim each new generation of children who are happy and innocent.

Little People

Traditional folktales and fairy tales describe the kingdoms of small trolls, gnomes, and fairies; Hans Christian Andersen wrote about tiny Thumbelina, who sleeps in a walnut shell; and J. R. R. Tolkien created a believable world for the hobbit. Eloise McGraw in *The Moorchild* creates a world in which the Folk, or fairy people, live in their own world near that of the human occupants of the moor. Saaski, the heroine of the story, cannot survive with the Folk because she does not have their ability to make herself invisible to humans. McGraw creates her fantasy plot when the Folk exchange Saaski for a human child. The author creates tension between the villagers and Saaski's parents when the villagers blame Saaski for various misfortunes and threaten the child. Now Saaski must discover who she is and try to save the human child and the foster parents she has grown to admire. Contemporary authors of fantasy satisfy children's fascination with people who are a lot like them, only much smaller.

Carol Kendall. In *The Gammage Cup,* Carol Kendall creates a new world, the Land between the Mountains, in which little people in the valley of the Watercress River live in twelve serene towns with names like Little Dripping, Great Dripping, and Slipper-on-the-Water. Kendall gives credibility to this setting by tracing its history, carefully describing its buildings, and creating inhabitants who have lived in the valley for centuries.

The valley has two types of residents. The Periods display smug conformity in their clothing, their insistence on neat houses, and their similar attitudes and values. In contrast, the five Minnipins—whom the Periods refer to as "Oh Them"—insist upon being different. Gummy roams the hills rather than working at a suitable job; Curley Green paints pictures and wears a scarlet cloak; Walter the Earl digs for ancient treasure; Muggles refuses to keep her house organized; and Mingy questions the rulers' authority.

The conflict between the two sides reaches a climax when the five Minnipins refuse to conform to one standard and decide that they would rather outlaw themselves, leave their homes, and become exiles in the mountains than conform to the Periods' wishes. However, Kendall allows nonconformity to save the valley; the Minnipins discover the ancient enemy, the Mushrooms, or Hairless Ones, who have tunneled a way into the valley through an old gold mine. The five exiles rally the villagers and lead the Periods in a glorious victory over the enemy. At this point, the exiles return to their homes as heroes.

Mary Norton. The little people in Mary Norton's stories do not live in an isolated kingdom of their own. Instead, they are found in "houses which are old and quiet and deep in the country—and where the human beings live to a routine. Routine is their safeguard. They must know which rooms are to be used and when. They do not stay long where there are careless people, or unruly children, or certain household pets" (p. 9). In *The Borrowers,* Norton persuades readers to suspend disbelief by developing a foundation in reality. She describes an old country house in detail, including a clock that has not been moved for over eighty years. Realistic humans living in the house see and believe in the little people.

Norton describes normal-sized people through the eyes of the Clock family, who are only six inches

In The Moorchild, *fairy people live in their own world alongside that of the humans. (Reprinted with permission of Margaret K. McElderry Books for Young Readers, an imprint of Simon & Schuster Children's Publishing Division from* The Moorchild *by Eloise McGraw. Jacket illustration copyright © 1996 Eloise McGraw.)*

tall. The Clocks' size forces them to lead precarious lives. They borrow their furnishings from the human occupants of the house.

Norton further encourages readers to suspend disbelief through the effort made to catch the little people. *The Borrowers* reaches an exciting climax when the housekeeper vows to have the borrowers exterminated by all available means: The rat-catcher arrives, complete with dogs, rabbit snares, sacks, spade, gun, and pickax. When a human boy takes an ax and desperately tries to dislodge the grating from the brick wall so that the little people can escape, readers have no doubt that those extraordinary beings are waiting in the shadows for his aid.

The Borrowers Afloat, The Borrowers Afield, The Borrowers Aloft, and *The Borrowers Avenged* continue the Clocks' adventures in fields and hedgerows. Sights, sounds, smells, and experiences seem original and authentic as readers look at the world from this unusual perspective.

Spirits Friendly and Frightening

Most children love good ghost stories or tales about beings from the spirit realm, whether frightening or friendly. Authors who write about these subjects may develop elements from folklore and the historic past. Older children who enjoy stories about ghosts and goblins like the suspense and humor of Mollie Hunter's *The Wicked One*. They also like Paul Fleischman's three short tales of the supernatural in *Graven Images*. Fleischman's tales are successful because they build upon suspenseful turns of events, human folly, and comic mishaps. In *Seven Strange & Ghostly Tales,* Brian Jacques develops strange and unexpected stories featuring ghosts, demons, and vampires. To entice readers, Jacques introduces each of his stories with a poem.

In a ghost story, Mary Downing Hahn helps present-day characters deal with their problems. In *Wait till Helen Comes,* Hahn's characters overcome their resentment against their stepfather and stepsister when they help the stepsister overcome her fascination with a ghost who is trying to lure the girl to her death. In *Ghost Abbey,* by Robert Westall, an abbey plays two different roles: (1) it protects those who care for it and (2) it threatens those who harm it. In *Whispers from the Dead,* by Joan Lowery Nixon, the ghost of a murdered character helps solve a mystery and prevent a second murder.

Patricia Wrightson develops a contest of wills between an elderly woman and an otherworld creature in *A Little Fear.* The conflict occurs when the Njimbin, an otherworld creature who can influence nature, challenges old Mrs. Tucker by trying to force her from her cottage in rural Australia. Wrightston's strong female character finally outwits the ancient being. *Balyet,* also by Wrightson, centers on another aboriginal spirit. In *Balyet,* the conflict is between an older woman, a girl, and the spirit.

In *The Boggart,* Susan Cooper develops a conflict of wills between the Boggart, an ancient spirit, and the children who visit a castle in the western highlands of Scotland. The conflict increases when the spirit accidentally accompanies the children to their home in Toronto, Canada. There, the children must use modern technology to return the spirit to his castle home. In Cooper's sequel, *The Boggart and the Monster,* the spirit interacts with the Loch Ness Monster.

Demonic forces, incantations, and vanishing humans provide the suspense in *The Spell of the Sorcerer's Skull,* by John Bellairs. A ghost plays a benevolent role in Sid Fleischman's *The Midnight Horse.* In this story, the Great Chaffalo, the ghost of a magician, helps Touch, an orphan boy, flee from his wicked great-uncle. Fleischman's use of similes and other figurative language creates an 1800s New Hampshire setting that seems suitable for such ghostly occurrences.

For older readers, *Silver Kiss* by Annette Curtis Klause has a mysterious teenage boy help a girl face her own problems and acquire self-realization. In this book, Zoe, a contemporary girl, and Simon, a three hundred-year-old vampire, help each other accept what has happened in their lives. In Francesca Lisa Block's *Missing Angel Juan,* the ghost of Witch Baby's grandfather helps her find her missing boyfriend. Authors of fantasy frequently help characters face issues and overcome problems that could be self-destructive. In Peter Dickinson's *The Lion Tamer's Daughter: And Other Stories* teenagers are helped by supernatural friends, while Patricia Windsor's *The Blooding* is a story of good versus evil.

Lucy Boston. The winner of the Lewis Carroll Shelf Award for *The Children of Green Knowe,* Lucy Boston uses her own historic manor house at Hemingford Grey near Cambridge, England, as the setting for her stories. The house and the way of life that past generations experienced in it provided Boston with ideas for a series of stories written about an old manor house and the friendly presences who return there from generations past.

The first book of a series, *The Children of Green Knowe* introduces the house, its owner Mrs. Oldknowe, her great-grandson Tolly, and the children who have previously lived in the house. Boston describes the house through the eyes of Tolly, a lonely, shy boy who comes to live in this old house with furnishings similar to those found in a castle. The past comes alive for Tolly as children who have lived there in previous generations come back to play with each other and bring vitality to the house and gardens. Readers are not surprised by these actions because Great-grandmother Oldknowe expects the children to return and enjoys having them visit. Boston allows readers to learn more about the people in the past through the stories that Mrs. Oldknowe tells Tolly.

Other books in this series include *The Treasure of Green Knowe, The River at Green Knowe, A Stranger at Green Knowe,* and *An Enemy at Green Knowe.* In all of the stories, ancestors return because someone wanted to keep their memories alive.

Time Warps

Children who read time-warp stories discover that there are more things in this world than progress and theories about the future. Time-warp stories encourage children to consider what might have happened in their own towns or geographic locations hundreds of years ago, as well as what the future might hold in centuries to come. Symbols and tangible objects unite past, present, and future. Believable characters travel to a distant past or see a future yet to materialize. Unlike many of the modern fantasies that bridge the world between old and new fantasy, time-warp stories focus on human development rather than on the forces of good and evil. The problems are solved by the characters, not by supernatural powers.

Authors frequently use the time-warp technique to allow their characters to make discoveries about themselves, their families, or the past. These discoveries usually allow the characters to gain new understandings. In *A Dig in Time,* Peni R. Griffin uses artifacts found in the backyard to allow a boy and a girl to go back to a time when their grandparents and parents were much younger. During this process, the protagonists make discoveries that help them in their contemporary world. In *Switching Well,* Griffin uses an old well to allow her thirteen-year-old heroine to wish herself one hundred years into the future. This becomes a dual exchange as a contemporary girl wishes herself back one hundred years to a past that she believes is simpler. Through their experiences, both girls discover that no time period is without problems.

Detailed descriptions of a farm and countryside in the twentieth century and during the American Civil War create a believable story in Janet Lunn's time-warp fantasy *The Root Cellar.* In this book, the problems that an unhappy orphan confronts in both the present and the past encourage her personal development. Time-warp experiences help children overcome problems related to growing up and to family in Ruth Park's *Playing Beatie Bow* and Cynthia Voigt's *Building Blocks.* In *Stonewords: A Ghost Story* and the sequel, *Zoe Rising,* Pam Conrad develops a theme of friendship. A contemporary girl interacts with a girl who lived in the same house during a different time. In *Zoe Rising,* fourteen-year-old Zoe goes back in time to solve a mystery in her estranged mother's past.

Belinda Hurmence uses a historical time and person-against-society conflict to help her protagonist understand a conflict that influenced her family. In *A Girl Called Boy,* Hurmence has a contemporary girl go back in time and experience slavery in 1853. Jane Yolen uses a similar approach in *The Devil's Arithmetic.* In this book, a contemporary Jewish girl faces the Holocaust. Both books are believable because the authors develop historical backgrounds that are authentic and characters who are changed by their experiences. In *The Pit,* Ann Cheetham takes her protagonist back to the plague-torn London of 1665. Cheetham's endnotes reveal that the story was inspired by historical documents disclosing both the horrors of the period and the heroism and the courage of some of the people. These books may seem real because the authors allow their contemporary protagonists to experience the problems of another time.

Margaret J. Anderson's characters and settings help readers understand changes that take place over time. Love, understanding, and friendship, even across years, are strong themes in Anderson's stories.

What is the influence on children when they read censored or watered-down materials? Does it affect their college educations? Joan DelFattore[1] identifies some of the possible influences of textbook censorship on college education. She states, "College professors' relative freedom to select and shape course material does not mean that textbook censorship does not affect college education. When students have spent twelve years reading books based more on market forces than on scholarly excellence, they may not come to college prepared to do college-level work. The increasing use of short sentences and simple words—often called 'dumbing down'—in elementary and secondary school textbooks has generated a great deal of print since the mid-1970s, but the watering down of ideas is at least equally dangerous" (p. 9).

In an earlier publication, Mark I. West[2] expands on the idea that censorship may prevent children from obtaining a quality education. He identifies the following five conclusions that he has reached about censorship: (1) The future of education in America rests with the future of public education. (2) Our schools must link the goals of equality and excellence by demanding the best of students. (3) Our schools must do more than convey a set of facts or even a set of basic skills; they must teach young people to think. (4) In order to learn to think, students must have something to think about, which means they should be exposed to scientific theories, literary classics, and the study of history. (5) Education should be governed by standards of excellence, not orthodoxy, timidity, or intolerance.

As you read these comments by DelFattore and West, do you agree or disagree with their concerns? What do you believe are the consequences of watered-down texts and content censorship? Do you believe that either one has influenced your education? If so, what were the influences?

---

[1] DelFattore, Joan. *What Johnny Shouldn't Read: Textbook Censorship in America.* New Haven: Yale University Press, 1992.

[2] West, Mark I. *Trust Your Children: Voices Against Censorship in Children's Literature.* New York: Neal-Schuman, 1988.

Anderson's *In the Keep of Time* takes place in Scotland. Tangible objects have an aura that seems to transcend time, and the ancient Smailholm Tower, a border keep built when Scotland was at war with England, allows children access to the past and future. In this story, a child is touched by a person from another time and a key glows when the moment is right for the children to walk through a door and enter another time period.

Science Fiction

Writers of science fiction rely on hypothesized scientific advancements and imagined technology to create their plots. In order to achieve credibility, they provide detailed descriptions of this technology, portray characters who believe in the technology or the results of the technology, and create a world where science interacts with every area of society. Like other modern fantasies, science fiction relies on an internal consistency among plot, characters, and setting to encourage readers' suspension of disbelief. Science fiction written for young children often emphasizes the adventure associated with traveling to distant galaxies or with encountering unusual aliens. Stories for older readers often hypothesize about the future of humanity and stress problem solving in future societies.

Critics do not agree on the identity of the first science fiction novel. Margaret P. Esmonde (1984) identifies Mary Godwin Shelley's *Frankenstein,* published in 1817, as the earliest science fiction story because the protagonist is a scientist, not a wizard, and the central theme is the proper use of knowledge and the moral responsibility of a scientist for his discovery.

Roland J. Green (1977) traces the emergence of the popularity of science fiction from the mid-1800s through the present explosion of interest. Jules Verne published the first major science fiction novel, *Five Weeks in a Balloon,* in 1863. Verne focused that book and later famous books enjoyed by older children and adults, such as *Twenty-Thousand Leagues Under the Sea,* on technology and invention but did not develop a society around them. Later in the nineteenth century, H. G. Wells began writing science fiction novels, such as *War of the Worlds,* that had a strong influence on the genre. According to Green, the writings of Wells differed from those of Jules Verne in that they included the systematic "extrapolation of social trends to create a detailed picture of a future society, revolutionary inventions, interplanetary warfare, and time travel" (p. 46).

After World War I, as technology advanced at an even faster pace, science fiction writing was influenced by the growth of magazines, such as *Amazing Stories.* John W. Campbell, Jr.'s, editorship of *Astounding Science Fiction,* beginning in 1938, was highly influential. Campbell insisted that the authors of stories he published develop strong characters, plausible science and technology, and logical speculation about future societies. He encouraged such talented science fiction writers as Robert A. Heinlein and Isaac Asimov.

In the 1960s, an increasing number of authors began to write science fiction stories. These stories were more suited to older children and young adults than to young children because the plots often relied on a developed sense of time, place, and space. Science fiction became a topic of interest for university and high-school courses. The media were extremely influential during this period. The movie *2001: A Space Odyssey* and the television program "Star Trek" created a devoted science fiction audience and suggested the imaginative potential of science fiction subjects. In the 1970s and 1980s, audiences flocked to such pictures as *Star Wars* and *E.T.* In the 1990s, the possible cloning of dinosaurs became a debated issue in *Jurassic Park.* Young people today read and reread the paperback versions of these movies.

Many writers are creating high-quality science fiction for young people and are considering responses to future catastrophes or scientific possibilities in their plots. The years following the destruction of modern civilization due to the Flash provide the setting for Caroline Stevermer's *River Rats.* In this story, a group of teenagers crew an old salvaged paddle-wheel steamer on the toxic Mississippi River. Their fight for physical survival is increased after they rescue a man who is being chased because he knows the location of a hoard of weapons. Stevermer pre-

sents a setting filled with ruined cities and the consequences of toxic pollution. The protagonists work together and survive in this desolate environment.

Authors who place their characters in science fiction environments tend to develop strong survival stories in addition to cautionary tales. The future aboard a space freighter is the setting for Annette Curtis Klause's *Alien Secrets.* While en route to the planet where her parents are based, the heroine makes friends with an alien and becomes involved in a mystery that allows her to make discoveries about the alien beings and their culture. Vivid descriptions of the characters and space travel create believable situations and settings. Interactions with aliens also provides the conflict in Neal Shusterman's *The Dark Side of Nowhere* as the protagonist must decide where to place his loyalties.

In *The Giver,* Lois Lowry develops a future in which poverty, inequality, and unemployment have been eliminated. This society, however, is devoid of conscience, emotion, and even color. Accompanying twelve-year-old Jonas as he discovers the truth about his society, readers must ponder and reexamine many of their own beliefs.

Gains in time research form the scientific probability and provide the plot in Robert Silverberg's *Letters from Atlantis.* Possible breakthroughs in time research in the twenty-first century allow a scientist to go back in time to the island of Atlantis by transferring the scientist's mind into the mind of a royal prince who lived in Atlantis. The scientist writes letters to another scientist, who also went back in time, and these letters detail what Atlantis might have been like 180 centuries ago.

In *Invitation to the Game,* Monica Hughes speculates about what might happen in the year 2154 if there is high unemployment, if workers have been replaced by robots, and if teenagers, after graduating from high school, are given permanent unemployed status rather than jobs. This is the predicament of eight teenagers who are relegated to a Designated Area. As they investigate their area, they discover not only the harsh realities of perpetual unemployment but also the mysterious something referred to as "The Game." When they receive an invitation to participate in the game, they experience lifelike computer simulations that place them in unfamiliar settings and give them challenges in which they must work together. The group discovers that each has unique capabilities.

Hughes provides the ultimate answer to unemployment and overcrowding when the members of the group find themselves on a distant planet and realize that they will not be going back to Earth. In a survival story, the members of the group must use the training that they gained during the simulation sessions and their unique skills to work together and to survive. As in her other science fiction books, Hughes considers the consequences of projected contemporary issues and provides at least a glimmer of hope for the future.

Madeleine L'Engle. Do we all need each other? Is every atom in the universe dependent on every other? Questions like these confront Madeleine L'Engle's characters as they travel the cosmos, face the problem of being different, fight to overcome evil, understand the need for all things to mature, and discover the power of love.

It is interesting to note L'Engle's thoughts about herself as she wrote *A Wrinkle in Time:*

I was trying to discover a theology by which I could live, because I had learned that I cannot live in a universe where there's no hope of anything, no hope of there being somebody to whom I could say, "Help!" (p. 254)

In *A Wrinkle in Time,* L'Engle creates characters who are different from the people around them but have high intelligence and strong bonds of love and loyalty to one another. Meg Murry and Charles Wallace are the children of eminent scientists. Meg worries about the way the people in their town make fun of her brother as backward and strange. Her father consoles her by telling her that her brother is doing things in his own way and time. In fact, Charles Wallace has very special powers: He can probe the minds of his mother and sister, and he is also extremely bright.

L'Engle's development of the characters provides a realistic foundation for the science fiction fantasy that follows. The children discover that their scientist father is fighting the "dark thing"—a thing so evil that it could overshadow a planet, block out the stars, and create fear beyond the possibility of comfort. The children travel in the fifth dimension to a far-distant planet, where their father has been imprisoned by the evil power of "It." L'Engle states that this villain is a naked brain because "the brain tends to be vicious when it's not informed by the heart"

(Wintle and Fisher, 1974, p. 254). The heart proves more powerful than the evil It in this story: Meg's ability to love deeply saves her father and Charles.

The battle against evil continues in *A Wind in the Door,* in which Charles appears to be dying. In *A Swiftly Tilting Planet,* readers discover the climactic purpose of Charles's special abilities. L'Engle creates a realistic foundation for the science fiction when fifteen-year-old Charles and his father construct a model of a tesseract, a square squared and then squared again, which is considered the dimension of time. Because Charles and his father can construct the tesseract, readers feel that the story must be true.

Another credible character adds realism to the story: The president of the United States asks for help. Elements of traditional fantasy enter this science fiction story in the form of an ancient rune designed to call the elements of light and hold back evil and a unicorn that aids Charles in a perilous journey. In all of her books, L'Engle emphasizes the mystery and beauty of the cosmos and the necessity of maintaining a natural balance in the order of the universe.

Anne McCaffrey. In Anne McCaffrey's *Dragonsong,* Pern is the third planet of Rukbat, a golden G-type star in the Sagittarian sector. When a wildly erratic bright red star approaches Pern, spore life, which proliferates at an incredible rate on the red star's surface, spins into space and falls in thin threads toward Pern's hospitable earth. The spore life is not hospitable to life on Pern, however. In order to counteract this menace, the colonists enlist a life form indigenous to the planet. These creatures, called dragons, have two remarkable characteristics: (1) they can travel instantly from place to place by teleportation and (2) they can emit flaming gas when they chew phosphine-bearing rock. When guided by dragonriders, they can destroy the spore before it reaches the planet.

In this setting, a young girl fights for her dream to become a harpist. Because her father believes that such a desire is disgraceful for a female and forbids her to play her music, Menolly runs away and makes friends with the dragons. After a series of adventures in both *Dragonsong* and *Dragonsinger,* Menolly learns that she need no longer hide her skill or fear her ambitions:

The Search for Truth

Recipient of the Newbery Medal
and the Louis Caroll Shelf
Award, MADELEINE L'ENGLE
discusses stories as vehicles of
truth and scientific theories in
science fiction.

Long ago when I was just learning to read, and the world was (as usual) tottering on the brink of war, I discovered that if I wanted to look for the truth of what was happening around me, and if I wanted to know what made the people tick who made the events I couldn't control, the place to look for that truth was in story. Facts simply told me what things were. Story told me what they were about, and sometimes even what they meant. It never occurred to me then, when I was little, nor does it now, that story is more appropriate for children than for adults. It is still, for me, the vehicle of truth.

As for writing stories for children, whether it's fantasy or "slice-of-life" stories, most people are adults by the time they get published. And most of us adults who are professional writers are writing for ourselves, out of our own needs, our own search for truth. If we aren't, we're writing down to children, and that is serving neither children, nor truth.

I'm sometimes asked, by both children and their elders, why I've written approximately half of my books for children, and I reply honestly that I've never written a book for children in my life, nor would I ever insult a child by doing so. The world is even more confused now than it was when I first discovered story as medium for meaning, and story is still, for me, the best way to make sense out of what is happening, to see "cosmos in chaos" (as Leonard Bernstein said). It is still the best way to keep hope alive, rather than giving in to suicidal pessimism.

Books of fantasy and science fiction, in particular, are books in which the writer can express a vision, in most cases vision of hope. A writer of fantasy usually looks at the seeming meaninglessness in what is happening on this planet, and says, "No, I won't accept that. There has got to be some meaning, some shape and pattern in all of this," and then looks to story for the discovery of that shape and pattern.

In my own fantasies I am very excited by some of the new sciences; in *A Wrinkle in Time* it is Einstein's theories of relativity, and Planck's Quantum theory; tesseract is a real word, and the theory of tessering is not as far fetched as at first it might seem. If anyone had asked my grandfather if we'd ever break the sound barrier, he'd have said, "Of course not." People are now saying "Of course not" about the light barrier, but, just as we've broken the sound barrier, so, one day, we'll break the light barrier, and then we'll be freed from the restrictions of time. We will be able to tesser.

In *A Wind in the Door*, I turn from the macrocosm to the microcosm, the world of the cellular biologist. Yes, indeed, there are mitochondria, and they live within us; they have their own DNA, and we are their host planet. And they are as much smaller than we are as galaxies are larger than we are. How can we—child or adult—understand this except in story?

Concepts which are too difficult for adults are open to children, who are not yet afraid of new ideas, who don't mind having the boat rocked, or new doors opened, or mixing metaphors! That is one very solid reason my science fiction/fantasy books are marketed for children; only children are open enough to understand them. Let's never underestimate the capacity of the child for a wide and glorious imagination, an ability to accept what is going on in our troubled world, and the courage to endure it with courage, and respond to it with a realistic hope.

The last vestige of anxiety lifted from Menolly's mind. As a journeyman in blue, she had rank and status enough to fear no one and nothing. No need to run or hide. She'd a place to fill and a craft that was unique to her. She'd come a long, long way in a sevenday. (*Dragonsinger,* p. 264)

Nancy Farmer. The year is 2194; the location is Harare, Zimbabwe. By analyzing the 1995 Newbery Honor book, Nancy Farmer's *The Ear, the Eye and the Arm,* you will discover several of the themes frequently developed in science fiction: Toxic contamination can change lives, the world of the future may be influenced by technology, and some members of the society search for their traditional heritage. The three main characters have unique characteristics that make them ideal detectives. Arm has a long snaky arm that can outreach all other arms. Ear has extremely sensitive hearing, and Eye has excellent vision. These detectives use their unique abilities to search for the three kidnapped children of the general.

In addition to unusual characters, the text includes both technology and mythology. For example, an automatic doberman guards the mansion, robot gardeners clip the grass, and a programmed pantry prepares the food. The author also uses ancient customs and references to mythology to create a credible history for the country. The author develops two quite different settings. One is the toxic dump where outcasts live. This setting is developed in the first half of the book when the children are kidnapped and forced to work in the mines by digging out refuse that can be sold. Resthaven, a compound in which people live by the ancient rules and customs, is developed in the second half of the book when the children are brought into the compound. In the compound they learn not only about the history of their country but also what it is like to live under separate roles and rules for males and females, to believe in superstitions such as witchcraft, and to live without modern medical knowledge. As in all good science fiction, the author provides detailed descriptions for her futuristic environment.

John Christopher. The future world that John Christopher envisions in *The White Mountains* is quite different from the world hoped for by people today. In Christopher's future, people have lost free will, and machines called Tripods have taken over. These machines maintain control through a capping

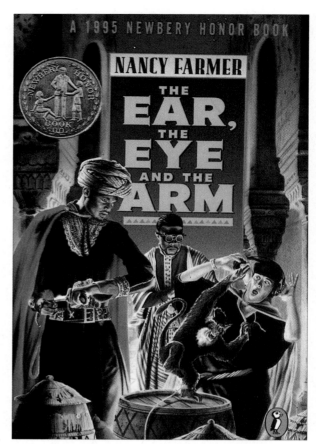

Toxic contamination in a future world changes lives in Nancy Farmer's The Ear, the Eye and the Arm. *(Illustration from* The Ear, the Eye and the Arm *by Nancy Farmer, copyright © 1995. Puffin Books. Used by permission of Penguin Books.)*

ceremony that places a steel plate on the skull, making the wearer docile and obedient. Fourteen-year-old Will Parker, who is angered by the prospect of an inescapable voice inside his head, discovers that a colony of free people lives in the White Mountains, which are far to the south. Will escapes with two other young people, but the Tripods follow them. Will discovers that freedom and hope are the most important luxuries in life.

In *The City of Gold and Lead* and *The Pool of Fire,* the free humans plan battle against the Tripods and then defeat them. Yet, quarreling factions defeat Will's attempts to plan for new unity among the victorious humans. Christopher's stories are exciting, but they are also sober reminders of what can happen if humanity allows itself to lose free will.

SUGGESTED ACTIVITIES

for Adult Understanding of Modern Fantasy

■ Read Hans Christian Andersen's "The Wild Swans." Compare the plot, characterizations, and setting with the Grimms's "The Six Swans." What are the similarities and differences?

■ Read Gail Carson Levine's *Ella Enchanted* and analyze the author's use of Cinderella elements.

■ Choose a book written from the point of view of someone who is different from a normal person. What techniques does the author use to encourage readers to suspend disbelief?

■ Discuss C. S. Lewis's "The Chronicles of Narnia" with another adult who has read the books and with a child who has read them. What are the differences, if any, in the interpretations of the two people?

■ After reading J. R. R. Tolkien's *The Hobbit* or *The Lord of the Rings,* identify common elements and symbols in Tolkien's work and mythology. Consider the use of fate, subterranean descents, denial of death, mortals and immortals, supernatural beings, and power granted to objects.

■ Authors who write believably about articulate animals balance reality and fantasy by allowing the animals to talk but still retain some animal characteristics. Choose an animal character such as Beatrix Potter's Peter Rabbit, Little Georgie from Robert Lawson's *Rabbit Hill,* or Mole from Kenneth Grahame's *The Wind in the Willows.* What human characteristics can you identify? What animal characteristics can you identify? Has the author developed a credible character? Why or why not?

■ This text discusses Susan Cooper's use of English, Celtic, and Welsh legends and myths in her fantasies. After reading Pat O'Shea's *The Hounds of the Morrigan,* investigate and identify elements from Irish legends and myths.

■ Use the database to prepare a list of suitable fiction to support a middle school unit on astronomy. Describe how you might use one or more of the books on this list to promote creative writing and critical thinking skills.

■ A sixth-grade boy who is having trouble reading expresses an interest in books about robots. Use the database to prepare a list of appropriate books for this student.

■ Your middle school class is creating a map of an imaginary world. Prepare a list of books that will help them with this task.

Involving Children in Modern Fantasy

You can extend the magic that children gain from modern fantasy by providing varied opportunities to interact with the plots, characters, and settings of such stories. Thus, you should give children opportunities to understand elements in fantasy, interpret modern fantasy through art, develop a fantasy interest center, and make connections between science and science fiction and between social studies and science fiction.

HELPING CHILDREN RECOGNIZE, UNDERSTAND, AND ENJOY ELEMENTS IN FANTASY

Fantasy is a worthy genre of literature for all children. It challenges the intellect, reveals insights, stimulates the imagination, and nurtures the affective domain. However, many children have difficulty comprehending modern fantasy. Unlike realistic fiction, which mirrors a more or less real world, modern fantasy presents an altered picture. One of the first ways to help children understand and appreciate modern fantasy is to read several fantasy selections and encourage the students to identify and discuss what makes each story modern fantasy. The following questions address the altered literary elements in the stories (Norton, 1992):

1. How has the author manipulated or altered the literary elements so that the story takes place in a world other than the real world of today?
2. What is the evidence that the setting has been altered? How was the setting altered? How does this setting differ from the real world? (The author does not need to alter all of these elements.)
3. What is the evidence that the characters are different from characters living in the real world? How are the characters altered? How do these characters differ from characters that you know in the real world?
4. What is the evidence that time has been altered? How was time altered? How is this experience with time different from experiences with time in the real world?
5. How did the author suspend disbelief and encourage readers to believe in the fanciful experience?

Again, be sure to remind students that they will not find all of these altered elements in every piece of modern fantasy.

Books that vividly describe settings encourage children to visualize the settings, respond to the language, and understand why authors must select words carefully to set the stage for their books. One of the ways to help students recognize the importance of setting in fantasy is to ask them to close their eyes and to listen to a passage (Norton, 1992). As they listen to the passage, have them try to visualize the setting and then describe what they see.

Numerous books have vivid paragraphs that can be used for visualization and discussion. In *The Wish Giver*, Bill Brittain uses rich and colorful imagery to create a memorable story. Fantasies in picture-book format written for younger children are also excellent selections for this type of activity. For example, have children visualize and describe the settings and the personified characters in Virginia Lee Burton's *The Little House*, Munro Leaf's *The Story of Ferdinand*, and Leo Lionni's *Swimmy*. Pointing out the author's use of similes and metaphors helps students understand the story.

Authors often enrich their fantasies with allegory, irony, figurative language, and traditional elements. Such elements may increase the appreciation of the stories for gifted children but cause confusion for less able readers. Susan Swanton's (1984) survey of the literary choices of gifted students supports this contention. Gifted students indicated that they liked science fiction and fantasy because of the challenges presented. While almost half of the books preferred by gifted students were classified as modern fantasy (29 percent science fiction, 18 percent other fantasy), none of the top choices of other students were similarly classified. Because modern fantasy can be pleasurable for all readers, the difference in the reading preferences is unfortunate.

With detailed illustrations and simple plots, picture books can help children understand the more complex elements found in modern fantasy. Picture books can stimulate discussion, illuminate meanings, and form bridges between illusion and understanding. Chart 7–1 identifies elements in modern fantasy and selections that develop and illustrate the elements. The picture books include both modern fantasy and traditional tales (see the Children's Literature for chapter 6 for the traditional tales). Have the children read and discuss the picture books in each category before they read and discuss the fantasy. After children can recognize the literary elements in picture books, they find it easier to identify similar elements in fantasy selections.

For example, illustrated fables with animal characters who talk, behave like humans, and possess human traits provide excellent examples of allegory. A background in fables can help older children answer the following questions after they read W. J. Corbett's *The Song of Pentecost:* What does the title mean? Why is the leader of the mice named Pentecost? What allegorical implications are found in the author's characterizations, settings, problems, resolutions of problems, and morals?

Each of the other picture books in Chart 7–1 illustrates an important element in fantasy. For example, Hugh Lewin's highly illustrated *Jafta* and *Jafta's Mother* are excellent sources for figurative language. Lewin describes and illustrates Jafta's feelings by comparing them to the feelings and actions of animals in Jafta's African environment. The double-spread illustrations show both the boy and the particular animal demonstrating such actions as skipping (like a spider), stamping (like an elephant), and grumbling (like a warthog). In the modern fantasy *The Wish Giver*, Bill Brittain also uses figurative language to suggest character traits and to enhance the rural setting.

CHART 7–1 Books for helping children understand modern fantasy

Elements	Picture Books	Modern Fantasy
Allegory	Holder's *Aesop's Fables* Lobel's *Fables*	Lewis's "Chronicles of Narnia"
Irony	Gage's *Cully, Cully and the Bear*	Brittain's *The Wish Giver*
Figurative language	Lewin's *Jafta* and *Jafta's Mother*	Brittain's *The Wish Giver* and *Dr. Dredd's Wagon of Wonders*

Folklore elements
  Power in tangible objects
  A quest
 	
  Magical powers
 	
  Transformations
 	
  Punishment for misused ability
	Marshak's *The Month Brothers*
	Severo's *The Good-Hearted Youngest Brother*
	Hodges's *Saint George and the Dragon*
	Grimms's *The Devil with the Three Golden Hairs*
	Andersen's *The Wild Swans*
	Williams's *The Velveteen Rabbit*
	Van Allsburg's *The Wreck of the Zephyr*
		Lunn's *The Root Cellar*
		Cooper's *Seaward*
		
		McKinley's *The Hero and the Crown*
		McKinley's *The Blue Sword*
		
		Cooper's *Seaward*
		Brittain's *The Wish Giver*

Older students may discover the mythological and legendary foundations of Tolkien's modern fantasy by tracing the important motifs in J. R. R. Tolkien's *The Hobbit* back to Norse myths and legends. Have older students identify the elements and motifs in Padraic Colum's *The Children of Odin,* Kevin Crossley-Holland's *The Faber Book of Northern Legends* and *The Norse Myths,* and Michael Harrison's *The Curse of the Ring.* Children who identify the important motifs in Colum's *The Children of Odin* will discover a constant battle between forces of good and evil for the control of humanity. Children also will discover that the remote past is considered a golden age, that there is a magical significance for runes, that the ring is a symbol of power, that a dragon must be slain, that promises are contracts to be kept, that fate governs the lives of all beings, that tricksters may help or hinder, and that heroes frequently make personal sacrifices for common good. (See also chapter 6.)

In addition to identifying the important motifs in *The Children of Odin,* ask older students to identify quotes that show these elements. For example, following are a few of the quotes showing that Norse mythology includes a constant battle between good and evil: "Always there had been war between the Giants and the Gods—between the Giants who would have destroyed the world and the Gods who would have protected the race of men and would have made the world more beautiful" (p. 6), the dwarf Brock's bargain with Loki was an evil bargain and "all its evil consequences you must bear" (p. 42), and "East of Midgard there was a place more evil than any region in Jotunheim. It was Jarnid, the Iron Wood. There dwelt witches who were the most foul of all witches. The son of the most evil witch would be the wolf who would swallow up the Moon and stain the heavens and earth with blood" (p. 168).

After Norse mythology, have the students identify similar elements in *The Hobbit* and provide evidence for those elements. The following examples show the battle between good and evil in *The Hobbit:* The evil goblins battle against the good dwarfs, Bilbo verbally battles against the Gollum, the evil forces lie to the east, evil wolves threaten the dwarfs, Bilbo battles against the dragon Smaug, evil Smaug battles the Lake Men, and the battle of the Five Armies has good and evil forces.

 ## INTERPRETING MODERN FANTASY THROUGH ART

The strange and curious worlds, imaginary kingdoms, animal fantasy, and preposterous situations found in modern fantasy lend themselves to artistic discussions of illustrated books, comparisons of illustrated books, and artistic interpretations created by children.

Responding to Illustrated Books

Numerous highly illustrated fantasy selections provide opportunities for children to respond to the illustrations, compare different illustrations of the same story, and critically evaluate why they like or do not like certain versions. John Warren Stewig (1993) states, "The ability to receive, process, reflect on, and respond to pictures is a critical but often overlooked aspect of children's response to literature" (p. 35). Stewig suggests giving children opportunities to observe, compare, and talk about the different illustrations. Stewig recommends a three-stage process, in which children describe, compare, and value. During the describing experience, have the children describe what is happening in the illustrations and how the artists present the story. While comparing, have the children consider how different artists approach the same point in the story—for example, the number of characters portrayed, the location of the action, and the background detail. Finally, in the valuing part of the process, have the children decide which of the versions they prefer and why. Stewig states that why is critical because "it is more important that children articulate their reasons than that they make a particular aesthetic choice. Children develop more effective speaking and writing techniques when they are engaged in this kind of critical thinking strategy" (p. 35).

For example, if choosing "The Emperor's New Clothes," Stewig recommends describing, comparing, and valuing the following books because the illustrations are quite different: *The Emperor's New Clothes,* retold by Riki Levison and illustrated by Robert Byrd; *The Emperor's New Clothes,* illustrated by Janet Stevens; *The Emperor's New Clothes,* illustrated by Dorothee Duntz; and *The Principal's New Clothes,* adapted by Stephanie Calmenson and illustrated by Denise Brunkus. Another choice might be *The Emperor's New Clothes,* illustrated by S. T. Mendelson. Because there are numerous illustrated versions of various Hans Christian Andersen tales, this activity may accompany other tales.

Also let children extend their appreciation of a fantasy selection through various art activities. Note, however, that art should allow children to expand their enjoyment of a story through self-expression; it should not be forced following the reading of every story.

Modern fantasy selections that can stimulate artistic interpretations range from books for preschool children through books appropriate for upper-elementary and middle-school children. You can explore a wide variety of art media in relation to modern fantasy selections, as well as to other literary genres.

Murals and Friezes

Mural and frieze interpretations of literature encourage children to work in a group in order to create a large picture. A mural is usually made by designing and creating a picture on a long piece of paper placed on the floor or long tables so that children can work together on it. A frieze is similar to a mural, but it consists of a long narrow border or band of paper.

The children can observe and "read" wordless books that look like murals to stimulate possible ideas. For example, if the illustrations for David Wiesner's wordless fantasy *Free Fall* were laid side by side, the results would be a mural depicting a young boy's dream.

Have the children plan the content of a mural and decide the responsibilities of each individual. Let the children create drawings on the mural with paints, chalk, or crayons. Finally, let the children add objects cut out of construction paper on top of background paintings. Place the finished mural on a large bulletin board or whole sections of a wall or hallway. Murals can depict one setting suggested by a book or can be divided into segments to illustrate different parts of a story.

Stories with vivid settings are enjoyable sources of mural subjects for young children. Beatrix Potter's *The Tale of Squirrel Nutkin* contains a descrip-
tion of the island in the middle of the lake where the squirrels go to gather nuts. Children have created murals showing a large lake surrounded by a woods, with a tree-covered island in the center. The largest tree is the hollow oak tree, the old brown owl's home. Because the story takes place in the autumn, have children create trees and bushes covered with shades of red, gold, and orange. On the lake, have them paint squirrels sailing toward the island on rafts. One group of children gathered real acorns, autumn leaves, and twigs to add to the mural. Other stories that suggest scenic murals include scenes in the hundred-acre wood in A. A. Milne's *Winnie-the-Pooh;* the river world of Mole, the Wild Wood, and Toad's home at Toad Hall in Kenneth Grahame's *The Wind in the Willows;* and the barnyard world of E. B. White's *Charlotte's Web.*

Children have also drawn in large mural format to show the travels of various characters in stories. They have illustrated Little Georgie's journey as he travels across the countryside in search of Uncle Analdas's home in chapters three and four of Robert Lawson's *Rabbit Hill.* Little Georgie travels to the Twin Bridges, walks briskly down the Hill, moves quietly past the home of the Dogs of the Fat-Man-at-the-Crossroads, runs happily across the High Ridge, leaps over Deadman's Brook, and eventually finds Uncle Analdas's disorderly burrow. Children may also create murals to contrast the city and rural settings found in Ursula K. LeGuin's *Catwings* and *Catwings Return.*

An illustration of an actual frieze of richly carved people and animals that decorated Greek architecture often interests children and helps them create their own friezes depicting the important characters and events in a story. After reading Carl Sandburg's *Rootabaga Stories,* one group of children created a humorous frieze. They showed the train and its occupants traveling toward Rootabaga Country through the land of Over and Under, the country of balloon pickers, and the country of circus clowns; the tracks running in zigzags in the land where pigs wear bibs; and the final destination of the village of Liver and Onions. The characters and their adventures found in J. R. R. Tolkien's *The Hobbit* and Lloyd Alexander's Prydain chronicles are fine inspirations for other friezes by older children.

Collages, Montages, and Mosaics

Three types of art involve gluing other materials onto flat surfaces. All three are also enjoyable ways to interpret literature. A collage is a picture made by pasting different shapes and textures of materials onto a surface (see Figure 7–1). Collect many materials—including newspapers, lace paper doilies, velvet, burlap, felt, satin, yarn, aluminum foil, rope, buttons, toothpicks, twigs, bark, corrugated paper, tissue paper, and paints—so that children have many things to choose from to achieve the effects that they desire when they are creating collages.

Young children like working with texture and then feeling the results of the different materials on their collages. Beatrix Potter's *The Tale of Peter Rabbit* is an excellent inspiration for collage interpretations. Some young children created Peter by cutting a jacket out of material and shoes out of construction paper and then adding a cotton-ball tail and string whiskers. They portrayed him in a gooseberry net made from string and had him peering forlornly at a scarecrow complete with brass-buttoned jacket, hanging shoes, and three-dimensional lettuce plants. Russell Erickson's various Warton the Toad books, Roald Dahl's *James and the Giant Peach,* Brian Jacques's various books about the animals of Redwall, and Keith Baker's *The Magic Fan* are other excellent inspirations for collage.

A montage is a composite created by bringing together into a single composition a number of different pictures or parts of pictures and arranging them to form a blended whole. Have children create a montage by cutting pictures from magazines or other sources and then mounting them so that the surfaces overlap. The pictures and their arrangement may suggest feelings, themes, moods, or concepts. Further, the pictures may be concrete or abstract in nature. Montage may be the first art form some children experience that is not necessarily realistic. Through montage, however, children find that they can select and rearrange pictures and parts of pictures to express their feelings.

E. B. White's *Charlotte's Web* has stimulated the creation of montage. Throughout the book, Templeton the rat is portrayed as an animal who "had a habit of picking up unusual objects around the farm and storing them in his home" (p. 45). He collected food scraps: part of a ham sandwich, a chunk of Swiss cheese, and a wormy apple core. Have chil-

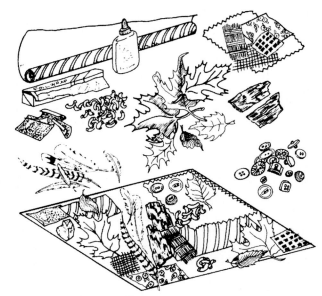

FIGURE 7–1 *Collage*

dren develop a montage that suggests the essence of the material objects that Templeton prizes.

After reading Ian Fleming's *Chitty Chitty Bang Bang,* children created a montage of antique cars and a candy factory. Older children have created more complex themes. They have used the montage process to suggest the battles between good and evil in J. R. R. Tolkien's *The Hobbit* and *The Lord of the Rings* and in Lloyd Alexander's Prydain chronicles. They have created montages of symbols representing past, present, and future inspired by the time-warp fantasies of Margaret J. Anderson and others. They have used montage to create worlds of friendly ghosts, such as those found in Lucy Boston's *The Children of Green Knowe,* and of less benevolent spirits, such as Mollie Hunter's *The Wicked One.*

A mosaic is a design or picture that results from gluing small objects of different colors onto a surface. Have children select a favorite character from literature; draw the character on a surface of heavy paper, cardboard, or wood; select appropriate small objects to fill in the lines—such as seeds, stones, or small bits of paper; place glue inside the shape; and then attach the objects to the surface. Have them fill in the background with color or drawings if they wish. Favorite characters for this activity include Margery Williams's *The Velveteen Rabbit,* A. A. Milne's characters in *Winnie-the-Pooh,* and Lewis Carroll's characters in *Alice's Adventures in Wonderland.*

Shadowboxes

Many stories lend themselves to miniature recreations of settings inside boxes or framed on shelves. Stories about small people or dolls, such as Mary Norton's *The Borrowers* or Rumer Godden's *The Dolls' House* are obvious sources of inspiration for such shadowboxes. Children of many ages, and adults as well, are often fascinated by miniatures.

Children enjoy collecting small items around their own homes, such as spools, thimbles, bottle caps, and boxes, and then turning them into furniture for Norton's Clock family. After reading *The Dolls' House,* children may wish to learn more about the elegant dollhouse described in the book and then to choose and recreate a favorite room from the house. Robert O'Brien's *Mrs. Frisby and the Rats of NIMH* can inspire children to recreate the inside of the laboratory, the rats' new colony in Thorn Valley, and other scenes. The strange and curious world of Lewis Carroll's *Alice's Adventures in Wonderland* provides many exciting scenes, such as Alice's tea party with the Mad Hatter. James Barrie's Never Land in *Peter Pan* provides other rewarding subjects, including the Darling children's nursery and Captain Hook's ship.

The preceding settings are merely suggestive of the many settings that you can use to stimulate artwork. For many children, art interpretation allows interaction with favorite characters in new ways. As suggested earlier, however, children do not need to interpret all of their reading with art projects. For young children, art should be an enjoyable extension of a story, not a general assignment. Classrooms and homes that provide rich backgrounds of art materials encourage children to create interpretations of their favorite storybook settings and characters.

 DEVELOPING A FANTASY INTEREST CENTER: A MODERN FANTASY WEB

University students in children's literature classes can use the webbing process suggested by Donna Norton (1977) to identify topics related to a central theme or subject, identify children's books related to the topic, and then develop activities that stimulate children to interact with the characters and situations in these books. One group chose this technique to help formulate and develop a children's literature interest center for the middle-elementary grades around the central subject "Imagine That."

After choosing their subject, the university students identified six major categories of modern fantasy that would be appropriate for their "Imagine That" theme. Next, they identified children's modern fantasy selections suitable for each category. In order to satisfy the interests and reading needs of different students, they identified books on several different reading levels that, like *Pinocchio,* had been published in various versions with different levels of reading difficulty. Following a search of the literature, the university students completed a literature web by identifying the books that they would use (see Figure 7–2).

With these books in hand and the web developed, the group divided its responsibilities. Each student wrote motivational paragraphs to introduce the books, to captivate children's interests, and to encourage the children to read the books. Next, the students developed four or five different activities to encourage children to interact with each book, including art interpretations, creative dramatizations, oral discussions, and creative writings. The students shared their paragraphs and activities in order to receive feedback from each group member. They placed the motivational paragraphs and directions for the suggested activities on large cards and put them into an attractive fantasy-land interest center complete with the books, necessary materials, and room to display the completed activities. Examples of motivational paragraphs and book-related activities developed around three of the six categories in the literature web of interest are shown in Figure 7–3.

Because several students were student teaching at the time, these student teachers placed an interest center in each of their classrooms and shared it with children. The students who developed and used the literature interest centers with children found that other children in a class wanted to read books because of the interest that the center generated. The student teachers led or motivated some activities, while the children did others independently.

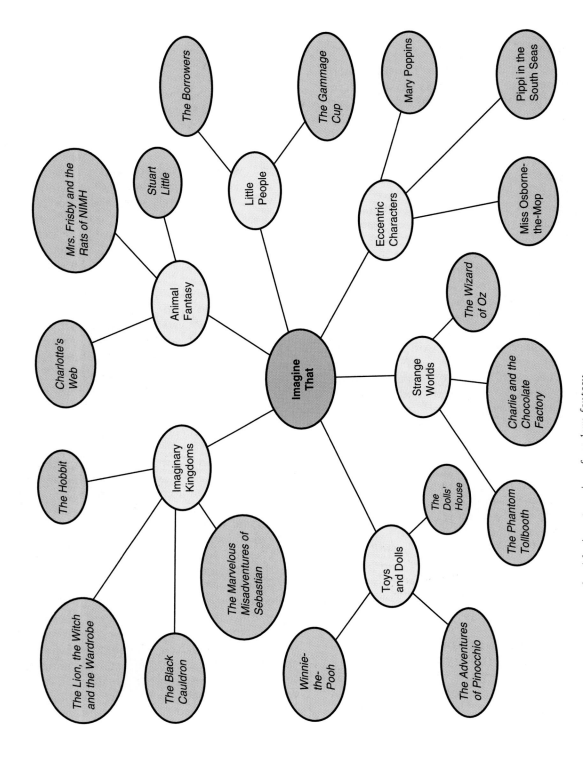

FIGURE 7–2   A literature web with six categories of modern fantasy

IMAGINARY KINGDOMS

> **The Lion, the Witch and the Wardrobe by C. S. Lewis.**
> It's true! A wardrobe leads to another land called Narnia, a land where it always snows but it's never Christmas. Peter, Susan, Edmund, and Lucy discover Narnia and must help break the wicked Snow Queen's spell. The centaurs, beavers, unicorns, and talking horses depend on the Pevensie children and on Aslan, the noble lion.

EXAMPLES OF ACTIVITIES

> Pretend you are Edmund's shadow. You are right there with him in all his adventures. You hear what he says and you know how he feels. Write a character sketch about Edmund from the viewpoint of his shadow. Include the things he does and why you, his shadow, think he does them. How and why does Edmund change? How do you feel about being his shadow? What would you say if you could talk?

> With a group of classmates who have read this book, act out "what happened about the statues" for the rest of the class. Refer to Chapter 16 for this exciting adventure.

> Choose your favorite part in *The Lion, the Witch and the Wardrobe* (about three pages). Practice reading it; when you are ready, record your selection. Following your recording, tell why this was your favorite part in the book. After everyone is finished, we will all listen to the tapes of *The Lion, the Witch and the Wardrobe.*

> Create and construct a box movie using ten scenes in proper sequence from *The Lion, the Witch and the Wardrobe.* Write an accompanying script to narrate the movie. Present your movie to the class.

ANIMAL FANTASY

> **Mrs. Frisby and the Rats of NIMH by Robert O'Brien**
> "You must go, Mrs. Frisby," said the owl, "to the rats under the rosebush. They are not, I think like other rats."
> The rats under the rosebush are *not* like other rats. Mrs. Frisby, a mouse, did go to the rats for help, and she did discover their secret. Mrs. Frisby found rats that could read, use machines, and plan a self-supporting rat society. She also found rats that were in great danger. Could tiny Mrs. Frisby help them? Read the book and find out for yourself.

EXAMPLES OF ACTIVITIES

> The publisher is searching high and low—it doesn't know what to do. The public is going wild and wants a sequel to *Mrs. Frisby and the Rats of NIMH.* Please help this publisher. Write to the publisher, and tell the editor why you should write *Mrs. Fribsy and the Rats of NIMH, Part II.* In your letter tell what you would include in your story. (Compare your ideas with Jane Leslie Conly's *Racso and the Rats of NIMH.*)

> Choose a friend who has read *Charlotte's Web.* Pretend that you are Nicodemus and your friend is Charlotte. Have a conversation in which you tell each other what it is like to live the life of a rat or a spider. Tell about your best friends, your adventures, and the advantages and disadvantages of being the kind of creature you are. During your conversation, tell each other why you think humans dislike spiders and rats.

> Pretend that you are a mouse or a rat. Somehow you have found your way into Ms. *(teacher's name)*'s classroom. You have never seen anything like it. Write about your adventures as you journey through the classroom and meet the people or objects in the room.

STRANGE WORLDS

> **The Phantom Tollbooth by Norton Juster**
> Inside the mysterious package that Milo found in his room was what looked like a genuine turnpike tollbooth. But Milo was in for an even bigger surprise when he drove his small electric car through the tollbooth gate. Suddenly, he found himself in The Lands Beyond, the enchanted home of some of the craziest creatures ever imagined. As Milo traveled through this confusing world, he was joined by an ill-mannered little Humbug and a ticking watchfob named Tock. The three characters found themselves drawn into a chain of adventures that led them closer and closer to the forbidden Mountains of Ignorance and black-hearted demons that awaited them there.

EXAMPLES OF ACTIVITIES

> Pretend that you are Milo: you just can't believe that you have found The Lands Beyond. You don't want to forget this crazy world that is so different from the one that you know. There must be a way to record your adventures. You decide to keep a diary. Write seven entries in your diary telling about different adventures in the enchanted and confusing world of The Lands Beyond. In your final entry, include any important lessons that you have learned. Bind your entries together and design a cover for your diary.

> Choose a friend who has also read *The Phantom Tollbooth* and together prepare a debate to present to the class. One of you is a faithful citizen of Dictionopolis and the other is from Digitopolis. Each of you must try to convince the class that your kingdom is better. Tell the class about the advantages of living where you live and the disadvantages of living in the other place. Defend your own kingdom so that your classmates will choose to live there.

FIGURE 7–3 *Motivational paragraphs and activities for three categories of modern fantasy*

INVOLVING CHILDREN WITH SCIENCE FICTION

Science fiction stories have inspired children to become scientists and writers. Scientist Carl Sagan (1980), of the popular "Cosmos" television series, credits the science fiction stories of H. G. Wells with stimulating his boyhood dreams of flying to the moon and Mars and with eventually leading him to become an astronomer. Robert Goddard, the inventor of modern rocketry, read *War of the Worlds* by Wells. Stories about the space traveler Buck Rogers influenced George Lucas, the creator of the movies *Star Wars* and *The Empire Strikes Back*. Science fiction provides enjoyment but it can also stimulate interaction between science fiction and science or social studies.

Interaction Between Science and Science Fiction

Many science fiction books are based on scientific principles and can be used as springboards for discussions involving creative thinking, critical thinking, and reinforcement of scientific facts. Children can sharpen their research skills by verifying scientific information in fantasies. Children also can enhance their appreciation and evaluation of settings in science fiction by discussing various books. Interaction between science and science fiction is highly motivating for gifted and talented students.

Several children's literature students and upper-elementary and middle-school teachers have developed activities that stress interaction between the science curriculum and science fiction. One class of teachers divided into small groups, each of which chose the study of astronomy; the human body; inventions; or changes in nature, including environmental problems, weather, ecosystems, or time. Next, the groups identified science fiction books to share orally with children or to display in the library for children to read independently. Then, the groups investigated the science curriculum and discovered science-related materials, scientific principles, and topics in current science magazines to stimulate interest in upper-elementary students. Finally, the groups shared their activities with children. Chart 7–2 contains examples of books, discussion topics, and related activities that proved rewarding.

Interdisciplinary Studies: Interaction Between Social Studies and Science Fiction

Science fiction relates to not only scientific principles and technology but also the possible impacts of technological changes, such as mechanization, space travel, and life on other planets, upon people and societies. Because science fiction is of high interest to many upper-elementary students, you can use it to help relate activities to meet the following four motivational recommendations for social studies recommended by John P. Lunstrum and Bob L. Taylor (1978):

1. Use materials and approaches that are responsive to and built on student interests.
2. Design and/or use strategies that demonstrate the relevance of the reading task in social studies, focusing on the study and discussion of controversy and the clarification of values.
3. Help students who have negative attitudes toward reading in the social studies and little confidence in their ability to experience success in this area.
4. Encourage students to use language activities, such as role-playing games and listening more effectively. Arouse curiosity about the communication process, of which reading is an integral part, and develop interpersonal communication skills. (p. 21)

Using science fiction in social studies classrooms allows students to understand and discuss broad themes like the nature of government, the merits of different types of social organization, and cultural differences. Science fiction can stimulate debate that is unhindered by children's stereotypes. Science fiction also encourages children to acquire a sense of the relationship between cause and effect, and in so doing, children can begin to grasp the sweep of history that is important to any study of social studies.

Many science fiction books lend themselves to debates on issues related to society and social studies. Classroom teachers have successfully used the issues and books in Chart 7–3 to motivate children to consider different viewpoints during social studies classes.

Because science fiction stories often describe futuristic cities on earth or other inhabited planets, they can inspire children to create their own model

CHART 7–2 Books, discussion topics, and activities relating to science and science fiction

Astronomy and Science Fiction	Changes in Natural Events or Environments That Could Affect the Future of Earth or Another Planet	Influences of Inventions, Machines, and Computers

Science Fiction to Share with Children

1 Cameron, Eleanor. *The Wonderful Flight to the Mushroom Planet.* With the help of a friend, two boys construct a spaceship and travel to a strange planet.

2 Lawrence, Louise. *Dream-Weaver.* A spaceship from earth is carrying colonists to a distant planet.

(See chapter 12 for nonfiction books about planets and space flights.)

Discussion Topics and Related Activities

1 Have the children discuss the possibility of living in a space colony. How would colonists control their environment? How would they communicate with other colonies? How would they travel between colonies? During the discussions, encourage the children to let their imaginations soar. Also, have them consider scientific principles and the ways authors of science fiction stories solve these problems. Discuss films and television programs as well.

2 Because many science fiction stories take place on other planets, have the children consider the possibilities of discovering a new planet. Share excerpts from nonfictional books that discuss searching for new planets.

3 Use the discussion on astronomers' searching for new planets to lead to a discussion about NASA's 430-foot-long orbiting space telescope.

4 Use the latest discoveries about the characteristics of other planets and the sun, as discovered by the *Voyager 1* and *2* explorations of the solar system and orbiting telescope, to stimulate discussions about science fiction and about how these characteristics would affect possible life on the planets or the development of space colonies.

Science Fiction to Share with Children

1 Doyle, Arthur Conan. *The Lost World.* People on earth discover a lost land in which prehistoric animals still live.

2 Hamilton, Virginia. *Dustland.* The air in a future earth time supports only dust and mutant animals and humans.

3 McCaffrey, Anne. *Dragonsong, Dragonsinger,* and *Dragonquest.* Colonists on Pern create a life form to destroy the spore life that invades the planet and has the ability to destroy all living matter.

Discussion Topics and Related Activities

1 Have the children discuss what could happen on earth if prehistoric animals were discovered and then began to multiply rapidly. Have the children consider competition for food, the eating habits of various prehistoric animals, conditions necessary for rapid reproduction, and possible consequences for plants, smaller animals, and human life. Also, have the children consider what could happen if species that are now considered endangered were to multiply rapidly. What changes in the environment might account for the reversal? What would be the consequences for other life?

2 Several science fiction books develop plots around consequences of changes in the earth because of pollution and overpopulation. Have the children develop discussions and writings around nonfictional books on pollution and overpopulation.

3 Have the children consider various environmental problems on earth today or problems that could develop due to litter from disabled space ships or other space-traveling vehicles, such as *Voyager 1.* Through discussions, have the children try to predict and provide various solutions to these problems.

Science Fiction to Share with Children

1 Christopher, John. *The White Mountains.* A futuristic mechanized society forms the setting for the story.

2 Hamilton, Virginia. *The Gathering.* A computer programmed by survivors helps rehabilitate a wasteland.

Discussion Topics and Related Activities

1 Have the children consider changes that have occurred in the world over the last one hundred years due to inventions, such as airplanes, automobiles, calculators, computers, and even light bulbs. Encourage the children to speculate about a world without these inventions and a world in which any of these inventions could become too powerful.

2 Have the children make their own inventions, draw and create models of them, describe the purposes and advantages of their inventions, share them with other children, and speculate what might happen if their inventions became too powerful.

3 Robots such as R2D2 and C3PO in *Star Wars* also fascinate children. Have the children design their own robot models, describe capabilities of the robots, and contemplate what other worlds or earth might be like if robots were plentiful or if they became more powerful than their human inventors.

Issue: *People who differ from those around them are often misunderstood, feared, and even hated. This treatment is inconsistent with the prevalent belief that fellowship and love are essential if society is to survive. How should people deal with those who are different? What could happen if fellowship and love are not emphasized by society?*

Science Fiction to Share with Children

1 Lowry, Lois. *The Giver*. This world of the future has solved many problems but the inhabitants appear to be devoid of conscience.
2 L'Engle, Madeleine. *A Wrinkle in Time*. People fear and whisper about Charles Wallace because he is different from the other children in the town: He can communicate without speaking.

Issue: *Should society allow its members to have free will? What could happen if people do not strive to retain freedom of choice?*

Science Fiction to Share with Children

1 Christopher, John. *The White Mountains*. People in the twenty-first century are controlled by machines called Tripods. When human members of the society reach the age of fourteen, steel plates are inserted into their skulls so that they can be controlled by the state.
2 Christopher, John. *The City of Gold and Lead*. Will tries to discover the secrets of the Tripod culture by spying inside the major Tripod city.
3 Christopher, John. *The Pool of Fire*. People try to set up a new government after defeating the Tripods; dissident groups, however, cannot agree on a unified approach.

cities. Have children consider what a city of the future would look like and how it would function if they could build it any way that they wished. One sixth-grade class designed such a city. The children researched known design possibilities and used their imaginations.

For the project, the children investigated energy-efficient buildings, transportation systems, sanitation systems, and suburban/urban growth before they began to build. They chose high-rise office and apartment buildings for their efficient use of urban space. For energy efficiency and beauty, their suburban homes were partially or totally below ground and had solar collectors. Shopping centers used below- and above-ground space, and they utilized light shafts to bring in light for plants and people. The children's transportation included clean, electric mass transit; computerized road systems for private cars to ensure safe, steady traffic; and moving sidewalks. Their sanitation system used a three-phase treatment process that produced drinkable water, and their power plant incinerated garbage to provide recycled power. The children planned museums and recreational facilities, including parks,

trees, and an arboretum. They considered the issues of controlling growth, providing an ideal number of people for their city, and satisfying their city's future energy needs.

Have children think about the impact on their own lives and society if an alien people landed on earth or if space exploration discovered life forms on other planets. Through role playing, have them imagine a first meeting, ways in which they might communicate, and ways in which humans and aliens could function together without destroying either culture. Television programs such as "Star Trek" can lead to the issue of interfering with another culture. Have children consider the possibility of earth's being invaded or colonized by aliens who are far superior intellectually to people on earth or a space exploration's discovering human life forms who have not progressed as far as those on earth.

Have children discuss the impact of various environments on space travelers who are trying to colonize them. Have the children construct whole new environments in their classrooms. Have them design settings that include atmosphere, plants, animals, and land characteristics; create new languages; develop communication systems; and suggest fine arts possibilities.

 ## UNIT PLAN: USING ONE BOOK OF MODERN FANTASY

Teachers and librarians can develop numerous enjoyable activities around one book of modern fantasy. Madeleine L'Engle's *A Wrinkle in Time*, for example, is a popular science fiction book. It has a plot, characters, settings, and themes that stimulate discussion, artwork, and creative dramatization. Many outstanding books can serve as bases for such activities. Therefore, you may wish to use the suggestions related to L'Engle's book as guidelines for activities in connection with other books.

Oral Discussion

Some of the suggestions for discussion of L'Engle's text involve questions that require children to consider information presented at different points in the text and then to integrate this information. Leading a discussion, interject appropriate text passages as the children consider their answers. Listen to the children's responses and, if appropriate, ask divergent questions. Divergent questions encourage more than one "correct" answer. Let the children verbalize different interpretations to the story. Encourage the children to consider their own experiences and reactions and thus to interact with the text.

Your discussion of L'Engle's text can focus on plot, characterization, setting, theme, and style, too. The following questions and suggestions are listed in the order of the material in the book (which is indicated by page or chapter). If you wish to focus on plot, characterization, setting, theme, or style at one time, group the following suggestions accordingly:

1. *Characterization.* What did Meg's father mean when he told Meg not to worry about Charles Wallace because "he does things in his own way and in his own time"? Was her father right? What exceptional behavior does Charles Wallace display? Why is Charles Wallace considered strange by the villagers? Why doesn't he want the people in the village to know his real capabilities? (chapter 2)

2. *Plot.* A tesseract is mentioned in several places in the book. Present ideas about what students think is meant by a tesseract. For example, Mrs. Whatsit informs Mrs. Murry that there is such a thing as a tesseract (p. 21). Mrs. Murry tells the children that she and their father used to have a joke about a thing called a tesseract (p. 23). The term *tessering* is described as traveling in the fifth dimension—going beyond the fourth dimension. The five dimensions are described as first, a line; second, a flat square; third, a cube; fourth, time; and fifth, the square of time, a tesseract in which people can travel through space without going the long way around (p. 76).

3. *Style: emotional response to language.* Throughout the book, L'Engle makes associations between smells and emotions. Discuss some of these associations: Mrs. Whatsit's statement that she found Charles Wallace's house by the smell; and then her reaction in which she describes how lovely and warm the house is inside (p. 17); or the delicate fragrance that Meg smells when the gentle beast with tentacles relieves her of her pain (p. 175). Express your associations between smells and emotions.

4. *Theme.* Mrs. Who tells Meg that if she wants to help her father, she will need to stake her life on the truth. Mrs. Whatsit agrees and tells the children that their father is staking his life on the truth. What do Mrs. Who and Mrs. Whatsit mean by their remarks (p. 92)? How does Mrs. Whatsit stake her life in the battle against evil (p. 92)?

5. *Characterization, theme.* Throughout the book, L'Engle develops descriptions and associations around "It." Discuss these associations and meanings:

   p. 72 It is described as a dark thing that blotted out the stars, brought a chill of fear, and is the evil that their father is fighting.

   p. 88 It is described as evil; It is the powers of darkness. It is being fought against throughout the universe. The great people of the earth who have fought against It include Jesus, Leonardo da Vinci, Michaelangelo, Madame Curie, Albert Einstein, and Albert Schweitzer. Discuss how these people fought against darkness, and identify other people who fought or are fighting against darkness.

p. 108 It makes its home in Camazotz, the most oriented city on the planet, the location of the Central Intelligence Center.

p. 118 The man is frightened about the prospect of being sent to It for reprocessing.

p. 141 It sometimes calls itself "The Happiest Sadist."

p. 158 It is a huge brain.

p. 170 Meg feels iciness because she has gone through the dark thing.

6. *Characterization, plot.* Mrs. Whatsit gives each child a talisman to strengthen the child's greatest ability: For Calvin, it is the ability to communicate with all kinds of people; for Meg, it is her faults; and for Charles Wallace, it is the resilience of his childhood (p. 100). How do the children use these abilities throughout the story in their fight against It and in their endeavors to free Mr. Murry? Which ability is most important? Why?

7. *Characterization, theme, setting.* Why did L'Engle introduce Camazotz by showing the children skipping and bouncing in rhythm, identical houses, and women who opened their doors simultaneously (p. 103)? Why is the woman so frightened about an Aberration? What eventually happened to the Aberration? What is the significance of these actions?

8. *Characterization, theme.* Compare the people living in Camazotz with Meg, Charles Wallace, and Calvin. How do you account for these differences (p. 118)? Could the people living in a city on earth become like the people in Camazotz? Why or why not? Why does the man at Central Intelligence Center tell the children that life will be easier for them if they don't fight It? What would happen if everyone took the man's suggestion (p. 121)? What are the consequences of allowing someone to accept all the pain, the responsibility, and the burdens of thought and decision? Would this be good or bad? Give a reason for your answer.

9. *Plot.* What is Meg's reason for saying the periodic table of elements when she is standing before It (p. 161)?

10. *Characterization, plot, theme.* What characteristics does Meg have that make her the only one who is able to go back to Camazotz and try to save Charles Wallace from the power of It

(p. 195)? What is the only weapon that Meg has that It does not possess (p. 203)? How does Meg use this weapon to free Charles Wallace? Do any people ever use this weapon? Has anyone here ever used this weapon? Is it a weapon for good or for bad?

Artwork

Art activities accompanying *A Wrinkle in Time* can stimulate children's interpretations of setting and characters. Ideally, children can demonstrate their divergent thinking as they interpret the author's descriptions. Following are several suggestions for art interpretations:

1. *Characterization.* Mrs. Whatsit goes through several different transformations in the course of the book. Encourage your students to illustrate these transformations. Suggestions include Mrs. Whatsit's appearance as a plump, tramplike character in her blue and green paisley scarf, red and yellow flowered print, red and black bandanna, sparse grayish hair, rough overcoat, shocking pink stole, and black rubber boots (pp. 16–17). Readers then see her transformed from this comical character into a beautiful winged creature with "wings made of rainbows, of light upon water, of poetry" (p. 64). Readers also discover that Mrs. Whatsit had been a star who gave her life in the battle against It (p. 92).

2. *Setting.* The medium is able to show the children visions through her globe. Ask your students to pretend to be sitting before a magical globe and to draw either the series of visions that the children see or the visions that people would like to see if they could ask the globe to show them anything.

3. *Setting.* Meg, Mr. Murry, and Calvin travel to a planet inhabited by creatures with four arms and five tentacles attached to each hand. The planet also has a different appearance from earth or Uriel. Ask your students to create a shadowbox showing the inhabitants and their planet.

Creative Dramatization

Creative drama allows children to interact with the characters in a story, interpret aspects of plot, and express their reactions to the author's style.

Following are several suggestions for creative dramatizations:

1. *Characterization.* Have your students role-play Mrs. Whatsit's first visit to Charles Wallace's home and Meg's and Mrs. Murry's reactions to her.

2. *Setting, style.* Use chapter 4 to create a Reader's Theater presentation for upper-elementary classes. Have your students accompany their oral readings with music that depicts the mood as Meg describes the light disappearing (p. 56); the sensations of moving with the earth (p. 58); leaving the silver glint of autumn behind and arriving in a golden field filled with light, multicolored flowers, singing birds, and an air of peace and joy (pp. 59–61); the transformation of Mrs. Whatsit into a beautiful winged creature with a voice as warm as a woodwind, with the clarity of a trumpet, and the mystery of an English horn; and ascending into the atmosphere to observe the moon and then seeing the dark ominous shadow that brought a chill of fear—the dark thing that their father was fighting.

3. *Style.* Have your students pantomime the passages on pages 56 and 57, when Meg experiences the black thing, complete with darkness, the feeling of her body's being gone, legs and arms tingling, traveling through space, and reuniting with Charles and Calvin on Uriel.

4. *Theme.* Have your students debate the argument between Meg and It, talking through Charles Wallace, found on page 160. Have them consider the question, and encourage one group to take It's view—like and equal are the same thing; people will be happy if they are alike—while another group argues Meg's point—like and equal are two different things; people cannot be happy if they are the same.

5. *Characterization, plot extension.* Have your students pretend that the story continues and role-play the scene in the kitchen after Mr. Murry, Charles Wallace, Meg, and Calvin return home. What would they say to Mrs. Murry and the two boys? What would Mrs. Murry and the boys say to them?

Many science fiction books encourage creative thinking and imagination. If science fiction can inspire children as it did Carl Sagan, then it can open new universes for other children.

SUGGESTED ACTIVITIES

for Involving Children in Modern Fantasy

- Develop a story-hour program that includes several short stories, a major story, and connecting materials appropriate for sharing with a designated group of children. Decide on a unifying theme within a modern fantasy topic. Combine modern fantasy and traditional literature.

- Investigate one of the methods for artistic interpretation discussed in this chapter—mural, frieze, collage, montage, mosaic, or shadowbox. Demonstrate use of the method.

- Share a modern fantasy selection that lends itself to artistic interpretations. Interact with a group of children as they interpret the story through a mural, frieze, collage, montage, mosaic, or shadowbox. How did various children decide to interpret the story? Did they interact with the plot, characters, or setting? Did they account for all three of these aspects of the story? Did they develop a mood, or did they create concrete images? Encourage the children to tell about their artistic interpretations.

- With a peer group, develop a modern fantasy web of interest around children's literature. For example, develop webs around such topics as "Travels in Time, Space, and Imagination" or "Animals as People." Identify books appropriate for the topics. Develop an introduction for each book to stimulate interest in the book. Suggest activities to encourage children to interact with the stories in a variety of ways.

- Search the science curriculum for topics that relate to science fiction. Identify appropriate children's science fiction for one of the topics. Develop an oral discussion lesson to share with children. In the lesson, suggest discussion questions and issues to stimulate creative and critical thinking. Relate the science content to the science fiction story.

- Choose a science fiction book and develop an in-depth plan for sharing the book with children. In the plan, include discussion questions, activities that relate to science or social studies, creative dramatizations, artistic interpretations, and creative writing suggestions.

 ## CHILDREN'S LITERATURE

Aiken, Joan. *The Wolves of Willoughby Chase.* Illustrated by Pat Marriott. Doubleday, 1963 (I:7–10 R:5). An English country house is the setting for a Victorian melodrama.

Alexander, Lloyd. *The Arkadians*. Dutton, 1995 (I:10+ R:6). The author develops his fantasy on foundations of Greek mythology.

_____. *The Beggar Queen*. Dutton, 1984 (I:10+ R:7). This is the climax to the Westmark trilogy.

_____. *The Black Cauldron*. Holt, Rinehart & Winston, 1965 (I:10+ R:7). Taran and his companions seek to find and destroy the evil cauldron.

_____. *The Book of Three*. Holt, Rinehart & Winston, 1964 (I:10+ R:5). This is the first of the Prydain chronicles.

_____. *The Castle of Llyr*. Holt, Rinehart & Winston, 1966 (I:10+ R:5). The adventure increases when Princess Eilonwy is abducted by the forces of evil.

_____. *The High King*. Holt, Rinehart & Winston, 1968 (I:10+ R:5). This is the final book in the Prydain chronicles.

_____. *The Iron Ring*. Dutton, 1997 (I:10+ R:6). This fantasy has elements from the myths from India.

_____. *The Marvelous Misadventures of Sebastian*. Dutton, 1970 (I:10+ R:6). A young musician living in the eighteenth century has a series of adventures.

_____. *The Remarkable Journey of Prince Jen*. Dutton, 1991 (I:10+ R:6). A prince journeys on a quest for learning.

_____. *Taran Wanderer*. Holt, Rinehart & Winston, 1967 (I:10+ R:5). This is the fourth book of the Prydain chronicles.

_____. *Westmark*. Dutton, 1981 (I:10+ R:7). Moral dilemmas and adventure combine to give a story of good versus evil.

Andersen, Hans Christian. *The Emperor's New Clothes*. Retold by Anne Rockwell. Translated by H. W. Dulcken. Illustrated by Anne Rockwell. Harper & Row, 1982 (I:6–9 R:6). Everyone except a child is afraid to tell the emperor the truth about his clothes.

_____. *The Emperor's New Clothes*. Retold by Riki Levison. Illustrated by Robert Byrd. Dutton, 1991 (I:6–9 R:6). Watercolors present the emperor as a lion.

_____. *The Emperor's New Clothes*. Illustrated by Dorothee Duntz. North-South Books, 1986 (I:6–9 R:6). The illustrations depict French-style costumes.

_____. *The Emperor's New Clothes*. Illustrated by S. T. Mendelson. Stewart, Tabori & Chang, 1992 (I:6–9 R:6) The characters in the fantasy are animals.

_____. *The Emperor's New Clothes*. Illustrated by Janet Stevens. Holiday, 1985 (I:6–9 R:6). The humorous illustrations depict the emperor as a pig.

_____. *Hans Andersen: His Classic Fairy Tales*. Translated by Erik Haugaard. Illustrated by Michael Foreman. Doubleday, 1974 (I:7–10 R:7). This collection contains eighteen Andersen tales.

_____. *Michael Hague's Favorite Hans Christian Andersen Fairy Tales*. Illustrated by Michael Hague. Holt, Rinehart & Winston, 1981 (I:5–8 R:7). A collection of nine stories is printed in fairly large type.

_____. *The Nightingale*. Illustrated by Alison Claire Darke. Doubleday, 1989 (I:6–12 R:5). The illustrations, which show a Chinese court setting, surround the text.

_____. *The Nightingale*. Translated by Eva Le Gallienne. Illustrated by Nancy Ekholm Burkert. Harper & Row, 1965 (I:all R:7). The emperor learns to value the real nightingale more than a jeweled mechanical bird.

_____. *The Principal's New Clothes*. Adapted by Stephanie Calmenson. Illustrated by Denise Brunkus, Scholastic, 1989 (I:6–12 R:6). In this version of "The Emperor's New Clothes," a contemporary principal becomes the leading character.

_____. *The Snow Queen*. Retold by Amy Ehrlich. Illustrated by Susan Jeffers. Dial, 1982 (I:6–9 R:6). Detailed line drawings suggest a wintry world.

_____. *The Snow Queen*. Adapted by Naomi Lewis. Illustrated by Errol LeCain. Viking, 1979 (I:6–9 R:6). An icy Snow Queen is shown against a dark blue background.

_____. *The Snow Queen*. Adapted by Naomi Lewis. Illustrated by Angela Barrett. Holt, Rinehart & Winston, 1988 (I:6–9 R:6). The illustrations in this version are interesting for comparisons.

_____. *The Steadfast Tin Soldier*. Illustrated by Thomas DiGrazia. Prentice-Hall, 1981 (I:6–8 R:6). The toy soldier falls in love with a paper ballerina.

_____. *The Steadfast Tin Soldier*. Retold and illustrated by Rachel Isadora. Putnam's, 1996 (I:6–10 R:5). The toy soldier falls in love with a paper ballerina.

_____. *The Steadfast Tin Soldier*. Translated by Naomi Lewis. Illustrated by P. J. Lynch. Gulliver, 1992 (I:6–9 R:6). This classic tale is about the toy soldier.

_____. *The Steadfast Tin Soldier*. Retold by Tor Seidler. Illustrated by Fred Marcellino. HarperCollins, 1992 (I:6–9 R:6). A Christmas setting is used for the story.

_____. *Thumbelina*. Retold by Amy Ehrlich. Illustrated by Susan Jeffers. Dial, 1979 (I:6–8 R:6). In a beautifully illustrated version, a girl is only one inch tall.

_____. *Thumbelina*. Retold by Jane Falloon. Illustrated by Emma Chichester Clark. Simon & Schuster, 1997 (I:6–8 R:6). A determined protagonist overcomes her small size.

_____. *The Tinderbox*. Adapted and illustrated by Barry Moser. Little, Brown, 1990 (I: 4–9 R:5). Moser changes the setting for the fantasy to Tennessee after the Civil War.

_____. *The Ugly Duckling*. Retold and illustrated by Lorinda Bryan Cauley. Harcourt Brace Jovanovich, 1979 (I:6–8 R:2). An ostracized duckling turns into a beautiful swan.

_____. *The Wild Swans*. Retold by Amy Ehrlich. Illustrated by Susan Jeffers. Dial, 1981 (I:7–12 R:7). Finely detailed illustrations develop a fantasy setting.

Anderson, Margaret J. *In the Keep of Time*. Knopf, 1977. (I:9+ R:6). Children step first into the past of the Middle Ages and then into the twenty-second century.

Armstrong, Jennifer. *Wan Hu Is In the Stars*. Illustrated by Barry Root. Tambourine, 1995 (I:5–9 R:5). An absent-minded Chinese poet finds a way to travel among the stars.

Atwater, Richard, and Florence Atwater. *Mr. Popper's Penguins*. Illustrated by Robert Lawson. Little, Brown, 1938 (I:7–11 R:7). Excitement develops when Captain Cook, an Antarctic penguin, is sent to a quiet, dreaming housepainter who longs for adventure.

Babbit, Natalie. *Tuck Everlasting*. Farrar, Straus & Giroux, 1975 (I:8–12 R:6). A fantasy story is about everlasting life.

Baker, Keith. *The Magic Fan*. Harcourt Brace Jovanovich, 1989 (I:5–8 R:4). A Japanese man saves his village when he is guided by a magic fan.

Barber, Antonia. *The Enchanter's Daughter*. Illustrated by Errol LeCain. Farrar, Straus & Giroux, 1987 (I:6–9 R:5). This story contains many folktale elements.

I = Interest by age range.

R = Readability by grade level.

Barrie, James. *Peter Pan*. Illustrated by Nora S. Unwin. Scribner's Sons, 1911, 1929, 1950 (I:8–10 R:6). Wendy, Michael, and John accompany Peter Pan to Never Land.

Baum, L. Frank. *The Wizard of Oz*. Illustrated by W. W. Denslow. Reilly, 1956 (I:8–11 R:6). This book contains many illustrations of the original 1900 edition.

———. *The Wizard of Oz*. Illustrated by Michael Hague. Holt, Rinehart & Winston, 1982 (I:8–11 R:6). This is a newly illustrated version of Oz.

Bellairs, John. *The Spell of the Sorcerer's Skull*. Dial, 1984 (I:8–12 R:4). A professor disappears and a boy fights evil forces.

Billingsley, Fanny. *Well Wished*. Simon & Schuster, 1997 (I:10+ R:5). The town has a wishing well that grants each person one wish.

Block, Francesca Lisa. *Missing Angel Juan*. HarperCollins, 1993 (I:12+ R:6). Her grandfather's ghost helps Witch Baby.

Bond, Michael. *A Bear Called Paddington*. Illustrated by Peggy Fortnum. Houghton Mifflin, 1960 (I:6–9 R:4). This book begins a series of adventures after a bear joins a human family.

———. *Paddington Abroad*. Illustrated by Peggy Fortnum. Houghton Mifflin, 1972 (I:6–9 R:4). Paddington plans the family vacation.

———. *Paddington Helps Out*. Illustrated by Peggy Fortnum. Houghton Mifflin, 1961 (I:6–9 R:4). The bear's actions provide humorous episodes.

———. *Paddington Marches On*. Illustrated by Peggy Fortnum. Houghton Mifflin, 1965 (I:6–9 R:4). The bear's adventures continue.

Boston, Lucy M. *The Children of Green Knowe*. Illustrated by Peter Boston. Harcourt Brace Jovanovich, 1955 (I:8–12 R:6). An old English house, a great-grandmother, and children who lived in the house during past generations make life happy again for a lonely boy.

———. *An Enemy at Green Knowe*. Illustrated by Peter Boston. Harcourt Brace Jovanovich, 1964 (I:8–12 R:6). A psychology researcher and an evil spirit threaten Green Knowe.

———. *The River at Green Knowe*. Illustrated by Peter Boston. Harcourt Brace Jovanovich, 1959 (I:8–12 R:6). Ancestors from the past visit Green Knowe again.

———. *A Stranger at Green Knowe*. Illustrated by Peter Boston. Harcourt Brace Jovanovich, 1961 (I:8–12 R:6). An escaped gorilla seeks sanctuary at Green Knowe.

———. *The Treasure of Green Knowe*. Illustrated by Peter Boston. Harcourt Brace Jovanovich, 1958 (I:8–12 R:6). Tolly finds a treasure hidden in his great-grandmother's house.

Brittain, Bill. *The Devil's Donkey*. Illustrated by Andrew Glass. Harper & Row, 1981 (I:9–12 R:5). A boy is changed into a donkey when he comes under the spell of Old Magda.

———. *Dr. Dredd's Wagon of Wonders*. Illustrated by Andrew Glass. Harper & Row, 1987 (I:9–12 R:6). A power struggle results between a boy with rainmaking power and Dr. Dredd.

———. *The Wish Giver*. Illustrated by Andrew Glass. Harper & Row, 1983 (I:8–12 R:5). Three children have surprising experiences when their wishes are granted.

Burton, Virginia Lee. *The Little House*. Houghton Mifflin, 1942 (I:3–7 R:3). The author personifies a house.

Cameron, Eleanor. *The Wonderful Flight to the Mushroom Planet*. Illustrated by Robert Henneberger. Little, Brown, 1954 (I:8–10 R:4). Two boys construct and fly a spaceship.

Carris, Joan. *Aunt Morbelia and the Screaming Skulls*. Illustrated by Doug Cushman. Little, Brown, 1990 (I:8+ R:5). Ghost stories told by a great aunt change the life of a boy with dyslexia.

Carroll, Lewis. *Alice's Adventures in Wonderland*. Illustrated by S. Michelle Wiggins. Ariel/Knopf, 1983 (I:8+ R:6). Two-page illustrations accompany the classic.

———. *Alice's Adventures in Wonderland*. Illustrated by Justin Todd. Crown, 1984 (I:8+ R:6). Photographs of Alice Liddell provided models for Todd's depiction of Alice.

———. *Alice's Adventures in Wonderland*. Illustrated by John Tenniel. Macmillan, 1866; Knopf, 1984 (I:8+ R:6). This is a facsimile edition.

———. *Through the Looking-Glass, and What Alice Found There*. Illustrated by John Tenniel. Macmillan, 1872; Knopf, 1984 (I:8+ R:6). This is a facsimile edition.

———. *Alice's Adventures in Wonderland*. Illustrated by John Tenniel. Macmillan, 1865, 1963 (I:all R:6). The classic tale begins as Alice falls down a rabbit hole.

———. *Alice's Adventures in Wonderland, Through the Looking Glass, and the Hunting of the Snark*. Illustrated by Sir John Tenniel. Chatto, Bodley Head & Jonathan Cape, 1982 (I:all R:6). This reissue of the classic stories celebrates Carroll's 150th anniversary.

———. *The Nursery "Alice."* Illustrated by John Tenniel. Macmillan, 1890, 1979 (I:6–10 R:5). Lewis Carroll prepared a version of *Alice's Adventures in Wonderland* for young children.

Cheetham, Ann. *The Pit*. Holt, 1990 (I:10+ R:6). In time-warp story, a boy goes back to the time of the plague in London.

Christopher, John. *The City of Gold and Lead*. Macmillan, 1967 (I:10+ R:6). In this science fiction story, Will wins an athletic contest so that he may go to the city of the Tripods.

———. *The Pool of Fire*. Macmillan, 1968 (I:10+ R:6). The Tripods are finally defeated, but Will's plans for world unity are hindered by quarreling factions among the people.

———. *The White Mountains*. Macmillan, 1967 (I:10+ R:6). A boy questions the Tripods' control over humans.

Cleary, Beverly. *The Mouse and the Motorcycle*. Illustrated by Louis Darling. Morrow, 1965 (I:7–11 R:3). Ralph makes friends with a boy who owns a toy motorcycle.

———. *Ralph S. Mouse*. Illustrated by Paul O. Zelinsky. Morrow, 1982 (I:7–11 R:3). Ralph finds himself in school.

———. *Runaway Ralph*. Illustrated by Louis Darling. Morrow, 1970 (I:7–11 R:3). Ralph is an unusual mouse who rides a motorcycle and doesn't like his life in an old hotel.

Collodi, Carlo. *The Adventures of Pinocchio*. Illustrated by Naiad Einsel. Macmillan, 1892, 1963 (I:7–12 R:7). A disobedient marionette eventually learns to be a real boy.

———. *The Adventures of Pinocchio*. Retold by Neil Morris. Illustrated by Frank Baber. Rand McNally, 1982 (I:7–12 R:7). This is a recent version of the classic story.

———. *The Adventures of Pinocchio*. Illustrated by Roberto Innocent. Knopf, 1988 (I:4–12 R:7). This is a nicely illustrated version.

———. *The Adventures of Pinocchio: Tale of a Puppet*. Translated by M. L. Rosenthal. Illustrated by Troy Howell. Lothrop, Lee & Shepard, 1983 (I:9+ R:7). This is a newly translated version of the classic.

Conly, Jane Leslie. *Racso and the Rats of NIMH*. Harper & Row, 1986 (I:8–12 R:5). This is a sequel to O'Brien's *Mrs. Frisby and the Rats of NIMH*.

Involving Children in Modern Fantasy   401

Conrad, Pam. *Stonewords: A Ghost Story*. HarperCollins, 1990 (I:10+ R:6). In a time-warp story, a girl goes back to 1870.

_____. *Zoe Rising*. HarperCollins, 1996 (I:10+ R:6). In a time-warp story, a girl goes back in time to save her mother.

Cooper, Susan. *The Boggart*. Macmillan, 1993 (I:10+ R:5). A spirit leaves his home in Scotland and is helped to return by children in Canada.

_____. *The Boggart and the Monster*. Simon & Schuster, 1997 (I:10+ R:5). The setting is a Scottish estate and the characters include the Loch Ness Monster.

_____. *The Dark Is Rising*. Illustrated by Alan E. Cober. Atheneum, 1973 (I:10+ R:8). The last of the Old Ones goes on a quest to overcome the forces of evil.

_____. *Greenwitch*. Atheneum, 1974 (I:10+ R:8). The quest continues for the key to the inscriptions on the Grail.

_____. *The Grey King*. Atheneum, 1975 (I:10+ R:8). Will Stanton sets out on a dangerous quest to regain the golden harp.

_____. *Over Sea, Under Stone*. Illustrated by Margery Gill. Harcourt Brace Jovanovich, 1965 (I:10+ R:8). Three children go on a quest for the Grail.

_____. *Seaward*. Atheneum, 1983 (I:10+ R:5). A boy and a girl face perils as they travel from the real world into a complex world filled with good and evil.

_____. *Silver on the Tree*. Atheneum, 1977, 1980 (I:10+ R:8). The final battle between the forces of good and evil takes place.

Corbett, W. J. *The Song of Pentecost*. Illustrated by Martin Ursell. Dutton, 1983 (I:9+ R:6). The Pentecost mouse leads his followers to safety in an allegorical tale.

Dahl, Roald. *James and the Giant Peach*. Illustrated by Nancy Ekholm Burkert. Knopf, 1961 (I:7–11 R:7). A boy's unhappiness changes when a peach grows large enough for him to enter.

Darling, Christina. *Mirror*. Illustrated by Alexandra Day. Farrar, Straus & Giroux, 1997 (I:5–9 R:4). A mirror provides a fantasy world.

Dengler, Marianna. *The Worry Stone*. Illustrated by Sibyl Graber Gerig. Northland, 1996 (I:8+ R:5). The author uses many folktale elements.

Dickinson, Peter. *A Box of Nothing*. Delacorte, 1985 (I:8+ R:5). A ten-year-old is in a strange land created from junk.

_____. *Eva*. Delacorte, 1989 (I:10+ R:6). In a future world, a girl lives in a chimpanzee's body after an accident.

_____. *The Lion Tamer's Daughter: And Other Stories*. Delacorte, 1997 (I:10+ R:5). These stories are about teenagers and their supernatural friends.

Doyle, Arthur Conan. *The Lost World*. Random House, 1959 (I:10+ R:7). Prehistoric animals live in a hidden land.

Erickson, Russell E. *A Toad for Tuesday*. Illustrated by Lawrence DiFiori. Lothrop, Lee & Shepard, 1974 (I:6–9 R:4). An owl captures Warton, but Warton becomes his friend rather than his dinner.

Farmer, Nancy. *The Ear, the Eye and the Arm*. Orchard, 1994 (I:12+ R:6). In a science fiction story set in the future, three mutant detectives search for three kidnapped children.

Fleischman, Paul. *Graven Images*. Illustrated by Andrew Glass. Harper & Row, 1982 (I:10+ R:6). This book contains three stories of the supernatural.

Fleischman, Sid. *The Midnight Horse*. Illustrated by Peter Sís. Greenwillow, 1990 (I:8–12 R:5). A ghostly magician helps an orphan boy.

Fleming, Ian. *Chitty Chitty Bang Bang*. Illustrated by John Burmingham. Random House, 1964 (I:7–11 R:6). A restored car has remarkable properties.

Garner, Alan. *Elidor*. Walck, 1967 (I:10+ R:7). Four children explore an old church in England and are drawn into a world in the grip of an evil power.

_____. *The Owl Service*. Walck, 1968 (I:10+ R:5). The discovery of an old set of dishes decorated with an owl pattern marks the beginning of some strange events.

_____. *The Weirdstone of Brisingamen*. Walck, 1969 (I:10+ R:5). Two modern English children discover the truth about an ancient legend as they battle witches and wolves.

Gerstein, Mordicai. *The Mountains of Tibet*. Harper & Row, 1987 (I:6–8 R:4). Elements of Asian folklore occur in this story of reincarnation.

Godden, Rumer. *The Dolls' House*. Illustrated by Tasha Tudor. Viking, 1947, 1962 (I:6–10 R:2). Three dolls want a home of their own.

Gogol, Nikolai V. *Sorotchintzy Fair*. Adapted by Countess Sybil Schonfeldt. Illustrated by Gennadij Spirin. Translated by Daniel Reynolds. Godine, 1991 (I:all R:5). A Russian fantasy has many characteristics of folklore.

Grahame, Kenneth. *The Wind in the Willows*. Illustrated by E. H. Shepard. Scribner's Sons, 1908, 1940 (I:7–12 R:7). Mole, Water-Rat, and Toad have a series of adventures along the river, on the open road, and in the wild wood.

Griffin, Peni R. *A Dig in Time*. Macmillan, 1991 (I:8+ R:5). Personal artifacts found in a yard allow children to have a time-warp experience in which they discover information about family members.

_____. *Switching Well*. Macmillan, 1993 (I:10+ R:6). One girl travels back in time, while another girl travels into her future.

Hahn, Mary Downing. *Wait till Helen Comes*. Clarion, 1986 (I:8–12 R:5). A ghost from the 1800s haunts a young child.

Hamilton, Virginia. *Dustland*. Greenwillow, 1980 (I:10+ R:7). The psychic unit travels into a future time, when earth supports only dust and mutant forms of animal and human life.

_____. *The Gathering*. Greenwillow, 1981 (I:10+ R:7). The psychic friends go into a domed city of the future.

_____. *Justice and Her Brothers*. Greenwillow, 1978 (I:10+ R:7). Justice and her brothers have psychic powers.

_____. *The Magical Adventures of Pretty Pearl*. Harper & Row, 1983 (I:10+ R:5). Pretty Pearl comes to earth to help former slaves journey from Georgia to Ohio.

Howe, James. *The Celery Stalks at Midnight*. Illustrated by Leslie Morrill. Atheneum, 1983 (I:8–10 R:5). This animal fantasy is a sequel to *Bunnicula* and *Howliday Inn*.

Hughes, Carol. *Toots and the Upside-Down House*. Illustrated by Garrett Sheldrewnson and Anthony Stacchi. Random, 1997 (I:8+ R:5). A girl finds herself as part of a group of fairies who combat goblins.

Hughes, Monica. *Invitation to the Game*. Simon & Schuster, 1991 (I:10+ R:7). Eight teenagers learn to work together and finally discover that they have been moved to a distant planet.

Hunter, Mollie. *The Mermaid Summer*. Harper, 1988 (I:10+ R:6). In a Scottish fantasy, two children gain three wishes from a mermaid.

_____. *The Wicked One*. Harper & Row, 1977 (I:10+ R:7). A hot-tempered Scotsman and a Grollican have an adventure filled with suspense and humor.

Hurmence, Belinda. *A Girl Called Boy.* Houghton Mifflin. 1982 (I:10+ R:6). A black girl goes back in time to 1853 and experiences slavery.

Jacques, Brian. *Mariel of Redwall.* Philomel, 1991 (I:10+ R:7). A mousemaid battles a pirate rat.

_____ . *Martin the Warrior.* Illustrated by Gary Chalk. Philomel, 1994 (I:10+ R:7). Martin ends the slavery caused by the ruthless stoat, Badrang.

_____ . *Mattimeo.* Putnam, 1990 (I:10+ R:7). This is a sequel to *Redwall.*

_____ . *Mossflower.* Putnam, 1988 (I:10+ R:7). This is a prequel to *Redwall.*

_____ . *Pearls of Leitra.* Philomel, 1997 (I:10+ R:7). In this tale of Redwall, the Abbot is kidnapped and his friends save him.

_____ . *Redwall.* Philomel, 1986 (I:10+ R:7). Matthias, a young mouse, seeks the legendary sword of Martin the Warrior.

_____ . *Seven Strange & Ghostly Tales.* Putnam, 1991 (I:8+ R:6). These short stories emphasize strange and unexpected occurrences.

James, Mary. *Shoebag.* Scholastic, 1990 (I:8+ R:4). A cockroach changes into a person.

Jennings, Patrick. *Faith and the Electric Dogs.* Scholastic, 1996 (I:8–12 R:5). A dog narrates an adventure that includes a rocket and a desert island.

Juster, Norton. *The Phantom Tollbooth.* Illustrated by Jules Feiffer. Random House, 1961 (I:9+ R:8). Milo enters a tollbooth and finds himself in the Kingdom of Wisdom.

Kendall, Carol. *The Gammage Cup.* Illustrated by Erik Blegvad. Harcourt Brace Jovanovich, 1959 (I:8–12 R:4). The peaceful existence of a land inhabited by little people is challenged by five nonconformists and an outside enemy.

Key, Alexander. *The Forgotten Door.* Westminster, 1965 (I:8–12 R:6). A boy from another planet is not understood by people.

Kimmel, Eric A. *Hershel and the Hanukkah Goblins.* Illustrated by Trina Schart Hyman. Holiday, 1989 (I:all). The goblins are defeated through wits.

King-Smith, Dick. *Martin's Mice.* Illustrated by Jez Alborough. Crown, 1989 (I:8–12 R:6). An animal fantasy explores animal nature and freedom.

_____ . *Pigs Might Fly.* Illustrated by Mary Rayner. Viking, 1982 (I:9–12 R:6). The runt of the litter helps his fellow pigs in their time of need.

Kipling, Rudyard. *The Elephant's Child.* Illustrated by Lorinda Bryan Cauley. Harcourt Brace Jovanovich, 1983 (I:5–7 R:7). This is a highly illustrated version of one of the *Just So Stories.*

_____ . *The Jungle Book.* Doubleday, 1894, 1964 (I:8–12 R:7). A collection of jungle stories includes "Mowgli's Brothers," "Tiger-Tiger!" "Rikki-Tikki-Tavi," and "Toomai of the Elephants."

_____ . *Just So Stories.* Doubleday, 1902, 1907, 1952 (I:5–7 R:5). This is a collection enjoyed by young children.

_____ . *Just So Stories.* Illustrated by Victor G. Ambrus. Rand McNally, 1982 (I:5–7 R:5). The classic stories are newly illustrated.

Klause, Annette Curtis. *Alien Secrets.* Delacorte, 1993 (I:12+ R:6). A science fiction story is set on a space freighter.

_____ . *Silver Kiss.* Delacorte, 1990 (I:12+ R:6). A vampire helps a girl gain understanding.

Lawrence, Louise. *Dream-Weaver.* Clarion, 1996 (I:12+ R:7). This science fiction includes weaving dreams and spaceships.

Lawson, Robert. *Ben and Me.* Little, Brown, 1939 (I:7–11 R:6). This is the autobiography of Benjamin Franklin's friend, Amos Mouse.

_____ . *Rabbit Hill.* Viking, 1944 (I:7–11 R:7). The animals on the hill wait expectantly for the new folks.

Leaf, Monro. *The Story of Ferdinand.* Illustrated by Robert Lawson. Viking, 1936 (I:4–10 R:6). Ferdinand would rather smell the flowers than fight the matador.

LeGuin, Ursula K. *Catwings.* Illustrated by S. D. Schindler. Watts, 1988 (I:3–8 R:4). Four winged kittens escape from the city slums.

_____ . *Catwings Return.* Illustrated by S. D. Schindler. Watts, 1989 (I:3–8 R:4). Two winged cats return to their city home.

_____ . *The Farthest Shore.* Illustrated by Gail Garraty. Atheneum, 1972 (I:10+ R:6). Ged, the Archimage of Roke, is placed in final combat against an evil wizard.

_____ . *A Ride on the Red Mare's Back.* Illustrated by Julie Downing. Orchard, 1992 (I:6–10 R:5). A toy horse comes to life and helps a girl recover her brother from trolls.

_____ . *Tehanu: The Last Book of Earthsea.* Atheneum, 1990 (I:10+ R:6). This book concludes the stories of Earthsea.

_____ . *A Wizard of Earthsea.* Illustrated by Ruth Robbins. Parnassus, 1968 (I:10+ R:6). Young Sparrowhawk shows great powers of enchantment.

L'Engle, Madeleine. *A Swiftly Tilting Planet.* Farrar, Straus & Giroux, 1978 (I:10+ R:7). Charles Wallace travels a perilous journey through time to keep a mad dictator from destroying the world.

_____ . *A Wind in the Door.* Farrar, Straus & Giroux, 1973 (I:10+ R:7). Strange beings come to enlist the children's aid in the galactic fight against evil.

_____ . *A Wrinkle in Time.* Farrar, Straus & Giroux, 1962 (I:10+ R:5). A search for Meg and Charles's father takes them across the galaxy into combat with an evil darkness that is threatening the cosmos.

Levine, Gail Carson. *Ella Enchanted.* HarperCollins, 1997 (I:8+ R:5). This original fantasy is based on the Cinderella tale.

Lewis, C. S. *The Last Battle.* Illustrated by Pauline Baynes. Macmillan, 1956. The final book of Narnia sees Aslan lead his people into paradise.

_____ . *The Lion, the Witch and the Wardrobe.* Illustrated by Pauline Baynes. Macmillan, 1950 (I:9+ R:7). Four children enter the magical kingdom of Narnia through a wardrobe.

_____ . *The Magician's Nephew.* Illustrated by Pauline Baynes. Macmillan, 1955 (I:9+ R:7). This sixth book in the chronicles explains how Aslan created Narnia.

_____ . *Prince Caspian, the Return to Narnia.* Illustrated by Pauline Baynes. Macmillan, 1951 (I:9+ R:7). The prince leads his army of talking beasts against the Telmarines.

_____ . *The Silver Chair.* Illustrated by Pauline Baynes. Macmillan, 1953 (I:9+ R:7). The children complete Aslan's mission.

_____ . *The Voyage of the Dawn Treader.* Illustrated by Pauline Baynes. Macmillan, 1952 (I:9+ R:7). Lucy and Edmund are reunited with King Caspian of Narnia.

Lewis, Naomi, trans. *Proud Knight, Fair Lady: The Twelve Lais of Marie de France.* Viking/Kestrel, 1989 (I:10+ R:6). This text includes stories of love, honor, and chivalry.

Lindgren, Astrid. *Pippi Longstocking.* Illustrated by Louis S. Glanzman. Viking, 1950 (I:7–11 R:5). Pippi does some very unusual things, such as scrubbing the floor with brushes tied onto her feet.

_____ . *Pippi in the South Seas.* Illustrated by Louis S. Glanzman. Viking, 1959 (I:7–11 R:5). Pippi continues her hilarious adventures on a South Seas island.

Lionni, Leo. *Swimmy.* Pantheon, 1963 (I:2–6 R:3). A little fish learns about the marvels of the sea.

Lowry, Lois. *The Giver.* Houghton Mifflin, 1993 (I:10+ R:5). In a science fiction story, a boy changes a world that is devoid of conscience.

Lunn, Janet. *The Root Cellar.* Scribner's Sons, 1983 (I:10+ R:4). A girl has a time-warp experience that sends her back to Canada in the 1860s.

McCaffrey, Anne. *Dragonquest.* Ballantine, 1981 (I:10+ R:6). This book contains continued adventures on a distant planet.

_____ . *Dragonsinger.* Atheneum, 1977 (I:10+ R:6). Menolly studies under the masterharper of the planet Pern.

_____ . *Dragonsong.* Atheneum, 1976 (I:10+ R:6). The planet Pern must be protected from spores that can destroy all living matter.

MacDonald, George. *At the Back of the North Wind.* Illustrated by Arthur Hughes. Dutton, 1871, 1966 (I:10+ R:6). In an allegorical story, a poor boy travels to the back of the North Wind.

_____ . *The Princess and the Goblin.* Illustrated by Nora S. Unwin. Macmillan, 1872, 1951 (I:10+ R:9). Princess Irene discovers her fairy godmother spinning magical thread.

McGraw, Eloise. *The Moorchild.* Simon & Schuster, 1996 (I:10+ R:5). A changling learns her true identity in this story of the fairy folk.

McKinley, Robin. *The Blue Sword.* Greenwillow, 1982 (I:10+ R:7). A girl discovers her mysterious powers and her heritage.

_____ . *The Hero and the Crown.* Greenwillow, 1984 (I:10+ R:7). Aerin faces the forces of evil during her quest for the crown.

Mahy, Margaret. *The Changeover.* Atheneum, 1984 (I:10+ R:7). A girl discovers her supernatural powers and saves her brother.

_____ . *The Five Sisters.* Illustrated by Patricia MacCarthy. Viking, 1997 (I:7–9 R:5). A chain of paper dolls visit unusual places and influence people's lives.

Mills, Lauren. *Fairy Wings.* Illustrated by Dennis Nolan. Little, Brown, 1995 (I:7–9 R:4). This is a highly illustrated story about a fairy who does not have wings.

Milne, A. A. *The House at Pooh Corner.* Illustrated by Ernest H. Shepard. Dutton, 1928, 1956 (I:6–10 R:3). Pooh builds a house.

_____ . *Winnie-the-Pooh.* Illustrated by Ernest H. Shepard. Dutton, 1926, 1954 (I:6–10 R:5). Pooh has adventures with his nursery friends and Christopher Robin.

Myers, Walter Dean. *The Story of Three Kingdoms.* Illustrated by Ashley Bryan. HarperCollins, 1995 (I:7+ R:5). This is a literary folktale.

Nix, Garth. *Sabriel.* HarperCollins, 1996 (I:12+ R:7). The heroine is the daughter of a necromancer.

Nixon, Joan Lowery. *Whispers from the Dead.* Delacorte, 1989 (I:10+ R:6). A girl receives messages from a murder victim.

Norton, Mary. *Bed-Knob and Broomstick.* Illustrated by Erik Blegvad. Harcourt Brace Jovanovich, 1943, 1971 (I:7–11 R:6). An old brass bed becomes a flying machine.

_____ . *The Borrowers.* Illustrated by Beth and Joe Krush. Harcourt Brace Jovanovich, 1952, 1953 (I:7–11 R:3). Three little people survive by borrowing items from the human household above.

_____ . *The Borrowers Afield.* Illustrated by Beth and Joe Krush. Harcourt Brace Jovanovich, 1955 (I:7–11 R:4). The Clock family leaves their home under the floorboards and escapes into the fields.

_____ . *The Borrowers Afloat.* Harcourt Brace Jovanovich, 1959 (I:7–11 R:4). The fantasy about little people continues.

_____ . *The Borrowers Aloft.* Harcourt Brace Jovanovich, 1961 (I:7–11 R:4). These are additional tales about small people in a normal world.

_____ . *The Borrowers Avenged.* Illustrated by Beth and Joe Krush. Harcourt Brace Jovanovich, 1982 (I:7–11 R:4). This is a new book in the Borrowers series.

O'Brien, Robert C. *Mrs. Frisby and the Rats of NIMH.* Illustrated by Zena Berstein. Atheneum, 1971 (I:8–12 R:4). A group of superior rats escape from a laboratory.

Oppenheim, Shulamith Levy. *The Hundredth Name.* Illustrated by Michael Hays. Boyd Mills, 1995 (I:4–8 R:5). An Egyptian boy tries to discover the hundredth name for Allah.

O'Shea, Pat. *The Hounds of the Morrigan.* Holiday House, 1986 (I:10+ R:6). Irish traditional literature influences this modern fantasy.

Park, Ruth. *Playing Beatie Bow.* Atheneum, 1982 (I:10+ R:6). A girl from Sydney, Australia, travels in time back to the 1870s.

Pearson, Kit. *Awake and Dreaming.* Viking, 1997 (I:8+ R:5). A nine-year-old becomes part of a dream world.

Potter, Beatrix. *The Tailor of Gloucester, from the Original Manuscript.* Warne, 1969, 1978 (I:5–9 R:8). This text is illustrated with Potter's original drawings.

_____ . *The Tale of Peter Rabbit.* Warne, 1902. This is the original tale of the mischievous rabbit.

_____ . *Tales of Peter Rabbit and His Friends.* Chatham, 1964 (I:3–9 R:6). The collection includes thirteen tales accompanied by Potter's illustrations.

_____ . *The Tale of Squirrel Nutkin.* Warne, 1903 (I:3–9 R:6). This is the original tale of the impertinent squirrel.

_____ . *A Treasury of Peter Rabbit and Other Stories.* Avenel, 1979 (I:3–7 R:6). A collection of favorite stories includes "Peter Rabbit," "Benjamin Bunny," "Squirrel Nutkin," "Two Bad Mice," and "Jeremy Fisher."

Pullman, Philip. *The Golden Compass.* Knopf, 1995 (I:10+ R:7). In a high fantasy, a girl battles forces that experiment on children.

_____ . *The Subtle Knife.* Knopf, 1997 (I:10+ R:6). This is a sequel to *The Golden Compass.*

Rodgers, Mary. *Summer Switch.* Harper & Row, 1982 (I:8–12 R:6). A father and son switch identity in this humorous fantasy.

Rodowsky, Colby F. *The Gathering Room.* Farrar, Straus & Giroux, 1981 (I:10+ R:7). Spirits of people buried in the cemetery are friends of a nine-year-old boy.

Sandburg, Carl. *More Rootabagas.* Illustrated by Paul O. Zelinsky. Knopf, 1993 (I:8–11 R:7). The text includes 10 previously unpublished stories.

_____ . *Rootabaga Stories.* Illustrated by Maud and Miska Petersham. Harcourt Brace Jovanovich, 1922, 1950 (I:8–11 R:7). This is a series of short nonsense stories.

_____ . *Rootabaga Stories.* Illustrated by Michael Hague. Harcourt Brace Jovanovich, 1922, 1988 (I:8–11 R:7). This is a newly illustrated text.

Selden, George. *Chester Cricket's Pigeon Ride.* Illustrated by Garth Williams. Farrar, Straus & Giroux, 1981 (I:6–9 R:4). Chester goes on a night tour of Manhattan because he misses his country home.

_____ . *The Cricket in Times Square*. Illustrated by Garth Williams. Farrar, Straus & Giroux, 1960 (I:7–11 R:3). Chester the cricket accidentally finds himself in a subway station below Times Square.

_____ . *Harry Cat's Pet Puppy*. Farrar, Straus & Giroux, 1975 (I:7–11 R:3). Harry experiences problems after he adopts a dog.

_____ . *Tucker's Countryside*. Farrar, Straus & Giroux, 1969 (I:7–11 R:3). The friends come to Connecticut to help Chester save the meadow.

Sherman, Josepha. *Child of Faerie, Child of Earth*. Illustrated by Rick Farley. Walter, 1992 (I:10+ R:5). This is a fantasy set in twelfth-century France.

Shusterman, Neal. *The Dark Side of Nowhere*. Little, Brown, 1997 (I:12+ R:6). This science fiction includes extraterrestrial families.

Silverberg, Robert. *Letters from Atlantis*. Illustrated by Robert Gould. Atheneum, 1990 (I:10+ R:6). In a science fiction story, a scientist goes back to Atlantis.

Sleator, William. *Interstellar Pig*. Dutton, 1984 (I:10 R:8). A game becomes a real experience in a science fiction story.

Smith, Sherwood. *Wren's Quest*. Harcourt Brace Jovanovich, 1993 (I:10+ R:6). A magician searches for her parentage.

Steig, William. *The Amazing Bone*. Farrar, Straus & Giroux, 1976 (I:6–9 R:3). This fantasy includes folklore elements.

Stevermer, Caroline. *River Rats*. Harcourt Brace Jovanovich, 1992 (I:10+ R:6). In a futuristic story, a group tries to survive after the Flash.

Thurber, James. *Many Moons*. Illustrated by Marc Simont. Harcourt Brace Jovanovich, 1990. Thurber's original copyright, 1943 (I:6–9 R:4). The court jester fulfills the princess's wish for the moon.

Tolkien, J. R. R. *Farmer Giles of Ham*. Illustrated by Pauline Baynes. Houghton Mifflin, 1978 (I:7–10 R:6). Farmer Giles becomes a hero when he accidentally fires his blunderbuss into a giant's face.

_____ . *The Fellowship of the Ring*. Houghton Mifflin, 1967 (I:12+ R:8) This is part of a trilogy enjoyed by older readers.

_____ . *The Hobbit*. Houghton Mifflin, 1938 (I:9–12 R:6). Bilbo Baggins, a hobbit, joins forces with thirteen dwarfs in their quest to overthrow the evil dragon.

_____ . *The Lord of the Rings*. Houghton Mifflin, 1974 (I:12+ R:8). This is part of a trilogy enjoyed by older readers.

_____ . *The Return of the King*. Houghton Mifflin, 1967 (I:12+ R:8). This is part of a trilogy enjoyed by older readers.

_____ . *The Two Towers*. Houghton Mifflin 1965 (I:12+ R:8). This is the second book in "The Lord of the Rings" trilogy.

Travers, Pamela L. *Mary Poppins*. Illustrated by Mary Shepard. Harcourt Brace Jovanovich, 1934, 1962 (I:7–11 R:7). An unusual nanny arrives with the east wind and changes the life of the Banks family.

Turner, Megan Whalen. *The Thief*. Greenwillow, 1996 (I:10+ R:6). This fantasy includes foundations in Greek mythology.

Van Allsburg, Chris. *The Wreck of the Zephyr*. Houghton Mifflin, 1983 (I:5–8 R:6). This is a picture storybook fantasy in which a boy tries to become a great sailor.

Vande Velde, Vivian. *Curses, Inc.: And Other Stories*. Harcourt Brace, 1997 (I:10+ R:6). This is a collection of stories with surprise endings.

Voigt, Cynthia. *Building Blocks*. Atheneum, 1984 (I:9 R:7). A time-warp experience helps a boy understand his father.

Westall, Robert. *Ghost Abbey*. Scholastic, 1989 (I:10+ R:6). The abbey protects those who care for it and threatens those who would harm it.

White, E. B. *Charlotte's Web*. Illustrated by Garth Williams. Harper & Row, 1952 (I:7–11 R:3). Charlotte, with the help of Templeton the rat, saves Wilbur's life and creates a legend.

_____ . *Stuart Little*. Illustrated by Garth Williams. Harper & Row, 1945 (I:7–11 R:6). Mrs. Little's second son is quite different from the rest of the family: He is a mouse.

Wiesner, David. *Free Fall*. Lothrop, Lee & Shepard, 1988 (I:all). A fantasy wordless book tells the story of a boy's dream.

Williams, Margery. *The Velveteen Rabbit*. Illustrated by Allen Atkinson. Knopf, 1984 (I:6–9 R:5). This is another newly illustrated version of the 1922 classic.

_____ . *The Velveteen Rabbit*. Illustrated by Michael Hague. Holt, Rinehart & Winston, 1983 (I:6–9 R:5). The drawings emphasize the boy.

_____ . *The Velveteen Rabbit*. Illustrated by Ilse Plume. Godine, 1982 (I:6–9 R:5). This book contains new illustrations with a classic tale.

_____ . *The Velveteen Rabbit: Or, How Toys Become Real*. Illustrated by Michael Green. Running Press, 1982 (I:6–9 R:5). Drawings in brown tones create a newly illustrated version of the story.

_____ . *The Velveteen Rabbit: Or How Toys Become Real*. Illustrated by William Nicholson. Doubleday, 1958 (I:6–9 R:5). A toy rabbit is given life after his faithful service to a child.

Windsor, Patricia. *The Blooding*. Scholastic, 1996 (I:12+ R:7). This supernatural story develops good versus evil.

Wolff, Ferida. *Seven Loaves of Bread*. Illustrated by Katie Keller. Tambourine, 1993 (I:4–8 R:4). The author uses the pattern of a cumulative folktale.

Wright, Betty Ren. *The Ghosts of Mercy Manor*. Scholastic, 1993 (I:10+ R:6). A girl tries to prove that she has seen ghosts.

Wrightson, Patricia. *A Little Fear*. Hutchinson, 1983 (I:9 R:6). An old woman outwits the Njimbin, a creature from Australian folklore.

_____ . *Balyet*. McElderry, 1989 (I:10+ R:6). An aboriginal spirit, an older woman, and a girl share an experience.

Yolen, Jane. *The Devil's Arithmetic*. Viking/Kestrel, 1988 (I:8+ R:5). In a time-warp story, a Jewish girl finds herself in World War II.

_____ . *Dragon's Blood*. Delacorte, 1982 (I:10+ R:5). On the planet Austar IV, a boy raises a dragon to be a fighter.

_____ . *The Girl Who Loved the Wind*. Illustrated by Ed Young. Crowell, 1972 (I:7–10 R:6). The wind visits a girl and sings to her about life.

_____ . *Here There Be Witches*. Illustrated by David Wilgus. Harcourt Brace, 1995 (I:8+). This is a collection of seventeen stories and poems about witches.

Illustration from *Pish, Posh, Said Hieronymus Bosch* by Nancy Williard. Illustration copyright © 1991 by Leo, Diane, and Lee Dillon. Used by permission of Harcourt Brace Jovanovich.

8 *Poetry*

Rhythmic Patterns of Language

According to Eve Merriam (1976), poetry is "Rainbow Writing" because it colors the human mind with the vast spectrum of human experience:

> *Rainbow Writing*
>
> Nasturtiums with
> their orange cries
> flare like trumpets;
> their music dies.
> Golden harps
> of butterflies;
> the strings are mute
> in autumn skies.
> Vermillion chords,
> then silent gray;
> the last notes of
> the song of day.
> Rainbow colors
> fade from sight,
> come back to me
> when I write.
>
> Eve Merriam
> *Rainbow Writing*, p. 3

As a rainbow inspires an awe of nature, so may a poem inspire an awe for words and the expression of feelings. Poetry often has a musical quality that attracts children and appeals to their emotions. The poet's choice of words can suggest new images and create delightful word plays.

Many poems allow children to see or feel with fresh insights. The first section of this chapter discusses the values of poetry, the characteristics of poems that children prefer, criteria for selecting poetry, elements of poetry, and forms of poetry. It concludes with a discussion of children's poem classifications and poets.

THE VALUES OF POETRY FOR CHILDREN

Children can share feelings, experiences, and visions with poets. Poetry also brings new understandings of the world. It encourages children to play with words and to realize some of the images possible when words are chosen carefully. Through poetry, children may discover the power of words, a power that poets can release. Poet Lilian Moore (1988) describes this power when she relates her reactions to the poetry of Valerie Worth. She states that she "felt a delicious shock, a pleasure at the clarity with which real things were seen" (p. 470). She continues to compare reading poetry to taking a field trip with binoculars that allow readers to look in new ways at the details of the world, at the bugs, the earthworms, and the dandelions. Moore (1993) also reveals, "The response to what is genuine in a poem is a kind of happiness" (p. 303). Poet Valerie Worth (1992) describes the impact of poetry for her when she states that poetry has such power that it can "reveal, extol, and even preserve the many beauties of the world" (p. 568).

Rumer Godden (1988) equates giving a child a love of poetry to giving a child the ability to enjoy life. She states:

To give a child a love of poetry is like instilling a spring or fountain of perpetual private refreshment—and not only refreshment; a love and understanding of poetry brings a perception, a sort of sixth sense that makes its possessor quick to life—quick in the sense of being very much alive—quick to the world around him; it rescues him from dullness, gives him a sense of form, a mental discipline, and because it is limitless it will grow as he grows. (p. 306)

Poet Charles Causley (Merrick, 1988) emphasizes the illuminating quality of poetry. He believes that one of the values of poetry is that a poem may suggest something different each time it is read.

During a stimulating address to the International Reading Association, Jean Le Pere (1980) identified six reasons for sharing poetry with children. First, poetry provides enjoyment. Young children begin to discover the enjoyment in poetry by hearing and sharing nonsense poems, Mother Goose rhymes, and tongue twisters. They grow into poetry through story poems, such as those written by A. A. Milne, and they gradually discover the many exciting forms available to poets. Second, poetry provides children with knowledge about concepts in the world around them: size, numbers, colors, and time. Third, because precise and varied words play such important roles in poetic expression, poetry encourages children to appreciate language and to expand their vocabularies. Horses not only run, they clop; kittens jump, but they also pounce; and the moon may be not only bright but also a silver sickle. Fourth, poetry helps children identify with people and situations. With Robert Louis Stevenson, they go up in a swing; with Robert Frost, they share a snowy evening in the woods; and with Mike Makley, they are "The New Kid" on the baseball team who plays just as well as Dutch, PeeWee, or Earl, even though she is a girl. Fifth, poetry expresses moods familiar to children and helps children understand and accept their feelings. Other children empathize with the child in Charlotte Zolotow's "Nobody Loves Me." Sometimes, it seems as if nobody loves the speaker, and sometimes it seems as if everybody loves him—feelings common to all children. Finally, poetry grants children insights into themselves and others, developing their sensitivity to universal needs and feelings. Through poems written by other children, as well as by adults, children discover that others have feelings similar to their own.

WHAT POETRY IS

What is this literary form that increases enjoyment, develops appreciation for language, and helps children gain insights about themselves? Poetry is not easily defined nor is it easily measured or classified. There is no single accepted definition of poetry.

Some definitions specify the characteristics of poetry, including the poetic elements and the functions of words, while other definitions emphasize the emotional impact of poetry. Try to develop your own definition of poetry as you read the following definitions by poets, critics, and children. Author Rumer Godden (1988) states, "True poetry, even in its smallest shape, should have form, meter, rhythm bound into a whole with words that so match and express its subject they seem inevitable" (p. 310).

Critic Patrick Groff (1969) maintains that poetry for children is writing that, in addition to using the mechanics of poetry, transcends literal meaning. He explains:

The use of original combinations of words is probably the easiest, the best, and the most obvious way to write poetry that transcends the literal and goes beyond a complete or obvious meaning. Consequently, in poetry a word has much more meaning than a word in prose. In the former the emphasis is connotative rather than denotative. Words possess suggested significance apart from their explicit and recognized meanings. It is the guessing element that requires the reader to go below the surface of words, to plumb their literal meanings. Figurative language most often provides the guessing element. (p. 185)

Emotional and physical reactions defined poetry for poet Emily Dickinson, who related poetry to a feeling: If she read a book that made "her body so cold no fire could warm" her, she knew it was poetry; if she felt physically as if the top of her head were taken off, she also knew it was poetry. Michael Bedard's *Emily* (1992) is a picture storybook in which a father gives his daughter a similar definition for poetry:

Listen to Mother play. She practices and practices a piece, and sometimes a magic happens and it seems the music starts to breathe. It sends a shiver through you. You can't explain it, really; it's a mystery. Well, when words do that, we call it poetry. (p. 12, unnumbered)

Poet Valerie Worth (1992) also talks about the power and magic of poetry and the need to select the right words, "the right verbs, the right adjectives, or the precious image would fade away and be gone—and the magic as well" (p. 569). Judson Jerome (1968) contends that poetry is words performed. He stresses that meaning cannot be separated from the sounds of words. As visual shape is important to sculptors or painters, tonal shape is important to poets. Jerome compares the work of poets to the composition of musicians; in both forms, tonal quality is essential.

Lee Bennett Hopkins's (1987) interviews with poets in *Pass the Poetry, Please!* include numerous and varied definitions of poetry. Poets express such phrases as "music of words," "celebration of life," and "revelation of feelings." Poet David McCord (1977) provides definitions such as the shiver down the spine, the translation of words that do not exist, the dripping of hot coffee from an icicle, and a calculus of the imagination.

Poet Harry Behn (1968) reports a thought-provoking example of what children think poetry is or is not. When he asked children to tell him what poetry should be, one boy replied, "Anything that recites nicely without people. . . . People are stories. A poem is something else. Something way out. Way out in the woods. Like Robert Frost waiting in a snowstorm with promises to keep" (p. 159). Other answers suggest a wide range of definitions of poetry, such as, "A poem should be about animals, what you feel, springtime, something funny, anything you see and hear, anything you can imagine. Anything. Even a story!" (p. 159).

Teacher Anne Clark (1992) identifies poetry as one of the purest literary art forms, in which "Capturing a moment, a glimpse, a sensation in a handful of words was magic to me" (p. 624).

Author Margaret Mahy presents a definition of poetry in her short story, "The Cat Who Became a Poet," found in *Nonstop Nonsense*. After the cat cannot stop himself from speaking in poetic form, he thinks, "I became a poet through eating the mouse. Perhaps the mouse became a poet through eating seeds. Perhaps all this poetry stuff is just the world's way of talking about itself" (p. 19). Following the cat's rendition of a poem that tricks a dog, the cat concludes, "If only he knew. I wasn't meaning to praise him. Poetry is very tricky stuff and can be taken two ways" (p. 19).

Overall, the various definitions of poetry highlight the importance of original combination of words, distinctive sound, and emotional impact. Visual elements are also significant in poetry. Some poems are like paintings; they must be seen to be appreciated. Poets may use shape and space to increase the impact of their words. They may group lines into stanzas, use open spaces to emphasize words, capi-

talize important words, or arrange a whole poem to suggest the subject matter.

The essential elements of poetry must be savored to be enjoyed. Like painting or sculpture, poetry cannot be experienced rapidly. It must be read slowly, even reread several times to immerse its readers or listeners in its sounds and imagery. In other words, children must have time to see, hear, and feel the world of poets.

CHARACTERISTICS OF POEMS THAT CHILDREN PREFER

Consider children's individual interests when choosing poetry for them. When children honestly judge what speaks to their imaginations, their judgments must be respected. Even though children's interests and experiences vary widely, research into children's poetry choices contains valuable information. Several researchers have identified poems that children generally enjoy and have analyzed the subjects and elements in these poems.

Carol Fisher and Margaret Natarella (1982) examined poetry preferences in the first through the third grades. They found that the children preferred narrative poems and limericks, poems about strange and fantastic events, traditional poems, and poems that rhymed or used alliteration and onomatopoeia to create sound patterns.

Karen Sue Kutiper (1985) surveyed preferences of students in the seventh, eighth, and ninth grades. She concluded that these students prefer rhyme, humorous narrative, and content based on familiar experiences.

Ann Terry (1974) investigated the poetry preferences of children in the fourth, fifth, and sixth grades. She also analyzed poetic elements in the poems that the children preferred. She concluded the following:

1. Children's enthusiasm for poetry declines as children advance in the elementary grades.
2. Children respond more favorably to contemporary poems than to traditional ones.
3. Children prefer poems dealing with familiar and enjoyable experiences.
4. Children enjoy poems that tell a story or have a strong element of humor.

5. Children prefer poems that feature rhythm and rhyme.

6. Among the least popular poems are those that rely too heavily on complex imagery or subtly implied emotion.

7. The majority of teachers in the fourth, fifth, and sixth grades pay little attention to poetry, seldom read it to children, and do not encourage them to write their own poems.

When Terry analyzed the forms of poetry that the children preferred or disliked, she found that narrative poems and limericks were among the most preferred, while haiku and free verse were among the least popular. The most popular poems were humorous, even nonsensical, about familiar experiences or animals. In a study based on Terry's earlier research, Carol Fisher and Margaret Natarella (1982) reported that children prefer rhythm, rhyme, alliteration, and onomatopoeia.

Terry stresses that adults should provide children with many experiences with poetry and should include a wide range of poetry. Terry also recommends that books of poetry be made accessible to children, that listening centers include tapes and records of poetry, and that a rich poetry environment be used to stimulate children to write their own poetry.

One reason for the narrow range of poems that children enjoy may be that adults infrequently share poetry with children. The enjoyment of poetry, like the enjoyment of other types of literature, can be increased by an enthusiastic adult who reads poetry to children. Because Terry's research indicates that teachers of older children seldom use poetry with them, enthusiasm for poetry first must be stimulated among teachers themselves.

The need for and the advantages of longer interactions with poetry are indicated by an analysis of poetry included in the International Reading Association's Children's Choices. Sam Sebesta (1983) reports, "serious poetry, blank and free verse, and extended imagery—all qualities that children disapproved of in other preference studies—are present on the lists of Children's Choices" (p. 67). For example, children liked serious traditional poems, such as Robert Frost's "Stopping by Woods on a Snowy Evening" and the poems of Arnold Adoff's *My Black Me: A Beginning Book of Black Poetry.* They liked the personified desert in Byrd Baylor's *The Desert Is Theirs.* They chose the imagistic poems about everyday things in Valerie Worth's *More Small Poems.* In addition, Sebesta found that the number of poetry books included in children's literary preferences implied a greater affection for poetry than was found in many previous studies.

Sebesta's conclusions about the reasons for the discrepancies between the previous studies and the Children's Choices provide valuable insights for anyone responsible for selecting and sharing poetry. First, unlike many of the research studies that present poetry in a brief fashion, the poetry on the Children's Choices is available in the classroom and is shared with children over a two- to six-week period. Second, unlike most of the studies that present poetry orally, the poetry on the Children's Choices includes books that emphasize the visual aspects of poetry. The selections frequently develop unique arrangements on the page, and the illustrations arouse interests and feelings. Third, recent developments in teaching poetry emphasize both the study of the structure of poetry and readers' responses to poetry. A merger of the two approaches may expand the range of poetry that children enjoy.

As you begin the study of poetry, you should also heed a warning given by William and Betty Greenway (1990). They state, "We may be teaching students the poetry they like as children, but not the poetry they'll like as adults" (p. 138).

 ### CRITERIA FOR SELECTING POETRY FOR CHILDREN

The criteria in the Evaluation Criteria box on page 413 are for selecting poetry for children. The criteria are compiled from recommendations by Leonard Clark (1969), Patrick Groff (1969), Harry Behn (1968), Samuel Morse (1969), Myra Cohn Livingston (1969), Kinereth Gensler and Nina Nyhart (1978), and Rumer Godden (1988).

Both Rumer Godden (1988) and Charles Causley (Merrick, 1988) emphasize that a good poem need not be understood all at once. Godden states that a good poem "has a mysterious capacity for growing, unfolding more and more of itself in the mind, and very soon a child whose ear is tuned, mind made alert, is ready to go beyond children's poets and the lively, quickly assimilable poems—far, far beyond" (p. 310). Liz Rosenberg (1991) stresses that the best children's poems accompany you through life, growing with you. Consequently, poetry "must be vibrant, skillful, mysterious, thrilling" (p. 55).

ELEMENTS OF POETRY

How important to you is a knowledge of the literary elements found in poetry? Avi (1993) states that of the various criteria, "only knowing the elements of good prose and poetry contributes meaningfully to an understanding of what is children's literature" (p. 42).

Poets use everyday language in different ways to encourage readers to see familiar things in new lights, to draw on their senses, and to fantasize. Poets also use certain devices to create medleys of sounds, suggest visual interpretations, and communicate messages. The criteria for selecting poetry for children suggest the importance of such poetic elements as rhythm, rhyme and other sound patterns, repetition, imagery, and shape in the creation of poetry.

Rhythm

The word *rhythm* is derived from the Greek *rhythmos,* meaning to flow. In poetry, this flowing quality refers to the movement of words in the poem. Stress, the number of syllables, and the pattern of syllables direct the feelings expressed in a poem. Many poems have a definite, repetitive cadence, or meter, with certain lines containing a certain number of pronounced beats. For example, limericks have a strict rhythmic structure easily recognizable even when one is hearing them in a foreign language. Free verse, however, usually has a casual, irregular rhythm similar to that of everyday speech.

Poets use rhythm for four specific purposes. First, they use rhythm to increase enjoyment in hearing language. Young children usually enjoy the repetitive cadences of nursery rhymes, chants, and nonsensical verses. Rhythm encourages children to join in orally, experiment with language, and move with it. Second, poets use rhythm to highlight and emphasize specific words. Poets often use stress to suggest the importance of words. Third, poets use

rhythm to create dramatic effects. Irregular meter or repeatedly stressed words may immediately attract attention. Fourth, poets use rhythm to suggest mood. For example, a rapid rhythm can suggest excitement and involvement, while a slow, leisurely rhythm can suggest laziness and contemplation. David McCord uses rhythm to suggest the sounds that a stick might make if a child dragged it along a fence. Rhythm in the following poem emphasizes specific words, attracts and holds attention, and suggests a certain mood.

The Pickety Fence

The pickety fence
The pickety fence
Give it a lick it's
The pickety fence
Give it a lick it's
A clickety fence
Give it a lick it's
A lickety fence
Give it a lick
Give it a lick
Give it a lick
With a rickety stick
Pickety
Pickety
Pickety
Pick

From Poem "The Pickety Fence" from *Far and Few: Rhymes of the Never Was and Always Is,* p. 7 by David McCord. Copyright © 1974, Little, Brown & Company.

As you share poetry with children you will notice that the rhythm of a poem works particularly well when it reinforces the content of the poem. Consider, for example, Robert Louis Stevenson's "From a Railway Carriage." The rhythm suggests the dash and rattle of a train as it crosses the country. You can easily imagine yourself peering out the window as the scenery rushes by.

From a Railway Carriage

Faster than fairies, faster than witches,
Bridges and houses, hedges and ditches;
And charging along like troops in a battle,
All through the meadows the horses and cattle:
All of the sights of the hill and the plain
Fly as thick as driving rain;
And ever again, in the wink of an eye,
Painted stations whistle by.
Here is a child who clambers and scrambles,
All by himself and gathering brambles;

Here is a tramp who stands and gazes;
And here is the green for stringing the daisies!
Here is a cart run away in the road
Lumping along with man and load;
And here is a mill and there is a river:
Each a glimpse and gone forever!

Robert Louis Stevenson
A Child's Garden of Verses, 1883

Rhythm and the sounds of language are important elements in *Talking Like the Rain: A First Book of Poems* selected by X. J. and Dorothy M. Kennedy. The book is introduced with a quote from Isak Dinesen's *Out of Africa,* in which the workers ask Dinesen to "Speak again. Speak like rain." The poems in the anthology are meant to be read aloud to children and to bring them rhythm and pleasure.

Rhythm and repetition are important poetic elements in Lee Bennett Hopkin's *Good Rhymes, Good*

Times. There is the rhythm and sound of the city as "Quiet rumbling/traffic/roars" (p. 8); the rhythm and feel of valentine feelings that go "flippy/fizzy, whoopy, whizzy" (p. 12); and the motion and rhythm of a kite that "flitters/twirls/tumbles/twitters" (p. 14). The repeated line "Sing a song of cities" (p. 5) emphasizes the sound of the city. The repetition of the word "good" in the poem "Good Books, Good Times!" (p. 28) emphasizes the importance of the things that are good in children's lives. The poems and songs in Alvin Schwartz's *And the Green Grass Grew All Around: Folk Poetry from Everyone* include the rhythms that children chant in games and sing in songs.

Rhyme and Other Sound Patterns

Sound is an important part of the pleasure of poetry. One of the ways in which poets can emphasize sound is rhyming. Many beloved traditional poems for children—such as Edward Lear's "The Owl and the Pussy-Cat"—use careful rhyme schemes. The twenty-five most preferred poems in Ann Terry's (1974) study of children's poetry preferences contain rhyming patterns.

Rhyming words may occur at the ends of lines and within lines. Poets of nonsense verse even create their own words to achieve humorous, rhyming effects. Consider, for example, Zilpha Keatley Snyder's use of rhyme in "Poem to Mud." The end rhymes—*ooze–slooze, crud–flood,* and *thickier–stickier*—suggest visual and auditory characteristics of mud. The internal rhymes—*fed–spread, slickier–stickier–thickier*—create a tongue-twisting quality.

*E*VALUATION CRITERIA

Literary Criticism: Selecting Poetry for Children

1. Poems that are lively, with exciting meters and rhythms, are most likely to appeal to young children.

2. Poems for young children should emphasize the sounds of language and encourage play with words.

3. Sharply cut visual images and words used in fresh, novel manners allow children to expand their imaginations and see or hear the world in a new way.

4. Poems for young children should tell simple stories and introduce stirring scenes of action.

5. The poems selected should not have been written down to children's supposed level.

6. The most effective poems allow children to interpret, to feel, and to put themselves into the poems. They encourage children to extend comparisons, images, and findings.

7. The subject matter should delight children, say something to them, enhance their egos, strike happy recollections, tickle their funny bones, or encourage them to explore.

8. Poems should be good enough to stand up under repeated readings.

Poem to Mud

Poem to mud—
Poem to ooze—
Patted in pies, or coating the shoes.
Poem to slooze—
Poem to crud—
Fed by a leak, or spread by a flood.
Wherever, whenever, whyever it goes,
Stirred by your finger, or strained by your toes,
There's nothing sloopier, slipperier, floppier,
There's nothing slickier, stickier, thickier,
There's nothing quickier to make grown-ups
   sickier,
Trulier coolier,
Than wonderful mud.

Zilpha Keatley Snyder
Today Is Saturday, pp. 18–19

THROUGH THE EYES OF A POET

Poetry Doesn't Have to Be Boring!

Creator of strange beasts and fanciful worlds of humorous incidents, JACK PRELUTSKY shares his views on making poetry exciting.

Once there was a teacher who had charge of thirty-three open and eager young minds. One Monday morning, the teacher opened her curriculum book, which indicated that she should recite a poem to her students. She did, and it came out something like this:

> Blah blah the flower,
> blah blah the tree,
> blah blah the shower,
> blah blah the bee.

When she had finished her recitation she said, "Please open your geography books to page one-hundred-thirty-seven."

On Tuesday morning, the teacher (a wonderful person who happened to be rather fond of poetry) decided, on her own initiative, to read another poem to her class. This poem, which was somewhat longer than the first, came out something like this:

> blah blah blah blah blah blah hill,
> blah blah blah blah blah blah still,
> blah blah blah blah blah blah mill,
> blah blah blah blah daffodil.

Then she said, "Please open your history books to page sixty-two."

She went on like this for the entire week, and by Friday, the children (who knew what was coming when she opened her book of verse) began making peculiar faces and shifting restlessly in their seats. The staunchest aesthetes in the group had begun to lose interest in flowers, bees, and hills, etc. Many of the children were harboring strange feelings about poetry.

Numerous internal rhymes are found in Robert Southey's classical poem, "The Cataract of Lodore." In the following excerpt from the poem, notice how internal rhymes create the sound and feel of the water as it flows toward a waterfall in the Lake District of England.

> Retreating and beating and meeting and sheeting,
> Delaying and straying and playing and spraying,
> Advancing and prancing and glancing and dancing,
> Recoiling, turmoiling and toiling and boiling,
> And gleaming and streaming and steaming and
>   beaming,
> And rushing and flushing and brushing and gushing,
> And flapping and rapping and clapping and slapping,
> And curling and whirling and purling and twirling,
> And thumping and plumping and bumping and
>   jumping,
> And dashing and flashing and splashing and
>   clashing; . . .

Robert Southey, 1774–1843.

A humorous picture-book version of the total poem is illustrated by David Catrow. Catrow's illustrations for *The Cataract of Lodore* present the English countryside as a Georgian gentleman and his family descend the river toward the mighty waterfall.

The poems in Jane Dyer's *Animal Crackers: A Delectable Collection of Pictures, Poems, and Lullabies for the Very Young* include many examples of rhyme. This selection includes both traditional sources and contemporary poets. Within the text are works by classic poets such as Alfred Lord Tennyson and Eugene Field and contemporary poets such as Jane Yolen and David McCord.

Poets also use alliteration, the repetition of initial consonants or groups of consonants, to create sound patterns. In "The Tutor," Carolyn Wells uses repetition of the beginning consonant *t* to create a humorous poem about a teacher trying to teach "two young tooters to toot." "The Tutor" is one of the poems selected by Isabel Wilner for *The Poetry Troupe*, a collection of

They began saying things about poetry to themselves and to each other. Here are some of the things they said:

"Poetry is boring."

"Poetry is dumb."

"Poetry doesn't make any sense."

"Poetry is about things that don't interest me."

"I hate poetry."

Once there was another teacher with a class of thirty-three young students. She was also a wonderful person with a fondness for poetry. One Sunday evening, she opened her curriculum book and saw that a unit of poetry was scheduled for the next day's lesson. "Hmmm-mmm," she mused. "Now what poem shall I share with them tomorrow?" After giving it some careful thought, she settled on a poem about a silly monster, which the poet had apparently created out of whole cloth, and which she thought might stimulate her pupils' imagi-nations. "Hmmmmmm," she mused again. "Now how can I make this poem even more inter-esting?" She deliberated a bit more and, in the course of memorizing the poem, came up with several ideas. The next morning, this is what happened:

"Children," she said. "Today is a special day. It is the first day of silly monster week, and to honor the oc-casion, I am going to share a silly monster poem with you." She held up a small tin can, and continued. "The monster lives in this can, but I am not going to show it to you yet, because I would like you to imagine what it looks like while I'm reciting the poem."

She then recited the poem, and upon reaching the last word in the last line, suddenly unleashed an ex-panding snake from the can. The children reacted with squeals of mock terror and real delight. Then they asked her to recite the poem again, which she did. Afterward, she had them draw pictures of the silly monster. No two interpretations were alike.

The drawings were pho-tographed and later presented in an assembly as a slide show, with the children reciting the poem in cho-rus. She shared a number of other poems during "silly monster week," always showing her honest enthusiasm and finding imagina-tive methods of presentation. She used masks, musical instruments, dance, sound-effects recordings, and clay sculpture. The children grew so involved that she soon was able to recite poems with no props at all. At the end of the week, these are some of the things her students said about poetry:

"Poetry is exciting."

"Poetry is fun."

"Poetry is interesting."

"Poetry makes you think."

"I love poetry."

over two hundred poems that children have selected for reading aloud. Mary Ann Hoberman's four-line poem "Gazelle," also in Wilner's collection, contains fifteen words beginning with *g*. If a poem contains a great deal of alliteration, a tongue twister results.

Assonance, the repetition of vowel sounds, is an-other means of creating interesting and unusual sound patterns. Jack Prelutsky uses the frequent rep-etition of the long *e* sound in the following poem.

> *Don't Ever Seize a Weasel by the Tail*
>
> You should never squeeze a weasel
> for you might displease the weasel,
> and don't ever seize the weasel by the tail.
> Let his tail blow in the breeze;
> if you pull it, he will sneeze,
> for the weasel's constitution tends to be a little frail.
> Yes the weasel wheezes easily;
> the weasel freezes easily;

> the weasel's tan complexion rather suddenly turns pale.
> So don't displease or tease a weasel,
> squeeze or freeze or wheeze a weasel
> and don't ever seize a weasel by the tail.

Jack Prelutsky
A Gopher in the Garden and Other Animal Poems, p. 19

The sounds of some words suggest the mean-ings that they are trying to convey. The term *onomatopoeia* refers to words that imitate the ac-tions or sounds with which they are associated. Words such as *plop, jounce,* and *beat* suggest the loud sound of rain hitting the concrete in Aileen Fisher's "Rain."

Young children who like to experiment with lan-guage may develop their own nonsense words to suggest certain sounds or meanings. In Kinereth Gensler and Nina Nyhart's (1978) *The Poetry Connection,* two poems written by second graders

The illustrations provide an appropriate setting for a poem about the Lake District in England.
(From The Cataract of Lodore *by Robert Southey. Illustrated by David Catrow. Illustrations copyright © 1992 by David Catrow. Reprinted by permission of Henry Holt and Company, Inc.)*

incorporate onomatopoeic language. One boy uses consecutive letter *d*'s to suggest that rain sounds like a machine gun. A girl uses repetitive words—*lip–lap* and *slip–slap*—to suggest sounds of a waterfall.

Eve Merriam effectively uses onomatopoeia in her poem "Owl," found in *Halloween ABC*. Merriam's repeated use of "who" sounds like the subject of her poem. One of her other poems, "Weather," found in Beatrice Schenk de Regniers's *Sing a Song of Popcorn*, begins with "Dot a dot dot" and continues with words like "spack a spack speck" to sound like rain. In *Earth Verses and Water Rhymes*, poet J. Patrick Lewis suggests in "Sounds of Winter" that October Ogres lumber in with a "tum-tum-titum."

Repetition

Poets frequently use repetition to enrich or emphasize words, phrases, lines, or even whole verses in poems. David McCord uses repetition of whole lines in "The Pickety Fence," and Lewis Carroll uses repetition to accent his feelings about soup.

Beautiful Soup

Beautiful Soup, so rich and green,
Waiting in a hot tureen!
Who for such dainties would not stoop?
Soup of the evening, beautiful Soup!
Soup of the evening, beautiful Soup!
Beau—ootiful Soo—oop!
Beau—ootiful Soo—oop!
Soo—oop of the e—e—evening,

Beautiful, beautiful Soup!
Beautiful Soup! Who cares for fish,
Game, or any other dish?
Who would not give all else for two
Pennyworth only of beautiful Soup?
Beau—ootiful Soo—oop!
Beau—ootiful Soo—oop!
Soo—op of the e—e—evening,
Beautiful, beauti—FUL SOUP!

Lewis Carroll
Alice's Adventures in Wonderland, 1865

"Beautiful Soup" is another favorite for oral reading because children find that they can recreate that marvelous sound of rich, hot soup being taken from the spoon and placed into their mouths.

Lullabies shared with young children are often enhanced by repetition. Christina G. Rossetti's "Lullaby" uses repetition to suggest a musical quality.

Lullaby

Lullaby, oh, lullaby!
Flowers are closed and lambs are sleeping;
Lullaby, oh, lullaby!
Stars are up, the moon is peeping;
Lullaby, oh, lullaby!
While the birds are silence keeping,
(Lullaby, oh, lullaby!)
Sleep, my baby, fall a-sleeping,
Lullaby, oh, lullaby!

Christina Rossetti
Sing-Song, 1872

Young children enjoy the numerous poems that contain repetition in Jane Yolen's *The Three Bears Rhyme Book*. Poems that are especially strong in repetition include "Three Bears Walking," "Photographs," "Bears' Chairs," and "Poppa Bear's Hum."

Imagery

Imagery is a primary element in poetry. It encourages children to see, hear, feel, taste, smell, and touch the worlds created by poets. You have already seen how rhythm, sound patterns, and repetition cause readers to experience what poets describe. Poets also use figurative language (language with nonliteral meanings) to clarify, add vividness, and encourage readers to experience things in new ways. Several types of figurative language are used in poetry. This discussion looks at metaphor, simile, personification, and hyperbole.

Metaphors are implied comparisons between things that have something in common but are essentially different. Metaphors highlight certain qualities in things to make readers see them in new ways. In the introduction to *Flashlight and Other Poems*, Judith Thurman (1976) uses metaphor when she asserts that a "poem is a flashlight, too: the flashlight of surprise. Pointed at a skinned knee or at an oil slick, at pretending to sleep or at kisses, at balloons, or snow, or at the soft, scary nuzzle of a mare, a poem lets us feel and know each in a fresh, sudden and strong light" (introduction). Thurman demonstrates her command of metaphor when she

compares the Milky Way to thick white breath in cold air, or clay to a clown without bones. In "Spill," Thurman compares a flock of flying sparrows to loose change spilling out of a pocket.

Spill

the wind scatters
a flock of sparrows—
a handful of small change
spilled suddenly
from the cloud's pocket

Judith Thurman
Flashlight and Other Poems,
p. 16

While metaphors are implied comparisons, similes are direct comparisons between things that have something in common but are essentially different. The comparisons made by similes are considered direct because the word *like* or *as* is included in the comparison. In "The Path on the Sea," a thirteen-year-old Russian child uses simile to capture the mystery and allure of moonlight on the ocean. Notice the use of the word *like* in the first line. What are the commonalities between a silver sickle and a new moon?

The Path on the Sea

The moon this night is like a silver sickle
Mowing a field of stars.
It has spread a golden runner
Over the rippling waves.
With its winking shimmer
This magic carpet lures me
To fly to the moon on it.

From the poem "The Path on the Sea" by Inna Miller,
from *The Moon Is Like a Silver Sickle* by
Miriam Morton. Reprinted by permission.

Insightful comparisons can develop meaning that transcends words. Poetic imagery can open the minds of children to new worlds and can allow children to ascend to different levels of consciousness.

Personification allows poets to give human emotions and characteristics to inanimate objects, abstract ideas, and nonhuman living things. For example, personification is an important element in Byrd Baylor's poetry about Native Americans and Native American legends. In *Moon Song*, Baylor personifies the moon as a mother who gives birth to Coyote Child, wraps him in her magic, caresses him with pale white mist, and shines on him with love. In Jamake Highwater's *Moonsong Lullaby,* the moon "sings," "smiles," "caresses," and "watches over us." In Myra Cohn Livingston's "Moon," found in her *Space Songs,* the moon "remembers" and "thinks" about space explorers. In J. Patrick Lewis's "Fog," found in *Earth Verses and Water Rhymes,* the fog arrives at night, allowing the night to slip "into her white silk shawl." Kaye Starbird uses personification in the following poem to encourage readers to visualize a wind with human characteristics.

The Wind

In spring, the wind's a sneaky wind,
A tricky wind,
A freaky wind,
A wind that hides around the bends
And doesn't die, but just pretends;
So if you stroll into a street
Out of a quiet lane,
All of a sudden you can meet
A smallish hurricane.
And as the grown-ups gasp and cough
Or grumble when their hats blow off,
And housewives clutch their grocery sacks
While all their hairdos come unpinned . . .
We kids—each time the wind attacks—
Just stretch our arms and turn our backs,
And then we giggle and relax
And lean against the wind.

Kaye Starbird
The Covered Bridge House and Other Poems,
p. 11

Hyperbole is exaggeration that creates specific effects. John Ciardi's humorous "Mummy Slept Late and Daddy Fixed Breakfast" says that a waffle is so tough that it cannot be dented by a hacksaw.

Mummy Slept Late and Daddy Fixed Breakfast

Daddy fixed the breakfast.
He made us each a waffle.
It looked like gravel pudding.
It tasted something awful.

"Ha, ha," he said, "I'll try again.
This time I'll get it right." But what I got was in
       between
Bituminous and anthracite.

"A little too well done? Oh well,
I'll have to start all over."
That time what landed on my plate
Looked like a manhole cover.

I tried to cut it with a fork:
The fork gave off a spark.

I tried a knife and twisted it
into a question mark.
I tried it with a hack-saw.
I tried it with a torch.
It didn't even make a dent.
It didn't even scorch.

The next time Dad gets breakfast
When Mommy's sleeping late,
I think I'll skip the waffles.
I'd sooner eat the plate!

John Ciardi
You Read to Me, I'll Read to You, p. 18

Many of the poems in Shel Silverstein's *Where the Sidewalk Ends* also include exaggeration.

Shape

Poets may place their words on pages in ways designed to supplement meaning and to create greater visual impact. Word division, line division, punctuation, and capitalization can emphasize content, as when Lewis Carroll writes about "Beau—ootiful Soo—oop!"

The shape of a poem may represent the thing or the physical experience that the poem describes. In Regina Sauro's "I Like to Swing," the poem becomes wider and wider toward the bottom, as the sweep of the swing becomes wider and wider. In "Seals," by William Jay Smith (anthologized in Stephen Dunning, Edward Lueders, and Hugh Smith's excellent *Reflections on a Gift of Watermelon Pickle . . . and Other Modern Verse*), the poem forms the shape of a supple seal and is reinforced by an accompanying photograph of a seal. Several of the poems in Myra Cohn Livingston's *Space Songs* are shaped like objects in space. For example, "Moon" looks like a crescent, "Meteorites" has a tail, and "Satellites" looks like a mechanical object. Children enjoy discovering that shape may be related to the meaning of a poem and experimenting with shape in their own poetry writing.

 ## FORMS OF POETRY

Some children do not believe that they are reading a poem unless the lines rhyme. While adults should not spend time with young children analyzing the form of a poem, children should realize that poetry has many different forms and that, as poet Amy Lowell (1971) once remarked, "every form is proper to poetry" (p. 7).

Children should be encouraged to write their own poetry. When they write poetry, they enjoy experimenting with different forms. For such experiments, however, they must be immersed in poetry and led through many enjoyable experiences with poems. This section takes a brief look at various forms of poetry, including lyric, narrative, ballad, limerick, concrete, and haiku.

Lyric Poetry

According to Northrop Frye, Sheridan Baker, and George Perkins (1985), a lyric poem is "a poem, brief and discontinuous, emphasizing sound and picture imagery rather than narrative or dramatic movement. Lyrical poetry began in ancient Greece in connection with music, as poetry sung, for the most part, to the accompaniment of a lyre" (p. 268). The epic poems of the Greeks were narratives emphasizing heroic deeds. Now, as in the past, lyric poems emphasize musical, pictorial, and emotional qualities. The musical roots of lyric poetry are indicated by the fact that the words of songs are now termed *lyrics*.

Poet Jose Garcia Villa's description of poetry (Cowen, 1983) emphasizes the importance of a lyrical quality. According to Villa, a poem must be magical, must be musical, and must fly like a bird. Many of the poems discussed in this chapter have lyrical quality.

Children's early experiences with poetry may be through Mother Goose rhymes sung to music and traditional lullabies sung at bedtime. Consider the melody associated with the words in the following traditional lullaby.

Hush, Little Baby

Hush, little baby, don't say a word,
Mama's going to buy you a mocking bird.
And if that mocking bird don't sing,
Mama's going to buy you a diamond ring.
And if that diamond ring turns to brass,
Mama's going to buy you a looking glass.
And if that looking glass gets broke,
Mama's going to buy you a billy goat.
And if that billy goat won't pull,
Mama's going to buy you a cart and bull.
And if that cart and bull turn over,
Mama's going to buy you a dog named Rover.
And if that dog named Rover won't bark,
Mama's going to buy you a horse and cart.
And if that horse and cart fall down,
You'll still be the sweetest little baby in town.

Traditional poem

Dan Fox's *Go In and Out the Window: An Illustrated Songbook for Young People* contains numerous traditional lyrics. Ashley Bryan's *I'm Going to Sing: Black American Spirituals* and John Langstaff's *What a Morning! The Christmas Story in Black Spirituals* show the emotional power associated with some lyrics. Jane Yolen's *Hark! A Christmas Sampler* includes many of the best-loved holiday lyrics.

Children's favorite storybook characters make up verses and sing their poems—as does A. A. Milne's Winnie-the-Pooh, for example. Many poets write poems that have singing qualities. Jack Prelutsky's anthology *The Random House Book of Poetry for Children* contains, for example, Lois Lenski's "Sing a Song of People," which recreates the tempo of people traveling through a city. John Ciardi's "The Myra Song" captures the personality of a little girl who enjoys singing, skipping, chattering, and playing. William Blake's "Introduction to 'Songs of Innocence'" has its piper of "happy songs/Every child may joy to hear."

The universality of songs and chants are shown through Nikki Siegen-Smith's *Songs for Survival: Songs and Chants from Tribal Peoples Around the World*. The anthology includes selections from six continents. The anthology is divided according to songs about beginnings, songs about the living world, songs that discuss the elements, and songs about survival. An introduction and an appendix present information about the importance of songs and customs of tribal groups.

Narrative Poetry

Poets may be expert storytellers. A poem that tells a story is narrative poetry. With rapid action and typically chronological order, story poems have long been favorites of children. They are excellent for increasing children's interest in, and appreciation of, poetry. Robert Browning's "The Pied Piper of Hamelin," first published in 1882, contains many of the characteristics that make narrative poems appealing to children. The actions of the villainous rats, for example, are easy to visualize.

Rats!
They fought the dogs, and filled the cats,
And bit the babies in the cradles,
And ate the cheeses out of the vats,
And licked the soup from the cook's own ladles,
Split open the kegs of salted sprats,

Made nests inside men's Sunday hats,
And even spoiled the women's chats
By drowning their speaking
With shrieking and squeaking
In fifty different sharps and flats.

The plot develops rapidly, as the townspeople approach the mayor and the town council demanding action. Into this setting comes the hero.

And in did come the strangest figure!
His queer long coat from heel to head
Was half of yellow and half of red;
And he himself was tall and thin,
With sharp blue eyes, each like a pin,
And light, loose hair, yet swarthy skin,
No tuft on cheek nor beard on chin,
But lips where smiles went out and in—
There was no guessing his kith and kin!
And nobody could enough admire
The tall man and his quaint attire:

With rapidity, the council offers the stranger a thousand gilders to rid the town of its rats, and the piper places the pipe to his lips. At this point, the tempo of the poem resembles the scurrying of rats.

And out of the house the rats came tumbling.
Great rats, small rats, lean rats, brawny rats,
Brown rats, black rats, gray rats, tawny rats,
Grave old plodders, gay young friskers,
Fathers, mothers, uncles, cousins,
Cocking tails and pricking whiskers,
Families by tens and dozens,
Brothers, sisters, husbands, wives—
Followed the piper for their lives.
From street to street he piped advancing,
And step for step they followed dancing,

Robert Browning
The Pied Piper of Hamelin, 1882

After the efficient disposal of the rats comes the confrontation, when the mayor refuses to pay the thousand gilders. In retribution, the piper puts the pipe to his lips and blows three notes. At this point, the tempo of the poem resembles the clapping of hands and the skipping of feet. Every child in the town merrily follows the piper through a wondrous portal into the mountain.

Other narrative poems long popular with children include Clement Moore's "A Visit from St. Nicholas" (now better known as "The Night Before Christmas"), which has been produced as books illustrated by Tomie dePaola and by Tasha Tudor; Lewis Carroll's delightful "The Walrus and the Carpenter,"

in which some young oysters go for a walk on the beach with one hungry animal and one hungry human; and Henry Wadsworth Longfellow's romantic dramas from early American history, "The Song of Hiawatha" and "Paul Revere's Ride." In Reeve Lindbergh's *Johnny Appleseed,* based on the legend of John Chapman, the text and the illustrations create a feeling of pioneer America. John Greenleaf Whittier's *Barbara Frietchie* also is about an earlier time in American history.

Many contemporary poets—including John Ciardi, Jack Prelutsky, and Beatrice Curtis Brown—write narrative poems. Their topics are both nonsensical and realistic. Several contemporary poets have written highly illustrated narrative poems. In *The Voyage of the Ludgate Hill: Travels with Robert Louis Stevenson,* Nancy Willard uses the poetic form to retell Stevenson's adventures on a tramp steamer. Her fanciful narrative poem explores what might have happened if Stevenson had interacted with the animals in the cargo hold. In *A Starlit Somersault Downhill,* also by Willard, a bear invites a rabbit to share his long winter nap.

Roy Gerrard's *Sir Francis Drake: His Daring Deeds* tells a lively story about the explorer. Gerrard's *Sir Cedric* is a heroic tale of Cedric the Good and Matilda the Pure. Gerrard's *Wagons West!* tells the story of a group of pioneers as they live their adventures on a wagon train heading westward to Oregon. The adventures along the way are developed through both the narrative poem and the illustrations. Along the way, the pioneers experience inclement weather, cattle thieves, and frontier entertainment.

Julia Fields's *The Green Lion of Zion Street* follows the exploits of a group of urban children as they wait for a bus on a foggy morning. In epic fashion, the children decide to challenge their fears and approach the dangerous lion that crouches "Fierce/Smirking/Vain" on Zion Street. Thankfully, they are able to walk through the frightening mists, face the lion, and laugh at their fears. After all, the scowling lion is made of stone.

Ballads

The ballad is a form of narrative folk song developed in Europe during the Middle Ages. Minstrels and bards (*bard* is the Welsh word for poet) sang the tales of legend or history, often accompanying themselves on stringed instruments. Modern poets have used the ballad form for poems to be read rather than sung. However, traditional ballads are part of the oral literary heritage of European culture, passed on by word of mouth.

Action, usually heroic or tragic, is the focus of such traditional ballads as "Tom Dooley" and "Barbara Allen." Cecil Day-Lewis (1947) says:

The meter is simple because the ballads were composed by simple people, and often members of the audience liked to make up additional stanzas. It is a fast-moving meter because a ballad generally had quite a long story to tell, and it was necessary to keep it on the go so that listeners shouldn't get bored. (p. 57)

Day-Lewis compares ballads to movies because both are highly dramatic and both rely on fast-paced incidents and dialogue.

Samuel Taylor Coleridge's "The Rime of the Ancient Mariner," a sea ballad published in 1798, was based on the legend that it is fatal to shoot an albatross. The text is dramatic, including memorable lines that are frequently quoted. Notice the drama in the following excerpt from the longer poem.

> The fair breeze blew, the white foam flew,
> The furrow follow'd free;
> We were the first that ever burst
> Into that silent sea.
>
> Down dropt the breeze, the sails dropt down,
> 'Twas sad as sad could be;
> And we did speak only to break
> The silence of the sea!
>
> All in a hot and copper sky,
> The bloody Sun, at noon,
> Right up above the mast did stand,
> No bigger than the Moon.
>
> Day after day, day after day,
> We stuck, nor breath nor motion;
> As idle as a painted ship
> Upon a painted ocean.
>
> Water, water, everywhere,
> And all the boards did shrink;
> Water, water, everywhere
> Nor any drop to drink.

Samuel Taylor Coleridge
From "The Rime of the Ancient Mariner," 1798

Salt-Sea Verse, compiled by Charles Causley, contains a number of sea ballads, including portions of Coleridge's "The Rime of the Ancient Mariner." Gene Kemp's anthology *Ducks and Dragons: Poems*

for Children contains a variety of English, Scottish, and American ballads that children enjoy reading or hearing read aloud. Jane Yolen's *The Ballad of the Pirate Queens* is the story of Anne Bonney and Mary Reade, two women aboard the *Vanity.* This ballad is full of adventure. Yolen provides notes about the history. Steven Kellogg's *I Was Born About 10,000 Years Ago* is an illustrated version of a ballad that includes considerable exaggeration.

Limericks

The short, witty poems called limericks are popular with children. Four of the best-liked poems in Ann Terry's (1974) study of children's poetry preferences are limericks. All limericks have the same basic structure and rhythm: They are five-line poems in which the first, second, and fifth lines rhyme and have three pronounced beats each, and the third and fourth lines rhyme and have two pronounced beats each. The limerick form was popularized by Edward Lear in the nineteenth century. Following is an example of humorous verse from Lear's *A Book of Nonsense.*

> There was an Old Man with a beard,
> Who said, "It is just as I feared!—
> Two Owls and a Hen,
> Four Larks and a Wren
> Have all built their nests in my beard."

Edward Lear
A Book of Nonsense, 1846

Children enjoy the visual imagery that this poem creates. They can see and laugh at the predicament of having those fowl nesting in a beard. They also enjoy reciting the definite rhythm and rhyme found in the limerick.

David McCord (1977), who has written numerous contemporary limericks himself, says that for a limerick to be successful, it must have perfect rhyming and flawless rhythm. McCord's amusing limericks in his *One at a Time: Collected Poems for the Young* illustrate the author's ability to play with words and the sounds of language. These limericks may also stimulate children to experiment with language by writing their own limericks.

Concrete Poems

Concrete is something that can be seen or touched, something that is physically real. When a poet emphasizes the meaning of a poem by shaping it into

"Dead Tree" (From Seeing Things: A Book of Poems, Robert Froman, "Dead Tree," Crowell, 1974, p. 9. Reprinted by permission of HarperCollins.)

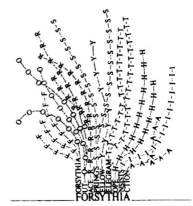

"Forsythia" (From Mary Ellen Solt, ed. "Forsythia." Concrete Poetry: A World View. Copyright © 1969. Reprinted by permission of Indiana University Press.)

the form of a picture, concrete poetry results. Robert Froman's poem "Dead Tree," from *Seeing Things: A Book of Poems,* is lettered in the shape of a dead tree trunk. Mary Ellen Solt was inspired to create both a poem and a picture about the promise of spring in a forsythia bush. Children should turn this poem on its side to read the thoughts of the author.

Children find concrete poetry exciting to look at. Observing concrete objects and writing picture poems about them also stretches children's imaginations.

Haiku

Haiku is a very old form of Japanese poetry. A haiku has three lines. The first line has five syllables, the second line has seven, and the final line has five. According to Ann Atwood (1971), a modern writer of haiku, the seventeen syllables of a haiku require a discipline that ideally results in a poem "both simple and profound, constructive and expansive, meticulously descriptive yet wholly suggestive" (introduction, unnumbered). Such a poem must be savored, not read hurriedly.

Poets of haiku link themselves with nature and the cycle of the seasons. A photograph of a beach scene, in which a stream of water is placing its mark upon the land, accompanies the following example of Atwood's haiku.

> A blank page of sand—
> at the water's cutting edge
> the pattern shaping.

From poem *Haiku: The Mood of Earth,*
by Ann Atwood,
Scribner's Sons, copyright 1971.
p. 4, unnumbered

Haiku by the great Japanese poet Issa, among other geniuses of this art, illustrate how this ancient form of verse has been used to express feelings, experiences, and visions in just the right words. Poems by Issa and important information about his life are included in Richard Lewis's *Of This World: A Poet's Life in Poetry.* Ann Atwood's haiku are collected in her *Haiku: The Mood of the Earth* and other books. Demi's collection of poems in *In the Eyes of the Cat: Japanese Poetry for All Seasons* includes a selection of Japanese poetry that has been translated by Tze-si Huang. Demi's illustrations combine with the poetry to provide a feeling for nature. Myra Cohn Livingston's *Cricket Never Does: A Collection of Haiku and Tanka* provides an introduction to the traditional Japanese forms of poetry.

POEMS AND POETS

To share poetry with children, you may select from many classic and contemporary poems. Poets who write for children use subject matters interesting to children. Children's poets write humorous poems; nature poems; poems that encourage children to identify with characters, situations, and locations; poems that suggest moods and feelings; animal poems; and poems about witches and ghosts. Although these categories sometimes overlap and some poets write about many different topics, many children's poets focus on certain subjects and types of poetry.

Nonsense and Humor: Poems for Starting Out Right

Nonsense rhymes are logical successors to Mother Goose rhymes for enjoyably introducing children to poetry. The nonsense poems of such great poets as Edward Lear and Lewis Carroll are ideal: They suggest spontaneous fun through emphatic, regular rhythms that are heightened by alliteration. Nonsense verses convey absurd meanings or even no meaning at all.

Humorous poetry, while closely related to nonsense poetry, deals with amusing happenings that might actually befall a person or an animal. Numerous contemporary poets also write nonsensical or humorous verse to entice children into the fun and life-enriching world of poetry.

The poems in *Animals That Ought to Be: Poems About Imaginary Pets,* written by Richard Michelson, provide humorous viewpoints about animals that "ought to be" because they could be of great service. For example, there is a poem about a "Roombroom" that cleans up messes. Other poems such as the "Nightmare Scarer" suggest that some of these pets might be difficult to control. Bonnie Christensen's *Rebus Riot* with its humorous content, puns, and word play is another book of poetry that appeals to younger children.

Samuel Marshak's *The Pup Grew Up* presents the comical dilemma of a lady's placing a Pekingese on a train and collecting a Great Dane when she gets off the train. The poem, written by a famous Russian poet, is a dig at bureaucracy.

An early love of William Blake's *Songs of Innocence* and *Songs of Experience* inspired Nancy Willard's *A Visit to William Blake's Inn: Poems for Innocent and Experienced Travelers.* The nonsense and lyric poems in the book, evocatively illustrated by Alice and Martin Provensen, present an odd assortment of guests and workers at the inn, including a rabbit that makes the bed and two dragons that bake the bread. "The Man in the Marmalade Hat Arrives" shows another of the guests.

> The man in the marmalade hat
> arrived in the middle of March,
> equipped with a bottle of starch
> to straighten the bends in the road, he said.
> He carried a bucket and mop.
> A most incommodious load, he said,
> and he asked for a room at the top.
>
> Now beat the gong and the drum!
> Call out the keepers
> and waken the sleepers.
> The man in the marmalade hat has come!
>
> The man in the marmalade hat
> bustled through all the rooms,
> and calling for dusters and brooms
> he trundled the guests from their beds,
> badgers and hedgehogs and moles.
> Winter is over, my loves, he said.
> Come away from your hollows and holes.
>
> Now beat the gong and the drum!
> Call out the keepers
> And waken the sleepers.
> The man in the marmalade hat has come!
>
> Nancy Willard
> *A Visit to William Blake's Inn,* p. 22

Humor is also found in the imagery, situations, and descriptive language in Willard's *Pish, Posh, Said Hieronymus Bosch,* inspired by the odd creatures found in artist Hieronymus Bosch's paintings. The artist, who painted in the late 1400s and early 1500s, was known for his bizarre creatures. When writing this poetry, Willard speculated about what it would be like to live and work in a household filled with Bosch's creatures. Consequently, the poetry is filled with three-legged thistles, pickle-winged fish, pigeon-toed rats, and a troop of jackdraws.

William Cole's *Poem Stew* includes humorous poems. Two larger anthologies contain sections of nonsense poetry. Jack Prelutsky's *The Random House Book of Poetry for Children* contains a section titled "Nonsense! Nonsense!" *Sing a Song of Popcorn: Every Child's Book of Poems,* by Beatrice Schenk de Regniers et al., includes poems categorized "Mostly Nonsense."

Edward Lear. Edward Lear, introduced earlier as the popularizer of the limerick form, had many loyal friends among the leaders and creative artists of

The humor of bizarre situations is found in both the poetry and the illustrations from Pish, Posh, Said Hieronymus Bosch by Nancy Willard, illustration copyright © 1991 by Leo, Diane, and Lee Dillon, reproduced by permission of Harcourt Brace & Company.

Great Britain in the nineteenth century. He was welcomed into their homes and became an "Adopty Duncle" to their children, for whom he wrote and illustrated the nonsense verses collected in *A Book of Nonsense* and *Nonsense Songs and Stories:* limericks, narrative poems, tongue twisters, and alphabet rhymes.

Lear's nonsense poems can be found in many anthologies. They have also been illustrated in single editions by several well-known illustrators. *Hilary Knight's The Owl and the Pussy-Cat* is an excellent choice for young children. The highly illustrated text begins with a fantasy situation and presents the poem as a story told by Professor Comfort. A careful search of the illustrations reveals numerous references to Lear's works and interests. Compare Knight's illustrated version with Jan Brett's illustrations for Lear's *The Owl and the Pussycat*. Brett places her characters in a Caribbean setting. Fred Marcellino's illustrated version of *The Pelican Chorus and Other Nonsense* written by Edward Lear includes "The New Vestments," "The Owl and the Pussycat," and "The Pelican Chorus." The delightfully humorous illustrations make interesting comparisons with other illustrated versions of Lear's poetry.

Lewis Carroll.   Lewis Carroll was the pen name for Charles Lutwidge Dodgson, a mathematician. Carroll's works are historical milestones of children's literature. His nonsense verses are found in *Alice's Adventures in Wonderland* and *Through the Looking Glass.* One of Carroll's most famous poems is "Jabberwocky," from *Through the Looking Glass,* which introduces the marvelous nonsense words *brillig, slithy toves,* and *borogoves.* This poem has been published as a lovely book illustrated by Jane Breskin Zalben.

Laura E. Richards.   Contemporary children may be surprised to discover that a well-known author of nonsense poetry is the daughter of Julia Ward Howe, who wrote a beautiful but somber poem, "The Battle Hymn of the Republic." Like Lear and Carroll, Richards has shared marvelous words and sounds with children. There are *wizzy wizzy woggums, ditty dotty doggums,* and *diddy doddy dorglums.* There are *Rummy-jums, Viddipocks,* and *Orang-Outang-Tangs.* Richards's collection *Tirra Lirra, Rhymes Old and New* contains many rhymes that emphasize the sound of language and encourage children to play with words. One of her best-loved nonsense poems follows.

Eletelephony

Once there was an elephant,
Who tried to use the telephant—
No! No! I mean an elephone
Who tried to use the telephone—
(Dear me! I am not certain quite
That even now I've got it right.)

Howe'er it was, he got his trunk
Entangled in the telephunk;
The more he tried to get it free,
The louder buzzed the telephee—
(I fear I'd better drop the song
Of elephop and telephong!)

From poem "Eletelephony" from *Tirra Lirra, Rhymes Old and New,* p. 31, by Laura E. Richards. Copyright © 1955, Little, Brown & Company.

Shel Silverstein.   One of the most popular children's poets, Shel Silverstein writes much nonsense and humorous poetry. Librarians report that Silverstein's *Where the Sidewalk Ends* and *A Light in the Attic* are in much demand by young readers. Improbable characters and situations in *A Light in the Attic* include a Quick-Digesting Gink, Sour Ann, and a polar bear in the Frigidaire. Silverstein covers slightly more realistic topics in poems like "The Boa Constrictor," from *Where the Sidewalk Ends*. In this poem, the narrator describes the experience of being swallowed by a boa constrictor. Children enjoy dramatizing this popular action poem. Silverstein's *Fall Up* includes poems about additional humorous situations.

Consider Silverstein's use of rhythm, rhyme, sound patterns, and repetition in "Ickle Me, Pickle Me, Tickle Me Too."

Ickle Me, Pickle Me, Tickle Me Too

Ickle Me, Pickle Me, Tickle Me too
Went for a ride in a flying shoe.
"Hooray!"
"What fun!"
"It's time we flew!"
Said Ickle Me, Pickle Me, Tickle Me too.

Ickle was captain, and Pickle was crew
And Tickle served coffee and mulligan stew
As higher
And higher
And higher they flew,
Ickle Me, Pickle Me, Tickle Me too.

Ickle Me, Pickle Me, Tickle Me too,
Over the sun and beyond the blue.
"Hold on!"
"Stay in!"
"I hope we do!"
Cried Ickle Me, Pickle Me, Tickle Me too.

Ickle Me, Pickle Me, Tickle Me too
Never returned to the world they knew,
And nobody
Knows what's
Happened to
Dear Ickle Me, Pickle Me, Tickle Me too.

From poem "Ickle Me, Pickle Me" by Shel Silverstein.
Copyright 1974. Reprinted by permission of
HarperCollins.

Jack Prelutsky.

The world created by Prelutsky's nonsense and humorous poetry for children could be described as the kingdom of immortal zanies and improbable situations such as those already shown in his poem "Don't Ever Seize a Weazel by the Tail." Within the pages of *The Queen of Eene* are preposterous characters, such as peculiar Mister Gaffe, Poor Old Penelope, Herbert Glerbertt, and the Four Foolish Ladies (Hattie, Harriet, Hope, and Hortense).

Rolling Harvey Down the Hill describes the humorous experiences of a boy and his four friends. In *The Sheriff of Rottenshot*, eccentric characters include Philbert Phlurk, Eddie the spaghetti nut, and a saucy little ocelot. *The Baby Uggs Are Hatching* contains poems about oddly named creatures, such as Sneepies and Slitchs. Prelutsky's *The Dragons Are Singing Tonight* contains poems about all types of dragons, and Peter Sis's illustrations add to the believability. Prelutsky's *Monday's Troll* features poems about enchanted characters such as witches and ogres. Other improbable creatures are found in *A Pizza the Size of the Sun*.

William Jay Smith.

Smith's *Laughing Time* contains many funny and entrancing poems, including limericks similar to those of Edward Lear. Smith's poem about escape to a strange land illustrates the spirit of fun that makes his poetry appealing to children.

The Land of Ho-Ho-Hum

When you want to do wherever you please,
Just sit down in an old valise,
And fasten the strap
Around your lap,
And fly off over the apple trees.

And fly for days and days and days
Over rivers, brooks, and bays
Until you come
To Ho-Ho-Hum
Where the Lion roars, and the Donkey brays.

Where the unicorn's tied to a golden chain,
And Umbrella Flowers drink the rain.
After that,
Put on your hat,
Then sit down and fly home again.

William Jay Smith
Laughing Time, p. 8

John Ciardi.

A poet who has been both a professor of English and a columnist for *Saturday Review World*, Ciardi has written two books with a simple vocabulary to appeal to children with beginning reading skills: *I Met a Man* and *You Read to Me, I'll Read to You*. In the second book, Ciardi tells readers, "All the poems printed in black, you read to me, and all the poems printed in blue, I'll read to you." This collection contains "Mummy Slept Late and Daddy Fixed Breakfast." Other popular poems in this book tell about such characters as Change McTang McQuarter Cat and Arvin Marvin Lillisbee Fitch.

Ciardi's *The Hopeful Trout and Other Limericks* contains numerous poems about funny situations supplemented by tongue-twisting sounds. However, some of Ciardi's poems are better understood by older children. Poems by Ciardi often contain satirical observations about human behavior or problems of society, and the humorous poems in *Doodle Soup* tend to be caustic.

N. M. Bodecker.   Poems suggesting that children should wash their hands with number-one dirt, shampoo their hair with molasses, and rinse off in cider are welcomed by young readers. Bodecker uses word play in "Bickering" to create humorous verse enjoyed by older children.

Bickering

The folks in Little Bickering
they argue quite a lot.
Is tutoring in bickering
required for a tot?
Are figs the best for figuring?
Is pepper ice cream hot?
Are wicks the best for wickering
a wicker chair or cot?
They find this endless dickering
and nonsense and nit pickering
uncommonly invigor'ing
I find it downright sickering!
You do agree!

From poem "Bickering" from *Hurry, Hurry Mary Dear,* by N. M. Bodecker, copyright 1976. Reprinted by permission of Athenaeum/MacMillan/Simon & Schuster, Inc.

In *Hurry, Hurry Mary Dear,* the title poem has a harassed woman who is told to pick apples, dill pickles, chop trees, dig turnips, split peas, churn butter, smoke hams, stack wood, take down screens and put up storm windows, close shutters, stoke fires, mend mittens, knit sweaters, and brew tea. This might not be so bad, but the man who is giving the orders sits in a rocking chair all of the time. Finally, Mary has enough: She places the teapot carefully on the demanding gentleman's head.

Nature Poems

Like children, poets have marveled at the opening of the first crocus, seen new visions in a snowflake, or stopped to watch a stream of crystal-clear water tumbling from a mountaintop. They have understood that people should feel reverence and respect for nature.

Such reverence and respect require special ways of hearing as well as special ways of looking. In *The Great Frog Race and Other Poems,* Kristine O'Connell George captures not only frogs but also Canada geese and other pleasures associated with a rural setting. In *Earth Verses and Water Rhymes,* J. Patrick Lewis encourages readers to try to catch the first snowflake on the tongue, feel the wind, and see the rays of a lighthouse. In *I'm Going to Pet a Worm Today and Other Poems,* Constance Levy encourages readers to explore many things in nature, including bees, old leaves, and water.

Charlotte Zolotow's poetry is about childhood experiences and nature. Two different editions of Zolotow's *River Winding* make possible interesting comparisons of the effects of illustrations. Children may enjoy evaluating the illustrations by Regina Shekerjian (1970 edition) and by Kazue Mizumura (1978 edition). The poem "Change" demonstrates how Zolotow is able to bring nature and children's experiences together in poetry.

Change

The summer
still hangs
heavy and sweet
with sunlight
as it did last year.

The autumn
still comes
showering gold and crimson
as it did last year.

The winter
still stings
clean and cold and white
as it did last year.

The spring
still comes
like a whisper in the dark night.

It is only I
who have changed.

From poem "Change" from *River Winding,* by Charlotte Zolotow. Copyright 1978. Reprinted by permission of Crowell/HarperCollins.

Creation and the ancient world are also subjects for poets. James Weldon Johnson's *The Creation,* newly illustrated by Carla Golembe, develops feelings of mystery and majesty. Douglas Wood's *Old Turtle* develops an understanding of the earth and our relationship with the beings who inhabit it. Cheng-Khee Chee's watercolors reinforce this fragility.

The ancient stories of Native Americans provide the inspiration for Jamake Highwater's *Moonsong Lullaby*. Highwater uses images such as grasslands that echo the moon's music. Nature also provides the focus for many of the selections included in John Bierhorst's *The Sacred Path: Spells, Prayers & Power Songs of the American Indians*. Seymour Simon's *Star Walk* is a collection of poetry about astronomy. The collection includes poems by poets such as Archibald MacLeish, Sara Teasdale, and May Swenson. Several Native American poems are included. The anthology is illustrated with photographs. *The Mermaid: And Other Sea Poems*, selected by Sophie Windham, is a collection of poems about both real and mythical sea creatures. Examples of poems include Rudyard Kipling's "Seal Lullaby," E. V. Rieu's "The Flattered Flying Fish," and Ted Hughes's "My Other Granny."

Nature poems frequently stimulate artists to create the settings described by poets. Ed Young illustrated Robert Frost's poem "Birches." Marcia Brown illustrated a series of "Mostly Weather" poems in de Regniers's *Sing a Song of Popcorn: Every Child's Book of Poems*. Wendell Minor's illustrations for Diane Siebert's *Mojave* illuminate the desert landscape, his illustrations in *Heartland* illuminate the land and people of the Midwest, and his illustrations for *Sierra* show the grandeur of the mountains. The poems in Myra Cohn Livingston's *Light & Shadow* are accompanied by Barbara Rogasky's photographs of many aspects of nature.

In Kenneth Koch and Kate Farrell's *Talking to the Sun*, an anthology containing artwork from the Metropolitan Museum of Art, many of the poems are nature poems. Likewise, *Who Has Seen the Wind? An Illustrated Collection of Poetry for Young People*, edited by Kathryn Sky-Peck, contains illustrations of paintings from the Museum of Fine Arts, Boston. For example, Jacob Abraham Camille Pissarro's "Morning Sunlight on the Snow" appears with Rudyard Kipling's "The Way Through the Woods" and Winslow Homer's "Boys in a Pasture" appears with Robert Frost's "The Pasture." Such illustrated versions help children discover new ways to look at nature.

Robert Frost.

The nature poems of Robert Frost are frequently included in anthologies of children's literature or are heavily illustrated in versions containing only one poem. As you read one of Frost's most famous poems, "Stopping by Woods on a Snowy Evening," try to visualize nature through the viewpoint of the poet. What emotions do you believe that the poet is experiencing?

Stopping by Woods on a Snowy Evening

Whose woods these are I think I know.
His house is in the village though;
He will not see me stopping here
To watch his woods fill up with snow.

My little horse must think it queer
To stop without a farmhouse near
Between the woods and frozen lake
The darkest evening of the year.

He gives his harness bells a shake
To ask if there is some mistake.
The only other sound's the sweep
Of easy wind and downy flake.

The woods are lovely, dark and deep,
But I have promises to keep,
And miles to go before I sleep,
And miles to go before I sleep.

Robert Frost, 1923

Aileen Fisher.

Fisher's poetry communicates the excitement and wonder of discovering nature. Her vision is fresh and full of the magic possible when a person really looks at the natural world. Fisher creates images that are real to children and that children may extend to other observations. In her poems about insects, found in *When It Comes to Bugs*, and her poems about seasons and rabbits, found in *Listen, Rabbit* and *Rabbits, Rabbits*, Fisher encourages readers to closely observe nature.

In Fisher's poems about winter, evergreens after a snowfall wear woolly wraps and snow fills the garden chairs with teddy bears. Fisher's "Frosted-Window World" allows children to visit Winter's house by going inside a frosted windowpane.

Frosted-Window World

The strangest thing,
the strangest thing
came true for me today:
I left myself beneath the quilt
and softly slipped away.

And do you know
the place I went
as shyly as a mouse,
as curious as a cottontail,
as watchful as a grouse?
Inside the frosted windowpane

(it's rather puzzling to explain)
to visit Winter's house!

How bright it was.
How light it was.
How white it was all over,
with twists and turns
through frosted ferns
and crusted weeds and clover,
through frost-grass
reaching up to my knees,
and frost-flowers
thick on all the trees.

The brightest sights,
the whitest sights
kept opening all around,
for everything
was flaked with frost,
the plants, the rocks,
the ground,
and everything was breathless-still
beneath the crusty rime—
there wasn't any clock to tick
or any bell to chime.
Inside the frosted windowpane
(it's rather puzzling to explain)
there wasn't any Time.

How clear it was.
How queer it was.
How near it was to heaven!
Till someone came
and called my name
and said, "It's after seven!"
And heaven vanished like an elf
and I whisked back, inside myself.

From poem "Frosted-Window World" from
In One Door and Out the Other:
A Book of Poems, by Aileen Fisher, copyright 1969.
Reprinted by permission of Crowell.

Byrd Baylor. The closeness between the land and the creatures who live upon it is strikingly presented in Baylor's poetry. Baylor tells readers that they must learn *The Other Way to Listen* if they are to be fortunate enough to hear corn singing, wildflower seeds bursting open, or a rock murmuring to a lizard. The old man in the poem teaches the child that nature will not talk to people who feel superior. A person must respect every aspect of nature, humble as well as grand, and must begin with the small things: one ant, one horned toad, one tree. In several of Baylor's books, Peter Parnall's sensitive illustrations are attuned to both nature and Baylor's words.

The poems in *Desert Voices* are written from the viewpoints of various inhabitants of the desert, animal and human. In *The Desert Is Theirs,* a poem about Native Americans, the poetry and accompanying illustrations develop the theme that the land is meant to be shared; it belongs to not only people but also spiders, scorpions, birds, coyotes, and lizards. This beautifully illustrated poem tells how Earthmaker created the desert, Spider People sewed the sky and earth together, and Elder Brother taught the people to live in the sun and to touch the power of the earth. Readers discover that the Papagos know how to share the earth. Baylor develops the close relationship between people and nature through terms such as *brother* and actions that emphasize respect:

Papagos try
not to anger
their animal brothers.

They don't
step on
a snake's track
in the sand.

They don't disturb
a fox's bones.
They don't shove
a horned toad
out of the path.

They know
the land belongs
to spider and ant
the same as it does
to people.

They never say,
"This is my land
to do with as I please."
They say,
"We share . . .
we only share."

From poem *The Desert Is Theirs,*
by Byrd Baylor. Reprinted by permission
of Simon & Schuster, Inc.

Paul Fleischman. Sound and motions in nature are strongly depicted in Paul Fleischman's *Joyful Noise: Poems for Two Voices* and *I Am Phoenix: Poems for Two Voices.* The texts are designed to be read aloud by two readers, one taking the left side, the other taking the right side. The poems are read from top to bottom, with some parts solo and some parts duet. For example, read aloud the poem, "Cicadas" in Figure 8–1

FIGURE 8–1 *"Cicadas" (From Paul Fleischman. "Cicadas."* Joyful Noise: Poems for Two Voices. *Text © 1998 by Paul Fleischman. Illustrations © by Eric Beddows. Harper & Row Publishers, Inc. Reprinted by permission of HarperCollins.)*

Cicadas

Afternoon, mid-August Two cicadas singing	
	Two cicadas singing Air kiln-hot, lead-heavy
Five cicadas humming Thunderheads northwestward Twelve cicadas buzzing	Five cicadas humming
	Twelve cicadas buzzing Up and down the street
the mighty choir's assembling Shrill cica- das droning	the mighty choir's assembling Ci- cadas droning in the elms
Three years spent underground	*Three years*
	among the roots
in darkness Now they're breaking ground	in darkness
	and climbing up the tree trunks
splitting skins and singing	and singing Jubilant cicadas
rejoicing	pouring out their
fervent praise	fervent praise for heat and light
their hymn sung to the sun Cicadas whin- ing	their hymn Cicadas whining ci- cadas whirring
whir- ring	ci- cadas pulsing
pulsing chanting from the treetops sending forth their booming boisterous joyful noise!	chanting from the treetops sending forth their booming joyful noise!

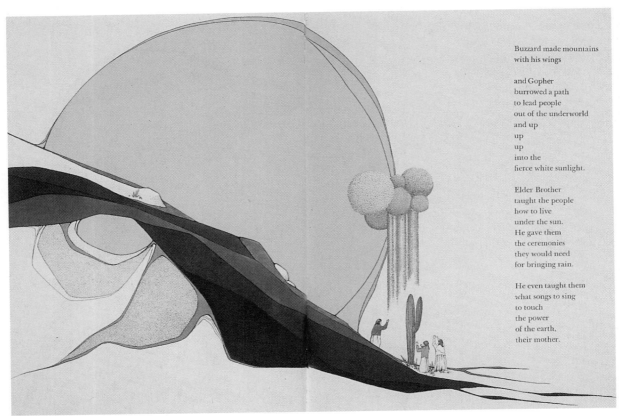

Buzzard made mountains
with his wings

and Gopher
burrowed a path
to lead people
out of the underworld
and up
up
up
into the
fierce white sunlight.

Elder Brother
taught the people
how to live
under the sun.
He gave them
the ceremonies
they would need
for bringing rain.

He even taught them
what songs to sing
to touch
the power
of the earth,
their mother.

Flowing lines in the illustrations create the mood for poems about the desert. (From The Desert Is Theirs *by Byrd Baylor. Text copyright © 1975 by Byrd Baylor; illustrations copyright © 1975 by Peter Parnall. Charles Scribner's Sons. Reprinted by permission of Simon & Schuster, Inc.)*

with another reader. Notice the effect created by the solo parts and the two voices.

Characters, Situations, and Locations

Poems about experiences that are familiar to children make up a very large category of poetry for children. Familiar experiences may be related to friends or family, may tell about everyday occurrences, or may provide insights into children's environments.

Eloise Greenfield illuminates life in the Bahamas in *Under the Sunday Tree.* The poems in this book develop positive images of life. Greenfield's *Honey, I Love* emphasizes the things a young girl loves, such as the way her cousin talks, the hose on a hot day, riding in a crowded car, and mama's soft and warm arm. The poems selected by Javaka Steptoe in *In Daddy's Arms I Am Tall: African Americans Celebrating Fathers* explore the bond between fathers and their children. Jo Carson's *Stories I Ain't Told Nobody Yet* is a collection of poetry written by people from the Appalachian region of the United States. Walter Dean Myers' *Harlem* celebrates the people, their dreams, and their environment.

Both realistic and fanciful experiences related to growing up contribute the subjects for X. J. Kennedy's poems in *The Forgetful Wishing Well: Poems for Young People.* Developing an understanding of poetry is the motivation for the poems in Kennedy's anthology *Knock at a Star: A Child's Introduction to Poetry.* The poems in the text are organized to help readers understand types and elements of poetry.

R. R. Knudson and May Swenson's *American Sports Poems* is a large anthology that includes poems about both specific sports and well-known athletes. *At the Crack of the Bat* is a collection of baseball poems compiled by Lillian Morrison. The poems in Barbara Esbensen's *Who Shrank My Grandmother's House: Po-*

ems of *Discovery* explore childhood discoveries about everyday objects, such as pencils, clouds, and doors.

Myra Cohn Livingston.

Whether about whispers tickling children's ears or celebration of such holidays as Thanksgiving, Christmas, and Martin Luther King Day, Livingston's verses create images and suggest experiences to which children can relate. One child felt his mouth puckering as he read Livingston's poem about learning to whistle.

I Haven't Learned to Whistle

I haven't learned to whistle.
I've tried—
But if there's anything like a whistle in me,
It stops
Inside.

Dad whistles.
My brother whistles
And almost everyone I know.

I've tried to put my lips together with wrinkles,
To push my tongue against my teeth
And make a whistle
Come
Out
Slow—

But what happens is nothing but a feeble gasping
Sound
Like a sort of sickly bird.

(Everybody says they never heard
A whistle like *that*
And to tell the truth
Neither did I.)

But Dad says, tonight, when he comes home,
He'll show me again how
To put my lips together with wrinkles,
To push my tongue against my teeth,
To blow my breath out and really make a whistle.

And I'll *try!*

Myra Cohn Livingston
O Sliver of Liver, p. 12

In additional poems, Livingston deals with characters, situations, and locations. Livingston's books of poems include *Celebrations, Sea Songs, Sky Songs,* and *Space Songs.*

Valerie Worth.

In *More Small Poems,* Valerie Worth poetically describes looking at a moth's wing through a magnifying glass, observing a kitten with a stiffly arched back, and seeing fireworks in the night sky. Something as simple as taking off one's shoes becomes a sensual experience for Worth, as in the following poem:

Barefoot

After that tight
Choke of sock
And blunt
Weight of shoe,

The foot can feel
Clover's green
Skin
Growing,

And the fine
Invisible
Teeth
Of gentle grass,

And the cool
Breath
Of the earth
Beneath.

Valerie Worth
Still More Small Poems, p. 13

In the poems of Valerie Worth, common things in the worlds of children contain magical qualities. In *Still More Small Poems,* Worth sees common objects with uncommon insights: Grandmother's door with the fancy glass pattern, a kite riding in the air, and rags that are no longer faithful pajamas but crumpled cloths used to wash windows. The poems from all four of Valerie Worth's series of small poems appear in *All the Small Poems.*

David McCord.

The poetic genius of McCord has won him numerous honors, including the Sarah Josepha Hale Medal, a Guggenheim Fellowship, and, in 1977, the first national award for excellence in children's poetry awarded by the National Council of Teachers of English. Clifton Fadiman (McCord, 1977) said, "David McCord stands among the finest of living writers of children's verse. He is both an acrobat of language and an authentic explorer of the child's inner world" (coverleaf).

One at a Time: Collected Poems for the Young contains over two hundred of McCord's poems: favorite chants, such as "Song of the Train," alphabet verses, riddles, poetic conversations, and numerous poems about animals, children's experiences, nature, and nonsense. The last section of the book, "Write Me

Another Verse," attempts to show readers how to write different poetry forms, including the ballad, the tercet, the villanelle, the clerihew, the cinquain, and the haiku. Earlier in the book, McCord gives directions for writing the couplet (two-line verse), the quatrain (four-line verse), the limerick (five-line verse), and the triolet (eight-line verse).

McCord's skill in using shape to supplement meaning is illustrated in the following poem.

The Grasshopper

Down
a
deep
well
a
grasshopper
fell.

By kicking about
He thought to get out.
He might have known better,
For that got him wetter.

To kick round and round
Is the way to get drowned,
And drowning is what
I should tell you he got.

But
the
well
had
a
rope
that
dangled
some
hope.
And sure as molasses
On one of his passes
He found the rope handy
And up he went, *and he*

it
up
and
it
up
and
it
up
and
it
up
went

And hopped away proper
As any grasshopper.

From poem "The Grasshopper" from
*One at a Time: Collected Poems
for the Young,* pp. 28–30 by David McCord.
Copyright © 1980, Little, Brown & Company.

Moods and Feelings

Children can learn through poets' descriptions of everyday life, dreams, and nostalgia that others experience many moods and feelings like their own. Arnold Adoff's *All the Colors of the Race* contains poems written from the viewpoint of a girl who has one black parent and one white parent. The poems reflect her thoughts and moods as she contemplates her heritage and other experiences in her life. Adoff's *Sports Pages* presents the exhilarations and the disappointments expressed by young athletes, while his *Love Letters* expresses often contrasting feelings.

A bedtime fantasy forms the setting for the adventures in David McPhail's *The Dream Child*. McPhail's selection of incidents in the world of

Illustrations support the mood of a lullaby. Illustrations by Holly Meade in Minfong Ho's Hush! A Thai Lullaby. *From* HUSH! *by Minfong Ho, illustrated by Holly Meade. Illustrations copyright © 1996 by Holly Meade. Reprinted by permission of Orchard Books, New York.*

Dream Child and Tame Bear creates a happy and dreamlike mood. Adventures that could be frightening or disruptive transform discord into harmony. Other moods and feelings related to nighttime, bedtime, and happy dreams are the focus of Thomas Hood's *Before I Go to Sleep* and Kay Chorao's anthology *The Baby's Bedtime Book,* in which a full-page painting accompanies each selection. Fantastic events in a dream world create a happy, imaginative setting in Nancy Willard's *Night Story.*

Moods and feelings in poems for older students are found in anthologies by Paul B. Janeczko. *Going over to Your Place: Poems for Each Other* includes over one hundred poems dealing with love and loss. *The Music of What Happens: Poems That Tell Stories* includes poignant poems about such emotional experiences as killing a rabbit or reading a grandfather's last letter. *I Feel a Little Jumpy Around You: A Book of Her Poems and His Poems Collected in Pairs,* selected by Naomi Shihab Nye and Janeczko, includes poems written from a female and a male perspective. Moods and feelings also provide the focus in Carol Ann Duffy's *I Wouldn't Thank You for a Valentine: Poems for Young Feminists.* These poems express a variety of feelings such as humor, anger, and conflict.

In a book of poetry for older readers, *Pierced By a Ray of Sun: Poems About the Times We Feel Alone,* Ruth Gordon selects poems that emphasize various moods and feelings from alienation through hope. The note to the reader provides an introduction to the various moods reflected in the poems as the poet asks, "Am I the only such person on Earth? . . . This collection was put together with the thought that throughout time and history many have felt as we feel. If we realize that we are not the only such people on Earth, perhaps poets' words of the distant past and recent present will help us face not only our differences, but also our sameness" (p. xvii).

Some of the poems written by children may reveal very emotional experiences or times of great unhappiness or fear in their lives. For example, the poems that are included in . . . *I Never Saw Another Butterfly* . . . , edited by Hana Volavkova were written in the Terezin Concentration Camp from 1942 through 1944. As you read the following poem, try to imagine the experiences of and the mood felt by the author, who was also a child.

The Butterfly

The last, the very last,
So richly, brightly, dazzlingly yellow.
Perhaps if the sun's tears would sing
    against a white stone. . . .

Such, such a yellow
Is carried lightly 'way up high.
It went away I'm sure because it wished to
    kiss the world good-bye.

For seven weeks I've lived in here,
Penned up inside this ghetto.
But I have found what I love here.
The dandelions call to me
And the white chestnut branches in the court.
Only I never saw another butterfly.

That butterfly was the last one.
Butterflies don't live in here, in the ghetto.

Pavel Friedman, 1942

Langston Hughes.

Although Hughes is not considered primarily a children's poet, his poetry explores feelings, asks difficult questions, and expresses hopes and desires that are meaningful to readers of any age. Some of his poems—such as "Merry-Go-Round"—can be used to help children understand and identify with the feelings and experiences of African Americans in earlier eras of American history. In another poem, Hughes vividly describes what life would be like without dreams.

Dreams

Hold fast to dreams
For if dreams die
Life is a broken-winged bird
That cannot fly.
Hold fast to dreams
For when dreams go
Life is a barren field
Frozen with snow.

Langston Hughes
The Dream Keeper, 1932, 1960

The photograph that accompanies "Dreams" in the anthology *Reflections on a Gift of Watermelon Pickle . . . and Other Modern Verse,* edited by Dunning, Lueders, and Smith, shows a solitary dried weed surrounded by ice crystals. When this poem was shared with a group of fifth graders, one of the students reminded the class that dreams do not need to die: Like the weed, they can be reborn in the spring.

Cynthia Rylant.   Moods and feelings related to growing up form the unifying theme in Rylant's *Waiting to Waltz: A Childhood*. Rylant's poems paint word pictures of a young girl feeling pride in her small town, pondering the relationships within the town, and revealing the experiences that influence her own maturation. In "Teenagers," for example, Rylant explores the longings of a child who is too big for some things and not big enough for others.

Teenagers

Watching the teenagers
in Beaver
using hairspray and
lipstick.
Kissing at ballgames.
Going steady.
And wanting it fast,
wanting it now.
Because all my pretend
had to be hidden.
All my games
secret.
Wanting to be a wide-open child
but too big,
too big.
No more.
Waiting to shave
and wear nylons
and waltz.
Forgetting when
I was last time
a child.
Never knowing
when it
ended.

Cynthia Rylant
Waiting to Waltz: A Childhood, p. 44

A combination of sadness and nostalgia is created in Patricia MacLachlan's *What You Know First*. The poem has an historical setting of a prairie farm during the Depression. As readers follow the girl's last tour of the farm they realize how important are these early experiences and keeping the memories even as you are forced to move to a new location. The mood of this poem could be compared with the mood created by the rhythmic language and the choice of experiences in Cynthia Rylant's *When I Was Young in the Mountains*.

Animals

When reporting a summary of the studies that investigated children's poetry preferences, Dianne Monson and Sam Sebesta (1991) concluded, "The popularity of humorous poems and poems about animals is evident from responses by English as well as U.S. children" (p. 668). Animals, whether teddy bears, cuddly puppies, purring kittens, or preposterous beasts of imagination, hold special places in the hearts of both children and adults. Therefore, it is not surprising that many poets write about animals. In *Feathered Ones and Furry*, Aileen Fisher shares with children her love for all types of animals, including the furry.

The Furry Ones

I like
the furry ones—
the waggy ones
the purry ones
the hoppy ones
that hurry,

The glossy ones
the saucy ones
the sleepy ones
the leapy ones
the mousy ones
that scurry,

The snuggly ones
the huggly ones
the never, never
ugly ones . . .
all soft
and warm
and furry.

Aileen Fisher
Feathered Ones and Furry, p. viii

The best-known collection of cat poems by a single author is probably T. S. Eliot's *Old Possum's Book of Practical Cats*. These poems, which were composed for Eliot's godchildren, are full of vivid language, interesting characterizations, and lyrical quality, as revealed when the poems were set to music in the Broadway show, *Cats*. Errol Le Cain has illustrated two poems from *Old Possum's Book of Practical Cats* in *Mr. Mistoffelees with Mungojerrie and Rumpelteazer*. It is interesting to compare the original illustrations by Edward Gorey with the new illustrations by Le Cain.

William Blake's "The Tyger," written in the eighteenth century, begins with the memorable lines "Tyger, Tyger, burning bright/In the forests of the night." In *The Tyger*, newly illustrated in a single volume, the paintings by Neil Waldman add to the energy, mood, and animals depicted in the poem.

Several anthologies about animals offer works by various poets. Laura Whipple's *Eric Carle's Animals, Animals*, an anthology, includes poems about a variety of animals. Carle's collage illustrations are vivid. Myra Cohn Livingston's *Cat Poems* explores all types of cats, from T. S. Eliot's humorous "The Song of the Jellicles" to Karla Kuskin's sad remembrances of a lost cat, "In August Once."

Anne Carter selected the poems for *Birds, Beasts, and Fishes: A Selection of Animal Poems*, a large-format book illustrated by Reg Cartwright and in-cluding more than fifty poems, ranging from the classic works of Boethius, Alfred Lord Tennyson, and Robert Louis Stevenson to the contemporary poems of Ted Hughes. The book also has a glossary of definitions for words that might not be known by contemporary readers, an index of first lines, and an index of titles. *The Beauty of the Beast: Poems from the Animal Kingdom*, selected by Jack Prelutsky, provides an interesting comparison.

Laura Whipple selected poems about mythical creatures for *Eric Carle's Dragons Dragons & Other Creatures That Never Were*. Eric Carle's large, colorful collages created from painted tissue paper introduce the right mood for poems about dragons, minotaurs, griffins, unicorns, krackens, and manticores. A detailed glossary contains information about these fabulous beasts and their origins. In addition, there are an index of poets and an index of creatures. Compare Whipple's collection with *The Dragons Are Singing Tonight*, written by Jack Prelutsky and illustrated by Peter Sis.

Two poetry collections are about dinosaurs. Compare the mood of the poems and the influence of Arnold Lobel's watercolor illustrations that accompany Jack Prelutsky's poems in *Tyrannosaurus Was a Beast: Dinosaur Poems* with the influence of Murray Tinkelman's black-and-white illustrations in Lee Bennett Hopkins's *Dinosaurs*.

Snail

Snail upon the wall,
Have you got at all
Anything to tell
About your shell?

Only this, my child—
When the wind is wild,
Or when the sun is hot,
It's all I've got.

John Drinkwater

Eric Carle's collage illustrations add to the beauty in a poetry collection about animals. (From Eric Carle's Animals, Animals. *Illustrations copyright © 1989 by Eric Carle. Philomel Books. Snail by John Drinkwater, © 1929. Reprinted by permission of Samuel French, Inc.)*

Witches and Ghosts

Haunted houses, ghostly appearances, mysterious happenings, and diabolic demons are found in Eve Merriam's *Halloween ABC*. The spooky nature of the poems is intensified by Lane Smith's dark, dramatic illustrations. Merriam uses repetition, alliteration, and vivid imagery to capture the essence of witches and other ghostly creatures. Henry Treece's *The Magic Wood*, in which a boy explores a wood that is full of shining eyes, creeping feet, and tiny cries, develops a frightening mood through repetition. Barry Moser's dark, somber paintings help to develop a wood that must not be entered at night.

Alfred Noyes's classic poem *The Highwayman* has a ghostly conclusion to a tale of love, horror, and unselfish motives. Charles Keeping's black-and-white illustrations in *The Highwayman* reinforce the drama in this poem for older readers. Prior to death, the characters are sketched in black. Following death, the horseman becomes a

The illustrations reinforce the spooky mood of the poems. (From Poems of Halloween Night: Ragged Shadows *by Lee Bennett Hopkins. Illustrated by Giles Laroche. Copyright © 1993 by Giles Laroche. Reprinted by permission of Little, Brown and Company.)*

predominantly white figure, who rides through ghostly trees, approaches the old inn door, and finds the landlord's daughter, who is now a ghostly figure herself.

Other vivid poems about ghoulies, ghosties, and graveyards are found in Daisy Wallace's collection, *Ghost Poems*, illustrated by Tomie dePaola. The world of spirits and eerie images is also evoked by Blaise Cendrar's words and Marcia Brown's illustrations in *Shadow*. Cendrar's carefully chosen words suggest a shadow that prowls, mingles, watches, spies, and sprawls in silence. Brown's collages reinforce this ghostly world. Several more ghostly poems are found in the section of poems titled "Spooky Poems" in *Sing a Song of Popcorn: Every Child's Book of Poems* by de Regniers, Moore, White, and Carr. *Poems of Halloween Night: Ragged Shadows* is a collection of poems selected by Lee Bennett Hopkins. Artist Giles Laroche used the setting of Salem, Massachusetts, for collage illustrations about Halloween and the creatures who inhabit the night.

 SUGGESTED ACTIVITIES

for Adult Understanding of Poetry

■ Compare the poetry selections chosen in the Children's Choices, published each year in the October issue of *The Reading Teacher*. What types of poetry are children selecting? Has the poetry changed throughout the years? The listing for all ages in the Children's Choices (1993) includes *And the Green Grass Grew All Around: Folk Poetry from Everyone*, collected by Alvin Schwartz; *Gonna Sing My Head Off!*, collected by Kathleen Krull; and *Jane Yolen's Mother Goose*, selected by Jane Yolen.

■ Read a poem that relies heavily on rhyming elements. Find the location of the rhyming words (at the ends of lines, at the beginnings of the lines, and within the lines). Read the poem orally. What feelings do the rhyming elements suggest?

■ Look through an anthology of poetry and find some poems that rely on sound patterns to create excitement. Prepare for oral presentation a poem that relies on alliteration (the repetition of initial consonant sounds) or assonance (the repetition of vowel sounds). Share the poem orally with a peer group.

■ Locate several poems that develop images literally and several poems that develop images figuratively. Is there a difference in your interest in the two types of imagery? Share the poems with a child. Does the child respond in the same ways to these types?

■ Compile a list of similes and metaphors found in a poem. What images does the poet suggest? Are similes or metaphors more effective or more easily visualized in word pictures than are realistic words?

■ Compare the subject matter of limericks written by Edward Lear with the subject matter of limericks written by such contemporary poets as N. M. Bodecker and William Jay Smith. How are they similar? How do they differ?

■ Read several collections of haiku. Based on your reading, tell what Ann Atwood meant when she said that haiku is "begun by the writer and completed by the reader."

■ Select and read several poems by one poet of humorous verse—such as Edward Lear, Lewis Carroll, Laura

E. Richards, Jack Prelutsky, Shel Silverstein, William Jay Smith, John Ciardi, or N. M. Bodecker. What poetic elements does the poet use? What subjects does the poet write about?

■ Compare the content and style of a poet who wrote humorous verse in the nineteenth century (such as Lewis Carroll or Edward Lear) with those of a contemporary author (such as Jack Prelutsky or N. M. Bodecker). What are the similarities and differences between the writers in the two time periods?

■ After reading some poetry, a primary class is interested in writing poetry about nature. Develop a list of appropriate books for a classroom library that will support their interest. Did you include nonfiction books? Why or why not?

■ You are preparing a letter for the parents of your third-grade class describing an upcoming poetry unit. You want to encourage the parents to help their children find poetry books in the library. Use the database to develop a book list to include in your letter.

■ You need to find books with poetry suitable for choral reading. Use the database to help you prepare such a list.

Involving Children in Poetry

Appreciation for language, knowledge about concepts, empathy with characters and situations, insights about oneself and others, self-expression, and enjoyment are values of poetry for children. Unfortunately, however, research supports Jon E. Shapiro's (1979) assertion that "poetry has often been the most neglected component of the language arts curriculum" (p. 91).

Over 75 percent of the middle-elementary teachers in Ann Terry's (1974) study of children's poetry preferences read poetry to their children less than once a month. This finding may also relate to the fact that the children in Terry's study reported a decreased interest in poetry as they progressed through the elementary grades. Gwendda McKay (1986) reported a similar finding in Australia. She concluded that children at all levels heard stories daily, whereas poetry received little attention. A review of the Children's Choices (1993) shows that very few of the books selected by children are poetry texts or poetry anthologies.

Shapiro maintains that adults' own lack of interest in poetry causes them to neglect it in the classroom. The only way for adults to feel comfortable sharing poetry with children is to read poetry written by many fine authors and thus discover a new or revitalized delight in poetry.

According to John Gough (1988), "Poetry is an acquired taste, and the taste can only be acquired by using poetry, rolling it around the tongue, spitting out words, chewing ideas, putting oneself into the action, taking risks, allowing oneself to be disturbed" (p. 194). Gough maintains that the disturbing aspect of poetry is especially important because "good poetry is disturbing. That is, it challenges our sense of reality, and breaks down our complacency with strange ideas, new feelings and alternative pictures of the world" (p. 194).

Gough (1984) also argues that the anthology format of many poetry collections discourages enjoyment. Individual poems are presented in isolation, rather than in a continuity that sustains interest. Gough believes that appreciation of poetry should be carefully developed and nurtured through a logical sequence: nursery rhymes and songs; rhymed stories, such as Dr. Seuss's *The Cat in the Hat;* narrative poems that are highly but carefully illustrated; stories, such as A. A. Milne's *Winnie-the-Pooh,* in which characters, adventures, and poems are strongly interrelated; narrative poems that give contextual support to the poetry; and then a coherent, related sequence of poems by one poet to encourage understanding of the personality of the poet and appreciation of the poems.

Rumer Godden (1988) stresses that children can be enticed with good poetry. She believes that children should proceed from singing and saying nursery rhymes to exploring lively poems that emphasize movement and rhythm, such as Stevenson's "Windy Nights," to hearing and reading small anthologies of poems to sharing poetry in which poets tell stories, such as Browning's "The Pied Piper of Hamelin," Rossetti's "Goblin Market," Noyes's "The Highwayman," and Scott's "Lochinvar."

University students in this author's classes often say that their aversion to poetry stems from the way in which it was presented in their elementary, middle-school, and high-school classrooms. They fondly remember the rhymes and jingles shared in kindergarten and first grade, but the pleasant associations are undercut by later forced memorization of poems and exercises in which everyone had to agree with the teacher's analysis of a poem. One student recalled her feelings of terror every Friday when she had to recite a memorized poem in front of the class and then had points deducted from her presentation for each error that she made.

Other university students, however, describe more positive memories of poetry in their elementary classrooms. The students remembered teachers who spontaneously shared a wide variety of poetry with their classes; who encouraged students to write poems and share them with an appreciative audience; and who had their students experiment with choral readings of poetry, sometimes accompanied by rhythm instruments. One student remembered a teacher who always had a poem to reflect the mood of a gentle rain, a smiling jack-o-lantern, or a mischievous child. Another remembered going outside on a warm spring day, looking at the butterflies and wildflowers in a meadow, listening to the world around her, sharing her feelings with the class, and then writing a poem to express the promise of that beautiful day. Yet another remembered a librarian who always included poetry in story-hour presentations.

After university students explore the various ways of sharing poetry with children, many of them sadly conclude that something was left out of their own educations. This section considers some ways that you may encourage children to enjoy and experience poetry by listening to poetry, moving to poetry, using poetry as the basis for creative dramatizations, developing choral speaking, combining music and poetry, combining art and poetry, and writing poetry themselves.

 ### LISTENING TO POETRY

Poetry is meant to be read, reread, and shared. The sounds, the rhythms, the vivid words, and the unexpected phrases lend themselves to oral reading. Research shows that poetry is rarely shared with children, and even when poetry is shared, it is often isolated from other experiences. Poet Lee Bennett Hopkins (1987) argues that poetry may be disliked by children because it is frequently taught as an isolated unit instead of shared at appropriate times throughout the day. Hopkins maintains that poetry deserves to be added to the total curriculum, not limited to the language arts. Hopkins provides the following guidelines for reading poetry orally to children, whether you are a parent, teacher, or librarian:

1. Before reading a poem to an audience, read it aloud several times to get the feel of the words and rhythm. Mark the words and phrases that you would like to emphasize.
2. Read the poem naturally, following the rhythm of the poem. Allow the physical appearance of the poem to dictate the rhythm and mood of the words. Some poems are meant to be read softly and slowly; others must be read at a more rapid pace.
3. Make pauses that make sense and that please you.
4. When reading a poem aloud, speak in a natural voice. Read a poem as though you were interested in the subject.

Reading poetry aloud is also an excellent activity for children. Teacher Lisa Lenz (1992) describes the benefits of immersing her elementary students in reading poetry aloud when she states:

Listening to poetry and reading it aloud has helped my first and second graders develop a feel for the texture and power of language. The poetry they've read has stepped off the printed page and become part of their lives. The poetry they've written continues to spill out of their own hearts and into those of their listeners. (p. 597)

Lenz describes the process that she used with her students to help them prepare for reading aloud their poems. They chose poems they loved and then progressed through a series of rehearsals with peer coaches. These coaches helped them listen to themselves and consider how they wanted each poem to sound. After they could read the poems smoothly, they listened for words or phrases that had interested them and marked up a photocopy of the poem by circling special words and making notes in the margins. When they felt prepared, they videotaped their presentations. In *Let's Do a Poem* (1991), Nancy Larrick emphasizes introducing poetry through such activities as listening, singing, and body movement.

 ### MOVING TO POETRY

The rhythms, sounds, characters, and images in many poems encourage physical responses from children. An observer of children on a playground is likely to see two children swinging a rope while a third child jumps to the rhythm and the actions described in a chant such as the following:

> Teddy bear, teddy bear, turn around.
> Teddy bear, teddy bear, touch the ground.
> Teddy bear, teddy bear, close your eyes.
> Teddy bear, teddy bear, be surprised.
> Teddy bear, teddy bear, climb up the stairs.
> Teddy bear, teddy bear, say your prayers.
> Teddy bear, teddy bear, turn out the light.
> Teddy bear, teddy bear, say good night.

In a similar way, children may be inspired to move when you slowly read a poem aloud. Valerie Worth's *More Small Poems* provides children with an opportunity to become a "Kitten," arching their backs, dancing sideways, tearing across the floor, crouching against imagined threats, and pouncing with claws ready, or to become "Fireworks," exploding in the air, billowing into bright color, and spilling back down toward earth in waterfalls. They can be spectacular in a much quieter way as a "Soap Bubble" that bends into different shapes, rises shimmering into the air, then pops and disappears. Worth's *Still More Small Poems* encourages children to experience the free flight of a "Kite" as the wind tears it from a hand and sends it soaring; to become a "Mushroom" pushing up through the soil; or to go "Barefoot," as their feet emerge from choking socks

and they feel cool clover and gentle blades of grass between their toes.

Sports enthusiasts can move to poetry that emphasizes the movements and tensions of various sports. Edwin Hoey's "Foul Shot" and Eve Merriam's "Cheers," both found in Stephen Dunning, Edward Lueders, and Hugh Smith's *Reflections on a Gift of Watermelon Pickle . . . and Other Modern Verse,* inspire children to recreate the rhythms and tensions of a basketball game and the sounds of cheerleaders at a football game. Several poems in R. R. Knudson and May Swenson's *American Sports Poems* lend themselves to acting out through movement. Joseph Colin Murphy's "The Skydivers" encourages children to experience the feel of wind, Arnold Adoff's "Point Guard" simulates passing and scoring, and Maxine Kumin's "400-Meter Freestyle" explores the excitement of a swimming match. Many of the poems in Lillian Morrison's *At the Crack of the Bat* lend themselves to movement. For example, children can pretend to be a baseball player who is experiencing tension in Jacqueline Sweeney's "First Time at Third."

Poetry anthologies, especially if they group poems according to theme, provide numerous opportunities for moving to poetry. For example, Jack Prelutsky's anthology *The Random House Book of Poetry for Children* allows children to become Stanley Kunitz's

ISSUE   Analyzing Poetry: Help or Hindrance?

Will Children enjoy poetry more and understand it better if they analyze the meaning and meter, identify figurative language, and define terminology and poetic devices? The activities suggested in basal readers that include poetry and in literature anthologies designed to be shared with children frequently suggest such analysis. Teachers or librarians may ask children to read or listen to a poem to identify the meaning and theme, locate the similes and metaphors, or identify the rhyming schemes. Adults encourage such activities in the belief that analyzing poetic devices im-

proves children's understanding, enjoyment, and writing of poetry.

Louise M. Rosenblatt takes a contrasting viewpoint.[1] She maintains that reading poetry should be an aesthetic experience in which children focus upon cognitive and affective elements, such as sensations, images, feelings, and ideas that allow them to have a "lived-through" experience. She believes that focusing children's attention on analysis is detrimental when children have not yet had many opportunities to experience poetry on their own terms. Adults should first encourage children to savor what

they visualize, feel, think, and enjoy while hearing or reading poetry.

Myra Cohn Livingston also dislikes analysis.[2] She states that she is unhappy when authors of basal readers use her poem "Whispers" to teach about rhyming words or punctuation, or to ask such questions as "What color is a whisper?"

---

[1] Rosenblatt, Louise M. "What Facts Does This Poem Teach You?" *Language Arts* 57 (April 1980): 386–394.

[2] Livingston, Myra Cohn. "An Unreasonable Excitement." *The Advocate* (Spring 1983).

"The Waltzer in the House" and William Jay Smith's "Seal." The grouping according to types of movements in some anthologies allows students to compare the feelings and the movements created by various poets.

DRAMATIZING POETRY

One of the values of poetry for children noted by Jean Le Pere (1980) is encouragement to identify with characters and situations. Narrative poetry is especially good for helping children identify with characters and situations. In addition, narrative poetry is a favorite among children. In their summary of research that analyzed children's responses to poetry, Dianne Monson and Sam Sebesta (1991) found that narrative poetry is preferred by many children. Creative dramatization is one of the ways that you can enhance children's enjoyment of the situations found in poetry.

Clement C. Moore's narrative poem "A Visit from St. Nicholas" (now familiarly known as "The Night Before Christmas") suggests several scenes to dramatize. Children can prepare for the Christmas celebration by trimming the tree and decorating the room. They can imagine the sugarplum dreams and act them out. They can reenact the father's response to hearing the clatter of hoofs. They can be reindeer pulling the loaded sleigh or St. Nicholas as he comes down the chimney, fills the stockings, and then bounds up the chimney and drives out of sight.

The poem has many other dramatic possibilities. Children have created the dialogue for an imaginary meeting between the father and St. Nicholas or the children and St. Nicholas. What would they say to each other? How would they act? If the children could ask St. Nicholas questions, what would they ask? If St. Nicholas could ask questions, what would he want to know? Children have imagined themselves as St. Nicholas going into many homes on Christmas Eve. What was the most unusual experience they had? They also have imagined themselves going back to St. Nick's workshop at the North Pole. What kind of a welcome did they receive?

Adults have used the nonsensical situations found in Jack Prelutsky's poems in *The Queen of Eene* to stimulate humorous dramatizations. One group, for example, dramatized the conversation and actions of the four foolish ladies (Hattie, Harriet, Hope, and Hortense) as they roped a rhinoceros and took him to tea. Then, the group imagined and acted out other predicaments that could have been created by the actions of the foolish ladies. "Gretchen in the Kitchen" can stimulate spooky dramatizations at Halloween. The quarts of curdled mud, salted spiders, ogre's backbone, and dragon's blood provide a setting appealing to children who are preparing to be spooks, witches, and black cats.

Other poems can be used to stimulate creative dramatizations, including the following:

1. "The Pied Piper of Hamelin," by Robert Browning, located in numerous sources, including Iona and Peter Opie's *The Oxford Book of Children's Verse.* The piper lures rats to their deaths. Then, after the mayor refuses to pay for his services, the piper entices the children of the town to follow him.
2. "The Adventures of Chris," by David McCord, found in *One at a Time: Collected Poems for the Young.* A toad and a boy discuss arithmetic, spelling, and what not to miss on earth.
3. *Sir Cedric,* by Roy Gerrard. Cedric the Good, Black Ned, and Matilda the Pure have knightly adventures.
4. *Sir Francis Drake: His Daring Deeds,* by Roy Gerrard. This explorer has numerous adventures that can stimulate dramatizations.
5. *Night Story,* by Nancy Willard. A small boy has a series of adventures in dreamland.
6. *The Voyage of the Ludgate Hill: Travels with Robert Louis Stevenson,* by Nancy Willard. Travelers on a steamship interact with the animals in the cargo hold.
7. *A Visit to William Blake's Inn: Poems for Innocent and Experienced Travelers,* by Nancy Willard. Many unusual characters, such as the man in the marmalade hat, visit the inn. The characters and incidents can stimulate many dramatizations.

 ## DEVELOPING CHORAL SPEAKING

Choral speaking, the interpretation of poetry or other literature by two or more voices speaking as one, is a group activity that allows children to experience, enjoy, and increase their interest in rhymes, jingles, and other types of poetry. During a choral-speaking or choral-reading experience, children discover that speaking voices can be combined as effectively as singing voices. Young children who cannot read can join in during repeated lines or can take part in rhymes and verses that they know from memory; older children can select anything suitable within their reading ability. Choral speaking is useful in a variety of situations: library programs, classrooms, and extracurricular organizations.

Increasing children's enjoyment of poetry and other literature, not developing a perfect performance, is the main purpose for using choral speaking with elementary children. Allow children to enjoy the experience and experiment with various ways of interpreting poetry. Donna Norton (1997) suggests the following guidelines for encouraging children to interact in choral arrangements:

1. When selecting materials for children who cannot read, choose poems or rhymes that are simple enough to memorize.
2. Choose material of interest to children. Young children like nonsense and active words; consequently, humorous poems are enjoyable first experiences and encourage children to have fun with poetry.
3. Select poems or nursery rhymes that use refrains, especially for young children. Refrains are easy for nonreaders to memorize and result in rapid participation from each group member.
4. Let children help select and interpret the poetry. Have them experiment with the rhythm and tempo of a poem, improvise the scenes of the selection, and try different voice combinations and various choral arrangements before they decide on the best structure.
5. Let children listen to each other as they try different interpretations within groups.

Barbara McIntyre (1974) maintains that adults should also understand the different phases through which children should be guided in their choral interpretations of poetry. First, because young children delight in the rhythm of nursery rhymes, encourage them to explore the rhythm in poetry. They can skip to the rhythm of "Jack and Jill," clap to the rhythm of "Hickory Dickory Dock," and sway to the rhythm of "Little Boy Blue." They can sense fast or slow, happy or sad rhythms through their bodies.

They can explore rhythm and tempo as they "hoppity, hoppity, hop" to A. A. Milne's poem "Hoppity" (found in *When We Were Very Young*).

Second, encourage children to experiment with the color and quality of voices available in the choral-speaking choir. McIntyre says that children do not need to know the meaning of *inflection* (rise and fall within a phrase), *pitch levels* (change between one phrase and another), *emphasis* (pointing out of the most important word), and *intensity* (loudness and softness of voices), but adults must understand these terms so that they can recommend materials that excite children and allow them to try different interpretations. Third, encourage children to understand and experiment with different choral arrangements, such as refrain, line, antiphonal, cumulative, and unison arrangements.

Refrain Arrangement

In refrain arrangement, an adult or a child reads or recites the body of a poem, and the other children respond in unison, repeating a refrain or chorus. Poems such as Maurice Sendak's *Pierre: A Cautionary Tale*, Lewis Carroll's "Beautiful Soup," and Jack Prelutsky's "The Yak" have lines that seem to invite group participation.

A nursery rhyme that encourages young children to participate is "A Jolly Old Pig."

Leader:	A jolly old pig once lived in a sty, And three little piggies she had, And she waddled about saying,
Group:	"Grumph! grumph! grumph!"
Leader:	While the little ones said,
Group:	"Wee! Wee!"
Leader:	And she waddled about saying,
Group:	"Grumph! grumph! grumph!"
Leader:	While the little ones said,
Group:	"Wee! Wee!"

The poetic retelling of "The Fox and the Grapes" in Tom Paxton's version of *Aesop's Fables* contains lines in parentheses such as "(A very high tree, Yes, a very high tree.)" that encourage group responses.

Line Arrangement

To develop a line arrangement, have one child or a group of children read the first line, another child or group read the next line, a third child or group read the next line, and so forth. Continue this arrangement with a different child or different group reading each line until the poem is finished. Use a familiar nursery rhyme to introduce this arrangement, such as:

Child 1 or Group 1:	One, two, buckle my shoe;
Child 2 or Group 2:	Three, four, shut the door;
Child 3 or Group 3:	Five, six, pick up sticks;
Child 4 or Group 4:	Seven, eight, lay them straight;
Child 5 or Group 5:	Nine, ten, a good fat hen.

Enjoyable poems for line-a-child arrangements include Zilpha Keatley Snyder's "Poem to Mud," Laura E. Richards's "Eletelephony," and Jack Prelutsky's "Pumberly Pott's Unpredictable Niece."

Antiphonal, or Dialogue, Arrangement

This arrangement highlights alternate speaking voices. Boys' voices may be balanced against girls' voices, or high voices may be balanced against low voices. Poems such as "Eskimo Chant," found in *The New Wind Has Wings: Poems from Canada,* compiled by Mary Alice Downie and Barbara Robertson, encourage children to respond in either joyful or fearful voices. Poems with question-and-answer formats or other dialogue between two people are obvious choices for antiphonal arrangements. Poems such as Kaye Starbird's "The Spelling Test" and the nursery rhyme "Pussy-Cat, Pussy-Cat" are enjoyable in dialogue arrangements. Paul Fleischman's *I Am Phoenix: Poems for Two Voices* includes poems about birds. Fleischman's *Joyful Noise: Poems for Two Voices* allows children to experiment with sounds and movements of insects. The poems are written to be read by more than one person. Children also enjoy chorally reading the lyrics from folk songs. The words of "Yankee Doodle," for example, can be used with one group of children reading each verse and another group responding with the chorus. Many traditional songs are found in Dan Fox's *Go In and Out the Window: An Illustrated Songbook for Young People.* The folk song "A Hole in the Bucket" presents an enjoyable dialogue between Liza and Henry for choral speaking activity.

Try the following Mother Goose rhyme as a dialogue arrangement:

Boys:	The man in the wilderness asked me
	How many strawberries grew in the sea.
Girls:	I answered him as I thought good,
	As many red herrings as grew in the wood.

Cumulative Arrangement

A crescendo arrangement may be used effectively to interpret a poem that builds to a climax. Have the first group read the first line or verse; the first and second groups read the second line or verse; the first, second, and third groups read the third line or verse; and so forth, until the climax. Then, have all of the groups read together.

Edward Lear's "The Owl and the Pussy-Cat" may be read in a cumulative arrangement by six groups; John Ciardi's "Mummy Slept Late and Daddy Fixed Breakfast" is also fun for six groups to develop into a climax, as Daddy's waffles become impossible to eat. Other poems appropriate for cumulative reading include Arnold Lobel's *The Rose in My Garden.* The nursery rhymes "There Was a Crooked Man" and "This Is the House That Jack Built" are also enjoyable.

Try the following traditional folk song, "Skin and Bones," as a cumulative arrangement:

Group 1:	There was an old woman all skin and bones, Oo—oo—oo!
Groups 1 and 2:	She lived down by the graveyard, Oo—oo—oo!
Groups 1, 2, and 3:	One night she thought she'd take a walk, Oo—oo—oo!
Groups 1, 2, 3, and 4:	She went to the closet to get a broom, Oo—oo—oo!
Groups 1, 2, 3, 4, and 5:	She opened the door and BOO!

As a variation, develop a reverse arrangement. Have all groups begin together; then, with each subsequent line or verse, have a group drop out until only one group remains. This arrangement works well with such poems as Barbara Kunz Loots's "Mountain Wind" and James Reeves's "The Wind." Both poems begin with louder expressions and end in silence or quiet. These poems are found in Jack Prelutsky's *The Random House Book of Poetry for Children.*

Unison Arrangement

In unison arrangement, the entire group or class reads or speaks a poem together. This arrangement is often the most difficult to perform, because it tends to create a singsong effect. For this reason, shorter poems, such as Myra Cohn Livingston's "O Sliver of Liver," Lillian Morrison's "The Sidewalk Racer" or "On the Skateboard," and Judith Thurman's "Campfire," are appropriate.

Additional Suggestions

Fran Tanner (1979) recommends that older children experiment with the effects of grouping their voices according to resonance, with light, medium, and dark voices. Through experimentation, children discover that light voices may effectively interpret happy, whimsical, or delicate parts; medium voices may add to descriptive and narrative parts; and dark voices may interpret robust and tragic material. Tanner recommends the following classic poem for such an experiment.

The Brook

(light)	I slip,
(medium)	I slide,
(dark)	I gloom.
(medium)	I glance.
	Among my skimming swallows;
(light)	I make the netted sunbeams dance
	Against my sandy shallows.
(dark)	I murmur under moon and stars
	In brambly wildernesses;
(medium)	I linger by my shingly bars,
(light)	I loiter round my cresses;
(medium)	And out again I curve and flow
	To join the brimming river,
(dark)	For men may come
(dark and medium)	and men may go,
(all)	But I go on forever.

Alfred Lord Tennyson

The poems in a single poetry collection may be read, discussed, and developed into various choral-speaking arrangements. For example, this activity can accompany Nancy Larrick's anthology, *When the Dark Comes Dancing: A Bedtime Poetry Book*. The poems may be presented in the following ways: Martin Brennan's "Benue Lullaby," refrain; Margaret Wise Brown's "Little Donkey Close Your Eyes," line-a-group; Arthur Guiterman's "Nocturne," antiphonal

between lighter voices and heavier voices; Felice Holman's "Night Sounds," antiphonal between male and female voices; Sabine Baring-Gould's "Now the Day Is Over," reverse cumulative; Vachel Lindsay's "The Moon's the North Wind's Cooky," reverse cumulative followed by cumulative; Myra Cohn Livingston's "The Night," unison; and Eve Merriam's "Lullaby," unison.

 ## WRITING POETRY

Research into the development of the writing process of children, conducted by Donald Graves (1988) and George Hillocks (1986), suggests that adults should work with children during the writing process rather than after the materials are completed. Current research emphasizes using phases in the writing process to encourage students to explore, plan, draft, and revise. For example, Proett and Gill (1986) report a sequence of events and recommend activities from experiences at the Bay Area Writing Project and the University of California. These educators sequence the process according to activities that should be done (a) before the students write (content and idea building through observing, remembering, imagining, experiencing, logging, reading, brainstorming, listing, dramatizing, developing details, and structuring), (b) while the students write (developing rhetorical stance and linguistic choices by deciding voice, audience, purpose, form, word choice, figurative language, structure, and syntax), and (c) after the students write (encouraging revision and highlighting by sharing with editing groups, raising questions, expanding, clarifying, proofreading, sharing, reading, and publishing).

The various phases are certainly crucial to poetry writing. By reading or listening to poetry, children obtain motivational and observational opportunities to develop their awareness and to stimulate their imaginations. Children require opportunities to incubate and clarify ideas, to compose and revise their poetry, and to share their poetry with an appreciative audience. To share poetry writing experiences with children, use the sequence in Chart 8–1, adapted from research by Donna Norton (1997).

Motivations

The three categories of motivational activities outlined in Chart 8–1 suggest that numerous topics can stimulate the writing of poetry. Many activities already occurring in classrooms, libraries, or extracurricular organizations are natural sources of topics for self-expression through poetry. For example, while teaching a social studies unit, a second-grade teacher showed a film about farm life. The teacher encouraged the children to observe the characteristics and actions of the farm animals and then to write about them in poetic form. A Girl Scout leader encouraged children to describe and write about their feelings following a soccer game. A librarian asked children to write their own color poems after they heard Mary O'Neill's poems about colors in *Hailstones and Halibut Bones*.

CHART 8–1   An instructional sequence for poetry writing

I. Motivation
   A. Ongoing activities
   B. Everyday experiences
   C. New, adult-introduced experiences
II. Oral exchange of ideas
   A. Questions and answers to extend stimulation activities
   B. Brainstorming of subjects, vocabulary, images, and such
   C. Idea clarifications
III. Transcription
   A. Individual dictation of poems to adults
   B. Individual writing
   C. Teacher interaction to help development
   D. Adult assistance when required
   E. Revision and editing through small-group interaction and teacher interaction during individual writing
IV. Sharing
   A. Reading of the poetry to a group
   B. Audience development
   C. Permanent collections
   D. Poetry extensions, if desired, to poetry dramatizations, choral reading, art interpretations, and so forth
V. Post-transcription
   A. Permanent writing folders
   B. Writing conferences
   C. Modeling of the writing process

Gerald Duffy (1973) identified frequent sharing of poetry as effective in motivating children to write poetry. University students have used both poetry written by adult authors and poetry written by children as ways of stimulating children to write their own poems. For example, they have used Kenneth Koch's *Wishes, Lies, and Dreams* (1970), reading the poems under a certain topic to children and then using the suggestions developed by Koch to encourage the children to write their own poems. Several of the categories include experiences that are common to children but allow the children to think of these experiences in new ways. A third-grade teacher encouraged his students to consider the wishes that they might make if they had the opportunity and then asked them to write a poem expressing those wishes. The following is an example of a third grader's wishes.

> I wish I had a puppy,
>   not a dog, a puppy
>   not a cat, a puppy
>   not a kitten, a puppy.
> I wish I was rich
>   not poor, but rich
>   not a little bit of money, a lot
>   so I'm really rich.
> I wish I had a Genie
>   not a pony, a Genie
>   not a pig, a Genie
>   not a pig or a pony
>   a Genie.
> I wish I could
>   have anything
>   know anything
>   be anything
>   see anything
>   and do anything
>   I wish.
>
>   Eight-year-old

Many adults encourage children to write poetry by introducing them to experiences that allow the children to nurture their awareness and their observational powers. The children may go for a walk in a flowering park or meadow, listen to the noises around them, smell the air in spring, touch trees and flowers, describe their sensations with new feelings, and then write poems about their experiences. The following poem resulted from a sixth grader's visual experiences out-of-doors.

Woodland

Cool crisp air calls me
Late September afternoon
Crimson, gold, green, rust
Falling leaves whisper softly
Come look, what's new in the woods?

Eleven-year-old

Even the sun's shining through a window can be used to inspire a poem.

The Sunshine

The sunshine entered the morning
And birds began to sing.
The sunshine entered the clouds
And a rainbow appeared.
The sunshine entered the afternoon
And made the evening clear.
Your smile entered the room
And sunshine entered my heart.

Eleven-year-old

Other activities found to be successful stimuli for poetry include listening to music, becoming involved in art projects, closely observing and touching objects, considering the various uses for unique objects, and looking at and discussing pictures. One girl described very well how music affected her.

A Song

Something I want to say
But haven't got the words
To say what I feel
The music makes it easy
The music sets me free.

Nine-year-old

A sixth-grade teacher found music to be especially stimulating for her students. She says, "We spent several sessions writing to music such as *Icarus* by Winter Consort and *Night on Bald Mountain* by Mussorgsky. The children let their imaginations soar, they visualized the images created by the music, and wrote their impressions. They especially enjoyed sharing their impressions with each other" (personal communication to author).

A class of older students studied possible relationships between art and poetry. First, the students viewed and discussed art chosen from the Metropolitan Museum of Art to illustrate the poems in Kenneth Koch and Kate Farrell's anthology *Talking to the Sun*. The students shared their feelings about the art, the poetry, and the appropriateness or inappropriateness of the matches between the art and poetry. Then, the students wrote their own poems about their moods and feelings, the settings in the paintings, or the characters in the paintings. The purpose for this activity was to enhance the enjoyment of the viewing and the writing, not to create literal interpretations of the artworks.

Oral Exchanges of Ideas

During an oral exchange of ideas, encourage children to think aloud about a subject. For example, through brainstorming, children may gain many ideas from each other and look at old ideas in new ways. Susan Nugent Reed (1979) describes how a poet in the schools, Bill Wertheim, encouraged discussion before writing:

The figure of a skeleton in one of the classrooms evolved into a lesson about death. Wertheim wrote, "The discussion went from Halloween to skeletons, to fear of skeletons, to monsters, to dying: loss of something and/or someone we love. How it feels to die, how it feels to lose someone you care about." He indicated that the topic first was discussed aloud, then later on paper. For those children who preferred an alternative topic, he suggested writing about coming back to life. Wertheim said it was the most touching lesson he had ever taught and that some children cried. This led to a discussion about crying, trust, and kindness. He took this opportunity to express the idea that "crying is OK, even for boys." He said that the children were kind and supportive of one another. (p. 110)

During an outside observational session, have children look at clouds and share their impressions, describe the ways the light filters through the leaves, or close their eyes and describe the sounds they hear. The librarian who encouraged children to write color poems after listening to Mary O'Neill's poems in *Hailstones and Halibut Bones* asked the children to observe the colors around them. They searched for objects that reminded them of the colors in the poems and talked about their moods as reflected by colors. For example, brainstorming the color white produced the following associations, and more: snowflakes, winter silence, puffy clouds, a wedding veil, the flash of winning, a frost-covered window, quivering vanilla pudding, heaps of popcorn, a plastered wall, apple blossoms, pale lilac blossoms, sails skimming across a lake, a forgotten memory, fog rising from a marsh, a polar bear, and a gift wrapped in tissue paper. After this experience, the children began to look at common objects and feelings with new awareness.

Transcriptions

You can help young children compose by taking dictation. Encourage the children to tell you their thoughts while you write them down. Parents indicate that even very young children enjoy seeing their creative jingles, rhymes, and poems in print. Children enjoy playing with language and feeling the tickle of new ways of expression falling off their tongues.

One university student found it meaningful that her mother had kept a notebook of her early experiences writing poetry. Another university student, who had several poems published, felt that his early spontaneous poetry, written down by his mother, had stimulated his desire to become a professional writer. Parents who have been successful in this type of dictation have been careful not to force dictation upon a child or to criticize any thoughts or feelings expressed. The experiences have been warm, trusting relationships, in which children discover that their thoughts can be written down and saved for themselves and for sharing with others.

When children have mastered the mechanics of writing, they usually write their own poems. However, when working with children, continue to interact with them as they progress with their writing. Encourage them to reread their poems aloud, ask questions to help clarify a problem or an idea, or answer questions pertaining to spelling and punctuation.

Sharing

The ideal way to share poetry is to read it to an appreciative audience. Consequently, many adults encourage children to share their creations with others. Attractive bulletin boards of children's poems may also stimulate children to read one another's poems and write more poems.

Children enjoy making permanent collections of their poems. One teacher had each child develop an accordion-pleated poem book (see Figure 8-2). To construct their books, the children folded large sheets of heavy drawing paper in half, con-

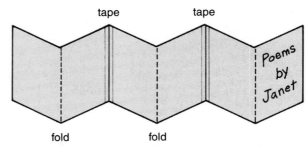

FIGURE 8-2 *An accordion-pleated poem book*

nected several sheets with tape, and printed an original poem and an accompanying illustration on each page.

Other classes have made their own books by constructing covers in various appropriate shapes, cutting paper to match the shapes, and binding the covers and pages together. A group of second graders placed Halloween poems inside a jack-o-lantern book, fourth graders wrote city poems inside a book resembling a skyscraper, and third graders placed humorous mythical animal poems inside a book resembling a beast from Dr. Seuss (see Figure 8-3). Although it is not necessary to extend writing of poetry to other activities, children often enjoy using their own poetry for choral reading, art interpretations, or dramatizations.

Various Forms of Poetry

Many children enjoy experimenting with writing different types of poems, such as limericks, cinquains, and diamantes. Limericks, for example, were among the poetry most enjoyed by children in Ann Terry's (1974) study of children's poetry preferences. David McCord's *One at a Time: Collected Poems for the Young* describes the content and form of limericks and provides examples that you can share with children. Use the nonsense limericks of Edward Lear, N. M. Bodecker, and William Jay Smith to stimulate these five-line poems. Follow this form: Lines 1, 2, and 5 rhyme and have a three-beat rhythm; lines 3 and 4 rhyme and have a two-beat rhythm. Brainstorming words that rhyme helps children complete their rhyming lines. After reading and listening to a number of limericks, a sixth grader wrote about and illustrated the following predicament.

Involving Children in Poetry **447**

FIGURE 8–3 *Shapes of various poetry books*

There once was a girl named Mandy
Whose hair was dreadfully sandy
She never did wash it
Instead she did frost it
The icing made Mandy smell dandy

Eleven-year-old

Cinquains are another form of poetry having specific structural requirements. These poems help children realize that descriptive words are important when expressing feelings in poetry and that rhyming words are not necessary. A cinquain uses the following structure.

Line 1:   One word for the title.
Line 2:   Two words that describe the title.
Line 3:   Three words that express action
            related to the title.
Line 4:   Four words that express a feeling about
            the title.
Line 5:   One word that either repeats the title or
            expresses a word closely related to the
            title.

Brainstorming descriptive words and action words adds to children's enjoyment in writing and sharing their cinquains. The following cinquains were written by middle-school children.

Tree
Huge,   woody
Expanding,   reproducing,   entertaining
Leaves   are   colorfully   crisp
Oak

Eleven-year-old

Lasagna
Hot,   delectable
Steaming,   bubbling,   oozing
Always   great   on   Fridays
Paisans

Eleven-year-old

A diamante is a diamond-shaped poem. Poems written in the diamante format progress from one noun to a final noun that contrasts with the first noun. Because this form is more complex than the cinquain is, you should describe each line and draw a diagram of the diamante to help children see the relationships among the lines. Diamantes have the following structure.

Line 1:   One noun.
Line 2:   Two adjectives that describe the noun.
Line 3:   Three words that express action
            related to the noun.
Line 4:   Four nouns or a phrase that expresses a
            transition in thought between the first
            noun and the final contrasting noun.
Line 5:   Three words that express action
            related to the contrasting noun.
Line 6:   Two adjectives that describe the contrasting noun.
Line 7:   One contrasting noun.

Diagramming this type of poem as follows is also helpful:

noun
describing describing
action   action   action
transition nouns or phrase
action   action   action
describing describing
noun

Children find it helpful to brainstorm suggestions for contrasting nouns to form the framework for the ideas developed in a diamante. One teacher brainstormed with upper-elementary students and developed the following contrasts.

sun—moon	tears—smiles
day—night	young—old
life—death	happy—sad
friends—enemies	man—woman
summer—winter	war—peace
sky—ground	love—hate
angel—devil	darkness—light
boredom—excitement	dreams—reality

Next, each group wrote a poem. The following poems were created by this experience.

Light

Beautiful, bright
Seeing, glistening, refreshing
Light is sometimes blinding
Groping, cautioning, frightening
Evil, insecure
Dark

Ten-year-old

Friends

Happiness, security
Understanding, caring, laughing
Reaching out your hand
Hating, hurting, fighting
Silence, tension
Enemies

Ten-year-old

An excellent source of ideas and suggestions for poetry writing is Stephen Dunning and William Stafford's *Getting the Knack: 20 Poetry Writing Exercises* (1992). Each of the exercises includes an introduction, steps to follow, and examples of poems that were written using the writing exercise.

SUGGESTED ACTIVITIES

for Involving Children in Poetry

- Develop a card file of poetry appropriate to use with children. Type the poems on cards using a primary-type typewriter. On the back of each card, list several suggestions for sharing the poem with children. Put the cards into logical categorizations.

- Ask some children to tell their favorite jumping-rope chants. Collect as many of these chants as possible.

Share any new chants with other children. Ask the children why they like and remember such chants.

- Select a series of poems that encourage physical responses from children. Share the poems with a group of children or a peer group. Include poems to encourage children to move through the air, mimic the movements of an animal, or become something other than themselves.

- Select a poem or a series of poems that encourage creative dramatizations. Plan the steps needed to encourage children to interpret the poetry.

- Select poems that can be interpreted through choral-speaking arrangements: refrain, line, antiphonal, cumulative, and unison. Share the poems with a group of children or a peer group.

- Following an instructional sequence for poetry writing, develop a lesson plan designed to stimulate children's writing of poetry.

- Try one of the activities developed in Stephen Dunning and William Stafford's *Getting the Knack: 20 Poetry Writing Exercises* (1992), Myra Cohn Livingston's *Poetry-Making: Ways to Begin Writing Poetry* (1991), or Beatrice Cullinan, Marilyn C. Scalo, and Virginia Schroeder's *Three Voices: An Invitation to Poetry Across the Curriculum*. Share the results of the activity with your children's literature class.

CHILDREN'S LITERATURE

Adoff, Arnold. *All the Colors of the Race*. Illustrated by John Steptoe. Lothrop, Lee & Shepard, 1982. A girl from a mixed racial parentage reflects on tolerance.

———. *Love Letters*. Illustrated by Lisa Desimini. Scholastic, 1997. The poems are messages that might be sent.

———. *My Black Me: A Beginning Book of Black Poetry*. Dutton, 1974. This is a collection of black poetry.

———. ed. *The Poetry of Black America: Anthology of the 20th Century*. Harper & Row, 1973. This text includes over three hundred poems by black poets.

———. *Sports Pages*. Illustrated by Steve Kuzma. Lippencott, 1986. This text includes poems about experiences of athletes.

Aesop. *Aesop's Fables*. Retold by Tom Paxton. Illustrated by Robert Rayevsky. Morrow, 1988. This is a poetic version of the fables.

Alarcon, Francisco X. *Laughing Tomatoes*. Illustrated by Maya Christina Gonzalez. Children's, 1997. The poems are presented in both English and Spanish.

Atwood, Ann. *Haiku: The Mood of Earth*. Scribner's Sons, 1971. Beautiful photographs accompany haiku nature poems.

Baylor, Byrd. *The Desert Is Theirs*. Illustrated by Peter Parnall. Scribner's Sons, 1975. A poem stresses the love the Papago Indians have for their desert home.

_____. *Moon Song.* Illustrated by Ronald Himler. Scribner's Sons, 1982. A Pima Indian legend, in poetic text, tells how Coyote was born and survived.

_____. *The Other Way to Listen.* Illustrated by Peter Parnall. Scribner's Sons, 1978. You have to be patient to hear cactuses blooming and rocks murmuring, but it's worth it.

Baylor, Byrd, and Peter Parnall. *Desert Voices.* Scribner's Sons, 1981. Ten creatures from the desert give their viewpoints on their surroundings.

Bechely, Paddy, ed. *Drumming in the Sky: Poems from 'Stories and Rhymes.'* Illustrated by Priscilla Lamont. British Broadcasting, 1981. The poems are selected from the BBC Radio series.

Berry, James. *Everywhere Faces Everywhere.* Illustrated by Reynold Ruffins. Simon & Schuster, 1997. Five sections divide the poetry into various subjects.

Bierhorst, John, ed. *The Sacred Path: Spells, Prayers & Power Songs of the American Indians.* Morrow, 1983. This collection is from sources across North America.

Blake, William. *The Tyger.* Illustrated by Neil Waldman. Harcourt Brace Jovanovich, 1993. This is a newly illustrated edition of the eighteenth-century poem.

Bodecker, N. M. *Hurry, Hurry Mary Dear.* Atheneum, 1976. A collection of forty-three humorous poems is accompanied by pen sketches.

Bouchard, David. *Voices From the Wild: An Animal Sensagoria.* Illustrated by Ron Parker. Chronicle, 1996. The poems depict twenty-five wild animals.

Brooks, Gwendolyn. *Bronzeville Boys and Girls.* Illustrated by Ronni Solbert. Harper & Row, 1956. This book explores children and their feelings.

Browning, Robert. *The Pied Piper of Hamelin.* Illustrated by Kate Greenaway. Warne Classic, 1888. This reissue of the original poem has delightful illustrations of children by Greenaway.

Bryan, Ashley. *I'm Going to Sing: Black American Spirituals.* Vol. 2. Atheneum, 1982. This text includes musical arrangements.

_____. *Sing to the Sun.* HarperCollins, 1992. African American poems reflect the Caribbean.

Burkert, Nancy Ekholm. *Valentine and Orson.* Farrar, Straus & Giroux, 1989. A tale of twins separated at birth is told in poetry.

Carroll, Lewis. *Jabberwocky.* Illustrated by Jane Breskin Zalben. Warne, 1977. This picture interpretation of Carroll's poem is in watercolors.

_____. *Poems of Lewis Carroll.* Selected by Myra Cohn Livingston. Crowell, 1973. This collection of poems is from *Alice's Adventures in Wonderland* and *Through the Looking-Glass.*

Carson, Jo, ed. *Stories I Ain't Told Nobody Yet.* Watts, 1989. This anthology includes a collection of poems written by people in Appalachia.

Carter, Anne, compiled by. *Birds, Beasts, and Fishes: A Selection of Animal Poems.* Illustrated by Reg Cartwright. Macmillan, 1991. This is a collection of poems about animals.

Causley, Charles, ed. *Salt-Sea Verse.* Illustrated by Antony Maitland. Kestrel, Puffin, 1981. This anthology of poems is about the sea.

Cendrars, Blaise. *Shadow.* Translated and illustrated by Marcia Brown. Scribner's Sons, 1982. An eerie poem talks about the world of spirits.

Chorao, Kay. *The Baby's Bedtime Book.* Dutton, 1984. This is a collection of lullabies.

Christensen, Bonnie. *Rebus Riot.* Dial, 1997. This is a collection of humorous poems.

Ciardi, John. *Doodle Soup.* Illustrated by Merle Nacht. Houghton Mifflin, 1985. This is a collection of humorous poems.

_____. *The Hopeful Trout and Other Limericks.* Illustrated by Susan Meddaugh. Houghton Mifflin, 1989. This text includes humorous limericks.

_____. *You Read to Me, I'll Read to You.* Illustrated by Edward Gorey. Lippincott, 1962. Poems for a child to read are followed by poems for an adult to read.

Cole, William, ed. *Poem Stew.* Illustrated by Karen Ann Weinhaus. Lippincott, 1981. This collection of humorous poems is related to food.

Demi, ed. *In the Eyes of the Cat: Japanese Poetry for All Seasons.* Illustrated by Demi, translated by Tze-si Huang. Holt, 1992. This is a collection of classic Japanese poetry.

de Regniers, Beatrice Schenk, Eva Moore, Mary Michaels White, and Jean Carr. *Sing a Song of Popcorn: Every Child's Book of Poems.* Scholastic, 1988. An anthology of poems is illustrated by nine Caldecott Medal artists.

Downie, Mary Alice, and Barbara Robertson, eds. *The New Wind Has Wings: Poems from Canada.* Illustrated by Elizabeth Cleaver. Oxford University Press, 1984. This is a collection of poems.

Duffy, Carol Ann, ed. *I Wouldn't Thank You for a Valentine: Poems for Young Feminists.* Illustrated by Trisha Rafferty. Holt, 1994. These poems explore many feelings and emotions.

Dunning, Stephen, Edward Lueders, and Hugh Smith, eds. *Reflections on a Gift of Watermelon Pickle . . . and Other Modern Verse.* Lothrop, Lee & Shepard, 1967. An anthology of one hundred and fourteen poems is accompanied by photographs.

Dyer, Jane. *Animal Crackers: A Delectable Collection of Pictures, Poems, and Lullabies for the Very Young.* Little, Brown, 1996. A collection of poems for young children.

Eliot, T. S. *Mr. Mistoffelees with Mungojerrie and Rumpelteazer.* Illustrated by Errol Le Cain. Harcourt Brace Jovanovich, 1991. These poems were selected from *Old Possum's Book of Practical Cats.*

_____. *Old Possum's Book of Practical Cats.* Illustrated by Edward Gorey. Harcourt Brace Jovanovich, 1939, 1967, 1982. This book includes such poems as "Mr. Mistofelees," "The Rum Tum Tugger," and "Macavity: The Mystery Cat."

Esbensen, Barbara. *Who Shrank My Grandmother's House? Poems of Discovery.* Illustrated by Eric Beddows. HarperCollins, 1992. The poems emphasize childhood discoveries.

Ferris, Helen, ed. *Favorite Poems Old and New.* Doubleday, 1957. This is an anthology.

Field, Eugene. *Wynken, Blynken and Nod.* Illustrated by Susan Jeffers. Dutton, 1982. The classic poem appears in a newly illustrated edition.

Fields, Julia. *The Green Lion of Zion Street.* Illustrated by Jerry Pinkney. Macmillan, 1988. In this poem, children conquer their fears.

Fisher, Aileen. *Feathered Ones and Furry.* Illustrated by Eric Carle. Crowell, 1971. Fifty-five poems are about furry animals and feathery birds.

_____. *In One Door and Out the Other: A Book of Poems.* Illustrated by Lillian Hoban. Crowell, 1969. A collection of poems tells about childhood experiences.

——— . *Listen, Rabbit.* Illustrated by Simeon Shimin. Crowell, 1964. These verses follow a boy through the seasons as he tries to befriend a rabbit.

——— . *Rabbits, Rabbits.* Illustrated by Gail Nieman. Harper & Row, 1983. These poems tell about rabbits during different times of the year.

——— . *When it Comes to Bugs.* Illustrated by Chris and Bruce Degen. Harper & Row, 1986. This text includes eighteen poems about bugs.

Fleischman, Paul. *I Am Phoenix: Poems for Two Voices.* Illustrated by Ken Nutt. Harper & Row, 1985. Poems about birds are designed to be read by two readers.

——— . *Joyful Noise: Poems for Two Voices.* Illustrated by Eric Beddows. Harper & Row, 1988. Poems written in two parts are designed to be read concurrently by two readers.

Fox, Dan, ed. *Go In and Out the Window: An Illustrated Songbook for Young People.* Metropolitan Museum of Art and Holt, Rinehart & Winston, 1987. This is a beautifully illustrated collection of songs.

Froman, Robert. *Seeing Things: A Book of Poems.* Crowell, 1974. Several concrete poems are in this collection.

Frost, Robert. *Birches.* Illustrated by Ed Young. Holt, Rinehart & Winston, 1988. This is a highly illustrated version of Frost's classic poem.

——— . *Stopping by Woods on a Snowy Evening.* Illustrated by Susan Jeffers. Dutton, 1978. Large pictures illustrate Frost's poem.

George, Kristine O'Connell. *The Great Frog Race and Other Poems.* Illustrated by Kate Kiesler. Clarion, 1997. The poems stress the natural world.

Gerrard, Roy. *Sir Cedric.* Farrar, Straus & Giroux, 1984. The heroic deeds of a bold knight are told in poetic form.

——— . *Sir Francis Drake: His Daring Deeds.* Farrar, Straus & Giroux, 1988. This poem tells about the exploits of the explorer.

——— . *Wagons West!* Farrar, Straus & Giroux, 1996. The poem tells the adventures experienced by a wagon train.

Gordon, Ruth, selected by. *Pierced By A Ray of Sun: Poems About the Times We Feel Alone.* HarperCollins, 1995. A collection of poems that express feelings.

Greenfield, Eloise, *Honey, I Love.* Illustrated by Jan Spivey Gilchrist. HarperCollins, 1995. The things a young girl loves.

——— . *Nathaniel Talking.* Illustrated by Jan Gilchrist. Black Butterfly Children's Books, 1989. The life of a nine-year-old is told in rap and verse.

Grimes, Nikki. *Come Sunday.* Illustrated by Michael Bryant. Eerdmans, 1996. The poems capture the spirit of a young girl and an African American congregation.

——— . *Under the Sunday Tree.* Illustrated by Amos Ferguson. Harper & Row, 1988. Poems explore life in the Bahamas.

Heide, Florence Parry. *Grim and Ghastly.* Illustrated by Victoria Chess. Lothrop, Lee & Shepard, 1992. A collection of monster poems.

Highwater, Jamake. *Moonsong Lullaby.* Photographs by Marcia Keegan. Lothrop, Lee & Shepard, 1981. A poem is inspired by ancient Native American stories.

Hood, Thomas. *Before I Go to Sleep.* Illustrated by Mary Jane Begin-Callanan. Putnam, 1990. Nighttime verse is by Thomas Hood.

Hopkins, Lee Bennett, ed. *Click, Rumble, Roar.* Photographs by Anna Held Audette. Crowell, 1987. This text includes eighteen poems about machines.

——— , ed. *Dinosaurs.* Illustrated by Murray Tinkelman. Harcourt Brace Jovanovich, 1987. Eighteen poems are about dinosaurs.

——— . *Good Rhymes, Good Times.* Illustrated by Frane Lessac. HarperCollins, 1995. This is a collection of twenty-one poems.

——— , ed. *Poems of Halloween Night: Ragged Shadows.* Illustrated by Giles Laroche. Little, Brown, 1993. This book contains fourteen Halloween poems.

——— , ed. *Surprises.* Illustrated by Megan Lloyd. Harper & Row, 1984. This is a collection of easy-to-read poems.

Hughes, Langston. *The Dream Keeper.* Knopf, 1932, 1960. This is a collection of poems by the black poet.

——— . *Selected Poems of Langston Hughes.* Knopf, 1942, 1959. Many poems relate to Hughes's black heritage.

Janeczko, Paul B., ed. *Going Over to Your Place. Poems for Each Other.* Bradbury, 1987. A collection of poems explores the feelings of young adults.

——— , ed. *The Music of What Happens: Poems That Tell Stories.* Watts, 1988. A collection of poems tells about serious occurrences in the lives of young adults.

Johnson, James Weldon. *The Creation.* Illustrated by Carla Golembe. Little, Brown, 1993. This poem is based on the creation story from the Bible.

Katz, Bobbi. *Truck Talk: Rhymes on Wheels.* Scholastic, 1997. The poems describe different kinds of trucks.

Kemp, Gene, ed. *Ducks and Dragons: Poems for Children.* Illustrated by Carolyn Dinan. Faber & Faber, 1980; Puffin, 1983. This is an anthology of poems about seasons, reality, animals, fantasy, fear, and old songs.

Kellogg, Steven. *I Was Born About 10,000 Years Ago.* Morrow, 1996. Kellogg illustrates the ballad.

Kennedy, X. J. *The Beasts of Bethlehem.* Illustrated by Michael McCurdy. Macmillan, 1992. The poems reflect possible feelings expressed by the animals present at the birth of Christ.

——— . *The Forgetful Wishing Well: Poems for Young People.* Illustrated by Monica Incisa. Atheneum, 1985. A collection of poems tells about meaningful experiences.

——— , and Dorothy M. Kennedy, eds. *Knock at a Star: A Child's Introduction to Poetry.* Illustrated by Karen Ann Weinhaus. Little, Brown, 1982. The anthology is organized to help children understand poetry.

——— , and Dorothy M. Kennedy, eds. *Talking Like the Rain: A First Book of Poems.* Illustrated by Jane Dyer. Little, Brown, 1992. This is an anthology of poetry from both classic and contemporary poets.

Kipling, Rudyard. *Gunga Din.* Illustrated by Robert Andrew Parker. Harcourt Brace Jovanovich, 1987. The poem is set in nineteenth-century India.

Knudson, R. R., and May Swenson, eds. *American Sports Poems.* Watts, 1988. An anthology of poems is about sports and athletes.

Koch, Kenneth, and Kate Farrell, eds. *Talking to the Sun.* Metropolitan Museum of Art/Holt, Rinehart & Winston, 1985. Reproductions from the Metropolitan Museum illustrate this anthology.

Lalicki, Barbara, ed. *If There Were Dreams to Sell.* Illustrated by Margot Tomes. Lothrop, Lee & Shepard, 1984. The poems follow an alphabetical format.

Langstaff, John, ed. *What a Morning! The Christmas Story in Black Spirituals.* Illustrated by Ashley Bryan. Macmillan, 1987. Black spirituals and illustrations tell the Christmas story.

Larrick, Nancy, ed. *Songs from Mother Goose.* Illustrated by Robin Spowart. Harper & Row, 1989. A collection of nursery rhymes is accompanied by music.

_____ , ed. *When the Dark Comes Dancing: A Bedtime Poetry Book.* Illustrated by John Wallner. Philomel, 1982. This poetry is to be read aloud at bedtime.

Lear, Edward. *A Book of Bosh.* Compiled by Brian Alderson. Penguin, 1982. This is a collection of Lear's poetry.

_____ . *The Complete Nonsense Book.* Dodd, Mead, 1946. This book includes *A Book of Nonsense,* originally published in 1846, and *Nonsense Songs and Stories,* originally published in 1871.

_____ . *Hilary Knight's The Owl and the Pussy-Cat.* Illustrated by Hilary Knight. Macmillan, 1983. Knight creates a fantasy around Lear's poem.

_____ . *The Nonsense Books of Edward Lear.* New American Library, 1964. These nonsense poems are still enjoyed by children.

_____ . *Nonsense Omnibus.* Warne, 1943. Original illustrations and verses are from four of Lear's collections.

_____ . *Nonsense Songs.* Illustrated by Bee Willey. Simon & Schuster, 1997. This is an illustrated version of four of Lear's poems.

_____ . *The Owl and the Pussycat.* Illustrated by Jan Brett. Putnam's, 1991. The classic poem is set in the Caribbean.

_____ . *The Pelican Chorus and Other Nonsense.* Illustrated by Fred Marcellino. HarperCollins, 1995. Three of Lear's poems are illustrated.

Lee, Dennis. *The Ice Cream Store.* Illustrated by David McPhail. HarperCollins, 1991. This is a collection of humorous poems.

Levy, Constance. *I'm Going to Pet a Worm Today and Other Poems.* Illustrated by Ronald Himler. Macmillan, 1991. This is a collection of nature poems.

Lewis, J. Patrick. *Earth Verses and Water Rhymes.* Illustrated by Robert Sabuda. Atheneum, 1991. This is a collection of nature poems.

Lewis, Richard. *Of This World: A Poet's Life in Poetry.* Photographs by Helen Buttfield. Dial, 1968. This book includes poems by the Japanese poet Issa and information about his life.

Lindbergh, Reeve. *Johnny Appleseed.* Illustrated by Kathy Jakobsen. Little, Brown, 1990. The poem is based on the life of John Chapman.

Little, Jean. *Hey World, Here I Am!* Illustrated by Sue Truesdell. Harper & Row, 1989. Poems and short stories are told from a teenage girl's viewpoint.

Livingston, Myra Cohn, ed. *Cat Poems.* Illustrated by Trina Schart Hyman. Holiday House, 1987. Nineteen poems are about cats.

_____ . *Celebrations.* Illustrated by Leonard Everett Fisher. Holiday House, 1985. A collection of sixteen poems is about holidays.

_____ . *A Circle of Seasons.* Illustrated by Leonard Everett Fisher. Holiday House, 1982. Poems are about the four seasons.

_____ . *Cricket Never Does: A Collection of Haiku and Tanka.* Illustrated by Kees de Kiefte. McElderry, 1997. The poems present the Japanese forms of poetry.

_____ . *Light & Shadow.* Photographs by Barbara Rogasky. Holiday House, 1992. These poems are accompanied by color photographs.

_____ . *O Sliver of Liver.* Illustrated by Iris Van Rynbach. Atheneum, 1979. This book contains a variety of poems, including cinquains, haiku, and poems about nature, holidays, daily life, human relationships, and emotions.

_____ . *Sea Songs.* Illustrated by Leonard Everett Fisher. Holiday House, 1986. A collection of poems is about the sea.

_____ . *Sky Songs.* Illustrated by Leonard Everett Fisher. Holiday House, 1983. These poems are about the sky.

_____ . *Space Songs.* Illustrated by Leonard Everett Fisher. Holiday House, 1988. These poems are about elements in space.

_____ , ed. *Thanksgiving Poems.* Illustrated by Stephen Gammell. Holiday House, 1985. This book contains contemporary and traditional holiday poems.

Lobel, Arnold. *The Rose in My Garden.* Illustrated by Anita Lobel. Greenwillow, 1984. A cumulative poem traces the flowers in the garden.

_____ . *Whiskers and Rhymes.* Greenwillow, 1985. These are rhyming poems for young children.

Longfellow, Henry Wadsworth. *Hiawatha.* Illustrated by Susan Jeffers. Dutton, 1983. Hiawatha's boyhood is illustrated in detailed artwork.

_____ . *Hiawatha.* Illustrated by Keith Mosely. Putnam, 1988. This is an abridged, pop-up version of the poem.

_____ . *Hiawatha's Childhood.* Illustrated by Errol LeCain. Farrar, Straus & Giroux, 1984. This winner of the 1985 Greenaway Medal provides a mystical setting.

_____ . *Paul Revere's Ride.* Illustrated by Paul Galdone. Crowell, 1963. The classic poem is illustrated for younger children.

_____ . *Paul Revere's Ride.* Illustrated by Ted Rand. Dutton, 1990. This is a narrative poem about the historical happening.

Loveday, John, ed. *Over the Bridge: An Anthology of New Poems.* Illustrated by Michael Foreman. Kestrel, Penguin, 1981. This anthology of poetry is by British poets.

MacLachlan, Patricia. *What You Know First.* Illustrated by Barry Moser. HarperCollins, 1995. A girl expresses her feelings about the farm.

McCord, David. *Far and Few: Rhymes of the Never Was and Always Is.* Illustrated by Henry B. Kane. Little, Brown, 1952. This book includes the popular nonsense poems found in "Five Chants."

_____ . *One at a Time: Collected Poems for the Young.* Illustrated by Henry B. Kane. Little, Brown, 1977. A large collection of poems is on many subjects.

McPhail, David. *The Dream Child.* Dutton, 1985. The poetic text follows a child's imaginative journey.

Mahy, Margaret. *Nonstop Nonsense.* Illustrated by Quentin Blake. Macmillan, 1989. This text contains nonsense poetry as well as short stories.

Marshak, Samuel. *The Pup Grew Up.* Translated by Richard Pevear. Illustrated by Vladimir Radunsky. H. Holt, 1989. Translated from Russian, this poem develops a comical incident on a train.

Merriam, Eve. *Halloween ABC.* Illustrated by Lane Smith. Macmillan, 1987. This is a collection of spooky Halloween poems.

_____ . *Rainbow Writing.* Atheneum, 1976. This poetry is designed to color our minds with the vast spectrum of human experience.

_____. *The Singing Green: New and Selected Poems for All Seasons*. Illustrated by Kathleen Collins Howell. Morrow, 1992. This is a collection of fifty poems.

Michelson, Richard. *Animals That Ought to Be: Poems About Imaginary Pets*. Illustrated by Leonard Baskin. Simon & Schuster, 1996. The collection includes fourteen poems about imaginary animals.

Milne, A. A. *When We Were Very Young*. Illustrated by Ernest H. Shepard. Dutton, 1961. Delightful poems are about Winnie-the-Pooh and the hundred-acre wood.

_____. *Winnie-the-Pooh*. Illustrated by Ernest H. Shepard. Dutton, 1954. This is the classic story, with poems, about Christopher Robin's friend, the bear.

_____. *The World of Christopher Robin*. Illustrated by E. H. Shepard. Dutton, 1958. Poems tell about a boy and his toy animal friends.

Moore, Clement. *The Night Before Christmas*. Illustrated by Tomie dePaola. Holiday House, 1980. Large, brightly colored illustrations appear in picture-book format.

_____. *The Night Before Christmas*. Illustrated by Tasha Tudor. Rand McNally, 1975. This book contains large illustrations of the popular Christmas poem.

Moore, Lilian. *Adam Mouse's Book of Poems*. Illustrated by Kathleen Garry McCord. Atheneum, 1992. These poems are about the adventures of a mouse.

_____. *Something New Begins*. Atheneum, 1982. This book contains fifteen new poems as well as selections from her previous poems.

_____. *Sunflakes: Poems for Children*. Illustrated by Jan Ormerod. Clarion, 1992. These poems are of interest to young children.

Morrison, Lillian, ed. *At the Crack of the Bat*. Illustrated by Steve Cieslawski. Hyperion, 1992. This is a collection of baseball poems.

Morton, Miriam, ed. *The Moon Is Like a Silver Sickle: A Celebration of Poetry by Russian Children*. Illustrated by Eros Keith. Simon & Schuster, 1972. This is a collection of ninety-two poems written by Russian children.

Myers, Walter Dean. *Harlem*. Illustrated by Christopher Myers. Scholastic, 1997. The poem celebrates the sights, sounds, and dreams of people in Harlem.

Noyes, Alfred. *The Highwayman*. Illustrated by Charles Keeping. Oxford University Press, 1981. A story poem is about a highwayman who risked his life every evening to visit the innkeeper's daughter.

Nye, Naomi Shihab, ed. *This Same Sky: A Collection of Poems from Around the World*. This collection includes poems from sixty-eight countries.

_____, and Paul B. Janeczko. Selected by. *I Feel a Little Jumpy Around You: A Book of Her Poems and His Poems Collected in Paris*. Simon & Schuster, 1996. The pairs of poems in this anthology examine subjects from a male and a female perspective.

O'Neill, Mary. *Hailstones and Halibut Bones*. Illustrated by Leonard Weisgard. Doubleday, 1961. Poems describe the basic colors.

Opie, Iona, and Peter Opie, eds. *The Oxford Book of Children's Verse*. Oxford University Press, 1984. This anthology includes poems from the medieval period through the twentieth century.

_____. *Tail Feathers from Mother Goose: The Opie Rhyme Book*. Little, Brown, 1988. A large collection of verses is illustrated by various artists.

Pooley, Sarah, ed. *A Day of Rhymes*. Knopf, 1988. A collection of sixty-one poems and fingerplays is for preschool children.

Prelutsky, Jack. *The Baby Uggs Are Hatching*. Illustrated by James Stevenson. Greenwillow, 1982. Humorous poems are about Grebles, Sneepies, and Slitchs.

_____. ed. *The Beauty of the Beast: Poems from the Animal Kingdom*. Illustrated by Meilo So. Knopf, 1997. A collection of animal poems from contemporary poets.

_____. *The Dragons Are Singing Tonight*. Illustrated by Peter Sis. Greenwillow, 1993. The poems are about dragons.

_____. *A Gopher in the Garden and Other Animal Poems*. Illustrated by Robert Leydenfrost. Macmillan, 1966, 1967. Humorous poems are about animals.

_____. *The Headless Horseman Rides Tonight*. Illustrated by Arnold Lobel. Greenwillow, 1980. Twelve scary poems are about giants, banshees, poltergeists, and zombies.

_____. *Monday's Troll*. Illustrated by Peter Sis. Greenwillow, 1996. Humorous rhymes about enchanted characters.

_____. *A Pizza the Size of the Sun*. Illustrated by James Stevenson. Greenwillow, 1996. A collection of humorous poems about zany creatures.

_____. *The Queen of Eene*. Illustrated by Victoria Chess. Greenwillow, 1978. Fourteen humorous poems have funny illustrations.

_____, ed. *The Random House Book of Poetry for Children*. Illustrated by Arnold Lobel. Random House, 1983. An anthology of over five hundred poems is divided according to themes.

_____, ed. *Read-Aloud Rhymes for the Very Young*. Illustrated by Marc Brown. Knopf, 1986. An attractive collection of poems stresses vivid language.

_____. *Rolling Harvey down the Hill*. Illustrated by Victoria Chess. Greenwillow, 1980. Humorous poems are about the adventures of five boys.

_____. *The Sheriff of Rottenshot*. Illustrated by Victoria Chess. Greenwillow, 1982. Humorous poems use strong rhyming patterns.

_____. *Tyrannosaurus Was a Beast: Dinosaur Poems*. Illustrated by Arnold Lobel. Greenwillow, 1988. Fourteen poems are about characteristics of dinosaurs.

Richards, Laura E. *Tirra Lirra, Rhymes Old and New*. Illustrated by Marguerite Davis. Little, Brown, 1955. Over one hundred humorous poems include "Eletelephony" and "Bobbily Boo and Wollypotump."

Rosen, Michael, edited by. *Poems for the Very Young*. Illustrated by Bob Graham, Kingfisher, 1993. This is a collection of poems chosen to help children discover the wonder of poetry.

Rossetti, Christina. *Goblin Market*. Illustrated and adapted by Ellen Raskin. Dutton, 1970. This is a picture-book version of the poem originally published in 1862.

_____. *Sing-Song*. Illustrated by Arthur Hughes. Routledge, 1872. This is a classic poem.

Rylant, Cynthia. *Waiting to Waltz: A Childhood*. Illustrated by Stephen Gammell. Bradbury, 1984. This is a collection of poems about growing up in a small Appalachian town.

Schwartz, Alvin. *And the Green Grass Grew All Around: Folk Poetry from Everyone*. Illustrated by Sue Truesdell. HarperCollins, 1992. This is a collection of folk poetry.

Seeger, Ruth Crawford. *American Folksongs for Children—In Home, School, and Nursery School*. Illustrated by Barbara Cooney. Doubleday, 1948. This book contains words and music to numerous folk songs, plus suggestions for using them with young children.

Sendak, Maurice. *Pierre: A Cautionary Tale*. Harper & Row, 1962. A boy learns that he should sometimes care.

Seuss, Dr. *The Cat in the Hat*. Random House, 1957. This is an illustrated humorous poem.

Siebert, Diane. *Heartland*. Illustrated by Wendell Minor. Crowell, 1989. The poem and illustrations describe the Midwest.

_____ . *Mojave*. Illustrated by Wendell Minor. Crowell, 1988. This poem and the illustrations show the landscape and the inhabitants of the Mojave Desert.

_____ . *Sierra*. Illustrated by Wendell Minor. HarperCollins, 1991. The poem and illustrations show the landscape of the Sierra Mountains.

Siegen-Smith, Nikki. *Songs for Survival: Songs and Chants from Tribal Peoples Around the World*. Illustrated by Bernard Lodge. Dutton, 1996. This is an anthology of songs and chants from peoples of six continents.

Silverstein, Shel. *Fall Up*. HarperCollins, 1996. This is a collection of humorous poems.

_____ . *A Light in the Attic*. Harper & Row, 1981. Humorous poems tell about such situations as the polar bear in the Frigidaire.

_____ . *Where the Sidewalk Ends*. Harper & Row, 1974. This is a collection of humorous poems.

Simon, Seymour, ed. *Star Walk*. Morrow, 1995. Photographs illustrate a book of poetry about astronomy.

Sky-Peck, Kathryn, edited by. *Who Has Seen the Wind? An Illustrated Collection of Poetry for Young People*. Museum of Fine Arts, Boston, and Rizzoli, 1991. Appropriate art accompanies a collection of poems.

Smith, William Jay. *Laughing Time*. Illustrated by Juliet Kepes. Little, Brown, 1955. Humorous poems tell about animals and people.

Snyder, Zilpha Keatley. *Today Is Saturday*. Illustrated by John Arms. Atheneum, 1969. This is a collection of poems written by Snyder.

Solt, Mary Ellen, ed. *Concrete Poetry: A World View*. Indiana University Press, 1980. This text includes poetry written in forms that relate to the meanings.

Southey, Robert. *The Cataract of Lodore*. Illustrated by David Catrow. Holt, 1992. This is a highly illustrated version of a classic poem.

Spivak, Dawnine. *Grass Sandals: The Travels of Basho*. Illustrated by Demi. Simon & Schuster, 1997. The story of the Japanese poet includes a series of his poems.

Starbird, Kaye. *The Covered Bridge House and Other Poems*. Illustrated by Jim Arnosky. Four Winds, 1979. Thirty poems tell about childhood experiences, such as jumping rope, hopping after falling on a ski slope, and wondering why no one can get rags from ragweed.

Steptoe, Javaka, ed. And Illustrated by. *In Daddy's Arms I Am Tall: African Americans Celebrating Fathers*. Lee & Low, 1997. An anthology of poems about fathers

Stevenson, Robert Louis. *A Child's Garden of Verses*. Longmans, Green 1885. This is a classic book of poetry.

Thurman, Judith. *Flashlight and Other Poems*. Illustrated by Reina Rubel. Atheneum, 1976. Poems describe such familiar things as balloons, closets, and going barefoot.

Tiller, Ruth. *Cats Vanish Slowly*. Illustrated by Laura Seeley. Peachtree, 1995. Twelve verses about cats.

Treece, Henry. *The Magic Wood*. Illustrated by Barry Moser. HarperCollins, 1992. The poem and the illustrations create a frightening mood.

Turner, Ann. *Mississippi Mud: Three Prairie Journals*. Illustrated by Robert J. Blake. HarperCollins, 1997. The poems express the feelings of three pioneer children.

Viorst, Judith. *If I Were in Charge of the World and Other Worries: Poems for Children and Their Parents*. Illustrated by Lynne Cherry. Atheneum, 1981. The poems are about everyday situations that frustrate.

Volavkova, Hana, ed. *. . . I Never Saw Another Butterfly. . . .* Schocken, 1993. This is a collection of children's poems and drawings by children in the Terezin Concentration Camp, 1942–1944.

Wallace, Daisy. *Fairy Poems*. Illustrated by Trina Schart Hyman. Holiday House, 1980. A collection of poems is about leprechauns and fairies.

_____ . *Ghost Poems*. Illustrated by Tomie dePaola. Holiday House, 1979. A collection of seventeen poems is about ghosts.

Westcott, Nadine Bernard. *Peanut Butter and Jelly: A Play Rhyme*. Dutton, 1987. The text includes suggested hand and body actions.

Whipple, Laura, ed. *Eric Carle's Animals, Animals*. Illustrated by Eric Carle. Philomel, 1989. This text includes an anthology of poems about animals.

_____ . *Eric Carle's Dragons Dragons & Other Creatures That Never Were*. Philomel, 1991. A large-format book illustrated with collage.

Whittier, John Greenleaf. *Barbara Frietchie*. Illustrated by Nancy Winslow Parker. Greenwillow, 1992. The classic poem set in the Civil War.

Willard, Nancy. *Night Story*. Illustrated by Ilse Plume. Harcourt Brace Jovanovich, 1986. A small boy has an adventure in dreamland.

_____ . *Pish, Posh, Said Hieronymus Bosch*. Illustrated by Leo and Diane Dillon. Harcourt Brace Jovanovich, 1991. A humorous poem is motivated by paintings.

_____ . *A Starlit Somersault Downhill*. Illustrated by Jerry Pinkney. Little, Brown, 1993. This narrative poem tells the story of a bear and a rabbit.

_____ . *A Visit to William Blake's Inn: Poems for Innocent and Experienced Travelers*. Illustrated by Alice and Martin Provensen. Harcourt Brace Jovanovich, 1981. Poems describe a menagerie of guests.

_____ . *The Voyage of the Ludgate Hill: Travels with Robert Louis Stevenson*. Illustrated by Alice and Martin Provensen. Harcourt Brace Jovanovich, 1987. A poem tells about Stevenson's adventures on a cargo steamer.

Wilner, Isabel, ed. *The Poetry Troup: An Anthology to Read Aloud*. Scribner's Sons, 1977. An anthology of over two hundred poems is selected for reading aloud.

Windham, Sophie. Selected by. *The Mermaid: And Other Sea Poems*. Scholastic, 1996. A collection of poems about real and mythical sea creatures.

Wood, Douglas. *Old Turtle*. Illustrated by Cheng-Khee Chee. Pfeifer-Hamilton, 1992. This poem emphasizes the importance of the earth.

Worth, Valerie. *All the Small Poems*. Illustrated by Natalie Babbitt. Farrar, Straus & Giroux, 1987. This is a collection of Worth's previously published "Small Poems."

———. *At Christmastime*. Illustrated by Antonio Frasconi. Harper Collins, 1992. These are poems about the Christmas season.

———. *More Small Poems*. Illustrated by Natalie Babbitt. Farrar, Straus & Giroux, 1976. Ordinary objects, such as acorns, soap bubbles, and Christmas lights, are the subjects of short poems.

———. *Still More Small Poems*. Illustrated by Natalie Babbitt. Farrar, Straus & Giroux, 1978. Twenty-five poems are about such ordinary objects as doors, rocks, slugs, and mushrooms.

Yolen, Jane. *The Ballad of the Pirate Queens*. Illustrated by David Shannon. Harcourt Brace, 1995. This is an adventurous poem.

———. *Hark! A Christmas Sampler*. Illustrated by Tomie dePaola, Music and arrangements by Adam Stemple. Putnam's, 1991. This is a collection of stories and songs.

———. ed. *The Lullaby Songbook*. Illustrated by Charles Mikolaycak. Harcourt Brace Jovanovich, 1986. This is a collection of lullabies from various cultures.

———. *The Three Bears Rhyme Book*. Illustrated by Jane Dyer. Harcourt Brace Jovanovich, 1987. Fifteen poems are about the three bears and Goldilocks.

Zolotow, Charlotte. *River Winding*. Illustrated by Kazue Mizumura. Crowell, 1978. Poems for young children paint images of things seen and remembered.

———. *River Winding*. Illustrated by Regina Shekerjian. Abelard-Schuman, 1970. These poems are for young children.

Illustration from *Smoky Night* by Eve Bunting, text copyright © 1994 by Eve Bunting, illustrations copyright © 1994 by David Diaz. Used by permission of Harcourt Brace & Company.

9 *Contemporary Realistic Fiction*

 Window on the World

- What Contemporary Realistic Fiction Is
- Values of Realistic Fiction
- How Realistic Fiction Has Changed
- Literary Criticism: New Realism and the Problem Novel
- Controversial Issues
- Literary Criticism: Guidelines for Selecting Controversial Fiction
- Literary Elements
- Subjects in Realistic Fiction
- Animal Stories, Mysteries, Sports Stories, and Humor

 Involving Children in Realistic Fiction

- Using Role Playing
- Using Bibliotherapy
- Using Survival Stories to Motivate Reading and Interaction with Literature
- Improving Self-Esteem and Understanding of Individuals
- Developing Questioning Strategies

Window on
the World

 ew terminology enters the discussion of children's books as you leave the realm of Mother Goose, most picture storybooks, traditional literature, and modern fantasy. Such terms as *relevant books, extreme realism, problem novel,* and *everyday occurrences* are found in critiques and discussions of contemporary realistic fiction.

While some of the books in this genre are among the most popular with older children, they are also among the most controversial. Interest groups, educators, and parents criticize and debate the value of some realistic stories for children. Many adults are concerned about such issues as censorship, sexism, promiscuity, violence, profanity, alienation from society, and racism. This chapter discusses what contemporary realistic fiction is, why it should be shared with children, how realistic fiction has changed, issues related to realistic fiction, and criteria for evaluating realistic fiction.

WHAT CONTEMPORARY REALISTIC FICTION IS

The term *contemporary realistic fiction* implies that everything in a realistic story—including plot, characters, and setting—is consistent with the lives of real people in our contemporary world. The word *realistic* does not mean that the story is true, however; it means only that the story could have happened.

Use of the words *realistic* and *fiction* together is confusing to some children, who have trouble distinguishing contemporary realistic fiction from modern fantasy or from stories that really happened. Certainly, authors of modern fantasy attempt to make their stories realistic in the sense that they try to create believable plots, characters, and settings; to make their stories as internally consistent as possible; and to ground their stories in familiar reality before introducing elements of fantasy. Contemporary realistic fiction, however, requires that plots deal with familiar, everyday problems, pleasures, and personal relationships and that characters and settings seem as real as the contemporary world we know. The supernatural has no part in such stories, except occasionally in the beliefs of realistic human characters.

Two popular animal stories demonstrate the differences between modern fantasy and contemporary realistic fiction. These differences are summarized in Chart 9–1. In Beatrix Potter's fantasy *The Tale of Peter Rabbit,* Peter talks, thinks, acts, and dresses like an inquisitive, sometimes greedy, sometimes frightened human child who needs his mother's love and care. While the story's garden setting is realistic, Peter's home is furnished with human furniture. In this fantasy, conflict develops because Peter demonstrates believable childlike desires.

In contrast, the three animals in Sheila Burnford's *The Incredible Journey* retain their animal characteristics as they struggle for survival in a realistically depicted Canadian wilderness. A trained hunting dog leads his companions across the wilderness; an English bull terrier, who is a cherished family pet, seeks people to give him food; and a Siamese cat retains her feline independence. Conflict in this realistic story develops as the animals become lost and face problems while trying to return to their home. Burnford does not give the animals human thoughts, values, or other human characteristics. The characters and settings are not only believable but also completely realistic in our everyday world.

CHART 9-1 Differences between modern fantasy and contemporary realistic fiction

	Modern Fantasy	Contemporary Realistic Fiction
Believable stories	Authors must encourage readers to suspend disbelief	Authors may rely on "relevant subjects," everyday occurrences, or extreme realism
Plot	Conflict may be against supernatural powers Problems may be solved through magical powers	Conflict develops as characters cope with such problems as growing up, survival, family discord, and inner-city tensions Antagonists may be self, other family members, society, or nature
Characters	Personified toys, little people, supernatural beings, real people who have imaginary experiences, animals who behave like people	Characters act like real people Animals always behave like animals
Setting	Past, present, or future Imaginary world May travel through time and space	The contemporary world is as we know it

 ## VALUES OF REALISTIC FICTION

One of the greatest values of realistic fiction for children is that many realistic stories allow children to identify with characters of their own age who have similar interests and problems. Children like to read about people whom they can understand. Thus, their favorite authors express a clear understanding of children. For example, one girl said about Judy Blume's *Are You There God? It's Me, Margaret,* "I've read this book five times; I could be Margaret."

Realistic fiction can help children discover that their problems and desires are not unique and that they are not alone in experiencing certain feelings and situations. Children who are unhappy about the death of a loved one may identify with Marvis Jukes's *I'll See You in My Dreams,* for example, or children who are having preadolescent anxieties, especially about boy–girl relationships, may find a comrade in Phyllis Naylor's *Alice in Rapture, Sort Of.* The young characters in these books face and overcome their problems while remaining true to themselves.

Realistic fiction also extends children's horizons by broadening their interests, allowing them to experience new adventures, and showing them different ways to view and deal with conflicts in their own lives. Children can vicariously live a survival adventure and mature in the process as they read Scott O'Dell's *Island of the Blue Dolphins,* for example, or experience the death of a father in Vera and Bill Cleaver's *Where the Lilies Bloom.*

According to Joanne Bernstein (1989), reading about children who are facing emotional problems can help other children discharge repressed emotions and cope with fear, anger, or grief. For example, books about divorce or abuse may help children cope with a traumatic period in their lives. In Beverly Cleary's *Dear Mr. Henshaw,* readers discover that parents as well as children are hurt by divorce. Children may realize the consequences of wife and child abuse by reading Betsy Byars's *Cracker Jackson.* (*A word of caution:* realistic fiction should *not* be used to replace professional help in situations that warrant such intervention. Children experiencing severe depression, anger, or grief may require professional help.) Many of the books discussed in this chapter can stimulate discussion and help children share their feelings and solve their problems. Of course, realistic fiction also provides children with pleasure and escape. Realistic animal stories, mysteries, sports stories, and humorous stories are enjoyable getaways for young people.

 ## HOW REALISTIC FICTION HAS CHANGED

Synonyms for *realistic* include other adjectives, such as *lifelike, genuine,* and *authentic.* Of course, what people consider lifelike depends upon the social context. What seems realistic to us might seem fantastic to people in different societies or other eras.

In the Victorian era of the late nineteenth and early twentieth centuries, realistic fiction emphasized traditional family roles and ties in warm, close, and stable family units that lived in one place for generations; strict roles for males and females, stressing higher education and careers for males and wifehood and motherhood for females; respect for law and adult authority; strong religious commitment; duty to educate, Christianize, or care for the poor; and problems related to overcoming sinfulness and becoming good.

Realistic fiction continued to emphasize many of these values well into the second half of the twentieth century, although the literature began to depict both female and male children gaining more independence. The characters in realistic children's fiction were usually white, middle-class, and members of stable families consisting of a father, a mother, and their children. Nontraditional families and family disturbances were virtually unrepresented in this literature.

Beginning roughly in the 1960s, however, the content of contemporary realistic fiction became more diverse—no doubt reflecting the increasingly diverse and complex social life in the United States and elsewhere. Contemporary realistic stories for children depict some unhappy and unstable families, single-parent families, and families in which both parents work outside the home. Career ambitions are not as confined to traditional gender roles as they were in the past. Children often have much responsibility and independence. Fear of or disrespect for law and authority is more common. Edu-

cation and religion receive less stress. Ethnic and racial minorities are more in evidence, and in general, people's economic, emotional, and social problems receive more emphasis.

John Rowe Townsend (1974) is among the researchers who have pointed out the striking contrasts between children's realistic fiction of the 1950s and the late 1960s. The 1950s was one of the quietest decades in children's literature: In keeping with traditional values, children were pictured as part of a stable community—grandparents were wise, parents were staunch and respected, and childhood was happy and secure. In contrast, children's literature of the late 1960s implied an erosion of adult authority and an apparent widening of the generation gap. It was no longer self-evident that parents knew best and that children could be guided into accepting the established codes and behavior.

Author Betsy Byars (1993), who has been writing for thirty years, states that children's publishing has changed a great deal. She says,

> I think there's been a great evolution. When I first started writing, children's books had to be nice. I can remember some editor writing in the margin, "Don't have him lie" or something like that. And now you're very free. You don't feel any pressure, you don't find yourself thinking things like, "I can't say this" or "This will be too tough a subject for kids." (p. 906)

In a study of themes found in contemporary realistic fiction published in the late 1970s, Jane M. Madsen and Elaine B. Wickersham (1980) found that popular themes for young children were overcoming fear and meeting responsibility and that stories about problems related to adoption, divorce, disabilities, and minority social status were more common than in the past. In the 1980s, contemporary realistic fiction for older children often depicted children overcoming family and personal problems. Children confronted quarreling or divorcing parents, deserting or noncaring parents, cruel foster families, conflicts between personal ambitions and parental desires, and death of loved ones. Discovery of self and development of maturity as children face and overcome their fears were other popular themes in stories written for older children. Such stories often stressed the importance of self-esteem and being true to oneself.

Contemporary realistic fiction in the 1990s reflects both the mirror of society's problems and changes that have occurred in books because of past criticisms. According to Aleen Pace Nilsen and Kenneth L. Donelson (1993), current realistic fiction novels for young adults have

less reliance for interest on shock and titillation; more excitement, romance, and optimism; more of a world view; less stereotyping of characters, plots, and settings; a more balanced and convincing view of parents; and more sophisticated and varied approaches to problems connected with racism and ethnic identification. (p. 112)

An introduction to recommended books titled "Curriculum Connectors: Family Secrets" in *School Library Journal* (1997) highlights many of the characteristics of current realistic fiction: "All of the families in the books listed below harbor secrets. Some are dark and grim; others are quirky and quite funny. Abuse, desertion, hidden pasts, feuds, and even a grandmother's elopement play a part. Some of the young protagonists draw on inner strengths they didn't know they had; others turn to siblings and friends for help. What these young people have in common is resilience, resourcefulness, and a feeling of hope for the future" (p. 112).

 LITERARY CRITICISM: NEW REALISM AND THE PROBLEM NOVEL

New realism is the term that Shelton L. Root (1977) applies to certain segments of contemporary realistic fiction. He describes new realism as

that fiction for young readers which addresses itself to personal problems and social issues heretofore considered taboo for fictional treatment by the general public, as enunciated by its traditional spokesmen: librarians, teachers, ministers, and others. The new realism is often graphic in its language and always explicit in its treatment. (p. 19)

Some literary critics question the merit of at least portions of this new realism. Sheila Egoff (1980), for example, applauds realistic novels that have strong literary qualities, including logical flow of narrative, delicate complexity of characterization, insights that convey the conduct of life as characters move from childhood to adolescence and to adulthood, and a quality that touches both the imagination and the emotions. In an outstanding realistic novel, says Egoff, conflict is integral to the plot and characters,

and resolution of conflict has wide implications growing out of the personal vision or experience of the writer. In contrast, Egoff maintains, conflict in a problem novel stems from the writer's social standards more than from personal feelings and emotions. The author's intentions may be good, but in an effort to make a point or argue a social position, the author creates a cardboard story instead of one that really comes alive. The conflict is specific rather than universal and narrow rather than far-reaching in its implications. Egoff identifies other typical characteristics of the problem novel:

1. Concern is with externals, with how things look rather than how things are. The author begins with a problem rather than with a plot or characters.
2. The protagonist is burdened with anxieties and grievances that grow out of alienation from the adult world.
3. The protagonist often achieves temporary relief through association with an unconventional adult from outside the family.
4. The narrative is usually in the first person, and its confessional tone is self-centered.
5. The vocabulary is limited, and observation is restricted by the pretense that an ordinary child is the narrator.
6. Sentences and paragraphs are short, the language is flat, without nuance, and the language may be emotionally numb.
7. Inclusion of expletives seem obligatory.
8. Sex is discussed openly.
9. The setting is usually urban.

Jack Forman (1985) adds that in contrast to the fully developed characters in books of literary quality, many topical novels "are peopled with characters who are more mouthpieces of a particular point of view than fully developed protagonists" (p. 470). Beverly Cleary (Connell, 1984) further articulates the difference between stories that focus on problems and stories that focus on people:

I'm more interested in writing about people than problems. *Dear Mr. Henshaw* [the winner of the 1984 Newbery Medal] is about a boy that had a problem, not a problem that had a boy. I don't search for a new problem. (p. 1F)

Educators and critics of children's literature in the mid-1980s disagreed, however, about how prominent new realism and problem novels actually are in contemporary realistic fiction for children. Critics such as Bertha M. Cheatham (1985) maintained that novels "mirroring real-life situations and tackling controversial subjects (drugs, sex, suicide) are increasing in numbers" (p. 25), while critics such as Marilyn F. Apseloff (1985) saw "a definite swing away from the serious 'new realism' which dominated the lists half a decade ago" (p. 32) in the United States, Europe, and Japan. Apseloff noted an apparently increasing demand for adventure stories, humorous stories, and realistic fiction of high literary quality.

Nancy Vasilakis (1985) maintains that in the late 1960s taboos began "falling like dominoes. . . . No subject was too lurid, no language too explicit, and no outlook too bleak"; but by the mid-1980s "librarians were questioning the existence of too many books that are poorly written, dishonest, and manipulative, simply because they are destined to be popular" (p. 768). Vasilakis concludes that controversial books are no longer automatic bestsellers. Instead, "the fear of censorship, concern over declining standards, and the economic recession of the early eighties forced publishers and librarians alike, after the first few tremors, to hunker down and become more discriminating in their choices of what to publish and what to buy" (p. 769).

Today's students of children's literature are living in an interesting era of book publishing for children. They may analyze new books of contemporary realistic fiction and contemplate the different directions that authors can choose to pursue.

CONTROVERSIAL ISSUES

Barbara Feldstein (1993) identifies the major controversies in children's books as political views that differ from those of censors, treatment of minorities, stereotyped roles of women, problems of contemporary society, and profane language. When any of these subjects are in books, you may expect varied reactions. The degree to which realistic fiction should reflect the reality of the times leads to controversy when writers create characters who face problems relating to sexism, sexuality, violence, and drugs. There is no simple solution: What one group considers controversial, another does not. Realistic

fiction has resulted in more controversy and calls for censorship than has any other genre. Therefore, educators must be aware of some concerns in this area of literature, including sexism, sexuality, violence, profanity, and family problems.

Sexism

Sexism has been a major concern for the past few decades. The following position statement by the Association of Women Psychologists (1970), written more than twenty-five years ago, stresses the dangers of the traditional roles created by society and reflected in literature:

Psychological oppression in the form of sex role socialization clearly conveys to girls from the earliest ages that their nature is to be submissive, servile, and repressed, and their role is to be servant, admirer, sex object and martyr. . . . The psychological consequences of goal depression in young women . . . are all too common. In addition, both men and women have come to realize the effect on men of this type of sex role stereotyping, the crippling pressure to compete, to achieve, to produce, to stifle emotion, sensitivity and gentleness, all taking their toll in psychic and physical traumas.

Feldstein (1993) brings this issue into current times by stating:

Over the past twenty years, no doubt as a result of the efforts of feminist groups, there has been an increase in the number of positive role models in children's literature. Nonetheless, there are still objections to passive female characters who do not take control over their own destiny. (p. 148)

The controversial issue of sexism in children's literature involves not only the exclusion of females from many children's books but also the stereotyped roles in which children's books often depict females. Female characters are often shown as homemakers or employees in "feminine" occupations. Often, female characters are passive, docile, fearful, and dependent. Children's books do not necessarily depict the roles of homemakers and of employees in traditionally female occupations in a condescending or demeaning light, but the implication that these are the *only* roles open to females is harmful to the girls and boys who read these stories.

People concerned with sexism have evaluated the roles of males and females in children's literature and in elementary classrooms. The evaluations are usually harshly critical of the negative forces of sex-role stereotyping. Ramona Frasher (1982), for example, reviewed research on sexism and sex-role stereotyping in children's literature and identified some trends. In Newbery Award-winning books published prior to the 1970s, male main characters outnumbered female main characters by about three to one. In addition, negative comments about females and stereotyping were common. Frasher's analysis of Newbery Award winners published between 1971 and 1980 showed the ratio of male characters to female characters was about equal. In addition, female characters tended to be portrayed with more positive and varied personality characteristics and to exhibit a greater variety of behaviors.

Even though these changes reflect a heightened sensitivity to feminist concerns, Frasher's article identifies three areas still of major concern: (1) changes are found predominantly in books written for children in middle- and late-childhood years, (2) the rush to respond to criticism resulted in too many examples of poor or marginal literature, and (3) until more authors are able to write with ease about both sexes engaged in a broad scope of activities and exhibiting a range of characteristics, children's literature will remain stereotyped. Frasher's conclusion emphasizes the need for critical evaluation in this area: "The number of books accessible to children is immense; it will take many years of publishing quality nonsexist literature to insure that a random selection is as likely to be nonstereotyped as it is to be stereotyped" (p. 77).

Educators, psychologists, and other concerned adults also criticize the sexism and sex-role stereotyping in realistic picture books. In an earlier study, Aleen Pace Nilsen (1971) analyzed the role of females in eighty Caldecott Medal winners and honor books. She chose picture books because illustrated books are "the ones influencing children at the time they are in the process of developing their own sexual identity. Children decide very early in life what roles are appropriate to male and female" (p. 919). Of the books that were realistic (as compared with fantasy), she found fewer stories having girls as the leading characters. She also compared the number of girl- and boy-centered stories over a twenty-year period; the percentage of girl-centered stories had decreased from a high of 46 percent in 1951–1955 to a low of 26 percent in 1966–1970.

Nilsen does not recommend that children not read these books, but she does suggest providing children with equally interesting books that have female main characters. She also recommends that artists become aware of the stereotypes that they can perpetuate in illustrating books. She points out that in Ezra Jack Keats' *Goggles,* Peter's sister sits on the sidewalk beside a baby and draws pictures while the boys' excitement rages around her. Likewise, in *A Tree Is Nice,* the boys are pictured in the upper branches of the trees, while the girls are pictured sitting in the lowest branches, waving to boys climbing trees, or sprinkling plants with a watering can.

Many female protagonists in books for older children behave in ways quite different from those of the heroines of traditional literature. They reflect the fairly recent realization that females are also *heroes,* with intellectual, emotional, and physical potential in their actions. Some of the most memorable girl characters—including Karana in Scott O'Dell's *Island of the Blue Dolphins,* Queenie in Robert Burch's *Queenie Peavy* (who insisted that she would grow up to be a doctor, not a nurse), Harriet in Louise Fitzhugh's *Harriet the Spy,* and even Jo in Louisa May Alcott's Victorian novel, *Little Women*—are believable and exciting because they do not follow stereotypical behavior patterns.

Anne Scott MacLeod (1994) analyzes changes in sexism in children's literature since the nineteenth century and concludes: "At their best, recent portraits of girls have a variety, individuality, and ease that contrasts with the narrowness of pre-1970s literature and equally with the self-consciousness of many early efforts to strengthen girls' literary images. Girls can be non-conformist now without being condemned, subtly or otherwise. Girls can know their own minds and act with courage and initiative without either apology or defiance and can even accept help or comfort without thereby backing into secondary roles. Rarest, but perhaps most significant, is the fictional adolescent girl who can move toward self-knowledge without taking male attention as the measure of her worth. It does not happen often, but it does happen in post-1970s literature" (p. 214). As you read the contemporary realistic literature published during different time periods, identify the various roles of females in the stories and analyze how those roles may have changed.

Nontraditional behaviors can, of course, also result in controversy. Women's roles and women's rights are political issues. Advocates express strong opinions on both sides. One of the areas that illustrates women's changing roles is the portrayal of the minor characters in stories. Mothers may be photographers who travel on assignments and join peace marches accompanied by their daughters, as in Norma Klein's *Mom, the Wolf Man and Me;* book illustrators who travel on consulting contracts, as in Lois Lowry's *Anastasia on Her Own;* and authors whose children consider them eccentric, as in Patricia MacLachlan's *The Facts and Fictions of Minna Pratt.* Recent books suggest that the roles of males and females may be changing, as increasingly varied occupations and behavior patterns are found in the books. Teachers, librarians, and parents should be aware, however, that not all people look on these changes favorably.

Sexuality

Today is a time of increasing sophistication and frankness about sexuality. Television programs and movies portray sexual relationships that would not have been shown to earlier generations of adults, let alone children. Premarital and extramarital sex, sexual development, homosexual experiences, and sex education are controversial topics in children's literature. The subjects of books written for older readers may be particularly controversial. For example, M. E. Kerr's *"Hello," I Lied* deals with problems associated with being gay; Suzanne Fisher Staples's *Dangerous Skies* deals with sexual abuse; and Francesca Lisa Block's *Girl Goddess #9: Nine Stories* describes a peer world that includes casual sex, drugs, and alcohol.

Several books written for older children describe nontraditional living situations in which a child's mother lives with a male friend. In Norma Klein's controversial *Mom, the Wolf Man and Me,* Theodore spends weekends with Brett's mother, which leads eleven-year-old Brett to ask her mother if she is having sexual relations with him. This results in a frank discussion about sexual intercourse. As might be expected, this book has met with varying reactions. John M. Kean and Carl Personke (1976) point out that numerous children today are living in one-parent households and that such children should have opportunities to read about "a warm home environment that differs from the usual pattern" (p. 334). In contrast, several librarians and literature

professors at one reading conference (Sam Houston, 1981) reported receiving many negative comments from parents and college students about the sexual discussions and unconventional life-styles described in Klein's book.

In a book for older audiences, *Dear Nobody,* Berlie Doherty explores feelings and issues associated with the pregnancy of an unmarried high school girl. The author explores the unhappiness and confusion that surround the decision to keep the baby as well as the responses of the mother, the baby's father, and their families.

Books describing children's concerns about their developing sexuality may also be controversial. For example, Judy Blume's popular *Are You There God? It's Me, Margaret* has been reviewed favorably as a

The author explores the various conflicts and emotions associated with teenage pregnancy. (From Dear Nobody *by Berlie Doherty. Jacket illustration copyright © 1992 by Diane Paterson. Reprinted by permission of Orchard Books, New York.)*

book that realistically conveys preadolescent girls' worries over menstruation and body changes. Yet in 1981, this book was one of several taken from library shelves and burned because some adults viewed it as a negative influence on children. In that same year, the national television news showed angry adults criticizing the morality of this book, as well as the morality of many other books, and the resulting flames of protest.

The results of a censorship survey may surprise many students of children's literature. Ken Donelson (1985) reports that Judy Blume, with five titles and thirty-three protests, is the second most widely protested author. (John Steinbeck, with seven titles and forty-five protests, is the most widely protested author.) In addition to *Are You There God? It's Me, Margaret,* Blume's *Then Again, Maybe I Won't; Deenie; Forever; It's Not the End of the World;* and *Blubber* have been strongly criticized or censored because of their sexual content or strong language.

Violence

Television, movies, and books have been accused of portraying too much violence. Children's cartoons are often criticized for their excessive violence. Children's books become the object of controversy when they portray what some people define as inappropriate behavior or excessive violence. Many realistic books containing violence have inner-city settings. For example, Frank Bonham's *Durango Street* describes the hero's bid for survival in a world of grim gang violence and drugs, a world where he could be used for "bayonet practice." Drugs also play a significant role in Walter Dean Myers's *Scorpions.* Some people believe that children should read about the reality of drugs in the world around them, while others believe that the minds of children should not be contaminated by the mention of drugs.

Shannon Maughan (1992) discusses the controversy around Clark Taylor's picture book, *The House That Crack Built.* Maughan states that much of the controversy centers around the appropriate age for this book, which is based on the nursery rhyme "The House That Jack Built." People living in suburban neighborhoods believe that the book is appropriate for students in high school and maybe junior high. In contrast, those living in urban environments see the

book as appropriate for children as young as first grade and extending through high school.

Profanity

Profanity and other language objectionable to some people are also controversial. What is considered objectionable has changed over the years, however. Mary Q. Steele (1971) describes her own experiences with writing. In the 1950s, editors deleted "hecks" and "darns" from manuscripts written for children, but now, authors can write relevant dialogue. Ken Donelson's (1985) survey on censorship reports that a committee unsuccessfully challenged the placement of Katherine Paterson's *The Great Gilly Hopkins* in an elementary library because the author used language that the committee members considered objectionable.

In 1990, a teacher in Donna Norton's children's literature class successfully met a challenge to Paterson's *Bridge to Terabithia.* One parent wanted the book removed from the class reading list because of mild profanity. The teacher successfully defended the book for literary merit, especially the importance of its themes.

Family Problems and Other Controversial Issues

Strong young protagonists in contemporary novels frequently overcome obstacles related to family problems caused by adult family members. The antagonists are frequently adults who have less than desirable qualities. The lack of strong adult role models in many contemporary books is also controversial. For example, Robert Unsworth (1988) praises the fully developed fathers in several recently published books, but he also states, "The bad news is the portrayal of that Dad at home. A grander group of adulterers, philanderers, child abusers, wife-beaters, drunks, and all-around ne'er-do-wells hasn't been seen since the fall of Rome" (p. 48).

Abandonment of children is another family problem that is depicted in many contemporary stories. According to Marilyn Fain Apseloff (1992), there are three types of abandonment:

Newer books portray mothers so intent upon finding themselves and doing their own thing that they are willing to leave their families in the process. . . . In other novels the abandonment is temporary. . . . Still another kind of abandonment occurs in books for older readers: the desertion of the mother when the child is still an infant. (pp. 102–103)

Apseloff concludes:

Here is unsoftened realism, an indictment of contemporary society, where adults no longer want to assume the traditional roles of protectors and nurturers of children. Such people have always existed, of course, but their numbers seem to be increasing, more adults being concerned with their own welfare and well-being first, before those of the rest of the family. (p. 105)

The role of the absent parent is highlighted in a review of *The Goats*. In a review of Brock Cole's *The Goats*, Anita Silvey (1988) states:

Like all powerful books, *The Goats* will repel some readers and attract others. Critics of the book are concerned with the absence of positive adult characters—as was the case with *Harriet the Spy*—and the change in the young protagonists from innocents to thieves. (p. 23)

Silvey goes on to praise the book, saying that the publication of the novel "signifies that we are still creating children's books that affirm the human spirit and the ability of the individual to rise above adversity" (p. 23).

The controversy surrounding the award given to a book in England illustrates issues in contemporary realistic fiction. According to Julie Eccleshare (1997), "The prestigious Carnegie Medal was awarded last month to Melvin Burgess for *Junk* (Andersen Press). A novel about a group of teenage drug addicts who think that they can handle heroin, *Junk* has attracted enormous media coverage, ranging from adults who find it frightening and even morally wrong that a children's book should deal with these issues, to those who see it as 'a book waiting to be written.' Holt will publish the book in the U.S. in spring '98" (p. 25). As you read *Junk* and books with similar content, ask yourself, "What is my own response to this content? Is it beneficial? Is it harmful?"

According to Michelle Mittelstadt (1993), "Increasingly, the schools are the battle ground for struggles mirroring broader societal debates collectively known as the 'cultural war' " (p. A9). Other issues that can be controversial in children's books are viewpoints on war and peace, religion, death, and racial matters. (Chapter 11 discusses critics' concerns about books related to African Americans, Hispanic Americans, Native Americans, and Asian Americans.)

 LITERARY CRITICISM: GUIDELINES FOR SELECTING CONTROVERSIAL FICTION

The question of how "realistic" realistic fiction should be is answered differently by various groups. Historically, schools have often been under the pressures of censorship because different groups have tried to impose their values. While modern censors might laugh at the literary concerns of the Puritans, there is still concern over appropriate subjects for children's literature. Children's books that explore sexuality, violence, moral problems, racism, and religious beliefs are likely to be thought objectionable by individuals and groups who believe that children should not be exposed to such ideas. Arbuthnot Lectures recipient Dorothy Butler (1990) warns:

we must confront those who would cut wild swaths through the body of children's books, rejecting some because they believe them to advance ideas which are in conflict with ones they wish children to espouse, embracing others because they appear to recommend currently approved attitudes—and all with little or no regard to literary merit, or reference to the opinions of those who might advise. We are in danger, in the hands of these well-meaning but misguided evangelists, of banishing at least half the classics of the English language; in vain to protest that the real liberators of the world have always been the informed, the readers; that the burning of books has always been in the cause of human oppression. The dictates of such critics, whether in the cause of antiracism, antisexism, or any other philosophy, denote an arrogance which may be excused as ignorance, but must not be tolerated. Good and true books engender true thought and feeling, and so allow children to think clearly and to feel deeply. (p. 37)

Teachers and librarians need to be knowledgeable about their communities, subjects that may prove controversial, and the merits of controversial books that they would like to share with children. Day Ann K. McClenathan (1979) suggests that wholesale avoidance of books containing controversial topics, in addition to encouraging overt censorship, is inappropriate because (1) books about relevant sociological or psychological problems can give young people opportunities to grow in their thinking processes and to extend their experiences; (2) problems in books can provide some children with opportunities for identification and allow other children opportunities to empathize with their peers; and (3) problems in books invite decisions, elicit opinions, and afford opportunities to take positions on issues.

Given the controversial issues and the need for books that are relevant to the interests, concerns, and problems of today's children, you should consider some guidelines when choosing realistic fiction for children. McClenathan provides teachers a useful guide for selecting books that might be considered controversial. (See the Evaluation Criteria box on this page for a summary of her guidelines.)

Dianne McAfee Hopkins (1993) provides useful recommendations for librarians who face challenges to literature. She recommends that you examine your district's materials selection policy carefully, ensure that principals and teachers are aware that the policy is intended for all who challenge the appropriateness of materials, take every challenge seriously, follow the

*E*VALUATION CRITERIA

Literary Criticism: Controversial Books

1. Know what might be considered controversial.

2. Determine the author's viewpoint and weigh the positive influences against perceived negative influences.

3. Be sure that the book meets normal literary criteria and is not chosen merely for its high interest and possibly controversial topic.

4. Know and be able to explain your purpose for using a particular book.

5. Review and be able to discuss both sides of the censorship question.

*I*SSUE Freedom to Read versus Censorship of Literature

Research articles, such as those written by Ken Donelson,[1] show that censorship of children's books is increasing. Organized group efforts are focusing on both children's literature and school textbooks.

Some groups want censorship and some groups advocate freedom of choice. Patrick Shannon[2] identifies several positions that are currently influencing children's literature. First is the position on censorship reflected in Mel and Norma Gabler's *What Are They Teaching Our Children?*[3] This position encourages parents to identify materials that they consider antifamily, anti-Christian, or anti-American, and then to force objectionable books off the shelves. Second is the position expressed in Cal Thomas's *Book Burning.*[4] Thomas accuses librarians, publishers, and school officials of censoring Christian and traditional content from school curricula and library shelves. Third is the position of the American Library Association,[5] which argues for the end of all cen-

sorship of books, for the readers' right to choose, and for the selection of books to be based on literary merit. Fourth is the position of the Council on Interracial Books for Children,[6] which objects to the biases in school textbooks. This group recommends basing library book selection on social concerns for equality and justice as well as for literary merit.

Author Richard Peck,[7] describing his recent experiences with censorship, concludes:

We have to use aggressive, public ways to point out to people hungry for power that we aren't powerless. . . . They need to see librarians and teachers and administrators grouped and united. And just at eye-level on the wall of the conference room, there should be a clearly lettered poster stating: READERS HAVE NOTHING TO FEAR; NONREADERS, EVERYTHING. (p. 817)

In all likelihood, the issue of censorship will continue through the next century, as concerned adults on both sides of the question argue whether lit-

erature and educators should indoctrinate the mores and morals of a community or should expand the ideas and understandings of children through exposure to and discussion of a variety of books and ideas.

---

[1]Donelson, Ken. "Almost 13 Years of Book Protests—Now What?" *School Library Journal* 31 (March 1985): 93–98.

[2]Shannon, Patrick. "Overt and Covert Censorship of Children's Books." *The New Advocate* 2 (Spring 1989): 97–104.

[3]Gabler, Mel, and Norma Gabler. *What Are They Teaching Our Children?* Wheaton Ill.: Victor, 1985.

[4]Thomas, Cal. *Book Burning.* Westchester, Ill.: Crossways, 1983.

[5]American Library Association. "The Freedom to Read." *Bill of Rights.* Chicago, Ill.: American Library Association, 1972.

[6]Council on Interracial Books for Children. *Human (and Anti–Human) Values in Children's Books.* New York: Council on Interracial Books for Children, 1976.

[7]Peck, Richard. "The Great Library-Shelf Witch Hunt." *Booklist* 88 (January 1, 1992): 816–817.

The title of an article by Leigh Ann Jones,[1] "Better Libraries Through Censorship," seems at first to be an oxymoron. How could there be a positive side for censorship? Jones, a school librarian, argues that in her school district a censorship controversy changed the district for the better because "it prompted us to examine current practices and policies, and provided impetus for us to" (p. 54) make the following changes: (1) to strengthen selection policy by adding parents to the committee, creating a district-level review committee for appeals, and adding a time frame with deadlines for responses; (2) to broaden library support by mobilizing parents into "Friends" groups and other supportive organizations for the library; (3) to affirm intellectual freedom by articulating the importance of the right to read; (4) to empower librarians by reaffirming the role of professional personnel in the careful selection of materials; and (5) to enhance the library role by stressing access to all library books through a policy of intellectual freedom.

As you read about the experiences of this school district, consider both the positive and potentially negative impact of censorship. Why do you believe that this challenge to books was handled successfully? Why does Jones claim that censorship created a climate for positive change? Interview librarians and other personnel associated with selecting books. How have they approached issues related to censorship?

---

[1] Jones, Leigh Ann. "Better Libraries Through Censorship." *School Library Journal* 42 (October 1996): 54.

---

reconsideration section of the policy fully, seek support when an oral or written challenge occurs, communicate at all levels to ensure that challenges are handled in an effective and objective manner, and recognize that you can be the key person in shaping the outcome of challenges to library materials.

Author Richard Peck (1992) provides an excellent observation for all of those who are developing defenses for books. Peck states, "Only the nonreader fears books" (p. 816).

In addition to the basic literary criteria, high-quality contemporary realistic fiction should satisfy the following requirements.

Know exactly what might be considered controversial. This means that you have to really read the book. You can't rely on the opinion of someone else or even on a good review. As a member of a school and a community, you must be able to appraise specific content. What offends in one community might go unnoticed or unchallenged in another.

Ascertain the author's point of view and weigh the power of the positive influence against exposure to a theme that some people perceive negatively. For example, if an author writes about the drug culture but events in the story clearly point to harmful effects of drug use, then you may miss an opportunity for shaping healthy attitudes.

Apply literary criteria to the selection of library books so that vulnerability to the arguments of would-be censors is at least partially reduced by the obvious overall quality of the book choices. Occasionally, teachers and librarians select books of inferior quality because they deal with topics having high interest for middle-grade or older children (for example, books involving experimentations with sex). The information in such books may be harmless (or even useful), but the books may fall short of accepted literary criteria. Then, if a book is targeted because it offends community groups, you will have difficulty defending it, and having it in your school collection will suggest that considerations other than literary quality determine choices. In addition, examine books that attempt to counter stereotypes for what can be thought of as overcorrection. Sometimes, in a passion to change images, authors work too hard on issues and neglect plot and characterizations.

Know and be able to explain your purpose for using a particular book. Have answers ready to the following questions:

1. Will the topic be understood by the students with whom I intend to use the book?
2. What merits of this particular book have influenced me to use it rather than another book of comparable literary, sociological, or psychological importance?
3. Is the book an acceptable model in terms of writing style and use of language?
4. Are my objectives in using this book educationally defensible (for example, refinement of attitudes, promotion of reading habits)?

In order to clarify and maintain your objectivity, review and be prepared to discuss both sides of the censorship question.

 LITERARY ELEMENTS

Contemporary realistic fiction should meet the basic literary criteria discussed in chapter 3. Conflicts that could really occur in our contemporary world should be integral to the plot, characterization, setting, and theme. In realistic contemporary settings, authors should thoroughly develop internal and external conflicts, developing credible stories through credible plots, good characterizations, meaningful themes, and effective styles. (See the Evaluation Criteria box on this page.)

Plot

Conflicts at the center of plots in contemporary realistic fiction may arise from external forces, with characters trying to overcome problems related to families, peers, or the society around them, or conflicts may arise with characters trying to overcome problems related to inner conflicts. However, internal conflicts often result from conflict with external forces. Consequently, person-against-self conflicts are common in contemporary realistic fiction.

As in traditional literature, conflict in contemporary realistic fiction may involve protagonists in quests (Henke, 1985). Caron Lee Cohen (1985) identifies four major components in person-against-self conflicts: (1) problem, (2) struggle, (3) realization, and (4) achievement of peace or truth. She says:

The point at which the struggle wanes and the inner strength emerges seems to be the point of self-realization. That point leads immediately to the final sense of peace or truth that is the resolution of the quest. The best books are those which move readers and cause them to identify with the character's struggle. (p. 28)

Of course, if readers are to understand conflicts and empathize with characters' responses, the characters themselves must be convincingly developed. The pressures that characters experience and the motives that characters act upon must be very clear. According to Hazel Rochman (1985), the age of protagonists in realistic fiction for older children is not so important as are convincing depictions of common hopes, fears, and important choices.

As an example of credible conflict, consider the person-against-self conflict that Paula Fox develops in *One-Eyed Cat*. Fox sets the stage for the forthcoming conflict by describing an incident in which Uncle Hilary gives Ned a loaded Daisy air rifle for his eleventh birthday. Ned's father, the Reverend Wallace, forbids Ned to use the gun until he is at least fourteen. Instead of hiding the gun, Ned's father takes it to the attic, where Ned can easily find it. A conflict is developed as Ned considers, "The painful thing was that, though Ned didn't always trust his father, his father trusted him, and that seemed to him unfair, although he couldn't explain why it was so" (p. 40).

Ned cannot resist the temptation of the gun, and fires it, shooting a wild stray cat. Then the person-against-self conflict deepens. Fox vividly describes Ned's fear and accompanying guilt when he sees the "gap, the dried blood, the little worm of mucus in the corner next to the cat's nose where the eye had been" (p. 70). Metaphor explains Ned's emotional response as "the gun was like a splinter in his mind" (p. 90). Ned's quest becomes to save the wild cat from sickness and starvation during the approaching winter. It also becomes a quest to overcome his sense of guilt and remorse and to tell the truth about what has happened.

Fox's novel follows Cohen's four major components. The problem results because Ned betrays his parent's trust; the struggle continues when Ned feels increasingly guilty because of his lies as he tries to save the wounded animal; the point of self-realization begins when Ned feels relief by confessing his guilt to a critically ill older neighbor; and peace and truth finally result on a moonlit night when Ned confesses his actions to his mother after they see a one-eyed cat and kittens emerging from the woods. In a satisfying conclusion, Ned and his mother exchange revealing confessions.

This book may be successful because the conflict appeals to more than one age or ability group. Most readers can empathize with the desire to commit a forbidden action and the terror of the consequences. More mature readers can appreciate the portrayal of a boy who successfully overcomes a hurdle in the maturation process.

Marion Dane Bauer's *On My Honor* develops a person-against-self conflict that is similar to the conflict in *One-Eyed Cat*. Consequently, the two books are excellent for comparisons. For example, the problem results for Bauer's character, Joel, because Joel betrays his parents' trust and swims with his friend in a treacherous river. The struggle continues when Joel feels increasing guilt, tries not to accept his friend's disappearance and probable death, and blames his father for allowing the two boys to go on a bike ride in the first place. Self-realization begins when Joel admits that Tony drowned and realizes that his father is not the cause of his problem. Although the seriousness of the problem does not allow complete resolution, peace begins after Joel sobbingly tells his father the whole truth. One of Bauer's themes, we have to live with our choices, is revealed when Joel's father says, "But, we all made choices today, Joel. You, me, Tony. Tony's the only one who doesn't have to live with his choice" (p. 88). Claudia Lepman-Logan (1989) maintains that books with such strong moral choices are excellent because "young readers need books that do more than entertain them. Books like *On My Honor* use readers as active participants, drawing them in on both emotional and intellectual levels" (p. 110).

Characterization

The characterization of Ned in Fox's *One-Eyed Cat* is an integral part of the conflict. For example, Fox describes Ned's actions, clarifies his response to his parents and to the wounded cat, and reveals his thoughts during his traumatic experiences. Readers know Ned intimately. They understand his hopes, his fears, his past, his present, and his relationships with his parents.

Complex characterizations that lead to self-discovery and personal relationships are also important in Cynthia Voigt's books about the Tillerman family. In *Homecoming*, Voigt focuses on the children's experiences after their emotionally ill mother deserts them. In the sequel, *Dicey's Song*, Voigt focuses on the four children and their grandmother: a young girl who is trying to hold her family together, a learning-disabled girl who has a gift for music, a gifted boy who tries to hide his giftedness because he does not want to be different, a younger brother who strikes out in anger, and a grandmother whom the townspeople consider eccentric. In all of Voigt's books, as in Fox's *One-Eyed Cat*, readers discover that the protagonists have many-sided personalities, like their own. Readers come to know these characters intimately, sharing their hopes, fears, pasts, and presents.

Throughout her books, Voigt effectively uses symbolism in her characterizations. Her use of symbolism associated with the blue heron is especially meaningful in *A Solitary Blue*. Consider the implications for Jeff's character in the following examples. When Jeff has low self-esteem, he views the heron as a creature that occupies "its own insignificant corner of the landscape in a timeless, long-legged solitude" (p. 45). Later, when Jeff feels angry, broken, and bruised due to his mother's behavior, he again views the heron; " 'Just leave me alone,' the heron seemed to be saying. Jeff rowed away, down the quiet creek. The bird did not watch him go" (p. 91). Finally, when Jeff discovers that he is a worthwhile person, he realizes that the solitary heron reminds him of his best friend, Dicey Tillerman. When Dicey laughingly states that she was thinking that the bird reminded her of Jeff, Jeff is flattered by the comparison. Jeff knows that he, like the heron, is a "rare bird," with staying power and a gentle spirit.

The synthesis of symbolism and character traits is equally important in *Dicey's Song*. For example, a careful tracing of musical selections, including the title, shows that Voigt uses music to develop character and to illustrate changes in personal development. Likewise, a dilapidated boat and a tree have important symbolic meanings.

Norma Fox Mazer also synthesizes symbols and characters in *After the Rain*. Mazer uses the symbolism of rain at the end of the book both to reveal and to review Rachel's changing feelings for her grandfather, Izzy. For example, after Izzy's death, Mazer states:

Symbolism enhances the characterization of a girl who makes discoveries about herself. (Illustration by James Shefcik from Dicey's Song *by Cynthia Voigt. Illustrations copyright © 1982 James Shefcik. Antheneum Publishers. Reprinted by permission of Simon & Schuster, Inc.)*

Then, behind her closed eyes, she sees a road, a narrow sandy road with tall trees on both sides, and she sees herself walking down this road in the rain . . . dark, blue-green of the trees . . . hard, dark lines of water sleeting down . . . nothing else exists but the wet road, the trees lashed by wind, and herself, a solitary figure walking in the rain. (p. 267)

Later, Rachel uses these words when talking about Izzy to her brother Jeremy:

"Anyway, I'm glad that I finally _____ ," she begins, and then she can't say it, can't say she's finally glad she got to know him. The sky is clear and cloudless, the trees are blazing purely with autumn color, but she is all at once in a storm. Hard rain again, this time with thunder and lightening. This time, not grief but anger. Anger at Izzy, hard strikes of anger splitting the blue sky she's created out of their feeling for each other. Anger for all those years he let slip by when they could have been knowing each other, when she could have loved him so much. (p. 278)

After Rachel has spent days searching for and finally finding Izzy's handprint and initials on the bridge he helped construct, "They are here now she thinks, and they will still be here years from now, when she, herself, is old. And then, though today the whole sky is covered by gray clouds, for a moment she feels the sun on her head, as warm as a loving hand" (p. 288). Mature readers enjoy the development of and the interactions with such characters as Dicey, Jeff, and Rachel. The symbolism makes the reading experience even more vivid and meaningful.

Cynthia Rylant develops both credible characters and the need to overcome personal sorrow after death in *Missing May*. By allowing Summer and Uncle Ob to remember May, Rylant allows readers to understand this remarkable woman. For example, notice how Rylant encourages readers to visualize May by contrasting her with other people:

May was gardening when she died. That's the word she always used: gardening. Everybody else in Fayette County would say they were going out to work in the garden, and that's the picture you'd get in your mind—people out there laboring and sweating and grunting in the dirt. But Aunt May gardened, and when she said it your mind would see some lovely person in a yellow-flowered hat snipping soft pink roses, little robins landing on her shoulders. (p. 9)

Throughout the book, Rylant develops May's character through such memories. By sharing their memories, both Summer and Uncle Ob can bury their sorrow and finally go on with the life that May would have wanted.

Theme

The underlying ideas that tie the plot, characters, and settings together in contemporary realistic fiction are closely related to the needs of modern children. For example, authors frequently show that children become stronger as they make discoveries about themselves. In *What Hearts,* Bruce Brooks's protagonist, Asa, learns that he needs to receive and give love if he is to be a total person. In *Western Wind,* Paula Fox's heroine, Elizabeth, makes discoveries about herself and develops important understandings as she interacts with her eccentric artist grandmother, with whom she spends the summer on an island off the coast of Maine.

When four sixth-grade students became the Academic Bowl team for their school in E. L. Konigsburg's *The View from Saturday,* they discover several important meanings in their own lives. For example, they discover the importance of expressing courtesy to one another, the importance of kindness, the importance of sharing, and the need to take careful notice of their actions and surroundings. By tracing the changes in the students as they interact with the team, Konigsburg develops the importance of these themes for each of the students and for their teacher, who needs to regain her confidence after an automobile accident.

As developed in contemporary realistic fiction, self-discovery is not always easy. In *T-Backs, T-Shirts, Coat, and Suit,* E. L. Konigsburg's twelve-year-old heroine discovers her values when she watches her aunt stand up for her own beliefs.

The books in this chapter develop many additional themes, such as children have common hopes and fears, life is filled with important choices that must be carefully considered, and friends should support rather than hurt each other.

Style

An effective literary style greatly enhances plot, characterization, and theme in realistic fiction. Vivid descriptions, believable dialogue, symbolism, figures of speech, and other stylistic techniques subtly provide readers with in-depth understanding of characters and situations. In *Dicey's Song,* for example, Cynthia Voigt develops a synthesis of symbols and character traits. Allusions to familiar music are among Voigt's symbolic means of emphasizing changes in the character.

In *Walk Two Moons,* Sharon Creech develops two parallel stories. As the heroine tells the story of her best friend Phoebe and her experiences when her mother left, Sal makes discoveries about her own life and learns to accept her own mother's actions. The author uses considerable symbolism to develop the feelings and characterizations in the story. For example, smoke symbolizes her feelings after her mother leaves: "There goes my mother" and "I watched the trail of smoke disappearing in the air" (p. 74). There is the symbolism of a dream about mother climbing a ladder and never coming down (p. 169). There is also the story of the mother dog as she weans and trains her children to be independent (pp. 257–258) and the symbolism of the singing trees that ends on page 268 at Sal's mother's grave.

Anne Fine's *Step by Wicked Step* provides an interesting book for analyzing an author's style that not only grabs the reader's attention, but also changes the plot in an unpredictable way. For example, the introductory chapters lead readers to believe that they may be approaching a mystery. Fine's first paragraph states: "Even before they reached the haunted house, the night had turned wild. The face of the minivan driver flicked from blue to white under the lightning. Each peal of thunder made the map in Mr. Plumley's hand shiver. The five leftover pupils from Stagfire School peered anxiously through the rain-spattered windows into the storm and the black night" (p. 3). As the minivan approaches Old Harwick Hall in England, the children comment on the forlorn appearance of the towering mansion with its turrets standing black against storm clouds. When they enter and go to their rooms they see a mark on the wall and find a hidden door with stretched and broken cobwebs. As they cautiously go through the door they find a hidden room with a book on the table titled: *Richard Clayton Harwick—My Story, Read and Weep.*

Now the children who are on a school field trip read the mysterious journal and discover the story of a boy who runs away from home after his father dies and he finds himself under the sinister influence of a stepfather. Fine changes the plot from an obvious mystery to one of self-discovery as each of the students realize that if Richard Clayton Harwick can tell his story, so can they. The remainder of the chapters focus on each child's telling his own story about divorce. The stories include sad, happy, and even humorous experiences. By the end of their stories, they discover that they are not alone and that someone has to make the effort because "as we all know, the ones who mess everything up in the first place aren't quite so good at fixing things again after" (p. 136).

In *Anastasia on Her Own,* Lois Lowry does not rely on preposterous situations to develop humor. Instead, she highlights the humor in a realistic contemporary situation. Two busy professional parents are trying to manage a household and to raise two children, and an enthusiastic, determined young protagonist believes that housekeeping can be easy if the family can only develop and closely follow a nonsexist household schedule. An unexpected consulting contract temporarily removes Anastasia's mother from the household and allows Anastasia an opportunity to test her theories.

Lowry develops humor by contrasting Anastasia's dream world with the world of reality; by describing the consequences when a naive but determined young girl approaches household tasks that are beyond her ability; and by describing the consequences of unexpected interruptions. Chapter one, for example, contains Anastasia's full-page schedule, which details hourly tasks from 7:00 A.M. to 8:00 P.M. In contrast, the eighth schedule in the book reads simply:

Housekeeping Schedule

Aftermath
Clean up. For hours and hours and hours.
Cry. (p. 122)

In *Missing May,* Cynthia Rylant uses contrasts to encourage readers to understand the treatment of Summer in two locations, to emphasize how Summer felt about this treatment, and to introduce the special bond that develops between May and Summer. Notice the impact of the following contrasting situations:

I stood there before those shelves, watching these wonders begin to spin as May turned on the fan overhead, and I felt like a magical little girl, a chosen little girl, like Alice who had fallen into Wonderland. This feeling has yet to leave me.

And as if the whirligigs weren't enough. May turned me to the kitchen, where she pulled open all the cabinet doors, plus the refrigerator, and she said, "Summer, whatever you like you can have and whatever you like that isn't here Uncle Ob will go down to Ellet's Grocery and get you. We want you to eat, honey."

Back in Ohio, where I'd been treated like a homework assignment somebody was always having to do, eating was never a joy of any kind. Every house I had ever lived in was so particular about its food, and especially when the food involved me. There's no good way to explain this. But I felt like one of those little mice who has to figure out the right button to push before its food will drop down into the cup. Caged and begging. That's how I felt sometimes. (p. 7)

As you read this quote, notice the emotional impact of the comparison between the magical girl in Alice in Wonderland and the caged mouse who must beg for every morsel.

 ## SUBJECTS IN REALISTIC FICTION

In order to help you recommend or choose specific books for children, this section emphasizes personality and social development in children. The various subject matters within the genre of contemporary realistic fiction encompass a wide range of themes.

Family Life

The family stories of the late 1930s through the early 1960s depict some of the strongest, warmest family relationships in contemporary realistic fiction for children. Today's children still enjoy the warmth and humor represented by the families in Elizabeth Enright's *Thimble Summer,* Eleanor Estes's *The Moffats,* Sydney Taylor's *All of a Kind Family,* and Madeleine L'Engle's *Meet the Austins.* The actions of the characters suggest that security is gained when family members work together, that each member has responsibility to other members, that consideration for others is desirable, and that family unity and loyalty can overcome hard times and peer conflicts.

Since the early 1960s, many changes have taken place in the characterizations of the American family in realistic fiction. Authors writing in the 1970s, 1980s, and 1990s often have focused on the need to overcome family disturbances, as children and adults adjust to new social realities. Death of one or both parents, foster families, single-parent families, children of unmarried females, the disruptions caused by divorce and remarriage, and child abuse are some of the issues related to children and their families that now appear in contemporary realistic fiction for children.

Such literature may help children realize that many family units other than the traditional one are common and legitimate in society today. Children

Sydney Taylor creates family stories that show warmth, humor, and strong family relationships. (From Ella of All of a Kind Family, by Sydney Taylor. Copyright © 1978 by Sydney Taylor. Illustrations copyright © 1978 by Gail Owens. Reprinted by permission of E. P. Dutton.)

may also see that problems often can be solved if family members work together. Even when depicting the most disturbing of relationships, authors of realistic fiction may show a strong need for family unity and a desire to keep at least some of the members together.

Authors of realistic stories about family disturbances use several literary techniques to create credible plots and characters. Often, they look at painful and potentially destructive situations and feelings that are common in society today. These situations are usually familiar to readers, who may have experienced similar situations, who may have known someone who had such experiences, or who may fear that they will have similar experiences. Authors often tell such stories from the perspective of a child or children involved. First-person or limited omniscient point of view from a child's perspective can successfully depict the emotional and behavioral reactions as the children first discover a problem, experience a wide range of personal difficulties and emotions when they try to change or understand the situation, and finally arrive at acceptance of the situation.

The characterizations may portray the vulnerability of the characters, create sympathy for them, and describe how they handle jolting disruptions and personal discoveries that affect their lives. Symbolism and allusion may emphasize conflicts and characters. Authors often use characters' reactions to change, trouble, and new discoveries to trace the development of better relationships with others or positive personal growth.

Some authors, however—such as those trying to make a point about child abuse—use specific situations or discoveries to allow children to escape from all reality. In realistic stories about family life, the antagonist may be a family member or an outside force, such as death of a parent, divorce, or moving to a new location. To relieve the impact of painful situations, authors may add humor. Humor can make situations bearable, create sympathy for characters, or clarify the nature of confrontations.

Desertion, Divorce, and Remarriage. In *Dear Mr. Henshaw,* Beverly Cleary effectively uses letters and diary entries written by her sixth-grade hero, Leigh Botts, to develop believable characters and plot and to show changes in Leigh as he begins to accept the actuality of his parents' divorce. As a classroom assignment, Leigh sends his favorite author a list of ten questions. Mr. Henshaw answers Leigh's questions and sends Leigh a list of ten questions that he wants Leigh to answer about himself.

At first, Leigh refuses to answer the questions. Then, his mother insists that because Mr. Henshaw answered Leigh's questions, Leigh must answer Mr. Henshaw's questions. The answers to the questions allow Cleary to provide important background information and to reveal Leigh's feelings about himself, his family, and his parents' divorce. Eventually, Leigh begins to write a diary—both because Mr. Henshaw suggests it and because Leigh's mother refuses to fix the television.

By midpoint in the book, the diary entries begin to change and Leigh realizes changes in his own character:

I don't have to pretend to write to Mr. Henshaw anymore. I have learned to say what I think on a piece of paper. And I don't hate my father either. I can't hate him. Maybe things would be easier if I could. (p. 73)

The entries seem believable because Cleary includes both humorous and painful experiences that are important in Leigh's life.

In *Strider,* the sequel to *Dear Mr. Henshaw,* Cleary again uses a series of diary entries to reveal changes in character. By caring for an abandoned dog, fourteen-year-old Leigh Botts finally learns to accept his parents' divorce and gains self-confidence. Cleary develops parallels to Leigh's divorced parents as Leigh and his best friend argue over the custody of the dog.

In *Thunderwith,* Libby Hathorn also uses a dog to help her heroine, Lara, gain strength and the ability to respond to her father's new family. The author develops person-versus-self conflict when Lara faces the death of her mother and person-against-person conflict when Lara must live with her father's second wife and children. By the end of the story, both Lara and her new family have gained understanding and made important discoveries about love. In *A Question of Trust,* Marion Dane Bauer uses a mother cat and her kittens to develop symbolism and create parallels in the lives of two boys who are facing the separation of their parents.

Mother-child relationships and the consequences that occur when mothers are no longer with their children are common plots in current realistic fiction. The plot in Creech's *Walk Two Moons* develops as Sal tries to discover why her mother left. In *Belle Prater's Boy,* Ruth White also deals with the loss of a parent. Notice in the following quote how White uses nature to reveal what the son has learned: "When I first came here, the trees were all in bloom. I never had seen anything so pretty, and thought nothing could ever hurt people who lived in such a beautiful place. Now the summer is gone. The apples are ripe, and I have learned . . . well, I have learned a beautiful place can't shelter you from hurt any more than a shack can" (p. 192). In both of these books, the protagonists make discoveries about tragedy and courage. Through their experiences they learn to face their problems and realize their personal strength.

In Carol Lea Benjamin's *The Wicked Stepdog,* twelve-year-old Lou is afraid of losing her father's love when he presents her with a new stepmother and a new "stepdog." Benjamin's first-person narrative from Lou's viewpoint emphasizes Lou's sometimes painful and sometimes humorous reactions to her changed family. Lou's changing responses to her stepmother's golden retriever symbolize her gradual acceptance of new circumstances. At first, she hates to walk the dog, but by the end of the story, when she meets a boy who also walks a dog, stepdog-walking has become one of Lou's favorite pastimes.

Single-Parent Families. Single-parent families have always existed, but recent realistic fiction for children portrays such families more often and sometimes more candidly than did most realistic fiction in the past. In contemporary novels for children, some of the families are doing quite well, while others face serious problems due to the lack of emotional and economic support from a mother or father.

A family's struggle to survive without one parent is popular in contemporary realistic fiction. Authors may suggest that the experience strengthens the children in the family or that the experience causes so many difficulties that the children find coping impossible. In Vera and Bill Cleaver's *Where the Lilies Bloom,* a fourteen-year-old girl experiences conflict between her desire to keep a promise that she made to her dying father and her developing realization that she must break the promise in order to ensure her family's survival.

Although Mary Call's father dies early in the story, the Cleavers characterize him plausibly, as a person who lives by a strong moral and family code. He demands that his daughter take pride in the family name, instill that pride in her brothers and sisters, and hold the family together without accepting charity. Later, this promise becomes a crucial element in the plot and in Mary Call's character development. The Cleavers develop a believable and interesting conflict. Mary Call tries to do as her father demanded, but she gradually realizes that she must accept help if she is to gain the knowledge that she needs and improve her family's welfare.

Jenny Davis's *Good-Bye and Keep Cold* begins with death and continues with adjustments to a single-parent family. Edda, a girl in the Kentucky mining area, first faces her father's accidental death in a strip mine and then grows up as her mother and younger brother must also face the traumatic changes in their lives. Davis uses nature to introduce the conflicting emotions. On the day of the funeral, young Edda retreats to Heaven, the favorite forest sanctuary of Edda and her father. The conflict and grief build as Edda first watches the glasslike water splash and glide over flat rocks and then:

Suddenly there were birds screaming overhead, loud, horrible screams, like people in pain. I started screaming back at them. . . . Mama was sleeping in her dark room up at the house, and Daddy was dead. There was no one to stop me, and that in itself made it all the more frightening and necessary to do. (p. 22)

Davis's story follows a family's healing process and deals with mature problems. Analyze the symbolic meaning of Davis's title, which is based on Robert Frost's poem, "Good-Bye and Keep Cold." Consider the meaning for Edda in the final paragraph. What does Edda mean when she thinks the following to herself?

Mama walked off from the people who raised her and never looked back. I don't want to do that. But I do want to be free of them, want them in perspective, want myself apart. I need to shake them loose, let go. Charlie says everybody has to raise their parents. Is that true? He says the time comes for all of us when we have to kiss them good-bye and trust them to be okay on their own. I've done the best I could with mine. Good-bye, you all, and good luck. Good-bye and keep cold. (p. 210)

In Marilyn Sachs's *The Bears' House,* detailed portrayal of a harsh reality gives the plot and the protagonist's responses full credibility. Five children live in a crowded apartment, their mother is emotionally disturbed, and their father deserts the family. The children's distrust of the adult world is expressed through their fears of being placed in foster homes and their lies to their social worker. Sachs contrasts the harsh reality of nine-year-old Fran Ellen's life with the beautiful make-believe place of her fantasies. When Fran Ellen sits in front of the dollhouse in her fourth-grade classroom, she can visit the Bear family and sit on Pappa Bear's lap when she feels unhappy. The conclusion of the story illustrates that contemporary realistic fiction may not have a happy-ever-after ending: Fran Ellen withdraws into her make-believe world, where she has found a way to survive in frightening and bewildering circumstances.

Numerous contemporary realistic fiction novels explore themes related to both the need for strong family loyalty during times of severe emotional strain and the person-versus-society conflict that re-

A child leaves her own harsh reality for a make-believe dollhouse world. (From The Bears' House, *by Marilyn Sachs. Copyright © 1971 by Marilyn Sachs. Reprinted by permission of Doubleday & Company, Inc.)*

sults when children fear the possible actions of people in social services. In *Mama, Let's Dance,* by Patricia Hermes, three children fear that they will be separated after their mother deserts them. Consequently, they try to keep the desertion a secret. Compare this book and additional books, such as Janet Taylor Lisle's *Afternoon of the Elves* and Paula Fox's *Monkey Island,* in which children are deserted by a parent.

Authors who place their protagonists in single-parent families frequently develop plots in which the characters go through unusual circumstances to learn about themselves or their parents. For example, in *The Moonlight Man,* Paula Fox places Catherine in the summer care of her father. As Catherine goes through a series of adventures with her novelist father, who is often intoxicated, she learns to accept his foibles and discovers characteristics about her mother and herself that she had never realized. By the end of the story, she realizes that it is sometimes very difficult to love someone, but we may still love someone if we dislike him. This theme is reinforced when Catherine realizes:

She had disliked her father that day. Yet she loved him. She went to bed and hit the pillow hard. Love, love, love, everyone was always saying. As though it were the easiest thing! The words she had shouted at him in the swing came back to her. Her father had been right; she hadn't known she had it in her to be so mean. (p. 149)

In *Pick-up Sticks* Sarah Ellis develops stronger relationships between a mother and daughter, thirteen-year-old Polly. As you read the following quotation, notice the changes that occur in the main character:

Polly studied her and saw, superimposed on the Mum of right now, a thirteen-years-younger Mum, eating pie, giggling with Marcie, finding the world suddenly beautiful. She realized that she had never put any energy into imagining Mum back then. She had used all her imaginings trying to visualize her father. She had made him up, again and again, handsome, rich, understanding, the father who never got older. And she would, no doubt, make him up again. She needed something to fill the father-shaped hole. But just at the moment, she didn't need him. He wasn't the point. (p. 123)

It is common in many stories about single-parent families for children to dream about the missing parent and not to appreciate the parent they have.

Many of the stories written about single-parent families develop themes in which children become stronger as they make discoveries about themselves and the adults in their lives. As in *The Moonlight Man,* some protagonists learn to accept the foibles of separated fathers or mothers and even grow closer to their parents, a change from the realistic fiction of the 1950s. The family structures, life-styles, values, and problems reflect contemporary concerns and issues.

Child Abuse and Foster Homes.

According to Eva-Maria Metcalf and Michael J. Meyer (1992), child abuse referrals in society are increasing rapidly. They state:

> The movement toward the recognition of children as people with individual rights who are thus entitled to a life of justice and happiness has undoubtedly both been affected by and contributed to the redefinition of child abuse. It is no surprise that much of recent children's literature is based on that very premise of entitlement. . . . We can only hope that the defense of the powerless and the outrage at their abuse in many recent children's books will bear a message that is heard by those readers who struggle or have struggled with abusive situations and by all who are today, or some day will be, parents. (p. 3)

As reflected in children's literature, the adult world may provide cruel experiences rather than happy and secure environments for development. The American Library Association's bibliography of literature related to child abuse includes thirty-nine titles that reflect chronic child abuse, relating to violence, sexual harassment, or neglect. According to Betsy Hearne (1985):

> Some of the books are grim, but most offer the hope or outright assertion that children can break out of tormenting situations through determined, independent actions. Sharing these books with children encourages exactly the kind of awareness that might help a victim of child abuse or help a friend help out. (p. 1261)

More hopeful treatments of foster care and child abuse appear in Patricia MacLachlan's *Mama One, Mama Two,* a picture storybook that depicts the warm, loving relationship between a foster mother and her foster child, and in Betsy Byars's *Cracker Jackson,* in which an eleven-year-old boy manages to convince adults that his former babysitter and her daughter are being abused by the husband and father. As in her other books, Byars uses humor and compassion to lighten the fear in the situation. As you read MacLachlan's *Mama One, Mama Two* and Byars's *Cracker Jackson,* consider each author's possible purpose. Consider, too, how each author develops plots, characters, settings, and themes. In addition, consider the possible responses of young readers.

Growing Up

Children face numerous challenges when they venture from the family environment and begin the often difficult process of growing up. Forming and maintaining relationships with peers is one important task. In addition, children may need to overcome emotional problems, to develop or recover self-esteem, and to identify their roles in their widening world. As children grow older, they may feel self-conscious about their changing bodies and developing sexuality. They must confront other facts of life as well, including survival and the inevitability of death. Books that explore children's concerns can stimulate discussion with children who are facing these same concerns. Such books also let children know that they are not alone, that other children experience the same problems and overcome them.

Peer Relationships.

Children, like adults, need the shared understanding, pleasure, challenge, sense of equality, and security that friendship with peers provides. Peer relationships involve many of the joys and sorrows with which children become familiar in family life, but peer relationships also expand understandings of other people and the world in ways that familiar family ties cannot. Contemporary realistic fiction portrays children who are forming friendships with peers much like themselves in certain ways and with peers who at first seem strange. Books that explore the meaning of real friendship and suggest that best friends should support, rather than hurt, each other may help children overcome the disappointment that results when friends move or may stimulate a discussion about the meaning of friendship.

Relationships between siblings and friends provide frequent plots in realistic fiction. Humorous sibling relationships are developed in Jane Cutler's *Rats!,* a collection of five stories about Jason, a fourth grader, and Edward, a first grader. These are lighthearted stories about the brothers' antics.

In *Bad Girls,* Cynthia Voigt uses the setting of a fifth-grade classroom and focuses attention on the behaviors of two girls who become best friends. Voigt introduces their attraction to each other early in the book and sets the stage for the mischief to follow: "When Mikey smiled that way, she looked mean, and dangerous—maybe evil. Margalo wanted to be her friend" (p. 11). Quickly, readers discover

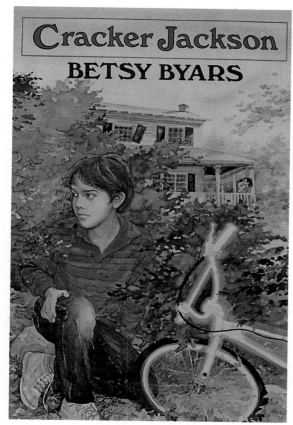

Humor and compassion lighten a story about child abuse. (From Cracker Jackson *by Betsy Byars. Jacket illustration by Diane de Groat. Text copyright © Betsy Byars, 1985. Jacket illustration copyright © Viking Penguin, Inc., 1985. Reprinted by permission of Penguin Books.)*

that Mikey has a closetful of smiles, one appropriate for every occasion. Voigt introduces the title of the book and the plot to follow as the girls are sure that the teacher is saying to herself, "How bad can two fifth-grade girls be?" (p. 23). Through their interactions with each other, their classmates, and their teacher, they learn a great deal about each other, but they really do not change from their original characters. The antics do seem real as one teacher commented, "I'm not sure I want my students to read this. It might give them ideas."

Authors often develop conflict in stories about interpersonal relationships by using person-against-self or person-against-person conflicts. In credible person-against-self conflicts, authors enable readers to identify inner conflicts and to understand why the

characters have the conflicts, how the characters handle the conflicts, and what things enable resolution of the conflicts. Resolutions should not be contrived; they should appear as natural outcomes. Contrived endings result when authors try too rapidly or too conveniently to create happy endings for serious and hurtful situations.

In credible person-against-person conflicts, authors develop both believable protagonists and believable opposing forces that serve as antagonists. Readers need to understand why conflicts occur between the forces. Do differences in values, personalities, or character traits cause conflict? An author's development of character should reflect such differences and encourage readers to understand why the characters act and react as they do. The conflicts that authors identify and the ways in which the characters overcome these conflicts usually communicate unifying themes about interpersonal relationships. The most successful themes develop naturally. The least successful themes are created solely for didactic purposes.

A person-against-self conflict and carefully developed character create a credible story in E. L. Konigsburg's *Jennifer, Hecate, Macbeth, William McKinley, and Me, Elizabeth.* Konigsburg encourages understanding of Elizabeth's inner conflict and need for a friend by emphasizing her shyness. She is a new girl in school, she goes to school alone, and she is afraid that she will cry when she walks into her classroom. Elizabeth's shyness and need for a friend are reemphasized through her responses when she meets Jennifer, a very imaginative girl. At first, Elizabeth complies with Jennifer's demands and suggestions even when she does not want to do what her new friend asks of her. Later, as she gains confidence in herself, Elizabeth becomes assertive. Her inner conflict is resolved when the friends no longer need the support of the game in which they pretend to be witch and assistant witch. Then, they can be just good friends and act as equals.

In *Words of Stone,* Kevin Henkes develops indepth looks at Blaze, who is still grieving for his dead mother, and Joselle, an unhappy and tough ten-year-old who decides to increase the excitement in her summer by playing malicious tricks on Blaze. Henkes focuses on each of the main characters in alternate chapters. This technique allows readers to understand the needs and conflicts within each of the characters. In a satisfying ending, each character forgives the other and realizes the value of true friendship.

The consequences of being different, having unusual responsibilities, and needing friendship and understanding are effectively developed in Janet Taylor Lisle's *Afternoon of the Elves*. Even though the two main characters are almost opposite in backgrounds and personalities, they are drawn together by Sara-Kate's insistence that she has an elfin village in her backyard. By working together in the village, Hillary gains new respect for Sara-Kate's differences and independence. Hillary discovers that Sara-Kate is responsible for nursing an invalid mother and holding the family together. Hillary concludes, "Perhaps being hungry and cold and angry and alone didn't mean you couldn't still be an elf. In fact, maybe those were exactly the things elves always were" (p. 119).

Stories about growing up frequently deal with problems associated with moving to new locations. Barbara Park's *The Kid in the Red Jacket* explores the problems faced by a fifth-grade boy when he moves to a different city. Making life more difficult for him is the first-grade girl who lives across the street and wants to be his best friend. Park uses a humorous approach to reveal many of the fears and problems associated with making new friends. In *The Broccoli Tapes*, Jan Slepian uses the concept of sending tapes from Hawaii back to friends in Boston to reveal a twelve-year-old girl's experiences as she adjusts to being away from her friends. In *Next-Door Neighbors*, Sarah Ellis's heroine discovers that new neighbors may help make a move bearable when her minister father is transferred to a new location in Western Canada. In *Amber Brown Is Not a Crayon*, Paula Danziger explores adjustments when a third-grade girl's best friend moves.

In *The Good Fortunes Gang*, Margaret Mahy's hero, Peter Fortune, moves from Australia to New Zealand and meets his hostile cousins. Mahy uses humor to lighten what Peter at first believes to be a disaster.

Physical Changes.
In order to develop credible problems, authors who write about physical maturity often describe embarrassing physical characteristics and explore ways in which the characters, friends, and family members respond to the characteristics. The stories may depict both person-against-self and person-against-person conflicts. Person-against-person conflicts include peer victimization of a main character, with the story told from the viewpoint of either the victimized child or a child who is part of the peer group. In the case of a main character who is part of a victimizing peer group, the author may develop the consequences of peer victimization by having the peer group turn against the main character. Some problems have simplistic or humorous resolutions, while other resolutions are complex and express the extreme sensitivity of children who are experiencing changes in their bodies and increased self-consciousness about their appearance as they grow up.

In *The Real Plato Jones*, Nina Bawden combines a thirteen-year-old boy's concerns over his short stature and his problems reconciling his heritage. Plato Constantine Jones has a Welsh grandfather who fought in World War II and a Greek grandfather who might have been a traitor, conflicts that provide numerous subplots in this coming-of-age story.

In *Are You There God? It's Me, Margaret*, Judy Blume explores a young girl's developing sexuality. Eleven-year-old Margaret has many questions about the physical changes occurring in her body, including breast development and the onset of menstruation. This book discusses a topic that is very serious to girls who are approaching physical maturity.

Emotional Changes.
Books that develop plots around emotional maturity—and physical maturity as well—differ in several important ways from the realistic fiction of the past. For example, several authors imply that parents are ineffective in helping a child cope with emotional changes and problems, are unavailable, or are unable to understand the child. Current realistic fiction often suggests that a person outside the family, an understanding grandparent or a knowledgeable friend, is the most important influence in a child's discovery of self—in contrast to the literature of the past, in which strong parents and caring brothers and sisters provide necessary support. Unlike many family stories in the past, current stories also suggest that children who are struggling toward emotional maturity have numerous problems.

Children confront a wide range of emotional issues while growing up. For example, in Lois Lowry's *Anastasia Krupnik*, a ten-year-old girl begins to overcome her desire to be the center of attention and her jealousy when she is able to place her family's new baby on her list of loves instead of her list of hates. Lowry extends the story of the Krupnik family in *Attaboy, Sam!,* focusing on Anastasia's little brother, Sam. The precocious boy's actions result in situations that are both hilarious and disastrous. Sam's story continues in *See You Around, Sam!* when Sam decides that he should run away to Alaska.

In *Bingo Brown and the Language of Love,* Betsy Byars uses lists to reveal a boy's growth, self-realization, and emotional maturity. For example, early in the novel, Bingo's lists include "Trials of Today" but no "Triumphs of Today." By the end of the novel, the trials are listed as "none!" and the triumphs include entries such as the following: "Attaining the mainstream of life and despite the unexpected strength of the current, not paddling in panic for shore" (p. 125). Through his summer ordeals and his reactions to a girlfriend who has moved, Bingo discovers that he can successfully face life. Lois Lowry's *Your Move, J. P.!* follows a seventh grader who is hopelessly in love.

In *Sydney, Herself,* Colby Rodowsky develops themes related to the importance of self-awareness through creative writing assignments. As a result of keeping a writing journal, Sydney learns to accept her heritage and respect her mother's needs.

The main character in Phyllis Reynolds Naylor's *Alice in Rapture, Sort Of* faces emotional changes caused by boy–girl relationships. Alice and her father live through what the father refers to as the summer of the first boyfriend. Naylor's figurative language effectively introduces the emotional conflict: The summer "stretched out before me like a roller coaster. I didn't want to get off, but I was terrified of what was over the next hill" (p. 2). By the end of the story, Alice concludes that it is more enjoyable to have male friends than boyfriends. In this humorous story, Naylor explores fears and issues associated with relationships, peer pressures, and growing up. Naylor's heroine, Alice McKinley, undergoes both humorous and painful experiences when she enters junior high in *Reluctantly Alice* and *All but Alice.* In *Reluctantly Alice,* she causes difficulties when she decides that it is her responsibility to advise her father and her older brother on their love lives. In *All but Alice,* she continues her meddling into her father's and brother's lives and decides that she needs to become involved in female relationships. Both books deal with emotional development through humorous experiences.

Martin, the twelve-year-old protagonist in Barbara O'Connor's *Beethoven In Paradise,* faces problems because he loves music. His father, however, wants him to play sports rather than play the violin. Through his experiences Martin begins to understand himself and his own desires.

The more serious consequences of growing up are explored in Neal Shusterman's *Speeding Bullet.* The hero, Nick Herrara, is a below-average student who has not received much attention until he saves a young girl from being hit by a subway train. The media and other people in New York City consider him a hero, and he receives all of the attention that he desires. The risks increase, however, when Nick begins to look for other people to rescue. By the end of the book, Nick gains understanding of his needs and reaches self-realization.

Changes in a boy's life from ages seven through twelve are developed in Bruce Brooks's *What Hearts.* This book includes four stories of experiences in Asa's life and shows how he overcomes his emotional problems and grows up along the way. At seven, Asa faces the divorce of his parents; at nine, he must choose between a good friend and a bad poem; at eleven, Asa faces problems associated with baseball; and at twelve, he experiences love. By the end of the story he understands:

He had the hearts, after all; he had the words, I love you I love you, printed clean. He had gotten them in what was suddenly his past, but they needn't stay there. . . . He had the words. There was a good thing about words: they could rise away from circumstances, they could take their meaning with them, they could move right along with you. And if a fellow had these words, these above all, then surely, something was in store in the future. Somewhere down the road, surely, these words would be made good. (p. 194)

In Katherine Paterson's *Come Sing, Jimmy Jo,* painful shyness causes person-against-self conflict, and the demands of a gifted but often selfish family create person-against-person conflicts for a gifted eleven-year-old boy. Paterson explores a young singer's fears after he reluctantly joins his Appalachian family's musical group and moves away from the protection of his beloved grandmother. Paterson describes changes in attitudes toward his gift in Jamie's changing responses to the audiences. Jamie proceeds from being a frightened boy who feels sick when he plays in front of people; to a bewildered boy who believes that his father, but not his mother, will protect him from the aggressive fans; to an entertainer who accepts his gift and discovers pleasure in sharing music. Readers can identify with Paterson's character because his fears about growing up and the changes that he faces are universal.

Cynthia Rylant's *A Fine White Dust* explores equally traumatic person-against-self conflicts. Pete, a thirteen-year-old boy, becomes involved with an unscrupulous traveling evangelist and struggles to understand his own religious beliefs. In a strong conclusion, Pete discovers that "the Preacher Man is behind me. But God is still right there, in front" (p. 106).

Survival

Physical and emotional survival are fundamental challenges for all humans. Confrontations with dangers in nature, society, or oneself require and, ideally, develop strength of character in young people and adults. The strong personalities in survival literature are especially popular with older children, who enjoy adventure stories.

Authors of survival literature use several literary techniques to create credible plots and characters. Person-against-nature, person-against-society, and person-against-self conflicts are often the stimuli for complex and exciting plots. Authors may develop forceful natural or social settings as antagonists in stories, clarifiers of conflicts, or means of developing desired moods. Style is also important in survival literature. Careful word selection, imagery, and rhythm patterns can heighten the emotional impact and credibility of adventures outside the realms of experience of most readers. Authors of survival literature usually rely on consistent point of view—often first-person or limited omniscient—to encourage the readers to identify with and believe in the protagonists and their experiences.

Surviving in Nature. In Jean Craighead George's *My Side of the Mountain,* Sam Gribley leaves his home in New York City to live off the land in the Catskill Mountains. George tells part of the story in the form of Sam's diary, which adds a sense of authenticity to the story and creates the feeling that the readers are sharing an autobiographical account of Sam's experiences. Detailed descriptions of Sam's preparing and storing food, tanning and sewing a deerhide suit, and carving and firing the interior of his home in a hemlock tree are told in a

Paterson develops credible characters in her novels. (From Park's Quest *by Katherine Paterson, jacket illustration by Ellen Thompson. Copyright © 1988 by Katherine Paterson. Lodestar Books, an affiliate of Dutton Children's Books, a division of Penguin Books USA, Inc. Reprinted by permission of Penguin Books USA, Inc.)*

matter-of-fact manner, which resembles the writing of someone who is keeping a log of his experiences and observations. The detailed descriptions of wild edible plants and important survival techniques also suggest that Sam prepared carefully for his experiment in the wild. George creates another exciting survival-in-nature story in *Julie of the Wolves.* In this story, a thirteen-year-old girl lost in the arctic tundra develops a friendship with wolves.

The consistent first-person point of view used by Scott O'Dell in *Island of the Blue Dolphins* creates a plausible plot, main character, and setting. When Karana, a young Indian girl who survives years alone on a Pacific Island, says, "I will tell you about my island," readers visualize the important features from her viewpoint and believe the description. When she says, "I was afraid," the fear seems real. Later, her discovery of her brother's body justifies her fear. This first-person point of view increases the readers' belief in Karana's personal struggles as she is torn between two forces. Will she adhere to the tribal law that prohibits women from making weapons? Or will she construct the weapons that will probably mean the difference between her life or death? Her inner turmoil heightens the suspense, as suggested by the following quote:

Would the four winds blow in from the four directions of the world and smother me as I made the weapons? Or would the earth tremble, as many said, and bury me beneath its falling rocks? Or, as others said, would the sea rise over the island in a terrible flood? Would the weapons break in my hands at the moment when my life was in danger, which is what my father had said? (p. 54)

Other major decisions are more meaningful, too, because they are told through Karana's point of view. When Karana decides to take a tribal canoe and sail in the direction that her people sailed, readers believe her turmoil as the canoe begins to leak and she must make another difficult decision: Should she go back and face loneliness or go on and face probable disaster? Karana decides to return to her island and make it as much of a home as she can.

O'Dell emphasizes the small details of days filled with improving shelter, finding food, and hiding supplies against the possibility of Aleut enemies' returning to the island. Karana's need for companionship is shown when she cannot kill the leader of the wild dogs after wounding him. Instead, she takes him to her shelter, cares for him, and names him Rontu. Returned to health, Rontu becomes her constant companion and defender. After Rontu's death, Karana tames another dog, who eventually sails with her to the mainland when her long years on the island are finally over.

In the survival story *Hatchet,* Gary Paulsen carefully documents Brian's problem-solving approaches. Each time that Brian faces a critical, often life-and-death problem, Paulsen reveals Brian's reasoning processes. Brian thinks about the pros and cons of various actions. For example, Brian thinks through the various actions that he could take after the pilot has a heart attack and Brian realizes that he is alone (pp. 17–30), the reasons that he should have no fear of the bear and return to the raspberry patch (p. 75),

the reasons that a water animal would come up to the sand (pp. 98–99), a way to create a weapon to effectively catch fish (pp. 111–115), ways to capture birds for meat (pp. 140–141), and a way to make a craft and reach the plane after a tornado reveals the location of the plane (pp. 166–183). Memories of books that Brian has read or television programs that he has seen frequently help him solve what otherwise would be impossible problems.

Paulsen uses contrasts to encourage readers to understand both the gravity and the consequences of many of the problems. For example, Brian compares his experiences in the wilderness with experiences that he has had at home. Readers understand that the search for and the storage of food is more than a simple trip to the grocery store. Unlike Brian's home experiences, his actions in the wilderness are life-and-death matters. You may compare Paulsen's survival story with Alden R. Carter's *Between a Rock and a Hard Place* and with Tim Wynne-Jones's *The Maestro.*

Surviving Inner-City Reality.

Dangerous, polluted, and economically deprived inner cities are the environments in which many American children face the challenges of growing up. Several authors of realistic fiction portray the problems of overcoming poverty, gang violence, and living without the security of strong, supportive family members. Many of these characters live in homeless situations. It is easy to rely on sensationalism for such stories, and numerous authors do. However, Virginia Hamilton, Walter Dean Myers, and Paula Fox, for example, create inner-city stories with literary merit.

One of the strongest inner-city stories is Virginia Hamilton's *The Planet of Junior Brown.* Hamilton's memorable characters enliven a complex story about friendship, loyalty, and learning to live together. The three main characters, all outcasts, live on the fringe of busy New York City. Junior Brown is a talented pianist who should be recognized for his skill, but the fact that he weighs almost three hundred pounds causes people to leave him alone. Consequently, he feels ugly and is afraid of being trapped in small spaces. Buddy Clark is an intelligent street boy who has lived on his own since the age of nine. The third outcast is Mr. Pool, a former teacher, who is a school custodian.

Mr. Pool feels that tough black children who know the city streets should be given opportunities to

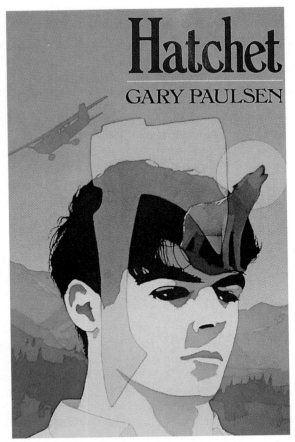

Gary Paulsen develops strong person-versus-nature and person-versus-self conflicts in Hatchet. *(From* Hatchet *by Gary Paulsen. Jacket cover by Neil Waldman. Copyright © 1987 by Neil Waldman. Reprinted by permission of Neil Waldman.)*

learn, but the rigid school regime causes him to lose heart, give up his teaching job, and move to the school basement. In this basement, however, Mr. Pool has a secret room where he can teach Junior Brown and Buddy Clark. Hamilton uses the symbolism associated with the word *planet* to develop each character's place in the story. Junior Brown's planet is an artistic creation that hangs suspended from metal rods and spherical tracks attached to the ceiling of the hidden room. While the children in the rooms above go through their normal days, the three outcasts build their solar system, create their planets, and learn about science and each other. Hamilton develops a strong theme when Buddy Clark takes the other outcasts to his own planet in

the basement of a deserted house and shares with them his own views of life:

"We are together," Buddy told them, "because we have to learn to live for each other. . . . If you stay here, you each have a voice in what you will do here. But the highest law for us is to live for one another. I can teach you how to do that." (p. 210)

In *Scorpions,* Walter Dean Myers creates a less hopeful and more tragic story. Conflict begins when Jamal's older brother, who is in jail, wants Jamal to take over leadership of a gang. Jamal is torn between worry over his mother, who works too hard, and indecision over his role in the gang. Jamal's person-against-self conflict increases when he is given a gun. Should he keep it even though his best friend warns him against having a gun? Should he use it to make his position strong within the gang? Should he use it to frighten a bully at school who has always tormented him? When the gun is used at the end of the story, Myers shows the tragic consequences of Jamal's decision. Because of the gun, Jamal loses his best friend. Readers of this story will understand the author's theme: There is danger when people are involved with violent gangs, drugs, and guns. *Somewhere in the Darkness,* also by Myers, is a story in which a boy learns about the harsh realities of life when he accompanies his convict father on a search for truth and respect.

Homelessness in America is a major social problem. According to Nel Ward and Patrick Jones (1992):

Increasingly, literature for children and young adults has addressed the problem of those who are forced to live in homeless shelters or in makeshift homes. . . . Books centering on homelessness focus on the impact of homelessness on children and young adults through friendships with homeless people, their attempts to help the homeless, and their experiences of being homeless themselves. (p. 340)

A picture book for younger children, *Mr. Bow Tie* by Karen Barbour, is the story of two children who befriend a homeless man and reunite him with his own family. This gentle story, written for younger readers, focuses on the positive interactions between a family and a homeless person.

Stories written for older audiences tend to depict the harsher realities of homelessness. For example, in *Monkey Island,* Paula Fox uses numerous con-

Gang violence and guns create conflict in this inner-city setting. (From Scorpions by Walter Dean Myers, copyright © 1988 by Walter Dean Myers. Cover art: Copyright © 1988 by Bradford Brown. Reprinted by permission of HarperCollins.)

Strong characters emerge in this survival story set in a large city. (From Monkey Island by Paula Fox. Copyright © 1991 by Paula Fox. Used by permission of Orchard Books.)

trasts between Clay's former life with his parents and his life as a homeless boy after his mother's desertion. In the following quotation, Fox depicts Clay's memories:

Standing there, hidden from the street, trying to breathe shallowly, he had what was almost a vision, or a kind of mist of memory, of being lifted up by his father in the dark warmth of a room, of being carried to the bathroom, where a tiny night-light in a floor socket gave off an amber glow and his father murmuring, "That's good my sweetheart. You can sleep right through now." (p. 26)

On the following page, Fox describes the reality of the streets through Clay's point of view,

He crossed a street and waited a moment as he heard a very faint murmur—there, and not there—whispers fading into nothing. Now he could see that the black patches were cardboard boxes and heaps of bundles and that there were many long pieces of cardboard lying about on the ground and beneath benches. There were people in the park. On a nearby bench, an old woman lay doubled over, apparently asleep, black plastic bags gathered around her on the bench and on the ground, like big black stones. (p. 27)

From this point on, Clay enters the world of New York City's homeless population and learns that the streets are dangerous. Happily, he is befriended by two homeless men who help him survive.

As in many stories of homeless people, Fox describes the dangers in the street and develops person-versus-society conflicts. Clay thinks about his negative associations with social services, Clay describes his fear of having an agency take him away so that he cannot find his mother, a character tells Clay that most people think of homeless people as nasty stains on the sidewalk, and Clay realizes that families can let you down. The story concludes happily when Clay finds his mother and then forgives her for her actions.

In *The Beggars' Ride,* Theresa Nelson develops the story of a runaway twelve-year-old girl who leaves her unhappy home to try to survive on the streets of Atlantic City. Nelson also depicts a person-versus-society conflict by developing stories of the various gang members who take Clare into their group. A kind older man helps Clare survive in this homeless environment.

You may want to compare the inner-city survival stories set in the United States with one set in Ankara, Turkey, the setting for Gaye Hicyilmaz's *Against the Storm.* This story shows the consequences of urban poverty. Hicyilmaz's story is vivid because she lived in Turkey for many years. According to the endnotes, "It was here that she was struck by the way children in particular are forced to suffer the effects of poverty and how poverty destroys the very fabric of society. Her novel was inspired by a true incident reported in the Turkish press" (endnotes).

To gain more insights into the world of homelessness and city poverty and to evaluate the authenticity of the conflict in these stories, read Judith Berck's nonfictional book *No Place to Be: Voices of Homeless Children.* Berck includes interviews with homeless children living in New York City's shelters and welfare hotels.

Surviving in a Dangerous World. A new type of survival literature is emerging in both American and British children's literature: realistic fiction that mirrors international headlines about new dangers in our modern age. In the person-against-society conflicts of this survival literature, the protagonists are usually innocent children and the antagonists are terrorist groups, oppressive military governments, and mass violence.

Terrorists create the person-against-society conflicts in Gillian Cross's *On the Edge.* In this book, the hostage is the kidnapped son of a journalist. Cross explores important choices. For the mother, it is complying with the terrorists' demands for the release of her son versus revealing information that could save the life of a world leader and destroy the assassination plot of the terrorists. For the son, it is what to do with the last few moments of his life.

In *AK,* Peter Dickinson develops the conflicts faced by Paul Kagomi, an orphan and a child guerrilla, who tries to survive in a war-torn African setting. Dickinson develops strong themes related to peace and war. Notice the impact of the following quote:

Now, you can't just say, "Let there be peace and happiness." It has to be built, by men and women working together. And even when it is built you can't leave it alone. It has to be tended, it has to be fed and repaired and altered to fit with changing times. It's like a railway, an engine on the railway. That doesn't run by itself. It has to be stoked and driven, its track must be kept sound and the signals working and the bridges inspected—all that. (p. 15)

Dickinson's conclusions are interesting for discussion and responses. Dickinson develops two contrasting scenarios for twenty years after the conclusion of the book. One is a very positive prediction in which the forces for freedom and peace have won. The other scenario is that guerrilla warfare and hatred are still the major way of life.

Other authors place their characters in the political turmoil of South America or Syria. James Watson's *Talking in Whispers,* a 1983 British Carnegie Honor book for older children, is a survival story in which the main character is hunted by the security forces of a South American government that denies basic human rights. Rafik Schami's *A Hand Full of Stars* places the hero in the political turmoil of modern Damascus. Showing how dangerous society can be, the story follows a teenager who wants to become a journalist within this suppressed society. His wishes come true when he and his friends begin an underground newspaper. After reading this book, you may speculate about the symbolism in the title. The author states at the end of the book what *A Hand Full of Stars* means: "The Hand is the hand of Uncle Salim, always there to guide the narrator; in the saddest moments, it points the way out of despair. Like the stars that illuminate the dark night sky, the Stars in the hand stand for hope" (endnote).

The political turmoil of Romania provides the setting and conflict in Bel Mooney's *The Voices of Silence.* The major conflict results when a girl betrays her parents to her friend.

In Lois Duncan's *Don't Look Behind You,* a family is threatened by hired assassins. Duncan develops the frightening adjustments that the family must make when it is placed under the federal witness security program. Older readers will understand the conflicts of the teenage girl who tries to salvage parts of her former life.

Death

Part of growing up is realizing and gradually accepting the fact of death. An increasing number of realistic fiction stories develop themes related to the acceptance of death and the overcoming of emotional problems following the death of a loved one. Louis Rauch Gibson and Laura M. Zaidman (1992) identify the importance of literature that deals with death:

Since children, like adults, are so deeply affected by the loss of a relative or friend, contemporary realistic fiction and biography help resolve some of the conflicts death presents. Literature about real and fictional people satisfies a desperate need to comfort children who are justifiably bewildered and fearful about death. (p. 233)

As might be expected, different authors treat the subject differently. Treatments also depend on the developmental levels of their intended readers.

Differences in cause of conflict, resolution of conflict, and depth of emotional involvement are apparent in books of realistic fiction about death. Consider how several authors develop these areas in books written for younger readers, preadolescents, and teenagers. For comparative purposes, consider Charlotte Graeber's *Mustard,* written for younger readers; Constance C. Greene's *Beat the Turtle Drum,* written for ten- to twelve-year-olds; Richard Peck's *Remembering the Good Times* and Judy Blume's *Tiger Eyes,* written for readers in their early teens; and Robert Cormier's *The Bumblebee Flies Anyway,* written for teenagers and young adults.

In Charlotte Graeber's *Mustard,* a book for young children, members of a family share the sorrow following a fourteen-year-old cat's heart attack and their decision to let the veterinarian help the cat die in peace. Graeber looks at the importance of a pet to a young boy and encourages readers to understand the boy's relationship to the cat by describing the boy's disbelief in the cat's ailments and his reactions after the pet dies. When Alex and his father go to the pet shelter to donate some of Mustard's things, Alex declines the offer of a kitten because he does not have room at the moment for anything but memories of Mustard. In another year, he may be ready for a pet, he says. This resolution encourages readers to

understand that healing takes time, memories are worth retaining, and family members can help each other in times of sadness.

Stories written for ten- through twelve-year-olds have more fully developed characters and deal with more difficult emotions, those related to adjusting to the death of a family member. Constance C. Greene's *Beat the Turtle Drum* develops the basis for a girl's reactions to her sister's accidental death by describing the warm relationship between ten-year-old Joss and her twelve-year-old sister, Kate. Kate believes that her parents prefer her younger sister. After Joss dies as a result of a fall from a tree, Kate faces both the sorrow of losing a sister and the inner conflict resulting from her belief that her sister was the favorite. Readers glimpse Kate's inner turmoil when she finally admits her feelings to an understanding relative, who responds:

I bet Joss would've felt the same way. If it'd been you, she might've said the same thing. And both of you would've been wrong. I think when a child dies, it's the saddest thing that could ever happen. And the next saddest is the way the brothers and sisters feel. They feel guilty, because they fought or were jealous or lots of things. And here they are, alive, and the other one is dead. And there's nothing they can do. It'll take time, Kate. (p. 105)

Kate gradually understands that overcoming her grief and conflicting emotions will take more than a moment but that she will receive pleasure from her memories of Joss.

The believable characters in Richard Peck's *Remembering the Good Times* helps readers in their teens identify with this story about the suicide of a best friend. Peck first carefully develops the distinct personalities of two boys and a girl in their junior-high years. Kate is involved with people and believes in herself; Buck does not know which group he belongs with; and Trav is angry, unsure of himself, and afraid of the future. Peck develops the main person-against-self conflict by describing Trav's increasing fears as he discusses current events and as he reacts to evidence that he is expected to grow up to be like his successful parents. Trav becomes angry when he feels that he is not being prepared for the realities of life.

Peck develops a strong relationship among the three friends. After Trav's suicide, Kate admonishes herself because she did not notice the little things that should have warned them about Trav's approaching suicide. Peck explores various responses to Trav's death, as high-school administrators blame the parents, the parents blame the school, a knowledgeable older friend states the community's responsibility, and Kate and Buck discover that they can remember the good times of their friendship.

The causes of the conflict in Blume's story for older readers, *Tiger Eyes*, are the sudden, violent death of a parent and a society that creates such violence. Blume develops a person-against-self conflict as a teenage girl, Davey, tries to adjust emotionally and physically to the death of her father, who was a robbery victim. Blume also develops a person-against-society conflict as the characters respond to and reflect about a society in which there is violent death, vandalism, excessive teenage tension, and powerful weapons. Blume's characterization encourages readers to understand Davey's turmoil. Blume shows Davey's emotional ties with her father, Davey's physical reactions when she faces her peers (she faints at school but cannot tell the nurse her problem), Davey's need for a quiet place to reflect, Davey's interactions with a man who is dying from cancer and an uncle who will not allow her to take chances but designs weapons at Los Alamos, and Davey's interactions with two friends who are also facing inner conflicts. The resolutions of the conflicts require much time, but Davey can finally face what happened, tell new friends how her father died, and consider her own future.

The setting in *The Bumblebee Flies Anyway*, Robert Cormier's psychological novel for teenagers and young adults, is a terminal care facility in which a sixteen-year-old boy, Barney, realizes that his treatment is only experimental and that he is actually dying. Cormier uses symbolism to convey Barney's feelings about being a terminally ill guinea pig: The complex is a facility for experimental medicine; "the Handyman" is a doctor who treats the patients and creates illusions; "the merchandise" is special medicines, chemicals, and drugs that are calculated to produce expected responses; and "the bumblebee" is a sportscar in a junkyard that at first appears to be shining and new but is actually only a cardboard mockup of reality.

Stories about death deal with irreversible problems that are difficult to accept and resolve. Consequently, the responses of individual children to the books may be very personal. An eight-year-old said that he felt better after reading *Mustard* because it helped him feel better after the death of his pet. An eleven-year-old, however, did not want to read Cynthia Rylant's book about the death of a great-aunt, *Missing May*, because she did not want to be reminded that someone she loved might die.

Several responses by fourteen-year-olds to *Tiger Eyes* demonstrate how personal the reactions to realistic fiction can be. One reader said, "This is not a good book to read in class. You need to be by yourself so you can cry if you want to." Another child said, "It's great. You get into the story and forget everything. I was afraid Davey was going to kill herself, but I thought, Judy Blume wouldn't kill her main character." A third reader said that the story was sad but its moral was happy: "Take a chance on your talents; planning someone's life for them doesn't make them happy; it's always better to face the truth rather than run from it; life is a great adventure; you can't go back in time. So pick up the pieces and move ahead; and some changes happen down inside of you and only you know about them." These responses indicate that a fourteen-year-old grasped many of the complex themes that Blume wove into her novel. It is also interesting to note that the themes identified are positive rather than negative.

As seen from the previous discussion, books on death focus on various aspects of death. Books such as Sharon Creech's *Chasing Redbird* deal with a child's struggle to accept her aunt's death. Two recent books deal with responses to death through violence. In Colby Rodowsky's *Remembering Mog*, the author proceeds through a series of family reactions to Mog's murder. The contemporary nightmare of dealing with a missing relative is also developed in Michael Cadnum's *Zero to the Bone*, a book for older readers.

People as Individuals, not Stereotypes

Stereotypical views of males and females, people with disabilities, and the elderly are becoming less prevalent than they once were in children's literature. Chapter 11, "Multicultural Literature," also discusses contemporary realistic fiction that portrays racial and ethnic minorities in unstereotyped ways.

Male and Females. Publishers are becoming sensitive to the need for literature that does not portray either sex in stereotypical roles. For example, since 1981, the Houghton Mifflin Publishing Company has had guidelines for eliminating sex stereotypes in materials that it publishes. Following are several guidelines:

1. Published materials should balance female and male protagonists and female and male contributors to society, and should present females and males in a variety of jobs. Stories should suggest that both females and males can prepare for and succeed in a variety of occupations.
2. Literature should recognize that males and females share the same basic emotions, personality traits, and capabilities. Both sexes should be portrayed in active pastimes and in solitary pursuits.
3. Sensitivity, taste, and nonstereotypic images should be employed in humor used to characterize the sexes.
4. Literature should present a broad range of historical references to women, including women whose contributions are well-known and less well-known.
5. Where appropriate, literature should include reference to legal, economic, and social issues related to women.
6. Historical books should include coverage of the roles and activities of women in past centuries.

As the roles of females in our society shift away from the stereotypes of the past, female characters in children's literature reflect these changes. Contemporary realistic fiction contains more girls who are distinct individuals. Girls may be brave, they may be tomboys, and they may be unorthodox. Mothers in realistic fiction are also taking on different roles. Often, they work outside the home; they may even have jobs more demanding than those of their husbands. Whatever roles females in recent realistic fiction play, the female characters are quite different from the female characters in earlier children's literature, even literature of the fairly recent past.

Consider, for example, the popular contemporary character Ramona, created by Beverly Cleary. Stories of her exploits span the years from the early 1950s into the 1980s. In *Henry and Beezus*, published in 1952, readers discover that the girls, Beezus and Ramona, are considered worthy playmates *even* by an active boy, such as Henry Huggins. These thoughts at least imply that active pastimes are not usually considered appropriate for girls; girls may not be considered creative playmates.

In later books, however, Ramona comes into her own. In *Ramona the Pest* (1968), she is not the stereotypical quiet girl; instead, she is the "worst rester" in kindergarten. By the time *Ramona and Her Father* was published in the late 1970s, the roles in her family have changed: Her father loses his job and stays home, while her mother returns to work on a full-time basis. Ramona humorously tries to help her father through this change in his life. *Ramona and Her Mother* explores a working mother's life as viewed by her seven-year-old daughter. By 1981, *Ramona Quimby, Age 8* is helping her family while her father returns to college. The Ramona books are popular with children who enjoy reading about the exploits of a spunky, humorous girl.

Louise Fitzhugh's hero in *Harriet the Spy* is an eleven-year-old girl whom other characters describe as exceptional, intelligent, and curious. Harriet's actions support these descriptions. Harriet hides in her secret places, observes her neighbors and classmates, and writes down her observations. The extent of this popular character's resourcefulness and self-confidence is revealed when her classmates find her notebook and organize "The Spy Catcher Club." Harriet uses all of her creativity to devise a plan that will convince her friends to forgive her. She is far from the fainting female of most traditional literature and Victorian fiction, who must be rescued from her failures by the males in the story. She is even able to return to her real loves, spying and writing. More tales about Harriet are found in *The Long Secret*.

E. L. Konigsburg's *From the Mixed-up Files of Mrs. Basil E. Frankweiler* is another book of realistic fiction in which a female protagonist belies the traditional stereotypes about passive femininity. Claudia Kincaid leads her brother in running away from home and hiding out in the Metropolitan Museum of Art. When the two children are given one hour to search the files and discover the answer to a mystery involving a statue of an angel, Claudia tells her impatient brother that five minutes of planning are worth fifteen minutes of haphazard looking. Her techniques prove successful, and they discover the answer.

Stereotyped views of males are also changing in our society and children's literature. In Katherine Paterson's *Bridge to Terabithia*, for example, a boy hates football, aspires to be an artist, and feels pressured by his father's traditionally masculine expectations of him. Although the father is afraid that Jess is becoming a "sissy," Jess finds support for being himself in a strong friendship with the story's other protagonist, a girl named Leslie, who is also a nonconformist in their rural community.

One outstanding book of realistic fiction from the mid-1960s reveals that wider options for males are becoming more prevalent in children's literature today. In Maia Wojciechowska's *Shadow of a Bull,* the son of a famous and supposedly fearless bullfighter learns that a male doesn't have to prove his manliness through acts of physical daring or violence. Manolo's village expects him to follow in his dead father's footsteps. As the men of the village begin training him in the art of bullfighting, Manolo believes that he is a coward because he has no interest in being a bullfighter. Manolo eventually learns that in order to be truly brave, he must be true to himself and not attempt to satisfy others' expectations. Wojciechowska effectively resolves Manolo's person-against-self conflict when Manolo tells the waiting crowd in the bullring that he prefers medicine to bullfighting.

Individuals Who Are Physically Different or Disabled.

Most children and adults dislike standing out in a crowd because of their appearance or physical capabilities. They also may feel discomfort when they see someone who does not conform to the customary standards of appearance or who is physically disabled. Children's realistic fiction is becoming increasingly sensitive to the importance of overcoming cruel or condescending stereotypes.

In *Blubber,* Judy Blume shows how peer cruelty to someone who is physically different can have negative consequences for all concerned. Classmates torment a girl whom they consider grossly overweight. A strong peer leader manipulates her friends into composing a list entitled "How to Have Fun with Blubber" and forces the girl herself to make self-demeaning statements, such as "I am Blubber, the smelly whale of class 206" (p. 72). The main character realizes the crushing impact of what she has done when she tries to stop the cruelty and her classmates then turn on her.

Authors who develop realistic plots around credible characters who have physical disabilities often describe details related to a disability, the feelings and experiences of the person who has the disability, and the feelings and experiences of family members and others who interact with the character. Well-written books help other children empathize with and understand children with disabilities. While adults should evaluate such books by literary standards, they also should evaluate them by their sensitivity. Mary Sage (1977) recommends the following criteria when evaluating books concerning individuals with disabilities:

1. The author should deal with the physical, practical, and emotional manifestations of the disabling condition accurately but not didactically.
2. Other characters in the story should behave realistically as they relate to the individual with disabilities.
3. The story should provide honest and workable information about disabling conditions and the potential of individuals with disabilities.

The resolution of conflict can be a special concern in realistic fiction dealing with physical disabilities. Does the author concoct a happy ending because he or she believes that all children's stories should have happy endings, or does the resolution of conflict evolve naturally and honestly? Through fiction that honestly deals with disabilities, readers can empathize with children who are courageously overcoming their problems and who, with their families, are facing new challenges. Writers of such literature often express the hope that their stories will encourage positive attitudes toward individuals with physical disabilities. As mainstreaming brings more children with disabilities into regular classrooms, this goal becomes more important.

Stories set in different historical periods often reflect changing attitudes about physical disabilities and provide bases for discussion with children. Julia Cunningham's story of a mute boy in *Burnish Me Bright* takes place in a French village of the past. The boy encounters prejudice, misunderstanding, fear, and even hostility. Monsieur Hilaire, a retired performer who befriends the boy and brings him into his world of pantomime, clarifies the reasons behind society's prejudice:

These people you have known are no worse than the others that walk the world but they share with the others a common enemy, and the enemy is anyone who is different. They fear the boy who can't speak, the woman who lives by herself and believes in the curative power of herbs, the man who reads books instead of going to the café at night, the person like me who has lived in the distant differences of the theater. They are not willing to try to understand, so they react against them and occasionally do them injury. (p. 18)

Ellen Howard sets *Edith Herself* in the pioneer America of the 1890s. The girl, Edith, faces her own fears and the ignorance of others who do not understand her epileptic seizures. The story may seem realistic because the experience happened to a relative of the author. Carol Carrick's *Stay Away from Simon* shows the damage inflicted on a boy with mental disabilities in the early 1800s. Both texts develop strong themes about the consequences of prejudice caused by ignorance.

In *From Anna*, Jean Little develops a credible perspective on visual impairment by describing a girl's frightening experiences as a result of blurred letters, letters that look the same, or even appear to jiggle across the page. In *The Gift of the Girl Who Couldn't Hear*, Susan Shreve develops the interactions between Eliza and her best friend, Lucy, who has been deaf since birth. In this book, Lucy helps Eliza understand her own self-worth. The theme of the book may be used as a basis for students to ponder the role of real and self-imposed limitations and the courage to distinguish between the two.

Disabilities include mental capacities that are not up to the social norm. Authors who write plausible books about the relationships between mentally disabled children and their normal siblings often portray the conflicting emotions of normal characters who experience both protective feelings and feelings of anger toward children with disabilities. In Betsy Byars's *The Summer of the Swans*, Sara is a normal teenager who is discontented with her looks, sometimes miserable for no apparent reason, and often frustrated with her mentally retarded brother as she cares for him.

Byars encourages readers to understand and empathize with Charlie's gentle nature. He is fascinated by the swans who glide silently across the lake, but he becomes confused and terrified when he follows the swans and becomes lost. During a frantic search for Charlie, Sara forgets her personal miseries. When the siblings are reunited, Sara discovers that she feels better about herself and life in general than she had before.

Virginia Euwer Wolff's *Probably Still Nick Swansen* develops a many-sided character, Nick, who faces the realities of his learning disability. The author explores the similarities between sixteen-year-old Nick and other teens as well as individual differences among the students in Nick's special education class. In a strong ending, Nick learns to accept himself.

The Elderly. When children's literature students evaluate the characterizations of elderly people in children's books, they often discover stereotypes. Denise C. Storey (1979) describes a study in which fifth-grade children analyzed the elderly characters found in books from their classroom library. The children concluded that (1) some elderly people lead

Mazer develops a believable relationship between grandfather and granddaughter (Jacket illustration by Fredericka Ribes from Norma Fox Mazer's AFTER THE RAIN. Jacket illustration Copyright © 1987 by Fredericka Ribes. By permission of Morrow Junior Books, a division of William Morrow & Company, Inc.)

What happens to the content of books that are first published in a foreign country and then published by American publishers? If a book is revised, what are the effects of the changes? In a two-part series, Jane Whitehead discusses the impact of revisions that range from subtle changes in vocabulary to radical changes that alter the character of the book.

In her pursuit of the subject Whitehead[1] interviewed editors and authors in United States, Great Britain, and European countries. Whitehead asked: "What gets changed, and why are such changes thought necessary? How far will editors go in their efforts to naturalize foreign texts? How do authors feel about having their work altered, often after it had been published in Britain? What assumptions are being made about the ability and willingness of American children to deal with cultural differences?" (p. 688).

As a result of her investigation, Whitehead discovered that Americanized texts include changes in such areas as titles, settings, character names, cultural allusions, spelling, and punctuation.

Whitehead[2] quotes authors and editors on both sides of the controversy. For example, some editors believe that Americanization is crucial to the success of British books because they believe that foreignness is a barrier that causes readers to lose interest in a book. A contrasting opinion is expressed by a former member of the Batchelder Award committee who maintains that a book "should not be Americanized. The reader should still be able to tell that the book was written in another country" (p. 29). Whitehead summarizes the attitudes of many British authors when she states, "They feel that, in spite of lip service to multiculturalism, American children are being overprotected

from exposure to different cultures, and they suspect that booksellers and publishers collude to present shorter, simpler texts to American children than are available to their peers in Britain and the rest of Europe" (p. 31).

What do you believe are the consequences of rewriting foreign books for American audiences? Are they good? Are they detrimental? What messages are editors and publishers sending to consumers when the books are Americanized? Which version of a book would you rather read? Why?

---

[1]Whitehead, Jane. " 'This Is Not What I Wrote!': The Americanization of British Children's Books—Part I." *The Horn Book* (November/December 1996): 687–693.
[2]Whitehead, Jane. " 'This Is Not What I Wrote!': The Americanization of British Children's Books—Part II." *The Horn Book* (January/February 1997): 27–34.

---

boring, lonely lives where nothing changes; (2) grandparents in books look older than their own grandparents; (3) the elderly do not work, have fun, or do anything exciting; (4) young people are mean to elderly people; (5) book characters do not want to listen or talk to the elderly; (6) some elderly people are mean, crabby, overly tidy, fussy, and unfair; (7) the elderly like to remember the good old days or dream of better times; and (8) there are few happy books about the elderly. It is interesting to compare this study conducted in 1979 with books that are published more recently. It is also interesting to compare this study with the concerns expressed by Betty Friedan (1993), who would like to see active, intelligent older people portrayed in the press and the media.

Some authors of contemporary realistic fiction are exploring the problems related to old age with greater sensitivity than authors expressed in books

of the past. When evaluating books dealing with the elderly, you should select books that show elderly people in a wide variety of roles. Close experiences between grandparents and grandchildren are common in books for young children, such as Tomie dePaola's *Nana Upstairs & Nana Downstairs,* Sharon Bell Mathis's *The Hundred Penny Box,* and Benjamin Darling's *Valerie and the Silver Pear.* Books for older children, such as Susan Campbell Bartoletti's *Dancing with Dziadziu,* often stress the worthwhile contributions that are still being made by the elderly, the warm relationships that can develop between grandparents and grandchildren, and a desire of elderly people to stay out of nursing homes. Some books are very serious; others develop serious themes through humorous stories.

In *The Golden Days,* Gail Radley explores both the unhappy emotions and the unwanted feelings of a boy living with foster parents and of an elderly woman living in a nursing home. Through their interactions, the boy and the elderly woman discover that they have many feelings and needs in common. After they run away together, they discover what it means to be a family and to trust others who are really interested in becoming part of that family.

In *Old John,* Peter Hartling explores the need for independence and strong relationships between generations. When a seventy-five-year-old father and grandfather comes to live with his family, Hartling describes a strong elderly man who has not only idiosyncrasies but also needs for love and independence. In *Everywhere,* Bruce Brooks develops the strong bond between grandfather and grandson. This bond increases after the grandfather suffers a heart attack. The healing power of love is the theme.

The growing relationships and understandings between a girl and her grandfather form the basis for Norma Fox Mazer's *After the Rain.* At first, Rachel resents the time that she is asked to spend with her ailing grandfather, but she mourns the loss of their precious moments together after his death. Well-developed characters help readers understand the needs of the two different generations and the changes that can result because people learn to understand each other.

Other outstanding books about the elderly and young people who love and respect them include Gary and Gail Provost's *David and Max* and Patricia MacLachlan's *Journey.* With their diverse, nonstereotyped depictions of elderly people, such books provide discussion materials that encourage older children to explore the roles of elderly people in literature and their own feelings about the elderly. Additional books about the elderly are found in Sandra McGuire's bibliography, "Promoting Positive Attitudes Toward Aging" (1993).

 ## ANIMAL STORIES, MYSTERIES, SPORTS STORIES, AND HUMOR

Animal stories include stories about dogs, horses, and birds. Mysteries use clues and suspense to help readers develop their powers of observation. Sports stories may be about baseball, football, or flying. Humorous stories use ridiculous situations, exaggeration, and the unexpected to create humor.

Animals

The animals in contemporary realistic fiction are quite different from the animals in traditional literature and modern fantasy. In traditional literature and modern fantasy, animals talk and act like people or have other magical powers. The animals in realistic fiction have a strong sense of reality and sometimes tragedy. Realistic animal stories place specific demands upon authors. When evaluating realistic animal stories for children, you should consider the following questions:

1. Does the author portray animals objectively, without giving them human thoughts or motives?
2. Does the behavior of the animal characters agree with information provided by knowledgeable observers of animals and authorities on animal behavior?
3. Does the story encourage children to respond to the needs of animals or the need of people to love animals without being too sentimental or melodramatic?

Authors who write credible animal stories often depict warm relationships between children and pets. The conflict in such stories usually occurs when something happens to disrupt the security of a pet's life. The antagonist may be a physical change in the animal, an environment different from the pet's secure home, or a human character whose treatment of the animal is cruel or even life threatening. Detailed descriptions of physical changes, settings that become antagonists, or cruel human characters may encourage children to understand the vulnerability of animals to such forces.

Credible stories about wild animals usually reflect research about animal behavior and natural habitats. Conflict may arise when animals face natural enemies, when humans take them from natural surroundings and place them in domestic environments, or when humans hunt or trap them.

Some authors use animal-against-society or animal-against-person conflicts to advocate protection of animals. Other authors stress the human development made possible by interaction with animals. Many authors also stress the positive effects of loyalty and devotion between humans and animals.

Consider, for example, the various techniques used by Theodore Taylor in *The Trouble with Tuck.* Taylor first develops a believably close relationship between Helen and her golden Labrador. Helen's love for Tuck and her family's devotion to the dog are strengthened by two incidents in which Tuck saves Helen from harm or possible death. The reactions of the family members when the veterinarian declares that Tuck is going blind and cannot be helped reflect their devotion to the dog and make plausible their acceptance of Helen's resolution of the problem. She calls a trainer for Seeing Eye dogs and makes an appointment for her parents without telling the trainer that the blind individual is a dog.

Although the trainer's initial reaction is negative, the family is finally offered an older Seeing Eye dog whose master has died. Taylor describes Helen's trials and frustrations as she tries to train Tuck to follow the Seeing Eye dog. After weeks of disappointment, she is rewarded when Tuck accepts and follows the older dog. This story, based on a true incident, emphasizes determination, loyalty, and self-confidence that may develop because of animal and human interaction.

In *Shiloh,* Phyllis Reynolds Naylor uses several techniques to develop the theme that cruelty to animals is wrong. For example, Marty thinks that something really hurts inside when a dog cringes like that. The theme is emphasized when the author compares a jar of lightning bugs to a chained dog: both are prisoners. The thoughts of others reveal the theme when Marty's father tells Marty to open his eyes and understand that there are many hard-hearted people. In the end, Marty is able to bargain for Shiloh because Judd, Shiloh's cruel owner, illegally killed a deer and Marty saw him. *Shiloh Season* is a sequel to the book and extends the conflict between Marty and Judd.

A classic book with a notable dog as the main character is Jack London's *Call of the Wild,* first published in 1903. This story depicts life in the Klondike during the Alaskan gold rush. London develops a credible story of transformation. Buck progresses from a docile pet to a rugged work dog and finally to an animal who is inescapably drawn by the wild cries of the wolf pack. London develops these remarkable changes in Buck by providing details of his life before and after he is stolen from his home in California and brought, raging and roaring, to face the primitive law of the Klondike. Buck changes as he reacts to a beating and the fierce fangs of fighting dogs, but he retains his spirit.

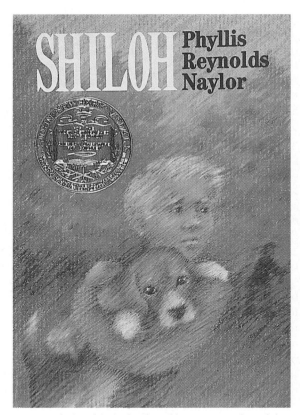

A strong relationship is developed between an abused dog and a boy. (From Shiloh *by Phyllis Reynolds Naylor. Copyright © 1991 by Phyllis Reynolds Naylor. Published by Atheneum, an imprint of Macmillan Publishing Company. Reprinted by permission of Dillys Evans Fine Illustrations.)*

While crossing the countryside in a dogsled harness, his long-suppressed instincts come alive.

This is also the story of strong bonds between dog and human. After a succession of sometimes cruel owners, Buck is purchased by kind John Thornton. Buck apparently feels an adoration for John that causes him continually to return from his wilderness treks until the terrible day when he returns to camp to find that John has been killed. Only then are the bonds between man and dog broken, allowing Buck to roam with the wolf pack:

His cunning was wolf cunning, and wild cunning; his intelligence shepherd intelligence and St. Bernard intelligence; and all this, plus an experience gained in the fiercest of schools, made him as formidable a creature as any that roamed the wild. (p. 114)

Other well-known books about dogs that have been popular in the last few decades include Jim Kjelgaard's *Big Red,* in which a mountain boy raises a dog that wins a prize in a big-city dog show; Fred Gipson's *Old Yeller,* the story of a boy and his dog in the Texas hill country of the 1860s; and Sheila Burnford's *The Incredible Journey,* an outstanding realistic story about a Labrador retriever, an English bull terrier, and a Siamese cat that travel 250 miles through the Canadian wilderness in search of their human family.

Horse stories also have qualities that make them marvelous for children. The horses and their owners, or would-be owners, usually have devoted relationships. Often, the little horse, which may have been laughed at or scorned, becomes the winner of a race and begins a famous line of horses. Sadness in many of these stories results when both horse and owner must overcome severe obstacles and even mistreatment.

Two outstanding authors of horse stories are Marguerite Henry and Walter Farley. Henry's stories reflect research and knowledge about horses and their trainers, and several of them report the history of a breed of horses. One memorable story narrates the ancestry of Man o' War, the greatest racehorse of his time. In *King of the Wind,* readers travel back two hundred years to the royal stables of a sultan of Morocco, where Agba, a young horse tender, has a dream of glory for a golden Arabian stallion with a white chest. The boy and horse travel from Morocco to France when the Sultan sends six of his best horses to King Louis XV, who rejects the horses, which have become thin from their voyage. Agba and the once-beautiful Sham are handed over to several degrading and even cruel masters before the English Earl of Godolphin discovers their plight and takes them home with him. In England, Agba's dream comes true. Three of the golden Arabian's offspring win various important races. When the great Arabian horse, renamed the Godolphin Arabian, stands before royalty, Agba's thoughts flash back to a promise that he made in Morocco:

"My name is Agba. Ba means father. I will be a father to you, Sham, and when I am grown I will ride you before the multitudes. And they will bow before you, and you will be the king of the Wind. I promise it." He had kept his word! (p. 169)

Other enjoyable books by Marguerite Henry include *Justin Morgan Had a Horse,* the story of the Morgan horse; *Black Gold,* the story of a racehorse and the jockey who brings him to winning form; *Misty of Chincoteague,* the story of the small, wild descendants of the Spanish horses shipwrecked off the Virginia coast; and *San Domingo: The Medicine Hat Stallion,* a story of a Nebraska frontier boy and his affection for an unusual horse. All of Henry's stories reflect an understanding of horses and the people who feel loving attachments to them.

A beautiful black stallion and his descendants are the chief characters in a series of books written by Walter Farley. The first, *The Black Stallion,* introduces a beautiful wild horse that is being loaded, unwillingly, onto a large ship. On this same ship is Alec Ramsay, who understands and loves horses. The two are brought together as the ship sinks, and the black horse pulls Alec through the waves to a small deserted island. Friendship develops as the two help each other survive, and Alec discovers the joy of racing on the back of the amazing horse.

Mysteries

Mysteries provide escape and enjoyable reading because of their suspense. They allow children to become involved in the solutions through clues. They also suggest that children themselves—if they are observant, creative, and imaginative—can solve mysteries.

Footsteps on a foggy night, disappearing people, mysterious strangers, and unusual occurrences woven together into exciting, fast-paced plots create mystery stories that appeal to older children. One eleven-year-old girl, an avid reader of mysteries, listed the following four characteristics that make a mystery exciting for her: (1) it should have an exciting plot that holds the interest of readers, (2) it should contain suspense, (3) it should have enough clues to allow readers to follow the action, and (4) the clues should be written in such a way that readers can try to discover "who done it." In answer to the question "What has caused your interest in mysteries?" she replied that she had read Donald J. Sobol's *Encyclopedia Brown* in third grade and enjoyed trying to follow the clues. She said that her favorite suspense story was Virginia Hamilton's *The House of Dies Drear,* a tale about the Underground Railroad.

The best-known mysteries for young readers are probably contained in Donald J. Sobol's "Encyclopedia Brown" series. In each of the books, ten-year-old

Leroy Brown helps his father, the police chief of Idvalle, solve crimes by figuring out the clues. For example, in *Encyclopedia Brown Tracks Them Down,* Leroy solves the case of a missing ambassador by reviewing the gifts presented to him at a birthday party. In another case in that book, Leroy solves the riddle of a flower can and discovers the identity of the boy who stole an 1861 Confederate coin worth $5,000. *Encyclopedia Brown Sets the Pace* contains ten more cases in which young readers can try to identify a thief or solve the problem of a bully who picks on smaller children. Sobol provides readers with the solutions and the reasoning behind them.

In *Roscoe's Leap,* Gillian Cross enhances mysterious elements by building suspense. Cross introduces fragments of memory that bring back feelings of terror in the protagonist. For example, Cross develops suspense associated with believable fear when Stephen hears words that trigger memories:

"Take them to see the Collection."

In Stephen's memory, something huge and dark moved suddenly out of the shadows. A pain along the side of his head and voices shouting and someone—himself?—screaming and screaming and screaming. . . . (p. 28)

The author gradually introduces new memories until the mystery of the French Terror is solved.

In *A Kind of Thief,* Vivien Alcock's introduction draws readers into the suspense. As you read the following quotes, notice how Alcock creates the mood and draws you into the conflict:

They came early, ringing at the bell, knocking at the door, and shouting. Elinor's room was at the back of the house. The noise disturbed her dreams, and she pulled her quilt over her head. Unlike her sister Judy, she was bad at waking up. It took her a long time to clear her mind of sleep. (p. 1)

There were two strange men in the hall, standing stiffly by the door. The older one was regarding her gloomily, as if he thought she only added to his troubles. The younger one was watching her father. Somehow they frightened her, coming here before the sun was properly up. She knew at once they meant her family no good. (p. 2)

The mystery deepens as Elinor's father is arrested. Before he is taken away, however, he slips a baggage claim receipt into her pocket and whispers words that she does not hear. When Elinor redeems the receipt and acquires her father's locked briefcase, she suspects the worst. The rest of the story accompanies Elinor through suspected family betrayal. Not until an accident occurs does Elinor learn the truth about her father and his interactions with his family.

Observation plays an important role in Robert Newman's mysteries, two of which are set in the London of Sherlock Holmes's time. *The Case of the Baker Street Irregular* and *The Case of the Vanishing Corpse* include suspense, sinister characters who must be outwitted, and several mysteries that seem not to be related but actually are.

In *The Original Freddie Ackerman,* Hadley Irwin introduces readers to the two personalities of Trevor Frederick Ackerman, who is going reluctantly to spend the summer with his great-aunts on an island off the coast of Maine. As you read the following quote, notice how Irwin separates the real experience from the imaginary one:

As they waited for the traffic light to turn green, he wondered what would happen if he opened the car door and disappeared. Great-Aunt Calla would probably be relieved, and Great-Aunt Louisa, sitting beside him, might not even notice, since she hadn't looked over at him yet and, besides that, seemed to have used up her quota of words for the day.

Freddie Ackerman, World War II ace, his B-24 Liberator bomber shot down in flames and his parachute buried deep in the Black Forest, would never allow himself to be captured alive with all the secret invasion plans he was carrying. Freddie Ackerman would fling open the car door, slide down into the river that bordered the autobahn, and fade like a ghost into the rain and mist of the German countryside. (p. 6)

Trevor's eccentric aunts provide mysterious quests for information to entice Trevor's interest. On the island, Trevor searches for physical evidence that will identify whether or not a book is a first edition. Strong relationships between the aunts and Trevor help him overcome feelings of alienation in his life.

Ellen Raskin's several books challenge readers to join often preposterous characters in working out puzzle clues. These clues include word puzzles, a series of obscurely written messages, and even observations gained through reading. *The Mysterious Disappearance of Leon (I Mean Noel)* is a humorous word puzzle, a game about names, liberally sprinkled with clues. As the story of Leon and Little Dumpling, the heirs to Mrs. Carillon's Pomato Soup fortune, proceeds, Raskin informs readers that there is a very important clue in a particular section or that they should mark the locations of Leon's fourteen messages because they contain important clues. Noel's final words, for example, as he bobs up and down in the water cause Little Dumpling years of searching. What is meant by "Noel glub C blub all . . . I glub new . . ."?

In *Figgs & Phantoms,* the clue that Raskin provides is "the bald spot." This clue eventually helps Mona Figg discover whether she has or has not actually visited Capri, the Figg family's idea of a perfect heaven. Raskin's *The Westing Game* includes many clues that must be worked through before the teams of players solve the mystery.

Zilpha Keatley Snyder's mysteries involve kidnapping, complex games, and mysterious secret environments. In *The Famous Stanley Kidnapping Case,* masked strangers kidnap five unusual children who accompany their parents to Italy. In *The Egypt Game,* six children create an ancient Egyptian world in an abandoned storage yard and solve a murder mystery.

Suspense, revenge, and mysterious happenings are all part of Robert Cormier's mystery for older readers, *In the Middle of the Night.* The novel begins with a foreshadowing of the suspense to follow: "Ten minutes later, Lulu was dead. And the nightmare began" (p. 9). Cormier uses several techniques to encourage readers to understand the conflict and its influence on the characters. For example, he described the son's reactions to his father as he burns letters, responds to reporters, and sees his face flashing on television. Tension builds as Cormier reviews old newspaper articles and relates telephone messages that change from calling the father in the middle of the night to calling the son in the afternoon. Now the tension increases as Cormier goes back and forth between Lulu, the child victim, and her brother and Denny, the son. In a dramatic ending, Denny's life is saved and he learns lessons about himself. Cormier's *Tenderness* is another taut mystery for older readers. This novel presents the portrait of a serial killer.

Sports

Sports stories rate highly with children who are sports enthusiasts. Some quite reluctant readers will finish a book about their favorite sport or sports hero. The majority of the sports stories are about boys, however, and few authors yet write about girls who enjoy participating in sports. Many stories deal with the ideal of fair play, the values of sports, the overcoming of conflicts between fathers and sons, and the overcoming of fears connected with sports. Unfortunately, many of the stories are didactic and have familiar plot lines and stock characters.

Sports stories for children are also apparently important to sport franchises. Karen Raugust (1997) reports a merger between major league sports teams and the publishing of sports-related books. According to a quote by the director of marketing for the National Hockey League, "The sport depends on the long-term development of fans. Publishing helps to support all of the other fan development programs" (p. 35). As these books become available, you may compare them with other books about sports and sports heroes.

Authors who write about baseball often imply that the sport has therapeutic values. Often, the emphasis in these books is on the role that baseball can play in helping children overcome problems at home, develop new friendships, face physical disabilities, or feel accomplishment. Matt Christopher's *The Fox Steals Home,* for example, tells the story of troubled Bobby Canfield, who is facing his parents' divorce and the prospect of his father's taking a job far from home. His father and his grandfather have coached him and nicknamed him "Fox." His proudest moment comes when he steals home and demonstrates to his father what a good player he has become.

In *Hang Tough, Paul Mather,* Alfred Slote writes about a leukemia victim whose greatest interest is baseball. The boy must face the knowledge that he has a short time to live and that his parents are trying to prevent him from playing to protect him. However, an understanding doctor helps him play his last season with dignity and courage. In *The Trading Game,* Slote's story is about a ten-year-old boy who matures during his interactions with his grandfather. The grandfather is a former baseball player.

In *Herbie Jones and the Monster Ball,* Suzy Kline humorously develops a story about a young boy who hates baseball until his uncle coaches a baseball team for eight- and nine-year-olds. The book does not stereotype girls, who play on the team. The boy's older sister also gives him baseball lessons.

Football is both the major interest and the cause of conflict between a father and son in Matt Christopher's *Football Fugitive.* Larry Shope loves football and longs for his father to leave his law practice long enough to watch Larry play. Larry and his father become closer when Mr. Shope provides legal assistance for a professional football star.

Written for older readers, Chris Crutcher's *Athletic Shorts* is a collection of six short stories about various types of athletes. The characters in many of these stories are taken from Crutcher's previous books.

The sport of flying provides the adventure in Betsy Byars's *Coast to Coast*. Developing a strong grandfather and granddaughter relationship, Byars takes readers on an adventurous trip in a Piper Cub when the grandfather and his granddaughter fly from South Carolina to California. This book shows that girls can be just as adventurous as boys.

Humor

Humorous stories, whether involving figures of fantasy or realistic people living in the contemporary world, are among children's favorites. Authors who write about humorous situations that could happen to real people (these situations and characters may stretch probability) allow children to understand that life can be highly entertaining and that it is not always serious. Writers may encourage readers to laugh at themselves and at numerous human foibles. Humorous situations and characters may highlight real problems and make reading about them palatable.

Authors of humorous realistic fiction use many of the sources of humor discussed in chapter 5— word play, surprise and the unexpected, exaggeration, and ridiculous situations. For example, authors may use a play on words or ideas to create humorous situations or clarify characters' feelings. Consider Betsy Byars's *The Cybil War*, an entertaining story about a fifth-grade boy who has a crush on a girl. The war develops as Cybil Ackerman responds in various ways to Simon's advances, which are intentionally misinterpreted by his best friend.

Beverly Cleary uses a twist on the words of a familiar television commercial to create a funny incident in *Ramona Quimby, Age 8*. When Ramona gives her book report, she presents it in the style of a television commercial. Her statement, "I can't believe I read the whole thing," causes a hilarious reaction among her classmates. In *The One in the Middle Is the Green Kangaroo*, Judy Blume uses a humorous analogy to clarify a middle child's feelings: "He felt like the peanut butter part of a sandwich squeezed between Mike and Ellen" (p. 7).

Judy Delton's *Angel's Mother's Wedding* presents the adventures of warm, humorous Angel O'Leary. Delton develops both humor and vivid characters by describing Angel's worries and imaginings. Misunderstandings provide a series of humorous incidents when five-year-old Rudy, Angel's brother, tries to give his new father a red paint job for a wedding pre-

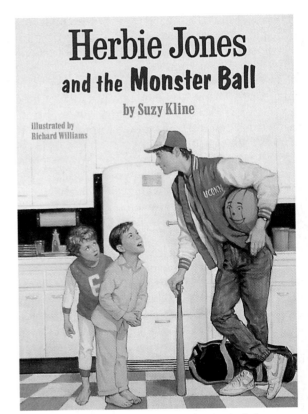

Humor is added to a story about a reluctant ballplayer. (From Herbie Jones and the Monster Ball *by Suzy Kline, illustrations by Richard Williams, copyright © 1988 by Richard Williams. Reprinted by permission of G. P. Putnam's Sons.)*

sent and then enacts how he believes a ring bearer should perform at the wedding.

Judy Blume uses a surprising and unexpected situation in *Tales of a Fourth Grade Nothing*. In this story, a humorous conflict between two brothers is brought to a climax when the younger boy swallows the older brother's pet turtle. An unexpected situation provides humor in Lois Lowry's *Anastasia on Her Own* when a naive cook, trying to prepare a gourmet dinner, asks for and receives cooking advice from a stranger who is calling to sell tap dancing lessons. In *Anastasia's Chosen Career*, Lowry uses excerpts from Anastasia's writings from a school assignment about careers.

An unexpected situation in Anne Fine's *Alias Madame Doubtfire* occurs when an ex-husband disguises himself as a cleaning woman and babysitter in his ex-wife's house. The humorous and surprising situations in Joan Bauer's *Squashed* occur when a

THROUGH THE EYES OF AN AUTHOR

The Laughter of Children

BEVERLY CLEARY, recipient of the Laura Ingalls Wilder Award, the Newbery Award, and many children's choice awards, discusses the importance of humor in children's realistic fiction.

Although for over thirty years I have been absorbed in stories that spring from the humor of everyday life, I try not to think about humor while writing, because of the sound advice given me by my first editor, Elisabeth Hamilton, whom I met after writing *Henry Huggins & Ellen Tebbits*. In discussing writing for children, I happened to mention humor. Elisabeth, a forceful woman, interrupted. "Darlin'," she said, "don't *ever* analyze it. Just do it." I have followed her advice. While I am writing, if I find myself thinking about humor and what makes a story humorous, I am through for the day; and that chapter usually goes into the wastebasket, for spontaneity has drained out of my work. Although introspection is valuable to every writer, I find that analyzing my own work is harmful because it makes writing self-conscious rather than intuitive. When I am not writing, however, I find myself mulling over the subject of humor, my kind of humor, and why so many children find it funny.

As a child I would have agreed that humor is "what makes you laugh." I could not find enough laughter in life or in books, so the stories I write are the stories I wanted to read as a child in Portland, Oregon—humorous stories about the problems which are small to adults but which loom so large in the lives of children, the sort of problems children can solve themselves. I agree with James Thurber's statement: "Humor is the best that lies closest to the familiar, to that part of the familiar which is humiliating, distressing, even tragic. . . . There is always a laugh in the utterly familiar."

My first book, *Henry Huggins,* a group of short stories about the sort of children I had known as a child, was written with a light heart from memories of Portland. As I wrote I discovered I had a collaborator, the child within myself—a rather odd, serious little girl, prone to colds, who sat in a child's rocking chair with her feet over the hot air outlet of the furnace, reading for hours, seeking laughter in the pages of books while her mother warned her she would ruin her eyes. That little girl, who has remained with me, prevents me from writing down to children, from poking fun at my characters, and from writing an adult reminiscence about childhood instead of a book to be enjoyed by children. And yet I do not write solely for that child; I am also writing for my adult self. We are collaborators who must agree. The feeling of being two ages at one time is delightful, one that surely must be a source of great pleasure to all writers of books enjoyed by children.

By the time I had published five books, several things had happened which forced me to think about children and humor: I had children of my own, twins—a boy and a girl; reviews said my books were hilarious or genuinely funny; a textbook of children's literature said my books were to be read "purely for amusement"; and enough children had written to me to give me some insight into their thoughts about my books.

One phrase began to stand out in these letters from children. Letter after letter told me my books were "funny and sad." Until these letters arrived, I had not thought of *Henry Huggins* as sad. The words, at that time never used by adults in reference to my books, began to haunt me. Funny and sad, or even funny and tragic, describes my view of life. To borrow another phrase from James Thurber, I had chosen "reality twisted to the right into humor rather than to the left into tragedy"—for that is my nature. I feel that comedy is as illuminating as tragedy—more so for younger readers who may be frightened or discouraged by tragedy in realistic fiction.

Abridged from "The Laughter of Children," *The Horn Book* (October 1982): 555–564. Copyright © 1982 by Beverly Cleary.

girl tries to grow the largest pumpkin for the Rock River Pumpkin Weigh-In. She tries everything including playing motivational tapes to make the pumpkin grow.

Comic twists, flamboyant characters, and humorous situations are part of the pleasure in reading Polly Horvath's *When the Circus Came to Town*. Although most of the incidents are humorous, the actions of the characters reflect and highlight human foibles, and the main characters learn something about themselves when they experience situations that are more humorous to readers than to them.

SUGGESTED ACTIVITIES

for Adult Understanding of Realistic Fiction

■ Sexism in literature, including the harmful sex-role socialization resulting from female- and male-role stereotyping, is a major concern of many educators and psychologists. In a school, public, or university library, choose a random sampling of children's literature selections. If these books were the only sources of information available about male and female roles, what information would be acquired from the books and their illustrations? Is this information accurate?

■ Read an earlier study that analyzes realistic fiction, such as Gloria Toby Blatt's "Violence in Children's Literature: A Content Analysis of a Select Sampling of Children's Literature and a Study of Children's Responses to Literary Episodes Depicting Violence" (1972); Carolyn Wilson Carmichael's "A Study of Selected Social Values as Reflected in Contemporary Realistic Fiction for Children" (1971); Ann E. Hall's "Contemporary Realism in American Children's Books" (1977); Alma Cross Homeze's "Interpersonal Relationships in Children's Literature from 1920 to 1960" (1963); or Judith Ann Noble's "The Home, the Church, and the School as Portrayed in American Realistic Fiction for Children 1965–1969" (1971). Read a sampling of the most current literature. How do the findings in this literature compare with the earlier findings?

■ Compile an annotated bibliography of books that shows both girls and boys in nontraditional sex roles. What is the greatest strength or weakness of each book? Read a sampling of books from Erica Bauermeister and Holly Smith's *Let's Hear It for the Girls* (1997). What messages about girls are developed in the books recommended by these authors?

■ Compare the professional roles of fathers and mothers in literature published in the 1970s, 1980s, and 1990s with the professional roles of fathers and mothers in literature published in earlier periods. Do the later books illustrate the changing family roles of both males and females? Is there conflict in a story if roles are reversed? How is this conflict handled?

■ Interview children's librarians in public or school libraries. Ask these librarians to state the guidelines used by the library when selecting books considered controversial for children. What issues, if any, do the librarians feel are relevant in the community? Can they identify any books that have caused controversy in the libraries? If there are such books, how did they handle the controversy?

■ Many realistic fiction stories deal with the problems that children must face and overcome when they experience separation from a friend, a neighborhood, or a parent, or they face the ultimate separation caused by death. Choose one area, read several books that explore the problem, and recommend books to share with younger children and books more appropriate for older children. Explain your decisions. Annotated bibliographies such as those found in Joanne E. Bernstein's "Bibliotherapy: How Books Can Help Young Children Cope" (1989) may be helpful in the search.

■ Read a survival story, such as Jean Craighead George's *My Side of the Mountain* or Scott O'Dell's *Island of the Blue Dolphins*. What writing style or technique does the author use to allow readers to understand the awesome power of natural enemies?

■ Compare the characteristics of a specific type of animal in a modern fantasy story with the characteristics of the same type of animal in a realistic animal adventure story.

■ You want to create a learning center featuring books that show both males and females in positive roles in nontraditional sex roles. Use the database to make a list of at least ten books that might be appropriate. List at least three criteria that you would use to determine whether each of these books would meet your goal. If possible, locate one of the books and based on your criteria, defend your reasons for including it or excluding it from the learning center.

■ Write step-by-step directions for conducting a search of the database that would result in a list of books that feature nontraditional families in a positive way. Print your list. See if another person can follow your directions and get the same results.

■ A student has requested more books by Walter Dean Myers. Write directions so that student could use the database and print a list of appropriate books.

Involving Children in Realistic Fiction

I f realistic fiction is to help children identify with others, extend their horizons, and gain personal insights, then adults who work with children must be aware of a wide range of realistic fiction and activities. It is not necessary, or even advisable, to attach literature-related activities to all realistic fiction that children read, but some activities are appropriate.

This section considers how you may use realistic fiction to stimulate role playing that strengthens understanding of the world and offers suggestions for handling real problems. This section also takes an in-depth look at children's literature units that stress the themes of island survival and survival in mountains, tundra, and the Canadian wilderness. In addition to activities and discussions stressing the influence of settings upon the conflicts in stories, a unit may relate literature to the science curriculum through activities that increase understanding of geography and botany. This section also tells you how to use literature to develop an appreciation for the contributions of females and an understanding of the various roles that both males and females can play in life. The section concludes with questioning strategies that can accompany realistic fiction or any other genre of literature.

Role playing is a creative dramatics activity in which children consider a problem, contemplate possible actions of people in reaction to the problem, and then act out the situation as they believe it might unfold in real life. According to child-development authorities, role playing fosters social development, increases problem-solving capabilities, and enhances creativity. Role playing helps children develop an understanding of the world around them and enhances children's understanding of various ways to handle common problems. Even young children can benefit from role-playing activities. Three- and four-year-olds can role-play experiences about family life while four- and five-year-olds can role-play situations that increase and extend their interests beyond family and school and into the world around them.

Shaffer (1989) provides guidelines that can help you select meaningful role-playing activities. He adapts Selman's stages of social perspective and describes characteristic student responses to others' perspectives. Understanding these typical responses can help you plan activities and observe or interact with students during role playing. For example, three- to six-year-olds are unaware of any perspective other than their own; six- to eight-year-olds recognize that people have perspectives different from theirs; eight- to ten-year-olds know that their points of view can conflict with others'; ten- to twelve-year-olds can consider their own and another person's point of view simultaneously; and twelve- to fifteen-year-olds attempt to understand another person's perspective by comparing it with that of the social system in which they operate.

Literature can be the stimulus for activities that satisfy the purposes of role playing. Use realistic picture books about doctors, dentists, and other neighborhood helpers to encourage young children to act out the roles of adults with whom they come in contact. Such role playing can decrease the fears of children by allowing them to experience a role before facing a real situation. Use books about families to encourage children to role-play interactions between different members of a family, nuclear or extended.

The plots in realistic fiction provide many opportunities for children to role-play problems. Zena Sutherland (1997) recommends that literature selected for stimulating, thought-provoking problem situations should (1) contain characters who are well developed and have clearly defined problems, (2) have plots that contain logical stopping places so that children can role-play the endings, (3) include problems, such as universal fears and concerns, that allow children to identify with the situations, and (4) present problems that help children develop their personal value systems. In role playing, you may either choose stories in which problems are developed to certain points and then have children role-play the unfinished situations or have children role-play various solutions to problems after they have read or listened to the whole stories.

Sutherland recommends the following procedures for role playing: First, encourage students to think about what will happen next in the story, to consider how the story might end, and to identify with the characters. Second, ask the students to describe the characters and then to play those roles. Third, ask the audience to observe and to decide if the solution is a realistic one. Fourth, ask the students who are role playing to decide what they will do to practice dialogue. Encourage them to describe the staging that they will use. Fifth, have the students role-play the situation, with each student playing the character that he or she represents. The focus should be solving a problem, not acting. Sixth, engage the players and the audience in a discussion of the role playing, the consequences of the actions, and alternative behaviors. Next, have the role players try new interpretations based on the ideas generated from the discussion. Finally, encourage students to assess the outcomes and determine the best ways to deal with the problems.

The books of realistic fiction discussed in this chapter offer many stimuli for role-playing situations. Because the books are categorized according to their content, you may refer to this chapter when searching for specific situations connected with family life, peer relationships, individuality, and so forth. The following books also contain problem situations that adults have used to stimulate children's role playing in connection with family life (Norton, 1992):

Family Life

1. *Responsibility toward family members (picture books).* Patricia Gauch's *Christina Katerina and the Time She Quit the Family. Problem:* What should happen in a family when a child wants to do only what pleases her and not what would make her part of the family? Mavis Jukes's *Like Jake and Me. Problem:* How should a stepfather and his new son adjust to each other? Phyllis Naylor's *Keeping a Christmas Secret. Problem:* How can a child redeem himself when he reveals an important family secret? How should the rest of the family respond? William Steig's *Spinky Sulks. Problem:* What should happen when a sulky boy discovers that his family really is trying to help him? Mildred Pitts Walter's *Two and Too Much. Problem:* What type of interaction should take place when a seven-year-old is asked to take care of his two-year-old sister?

2. *Interpersonal relationships.* Sharon Bell Mathis's *The Hundred Penny Box. Problem:* How should a boy respond when he makes friends with his great-great-aunt and tries to explain her feelings about an old box of pennies to his mother? How should the aunt and the mother interact with each other? Roni Schotter's *Captain Snap and the Children of Vinegar Lane. Problem:* How should children act and talk when they want to make friends with a lonely older man? How should the man respond to the children?

3. *Making difficult decisions.* Jeannie Baker's *Where the Forest Meets the Sea. Problem:* How can difficult ecological decisions be made so that the forest and seashore will be protected? How should the boy let his grandfather know that he understands the problem? Dayal Khalsa's *I Want a Dog. Problem:* How can you convince your family that you are responsible enough to own a pet? Theodore Taylor's *The Trouble with Tuck. Problem:* How should a family respond when the dog goes blind?

4. *Family disturbances.* Carol Lea Benjamin's *The Wicked Stepdog. Problem:* How should a girl, her father, and her new stepmother act when the father remarries? What can they each do to accept each other? Beverly Cleary's *Dear Mr. Henshaw. Problem:* How can a boy overcome his problems related to his parents' divorce? What should the mother, the father, and the boy say to each other? How can the parents help the boy understand what has happened to his family? Janet Taylor Lisle's *Afternoon of the Elves. Problem:* How should a family try to survive when a parent is mentally or physically incompetent? How can a friend help in this situation?

5. *Accepting others and overcoming prejudice.* Judy Blume's *Blubber.* *Problem:* How can students show sensitivity toward a student who is overweight? Betsy Byars's *The Summer of the Swans.* *Problem:* How should a sister and society respond to a child who is mentally retarded? Nicholasa Mohr's *Felita* and *Going Home.* *Problem:* In the first book, how can prejudice toward a Puerto Rican girl in New York be overcome? In the second book, how can the same girl overcome prejudice against a Puerto Rican American girl when she visits Puerto Rico?

Such stories allow children to empathize with characters who have problems that many children in elementary school experience. Through role playing, children may discover ways to handle problems and increase their sensitivity to the problems of others.

In addition to understandings gained through role playing, students gain understandings through discussions about books in which characters make moral choices. After reading Marion Dane Bauer's *On My Honor* with sixth- and seventh-grade students, Claudia Lepman-Logan (1989) states:

I was astonished at the response it provoked. I had thought that using a book with a moral choice as its theme might stimulate some interesting discussions, but I was quite unprepared for the intense and lively debates that engaged even the most passive students. . . . Throughout the reading of the book my students found themselves comparing and contrasting their own inclinations with Joel's motivations. The element of uncertainty is stretched out until the ending, which, interestingly enough, did not bring a close to either the events in the book or to our discussions. By following Joel's inner turmoil readers had to decide whether his final decision was indeed believable. (p. 108)

Lepman-Logan extended the initial discussion by asking her students to consider the choices that writers face when they resolve the problems that they create. Students who wanted more details to accompany *On My Honor* created additional dialogues among characters and explored further consequences that might result for the characters. Additional books that have moral choices and endings that lead to further consequences for the characters include Paula Fox's *One-Eyed Cat,* Walter Dean Myers's *Scorpions,* Gillian Cross's *On the Edge,* Cynthia Rylant's *A Fine White Dust,* Stephanie S. Tolan's *A Good Courage,* and Brock Cole's *The Goats.*

 ## USING BIBLIOTHERAPY

In recent years, librarians and educators have recommended reading and interacting with particular books as ways for individuals to gain insights into their own problems. According to the *Dictionary of Education* by Carter Good (1973), bibliotherapy is the "use of books to influence the total development, a process of interaction between the reader and literature which is used for personality assessment, adjustment, growth, clinical and mental hygiene purposes; a concept that ideas inherent in selecting reading material can have a therapeutic effect upon the mental or physical ills of the reader" (p. 58). By this definition, everyone can be helped through reading. Bibliotherapy is a process in which every literate person participates at some time.

According to Joanne Bernstein (1983), bibliotherapy is gaining insights from reading fiction or nonfiction that lead to self-examination. Bernstein suggests that to use books to help children gain insights into their own lives and to help them identify with others you must (1) know how and when to introduce the materials, (2) be sufficiently familiar with the materials, and (3) know each child's particular need.

Bernstein stresses that if you are using books to help children cope with their problems, you should not force the books upon them. Instead, you should provide a selection of materials from which the children can choose and then be patient until the children are ready to use them. After a child has read a book, be available for discussion or, more important, for listening. During a discussion, let children talk about the actions and feelings of the characters in the story, suggest areas in which they agree and disagree with the characters, consider the consequences of the characters' actions, and talk about other ways that a problem might be approached.

Many books provide additional resources for those who are interested in bibliotherapy. Bernstein's book contains a bibliography of adult references pertaining to bibliotherapy and an extensive annotated bibliography of children's books that deal with accepting a new sibling; going to a new school; getting used to a new neighborhood; coping with death, divorce, desertion, serious illness, and displacement due to war; and dealing with foster care, stepparents, and adoption.

Many realistic fiction adventure stories portray physical survival and increased emotional maturity of the main characters. The plots and strong characterizations in this type of realistic fiction encourage children to live the adventures vicariously. Physical characteristics that cause major conflicts may help children understand the importance of setting.

Two very interesting instructional activities developed by university students and then shared with classrooms of children centered on the survival theme. One group developed an in-depth literature unit around physical and emotional survival on islands. Another group chose physical and emotional survival in mountains, on arctic tundra, and in Canadian wilderness. Each group used the webbing process to organize its units.

Interdisciplinary Unit: Island Survival

The university students who chose the island survival theme identified the following books for ability to survive physically and grow in maturity because of the experiences:

Island of the Blue Dolphins, by Scott O'Dell
Call It Courage, by Armstrong Sperry
The Cay, by Theodore Taylor
The Swiss Family Robinson, by Johann David Wyss

The group read the books and identified the central themes and the main areas that challenged the physical survival: characteristics of the natural environment, including climatic conditions of the islands caused by their geographical locations, and survival needs related to other human needs. This central theme and six subtopics associated with survival were identified in the first phase of the island survival web (see Figure 9–1). During the next phase, the group identified subjects related to each subtopic on the web. The group developed the extended web shown in Figure 9–2.

After finishing the webs, the group planned activities to help children learn the importance of setting, realize that setting may cause major conflicts, and understand each identified physical survival topic. The university students also identified topics related to an upper-elementary science curriculum. They used interesting literature to increase children's understanding of scientific principles, and they developed activities to stimulate oral language, written language, and artistic interpretations of the plots and characters.

The examples in Chart 9–2 are taken from the physical survival activities developed around Scott O'Dell's *Island of the Blue Dolphins.* Several activities are included for each main subtopic in the web to allow you to visualize the types of physical survival activities that are possible in the classroom. Many of these activities are also appropriate for discussion in the library. The university students developed similar activities around each island survival book. Their

FIGURE 9–1 *Island survival web, first phase*

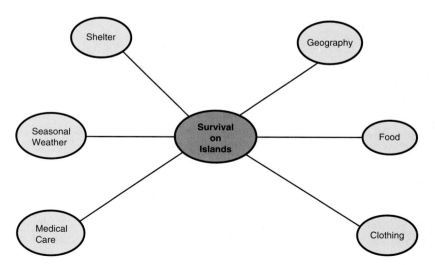

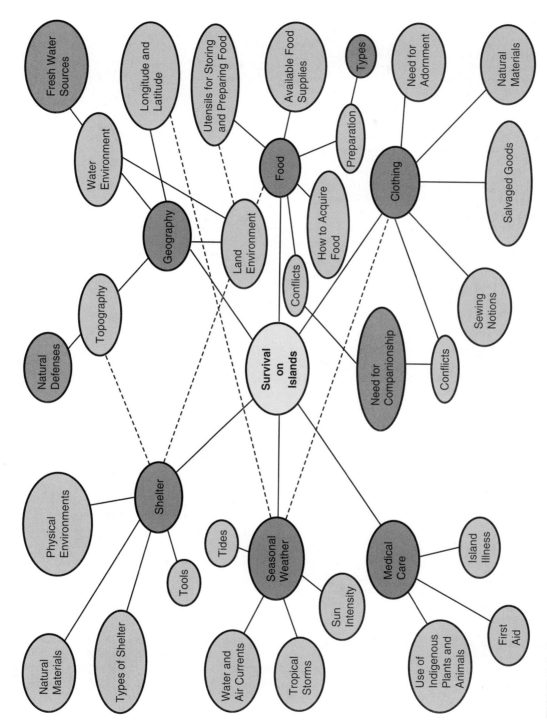

FIGURE 9–2 *Extended island survival web*

I. Seasonal weather
   A. Karana's life revolves around the seasons; she calculates time and the jobs that she must do according to the seasons. Identify the island seasons, the characteristics, and the reasons for Karana's total involvement in the seasons. O'Dell's text provides many clues to seasonal weather: The flowers are plentiful in the spring because of heavy winter rains; in the spring, the birds leave the island and fly to the north; Karana gathers food for the winter; seasonal storms have winds and high waves.
   B. On a large mural, draw the Island of the Blue Dolphins, depicting the different seasons and weather conditions described in the book.
   C. Pretend to be Karana and write a diary. Include five entries from each season on the island. In the entries, describe seasonal weather and activities during that season.

II. Medical care
   A. *Use of indigenous plants and animals:* In the wilderness, accidents or illnesses are dangerous; there are no doctors or drugstores. Read page 96 to find out what Karana used on Rontu's wound. Find this plant (coral bush) in a reference book and consider why it would help Rontu's wound.
   B. *First aid and use of indigenous plants and animals:* Pretend that you and your family are isolated on an island in the Pacific. Consider the minor illnesses or accidents that could easily occur while on the island. For example, sunburn is common in warm climates. Other problems might include poisonous stings, broken legs, stomach upsets, headaches, and wounds. Research some plants, herbs, and other first aid resources that might be found on the island. Make an illustrated island survival book for medical care. Include drawings of plants, their medical properties, and sketches of first aid measures. After this is finished, consider Karana's personal medical needs and how she handled her problems.

III. Clothing
   A. *Natural materials:* Karana and her people lived on an island where the only sources of clothing were natural materials, plant and animal, found on the island or in the sea. What garments did Karana make for herself? What natural materials did she use? Divide into groups and investigate the procedures Karana would need to use and the time that would be involved in making a skirt from yucca fibers, a belt or a pair of sandals from sealskin, an otter cape, or a skirt of cormorant skins. (Even the needle and thread were made from natural sources.) After describing the natural materials and the procedures, discuss the importance of obtaining clothing in an isolated area and the influence that the need to obtain clothing has on the actions of the characters.
      Consider how your life is different because clothing and materials for clothing are easy to obtain. In your environment, identify natural materials that you could use for clothing and consider what you would need to do to make clothing from them. If possible, try making a garment from natural materials.
   B. *Adornment:* Karana and the women of her island wanted flowers and jewelry that would improve their appearance. Consider why Karana found satisfaction in making a flower wreath for her hair and for Rontu's neck. Investigate the types of flowers that Karana might have used to make her wreath. If possible, make your own flower wreaths using flowers in your own locality.
      Karana was also fond of jewelry. Consider the implications of Karana's spending five nights to make a circlet of abalone shells as a present for the Aleut girl, Tutok. Examine jewelry made from seashells. If possible, make your own jewelry from seashells. This can also be an opportunity for investigating the types of seashells that might be available on Karana's island.

IV. Food
   A. *Food supplies:* List the foods Karana ate in the story. References are made to the scarlet apples that grow on cactus bushes (tunas) and foods from the sea, such as abalones and scallops. Research the possible sources that might be available on a Pacific Island. Investigate several cookbooks and make an Island of the Blue Dolphins cookbook using the foods and seasonings Karana might find.

CHART 9–2 *Continued*

B. *Utensils for storing and preparing food:* How did Karana fix her food? Where did she store the food to preserve it and protect it from animals? Karana had to make all of the utensils and storage containers for her food and water. Draw or make a list of five things Karana had to make in order to cook or store her food. Tell or show how she made these utensils or storage containers. Why was it important that Karana create each item? What could have happened if she had not created ways to store food? What impact did preparing and storing food have on her use of time and the plot of the story?

C. *Acquiring food:* Women in Karana's village were forbidden to make weapons. What is the significance for Karana when, in spite of her fear, she makes weapons to protect herself and to obtain food? Why did she think of destructive winds when she considered the advisability of making weapons? Draw several weapons that Karana created, explain how she made them, and identify the natural resources she used.

D. *Acquiring food and available food supplies:* Rontu and Karana encounter and later hunt a devilfish. From the description on pages 103–104 and 118–124, try to determine another name for a devilfish. Use reference books and pay close attention to the details. Why did Karana spend her whole winter crafting a special kind of spear to hunt the devilfish?

E. *Conflicts between food or clothing sources and need for companionship:* A conflict arises for Karana when she begins to make friends with some animals on the island. What is the significance of her statement on page 156 that she would never kill another otter, seal, cormorant, or wild dog? Debate this issue as it could relate to your own life. (Another topic for debate is the destruction of animals, such as the sea otter. Karana decided to stop killing the otters even for a cape and would not tell the white men where the otters were located. Investigate the controversy connected with killing or saving the sea otter and then, taking pro and con positions, debate the issue.)

V. Geography

A. *Topography:* Based on Karana's description of the Island of the Blue Dolphins in chapter two and other parts of the book, make a map of the island. The map should include a scale and symbols. To make the scale, you must determine the equivalent length of a league. In her descriptions of where the sun rises and sets, Karana has given the north, south, east, and west directions. Place these symbols on the map. Chart the wind directions on the map. (The island is two leagues long and one league wide. A league is equivalent to about three miles. The island looks like a dolphin lying on its side. The tail points toward sunrise, which is east, and the nose points toward sunset, which is west.)

B. *Physical environment, longitude and latitude:* The Island of the Blue Dolphins is real. On a large map or atlas that shows the California coastline, find San Nicolas, which is located about seventy-five miles southwest of Los Angeles. Identify the longitude and latitude of the island. What is the effect of this longitude and latitude upon the island? Compare a description of San Nicolas in a reference book with the description of the island in the story. Are there any similarities or differences?

If someone were marooned on an island, what longitude and latitude would that person choose in order to have a natural environment most advantageous to survival? Write a short story describing the setting and how one would survive on the island.

C. *Topography, physical environment:* Several geographical terms are used in *Island of the Blue Dolphins*. Following is a list of some of these terms. To develop an understanding of the geography of the island, define each term as used in the story, find pictures illustrating each term, and draw examples of the terms as they looked on Karana's island. Try to see each one through Karana's eyes. What was the significance of each feature for Karana's survival?

mesa	cliffs	ravine
harbor	canyon	spring
cove		

continues

CHART 9–2 *Continued*

VI. Shelter

    A. *Types of shelters:* In her struggles for survival, Karana constructed both a fenced-in house (pp. 74–76) and a cave dwelling (p. 89). Reread the descriptions of each house and consider Karana's needs when she constructed these shelters. What was the advantage of each type of shelter? How did each shelter relate to the natural materials found upon the island, the physical environment of the island, and the tools that Karana had available for her use? Why did the need for shelter play such an important part in the development of the story and in the use of Karana's time and energy? Choose one of her island shelters and build a model of the shelter.

    B. *Natural materials:* Look at our own environment. If people were isolated in their physical environments without the houses and other buildings they have now, what types of natural shelter would they construct? Write a short story describing the decision-making processes that people use as they think about the types of shelter they will construct. In this story, consider the need for protection against weather changes, natural predators that might harm individuals or take their food supplies, the topography of the land that could be used to advantage, the proximity of the shelter to life-sustaining food and water supplies, and the availability of building materials and tools needed for construction. Build a model of this shelter.

discussions and activities stressed the importance of setting in developing the conflict and the effects upon the growth of the characters as they overcame problems connected with setting or loneliness. The students also compared the various characters, their settings, and the physical and emotional strategies that led to survival.

In a final activity, the university students set up an elementary-school classroom as an island. They divided the class into groups according to shelter, food, clothing, geography, medical care, and seasonal weather. For Island Day, the elementary-school children chose and developed activities that represented their areas of interest. The children constructed shelters in which they located various interest centers. The children shared tool-making and cooking experiences. Art and science displays depicted weather, geography, clothing, food, and shelter. A special demonstration showed possible medical care for island survival. While learning about the impact of setting upon characters in survival literature, the children also discovered much about their own environments and how they might conquer their own worlds.

Survival in Mountains, on Tundra, and in Canadian Wilderness

Two books by Jean Craighead George stimulated interesting discovery activities related to survival. First, *My Side of the Mountain* portrays survival in the mountains of the northeastern United States. Second, *Julie of the Wolves* portrays survival on the arctic tundra. The stories also stress emotional and personal maturation. Gary Paulsen's *Hatchet* emphasizes survival in the Canadian wilderness. Like the characters in George's books, Paulsen's character also experiences emotional and personal growth.

After developing webs similar to the ones developed for island survival, upper-elementary students compared the three different settings according to their geographical locations, topography, longitude and latitude, and physical environments; their natural food supplies; the clothing required; medical care required and how characters in the books solved this problem; seasonal changes in weather that influenced the characters' actions; and the shelters that the characters made out of natural materials. The students compared the actions of the main characters in each story and identified the different ways in which the characters responded to personal and environmental problems.

The descriptions of edible foods and their growing locations found in *My Side of the Mountain* and *Hatchet* related to topics studied in the science curriculum. To highlight these relationships, students reviewed the environmental implications of the vegetation described in the books. They identified the edible plants and berries that the characters found in the northeastern part of the United States and in the Canadian wilderness and the procedures that the characters used to prepare and store the foods.

In *My Side of the Mountain,* students identified the larger trees that covered the slopes of a northeastern mountain: hemlock, oak, walnut, and hickory. They located references to plants that grew next to springs decorated with "flowers, ferns, moss, weeds—everything that loved water" (p. 30). Then, students followed the searches in the book for edible food, the steps in preparing the food, and methods of storing the food. Plant foods included hickory nuts and salt from hickory limbs (p. 23), apples (p. 24), walnuts, cattails, arrowleaf (p. 24), bulbs of dogtooth violets (pp. 27–28), dandelion greens (p. 28), strawberries (p. 35), wild garlic, jack-in-the-pulpit roots (p. 45), daisies, inner bark from the poplar tree, acorns (p. 62), sassafras roots (p. 66), pennyroyal, winterberry leaves (p. 67), arrowleaf bulbs, cattail tubers, bulrush roots, and wild onions (p. 81).

Referring to Laurence Pringle's *Wild Foods: A Beginner's Guide to Identifying, Harvesting and Preparing Safe and Tasty Plants from the Outdoors* (1978) and Euell Gibbons's *Stalking the Wild Asparagus* (1970), students investigated the wild plants mentioned in *My Side of the Mountain,* read suggestions for identifying and preparing them, compared these suggestions with the ways in which the book's main character identified and prepared them, and identified which plants might be found near their own homes. (Warnings were also stressed; many wild plants are dangerous to eat. Therefore, the teacher recommended that the children not eat any plant unless they were accompanied by someone who knew exactly which plants were safe and which were dangerous.)

Because cattails were mentioned and were available near the school, the students gathered them and tried grinding them into flour. They also followed Laurence Pringle's suggestions for boiling cattail rhizomes and using them as a potato substitute. This experience increased their empathy for the characters in the book, who had to work hard to survive on natural foods. The children related their research on natural foods and their preparation to the climatic conditions, geographical locations, and amount of water available for plants in *My Side of the Mountain.*

 ## IMPROVING SELF-ESTEEM AND UNDERSTANDING OF INDIVIDUALS

Researchers and writers in educational publications have found that until quite recently, children's textbooks lacked sufficient portrayals of positive female roles. In addition, Masha Kabakow Rudman (1984) concludes: "clinical psychologists have regularly defined anything but conventional gender role behavior as abnormal. This definition extends to characteristics beyond behavior and indicates that male characters are valued far above female" (p. 101). Research attests to the stereotyping of males and females in children's literature.

Students of children's literature have identified literature suggesting that females and males do not necessarily act in stereotypical ways. Books that illustrate nonstereotypical behavioral patterns can help teachers, librarians, and parents who wish to combat stereotypes. Following are several examples.

1. Both girls and boys can overcome great struggles in nature and survive.
   Female: Scott O'Dell's *Island of the Blue Dolphins* and Jean Craighead George's *Julie of the Wolves.*
   Male: Armstrong Sperry's *Call It Courage* and Gary Paulsen's *Hatchet.*
2. Both young girls and young boys can be brave and intelligent.
   Female: Beverly Cleary's *Ramona the Brave.*
   Male: Lois Lowry's *Attaboy, Sam!*
3. Girls can be independent and take care of their younger siblings or pets.
   Female: E. L. Konigsburg's *From the Mixed-up Files of Mrs. Basil E. Frankweiler* and Theodore Taylor's *The Trouble with Tuck.*
4. Both girls and boys can be intelligent and curious.
   Female: Louise Fitzhugh's *Harriet the Spy.*
   Male: Donald J. Sobol's *Encyclopedia Brown Sets the Pace.*
5. Boys can express feelings of fear; facing death is not the only way to demonstrate courage.
   Male: Maia Wojciechowska's *Shadow of a Bull* and Jean Little's *Different Dragons.*

These books have led to interesting discussions and comparisons. Children have learned that both boys and girls can demonstrate a wide range of acceptable behaviors—or have read stories that verified what their own experience has already taught them about the full range of feelings and behaviors available to girls and boys.

DEVELOPING QUESTIONING STRATEGIES

Not all literature selections should be accompanied by questioning. Nevertheless, librarians and teachers responsible for encouraging children to think about and react to literature in a variety of ways find a framework helpful for designing questions to help children examine certain aspects of a story and questions that require higher-level thought processes. Teachers and librarians who wish to develop such questioning strategies will find assistance in taxonomies of reading comprehension, such as those developed by Benjamin Bloom (1956) and Thomas C. Barrett (1972). For example, Barrett identifies four levels of reading comprehension: (1) literal recognition or recall, (2) inference, (3) evaluation, and (4) appreciation.

Develop questions related to levels of reading comprehension in relation to realistic fiction, such as Katherine Paterson's *Jacob Have I Loved,* which is used in the following extended examples. Paterson's book is appropriate for the upper-elementary and middle-school students. The following questions suggest only the types of questions that might be developed around any book. A librarian or teacher might choose to focus upon only a few of these questions. The questions simply illustrate a variety of examples from each subsection of the taxonomy. They are not meant to suggest that every question must be discussed.

Literal Recognition

Literal recognition requires children to identify information provided in the literature. You may require children to recall the information from memory after reading or listening to a story or to locate information while reading a literature selection. Literal-level questions, such as the following, often use the words *who, what, where, when,* and *how:*

1. *Recall of details:* Where does the story *Jacob Have I Loved* take place? When does the story take place? Who are the characters in the story?
2. *Recall of sequence of events:* What sequence of events led Louise to believe that Caroline was the favored child in the family? What sequence of events caused Louise to move from an island to a mountain community?
3. *Recall of comparisons:* Compare the author's physical descriptions of Louise and Caroline. Compare the way in which Louise thought the family treated her with the way in which she thought they treated her twin sister, Caroline.
4. *Recall of character traits:* Describe Louise's response to the story about the birth of the twins, Louise and Caroline. How does Grandma respond to Caroline, to Louise, to Captain Wallace, to her son, and to her daughter-in-law?

Inference

When children infer an answer to a question, they go beyond the information that the author provides and hypothesize about such things as details, main ideas, and cause-and-effect relationships. Inference is usually considered a higher-level thought process; the answers are not specifically stated within the text. Examples of inferential questions include the following:

1. *Inferring supporting details:* At the end of *Jacob Have I Loved,* Joseph Wojtkiewicz says, "God in heaven's been raising you for this valley from the day you were born." What do you believe he meant by this statement?
2. *Inferring main idea:* What do you believe is the theme of the book? What message do you think the author was trying to express? How does the author develop this theme?
3. *Inferring comparisons:* Think about Captain Wallace, who is such a part of Louise's story. Compare that character with the one who left the island when he was a young man. How do you believe they are alike and how do you believe they are different?
4. *Inferring cause-and-effect relationships:* If you identified any changes in Captain Wallace, what do you believe might have caused them? Why do you believe Louise dreamed about Caroline's death? Why do you believe that Louise felt wild exaltation and then terrible guilt after these dreams?
5. *Inferring character traits:* What do you believe caused Louise to change her mind about wanting Hiram Wallace to be an islander who escaped rather than a Nazi spy? What is Louise

saying about herself when she emphasizes the word *escaped?* Why do you believe Louise became so upset whenever she was called "Wheeze"? Why do you think Louise was so upset when Call invited Caroline to join them during their visit to the captain? At the end of the book, after Louise has delivered twins to a mountain family, she becomes very anxious over the healthier twin. Why do you think she gave this advice, "You should hold him. Hold him as much as you can. Or let his mother hold him" (p. 215)? What does this reaction say about Louise's own character and the changes in character that took place in her lifetime?

6. *Inferring outcomes:* There were several places in the book when the action and outcome of the story would have changed if characters had acted in different ways. Have students read or listen to the book up to a certain point. At various points, ask students to predict the outcomes. For example:

   a. At the end of chapter four, a mysterious man leaves the boat and walks alone toward an abandoned house. Who do you think he is? How do you think this man will influence the story?

   b. At the end of chapter twelve, Caroline finds and uses Louise's hidden hand lotion. What do you think will happen after Louise angrily breaks the bottle and runs out of the house?

   c. At the close of chapter fourteen, the captain has offered to send Caroline to Baltimore to continue her musical education. How do you think Caroline, her parents, and Louise will react to this suggestion?

   d. At the end of chapter seventeen, Louise and the captain are discussing what she plans to do with her life. Louise responds that she wants to become a doctor but cannot leave her family. Knowing Louise and her family, how do you think the story will end?

Evaluation

Evaluative questions require children to make judgments about the content of the literature by comparing it with external criteria, such as what authorities on a subject say, or internal criteria, such as experience or knowledge. The following are examples of evaluative questions:

1. *Judgment of adequacy or validity:* Do you agree that Louise in *Jacob Have I Loved* would not have been accepted as a student in a medical college? Why or why not? This story took place in the 1940s; would the author have been able to include the same scene between a woman and a university adviser if the story had taken place in the 1990s? Why or why not?

2. *Judgment of appropriateness:* What do you think the author meant by the reference to the quote, "Jacob have I loved, but Esau have I hated." How does this biblical line relate to the book? Do you think it is a good title for the book? Why or why not?

3. *Judgment of worth, desirability, or acceptability:* Was Louise right in her judgment that her parents always favored Caroline? What caused her to reach her final decision? Do you believe that Louise made the right decision when she left the island? Why or why not?

Appreciation

Appreciation of literature requires a sensitivity to the techniques that authors use in order to have emotional impact on their readers. Questions can encourage children to respond emotionally to the plot, identify with the characters, react to an author's use of language, and react to an author's ability to create a visual image through word choices in the text. The following are examples of questions to stimulate appreciation:

1. *Emotional response to plot or theme:* How did you respond to the plot of *Jacob Have I Loved?* Did the author hold your interest? If so, how? Do you believe the theme of the story was worthwhile? Why or why not? Pretend that you are either recommending this book for someone else to read or recommending that this book not be read; what would you tell that person?

2. *Identification with characters and incidents:* Have you ever felt, or known anyone who felt, like thirteen-year-old Louise or her twin sister, Caroline? What caused you or the person to feel that way? How would you have reacted if you had been thirteen-year-old Louise? How would you have reacted if you had been Caroline? Pretend to be a grown-up Louise in chapter eighteen talking with your mother about leaving the island. What emotions do you think your mother would

Involving Children in Realistic Fiction 🍃 **511**

feel when you responded, "I'm not going to rot here like Grandma" (p. 200)? How would you feel when she told you, "I chose to leave my own people and build a life for myself somewhere else. I certainly wouldn't deny you that same choice. But . . . oh, Louise, we will miss you, your father and I" (p. 201)?

3. *Imagery:* How did the author encourage you to see the relationship between the island setting and changes in Louise's character over her lifetime?

4. *Appreciative comprehension and identification with characters and incidents:* Have you ever felt or known anyone who felt like thirteen-year-old Louise when she listened to the story about her birth and thought, "I felt cold all over, as though I was the newborn infant a second time, cast aside and forgotten" (p. 15)? How would you have reacted if you had been Louise and had heard this story repeatedly? What do you think could make you feel cold all over if you were Caroline and heard this story?

 ## SUGGESTED ACTIVITIES

for Involving Children in Realistic Fiction

■ Using the criteria for selecting appropriate literature for role playing, develop a file of stories that have problem situations appropriate for elementary-school children. Include stories that can be used by reading to a certain point and allowing children to role-play possible solutions, as well as stories that are more appropriate for role playing after an entire story has been read. Choose a role-playing situation and lead a role-playing activity with either a group of children or a peer group.

■ Choose a survival book related to the survival on islands webs. Develop instructional activities for the book to correspond with the webs. Suggested books include *Call It Courage, The Cay, The Swiss Family Robinson, My Side of the Mountain, Hatchet,* and *Julie of the Wolves.*

■ Review the stories in a basal reader, and evaluate their content according to stereotypical roles for either males or females. Assume that some corrective action is required if a balanced portrayal of contributions of males and females is to occur, and identify several children's literature selections that could be used to balance a viewpoint. How could the literature be used in an instructional setting?

■ List children's literature sources that show many behavioral patterns for boys and girls, men and women.

■ Develop a bibliography of books that illustrate non-stereotypical behavioral patterns in boys and girls. Write a short summary to describe the behavioral patterns that are shown in each book.

■ Choose a realistic fiction book other than *Jacob Have I Loved.* Develop questioning strategies that follow a taxonomy of comprehension, such as that developed by Thomas C. Barrett or Benjamin Bloom.

 ## CHILDREN'S LITERATURE

Alcock, Vivien. *A Kind of Thief.* Delacorte, 1992 (I:10+ R:6). When Elinor's father is arrested for embezzlement, she reclaims his locked briefcase.

Alcott, Louisa M. *Little Women* (first published in 1868). Crowell, 1995 (I:10+ R:7). One of the early stories about a realistic family that focuses on female characters.

Anderson, Rachel. *The Bus People.* Holt, 1992 (I:10+ R:7). The bus people are a group of special education children.

Avi. *Nothing but the Truth: A Documentary Novel.* Orchard, 1991 (I:12+). The text is presented through various documents.

Baker, Jeannie. *Where the Forest Meets the Sea.* Greenwillow, 1988 (I:4–10). A boy and his grandfather experience changing environments in Australia.

Barbour, Karen. *Mr. Bow Tie.* Harcourt Brace Jovanovich, 1991 (I:4–8 R:4). A family befriends a homeless man.

Bartoletti, Susan Campbell. *Dancing with Dziadziu.* Illustrated by Annika Nelson. Harcourt Brace, 1997 (I:8–12 R:5). A Polish American family listen to their grandmother's remembrances of life in Poland and her journey to America.

Bauer, Joan. *Squashed.* Delacorte, 1992 (I:10+ R:5). In a humorous story, a girl tries to grow the largest pumpkin.

Bauer, Marion Dane. *On My Honor.* Clarion, 1986 (I:10+ R:4). A strong person-against-self conflict results when a friend drowns in a river.

———. *A Question of Trust.* Scholastic, 1994 (I:10+ R:5). Saving a kitten becomes the mission for a boy who is facing his parents' separation.

Bawden, Nina. *Humbug.* Clarion, 1992 (I:8+ R:5). An elderly woman teaches a girl how to survive cruelty and to recognize lies.

———. *The Outside Child.* Lothrop, Lee & Shepard, 1989 (I:10+ R:6). A thirteen-year-old girl discovers that her father has a second family.

———. *The Real Plato Jones.* Clarion, 1993 (I:12+ R:6). A thirteen-year-old boy who lives in a London suburb struggles to understand his family, which includes a Welsh grandfather and a Greek grandfather.

I = Interest by age range.

R = Readability by grade level.

Baylor, Byrd. *Hawk, I'm Your Brother.* Illustrated by Peter Parnall. Scribner's Sons, 1976 (I:all R:6). Rudy Soto would like to glide through the air like a hawk.

Benjamin, Carol Lea. *The Wicked Stepdog.* Crowell, 1982 (I:9–12 R:4). A twelve-year-old girl fears she is losing her father's love when he remarries.

Berck, Judith. *No Place to Be: Voices of Homeless Children.* Houghton Mifflin, 1991 (I:12+). Interviews with homeless children may be used to authenticate fictional literature on this topic.

Block, Francesca Lia. *Girl Goddess #9: Nine Stories.* HarperCollins, 1996 (I:14+ R:7). This book for older, mature readers tells about a peer world that is filled with casual sex and drugs.

Blume, Judy. *Are You There God? It's Me, Margaret.* Bradbury, 1970 (I:10+ R:6). Eleven-year-old Margaret wonders about the changes that are occurring in her body.

———. *Blubber.* Bradbury, 1974 (I:10+ R:4). The children in the fifth grade start a campaign against a heavier girl in the class.

———. *Deenie.* Bradbury, 1973 (young adult).

———. *Forever.* Bradbury, 1975 (young adult).

———. *It's Not the End of the World.* Bradbury, 1972 (young adult).

———. *The One in the Middle Is the Green Kangaroo.* Illustrated by Amy Aitken. Bradbury, 1981 (I:6–9 R:2). A middle child gains self-esteem when he gets a part in a play.

———. *Otherwise Known as Sheila the Great.* Dutton, 1972 (I:9–12 R:6). Ten-year-old Sheila experiences an exciting summer.

———. *Tales of a Fourth Grade Nothing.* Illustrated by Roy Doty. Dutton, 1972 (I:7–12 R:4). Peter's problem is his two-year-old brother, Fudge.

———. *Then Again, Maybe I Won't.* Bradbury, 1971 (young adult).

———. *Tiger Eyes.* Bradbury, 1981. (I:12+ R:7). A fifteen-year-old girl faces violence and fear.

Bonham, Frank, *Durango Street.* Dutton, 1965 (I:12+ R:5). Gang violence is realistically portrayed as two inner-city gangs cut out their territories.

Brooks, Bruce. *Everywhere.* HarperCollins, 1990 (I:8+ R:4). A boy tries to save his grandfather.

———. *The Moves Make the Man.* Harper & Row, 1984 (I:10+ R:7). Basketball develops understanding between a black and a white boy.

———. *What Hearts.* HarperCollins, 1992 (I:10+ R:5). Four short stories trace various stages in the life of a boy.

Burch, Robert. *Queenie Peavy.* Illustrated by Jerry Lazare. Viking, 1966 (I:10+ R:6). A strong female character longs for the day when her father will return from jail, but then she discovers his true nature.

Burnford, Sheila. *The Incredible Journey.* Illustrated by Carl Burger. Little, Brown, 1960, 1961 (I:8+ R:8). Three animals travel through 250 miles of Canadian wilderness.

Byars, Betsy. *After the Goat Man.* Illustrated by Ronald Himler. Viking, 1974 (I:9–12 R:7). An overweight boy meets a man who is trying to protect his home from an advancing interstate highway.

———. *The Animal, the Vegetable, and John D. Jones.* Illustrated by Ruth Sanderson. Delacorte, 1982 (I:9–12 R:5). Three children come into conflict when their single parents share a vacation.

———. *Bingo Brown and the Language of Love.* Viking, 1989 (I:10+ R:5). A fifth-grade boy experiences his first crush.

———. *The Burning Questions of Bingo Brown.* Viking Kestrel, 1988 (I:10+ R:6). A boy searches for answers to confusing questions.

———. *Coast to Coast.* Delacorte, 1992 (I:10+ R:5). A girl and her grandfather fly across the United States in a small airplane.

———. *Cracker Jackson.* Viking, 1985 (I:10+ R:6). An eleven-year-old boy tries to save his former babysitter from abuse by her husband.

———. *The Cybil War.* Illustrated by Gail Owens. Viking, 1981 (I:9–12 R:6). Two fourth graders battle for a girl's affections.

———. *The 18th Emergency.* Illustrated by Robert Grossman. Viking, 1973 (I:8–12 R:3). Problems arise from insulting the biggest boy in school.

———. *The Night Swimmers.* Illustrated by Troy Howell. Delacorte, 1980 (I:8–12 R:5). An older sister tries to care for her brothers while her father works nights.

———. *The Summer of the Swans.* Illustrated by Ted CoConis. Viking, 1970 (I:8–12 R:4). A mentally disabled boy goes out alone in search of the wild swans.

Cadnum, Michael. *Zero to the Bone.* Viking, 1996 (I:12+ R:7). A family faces a frightening experience when a girl is missing.

Carrick, Carol. *The Accident.* Illustrated by Donald Carrick. Seabury, 1976 (I:5–8 R:4). Christopher experiences a series of emotions after his dog is killed.

———. *Stay Away from Simon.* Clarion, 1985 (I:7–10 R:3). A mentally retarded boy helps two children discover that disabled people have great worth.

Carter, Alden R. *Between a Rock and a Hard Place.* Scholastic, 1995 (I:12+ R:7). This is a story of survival set in the Minnesota lake country.

Christopher, Matt. *Dirt Bike Racer.* Illustrated by Barry Bomzer. Little, Brown, 1979 (I:10+ R:4). Twelve-year-old Ron Baker restores a minibike.

———. *Face-Off.* Illustrated by Harvey Kidder. Little, Brown, 1972 (I:8–12 R:4). Scott Harrison must overcome a tremendous fear about a hockey player.

———. *Football Fugitive.* Illustrated by Larry Johnson. Little, Brown, 1976 (I:9–12 R:6). Larry wishes his father would take an interest in football.

———. *The Fox Steals Home.* Illustrated by Larry Johnson. Little, Brown, 1978 (I:8–12 R:6). Baseball helps a boy overcome his worries about his parents' divorce.

Cleary, Beverly. *Dear Mr. Henshaw.* Illustrated by Paul O. Zelinsky. Morrow, 1983 (I:9–12 R:5). Corresponding with an author helps a boy overcome problems related to his parents' divorce.

———. *Henry and Beezus.* Illustrated by Louis Darling. Morrow, 1952 (I:7–10 R:6). Henry and the girl he finds least obnoxious have a humorously good time.

———. *Mitch and Amy.* Illustrated by George Porter. Morrow, 1967 (I:7–10 R:6). A humorous story is about everyday experiences.

———. *Muggie Maggie.* Illustrated by Kay Life. Morrow, 1990 (I:7–10 R:5). A third grader decides that she does not want to learn cursive writing.

_____ . *Ramona the Brave*. Illustrated by Alan Tiegreen. Morrow, 1975 (I:7–10 R:6). Ramona has many difficulties until she finally wins a truce with the first-grade teacher.

_____ . *Ramona and Her Father*. Illustrated by Alan Tiegreen. Morrow, 1977 (I:7–10 R:6). Ramona tries to help her father through a trying period after he has lost his job.

_____ . *Ramona and Her Mother*. Illustrated by Alan Tiegreen. Morrow, 1979 (I:7–10 R:6). Ramona's mother goes to work.

_____ . *Ramona the Pest*. Illustrated by Louis Darling. Morrow, 1968 (I:7–10 R:4). Ramona enters kindergarten and spreads exasperation into a wider sphere.

_____ . *Ramona Quimby, Age 8*. Illustrated by Alan Tiegreen. Morrow, 1981 (I:7–10 R:6). Ramona faces new challenges when her father returns to college.

_____ . *Strider*. Illustrated by Paul O. Zelinsky. Morrow, 1991 (I:10+ R:5). This is a sequel to *Dear Mr. Henshaw*.

Cleaver, Vera, and Bill Cleaver. *Trial Valley*. Lippincott, 1977 (I:11+ R:5). In a sequel to *Where the Lilies Bloom,* Mary Call struggles to keep the family together.

_____ . *Where the Lilies Bloom*. Illustrated by Jim Spanfeller. Lippincott, 1969 (I:11+ R:5). Four children hide their father's death so that they can remain together.

Cole, Brock. *The Goats*. Farrar, Straus & Giroux, 1987 (I:10+ R:5). A boy and a girl survive a camp experience in which they are humiliated by their peers.

Conly, Jane Leslie. *Crazy Lady!* HarperCollins, 1993 (I:10+ R:5). Interactions with a retarded boy help a boy face the death of his mother and appreciate the support of his father.

Corcoran, Barbara. *The Potato Kit*. Atheneum, 1989 (I:10+ R:6). A girl from a poor rural family spends the summer with a wealthier family.

Cormier, Robert. *The Bumblebee Flies Anyway*. Pantheon, 1983 (I:14+ R:6). A sixteen-year-old boy faces illness in a terminal care facility.

_____ . *In the Middle of the Night*. Delacorte, 1995 (I:12+ R:6). A woman seeks revenge for an accident.

_____ . *Tenderness*. Delacorte, 1997 (I:12+ R:6). This is a chilling portrait of a serial murderer.

Creech, Sharon. *Chasing Redbird*. HarperCollins, 1997 (I:10+ R:6). Set in Appalachia, a thirteen-year-old girl struggles to accept herself.

_____ . *Walk Two Moons*. HarperCollins, 1994 (I:12+ R:6). Thirteen-year-old Sal and her grandparents take a car trip trying to trace the route of Sal's mother.

Cross, Gillian. *A Map to Nowhere*. Holiday House, 1989 (I:10+ R:5). A boy decides if he should betray his friend.

_____ . *On the Edge*. Holiday House, 1985 (I:10+ R:5). This is a gripping story of kidnapping and terrorism.

_____ . *Roscoe's Leap*. Holiday House, 1987 (I:10+ R:6). This mystery is about a collection of windup toys.

Crutcher, Chris. *Athletic Shorts*. Greenwillow, 1991 (I:10+ R:6). Six short stories are about athletes.

Cunningham, Julia. *Burnish Me Bright*. Illustrated by Don Freeman. Pantheon, 1970 (I:8–12 R:8). A mute boy in a French village is taught to pantomime by a retired actor and then is persecuted by the villagers.

Cutler, Jane. *No Dogs Allowed*. Farrar Straus & Giroux, 1992 (I:8+ R:4). Humor develops in stories about a five-year-old and his older brother.

_____ . *Rats!* Illustrated by Tracey Campbell Pearson. HarperCollins, 1996 (I:8+ R:4). This is a collection of five stories about two brothers.

Danziger, Paula. *Amber Brown Is Not a Crayon*. Illustrated by Tony Ross. Putnum, 1994 (I:6–9 R:4). A third-grade girl's best friend moves.

Danziger, Paula, and Ann M. Martin. *P. S. Longer Letter Later*. Scholastic, 1998 (I:10+ R:5). The story is built around the exchange of letters between two girls.

Darling, Benjamin. *Valerie and the Silver Pear*. Illustrated by Dan Lane. Four Winds, 1992 (I:5–8 R:3). A girl and her grandfather develop a close relationship as they harvest and cook the grandmother's fruit.

Davis, Jenny. *Good-Bye and Keep Cold*. Orchard, 1987 (I:12+ R:6). A girl looks back on the traumatic years after her father's death in a mining accident.

Delton, Judy. *Angel's Mother's Wedding*. Houghton Mifflin, 1987 (I:7–10 R:4). Angel worries that her mother is not taking the upcoming wedding seriously enough.

dePaola, Tomie. *Nana Upstairs & Nana Downstairs*. Putnam, 1973 (I:3–7 R:6). A boy has two beloved grandmothers.

Dickinson, Peter. *AK*. Delacorte, 1992 (I:12+ R:6). In this Whitbread Award winner, a boy is part of a guerrilla band in Africa.

Doherty, Berlie. *Dear Nobody*. Orchard, 1992 (I:12+ R:6). This 1992 Carnegie Medal winner is the story of a girl who struggles with her pregnancy.

Duncan, Lois. *Don't Look Behind You*. Delacorte, 1989 (I:12+ R:6). A family must move when the father is threatened.

Ellis, Sarah. *Next-Door Neighbors*. Macmillan, 1990 (I:10+ R:5). A girl has difficulty making friends her own age when she moves.

_____ . *Pick-up Sticks*. Macmillan, 1992 (I:10+ R:5). A girl learns to appreciate the things in life that really matter.

Enright, Elizabeth. *Thimble Summer*. Holt, Rinehart & Winston, 1938, 1966 (I:7–12 R:5). Nine-year-old Garnet spends the summer on her Wisconsin farm.

Estes, Eleanor. *The Moffats*. Illustrated by Louis Slobodkin. Harcourt Brace Jovanovich, 1941 (I:7–10 R:4). The happy Moffat children experience a series of adventures.

Farber, Norma. *How Does It Feel to Be Old?* Illustrated by Trina Schart Hyman. Dutton, 1979 (I:5–8 R:2). A grandmother tells her granddaughter about the good and bad experiences related to growing old.

Farley, Walter. *The Black Stallion*. Illustrated by Keith Ward. Random House, 1944 (I:8+ R:3). The black stallion saves Alec's life.

_____ . *The Black Stallion Picture Book*. Photographs furnished by United Artists. Random House, 1979 (I:6–8 R:2). This is a picture storybook version of *The Black Stallion*.

_____ . *The Black Stallion Returns*. Random House, 1945, 1973 (I:8+). Alec learns the history of the horse and finds himself in the center of a blood feud and an important race.

Fassler, Joan. *Howie Helps Himself*. Illustrated by Joe Lasker. Whitman, 1974 (I:4–8 R:2). A child with cerebral palsy tries very hard to move his wheelchair by himself.

Fine, Anne. *Alias Madame Doubtfire*. Little, Brown, 1988 (I:9+ R:5). A father in disguise becomes babysitter and cleaning woman in the home of his ex-wife.

_____ . *The Tulip Touch*. Little, Brown, 1997 (I:10+ R:6). A friendship results in dangerous games.

_____. *Step by Wicked Step.* Little Brown, 1996 (I:10+ R:6). Five classmates tell stories about their parents' divorces.

Fitzhugh, Louise. *Harriet the Spy.* Harper & Row, 1964 (I:8–12 R:3). Eleven-year-old Harriet keeps a notebook of observations about people.

_____. *The Long Secret.* Harper & Row, 1965 (I:8–12 R:3). This is a sequel to *Harriet the Spy.*

Fleischman, Paul. *Seedfolks.* Illustrated by Judy Pedersen. HarperCollins, 1997 (I:10+ R:6). A garden in Cleveland unites a community.

Foreman, Michael. *Seal Surfer.* Harcourt Brace, 1997 (I:5–9 R:4). A young boy in a wheelchair develops a strong bond with a seal.

Fox, Paula. *Monkey Island.* Orchard, 1991 (I:10+ R:6). A boy tries to survive in the inner city.

_____. *The Moonlight Man.* Bradbury, 1986 (I:12+ R:5). A girl makes discoveries about herself and her father after her parents' divorce.

_____. *One-Eyed Cat.* Bradbury, 1984 (I:10+ R:5). An eleven-year-old boy shoots a cat and then must face his guilt.

_____. *The Village by the Sea.* Watts, 1988 (I:10+ R:6). A girl discovers human foibles when she stays with an aunt while her father has surgery.

_____. *Western Wind.* Orchard, 1993 (I:9+ R:5). An eleven-year-old girl makes discoveries about herself when she spends time with her grandmother on an island off the coast of Maine.

Franklin, Kristine L. *Lone Wolf.* Candlewick, 1997 (I:9+ R:5). A boy living in the north woods faces his problems by learning about wolves.

Freeman, Suzanne. *The Cucoo's Child.* Greenwillow, 1996 (I:10+ R:6). Two girls leave Beirut to live with their aunt in Tennessee after their parents disappear.

Garland, Sherry. *The Silent Storm.* Harcourt, 1993 (I:10+ R:6). In this survival story, a girl, her brother, and her grandfather face a hurricane.

Gauch, Patricia. *Christina Katerina and the Time She Quit the Family.* Illustrated by Elise Primavera. Putnam's, 1987 (I:4–8). A young girl experiences humorous complications with her family.

George, Jean Craighead. *The Cry of the Crow.* Harper & Row, 1980 (I:10+ R:5). Mandy must make a choice when her pet crow attacks her brother.

_____. *Julie of the Wolves.* Illustrated by John Schoenherr. Harper & Row, 1972 (I:10+ R:7). An Eskimo girl lost on the North Slope of Alaska survives with the help of wolves.

_____. *My Side of the Mountain.* Dutton, 1959 (I:10+ R:6). Sam Gribley creates a home inside a rotted-out tree.

Gifaldi, David *Toby Scudder, Ultimate Warrior.* Clarion, 1993 (I:9+ R:5). A bully learns that he needs close relationships.

Gipson, Fred. *Old Yeller.* Illustrated by Carl Burger. Harper & Row, 1956 (I:10+ R:6). Old Yeller is bitten by a rabid wolf as he saves the lives of those he loves.

Godden, Rumer. *Listen to the Nightingale.* Viking, 1992 (I:10+ R:5). A puppy brings a solution to two girls, one of whom has a leg in a steel brace.

Graeber, Charlotte. *Mustard.* Illustrated by Donna Diamond. Macmillan, 1982 (I:7–10 R:4). A boy faces the death of his beloved fourteen-year-old cat.

Greenberg, Jan. *The Iceberg and Its Shadow.* Farrar, Straus & Giroux, 1980 (I:9–14 R:6). This story of peer manipulation and victimization is similar to Judy Blume's *Blubber.*

Greene, Constance. *Beat the Turtle Drum.* Illustrated by Donna Diamond. Viking, 1976 (I:10+ R:7). After an accident, the family must cope with Joss's death.

Greenwald, Sheila. *Give Us a Great Big Smile, Rosy Cole.* Little, Brown, 1981 (I:8–10 R:4). Rosy's uncle decides that he will base a book on his niece and her violin.

Haas, Jessie. *Keeping Barney.* Greenwillow, 1982 (I:9–12 R:5). A girl gets a chance to care for a horse and tries to win his devotion.

Hall, Lynn. *In Trouble Again, Zelda Hammersmith?* Harcourt Brace Jovanovich, 1987 (I:8–12 R:3). Five humorous episodes are about a fourth-grade girl.

Hamilton, Virginia. *The House of Dies Drear.* Macmillan, 1968 (I:11+ R:4). In a suspenseful story, a family lives in a home that was once a station on the Underground Railroad.

_____. *Plain City.* Scholastic, 1993 (I:10+ R:5). A twelve-year-old girl makes discoveries about her family when she searches for her father.

_____. *The Planet of Junior Brown.* Macmillan, 1971 (I:12+ R:6). The outcasts from society create their own world in a secret basement room.

Hanel, Wolfram. *Abby.* Illustrated by Alan Marks, North-South, 1996 (I:7–9 R:4). When a dog eats poisoned meat, her mistress cares for her and celebrates her recovery.

Harris, Rosemary. *Zed.* Farber & Farber, 1982 (I:12+ R:7). An eight-year-old boy is held by terrorists in London.

Hartling, Peter. *Old John.* Translated by Elizabeth D. Crawford. Lothrop, Lee & Shepard, 1990 (I:8+ R:5). A family must adjust when an elderly grandfather moves in.

Hathorn, Libby. *Thunderwith.* Little, Brown, 1991 (I:10+ R:5). In this book, set in Australia, a girl's experience with a dog helps her overcome her fear after her mother's death.

Haugen, Tormod. *The Night Birds.* Translated from the Norwegian by Sheila La Farge. Delacorte, 1982 (I:10+ R:3). A seven-year-old boy faces real and imagined terrors.

Hautzig, Esther. *A Gift for Mama.* Illustrated by Donna Diamond. Viking, 1981 (I:8–10 R:4). Sarah mends clothing to earn money for a Mother's Day gift.

Hayes, Daniel. *Flyers.* Simon & Schuster, 1996 (I:12+ R:7). The story about the escapades of a teenager take place in upstate New York.

Henkes, Kevin. *Words of Stone.* Greenwillow, 1992 (I:10+ R:5). This story shows the power of friendship between two children who have had difficulties in their lives.

Henry, Marguerite. *Black Gold.* Illustrated by Wesley Dennis. Rand McNally, 1957 (I:8–12 R:6). This is the history of a great racing horse named Black Gold and the trainer and jockey who loved him.

_____. *Justin Morgan Had a Horse.* Illustrated by Wesley Dennis. Rand McNally, 1954 (I:8–12 R:6). This is the story of how Little Bub inherited the name of his owner Justin Morgan.

_____. *King of the Wind.* Illustrated by Wesley Dennis. Rand McNally, 1948, 1976 (I:8–12 R:6). This is the story of the great Godolphin Arabian who was the ancestor of Man o' War.

_____ . *Misty of Chincoteague.* Illustrated by Wesley Dennis. Rand McNally, 1947, 1963 (I:8–12 R:6). Misty is the descendent of the Spanish horses that swam to Assateague Island after a shipwreck.

_____ . *San Domingo: The Medicine Hat Stallion.* Illustrated by Robert Lougheed. Rand McNally, 1972 (I:9–14 R:4). A boy's greatest joy is his foal with the markings believed sacred by the Indians.

Hermes, Patricia. *Mama, Let's Dance.* Little, Brown, 1991 (I:10+ R:5). Children try to keep the family together after their mother leaves them.

Hicyilmaz, Gaye. *Against the Storm.* Little, Brown, 1992 (I:10+ R:6). In this story, set in Ankara, a boy learns about survival in city poverty.

Honeycutt, Natalie. *Juliet Fisher and the Foolproof Plan.* Bradbury, 1992 (I:8–10 R:3). A third-grade girl tries to change a messy classmate.

_____ . *Twilight in Grace Falls.* Orchard, 1997 (I:10+ R:6). The family and the town experience hard times when the lumber mill closes.

Hopkins, Lee Bennett. *Mama.* Knopf, 1977 (I:7–10 R:6). A boy worries about his mother and tries to change her.

Horvath, Polly. *When the Circus Came to Town.* Farrar, Straus & Giroux, 1996 (I:9+ R:6). This humorous story also develops a theme about the importance of tolerance.

Howard, Ellen. *Edith Herself.* Atheneum, 1987 (I:7–10 R:4). A girl with epilepsy learns to value herself in the 1890s.

Hughes, Dean. *Family Pose.* Atheneum, 1989 (I:10+ R:6). An orphan boy discovers a new family among hotel workers.

_____ . *Team Picture.* Simon & Schuster, 1996 (I:10+ R:6). A foster child tries to form a family with a bellman who has had problems with alcohol abuse.

Hunt, Irene. *Up a Road Slowly.* Follett, 1966 (I:11+ R:7). This is the story of a girl's life and the influence of an aunt with whom she stays after her mother dies.

Hurwitz, Johanna. *Russell and Elisa.* Illustrated by Lillian Hoban. Morrow, 1989 (I:3–8 R:3). Six stories tell about a brother and sister.

Irwin, Hadley. *The Original Freddie Ackerman.* Macmillan, 1992 (I:10+ R:5). Two great aunts provide a mystery for a boy when he visits their home.

Johnson, Angela. *Toning the Sweep.* Orchard, 1993 (I:12+ R:4). A fourteen-year-old girl records the reminisces of her dying grandmother.

Jukes, Mavis. *I'll See You in My Dreams.* Illustrated by Stacey Schuett. Knopf, 1993 (I:5–8 R:4). A young girl copes with the death of a favorite uncle.

_____ . *Like Jake and Me.* Illustrated by Lloyd Bloom. Knopf, 1984 (I:6–8). A boy learns to appreciate his stepfather.

Keller, Beverly. *No Beasts! No Children!* Lothrop, Lee & Shepard, 1983 (I:8–12 R:4). A father, his children, and their pets cope by themselves.

Kerr, M. E. *"Hello," I Lied.* HarperCollins, 1997 (I:14+ R:7). A seventeen-year-old boy is in conflict over his admission that he is gay.

Khalsa, Dayal. *I Want a Dog.* Clarkson, 1987 (I:4–7). A girl discovers that having a dog includes responsibilities.

Kjelgaard, Jim. *Big Red.* Illustrated by Bob Kuhn. Holiday House, 1945, 1956 (I:10+ R:7). Danny trains a champion Irish setter.

Klein, Norma. *Mom, the Wolf Man and Me.* Pantheon, 1972 (I:12+ R:6). Eleven-year-old Brett loves her life with her lively unwed mother.

Kline, Suzy. *Herbie Jones and the Monster Ball.* Illustrated by Richard Williams. Putnam, 1988 (I:8+ R:4). A boy learns to play baseball when his uncle is the coach.

Koertge, Ron. *The Harmony Arms.* Little, Brown, 1992 (I:10+ R:5). Humor adds to this story of a boy and his recently divorced father.

Konigsburg, E. L. *About the B'nai Bagels.* Atheneum, 1969 (I:8–12 R:7). Mark Setzer has special problems with his little league baseball team: His mother is the manager, and his brother is the coach.

_____ . *From the Mixed-up Files of Mrs. Basil E. Frankweiler.* Atheneum, 1967 (I:9–12 R:7). Eleven-year-old Claudia and her younger brother run away to the Metropolitan Museum of Art.

_____ . *(George).* Atheneum, 1970, 1980 (I:10+ R:7). This is a story about a multiple personality and how the differences were resolved.

_____ . *Jennifer, Hecate, Macbeth, William McKinley, and Me, Elizabeth.* Atheneum, 1967, 1976 (I:8–12 R:4). Elizabeth becomes an apprentice witch in this story of interracial friendships.

_____ . *Journey to an 800 Number.* Atheneum, 1982 (I:10+ R:7). A boy learns to appreciate his father when he spends the summer with him.

_____ . *T-Backs, T-Shirts, Coat, and Suit.* Atheneum, 1993 (I:10+ R:5). A twelve-year-old girl discovers her own values.

_____ . *Throwing Shadows.* Atheneum, 1979 (I:11+ R:7). A collection of five short stories is about people making discoveries about themselves.

_____ . *The View from Saturday.* Atheneum, 1996 (I:9–12 R:5). Four sixth-grade students win a championship and gain their personal quests.

L'Engle, Madeleine. *Meet the Austins.* Vanguard, 1960 (I:10+ R:6). The six Austins have a family filled with spontaneous love, understanding, and personal discipline.

Lisle, Janet Taylor. *Afternoon of the Elves.* Watts, 1989 (I:10+ R:5). Two very different girls become friends as they work on a miniature village.

Little, Jean. *Different Dragons.* Illustrated by Laura Fernandez. Viking, 1986 (I:8–10 R:4). A boy overcomes his fear of dogs.

_____ . *From Anna.* Illustrated by Joan Sandin. Harper & Row, 1972 (I:8–12 R:5). Nine-year-old Anna lives in a world blurred by poor eyesight until she is placed in a special class.

London, Jack. *Call of the Wild.* Photographs by Seymour Linden. Harmony, 1903, 1977 (I:10+ R:5). This is the classic story of a brave dog and the Klondike gold rush.

Lowry, Lois. *All About Sam.* Illustrated by Diane deGroat. Houghton Mifflin, 1988 (I:8–12 R:5). This story is about Anastasia's little brother.

_____ . *Anastasia Again!* Illustrated by Diane deGroat. Houghton Mifflin, 1981. (I:8–12 R:6). Anastasia must adjust to living in the suburbs.

_____ . *Anastasia on Her Own.* Houghton Mifflin, 1985 (I:8–12 R:4). In a humorous tale, Anastasia takes over housekeeping when her mother leaves for a consulting job.

_____ . *Anastasia Krupnik.* Houghton Mifflin, 1979 (I:8–12 R:6). Ten-year-old Anastasia forms a hate list and a love list and discovers that eventually all of the items are on one list.

_____ . *Anastasia's Chosen Career.* Houghton Mifflin, 1987 (I:10+ R:6). Anastasia has humorous experiences when she takes a modeling course.

_____ . *Anastasia at Your Service.* Illustrated by Diane deGroat. Houghton Mifflin, 1982 (I:8–12 R:6). An older Anastasia becomes a household servant rather than a companion to a rich woman.

_____ . *Attaboy, Sam!* Illustrated by Diane deGroat. Houghton, 1992 (I:8+ R:5). The youngest Krupnik adds disastrous experiences.

_____ . *The One Hundredth Thing About Caroline.* Houghton Mifflin, 1983 (I:8–12 R:3). An eleven-year-old retaliates when she thinks she is to become the victim of murder.

_____ . *Rabble Starkey.* Houghton Mifflin, 1987 (I:10+ R:6). Set in an Appalachian town, a twelve-year-old girl learns to value a different type of family.

_____ . *See You Around, Sam!* Illustrated by Diane deGroat. Houghton Mifflin, 1996 (I:8+ R:5). Anastasia's younger brother decides that he should run away to Alaska.

_____ . *Your Move, J. P.!* Houghton Mifflin, 1990 (I:10+ R:6). A seventh grader experiences feelings of love.

Lynch, Chris. *Shadow Boxer.* HarperCollins, 1993 (I:12+ R:6). The story develops inner-city struggles as a fourteen-year-old boy tries to protect his younger brother.

McDonald, Joyce. *Comfort Creek.* Delacorte, 1996 (I:10+ R:5). A sixth-grade girl helps keep her family together after her mother runs off to play with a bluegrass band.

McKay, Hilary. *The Exiles.* Macmillan, 1992 (I:9+ R:5). Four sisters spend their summer vacation with their grandmother and learn some valuable lessons.

MacGregor, Rob. *Hawk Moon.* Simon & Schuster, 1996 (I:12+ R:6). This is a murder mystery set in Aspen, Colorado.

MacLachlan, Patricia. *The Facts and Fictions of Minna Pratt.* Harper & Row, 1988 (I:7–12 R:4). A girl learns to appreciate herself and her family.

_____ . *Journey.* Delacorte, 1991 (I:8+ R:4). Photographs and their grandparents help two children understand their lives and their mother's desertion.

_____ . *Mama One, Mama Two.* Illustrated by Ruth Lercher Bornstein. Harper & Row, 1982 (I:4–8 R:3). A child has a happy foster home experience.

Mahy, Margaret. *The Good Fortunes Gang.* Delacorte, 1993 (I:8–10 R:4). A boy must adjust when he moves from Australia to New Zealand.

Marino, Jan. *For the Love of Pete.* Little, Brown, 1993 (I:10+ R:5). Eleven-year-old Phoebe travels with her grandmother's servants to find Phoebe's father.

Mathis, Sharon Bell. *The Hundred Penny Box.* Puffin, 1986 (I:6–9 R:3). A boy loves to hear his aunt tell stories about each penny in a box.

Mauser, Pat Rhoads. *A Bundle of Sticks.* Illustrated by Gail Owens. Atheneum, 1982 (I:9–12 R:5). An eleven-year-old is humiliated by a bully and takes self-defense lessons.

Mazer, Norma Fox. *After the Rain.* Morrow, 1987 (I:12+ R:5). A fifteen-year-old girl faces her grandfather's death.

Mohr, Nicholasa. *Felita.* Illustrated by Ray Cruz, Dial, 1979 (I:9–12). A Puerto Rican girl experiences prejudice in New York.

_____ . *Going Home.* Dial, 1986 (I:10+). A Puerto Rican girl experiences prejudice when she returns to Puerto Rico.

Mooney, Bel. *The Voices of Silence.* Delacorte, 1997 (I:10+ R:6). This novel is set in Romania under Communist rule.

Mowry, Jess. *Babylon Boyz.* Simon & Schuster, 1997 (I:12+ R:7). This is a story of inner-city life set in Oakland, California.

Myers, Walter Dean. *Mop, Moondance, and the Nagasaki Knights.* Delacorte, 1992 (I:9+ R:5). Three boys must overcome language and cultural barriers when they play baseball in an international tournament.

_____ . *Scorpions.* Harper & Row, 1988 (I:10+ R:5). A boy becomes involved with a gang, and his best friend tries to stop his actions.

_____ . *Somewhere in the Darkness.* Scholastic, 1992 (I:12+ R:5). A fourteen-year-old boy discovers his father's harsh world.

Naylor, Phyllis Reynolds. *Alice in Rapture, Sort Of.* Atheneum, 1989 (I:10+ R:5). A girl discovers that it is better to be friends with a boy than to have a boyfriend.

_____ . *All but Alice.* Atheneum, 1992 (I:10+ R:5). The seventh grade provides additional humorous experiences for Alice.

_____ . *Josie's Troubles.* Illustrated by Shelley Matheis. Atheneum, 1992. (I:8+ R:4). Two friends try to earn money to pay for fixing a broken leg on a piano bench.

_____ . *Keeping a Christmas Secret.* Illustrated by Lena Schiffman. Atheneum, 1989 (I:5–8). A young boy discovers how hard it is to keep secrets.

_____ . *Reluctantly Alice.* Atheneum, 1991 (I:10+ R:5). In a humorous story, Alice experiences junior high school.

_____ . *Shiloh.* Atheneum, 1991 (I:10+ R:5). A boy saves an abused dog.

_____ . *Shiloh Season.* Atheneum, 1996 (I:8+ R:5). This is a sequel to *Shiloh.*

Nelson, Theresa. *The Beggars' Ride.* Orchard, 1992 (I:10+ R:5). A runaway girl tries to survive in Atlantic City.

Neville, Emily. *It's Like This, Cat.* Illustrated by Emil Weiss. Harper & Row, 1963 (I:8–12 R:6). David Mitchell has two best friends, an older boy and a stray tomcat.

Newman, Robert. *The Case of the Baker Street Irregular.* Atheneum, 1978 (I:10+ R:6). Kidnappings, bombings, and the mystery of the identity of Andrew's mother bring Andrew and Sherlock Holmes together.

_____ . *The Case of the Vanishing Corpse.* Atheneum, 1980 (I:10+ R:6). A series of incidents bring Andrew into contact with Constable Wyatt.

O'Connor, Barbara. *Beethoven In Paradise.* Farrar, Straus & Giroux, 1997 (I:10+ R:6). The hero of this story would rather play the violin than play on the Little League team.

O'Dell, Scott. *Island of the Blue Dolphins.* Houghton Mifflin, 1960 (I:10+ R:6). Twelve-year-old Karana survives alone for eighteen years before a ship takes her to the California mainland.

Park, Barbara. *Don't Make Me Smile.* Knopf, 1981 (I:9–12 R:5). A ten-year-old boy reacts to his parents' divorce.

_____ . *The Kid in the Red Jacket.* Knopf, 1987 (I:7–11 R:3). A ten-year-old boy faces humorous problems when he moves.

_____ . *Maxie, Rosie, and Earl—Partners in Crime.* Knopf, 1990 (I:8–12 R:5). A humorous story about three children who constantly get into trouble.

Paterson, Katherine. *Bridge to Terabithia.* Illustrated by Donna Diamond. Crowell, 1977 (I:10–14 R:6). Two nonconformists create their own magical realm.

_____. *Come Sing, Jimmy Jo*. Dutton, 1985 (I:10+ R:4). An eleven-year-old boy makes self-discoveries through his musical gift.

_____. *Flip-Flop Girl*. Lodestar, 1994 (I:10+ R:5). A girl faces the death of her father.

_____. *The Great Gilly Hopkins*. Crowell, 1978 (I:10+ R:6). A rebellious girl tries to adjust to abandonment and foster homes.

_____. *Jacob Have I Loved*. Crowell, 1980 (I:10+ R:7). A twin feels that her sister has deprived her of parental affection and schooling.

_____. *Park's Quest*. Lodestar Books, 1988. (I:10+ R:5+). A boy is on a quest to learn about his father, who died in Vietnam.

Patron, Susan. *Maybe Yes, Maybe No, Maybe Maybe*. Illustrated by Dorothy Donahue. Orchard, 1993 (I:7–10 R:4). A girl uses her artistic ability when her family moves to a new apartment.

Paulsen, Gary. *The Car*. Harcourt Brace Jovanovich, 1994 (I:10+ R:6). Two Vietnam veterans show that one can learn from experience.

_____. *Dancing Carl*. Bradbury, 1983 (I:10+ R:4). Two boys learn to respect a war veteran who had a traumatic experience.

_____. *Hatchet*. Bradbury, 1987 (I:10+ R:6). A thirteen-year-old boy learns personal and physical survival in the Canadian wilderness.

_____. *The Schernoff Discoveries*. Delacorte, 1997 (I:10+ R:6). A fourteen-year-old boy tells about his best friend.

Pearson, Gayle. *The Secret Box*. Atheneum, 1997 (I:8–12 R:5). This is a collection of stories about secrets.

Peck, Richard. *Bel-Air Bambi and the Mall Rats*. Delacorte, 1993 (I:10+ R:5). A sixth-grade girl tells the story of how a group of kids save the town from the local gang.

_____. *Remembering the Good Times*. Delacorte, 1985 (I:12+ R:4). A strong friendship develops among three students until one takes his own life.

Perkins, Lynne Rae. *Home Lovely*. Greenwillow, 1995 (I:6–9 R:3). A young girl keeps herself busy planting and caring for seedlings while her mother works.

Petersen, P. J. *The Sub*. Illustrated by Meredith Johnson. Dutton, 1993 (I:8–10 R:4). Two boys switch seats when they have a substitute teacher.

Phipson, Joan. *Hit and Run*. Atheneum, 1985 (I:10+ R:6). A survival story is set in Australia.

Powell, Randy. *My Underrated Year*. Farrar, Straus & Giroux, 1988 (I:10+ R:5). A boy discovers that a girl is one of his greatest competitors in sports.

Provost, Gary, and Gail Levine-Provost. *David and Max*. Jewish Publication Society, 1988 (I:10+ R:6). A twelve-year-old boy remembers the summer before his grandfather died.

Rabe, Berniece. *The Balancing Girl*. Illustrated by Lillian Hoban. Dutton, 1981 (I:7–9 R:4). A physically disabled girl proves she is a capable person.

Radley, Gail. *The Golden Days*. Macmillan, 1991 (I:10+ R:5). An eleven-year-old boy and an elderly woman run away and try to create their own life.

Rapp, Adam. *The Buffalo Tree*. Gront Street, 1997 (I:12+ R:6). The setting is a juvenile detention facility.

Raskin, Ellen. *Figgs & Phantoms*. Dutton, 1974 (I:10+ R:5). An unusual family is constantly searching for Capri, their idea of heaven.

_____. *The Mysterious Disappearance of Leon (I Mean Noel)*. Dutton, 1971 (I:10+ R:5). A word puzzle is used to solve the mystery of the disappearing Leon.

_____. *The Westing Game*. Dutton, 1978 (I:10+ R:5). Sixteen heirs are invited to solve a riddle.

Reuter, Bjarne. *Buster's World*. Translated by Anthea Bell. Dutton, 1989 (I:8+ R:5). The main character copes with an alcoholic father.

Riskind, Mary. *Apple Is My Sign*. Houghton Mifflin, 1981 (I:9–12 R:5). A deaf boy goes to a school for the deaf in the early 1900s.

Rocklin, Joanne. *For Your Eyes Only!* Illustrated by Mark Todd. Scholastic, 1997 (I:9–12 R:5). Sixth-grade students express many emotions through their journals.

Rodowsky, Colby. *Remembering Mog*. Farrar, Straus & Giroux, 1996 (I:12+ R:6). A girl and her family try to cope with the murder of her older sister.

_____. *Sydney, Herself*. Farrar, Straus & Giroux, 1989 (I:12+ R:6). A writing assignment helps a girl make discoveries about herself.

Rylant, Cynthia. *A Fine White Dust*. Bradbury, 1986 (I:11+ R:6). A thirteen-year-old boy faces challenges about his religious beliefs.

_____. *A Kindness*. Orchard, 1988 (I:12+ R:6). A teenage boy faces his mother's pregnancy in their single-parent home.

_____. *Missing May*. Orchard, 1992 (I:10+ R:6). Set in West Virginia, a girl and her uncle try to overcome the grief associated with the death of a beloved aunt.

Sachs, Marilyn. *The Bears' House*. Illustrated by Louis Glanzman. Doubleday, 1971 (I:8–11 R:6). An unhappy fourth grader tries to cope with a sick mother and desertion by her father.

_____. *A Secret Friend*. Doubleday, 1978 (I:8–12 R:4). Two best friends break their relationship after many years.

Savage, Deborah. *Under a Different Sky*. Houghton Mifflin, 1997 (I:12+ R:6). Two students from different social levels develop a relationship.

Schami, Rafik. *A Hand Full of Stars*. Translated by Rika Lesser. Dutton, 1990 (I:12+ R:6). In this story, set in Damascus, a boy becomes involved with an underground newspaper.

Schotter, Roni. *Captain Snap and the Children of Vinegar Lane*. Illustrated by Marcia Sewell, Orchard, 1989 (I:5–8). The children make friends with an older man.

Shreve, Susan. *The Gift of the Girl Who Couldn't Hear*. Tambourine, 1991 (I:9+ R:5). A deaf friend helps a girl overcome her self-doubts.

Shusterman, Neal. *Speeding Bullet*. Scholastic, 1992 (I:10+ R:6). A boy believes that he has special powers to rescue people.

Slepian, Jan. *The Broccoli Tapes*. Philomel, 1989 (I:10+ R:6). Twelve-year-old Sara sends tapes from Hawaii back to her friends in Boston.

Slote, Alfred. *Hang Tough, Paul Mather*. Lippincott, 1973 (I:9–12 R:3). Baseball helps Paul Mather face his death when he discovers that he has an incurable blood disease.

_____. *The Trading Game*. Lippincott, 1990 (I:10+ R:4). A ten-year-old boy grows up as he interacts with baseball and his grandfather.

Smith, Doris Buchanan. *Best Girl*. Viking, 1993 (I:10+ R:5). A girl makes discoveries about herself with the help of an understanding older person.

Smith, Janice Lee. *The Show-and-Tell War*. Illustrated by Dick Gackenbach. Harper & Row, 1988 (I:7–9 R:4). This is a series of humorous stories.

Snyder, Zilpha Keatley. *The Egypt Game*. Illustrated by Alton Raible. Atheneum, 1967 (I:10+ R:6). A group of sixth-grade children recreate the land of ancient Egypt.

———. *The Famous Stanley Kidnapping Case*. Atheneum, 1979 (I:10+ R:7). Kidnappers hold children for ransom in a deserted basement.

Sobol, Donald J. *Encyclopedia Brown Sets the Pace*. Illustrated by Ib Ohlsson. Scholastic/Four Winds, 1982 (I:7–10 R:5). This book contains a new series of cases to solve.

———. *Encyclopedia Brown Tracks Them Down*. Illustrated by Leonard Shortall. Crowell, 1971 (I:7–10 R:3). Clues and solutions make it possible for children to solve mysteries.

Sperry, Armstrong. *Call It Courage*. Macmillan, 1940 (I:9–13 R:6). A Polynesian boy travels alone in an outrigger canoe.

Spinelli, Jerry. *Wringer*. HarperCollins, 1997 (I:9+ R:4). A boy develops the courage to oppose violence.

Staples, Suzanne Fisher. *Dangerous Skies*. Farrar, Straus & Giroux, 1996 (I:12+ R:6). Characters face conflicts caused by racism in this story that includes a murder.

———. *Shabanu: Daughter of the Wind*. Knopf, 1989 (I:12+ R:6). A girl in Pakistan asserts her independence.

Steig, William. *Spinky Sulks*. New York: Farrar, Straus & Giroux, 1988 (I:3–8 R:5). A sulky boy discovers that his family is really trying to help him.

Stolz, Mary. *Stealing Home*. HarperCollins, 1992 (I:8–12 R:4). This is an extension of the story about a grandfather and grandson introduced in the picture book *Storm in the Night*.

Strachan, Ian. *Flawed Glass*. Little, Brown, 1990 (I:10+ R:6). In this book, set in Scotland, a girl with a physical handicap learns to adjust to her difficulties.

Sykes, Shelley. *For Mike*. Delacorte, 1998 (I:12+ R:6). A boy tries to discover the reasons for his best friend's disappearance.

Taylor, Clark. *The House That Crack Built*. Illustrated by Jan Thompson Dicks. Chronicle Books, 1992 (I:10+). This is a controversial book.

Taylor, Sydney. *All-of-a-Kind Family*. Illustrated by Helen John. Follett, 1951 (I:7–10 R:4). Five girls live with their parents on New York's East Side in 1912.

———. *Ella of All-of-a-Kind Family*. Illustrated by Gail Owens. Dutton, 1978 (I:10+ R:5). Ella is grown-up and must decide whether or not she wants a singing career.

Taylor, Theodore. *The Cay*. Doubleday, 1969 (I:10+ R:6). A blind American boy is stranded on a Caribbean cay with a West Indian.

———. *The Trouble with Tuck*. Doubleday, 1981 (I:6–9 R:5). Based on a true incident, the story follows a girl as she trains a blind Labrador to follow a guide dog.

Taylor, William. *Agnes the Sheep*. Scholastic, 1991 (I:8+ R:5). An eccentric older lady and a nasty sheep combine to create a humorous story.

Tolan, Stephanie S. *A Good Courage*. Morrow, 1988 (I:12+ R:6). A boy and his mother enter a commune only for the boy to discover dangers within the cult.

Voigt, Cynthia. *Bad Girls*. Scholastic, 1996 (I:9+ R:7). Two fifth-grade girls become best friends.

———. *Dicey's Song*. Atheneum, 1982 (I:10+ R:5). Dicey brings her brothers and sister to their grandmother's house after their mother abandons them.

———. *Homecoming*. Atheneum, 1981 (I:10+ R:5). The children survive as they try to reach their grandmother.

———. *A Solitary Blue*. Atheneum, 1983 (I:10+ R:6). A boy develops a loving relationship with his father after he faces his mother's desertion.

———. *Sons from Afar*. Atheneum, 1987 (I:10+ R:6). The youngest Tillerman brothers search for their father.

Walter, Virginia. *Making Up Megaboy*. Illustrated by Katrina Roeckelein. DK, 1998 (I:10+ R:6). Various people present their points of view about a tragic incident.

Watson, James. *Talking in Whispers*. Victor Gollancz, 1983 (I:12+ R:7). In a political thriller, a boy survives against an oppressive military government.

White, Ruth. *Belle Prater's Boy*. Farrar, Straus & Giroux, 1996 (I:10+ R:6). A boy faces the disappearance of his mother.

Williams, Carol Lynch. *The True Colors of Caitlynne Jackson*. Delacorte, 1997, (I:10+ R:5). A 12-year-old girl must take care of her sister after her mother leaves.

Wojciechowska, Maia. *Shadow of a Bull*. Illustrated by Alvin Smith. Atheneum, 1964 (I:10+ R:5). Manolo discovers that true bravery is not always in the bullring.

Wolff, Virginia Euwer. *Probably Still Nick Swansen*. Holt, Rinehart & Winston, 1988 (I:10+ R:6). A boy with learning disabilities learns to accept himself and his sister's death.

Woodson, Jacqueline. *Maizon at Blue Hill*. Delacorte, 1992 (I:10+ R:5). An African American girl faces challenges in a private girls' school where she is one of only five black students.

Wynne-Jones, Tim. *The Maestro*. Orchard, 1996 (I:11+ R:6). A fourteen-year-old boy runs away from his brutal father and learns to overcome his own conflicts in the Ontario wilderness.

Wyss, Johann David. *The Swiss Family Robinson*. Illustrated by Lynd Ward. Grosset & Dunlap, 1949 (I:10+ R:6). In a classic story, a family is shipwrecked.

Illustration from *Ox-Cart Man* by Donald Hall, illustrated by Barbara Cooney. Copyright © 1979 by Barbara Cooney Porter, illustrations. Used by permission of Viking Penguin, a division of Penguin Books USA, Inc.

10 *Historical Fiction*

The People and the Past Come Alive

The thread of people's lives weaves through the past, through the present, and into the future. Many Americans have a deep desire to trace their roots—here in this hemisphere or back to Europe, Asia, or Africa. What did their ancestors experience? Why did their ancestors travel to North America? What were their ancestors' personal feelings and beliefs? What was life like for the settlers who pioneered the American frontier and for the native North Americans who greeted them? Did people of the past have the same concerns as people of the present do? Can their experiences suggest solutions for today's problems?

Through the pages of historical fiction, the past comes alive. It is not just dates, accomplishments, and battles; it is people, famous and unknown. This chapter discusses the values of historical fiction for children, gives criteria for evaluating historical fiction, looks at the need for historical authenticity, and provides examples of historical fiction. Books of historical fiction are linked to a short discussion of events in the time period that they reflect in the hope that this chronological framework will give you a better understanding of the sweep of history as portrayed in these books. One way to evaluate the importance of historical fiction is to analyze the genre of books awarded the Batchelder Award presented to the best book translated into English. Over one-half of the awards presented since 1968 are for historical fiction.

VALUES OF HISTORICAL FICTION FOR CHILDREN

Children cannot actually cross the ocean on the *Mayflower* and see a new world for the first time, or experience the arrival of the first Europeans on their native shores, or feel the consequences of persecution during World War II. They can imagine these experiences, however, through the pages of historical fiction. With Patricia Clapp's *Constance: A Story of Early Plymouth,* they can imagine that they are standing on the swaying deck of the *Mayflower* and seeing their new home. With Scott O'Dell's *The Feathered Serpent,* they can imagine that they are witnessing Montezuma's tragic encounter with the Spanish conquistador Hernando Cortés. With Paul Fleischman's *Bull Run,* they can understand the various viewpoints associated with the Civil War. With Ida Vos's *Hide and Seek,* they can imagine that they are given sanctuary by Dutch gentiles during World War II.

As children read for enjoyment, they relive the past vicariously. Tales based on authentic historical settings or episodes are alive with adventures that appeal to many children. They may follow the adventures of a young girl living on the Wisconsin frontier in Carol Ryrie Brink's *Caddie Woodlawn.* They may follow the adventures of a girl in Victorian London, interacting with people in the sinister opium trade and conducting a quest for a missing ruby in Philip Pullman's *The Ruby in the Smoke.* They may discover that courage is required to take a stand during colonial times as they interact with the heroine in Ann Rinaldi's *The Fifth of March: A Story of the Boston Massacre.* They may follow the adventures of Jeff Bussey in Harold Keith's *Rifles for Watie* as Jeff tries to find information behind enemy lines during the Civil War. They may follow a family as the family prepares for an 1890s Christmas celebration in Virginia Hamilton's *The Bells of Christmas.* They may follow Patrick and his sister Keely as Keely tries to interest her polio-stricken brother in a challenge that sparks his interest in Julie Johnston's *Hero of Lesser Causes.* They may follow the rescue effort during the evacuation of Dunkirk in May, 1940 in Louise Borden's *The Little Ships: The Heroic Rescue at Dunkirk in World War II.*

Children who read historical fiction gain an understanding of their own heritage. The research that precedes the writing of authentic historical stories enables authors to incorporate information about the period naturally. Children gain knowledge about the people, values, beliefs, hardships, and physical surroundings common to various periods. They discover the events that preceded their own time and made the present possible. Through historical fiction, children can begin to visualize the sweep of history. As characters in historical fiction from many different time periods face and overcome their problems, children may discover universal truths, identify feelings and behaviors that encourage them to consider alternative ways to handle their own problems, empathize with viewpoints that are different from their own, and realize that history consists of many people who have learned to work together.

The journal of the National Council for the Social Studies, *Social Education* (1992), maintains that an emphasis on human relations is a primary criterion for selecting notable books. Through historical fiction, children can discover that in all times, people have depended upon one another and that they have had similar needs. Children can learn that when human relationships deteriorate, tragedy usually results. Historical fiction allows children to judge relationships and realize that their present and future are linked to the actions in the past. Outstanding books of historical fiction for children satisfy what Joan W. Blos (1980, p. 375) believes is a primary role of literature: "tying together the past, the present, and the promise of the future" in ways that "confirm human bonds."

 ## LITERARY CRITICISM: USING LITERARY ELEMENTS TO EVALUATE HISTORICAL FICTION

When evaluating historical fiction for children, adults must be certain that a story adheres to the criteria for excellent literature discussed in chapter 3. Historical fiction must also satisfy special requirements in terms of plot, characterization, setting, and theme. The questions in the Evaluation Criteria box on this page summarize the criteria that you should consider (in addition to considerations of literary quality raised in chapter 3) when evaluating historical fiction for children.

Plot

Credible plots in historical fiction emerge from authentically developed time periods. The experiences, conflicts, and resolutions of conflicts must reflect the times—whether the antagonist is another person, society, nature, or internal dilemmas faced by the protagonist. Conflict in historical fiction often develops when characters leave their environments and move into alien ones. Authors may highlight the problems, cultures, or diverse values of time periods by exploring the conflicts developed because of characters' inner turmoil or because of societal pressures. Author Russell Freedman (1992) presents interesting insights into the search for truth about the interactions between pioneers and Native Americans. He describes his own search for truth about the wagon-train journeys along the Oregon Trail. Freedman states:

Now, the movies and television have taught us that this journey was fraught with peril, since the hostile Indians were likely to attack at any moment. And yet, as I pursued my research, I found that Indian attacks were few

ℰVALUATION CRITERIA

Literary Criticism: Historical Fiction

1. Do the characters' experiences, conflicts, and resolutions of conflicts reflect what is known about the time period?

2. Do the characters' actions express values and beliefs that are realistic for the time period?

3. Is the language authentic for the period without relying on so many colorful terms or dialects that the story is difficult to understand?

4. Is the setting authentic in every detail?

5. Are details integrated into the story so that they do not overwhelm readers or detract from the story?

6. If the setting is the antagonist, are the relationships between characters and setting clearly developed?

7. Is the theme worthwhile?

8. Does the style enhance the mood and clarify the conflicts, characterizations, settings, and themes?

and far between. Attacks were infrequent. I began to wonder, how menacing were the Indians. (p. 2)

In his search for the truth, Freedman describes differences in the impressions gained from diaries written by men and by women. Whereas men always emphasized the dangers from Indians and described their battles with Indian war parties, women's diaries frequently showed initial fear of the Indians but usually described the Indians as friendly and helpful. Freedman speculates about the accuracy of the depiction of history for this period.

In Avi's *The True Confessions of Charlotte Doyle,* the conflicts develop after Charlotte leaves England to sail on the *Seahawk,* a merchant sailing ship crossing the Atlantic in 1832. Person-against-self conflicts develop when Charlotte faces her changing attitudes toward the captain and the crew and about her own family.

Scott O'Dell develops credible person-against-self conflict in *The Captive.* In this book, a young Jesuit seminarian faces moral dilemmas when he leaves his Spanish homeland in the early 1500s and accompanies an expedition to the Americas. O'Dell describes the Jesuit's faith and his desire to bring Christianity to the native Maya of New Spain, his turmoil when he discovers the real motives behind the Spaniards' actions, his refusal to betray the native people, his pondering over his inability to change them, and his justification for his own grasping for power by impersonating a Mayan god. The various characterizations help readers understand both good and bad human motives.

Circle of Fire, by William H. Hooks, explores the moral dilemmas created by prejudice. Hooks's story takes place in North Carolina in the 1930s. In this story, a white boy and his two black friends try to prevent a Ku Klux Klan attack on Irish gypsies. Hooks develops additional believable personal conflict when the eleven-year-old boy discovers that his father, whom he loves and respects, is probably involved in the Klan.

Historical fiction stories also develop plausible person-against-society conflicts. In Karen Cushman's *Catherine, Called Birdy* and *The Midwife's Apprentice,* both person-against-society and person-against-self conflicts develop as the heroines face conflicts caused by society in medieval England and their needs to overcome inner turmoils. The conflicts in *The True Confessions of Charlotte Doyle* are

credible because Avi convincingly develops Victorian attitudes about people in various social classes. The conflict in *The Captive* develops because of greed and the Spaniards' socially supported prejudice against non-Europeans, which O'Dell compellingly portrays. Likewise, conflict develops in *Circle of Fire* because of social prejudice.

Authors who develop credible person-against-society conflicts must describe the values and beliefs of the time period or the attitudes of a segment of the population so that readers understand the nature of the antagonist. In Kathryn Lasky's *The Night Journey,* deadly anti-Semitism is the antagonist that forces a Jewish family to plan and execute a dangerous flight from czarist Russia. The story seems more credible because a modern-day family in this book believes that these memories would be so painful that the great-grandmother should not be encouraged to remember the experiences. In Carolyn Reeder's *Shades of Gray,* a boy who is orphaned by the Civil War learns to live with his uncle who has pacifist convictions. To make a believable story, Reeder develops the values and beliefs that cause societal conflicts.

Well-developed person-against-self and person-against-society conflicts help readers understand the values expressed during a time period and the problems, moral dilemmas, and social issues faced by the people. Authors often use these conflicts and their resolutions to develop themes in historical fiction.

Characterization

The actions, beliefs, and values of characters in historical fiction must be realistic for the time period. Authors of historical novels admit that it is sometimes difficult not to give their historical characters contemporary actions and values. Historical fiction author Erik Haugaard (1988) emphasizes the need to accurately depict the beliefs and values of the time period. Haugaard differentiates between technical faults and spiritual errors in historical fiction. He contends that technical faults such as advancing the petroleum lamp by half a century do not bother him as much as do spiritual ones. He states:

The errors which I have dubbed spiritual I dislike much more, and I would be much harder on them than mere mistake of a date. By spiritual mistakes I mean giving people in one century the ideas and opinions of another. A citizen of Rome at the time of Christ might have considered slavery vile. But if he did, he was unique. There is no doubt that the vast majority did not even question the institution. If the author lets the character in his novel have extremely unorthodox views, he must explain why and how he came to hold those opinions. If the characters in a historical novel are merely twentieth century men and women dressed up to perform a masquerade, I see little point in applauding just because their dresses are described accurately. (p. 7)

Choosing the main and supporting characters can cause additional problems. For example, authors of historical fiction rarely use famous people as pivotal characters unless they can document evidence about specific dialogue or sentiments. Authors frequently place historical figures in the role of secondary characters. In Esther Forbes's *Johnny Tremain,* for example, a fictional silversmith's apprentice is the pivotal character, while Paul Revere and Samuel Adams are background characters.

Authors develop characters through dialogue, thoughts, actions, and descriptions. While all of these elements must appear authentic, the speech of the characters and the language of a period can cause problems for writers of historical fiction. For example, Harold Keith wanted one of his characters in *The Obstinate Land* to speak with a dialect: "Mattie Cooper's Arkansas dialect was hard to pin down until I had the good fortune to discover old files of the magazine *Dialect Notes,* containing several studies by Dr. J. W. Carr, associate professor of English and Modern Languages at the University of Arkansas, 1901–06" (1977, author's notes). This study provided Keith with the words and the pronunciations necessary to develop a character whose speech was realistic for the time and the location. Authors of children's historical fiction must be careful, however, not to use so many colorful terms from a period that the story is difficult for young readers to comprehend. Zena Sutherland (1997) agrees that creating natural conversations is one of the most difficult tasks for writers of historical fiction.

Literature critic Rebecca Lukens (1986) stresses the importance of believable characters in helping readers understand the differences and similarities between people in different times and places. Readers must believe that the characters in historical fiction are human beings like themselves. Belief in individual characters was one of the goals cited by Michael Dorris (1992) in his writing of *Morning Girl,* a story about the Taino people, who lived on the Bahama islands at the time of Columbus's arrival in 1492. Dorris states:

In the characters of Morning Girl and Star Boy, I allowed myself to speculate freely, to invite onto the page two fully invested children—curious, independent, self-analytical, strong, moving toward independence, whose flaws were the flaws of youth: redeemable with wisdom and maturity. (p. 3)

The resulting novel encourages readers to understand and believe in these characters who lived in a different time.

Setting

Because historical fiction must be authentic in every respect, the careful development of setting for a certain time period is essential. Historical fiction author Leon Garfield states that "historical fiction more than any other kind of fiction must be rooted in a particular place and time" (1988, p. 736). A setting this important to a story is called an integral setting.

Rebecca Lukens (1986) says that an integral setting must be described in details so clear that readers understand how the story is related to a time and place. This is of particular concern in historical fiction written for children, because children cannot draw on memory for historical periods. Writers must provide images through vivid descriptions that do not overpower plot and characterization. John Stewig (1989) also emphasizes the need for integral settings when he concludes, "One mark of a skilled writer in any genre is the ability to weave in details so they aren't noticed consciously, yet are available when needed later" (p. 135).

When writing lengthy books for older children, authors have more time to develop settings in which the actions and characters are influenced by both time and place. The setting in historical fiction may guide readers into the plot, create visual images that encourage them to accept a character's experiences, and encourage them to feel the excitement of a time period.

Setting plays the role of antagonist in many stories about exploration and pioneering. For example, in Honore Morrow's *On to Oregon!,* sleet storms, rugged mountains, swift streams, and natural predators act as antagonists. Morrow's descriptions leave little doubt that the children are confronting a beautiful but awesome adversary.

THROUGH THE EYES OF A CHILD

Responses to Jane Yolen's *Encounter*

JANE YOLEN'S *Encounter* is a highly illustrated story of the Taino people at the time of Christopher Columbus's expedition. Fifth-grade students in Carolyn Marek's language arts classes in Caldwell, Texas, generated the following reactions, writing responses and taking part in a lively discussion.

Most of the children were outraged at the treatment of the Taino people. Almost every child was drawn to the illustrations, especially to the final illustration, in which the old man's feet have disappeared. As you read the following responses, notice how the children responded to both the illustrations and the situations. Many of the children place themselves into the story.

Drew: "I think that *Encounter* on a scale of 1 to 10 would be an 11. . . . Think what would happen if aliens came down from space and made us wear their clothes and take us away. The illustrator made a good point of that on the last page. The man wasn't disappearing, his beliefs were. I would feel uncomfortable, angry, and afraid if I were a Taino back then. Not being able to believe what you want to is very wrong. I would surely have hated to be in his shoes. The worst part is, the boy knew that there was danger, but the other Taino wouldn't listen because he was a child. This reminded me of what happens to me all the time. It's stupidity that no one will listen to kids because they are kids."

Shana: "My reaction to the book is that I have learned not to welcome anyone who makes you do strange or uncomfortable things. If I were a Taino boy or girl I would have been very frightened. Having a dream like that and then having that happen would be absolutely frightening. One last thing about the book is at the end, when the old man said, 'May it be a warning to all the children and all the people in every land.' I think that means that you do not do anything that feels uncomfortable or strange to you. I also want to say that the reason I think the old man's feet are fading away in the last picture is he still believes in the culture but his faith is slowly fading away."

Jaime: "My reaction to the story *Encounter* was that it is a warning for other people. In the last picture it may symbolize that his people and their land are going or they may have lost the land and they have changed their culture. If I was a Taino boy I would be scared or maybe confused."

Jessica: "I tried to put myself into the little boy's shoes. . . . I wondered if somebody could have this much courage not to cry out when strangers took him away from his people, his very own family. At the end of the story, the little boy's, or now the old man's, feet weren't there. I think this is because his hope was lost for his tribe. If they would have listened to him and his dream, none of this would ever have happened."

Brian: "I think the book is interesting. If I was a child on that island, I wouldn't have trusted the strangers until I was certain that they weren't greedy. In my opinion, the last picture meant that the Taino's beliefs are being destroyed by the generations of greedy men. I think the moral of the story is that you should listen to children more often, because they might know more than you think."

Nick: "I think that the old man symbolizes a religion/race/family, a rapidly disappearing part of ourselves. It could also symbolize the multicultural world as a whole, the feet symbolizing the lost Taino tribes leaving an eternal scar . . . on our society today. The story also shows that thoughts and dreams matter, no matter what the age, race, or religion of the person who is thinking them."

Through their discussions, the children showed that they were also fascinated with the zemis, the religious statue to which the boy prayed and from which he received dreams. The book instigated many oral discussions, speculations, and searches for answers to questions. The teacher, Carolyn Marek, said, "I have yet to find another picture book that attracts as much attention again and again throughout the year as has *Encounter*. We have bestowed our own award on *Encounter* as our choice for best illustrated book of all time and best book in the category of historical fiction."

As you read *Encounter* and analyze the illustrations, compare your responses with those of these fifth-grade children.

Setting may also be the antagonist in a story set in a city. In *Anna, Grandpa, and the Big Storm,* Carla Stevens develops the 1888 blizzard in New York City into an antagonist.

Authors of historical fiction sometimes contrast settings in order to develop conflict. Both Ann Petry (*Tituba of Salem Village*) and Elizabeth George Speare (*The Witch of Blackbird Pond*) use this technique. Both authors have taken protagonists from the warm, colorful Caribbean and placed them in the bleak, somber surroundings of a Puritan village. Time and place then influence how other characters react to these protagonists and how these characters respond to their new environments.

Some settings in historical fiction create happy, nostalgic moods. In Cynthia Rylant's picture storybook *When I Was Young in the Mountains,* the illustrations and the text allow readers to glimpse a girl's happy years of growing up in the Appalachian mountains of Virginia. This peaceful setting includes swimming holes, country stores, and family evenings on the porch. The illustrations help integrate the details of the time period into the story. In contrast, the illustrations in Jo Hoestlandt's *Star of Fear, Star of Hope* reinforce a poignantly sad tale of separation in Nazi-occupied France in 1942.

Esther Forbes integrates many details of colonial life into the setting of her story for older readers, *Johnny Tremain.* The sights, sounds, and smells of revolutionary Boston are woven into the characters' daily routines. Readers know that Johnny sleeps in a loft, wears leather breeches and a coarse shirt, likes the bustling wharf, and is proud of his work in the silversmith's shop.

Smells, sounds, and light create believable settings in Gary Paulsen's *The Winter Room,* a story of farm life in an earlier American setting. Paulsen introduces *The Winter Room* by telling readers that if books could have smells, this book "would have the smell of new-mown hay as it falls off the oiled sickle blade when the horses pull the mower through the field, and the sour smell of manure steaming in a winter barn" (p. 1). If it could have sounds, it "would have the high, keening sound of the six-foot bucksaws as the men pull them back and forth through the trees to cut pine for paper pulp; the grunting-gassy sounds of the work teams snorting and slapping as they hit the harness to jerk the stumps out of the ground" (p. 2). And if the book could have light, it would have "the soft gold light—gold with bits of hay dust floating in it—that slips through the crack in the barn wall; the light of the Coleman lantern hissing flat-white in the kitchen; the silver-gray light of a middle winter day, the splattered, white-night light of a full moon on snow, the new light of dawn at the eastern edge of the pasture behind the cows coming in to be milked on a summer morning" (p. 2). But, Paulsen tells readers that because books cannot have smells, sounds, and light, the book needs readers who bring these sensations to the reading. Throughout his book, Paulsen's descriptions help readers visualize and vicariously experience details.

Theme

Themes in historical fiction, as in any literature, should be worthwhile and as relevant in today's society as they were in the historical periods represented. Many books of historical fiction have themes that have been relevant throughout history. The search for freedom is a theme in literature about all time periods. For example, Rosemary Sutcliff's

The illustrations reflect a happy setting in an Appalachian mountain community. (From When I Was Young in the Mountains, *by Cynthia Rylant, illustrated by Diane Goode. Illustrations © 1982 by Diane Goode. E. P. Dutton, Inc. Reprinted by permission of E. P. Dutton, Inc.)*

 The People and the Past Come Alive   527

Blood Feud tells about tribal Britons who are confronting the invading Vikings. Her *Frontier Wolf* tells about tribal Britons who are confronting Roman armies. Her *The Shining Company* is based on the development of a fighting brotherhood formed to battle the invading Saxons. Sutcliff's books develop stories in which searching for or defending freedom are primary goals. Sutcliff's books are memorable according to Sutherland (1997) because they are built around great themes. "Her characters live and die for principles they value and that people today still value" (p. 395). Freedom is one of the great themes in historical fiction. Elizabeth Yates's *Amos Fortune, Free Man* tells about an African slave searching for freedom in colonial Boston.

Love of the land and the independence that it provides are themes in books about the westward expansion of European settlers in North America and about the Native Americans that they displaced. Europeans leave relatives and established communities to face unknown dangers and acquire homesteads. Native Americans first attempt to share their beloved natural environment with the new arrivals. Then, they find themselves being pushed out of their homes. Love of land and the consequences caused by loss of land are developed by Scott O'Dell and Elizabeth Hall in *Thunder Rolling in the Mountains*. This book, told through the viewpoint of Chief Joseph's daughter, develops the conflict and pain associated with being forced to leave the Wallowa Valley. Children in both the westward expansion literature and the Native American literature inherit their parents' dreams and fight to retain the land.

Loyalty and honor are also common themes in stories about all time periods. People are loyal to friends and family members, following them on difficult quests and avenging their deaths or dishonor. They are loyal to their principles and defend them. Many books of historical fiction for children stress the cruelty and futility of war, even when adherence to loyalty and honor have helped cause the conflict. Novels about war in various historical periods often develop the themes of overcoming injustice. They also show ways in which people on both sides of a conflict have much in common. The beliefs of nonviolent people such as the Quakers are the bases of themes in some historical novels. Many themes are relevant to understanding, whether the stories in which they are developed take place in ancient Rome or contemporary America.

Style

An author's style influences the mood in historical fiction. For example, the repetition of the line "When I was young in the mountains" in Cynthia Rylant's text helps create a warm, nostalgic mood, in which harmful occurrences seem improbable. Brett Harvey introduces her mostly happy pioneer adventure *Cassie's Journey: Going West in the 1860s* with a description that suggests anticipation and security: "We're on our way to California! I'm riding up high with Papa, and the wind is rocking the wagon. When I look back I can see a long line of wagons curling behind us like a snake in the dust" (unnumbered).

In contrast, Patricia MacLachlan's introduction to *Sarah, Plain and Tall* suggests that the story will be about a family but that some unhappiness may have entered the family's life:

"Did Mama sing every day?" asked Caleb. "Every-single-day?" He sat close to the fire, his chin in his hand. It was dusk, and the dogs lay beside him on the warm hearthstones. "Every-single-day," I told him for the second time this week. For the twentieth time this month. The hundredth time this year? And the past few years? (p. 3)

If a historical fiction story has elements of suspense and adventure, the introduction frequently hints at the intrigue to follow. Leon Garfield's *The December Rose* and Philip Pullman's *The Ruby in the Smoke* develop mystery and adventure in Victorian England. Garfield introduces his mystery in a style that hints at intrigue:

Although the day was warm and sunny, she was dressed entirely in black . . . which served to set off the extreme pallor of her complexion and the brilliancy of her eyes. Her name was Donia Vassilovas. She was known as an enemy of the country and a grave risk to the security of the state. (p. 5)

In a fast-paced plot, Barnacle, a chimney sweep, accidentally lands in the midst of a conspiracy, grabs an important clue, and becomes a hunted individual.

Pullman uses a similar technique to introduce his novel about the sinister opium trade and the quest for a missing ruby:

On a cold, fretful afternoon in early October, 1872, a hansom cab drew up outside the offices of Lockhart and Selby, Shipping Agents, in the financial heart of London, and a young girl got out and paid the driver. She was a person of sixteen or so—alone, and uncommonly pretty. . . . Her name was Sally Lockhart; and within fifteen minutes she was going to kill a man. (p. 3)

Various forms of figurative language may clarify the conflicts, characters, settings, and themes in historical fiction. Figurative language is especially powerful when it provides insights into time, place, and conflict. For example, Rudolf Frank in *No Hero for the Kaiser* creates vivid images of World War I settings. In the following example, Frank makes readers understand both the physical and psychological settings and introduces the antiwar theme through his choice of words:

The distant thud of cannon came closer, like a thunderstorm brewing. And as if the storm had already broken, women, boys, girls, and soldiers began to rush around in confusion; trumpets sounded, and suddenly the Russians had swept out of the village like the wind. Now they were firing down from the low hills into the village. It sounded like the high-pitched whine of mosquitoes as they fly past your ear looking for a place to settle and bite: zzzzzz—a thin, sharp noise, full of sly malice. Jan knew that any one of these invisible whining bullets could kill man or beast on the spot. A dreadful feeling! But there was worse to come. (p. 2)

Allusions in historical fiction frequently provide insights into plots and characters. These same allusions, however, may require interpretation for less knowledgeable readers. For example, Frank uses allusions to the biblical flood, Napoleon, the skull of an African sultan, and the Maid of Orleans. Some of these allusions are explained in the text, while others are not. Karen Cushman identifies many of her journal entries in *Catherine, Called Birdy* with religious holidays that correspond with the dates. These "Feasts of Saint . . ." infer the importance of religion in medieval England.

In *The True Story of Spit MacPhee,* set in Australia in the 1920s, James Aldridge uses an unexplained allusion when Old Fyfe, the Scottish grandfather, looks at his grandson's friend, Sadie, and says with a grim laugh, "How are ye dressed, Jean Armour, aye sae clean and neat" (p. 37). This allusion depicts character and hints at possible conflict when readers understand that the grandfather is referring to poet Robert Burns's first real love. It is interesting to identify such allusions in historical fiction.

HISTORICAL AUTHENTICITY

In a review of the attitudes expressed by authors of historical fiction, Lawrence R. Sipe (1997) states, "The issue that receives the most attention from au-

thors of historical fiction is how to write authentically" (p. 246). This concern for authenticity emphasizes the use of language; the depiction of the details of everyday life; the faithfulness to the historical record; and the need for readers to perceive that the language, situations, and characters are "true."

The need for authentic historical detail places special demands on authors of historical fiction. Some authors actually lived through the experiences that they write about or knew someone who lived through them. Other authors write about historical periods far removed from their personal experiences. To gather their data, they must rely on sources of information far different from the people who remember vividly a historical period. Diane Stanley (1994) emphasizes that authors of historical fiction must set high standards in the hope of coming close to the truth.

Laura Ingalls Wilder, the author of the "Little House" books, lived in the big woods of Wisconsin, traveled by covered wagon through Kansas, lived in a sod house in Minnesota, and shared her life with Pa, Ma, Mary, and Carrie when they finally settled in South Dakota. Wilder's books sound as if they were written immediately after an incident occurred, but Wilder actually wrote the stories describing her life from 1870 through 1889 much later, between 1926 and 1943. Authors who write about their own past experiences need to have both keen powers of observation and excellent memories in order to share the details of their lives with others.

Predominantly happy experiences in the past may be easy to remember. For authors who write about painful experiences in their own lives, however, the doors of memory may be more difficult to open. Johanna Reiss found herself remembering things that she had preferred to forget when she began writing the story of her experiences as a Jewish child hidden by Dutch gentiles during the Holocaust and World War II. According to the publishers of *The Upstairs Room,* Reiss (1972) "did not set out to write a book about her experiences during the Second World War; she simply wanted to record them for her two daughters, who are now about the age she was when she went to stay with the Oastervelds" (p. 197). When Reiss started to write, she began remembering experiences that she had never talked about with anyone because they were too painful. To reinforce her memory, she took her children back to Usselo, Holland, where she visited the Dutch family who had protected her and looked again at the upstairs room and the closet in which she had hidden from the Nazis.

Authors such as Carol Ryrie Brink write about relatives' experiences. In *Caddie Woodlawn,* Brink recreates the story of her grandmother and her grandmother's family. In her author's note to the book, Brink (1973) tells how she lived with her grandmother and loved to listen to her tell stories about her pioneer childhood:

It was many years later that I remembered those stories of Caddie's childhood, and I said to myself, "If I loved them so much perhaps other children would like them too." Caddie was still alive when I was writing, and I sent letters to her, asking about the details that I did not remember clearly. She was pleased when the book was done. "There is only one thing that I do not understand," she said. "You never knew my mother and father and my brothers—how could you write about them exactly as they were?" "But, Gram," I said, "You told me." (p. 283)

Uri Orlev based his World War II story *The Man from the Other Side* on the memories of a journalist who as a child had lived on the outskirts of the Warsaw Ghetto and had helped his father provide assistance for the Jewish people in the ghetto. Consequently, the setting and the conflict seem very believable.

Of course, modern authors have no first-hand experience of some earlier times and cannot even talk to someone who lived during certain historical periods, so they must use other resources in researching their chosen time periods. Hester Burton (1973), a well-known writer of historical fiction with British settings, says:

Ideally I should be so knowledgeable that I have no need to turn to a book of reference once I have actually started writing the book. I should be able to see clearly in my mind's eye the houses in which my characters live, the clothes they wear, and the cars and carriages and ships in which they travel. I should know what food they eat, what songs they sing when they are happy, and what are the sights and smells they are likely to meet when they walk down the street. I must understand their religion, their political hopes, their trades and—what is most important—the relationships between different members of a family common to their particular generation. (p. 299)

To acquire this much knowledge about a time period demands much research. Some authors have chosen to research and write about one period; others have written books covering many different time periods. Rosemary Sutcliff has written several outstanding books of historical fiction, and John Townsend (1974) says that in the area of serious historical novels, Sutcliff stands above the rest. Sutcliff reveals her thorough knowledge of certain historical periods in both the stories themselves and her introductions to them. In the introduction to *Song for a Dark Queen,* for example, Sutcliff outlines the historical events that influence the incidents in the book, describes how the plot arose out of her reading certain scholarly works about the culture of the period, and then lists the sources that provided background information for the story.

Kathryn Lasky reveals the influence of extensive research in her author's note for *Beyond the Divide.* Lasky says that she based the book in part on Theodora Kroeber's biography of the last Yahi Indian, *Ishi: The Last of His Tribe,* and in part on J. Goldsborough Bruff's journal that describes his own experiences during the gold rush. Lasky (1983) describes her own discoveries about the West:

Mrs. Kroeber's story was the first true western tale I had ever read. This was not the West of television, nor was the gold rush the one written about in my school books. The bad guys were worse than I had ever imagined, and the greed for gold was pernicious and deadly to the human spirit. People did not just rob, they killed, and on occasion massacred. The conditions of survival were the most arduous imaginable, but there was one emigrant whose spirit was left miraculously intact. (p. 253)

These discoveries, characterizations, settings, and themes are apparent in her historical novel.

Lois Lowry based *Number the Stars* on the experiences of the Danish Resistance. Lowry reveals that she was determined to tell the story of the Danish people and the Danish Resistance after seeing a photograph of Kim Malthe-Bruun and reading about his helping Jewish residents of Denmark. The Nazis captured and executed this resistance leader when he was only twenty-one.

Reading about any of the well-known authors of historical fiction whose books are noted for authentic backgrounds reveals that the authors first spend hundreds of hours researching county courthouse records and old letters, newspapers, and history books; conducting personal interviews; and visiting museums and historical locations. Authors must then write stories that develop believable plots, characters, and settings without sounding like history textbooks. In doing so, they must carefully consider the many conflicting points of view that surround particular events. Writing excellent historical fiction is a very demanding task.

A CHRONOLOGY OF HISTORICAL FICTION

In sharing historical fiction with children, you must understand at least some of the history of a time period in order to evaluate stories reflecting that period. Following a three-year study, my own research (Norton, 1980) found that the understanding, evaluation, and utilization of historical fiction of students in children's literature courses improved if the students discussed books of historical fiction in a chronological order, briefly identified the actual historical happenings in each time period, identified major themes in literature written about a specific period (although, of course, some books have more than one theme), discussed the implications of recurring themes, identified how authors develop believable plots for a time period, and discussed the modern significance of the literature. To assist in the study of historical fiction, this chapter discusses books of historical fiction in an order similar to the one used during Norton's study. Ideally, this framework will assist you as you discuss the literature in children's literature classes and undertake individual studies of historical fiction for children. Chart 10–1 presents a simple chronology of Western and North American history and the main themes developed in books in each period.

Ancient Times Through the Middle Ages

Western culture began over five thousand years ago in the ancient Sumerian and Egyptian societies of the Middle Eastern "cradle of civilization." Absolute rulers directed vast numbers of slaves in constructing temples and pyramids in honor of themselves and their gods. In 332 B.C., Alexander the Great conquered most of the Middle East. Two hundred years later, the great military might of the Romans created an empire that eventually surrounded the Mediterranean Sea and covered most of Europe for hundreds of years. As the Roman Empire became larger, encompassing many different cultures and geographical areas, Roman rule became harsher and harsher.

In pre-Roman times, various Celtic peoples, including the Britons and Gaels, inhabited the British Isles. These people lived in tribes ruled by chiefs and often warred with one another over land and people. In 55 B.C., Julius Caesar failed in an attempt to add present-day England and Scotland to the Roman Empire. One hundred years later, Emperor Claudius succeeded in annexing Britain. Roman legions were left behind to subdue the people and to keep peace among the tribes.

The Roman dominance lasted throughout Europe until about A.D. 410, when fierce tribes of Teutonic peoples from northern Europe invaded and sacked Rome, beginning the long medieval period in European history that has sometimes been called the Dark Ages. In their great ships, Vikings from Norway were led by people such as Eric the Red. The Vikings raided the coasts of Europe and demonstrated their remarkable seafaring skills by exploring Greenland and Iceland. In about A.D. 1000, Norse explorers under Leif Ericson's command crossed the Atlantic Ocean and stayed briefly in a place in North America they called "Vinland."

Teutonic Saxons and Angles from the continent invaded and settled Britain. The once-unified Roman empire dissolved into many small domains ruled by competing feudal lords and the warrior nobility that served them in ongoing battles. The lords lived in fortified castles surrounded by cottages and fields in which enslaved peasants produced food and wealth for them. Constant warfare and rampant disease, such as the plague (also known as the Black Death), ravaged the developing towns of England, France, and elsewhere. The strong Christian beliefs of the Middle Ages led to the construction of magnificent cathedrals and to crusades in which Christian warriors attempted to capture Jerusalem for the Roman Catholic Church, which still survived in splendor and power after the fall of Rome.

Authors who write historical fiction about the ancient world and medieval times in Europe often tell their stories from the viewpoint of slaves or other people subjugated by the powerful. Other authors represent the perspectives of the mighty, such as Romans and Vikings, and show the ways in which all people have certain desires and fears in common and confront similar problems. Through these various perspectives, authors of historical fiction for children encourage young readers to imagine and empathize with the personal and social conflicts of

CHART 10–1   Eras and themes in historical fiction

Date	Period	Themes
3000 B.C.	Ancient times through the Middle Ages	Loyalty is one of the noblest human traits. Ignorance, prejudice, and hatred can have destructive consequences for all concerned. Hatred, not people, is the great enemy. Love is stronger than hatred and prevails through times of great trouble. People will always search for freedom and riches. Courage is more important than physical strength. A physical disability does not reduce a person's humanity. People can overcome their handicaps.
A.D. 1492	Changes in the Old World and discovery of the New World	Greed is a strong motivational force and can have destructive consequences. Moral dilemmas must be faced and resolved. People will face severe hardships to acquire the political and religious freedom that they desire. People must work together if they are to survive. Overcoming problems can strengthen character. War creates tragedy. Life is more than physical survival. Land is important: People will endure numerous hardships to acquire land for personal reasons or for the glory of their country.
1692	The Salem witch-hunts	Prejudiced persecution of others is a frightening and destructive social phenomenon. People seek freedom from persecution. Moral obligations require some people to defend the rights of others.
1776	The American Revolution	Freedom is worth fighting for. Strong beliefs require strong commitments.
1780	Early expansion of the United States and Canada	Friendship and faith are important. People long for their own land and the freedom that ownership implies. People will withstand great hardships to retain their dreams. Strong family bonds help physical and spiritual survival. Prejudice and hatred are destructive forces. The greatest strength comes from within. Moral obligations require personal commitment.

people in the distant past. Themes emerge as the characters fight for their beliefs and personal freedoms, follow their dreams, struggle with moral dilemmas, or overcome prejudices or self-doubts that could destroy them.

In *The Bronze Bow*, Elizabeth George Speare focuses upon Israel during Roman rule. She portrays the harshness of the Roman conquerors by telling the story through the eyes of a boy who longs to avenge the death of his parents. (His father was crucified by

CHART 10–1 *Continued*

Date	Period	Themes
1861	The Civil War	War creates tragedy. Moral obligations must be met even if one's life or freedom is in jeopardy. Moral sense does not depend on skin color, but on what is inside a person. People should take pride in themselves and their accomplishments. Prejudice and hatred are destructive forces. People search for freedom. Personal conscience may not allow some people to kill others. Strong family ties help people persevere.
1860s	The western frontier	People have moral obligations. People have strong dreams of owning land. Families can survive if they work together. People need each other and may work together for their mutual good. Battles can be won through legal means rather than through unlawful actions. Hatred and prejudice are destructive forces. Without spiritual hope, people may lose their will to live.
1900	The early twentieth century	People will strive for survival of the physical body and the spirit. Prejudice and discrimination are destructive forces. There is a bond between people who experience injustice. Monetary wealth does not create a rich life.
1939	World War II	People will seek freedom from religious and political persecution. Prejudice and hatred are destructive forces. Moral obligation and personal conscience are strong forces. Freedom is worth fighting for. Family love and loyalty help people endure catastrophic experiences.

Roman soldiers, and his mother died from grief and exposure.) Daniel bar Jamin's bitterness intensifies when he joins a guerrilla band and nurtures his hatred of the Romans. His person-against-self conflict comes to a turning point when he almost sacrifices his sister because of his hatred. Speare encourages readers to understand Daniel's real enemy. When Daniel talks to Jesus, both Daniel and readers realize

that hatred, not Romans, is the enemy. In fact, the only thing stronger than hatred is love. Speare shows the magnitude of Daniel's change when he invites a Roman soldier into his home at the close of the story.

Rosemary Sutcliff uses a real British mystery twenty centuries old as the basis for her historical novel *Sun Horse, Moon Horse.* The magical Uffington White Horse has raced across the Berkshire Downs in England for over two thousand years. What force, in approximately 100 B.C., motivated the carving of this beautiful animal into the hillside? What sculptor could create an earthen horse alive with movement and power? Sutcliff's novel about the Iceni, a tribe of early Britons before the Roman invasion, presents her version of how this horse, still visible today, came to be carved into the high downs.

Sutcliff's theme, that people will search for freedom, is developed through a comparison of the peaceful existence of the Iceni before their capture to the time of their subjugation by another tribe covetous of the Iceni's land and horses. An Iceni boy's desire for freedom for his people, combined with his artistic talent, gives the tribe their chance for liberation. The boy agrees to complete the carving of the conquering tribe's sun-horse symbol if, after he has completed the carving, his people can go free. He does not carve only the symbol of his enemies, however; he also carves the moon horse, symbol of his own tribe. His final actions express the depth of his tribal loyalty, desire for his tribe's freedom, and belief in the symbolism of the moon horse: Upon completion of the moon-horse carving, he asks that his own life be sacrificed upon the horse to give it necessary life and strength. Sutcliff reaffirms the tribe's loyalty to and admiration for the boy through the feelings expressed by the new leader:

Heart-brother . . . wait for me in the Land of Apple Trees. Whether it be tomorrow, or when I am Lord of many spears in the north, and too old to sit a horse or lift a sword, wait for me until I come. And do not be forgetting me, for I will not forget you. (p. 106)

The Iceni tribe's futile effort to stem the tide of Roman conquest is the subject of Sutcliff's *Song for a Dark Queen*. The year is A.D. 62, over 150 years after the Iceni left the Berkshire Downs in search of new horse runs. The leading character is a queen rather than a male chieftain. (The Iceni leadership did not go from father to son, but down the "moonside," from mother to daughters.) Through descriptions of the queen's early training and her reactions when her tribe is conquered by the Romans, Sutcliff shows the basis for the Iceni's belief in their strong female leader. She has been trained from early childhood to lead men in battle, and she heads a revolt that almost succeeds in overpowering the Roman rule and defending the ancient tribal culture. Her efforts fail, however. The Romans overpower the Iceni and place them firmly under Roman dom-

inance. Sutcliff emphasizes the theme that freedom is important to the Iceni by describing how the queen decides to sacrifice her life rather than to be a captive. In books about the Roman legions, such as *Frontier Wolf* and *The Lantern Bearers*, Sutcliff develops believable characters, whose desires and actions express such timeless themes as loyalty, honor, desire for freedom, and self-sacrifice.

Authors who write about the Viking period develop both honorable heroes who strive for human freedom and evil men who kill and enslave. Vivid descriptions are important for these characterizations. Sutcliff's description of the approaching Vikings is especially effective in *Blood Feud* because she tells the story from the viewpoint of Jestyn, an English boy who believes terrible stories about the Vikings:

The men who stood there glancing me over were the true Viking kind that I had heard of in stories and been told to pray God I might never see in life. Men with grey ring-mail strengthening their leather byrnies, iron-bound war-caps, long straight swords. One had a silver arm-ring, one had studs of coral in the clasp of his belt, one wore a rough wolf-skin cloak. (p. 14)

Sutcliff's vivid descriptions help readers understand Jestyn's reactions to being purchased for six gold pieces and a wolf skin and to wearing the hated thrall ring of a slave. When Jestyn concludes that his master is a good man, readers are encouraged to believe in his worth. The remainder of the book stresses the themes of honor toward parents and loyalty between friends as the Viking and his now-loyal friend search for the murderer of the Viking's father.

While the Vikings were roaming the seas, knights in armor all across Europe were challenging one another over land and power, and humble people were working in the fields of nobles or serving the mighty in the great halls of castles. In *The Door in the Wall*, Marguerite DeAngeli uses an English castle and its surroundings as the settings for her story about ten-year-old Robin, who is expected to train for knighthood. The plot has an unusual twist when Robin is stricken with a mysterious ailment that paralyzes his legs. The door in the title of the story becomes symbolic. A monk gives unhappy Robin difficult advice: "Thou hast only to follow the wall far enough and there will be a door in it" (p. 16).

This symbol is very important in the story. DeAngeli traces Robin's search for his own door and the preparation necessary to find it. The monk helps Robin by guiding his learning, encouraging him to carve and to read, and expressing the belief that Robin's hands and mind, if not his legs, must be taught because they represent other doors in the wall. Robin worries that as a person who walks with crutches, he will be useless as a knight. His father's friend Sir Peter reassures him by saying that if a person cannot serve in one way, another means of serving will present itself. Sir Peter is proven correct when Welsh forces attack the castle. Robin proves his worth to himself and the castle by escaping the enemy sentry and obtaining help from the neighboring castle.

DeAngeli encourages readers to understand the importance of accepting people for what they are, rather than rejecting them because of physical disability, when Robin's father congratulates him: "The courage you have shown, the craftsmanship proven by the harp, and the spirit in your singing all make so bright a light that I cannot see whether or not your legs are misshapen" (p. 120).

Many children enjoy this beautiful story about a child who finds a door in his wall. One girl said that it was her favorite book because she liked the way in which Robin overcame his problem and was happy with his life. The theme is especially appropriate for teaching positive attitudes about individuals with disabilities.

Elizabeth Alder's *The King's Shadow*, set in Saxon England prior to the Battle of Hastings in 1066, has two strong themes that are characteristic of literature set in the Middle Ages: Loyalty is one of the noblest human traits, and physical disability does not reduce a person's humanity. Both themes are developed as a Welsh boy named Evyn first experiences violence at the murder of his father and then has his tongue cut off by his father's murderers. Even though he is now speechless and sold into slavery, he eventually comes under the control and guidance of an honorable lady who begins to see his worth and sends him to an abbey where he eventually learns to read and write. Evyn discovers the importance of loyalty when he becomes squire to Harold Godwinson, England's last Saxon king. As Evyn rides at Harold's side, he learns the importance of both the loyalty to England expressed by Harold and his own growing loyalty to a man who Evyn believes is one of the most noble of men. During his experience, Evyn discovers that his physical disability does

not reduce his own humanity or value. Alder brings additional authenticity to her retelling of the time period through the inclusion of excerpts from *The Anglo Saxon Chronicle* and legends such as "The Song of Roland" and "Beowulf."

Two books by Karen Cushman have settings in medieval England in the thirteenth and fourteenth centuries. Interesting comparisons may be made among characteristics of the social levels, characterizations of the two different heroines, conflicts developed, and themes portrayed in *Catherine, Called Birdy,* and *The Midwife's Apprentice*. For example, readers may compare the social structure associated with a medieval English manor and the knight's family in *Catherine, Called Birdy* with the lowest level of poverty described in *The Midwife's Apprentice*. In the latter book, Cushman leaves no doubt about this lowly social level when she introduces both the setting and the heroine, Brat: "When animal droppings and garbage and spoiled straw are piled up in a great heap, the rotting and molding give forth heat. Usually no one gets close enough to notice because of the stench. But the girl noticed and, on that frosty night, burrowed deep into the warm, rotting muck, heedless of the smell. In any event, the dung heap probably smelled little worse than everything else in her life—the food scraps scavenged from kitchen yards, the stables and sties she slept in when she could, and her own unwashed, unnourished, unloved, and unlovely body" (p. 1).

Although the positions of Cushman's two heroines are very different, there are similarities between the two characters. Both Catherine and Brat are strong-willed females who must face conflicts caused by the social structure in order to succeed. There is Catherine's desire for independence and an adventurous life versus society's requirements for females and her father's desire to marry his daughter to a wealthy suitor. There is Brat's need to rise above the ignorance and superstition surrounding her and the antagonism of the village midwife in order to gain the skills and self-respect she needs to succeed.

There are also similarities in themes between Cushman's two books. In both books the heroines discover, through their own actions, that the world is full of possibilities. But in order to realize these possibilities, they must continue trying. Brat, now Alyce, states this very well when she declares, "' Jane Sharp! It is I, Alyce, your apprentice. I have come back. And if you do not let me in, I will try again and again. I can do what you tell me and take what you give me, and I know how to try and risk and fail and try again and not give up. I will not go away.' The door opened. Alyce went in. And the cat went with her" (pp. 116–117). This symbol of going through the door could be compared with DeAngeli's *The Door in the Wall* in which she traces a crippled boy's life as he searches for his own door and the preparation necessary to find it.

Books set in feudal Japan relate to the theme of overcoming racial and cultural conflict. Erik Christian Haugaard's *The Boy and the Samurai* is set in feudal Japan during the period of civil wars in the late 1400s and 1500s. As do the authors of many other stories with war-time settings, Haugaard emphasizes the search for peace and the painful realities resulting from war. Haugaard's settings and characters allow readers to visualize the world of street orphans, warlords, samurais, and priests.

The following themes are expressed in historical fiction about ancient and medieval times. Consider how these themes relate to specific happenings in the time periods. Are any of these themes significant in our modern world?

1. Loyalty is one of the noblest human traits.
2. Ignorance, prejudice, and hatred can have destructive consequences for all concerned.
3. Hatred, not people, is the great enemy.
4. Love is stronger than hatred and prevails through times of great trouble.
5. People will always search for freedom and riches.
6. Courage is more important than physical strength.
7. A physical disability does not reduce a person's humanity.
8. People can overcome their handicaps.

Changes in the Old World and Encounters with the New World

By the fifteenth century, Europe had entered the Renaissance, a time of cultural rebirth and great social change. Large cities were bustling with trade, and middle-class merchants had attained more social prominence. Protestant Christianity was arising out of medieval Catholicism and challenging the religious and political power of the established church. In Germany, Johann Gutenberg was inventing the printing press, which William Caxton soon used to publish the first printed books in England. Great

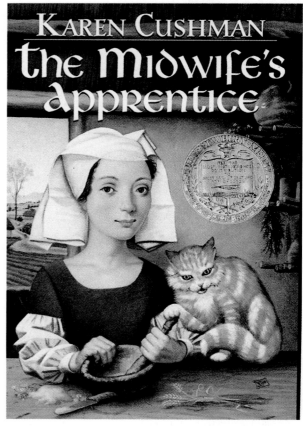

A book set in medieval England emphasizes the need to overcome person-versus-society and person-versus-self conflicts. (From The Midwife's Apprentice, *by Karen Cushman, text copyright © 1995, Clarion Books. Used by permission of E. P. Dutton, Inc.*)

artists such as Michelangelo and William Shakespeare began to raise the visual arts and literature to new heights of creative glory, inspired by the rediscovery of ancient Greek and Roman culture. Ordinary people were expecting and demanding greater economic, political, and religious freedom. Explorers were sailing off to prove their belief that the world was round and then to acquire great riches in the New World, a land that was inhabited by native peoples in the Western Hemisphere.

The arrival of Christopher Columbus on a Caribbean island in 1492 was soon followed by conquest of ancient Mayan and Aztec cultures in Central America by Spanish explorers. By the late sixteenth and the early seventeenth centuries, colonies were springing up along the Atlantic coast of North America. People followed their lust for wealth and adven-

The main character in Michael Dorris's Sees Behind Trees encounters "strangers" for the first time. (From Sees Behind Trees by Michael Dorris, text copyright © 1996. Reprinted by permission of Hyperion Books for Children.)

by the Spanish, and details describing trade between the explorers and the Taino people. Information provided in the author's notes indicate how disastrous this encounter was for the Taino people, who went from a population of 300,000 at the time of Columbus's landing to 500 only fifty years later. The book develops the theme that interaction with people who do not understand or respect your culture can have terrible consequences. As a result of this encounter, the Taino people lost their language, religion, and culture.

In *Morning Girl,* Michael Dorris writes from the perspective of Morning Girl and Star Boy, two Taino children who live on a Bahamian island at the time of Columbus's landing. By developing strong characters and detailing the settings, Dorris encourages readers to understand the nature of the Taino people and their culture. Unlike Yolen, Dorris concludes his book at the time of the first sighting of the Spanish sailors. Dorris includes an epilogue that quotes Columbus's journal on October 11, 1492, the day he first encounters the Taino people. Dorris's *Sees Behind Trees* is set in sixteenth-century America. The main character sees "strangers" for the first time and proves himself as he accompanies a village elder on a pilgrimage to find the land of the water.

Person-against-self conflicts, settings that depict Mayan and Aztec cultures, and themes that illustrate the consequences of greed are found in Scott O'Dell's historical novels based on the Spanish conquest of Mexico in the early 1500s. O'Dell's *The Captive, The Feathered Serpent,* and *The Amethyst Ring* focus not so much on the events of the time as on the moral dilemmas that a young priest faces in the New World.

A young, idealistic Jesuit seminarian, Julián Escobar, leaves his secure home in Spain and joins an expedition to Central America, inspired by the prospect of saving the souls of native peoples in New Spain. During the long voyage across the Atlantic, he begins to realize that the Spanish grandee leading the expedition actually intends to exploit and enslave the Maya and the Aztecs, rather than convert them to Christianity.

Later, Julián questions whether he has the spirit or the patience to spread the Christian faith within cultures so different from his own. O'Dell explores changes in Julián by stressing the changing conflicts in Julián's life: Should he take on the role of the mythical Kukulcán in order to save his life and make

ture or their desire for freedom from the religious persecution and political conflicts that were occurring in England and elsewhere.

Several books published in 1992, the five hundredth anniversary of Columbus's voyage, present the landing of Columbus from the viewpoint of the native peoples. Jane Yolen's picture storybook *Encounter* develops a hypothetical interaction between a Taino Indian boy and Columbus and his men on the island of San Salvador in 1492. The text is developed on the premise that dreams forewarn the boy about the disastrous consequences of interacting with the explorers, whom the people believe have flown down from the sky. Yolen includes descriptions of the Taino Indians and their beliefs, details about the loss of culture and human life that resulted because of the exploration and colonization

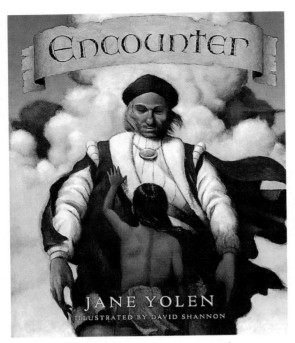

This text emphasizes the possible interaction between a Taino Indian boy and Columbus. (Illustration from Encounter by Jane Yolen, copyright © 1992 by David Shannon. Reproduced by permission of Harcourt Brace & Company.)

his views palatable to people with their own ancient beliefs? Should he advise attacking a neighboring city before his own Mayan city is attacked? How should he respond to the Mayan rites of sun worship? Why does God permit both good and evil? Julián's defense of his inability to change the Maya and of his own eventual grasping for power demonstrate changes in his character. In *The Feathered Serpent,* for example, Julián thinks back to Augustine's teachings and concludes that evil exists because God wills it. Therefore, idol worship and human sacrifice are beyond his control. Julián does admit, however, that this argument may be only a defense of his own actions.

O'Dell's descriptions of Mayan and Aztec cities and temples and other aspects of the cultures encourage readers to understand that an advanced civilization inhabited the Americas long before European exploration and settlement. Readers may also ponder the right of one culture to destroy another culture whose citizens worship different gods and possess riches desired by a foreign power.

In 1620, the *Mayflower* brought the first group of settlers to New England. The Pilgrims made no easy conquest of the wilderness. Their sponsors in England did not provide enough supplies, their first winter was filled with sickness and starvation, and the new settlers were apprehensive about the native peoples who lived beyond their settlement.

Authors who write about the settlement of Plymouth colony often look at the reasons for leaving England and the hardships faced by the Pilgrims. In *Constance: A Story of Early Plymouth,* for example, Patricia Clapp tells about the early settlement of New England from the viewpoint of a fourteen-year-old girl. Because Constance did not want to leave her cherished London, her first view of the new world from the deck of the *Mayflower* is an unpleasant one. Clapp encourages readers to understand the various viewpoints of the Pilgrims by contrasting Constance's view of a bleak and unfriendly land with the excitement and anticipation expressed by her father, William Bradford, John Alden, and Miles Standish.

Arnold Lobel's *On the Day Peter Stuyvesant Sailed into Town,* a picture storybook for young children, humorously brings the colonial setting of New Amsterdam to life. When Stuyvesant arrived on the shores of present-day New York in 1647, he found a town near collapse. The streets were reverting to weeds and were littered with garbage, animals ran freely, houses were falling into disrepair, and the walls of the fort were crumbling. Stuyvesant considered this abominable and quickly told the settlers to improve their town. He was so successful that within the next ten years the town doubled in size and became as neat as any Dutch community in Europe. The pictures in this book help children visualize the sailing ships, colonial dress and homes, and Dutch windmills.

While early colonists in North America were struggling to survive, ominous clouds were gathering over England. Conflict between Catholic King Charles I and the staunchly Protestant Parliament led to war in 1642. Authors who place their stories in England during this time frequently develop the theme that war is tragic and explore the influences that shape an awareness of the reality of war.

One of the strongest leaders to emerge during the English Civil War was Oliver Cromwell, an ordinary man but a great military organizer. In Erik Christian Haugaard's *Cromwell's Boy,* a thirteen-year-old boy

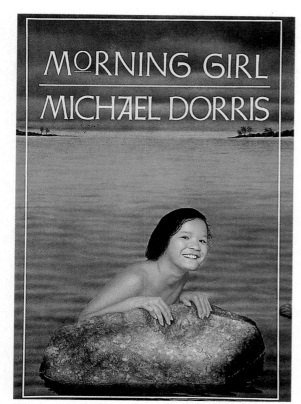

This text presents the perspective of two Taino Indian children. (From Morning Girl *by Michael Dorris, published by Hyperion Books for Children. Copyright © 1992 by Michael Dorris. Reprinted by permission of Hyperion/Disney, NY.)*

change in Europe and about early European settlement of the Western Hemisphere. Why and how are they related to specific happenings in the time periods? Do these themes have relevance in other periods of history? Do they have relevance for us today?

1. Greed is a strong motivational force and can have destructive consequences.
2. Moral dilemmas must be faced and resolved.
3. People will face severe hardships to acquire the political and religious freedom that they desire.
4. People must work together if they are to survive.
5. Overcoming problems can strengthen character.
6. War creates tragedy.
7. Life is more than physical survival.
8. Land is important: People will endure numerous hardships to acquire land for personal reasons or for the glory of their country.

The Salem Witch-Hunts

Belief in witchcraft was common in medieval Europe. Thousands of religious and political nonconformists, independent thinkers and artists, mentally ill persons, and other unusual people seemed to threaten the established social order. Such people were accused of witchcraft and were burned at the stake. Belief in witchcraft continued even in the relatively more enlightened sixteenth and seventeenth centuries and crossed the Atlantic with the first settlers of North America.

In the new England colonies of the late 1600s, strict Puritan religious beliefs governed every aspect of social life. Any kind of nonconformity was viewed as the work of the devil. The famous witch-hunts of 1692 in Salem, Massachusetts, began when a doctor stated that the hysterical behavior of several teenage girls was due to the "evil eye." Within six months, twenty persons had been sentenced to death and one hundred and fifty had been sent to prison.

Boston minister Cotton Mather was one of those who preached the power of the devil and the need to purge the world of witchcraft. People charged with witchcraft were pardoned in 1693 when Sir William Phipps, royal governor of the Massachusetts Bay Colony, said that the witch-hunt proceedings were too violent and not based upon fact. Belief in witchcraft faded in the 1700s as new scientific knowledge began to explain previously frightening phenomena.

The conflict in stories set in this short period of American history is usually person-against-society.

discovers the tragic reality of war. The boy, also named Oliver, rides a horse well, does not divulge secrets, and looks inconspicuous. His ability to serve Cromwell extends beyond messages. Oliver goes into the dangerous stronghold of the king's army as a spy. Haugaard suggests the lessons that Oliver has learned, using a flashback in which Oliver remembers his youthful experiences:

In my youth there was little time for dreams. Life challenged me early. The leisure to reflect was not my lot; tomorrow was ever knocking on the door of today with new demands. It made me resourceful and sharpened my wit, but the purpose of life must be more than just to survive. You must be able—at least for short moments—to hold your precious soul in your hands and to contemplate that gift with love and understanding. (p. 1)

Consider the following themes developed in historical fiction about the age of cultural and social

Authors often place their characters in a hostile environment, where their usual behaviors create suspicion. For example, is a person a witch because he or she brews tea from herbs to give to the ill? Does spinning thread faster and better prove that a person is a witch? Does speaking to a cat indicate witchcraft? These are the charges that face the protagonist in Ann Petry's *Tituba of Salem Village.*

Contrasts in setting suggest the drama that follows. Petry describes two slaves who are living in comparative freedom by a sparkling sea on the coral-encrusted coastline of Barbados. Tituba and her husband lose their fairly permissive owner in Barbados and in his place acquire a solemn, dark-clothed minister from Boston. The setting changes rapidly from the tropical home to a dark ship that is taking the slaves to New England.

Petry completes the change in setting when she describes the minister's house in Salem. Rotten eggs on the doorstep of the gloomy, neglected building greet Reverend Parris, his family, and the two slaves to their new home. Soon, people in the town are muttering threats, teenage girls are becoming hysterical, and townspeople are testifying that Tituba can transform herself into a wolf or travel without her body. Tituba's crime is not witchcraft. Instead, she is not only a strange black person in a predominantly white community but also a more capable and intelligent person than many of the people around her.

This book develops insights into the consequences of inhumanity, regardless of time or place. Readers are encouraged to see and feel danger in mass accusations and a fear in people to defend what they know is right. Compare Petry's characterization and plot development with Patricia Clapp's in *Witches' Children: A Story of Salem,* which relates the Salem experience through the eyes of a bound girl.

The free white protagonist in Elizabeth George Speare's *The Witch of Blackbird Pond* comes from Barbados, but Kit's life is quite different from Tituba's. Contrasts between the people in Kit's early childhood environment and the people in New England encourage readers to anticipate the conflict. On Barbados, Kit was raised by a loving grandfather, who encouraged her to read history, poetry, and plays.

After the death of her grandfather, Kit travels to New England to live with her aunt. Several experiences on the ship suggest that her former life-style will not be appropriate for her new world. For ex-

ample, when Kit tries to discuss Shakespeare with a fellow passenger, he is shocked because a girl should not read such things: "The proper use of reading is to improve our sinful nature, and to fill our minds with God's holy word" (p. 28). An even harsher response occurs after she jumps into a harbor and swims to rescue a child's doll. (The Puritans believe that only guilty people are able to stay afloat.)

When Kit's behavior in the Puritan village remains consistent with her earlier behavior, she raises the suspicions of the townspeople. When sickness breaks out in the town, the people believe that they are bewitched and blame Hannah, a Quaker believed to be a witch. Kit risks her life to warn her friend, and they escape before Hannah's cottage is burned by angry men.

Kit's action incurs the wrath of the settlement, and she is arrested for witchcraft. The charges brought against her are similar to those brought against Tituba. Unlike Tituba, however, Kit has friends and family who stand by her and assist in her acquittal. She learns that it is important to choose one's friends and then to stand by them.

The protagonists in Petry's and Speare's books have courage, high spirits, and honor in trying circumstances. Both remain true to their beliefs, even when faced with hostility and superstition. They cry out against injustices around them. Because of their actions, a few people realize the consequences of blind fear and hatred.

Various attitudes of the times and conflicts caused by the social and religious beliefs of Puritan Boston create person-against-society conflicts in Paul Fleischman's *Saturnalia.* Fleischman's characters strive to survive in a society that is suspicious of knowledge, education, and books; mistrustful of Native Americans; and filled with prejudice. Fleischman develops many of the same themes found in the stories about the Salem witch-hunts.

Consider the following themes developed in historical fiction about the Salem witch-hunts. What consequences of inhumanity and persecution are developed in other time periods? What historical events coincide with such persecution?

1. Prejudiced persecution of others is a frightening and destructive social phenomenon.
2. People seek freedom from persecution.
3. Moral obligations require some people to defend the rights of others.

The American Revolution

The inhabitants of the thirteen American colonies founded by the British came from different countries and had differing sympathies and practices. They did, however, have several strong antagonisms in common. They shared a fear of the native peoples of North America; they went through a period when they shared a dread of French conquest; and they came to conflict with their ruler, the British crown. Although British subjects, the colonists had no elected representatives in the British Parliament that made decisions affecting their lives. For example, the colonists were allowed to buy tea, a popular beverage, only from the British East Indian Company, and Parliament levied a heavy tax on that tea. By the mid-eighteenth century, an accumulation of such injustices united colonists from New Hampshire to Georgia in opposition to their common oppressor across the Atlantic.

A series of demands made by the British government hastened the uniting of the colonies. In 1765, Britain tried to raise money by passing the Stamp Act, which placed a tax on all paper used in the colonies and declared all unstamped documents to be legally void. Then, the British demanded that British soldiers in the colonies be quartered by the colonists themselves. In 1773, when several British ships bearing tea arrived in Boston Harbor, the Bostonians would not accept the shipment. They refused to pay taxes without the right to vote for those who would represent them. Colonists disguised as Indians boarded the ships and dumped the tea into the harbor. The British Parliament responded by closing Boston Harbor, blocking it from trade. The sympathies of many colonists were in accord with the goal of independence from Great Britain.

Samuel Adams and others like him rallied the colonists in support of this cause. The Declaration of Independence and the long years of the Revolutionary War soon followed—an exciting time in American history. We are all familiar with the famous leaders of this period, but as Elizabeth Yates (1974) points out, many other Americans whose names we do not know played dynamic roles in creating a new nation:

Those who lived in small towns and villages and on distant farms, who thought and talked about events and made their feelings known: men who left their stock and crops and marched off to fight because they were convinced of the rightness of the stand that had been made, women who took over the work of the farms along with the care of their homes and families. Their names made no news. They did no particular acts of heroism, except as the living of each day was heroic in itself. Hard work they knew well, and hardship they could endure. Giving their lives or living their lives, they were as much the foundation of the new nation as were those whose names have long been known. (p. 6)

While famous people are found in the backgrounds of much historical fiction about the American Revolution that has been written for children, everyday people are the heroes of most of such books. In general, two types of stories are written about the revolutionary period: (1) tales about those who defend the home front while others go off to war and (2) tales about males and females who become actively involved in the war itself.

The best-known children's story about this period is Esther Forbes's *Johnny Tremain*. Forbes creates a superbly authentic setting. Paul Revere and Samuel Adams play important parts in the story, but a silversmith's apprentice named Johnny and other boys like him are the heroes. Through Johnny's observations, actions, and thoughts, Forbes emphasizes the issues of the times, the values of the people, and the feelings about freedom. Johnny discovers the political thinking of the time when he hears a minister preach sermons filled with anger against taxation without representation, delivers messages for the secret anti-British Boston Observers, and rides for the Boston Committee of Correspondence.

Forbes's writing style creates believable action and dialogue, as in this excerpt from a speech calling the rebels to action:

Friends! Brethren! Countrymen! That worst of Plagues, the detested tea shipped for this Port by the East Indian Company, is now arrived in the Harbour: the hour of destruction, of manly opposition to the machinations of Tyranny, stares you in the Face; Every Friend to his Country, to Himself, and to Posterity, is now called upon to meet. (p. 107)

Johnny is one of the "Indians" who throw the tea into Boston Harbor. He experiences the anger and resulting unity when British troops close the harbor. He is there when British troops and colonial rebels clash at Concord. Unhappily, he is also there when his best friend dies. He makes the discovery that a sixteen-year-old is considered a boy in times of peace but a man in times of war. As a man, he has the duty to risk his life for what he believes.

The People and the Past Come Alive 541

Consider the themes and the historical facts from this period. Why do you think the following themes are developed in the literature? How and why are these themes similar to or different from themes in stories about other wartime periods?

1. Freedom is worth fighting for.
2. Strong beliefs require strong commitments.

Early Expansion of the United States and Canada

As more and more settlers came to America, a need for additional land became evident. Many settlers headed away from the Atlantic coastline into the rolling, tree-covered hills to the west, north, and south. These settlers had something in common: With courage, they sought freedom and land. Some settlers developed friendly relationships with the Native Americans,* and others experienced hostilities. It was not uncommon for settlers to be captured by Indians and taken into their tribes, sold as slaves, or held for ransom. Many abductions, however, were in retaliation for settlers' attacks.

Stories about early pioneer expansion are popular with children, who enjoy vivid characters and rapid action. The young characters may be popular with children because they often show extraordinary courage and prove that they can be equal to adults. Many of the stories depict strong family bonds. Vivid descriptions of the new land encourage readers to understand why a family is willing to give up a secure environment to live on a raw and dangerous frontier. Person-against-nature conflicts often appear in these stories. Person-against-self conflicts occur when characters face moral dilemmas, such as racial prejudice.

Themes of friendship, faith, moral obligation, working together, and love for land are found in Elizabeth George Speare's *The Sign of the Beaver*. The Maine wilderness in the 1700s can be either an antagonist or a friend. Matt, the thirteen-year-old main character, faces a life-and-death struggle when his father leaves him alone to guard their frontier cabin through the

*This book primarily uses the term *Native Americans* to denote the people historically referred to as *American Indians*. The term *Indian* is sometimes used interchangeably with *Native American* and in some contexts is used to name certain tribes of Native Americans.

Survival and friendship are important in this story set in the 1700s. (From The Sign of the Beaver, *by Elizabeth George Speare. Copyright © 1983 by Elizabeth George Speare. Reprinted by permission of Dell Publishing Company.*)

winter. Without food or a gun, Matt confronts a harsh natural environment, fear of the local Indians, and the possibility that he may never see his parents again. In spite of conflicts about the ways in which white settlers are changing their land, a Penobscot boy befriends Matt and teaches him how to survive.

The frontier of understanding rather than the frontier of physical expansion is the setting for Carol Carrick's *Stay Away from Simon!* Attitudes toward and fears about a mentally retarded boy provide the conflict in this story set on Martha's Vineyard in the 1830s. Carrick creates believable fear and misunderstanding when two children, Lucy and Josiah, risk getting lost in a snowstorm to avoid walking on the road with Simon. Carrick then encourages readers to understand how ridiculous these fears are by developing Simon as a caring individual who leads the children to safety.

The need to believe in oneself and the importance of retaining and respecting one's own beliefs are themes developed in Janet Lunn's person-against-society and person-against-self conflicts set in Hawthorn Bay, Ontario. Lunn's *Shadow in Hawthorn Bay,* winner of the Canadian children's literature award, follows fifteen-year-old Mary Urquhart as she leaves her Scottish highlands on the shores of Loch Ness to try to find and help her cousin in Canada. As Mary tends sheep in Scotland, she hears her cousin Duncan calling her to come to him. She does not consider this unusual, even though Duncan is over three thousand miles away. Her actions and the belief of her Scottish family make her ability to see into the future believable. This same ability, referred to as second sight, causes her conflict when she interacts with a society that not only does not believe in her special powers but also fears and distrusts them.

Lunn develops a related person-against-self conflict as Mary fights her powers and the consequences of her visions. As part of this inner conflict, Mary must overcome her fear of going into the forest, her fear of the black water, and her belief that something evil is trapped in the bay. Mary overcomes her fears and gains the insight that she needs to believe in herself and her powers. With this realization, Lunn develops the theme of the book: It is important to keep your beliefs and ways.

Joan W. Blos's *A Gathering of Days: A New England Girl's Journal, 1830–32* is the fictional journal of a thirteen-year-old girl on a New Hampshire farm. Blos (1980) says that she tried to develop three types of truthfulness: "the social truthfulness of the situation, the psychological truthfulness of the characters, and the literary truthfulness of the manner of telling" (p. 371). Consequently, the characters are similar to those who stare from New England portraits. Likewise, the tone of the story is similar to that in *Leavitt's Almanac,* written for farmers, with the form and style found in journal writings of that period.

Both Elizabeth George Speare's *Calico Captive* and Lois Lenski's *Indian Captive: The Story of Mary Jemison* are stories about white girls captured by native tribespeople. Both girls face difficult conflicts and harsh circumstances, but their experiences eventually cause them to question their former prejudices. Speare's Miriam learns more about the Indians from Pierre, a *coureur des bois.* Mary Jemison, after much inner turmoil, finally decides that the Seneca are her people:

At that moment she saw Old Shagbark looking at her, his brown eyes overflowing with kindness and understanding. He knew how hard it was for her to decide. . . . She saw the Englishman, too. His lips were smiling, but his eyes of cold gray were hard. Even if she were able to put all her thoughts into words, she knew he would never, never understand. Better to live with those who understood her because they loved her so much, than with one who could never think with her, in sympathy, about anything. . . . Squirrel Woman's scowling face and even Gray Wolf's wicked one no longer held any terrors, because she understood them. (p. 268)

Books written from Native American viewpoints describe the harmful influences of an expanding white population. In *Sweetgrass,* a winner of the Canadian Library Association's Book of the Year Award, Jan Hudson focuses on the struggle for maturity of a young Blackfoot girl as she faces a life-and-death battle in 1837. Smallpox, the "white man's sickness," results in hunger and death. The themes in *Sweetgrass* are that it is important to honor moral obligation toward others and that it is important to retain one's dreams.

Hudson employs figurative language involving signs and omens that are meaningful to the characters and that reinforce themes related to retaining one's identity and meeting obligations toward family members. For example, the main character considers the importance of her name. She believes that it is appropriate because sweetgrass is "ordinary to look at but it's fragrant as the spring" (p. 12). Later, her grandmother tells her that sweetgrass has the power of memories. As Sweetgrass considers her future, readers discover that she is joyfully approaching womanhood. She says, "I felt mightier than a brave. . . . I felt I was holding the future like summer berries in my hands" (p. 26). Instead of allowing the signs and omens to control her life, Sweetgrass uses them to overcome taboos and to help her family in a time of great trouble. She decides, "I would make Father do what I wanted. I would find the signs, the power to control my own days. I would make my life be what I wanted" (p. 15).

The themes in books of historical fiction about the early expansion of the United States vary considerably. Consider the following themes. Why do you think that authors who write stories about this period chose them? How do these themes compare to themes found in different time periods? Are the themes significant today?

Reporting of history may change depending upon the viewpoint of an author. This is also true in the writing of historical fiction. Too many frontier books are told from the perspective of the white settlers rather than from the perspective of the Native Americans. In this context, some critics fear that children will not realize the hardships experienced by the Native Americans or the contributions that the Native Americans made. Stories from the perspective of the white settlers emphasize kidnappings of white children, attacks on wagon trains by warring tribes, the burning of white settlements, and rescues of settlers by soldiers. Many frontier heroes created their reputations as Indian fighters.

Some critics believe that historical fiction about the settlement of North America should include more stories told from the native perspective. These stories might include kidnappings of Native American children by white settlers or emphasize the reasons for the kidnappings of white children. The stories might portray the numerous peaceful tribes, who lived in harmony with settlers. They might emphasize the diversity of the Native American cultures. Students of children's literature should consider the viewpoints of authors and the consequences of unbalanced narratives of other time periods, including narratives about early explorers, the Roman invasion of Britain, religious freedom and the settlement of America, the Revolutionary War, the Civil War, and World War II.

Unbalanced viewpoints may be particularly harmful when presenting stories with a World War II Holocaust setting. Leslie Barban[1] emphasizes the importance of viewpoint in this literature when she states:

George Santayana once said, "Those who cannot remember the past are condemned to repeat it." This famous adage has proved itself to be true in many ways. Children's rooms in public libraries and school media centers across the nation house many important and memorable books not only about the Holocaust but about all types of racial prejudice. However, the Holocaust is often not discussed: many parents believe the subject will depress children, librarians often choose non-controversial titles for booktalking, and teachers often feel that it's too disturbing or inappropriate to discuss in the classroom. Furthermore, some children are being told that the Holocaust is folklore and that the mass murder of 11 million people never happened. History textbooks mention it, but any true deliberation on the subject seems too much to ask of children. Is it? (p. 25)

In addition to evaluating the balance in historical fiction and in literary discussions, you should encourage students to evaluate and authenticate the historical accuracy in historical fiction. According to the findings of a study in *The Nation's Report Card,*[2] fourth-, eighth-, and twelfth-grade students "have a limited grasp of U.S. history." In addition, the study calls for assignments that encourage "thoughtful analytical essays" (p. 4). Evaluating and authenticating the historical accuracy in historical fiction and historical biography encourage thoughtful analytical essays.

As you consider the issue of unbalanced viewpoints and accuracy in historical fiction and the findings of *The Nation's Report Card,* what do you think is the role of historical fiction? What viewpoints should be expressed by the authors of historical fiction? How could you develop a balanced viewpoint of a historical time period through the use of historical fiction?

---

[1]Barban, Leslie. "Remember to Never Forget." *Book Links* 2 (March 1993): 25–29.

[2]Knight-Ridder News Service. "Most Students Have Limited Grasp of History, Study Finds." Bryan, College Station: *Eagle* (April 3, 1990): 1–4.

1. Friendship and faith are important.
2. People long for their own land and the freedom that ownership implies.
3. People will withstand great hardships to retain their dreams.
4. Strong family bonds help physical and spiritual survival.
5. Prejudice and hatred are destructive forces.
6. The greatest strength comes from within.
7. Moral obligations require personal commitment.

The Civil War

In the early centuries of American history, white slave traders brought hundreds of thousands of black Africans to this continent in chains and sold

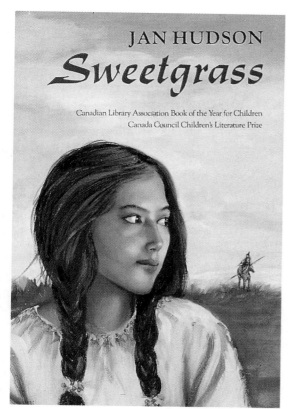

The language and setting reflect the Blackfoot culture. (From Sweetgrass *by Jan Hudson. Illustration copyright © 1989 by Jan Spivey Gilchrist. Reprinted by permission of Philomel Books, a division of Putnam & Grosset Group.)*

them on auction blocks as field workers, house servants, and skilled craftspeople. Many people in both the North and the South believed that slavery was immoral; therefore, unable to pass laws against it, they assisted slaves in their flight toward Canada and freedom.

Helping runaway slaves was a dangerous undertaking, especially after the passage of the Fugitive Slave Act in 1850 made it a crime. Handbills offering rewards for the return of certain slaves added to the danger by urging slave catchers to hunt for suspected runaways. Because of the dangers and the need for secrecy, an illicit network of people dedicated to assisting fugitive slaves linked the North and South. Free people led the fugitives from one safe hiding place to another on each part of their journey along the Underground Railroad to Canada.

Conflicts between northern and southern interests that had emerged during the Constitutional Convention increased in the 1850s and led to the outbreak of the Civil War in 1861. The United States was torn apart. In some cases, relatives were on opposite sides of the conflict and faced one another on the battlefields of Bull Run and Gettysburg.

Some authors examine slavery and the experiences of slaves during captivity or as fugitives seeking freedom. Other authors examine the impact of the Civil War on young soldiers or on the people who remained at home. Person-against-society and person-against-self conflicts are common in historical fiction covering this period. Some characters confront prejudice and hatred and others wrestle with their consciences and discover the tragedy associated with slavery and war. Authors who create credible plots consider not only the historical events but also the conflicting social attitudes of the times. The themes developed in this literature reflect a need for personal freedom, ponder the right of one person to own another, consider the tragedies of war, and question the killing of one human by another.

The attitudes expressed toward blacks create special problems for authors who write about slavery. How accurately should historical fiction reflect the attitudes and circumstances of the times? Should authors use terms of the period that are considered insensitive and offensive today? For example, in their authors' note to *Jump Ship to Freedom,* James and Christopher Collier consider use of the word *nigger.* Although the word is considered offensive today, would avoiding it in a novel about slavery distort history? The Colliers chose to use the term in order to illustrate their main character's change in attitude as he develops self-respect and self-confidence and to highlight the social attitudes of the other characters in the book.

In *Jump Ship to Freedom,* those who use the word *nigger* express racial bias toward blacks, and those who do not are concerned with the rights and self-respect of all humans. Consider, for example, how the slave Daniel uses the word. At first, he refers to himself as a nigger. He considers himself unintelligent, inferior to whites, and unable to think of himself as a person. He allows other people's opinions to reinforce these beliefs. Self-realization develops slowly. Daniel discovers that he can develop and carry out a plan to recover his father's confiscated funds and free himself, associate with people who

Fugitive slaves follow the Underground Railroad to freedom. (From The Drinking Gourd, *by F. N. Monjo. Pictures by Fred Brenner. An I CAN READ History Book. Pictures copyright © 1970 by Fred Brenner. Reprinted by permission of Harper & Row Publishers.)*

consider him capable and slavery immoral, meet his moral obligations to his mother, and fight for his rights. After he makes these personal discoveries, he refuses to call himself *nigger.*

A slave ship in which human cargo are chained together in cramped quarters provides the setting for Paula Fox's *The Slave Dancer.* The story is told from the point of view of a thirteen-year-old white boy from New Orleans who is kidnapped by slave traders to play his fife on their ship. When the ship reaches Africa, Jessie learns about the trade in human "Black Gold" and discovers that in their greed for trade goods, African chiefs sell their own people and people kidnapped from other tribes. For four long nights, longboats bring their cargoes to the slave ship: men and women who are half-conscious from the pressure of bodies and bruised by ankle shackles. The detailed descriptions of the conditions on the ship are believable. Jessie describes the holds as pits of misery, is horrified by the low regard for human life, and is shocked when prisoners who die are thrown overboard. Jessie learns the reason for having him aboard when slaves are dragged on deck and forced to dance. A dead or weak slave cannot be sold for profit, and the slave traders believe that dancing keeps their bodies strong.

This book has stirred much controversy. Some have criticized the fact that the slaves in the book are not treated like human beings or even given names. Many college students, however, say that while reading *The Slave Dancer,* they realized for the first time the true inhumanity of slavery. Fox reveals the impact of the experience on Jessie by flashing ahead in time to Jessie's memories:

At the first note of a tune or a song, I would see once again as though they'd never ceased their dancing in my mind, black men and women and children lifting their tormented limbs in time to a reedy martial air, the dust rising from their joyless thumping, the sound of the fife finally drowned beneath the clanging of their chains. (p. 176)

You may compare the descriptions in *The Slave Dancer* with Tom Feelings's illustrations in *The Middle Passage: White Ships/Black Cargo.*

A book written for young children explains the purposes of the Underground Railroad. F. N. Monjo's *The Drinking Gourd* tells of a family that is part of the Underground Railroad and the role of that family in helping a fugitive slave family escape. Even though this is an easy-to-read book, it illustrates the importance of one family's contributions. The dialogue between father and sons discloses the purpose of the railroad. Young readers also experience excitement and danger as Tommy accompanies his father and an escaping black family on the next part of their journey.

Kathryn Lasky and Katherine Paterson develop novels that also focus on the journey north. Lasky's *True North* develops themes related to moral obligations and the destructive forces of prejudice as a runaway slave dodges slave catchers as she travels the Underground Railroad on her way to Canada. After a white girl discovers the runaway hiding in her grandfather's house, the two girls join forces on this dangerous journey north. Lasky develops two strong heroines who are committed to the abolitionist movement. In addition, the author emphasizes the restrictive roles of women during the time period. In *Jip, His Story,* Paterson's hero escapes to Canada with the help of a Quaker neighbor when Jip discovers that his mother was a runaway slave.

The impact of the Civil War on free whites in the United States is the subject of several novels in which idealistic young men come to realize that war is not simply a glamorous time of brass bands and heroic battles led by banner-carrying leaders. Stories about fighting soldiers often show men realizing the true horrors of war. Paul Fleischman's *Bull Run* is a series of short descriptive pieces that characterize the reactions of sixteen people who were involved in the first battle of the Civil War. Eight of these people express the Northern point of view and eight express the Southern point of view. Fleischman's characters allow readers to understand the many viewpoints associated with the war. The book is an excellent source for evaluating the importance of point of view when writing about historical time periods and controversial issues. Different points of view are also developed by Carolyn Reeder in *Across the Lines* as Edward and his slave and friend, Simon, struggle with issues of freedom and friendship.

One of the finest books to depict the wartime hardships and conflicts of family members who remain at home is Irene Hunt's *Across Five Aprils*. The beginning conflict is effectively introduced as members of a family in southern Illinois debate the issues related to the Civil War and choose their allegiances: Matt Creighton, the head of the family, argues that a strong union must be maintained; the majority of his sons agree with him, but one son argues that people in the South should be able to live without Northern interference.

Hunt develops a strong personal conflict. Jethro, the youngest son, is emotionally torn between two beloved brothers, one who joins the Union Army and another who fights for the Confederacy. The consequences of hatred are illustrated when young toughs burn the Creightons' barn and put oil into their well because of the family's divided allegiances. Readers also glimpse a different view of people when neighbors guard the farm, help put in the crops, and rebuild the barn.

This is the touching story of a heroic family overcoming problems at home and awaiting news of fighting sons. In spite of disagreement, the Creightons maintain strong family ties. When the son fighting for the South learns that one of his brothers was killed at Pittsburgh Landing, he sends a message to his mother that he was not in that battle and did not fire the bullet that killed his brother. This story helps children understand the real tragedy of the Civil War: Brothers fought against brothers and neighbors against neighbors.

Consider the following themes developed around slavery and the Civil War. Why are so many of the themes related to overcoming great personal and

Sixteen different characters present their perspectives about the first battle of the Civil War. (From Bull Run, *text copyright © 1993 by Paul Fleischman. Jacket art copyright © 1993 by David Frampton/jacket copyright © 1993 by HarperCollins Publishers. Used by permission of HarperCollins Publishers.)*

social conflicts? How do these themes relate to the events and values of the times? Are they appropriate for the time period? What other time periods, if any, reflect similar themes, and what do they have in common with the Civil War period? Are any of these themes significant in contemporary life and literature?

1. War creates tragedy.
2. Moral obligations must be met even if one's life or freedom is in jeopardy.
3. Moral sense does not depend on skin color, but on what is inside a person.
4. People should take pride in themselves and their accomplishments.
5. Prejudice and hatred are destructive forces.
6. People search for freedom.

7. Personal conscience may not allow some people to kill others.
8. Strong family ties help people persevere.

The Western Frontier

The American frontier was extending farther and farther west in the 1800s. White Americans were giving up their settled towns and farms in the East to make their fortunes in unknown territories. Former slaves saw the frontier as a place to make a new start in freedom, and Asian immigrants to the West Coast moved inland to work on the railroads that were beginning to span the Great Plains. The Homestead Act of 1862 promised free land to settlers willing to stake their claims and develop the land. Stories of rich earth in fertile valleys caused families to travel thousands of miles over prairies and mountains to reach Oregon. Many women, according to Beth Blenz-Clucas (1993), were enticed to travel to Oregon because it was possible for them to retain title to their own lands whether they were single or married. Others dreamed of rich prairie land that did not need to be cleared of rocks or timber, and covered wagons carried many settlers into the Oklahoma Territory.

Whether the pioneers stopped in the Midwest or went along the Oregon Trail, the journey was perilous. They fought nature, battling blizzards, dust storms, mountain crossings, and swollen rivers. They fought people as they met unfriendly Native Americans, outlaws, and cattle ranchers who did not want them to farm. Some demonstrated noble qualities as they helped each other search for new land and made friends with the Native Americans whom they encountered. Others demonstrated greed and prejudice in their interactions with other pioneers and Native Americans.

Native peoples themselves were experiencing a time of trauma. Outsiders invaded their ancient territories, staking claims to land that had once been without ownership or boundaries, and killing the buffalo and other wild animals on which the people relied for sustenance. The American government had begun its campaign to relocate Native Americans onto reservations that were minuscule in size and resources compared with the rich stretches of prairie and mountain that had long been the native people's domain.

This period of American history—with its high hopes, dangers, triumphs, and tragic conflicts—still captures the imagination of Americans. Stories about pioneer America are popular with children, as exemplified by the continuing interest in books such as Laura Ingalls Wilder's "Little House" series. Historical fiction for children includes three general types of stories about this period: (1) adventure stories in which the characters cross the prairies and mountains, (2) stories about family life on pioneer homesteads, and (3) stories about interactions between Native Americans and pioneers or Native Americans and military forces.

Authors who write about crossing the continent explore people's reasons for moving and their strong feelings for the land. Self-discovery may occur in young characters who begin to understand their parents' motivations and values. Detailed descriptions allow readers to understand the awesome continent as both inspiration and antagonist. Stories set on homesteads often develop relationships in which families seek to achieve their dreams. Like earlier stories about Native Americans and colonial settlers, these stories include tales of captive children and of the harsh treatment of Native Americans by white people who alter a traditional way of life.

Moving West.

Barbara Brenner's *Wagon Wheels* is an enjoyable book for young readers. Based on fact, it tells about an African American pioneer family that leaves Kentucky after the Civil War and moves to Kansas to receive land under the Homestead Act. The family develops a friendly relationship with members of an Indian tribe, without whose help they would have starved. Young children enjoy the story because it shows that pioneer children were courageous: Three boys survive a prairie fire and travel over one hundred miles to join their father. This is one of the few books written about African Americans as a part of the frontier experience.

Two other books written for young readers follow pioneer families as they journey westward. Brett Harvey's *Cassie's Journey: Going West in the 1860s* develops the dangers and hardships as well as the close relationships of pioneers traveling from Illinois to California. The illustrations reinforce the need to work together if the families are to survive. Kerry Lydon's *A Birthday for Blue* tells about a pioneer boy who spends his seventh birthday traveling westward by covered wagon.

Honore Morrow tells the story of earlier pioneers to the far West in *On to Oregon!,* a book for older children. Morrow's novel about pioneers from Missouri in the 1840s is more than an adventure story about crossing the continent; it is also a psychological story about the challenge of surviving in harsh circumstances. After his parents die on the trail, thirteen-year-old John Sager becomes head of the family and leads his brothers and sisters on to Oregon over a thousand miles of treacherous mountains, canyons, and rivers. The people in the wagon train do not want responsibility for the Sager children and plan to send them back East.

Morrow shows the strength of the father's dream by describing John's actions. John refuses to forfeit his father's dream; he works out a scheme so that the people think that he and his siblings will be traveling with Kit Carson. The children secretly pack their goods on oxen and head out on the lonely trail. The natural environment becomes the chief antagonist against which the children must struggle before reaching a warm, gentle valley in the Oregon of their dreams.

Morrow looks at the contributions of people who made westward expansion possible. Consider, for example, the possible impact of Morrow's closing statements:

You and I will never hear that magic call of the West, "Catch up! Catch up!" We never shall see the Rockies framed in the opening of our prairie schooner and tingle with the knowledge that if we and our fellow immigrants can reach the valleys in the blue beyond the mountains and there plow enough acreage, that acreage will belong forever to America. (p. 235)

Kathryn Lasky's *Beyond the Divide,* a story of survival set in the ruggedness of the far West just before the Civil War, develops themes related to the destructive nature of greed and prejudice and the constructive power of dreams, hope, and moral obligations. Louise Moeri effectively develops similar themes in *Save Queen of Sheba,* as twelve-year-old King David and his young sister Queen of Sheba (named after biblical characters) survive a Sioux raid and set out alone across the prairie in hope of finding the wagons that separated from their portion of the wagon train. Moeri effectively demonstrates the strength of King David's feeling of responsibility by developing his varied emotional responses during several emotionally and physically draining experiences.

The western frontier of the 1820s is the focus for Robert McClung's fictionalized biography of a legendary trapper in *Hugh Glass, Mountain Man.* Maps help readers follow the expedition and trace the route of Hugh Glass after he is attacked by a grizzly bear and then left for dead by his fellow trappers. The story follows a sequence of betrayal, survival, search for revenge, and ultimate forgiveness. McClung develops contrasts through the use of flashbacks. For example, flashbacks help the protagonist understand and finally forgive the trappers who had left him for dead:

"We thought you was dead," Fitzgerald said stubbornly, his face flushing, "or next thing to it! We did our best fer you for five days, Hugh, but when Indian signs showed, we had to leave . . . we knowned you wouldn't want t'pull us under, too, would you?" . . . "You abandoned me!" Hugh growled again. "Robbed me and left. I wouldn't treat a dog thataway!" As he said it, he suddenly remembered the old hound dog that gunsmith Wolfson had abused in Pittsburgh. Many a time Hugh had stood between it and the gunsmith's kicks. That dog had worshipped Hugh, and yet he'd left it behind when he took off. Why? He'd always remember its mournful whine as he left. He sighed and was silent. (p. 145)

McClung develops a wide variety of characters, including both friendly and hostile Native Americans and loyal and greedy trappers.

Pioneer Family Life. Many stories about pioneer life depict the power of a family that is working to conquer outside dangers and build a home filled with love and decency. One author in particular has enabled children to vicariously experience family life on the frontier. Laura Ingalls Wilder, through her "Little House" books, recreated the world of her own frontier family from 1870 through 1889. The "Little House" books have sold in the millions and received literary acclaim. A popular television series introduced the Ingalls family to millions of new friends.

The first book, *Little House in the Big Woods,* takes place in a deep forest in Wisconsin. Unlike the settings in many other pioneer stories, this setting is not antagonistic. Although the woods are filled with bears and other wild animals, the danger never really enters the log cabin in the clearing. Any potential dangers are implied through Pa's stories about his adventures in the big woods, told in a close family environment inside the cabin. Other descriptions of family activities also suggest that the environment, while creating hard work for the pioneer family, is not dangerous. The family clears the land, plants and harvests the crops, gathers sap from the sugar bush, and hitches up the wagon and drives through the woods to Grandpa's house.

Wilder focuses upon the interactions of the family members. Pa's actions, for example, imply that he is a warm, loving father. After working all day, he has time to play the fiddle, play mad dog with the children, and tell stories. Likewise, Ma takes care of the physical needs of the children but also helps them create paper dolls. The impact of what it means to live in the relative isolation of the frontier, where a family must be self-sufficient, is also implied through the children's actions and thoughts: They feel secure when the attic is hung with smoked hams and filled with pumpkins, they are excited when they get new mittens and a cloth doll for Christmas, and they are astonished when they visit a town for the first time and see a store filled with marvelous treasures.

In other "Little House" books, Laura and her family leave the big woods of Wisconsin to live in the prairie states: Kansas, Minnesota, and South Dakota. The children go to a one-room school, build a fish trap, have a grasshopper invasion, worry when Pa must walk three hundred miles to find a job, and live through a blizzard. Wilder's description of the winter in *Little Town on the Prairie* encourages modern children to share the experience:

All winter long, they had been crowded in the little kitchen, cold and hungry and working hard in the dark and the cold to twist enough hay to keep the fire going and to grind wheat in the coffee mill for the day's bread. All that long, long winter, the only hope had been that sometime winter must end, sometime blizzards must stop, the sun would shine warm again. (p. 3)

When Laura gets her first job in the little town of De Smet, South Dakota, she earns twenty-five cents a day and her dinner for sewing shirts. Unselfishly, she saves this money to help send her sister Mary to a college for the blind in Vinton, Iowa. The series ends with stories about Laura's experiences as a school teacher, her marriage to Almanzo Wilder, and their early years together on a prairie homestead. One reason that children like these books so much is the feeling of closeness that they have with Laura.

Carol Ryrie Brink's *Caddie Woodlawn* presents another loving frontier family. The time and setting are similar to those of the first "Little House" book: the last half of the nineteenth century in Wisconsin. In fact, the real Caddie, Brink's grandmother, lived approximately thirty miles north of where Laura Ingalls Wilder was born. Caddie is a warm-hearted, brave, rambunctious girl who loves to play in the woods and along the river with her brothers. She is also a friend of Native Americans in the area.

In one dramatic situation, Caddie jumps on a horse and rides through the night woods to warn her friend Indian John about a plot by some settlers to attack John's people. Caddie's experiences differ from present-day ones, but her worries about growing up are similar to those of any girl, no matter when she lives. With Caddie, children know that everything will be all right:

When she awoke she knew that she need not be afraid of growing up. It was not just sewing and weaving and wearing stays. It was a responsibility, but, as Father spoke of it, it was a beautiful and precious one, and Caddie was ready to go and meet it. (p. 251)

Patricia MacLachlan's *Sarah, Plain and Tall* is a more recently published book about pioneer family life. In this book for younger readers, MacLachlan develops the strong need for a loving mother and a happy family life and introduces the children's need for singing in the home by contrasting the singing that took place before the mother's death with the quiet, sad atmosphere that dominates life after the mother's death. The father's needs are revealed through his actions: He places an advertisement for a wife in an eastern newspaper, in response to which "plain and tall" Sarah enters the family's life.

The children's need for a mother and a happy home is reflected in their desire for singing, in their rereading of Sarah's letters until the letters are worn out, their desire to be perfect for Sarah, their frightened reactions when Sarah misses the sea, their trying to bring characteristics of the sea into their prairie farm, and their complete happiness when they realize that Sarah will stay on the prairie. MacLachlan's Sarah is a strong, loving, independent pioneer woman who discovers that her love for her new family is stronger than her feelings of loneliness for the sea. Like Wilder's and Brink's, MacLachlan's characters may seem real because she drew them from her own family history.

Ellen Howard's *Edith Herself* is another book in which the author draws characters and conflicts from family history. The experiences, however, involve prejudice and fear. Misunderstandings and fear about epilepsy create person-against-society and person-against-self conflicts in Howard's story set in rural America of the 1890s. Edith leaves a loving home after her father's death and moves into the sterner environment of her older sister's family. At the same time, Edith experiences her first epileptic seizure. Howard reflects both the ignorance of the society and the fear of people who face circumstances that they do not understand. Howard creates a strong character, who overcomes her own fears, attends school, and learns to believe in herself. These actions emphasize the need to believe in oneself.

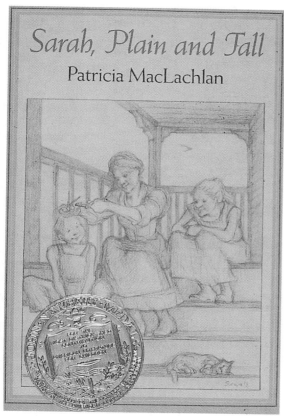

The need for warm family relationships provides the focus for this frontier story. (From Sarah, Plain and Tall, *by Patricia MacLachlan. Jacket art copyright © 1985 by Marcia Sewall. Reprinted by permission of HarperCollins.)*

Paul Fleischman's *The Borning Room* follows the happenings in a room on an Ohio farm. Family members experience both birth and death in a room set aside for such special occasions. Fleischman focuses on a baby born in 1851 and proceeds through her experiences on the Ohio frontier, through the life cycle of birth, marriage, and death. The time period between Georgina's birth and death allows Fleischman to include happenings that were influenced by changes in history, such as runaway slaves, the Civil War, and the introduction of chloroform. The book concludes as the now older lady, Georgina, awaits her own death in the borning room and thinks about the changes that have happened in the years between 1851 and 1918. In this conclusion, Fleischman encourages readers to understand the changes that have taken place in this one character's life and on the Ohio frontier:

I was born in this same month of January. The day might have looked precisely like this one. What a lot, though, has changed between that day and this. Automobiles, telephones, electric lights. And yet, nothing's changed. Here it is 1918 and a woman still can't vote. Over in Europe, we're fighting the Kaiser. A new set of buglers and battles. More dying. It's Shiloh and Vicksburg all over again. But you're too young to know that war. . . . I've got a grandson scuttling through the trenches and a daughter doctoring the wounded. And a son who teaches music at Princeton by day and writes pacifist pamphlets at night. That's Virgil you hear sawing wood. He alone of the four stayed here, as I did. (p. 100).

In *The Winter Room*, Gary Paulsen uses the stories told by family members through the long winter months on a northern farm. Paulsen encourages readers to see, hear, and feel the power of the stories and the memories revealed. He uses a sequence that follows the activities on a farm from spring through winter. The winter nights, however, bring out the stories. The family sits around the stove and watches the fire through the mica windows in the door and wait for the magic that begins, "It was when I was young . . . " (p. 69). Paulsen shows that stories provide a way to learn about others and to gain feelings of self-worth.

Another outstanding book about pioneer family life is Scott O'Dell's *Carlota*. This is the story of the strong and independent daughter of a Spanish landholder in early California. California is also the setting for Karen Cushman's *The Ballad of Lucy Whipple*. As in her other books, Cushman's heroine at first rebels against her life, but she finally discovers that she can create a home wherever she is.

Pioneers and Native Americans.

The West Texas frontier of the 1860s provides the setting for Patricia Beatty's *Wait for Me, Watch for Me, Eula Bee*. The book tells of the capture of two farm children by Comanche and Kiowa Indians, the subsequent escape of the older boy, the changing loyalties of the very young girl who learns to love her Comanche foster parent, and her rescue by her brother. Beatty's descriptions of camp life, food, travel, and behavior create a vivid picture of the period. The author's notes list the sources for her information on Comanche and Kiowa tribes and their treatment of captives.

While Beatty depicts the Comanche as leading a harsh life built on raiding and warfare, she also depicts the value that the Comanche place on children. The little girl and her Comanche foster parent develop a warm, loving relationship. Sadness in this book stems from the tragic results of the lack of understanding of two cultures.

A tragic period in Navaho history, 1863–1865, is the setting for Scott O'Dell's *Sing Down the Moon*. The story of the three-hundred-mile forced march that culminates in holding Navahos prisoner at Fort Sumner, New Mexico, is told through the viewpoint of a Navaho girl, Bright Morning. O'Dell effectively uses both descriptions of physical settings and characterizations to depict tragedy. The Navahos are forced to leave their home, the beautiful Canyon de Chelly, with its fruit trees, green grass, sheep, and cool water, for the harsh windswept landscape around Fort Sumner.

The greatest tragedy does not result from the loss of home, however, but from the loss of spiritual hope. Still, Bright Morning does not give up her dream of returning to her beautiful canyon, and O'Dell creates a thought-provoking, bittersweet ending. Bright Morning and her husband escape from the U.S. Army and return to her hidden valley. It is as she remembers it: The blossoms are on the trees, a sheep and a lamb are grazing on the green land, and the tools that she hid from the soldiers are waiting. However, a menacing shadow looms over their happiness. Readers cannot forget that the Navaho family is hiding from the soldiers whom they saw on the horizon.

In *Thunder Rolling in the Mountains*, Scott O'Dell and Elizabeth Hall write about another tragic Native American experience. The Nez Perce tribe and Chief Joseph are removed from their homeland in 1877. O'Dell and Hall develop the Nez Perce feelings for lost land and culture. The Nez Perce are moved from the Wallowa Valley in Oregon to Bear Paws in Montana and finally to reservation lands in Oklahoma. The story is told through the viewpoint of Chief Joseph's daughter.

In the foreword, Elizabeth Hall describes the immersion of Scott O'Dell in this story. O'Dell followed the trail taken by Chief Joseph in 1877 and researched the words, deeds, and recollections of the survivors who were part of this forced movement and the conflicts that occurred.

Many authors who write about the pioneer period stress the quest for and love of land and the conflicts between different cultures. Consider the following themes developed in historical fiction about pioneer America. How do the themes correspond with historical events? What other periods have similar themes? What are the similarities between times with similar themes?

1. People have moral obligations.
2. People have strong dreams of owning land.
3. Families can survive if they work together.
4. People need each other and may work together for their mutual good.
5. Battles can be won through legal means rather than through unlawful actions.
6. Hatred and prejudice are destructive forces.
7. Without spiritual hope, people may lose their will to live.

The Early Twentieth Century

Recent books of historical fiction with settings in the early 1900s often depict survival of immigrants who flee Europe or social conflicts and the Great Depression, which began in 1929. These stories stress both physical and spiritual survival as people strive to maintain pride and independence. Person-against-society and person-against-self conflicts develop when the characters experience or express racial prejudice and face financial hardships.

Even though Patricia Beatty's *Sarah and Me and the Lady from the Sea* takes place in 1894, shortly before the turn of the century, the father's bankruptcy caused by a flood is as devastating as the financial hardships caused by the Depression. Beatty shows the importance of family unity and a bond between people who are facing hardships. Beatty humorously contrasts the life of the family before and after the bankruptcy. For example, a family who has always had servants must learn to cook on a wood-burning stove, dress poultry, and wash clothes. At first, Beatty's family reflects prejudices against those who have less social standing than themselves. However, these characters show the family how to survive without servants and how to enjoy their new life.

Felice Holman's *The Wild Children* is set in Russia between 1917 and 1921, the time following the Bolshevik Revolution. The main characters are children who are left homeless because their parents are either dead or imprisoned. The antagonist is a society that fears political freedom. Holman's vivid descriptions of the living conditions of the children and their fear of authority create believable antagonists. The children's struggle for survival and their need for each other emphasize that love and loyalty help people endure and survive catastrophic experiences.

In *No Hero for the Kaiser,* Rudolph Frank develops a strong antiwar theme through depictions of World War I and person-against-society conflict. For example, Frank suggests the destructive nature of war when he compares the peaceful Polish hamlet before and after the desolation caused by war. Person-against-society conflict is seen in the main character's conflict with the German officers and the foot soldiers' conflicts as they follow orders while dreaming of homes and families. Frank characterizes soldiers who are caught up in actions that are not of their doing. The final actions of the main character are especially effective in supporting the antiwar theme. When the supreme commander wants to honor Jan and make him a symbol for the war effort, Jan disappears, even though he is giving up personal glory. Frank develops the importance of this action through the words of one of Jan's friends:

Then Father Distelmann stood up, looked around the circle of his friends, and spoke slowly, "I knew him from the very beginning, isn't that right, Hottenrot, when we were advancing near Lodz. He always showed us the right way, always the right way. . . . I believe he's done the same thing this time." (p. 220)

The impact of the antiwar theme is strengthened when readers discover that this book was banned by Hitler.

Historically accurate settings add to this World War I story. (From No Hero for the Kaiser *by Rudolf Frank, translated from the 1931 edition by Patricia Crampton, copyright © 1986. Illustrated by Klaus Steffens. Reprinted by permission of Lothrop, Lee & Shepard.)*

In Karen Hesse's *Letters from Rifka,* a Jewish family flees Russia in 1919. The plot unfolds as Rifka writes letters to her cousin Tovah. The details show that degrading experiences and terror do not overcome the family's will to escape and survive. Rifka experiences additional conflict when she is prohibited from sailing to America because she has ringworm. Later, she is kept in detention at Ellis Island. Finally, after months of separation, she is reunited with her family. The story may be so believable because it is based on the true experiences of the author's great-aunt.

Anna Myers's *Fire in the Hills,* set in rural Oklahoma during World War I, develops themes related to prejudice and discrimination. For example, during the interactions with a conscientious objector and a German immigrant family, the author develops the themes that prejudice and discrimination are destructive forces and that there is a bond between people who experience injustice. Through the actions of Hallie, the sixteen-year-old heroine, the author also develops themes related to the importance of dreams and working for a goal as Hallie discovers that her goal to become a teacher is possible, that women deserve to find a place for themselves in the world, and that women can work together to make their desires known.

Themes related to literature of the Depression suggest that people will strive for survival of the physical body and the spirit and that monetary wealth does not create a rich life. These themes are important in Mildred Ames's *Grandpa Jake and the Grand Christmas*. Through interactions with her grandfather, a girl, Lizzie, learns that life would have no meaning without dreams.

The survival of the spirit also is important in Garry Disher's *The Bamboo Flute*, set in the Australian depression of 1932. Through interactions with a flute-playing vagrant, twelve-year-old Paul understands the values of friendship and family, too.

Mildred D. Taylor's *Roll of Thunder, Hear My Cry* explores both the subtle and the explicit racial prejudice that many white Americans expressed toward African Americans in the early twentieth century. Consider, for example, the subtle discrimination developed by Taylor. Cassie and her brother, who live in rural Mississippi, excitedly await their new schoolbooks, only to receive badly worn, dirty castoffs from the white elementary school. When Cassie's brother looks at the inside cover of his book, he sees that on its twelfth date of issue—to him—it is described as being in very poor condition and the race of the student is listed as "nigra."

The warm family life of the children gives them the strength to confront such discrimination. First, they refuse the books. Then, they create a minor accident for the bus driver, who consistently and intentionally splashes the black children's clothes with dirty water as he drives the white children to their separate school. (There is no bus service for the black school.) After the children secretly deepen one of the puddles in the road, the bus breaks an axle and its riders must walk.

Other expressions of racism portrayed in this book are far less subtle, however, and they include the family's experiences with night riders and cross burnings. Understandably, the family feels fear as well as humiliation and indignation. In a sequel to this book, *Let the Circle Be Unbroken*, Taylor helps readers see how the estrangement of white and black people from each other results from ingrained social prejudices. The family in *Roll of Thunder, Hear My Cry* owns its own land, the mother has graduated from a teacher's college, and the children consistently attend school. The family experiences injustice, but a loving environment helps protect and strengthen the members.

The experiences in William H. Armstrong's *Sounder* are harsher and filled with tragedy. An early twentieth-

⟨ISSUE   Should Historical Fiction Reflect the Attitudes of the Time Period?

Should historical fiction reflect the attitudes and circumstances of the times? Or should historical fiction reflect the changing attitudes toward people of all races? These issues become especially critical when historical fiction is reviewed by literary critics and various interest groups.

Sounder, by William H. Armstrong, is an example of historical fiction that has been both acclaimed for literary merit and criticized for its portrayal of a black family. Literary acclaim is exemplified in the awarding of the Newbery Medal in 1970. However, *Sounder* has been denounced by some critics because they believe that it emasculates the black man and destroys the African American family by showing it as spiritless and submissive rather than actively fighting injustice. In contrast, other critics maintain that the book authentically depicts the poverty, ignorance, and attitudes of the times; consequently, the family members acted in the only way possible.

A similar debate centers on the depiction of African American characters in Paula Fox's 1973 Newbery Medal winner *The Slave Dancer*. Students of children's literature should consider this issue and the implications for writers, publishers, and selectors of literature when they read historical fiction that depicts African Americans, Asian Americans, and Hispanic Americans.

century family of African American sharecroppers lives in one of numerous ramshackle cabins scattered across the vast fields of the white landlord. When the poverty-stricken father steals a ham to feed his hungry family, he is handcuffed, chained, and taken to jail. The futility of protest is suggested as Sounder, the family's faithful coon dog, tries to save the father and is wounded by the white sheriff's shotgun.

Comparisons between the two incidents are developed as both the father and Sounder are gone: the father to jail and then to a succession of chain gangs, and Sounder to the woods to heal his wounds. A strong bond between man and dog is implied when Sounder returns, a crippled remnant of his former self. He does not bark until the father returns home, himself crippled by a dynamite blast in the prison quarry. The two old friends are physically and emotionally tired and have only a short life together. The final vision of the two friends is one of remembered strength, as the son, grown to manhood, recalls his father and the faithful dog as they were before the tragic happenings:

The pine trees would look down forever on a lantern burning out of oil but not going out. A harvest moon would cast shadows forever of a man walking upright, his dog, bouncing after him. And the quiet of the night would fill and echo again with the deep voice of Sounder, the great coon dog. (p. 116)

Critics of *Sounder* believe that because the dog is the only character in the book with a name, the book implies that the characters need not be respected as human beings. Critics also object to the black family's being characterized as submissive and spiritless. Others argue that the family should be nameless because the tragedy depicted in the story was one shared by many poor black sharecroppers during that period. In the later view, tragedy is seen as a strong bond between all people who experience injustice. Readers may consider both viewpoints and form their own evaluations of *Sounder*.

In *Circle of Fire*, William H. Hooks also explores the consequences of hatred and prejudice. The setting is North Carolina in the 1930s. The conflict is between the Ku Klux Klan and a group of Irish gypsies. Hooks creates a believable person-against-society conflict, telling the story through the viewpoint of an eleven-year-old boy that befriends the gypsies. Readers may wish to consider an assertion that Hooks makes in his endnote:

The Ku Klux Klan grows and expands, reaching even into the alien territory of the North. *Circle of Fire*, set in the 1930s, is about the turbulent drama that occurred when someone dared step outside that "rightful place." These same events could happen today. (p. 147)

The themes developed in historical fiction set in the early twentieth century highlight both negative and positive attitudes and values. Consider the following themes found in the literature. How do the themes relate to the historical events? Are these themes found during any other time period in historical fiction?

1. People will strive for survival of the physical body and the spirit.
2. Prejudice and discrimination are destructive forces.
3. There is a bond between people who experience injustice.
4. Monetary wealth does not create a rich life.

World War II

In 1933, Adolf Hitler took power in Germany, and Germany resigned from the League of Nations. In 1935, Hitler reintroduced conscription of German soldiers and recommended rearmament, contrary to the Treaty of Versailles. Along with a rapid increase in military power came an obsessive hatred of the Jewish people. In March 1938, Hitler's war machine began moving across Europe. Austria was occupied, and imprisonment of Jews began. World War II became a reality when the Germans invaded Poland on September 1, 1939.

The 1940s saw the invasions of Norway, Belgium, and Holland; the defeat of the French army; and the heroic evacuation of British soldiers from Dunkirk. From the start of the invasions through the defeat of Hitler's forces in 1945, these years have inspired many tales of both sorrow and heroism.

Authors who write children's historical fiction set in World War II often focus on the experiences of Jewish people in hiding and concentration camps, the experiences of Japanese Americans in internment centers in the United States, or the perseverance of people in occupied lands. Because some of these stories are written by people who lived similar experiences, the stories tend to be emotional. The authors often create vivid conflicts.

Authors explore the consequences of war and prejudice by having characters ponder why their lives are in turmoil, by describing the characters' fears and their reactions to their situations and to one another, and by revealing what happens to the characters or their families as a result of war. As might be expected, the themes of these stories include the consequences of hatred and prejudice, the search for religious and personal freedom, the role of conscience, and obligation toward others.

Some other World War II stories have adventurous plots. For example, Marie McSwigan's *Snow Treasure* is based on a true incident in 1940, in which $9 million in Norwegian gold bullion (thirteen tons) is slipped past Nazi sentries and shipped to Baltimore. The unusual twist is that children on sleds get the bullion past the Nazi troops to a boat hidden in a fjord. Children enjoy this story because it demonstrates how important even young children can be when they work together to preserve their country.

Louise Borden's *The Little Ships: The Heroic Rescue at Dunkirk in World War II* presents the rescue through the eyes of a young girl who joins her father in this rescue. Michael Foreman's illustrations of the fishing boats and the rescue adds drama to this story. In a book for older readers, *Wish Me Luck,* James Heneghan presents another type of rescue, as children are on a ship that is torpedoed on the journey from England to Canada.

Peter Hartling's *Crutches* develops a theme associated with the terrible consequences of war and the struggle for freedom. The protagonist in *Crutches* is separated from his mother as a consequence of World War II. Hartling develops strong bonds between the homeless boy and a survivor of the war who now walks on crutches. In a story that shows the importance of friendship and the triumph of family loyalty, the boy and the survivor eventually find the mother and reunite the family. Stressing the consequences of war on European families, Hartling shows the inhumanity associated with war and the spirits that survive even in war-torn countries.

Mary Downing Hahn develops person-versus-society and person-versus-self conflicts in *Stepping on the Cracks.* Person-versus-society conflicts emerge as children living in College Park, Maryland, discover a deserter from the army. Through various conversations and reactions, Hahn shows the attitudes of society toward a man who is an army de-

serter and a conscientious objector. Person-versus-self conflicts are explored as the children make decisions about helping the man. Hahn shows that moral obligations and personal conscience are strong forces, war is terrible, and friendship is powerful. The major conflict in Robert Cormier's *Other Bells for Us to Ring,* a story set in America, is person-versus-self for the protagonist, who faces questions about faith. The authors of both books develop numerous details about the war years in the United States to authenticate the settings.

The Holocaust. The Nazis' terrible crimes against Jewish people are familiar to adults and children alike. Stories about the Holocaust help children sense the bewilderment and terror of a time when innocent people were the subject of irrational hatred and persecution.

In a picture storybook for younger children, *Star of Fear, Star of Hope,* Jo Hoestlandt writes a poignant account of two friends who are separated in Nazi-occupied France in 1942. The story begins, "My name is Helen, and I'm nearly an old woman now. When I'm gone, who will remember Lydia? That is why I want to tell you our story" (unnumbered). The author places the Holocaust on a very personal level by telling the story of the two friends. The personal conflict begins on the eve of Helen's ninth birthday when her Jewish friend Lydia is invited to stay overnight. It is on this night when the Nazis begin their roundup of the Jews. Helen does not understand why her friend leaves hurriedly and responds with words she has always regretted: "You're not my friend anymore!" (unnumbered). Unfortunately, this is the last time that Helen sees her friend. The book ends on a hopeful note as Helen remembers the rhyme they used to say:

> "Stars at morning, better take warning.
> Stars at night, hope is in sight.
> I'll always have hope . . ." (unnumbered)

Johanna Reiss tells a fictional version of her own life in *The Upstairs Room.* Reiss allows readers to glimpse varying consequences of prejudice and hatred. A young girl, Johanna, hears news of the war and asks why Hitler hates her people. The girl is barred from restaurants and the public school, and she learns that many Jewish people are being taken to forced-labor camps. Reiss depicts the obligations of one person to another when a Dutch family offers, in spite of great danger, to hide Johanna and her sister on their farm. The farmer builds a secret space in an upstairs closet to provide a hiding place for the two girls. At first, Johanna does not understand why she and her sister must hide, but gradually, she realizes their serious predicament, as word of the Holocaust spreads.

In several scenes, Reiss's style and first-person point of view create the breathless fear of the children. For example, as the children hide in the cramped closet:

Footsteps. Loud ones. Boots. Coming up the stairs. Wooden shoes. Coming behind. Sini put her arms around me and pushed my head against her shoulder. Loud voices. Ugly ones. Furniture being moved. And Opoe's protesting voice. The closet door was thrown open. Hands fumbled on the shelves. Sini was trembling. She tightened her arms around me. I no longer breathed through my nose. Breathing through my mouth made less noise. (p. 149)

The girls and the family protecting them are brave during this unsuccessful search by Nazi troops. The story ends happily. Canadian troops liberate the town, and at last, Johanna and her sister may leave their room. This is a powerful story of the experiences of common people during the German occupation. (Some adults have criticized this book because of realistic dialogue, in which members of the farm family use swear words.)

Trust in and loyalty toward a parent are the motivational forces in Uri Orlev's story of survival set in the Jewish ghetto of Warsaw, Poland. *The Island on Bird Street* chronicles the experiences of Alex, who turns a bombed-out building into a refuge while he waits for his father's return. Surrounded by houses emptied of food, Alex feels that his refuge is similar to the desert island in his favorite book, *Robinson Crusoe*. Orlev develops the symbolism of a lonely island, on which Alex, like Robinson Crusoe, must learn how to survive, and the terrifying historical background of the Holocaust, in which Alex witnesses the capture of his Jewish family and friends, experiences fear and loneliness, and nurses a resistance fighter's wounds. The book concludes on a note of hope. Alex's father returns, finds Alex where he promised to wait, and takes Alex to the forest to be with the partisans who are resisting the Nazis.

Orlev also sets *The Man from the Other Side* in the Warsaw Ghetto during World War II. In this story, a

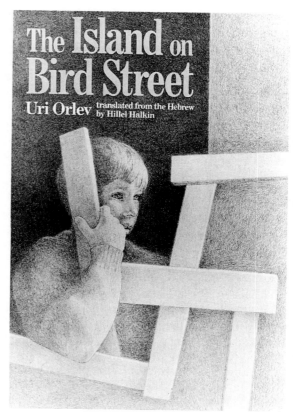

Symbolic and historical settings are integral to a story set in the Warsaw ghetto. (From The Island on Bird Street by Uri Orlev. Jacket illustration copyright © 1984 by Jean Titherington. Reprinted by permission of Houghton Mifflin Company.)

Polish boy and his father risk detection and punishment for taking supplies to the Jewish people who are enclosed on the other side of the walls. This gripping story ends with the Warsaw Ghetto uprising. Orlev presents much history of the Jewish people in Poland through dialogue. He also describes the feelings of anti-Semitism that were felt by many of the people.

In *The Lady with the Hat* and *Lydia, Queen of Palestine,* Orlev places his characters in a later time as they relocate in Palestine. In *The Lady with the Hat,* Orlev develops themes about faith and hope and the need to look after each other. The book is set in 1947 prior to the formation of the Jewish state. The main character is the only member of his immediate family to survive the German concentration camps. Now he tries to enter Palestine as an illegal immigrant. Orlev uses flashbacks to allow readers to understand Yulek's previous experiences. Orlev paints a portrait of people looking for freedom in their own land and of the search that survivors will conduct in order to locate missing relatives.

Orlev's *Lydia, Queen of Palestine* is a lighter story in which ten-year-old Lydia escapes from Romania to Palestine, where she becomes a resident of a kibbutz. Readers enjoy this often humorous story of a free-spirited child who considers herself "a terror." Lydia has many of the characteristics needed to be a survivor.

In *When Hitler Stole Pink Rabbit,* Judith Kerr uses personal experiences to provide details about a Jewish family that flees Germany just before the Nazis can arrest the father. Another family escapes in Sonia Levitin's *Journey to America.* In both books, the families show courage in times of great danger. Although they must leave their possessions and friends behind, the families feel that everything will be all right if the family can be together. Levitin extends the experiences of her family in *Silver Days.* In the latter book, Levitin develops the problems of living as refugees in America during World War II. This girl and her family face poverty and try to retain their roots.

Several books develop the role of the resistance or friendly gentile families in the Jewish struggle for survival. Ida Vos's *Hide and Seek* presents the cruel world of the Holocaust as it changes the lives of Jewish people living in the Netherlands under German occupation. Vos encourages readers to respond to the book in her foreword remarks:

Can you imagine how it feels when you find out that people you love are dead, all of a sudden? Imagine what it would be like not ever to be allowed to go outside, year after year. Imagine being able to do your shopping only between three and five o'clock. Imagine. . . . I know how difficult it is to imagine such things; that is the reason I wrote *Hide and Seek.* To let you feel how terrible it is to be discriminated against, and to let you know how terrible it was to be a Jewish child in Holland during those years. (p. ix)

Vos also encourages readers to understand both the courage of the Jewish people and the determination of the Dutch gentiles who risked their lives for their neighbors. Compare this book with Lois Lowry's *Number the Stars,* a book about the Danish endeavor to move Jewish residents to Sweden and safety.

After reading such stories, children often are concerned about the implications of not acting when other people are unjustly accused of crimes. Some books, such as Jane Yolen's *The Devil's Arithmetic,* discussed in chapter 7, have accurate historical settings. Even though its time-warp elements make it a fantasy, the book is historically correct.

Internment of Japanese Americans and the Pacific Conflict. The Jewish people weren't the only ones to live through persecution and fear during World War II. Many children are surprised to read stories about the American treatment of Japanese Americans during World War II. Two books by Yoshiko Uchida tell about a Japanese American family's experiences after the bombing of Pearl Harbor. (Although the stories are fictional, they are based on what happened to Uchida and her family.)

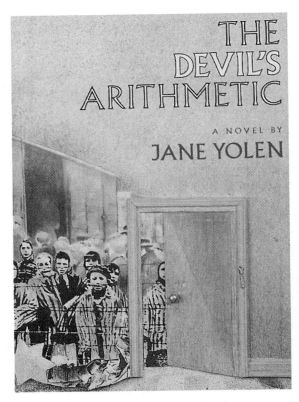

A time-warp experience develops a girl's understanding of the Holocaust. (From The Devil's Arithmetic *by Jane Yolen, copyright © 1988. Reprinted by permission of Viking Penguin.)*

In *Journey to Topaz,* the police take away Yuki's father, a businessman in Berkeley, California, and send Yuki, her mother, and her older brother to a permanent internment center in Utah, called Topaz. Uchida creates vivid pictures of the internment camp. She describes, for example, latrines without doors, lines of people waiting to use them, and the wind blowing across the desert into the barracks. The fear of the interned people and their wardens climaxes when the grandfather of Yuki's best friend goes searching for arrowheads and is shot by a guard who believes that he is trying to escape. Family members experience conflicting feelings when Yuki's brother, wishing to prove his loyalty to America, joins an army unit composed of Japanese Americans.

Yuki's story continues in *Journey Home,* in which the family returns to Berkeley, only to discover distrust, difficulty finding work, and anti-Japanese violence. The family feels hope and strength more than bitterness, however. Yuki discovers that coming home is having everyone she cares about around her.

Historical fiction set in World War II includes stories about the Pacific conflict. These books develop similar themes as those of other war texts. For example, *Shin's Tricycle,* by Tatsuharu Kodama, develops the theme that wars are brutal and we should try to keep the dream of peace alive for all children. In this true story, a young boy and his best friend are killed by the bomb while riding the prized tricycle. The tricycle is now located at the Peace Museum in Hiroshima.

The setting for Graham Salisbury's *Under the Blood Red Sun* is Hawaii at the time of the bombing of Pearl Harbor. In this story, a Japanese American and his best friend discover that their carefree life of school and baseball is disrupted by the bombing and the war. Most of the conflicts developed in the story are person-against-society as Japanese American families are subjected to suspicion by neighbors and the military. This is especially true after the father and grandfather are placed in internment camps. There are strong ties, however, developed between people of different racial origins. Two of the strongest themes developed in the book are the importance of retaining cultural values and beliefs even in times of great stress and the importance of having the freedom to make choices.

Laurence Yep's *Hiroshima* is set in Japan during the time of the dropping of the atomic bomb. Although most of the book is based on historical fact, there is an element of historical fiction in the development of the main character, Sachi, whom Yep describes as a composite of several children who experienced the bombing. Yep's descriptions of the setting and Sachi's responses at the time of the bombing are particularly vivid. The book includes a discussion of the test agreements and the working for peace. Yep concludes the text with the theme: "It must not drop again" (p. 49).

The themes in children's historical fiction with settings during World War II resemble themes found during other times of great peril. Consider the following themes. How do they relate to historical events? What are characteristics of other historical periods that have similar themes?

1. People will seek freedom from religious and political persecution.
2. Prejudice and hatred are destructive forces.
3. Moral obligation and personal conscience are strong forces.
4. Freedom is worth fighting for.
5. Family love and loyalty help people endure catastrophic experiences.

 SUGGESTED ACTIVITIES

for Adult Understanding of Historical Fiction

- Find an example of historical fiction written for beginning readers and another written for older readers. Compare the settings. Are they both integral settings? If the book written for younger children does not provide as many details as the one for older children, has the author used any other medium to relate details to the readers? For example, compare Arnold Lobel's setting in *On the Day Peter Stuyvesant Sailed into Town* with Esther Forbes's setting in *Johnny Tremain.*

- Locate a story in which the setting takes on the role of antagonist (for example, Honore Morrow's *On to Oregon!*). How has the author developed the setting as the antagonist? How do the characters overcome the obstacles of nature? What happens to the characters as they face and overcome the antagonist?

- Writers of historical fiction often place famous persons into the backgrounds of their stories but make the pivotal character fictional. Read a story such as Erik Christian Haugaard's *Cromwell's Boy* and compare the roles of the little-known eleven-year-old Oliver Cutter with the well-known Oliver Cromwell. Why did the author choose a little-known person as the main character?

- Writing an excellent historical fiction novel requires much research. Choose several authors of historical fiction and investigate the sources that they used.

- Read the acceptance speech of an author of historical fiction who has been awarded the Newbery Medal, such as Joan Blos (1980). What were the author's reasons for choosing to write about that period in history? Does the author discuss the sources used?

- Using Chart 10–1, "Eras and Themes in Historical Fiction," make a list of historical literature that develops each theme during a selected time period.

- Read an article on literature with wartime settings, such as Barbara Harrison's "Howl like the Wolves" (1987) or Winfred Kaminski's "War and Peace in Recent German Children's Literature" (1987). Summarize the points made by the author and provide your reactions to the article.

- A group of teachers in the same elementary school has decided to do a school-wide unit on American Westward Expansion. Develop a list of books for primary, upper elementary, and middle school students that would support the goals of these teachers. Print your lists.

- Your middle school class is studying the American Civil War. You want them to have resources in their classroom library that will help them write a one-act play about the war. Develop a list of books for this purpose and print your list.

- An upgraded elementary school has been studying ancient Egypt in preparation for an author visit by Aliki. Use the database to provide appropriate resource books. Print your list.

Involving Children in Historical Fiction

Children can learn to love and respect history when they vicariously share the experiences of a character with whom they identify. Surrounding themselves with the flavor and spirit of a historical period, they also can visualize how people are affected by the times in which they live. Historical fiction helps children acquire the idea that history is people rather than merely a series of events. You can bring history to life by guiding children toward individual reading selections, reading historical fiction aloud to students, encouraging dramatic presentations of short scenes from favorite books, and using literature in pleasant ways to develop attitudes and general concepts about history.

A writer of historical fiction, Geoffrey Trease (1977), makes a case for using the genre to add new meaning and excitement to social studies:

So even in the context of social studies, the historical story has an important part to play, and it would be wasteful not to utilize all that the writer has so painstakingly researched and made available to children in an attractive form. (p. 28)

Thus, historical fiction allows children to learn about the continuity of events, to understand human relationships, and to immerse themselves in the settings characteristic of specific times.

Joan Aiken (1985) emphasizes that writers must develop within children an awareness of the past, an appreciation for the past, and a feeling of indebtedness toward the past. Aiken believes that as children begin to value and appreciate the contributions of people before their own times, they may realize that they also have obligations to future generations.

Hazel Rochman (1989) states that she uses a subject or theme, such as war or survival, to interest readers and "to bring in a variety of reading levels, genres, and cultures; to appeal to a wide range of reading interests and to push readers a little beyond where they might go on their own" (p. 32). Rochman maintains that historical fiction is an excellent genre for interesting and exciting readers.

 PROVIDING BACKGROUND THROUGH ILLUSTRATIONS

Illustrations in picture storybooks are excellent for helping children visualize the settings for various time periods in historical fiction (Norton, 1992). If the illustrations have carefully researched details, children can both visualize the characteristics associated with the time period and authenticate the textual descriptions. The following picture storybooks reflect historical settings (many of these books are discussed in chapters 4, 5, and 11 in this text):

Middle Ages:	Jonathan Hunt's *Illuminations*
	David Macaulay's *Castle*
Early Native American cultures:	Marcia Sewall's *People of the Breaking Day*
	Stephen Trimble's *The Village of Blue Stone*
	Jane Yolen's *Encounter*
Pioneer America:	Jim Aylesworth's *The Folks in the Valley: A Pennsylvania Dutch ABC*
	Byrd Baylor's *The Best Town in the World*
	Donald Hall's *Ox-Cart Man*
	Brett Harvey's *Cassie's Journey: Going West in the 1860s*
	Brett Harvey's *My Prairie Year: Based on the Diary of Elenor Plaisted*
	Reeve Lindbergh's *Johnny Appleseed*
	Patricia MacLachlan's *Three Names*

Early 1900s:	Gloria Houston's *My Great-Aunt Arizona* Megan McDonald's *The Great Pumpkin Switch* Janice Shefelman's *A Peddler's Dream*
Mid-1900s:	Judith Hendershot's *In Coal Country* William Kurelek's *A Prairie Boy's Summer* Cynthia Rylant's *Appalachia: The Voices of Sleeping Birds* Jane Yolen's *Letting Swift River Go*
World War II:	Michael Foreman's *War Boy* Roberto Innocenti's *Rose Blanche*
Migrant families:	Sherley Anne Williams's *Working Cotton*

These picture storybooks will add background information as children read about or research various time periods.

UNIT PLAN: LOOKING AT COLONIAL TIMES

Celebrations throughout the United States commemorated the bicentennial of our country in 1976. The bicentennial stimulated interest in searching for our roots and learning more about the early colonial days and the Revolutionary War. Carol Gay (1976) says that the important task of sharing a sense of the colonial past with children can be effectively approached through the following activities: (1) sharing with children the same stories that colonial children read, (2) encouraging children to take a penetrating look at a historical figure, and (3) inviting students to compare the values and problems of colonial times with those of contemporary times. While these activities would be meaningful for any time period, this section considers some ways to accomplish each of these goals with historical fiction related to colonial days.

Books Read by Colonial Children

What books were available to children in the North American colonies of the 1600s and 1700s? What books did children read at school and at home? One of the books most commonly referred to in colonial literature and used in colonial education was the hornbook. (Reproductions are available through The Hornbook, Inc., Boston, Massachusetts.) The original hornbooks were thin pieces of three-by-five-inch wood onto which tacks attached a printed paper covered with a transparent sheet of yellowish horn. Hornbooks contained the alphabet, vowel–consonant and consonant–vowel combinations, the Lord's Prayer, and sometimes Arabic numerals. They were designed to teach colonial children to read and spell.

Another book mentioned often in the literature of colonial times is *The New-England Primer*. (This primer came out in many editions over the years and is available in a reissued text.) The chapbooks popular in England were also found in the colonies. Some of these had didactic messages; others contained entertaining traditional tales, such as "Tom Thumb," "Reynard the Fox," "Jack the Giant Killer," and "Robin Hood." These stories are available today. An influential book written during the seventeenth century was John Bunyan's *Pilgrim's Progress*. Both children and adults enjoyed following Christian on his perilous journey as he searched for salvation.

Other popular books of colonial times that contemporary children may enjoy include *Babes in the Woods* (reissued in Frederick Warne's edition of Randolph Caldecott's *Picture Book No. 1*), John Newbery's *History of Little Goody Two-Shoes*, and Daniel Defoe's *Robinson Crusoe*. Reading from these books or listening to stories read from them allows children to develop close relationships with characters from the past. Children are excited to discover that today they are fascinated by the same plots and characters that fascinated children over two hundred years ago. *Fifteen Centuries of Children's Literature: An Annotated Chronology of British and American Works in Historical Context* by Jane Bingham and Grayce Scholt (1980) is an excellent resource for locating books that were published during a specific time period.

Historical Figures

Older-elementary and middle-school children can learn about the process of scholarly research used by historical novelists or biographers when they recreate a day in the life of famous American colonists or Native Americans of the period, such as Benjamin Franklin, Pocahontas, George Washington, Betsy

Ross, Abigail Adams, or Paul Revere. While many books of historical fiction develop fictional stories about unknown people, many also refer to famous people and leaders. For example, Esther Forbes's *Johnny Tremain* includes frequent mention of well-known figures during the American Revolution. Children can do research on these historical figures because much information about them is available.

The first step is to identify a figure about whom there is sufficient source material. Then, divide the class into smaller research groups, each to work on a different aspect in the life of the person selected. Next, have the children accumulate as many reference materials as possible. Biographies, information about the person's home, speeches or writings by the person, reproductions of newspapers available at that time, and the weather conditions for the period (listed in almanacs) are valuable resources. Have each group develop a composite picture of what the historical figure did during the chosen period; this should include possible thoughts, writings, actions, associations, and concerns.

Children should gain two values from this activity. First, they should experience such an intimate look at a day from the past that the person and place come alive for them. Second, they should gain an awareness about how research uncovers the past.

Values and Problems of Colonial Times

Historical fiction set in colonial times presents problems and their associated values. Stories related to the early colonial period stress a search for religious and political freedom, as the colonists fight the tyranny of a hated government and brave the frequent miseries associated with starting over in a new land. The colonists face danger, disease, and even starvation in order to fulfill their dream. In some books, such as Patricia Clapp's *Constance: A Story of Early Plymouth,* people also make personal adjustments, longing to return to a beloved home, battling the role mandated by their society, and finally discovering love for their new land.

Much historical fiction set in the Revolutionary War period stresses the battle for freedom, as well as the tragedy of war and the personal and emotional problems associated with following one's conscience during wartime. Some books that develop similar problems and values have settings in different time periods. Have students discuss these prob-

lems and values and then compare and relate them to current experiences. Following are a few examples of historical fiction that may be used to stimulate such discussion.

- People need political and religious freedom, and they will go through many hardships in search of freedom. *Colonial times:* Patricia Clapp's *Constance: A Story of Early Plymouth;* Elizabeth George Speare's *The Witch of Blackbird Pond. Czarist Russia:* Kathryn Lasky's *The Night Journey. World War II:* Aranka Siegal's *Upon the Head of the Goat: A Childhood in Hungary 1939–1944;* Yoshiko Uchida's *Journey Home.*
- Sometimes people must fight or risk freedom to save what they believe in. *Colonial times:* Esther Forbes's *Johnny Tremain. Post-revolutionary times:* James and Christopher Collier's *Jump Ship to Freedom. Civil War:* Irene Hunt's *Across Five Aprils. World War II:* Marie McSwigan's *Snow Treasure;* Uri Orlev's *The Man from the Other Side.*
- War and hatred are destructive forces. *Colonial times:* Esther Forbes's *Johnny Tremain. English Civil War:* Erik Christian Haugaard's *Cromwell's Boy. Civil War:* Paul Fleischman's *Bull Run. World War II:* Johanna Reiss's *The Upstairs Room;* Uri Orlev's *The Island on Bird Street.*

When children see and discuss the relationships among values that have been held across historical periods, they begin to realize that these values are also important today.

The Salem Witch-Hunts

Incidents of unreasonable fears and unjustified persecutions appear throughout history. The historical fiction books written about the late 1600s provide stimulating sources for oral discussion, creative dramatizations, clarification of values, writing, understanding of setting and characterization, and comparing of literary works that develop similar themes. Ann Petry's *Tituba of Salem Village* is about an enslaved black woman, and Elizabeth George Speare's *The Witch of Blackbird Pond* is about a free teenaged white girl. Both protagonists experience the impact of witch-hunts and unjustified persecution. These stories are excellent for discussion and comparison. Chart 10–2 presents the discussion and learning possibilities that a sixth-grade teacher mapped for using these two books with her students.

CHART 10-2 Comparing Ann Petry's *Tituba of Salem Village* and Elizabeth George Speare's *The Witch of Blackbird Pond* for sixth graders

Tituba of Salem Village	The Witch of Blackbird Pond
Dramatization	
1. Dramatize the family's approaching the gloomy house in Salem Village and meeting Goody Good.	1. Dramatize Kit's first meeting with her relatives.
2. Recreate the scene in which the children bring in the fortune-telling cards and try to convince Tituba to read their fortunes.	2. Recreate the dame's school and Kit's providing instruction for her six students.
3. Dramatize the court scene, including the witnesses against Tituba and the appearance of Samuel Conklin, who comes to her defense.	3. Role-play the conversations between Kit and the Quaker woman, Hannah Tupper, who lives in the meadow.
4. Interview Tituba, her husband, the minister, Betsy, Abigail, and Samuel Conklin. How does each describe the experiences leading up to the trial? How do they feel about the results of the trial? Are they pleased when Tituba is freed?	4. Dramatize the scenes during which Kit is accused of witchcraft, is taken prisoner to the shed, stands trial for witchcraft, and is freed because Prudence demonstrates her reading skills.
Characterization	
How does each of the following people see Tituba and feel about her:	How does each of the following people see Kit and feel about her:
1. Her former owner on Barbados?	1. Kit's grandfather?
2. The minister?	2. Matthew Wood?
3. The minister's wife?	3. Aunt Rachel?
4. Betsy or Abigail?	4. Reverend Gershom Bulkeley?
5. Dr. Griggs?	5. William Ashby?
6. A resident of Salem Village?	6. Judith or Mercy?
7. Samuel Conklin?	7. Goodwife Cruff?
8. Tituba herself?	8. Hannah Tupper?
	9. Nat Eaton?
	10. Kit herself?

Setting

1. Compare the jewel-like setting of Barbados with Tituba's description of the house in Salem and Kit's description of the colorless Puritan village.
2. Why did both authors choose to take their heroines from tropical islands to very different locations?
3. What might have happened in each story if Kit and Tituba had remained in Barbados?

Values Clarification	
1. Why did Tituba's former owner decide to sell her two dear companions? Do you believe her reason was good? Why or why not?	1. Why did Kit's grandfather want her to read and discuss plays? Why do you think the Puritans reacted so differently to her desire to read such material?
2. Why do you believe that Abigail encouraged the other girls to try to put Betsy into a trance?	2. Why do you believe that Kit enjoyed going to the meadow and visiting Hannah Tupper? Why were the villagers afraid of both the meadow and Hannah Tupper?
3. What special skills did Tituba have that made her different from the people in Salem Village? Why would the people hate and fear her?	3. What makes Hannah Tupper different from the villagers? Why would people fear her?
4. Why do you believe that the minister did not come to Tituba's defense or pay her jail fees?	4. What made Kit Tyler different from the villagers? Why would people fear her?

CHART 10–2 *Continued*

Tituba of Salem Village	The Witch of Blackbird Pond

Values Clarification (Continued)

5. Why was Samuel Conklin the only one to come to Tituba's defense? How did he demonstrate his faith in her?

5. What was the difference between the way Goodwife Cruff felt about her daughter Prudence and the way that Kit felt about Prudence? Who was right?
6. How would Prudence's life have been different if Kit had not helped Prudence? Why do you think that Kit didn't speak out in court about Prudence, even if her answer might have helped her own case?
7. Why do you believe Kit's friend, "dear dependable William," did not come to her defense at the trial? Why did Nat Eaton risk his own liberty to testify for her?

Personal Response

1. How would you have felt if you had been Tituba and had been forced to leave your homeland? What would your reaction have been to your new family and the people of the village?

1. If you had been Kit, would you have risked your safety to help both Hannah Tupper and Prudence Cruff? Why or why not?
2. Have you ever felt like Kit? When?

2. Have you ever known anyone or read about anyone who was feared or disliked because that person was different from others? Has this ever happened to you? When? Who helped you when you needed help?
3. Compare both books. Which story did you like better? Why?
4. Were you satisfied with the ending of each story? Why or why not? If you could change either story, how would you change it?
5. Do you believe that a story about personal persecution could be written about a person today? What would be the cause of the persecution? How might the person solve his or her problem?

Writing

1. Pretend that you are either Tituba or Kit. Choose a period of time from the story and write your experiences in a journal format.
2. Pretend to be someone living in Salem Village who has relatives in England. Write a letter to these relatives telling them about what has been happening in Salem.
3. Pretend to be a twentieth-century writer developing a script for a television "You Are There" program. Write the script for a reenactment of the trial of either Tituba or Kit.

Compare the themes of fear and unjustified persecution in *Tituba of Salem Village* and *The Witch of Blackbird Pond* with those set in other time periods, such as (1) suspicion toward and the persecution of the Navaho Indians in Scott O'Dell's *Sing Down the Moon* and (2) suspicion toward and persecution of gypsies in William Hooks's *Circle of Fire.*

Compare the suspicion toward and persecution of Jewish people during World War II in the following books: Johanna Reiss's *The Upstairs Room,*

Esther Hautzig's *The Endless Steppe: A Girl in Exile,* Judith Kerr's *When Hitler Stole Pink Rabbit,* Sonia Levitin's *Journey to America,* Aranka Siegal's *Upon the Head of the Goat: A Childhood in Hungary 1939–1944,* Uri Orlev's *The Island on Bird Street* and *The Man from the Other Side,* Lois Lowry's *Number the Stars,* and Ida Vos's *Hide and Seek.* Compare the suspicion toward and persecution of people who are different in Janet Lunn's *Shadow in Hawthorn Bay,* Carol Carrick's *Stay Away from Simon!,* and Ellen Howard's *Edith Herself.*

INTERDISCIPLINARY UNIT: LOOKING AT PIONEER AMERICA

Most children are fascinated with the time in American history when courageous adults and children were struggling across the country on foot, on horseback, or in covered wagons. They like to hear about children who rode on canal barges, floated on rafts down the Ohio, or traveled on steamboats down the Mississippi. They also enjoy vicariously experiencing the frontier years after the covered wagons were unloaded and families began their new lives in sod houses or log cabins.

Teachers of social studies find this period exciting. They use the fiction of the pioneer period to help children develop closer ties with the past, understand the physical environment of the time, and discover the links between the pioneer past and the present. Ways of developing these understandings range from sharing an individual story with children to developing total units that encourage children to identify with the period through music, art, stories, games, foods, values, home remedies, and research of historic characters.

In order to immerse children in the physical environment of the time and to stimulate their curiosity, show them objects that were important, for both survival and pleasure, to a pioneer family: quilts, tools (hammer, nails, spade, hoe, grindstone), tallow candles, lengths of cotton cloth, wooden buckets, iron pots, skillets, earthenware jugs, tin lanterns, dried herbs, food (a barrel of flour; yeast; dried beans, peas, and corn; salt; sugar; dried apples; a slab of bacon), seed corn, cornhusk dolls, a china-head doll, a yoke, a churn, a spinning wheel, a fiddle, a log cabin (made from Lincoln Logs), and pictures of pioneers. Accompany these objects by displays of historical fiction, books that pioneer children might have read, and books about pioneer art, music, and crafts.

One teacher introduced some third-grade students to the pioneer period by dressing in pioneer style, greeting the students at the classroom door, and taking them on a classroom tour. By enthusiastically presenting artifacts, the teacher excited the children and made them want to know more.

Values from the Past

Children can learn about the past and relate it to the present when they identify the values held and problems overcome by people living in pioneer America. Children can compare these values and problems and the solutions of problems, as depicted in historical fiction, with those of today. The pioneer period is filled with stories that stress love of the land and the need for positive relationships among family members, neighbors, pioneers, and Native Americans, including the struggle for survival and the need for bravery. The following experiences encourage children to clarify their own values as well as those of others.

Love of the Land. Pioneers were drawn to the West because of the opportunity to own rich farmland. Some people left their homes in the East when their land no longer produced good crops. Others traveled to the West because they wanted more room or fewer neighbors. Still others acquired the free land provided under the Homestead Act (see Figure 10–1). After children have read one of the books that place this emphasis on the land (such as Honore Morrow's *On to Oregon!;* Barbara Brenner's *Wagon Wheels;* and Harold Keith's *The Obstinate Land*), ask them to identify the reasons of the pioneers for moving and conflicts that family members felt when they were deciding whether or not to move.

At this point, use role playing to help clarify the attitudes of pioneer family members. Ask the students to imagine that the year is 1866. The Civil War ended the year before. They are living on a small New England farm. They are sitting with their immediate family and their visiting aunt and uncle at the evening meal. Their aunt begins excitedly talking about an article in the paper telling how many people are going west to claim free land provided

FIGURE 10–1 A poster for the Homestead Act

under the Homestead Act of 1862. The aunt and uncle are ready to sell their farm, pack a few belongings, and travel to the West in a covered wagon. The aunt wants her brother's family to join them. Suggest that the students role-play the reactions of the different family characters and decide whether or not they should go. Based on characteristics found in historical fiction stories, the characters might express these concerns:

- *Mother:* She knows that her husband wants to own a better farm, but her family lives in the East and she doesn't want to leave it. In addition, she has lost one child, who is buried on the old farm. She is also concerned about living on the frontier away from a church, a school, and the protection of close neighbors.
- *Father:* He is unhappy with his rocky farm and the poor production it has provided. He has dreamed of a farm with rich soil to produce better crops and support his family.
- *Twelve-year-old daughter:* She is filled with the excitement of a new adventure. She wants to see new lands and Indians. In addition, she is not displeased with the prospect of leaving school for a while.
- *Seven-year-old son:* The farmhouse is the only home that he has ever known; his best friend and his relatives live in the surrounding countryside. He'd love to see some Indians and he wants to please his father but he doesn't know what to expect in a land that far from home.

Have the students consider each person's arguments and decide if they would have moved to a new land. Have the students continue by talking about what they would take with them if they decided to homestead.

Finally, draw the discussion into the present time. Do people still have a strong loyalty to the land? Do they want to own their own land? Encourage the students to provide reasons for their arguments. Place the desire for unspoiled land as well as adventure into a modern framework by having students pretend that their families are moving to a wilderness area in Alaska. Why would they want to move? Why would they not want to move? What problems do they think they would encounter before moving? How would they solve them? What problems would they encounter in the Alaskan wilderness? How would they solve them? Finally, do they believe that these problems and their solutions are similar to those experienced by pioneers?

Human Relations. Many stories about pioneer days present different ways of dealing with Native Americans and diverse attitudes toward them. The only solution that many books give is a battle between the Native Americans and whites. In contrast, Alice Dalgliesh's *The Courage of Sarah Noble* presents a family who settles on land for which the native people have been given a fair price, with the provision that they retain their right to fish in the river. Sarah's parents believe that all people must be treated fairly. Encourage children to discuss the reasons for various actions, the beliefs of the pioneers, and the consequences.

After children have read the "Massacre" and "Ambassador to the Enemy" chapters in Carol Ryrie Brink's *Caddie Woodlawn,* ask them to discuss the decision made by the settlers to attack the Indians because they thought the Indians were going to attack them. Why did the settlers reach their decision? Was it accurate? Why or why not?

Then, ask the students to place themselves in Caddie's role. If they were Caddie, would they have warned the Indians? Why or why not? What might have been the results if Caddie had not made her evening ride?

Finally, bring the discussion to contemporary times. Ask the students if there are times when people today might decide to act out of fright rather than out of knowledge. What events would they consider important enough to risk their own safety?

Books about pioneers also include many stories about need to help others. Neighbors and family members help each other and provide moral support during times of crisis. The "Little House" series, by Laura Ingalls Wilder, contains many incidents of family support and working with neighbors. *Sarah, Plain and Tall* by Patricia MacLachlan emphasizes the need for a mother and wife in pioneer times. Encourage children to discuss the values of positive relationships during both pioneer and contemporary times.

The Pioneer Environment

Pioneer stories are rich in descriptions of the homes, crafts, store goods, food, transportation, books, and pleasures of the pioneers.

Amusements of the Pioneer Family. Allowing children to take part in the same experiences that entertained pioneer children is a good way to help them feel closer to their counterparts in the past. For example, Laura Ingalls Wilder's *Little House in the Big Woods* describes happy moments that can be recreated with children:

1. For a special birthday treat, Pa played and sang "Pop Goes the Weasel" for Laura. Some of her happiest memories were related to Pa's fiddle. Other songs mentioned in the book are "Rock of Ages" (the fiddle could not play weekday songs on Sunday) and "Yankee Doodle."
2. The family traveled through the woods to a square dance at Grandpa's house. At the dance, the fiddler played and the squaredance caller called the squares for "Buffalo Gals," "The Irish Washerwoman," and "The Arkansas Traveler."
3. After the day's work was finished, Ma sometimes cut paper dolls for the girls out of stiff white paper and made dresses, hats, ribbons, and laces out of colored paper.
4. In the winter evenings, Laura and Mary begged Pa to tell them stories. He told them about "Grandpa and the Panther," "Pa and the Bear in the Way," "Pa and the Voice in the Woods," and "Grandpa's Sled and the Pig." Enough details are included in these stories so that they can be retold to children.

A School Day with the Pioneer Family. A day in school for pioneer children (if a school was available) was quite different from a contemporary day in school. Historical fiction and other sources provide enough information about schools attended, books read, and parables memorized to interest children and recreate a school day that emphasizes spelling, reading, and arithmetic.

Modern children may be surprised that Ma in Laura Ingalls Wilder's *On the Banks of Plum Creek* considered three books on the subjects of spelling, reading, and arithmetic among her "best things" and gave them solemnly to the girls with the advice that they care for them and study faithfully.

A number of early textbooks and other stories have been reissued in their original form and can be shared with children. For example, children can read the rhyming alphabet; practice their letters; and learn to read words of one, two, three, four, and five syllables from *The New England Primer* (Ford, 1962).

Pioneer children also read and wrote maxims to practice their handwriting or as punishment for bad behavior. Joan W. Blos's *A Gathering of Days: A New England Girl's Journal, 1830–32* tells of this experience in the 1830s and lists some maxims that were written, such as:

> Speak the truth and lie not.
> To thine own self be true.
> Give to them that want.

Additional methods of instruction are described in other stories. Carol Ryrie Brink's *Caddie Woodlawn* describes an 1860 method for memorizing the multiplication tables; the children sang them to the tune of "Yankee Doodle." Recreating a typical school day during which children read from the primer, recite and copy parables, have a spelling bee, and sing their multiplication tables would help them visualize the pioneer child's life and develop an understanding that education was considered important in earlier times.

A Day in the General Store. The country store was very different from the contemporary department store or large shopping mall. It fascinated children, however, just as malls create excitement in today's children. Laura Ingalls Wilder's first experience in a general store is described in *Little House in the Big Woods*. This store included bright materials, kegs of nails, kegs of shot, barrels of candy, cooking utensils, plowshares, knives, shoes, and dishes. In fact, it had just about everything.

A source of information about the kinds of materials that might be available to a pioneer family in the late 1800s is a reissue of an early Sears, Roebuck and Company catalogue (1970). Through these pages, children can acquire an understanding of the merchandise available and the fashions of the day. They can use the information found in such sources either to create a child-sized general store in one corner of the room or to create miniature stores in boxes.

While people may not keep the following kind of a work schedule today, the daily activities of the pioneer family associated with the house and other outside responsibilities are of interest to children.

Pioneer Chores

Wash on Monday
Iron on Tuesday
Mend on Wednesday
Churn on Thursday
Clean on Friday
Bake on Saturday
Rest on Sunday

Preparing food is mentioned in many stories. Because pioneer families could not go to the local store for supplies, they needed to prepare their own. Churning butter is one activity that children enjoy. A simple recipe for butter that children can make easily follows:

1/2 pint whipping cream
1/4 teaspoon salt
Pint jar with tight cover
Pour the 1/2 pint of whipping cream into the pint jar. Seal the cover tightly onto the jar. Shake the jar until the cream turns to butter. Remove the lid, pour off the liquid, and work out any excess liquid. Add salt and stir it into the butter. Remove the butter from jar and shape it.

According to Laura in *Little House in the Big Woods,* Ma was not always satisfied with white butter. Children may wish to experiment with the technique Ma used to add a yellow color to the butter. She rubbed a carrot over a pan that had nail holes punched across the bottom. She placed the soft, grated carrot into a pan of milk, then warmed the mixture and poured it into a cloth bag. When she squeezed the bag, bright yellow milk ran from the cloth and was added to the cream in the churn (p. 30).

Because pioneer families had no refrigerators or freezers, they had to find other ways to preserve their foods. If they lived in the North, they used nature's icebox in the winter. In Joan W. Blos's *A Gathering of Days: A New England Girl's Journal, 1830–32,* children read about chopping off a frozen wedge of soup and heating it in the kettle. Other stories describe the feeling of well-being when the pantry, shed, attic, and cellar were filled with food. In contrast, people experienced great concern when only seed corn remained between the family and starvation.

Children can learn about different ways that the pioneers preserved fruits and vegetables by reading Eliot Wigginton's *The Foxfire Book* (1972). Children enjoy drying their own apples and then having them for a special snack. Other books in this series provide details for many additional pioneer activities.

The people in pioneer fiction become alive for children who cannot actually live on a prairie homestead. Children can sing the same songs pioneer children sang, dance to the music of a pioneer fiddle, listen to the pioneer storyteller, imagine they attend a pioneer school, imagine they go to the general store, and do the chores of the homestead.

Trails in Westward Expansion

Deep ruts across a sea of prairie grass, markers along river crossings, and scars created by oxen hooves sliding down the rock sides of canyons were the pioneer equivalent of modern interstate highways. Like highways, these trails were important for moving people and commerce across the country; without them, the West could not have been opened for expansion. It is hard to imagine a thousand men, women, and children with two hundred covered wagons following such rough trails across prairies, deserts, and mountains to reach California or Oregon.

Have children discuss the purpose for the trails (such as cattle drives, wagon trails, fast movement of mail), the locations of the trails, the physical hardships found along the trails, forts built along the trails, and distances covered by the trails. Have them draw a large map of the United States, place on it the major westward trails, and then trace, using different colored pencils, the routes taken by pioneers in various books of historical fiction. The following books provide enough descriptions of locations to be of value in this activity:

1. Alice Dalgliesh, *The Courage of Sarah Noble.* Westfield, Massachusetts, to New Milford, Connecticut, by foot and horse backpack, 1707.

2. Brett Harvey, *Cassie's Journey: Going West in the 1860s*. Map shows the trail from Independence, Missouri, to Sacramento, California.
3. Honore Morrow, *On to Oregon!* Missouri to Oregon by covered wagon, horse, and foot, 1844.
4. Laura Ingalls Wilder, "Little House" books: Pepin, Wisconsin, to Kansas, to Minnesota, and to Dakota Territory near De Smet by covered wagon, 1870s.

Research Skills

Many historical fiction books describe the sources used by the authors to develop the settings and authenticity of periods. Encouraging children to choose a specific time period and location and then to discover as much as possible about the people and their times will help the children develop respect for research skills and gain new insights.

In one class, children researched their own small city during the late 1800s. The group investigated documents at the historical society; searched old newspapers; found old family albums, journals, and letters; searched documents at the courthouse; interviewed people whose relatives had lived in the town during that time; read references to discover information about fashions, transportation, and food; and located buildings that would have existed during that time. After they had gathered this information, they pretended that they were living a hundred years earlier and wrote stories about themselves. The stories contained only authentic background information.

Additional Activities

Have children pretend that they are newspaper reporters sent from an eastern paper to discover what living on the frontier is really like. Encourage them to write news stories to send back to the newspaper. In addition, have them pretend that they can take tintype pictures to accompany their stories; have them draw pictures of the scenes that they would like to photograph.

Many pioneers moved to the West because they received encouraging letters from friends and relatives. Have children write letters to friends or relatives telling the Easterners why they should or should not sell all their property and move to ____.

Several books of historical fiction, such as Joan W. Blos's *A Gathering of Days: A New England Girl's Journal, 1830–32*, are written in journal format. Have children select a character from a historical fiction story and write several journal entries for a specific period in the story.

Many scenes from historical fiction about the pioneer period can be dramatized. The experiences of Alice Dalgliesh's Sarah Noble in playing and living with the Indian family when her father leaves her to return for his wife are interesting to dramatize.

A Culminating Activity

Children enjoy sharing their knowledge about pioneer days with their parents or other children. Have a class plan a pioneer day in which the children display pioneer objects, food, arts, and crafts; demonstrate songs or dances learned; and share information gained, creative writing completed, and art projects made during their study of pioneer life and historical fiction.

 LOOKING AT AMERICAN HISTORY IN FOLK SONGS

Folk songs, like historical fiction, present a panorama of American history, creating a picture of the common people during different periods. The books discussed in this chapter often refer to characters who are listening to, singing, or playing music. Several songs have already been suggested as means of making the pioneer period come alive for today's children.

One very exciting historical unit used with children combined folk music, historical fiction, and social studies. Singing or square dancing to the music of the times allowed the children to share an experience that was similar to that of the characters in the books they were reading. The words of the songs helped convey the essence of certain periods.

Chart 10–3 lists folk songs from different historical periods. The folk songs in the chart, and information about the historical struggles of the times, can be found in the following books: C. A. Browne's *The Story of Our National Ballads* (1960), Edith Fowke and Joe Glazer's *Songs of Work and Protest* (1973), Tom Glazer's *A New Treasury of Folk Songs* (1961), and Carl Sandburg's *The American Songbag* (1927). Dan Fox's *Go In and Out the Window* (1987)

CHART 10–3 Folk songs

Year	Song
1754 and 1776	"Yankee Doodle"—symbolic of the struggle for freedom.
1796–1800	"Jefferson and Liberty"—Jefferson pledged to repeal the Sedition Act.
Early 1800s	"Blow Ye Wings in the Morning"—whaling industry along the eastern seaboard.
1825–1913	"Low Bridge Everybody Down"—mule drivers on the Erie Canal.
1841–1847	"Patsy Works on the Railroad"—Irish workers completing railroad in eastern United States.
1850s	"Sweet Betsy from Pike"—taking a covered wagon to California.
1850s	"Go Down Moses"—freedom song of the black slaves.
1850s	"Oh, Freedom"—freedom song of the slaves.
1859	"John Brown's Body"—attack on garrison at Harper's Ferry to capture arms and liberate slaves.
1861	"The Battle Hymn of the Republic"—Julia Ward Howe watched the campfires of the Union Army.
1872	"John Henry"—a steel-driving man drilling the Big Bend Tunnel on the Chesapeake and Ohio Railroad.
1888	"Drill, Ye Tarriers, Drill"—dynamiters blasting their way through the mountains as the railroads crossed the continent.
1870–1890	"The Old Chisholm Trail"—herding cattle from San Antonio, Texas northward.
1897	"Hallelujah, I'm a Bum"—hoboing on the open road.
Early 1900s	"Sixteen Tons"—coal mining song.

combines folk songs and art from the Metropolitan Museum of Art. Alvin Schwartz's *And the Green Grass Grew All Around* (1992) includes both folk poetry and music.

The teacher who developed this historical song and literature unit with fourth-grade children used the following time periods: Revolutionary War, early expansion, Civil War, and pioneer America. He collected many books at different levels of reading ability. Some, he shared orally with the group; others, the children read themselves. Esther Forbes's *Johnny Tremain* provided the major emphasis for the Revolutionary War period. Books of historical fiction related to the early expansion period included Honore Morrow's *On to Oregon!* and Joan Blos's *A Gathering of Days: A New England Girl's Journal, 1830–32.* Books related to the Civil War period included Harold Keith's *Rifles for Watie,* Paul Fleischman's *Bull Run,* and Irene Hunt's *Across Five Aprils.* Books about pioneer America included Carol Ryrie Brink's *Caddie Woodlawn,* all of Laura Ingalls Wilder's "Little House" series, and Patricia MacLachlan's *Sarah, Plain and Tall.*

In addition to books of historical fiction, the teacher used biographies of famous people from the time period and other informational books about the period from the Revolutionary War through the days of pioneer America. The students involved themselves in history; they sang the songs of the people, acted out scenes from the stories, made artifacts such as cornhusk dolls, wrote creative stories, and investigated the historical periods.

One day, the children sat in a circle on the floor and sang folk songs from the Civil War period. After they sang each song, some children pretended to be slaves, seeking freedom by way of the Underground Railroad; Separatists in Ohio deciding if they should or should not fight in the Civil War; and different members of the Creighton family, who were home from the war, sharing their experiences from Irene Hunt's *Across Five Aprils.* The teacher and the children thoroughly enjoyed the experience and gained much information about their American heritage and literature reflecting this heritage. When evaluating their experience, the children indicated that they had never had such an enjoyable time learning social studies. The characters of the past actually lived for these children, as they discovered the pleasures that may be gained from reading.

Students in one class used Susan M. Knorr and Margaret Knorr's *Books on the Move: A Read-About-It Go-There Guide to America's Best Family Destinations* (1993) to create their own "Books on the Move" source. First, they looked at and discussed the authors' chapter eight, "Stepping into the Past." In this chapter, the authors include children's books on such topics as history museums, dolls and toys, teddy bears, mummies, early American settlements, nineteenth-century New England, frontier living, the journey of Lewis and Clark, settling the West, gold rush days, cowhands and mountaineers, Native Americans, pueblo and cliff dwellers, striving for freedom, historic homes and sites, and various battles. In addition, the book includes destinations where people can go to see and discover more information about these time periods in history.

Next, the students conducted research on their own city and state. What historical sources did they have? What museums or other sites were found in their state? After selecting several of these sites, the students identified books that they could use to make connections with those sites and to learn more about the historic time period. They wrote to or visited various sites and wrote descriptions of the destinations that were similar to those developed by Knorr and Knorr. As a class, they read all of the material that they could find associated with a site near their school and then visited the site and wrote their impressions of the visit.

Finally, they published their own state source for historic sites and placed it in the school library. The activity and the book also provided motivation for family and group excursions.

 SUGGESTED ACTIVITIES

for Involving Children in Historical Fiction

- Historical fiction is a means of translating the information found in sterile textbooks into vivid spectacles of human drama. Choose a social studies or history text appropriate for children of a certain age, list the content and time periods covered in the text, and identify historical fiction to stimulate children's interest and understanding of that content or time period.

- With a group of children or a peer group, compare the information found in a textbook (see the first activity) with the background information discovered in the books of historical fiction. Do the two sources agree? If they do not, research other sources in order to discover which is correct. If they do agree, discuss which sources more vividly describe history and what makes those sources more meaningful.

- One value of reading historical fiction is the development of an understanding that certain human qualities persist through each century and tie the past to the present. Use Chart 10–1, "Eras and Themes in Historical Fiction," and share literature from several periods with children. Lead a discussion that helps the children identify the values expressed in those time periods. Allow the children to discuss whether these values are still accepted by people today and whether the values will still be important in the next century. Ask the children why or why not.

- Discussions of controversial issues create springboards that allow children to become involved in stimulating debates. Historical fiction has numerous characters who take stands on controversial issues. The plots of many historical fiction stories are based on issues considered controversial during a time period. Identify several books from a time period and find paragraphs that state these issues. Develop a list of provocative questions to use when sharing this material with children. For example, in the Revolutionary War period, some literary characters believed that freedom was worth fighting for, no matter what the consequences; others believed that the colonies should stay loyal to England; and still others felt that all killing was wrong.

- Encourage children to select one controversial issue found in historical fiction, pretend to be on the side of one group or another in the story, do additional research on the issue, and take part in a debate.

- In order to discover how vividly a setting can be presented in historical fiction, allow children to draw detailed pictures after they have read or listened to a story. To increase their appreciation of the settings described in some books, ask the children to draw the setting described in an excellent historical book as well as a setting that is inadequately described. Discuss the differences for the readers and for the writer. Which one is more meaningful to readers? Which one is more demanding on the author? Why?

- Select a scene from historical fiction that has both memorable characters and an exciting plot. With a group of children or peers, develop the scene into a creative dramatization.

- Select folk songs that were popular during a specific period in history. Listen to and read the words and sing the songs. What conflicts, problems, or values do the lyrics present? Are the same themes found in historical fiction of that time period?

CHILDREN'S LITERATURE

Alder, Elizabeth. *The King's Shadow*. Farrar, Straus & Giroux, 1995 (I:11+ R:7). The novel is set in England prior to the Battle of Hastings in 1066.

Aldridge, James. *The True Story of Spit MacPhee*. Viking Kestrel, 1986 (I:10+ R:6). An Australian story is set in the late 1920s.

Ames, Mildred. *Grandpa Jake and the Grand Christmas*. Scribner, 1990 (I:8+ R:5). In a Depression story, a girl makes discoveries about her grandfather.

Armstrong, Jennifer. *The Dreams of Mairhe Mehan: A Novel of the Civil War*. Knopf, 1996 (I:10+ R:6). A story of Irish immigrants living in Washington, D.C.

Armstrong, William H. *Sounder*. Illustrated by James Barkley. Harper & Row, 1969 (I:10+ R:6). An African American sharecropper's family experiences prejudice.

Avi. *The Fighting Ground*. Lippincott, 1984 (I:10+ R:6). A thirteen-year-old boy experiences the reality of war during the American Revolution.

_____. *The True Confessions of Charlotte Doyle*. Orchard, 1990 (I:10+ R:6). A girl is accused of murder when she travels on a sailing ship.

Beatty, Patricia. *Eight Mules from Monterey*. Morrow, 1982 (I:10+ R:6). The Ashmores cross the California mountains in 1916.

_____. *Sarah and Me and the Lady from the Sea*. Morrow, 1989 (I:10+ R:6). A family learns self-reliance following the father's business failures.

_____. *Wait for Me, Watch for Me, Eula Bee*. Morrow, 1978 (I:12+ R:7). Two white children are taken captive by Indians and the girl grows to trust an Indian brave.

Blos, Joan W. *A Gathering of Days: A New England Girl's Journal, 1830–32*. Scribner's Sons, 1979 (I:8–14 R:6). This book tells a thirteen-year-old girl's experiences on a farm.

Borden, Louise. *The Little Ships: The Heroic Rescue at Dunkirk in World War II*. Illustrated by Michael Foreman. Simon & Schuster, 1997 (I:8+ R:4). The rescue in 1940 is told through the eyes of a young girl.

Bradley, Kimberly Brubaker. *Ruthie's Gift*. Delacorte, 1998 (I:7–12 R:5). The setting is Indiana prior to WWI.

Branford, Henrietta. *Fire, Bed, and Bone*. Candlewick, 1998 (I:10+ R:5). The historical conflict and characterizations for 1381 Britain are developed through the point of view of a hunting dog.

Brenner, Barbara. *Wagon Wheels*. Illustrated by Don Bolognese. Harper & Row, 1978 (I:6–9 R:1). An easy-to-read story is about a real pioneer family.

Brink, Carol Ryrie. *Caddie Woodlawn*. Illustrated by Trina Schart Hyman. Macmillan, 1935, 1963, 1973 (I:8–12 R:6). Twelve-year-old Caddie lives with her family on the Wisconsin frontier in 1864.

Calvert, Patricia. *Bigger*. Scribners, 1994 (I:8+ R:5). Set after the Civil War, a boy searches for his father.

Carrick, Carol. *Stay Away from Simon!* Illustrated by Donald Carrick. Clarion, 1985 (I:7–10 R:3). A mentally retarded boy and a snowstorm help two children realize that disabled people can have great worth.

Clapp, Patricia. *Constance: A Story of Early Plymouth*. Lothrop, Lee & Shepard. 1968 (I:12+ R:7). This is the story of the first few years of the Plymouth Colony.

_____. *Witches' Children: A Story of Salem*. Lothrop, Lee & Shepard, 1982 (I:10+ R:7). A bound girl tells about the hysteria that takes over Salem in 1692.

Collier, James, and Christopher Collier. *Jump Ship to Freedom*. Delacorte, 1981 (I:10+ R:7). A slave obtains his freedom and that of his mother.

Conrad, Pam. *My Daniel*. Harper & Row, 1989 (I:10+ R:5). A grandmother relives her life on a pioneer Nebraska farm as she takes her grandchildren on a tour through the Natural History Museum.

Cormier, Robert. *Other Bells for Us to Ring*. Illustrated by Deborah Kogan Ray. Delacorte, 1990 (I:8+ R:5). A World War II story is set in the United States.

Cushman, Karen. *The Ballad of Lucy Whipple*. Clarion, 1996 (I:10+ R:8). This historical fiction is set in a small mining town during the Gold Rush.

_____. *Catherine, Called Birdy*. Clarion, 1994 (I:12+ R:9). Set in medieval England, the story centers around the life of the thirteen-year-old daughter of an English knight.

_____. *The Midwife's Apprentice*. Clarion, 1995 (I:12+ R:8). Set in medieval England, the story centers on a strong heroine who overcomes her problems with a society that does not care for its homeless.

Dalgliesh, Alice. *The Courage of Sarah Noble*. Illustrated by Leonard Weisgard. Scribner's Sons, 1954 (I:6–9 R:3). In 1707, Sarah keeps up her courage as she and her father go through the wilderness.

DeAngeli, Marguerite. *The Door in the Wall*. Doubleday, 1949 (I:8–12 R:6). Robin overcomes a mysterious ailment in England during the time of Edward III.

Disher, Garry. *The Bamboo Flute*. Ticknor & Fields, 1993 (I:10+ R:5). In the Australian depression of 1932, a boy develops understanding of others.

Dorris, Michael. *Morning Girl*. Hyperion, 1992 (I:8+ R:4). The story focuses on the life of a Taino Indian girl and boy in 1492.

_____. *Sees Behind Trees*. Hyperion, 1966 (I:9+ R:5). The story is set in pre-Colonial America.

Fleischman, Paul. *The Borning Room*. HarperCollins, 1991 (I:10+ R:5). Family life on the Ohio frontier follows the activities in a room set aside for births and deaths.

_____. *Bull Run*. HarperCollins, 1993 (I:10+ R:5). The book is told from the viewpoints of various people associated with the first battle of the Civil War.

I = Interest by age range.

R = Readability by grade level.

_____ . *Coming-and-Going Men: Four Tales.* Illustrated by Randy Gaul. Harper & Row, 1985 (I:10+ R:6). The text includes four short stories set in Vermont in 1800.

_____ . *Path of the Pale Horse.* Harper & Row, 1983 (I:10+ R:6). A fourteen-year-old boy helps a doctor treat yellow fever in Philadelphia in 1793.

_____ . *Saturnalia.* HarperCollins, 1990 (I:12+ R:6). This is the story of a printer in Boston, 1681.

Forbes, Esther. *Johnny Tremain.* Illustrated by Lynd Ward. Houghton Mifflin, 1943 (I:10–14 R:6). A silversmith's apprentice lives through prerevolutionary days and early wartime in Boston.

Fox, Paula. *The Slave Dancer.* Illustrated by Eros Keith. Bradbury, 1973 (I:12+ R:7). In 1840, a fife player witnesses the misery of the slave trade.

Frank, Rudolf. *No Hero for the Kaiser.* Translated by Patricia Crampton. Illustrated by Klaus Steffens. Lothrop, Lee & Shepard, 1986 (I:10+ R:7). The author develops an antiwar theme.

Garfield, Leon. *The December Rose.* Viking/Kestrel, 1986 (I:10+ R:7). A mystery is set in Victorian London.

Giff, Patricia Reilly. *Lily's Crossing.* Delacorte, 1997 (I:10+ R:6). The story is set in World War II.

Graham, Harriet. *A Boy and His Bear.* Simon & Schuster, 1996 (I:9+ R:6). This is the story of a boy who dislikes killing animals and is apprenticed to a tanner.

Gray, Elizabeth Janet. *Adam of the Road.* Illustrated by Robert Lawson. Viking, 1942, 1970 (I:8–12 R:6). A young minstrel has many adventures in the England of 1294.

Haas, Jessie. *Westminster West.* Greenwillow, 1997 (I:11+ R:6). The story is set in Vermont in 1884.

Hahn, Mary Downing, *Following My Own Footsteps.* Clarion, 1996 (I:10+ R:6). Set in the United States during World War II, a boy tries to break the cycle of violence in his own family.

_____ . *Stepping on the Cracks.* Clarion, 1991 (I:10+ R:6). Children face the issue of conscientious objectors in a World War II story set in the United States.

Hamilton, Virginia. *The Bells of Christmas.* Illustrated by Lambert Davis. Harcourt Brace Jovanovich, 1989 (I:8+ R:5). A prosperous African American family experiences Christmas in Ohio in the 1890s.

Hartling, Peter. *Crutches.* Translated by Elizabeth D. Crawford. Lothrop, Lee & Shepard, 1988 (I:10+ R:6). A boy searches for his mother in postwar Vienna.

Harvey, Brett. *Cassie's Journey: Going West in the 1860s.* Illustrated by Deborah Kogan Ray. Holiday House, 1988 (I:7–9 R:3). A young girl describes her experiences on a wagon train.

Haugaard, Erik Christian. *The Boy and the Samurai.* Houghton Mifflin, 1991 (I:11+ R:6). In feudal Japan, a young orphan helps a Samurai rescue his wife from a warlord.

_____ . *Cromwell's Boy.* Houghton Mifflin, 1978 (I:11+ R:5). Oliver is a messenger for Oliver Cromwell and Parliament.

Hautzig, Esther. *The Endless Steppe: A Girl in Exile.* Harper Junior Books, 1968 (I:12+ R:7). In a true story, a Jewish girl and her parents are exiled to Siberia during World War II.

Heneghan, James. *Wish Me Luck.* Farrar, Straus & Giroux, 1997 (I:12+ R:7). Set in World War II, a British child sails on a ship to Canada.

Hesse, Karen. *Letters from Rifka.* Holt, 1992 (I:10+ R:6). A Jewish girl and her family flee Russia in 1919.

_____ . *Out of the Dust.* Scholastic, 1997 (I:10 + R:6). The story is set in Oklahoma during the dust bowl and the Depression.

Hill, Susan. *The Glass Angels.* Illustrated by Valerie Littlewood. Candlewick, 1992 (I:8+ R:5). In post–World War II England, a girl and her mother discover that people can help.

Hoestlandt, Jo. *Star of Fear, Star of Hope.* Translated from the French by Mark Polizzotti. Illustrated by Johanna Kang. Walker, 1995 (I:7–10 R:3). Nine-year-old Helen tells the story of the disappearance of her friend during the Holocaust.

Holman, Felice. *The Wild Children.* Scribner's Sons, 1983 (I:10+ R:4). A group of homeless children strive to survive during the Bolshevik Revolution.

Holub, Josef. *The Robber and Me.* Translated by Elizabeth D. Crawford. Holt, 1997 (I:8 + R:6). The story is set in Germany during the mid 1800s.

Hooks, William H. *Circle of Fire.* Atheneum, 1983 (I:10+ R:6). A boy and his friends try to prevent a Ku Klux Klan attack.

Howard, Ellen. *Edith Herself.* Atheneum, 1987 (I:7–10 R:4). A girl with epilepsy learns to value herself in the 1890s.

Hudson, Jan. *Sweetgrass.* Tree Frog, 1984, Philomel, 1989 (I:10+ R:4). A young Blackfoot girl grows up during the winter of a smallpox epidemic in 1837.

Hunt, Irene. *Across Five Aprils.* Follett, 1964 (I:10+ R:7). Jethro Creighton must become the man of the family when his brothers go to war and his father has a heart attack.

Johnston, Julie. *Hero of Lesser Causes.* Little, Brown, 1993 (I:10+ R:5). In Canada in 1946, a girl tries to interest her polio-stricken brother in an intellectual challenge.

Keith, Harold. *The Obstinate Land.* Crowell, 1977 (I:12+ R:7). In 1893, thirteen-year-old Fritz Romberg and his family move to the Oklahoma prairie.

_____ . *Rifles for Watie.* Crowell, 1957 (I:12+ R:7). A Civil War story involves a Cherokee raider.

Kerr, Judith. *When Hitler Stole Pink Rabbit.* Coward, McCann, 1972 (I:8–12 R:3). Anna and her family escape from Hitler's Germany.

Kinsey-Warnock, Natalie. *The Canada Geese Quilt.* Illustrated by Leslie W. Bowman. Dutton, 1989 (I:8+ R:5). In 1940s Vermont, a girl and her grandmother make a quilt.

Kirkpatrick, Katherine. *Keeping the Good Light.* Delacorte, 1995 (I:12+ R:6). The setting is Stepping Stones Lighthouse, 1903.

Kodama, Tatsuharu. *Shin's Tricycle.* Illustrated by Noriyuki Ando. Walker, 1995 (I:all). A boy is killed while riding his tricycle at the time of the bombing of Hiroshima.

Lasky, Kathryn. *Beyond the Divide.* Macmillan, 1983 (I:9+ R:6). In 1849, a fourteen-year-old girl accompanies her father across the continent.

_____ . *The Night Journey.* Illustrated by Trina Schart Hyman. Warne, 1981 (I:10+ R:6). A nine-year-old girl learns about her great-grandmother's escape from Czarist Russia in 1900.

_____ . *True North.* Scholastic, 1996 (I:12+ R:7). A runaway slave and a white girl join forces.

Lenski, Lois. *Indian Captive: The Story of Mary Jemison.* Stokes, 1941 (I:10+ R:7). A captive white girl decides to stay with the Senecas.

Levin, Betty. *Brother Moose.* Greenwillow, 1990 (I:10+ R:6). Two orphans interact with a Native American boy and his grandfather in Maine in the 1800s.

Levitin, Sonia. *Annie's Promise*. Atheneum, 1993 (I:12+ R:6). This is the third book about the Platt family.

———. *Journey to America*. Illustrated by Charles Robinson. Atheneum, 1970 (I:12+ R:6). A Jewish family escapes from Nazi Germany.

———. *Silver Days*. Atheneum, 1989 (I:12+ R:6). Here are additional experiences of the family introduced in *Journey to America*.

Lobel, Arnold. *On the Day Peter Stuyvesant Sailed into Town*. Harper & Row, 1971 (I:4–8 R:3). A picture storybook tells about the New Amsterdam colony.

Longfellow, Henry Wadsworth. *Paul Revere's Ride*. Illustrated by Adrian J. Iorio and Frederick J. Alford. Houghton Mifflin (I:8+). This is the classic poem.

Lowry, Lois. *Number the Stars*. Houghton Mifflin, 1989 (I:10+ R:6). In Copenhagen, the Danes try to save their Jewish citizens in 1943.

Lunn, Janet. *Shadow in Hawthorn Bay*. Scribner's Sons, 1986 (I:10+ R:5). A girl with second sight experiences prejudice in Canada in the 1800s.

Lydon, Kerry Raines. *A Birthday for Blue*. Illustrated by Michael Hayes Albert. Whitman, 1989 (I:5–8 R:4). A pioneer boy spends his seventh birthday in a covered wagon.

Lyon, George Ella. *Borrowed Children*. Watts, 1988 (I:10+ R:5). This story is set in Kentucky during the Depression.

MacLachlan, Patricia. *Sarah, Plain and Tall*. Harper & Row, 1985 (I:7–10 R:3). A frontier family longs for a new mother.

McClung, Robert. *Hugh Glass, Mountain Man*. Morrow, 1990 (I:10+ R:6). This is a fictionalized biography of a fur trapper in 1823.

McGuigan, Mary Ann. *Where You Belong*. Simon & Schuster, 1997 (I:10+ R:6). Set in 1963, the story develops problems with interracial friendships.

McSwigan, Marie. *Snow Treasure*. Illustrated by Mary Reardon. Dutton, 1942 (I:8–12 R:4). This is a retelling of a real adventure against the Nazis in World War II Norway.

Moeri, Louise. *Save Queen of Sheba*. Dutton, 1981 (I:10+ R:5). A twelve-year-old boy and his young sister cross the prairie alone after their wagon train is attacked.

Monjo, F. N. *The Drinking Gourd*. Illustrated by Fred Brenner. Harper & Row, 1970 (I:7–9 R:2). An "I Can Read" history book about the Underground Railroad.

Morrow, Honore. *On to Oregon!* Illustrated by Edward Shenton. Morrow, 1926, 1948, 1954 (I:10+ R:6). Children travel alone to Oregon in 1844.

Myers, Anna. *Fire in the Hills*. Walker, 1996 (I:10+ R:8). The story is set in Oklahoma during World War I.

Namioka, Lensey. *The Coming of the Bear*. HarperCollins, 1992 (I:9+ R:6). The setting is Japan in the 1600s.

O'Dell, Scott. *The Amethyst Ring*. Houghton Mifflin, 1983 (I:10+ R:6). This is the final story of Julián Escobar.

———. *The Captive*. Houghton Mifflin, 1979 (I:10+ R:6). A young Spanish seminarian witnesses the exploitation of the Maya during the 1500s.

———. *Carlota*. Houghton Mifflin, 1977 (I:9+ R:4). A Spanish girl fights beside her father during the Mexican war.

———. *The Feathered Serpent*. Houghton Mifflin, 1981 (I:10+ R:6). This is a sequel to *The Captive*.

———. *Sing Down the Moon*. Houghton Mifflin, 1970 (I:10+ R:6). This is the forced march of the Navaho from a young girl's perspective.

———. and Elizabeth Hall. *Thunder Rolling in the Mountains*. Houghton Mifflin, 1992 (I:10+ R:6). The setting is the late nineteenth century when the Nez Perce are forced to leave their lands.

Orlev, Uri. *The Island on Bird Street*. Translated by Hillel Halkin. Houghton Mifflin, 1984 (I:10+ R:6). A twelve-year-old Jewish boy survives in the Warsaw ghetto.

———. *The Lady with the Hat*. Houghton Mifflin, 1995 (I:12+ R:5). A Holocaust survivor moves to a kibbutz in Israel.

———. *Lydia, Queen of Palestine*. Translated from the Hebrew by Hillel Halkin. Puffin, 1995 (I:10+ R:4). A ten-year-old girl describes her life in a kibbutz.

———. *The Man from the Other Side*. Houghton Mifflin, 1991 (I:10+ R:6). A boy and his father help bring supplies to the Jewish people in the Warsaw Ghetto.

Oughton, Jerrie. *The War in Georgia*. Houghton Mifflin, 1997 (I:12+ R:6). The story, set in Georgia during World War II, parallels two wars, one of which is in the neighborhood.

Paterson, Katherine. *Jip, His Story*. Dutton, 1996 (I:10+ R:6). The story is set in Vermont in the 1850s.

Paulsen, Gary. *The Winter Room*. Orchard, 1989 (I:8+ R:5). The plot follows the seasons of the year on a northern farm in which winter brings storytelling.

Pearson, Kit. *The Sky Is Falling*. Viking, 1989 (I:10+ R:6). A girl and her brother are sent to Canada to escape the bombing in England.

Petry, Ann. *Tituba of Salem Village*. Crowell, 1964 (I:11+ R:6). A talented slave becomes part of the famous Salem witch trials.

Pullman, Philip. *The Ruby in the Smoke*. Knopf, 1985 (I:10+ R:6). A girl is involved in a mystery in Victorian London.

Reeder, Carolyn. *Across the Lines*. Simon & Schuster, 1997 (I:9+ R:6). The story is set in the Civil War.

———. *Shades of Gray*. Macmillan, 1989 (I:10+ R:6). Set in the Civil War, a boy encounters pacifism.

Reiss, Johanna. *The Upstairs Room*. Crowell, 1972 (I:11+ R:4). This is the true story of a Jewish girl's experience hiding from the Nazis.

Rinaldi, Ann. *The Fifth of March: A Story of the Boston Massacre*. Harcourt Brace Jovanovich, 1993 (I:10+ R:6). This story is set in Boston in 1770.

Rylant, Cynthia. *When I Was Young in the Mountains*. Dutton, 1982 (I:4–9 R:3). This book contains memories of Appalachia.

Salisbury, Graham. *Under the Blood Red Sun*. Delacorte, 1995 (I:8+ R:6). A Japanese American boy and his best friend find their activities disrupted by the bombing of Pearl Harbor.

Sandin, Joan. *The Long Way to a New Land*. Harper & Row, 1981 (I:7–9 R:3). A Swedish family emigrates to America in 1868.

Siegal, Aranka. *Grace in the Wilderness: After the Liberation, 1945–1948*. Farrar, Straus & Giroux, 1985 (I:10+ R:7). This is a sequel to *Upon the Head of the Goat*.

———. *Upon the Head of the Goat: A Childhood in Hungary 1939–1944*. Farrar, Straus & Giroux, 1981 (I:10+ R:7). Nine-year-old Piri experiences the Holocaust.

Skolsky, Mindy Warshaw. *Love From Your Friend, Hannah*. DK, 1998 (I:8+ R:5). Letters and notes to friends and relatives develop life during the Depression.

Slepian, Jan. *Risk n'Roses*. Philomel, 1990 (I:10+ R:5). A story of peer pressure and family loyalties is set in New York after World War II.

Smucker, Anna Egan. *No Star Nights*. Illustrated by Steve Johnson. Knopf, 1989 (I:5–8 R:4). The text and illustrations show growing up in a West Virginia steel-mill town.

Snyder, Zilpha Keatley. *Gib Rides Home*. Delacorte, 1998 (I:9 + R:5). This is the story of an orphan boy set in the early 1900s.

Speare, Elizabeth George. *The Bronze Bow*. Houghton Mifflin, 1961 (I:10+ R:6). A boy's hatred of the Romans is affected after he meets Jesus.

_____ . *Calico Captive*. Illustrated by W. T. Mars. Houghton Mifflin, 1957 (I:10+ R:6). White people are forced to march north to Indian territories in Canada.

_____ . *The Sign of the Beaver*. Houghton Mifflin, 1983 (I:8–12 R:5). A boy survives in a frontier cabin after an Indian friend teaches him survival techniques.

_____ . *The Witch of Blackbird Pond*. Houghton Mifflin, 1958 (I:9–14 R:4). A flamboyant girl is accused of witchcraft in colonial New England.

Stevens, Carla. *Anna, Grandpa, and the Big Storm*. Illustrated by Margot Tomes. Houghton Mifflin, 1982 (I:6–9 R:3). Seven-year-old Anna experiences a blizzard in New York City in 1888.

Stolz, Mary. *Bartholomew Fair*. Greenwillow, 1990 (I:10+ R:6). Six diverse people attend a fair in London, 1597.

Sutcliff, Rosemary. *Blood Feud*. Dutton, 1976. An English boy is carried away in a Viking raid and sold into slavery.

_____ . *The Eagle of the Ninth*. Illustrated by C. Walter Hodges. Walck, 1954 (I:11+ R:8). A Roman officer's son discovers the mystery of his father's legion.

_____ . *Frontier Wolf*. Dutton, 1981 (I:10+ R:8). A Roman centurion leads a band of British warriors.

_____ . *The Lantern Bearers*. Illustrated by Charles Keeping. Walck, 1959 (I:11+ R:7). The Saxons invade Roman Britain.

_____ . *The Shining Company*. Farrar, Straus, Giroux, 1990 (I:11+ R:8). The story is set in seventh-century Britain at the time of the invading Saxons.

_____ . *The Silver Branch*. Illustrated by Charles Keeping. Walck, 1958 (I:10+ R:8). Two Romans uncover a plot to overthrow the emperor.

_____ . *Song for a Dark Queen*. Crowell, 1978 (I:10+ R:6). The queen of a tribe of Britains leads the fight against the Roman armies.

_____ . *Sun Horse, Moon Horse*. Illustrated by Shirley Felts. Dutton, 1978 (I:10+ R:6). A boy saves his people from slavery in pre–Roman Britain.

Taylor, Mildred D. *Let the Circle Be Unbroken*. Dial, 1981 (I:10 R:6). This is a sequel to *Roll of Thunder, Hear My Cry*.

_____ . *Roll of Thunder, Hear My Cry*. Illustrated by Jerry Pinkney. Dial, 1976 (I:10+ R:6). A black family suffers prejudice in rural Mississippi.

Uchida, Yoshiko. *Journey Home*. Illustrated by Charles Robinson. Atheneum, 1978 (I:10+ R:5). In a sequel to *Journey to Topaz*, twelve-year-old Yuki and her parents return to California and try to adjust.

_____ . *Journey to Topaz*. Illustrated by Donald Carrick. Scribner's Sons, 1971 (I:10+ R:5). A Japanese American family is held in an internment camp in Utah during World War II.

Vos, Ida. *Hide and Seek*. Translated by Terese Edelstein and Inez Smidt. Houghton Mifflin, 1991 (I:8+ R:5). A Jewish family is hidden by Dutch neighbors during the German occupation of the Netherlands.

Westall, Robert. *Time of Fire*. Scholastic, 1997 (I:10 + R:5). The setting is WWII England.

Wilder, Laura Ingalls. *By the Shores of Silver Lake*. Illustrated by Garth Williams. Harper & Row, 1939, 1953 (I:8–12 R:6). The Ingalls move again to the Dakota territory.

_____ . *The First Four Years*. Illustrated by Garth Williams. Harper & Row, 1971 (I:8–12 R:6). Laura and Almanzo spend their first four years of marriage on a South Dakota homestead.

_____ . *Little House in the Big Woods*. Illustrated by Garth Williams. Harper & Row, 1932, 1953 (I:8–12 R:6). This is the first in a series of books about a loving pioneer family.

_____ . *Little House on the Prairie*. Illustrated by Garth Williams. Harper & Row, 1935, 1953 (I:8–12 R:8). The Ingalls family moves to Kansas.

_____ . *Little Town on the Prairie*. Illustrated by Garth Williams. Harper & Row, 1941, 1953 (I:8–12 R:8). Laura has her first job.

_____ . *The Long Winter*. Illustrated by Garth Williams. Harper & Row, 1940, 1953 (I:8–12 R:6). A blizzard causes the Ingalls family great discomfort.

_____ . *On the Banks of Plum Creek*. Illustrated by Garth Williams. Harper & Row, 1937, 1953 (I:8–12 R:6). The Ingalls family moves to Minnesota.

_____ . *These Happy Golden Years*. Illustrated by Garth Williams. Harper & Row, 1943, 1953 (I:8–12 R:6). Laura becomes a teacher and meets her future husband.

Yates, Elizabeth. *Amos Fortune, Free Man*. Illustrated by Nora S. Unwin. Dutton, 1950 (I:10+ R:6). An African enslaved by white traders is educated by his Quaker owner in Boston.

Yep, Laurence. *Hiroshima*. Scholastic, 1995 (I:9+ R:4). The book tells the story of the dropping of the atomic bomb.

Yolen, Jane. *Encounter*. Illustrated by David Shannon. Harcourt Brace Jovanovich, 1992 (I:6–10 R:5). In this hypothetical story, a Taino boy tells about the landing of Columbus.

Illustration from *Grandfather's Journey.* Copyright © 1993 by Allen Say. Reprinted by permission of Houghton Mifflin Co. All rights reserved.

11 *Multicultural Literature*

 Our Rich Mosaic

- What Multicultural Literature Is
- Values of Multicultural Literature
- Images of Racial and Ethnic Minorities in the Past
- Literary Criticism: Evaluating Multicultural Literature
- African American Literature
- Native American Literature
- Hispanic American Literature
- Asian American Literature

 Involving Children in Multicultural Literature

- Developing an Appreciation for African American Culture
- Developing an Appreciation for Native American Culture
- Developing an Appreciation for Hispanic American Culture
- Developing an Appreciation for Asian American Culture
- Recognizing Similarities

*O*ur Rich Mosaic

 heightened sensitivity to the needs of all people in American society has led to the realization that reading and literature programs for children should include literature by and about members of all cultural groups. Literature is appropriate for building respect across cultures, sharpening sensitivity toward the common features of all individuals, and improving the self-esteem of people who are members of racial and ethnic minority groups. The English Journal Forum (1990) states: "We believe that one of our country's strengths is its diversity. We deplore the attitude that bilingualism and multiculturalism are problems to be solved rather than boons to be celebrated" (p. 15).

Educators such as Eileen Tway (1989) argue, "In a country of multicultural heritage, children require books that reflect and illuminate that varied heritage" (p. 109). Bruce Sealey (1984) emphasizes that education should encourage children to accept and be sensitive to cultural diversity, to understand that similar values frequently underlie different customs, to have quality contact with people from other cultures, and to role-play experiences involved with other cultures. David Piper (1986) recommends using traditional stories and fables from various cultural sources and focusing on children's cultural backgrounds. Educators and critics of children's literature maintain that children should be exposed to multicultural literature that

heightens respect for the individuals, as well as the contributions and the values, of cultural minorities.

Many of the multicultural literature programs that have met these goals have accomplished them through preservice or in-service education of teachers and librarians. Such education stresses evaluating, selecting, and sharing multicultural literature (Norton, 1984–1987). The tasks related to developing such programs are enormous. Universities are beginning to require courses that include selecting and using multicultural literature. Until all educators have been trained in this way, school districts must provide in-service instruction so that teachers and librarians can select and use materials that create an atmosphere of respect for all children. One of the most formidable tasks is becoming familiar with the available literature and other teaching materials. Library selection committees, teachers, and administrators must all become involved in this process.

This chapter is not intended to isolate the literature and contributions of racial and ethnic minorities from other literature discussed in this book. Instead, it tries to place multicultural literature in a context helpful to librarians, teachers, and parents who wish to select and share such materials with children or develop multicultural literature programs.

☙ WHAT MULTICULTURAL LITERATURE IS

Multicultural literature is literature about racial or ethnic minority groups that are culturally and socially different from the white Anglo-Saxon majority in the United States, whose largely middle-class values and customs are most represented in American literature. Violet Harris (1992) defines multicultural literature as "literature that focuses on people of color, on religious minorities, on regional cultures, on the disabled, and on the aged."

Although, of course, ethnic diversity in the United States is extremely great, multicultural literature is usually viewed as literature about African Americans; Native Americans*; Hispanic Americans, including Mexican Americans, Puerto Ricans, Cuban

---

*This book primarily uses the term *Native Americans* to denote the people historically referred to as *American Indians*. The term *Indian* is sometimes used interchangeably with *Native American* and in some contexts is used to name certain tribes of Native Americans.

Americans, and others of Spanish descent or cultural heritage; and Asian Americans, including Chinese Americans, Japanese Americans, Korean Americans, Vietnamese Americans, and others. This chapter focuses on the literature of these groups. Discussion of literature on religious minorities such as the Jewish people is found primarily in the traditional literature, historical fiction, and nonfiction chapters. Literature about individuals with disabilities and the elderly is found primarily in the contemporary realistic fiction chapter.

 ## VALUES OF MULTICULTURAL LITERATURE

Many of the goals for multicultural education can be developed through multicultural literature. For example, Rena Lewis and Donald Doorlag (1987) state that multicultural education can restore cultural rights by emphasizing cultural equality and respect, enhance the self-concepts of students, and teach respect for various cultures while teaching basic skills. These goals for multicultural education are similar to the following goals of the UN Convention of the Rights of the Child and cited by Doni Kwolek Kobus (1992):

1. understanding and respect for each child's cultural group identities;
2. respect for and tolerance of cultural differences, including differences of gender, language, race, ethnicity, religion, region, and disabilities;
3. understanding of and respect for universal human rights and fundamental freedoms;
4. preparation of children for responsible life in a free society; and
5. knowledge of cross-cultural communication strategies, perspective taking, and conflict management skills to ensure understanding, peace, tolerance, and friendship among all peoples and groups. (p. 224)

Through multicultural literature, children who are members of racial or ethnic minority groups realize that they have a cultural heritage of which they can be proud, and that their culture has made important contributions to the United States and to the world. Pride in their heritage helps children who are members of minority groups improve their self-concepts and develop cultural identity. Learning about other cultures allows children to understand that people who belong to racial or ethnic groups other than theirs are real people, with feelings, emotions, and needs similar to their own—individual human beings, not stereotypes. Through multicultural literature, children discover that while not all people may share their personal beliefs and values, individuals can and must learn to live in harmony.

Through multicultural literature, children of the majority culture learn to respect the values and contributions of minority groups in the United States and the values and contributions of people in other parts of the world. In addition, children broaden their understanding of history, geography, and natural history when they read about cultural groups living in various regions of their country and the world. The wide range of multicultural themes also helps children develop an understanding of social change. Finally, reading about members of minority groups who have successfully solved their own problems and made notable achievements helps raise the aspirations of children who belong to a minority group.

 ## IMAGES OF RACIAL AND ETHNIC MINORITIES IN THE PAST

Only recently have Americans begun to realize that certain books—because of their illustrations, themes, characterizations, and language—can perpetuate stereotypes and result in psychological damage or discomfort for children. In the late 1940s, Americans began to express publicly their growing objections to the use of certain stereotypes in literature. In 1965, Nancy Larrick's article, "The All-White World of Children's Books," had much impact because her research showed both that there was a lack of books about minorities and that stereotypes were found in the few available books (*Saturday Review,* 1965). Many changes in American social life and literature have occurred since then, but further improvements are needed.

Eleven years later, in 1976, Bettye Latimer cautioned that through selection of books and instructional materials, some educators continue to communicate negative messages about minorities to children. Latimer states, "If your bulletin boards, your models, and your authority lines are White, and I am Black, Latino or Native American, then you have telegraphed me messages which I will reject" (p. 156). Latimer maintains that white children are taught a distorted image of American society and are not prepared to value American society's multiracial character because they are surrounded with literature and other instructional materials that either present minorities stereotypically or make minorities invisible by omitting them entirely. Latimer also stresses that because of the comparatively small number of books written about members of racial and ethnic minorities, well-meaning librarians, teachers, and other adults are likely to accept any book that describes or pictures members of minority groups, without carefully evaluating the stories and the stereotypes that they might be fostering. She believes that adults who work with children and literature should reeducate themselves to the social values that books pass on to children. To do this, adults must learn to assess books written about children from all ethnic backgrounds.

Nine years later, in 1985, author Eloise Greenfield is even harsher in her criticism of authors who perpetuate racism and stereotypes in literature. She states that books that express racism or negative attitudes toward any group "constrain rather than encourage human development. To perpetuate these attitudes through the use of the written word constitutes a gross and arrogant misuse of talent and skill" (p. 19).

The topic of images and stereotypes in multicultural literature became an important area of research, especially in the 1970s. As you read the following sections, remember the conclusions of these researchers and consider how their research may have influenced later multicultural literature.

African Americans

Several researchers have investigated images of African Americans in children's literature, focusing on stereotypes, attitudes that white characters express toward black characters, and the importance of black characters in the literature. Dorothy May Broderick (1971), for example, analyzed American children's literature published between 1827 and 1967. She reports that the personal characteristics of African American people portrayed in these books suggested that they (1) are not physically attractive, (2) are musical, (3) combine religious fervor with superstitious beliefs, (4) are required to select life goals that benefit black people, and (5) are dependent upon white people for whatever good things they could hope to acquire. Broderick concluded that in the 140-year period she studied, African American children would find little in literature to enhance pride in their heritage and that if these books were white children's only contacts with black people, white children would develop a sense of superiority.

Beryle Banfield (1985) reviewed stereotypes found in pre–Civil War literature and found that stories set in the plantation South of the 1800s depicted slavery as idyllic, pastoral, and beneficial for the slave. In addition, these books frequently suggested that the slaves were so contented on the plantation that they were wretched when they tried to survive as free people.

In investigating whether or not changes in attitudes toward African Americans had occurred in more recent times, Julia Ann Carlson (1969) compared American children's literature of the 1930s with that of the 1960s. She discovered that many changes in the depiction of black characters occurred between the two time periods. Although 15 percent of the books from the earlier period mentioned African American characters, these characters tended to be stereotyped. Only 10 percent of the books in the later period mentioned African American characters at all, but when they did, they tended to present black people as individuals with either a racial problem or a universal problem. Betty M. Morgan (1973) reported that the number of books with African American people as the main characters has increased markedly. This chapter discusses numerous selections of excellent African American literature that do not perpetuate stereotypes from the past. In fact, there are more new African American selections than there are for any of the other peoples discussed in this chapter. In addition, fewer of the books go out of print.

Native Americans

Native Americans fared no better than African Americans in the literature of the past. According to Mary Gloyne Byler (1977):

There are too many books featuring painted, whooping, befeathered Indians closing in on too many forts, maliciously attacking "peaceful" settlers or simply leering menacingly from the background; too many books in which white benevolence is the only thing that saves the day for the incompetent childlike Indian; too many stories setting forth what is "best" for American Indians. (p. 28)

Researchers analyzing the images of Native Americans in children's literature written in the past have identified many negative stereotypes in a large percentage of the literature. According to Laura Herbst (1977), three of the most common stereotypes characterize Native Americans as (1) savage, depraved, and cruel; (2) noble, proud, silent, and close to nature; or (3) inferior, childlike, and helpless. Terms and comparisons suggesting negative and derogatory images often reinforce such stereotypes. A white family, for example, may be said to consist of a husband, a wife, and a child; members of Native American families, in contrast, may be called bucks, squaws, and papooses. White authors often dehumanize Native Americans by comparing them to animals. Even Native American language is often described as "snarling," "grunting," or "yelping." *The Matchlock Gun*, by Walter Edmonds, compares the nameless Indians to trotting dogs, sniffing the scent of food. Often, Native American characters are depersonalized by not being given names, which implies that they are not individuals, or even full-fledged human beings.

In addition to stereotypes about Native American people, Laura Herbst identifies three stereotypical ways in which Native American culture has been portrayed in children's literature. First, the culture may be depicted as inferior to the white culture, treating the abandonment of the Native American way of life as an improvement. Native American characters are often depicted as gaining by going to white schools or taking on the values of the white culture, leaving their culture and even their people behind. A common theme in such literature is that white people must be responsible for remaking Native Americans.

Second, the culture may be depicted as valueless, and thus not worthy of respect. Depicting the rich diversity of spiritual beliefs and ceremonies, moral values, artistic skills, and the life-styles in Native American cultures may be ignored in favor of depicting violence as the chief Native American value. Authors may be ignorant of the fact that Native American peoples have many different cultures.

Third, the culture may be depicted as quaint or superficial, without depth or warmth. White characters in children's literature of the past commonly ridicule or scorn customs that have spiritual significance to Native Americans. They disparage sacred ceremonies, medicine men, ancient artifacts, and traditional legends as belonging to "heathen savages." Any of these three stereotypical portrayals of a culture is offensive. More current books, however, especially those written by Native American authors or other authorities on Native American culture, are sensitive to the heritage and individuality of the native peoples of North America.

Hispanic Americans

Betty M. Morgan (1973) concluded that the number of children's books with members of minority groups as main characters has increased since World War II, but she also found that this is true only for books about either African Americans or Native Americans. Far fewer children's books have Hispanic Americans or Asian Americans as the main characters. Authors such as Gary Soto also lament the lack of Hispanic writers being published in the United States (Lodge, 1997).

Both the lack of children's literature about people of Hispanic descent and heritage and the negative stereotypes found in some of the literature have been criticized. At one children's literature conference, Mauricio Charpenel (1980), consultant to the Mexican Ministry of Education, reported that very few stories are written for or about Mexican or Mexican American children. He was especially concerned about poetry. While Latin American writers publish beautiful poetry, the poems are not shared with Mexican American children in the United States. Both teachers and librarians at the conference expressed concern for literature that would appeal to Hispanic American children and create positive images of their heritage.

The Council on Interracial Books for Children (1977a) has been critical of the depictions of Mexican Americans in children's literature of the past. After analyzing two hundred books, the council concluded that little in the stories would enable children to recognize a culture, a history, or a set of life circumstances. The council criticized the theme of poverty that recurs as if it is a "natural facet of the Chicano condition" (p. 57) and the tendency for Mexican American problems to be solved by the intervention of Anglo Americans. The council also felt that Mexican Americans' problems had been treated superficially in the books it studied. For example, many books suggest that if children learn English, all of their problems will be solved.

Even fewer books are being written about Puerto Rican Americans, Cuban Americans, and the many new Americans from Central American countries. The majority of books about Puerto Ricans, for example, lack literary merit and overuse a New York City ghetto setting. In addition to fewer books about Hispanic Americans, the available books tend to go out of print.

Asian Americans

Since few books about Asian Americans have been published for children, researchers who have tried to evaluate books about Asian Americans have had little to study. In 1976, the Asian American Children's Book Project (Council on Interracial Books for Children, 1977b) identified sixty-six books with Asian American central characters, and most of these books were about Chinese Americans. The members of the project concluded that with only a few exceptions the books were grossly misleading. They presented stereotypes suggesting that all Asian Americans look alike, choose to live in "quaint" communities in the midst of large cities, and cling to "outworn, alien" customs. The project also criticized the books because they tended to measure success by the extent to which Asian Americans have assimilated white middle-class values and because they implied that hard work, learning to speak English, and keeping a low profile would enable them to overcome adversity and be successful.

Stereotypes of Asian characters change slowly. Bu Kun-yu (1988) identifies past stereotypes of Chinese people and contrasts these stereotypes with current attitudes:

For hundreds of years, Chinese people have been described as diligent, conservative, obedient. In the wake of modernization, the three traditional words seem inappropriate. Today's students' slogan is: "Be a pioneer of reform, not a lamb of the traditional education system." Thus, three new words are used to describe the demands of modern society: *practical, efficient,* and *adventurous.* (p. 378)

 ### *LITERARY CRITICISM: EVALUATING MULTICULTURAL LITERATURE*

To develop positive attitudes about and respect for individuals in all cultures, children need many opportunities to read and listen to literature that presents accurate and respectful images of everyone. Because fewer children's books in the United States are written from the perspective of racial or cultural minorities and because many stories perpetuate negative stereotypes, you should carefully evaluate books containing nonwhite characters. Outstanding multicultural literature meets the literary criteria applied to any fine book, but other criteria apply to the treatment of cultural and racial minorities. The following criteria related to literature that represents African Americans, Native Americans, Hispanic Americans, and Asian Americans reflect the recommendations of the earlier cited research studies and evaluations compiled by Donna Norton (1997):

Are African, Native, Hispanic, and Asian Americans portrayed as unique individuals, with their own thoughts, emotions, and philosophies, instead of as representatives of particular racial or cultural groups?

Does a book transcend stereotypes in the appearance, behavior, and character traits of its nonwhite characters? Does the depiction of nonwhite characters and life-styles lack any implication of stigma? Does a book suggest that all members of an ethnic or racial group live in poverty? Are the characters from a variety of socioeconomic backgrounds, educational levels, and occupations? Does the author avoid depicting Asian Americans as workers in restaurants and laundries, Hispanic Americans as illegal alien unskilled laborers, Native Americans as bloodthirsty warriors, African Americans as menial service employees, and so forth? Does the author avoid the "model minority" and "bad minority" syndrome? Are nonwhite characters respected for themselves, or must they display outstanding abilities to gain approval from white characters?

Is the physical diversity within a particular racial or cultural minority group authentically portrayed in the text and the illustrations? Do nonwhite characters have stereotypically exaggerated facial features or physiques that make them all look alike?

Will children be able to recognize the characters in the text and the illustrations as African Americans, Hispanic Americans, Asian Americans, or Native American and not mistake them for white? Are people of color shown as gray—that is, as simply darker versions of Caucasian-featured people?

Is the culture of a racial or ethnic minority group accurately portrayed? Is it treated with respect, or is it depicted as inferior to the majority white culture? Does the author believe the culture worthy of preservation? Is the cultural diversity within African American, Asian American, Hispanic American, and Native American life clearly demonstrated? Are the customs and values of those diverse groups accurately portrayed? Must nonwhite characters fit into a cultural image acceptable to white characters? Is a nonwhite culture shown in an overly exotic or romanticized way instead of being placed within the context of everyday activities familiar to all people?

Are social issues and problems related to minority group status depicted frankly and accurately, without oversimplification? Must characters who are members of racial and cultural minority groups exercise all of the understanding and forgiveness?

Do nonwhite characters handle their problems individually, through their own efforts or with the assistance of close family and friends, or are problems solved through the intervention of whites? Are nonwhite characters shown as the equals of white characters? Are some characters placed in submissive or inferior positions? Are white people always the benefactors?

Are nonwhite characters glamorized or glorified, especially in biography? (Both excessive praise and excessive deprecation of nonwhite characters result in unreal and unbalanced characterizations.) If the book is a biography, are both the personality and the accomplishments of the main character shown in accurate detail and not oversimplified?

Is the setting of a story authentic, whether past, present, or future? Will children be able to recognize the setting as urban, rural, or fantasy? If a story deals with factual information or historical events, are the details accurate? If the setting is contemporary, does the author accurately describe the situations of nonwhite people in the United States and elsewhere today? Does a book rectify historical distortions and omissions?

If dialect is used, does it have a legitimate purpose? Does it ring true and blend in naturally with the story in a nonstereotypical way, or is it simply used as an example of substandard English? If non–English words are used, are they spelled and used correctly? Is offensive or degrading vocabulary used to describe the characters, their actions, their customs, or their life-styles?

Are the illustrations authentic and nonstereotypical in every detail?

Does a book reflect an awareness of the changing status of females in all racial and cultural groups today? Does the author provide role models for girls other than subservient females?

See the Evaluation Criteria list on this page.

ℰVALUATION CRITERIA

Literary Criticism: Multicultural Literature

1. Are the characters portrayed as individuals instead of as representatives of a group?
2. Does the book transcend stereotypes?
3. Does the book portray physical diversity?
4. Will children be able to recognize the characters in the text and illustrations?
5. Is the culture accurately portrayed?
6. Are social issues and problems depicted frankly, accurately, and without oversimplification?
7. Do nonwhite characters solve their problems without intervention by whites?
8. Are nonwhite characters shown as equals of white characters?
9. Does the author avoid glamorizing or glorifying nonwhite characters?
10. Is the setting authentic?
11. Are the factual and historical details accurate?
12. Does the author accurately describe contemporary settings?
13. Does the book rectify historical distortions or omissions?
14. Does dialect have a legitimate purpose and does it ring true?
15. Does the author avoid offensive or degrading vocabulary?
16. Are the illustrations authentic and nonstereotypical?
17. Does the book reflect an awareness of the changing status of females?

AFRICAN AMERICAN LITERATURE

Many fine books of traditional literature, contemporary realistic fiction, and nonfiction reflect the heritage and modern-day experiences of African Americans. Reading these enjoyable and well-written books will help children from all racial and cultural backgrounds identify with and appreciate the dreams, problems, and cultural contributions of black people on this continent. According to Hazel Rochman (1993):

African American literature is flourishing. In the last year, perhaps because African American history is now a required part of the curriculum in many states, there have been many new books about slavery and resistance, as well as several fine books about the civil rights movement. The focus has shifted from the role of the great leaders to the experience of ordinary people, including women and children. (p. 1052)

Traditional Literature

Traditional folk literature, the tales originally handed down through centuries of oral storytelling, includes many of the stories that children most enjoy. Through reading African and African American traditional tales, children discover a rich literary heritage, gain a respect for the creativity of the people who originated the stories, develop an understanding of the values of the originators, and share enjoyable experiences that have entertained others in centuries past. Modern writers of contemporary realistic fiction about African Americans often have their characters tell African tales in order to develop closer relationships to and understanding of the African heritage. Other authors write original modern fantasies based on African elements. The beliefs and values found in African and African American folklore are found in both poetry and contemporary stories; therefore, it is important to introduce a study of African American literature with traditional literature.

Traditional African and African American literature includes folktales that are indigenous to various countries on the African continent, African folk literature that was transported to one of the Caribbean islands and then altered in the new setting, and folk literature that originated in the American South. This final category includes many tales based on African themes and motifs or altered to meet the needs of southern African American storytellers.

African Tales. Africa has a long and rich history of oral literature. In 1828, the first known collection of African tales was published for European audiences. This collection, *Fables Sénégalaises Recueillies de l'Oulof,* was translated into French by le Bon Roger, the French Commandant of Senegal. More collections appeared as administrators, traders, and missionaries collected traditional African stories for various purposes. A brief review of these purposes shows how important an understanding of folklore is for understanding people. Daniel Crowley (1979) states:

Linguists collected tales as samples of language usage, teachers as a means of inculcating local languages, missionaries to study local values and beliefs, African elites in pursuit of vindication against colonialism, diffusionists in the search of distribution patterns on which to base migration theories, litterateurs and journalists looking for "authentic" themes. . . . (p. 11)

The collection of authentic folklore and artistic representations by ancient peoples is considered so important that Leo Frobenius and Douglas Fox (1983) state in the introduction to *African Genesis:*

Every fact, object, and belief which can help us to understand the growth of human culture should be recorded and indexed for use. . . . We will find that there are peoples of whom we do not know enough, and so it will be necessary to send out expeditions to find and gather the material we lack. (p. 16)

This is also a worthy attitude for students of children's literature, who can analyze the folklore to make discoveries about the types of stories represented, as well as the cultural patterns, values, and beliefs reflected in the ancient tales. Like other traditional lore, African folklore reveals ancient beliefs in the origins of the natural and tribal worlds, as well as certain physical and spiritual traits.

The beautifully expressed and illustrated traditional African tales discussed in this section represent some of the most noble values attributed to humanity: love of beauty, humor, work, courage, imagination, and perseverance. Children discover pride and hope in being black, as well as pleasure in the richness of cultural heritage.

Some tales explore societal problems and provide possible solutions. In the introduction to *The Dancing Palm Tree and Other Nigerian Folktales,* Barbara Walker (1990) describes this important role in Yoruba tales,

Many of the stories begin, "Far away and long ago in a small village," for this is a tradition in Yoruba storytelling. And somewhere in each story there is likely to be a "moral," a human truth which is taught through what happens in the story. For one of the main purposes of storytelling in Nigeria has always been to teach, to instruct, a very important function in a land where until just recently there were few schools and where many of the important lessons of life were learned at the knee of the storyteller. But you will find that the truths taught in these stories prevail not only in Nigeria but all around the world, truths that people must learn to live by no matter what country they call home. (p. 3)

As you read the stories in this section on African folklore, try to identify the truths, values, and beliefs that are important to the African people and to those from around the world.

Mabel Ross and Barbara Walker (1979) state, "The measure of a narrator's skill is indicated in the degree to which he can leave with the listener a valid key to acceptable moral and social behavior, a guide to the making of a responsible choice, within the framework of his own culture" (p. 236). For example, Verna Aardema's *Bringing the Rain to Kapiti Plain: A Nandi Tale* shows that individuals have obligations for the betterment of the people, the environment, and the animals that provide their welfare. Ashley Bryan's "The Husband Who Counted the Spoonfuls," found in *Beat the Story-Drum, Pum-Pum,* develops a need for stability in marital relationships. Solving family relationships is the theme found in Nancy Raines Day's *The Lion's Whiskers: An Ethiopian Folktale.* In this tale a caring stepmother discovers how to make her elusive stepson respond to her. In a varia-

tion of the "Lazy Jack" theme, *Gift of the Sun: A Tale from South Africa,* a man finds an occupation.

Ann Grifalconi's *The Village of Round and Square Houses* reveals how a social custom began. In this case, a volcanic eruption in the distant past leaves only two houses within the village: one round and one square. To meet the needs of the village, the women and children move into the round house while the men stay in the square house. According to the tale, the custom continues today because people "live together peacefully here—Because each one has a place to be apart, and a time to be together. . . . And that is how our way came about and will continue—Til Naka speaks again!" (unnumbered).

As you read collections of African folktales for children, notice how most of the values and beliefs identified by Ross and Walker in their adult collection are also found in folktales published for children: the importance of maintaining friendship, a need for family loyalty, the desirability of genuine hospitality, the use of wit and trickery in unequal relationships, a strict code for ownership and borrowing, gratitude for help rendered, high risk in excessive pride, care for the feelings of those in

⌐SSUE   Revision of a Controversial Book

One of the most controversial children's books is Helen Bannerman's *The Story of Little Black Sambo,* published by HarperCollins in 1899. Lambeth Hochwald[1] reviews the controversy about the original publication and discusses two new revisions of the book: *The Story of Little Babaji,*[2] illustrated by Fred Marcellino, and *Sam and the Tigers,*[3] retold by Julius Lester and illustrated by Jerry Pinkney.

In the discussion about the 1899 story, Hockwald points out the derogatory names of Black Mumbo and Black Jumbo and the stereotypical illustrations in which the family is depicted with full red lips and exaggerated white coloring for the

eyes. Even though the book remained controversial and was removed from many libraries in the 1970s, the original edition still sells about 20,000 copies a year.

The two new versions provide excellent discussion topics as students of children's literature compare the two new versions with the original text and illustrations. For example, Marcellino retains much of the original text, but gives the characters new names and places the illustrations in a setting from India. The Lester and Pinkney collaboration is set in the American South of the 1920s.

As you read the two new versions and compare them with the original

text, consider your responses to all three books. Did the new versions eliminate the reasons for the original controversy? If the reasons for the original controversy were not eliminated, how did the revisions change the stereotypical topic?

---

[1] Hockwald, Lambeth. "Little Book, Big Controversy." *Publishers Weekly* 243 (July 29, 1996): 32–33.

[2] Bannerman, Helen. *The Story of Little Babaji.* Illustrated by Fred Marcellino. HarperCollins, 1996.

[3] Lester, Julius. *Sam and the Tigers.* Illustrated by Jerry Pinkney. Dial, 1996.

authority, respect for individuality, and appropriate awe of the supernatural.

Notice that individuals who adhere to the values and beliefs are frequently rewarded, while individuals who reject the values and beliefs are usually punished. For example, traditional values reflected in the folklore of several African cultures are found in Harold Courlander's *The Crest and the Hide: And Other African Stories of Heroes, Chiefs, Bards, Hunters, Sorcerers, and Common People*. This collection of twenty tales from such cultures as the Ashanti, the Yoruba, the Swahili, and the Zulu emphasizes the values of wisdom, friendship, love, and heroism, as well as some behaviors that are not respected, such as foolishness and disloyalty.

Barbara K. Walker's *The Dancing Palm Tree and Other Nigerian Folktales* is a collection of eleven folktales told to Walker by Olawale Idewu, a Nigerian student. In addition to being an excellent source of tales that reflect the traditional values, this book includes a glossary of information to help readers interpret the stories. For example, the entry for NO-KING-IS-AS-GREAT-AS-GOD states: "Names such as this one are quite common in Yoruba life. In fact, the whole process of naming is an extremely interesting and complicated one. Each name which is used has a definite meaning and purpose, and it tells a great deal about its owner" (p. 95). The authors then explain that names may specify family positions, christening names, totem names, and pet names.

Wit and trickery are also appropriate actions in Gerald McDermott's retelling of *Zomo the Rabbit: A Trickster Tale from West Africa*. McDermott describes Zomo in this way:

> He is not big.
> He is not strong.
> But he is very clever. (p. 1, unnumbered)

In this tale, Zomo approaches Sky God because he wants more than cleverness—he wants wisdom. To acquire wisdom, however, he must earn it by bringing Sky God three items: the scales of Big Fish, the milk of Wild Cow, and the tooth of Leopard. Zomo is able to acquire these items through his wit and trickery. Consequently, Sky God tells him: "Three things in this world are worth having: courage, good sense, and caution. . . . Little rabbit, you have lots of courage, a bit of sense, but no caution. So next time you see Big Fish, or Wild Cow, or Leopard . . . better run fast!" (p. 26, unnumbered). This is an example of a folktale in which the advice given by Sky God reflects the beliefs and values of the people.

Additional folktales that develop the values of the people include John Steptoe's *Mufaro's Beautiful Daughters: An African Tale* which shows the importance of kindness and generosity toward others and

Detailed drawings place the setting for this tale in central Africa. (From The Fortune-Tellers *by Lloyd Alexander, illustrated by Trina Schart Hyman. Copyright © 1992 by Trina Schart Hyman, illustrations. Used by permission of Dutton Children's Books, a division of Penguin Books USA Inc.)*

the harmful results of greed and selfishness. The folktales in Brent Ashabranner and Russell Davis's *The Lion's Whiskers: And Other Ethiopian Tales* reveal important values such as courage and wisdom.

David Wisniewski's *Sundiata: Lion King of Mali,* a legend, is the tale of a ruler who lived in the late 1200s. The tale begins in this fashion: "Listen to me, children of the Bright Country, and hear the great deeds of ages past. The words I speak are those of my father and his father before him, pure and full of truth . . ." (p. 1, unnumbered). Sundiata's courage and leadership are especially valued in this tale. In addition, when he is returned to the throne, he tells his people that from that time on, no one shall interfere with another's destiny.

In endnotes, Wisniewski (1992) provides information about the source of this tale. For example, Wisniewski states:

The story of Sundiata has reached modern ears through the unbroken oral tradition provided by griots. Many African ethnic groups rely on the prodigious memories of these people, rather than written accounts, to preserve the history and wisdom of the past. This version of the Sundiata epic is distilled from the words of Djeli Mamoudou Kouyate, a griot of the Keita clan, in *Sundiata: An Epic of Old Mali,* a compilation written by Djibril Tamsir Niane and translated from the original Malinke by G. D. Pickett (London, 1965). (endnote)

This information is valuable because it allows you to compare Wisniewski's retelling and interpretation with the earlier version.

Verna Aardema's *Misoso: Once Upon a Time Tales from Africa* is another example of a collection of tales in which the reteller provides both background information and the original source for the tale. For example, the author's "Afterword" for "Kindai and the Ape" states, "This is a reciprocal tale with the universal theme of kindness rewarded, and it bears similarities to both Jewish and Roman legends. It originated with the Emo-Yo-Quaim, black Jews whose ancestors fled to northern Africa in A.D. 70, after the destruction of Jerusalem" (p. 85). Aardema identifies the source of this story as "The Man Who Thought He Was Foolish" in *Folktales of A Savage,* by Bata Kindai Amgoza Ibn Lobagola, published by Knopf in 1930.

Several myths from Virginia Hamilton's *In the Beginning: Creation Stories from Around the World* explore the origins of the natural world. For example, in "Spider Ananse Finds Something: Wulbarie the Creator," a myth from West Africa, Ananse brings the sun, moon, and darkness to earth. Unfortunately, he also causes blindness to come upon some of the people. The theme that weakness can overcome strength is developed as trickster Ananse outwits the more powerful sky god. In "Man Copies God: Nyambi the Creator," a myth from Zambia, Nyambi creates animals and man but is unhappy when man tries to copy god or disobeys his instructions. Consequently, Nyambi climbs into the sky and vanishes from earth. The only sign that god is still in the sky is the sun that rises every morning. The theme in this tale is that humans are at odds with the will of god.

Ruby Dee's *Tower to Heaven,* a tale from Ghana in West Africa, reveals why the great god of the sky, Onyankopon, no longer lives on the earth and why people tried to build a tower to communicate with him after he disappeared into the sky. Mary-Joan Gerson's *Why the Sky Is Far Away: A Nigerian Folktale* explains not only why the sky is far away but also why people have to plow the fields and hunt the forests rather than take food from the sky. The story contains the theme that people will be punished if they waste resources and take more than they need to satisfy hunger. The theme of the tale is very important in today's world, as it was in earlier times.

The ways in which animals and people acquired certain physical and spiritual traits are popular subjects in African tales. Barbara Knutson's *How the Guinea Fowl Got Her Spots: A Swahili Tale of Friendship,* the retelling of a Swahili tale, explains one such characteristic. In addition, the tale develops the relationships between cows and guinea fowl and shows the value of maintaining friendships and being loyal to friends. The tale reveals that wit and trickery are condoned when the unequal relationships are between the small guinea fowl and the much larger lion. Knutson's *Why the Crab Has No Head,* a tale from Zaire, explains two characteristics. First, Crab has no head because his pride offended the creator. Second, Crab walks sideways because he is filled with embarrassment instead of pride. A need to humble individuals who express excessive pride is a common theme in African folklore.

Two tales in Ashley Bryan's *Beat the Story-Drum, Pum-Pum* are also characteristic of explanation stories. "How Animals Got Their Tails" reveals not only how animals received their individual tails but also why there is animosity between rabbits and foxes.

THROUGH THE EYES OF A STORYTELLER

The Oral Tradition: People to People, Voice to Voice

ASHLEY BRYAN defines himself first and foremost as a painter, but anyone who has ever heard him tell a story or recite a poem would argue that he is also a premier storyteller. A true Renaissance man, Bryan is the author/illustrator of several books of tales from motifs discovered in African and Caribbean cultures. He has also collected and illustrated books of African American spirituals. Bryan was selected by the American Library Association to give the prestigious May Arbuthnot lecture in 1990.

The oral tradition in literature is not exotic or something found only in pre-literate societies. Just listening to people is listening to their stories. While many tales are presented in circumstances where the wise elders answer the questions of children, the oral tradition is not limited to that. All life experience is rich, whether it is children talking to other children on the playground or families talking around the dinner table. The oral tradition will never die, even in this age of television and videocassettes, because each family has its own oral tradition.

Whenever I speak to an audience, I remind listeners that they have an intrinsic art that they have spent years preparing to share with me—the art of listening. My art of storytelling is exchanged for their art of listening. And, believe me, there is excitement generated in that exchange!

I set aside the months of February to June each year to visit schools across the country. When I enter some schools, especially those with older students, I can see that some administrators and teachers fear for me, as I am armed only with the art of poetry. However, I always count on the courtesy and decency of the audience. When they find out how much the poetry means to me, the audience shares that.

Poetry always reminds me that language is man's greatest invention. The poet is more aware than most people of the wonder and mystery of language. Poetry deals with emotions, an area we are most ashamed of as human beings. But it is the emotion of poetry that allows it to reach out and touch the minds and hearts of the listeners in a way that no other medium can.

For this reason, I always begin each storytelling session by reciting a variety of poems written by black poets. I give most of my talks to adults. It is the adults who ask me to come and speak to the children. I try to prepare a range of material that cuts across all ages.

I believe if something is beautiful, it is for everyone. Beauty has no age restrictions. When I watch the evening sky from my island home in Maine, I ask myself, is this sunset meant for a certain age group? I think not.

Also, I never consider limiting the words I choose to tell my stories because children may not understand them. Children are always interested in what the voice is doing and children want to stretch. Whether or not they understand a

"Why Bush Cow and Elephant Are Bad Friends" reveals why animals fight in the bush.

Tololwa M. Mollel's *A Promise to the Sun: A Story of Africa* explains why bats live in caves and fly only at night. The tale also reveals the importance of keeping promises and the shame associated with broken promises.

Verna Aardema's *Why Mosquitoes Buzz in People's Ears* explains why mosquitoes are noisy. Written as a cumulative tale, it is excellent for sharing orally with children. It suggests a rich language heritage and a respect for storytelling. Ashley Bryan's retelling of Nigerian tales in *The Story of Lightning & Thunder* also reflects this rich language tradition. The oral language tradition is revealed in this introduction to the tale "Ma Sheep Thunder and Son Ram Lightning": "A long time ago, I mean a long, long, time ago, if you wanted to pat Lightning or chat with Thunder, you could do it. Uh-huh, you could . . ."

poem completely, even young children will attend to it.

I choose the words of poetry for my stories, too, using the tools of close rhyme, rhythm, repetition, and alliteration. I spend months and years preparing stories and poems. I need that time to make the story or the poem truly mine. I always encourage teachers to allow their students three to four weeks to prepare to recite a poem. No poem should ever be read aloud "cold."

By allowing students time to investigate and play with the language of the poem, one automatically sets up a spirit of cooperation in the classroom. By the time children are asked to recite the poem, they can do so with confidence because now they know all the words and can read with expression.

I like my school visits to be a reminder that reading aloud should be an integral part of the entire school year, no matter what the age of the students. No one is "too old" to be read to, or to be told a story. No one is too young to tell a story that he or she has practiced.

Children always ask me how old I am. I tell them I am four. I tell them I am six. I tell them I am ten. I am forty-six, and I am sixty-four. I ask them to choose the age they want

me to be. Invariably, young children will decide and be satisfied that I am four or six, close to their own age.

When I visit schools, I am often treated to wonderful performances of my stories, acted out by the children. It is important that the performance that I see not be the *only* performance. If students have taken time to prepare, they should be allowed to perform again and again. Why not repeat the story to another group a week later? Why not perform again in a month? That way the story will always be truly theirs to own, and there will not be that "emotional letdown" that often occurs after a single performance. Children will also learn each performance can be special. Each time one can embellish a story, and it will grow richer through the retelling.

It is so important to be rooted in who you are, and then all flows naturally from this source. I have always been a teacher. And, I have always earned money to meet my responsibilities from areas other than my art. I write for myself. Since I don't sign contracts before I begin working on a project, I can be patient with a project and release it only when I feel it is ready. That way, my publisher can *choose* to accept my work. I am al-

ways prepared to take the work back.

The stories I write often evolve from very spare motifs, sometimes only four or five lines from an ancient journal. I sometimes play with a story for up to ten years before I will focus on it and make it a book.

My challenge is to open up the story from the printed word and try to match the expressive style of illustration to the story itself. That is why I don't use just a single artistic medium or style. When I wanted to concentrate on the movement in the illustrations in *The Dancing Granny,* I used the brushstroke style of painting from the Japanese and Chinese traditions. The characters needed to tumble around the pages. Bright, fresh watercolors captured the mood I wanted to create in *Turtle Knows Your Name.* My current project is a child's book of spirituals. This time I am working with African textile and quilt patterns.

I hope that you will help the art of storytelling flourish in your own way—people to people, voice to voice.

Drawn from an interview, March 30, 1990, by Linda James Scharp.

Several beautifully illustrated books contain single African folktales or legends retold for children of all ages. Aardema's *Who's in Rabbit's House?* is an unusual and humorous Masai tale about tricky animals. This tale is written in the form of a play performed by villagers for their townsfolk. In this tale, Caterpillar, who is smaller, slower, and weaker than any of the other animals (including Rabbit, Jackal, Leopard, Elephant, and Rhinoceros), must use wit and trickery to correct the imbalance. In addition, repetition of words adds to the vivid descriptions, and the dialogue suggests the richness of African language. The jackal trots off "kpata, kpata," the leopard jumps "pa, pa, pa," and the frog laughs "dgung, dgung, dgung." This is an excellent tale to stimulate creative dramatizations by children, who enjoy repeating the sound effects and dialogues out loud and creating masks of the various animals.

Aardema's *How the Ostrich Got Its Long Neck* provides an example of both a traditional African oral storytelling style and a pourquoi tale that explains an animal characteristic. Aardema uses a repetitive language that reflects the sounds of the animals. For example, Crocodile's tears drip with tiny splashes, "tih tih tih"; Fish Eagle cries "Kwak! Kwak!"; and Kudo gallops, "ka-PU-tu, ka-PU-tu, ka-PU-tu." In a pourquoi fashion, the tale reveals how and why the ostrich gained his long neck and why they now live in the bush far from the river and the hungry crocodile. Aardema uses a similar language style in *The Lonely Lioness and the Ostrich Chicks: A Masai Tale* and in *This for That: A Tonga Tale.*

Another folktale rich in the language of the African storyteller is Gail E. Haley's *A Story, a Story.* This tale about Ananse, the spider man, repeats key words to make them stronger, as Ananse's wit helps him overcome serious difficulties. Ananse seeks stories from the powerful sky god, and the god laughs: "How can a weak old man like you, so small, so small, so small, pay my price?" (p. 6, unnumbered). Ananse fools the god and is able to capture the leopard-of-the-terrible-teeth; Mmboro, the hornet who stings like fire; and Mmoatia, the fairy whom people never see. As a reward for these gifts, the sky god gives Ananse the stories that previously belonged only to the god. From this tale, children can understand the importance of storytelling on the African continent as well as recognize the occurrences in which wit and trickery may be legitimately used in African folklore.

American Tales. New folktales developed when Africans became slaves in North America, as Virginia Hamilton (1985) points out in her introduction to *The People Could Fly: American Black Folktales:*

Out of the contacts the plantation slaves made in their new world, combined with memories and habits from the old world of Africa, came a body of folk expression about the slaves and their experiences. The slaves created tales in which various animals . . . took on characteristics of the people found in the new environment of the plantation. (p. x)

For example, the favorite Br'er Rabbit, who was small and apparently helpless when compared with the more powerful bear and fox, was smart, tricky, and clever, and usually won out over larger and stronger animals. The slaves, who identified with the rabbit, told many tales about his exploits.

Hamilton's collection of tales is divided into four parts: (1) animal tales, (2) extravagant and fanciful experiences, (3) supernatural tales, and (4) slave tales of freedom. The collection provides sources for listening, discussing, and comparing. For example, readers can compare the folklore elements, plot, and themes in Hamilton's "The Beautiful Girl of the Moon Tower," a folktale from the Cape Verde Islands, and Elizabeth Isele's retelling of the Russian tale "The Frog Princess."

The most famous collection of African American folktales originating in the southern United States are the stories originally collected and retold by Joel Chandler Harris's "Uncle Remus" in the late nineteenth century. Again, that "monstrous clever beast," Brer Rabbit, always survives by using his cunning against stronger enemies. William J. Faulkner's *The Days When the Animals Talked* (1977) presents background information on African American folktales about animals. Faulkner tells how the tales were created and what their significance is in American history.

Two authors, Van Dyke Parks and Julius Lester, have adapted highly acclaimed versions of the Uncle Remus stories originally written down by Joel Chandler Harris. The combination of Parks's text and Barry Moser's illustrations for *Jump! The Adventures of Brer Rabbit* and *Jump Again! More Adventures of Brer Rabbit* form highly readable and visually satisfying experiences. It is interesting to analyze the animal characters, to consider the social impact of slavery as depicted in the stories, to identify values that are similar to those found in African tales, to compare similar tales found in other cultures or in other versions of the Uncle Remus stories, and to consider the impact of the authors' styles.

For example, Brer Rabbit is considered a character who can use his head, outdo and outwit all other creatures, and rely on trickery if necessary. In this role, Brer Rabbit uses trickery if he is in conflict with bigger and more powerful characters, but Brer Rabbit also represents what happens when folks are full of conceit and proudness. They "are going to get it taken out of them. Brer Rabbit did get caught up with once, and it cooled him right off" (*Jump!,* p. 19). Notice that both of these values are also found in African folklore. In addition, the tales reflect changes caused by the new environment, where the storytellers are influenced by slavery and European colonization and the need to protect their families and develop friendships that are tempered with distrust.

Symbolism, onomatopoeia, and personification add to Parks's storytelling style. For example, Parks uses symbolic meaning to contrast the length of night and day in *Jump!*: "When the nights were long and the days were short, with plenty of wood on the fire and sweet potatoes in the embers, Brer Rabbit could outdo all the other creatures" (p. 3). Onomatopoeia is used to imitate actions. Brer Rabbit relies on his "lippity-clip and his blickety-blick" (p. 3). Personification is found in descriptions of nature: "Way back yonder when the moon was lots bigger than he is now . . ." (p. 3).

Make comparisons within and across cultures. For example, compare the stories retold in Parks's version, stories retold in Lester's *The Tales of Uncle Remus: The Adventures of Brer Rabbit,* and stories in earlier versions retold by Joel Chandler Harris. Make cross-cultural comparisons by analyzing "Brer Rabbit Finds His Match" *(Jump!)* and the Aesop fable, "The Tortoise and the Hare."

Stories such as these Brer Rabbit tales are filled with symbolism and alternate meanings. For example, in *The Adventures of High John the Conqueror,* Steve Sanfield states:

The slaves often told stories about Brer Rabbit, about how, through his cunning and his tricks, he would overcome all the might and power and meanness of Brer Fox and Brer Bear and Brer Wolf. Whites would hear those stories and think, "Oh, isn't that cute, little Brer Rabbit fooling big Brer Bear." But when the slaves told and heard them, they heard them differently. They saw themselves as Brer Rabbit and the slaveholders as Brer Wolf and Brer Fox, and the only way to defeat all that power and brute force was to be just a little bit more clever. (p. 5)

There are distinct oral storytelling styles in African American folktales. Current retellers of these tales frequently mention the influence of storytellers in their own youth. For example, Patricia McKissack introduces *Flossie & the Fox* by telling readers:

Here is a story from my youth, retold in the same rich and colorful language that was my grandfather's. He began all his yarns with questions. "Did I ever tell you 'bout the time lil' Flossie Finley come out the Piney Woods heeling a fox?" I'd snuggle up beside him in the big porch swing, then he'd begin his tale. . . . (author's note, unnumbered)

Interestingly, Julius Lester also introduces *The Tales of Uncle Remus: The Adventures of Brer Rabbit* with the information that his most "lasting memories of my grandmother are of her telling me sto-

ries. . . . My favorites, and I'm sure they were hers as well, were the Brer Rabbit stories" (p. vii). Look for, compare, and analyze the influence of the storyteller's style in these selections.

Robert D. San Souci's *The Talking Eggs* is adapted from a Creole folktale collected in Louisiana. The tale shows that kindness is a respected value, while greed is not rewarded. William H. Hooks's *The Ballad of Belle Dorcas* is a tale set in the tidewater section of the Carolinas during the time of slavery. The protagonists are a free issue woman and a slave who fall in love, but they are threatened with separation when the master wishes to sell the slave. In addition to revealing the consequences of social injustice, the tale reveals the power of love and belief in the magical ability of the spells created by conjurers. Robert D. San Souci's *Sukey and the Mermaid,* collected from the Sea Islands off South Carolina's coast, is a melding of story elements from West Africa and the Caribbean. Virginia Hamilton's *Her Stories: African American Folktales, Fairy Tales, and True Tales* includes "Mary Belle and the Mermaid," collected in South Carolina.

Three books develop stories based on supernatural events. Mary E. Lyons's *Raw Head, Bloody Bones: African-American Tales of the Supernatural* is a collection of stories about goblins, ghosts, monsters, and superhumans from the United States and the Caribbean countries. The author's introduction, notes, bibliography, and suggested readings provide useful information. Patricia C. McKissack's *The Dark-Thirty: Southern Tales of the Supernatural* is a collection of original tales that are rooted in African American history and the oral storytelling tradition. Lynn Joseph's *A Wave in Her Pocket: Stories from Trinidad* is a collection of stories, some of which originated in West Africa, some in Trinidad, and some in the author's imagination. Compare the three books for the storytelling styles and the subjects.

John Henry, a real person and the great black hero of American folklore, is characterized as a "steel-driving" man. Ezra Jack Keats has written and illustrated an attractive edition of John Henry's story, *John Henry: An American Legend.* "Born with a hammer in his hand," the John Henry of folklore accomplishes seemingly impossible tasks, such as turning a huge broken paddle wheel and saving a ship from sinking, laying more railroad track than many men combined, hammering out a dangerous dynamite fuse and saving the men from a cave-in, and challenging and beating a steam drill in a race until he

finally dies "with his hammer in his hand." The large, colorful illustrations in Keats's book suggest the power and heroism of this American legend.

Stories of another folk hero are retold by Steve Sanfield in *The Adventures of High John the Conqueror*. High John is similar to Brer Rabbit because he uses cleverness to outwit his more powerful adversary, the Old Master. The themes in these stories show that the spirit cannot be taken away even if people are living in the worst conditions. Sanfield's text includes factual information to help readers understand and interpret the tales.

Spirituals provide another source for understanding the values in the African American folktales. Spirituals provide the text to accompany Ashley Bryan's colorful illustrations in John Langstaff's *What a Morning! The Christmas Story in Black Spirituals*. The format of the book includes a colorful illustration and appropriate biblical text followed by the words and music for the accompanying spiritual. Another source for spirituals is Bryan's *All Night, All Day: A Child's First Book of African-American Spirituals*.

Fiction

There is currently an abundance of fiction written about the African American experience. This was not always the case. According to Ilene Cooper (1992):

Thirty years ago there were almost no picture books featuring African American children. Happily, this is no longer the case—throughout children's literature, there are now stories (and nonfiction) that examine the black experience, from both a particular and a universal perspective. This is especially true of picture books, where each publishing season seems to bring more titles featuring African American children as the protagonists, brought to life by talented writers and artists. (p. 1036)

Writing in *Publishers Weekly*, Bella Stander (1992) states, "Children's publishers are putting African American-themed books front and center in their catalogues these days, attesting to their growing importance" (p. 28). In a historical review of African American literature, Jean St. Clair (1989) comments on the increasing quality found in African American literature. St. Clair emphasizes that this is especially

Controversy surrounds Margot Zemach's 1982 book, *Jake and Honeybunch Go to Heaven,* a traditional tale with a "green pastures" depiction of heaven and African American characters. The *New York Times Book Review* found literary merit in the story. Public school library selection committees in Chicago, San Francisco, and Milwaukee, however, rejected the book as lacking literary merit and/or as containing racial stereotyping. The March 1983 issue of *American Libraries*[1] focused on this controversy, presenting both positive and negative points of view.

After reading the book, students of children's literature may decide which of the following viewpoints reflect their own beliefs and opinions:

1. "The book is offensive and degrading, wholly inappropriate for children whether they be black or white" (p. 130).
2. "I regret that a discussion between a library and a publisher on the merits of a book has become a library selection issue debated in the public press" (p. 131).
3. "The prejudice in this book is against portraying blacks in children's books in any but the most positive way; it is appropriate, too, to portray blacks in a realistic way using valid sources" (p. 131).
4. "Do some librarians seriously assert they will not purchase such material for children at least because that time in history is viewed as repellent? If so, isn't that like saying we have no past?" (p. 131).
5. "The shallow treatment of the story, the illustrations, the demeaning style of the writing brought a terrible sense of déjà vu" (p. 131).
6. "Any library or any children's department of a library has the right to select or reject materials based on that library's selection policy. The operative question here is one raised in a news program on the Public Broadcasting Service (PBS): What do you think of the notion that the publisher is charging censorship in order to sell books over librarians' protests?" (p. 132).

Denise Wilms[2] identified secondary controversies surrounding this book: "While the book's art and story are sound, its depiction of a certain segment of black culture will stir controversy. . . . In addition, its lighthearted view of heaven may be an affront to some groups who see heaven in a more somber light" (p. 619).

Beryle Banfield and Geraldine L. Wilson[3] identified and criticized symbolic misrepresentations and distortions in *Jake and Honeybunch Go to Heaven.* Banfield and Wilson state:

Significantly the book misrepresents the unique, culturally distinctive view of spiritual life held by people of African descent. . . . Zemach has not used one culturally authentic clue about heaven as understood by generations of black people. (pp. 197–198)

Banfield and Wilson conclude their article with a comparison of the cultural symbols as represented in *Jake and Honeybunch Go to Heaven* with the African American perspective of those same symbols.

---

[1] Brandehoff, Susan E. "Jake and Honeybunch Go to Heaven: Children's Book Fans Smoldering Debate," *American Libraries* 14 (March 1983): 130–132.

[2] Wilms, Denise. "Focus: Jake and Honeybunch Go to Heaven." *Booklist* 79 (January 1, 1983): 619.

[3] Banfield, Beryle, and Geraldine L. Wilson. "The Black Experience Through White Eyes—The Same Old Story Again." In *The Black American in Books for Children: Readings in Racism,* edited by Donnarae MacCann and Gloria Woodard. Metuchen, N.J.: Scarecrow, 1985,

---

true, beginning in the 1970s, with the books written by African American authors.

Fiction written about African American characters differs, depending on the age of the intended audience. Books for younger readers emphasize the universal needs of children. Books for children in the middle-elementary grades emphasize searching for the past and understanding one's ancestry. Books for older children often have the characters face severe personal and social conflicts.

Books for Young Children. Fictional stories about African Americans written for young children mainly depict black children facing situations and problems common to all young children: overcoming jealousy, adjusting to a new baby, expressing a need for attention, experiencing rivalry with siblings, developing personal relationships, and overcoming family problems. Children from all ethnic backgrounds can realize from these books that African American children have the same needs, desires, and problems that other children have and solve their problems in similar ways.

Books for younger children frequently depict warm relationships between children and their mothers or interracial experiences. Irene Smalls-Hector's *Jonathan and His Mommy* depicts a mother and her son walking in the neighborhood. On this walk, they try various movements, such as zigzag walking, making giant steps, and itsy-bitsy baby steps. Michael Hays's illustrations show the city neighborhood and the people who live there. The actions and the illustrations suggest warm relationships.

Rosa Guy's *Billy the Great* develops two universal themes: parents frequently plan the future for their children, even if they are very young, and developing interracial friendships is frequently easier for the children than for the parents. In a satisfying ending, the two boys show the strength of their friendship. In Mary Hoffman's *Amazing Grace,* Grace proves that race and gender do not matter. She can be the best Peter Pan in her class production. Andrea Davis Pinkney develops warm family relations associated with preparation for a celebration in *Seven Candles for Kwanzaa.* This story shows a family preparing for the seven-day African American holiday. Jane Resh Thomas's *Celebration!* focuses on an African American family's Fourth of July. In *Come Sunday,* Nikki Grimes depicts an exuberant African American congregation.

Sharon Bell Mathis depicts warm relationships between young children and elderly people in *The Hundred Penny Box.* In this book, Michael makes friends with his Great-great-aunt Dew and learns about the box in which she keeps a penny for every year of her life. "It's my old cracked-up, wacky-dacky box with the top broken," says Michael's Aunt Dew. "Them's my years in that box . . . . That's me in that box." (p. 19). *The Patchwork Quilt,* by Valerie Flournoy, tells the story of a developing relationship between a grandmother and granddaughter. Both books demonstrate the importance of intergenerational love and respect and of shared memories.

A grandfather and his grandson share stories and develop a closer relationship in Mary Stolz's *Storm in the Night.* In *Elijah's Angel: A Story for Chanukah and Christmas,* Michael J. Rosen develops a warm relationship between an elderly African American wood carver and a young Jewish boy through a gift of an angel.

Imagination and desire to win a cakewalk combine to make a girl try to capture the wind as her

Love and respect are essential emotions in a story that develops a relationship between two generations. (From The Patchwork Quilt, *by Valerie Flournoy, pictures copyright © 1985 by Jerry Pinkney. Reproduced by permission of Dial Books for Young Readers.)*

dancing partner in Patricia McKissack's *Mirandy and Brother Wind.* The story may be so believable because the author was influenced by a picture of her grandparents after they won a cakewalk. Imagination also plays a role in Faith Ringgold's *Tar Beach.* The illustrations show a girl lying on the rooftop of her apartment building and flying over Harlem in the late 1930s.

Happy childhood memories also form the background for Donald Crews's *Bigmama's,* a story about warm family relationships that increase as the children visit Bigmama's house in Florida. Crews uses the same Florida setting for *Shortcut.* In this story, the children have a frightening experience. On the railroad track that they choose for a shortcut home, they encounter an oncoming train that sounds "WHOO WHOO" and "KLAKITY KLAKITY KLAKITY KLAK" in the night. The story has a happy ending: The children reach the warmth of Bigmama's house and decide that they will not take the shortcut again.

The train whistle was much louder.

"Back to the cut-off!"   "RUN"

The language and the colors reinforce a frightening experience. (Illustration by Donald Crews from his Shortcut. *Copyright © 1992 by Donald Crews. Reprinted by permission of Green Willow Books/William Morrow and Company.)*

In *Working Cotton,* Sherley Anne Williams drew on her own childhood experiences in the cotton fields of Fresno, California. The text and the illustrations depict the hardworking life of a migrant family.

Several contemporary realistic picture books for younger children are set in Africa and focus on warm relationships between families and friends. Karen Lynn Williams's *When Africa Was Home* describes relationships between a white boy and his African neighbors. The strength of these relationships is shown when, after the family returns to America, they decide that their home is really in Africa. Consequently, they return to Africa and to their friends.

Virginia Kroll's *Masai and I* is an imaginative story in which a girl is learning about East Africa in her American school. The text describes and the illustrations show the girl thinking about what it would be like if she were Masai and were doing the same activities. For example, the text and illustrations contrast going home, eating dinner, getting dessert, playing at night, making the bed, looking at animals, running in the neighborhood, and attending a family dinner. Kroll's text stimulates readers to make other comparisons between their lives and those of people living in other countries.

Books with African settings may also show the consequences of segregated townships. Rachel Isadora's *At the Crossroads* follows South African children waiting to welcome their fathers, who are returning from working in the mines after being sep-

arated from their families for ten months. The text describes and illustrations show both the loving relationships between fathers and children, and the shanties in which they live. Catherine Stock's *Armien's Fishing Trip* is set in a South African fishing village. Stock's introduction informs readers that many families were forced to leave the village when it was declared white in 1967. Stock introduces the differences in setting when Armien breathes the fresh salty air and wishes "that he still lived here instead of on the hot and sandy Cape Flats" (p. 2, unnumbered). The rest of the book explores the warm relationships between Armien and his relatives and friends. Adventure is provided when Armien saves a man from drowning while on the fishing trip.

In *The Day Gogo Went to Vote: South Africa, April 1994,* Elinor Batezal Sisulu creates a picture storybook with a strong character who voices her needs to vote. Gogo, Thembi's one hundred-year-old great-great-grandmother, has not left her home in many years and now she explains why she is going out to vote: " 'Thembi, black people in South Africa have fought for many years for the right to vote. This is the first time we have a chance to vote for our own leaders, and it might be my last. This is why I must vote, no matter how many miles I have to stand in line!' " (unnumbered). The remainder of the book follows the process as the oldest woman in the township goes to vote and the township celebrates the election of Nelson Mandela.

Chapters 4 and 5 discuss additional picture story-books written from the African American perspective.

Books for Children in the Middle-Elementary Grades.

Many African American stories written for children in the middle-elementary grades are written by authors—black and white—who are sensitive to the black experience. Some themes—such as the discovery of oneself, the need to give and receive love, the problems experienced when children realize that the parents whom they love are getting a divorce, and the fears associated with nonachievement in school—are universal and suggest that all children have similar needs, fears, and problems. Other themes, such as searching for one's roots in the African past, speak of a special need by black children to know about their ancestry.

Virginia Hamilton's *Zeely* is a warm, sensitive story about an imaginative girl who makes an important discovery about herself and others when she and her brother spend the summer on their Uncle Ross's farm. Elizabeth is not satisfied with the status quo; she calls herself Geeder, renames her younger brother Toeboy, renames her uncle's town Crystal, and calls the asphalt highway Leadback. When the imaginative Geeder sees her uncle's neighbor, Miss Zeely Tayber, Hamilton describes Zeely's appearance in detail: Zeely is a thin and stately woman over six feet tall, with a calm and proud expression, skin the color of rich Ceylon ebony, and the most beautiful face that Geeder has ever seen. When Geeder discovers a photograph of a Watusi queen who looks exactly like Zeely, she decides that Zeely must have royal blood.

Geeder is swept up in this fantasy and shares her beliefs with the village children. Then, Zeely helps Geeder make her greatest discovery. As they talk, Geeder realizes that dreaming is fine, but being yourself is even better. This realization causes Geeder to see everything in a new way. She realizes that Zeely is indeed a queen, but not like the ones in books, with their servants, kingdoms, and wealth. Zeely is queen because she is a self-loving person who always does her work better than anybody else. Geeder realizes that what a person is inside is more important than how a person looks or what a person owns. When Hamilton shares Geeder's final thoughts about her wonderful summer and her discovery that even stars resemble people, readers understand just how much wisdom Elizabeth has gained:

Some stars were no more than bright arcs in the sky as they burned out. But others lived on and on. There was a blue star in the sky south of Hesperus, the evening star. She thought of naming it Miss Zeely Tayber. There it would be in Uncle Ross' sky forever. (p. 121)

Another book that explores a character's personal discovery and strength of character is *Sister,* by Eloise Greenfield. Sister, whose real name is Doretha, keeps a journal in which she records the hard times—and the good times that "rainbowed" their way through those harder times. Doretha's memory book helps her realize "I'm me." The words of the school song sung in *Sister* are characteristic of the themes found in this and other books by Greenfield:

> We strong black brothers and sisters
> Working in unity,
> We strong black brothers and sisters,
> Building our community,
> We all work together, learn together
> Live in harmony
> We strong black brothers and sisters
> Building for you and for me. (p. 69)

Another book with strong characters is John Steptoe's *Creativity,* a story of friendship.

Mildred Taylor's *The Gold Cadillac* is a fictionalized story based on Taylor's painful memories, a story about family unity and the consequences of racial prejudice. The prejudice occurs in 1950, when a northern black family buys a gold Cadillac and tries to drive to Mississippi. For the first time, the children experience segregation and racial hostility. As in other books by Taylor, the theme is that family love and unity help them overcome such terrible experiences. The characters in Vaunda Micheaux Nelson's *Mayfield Crossing* also overcome prejudice after they move from their old school to their new school.

Books for Older Children.

Outstanding realistic fiction written for older children is characterized by both strong characters and strong themes. The themes in these stories include searching for freedom and dignity, learning to live together, tackling problems personally rather than waiting for someone else to do so, survival of the body and the spirit, and the more humorous problems involved in living through a first crush.

Virginia Hamilton has written several fine novels that older children find engrossing. In her suspenseful contemporary story *The House of Dies Drear,* she skillfully presents historical information about slavery and the Underground Railroad through the conversations of a black history professor and his son who are interested in the history of the pre–Civil War mansion that they are about to rent. (Compare Hamilton's presentation of information about slavery with Belinda Hurmence's presentation of information in her time travel fantasy about slavery in *A Girl Called Boy*.) Hamilton provides details for a setting that seems perfect for the mysterious occurrences that begin soon after the family arrives:

The house of Dies Drear loomed out of mist and murky sky, not only gray and formless, but huge and unnatural. It seemed to crouch on the side of a high hill above the highway. And it had a dark, isolated look about it that set it at odds with all that was living. (p. 26)

Thomas learns that Dies Drear and two escaped slaves were murdered and that rumors say the abolitionist and the slaves haunt the old house and the hidden tunnels below. Mystery fans will enjoy this fast-paced book. In a sequel, *The Mystery of Drear House*, Hamilton answers questions that students may have after reading *The House of Dies Drear*. In this sequel, the characters protect the treasure accumulated by Dies Drear from nature and from the thieving Darrows.

In an interview conducted by Hazel Rochman (1992c), Virginia Hamilton discusses her interest in the Underground Railroad and mentions that her grandfather was a fugitive slave who came to Ohio from Virginia. She describes the houses in Ohio that are similar to the one in *The House of Dies Drear*. She states:

There are houses here with secret rooms and tunnels that were stations on the Underground going north into Oberlin and up to Shawnee territory. There's an octagonal house in Yellow Springs that was specifically designed to hide runaways. It had all these corners that could be cut off into little cubbyholes. (p. 1020)

Hamilton writes about the black experience with a universal appeal that speaks to readers of any heritage. Another of Hamilton's characters learns that choice and action lie within his power in *M. C. Higgins, the Great*. In this story, the enemy is the spoil heap remaining from strip mining of the mountains, an oozing pile that threatens to swallow a boy's home and even his mother's beloved sunflower. In *Cousins*, Hamilton explores interrelationships within an extended family.

In *Scorpions*, Walter Dean Myers's characters face person-against-society conflicts created by the contemporary world of drug dealers and gangs. They also face person-against-self conflicts created by inner fears and consequences related to owning a gun. The characters of Mama and her younger son Jamal are especially strong. Myers develops Mama's character through numerous contrasts. For example, when Mama thinks about her older son, who is in jail for robbery, she remembers looking at him as a baby and feeling great expectations because "You got a baby and you hope so much for it. . . . " (p. 54). Later, Mama is torn between her need to help this older son and to protect her younger children. Myers develops Mama's inner conflict as she discusses her problems with her minister:

"And I know they convicted him of taking somebody's life, but that don't mean he ain't my flesh and blood." The minister replies: "Sometimes the herbs we take are bitter, sister, but we got to take them anyway. . . . You got to hold your family here together too. We can't let the bad mess up the good." (p. 153)

In a tragic ending, Jamal discovers the consequences of having the gun and makes an even greater personal discovery. There was "the part of him, a part that was small and afraid, that still wanted that gun" (p. 214). This poignant story reveals the complex problems facing two generations of people who are fighting for personal and family survival in a dangerous world. In *Slam!*, Myers also uses contemporary urban locations. Now basketball helps the main character learn truths about himself.

A rural story for older children is much lighter in tone than are the previously discussed books. Bette Greene's humorous *Philip Hall Likes Me. I Reckon Maybe* is set in Arkansas. The eleven-year-old main characters are Philip Hall, the smartest boy in the class, and Beth Lambert, the girl who has her first crush. Greene creates humor as Beth tries to maneuver herself and Philip into shared experiences. Beth is a little suspicious that Philip may not be the smartest child in the class: She may be letting him win. The two work together to solve the mystery of her father's missing turkeys, but they are in direct competition when each of them raises a calf to show at the annual county fair. When Beth's calf wins, Philip's first reaction is shame. Then, he feels the unfamiliar emotions related to losing. Beth solves their problem when she invites him to be her partner in the square-dancing contest. As friends and partners, they can win or lose together. Philip finally admits what Beth has been longing to hear: "Sometimes I reckon I likes you, Beth Lambert" (p. 135).

In another book that is also lighter in tone, *The Mouse Rap,* Walter Dean Myers uses a style that many readers enjoy. Students of children's literature can analyze the impact of the language as the main character, fourteen-year-old Mouse, presents many of his views in rap. For example, Myers introduces his character in this way:

Ka-phoomp! Ka-Phoomp! Da Doom Da Dooom!
Ka-phoomp! Ka-phoomp! Da Doom Da Dooom!
You can call me Mouse, 'cause that's my tag
I'm into it all, everything's my bag
You know I can run, you know I can hoop
I can do it alone, or in a group
My ace is Styx, he'll always do
Add Bev and Sheri, and you got my crew
My tag is Mouse, and it'll never fail
And just like a mouse I got me a tale
Ka-phoomp! Ka-phoomp! Da Doom Da Dooom!
Ka-phoomp! Ka-phoomp! Da Doom Da Dooom! (p. 3)

Read portions of the book aloud to gain the greatest response to the text.

Chapter 10 discussed other stories about African Americans for older children, including Mildred D. Taylor's *Roll of Thunder, Hear My Cry,* James and Christopher Collier's *Jump Ship to Freedom,* and Kathryn Lasky's *True North.* Books such as Joyce Hansen's *Which Way Freedom* and *I Thought My Soul Would Rise and Fly: The Diary of Patsy, a Freed Girl,* and Colin A. Palmer's *The First Passage: Blacks in the Americas, 1502–1617* are based on historical information about African Americans during the Civil War and reconstruction. The characters in all of these stories meet the criteria for outstanding characterization in literature: They are memorable individuals who face the best and the worst that life offers. They are portrayed with dignity and without stereotype.

Characters such as the slave in Gary Paulsen's *Nightjohn* show both the ordeals experienced by the slaves and the hope and perseverance that kept them alive. Even though he is cruelly treated, Nightjohn brings his gifts of teaching reading and writing to the young slave children. Twelve-year-old Sarny reveals both his suffering and his personal value very well when she thinks:

In the night he come walking. Late in the night and when he walks he leaves the tracks that we find in the soft dirt down where the drive meets the road, in the soft warm dirt in the sun we see his tracks with the middle toe missing on the left foot and the middle toe missing on the right and we know.
We know.
It be Nightjohn.
Late he come walking and nobody else knows, nobody from the big house or the other big houses know but we do.

We know.
Late he come walking and it be Nightjohn and he bringing us the way to know. (p. 92)

Literature that shows the slaves' struggle for learning is important according to Cecelia McCall (1989), because:

Though the majority of slaves remained illiterate, some defied the prohibitions that decreed education illegal for those who were only three-fifths of a person. The history of learning among African-Americans is as old as their roots in this country and runs parallel to the struggle for freedom. (p. 3)

As in the literature for young readers, the stories for older readers reflect varied settings and socioeconomic levels. The main character may be the child of a highly educated college professor or the child of a destitute sharecropper. The realistic stories for older readers do, however, reflect a harsh realism in the African American experience, whether in the past or in contemporary life. Some of these stories—such as Virginia Hamilton's *The Planet of Junior Brown* and Walter Dean Myers's *Scorpions*—portray an economically disadvantaged inner-city existence and problems of survival very different from those of the middle-class experience. However, children in the stories reflect pride in their individuality and in their decisions to be themselves. The courage and determination of the characters are inspirational to all.

Authors of contemporary realistic fiction that emphasizes the black experience may focus on characters who try to survive in modern repressive environments. For example, Frances Temple (1992) describes her reasons for writing *Taste of Salt: A Story of Modern Haiti.* She says:

I read about the firebombing of the boys' shelter, Lafanmi Selavi, in Haiti, heard some of Jean-Bertrand Aristide's speeches, saw pictures of children and teenagers working, demonstrating. I wondered what it would be like to be one of them, called to be a mover and shaker in a country trying to make a new start, pitted against the giants of political terrorism and our global economy. (endcover)

The importance of becoming literate is developed in this story set in the time of slavery. (Jacket cover from Nightjohn *by Gary Paulsen. Copyright © 1993 by Lynn Brasswell. Used by permission of Delacorte Press, a division of Bantam Doubleday Dell Publishing Group, Inc.)*

Temple's novel for older readers is based on the lives of a fictional street urchin and a young woman who writes the story about their experiences. It is a dramatic story of survival, in which the characters conclude, " 'Is hope they want to kill, Jeremie.' 'Is hope we need to keep alive, then, Djo.' 'And we will, Jeri, don't you think?' " (p. 172). As in many of the African American stories, this book also concludes on a note of courage and determination.

Nonfiction

Because two of the strongest purposes for sharing literature by and about African Americans with chil-dren are to raise the aspirations of black children and to encourage understanding of the African American experience by nonblack children, biographies should be important in a multicultural literature program. Biographies of African American leaders and artists tell children about contributions to American society and the problems overcome.

Several biographies for children portray the life of nineteenth-century freedom fighter Frederick Douglass. For example, Lillie Patterson's *Frederick Douglass: Freedom Fighter* is a dramatic encounter with Douglass's life in slavery, protest against slavery, escape from the slave owners and then slave hunters, work on the Underground Railroad, and championing of the rights of not only black people but also the Chinese, the Irish, and females. Douglas Miller's *Frederick Douglass and the Fight for Freedom* covers similar events and is interesting for comparative study. Miller, a professor of American history, includes a valuable list of additional readings and discusses some of the problems in previous biographies. Michael McCurdy's *Escape from Slavery: The Boyhood of Frederick Douglass in His Own Words* preserves Douglass's original writings. Milton Meltzer's *Frederich Douglass: In His Own Words* is a collection of Douglass's speeches and writings. Through his writings students will discover attitudes toward slavery.

Virginia Hamilton's *Anthony Burns: The Defeat and Triumph of a Fugitive Slave* covers the life of a slave who is less well known than Frederick Douglass. However, the escape of Burns to Boston, his arrest, and trial had much impact on the abolitionists and advanced the antislavery movement. (See chapter 12 for a discussion of Hamilton's biography.) Gwen Everett's *John Brown: One Man Against Slavery* presents the story of the abolitionist through the viewpoint of Brown's sixteen-year-old daughter. The book is illustrated with a series of paintings drawn in 1941 by a prominent African American artist, Jacob Lawrence.

James T. DeKay's *Meet Martin Luther King, Jr.* stresses the magnitude of King's work and his reasons for fighting against injustice. Lillie Patterson's *Martin Luther King, Jr. and the Freedom Movement* begins with an account of the 1955–1956 Montgomery, Alabama, bus boycott and Martin Luther King, Jr.'s involvement in the boycott. Patterson then explores King's earlier background and discovers some of the influences that caused King to become a leader in the boycott and the civil rights movement.

James Haskins's *The Life and Death of Martin Luther King, Jr.* presents a stirring account of both King's triumphs and tragedies. Haskins's *I Have a Dream: The Life and Words of Martin Luther King, Jr.* focuses on King's involvement with the civil rights movement. Compare these biographies of Martin Luther King, Jr., with the revised edition of *My Life with Martin Luther King, Jr.* by Coretta Scott King.

Interesting comparisons may be made between two highly illustrated biographies of Martin Luther King, Jr. Faith Ringgold's *My Dream of Martin Luther King* develops the biography through a dream sequence. The text begins appropriately, "I've always been a dreamer. But the only dreams I can remember are the ones I dream with my eyes wide open. Once I go to sleep, I rarely remember my dreams. However, one day while watching a television program about Martin Luther King, Jr., I slept and had a dream that I will never forget" (unnumbered). From that point on, the text and illustrations present various stages in developing King's vision for a better world such as joining demonstrations, listening to his father's sermons, being influenced by the teachings of Mahatma Gandhi, becoming an adult minister, and finally dying from an assassin's bullet. The text and dream sequence end as people in a crowd scene trade bags filled with prejudice, hate, ignorance, violence, and fear for Martin Luther King's dream for the promised land.

Rosemary L. Bray's biography, *Martin Luther King,* is illustrated with folk-art paintings. Bray's biography includes more details about King's life. Neither book includes source notes. Students of children's literature can compare the impact of the illustrations and the depiction of King's life in these two highly illustrated biographies written to appeal to younger audiences.

Eloise Greenfield's *Rosa Parks* focuses on the life of the seamstress in Montgomery who refused to give up her seat on the bus. Judith Bentley's *Harriet Tubman,* the biography of a Civil War heroine, is supported with photographs, source notes, further reading, a bibliography, and an index.

Arnold Adoff's *Malcolm X* stresses how and why Malcolm X urged African Americans to be proud of their heritage and themselves. In books written for older readers, *Malcolm X: By Any Means Necessary,* by Walter Dean Myers, and Kevin Brown's *Malcolm X: His Life and Legacy* set their biographical character against the history of segregation and the civil rights movement. Compare the three books about Malcolm X. Patricia McKissack's *Jesse Jackson* focuses on the accomplishments of the first black man to run for president of the United States.

Several books reflect the contributions of African Americans to the fine arts. James Weldon Johnson's *Lift Every Voice and Sing* is often referred to as the African American national anthem. This book combines the song with linocut prints that were originally created in the 1940s by Elizabeth Catlett. *Sweet Words So Brave: The Story of African American Literature* by Barbara K. Curry and James Michael Brodie provides an introduction to authors and literature.

The contributions of African American people to the American theater are stressed in James Haskins's *Black Theater in America.* Haskins traces the American theater from minstrel shows through contemporary protest plays and drama, highlighting black writers, actors, and musicians. Glennette Tilley Turner's *Take a Walk in Their Shoes* includes short biographies of fourteen African Americans. The text includes skits that children can perform.

Mary E. Lyons's *Sorrow's Kitchen: The Life and Folklore of Zora Neale Hurston* describes the life of a black author who was part of the Harlem Renaissance and recorded and published folklore collected from the southern United States and the West Indies. Hurston's writings enrich the biography, which is supported with notes, suggested readings, and a bibliography. Many contributions of African Americans in the area of poetry are included in chapter 8, "Poetry."

Patricia and Frederick McKissack focus attention on the contributions of African Americans in the labor movement. Their *A Long Hard Journey: The Story of the Pullman Porter* chronicles the struggle for African Americans to form a union for railroad porters. Walter Dean Myers's *Now Is Your Time! The African-American Struggle for Freedom* includes shorter episodes that explore the African American experience from slavery through the civil rights movement and into contemporary times. This book includes sources, a bibliography, and an index. Patricia and Frederick McKissack have written a second edition of *The Civil Rights Movement in America from 1865 to the Present.* This large book is supported with numerous photographs and descriptions of people who influenced the civil rights movement. Virginia Hamilton's *Many Thousand Gone: African Americans from Slavery to Freedom* provides short accounts of people who were involved in the fight for freedom. The book is divided into three parts: Slavery in America, Running-Away, and Exodus to Freedom, and it includes a bibliography and an index. In a book about the civil rights movement, *The March on Washington,* James Haskins discusses not only the event but also the people who were influential in the organization.

The books discussed in this chapter have broad appeal for children and a wide range of content. The emergence of outstanding authors who write about the African American experience with sensitivity and honesty has provided more excellent books about African Americans than are available about other minorities in the United States. When shared with children, such books contribute toward positive self-images and respect for individuals across cultures. They also do much to lessen the negative stereotypes of African American people in American literature of the past.

 ## *NATIVE AMERICAN LITERATURE*

The copyright dates listed in the annotated bibliography at the end of this chapter show that the majority of recommended books about Native Americans have been published relatively recently. Few copyright dates precede the 1970s, which indicates a recent increase in the number of books written from a Native American perspective. Many of these books are beautifully illustrated traditional tales, and several have won the Caldecott Medal. Some are written by Native Americans themselves; others have been written by non–Native American writers, such as anthropologist Joyce Rockwood, who have used their knowledge of native cultures to authentically portray the Native American past.

The lovely poetry written by Byrd Baylor and the tales that she has collected increase understanding of Native American values and heritage, but there are still too few stories with contemporary settings and Native American main characters. Consequently, most children have few opportunities to read about Native American children facing the problems of today.

Jon C. Stott (1992) focuses on another problem faced by people seeking authentic Native American literature. He states, "Works by native authors generally appear on the lists of smaller, regional publishers, and, unfortunately, seldom reach a wide audience" (p. 374). Consequently, some Native American literature is not easily available.

In a bulletin published by the National Council for the Social Studies, Karen D. Harvey, Lisa D. Harjo, and Jane K. Jackson (1990) identify the following facts that you should consider when choosing and evaluating materials about Native Americans. First, Native American cultures span twenty or more millennia, from before written history to today. Second, most of the Native American history is tentative, speculative, and written by European or Anglo-American explorers or scholars, and much of the oral history of the Native peoples was lost. Third, widely diverse physical environments influenced the development of ancient and contemporary native American cultures, including Arctic tundra, woodlands, deserts, Mesoamerican jungles, prairies, plateaus, plains, swamps, and mountains. Fourth, linguists believe that at least two hundred languages were spoken in North America before European contact, and scholars estimate that seventy-three language families existed in North America at the time of European contact. Fifth, currently, there are about five hundred federally recognized tribes and about three hundred federal Indian reservations. Sixth, no one federal or tribal definition establishes a person's identity as an Indian. Consequently, Harvey, Harjo, and Jackson conclude, "the subject is vast, complicated, diverse, and difficult" (p. 2).

Traditional Tales

Native American tales show that the North American continent had traditional tales centuries old before the European settlers arrived. Traditional Native American tales make up a heritage that all North Americans should take pride in and pass on to future generations. Clifford E. Trafzer (1992), Director of Native American Studies at the University of California, Riverside, stresses the importance of these traditional tales. He says:

The words of the old stories are not myths and fairy tales. They are a communion with the ancient dead—the Animal, Plant, and Earth Surface Peoples who once inhabited the world and whose spirits continue to influence the course of Native American history. (p. 381)

Trafzer also emphasizes the importance of these stories for children, saying, "There is something sacred in the old texts, the ancient literature of America. . . . The accounts provide children with a better understanding of this land and its first people" (p. 393).

Critics and reviewers of multicultural literature emphasize the need for authenticity in texts and in illustrations. For example, Betsy Hearne (1993a, 1993b) emphasizes that not only should the reteller provide information about the original source for the tale but also a text adapted from folklore should be judged for its balance of two traditions: the one from which it is drawn and the one that it is entering. Texts and illustrations, then, should ring true for the culture from which they are adapted and be meaningful to the culture that is reading them. When evaluating the works of John Bierhorst, Barbara Bader (1997) also emphasizes the importance of authenticity. Notice what elements of Bierhorst's writing she stresses: "Authentic, accessible, and uncommonly attractive; also, fully documented, with historical introductions, source notes, and explanatory page notes. At a time when freeform, embellished retellings were the norm, with perhaps a nod to an eminent anthropologist or native informant, Bierhorst's work stood out for integrity and intrinsic quality" (p. 270).

In an evaluation of children's literature about Native Americans, Trafzer (1992) emphasizes the need for citing tribal sources and creating works that are culturally authentic for the tribe. Stott (1992) adds that critics of Native American literature must employ a complex set of guidelines, including:

If it is based on oral materials, how well is its orality transferred to the page? For whom is the book intended, and are the needs of audience met? If the writer is non-native, how well is the process of translation carried out? If it is by a native writer, is the book subject to different evaluative guidelines? Does the reviewer take into account the distance between a native author and a young, non-native reader? (p. 374)

In his collection of traditional Native American tales, *Anpao: An American Indian Odyssey,* Jamake Highwater compares tellers of Native American folktales to weavers whose designs are the threads of their personal sagas as well as the history of their people. Stories of the Native American oral tradition have been passed down and often mingled with tales from other tribes. Says Highwater:

They exist as the river of memory of a people, surging with their images and their rich meanings from one place to another, from one generation to the next—the tellers and the told so intermingled in time and space that no one can separate them. (p. 239)

Highwater recounts the task of preserving and transmitting traditional stories described by the Santee Dakota, Charles Eastman. Writing of his own boyhood, Eastman said that very early in life, Indian boys assumed the task of preserving and transmitting their legends. In the evening, a boy would listen as one of his parents or grandparents told a tale. Often, the boy would be required to repeat the story the following evening. The household became his audience and either criticized or applauded his endeavors.

Highwater has combined a number of traditional Indian tales in *Anpao: An American Indian Odyssey.* The story begins "In the days before the people fled into the water . . . [when] there was no war and the people were at peace" (p. 15). During this time, Anpao travels across the great prairies, through deep canyons, and along wooded ridges in search of his destiny. Along the way, he observes the cultures and customs of many different tribes. His odyssey illustrates the diversity of the land, life-styles, and history found within the Indian cultures of North America.

Native American traditional literature is an excellent source for identifying and understanding tribal traditional values and beliefs. Stephen Dow Beckham, (1997) in the introduction to *Echoes of the Elders: The Stories and Paintings of Chief Lelooska,* states:

The stories were the primary means of passing on the tribal memory. They recounted how the world had come to be, why things were named as they were, and how humans should act. They speak through time to listeners and readers today. (p. 5)

Several sources provide documentation for traditional Native American values and beliefs. For example, *Human Behavior and American Indians,* by Hanson and Eisenbise (1983), documents tribal traditional values and compares them to urban industrial values. *The Journal of American Indian Education* (Spang, 1965) identifies North American Indian cultural values and compares them to the values of the dominant non-Indian culture. The Coalition of Indian Controlled School Boards (Ross and Brave Eagle, 1975) identifies traditional Lakota values and compares them to non-Lakota values.

A review of these sources indicates that many of the traditional values, such as living in harmony with nature, viewing religion as a natural phenomenon closely related to nature, showing respect for wisdom gained through age and experience, acquiring patience, and emphasizing group and extended family needs rather than individual needs, are also dominant themes in the traditional tales from various tribal regions. As you read Native American tales, see if you can identify these values.

For example, living in harmony with nature is a dominant theme in Tomie dePaola's retelling of the Comanche tale, *The Legend of the Bluebonnet.* The theme is developed when selfishly taking from the land is punished by drought, while unselfishly giving of a prized possession is rewarded with bluebonnets and rain. The name change in the main character as she goes from She-Who-Is-Alone to One-Who-Dearly-Loved-Her-People supports the emphasis on extended family rather than the individual. Having reverence for animals is an important theme in Barbara Diamond Goldin's retelling of *The Girl Who Lived with the Bears,* a tale from the Pacific Northwest.

Paula Underwood Spencer's *Who Speaks for Wolf* develops the importance of living in harmony with nature through a "Native American Learning Story," told by her Oneida father, Sharp-Eyed Hawk. The story relates experiences of the Oneida as they move to a new location, only to realize that they forgot the rights of the animals. At the end of the tale, the wise storyteller gazes slowly around the council circle and asks the ancient question:

> Tell me now my brothers
> Tell me now my sisters
> Who speaks for Wolf? (p. 40)

The interactions between buffalo and Great Plains Indians are developed in both Olaf Baker's *Where the Buffaloes Begin* and Paul Goble's *Buffalo Woman.* In *Where the Buffaloes Begin,* Stephen Gammell's marvelous black-and-white drawings capture the buffaloes surging out of a mythical lake after their birth, rampaging across the prairie, and eventually saving Little Wolf's people from their enemies. In traditional tales from the Great Plains, the buffalo people frequently save those who understand and respect them. Goble's tale ends with why the relationship between the Great Plains Indians and the buffaloes is so important:

> The relationship was made between the People and the Buffalo Nation; it will last until the end of time. It will be remembered that a brave young man became a buffalo because he loved his wife and little child. In return the Buffalo People have given their flesh so that little children, and babies still unborn, will always have meat to eat. It is the Creator's wish. (unnumbered)

Showing respect for animals, keeping one's word, and listening to elders are interrelated themes in Frank Cushing's "The Poor Turkey Girl," found in *Zuni Folk Tales.* In this Cinderella-type tale, a Zuni maiden who cares for the turkeys is helped to go to a festival by old Gobble and the other turkeys. When the girl does not heed old Gobble's admonition and return on time to feed the turkeys, she loses everything because:

> After all, the gods dispose of men according as men are fitted; and if the poor be poor in heart and spirit as well as in appearance, how will they be aught but poor to the end of their days? Thus shortens my story. (p. 64)

You may compare "Poor Turkey Girl" with Penny Pollock's retelling of the same tale, *The Turkey Girl: A Zuni Cinderella Story.* Pollock identifies her original source as Cushing's *Zuni Folk Tales.*

Traditional tales of legendary heroes reflect important values and beliefs of the people. These heroes have many of the same characteristics found in heroic tales from other cultures. Like Beowulf in the Norse legend, an Inuit hero shows bravery, honor, and a willingness to avenge wrongs. In the introduction to one of the tales included in *Stories from the Canadian North,* Muriel Whitaker states:

> In order to understand fully the ending of "The Blind Boy and the Loon," one must realize that the Eskimo hero was predominantly an avenger. Just as the spirits of weather, thunder, lightning, and the sea took vengeance on those who mistreated them, so too was the mortal hero expected to have the will and the power to exact retribution for evil. (p. 20)

According to Robin McGrath (1988), the traditional tales in Inuit folklore can be divided into six classifications: creation myths or stories, which embody religious belief; stories of fabulous beings such as trolls, giants, or ghosts; tales of epic heroes; stories of murder and revenge; beast fables; and personal memoirs. Stories in these classifications can be found in the adult resource *The Eskimo Storyteller: Folktales from Noatak, Alaska* by Edwin S. Hall, Jr. (1976). Additional Inuit tales include John Bierhorst's *The Dancing Fox: Arctic Folktales,* Lydia Dabcovich's *The Polar Bear Son: An Inuit Tale,* and Howard Norman's *The Girl Who Dreamed Only Geese and Other Tales of the Far North.* Bierhorst and Norman include an introduction and notes that enhance understanding of the tales. Dabcovich discusses the background of the tale and her research into the subject.

Legends from the northwestern United States and Canada emphasize heroes who venture onto the unpredictable sea and overcome perils of the ocean wilderness. Christie Harris's *The Trouble with Adventurers* includes tales with representative themes. For example, "The Bird of Good Luck" shows that fame can arouse envy; "How Raven Gets the Oolikan" suggests that the deeds of heroes are not always to be admired; "Revenge of the Wolf Prince" suggests that heroes do not always survive to enjoy a happy future; and "Ghost Canoe People" shows that heroes often need supernatural help but that supernatural beings may not be inclined to offer assistance. Tales from British Columbia are found in *Kwakiutl Legends*, retold by Chief James Wallas, and in *Echoes of the Elders: The Stories and Paintings Chief Lelooska*, edited by Christine Normandin.

Native North Americans, like people everywhere, evolved mythology that explained the origins of the universe and natural phenomena. According to Virginia Haviland (1979), Native Americans believed in "supernatural forces and their legends told of culture heroes and shape-shifters who used magic. Animals had power to turn into people and people into animals. The animal stories, like animal folklore of many other countries, are often humorous, and the characters are accomplished tricksters" (p. 13).

Native Americans, Native Canadians, and the Inuit peoples developed a rich heritage of traditional myths and legends. John Bierhorst (1976) identifies the following four categories found in Native American mythology: (1) myths that emphasize "setting the world in order," in which the world is created out of or fashioned from the chaos of nature; (2) myths that emphasize "family drama" by centering on conflicts and affinities rising out of the kinship unit; (3) myths that emphasize "fair and foul," such as the trickster cycle tales, in which the hero progresses from a character of utter worthlessness to one that displays a gradual understanding of social virtue; and (4) myths that emphasize "crossing the threshold" by depicting the passage from unconsciousness to consciousness, the ordeal of puberty, the passage into and out of the animal world, the passage into and out of death, and the transition from nature to culture. In a book for adults, *The Red Swan: Myths and Tales of the American Indians*, Bierhorst presents and discusses examples of these various categories of myths. Bierhorst's categories are also found in single stories and anthologies that include several tales passed down in tribes across the North American continent.

Setting-the-World-in-Order Tales.

Traditional tales that emphasize setting the world in order tell about creating the earth and various animal and plant life. Earth-diver type myths are found in the literature of numerous North American Indians. For example, Virginia Hamilton includes two earth-diver myths in *In the Beginning: Creation Stories from Around the World*: (1) "Turtle Dives to the Bottom of the Sea: Earth Starter the Creator," a Maidu tale from California, and (2) "The Woman Who Fell from the Sky: Divine Woman the Creator," a Huron myth from the northeastern United States. Hamilton's collection also includes a Blackfoot myth in which Na'pi, or Old Man the Creator, travels around the world creating people and animals and an Eskimo myth in which Raven, a trickster god, travels around the world instructing people how to live. Amy L. Cohn's *From Sea to Shining Sea: A Treasury of American Folklore and Folk Songs* includes a creation story told by the Iroquois people, as well as tales from other Native American peoples.

Creation stories from several tribes are found in *Keepers of the Earth: Native American Stories and Environmental Activities for Children*, by Michael J. Caduto and Joseph Bruchac. An Onondaga tale from the northeastern woodlands, "The Earth on Turtle's Back," tells about how Great Turtle gives his shell to hold Earth and the seeds brought to Earth by the Great Chief's wife. In a Navajo tale, "Four Worlds: The Dine Story of Creation," the Holy People move from the first world to the fourth world by way of a female reed. This tale shows the disastrous consequences of not taking care of Earth. The tale concludes with a warning: "So the Fourth World came to be. However, just as the worlds before it were destroyed when wrong was done, so too this Fourth World was destined to be destroyed when the people do not live the right way. That is what the Dine say to this day" (p. 34).

Native American tales, such as Barbara Esbensen's *The Star Maiden*, account for the creation of plant life. In this lyrical rendition of an Ojibway tale, Star Maiden and her sisters leave their home in the sky and become the beautiful star-shaped water lilies. The Es-

KEEPERS OF THE EARTH
Native American Stories and Environmental Activities for Children

Michael J. Caduto and Joseph Bruchac

Foreword by N. Scott Momaday
Illustrations by John Kahionhes Fadden and Carol Wood

(From Keepers of the Earth: Native American Stories and Environmental Activities for Children *by Michael J. Caduto and Joseph Bruchac; illustrations by John Kahionhes Fadden and Carol Wood. Cover illustration copyright © 1989 John Kahionhes Fadden. Published by Fulcrum, Inc., 1989. Reprinted by permission.)*

kimo tale, "The Doll," found in Dale DeArmond's *The Boy Who Found the Light* is about a magical boy carved out of a tree, who comes to life and eventually locates and opens the covers over the sky wall. From these openings in the sky come the plants and animals that provide for the Eskimo people. Through the eastern hole emerge trees, bushes, and caribou. The second hole provides grasses, flowers, geese, and ptarmigan. Through the southern hole flow sea spray, seals, and whales. From the next hole, the western wind brings a rainstorm, sleet, and great walruses. From the final hole, the north wind brings blasts of ice and snow and two great white bears. When the boy returns to his village, he warns the people:

they must never kill for sport, but only for the meat they needed, and that meat must never be wasted. He taught the people that animals are just like people, and must be treated with respect. And he taught them that they should

This collection includes paintings about the Navajo Indians. (From Shonto Begay's Navajo: Visions and Voices Across the Mesa. *Scholastic, 1995.)*

make masks and pay honor to the inuas, spirits of the animals with songs and dances. (p. 58)

This tale provides both a creation story and a lesson about how to care for the animals.

Many of the Native American traditional tales explain the creation of something in nature. Nina Jaffe's *The Golden Flower* is adapted from a Taino myth. Both the text and the illustrations develop a creation story in which an arid desert is turned into a lush forest. When a child finds seeds, he plants them on a mountaintop until a forest grows. A beautiful flower grows with a golden ball (a pumpkin) in the center. This ball becomes a coveted object. When two men fight over its possession the pumpkin bursts open and the ocean comes forth. In addition to an explanatory tale, the story develops the importance of life and fertility even in once-harsh environments.

The creation of horses and the four sacred directions are very important in many Native American tales. For example, in *Turquoise Boy: A Navajo Legend,* Terri Cohlene reveals how the son of Changing

Our Rich Mosaic   607

Woman visits the four sacred mountains and gains gifts from the Talking Gods who live on the sacred White Shell Mountain of the East, the sacred Turquoise Mountain of the South, the sacred Abalone Shell Mountain of the West, and the sacred Black Jet Mountain of the North. These gifts are eventually used by Changing Woman to create horses, which are very important to the Navajo people. In addition to the tale, this book provides information about the Navajo homeland, the Navajo people, and the Navajo beliefs.

Lois Duncan's *The Magic of Spider Woman* is a creation tale, an explanatory tale, and a cautionary tale. It is a tale about how Wandering Girl came to be known as Weaving Woman and also about the consequences when she disobeys Spider Woman. The story begins "before the beginning of time" when there were only animal beings and insects in the Third World. One of these insects is Spider Woman, who knows the secret of how to spin and weave. As in other traditional Navajo tales, the Third World floods and the beings escape to the Fourth World through a hollow reed. It is in this world that Spirit Being creates the first people, the Navajo. Now the Great Spirit teaches the people all they need to know to survive including the songs and chants called the Blessing Way that keep the people healthy and in harmony with nature. Unfortunately, Wandering Girl does not receive the instructions. During the cold winter, Spider Woman takes pity on Wandering Girl and teaches her to weave blankets. Spider Woman also gives a warning that is a moral lesson or theme for the story: "But there is one danger that you always must be aware of. The Navajo People must walk the Middle Way, which means that they must respect the boundaries and try to keep their lives in balance. They should not do too much of anything. You must promise not to weave for too long, or a terrible thing will happen to you" (unnumbered).

From that time she becomes known as Weaving Woman. Unfortunately, she does not take Spider Woman's warning and becomes completely engrossed in weaving a beautiful blanket and her spirit becomes trapped in the blanket. To free the spirit, a spirit trail is created in the blanket by pulling a yarn from the finished weaving and pulling the strand through so that it is now less perfect. After Weaving Woman is freed, her words reinforce the moral she should have heeded earlier: " 'Oh, Spirit Being! I have learned my lesson!' she cried. 'Never again

will I weave for too long at a sitting and never again will I doubt the wisdom of my creators!' " (unnumbered). The tale concludes with a why explanation. Now every Navajo blanket includes a pathway so that the spirit of the weaver will not be imprisoned by the beauty of the rug.

Family Drama Tales.   Family drama tales focus on various family needs and conflicts, such as learning from elders, providing protection, obtaining food, and overcoming problems, including rivalry and aggression. The family in these stories may be the smaller tribal unit or the greater cosmos. If the tale deals with the greater world family, the storyteller may refer to Earth as mother, Sky as father, and humanity as children. Many of these stories reveal tribal standards.

Several tales in Jean Monroe and Ray Williamson's *They Dance in the Sky: Native American Star Myths* illustrate universal family concerns and appropriate behaviors. For example, "Bright Shining Old Man," an Onondaga tale from New York, shows that children will be punished if they ignore the warnings of their elders. In "The Little Girl Who Scatters the Stars," a tale from the Cochita Pueblo in New Mexico, a girl cannot overcome her curiosity. It is a universal family tale. In it, "Our Mother" tells the people that they are all brothers and sisters and instructs them to live as one large family. One of the tales in Joseph Bruchac's *The Boy Who Lived With the Bears and Other Iroquois Stories* is a teaching tale that shows parents how they should treat their children.

Michael Rosen's *Crow and Hawk: A Traditional Pueblo Indian Story* is a family drama tale in which a crow becomes tired of sitting on her eggs. Hawk finds the nest, hatches the eggs, and cares for the young birds. When Crow finally returns and wants her babies, Crow and Hawk take their quarrel to Eagle, King of the Birds. When Eagle asks the little ones which mother they want, they respond, "Hawk is the only mother we know" (unnumbered). Eagle then decides in Hawk's favor because Crow had left the nest and thus lost the children. In the author's notes, the original source is identified as a story collected in 1928 by Ruth Benedict and published in *Tales of the Cochiti Indians,* published in 1931 by the University of New Mexico Press.

Why there is chaos in the sky, society, and family life is revealed in Jerrie Oughton's *How the Stars Fell into the Sky: A Navajo Legend.* In this tale, First Woman wants to write the laws for the people to see. First Man makes several suggestions for places to write them, such as in the sand or on the water, but First Woman argues that they will be blown away or disappear into the water. Finally, First Man suggests that she take her jewels and write the laws in the sky. First Woman begins her mission by designing a pattern of stars so that all can read the laws. Coyote offers to help her complete her task, but he is unhappy when she tells him that writing the laws with the stars could take many moons. First Woman tries to convince Coyote that it is important to have the laws, so that the people will see them before they enter their hogans, mothers will sing of them to their children, and lonely warriors will warm themselves by them. However, Coyote impatiently gathers the corners of First Woman's blanket and flings the remaining stars out into the night, spilling them in disarray. The tale concludes: "As the pulse of the second day brought it into being, the people rose and went about their lives, never knowing in what foolish haste Coyote had tumbled the stars . . . never knowing the reason for the confusion that would al-ways dwell among them" (p. 30). According to Oughton, this is a retelling of a traditional tale told to the Navajo Indians by Hosteen Klah, their great medicine man, at the turn of the century.

Trickster Tales. Trickster tales reveal both good and bad conduct. John Bierhorst (1976) states, "The trickster tale affords the narrator an opportunity to flirt with immoral or antisocial temptations" (p. 6) in humorous ways. Trickster characters are found throughout North America. On the northwestern coast of the Pacific Ocean, the trickster is called Raven. When evaluating the role of Raven, Bierhorst (1993) states:

Raven is tough. Whatever is ascribed to him, he can survive it. And when we look back on what has been said of him, we may find that there is more wisdom to these tales than we had realized. As for Raven himself, he is always off on a new adventure. One of the old Tsimshian narrators used to say that after each scrape Raven doggedly "journeys on." Or as another of the old texts once phrased it, the trickster simply "put on his raven garment and flew away."

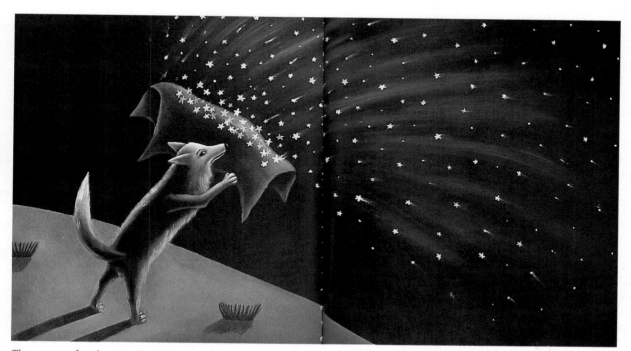

The reasons for chaos in the sky and society are revealed in this Navajo tale. (Illustration from How the Stars Fell into the Sky *by Jerrie Oughton. Illustrations copyright © 1992 by Lisa Desimini. Reprinted by permission of Houghton Mifflin Co. All rights reserved.)*

Raven the trickster is the central character in Gerald McDermott's *Raven: A Trickster Tale from the Pacific Northwest*. In this tale, to bring light from Sky Chief, Raven changes himself into a pine needle that is in a drinking cup of Sky Chief's daughter. After swallowing the needle, she eventually gives birth to a child that is really Raven in human form. Thus, Raven is able to acquire the sun that is in a set of nested boxes found in the sky lodge and bring light to the earth. Compare McDermott's version of this tale with Ann Dixon's *How Raven Brought Light to People*.

Iktomi is the Sioux name for trickster. In *Iktomi and the Boulder: A Plains Indian Story*, Paul Goble describes the fair and foul side of Iktomi, who is

beyond the realm of moral values. He lacks all sincerity. Tales about Iktomi remind us that unsociable and chaotic behavior is never far below the surface. We can see ourselves in him. Iktomi is also credited with greater things: in many of the older stories, the Creator entrusts him with much of Creation. People say that what seem to be the "mistakes" and "irrational" aspects of Creation, such as earthquakes, floods, disease, flies, and mosquitos, were surely made by Iktomi. (introduction)

In Goble's version of the Sioux tale, conceited Iktomi first gives his blanket to a boulder and then deceitfully takes the blanket back when he needs it for protection. Iktomi uses trickery to save himself from the angry boulder. Even though he eventually wins the confrontation, he is frightened and momentarily humbled by his experience. Goble's *Iktomi and the Berries* provides another humbling experience for the trickster character.

Another trickster character is Coyote, who may be a creator or a trickster in folklore from the Great Plains. In *Coyote Steals the Blanket: A Ute Tale,* a tale retold by Janet Stevens, Coyote repeatedly declares, "I go where I want, I do what I want, and I take what I want." Consequently, when Hummingbird warns him not to touch the blankets that cover the rocks, he does it anyway. When Coyote brags and disobeys, he is humbled. In Barbara Diamond Goldin's *Coyote and the Fire Stick: A Pacific Northwest Indian Tale,* the crafty character teaches the People to start a fire by rubbing sticks together.

Coyote also may be a changer. William Morgan's *Navajo Coyote Tales* includes six tales about Coyote as both a trickster and a changer. The stories include such additional characters as Crow, Horned Toad, and Rabbit.

Threshold Tales. Numerous Native American tales depict crossing various thresholds. Transformations that allow characters to go into and out of the animal world are especially popular in stories retold for children. Paul Goble's *Buffalo Woman* uses transformations to show the bond between Native Americans and animals. Goble's retelling of a tale from the Great Plains reflects a bond between the humans and the buffalo herds, essential if both the people and the buffaloes were to prosper.

In *Beyond the Ridge,* Goble's main character goes from the land of the living to the spirit world. An elderly Plains Indian experiences the afterlife as believed by her people. On her way, she discovers Owl Maker. The spirits of individuals who have led good lives pass Owl Maker to the right, toward Wanagiyata, Land of Many Tipis. However, Owl Maker pushes the spirits of those who have led bad lives to the left, along a short path where they fall off, landing back on earth to wander for a time as ghosts.

Combination Tales. Many traditional tales have elements that include several of the folklore types. For example, John Bierhorst's *The Ring in the Prairie: A Shawnee Legend* has elements related to fair and foul tricksters, to crossing thresholds, and to family drama. First, the Shawnee hunter plays the trickster, turning himself into a mouse and creeping close to a beautiful young woman who descends from the sky. Then, he returns to his human form and captures his heart's desire. The tale contains several crossing-the-threshold experiences. The hunter passes into and out of the animal world before he and his family are permanently transformed into animals. His captured bride crosses from the world of the star people to the world of humans and back to the world of the star people before she is permanently transformed into a white hawk. The story also reflects strong family ties. The hunter mourns the loss of his wife and son and then goes on a difficult quest so that he can be reunited with his family.

"The Boy Who Found the Light," adapted by Dale DeArmond in a book by that name, exemplifies an Eskimo story that has elements of setting the world in order, trickster tales, and threshold tales. First, the orphan boy, Tulugac, sets out on a quest to return light to the Eskimo people. On this quest, Tulugac is helped by his old aunt, who is considered a witch because she has special powers. On his travels, Tulugac is assisted by a rabbit, a bear, and an owl. As the tale continues, Tulugac finds the sun and the moon and tricks an old man so that he (Tulugac) may retrieve the sun and the moon and return the light to the people. Finally, Tulugac is assisted by a small bird-skin that he has been carrying with him. In his time of need, the birdskin surrounds him and he is transformed into a raven flying swiftly and smoothly through the air.

On Tulugac's return journey to his village, the story takes on setting-the-world-in-order elements. Tulugac, now the raven boy, breaks off pieces of the light and throws them away so that there is daylight everywhere. According to the tale, the intervals of darkness and light change throughout the year because, "Sometimes he waited a long time before he threw out another piece of light, and that is why we have the long nights of winter. Sometimes he threw out more light very soon, making the short nights and long days of summer" (p. 30).

In *Keepers of the Animals: Native American Stories and Wildlife Activities for Children,* Michael J. Caduto and Joseph Bruchac discuss the various circles found in "Salmon Boy," a Haida tale from the Pacific Northwest. They state:

"Salmon Boy" is an allegory of great importance, revealing a series of interlocking circles which, as the story proceeds, run progressively deeper into the life ways of the Haida. . . . There is an important, interdependent relationship here: The salmon give people food and the people show their appreciation through prayer and reverence. (p. 97)

Caduto and Bruchac identify the first circle as the great circle of life and death and as the reality of the spirit world. Another circle is transformation, depicted when Salmon Boy returns to his people as a healer and a teacher to instruct them in the ways of the Salmon People and to help them when they are sick. This circle shows the sense of interconnectedness between this world and the spirit world, and between animals and people. Finally, Salmon Boy's body is placed in the river, where it circles four times, a sacred number, and returns to the Salmon People.

In *Storm Boy,* Paul Owen Lewis also includes a combination of these characteristics in his original tale based on the mythology of the Northwest Coast of North America. For example, the author focuses on the motifs of separation, initiation, and return. Under separation are the motifs that wandering too far from the village invites supernatural encounters and there is a mysterious entrance into the Spirit World. Under initiation are the motifs that animals are encountered in human form and potlatching or exchanging of gifts and culture are important. Under return are the motifs that objects are given to assist in the return, a mysterious return is possible by wishing continually, there is a time disparity between two realms, and there is a claiming of a crest. As you read the Native American folklore, you will discover many of these combination tales.

Songs and Poetry

Songs, chants, and poems are very important in the various Native American cultures. Many poems express reverence for creation, nature, and beauty. Native Americans created poetry for a purpose; they believed that there was power in the word. Songs were often part of ceremonial rituals, with their symbolism portrayed through dance.

The beauty of both ancient Native American poetry and contemporary poetry about Native American experiences can be shared with children. An interesting resource book that shares the music of Native Americans with children of many cultures is John Bierhorst's *A Cry from the Earth: Music of the North American Indians.* According to Bierhorst, native peoples throughout North America shared a belief in the supernatural power of music to cure disease, bring rain, win a lover, or defeat an enemy.

Many Native Americans today sing the songs for pleasure and to express pride in their heritage. Bierhorst's book contains words and music for many songs, including songs of prayer, magic, and dreams, songs to control the weather, and music to accompany various dances. There are greeting songs, love songs, a Hopi flute song, a Hopi sleep song, a Cherokee lullaby, and a Kwakiutl cradlesong. Music, words, and dance steps are included so that children can recreate, experience, and respect this musical heritage.

The wide range of subjects around which songs were created suggests a Native American heritage that is richly various. Bierhorst's anthology *The Sacred Path: Spells, Prayers, and Power Songs of the American Indians* is organized according to themes. An introduction, a glossary, and a list of notes and sources add authenticity and additional information.

Byrd Baylor has expressed her love and concern for the Native American peoples and the land of the

Southwest in a series of books written in poetic form. One of them ponders the secrets of prehistoric people as seen through their drawings on pottery. In *When Clay Sings,* the designs on ancient shards of pottery created by the Anasazi, Mogollon, Hohokam, and Mimbres cultures of the Southwest are the models for Bahti's illustrations and suggest the inspiration for Baylor's poetry. According to Baylor:

Indians who find this pottery today say that everything has its own spirit—even a broken pot. . . . They say that every piece of clay is a piece of someone's life. They even say it has its own small voice and sings in its own way. (cover summary)

Poetry selections by Byrd Baylor and Jamake Highwater reflect foundations in traditional beliefs and mythological references. For example, Baylor's *The Other Way to Listen* and *The Desert Is Theirs* communicate to young readers the Native American closeness to nature. Peter Parnall's illustrations suggest the majesty of the desert and the respect of the Papago Indians for it. In *Moon Song,* Baylor presents a "why" tale in poetic form. She develops the closeness in nature between Moon and coyotes. Highwater's *Moonsong Lullaby* has foundations in traditional beliefs. The poem develops respect for nature, close relationships with animals, respect for older people, and belief in ancient knowledge.

Mythological references also abound in the poetry by Highwater and Baylor. For example, in *Moonsong Lullaby,* animals give their lives to the people who respect them, holy people have special powers, and Moon is wife to Sun. Virginia Driving Hawk Sneve's collection, *Dancing Teepees: Poems of American Indian Youth,* includes poems from various tribes, such as the Hopi, the Zuni, and the Lakota Sioux. The poems vary from the words of heroes, such as Black Elk, to the prayers of ancient peoples to the writings of contemporary tribal poets.

Susan Jeffers has adapted the words of Chief Seattle into a poetic text in *Brother Eagle, Sister Sky: A Message from Chief Seattle.* The text is based on the message that Chief Seattle supposedly presented in a speech describing his people's respect for the earth and his concern for the way the land will be treated in the future (There is some disagreement about the actual rendition of Chief Seattle's message, however.) Compare the text for Jeffers's book with the version provided by Joseph Campbell in *Transformations of Myth Through Time*

(1990). As you read both versions, analyze the variances, and consider any reasons for the variations.

Shonto Begay's *Navajo: Visions and Voices Across the Mesa* includes poems that reflect both an ancient past and a contemporary culture. Poems such as "Echoes" and "Creation" provide visions of the ancient culture of the Navajo. Poems such as "Into the New World" reflect contemporary concerns related to damages done to the earth and the environment.

Poetic texts reinforce the desirable understanding that Native American peoples have diverse cultures and great artistic traditions.

Historical Fiction

Themes and conflicts in historical fiction about Native Americans often emphasize the survival of the body or the spirit. Some authors emphasize periods in history in which contact with white settlers or cavalry resulted in catastrophic changes. Others emphasize growing interpersonal relationships between Native American and white characters. Four award-winning books provide examples for these two types of historical fiction.

Scott O'Dell's Newbery Honor Book, *Sing Down the Moon,* focuses on the mid-1860s, when the U.S. Cavalry forced the Navaho to make the three-hundred-mile Long Walk from their beautiful and productive home in Canyon de Chelly to stark Fort Sumner. O'Dell effectively develops the resulting conflict through descriptions of the contrasting settings. He provides detailed descriptions of Canyon de Chelly, a place of miracles. This idealistic setting does not last. It is followed by horror when Colonel Kit Carson's soldiers first destroy the crops and livestock in the canyon and then force the Navaho to walk through desolate country to a setting that is unconducive to physical or spiritual survival. Fifteen hundred Navaho die, and many others lose their will to live.

O'Dell's protagonist, a Navaho woman named Bright Morning, retains an inner strength based on hope for the future. While she is a captive, she hoards food and plans for the day when she and her husband will return to their canyon. Susan Naramore Maher (1992) states that O'Dell's female narrators are significant agents because as "strong, resistant purveyors of connection, they stand in opposition to the hermetic, invulnerable, unresponsive heroes of formulary westerns—the Orlovs and the Long Knives" (p. 226).

Jan Hudson's *Sweetgrass* is a story of a Blackfoot girl who survives a smallpox epidemic in the 1830s. Even though the girl does not interact with white characters, she battles the disease brought to her people. Hudson, the author of this Canadian Library Association Book of the Year Award winner, writes about native peoples with sensitivity. (See chapter 10 for a discussion of *Sweetgrass*.)

Farley Mowat's Canadian Library Association Book of the Year, *Lost in the Barrens*, takes place in the twentieth century in a remote arctic wilderness, hundreds of miles from the nearest town. The two main characters are Awasin, a Woodland Cree, and Jamie, a white Canadian orphan who moves north to live with his uncle. The setting becomes an antagonist for both boys when they accompany the Crees on a hunting expedition and then become separated from the hunters. Mowat vividly describes searching for food and preparing for the rapidly approaching winter. Through long periods of isolation, the boys develop a close relationship and an understanding of each other. Elizabeth George Speare's Newbery Honor Book, *The Sign of the Beaver*, focuses on the friendship between a Native American boy and a white boy in the Maine wilderness of the 1700s. (See chapter 10 for a discussion of *The Sign of the Beaver*.)

In his latest book, *Thunder Rolling in the Mountains*, Scott O'Dell, with the assistance of his wife Elizabeth Hall, again develops a story based on the removal of Indian peoples from their land. This time, the narrator is Chief Joseph's daughter, who tells from her point of view the story of the forced removal of the Nez Perce tribe from their homeland in 1877. In the foreword to the book, Hall describes O'Dell's fascination with this subject:

At the time of his death, Scott O'Dell was immersed in the story of Chief Joseph and his people. Their courage and determination in the face of cruelty, betrayal, and bureaucratic ignorance moved him deeply. So deeply that he continued to work on the manuscript in the hospital until two days before he died. (p. ix)

Readers will also experience O'Dell's fascination with this time period and the plight of these brave people.

Two historical fiction books about Native Americans are set in 1492 at the time of Columbus's first contact with the native peoples. Jane Yolen's *Encounter* is a picture book written for younger audi-ences. Michael Dorris's *Morning Girl* is a book for older readers. (See chapter 10 for a further discussion of these books.) Both books are written from the point of view of native children and both provide information about the beliefs and values of the Taino culture. Both authors also provide insights into their reasons for writing the stories and the research necessary for depicting the Taino culture, which was eliminated by the contact with Europeans. Yolen (1992) says:

In order to create and recreate the characters in *Encounter*, I did the kind of research one might ordinarily do for a non-fiction book. And once I had the outlines of the Taino culture down (or at least what we know from the shards left), I could write the story as if I were a child of that culture. (p. 238)

The resulting text and illustrations provide insights into how the Taino people may have reacted to Columbus and his men. The final illustration in the text is symbolic: An old Taino Indian is sitting on a stump, but, like his people and his culture, his legs are disappearing. You may also find it interesting to compare *Encounter* and *Morning Girl*. In *Sees Behind Trees* Dorris places his characters in sixteenth-century America. Now a partially sighted boy discovers the importance of his other senses.

Through all of these stories, children can experience Native American characters who have personal thoughts and emotions and who live within a family as well as within a tribe. In addition, children will begin to understand the impact of white people on the Native American way of life. (Additional historical stories are discussed in chapter 10.)

Contemporary Realistic Fiction

Little contemporary realistic fiction for children focuses on Native Americans. In the books that are available, Native Americans often express conflict between the old ways and the new ones. Characters must decide whether to preserve their heritage or to abandon it. Many of the stories allow Native Americans to honor the old ways but to live with the new ones. Some stories show life on modern reservations; others depict families who have left the reservation to live in cities. The needs of all individuals are shown: Characters search for their identities or express a desire for love. The Native American characters often express hostility toward white characters who have been unfair to them, but some stories develop strong friendships between people from different backgrounds.

Like other contemporary realistic fiction for younger children, stories about Native Americans for young audiences frequently develop themes related to love and family relationships. Barbara Joosse's *Mama, Do You Love Me?* and Nancy Luenn's *Nessa's Fish* are picture books set in the Arctic regions. In *Mama, Do You Love Me?* a young child tests her mother's love. Through satisfactory responses, the girl discovers that her mama loves her "more than the raven loves his treasure, more than the dog loves his tail, more than the whale loves his spout" (pp. 4–5). Each of the questions and responses relates to the culture. In *Nessa's Fish,* a young girl not only protects her ailing grandmother but also saves the fish that they caught from hungry arctic animals.

A loving relationship between a Navaho girl and her grandmother provides the foundation in Miska Miles's *Annie and the Old One.* The conflict in the story develops because Annie does not want to accept the natural order of aging and death. In an effort to hold back time, Annie tries to prevent her grandmother from completing the rug that she is weaving because her grandmother has said, "My children, when the new rug is taken from the loom, I will go to Mother Earth" (p. 15). The author emphasizes the way that Annie's inner conflict ends, and the theme that we are all part of nature emerges when Annie finally realizes:

The cactus did not bloom forever. Petals dried and fell to earth. She knew that she was a part of the earth and the things on it. She would always be a part of the earth, just as her grandmother had always been, just as her grandmother would always be, always and forever. And Annie was breathless with the wonder of it. (p. 41)

Annie's actions show that she has accepted nature's inevitable role. Annie picks up the weaving stick and begins to help her grandmother complete the rug.

Symbolism, ancient traditions, and person-against-self conflicts are important elements in two books. In Jean Craighead George's *The Talking Earth,* a book for middle-elementary readers, a Seminole girl who lives on the Big Cypress Reservation questions the traditions of her people and searches for her heritage as she travels alone through the swamp. In Joseph Bruchac's *Eagle Song,* a Mohawk boy faces conflict when he moves from the reservation to Brooklyn. The author uses the legend of a peacemaker who united the Iroquois Confederacy to help the boy overcome his problems.

In a novel written for older readers, conflicting settings provide problems in Robert Lipsyte's *The Brave.* When Sonny Bear, a Moscondaga Indian, leaves the reservation and his great-uncle to try to become a boxer in Manhattan, he experiences the harsh underworld of violence, drugs, gangs, and prison. His heritage, however, with his uncle's teachings about the Running Braves, and the help of a policeman make it possible for Sonny Bear to channel the hawk inside himself, face his problems, and control his life.

Authors of contemporary stories about Native Americans frequently develop understandings about the past to help their characters respect their

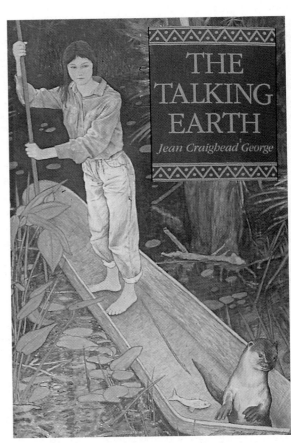

A contemporary Seminole girl searches for her heritage. (From The Talking Earth *by Jean Craighead George. Jacket art copyright © 1983 by Bob Marstall. Reprinted by permission of HarperCollins Publishers.)*

heritage. For example, in *High Elk's Treasure*, Virginia Driving Hawk Sneve ties the past to the present with a flashback to the year 1876, when the Sioux were taken to the reservation following the defeat of General Custer at the Battle of the Little Big Horn. One hundred years later, High Elk's descendants excitedly discover a pictograph of the Battle of the Little Big Horn. This pictograph is later authenticated by an expert from the university. Sneve develops a feeling for the past and pride in Native American heritage throughout this book. In *Bearstone*, Will Hobbs uses an ancient turquoise bear to help a Ute Indian boy clarify his beliefs and overcome his personal problems.

Three stories with Eskimo protagonists show the range of subjects and conflicts that are covered in contemporary literature. In Jean Craighead George's *Water Sky*, Lincoln, a boy from Massachusetts, journeys to Barrow, Alaska, in search of his uncle. The conflict between cultures is reinforced by the boy's mother, who does not want Lincoln to make this journey. During his quest, Lincoln lives at a whaling camp, where he learns to understand and respect his Eskimo heritage. Throughout this story, George combines vivid settings and information about Eskimo values and beliefs.

In Gary Paulsen's *Dogsong*, Russel, a contemporary Eskimo boy, leaves the mechanized world in which his people hunt seal and caribou by snowmobiles to discover the ways and beliefs that were there in the days of dogsleds. Russel's mentor is an elderly Eskimo who believes that the Eskimo people have lost the songs that made the whales and other animals come to the people in times of need. Russel's search for his own song takes him on a 1,400-mile dogsled trek across the isolated ice and tundra. In a traditional manner, dreams and visions become part of the learning experience. In a dream, Russel goes back in time, faces his fear, kills a mammoth, and sings a song in exultation. Through his ordeal with nature, Russel discovers the power of the old Eskimo ways.

In Scott O'Dell's *Black Star, Bright Dawn*, an Eskimo girl drives a dogsled team in the Iditarod Trail Sled Dog Race from Anchorage to Nome. Through her experiences, the girl learns to depend on her dogs and herself. In addition, she discovers the strength in her Eskimo heritage, values, and beliefs. Realistic fictional stories portray some conflicts in contemporary Native American children's lives, as well as some resolutions that reflect self-esteem and respect for an ancient heritage.

Nonfiction

Authors of informational books about Native Americans for young children often use illustrated texts to encourage identification with traditional ways of life and cultural contributions made by Native Americans. Authors of informational books for older readers often stress history, the struggle for survival, and various contemporary conflicts.

Art works of Native American children in Bruce Hucko's *A Rainbow at Night: The World in Words and Pictures by Navajo Children* present a view of the children's life and culture through their drawings and paintings. George Littlechild's *This Land Is My Land* presents an illustrated history of Littlechild's ancestors. The illustrations by this well-known Cree artist provide an interesting subject for discussion and enjoyment.

Sandra DeCoteau Orie's *Did You Hear Wind Sing Your Name?: An Oneida Song of Spring* presents the Oneida Indians' view of nature. The author's note explains the symbolism of the pine tree as it represents the unity of the six nations of the Iroquois Confederacy; hawk, as the bringer of good news; the three sisters of corn, beans, and squash as sustaining staples; the flowers that give beauty; and the celebration of the circle of life.

In *People of the Breaking Day*, Marcia Sewall takes readers back to the Wampanoag nation of southeastern Massachusetts before the English settlers arrive. The text, which is divided into sections, presents information about the tribe, the belief in the Great Spirit, the celebrations, the role of warriors and other members of the tribe, and the family.

Paul Goble's *Death of the Iron Horse* and Russell Freedman's *Buffalo Hunt* and *An Indian Winter* also provide historical perspectives. Goble uses an actual incident in 1867, when a Union Pacific train was derailed by the Cheyenne. In this fictionalized story, Goble shows that the Cheyenne fought the encroaching white culture by attacking the railroad. In *Buffalo Hunt*, Freedman shows the importance of the buffaloes to the Indians living on the Great Plains. His text includes descriptions of the hunts, attitudes of the Indians toward the buffaloes, and the consequences to the Indians when the white culture all but eliminated the buffaloes. The text is illustrated with reproductions of paintings by such artists as George Catlin and Karl Bodmer, who actually saw the buffalo hunts. The titled and dated illustrations add interest to the text. Freedman uses a similar approach in *An Indian Winter,* accompanying his description of traditional Mandan life in the 1800s with paintings and drawings created by Karl Bodmer in 1832.

Diane Swanson's *Buffalo Sunrise: The Story of a North American Giant* includes a section on how the buffalo (bison) provided for the Blackfoot families living on the Alberta-Montana plains in the 1870s. According to the text, the buffalo provided a variety of activities and materials including laughter of children caused by antics of the young calves and the uses for the buffalo including hides for tipis and clothing, rattles from the hooves, and food. A chart shows examples of the more than one hundred uses for various parts of the buffalo including hides, horns, hooves, sinew, tails, bones, organs, fat, and hair. The author uses boxed materials that add to readers' understanding. For example, a boxed section tells about the importance of the birth of a white buffalo in 1994 and the belief in the miracles possible. Swanson quotes one of the Aani people who said, "Everything is reborn: thought, hope, life, all of these things" (p. 16). The text is illustrated with both early drawings and paintings and with contemporary photographs.

Caroline Arnold's *The Ancient Cliff Dwellers of Mesa Verde* describes the lives of the Anasazi, or ancient ones, through color photographs and text describing the cliff dwellings found in Mesa Verde National Park. Topics covered by Arnold include the discovery of Mesa Verde, uncovering the past, the history of the

Illustration, "Mih-Tutta-Hang-Kusch, Mandan Village" by Karl Bodmer. *(From* An Indian Winter *by Russell Freedman, illustration of "Mih-Tutta-Hang-Kusch, Mandan Village by Karl Bodmer. Copyright © 1992. Reprinted by permission of Joslyn Art Museum, Omaha, Nebraska; gift of Enron Art Foundation.)*

Chapter 11   *Multicultural Literature*

Anasazi, the daily life of the Anasazi, and speculations about why the Anasazi left Mesa Verde.

Nonfictional books also provide information about the Arctic regions and the native peoples who live there. Normee Ekoomiak's *Arctic Memories* is written in both English and Inuktitut, the Inuit language. The illustrations by the Inuk artist also provide information about the culture, including the iglu, ice fishing, Okpik, traveling, games, and ancestral hunters. Diane Hoyt-Goldsmith's *Arctic Hunter* uses photographs to show aspects of contemporary life of the Eskimo people.

Contemporary books about Native Americans frequently discuss both the advantages and problems related to growing up in two cultures. Books for younger readers usually present a positive view of these interactions. In *Pueblo Boy: Growing Up in Two Worlds*, Marcia Keegan depicts the life of a Pueblo Indian boy living in New Mexico. The text, in the form of a photographic essay, follows the boy as he learns to live in two cultures.

Biographies

Biographies are important reading for children because they encourage high aspirations and respect for the social contributions of outstanding people. However, there are fewer biographies about Native Americans than there are about African Americans.

Several biographies look at famous Native Americans who interacted with white settlers of this continent. For example, *Sacajawea, Wilderness Guide*, by Kate Jassem, is the biography of the Shoshone woman who guided the Lewis and Clark expedition across the Rocky Mountains to the Pacific Ocean. This book is appropriate for young readers.

Dennis Brindell Fradin's *Hiawatha: Messenger of Peace* is also appropriate for younger children. Fradin uses information that is known about the Iroquois who lived about five hundred years ago to recreate the role of Hiawatha as one of the founders of the Iroquois Confederacy. Fradin clearly separates what is actually known from the legend of Hiawatha. For example, Fradin states:

It is also said that around this time the Peacemaker chose the pine tree as a symbol of peace between the five Iroquois tribes and that Hiawatha invented a way to record important events. Hiawatha took large numbers of purple and white wampum beads and used them to make pictures that told a story. The Iroquois then began to record their major events on wampum belts in picture form.

Some of these belts are now in museums, but they are not our main sources of information about Hiawatha. Our primary sources are the stories that the Iroquois elders have handed down to their young people for generations. (p. 30)

The title of Judith St. George's *To See With the Heart: The Life of Sitting Bull* is based on the Sioux Chief's ability to see "with the eyes in his heart rather than the eyes in his head." The biography covers his life on the Great Plains as he first leads raids against his people's enemies and later leads the fight against the European advancement that culminated in the Battle of Little Bighorn. St. George uses interviews found in archives to reconstruct Sitting Bull's life.

Laurie Lawlor's *Shadow Catcher: The Life and Work of Edward S. Curtis* is a biography of the man who documented North American Indian culture beginning in 1898 and continuing for thirty years. The biography is illustrated with reproductions of Curtis's photographs that provide readers with a vivid view of Native American culture. The text includes a listing of Curtis's twenty volumes of the North American Indian, a bibliography of books for children, a bibliography of books by or about Edward Curtis, and an index.

Conflicts between worlds provide numerous opportunities for character and plot development in Jean Fritz's *The Double Life of Pocahontas*. Fritz effectively develops a character who is torn between loyalty to her father's tribe and to her new friends in the Jamestown colony. As in her other biographies, Fritz documents her historical interpretations. Notes, a bibliography, an index, and a map add to the authenticity.

Russell Freedman's *Indian Chiefs* includes short biographies about Red Cloud, Satanta, Quanah Parker, Washakie, Joseph, and Sitting Bull. The text is supported with photographs, a bibliography, and an index. Biographies of the various Native American leaders include Albert Marrin's *Plains Warrior: Chief Quanah Parker and the Comanches* and Russell Freedman's *The Life and Death of Crazy Horse*. Dorothy Morrison's *Chief Sarah: Sarah Winnemucca's Fight for Indian Rights* is one of the strongest biographies of this period. Morrison develops conflicts through contrasts when she describes Sarah's confusion:

The whites killed—but they had made her well. They took the Indians' meadows—but gave them horses and presents. They burned stores of food—but they gave food, too. Would she ever understand these strange people who were overrunning the land? (p. 31)

Morrison shows Sarah's battle for retention of Paiute culture when she describes Sarah's dream:

All this time Sarah had been lecturing and saving every penny, for she had another dream—of a school for Indian children, taught by Indians themselves, a school that would train its students as teachers for their own people. Up to then, Indian schools, both private and under the Bureau, had been taught and managed by white people who tried to "civilize" the students by wiping out native language and culture. Sarah, however, was sure her people's culture was worth preserving. (p. 149)

Additional Native American biographies are discussed in chapter 12.

 ### HISPANIC AMERICAN LITERATURE

Surprisingly, there are far fewer books about Hispanic Americans than there are books about either African Americans or Native Americans. In addition, the books about Hispanic Americans tend to go out of print faster than do the books about the other cultures. This phenomenon is readily seen between the third edition of this textbook (Norton, 1991) and the fourth edition published in 1995. A search of *Books in Print* disclosed that the following percentage of books from the 1991 text were no longer in print: 14 percent of African American, 25 percent of Asian American, 35 percent of Native American, and over 50 percent of Hispanic American books. This trend continues into the fifth edition, published in 1999. More than 50 percent of the books are again out of print. Numerous new books about African Americans and Native Americans replaced most of the books that were out of print, but new books did not always replace the books about Hispanic Americans. Consequently, some out-of-print books about Hispanic Americans appear in the bibliography for this edition.

Most children's books about Hispanic Americans depict people of Mexican or Puerto Rican heritage, although the United States population contains numerous other Hispanic groups. People of Hispanic descent are the largest minority group in the United States, but relatively few children's books have been written about them. There is also an imbalance in the types of stories available. Award-winning picture storybooks about Hispanic Americans tend to examine Christmas celebrations. Award-winning novels are about a small segment of the Hispanic American population, the sheepherders of Spanish Basque heritage, whose ancestors emigrated to parts of North America before those parts came under United States control. Although folktales and poetry are available for adults, a shortage of children's literature exists.

Many books for children about Hispanic Americans develop connections between the people and their religious faith. Celebrations, such as La Posada, suggest this cultural heritage. The respect for freedom is stressed through the celebration of Cinco de Mayo. Spanish vocabulary is also interspersed throughout many stories, allowing children to associate with a rich language heritage. (Misspelled and incorrectly used Spanish words have appeared all too often in this type of book, however. These errors have, understandably, caused criticism.) Several books are more factual, presenting the Spanish heritage that existed on the North American continent long before the United States became a nation. These stories suggest that Americans with Spanish ancestry have a heritage worthy of respect and of sharing with others.

Folklore

The wide cultural areas for Hispanic folklore include Mexico, South and Central America, Cuba, and the American Southwest. The folklore incorporates pre-Spanish tales of the Aztecs, Maya, and Incas. The Spaniards colonized the earlier populations, and different groups, such as the Apache and Pueblo Indians, interacted. As in other cultures, there are myths that explain (*ejemplo*), as well as folktales and fairy tales (collectively called *cuento*).

Many of the early Aztec and Mayan tales were recorded for European audiences by Spaniards in the sixteenth century. Others were written down by Aztecs who learned to read and write in the Texcoco Seminary. These tales were illustrated in pictographic forms on codices and provide many of the sources used by current folklorists and retellers of the tales.

Tales in John Bierhorst's *The Monkey's Haircut and Other Stories Told by the Maya,* collected from the Maya in Guatemala and southeastern Mexico, indicate many of the traditional Mayan values and cultural characteristics. For example, the extensive use of riddles in the folklore shows that the people value cleverness. In "Rabbit and Coyote," double meanings allow Rabbit to dupe Coyote and to escape from his cage. The plot of "Tup and the Ants" hinges on a pun. Cultural characteristics are shown in other tales, such as "The Mole Catcher," in which a husband must pay a price for his wife through a bride service. In *Song of Chirimia—A Guatemalan Folktale*, Jane Anne Volkmer retells the story of a young man who goes on a quest to win a Mayan princess. The illustrations, based on ancient stone carvings, provide a feeling for the Mayan civilization. The text is also printed in both English and Spanish.

Values and beliefs from numerous Hispanic cultures are reflected in *The King of the Mountains: A Treasury of Latin American Folk Stories* collected by M. A. Jagendorf and R. S. Boggs. This collection contains stories from twenty-six countries. Stories such as the Mexican "The Sacred Drum of Tepozteco" show that wisdom, understanding, and virtuous living are respected values because they lead to rewards. In contrast, attacking a revered king and putting on a display for the sake of appearance only are despised actions because they lead to punishment. Additional Mexican folktales are found in Francisco Hinojosa's *The Old Lady Who Ate People*, a collection of frightening stories from Mexico.

Legends, myths, and riddles from South America are found in collections by John Bierhorst and Natalia M. Belting. Bierhorst's *The Mythology of South America* provides scholarly background and selections that reflect the creation of the world and the origins of civilization as well as the conflicts between people. Bierhorst divides the stories and the discussions according to Greater Brazil, Guiana, Brazilian Highlands, Gran Chaco, Far South, Northwest, and Central Andes. Extensive notes on sources and references add to the text. Bierhorst's *Lightning Inside You and Other Native American Riddles* includes 150 riddles from several North and South American cultural regions, including southern Mexico and western South America. An annotated list of sources is helpful for students of children's literature. Belting's *Moon Was Tired of Walking on Air* is a collection of creation myths told in South American Indian cultures. Belting introduces her selections by describing the scattering of the Ancestors, who:

looked at the earth and wondered at the sky, and the animals, the birds and the fishes. How was the earth made?

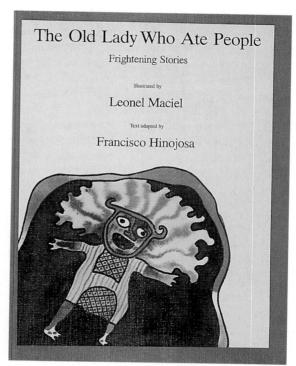

The illustrations enhance the frightening quality of these folktales. (From The Old Lady Who Ate People *by Francisco Hinojosa, illustrated by Leonel Maciel. Copyright © 1981. Reprinted by permission of Organization Editorial Novaro, S.A.)*

How did Sun and Moon, how did the stars, get into the sky? Where did they themselves come from, and where had the animals lived before? How was night made, and the seasons? Why was Rainbow bent? They wondered, dreamed, asked one another, told their children what they knew, what they learned: this is the way, they told them, that things came to be. (introduction)

Belting includes a map of South America, in which she locates the sources for the tales.

Lois Ehlert's *Moon Rope* is adapted from a Peruvian tale called "The Fox and the Mole," in which Fox convinces Mole that they should try to climb to the moon on a rope woven of grass. The story ends as a pourquoi tale because, after falling off the rope, Mole prefers to stay in the earth and come out only at night, avoiding other animals and never having to listen to Fox. Fox, however, may have made it to the moon because "The birds say that on a clear night they can see him in the full moon, looking down on earth. Mole says he hasn't seen him. Have you?"

(unnumbered). The text, written in both English and Spanish, is illustrated with pictures that were inspired by ancient Peruvian textiles, jewelry, ceramics, sculpture, and architectural detail. Ehlert's *Cuckoo: A Mexican Folktale* is another pourquoi tale written in both English and Spanish.

Many of the folktales from Mexico, South and Central America, and Hispanic cultures in the United States reflect a blending of cultures as stated in the introduction to José Griego y Maestas and Rudolfo A. Anaya's *Cuentos: Tales from the Hispanic Southwest:*

The stories also reflect a history of thirteen centuries of cultural infusing and blending in the Hispan mestizaje, from the Moors and Jews in Spain, to the Orientals in the Philippines, Africans in the Caribbean, and the Indians in America—be they Aztec, Apache or Pueblo. (p. 4)

For example, "The Man Who Knew the Language of the Animals," a folktale in *Cuentos: Tales from the Hispanic Southwest,* is based on a Moorish tale from "A Thousand and One Nights." The tale is also simi-lar to Verna Aardema's African tale, *What's So Funny, Ketu?* Differences between the African and Hispanic tales reflect cultural values. The main character in the Hispanic tale portrays a stronger masculine role.

John Bierhorst's *Doctor Coyote: A Native American Aesop's Fables,* a retelling, also indicates cultural infusion. Bierhorst identifies the text as Mexican in origin and shows the strong Spanish–Aztec connection. It is interesting to compare these fables with Aesop's fables and with coyote trickster tales.

Bierhorst's *Spirit Child: A Story of the Nativity* shows the infusion of Christian and Aztec beliefs. The text describes and Barbara Cooney's illustrations depict an Aztec setting for the birth of the Christ child. Extensive Aztec beliefs are infused. Likewise, various versions of "The Virgin of Guadalupe" represent the merger of Spanish–Catholic and Aztec Indian heritages.

Tomie dePaola's *The Lady of Guadalupe,* a retelling of a Mexican tale, develops the connection between the people and their religious faith. According to legend, the Lady of Guadalupe, now the patron saint of Mexico, appeared to a poor Mexican Indian on a De-

This pourquoi tale explains the actions of Mole and Fox. (Illustration from Moon Rope: A Peruvian Folktale, *copyright © 1992 by Lois Ehlert. Reproduced by permission of Harcourt Brace & Company.)*

cember morning in 1531. Juan Diego, "He-who-speaks-like-an-eagle," was walking toward the Church of Santiago when he saw a hill covered with a brilliant white cloud. Out of the cloud came a gentle voice calling Juan's name and telling him that a church should be built on that site so that the Virgin Mary could show her love for Juan's people, the Indians of Mexico. On Juan's third visit to the bishop, he was believed because he brought with him a visual sign from the Lady of Guadalupe: His rough cape had been changed into a painting of the lady. The church was built on the location, and the cape with its miraculous change was placed inside the structure. DePaola says that he has had a lifelong interest in the legend of the Lady of Guadalupe. His drawings, based on careful research, depict the dress and architecture of sixteenth-century Mexico.

Two traditional tales adapted by Harriet Rohmer originate with the Miskito Indians of Nicaragua. *The Invisible Hunters* reflects the impact of European cultures on the Miskito people. The three hunters are punished when they break their promise and forsake their people. European traders influence the hunters' actions and create and expand their greed. *Mother Scorpion Country* is a tale of love. In this tale, a husband tries to accompany his wife into the land of the dead. According to the author's notes, "the compassionate figure of Mother Scorpion reflects a pre–Christian matriarchal past" (p. 32).

Both of Rohmer's texts include information about the author's research. For example, Rohmer began her research for *The Invisible Hunters* in anthropological archives, visited the Miskito communities in the company of an Afro-Indian Catholic priest, learned more details of the story from an elder Miskito Catholic deacon, and finally met a Miskito bishop of the Moravian Church, who provided many additional details. During this final contact, Rohmer was told, "According to the stories I heard as a child the Dar has a voice. I can take you to people who say they have heard that voice" (p. 31). In *Mother Scorpion Country,* Rohmer traces the story to the endeavors of a young Moravian minister who recorded the stories and customs of the Miskito Indians in the early 1900s. Early Inca life is reflected in Jane Kurtz's *Miro in the Kingdom of the Sun.*

Two retellers of Hispanic folklore have chosen to retell various versions of "La Llorona," the woman who killed her children and now wanders crying through the night. Because of loneliness, it is be-

lieved that she kidnaps children. *Prietita and the Ghost Woman,* by Gloria Anzaldua, is a story about a girl who goes in search of herbs to cure her mother and becomes lost in the woods. She has always heard about the ghost woman who steals children. Now she may be meeting the ghost woman. Rudolfo Anaya's *Maya's Children: The Story of La Llorona* tells about a Mayan woman who is immortal. When the god is angered by her immortality, he threatens to destroy her children. When she tries to trick the god, her children perish. Readers can compare the retellings and the illustrations in these two books.

Picture Storybooks

Listening to and saying rhymes from various cultures encourage children to interact with language as well as to discover the joy in language and in word play. Margot Griego's *Tortillitas Para Mama and Other Spanish Nursery Rhymes* and Lulu Delacre's *Arroz Con Leche: Popular Songs and Rhymes from Latin America* are written in both English and Spanish. These texts provide sources for sharing literature in either language.

My First Book of Proverbs by Ralfka Gonzalez and Ana Ruiz includes simple proverbs such as "A good listener needs few words." Each of the proverbs is illustrated in colorful illustrations that have the flavor of folk art. Jeanette Winter's *Josefina* is a counting story in which the illustrations also have the flavor of folk art. The illustrations include numerous Mexican motifs.

Deborah Lattimore's *The Flame of Peace: A Tale of the Aztecs* is a literary fairy tale based on the Aztec nine evil lords of darkness and the god of peace. Lattimore uses information from Aztec myth and hypothesizes about what might have caused the Alliance of Cities during the time of Itzcoatl. In the resulting story, a young boy uses his wits against the evil lords and brings peace to the cities. The illustrations reflect Aztec settings and characters.

Richard Garcia's *My Aunt Otilia's Spirits,* a fictional story set in contemporary San Francisco, includes elements of the supernatural. Garcia bases the story on a visit from a Puerto Rican relative. Consider the interrelationships between reality and fantasy as Garcia describes the story in the endnotes:

Like all stories, this one is based on a kernel of fact—that is that my Aunt Otilia was accompanied by bed shakings and wall knockings wherever she went. However, this was not regarded as unusual in my family, or a cause for much concern. The supernatural had a natural place in our life. Most of the time we ignored it—sometimes it meant something—as in the case of an omen or a dream. We had a large and well-worn copy of an old dream book—and this was often consulted in the morning if a dream seemed significant. . . . And those who had died were never thought of as being very far away—and were often spoken to as if they were in the room. (p. 24)

Leo Politi has written and illustrated a number of award-winning picture storybooks about Mexican American children living in southern California. His *Song of the Swallows* tells the story of a young boy whose dear friend is the gardener and bell ringer at the mission of San Juan Capistrano. Politi shares Mexican American history with readers as the gardener tells Juan the story of the mission and of *las golondrinas,* the swallows who always return to the mission in the spring, on Saint Joseph's Day, and remain there until late summer. Politi's illustrations recreate the Spanish architecture of the mission and demonstrate a young boy's love for plants and birds.

Marie Hall Ets and Aurora Labastida's *Nine Days to Christmas: A Story of Mexico* tells of a kindergarten child who is excited because she is going to have her own special Christmas party, complete with a piñata. In the midst of numerous other everyday activities, Ceci chooses her piñata at the market, fills it with toys and candy, and joins the La Posada procession. After Ceci sees her beautiful piñata being broken at the party, she is unhappy until she sees a star in the sky that resembles her piñata. Children relate to the girl's feelings and learn about the Mexican celebration of Christmas when they read this book. This story depicts a middle-class family that lives in an attractive city home. Children can see that poverty is not the condition of all people with a Spanish heritage.

Mexican motifs are also important in Gerardo Suzan's illustrations for Virginia Kroll's *Butterfly Boy.* Suzan uses bright colors to develop the mood and setting for this tender story of a boy and his invalid grandfather as the boy tries to ensure that the red admiral butterflies will return.

Historical and Contemporary Realistic Fiction

Only a few books of historical and contemporary realistic fiction for children portray Hispanic Americans in suitably positive ways or as the main characters. Marian L. Martinello and Samuel P. Nesmith's

With Domingo Leal in San Antonio 1734 takes a documentary approach to Hispanic American history and life in the United States. Published by the University of Texas Institute of Texas Cultures at San Antonio, this carefully researched book describes a day in the life of a young Spanish boy who travels with his family from the Canary Islands through Mexico to the Villa de San Fernando on the banks of the Rio San Antonio de Padua in present-day Texas. This historical novel can strengthen children's understanding of a lengthy Hispanic heritage in the southwestern United States. It also demonstrates that people of Spanish ancestry were living on the North American frontier before English-speaking settlers claimed it.

Another book of historical fiction depicting the early Spanish presence in western North America is Scott O'Dell's *Carlota.* In this story set in Spanish California in the mid-1800s, O'Dell explores the conflicts that occur between people who expect females to play a traditionally feminine role and others who encourage a different type of behavior. Carlota is the strong and independent daughter of Don Saturnino, a native Californian whose ancestors came from Spain. Her father supports her brave and adventurous inclinations.

Joseph Krumgold's *. . . And Now Miguel,* based on a full-length documentary film feature, is the story of the Chavez family, which has been raising sheep in New Mexico since before their region became part of the United States. Their ancestors raised sheep in Spain. Krumgold tells the story from the viewpoint of the middle child, Miguel, who unlike his older brother is too young to get everything he wants and, unlike his younger brother, is too old to be happy with everything he has. Miguel has a secret wish to accompany the older family members when they herd the sheep to the summer grazing land in the Sangre de Cristo Mountains. With the help of San Ysidro, the patron saint of farmers, Miguel strives to make everyone see that he is ready for this responsibility. When he is allowed to accompany his elders on the drive and reaches the summer camp, he feels pride in his family's traditions and in his own accomplishments:

In this place many men named Chavez had come. Those I could remember, and then my grandfather as well. And my father, Blas, and my uncles, Eli and Bonifacio. And my brothers, Blasito and Gabriel. And now, watching the shining world as I knew it would look when I came to this place, I stood, Miguel. (p. 244)

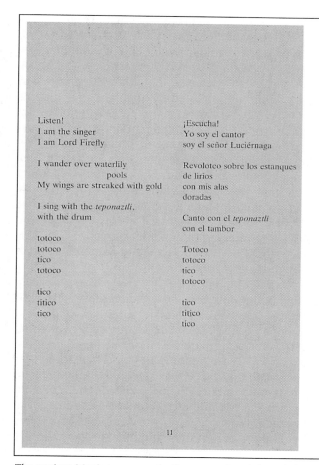

Listen!	¡Escucha!
I am the singer	Yo soy el cantor
I am Lord Firefly	soy el señor Luciérnaga
I wander over waterlily	Revoloteo sobre los estanques
pools	de lirios
My wings are streaked with gold	con mis alas
	doradas
I sing with the *teponaztli*,	Canto con el *teponaztli*
with the drum	con el tambor
totoco	
totoco	Totoco
tico	totoco
totoco	tico
	totoco
tico	
titico	tico
tico	titico
	tico

11

The ancient Mexican source for the poetry is reinforced through the illustrations in My Song Is a Piece of Jade: Poems of Ancient Mexico in English and Spanish *adapted by Toni de Gerez, illustrated by William Stark. (Copyright © 1981, English translation copyright © 1984 by Organización Editorial Novaro, S. A. Reprinted by permission of Little, Brown and Company.)*

Krumgold visited the real Miguel and his family when the film was produced. Krumgold celebrated Saints' Day with them and observed all of the important functions of a sheep ranch. He grew to know a closely knit family with a heritage going back to ancient Spain.

The eight-year-old in Nicholasa Mohr's *Felita* has lived in her Puerto Rican neighborhood of New York City for as long as she can remember. Mohr depicts the reasons for Felita's great love of her neighborhood. When Felita walks down the street, she can greet everyone by name. Her dearest friends live in the apartments on the block, and her grandmother, Abuelita, lives nearby. Conflict results when Felita's father decides that the family must move to a neighborhood where the schools are better and the threats of gang violence are fewer. In the new neighborhood, Anglo children call Felita names, tear her clothes, and tell her to move away. Felita's mother is shocked by the attitudes of the children and tells Felita that she must not hate, because that could make her as mean inside as the people who are attacking her:

Instead you must learn to love yourself. This is more important. To love yourself and feel worthy, despite anything they might say against you and your family! That is the real victory. It will make you strong inside. (p. 39)

When violence against the family continues and no neighbors offer help, Felita's family moves back to the old neighborhood. Felita experiences anger, sorrow, and humiliation, but she finally regains her feeling of self-worth. With her grandmother's help,

Felita returns to her happy, lively self, secure in the surroundings of her warm, loving family and friends. Perhaps the neighborhood and the people in *Felita* seem so real because Mohr herself was born and grew up in a similar neighborhood in New York City.

Mohr's *Going Home* provides additional adventures for Felita. Twelve-year-old Felita finds that she must face and overcome new person-against-self and person-against-society conflicts. During a trip to visit relatives in Puerto Rico, Felita finds that she is the object of attack because she is the gringa and not accepted by some of the Puerto Rican girls.

Hispanic American author Gary Soto has several current texts that appeal to readers. *Taking Sides* is a realistic fiction story about a Hispanic American boy who moves from the barrio to the suburbs. The protagonist, who is a basketball player, must decide how he will respond when his new team plays his old team in a league game. Soto develops themes related to loyalty and friendship. In *Pacific Crossing,* the boys from the barrio participate in an exchange program in Japan. *Too Many Tamales* is the story of a girl who faces a dilemma on Christmas Eve when she misplaces her mother's diamond ring. *Neighborhood Odes* is a collection of twenty-one poems about a Hispanic American neighborhood and the people who live in the neighborhood. *Snapshots from the Wedding* tells the story of a wedding through the point of view of the young flower girl.

Ben Mikaelsen and Frances Temple develop faster and more dangerous plots in books for older readers. Mikaelsen's *Sparrow Hawk Red* is a story of survival in the streets and drug traffic of Mexico. Thirteen-year-old Ricky Diaz discovers that his mother was murdered by drug smugglers because of his father's work for the Drug Enforcement Agency. In an effort to avenge his mother, Ricky disguises himself as a Mexican street urchin. With the help of Soledad, another street urchin, he enters the smugglers' compound, steals a plane containing the missing radar that allows smugglers to escape detection, and narrowly escapes. Through his adventures, Ricky discovers the importance of his heritage. Temple's *Grab Hands and Run* is set in El Salvador. The plot follows a family who tries to leave El Salvador after the father disappears.

Several books published by Pinata Books, a division of Arte Publico Press, provide interesting reading sources for older students. For example, *Hispanic, Female and Young: An Anthology* edited by Phyllis Tashlik is an example of a writing and literature project completed by young Latino students in New York City's El Barrio. The anthology includes interviews with both parents of the students and with Hispanic authors. In addition, the text includes poetry and other selections written by Hispanic female authors. Students of children's literature may be especially interested in an interview with Nicholasa Mohr in which she tells readers to "Hold Fast to Your Dreams." In this interview she discusses career choices for Hispanic women. This book could be used to motivate students to write similar texts.

Two additional books by the same publisher, Anilu Bernardo's *Jumping Off to Freedom* and Victor Villasenor's *Walking Stars: Stories of Magic and Power,* are stories in which young people overcome odds and succeed. *Jumping Off to Freedom* is the story of a fifteen-year-old boy and his father who seek freedom from Cuba's government by heading for Miami on a raft. This story includes both person-against-society and person-against-nature conflicts as the protagonists must escape the repressive Communist government and the dangerous ocean. *Walking Stars: Stories of Magic and Power* is a selection of stories about the author's family. Some of these stories are about escaping from persecution, while others are about more common occurrences. In the preface, the author explains that he wrote the book in order to tell children "that there's a way to live life, la viva, with power and magic, a way of triumphing over all odds and living life like a superhuman being" (p. 7).

Nonfiction

High-quality informational books about Hispanic Americans include books on history, geography, culture, and people. For example, several recently published books look at the discoveries about and the accomplishments of the ancient native cultures of the Western Hemisphere. Carolyn Meyer and Charles Gallenkamp's *The Mystery of the Ancient Maya* provides a thoroughly documented presentation of Mayan history and accomplishments. The authors' writing style creates interest in the subject, and early photographs and drawings add to the authenticity. Compare the content in Meyer and Gallenkamp's book with Irene Flum Galvin's *The Ancient Maya*. Jean Fritz et al. develop the history of various parts of the world at the time of Columbus in *The World in 1492*. The section titled "The Americas in 1492" is written by Jamake Highwater. This chapter includes information on the Aztecs, the Incas, and other native peoples. Maps show the Aztec and Inca empires, and illustrations show art from the time period. Judy Cozzen's *Kids Explore America's Hispanic Heritage* was written as a school project and provides interesting ideas for a study of Hispanic cultures.

While the majority of books about Spanish American celebrations for young children concentrate on the Christmas holidays, Cinco de Mayo, the commemoration of the Mexican army's defeat of the French army on May 5, 1862, is also a major holiday for Mexican Americans. June Behrens's *Fiesta!* is an informational book describing the modern-day celebration of this holiday. Photographs show a Mexican American festival in which music is played by a mariachi band, costumed dancers perform traditional Mexican dances, and young and old enjoy the celebration. Photographs also show children at school as they learn about and participate in the Cinco de Mayo activities. The book closes with a message from the author, who suggests that Americans of all heritages have become good amigos.

Information on the history of the Spanish involvement in the Americas is discussed in Albert Marrin's *Empires Lost and Won: The Spanish Heritage in the Southwest*. The history begins in 711 A.D. when the Moors told stories about the cities of gold. The text continues through the Middle Ages, into Coronado's expedition, and the westward expansion. The author includes maps and drawings.

Several nonfiction books provide information about Hispanic American children and families. Tricia Brown's *Hello, Amigos!* is a photo essay for younger children. It chronicles a special day in the life of six-year-old Frankie Valdez, a Mexican American boy whose family lives in San Francisco's Mission District. Fran Ortiz's photographs show the boy as he goes to school, attends classes, plays with friends, reacts to a classroom birthday

Information about the Aztecs and Incas focuses on the accomplishments of the native peoples. (From The World in 1492. *Copyright © 1992 by Henry Holt and Company, Inc. Illustrations copyright © 1992 by Stefano Vitale. Reprinted by permission of Henry Holt and Company, Inc.)*

cake, goes to the boys' club, and shares his birthday celebration with his family. In *Calling the Doves*, Juan Felipe Herrera tells a story about his childhood as a migrant farmworker. The story develops a strong relationship between the family and the land as well as depicts the grueling nature of farm labor. Maria Cristina Brusca's *On the Pampas* is a highly illustrated book that describes a girl's experiences during a summer spent with her grandparents on their ranch in Argentina. The watercolor paintings provide visual images of the settings.

Two books for older children, Larry Dane Brimner's *A Migrant Family* and S. Beth Atkin's *Voices from the Fields: Children of Migrant Farmworkers Tell Their Stories*, tell about the lives of children of migrant laborers. Both books are illustrated with photographs. Atkin uses introductions and interviews to develop the stories of the children, who tell about

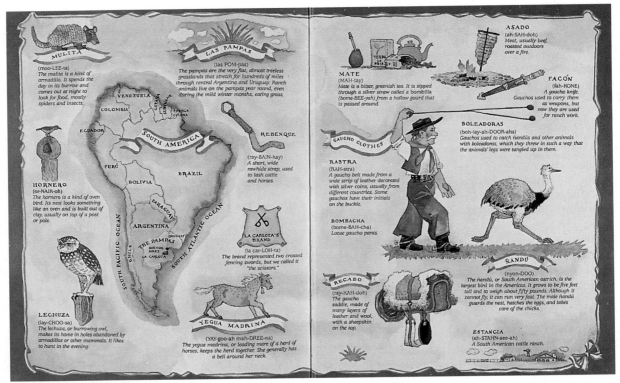

A map and an illustrated glossary add to understanding. (From On the Pampas *by Maria Cristina Brusca. Copyright © 1991 by Maria Cristina Brusca. Reprinted by permission of Henry Holt and Company.)*

their dreams and the joys of family relationships, as well as their hardships.

 ## ASIAN AMERICAN LITERATURE

Few highly recommended books for children represent an Asian American perspective. Folktales from several Asian countries can help Asian American children and children from other ethnic backgrounds appreciate the traditional values and creative imagination of Asian peoples (see chapter 6). Folktales, such as those found in *The Rainbow People,* retold by Laurence Yep, are especially good because they were collected from Chinese Americans living in California.

The widest range of Asian American experiences in current children's literature is found in the works of Laurence Yep, who writes with sensitivity about Chinese Americans who, like himself, have lived in San Francisco, California. His characters overcome the stereotypes associated with literature about Asian Americans, and his stories integrate information about Chinese cultural heritage into the everyday lives of the people involved. Yep has received the International Reading Association's 1976 Children's Book Award and a Newbery Honor Book award.

Mingshui Cai (1992) discusses examples of acculturation found within three of Yep's novels: *Dragonwings, Child of the Owl,* and *Star Fisher.* Cai states:

Although set in different times, these three novels have something in common: They cover themes like poverty, racial discrimination, marginalization, and loss of identity, which are typical of multicultural literature; and most significantly, they represent Chinese Americans' process of acculturation as a way out of the dilemma of being caught between two worlds. (p. 108)

Cai argues that Yep's novels contain two aspects of acculturation, "assimilating to the mainstream culture while maintaining Chinese identity" (p. 109).

ISSUE   Who Should Write Multicultural Literature?

At a recent multicultural roundtable attended by various leaders in multicultural literature and education,[1] one of the debated questions was, Who Should Write Multicultural Literature? Many of the participants felt strongly that only members of an ethnic group should have ownership of the literature and be encouraged to write the literature and critique the literature written by others. According to this viewpoint, only African Americans, for example, have the experience and the perception to write authentically about the black experience. Others argued the viewpoint that anyone who writes with sensitivity and does the required research into the subject and the culture should be able to write about the culture.

Jane Yolen[2] maintains that demanding that only a person from a culture may write about that culture is "creating a kind of literature apartheid. Think of it: if I, a careful artist, am only allowed to write about the culture I grew up in—Jewish, Manhattan, Virginia, and Westport, Connecticut, 1940s–1960s—I could have written *The Devil's Arithmetic*, but not *Passager;* I could have created *All Those Secrets of the World*, but not *Piggins*. I could have made *And Twelve Chinese Acrobats*, but not *The Emperor and the Kite*" (p. 289).

Betsy Hearne provides interesting thoughts about this issue in a recent article in *School Library Journal*.[3] Hearne states:

What defines an authority in creating or evaluating picture-book folklore? A well-read expert? Someone raised in the culture represented by the story? Can only members of an ethnic group truly represent the lore of that group? How can we tell? By the name? The skin color? Does the absence of an author or artist's photograph mean an African-American folktale has been adapted by a WASP? If so, does that mean a majority is ripping off a minority, or honoring it? Graciela Italiano has addressed this controversy in a paper delivered at the 1992 Allerton Institute.[4]

She underscores the importance of knowing a cultural tradition, from the standpoint of both experience and study, over the formal qualification of being a card-carrying member of the culture. At the same conference Hazel Rochman[5] argued eloquently against the misconception that "only Indians can really judge books about Indians, Jews about Jews . . . locking us into smaller and tighter boxes" (p. 34).

As you read Hearne's questions and concerns, ask yourself the same questions. What is your viewpoint on this important issue? What should be the qualifications of a person writing about a culture or evaluating the books written about that culture? Who should write and evaluate the books? What criteria should you use when selecting and evaluating the books about a culture that is different from your own?

[1] Roundtable on Multicultural Education, New York City, May 1993.

[2] Yolen, Jane. "Taking Time: Or How Things Have Changed in the Last Thirty-Five Years of Children's Publishing." *The New Advocate* 10 (Fall 1997): 285–291.

[3] Hearne, Betsy. "Respect the Source: Reducing Cultural Chaos in Picture Books, Part Two." *School Library Journal* 39 (August 1993): 33–37.

[4] Italiano, Graciela. "Reading Latin America: Issues in the Evaluation of Latino Children's Books in Spanish and English." In *Evaluating Children's Books: A Critical Look*, edited by Betsy Hearne and Roger Sutton. Champaign: University of Illinois Graduate School of Library and Information Science, 1993.

[5] Rochman, Hazel. "And Yet . . . Beyond Political Correctness." In *Evaluating Children's Books: A Critical Look*, edited by Betsy Hearne and Roger Sutton. Champaign: University of Illinois Graduate School of Library and Information Science, 1993.

Yep's *Dragonwings*, set in 1903 San Francisco, is based on a true incident in which a Chinese American built and flew an airplane. The characters are people who retain their values and respect for their heritage while adjusting to a new country. The "town of the Tang people" is eight-year-old Moon Shadow's destination when he leaves his mother in the Middle Kingdom (China). He is filled with conflicting emotions when he first meets his father in the country that some call the "Land of the Demons" and others call the "Land of the Golden Mountain."

The Tang men in San Francisco give Moon Shadow clothing and things for the body, but his father gives him a marvelous, shimmering kite shaped like a butterfly, a gift designed to stir the soul. Moon Shadow joins his father in his dream to build a flying machine. Motivated by the work of Orville and Wilbur Wright, Moon Shadow's father builds an airplane, names it *Dragonwings*, and soars off the cliffs overlooking San Francisco Bay. Having achieved his dream, he decides to return to work so that his wife can join him in America.

In the process of the story, Moon Shadow learns that his stereotype of the white demons is not always accurate. When he and his father move away from the Tang men's protection, Moon Shadow meets and talks to his first demon. Instead of being ten feet tall, with blue skin and a face covered with warts, she is a petite woman who is very friendly and considerate. As Moon Shadow and his father get to know this Anglo-Saxon woman and her family, they all gain respect for one another. When they share knowledge, the father concludes: "We see the same thing and yet find different truths."

Readers also discover that many stereotypes about Chinese Americans are incorrect. This book is especially strong in its coverage of Chinese traditions and beliefs. For example, readers learn about the great respect that Chinese Americans feel for the aged and the dead. Family obligations do not end when a family member has retired or died. As Moon Shadow seeks to educate his white friend about the nature of dragons, readers discover traditional Chinese tales about a benevolent and wise dragon who is king among reptiles and emperor of animals. Readers realize the value of honor as the doubting Tang men pull *Dragonwings* up the hill for its maiden voyage. If the Tang men laugh at Moon Shadow's father, they laugh at a body of people who stand beside each other through times of adversity and honor. Children who read this story learn about the contributions and struggles of the Chinese Americans and the prejudice that they still experience.

The Serpent's Children is set in a time when China was battling both Manchu and British domination. In *Child of the Owl,* young Casey discovers that she knows more about racehorses than about her own Chinese heritage. *Star Fisher* is a story about a Chinese family overcoming prejudice in West Virginia during the late 1920s. The protagonists in all of these books by Yep are distinct and believable individuals, far from the conventional stereotypes of Asian people.

Two novels by Laurence Yep provide insights in Chinese American and white attitudes. In *Thief of Hearts,* a sequel to *Child of the Owl,* Yep writes another novel in which the main character develops cross-cultural understanding. Yep's *Later, Gater* develops themes related to sibling rivalry.

Stories about early immigration experiences in the New World are popular subjects in children's books. Allen Say's *Grandfather's Journey* is an immigration story that includes two journeys: one to California and then, many years later, one back to visit the Japan of his youth. The story also covers the time of World War II, when Grandfather cannot return to California again, but he tells his grandson, Allen Say, stories about America. *Grandfather's Journey* is an excellent companion for Say's *Tree of Cranes,* which is set in Japan. The story shows the melding of two cultures. The boy's mother, who was born in America, prepares a Christmas celebration that combines the Japanese and American cultures.

Paul Yee's *Tales from Gold Mountain: Stories of the Chinese in the New World* includes eight stories about Chinese immigrants in the United States and Canada. Compare Yee's stories with those developed in Yep's *Dragonwings* and the following book, written about contemporary experience.

Bette Bao Lord, the author of *In the Year of the Boar and Jackie Robinson,* created a story that reflects her own experiences and beliefs. Like her pro-

The Japanese and American cultures combine in this book about the Christmas celebration. (Illustration from Tree of Cranes *by Allen Say. Copyright © 1991 by Allen Say. Reprinted by permission of Houghton Mifflin Company. All rights reserved.)*

tagonist Shirley Temple Wong, Lord was a Chinese immigrant to America. Lord says:

Many feel that loss of one's native culture is the price one must pay for becoming an American. I do not feel this way. I think we hyphenated Americans are doubly blessed. We can choose the best of both. (endcover)

In 1947, Shirley discovers that she can adore baseball, the Brooklyn Dodgers, and Jackie Robinson and still maintain the bond of family and the bond of culture.

Numerous experiences in the life of a Vietnamese American are shown through a photographic essay in Diane Hoyt-Goldsmith's *Hoang Anh: A Vietnamese-American Boy.* Lawrence Migdale's photographs show the daily activities of Hoang Anh and his family in San Rafael, California, as they work on their fishing boat, live and play at home, prepare for the New Year, and experience the Tet Festival. Patricia McMahon's *Chi-Hoon: A Korean Girl* is a photographic essay that presents one week in the life of a Korean girl.

Although Takaaki Nomura's picture storybook *Grandpa's Town* is set in Japan rather than North America, the themes of the story relate to the universality of loving relationships between grandfathers and grandsons, possible loneliness after the death of a loved one, and preferences for staying with old friends. This story, written in both Japanese and English, includes much cultural information. A young boy accompanies his grandfather around town, meets his grandfather's friends, and discovers

that his grandfather is not willing to leave these friends to move in with the boy and his mother.

Eleanor Coerr's *Mieko and the Fifth Treasure,* a book for older children, is also set in Japan. Mieko's talent for painting, called "the fifth treasure," brings her great joy until her hand is damaged by a piece of glass when the bomb drops on Nagasaki. Mieko experiences a great sense of loss until she overcomes her unhappiness and discovers that she can still paint. Coerr develops the themes of the importance of friendship and the need for self-confidence. The setting allows Coerr to provide much information about the Japanese people, their customs, and their beliefs. You may compare Coerr's experiences with the atomic bomb with those developed in Tatsuharu Kodama's *Shin's Tricycle* and Laurence Yep's *Hiroshima.*

The setting for Sook Nyul Choi's *Year of Impossible Goodbyes* is Japanese-occupied Korea at the close of World War II. The author develops the person-versus-society conflict experienced by Sookan, a ten-year-old Korean girl, and her family, who experience the oppressive treatment of both the Japanese and Russian occupation of North Korea. The author uses many small details and incidents to symbolize the oppression experienced by the family and the family's longing for freedom. For example, they are forbidden to grow flowers. In one incident, when the family manages to have a tiny patch of flowers, the Japanese police captain and his men trample the flowers. After that, the mother puts her packets of seeds carefully

This photographic essay captures many experiences in the life of a Vietnamese American. (From Hoang Anh: A Vietnamese-American Boy *by Diane Hoyt-Goldsmith. Photographs copyright © 1992 by Lawrence Migdale. Reprinted by permission of Holiday House.)*

Our Rich Mosaic 629

away. Each time she looks at them, she wonders if they will ever be able to plant the seeds. After another incident, the police punish the grandfather by chopping down his favorite pine tree. Shortly after the loss of the tree, the grandfather dies. After many dangerous experiences, the children and the mother escape to South Korea. In her endnotes, the author states her reasons for writing this book:

Having lived through this turbulent period of Korean history, I wanted to share my experiences. So little is known about my homeland, its rich culture and its sad history. My love for my native country and for my adopted country prompted me to write this book to share some of my experiences and foster greater understanding. (unnumbered)

Seeds and memories and the future they represent are important in *Year of Impossible Goodbyes,* as they are in Sherry Garland's *The Lotus Seed,* written for younger children. In this story, a Vietnamese family resettles in America. During happier days in Vietnam, the grandmother picks a seed from a lotus plant in the emperor's garden to remember the special occasion. Throughout her life, she looks at this seed during important moments in her life or when she feels sad. The seed is so important that she brings it to America when her family escapes the war. Years later, a grandson carelessly throws out the seed, which saddens his grandmother tremendously. Luckily, the seed is thrown where it eventually grows into a lotus plant. When the blossom fades, the grandmother gives a seed to each of her grandchildren. Garland develops a universal theme: Small things and the memories that they evoke are important in our lives.

Huynh Quang Nhuong's *The Land I Lost: Adventures of a Boy in Vietnam* is also a story set in Vietnam. In this story, Nhuong takes readers back to a time of family and village experiences. Nhuong's *Water Buffalo Days: Growing up in Vietnam* tells about the author's boyhood. Traditions and beliefs are important elements in the stories of both Nhuong and Garland.

Adjusting to a new culture and developing understanding of oneself and others are problems faced by many new Americans. Lensey Namioka's *Yang the Youngest and His Terrible Ear* is a humorous contemporary realistic fiction story that speaks to the needs of many readers. The author develops a protagonist, nine-year-old Yingtao, who is out of place in his musical family. Although he has a great eye, he has a terrible ear. Students of children's literature can analyze Yingtao's reactions to both learning about English and trying to make his family understand that he is not, and will never be, a talented musician. The author helps readers visualize the problems by relating them to Yingtao's Chinese background. When Yingtao tries to work out inconsistencies in English, he states: "Talking to Americans is like walking along a country footpath in China. You think the path is nice and firm, but your foot suddenly slips on a muddy stretch and you land with a big splash in a wet rice paddy" (p. 60). In a satisfying ending, both the family of his American friend and Yingtao's own family realize the importance of honoring one's gifts. Michele Surat's *Angel Child, Dragon Child* is a realistic story about a young Vietnamese girl's difficulties developing associations with her classmates after her family moves to the United States. The plots, characters, and themes in these books may encourage discussion and promote understanding.

The importance of even small cultural artifacts, such as eating utensils, stimulates a humorous plot in Ina R. Friedman's *How My Parents Learned to Eat.* Friedman suggests the solution to a problem on the first page of this picture storybook: "In our house, some days we eat with chopsticks and some days we eat with knives and forks. For me, it's natural" (p. 1, unnumbered). The rest of the story tells how an American sailor courts a Japanese girl, and each secretly tries to learn the other's way of eating. The couple reaches a satisfactory compromise because each person still respects the other's culture.

Yoshiko Uchida, the author of several historical fiction novels about the Japanese American experience during World War II (see chapter 10), tells her personal experiences in *The Invisible Thread.* Students of children's literature may compare experiences described by Uchida in her autobiography with her historical fiction.

If children are to learn about the cultural heritage and the contributions of Asian American people, as well as discover the similarities between Asian and non–Asian Americans, more high-quality literature about Asian Americans is needed. Because biographies and autobiographies are especially good for raising children's aspirations and increasing understanding of the contributions and problems of individuals, multicultural literature programs need biographies about Asian Americans.

SUGGESTED ACTIVITIES

for Adult Understanding of Multicultural Literature

- Collect several examples of children's literature written before 1960 that contain African American characters. Compare these books with books written after 1975. Using the Evaluation Criteria for multicultural literature, compare the images of black people reflected in the literature of the two time periods.

- Bettye I. Latimer (1976) surveyed trade books published in the mid-1960s and the 1970s and concluded that about 1 percent of the books involved African American characters. Choose a recent publication date, and select books that have been chosen as the best books of the year by the School Library Journal Book Review Editors or some other group that selects outstanding books. Tabulate the number of books that are about African Americans, Native Americans, Hispanic Americans, and Asian Americans. What percentage of the books selected as outstanding literature include characters who are members of minority groups?

- Many African tales have characteristics, such as repetition of words, that make them appealing for oral storytelling. Select several traditional African tales and identify the characteristics that make them appropriate for storytelling or oral reading.

- Choose one of the cultural groups discussed in the chapter. Read a number of myths, legends, and folktales from that culture. Summarize the traditional beliefs and values. Provide quotations from the tales to show the beliefs and values. Try to identify those same beliefs and values in other genres of literature depicting the same culture. What conclusions can you reach about the importance of traditional literature?

- Read James Taggart's " 'Hansel and Gretel' in Spain and Mexico" (1986). How are the versions the same? How are they different? How do the versions compare with the Grimms's version? Why are the versions different? How does each version relate to traditional cultural values?

- Choose an outstanding author, such as Virginia Hamilton or Laurence Yep, and read several books by that author. What makes the plot and the characters memorable? What are the themes in the writer's work? Is there a common theme throughout the writing?

- With a group of your peers, choose an area of literature discussed in this chapter. Select five books that develop the values of multicultural literature discussed in this chapter. Also select five books that do not develop the values. Share the books and your rationales for selecting them with the rest of the class.

- Compare the characterizations of Native Americans in children's literature published before 1960 with the characterizations of Native Americans in books published after 1975. How would readers describe Native Americans if this literature were their only contact with Native Americans? Has there been a change in characterizations between the literature of the two periods?

- Several classics, or old standards, in children's literature have been praised by some but criticized by others. In the area of literature referring to African American experiences, Marguerite De Angeli's *Bright April* has been criticized because of the way April is subjected to prejudice and because of the prescribed formula for success that the story implies. Likewise, Ingrid and Edgar D'Aulaire's *Abraham Lincoln* has been criticized for overromanticizing Lincoln's life and depicting both African American and Native American people as the "white man's burden." Read one of these books. Discuss your reactions with your peers.

- Select an ethnic group of which you are not a member and develop a list of books that will help an upper elementary class build a timeline that will identify important contributions of individuals from that ethnic group to American culture. Print your list and share copies of it with classmates.

- A teacher comes to you and wants suggestions for a learning center about Asian cultures. Write a step-by-step explanation for using the database to narrow down her search to a list of folktales and nonfiction books about a single Asian culture, e.g., Japan or China. Give your directions to another student and have them print their list.

- Choose a traditional folktale. Use the database to locate books from different cultures that tell the same tale. Write an activity that fifth graders could do using the books as a resource for a writing workshop.

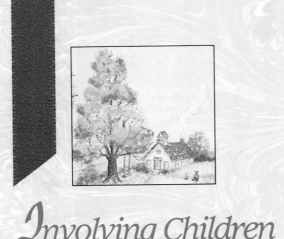

Involving Children in Multicultural Literature

Educators are concerned about the quality and the quantity of multicultural materials available for sharing with children. They are also concerned about the teaching strategies used in developing understanding of and positive attitudes toward various cultural groups. Across the decades, educators have called for more involvement with multicultural concepts. For example, in the 1970s, Gwendolyn Baker (1978) argued that little planning had been given to the process of multicultural education. She maintained that both college students and teachers required training in the concepts to be developed, the objectives to be achieved, the knowledge about various cultures, and the integration of multicultural concepts at all levels of education.

In 1989, educators such as Cathy Roller (1989) argued, "Reading instruction as presently delivered has, probably unintentionally, been instrumental in perpetuating and maintaining our class- and race-stratified society" (p. 492). Educators such as D. Bruce Sealey (1984) were also critical of current instructional practices. They emphasized that instruction should encourage students to accept and be sensitive to cultural diversity, to understand that similar values frequently underlie different customs, to have quality contact with people from other cultures, and to role-play experiences in order to involve students with other cultures.

In 1993, educators were still critical of the quality of multicultural education. For example, Lily Wong Fillmore (1993) discussed the issues involved in educating citizens for a multicultural twenty-first century and presented some ideas for change. Kathryn H. Au (1993) stated:

Clearly, there is a need for schools to improve the literacy instruction of students of diverse backgrounds. This need is becoming even more urgent given the population trends in the United States. In 1982 nearly three of four American young people (ages 0 to 17) were European American, but by 2020 only one of two young people will be European American. In 1982 only one of 10 young people was Hispanic, while it is estimated that this figure will change to one of four in 2020. (p. 3)

Au also argued for the inclusion of multicultural literature in the classroom when she stated:

Multiethnic literature can be used in the classroom to affirm the cultural identity of students of diverse backgrounds, and to develop all students' understanding and appreciation of other cultures. This view of literature is one of the new patterns of instruction that can help to support the school literacy development of students of diverse backgrounds. (p. 176)

Many educators recommend using multicultural literature and literature-related activities to improve children's understandings. For example, Eileen Tway (1989) maintains that multicultural literature and literature-related activities are essential in the classroom because they meet the needs of children and help the children understand themselves and others. Likewise, David Piper (1986) recommends using the traditional stories and fables from various cultural sources and creating awareness of different language and cultural backgrounds.

Sources such as Judy Sierra's *Multicultural Folktales for the Feltboard and Readers' Theater* (1996) and Pamela Gerke's *Multicultural Plays for Children, Volume II, Grades 4–6* (1996) provide materials and ideas that are useful for the multicultural literature program. Sierra's text includes twenty tales and directions for using them in various forms such as flannelboards and reader's theater. Gerke's book includes ten folktales that are presented in the form of plays. The plays have directions for creating props, sets, and costumes. Sources such as Herman L. Totten, Carolyn Garner, and Risa W. Brown's *Culturally Diverse Library Collections for Youth* (1996) and Katherine Gleason's *Native American Literature* (1996) provide additional sources for materials. *Culturally Diverse Library Collections for Youth* includes recommended literature about African Americans, Native Americans, Hispanic Americans, and Asian Americans. In addition to books, there is a guide to videos. *Native American Literature* includes an introduction to the oral tradition and chapters that highlight the writings of various Native American authors.

This section considers many types of activities that can heighten the value of excellent multicultural literature. Many of the teaching models and instructional ideas evolved from Donna Norton's (1984–1987; Norton and McNamara, 1988; Norton and Norton, 1994) research during the past ten years, including different approaches with undergraduate and graduate classes, research in elementary and middle school classes, multicultural literature evaluations, and development of multicultural literature curriculum and inservice activities.

Portions of the sequence of study that are recommended in this chapter were published in Norton's "Teaching Multicultural Literature in the Reading Curriculum" (1990). The journal article received the 1992 Virginia Hamilton Essay Award, which is presented by the Virginia Hamilton Conference Advisory Board at Kent State University. This annual award recognizes an article that "makes a significant contribution to the professional literature concerning multicultural literary experiences for youth." I was very honored to be the recipient of this award, and I hope the sequence of study will help you as you prepare to use multicultural literature.

Research and experience as well as a search through the scholarly literature support a sequence of study in multicultural literature that proceeds from the ancient literature of a culture to the contemporary literature. For example, both Franchot Ballinger (1984) and Michael Dorris (1979) recommend a sequence of study of Native Ameri-

can literature that begins with a study of broad oral traditions, narrows to specific tribal experiences as expressed in mythology, continues with biographical and autobiographical study of specific cultural areas, and concludes with a study of contemporary Native American literature. Dorris supports this sequence because:

To investigate any Native American literature one must examine its evolution and development through time; one must know something of the language—its rules, its implied world view—of its creation; one must know something of the culture's history of contacts with other peoples, both Native American and Euro-American; and one must know something of the modern social setting of the culture. (p. 157)

The sequence of study used in Chart 11–1 modifies the Ballinger and Dorris models and emphasizes literature written for children. This study is a five-phase approach. It begins with a broad awareness of myths, legends, and folktales from one cultural group (for example, Native American). Then, it narrows to the myths, legends, and folktales of one or two tribal or cultural areas (for example, Native American myths and legends from the Plains Indians or Indians of the northwestern coast). It proceeds to autobiographies, biographies, and other informational literature about an earlier time in history, continues with historical fiction, and concludes with literature written for children by authors whose work represents that cultural group and contemporary time.

Follow the total sequence with one cultural group before proceeding to another cultural group. As you work through each phase, you are developing understandings that build upon each other. For example, after students can identify the traditional values and beliefs of the people as represented in their folktales, myths, and legends, they find it easier to identify values and beliefs in historical nonfiction. Students can use the knowledge gained from analyzing historical nonfiction, including autobiographies and biographies, to evaluate the appropriateness and authenticity of historical fiction and contemporary literature. As you proceed through the study, make cross-cultural comparisons. This series of activities can easily take the form of a unit.

CHART 11-1   Sequence for Multicultural Literature Study

Phase I: Traditional Literature (Generalizations and Broad Views)
A. Identify distinctions among folktales, myths, and legends.
B. Identify ancient stories that have common features and that are found in many regions.
C. Identify types of stories that dominate a subject.
D. Summarize the nature of oral language, the role of traditional literature, the role of an audience, and the literary style.

Phase II: Traditional Tales from One Area (Narrower View)
A. Analyze traditional myths and other story types and compare findings with those in Phase I.
B. Analyze and identify values, beliefs, and themes in the traditional tales of one region.

Phase III: Historical Nonfiction
A. Analyze nonfiction for the values, beliefs, and themes identified in traditional literature.
B. Compare adult autobiographies and children's biographies (if possible).
C. Compare information in historical documents with autobiographies and biographies.

Phase IV: Historical Fiction
A. Evaluate historical fiction according to the authenticity of the conflicts, characterizations, settings, themes, language, and traditional beliefs and values.
B. Search for the role of traditional literature in historical fiction.
C. Compare historical fiction with autobiographies, biographies, and historical information.

Phase V: Contemporary Literature
A. Analyze the inclusion of any beliefs and values identified in traditional literature and nonfictional literature.
B. Analyze contemporary characterizations and conflicts.
C. Analyze the themes and look for threads that cross the literature.

 DEVELOPING AN APPRECIATION FOR AFRICAN AMERICAN CULTURE

To help students develop an appreciation of the culture of African Americans, encourage the students to read a number of literature selections in various genres. Use the following activities to develop higher comprehension abilities in literature-based reading programs and to add understanding to other areas of the curriculum, such as social studies.

Phase One: Traditional Literature

Before beginning a study of the folktales, myths, and legends from Africa, discuss the importance of the oral tradition in transmitting the beliefs and values of all people. Make sure that students know the background of the oral tradition and that tales were handed down for many generations before they were transcribed into written form. Share with the students that many contemporary storytellers pre-fer the stories that were part of the oral tradition. For example, Jack Maguire (1988) emphasizes that many storytellers and storylisteners "prefer tales that developed within a predominately oral culture, such as the 'Ananasi the Spider' stories of Central America, the myths and legends of ancient Greece and Scandinavia, or the 'Jack Tales' of pioneer Appalachia" (p. 7). Also show and discuss a map of the African continent so that students understand the diversity of locations for folklore.

To help students understand the importance of oral language in transmitting cultural information, begin with a study of African folklore. Emphasize the power of oral storytellers and the impact of the language. Share with students that ancient Africans depended on oral storytellers to keep alive the cultural past. Storytellers chanted and sang, interacted with the audience, and acted out story elements. The art of storytelling was so highly valued that storytelling competitions were held to encourage the most vivid and entertaining stories. Tell the students

CHART 11-2 Introducing Traditional Tales with Objects

Object	Association	Traditional Tales
1. A rabbit	The importance of sense	Gerald McDermott, *Zomo the Rabbit*
2. A cardboard rainbow	Pia is trying to bring harmony to human world, while his mother weaves curtains from rainbows.	Jan Carew, *Children of the Sun*
3. A rabbit and a hut	Someone has taken possession of rabbit's house.	Verna Aardema, *Who's in Rabbit's House?*
4. A mosquito	The mosquito was not always noisy.	Verna Aardema, *Why Mosquitoes Buzz in People's Ears*
5. A crab	Pride causes Crab to be left without a head.	Barbara Knutson, *Why the Crab Has No Head*
6. A box containing stories	How did stories come to earth?	Gail Haley, *A Story, a Story*
7. Round and square houses	Why do men live in square houses and women live in round houses?	Ann Grifalconi, *The Village of Round and Square Houses*

that they will be listening to oral storytellers, identifying oral storytelling styles, and creating their own storytelling experiences.

Storytelling. Begin this enjoyable study by investigating how authentic storytellers selected their stories, what story openings were found in African folklore, what styles were common in storytelling, and how storytellers ended their stories. Relate to the students information about how contemporary storytellers such as Gail E. Haley (1986) find and retell their folktales. For example, Haley researches as far back as she can, to the earliest known version, and attempts to immerse herself in the culture that created the story. Haley states:

In the case of *A Story, a Story,* I took a course in African dance. I learned to prepare African food. I haunted museums and private collections of African artifacts. I even befriended a stranded African magic woman who shared our New York apartment for almost a year, imbuing me with her country and culture. But the basis remains the search for the primal roots of the story, the original tale. (p. 120)

Story Selections. Descriptions of storytellers from West Africa provide ideas for selecting a story from a number of possibilities. During her travels through Africa in the nineteenth century, Mary Kingsley (1964) discovered story minstrels who carried nets resembling fishing nets that contained such objects as bones, feathers, and china bits. When a listener chose an object, the storyteller would tell a story about it. Another interesting technique required storytellers to wear hats with articles suspended from the brims. A listener again would select an intriguing item, and the story would begin.

Teachers and librarians can easily use these techniques to help children select the story or stories to hear and to stimulate their interest. Cardboard cutouts, miniature objects, or real things that suggest a character or animal in a story can be chosen. Chart 11-2 gives examples of objects and the stories that they represent.

Story Openings. Storytellers from several African countries introduce stories by calling out sentences that elicit responses by the audiences. For example, Philip Noss (1972) relates that the following is a common story starter from Cameroon:

Storyteller: Listen to a tale! Listen to a tale!

Audience: A tale for fun, for fun. Your throat is a gong, your body a locust; bring it here for me to roast!

Storyteller: Children, listen to a tale, a tale for fun, for fun.

If you prefer to use an opening statement and response in an African language, use the following

Hausa opening from Nigeria, identified by A. J. Tremearne (1970):

Storyteller: Ga ta, ga ta nan. (See it, see it here.)
Audience: Ta zo, muii. (Let it come, for us to hear.)

If the stories are from the West Indies, one of the introductions identified by Elsie Clews Parsons (1918) would be appropriate:

1. Once upon a time, a very good time
   Not my time, nor your time, old people's time
2. Once upon a time, a very good time
   Monkey chew tobacco and spit white lime

Use these openings with any of the traditional African tales previously described, or use them to introduce a series of folktales. For example, Verna Aardema's humorous *Who's in Rabbit's House?* seems particularly appropriate for an introduction stressing a tale for fun. An enjoyable series of folktales might include "why" tales such as Aardema's *Why Mosquitoes Buzz in People's Ears* and Ashley Bryan's *The Cat's Purr* and "Why Frog and Snake Never Play Together" in *Beat the Story-Drum, Pum-Pum*. Another series might include hero or trickster tales.

Storytelling Styles. Listening to Ashley Bryan's tape, *The Dancing Granny and Other African Stories* (1985), is an excellent way to introduce storytelling styles. Have students listen to the tape and then describe this very vivid style. Have them search other sources for descriptions of storytelling styles. They will discover that the style of the traditional African storyteller, still found in many African countries today, can be characterized as a lively mixture of mimicking dialogue, body action, audience participation, and rhythm. Storytellers mimic the sounds of animals, change their voices to characterize both animal and human characters, develop dialogue, and encourage their listeners to interact with the story. Usually, they also add musical accompaniment with drums or other rhythm and string instruments such as thumb pianos. Anne Pellowski (1977) says that music and rhythm are important additions to African storytellers:

Taken as a whole, all storytelling in Africa, whether folk, religious, or bardic, whether in prose or poetry, seems to be strongly influenced by music and rhythm. It is rare to find stories that do not have some rhythmical or musical interlude or accompaniment, using either the voice, body parts, or special instruments. (p. 116)

Because children enjoy interacting with storytellers and interpreting tempos with drums or other musical instruments, such additions to storytelling can increase appreciation and understanding of traditional African tales. Stories such as Aardema's *Why Mosquitoes Buzz in People's Ears* and *Who's in Rabbit's House?*, with their strong oral language patterns and varied animal characterizations, can effectively introduce traditional African style.

Story Endings. Just as African storytellers use interesting story beginnings, they also often use certain types of story endings. A dramatic story could end with the Hausa *Suka zona* (they remained) or the Angolan *Mahezu* (finished). For an obvious exaggeration from the West Indies, the storyteller might choose this ending:

Chase the rooster and catch the hen
I'll never tell a lie like that again.

Storytellers from the West Indies also provide an appropriate ending for humorous folktales:

They lived in peace, they died in peace
And they were buried in a pot of candle grease.

A folktale from the West Indies, such as Ashley Bryan's retelling of *Turtle Knows Your Name,* is appropriate. Bryan's rhythmic language makes this tale an enjoyable choice for an oral experience.

Children enjoy recreating the atmosphere of traditional African tales. African American children take special pride in the stories and the exciting ways in which the stories can be presented to an audience. Both adults and children can tell stories and then discuss the traditional African approaches to storytelling and the ways in which these approaches enhanced the enjoyment for both storyteller and listeners. After the stories are told, students may read them constantly. Conclude by asking students to identify and summarize the oral language styles that are found in traditional African folklore.

Values and Beliefs. After students consider the impact of the language on the folklore of Africa, ask them to read numerous examples of folklore from Africa to identify values and beliefs found in the tales. You may use several approaches to help students identify values and beliefs. Because themes are closely related to values and beliefs, have students search for themes in the folklore. Asking students to provide support for the themes helps them develop higher comprehension and cognitive skills.

In the following example, the themes in John Steptoe's *Mufaro's Beautiful Daughters: An African Tale* also illuminate values and beliefs. First, help students search for themes by asking them to listen to or to read the story and ask themselves: What is the author trying to tell me that would make a difference in my life? How do I know that the author is telling me _____ ? Remind the students that proof of theme may include many elements in the story, such as the characters' actions, the characters' thoughts, the interaction of characters as shown through dialogue, the rewards and punishments that end the story, a statement of theme by the author, and illustrations.

Next, read *Mufaro's Beautiful Daughters* as students listen to answer the first question: What is the author trying to tell me that would make a difference in my life? After you complete the story, ask the students to provide at least two important themes in this book. They may say, for example, greed and selfishness are harmful, or bad, personal characteristics and that kindness and generosity are beneficial, or good, personal characteristics. The wording of these themes will differ depending on the age of the students.

Reread *Mufaro's Beautiful Daughters,* asking the students to identify support for each theme within the tale. Remind them of the different ways in which authors develop and support a theme. As support for "greed and selfishness are harmful personal characteristics," students may identify some of the following examples:

1. Illustrations show a bad-tempered girl (illustrations).
2. Manyara tries to trick her sister so that only Manyara will visit the king (actions).
3. Greed causes Manyara to leave the village secretly (actions).
4. Manyara refuses to give a hungry boy food and responds, "I have brought only enough for myself" (actions and dialogue).
5. Manyara shows anger when she says, "Out of my way, boy!" (actions and dialogue).

6. Manyara refuses to take advice from an older woman (actions that show disrespect for older people).
7. Manyara sees a monster snake with five heads (punishment as part of the ending).
8. Manyara becomes a servant to her sister, the queen (punishment as part of the ending).
9. Greed is punished (represented by the ending).

As support for "kindness and generosity are beneficial personal characteristics," students may identify some of the following examples:

1. Nyasha sings while she works, causing people to think that her singing makes the plants bountiful (actions).
2. Nyasha is kind to a garden snake (actions).
3. Nyasha does not complain because she is considerate of her father's feelings (actions and the author tells us).
4. Illustrations show Nyasha as a happy, thoughtful girl (illustrations).
5. Nyasha gives food to a hungry boy; she says, "You must be hungry," . . . and handed him a yam that she had brought for her lunch (actions and dialogue).
6. Nyasha takes advice from the older woman (actions show respect for older people).
7. Nyasha bravely approaches the chamber in which she is to meet the king (actions).
8. Nyasha sees a little snake and then the king (reward as part of the ending).
9. Nyasha proves herself to be both most worthy and most beautiful (ending).
10. Kindness and generosity are rewarded as Nyasha becomes queen (reward as ending).

After completing this activity, ask the students to identify any additional values and beliefs that they discovered. For example, in addition to admiring generosity and kindness and despising greed and selfishness, the African people represented in this tale value the advice of older people and consider worthiness to be more important than beauty. Again, students should support these values and beliefs with evidence from the tale.

Charting answers to questions related to folk characteristics is another technique that helps students identify values in folklore (Norton, 1994). First, discuss various ways in which students can identify traditional values found in folklore. For example, they can read the folklore to discover answers to each of the following questions:

1. What reward or rewards are desired?
2. What actions are rewarded or admired?
3. What actions are punished or despised?
4. What rewards are given to the heroes, the heroines, or the great people in the stories?
5. What are the personal characteristics of the heroes, the heroines, or the great people in the stories?

Next, print each of these questions on a chart. Allow room to include several African tales. When students read various African tales, have them use the chart to identify and discuss traditional values and beliefs.

Introduce the first book on the chart, Gail Haley's *A Story, a Story*. It is advisable to complete the first example together. Ask the students to listen carefully so that they will be able to answer the questions and identify the values on the chart. After reading *A Story, a Story* aloud, ask the students to identify the answers to the questions and to place them in the proper location on the chart. Chart 11–3 shows the results of this activity using *A Story, a Story*, Gerald McDermott's *Zomo the Rabbit: A Trickster Tale from West Africa*, and Jan Carew's *Children of the Sun*. For additional books, use a similar listening, listing, and discussing procedure, or have the students read these books independently and then discuss their results.

After each reading activity, discuss the values and beliefs that are developed in the story. Ask the students to notice ways that some of the values and beliefs express the importance of oral language discussed earlier. Ask the students to notice how the theme in *Mufaro's Beautiful Daughters: An African Tale* is similar to that in *Children of the Sun*. Read as many African tales as possible to find additional values and beliefs and to discover common values and beliefs in various folklore selections.

Notice that within these tales are many trickster tales. Tricksters may win or lose. Explain to students that in folklore, trickery is often considered necessary to create a balance. Consequently, students should consider what forces are out of balance.

Before leaving Phase One, review discoveries about oral storytelling and summarize the values and beliefs that the students discovered in reading African folklore.

Phase Two: Folklore of the American South

African American folktales and legends include many of the values and characteristics of the African tales. The resulting tales combine a past culture, a new en-

CHART 11–3   Values Identified in African Folklore

Questions for Values	A Story, a Story	Zomo the Rabbit	Children of the Sun
What reward is desired?	Stories from the powerful sky god	Wisdom	Peace and harmony
What actions are rewarded or admired?	Outwitting the leopard, the hornet, and the fairy	Using wit, trickery, and courage	Being good and searching for peace and harmony
What actions are punished or despised?	—	Lacking caution	Disobeying one's father, haughtiness, and rebelliousness
What rewards are given to heroes, heroines, or great people?	Oral stories to delight the people	Advice (the three things that are worth having are courage, good sense, and caution)	Patience and life
What are the personal characteristics of heroes, heroines, or great people?	Intelligence and verbal ability (in the small old man)	Courage and cleverness	Goodness, patience, the desire to serve, and humanity

vironment, and new experiences. Many of the traditional values, including love for language, respect for wit, hospitality, generosity, gratitude, and reverence for elderly people, are also found in African American folklore. During Phase Two, identify the philosophy, values, and beliefs of the people as reflected in African American folklore. Have students identify similarities between the African folklore and the American folklore. Also, help students identify any differences that reflect the new environment and experiences.

Begin the study by sharing and discussing the stories found in Virginia Hamilton's *The People Could Fly: American Black Folktales*. Identify the types of tales, such as animal tales, supernatural tales, and slave tales of freedom. As you continue your study, encourage your students to identify values, beliefs, and language styles. Use the same techniques that encouraged students to search for values, beliefs, and themes in African folklore. For example, trace themes in several African American folktales and compare those themes with the themes found in African folklore. Develop charts that are similar to Chart 11–3. Analyze numerous African American folktales and compare the values. Read African American folktales aloud. Are there any similarities in language style? Identify stories that have similar story structures and discuss the similarities but also consider why there might be differences. In addition to Hamilton's book, the following books are excellent sources of tales: Julius Lester's adaptations of Joel Chandler Harris's tales in *The Tales of Uncle Remus: The Adventures of Brer Rabbit* and *More Tales of Uncle Remus: Further Adventures of Brer Rabbit, His Friends, Enemies, and Others;* Lester's *The Knee-High Man and Other Tales;* Van Dyke Parks's adaptation of Joel Chandler Harris's tales in *Jump! The Adventures of Brer Rabbit* and *Jump Again! More Adventures of Brer Rabbit;* Patricia McKissack's *Flossie & the Fox;* William H. Hooks's *The Ballad of Belle Dorcus;* Steve Sanfield's *The Adventures of High John the Conqueror;* and Robert D. San Souci's *Sukey and the Mermaid*.

Activities developed around John Henry, the tall tale hero, provide opportunities for creative dramatizations, discussions about values, learning about history, and writing. As a poem, a song, or a longer narrative, the tale can stimulate many creative activities. Because there are several versions of the John Henry tale, compare the books, poem, and song. Is the story the same in each version? Are the illustrations alike or different? Which version is the most effective? Why?

Teachers have used the tale in its various forms with children in all of the elementary grades. In the lower grades, children can listen to the story and discuss the large illustrations in the picture book *John Henry,* by Ezra Jack Keats, or in *John Henry,* by Julius Lester. The language of the books make pleasant listening while children discover that American folk heroes are from different ethnic backgrounds. Through the story and pictures, children can gain an understanding of tall tales and the actions that heroes are supposed to perform. Discuss other folk heroes, such as Davy Crockett and Paul Bunyan. Have the children compare the remarkable feats of each hero and decide how much of each hero's story is exaggerated.

In poetic form, John Henry makes a good choral presentation. Classes have tried the poem as a refrain in which a leader reads the opening lines of each verse and the class enters in on each of the repetitive lines, such as "He laid down his hammer and he died." Alternatively, have students read each verse in a cumulative arrangement, in which one group begins the first verse, the second joins the second verse, and a third joins the third verse. This arrangement continues until the poem is complete.

Encourage creative writing by asking children to write their own work chants and tall tales. One class pretended that John Henry was a contemporary hero and wrote about the heroic deeds that he could do if he lived in their lifetime. Stories described him saving the nuclear reactor at Three Mile Island, rescuing people from the upper floors during a hotel fire, and completing work on a superhighway or a skyscraper. Illustrations accompanying the stories showed John Henry as a strong man who was also concerned with the lives of the people around him. Other classes have used tales about John Henry to stimulate creative drama.

As a conclusion to Phase Two, summarize the likenesses and differences between African and African American folklore. Identify stories that have close similarities, and consider any reasons for the similarities. Also consider reasons for the differences within the tales.

Phase Three: Historical Nonfiction

By this time, students should have gained understanding that they can use as they read, analyze, and evaluate both nonfictional and fictional literature. During Phase Three, have students read, discuss, and evaluate nonfictional literature that reflects a historical perspective. For example, as students read biographies and autobiographies, have them analyze the inclusion of values, beliefs, and philosophies found in the traditional literature. Have the students read a number of sources, evaluate the accuracy of the information, and identify historical happenings that influenced the culture. Include other types of nonfictional informational texts so that students may critically evaluate the accuracy of settings, happenings, and sources of conflict.

Use Chart 11–4 to help students as they proceed with this evaluation. Note, however, that the material included in Chart 11–4 is only a partial listing of the information that may be included. Notice a continuity within the literature of the language style, theme, and values found in earlier traditional literature. Also notice that the sources of conflict are authentic for this time period. The students who evaluated *Amos*

Fortune, however, concluded after reading other non-fictional sources that many of the horrors of the period were not included in this biography.

Additional biographies that are excellent for analyzing during Phase Three include Lillie Patterson's *Frederick Douglass: Freedom Fighter,* Douglas Miller's *Frederick Douglass and the Fight for Freedom,* and Virginia Hamilton's *Anthony Burns: The Defeat and Triumph of a Fugitive Slave.* Milton Meltzer's *The Black Americans: A History in Their Own Words, 1619–1983* is an excellent source for shorter autobiographical sketches and information. Virginia Hamilton's *Many Thousand Gone: African Americans from Slavery to Freedom* also provides shorter sketches of people.

Another type of activity using historical nonfiction is recommended by Wynell Burroughs Schamel and Jean West (1992). These educational specialists at the Education Branch, National Archives and Records

CHART 11–4 Analyzing Historical Biography and Autobiography

Literature	Evidence of Philosophy, Values, Beliefs, and Language from Phases One and Two	Sources of Conflict	Historical Happenings and Evaluations
Yates's *Amos Fortune, Free Man*	African story told by Amos is in the style of African storytellers, using repetition, chants, and audience participation. *Theme:* Freedom is important. *Values:* Work, family, retribution, generosity, love of nature.	Person against society, as Amos fights mistreatment, injustice, and separation. Person against self, as Amos considers consequences of his actions.	New Hampshire, 1725–1801. Blacks are taken from Africa and sold as slaves. The horrors of the slave block are avoided in the text, so acceptance of the situations may be too easy.
Ferris's *Go Free or Die: A Story of Harriet Tubman*	*Themes:* Freedom is worth risking one's life. We must help others obtain their freedom. *Values:* Obligations to family and people, wit, trickery when needed for balance, responsibility, and gratitude.	Person against society, as Harriet fights to free blacks and to combat injustice.	America, mid-1800s to the end of the Civil War. This story is based on facts related to slavery, the Underground Railroad, the 1850 Fugitive Slave Act, and the 1863 Emancipation Proclamation. Tubman freed more than three hundred slaves in ten years.

Administration in Washington, D. C., recommend teaching about the Civil War and the fight for equal rights by analyzing documents from the time period, such as a recruiting poster for black soldiers in the Civil War. They provide a copy of a poster and recommend questions to analyze the poster, such as

Who do you believe is the intended audience for the poster? What does the government hope the audience will do? What references to pay do you find in this document? What references to treatment of prisoners of war do you find in this document? What evidence of government efforts to improve conditions for black soldiers do you find in this document? What purpose(s) of government is/are served by this poster? How is the design of this poster different from contemporary military recruitment posters? (p. 120)

Schamel and West also provide suggestions for creative writing, oral reports, and further research.

Phase Four: Historical Fiction

During Phase Four, have students read, analyze, and evaluate historical fiction and fiction with historical backgrounds according to credibility of conflict, believability of characterization, authenticity of setting, authenticity of traditional beliefs expressed by the characters, appropriateness of themes, and appropriateness of the author's style. Understandings gained from the previously studied biographies, autobiographies, and informational books are especially important during Phase Four. For example, if students have read a number of biographies and other nonfictional texts about the time of slavery, then they can analyze a fictional book, such as Belinda Hurmence's *A Girl Called Boy*. Even though there is a time-warp experience in this story, the major portion of the story is set in North Carolina in the 1850s.

Have students evaluate the authenticity of the 1850s North Carolina plantation setting. Also, have them use the knowledge that they gained while reading biographies of this time period to analyze the credibility of the conflict. Have students provide evidence for answers to the following questions: Is the setting authentic for a plantation that included numerous slaves? If the setting is authentic, what makes it authentic? What proof do you have that this setting is or is not authentic? Does the plot parallel stories of actual slaves? How? Is the person-against-society conflict as believable as are the conflicts in biographies and autobiographies? What are the comparisons? Why is the conflict be-

lievable? How does the author develop believable characters?

Relate instances of characterization with examples from biographies and autobiographies. Are any of the traditional beliefs, themes, and language styles that were found during Phases One and Two also found in this book? Which ones? How are these beliefs developed in the story? Are any of the themes identified in biographies also found in this book? If so, how does the author develop these themes? Do you believe that the themes are appropriate for this story? Why or why not? Is the author's style appropriate for the story? Why or why not? Find examples of author's style that you think are either very good or inappropriate. What, if any, is the relationship of this book to the findings from Phases One, Two, and Three of this study? Defend your answer.

You may use numerous books for Phase Four. Additional books with historical settings about slavery include N. Monjo's *The Drinking Gourd,* Paula Fox's *Slave Dancer,* James and Christopher Collier's *Jump Ship to Freedom,* James Berry's *Ajeemah and His Son,* Gary Paulsen's *Nightjohn,* and Mary Stolz's *Cezanne Pinto: A Memoir.* Mildred Taylor's family survival stories set in the 1900s, *The Gold Cadillac, Roll of Thunder, Hear My Cry,* and *Let the Circle Be Unbroken,* are excellent sources for analysis and comparison. The themes related to family, physical, and spiritual survival have threads that may be traced to the earlier studies.

Phase Five: Contemporary Literature

During the final phase, have students read, analyze, and evaluate contemporary literature, including poetry, fiction, and biography. Have the students search for continuity within the literature as reflected in the images, themes, values, and sources of conflict. Also, have them reflect on changes that have taken place. For example, ask the students to read the poetry of Langston Hughes, Gwendolyn Brooks, and Tom Feelings. Poetry selections such as Hughes's "Dreams" and "Merry-Go-Round" should have special significance because the students should understand both the pain of prejudice and the joy of life experienced by people earlier in American history. Students also should gain respect for the poets who created such vivid images within their poems.

Some books are especially good for relating the past and the present. For example, ask students to read such contemporary realistic fiction selections as Sharon Bell Mathis's *The Hundred Penny Box* and Virginia Hamilton's *The House of Dies Drear*. The students should understand Mathis's characterization when Aunt Dew excitedly says, "18 and 74. Year I was born. Slavery over! Black men in Congress running things. They was in charge. It was the Reconstruction" (p. 26). In Hamilton's book, they should understand the pride in the African American family as it tries to unravel a mystery related to a home on the Underground Railroad.

Strong family relationships and respect for elders are found in books that span all five phases of this study. Ask students to search for support for these themes in such books as Valerie Flournoy's *The Patchwork Quilt,* Lucille Clifton's *Everett Anderson's Goodbye,* Mildred Pitts Walter's *Justin and the Best Biscuits in the World,* and Mary Stolz's *Storm in the Night*. Pride in heritage and strength in character are also frequent themes and values. Ask the students to trace these themes and values in books such as Eloise Greenfield's *Sister* and Virginia Hamilton's *Zeely* and *Junius Over Far*.

Finally, ask the students to read biographies of contemporary African American people, such as Martin Luther King, Jr., Barbara Jordan, Malcolm X, Langston Hughes, and Arthur Mitchell. Ask them to search for conflicts, characterizations, values, and themes. Is there any evidence of continuity within the literature? If so, what aspects are also found in the other phases?

Comparisons between the more historical biographies and the contemporary biographies are especially interesting. Biographies lend themselves to numerous activities in the curriculum. The following activities include a study of biographies in history, science, literature, reading, art, music, and sports:

1. Have the children search the literature and develop a time line illustrating the contributions of famous African Americans in history. Develop the time line on a bulletin board and display literature selections that tell about the people.
2. Ask the children to share their reactions after reading a biography about Martin Luther King, Jr. Have them interview parents and other adults about the goals of the late civil rights leader.
3. After reading a biography, perform "A Day in the Life of _____ ."

4. Share literature written by African American authors. Discuss the contributions and styles of such authors as John Steptoe, Sharon Mathis, Eloise Greenfield, and Virginia Hamilton.
5. After reading biographies or stories about African American musicians, share and discuss their music.
6. Read biographies of African American athletes and discuss records set or other contributions.
7. After reading literature about the contributions and lives of African Americans, create a "What's My Line" game in which a panel of children asks questions while another group answers.
8. Using a "Meet the Press" format, ask children to take roles of famous African Americans or reporters who interview them. Prepare for the session by reading literature.

You can use similar activities to highlight the contributions of Native Americans, Hispanics, and Asian Americans. However, before proceeding to the literature of another cultural group, review what the students have learned from this five-phase study. Review the evidence of both continuity and change. What do the students know about the literature of the African American culture that will make a difference in their lives?

 ## DEVELOPING AN APPRECIATION FOR NATIVE AMERICAN CULTURE

To study Native American cultures, use many of the same techniques that you used for African American culture. Begin with Native American folklore, in general. Then, narrow the study to the folklore of specific peoples. Proceed to historical nonfiction. Follow historical nonfiction with historical fiction, and end with contemporary literature.

Phase One: Native American Folklore

Before beginning a study of Native American culture, show and discuss a map of the North American continent to reveal to students the diversity of locations for Native American peoples. John Bierhorst's *The Mythology of North America* (1985) includes a useful map of North American mythological regions. A map is also located in Michael J. Caduto and Joseph Bruchac's *Keepers of the Ani-*

mals: *Native American Stories and Wildlife Activities for Children* (1991). According to the authors, this map indicates the cultural areas and tribal locations of Native North Americans as they appeared around 1600. Have students begin their study of Native American folklore with an investigation of the oral language.

Storytelling. Native American storytellers, like African storytellers, developed definite styles in their storytelling over centuries of oral tradition. Storytelling was an important part of early Indian life, and stories were carefully passed down from one generation to the next. It was quite common for Indians to gather around a fire or sit around their homes while listening to stories. The storytelling sessions often continued for long periods of time, with each person telling a story. Children have opportunities to empathize with members of Native American culture when they take part in storytelling activities that closely resemble the original experience. According to Michael J. Caduto and Joseph Bruchac (1989), "Stories form a link between our imagination and our surroundings. They are a way of reaching deep into a child's inner world, to the places where dreams and fantasies are constantly sculpting an ever-growing world view" (p. 7).

Caduto and Bruchac also emphasize the importance of the setting for the storytelling. They state:

In the American Indian culture, everyone was allowed to have their say and people listened with patience. People would sit in a circle during the time of storytelling because in a circle no person is at the head. All are "the same height." Remembering this may help you and it is good to remind your listeners—who are not just an audience but part of the story—of that. (p. 8)

Story Openings. Several collectors of Native American tales and observers of Native American storytellers have identified characteristic opening sentences that you may use when presenting Native American stories to children. Franc Newcomb (1967), for example, found that many Navaho storytellers opened their stories with one of the following tributes to the past:

In the beginning, when the world was new

At the time when men and animals were all the same and spoke the same language

A popular beginning with the White Mountain Apache was "long, long ago, they say." According to Caduto and Bruchac (1989), the Abenaki people begin a story with, "Here my story camps." The Iroquois often begin by saying, "Would you like to hear a story?"

Have the children search through stories from many Native American tribes and discover how interpreters and translators of traditional Indian folktales introduced their stories. Have the children investigate further and find the exact story openers a certain tribe would be likely to use so that they can use those openings when telling stories from that tribe.

Storytelling Styles. The storytelling styles used by various Indians of North America were quite different from the styles for African storytellers. Melville Jacobs (1959) describes the storytelling style of Northwest Indians as being terse, staccato, and rapid. It was usually compact, with little description, although storytellers might use pantomime and gestures to develop the story. Gladys Reichard (1974) found that the Coeur d'Alene Indians used dramatic movements to increase the drama of their tales.

The listening styles of the Native American audiences were also quite different. Native American children were expected to be very attentive and not to interrupt the storyteller. Their only response might be the Hopi's repetition of the last word in a sentence, or the Crow's responsive "E!" (yes) following every few sentences. According to Byrd Baylor (1976), this response was a sign that the audience was attentive and appreciative. Children in classroom and library story times may also enjoy using these signs to show that they are listening.

Morris Opler (1938) discovered an interesting detail about Jicarilla Apache storytellers that can be used to add authenticity and cultural understanding to Native American storytelling. Storytellers gave kernels of corn to children during story time. Because corn was very important, it was believed that if children ate the corn during the storytelling they would remember the content and the importance of the stories.

Story Endings. Melville Jacobs (1959) says that Clackama Indians ended many stories by telling an epilogue about an Indian's metamorphosis into an animal, bird, or fish. Most of the stories also had a final ending that meant "myth, myth" or "story, story." Jicarilla Apache storytellers sometimes ended their stories by giving gifts to the listeners because they had stolen a night from their audience. Caduto and Bruchac (1989) say that the Abenaki people closed their stories with phrases such as "That is the end" or "Then I left." The Iroquois often ended their stories with "Da neho!" which means, "That is all."

Teachers and librarians have found that adding authentic storytelling techniques increases understanding and respect for a cultural heritage and stimulates discussions about traditional values. Before leaving this portion of Phase One, ask students to summarize what they have learned about Native American folklore styles.

Types of Tales. Collect as many examples of North American Indian folklore as possible. Have the students use these tales to categorize stories that meet Bierhorst's story types found in Native American folklore: (1) setting-the-world-in-order tales, (2) family drama tales, (3) trickster tales, and (4) threshold tales. Chart 11–5 includes examples of literature that you may use for this purpose. Before leaving Phase One, summarize your generalizations about Native American folklore and review your discoveries about oral storytelling.

Phase Two: Folklore from Specific Peoples

During Phase Two, narrow the emphasis to the folklore of one or two Native American peoples. If the students work well in groups, you may choose several tribal regions and allow each group to do an indepth study of the folklore of that region. For example, there are many stories from the Plains Indians, from the Southwest Pueblo peoples, and from Indians of the Pacific Northwest. Have students search for similarities in story types found in Phase One and analyze the literature for values and beliefs of the specific people. Have them consider the importance of variants in the story types and search for cultural and geographical reasons for these variants.

Locate as many folktales, myths, and legends as possible from the specific regions to be studied. Several documented sources of Native American traditional values will help students as they search for evidence of those values. For example, Hanson and Eisenbise's *Human Behavior and American Indians* (1983) documents traditional values and compares them to urban industrial values. Ross and Brave Eagle (1975) identify traditional Lakota values. These Lakota values are especially important if the stu-

CHART 11–5 Literature for a Study of Native American Folklore

Setting the World in Order
Duncan's *The Magic of Spider Woman*
Esbensen's *The Star Maiden*
Hamilton's "Turtle Dives to the Bottom of the Sea" in *In the Beginning: Creation Stories from Around the World*
Monroe and Williamson's *They Dance in the Sky: Native American Star Myths*

Family Drama
Metayer's *Tales from the Igloo*
Monroe and Williamson's *They Dance in the Sky: Native American Star Myths*
Spencer's *Who Speaks for Wolf*

Tricksters
Goble's *Iktomi and the Boulder: A Plains Indian Story*
Lame Deer's "Iktoml and the Ducks" in Cohn's *From Sea to Shining Sea: A Treasury of American Folklore and Folk Songs*
McDermott's *Raven: A Trickster Tale from the Pacific Northwest*

Thresholds
Bierhorst's *The Ring in the Prairie: A Shawnee Legend*
Goble's *Buffalo Woman*
Steven's *Coyote Steals the Blanket: A Ute Tale*

dents are reading and analyzing literature from various Great Plains peoples.

Numerous collections of folklore contain selections from various tribal areas. These sources include Michael J. Caduto and Joseph Bruchac's *Keepers of the Earth: Native American Stories and Environmental Activities for Children* and *Keepers of the Animals: Native American Stories and Wildlife Activities for Children,* and Virginia Hamilton's *In the Beginning: Creation Stories from Around the World.* Chart 11–6 presents a few additional sources of folklore from the Great Plains, the Southwest, and the Northwest. Have students summarize the values, beliefs, and themes found in the traditional literature of a specific people and compare the types of stories found in Phase One and Phase Two. (Use similar techniques to help students discover themes and values like those developed under Phases One and Two of African American literature.)

CHART 11–6   Folklore Sources for a Study of Literature from the Great Plains, the Southwest, and the Northwest

Great Plains	Southwest	Northwest
Baker's *Where the Buffalos Begin* Bierhorst's *The Ring in the Prairie* dePaola's *The Legend of the Blue-bonnet* Goble's *Buffalo Woman*	Baylor's *Moon Song* Cohlene's *Turquoise Boy: A Navajo Legend* Cushing's *Zuni Folk Tales*	Bierhorst's *The Girl Who Married a Ghost* McDermott's *Raven: A Trickster Tale from the Pacific Northwest* Normandin's *Echoes of the Elders: The Stories and Paintings of Chief Lelooska* Wallas's *Kwakiutl Legends*

At the conclusion of Phase Two, have older students analyze Jamake Highwater's *Anpao: An American Indian Odyssey*. This story combines a number of traditional Native American tales.

Many additional activities that you may develop with Native American folklore are found in Caduto and Bruchac's *Keepers of the Earth: Native American Stories and Environmental Activities for Children* and *Keepers of the Animals: Native American Stories and Wildlife Activities for Children*. The activities in these books encourage children to integrate science, geography, and environmental studies into the reading of Native American folklore.

Phase Three: Historical Nonfiction

As in the study of African American literature, students' previous knowledge should help them evaluate the inclusion of accurate values, beliefs, and philosophies in historical nonfiction. Have students read a number of sources to evaluate the authenticity of historical information and to identify the historical happenings that influenced the culture. Have the students develop a chart similar to Chart 11–4. This time, the sources should be Native American biographies and autobiographies from the particular region that the students are studying.

Historical literature frequently includes personal conflict. The individuals must overcome problems because of differences between their own Native American beliefs and values and those of the Euro–American culture. As part of the Phase Three study, have the students search for evidence of such conflicts. Are the beliefs, values, customs, and religion in conflict with the different culture? As might be expected, adult autobiographies reflect much cultural conflict. Have students use data from a study of adult autobiographies to analyze what percentage of their biographies correspond with the findings from adult texts. See Chart 11–7 for a calculation from a study by Donna Norton (1987).

Have students also search for the development of conflicts caused by differences of opinion over land. For example, does the biographer emphasize conflicts because the people were displaced? Is the impoverishment of the people of concern? Or does the

CHART 11–7   Percentages of Adult Autobiographies That Include Conflicts Caused by Cultural Beliefs

Tribal Location	Beliefs	Values	Customs	Religion
Great Plains	46%	85%	54%	85%
Great Basin	50	50	50	—
Southwest	50	75	50	63

CHART 11-8 Percentages of Adult Autobiographies That Deal with Conflicts Over Land

Tribal Location	People Displaced	People Impoverished	Leaders Emerging
Great Plains	61 %	77 %	38 %
Great Basin	100	100	50
Southwest	50	25	38

biographer emphasize the emergence of leaders who try to regain or keep the land? Chart 11–8 identifies percentages of conflicts over land found in adult texts. In addition, have students compare the types of conflicts found in children's biographies with the types of conflicts found in adult autobiographies.

Comparison encourages students to consider the credibility of biographies from different regions. Nonfictional sources, such as Russell Freedman's *Buffalo Hunt, The Life and Death of Crazy Horse,* and *An Indian Winter* and Rayna Green's *Women in American Indian Society,* provide historical perspectives. Byrd Baylor's *When Clay Sings* is a poetic telling of the ancient way of life of Native Americans living in the Southwest desert.

Native American nonfiction is also an excellent source of material for integrating literature and geography. Books such as Marcia Sewall's *People of the Breaking Day* and Jane Yolen's *Encounter* present stories about the native peoples before or just at the time of Columbus. Use these books to help students analyze literature according to the five themes of geography (see below), to integrate the study of literature and geography, to increase understanding of Native American peoples before and at the time of Columbus, and to motivate discussions related to geography and nonfiction literature (Norton and Norton, 1999).

Before reading either of these books to the students, provide some historical background about the time period and the locations. For *People of the Breaking Day,* explain that this story takes place before the English settlers arrive and change the lives of the people. Using a map or a globe, show and discuss the location of the story. For *Encounter,* explain that this is a story about what might have happened when the Taino Indians of the West Indies met Christopher Columbus and his Spanish explorers for the first time. Also show and discuss the location of San Salvador in the West Indies.

Introduce the five themes of geography that students will use to analyze and discuss the information in these books. Tell the students that geographers have developed this procedure to allow students to inquire about places on the earth and to analyze the relationships of these places to the people who live there. The following five fundamental themes in geography were developed by the Committee on Geographic Education (1983) and are also discussed in *GEO News Handbook* (1990):

1. *Location, including where and why:* Where does the story take place as far as city, country, continent, longitude, latitude, and so forth? Why does the story take place in this location?
2. *Place, including physical and human characteristics:* What are the physical features and characteristics? What are the characteristics of the people, including distinctive cultural traditions?
3. *Relationships within places, including cultural and physical interactions and how relationships develop:* How do human–environmental relationships develop and what are the consequences? What is the primary use of land? How have the people altered the environment? Where do most people live?
4. *Movement, including people, ideas, and materials:* How are the movements of people, ideas, and materials influenced and accomplished? What are the consequences of such movements?
5. *Regions, including how they form and change:* What are the major languages? What are the vegetation regions? What are the country's political divisions? How do the regions change?

Discuss these themes using language that is appropriate for student understanding. Develop a chart

CHART 11–9   Book Title: *People of the Breaking Day*

Location	Place	Relationships	Movement	Regions
East Coast. Small settlement. "Where the sun rises." Close to the sea. Away from Mohawks, Penacooks, and Abanakis.	Climate has four seasons. Plentiful food. Cold winters. Wampanoag tribe. Hunt, fish, plant. Father is teacher. Ceremonies for war and death. Animals: fox, bear, deer, hawk.	Great Sachem or leader knows fields, forests, and water. He decides just punishments. Council decides issues of war. Men make arrows, build fences and canoes. Women garden, tend fields, care for needs. Relationships with Mother Earth.	Paths bind villages. Trade with Narragansetts for soapstone, pipes, bowls, and beads. Trade pipes, bowls, beads, and corn with Abanakis for birchbark. Make [birchbark] into canoes. Play games with other nations. Move for survival.	Vegetation: woods, fields, and forests. Regions divided according to hunting grounds. May fight over fishing and hunting grounds.

From Donna E. Norton and Saundra E. Norton, *Language Arts Activities for Children,* 3rd ed. Upper Saddle River, N.J.: Merrill/Prentice Hall, 1999.

for each of the books. On this chart, place the five themes of geography. As the students read or listen to each book, ask them to identify and discuss the information appropriate for each of the categories. See Chart 11–9 for an example of this analysis using *People of the Breaking Day.* You may use many additional books for this activity, including Francine Jacobs's *The Tainos: The People Who Welcomed Columbus* and George DeLucenay Leon's *Explorers of the Americas Before Columbus.*

Phase Four: Historical Fiction

If students are examining literature from the Great Plains, Jan Hudson's *Sweetgrass* is excellent for analyzing historical fiction according to authenticity of setting, credibility of conflict, believability of characterization, authenticity of traditional beliefs, appropriateness of themes, and the author's style. The setting is among the Blackfoot people in southern Canada. The conflict develops a person-against-society problem. European expansion and smallpox cause the Native American characters to face disruption of their lives. The person-against-self conflicts result when characters must overcome differences in belief systems or taboos to survive within

their cultures. Without an understanding of Blackfoot values and beliefs, these conflicts would not seem believable. *Sweetgrass* is especially effective for showing students that language should reflect the people, the setting, and the time period. Have students consider the effectiveness of the figurative language and prairie symbolism to describe characters, setting, and conflict.

In Paul Goble's *Beyond the Ridge,* students should discover a belief in the afterlife as experienced by an elderly Indian woman from the Great Plains. This belief is also found in traditional literature.

The following example shows how to present a historical fiction text from the Southwest. Scott O'Dell's *Sing Down the Moon* is based on a tragic time in Navaho history, spanning 1863 to 1865. The story begins during a beautiful spring in Canyon de Chelly. Life seems promising. Then, the United States government sends Colonel Kit Carson to the canyon to bring the Navahos to Fort Sumner, New Mexico. In order to force the Indians' surrender, the troops destroy the crops and livestock. Then, they drive the Navahos to the fort. This three-hundred-mile journey is known as The Long Walk. While at Fort Sumner, more than fifteen hundred Indians died, and many others lost their will to live.

The creation stories of the Navahos refer to creating the mountains as "singing up the mountains." Ask students: What is the significance of Scott O'Dell's title *Sing Down the Moon*? What happened to the Navaho way of life during the years depicted in the story? Why did the government force the Indians to leave their home? If people today were Navahos living at that time, how might they feel? How might a soldier feel?

When it was time for Bright Morning to become a woman, the tribe prepared for the Womanhood Ceremony. Have students investigate the ceremonies celebrated by Navaho Indians. In groups, have students demonstrate one ceremony to the rest of the class and explain its purpose.

Tall Boy made a lance to use against the Long Knives. The only materials with which he had to work were those available in nature. Have students investigate other weapons and tools that Native Americans used, review how the people made the weapons and tools, and draw a picture of each.

In *Sing Down the Moon,* Bright Morning steps on a spear and breaks it when her son reaches out toward a young lamb. Discuss the symbolic meaning of this action.

Many clues in *Sing Down the Moon* suggest the environment in which Bright Morning and her tribe live. For example, O'Dell develops a visual image, describing the canyons: "The stone walls of the canyons stand so close together that you can touch them with your outstretched hand" (p. 1). He describes the rain through Bright Morning's thoughts: "At first it was a whisper, like a wind among the dry corn stalks of our cornfield" (p. 2). O'Dell suggests that even the streams have a voice of their own: "The stream sounded like men's voices speaking" (p. 53). These descriptions also suggest characteristics of the Navahos' environment, as well as their respect for nature, and whether they were a hunting or a farming tribe.

Discuss the significance of the descriptions in O'Dell's language. How does O'Dell feel about the Navahos? Have students search for other visual language that describes the various environments experienced by the Navahos as they leave their canyon and go to Fort Sumner. Compare the canyon environment with that at Fort Sumner and draw pictures of both locations.

For creative writing, have the students describe two environments, one that is lovely and enjoyable to live in and one that is not. Have the students draw a picture illustrating each and describe the pictures using language that will allow someone else to visualize them. Before completing Phase Four, ask the students to summarize their findings and to trace any threads that continue through Phases One through Four.

Phase Five: Contemporary Literature

Contemporary Native American poetry is especially rich in symbolism and mythological references. Allow students to discover the close relationships between the folklore read in Phases One and Two and contemporary texts. For example, ask students to read Jamake Highwater's *Moonsong Lullaby* and to identify mythological references, personification of nature, and foundations in traditional beliefs. A cognitive web such as Figure 11–1 is an excellent way to help students identify relationships.

Read the poem *Moonsong Lullaby* for the enjoyment of the words and the imagery. Draw a web on the board with the title in the center and the circled topics extending from the center. Tell the students that *Moonsong Lullaby* shows very close relationships between nature and the people. Ask the students to identify evidence of these close relationships through such topics as the personification of nature, mythological references within the poem, and foundations on traditional beliefs. Tell the students that they will need to use the knowledge that they have acquired about Native American peoples in the previous phases of their study. After the students complete the web, have them analyze the appropriateness of the language for a Native American poem that emphasizes traditional beliefs. If the students are studying the Southwest, Byrd Baylor's poem about the Papago Indians, *The Desert Is Theirs,* is an excellent choice for a similar activity.

Several contemporary fiction books are interesting for analysis and comparison. For example, younger students may search for any evidence of continuity in the writings of Virginia Driving Hawk Sneve while older students analyze Robert Lipsyte's *The Brave.* White Deer of Autumn's contemporary story *Ceremony—In the Circle of Life* is an excellent book for comparing the values in realistic fiction and folklore. For example, ask the students to compare

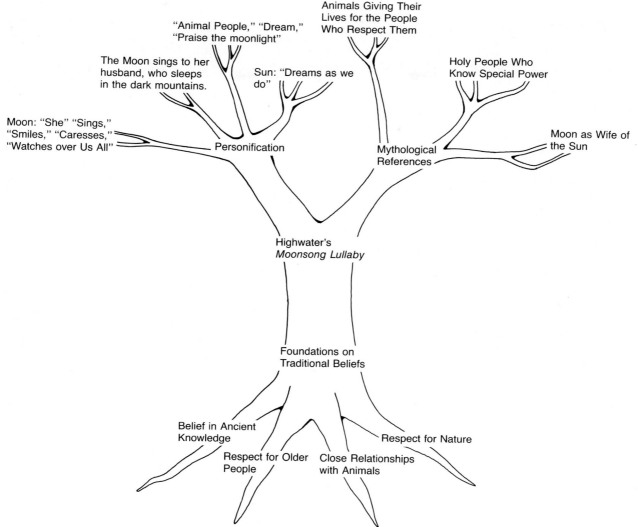

FIGURE 11–1 *Relationships between folklore and Jamake Highwater's* Moonsong Lullaby

The following labels appear on the tree diagram:

"Animal People," "Dream," "Praise the moonlight"

Animals Giving Their Lives for the People Who Respect Them

The Moon sings to her husband, who sleeps in the dark mountains.

Sun: "Dreams as we do"

Holy People Who Know Special Power

Moon: "She" "Sings," "Smiles," "Caresses," "Watches over Us All"

Personification

Mythological References

Moon as Wife of the Sun

Highwater's *Moonsong Lullaby*

Foundations on Traditional Beliefs

Belief in Ancient Knowledge

Respect for Older People

Close Relationships with Animals

Respect for Nature

Ceremony and *The Legend of the Bluebonnet.* (Chart 11–10 compares these books.) Have the students discuss the results of the comparison and consider the reasons for the similarities between the values in the traditional tale and the contemporary story.

Byrd Baylor's contemporary story from the Southwest, *Hawk, I'm Your Brother,* is another excellent choice for comparative studies. Through this book, students can visualize the close relationships between a Native American boy and a hawk. There are also frequent references to dreams of flying and ancient knowledge. In addition to identifying relationships between traditional folklore and contemporary stories, you may use *Hawk, I'm Your Brother* to help children recognize differences in point of view and to motivate the writing of a story from another point of view. Such activities help students analyze the characterizations within the book. Use the

CHART 11–10 A Comparison of Values in Traditional and Contemporary Native American Literature

Comparisons	Traditional Folklore *The Legend of the Bluebonnet*	Contemporary Fiction *Ceremony—In the Circle of Life*
What is the problem?	Drought and famine that are killing the Comanche	Destruction of the land by humans
What reward is desired?	To end the drought and famine To save the land and people	To comfort and honor Mother Earth To teach humans about Mother Earth
What actions (or values) are rewarded or admired?	Sacrifice to save the land and tribe Belief in the Great Spirit	Honor and care for Mother Earth Living in harmony with nature Knowledge, truth, and belief
What actions are punished or despised?	Selfishness Taking from Earth without giving back	Pollution and destruction of Mother Earth
What rewards are given?	Bluebonnets, as a sign of forgiveness Rain to end the drought A name change	A living pipe to symbolize the vision of Mother Earth New strength, knowledge, and understanding
What are the personal characteristics of heroes, heroines, or great people?	Unselfish love of the people and land Respect for the Great Spirit Willingness to sacrifice to benefit others	Love of animals and the land Respect for the Star Spirit and the ways of the people Desire for knowledge and truth

following instructional sequence for developing understanding of point of view:

1. Introduce the story and tell the students that they will be listening to a story in which the author describes and develops the hero's aspirations. Ask the students to consider how they would feel as Rudy Soto. Also, ask them to consider the feelings and desires of the hawk.
2. After reading *Hawk, I'm Your Brother* aloud, lead a discussion in which the students characterize Rudy and the hawk, and identify the major sequence of events leading up to Rudy's decision to release the hawk.
3. Ask the students to consider the significance of the title of the book. Why did Baylor choose *Hawk, I'm Your Brother?* Is it an accurate description of Rudy Soto's relationship to the hawk? How are Rudy and the hawk alike? How are they different? Why did Rudy release the hawk? How do you think Rudy felt after releasing the hawk? How do you think the hawk felt after being released? What would you do if you were Rudy Soto? How would you react if you were the hawk?

4. Tell the students that an incident may be described in different ways by several people who have the same experience. The details that characters describe, the feelings that they experience, and their beliefs in the right or wrong of an incident may vary. Consequently, the same story could change drastically, depending on the point of view of the storyteller. Ask the students to tell you whose point of view Baylor develops in *Hawk, I'm Your Brother.* How did they know that the story was told from Rudy Soto's point of view? Then, ask the students to consider how the story might be written if the author chose the hawk's point of view.

5. Ask the students to imagine that they are the hawk that Rudy captured. Have them write a story about what happened to them, beginning

from the time of the capture from the nest high on Santos Mountain.

As a conclusion to Phase Five, summarize the findings and the threads discovered across the ages of literature. Review examples of continuity and evidences of change. What do the students know about the literature of Native Americans that will make a difference in their lives?

 ### DEVELOPING AN APPRECIATION FOR HISPANIC AMERICAN CULTURE

Hispanic literature and culture are very complex. This complexity results from the infusion of numerous influences. Jose Griego y Maestas and Rudolfo A. Anaya (1980) reinforce the importance of the traditional literature in understanding the culture and show the complexity of such a study. They say that the tales

are a great part of the soul of our culture, and they reflect the values of our forefathers. . . .

The stories reflect a history of thirteen centuries of infusing and blending from the Moors and Jews in Spain, to the orientals in the Philippines, Africans in the Caribbean, and the Indians in America—be they Aztec, Apache or Pueblo. (p. 4)

This chapter includes the ancient literature of the Aztecs and Maya, proceeds to the more recent folklore of Mexico and America, and then concludes with contemporary Hispanic American poetry and fiction.

Phase One: Ancient Aztec and Mayan Folklore

Ancient folklore was first recorded for European audiences by the Spaniards in the sixteenth century. Introduce the folklore by showing students a map of Mexico and Central America that indicates locations of Aztec and Mayan peoples, such as those found in various adult sources, including *Atlas of Ancient America,* by Michael Coe, Dean Snow, and Elizabeth Benson (1986); *The Maya,* by Michael Coe (1984); and *The King Danced in the Marketplace,* by Frances Gillmor (1977). These books are also excellent sources for additional information about these ancient cultures.

Myths found in Carleton Beals's *Stories Told by the Aztecs: Before the Spaniards Came* allow students to identify characteristics of Aztec folklore and to discover the importance of the three gods that dominate much of the mythology and other literature:

(1) Quetzalcoatl, the Plumed Serpent, who drove out earlier animal gods and led the Toltecs in the Central Valley of Mexico; (2) Tezcatlipoca, the Black Mirror that Smokes, leader of the Chichimeca, or Stone Men; (3) and Huitzilopochtli, the Left-legged Hummingbird, the Aztec war god also known as Mexitli, Heart of the Maguey, after whom modern Mexico is named. (p. 10)

John Bierhorst's *The Hungry Woman: Myths and Legends of the Aztecs* is another source for Aztec literature.

After students read or listen to some of the Aztec tales and look at Aztec art in such sources as the *Atlas of Ancient America,* have them analyze the inclusion of Aztec tales and art in Deborah Nourse Lattimore's *The Flame of Peace: A Tale of the Aztecs.* Lattimore states that she combined "the known elements and the lively, authentic art with some educated guesses based on my research and knowledge of the period—to create a story with pictures that I hope will satisfy those two most critical audiences: scholars and children" (endcover). Students should use their own research abilities to decide if she reached her goal. What evidence do they have that Lattimore based her story on research and knowledge?

John Bierhorst's *The Monkey's Haircut and Other Stories Told by the Maya* provides a source for students to identify characteristics of and values in Mayan folklore. For example, have students search for stories that have the following values and characteristics identified by Bierhorst: (1) cleverness, as shown by stories that include riddles, puns, double meanings, and tricksters; (2) culture, such as paying a bride service and being godparents; (3) corn and farming practices.

Have students search for characteristics and values in other tales from before interaction with the Spanish culture. They will discover many of the values previously discussed. In addition, they will find stories that reflect such values as need to sacrifice for the betterment of the group and the worthiness of bravery and honor. Good choices for this activity include Francisco Hinojosa's *The Old Lady Who Ate People,* Harriet Rohmer and Dorminster Wilson's *Mother Scorpion Country,* and Vivien Blackmore's *Why Corn Is Golden: Stories About Plants.*

Ask the students to use all of the information that they have gained from a study of ancient folklore to analyze and interpret Toni de Gerez's adaptation of an ancient Toltec poem, *My Song Is a Piece of Jade*. Ask the students to identify the values, characters, and mythological references that they discover in the folklore. Ask them to identify any additional information that the poetry reveals about the culture. Also, ask them to consider how and why a study of the mythological foundations of the people has made this poem more interesting and understandable. Before leaving Phase One, have the students summarize their findings.

Phase Two: Stories That Reflect Interaction with Other Cultures

Many of the values, beliefs, and characteristics of ancient literature are found in more recent traditional literature. The most dramatic difference coincides with the arrival of Cortés and the Spanish. A large body of folklore reflects the interactions between the ancient peoples and Christianity. Some tales show the clash of cultural values while others reflect stories that changed because of the settings. Teachers should choose tales according to the appropriateness for the ages of their students. For example, tales that reflect interactions between the people and Christianity include Tomie dePaola's *The Lady of Guadalupe* and John Bierhorst's *Spirit Child: A Story of the Nativity*, a translation. *The Invisible Hunters*, by Harriet Rohmer, Octavio Chow, and Morris Vidaure, may help students understand what happens when cultures clash.

Changes due to place are easy to identify in *Doctor Coyote: A Native American Aesop's Fables*, Bierhorst's retelling from an Aztec manuscript. Have students identify the relationships with the earlier Aesop and the trickster characters of Indian lore.

José Griego y Maestas and Rudolfo A. Anaya's *Cuentos: Tales from the Hispanic Southwest* includes numerous tales that are valuable for Phase Two. For example, students enjoy comparing one of the tales, "The Man Who Knew the Language of the Animals," with Verna Aardema's *What's So Funny, Ketu?*, which is based on an African tale. Have the students identify the similarities and differences and note ways in which the differences reflect cultural differences.

Older students may compare the "Hansel and Gretel" variants from Spain and Mexico found in James Taggart's article, " 'Hansel and Gretel' in Spain and Mexico" (1986). Have them compare these versions with the Grimms's tales. These variants are more complex and include changes in the tales due to male or female storytellers.

Before leaving Phase Two, have the students summarize similarities and differences between Phases One and Two and consider reasons for the stories to be either alike or different.

Phase Three: Historical Nonfiction

Several books can help students understand the Aztecs and Maya. For example, Cottie Burland's *An Aztec Town* provides background information and drawings of different parts of a city. Albert Marrin's *Aztecs and Spaniards: Cortés and the Conquest of Mexico* describes the culture and the conquest. *The Mystery of the Ancient Maya*, by Carolyn Meyer and Charles Gallenkamp, explores the ancient culture. Albert Marrin's *Empires Lost and Won: The Spanish Heritage in the Southwest* traces the history of Spanish involvement.

Phase Four: Historical Fiction

An understanding of history is important for students to analyze historical fiction about the Spanish conquest. Older students may read and analyze the historical accuracy and trace the traditional beliefs in such books as Scott O'Dell's *The Captive, The Feathered Serpent*, and *The Amethyst Ring*. In *The King's Fifth*, O'Dell accompanies Coronado's army as it searches for the golden cities of the Southwest.

Ann Nolan Clark's historical fiction provides gentler sources for analysis. For example, *Secret of the Andes* is an Inca story that reveals the importance of respecting elders, giving and sharing oneself, and making discoveries.

Phase Five: Contemporary Literature

Of the groups studied thus far, there are fewer contemporary Hispanic literature selections available for children. Likewise, contemporary study may require broadening the base of Hispanic literature to include authors of Cuban or Puerto Rican ancestry. Authors who may be analyzed include Pura Belpre, Nicole DeMessieres, Francisco Hinojosa, Nicholasa Mohr, Sandra Cisneros, Gary Soto, and Richard García.

Many stories, such as Cisneros's *The House on Mango Street*, express the pain and fear of characters who struggle to find themselves in a world that is often alien. In books such as Nicholasa Mohr's *Going Home,* have students analyze the forces that cause an American girl from Puerto Rican ancestry not to be accepted by Puerto Rican girls.

The Newbery Medal winner, . . . *And Now Miguel,* by Joseph Krumgold, includes many cultural values and beliefs. In addition, the book provides insights into a young boy's development. The following example shows how you might share and discuss this book.

Ask students if there has ever been anything they wanted to do very badly but were told by their parents that they couldn't do until they were older. Talk about some of the things that the students mention. Discuss the possible reasons why the students would have to be older to do those things. Then explain that this book is about a twelve-year-old boy who wants something and that the story is about how he goes about getting what he wants.

The book can be read aloud to children or individually by children, if there are enough copies. If each child has a copy, read the beginning of a chapter aloud and have the students read the remainder of the chapter silently.

Chapter one describes the setting in detail. Prepare a map of New Mexico showing the Sangre de Cristo mountain range, the Rio Grande River, the city of Taos, and the San Juan mountain range. Show the cliffs of the San Juan range going down to the Rio Grande. Have the children locate and label each detail on the map. Then, have them trace the migration of the sheep as described by Miguel in chapter one. The beginning chapters also mention the following landforms: cliff, mountain, mesa, plain, canyon, and arroyo. Collect pictures to show examples of each type of landform. Discuss characteristics of each picture and ways in which the characteristics relate to the section in the story.

In chapter two, Miguel says that he must take his winter clothes to wear in the mountains even though it will be summer. Have the children speculate about the reasons for the differences between the temperature on the plain and in the mountains. Using reference books, have a group of children find the temperature ranges for New Mexico. Have them check other areas where there is a plain and there are nearby mountains. Have them check differences in temperature according to elevation. Lead them into a generalization on the effect of elevation on temperature and on Miguel's plans.

Miguel comes from a large, multigenerational family. Starting with Grandfather Chavez, have the children make a genealogical chart of the Chavez family. Then have them make charts of their own families.

The life of the Chavez family revolves around the life cycle of the sheep. Review the cycle with the children: winter on the mesa, back to the ranch in early spring for the birth of the lambs and the shearing, and into the mountains for the summer. Discuss the importance of sheep to the Chavez family and the ways in which the sheep influence the life-style and desires of each family member.

Ask the children to imagine that they are Miguel and are planning their trip into the mountains. They will be gone all summer, so they must take everything with them. Have them list everything that they will need and give reasons for using valuable space on the pack mule to take each item. In addition, ask the children to pretend that they are Miguel and use a diary format to write their feelings and experiences as they try to convince the family that they are old enough to accompany the men to the summer pasture.

Mutual cooperation within the family is an important value stressed in the book. Discuss how each family member contributes to the family's welfare.

Another value is the strong integration of religious beliefs into daily life. There are references to this value throughout the book, but this value is particularly strong beginning with chapter eight, in which Miguel explains about San Ysidro to the readers. Grandfather Chavez is the embodiment of the values, whereas Eil has seemingly rejected the religious values. Ask the students to identify values, beliefs, and themes in . . . *And Now Miguel* that are similar to the values, beliefs, and themes discovered in other Hispanic American literature. Ask the students to account for any similarities and differences.

 ### DEVELOPING AN APPRECIATION FOR ASIAN AMERICAN CULTURE

Because there are so many different Asian groups, a thorough study would require investigating the folklore from Japan, China, Vietnam, and other Eastern countries and then extending that analysis into historical and contemporary works. (See chapter 6 for a unit that emphasizes developing understandings of the Chinese culture.) Such an investigation is much too extensive for this chapter. However, if you are planning such a study, the writings of the following authors will be beneficial: Sumiko Yogawa, Taro Yashima, Laurence Yep, Paul Yee, Yoshiko Uchida, Yozo Otsuki, He Liyi, Huynh Quang Nhuong, Allen Say, Shizuye Takashima, and Toshi Maruki.

Traditional Tales

A Japanese style of storytelling that is especially interesting to children is the *kamishibai*—an outdoor form of storytelling with pictures. Although it is not so old as the African and Native American techniques discussed earlier, it is different from either the African or the Native American traditions.

Story Opening.
Keigo Seki (1963) identifies an opening sentence that is often used in Japanese storytelling. The following opening can add an authentic flavor to storytelling in classrooms, especially if the storyteller begins the story in Japanese:

> Mukashi, mukash (Long, long ago)
> Aro tokoro ni (In a certain place)

Storytelling Style.
Kamishibai was performed by men who had a collection of about four stories that were illustrated on cards and shown in a wooden boxholder resembling a miniature stage. The stories were illustrated on a series of picture cards and then placed in a wooden holder about one foot high and eighteen inches wide. The front of the theater had flaps that opened to reveal the stage. The cards fit into a slot in the side of the box. The storyteller pulled the sequentially placed cards out of the box. The text was written on the back of the card that preceded the picture that was currently showing on the stage. (The title was the first card removed and placed in the back of the box; the text that accompanied the next picture was on the back of the title card. This procedure continued with each card as the story unfolded in pictures and words.)

Anne Pellowski (1977) describes how influential kamishibai storytelling has been in Japan:

Considering the impact that the kamishibai had on children's literature and the fact that the same publishers who produced the cards were also later producing children's books, it is no wonder that one of the most popular formats for children's picture books in Japan is the horizontal style reminiscent of the kamishibai. (p. 145)

A Japanese Kamishibai Presentation

A kamishibai storytelling experience with its box-holder and picture cards is an enjoyable way for children to illustrate a story, retell the story, and also experience the way in which Japanese children enjoy folktales. One group of children created a kamishibai theater out of a heavy cardboard box. First, they cut a viewing opening in the front of the box. Next, they cut flaps that could open and close across the front of the stage and attached them to the front sides of the box so the flaps could be in either an open position or a closed position. Then, they cut openings in the sides of the box so that the cards could be placed inside. They placed identical openings on either side so that the openings would provide support for the pictures viewed on the stage. They made the side openings a little taller than the front openings so that each card would be framed by the center stage.

Next, they cut tagboard cards to fit inside the theater. The cards were a few inches wider than the theater so that the storyteller could grasp them easily and remove them at the proper time. They were also slightly shorter than the side opening so that they would go in and out easily (see Figure 11–2).

The group chose a Japanese folktale, Arlene Mosel's *The Funny Little Woman,* to illustrate on the kamishibai picture cards. The group liked the story and wanted to illustrate the characters, including the wicked Oni (demons who live in underground caverns) and the old woman whom they kidnap and force to cook for them. The children selected the scenes that they wanted to illustrate, selected from this list the scene or scenes each one would draw (the original kamishibai presentations usually ranged from six to twenty scenes), and completed the drawings. They put the cards into sequence, including a title card for an introduction. Then, like authentic kamishibai storytellers, they wrote the dialogue for each card on the back of the card preceding it. They placed the cards in the theater and told the story to an appreciative audience. (As they removed each card, they placed it at the back of the box, so that the storytellers would have their cues in front of them.)

This activity is especially appropriate for small groups, because each group can select a particular

FIGURE 11–2 A kamishibai theater

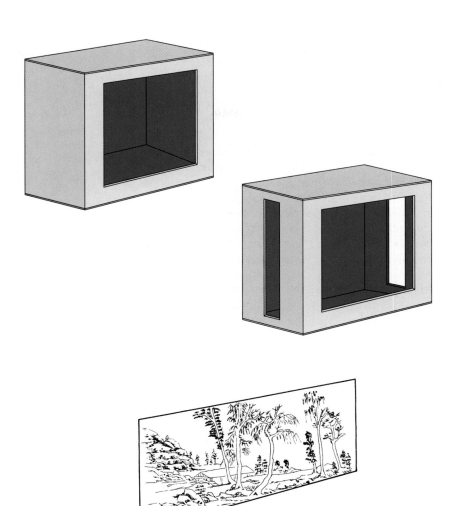

Japanese tale, prepare it for presentation, and present the story to the other groups. In that way, children can be both storytellers and audience. Arthur Levine's *The Boy Who Drew Cats: A Japanese Folktale* is another story excellent for kamishibai presentations.

 RECOGNIZING SIMILARITIES

One value of sharing multicultural literature with children is increasing the understanding of the children that those who belong to groups other than their own are real people, with feelings, emo-

tions, and needs similar to theirs. M. Elaine Aoki (1981) says that literature also can contribute to children's development of values. Consequently, she feels that adults must lead children in active discussions about those values. She says that this discussion should not be a didactic lesson, but it should help children gain positive attitudes toward all people. She identifies two steps that should be included in such discussion. First, children can take the viewpoint of a character in a story. When they are that character, they can consider what they would have done under similar circumstances and how they would have felt. Second, children can search for elements within the story that are related to their own experiences. They can identify times when they had feelings or needs like those the characters in the story express.

Many multicultural books, especially those written for young children, have themes suggesting that children everywhere have more similarities than differences. These books can stimulate discussions in which children relate similar experiences they have had, tell how they handled similar problems, suggest how they would feel if they had a similar experience, or relate ways they might respond to similar circumstances. For example, after reading John Steptoe's *Stevie,* children can talk about how they would feel if a younger child came to their room and broke their toys, how they would solve this problem if they were Stevie, and the feelings that they might experience if the child were no longer there. They can discover from discussing Valerie Flournoy's *The Patchwork Quilt* that love between grandparents and grandchildren is universal. Such love is also depicted in Takaaki Nomura's Japanese story, *Grandpa's Town,* and in Miska Miles's Native American story, *Annie and the Old One.*

Many books for older readers also suggest universal needs and emotions. You can use the following books to stimulate discussions on the topics suggested:

1. *Experiencing prejudice creates strong emotions:* Laurence Yep's *Dragonwings* (Chinese American), Nicholasa Mohr's *Felita* (Puerto Rican), Scott O'Dell's *Sing Down the Moon* (Native American), and Mildred Taylor's *Roll of Thunder, Hear My Cry* (African American).
2. *All people have dreams that influence their lives:* Laurence Yep's *Dragonwings* (Chinese American), Joseph Krumgold's *. . . And Now Miguel* (Spanish American-Basque), Robert Lipsyte's *The Brave* (Native American), and Paula Fox's *How Many Miles to Babylon?* (African American).
3. *Discovering one's own heritage brings pride:* Laurence Yep's *Child of the Owl* (Chinese American), Scott O'Dell's *Black Star, Bright Dawn* (Native American), and Virginia Hamilton's *Zeely* (African American).
4. *People can have strong feelings of love toward older family members:* Sook Nyul Choi's *Year of Impossible Goodbyes* (Korean), Miska Miles's *Annie and the Old One* (Native American), Sharon Bell Mathis's *The Hundred Penny Box* (African American), and Valerie Flournoy's *The Patchwork Quilt* (African American).

 SUGGESTED ACTIVITIES

for Involving Children in Multicultural Literature

- Choose African, Native American, or Asian traditional tales. Prepare a story opening, storytelling style, and story ending that reflect the authentic traditional presentation of the tales. Share the stories with a group of children or a peer group.

- Choose an African people other than the Ashanti. Suggest stories and other learning experiences that would allow children to develop an appreciation for the culture.

- Search a social studies or history curriculum and identify African Americans, Native Americans, Hispanic Americans, or Asian Americans who have made contributions during the time periods or subjects being studied. Identify literature selections that include additional information about those individuals and their contributions.

- Develop a time line showing the chronology of famous African Americans, Native Americans, Hispanic Americans, and Asian Americans. Identify literature that may be used with the time line.

- Develop a "What's My Line" program, round-table discussion, or a "Meet the Press" activity that stresses the contributions of famous African Americans, Native Americans, Hispanic Americans, or Asian Americans.

- Choose a multicultural story and develop a series of discussion questions that would allow children to gain insights into the culture portrayed in the book.

- Choose an Asian culture and develop a five-phase study that proceeds from traditional literature to contemporary Asian American literature.

- Read a book such as Hazel Rochman's *Against Borders: Promoting Books for a Multicultural World* (1992) or Carla Hayden's *Venture into Cultures: A Resource Book of Multicultural Materials and Programs* (1992). Rochman's book is a joint ALA and *Booklist* publication that expands *Booklist* bibliographies focusing on specific groups. The text includes essays on cultural issues and booktalks that explore various themes such as friends, love, and survival. Hayden's book includes an annotated list of books and program ideas for using multicultural literature. The cultures discussed in the book include African American, Arabic, Asian, Hispanic, Jewish, Native American, and Persian. Give a short report on the book to your children's literature class.

CHILDREN'S LITERATURE

ASIAN AMERICAN LITERATURE

Allen, Judy. *Tiger.* Illustrated by Tudor Humphries. Candlewick, 1992 (I:5–8 R:4). A hunter saves a South Chinese tiger by taking its picture rather than killing it.

Asian Culture Centre for UNESCO. *Folktales from Asia for Children Everywhere.* 3 vols. Weatherhill, 1976, 1977 (I:8–12 R:6). The folktales come from many Asian countries.

Choi, Sook Nyul. *Year of Impossible Goodbyes.* Houghton Mifflin, 1991 (I:10 R:5). A ten-year-old tells about her Korean family's experiences during the Japanese occupation in World War II.

Coerr, Eleanor. *Mieko and the Fifth Treasure.* Putnam, 1993 (I:8+ R:5). A young Japanese girl almost loses her gift for drawing when her hand is cut during the bombing of Nagasaki.

Czernecki, Stefan, retold by. *The Cricket's Cage: A Chinese Folktale.* Hyperion, 1997 (I:5–8 R:4). This is an illustrated version of the legend of the Forbidden City.

Friedman, Ina R. *How My Parents Learned to Eat.* Illustrated by Allen Say. Houghton Mifflin, 1984 (I:6–8 R:3). A humorous story is about eating with chopsticks or knives and forks.

Garland, Sherry. *The Lotus Seed.* Illustrated by Tatsuro Kivchi. Harcourt Brace Jovanovich, 1993 (I:5–8 R:4). A Vietnamese woman brings an important lotus seed with her when she and her family resettle in America.

Ho, Minfong. *Hush! A Thai Lullaby.* Illustrated by Holly Meade. Orchard, 1996 (I:all). A mother tries to quiet the animals so that her baby can sleep.

Hoyt-Goldsmith, Diane. *Hoang Anh: A Vietnamese-American Boy.* Photographs by Lawrence Migdale. Holiday, 1992 (I:5–9 R:4). Text and photographs describe the daily activities of a boy and his family who now live in San Rafael, California.

Huynh, Quang Nhuong. *Water Buffalo Days: Growing Up in Vietnam.* Illustrated by Jean and Mou-sien Tseng. HarperCollins, 1997 (I:8+ R:4). The author tells about his boyhood in Vietnam.

Hyun, Peter, ed. *Korea's Favorite Tales and Lyrics.* Illustrated by Dong-il Park. Tuttle/Seoul International, 1986 (I:5–10 R:6). This is a collection of folktales, poems, and stories.

Kim, Helen. *The Long Season of Rain.* Holt, 1996 (I:12+ R:6). Written from the point of view of an eleven-year-old Korean girl, the story tells about life in the 1960s.

Kodama, Tatsuharu. *Shin's Tricycle.* Illustrated by Noriyuki Ando. Walker, 1995 (I:all). This is a true story about an atomic bomb victim.

Levine, Arthur. *The Boy Who Drew Cats: A Japanese Folktale.* Illustrated by Frédéric Clément. Dial, 1993 (I:8+ R:5). The folktale is based on a version printed in Tokyo in 1898.

Lord, Bette Bao. *In the Year of the Boar and Jackie Robinson.* Illustrated by Marc Simont. Harper & Row, 1984 (I:8–12 R:4). Developing a love for baseball helps a Chinese girl make friends in America.

McCully, Emily Arnold. *Beautiful Warrior: The Legend of the Nun's Kung Fu.* Scholastic, 1998 (I:6-10 R:5). The art reflects classic Chinese painting in this story of kung fu masters.

McMahon, Patricia. *Chi-Hoon: A Korean Girl.* Photographs by Michael O'Brien. Caroline House, 1993 (I:8+ R:4). The text presents one week in the life of a Korean girl.

Melmed, Laura Krauss. *The First Song Ever Sung.* Illustrated by Ed Young. Lothrop Lee & Shepard, 1993 (I:4–8). In a Japanese setting, the illustrations and poetic text follow a boy as he poses the question, What was the first song ever sung?

Mosel, Arlene. *The Funny Little Woman.* Illustrated by Blair Lent. Dutton, 1972 (I:6–8 R:6). In a Japanese folktale, a woman steals a magic paddle.

Namioka, Lensey. *Yang the Youngest and His Terrible Ear.* Illustrated by Kees de Kiefe. Little, Brown, 1992 (I:8+ R:4). A nine-year-old moves with his musical family from China to Seattle.

Nhuong, Huynh Quang. *The Land I Lost: Adventures of a Boy in Vietnam.* Illustrated by Vo-Dinh Mai. Harper & Row, 1982 (I:8–12 R:6). The author tells about his boyhood experiences in Vietnam.

Nomura, Takaaki. *Grandpa's Town.* Translated by Amanda Mayer Stinchecum. Kane-Miller, 1991 (I:3–7 R:4). The text written in both Japanese and English follows a boy and his grandfather around the grandfather's town.

Salisbury, Graham. *Under the Blood Red Sun.* Delacorte, 1995 (I:8+ R:6). A Japanese American boy and his best friend find their activities disrupted by the bombing of Pearl Harbor.

Say, Allen. *Grandfather's Journey.* Houghton Mifflin, 1993 (I:all). The illustrations and text cover the immigration story of a Japanese American.

_____. *Tree of Cranes.* Houghton Mifflin, 1991 (I:5–8 R:4). A Japanese boy's mother shares her California Christmas with her son.

Spivak, Dawnine. *Grass Sandals: The Travels of Basho.* Illustrated by Demi. Simon & Schuster, 1997 (I:8+). This picture book is set in seventeenth-century Japan.

Surat, Michele Maria. *Angel Child, Dragon Child.* Illustrated by Vo-Dinh Mai. Carnival/Raintree, 1983 (I:6–8 R:4). A young Vietnamese child learns to adjust to her American home.

Uchida, Yoshiko. *Invisible Thread.* Messner, 1992 (I:10+ R:6). A Japanese American tells her own experiences in this autobiography.

Waters, Kate, and Madeline Slovenz-Low. *Lion Dancer: Ernie Wan's Chinese New Year.* Photographs by Martha Cooper. Scholastic, 1990 (I:5–8 R:3). A six-year-old boy performs his first lion dance.

Yagawa, Sumiko. *The Crane Wife.* Illustrated by Suekichi Akaba. Morrow, 1981 (I:all R:6). A traditional Japanese tale depicts the consequences of greed.

Yee, Paul. *Tales from Gold Mountain: Stories of the Chinese in the New World.* Macmillan, 1990 (I:10+ R:5). Eight original stories are based on the experiences of Chinese immigrants.

Yep, Laurence. *The Case of the Goblin Pearls.* HarperCollins, 1997 (I:8+ R:4). This is a mystery set in San Francisco's Chinatown.

_____. *Child of the Owl.* Harper & Row, 1977 (I:10+ R:7). Casey learns to respect her heritage and to look deep inside herself.

_____. *Dragonwings.* Harper & Row, 1975 (I:10+ R:6). In 1903, eight-year-old Moon Shadow helps his father build a flying machine.

_____. *Hiroshima.* Scholastic, 1995 (I:9+ R:4). The book tells the story of the dropping of the atomic bomb.

I = Interest by age level.

R = Readability by grade level.

_____ . *Later, Gater*. Hyperion, 1995 (I:9+ R:4). Sibling rivalry is the focus of the book.

_____ . *The Man Who Tricked a Ghost*. Illustrated by Isadore Seltzer. Troll, 1993 (I:5–8 R:4). Set in medieval China, the story tells about a boy who outwits a ghost.

_____ . *The Rainbow People*. Illustrated by David Wiesner. Harper & Row, 1989 (I:8+ R:5). This text includes Chinese folktales that were collected from Asian Americans.

_____ . *The Serpent's Children*. Harper & Row, 1984 (I:10+ R:6). In nineteenth-century China, a girl finds that she has strength to protect her family.

_____ . *Star Fisher*. Morrow, 1991 (I:10+ R:6). In 1927, a Chinese American family experiences prejudice when they move to West Virginia.

_____ . *Thief of Hearts*. HarperCollins, 1995 (I:10+ R:6). This is a sequel to *Child of the Owl*.

AFRICAN AMERICAN LITERATURE

Aardema, Verna. *Bringing the Rain to Kapiti Plain: A Nandi Tale*. Illustrated by Beatriz Vidal. Dial, 1981 (I:5–8). This is a cumulative tale from Kenya.

_____ . *How the Ostrich Got Its Long Neck*. Illustrated by Marcia Brown. Scholastic, 1995 (I:4–7 R:6). A pourquoi tale from Kenya.

_____ , retold by. *The Lonely Lioness and the Ostrich Chicks: A Masai Tale*. Illustrated by Yumi Heo. Knopf, 1996 (I:5–8 R:4). Clever actions overcome strength.

_____ . *Misoso: Once Upon a Time Tales from Africa*. Illustrated by Reynold Ruffins. Knopf, 1994 (I:8+ R:3). This is a collection of twelve tales.

_____ . *This For That: A Tonga Tale*. Illustrated by Victoria Chess. Dial, 1997 (I:5–8 R:5). The tale develops the moral that truth will overtake lies.

_____ . *What's So Funny, Ketu?* Illustrated by Marc Brown. Dial, 1982 (I:all R:4). This is a tale from Sudan.

_____ . *Who's in Rabbit's House?* Illustrated by Leo and Diane Dillon. Dial, 1977 (I:7+ R:3). A Masai folktale is illustrated as a play performed by villagers wearing masks.

_____ . *Why Mosquitoes Buzz in People's Ears*. Illustrated by Leo and Diane Dillon. Dial, 1975 (I:5–9 R:6). An African folktale explains why mosquitoes buzz.

Adoff, Arnold. *In for Winter, Out for Spring*. Illustrated by Jerry Pinkney. Harcourt Brace Jovanovich, 1991 (I:all). Beautiful illustrations accompany poetry that shows the four seasons.

_____ . *Malcolm X*. Crowell, 1970 (I:7–12 R:5). This is a biography of the African American leader.

_____ , ed. *The Poetry of Black America: Anthology of the 20th Century*. Harper & Row, 1973. This text includes over six hundred poems by African American poets.

Alexander, Lloyd. *The Fortune-Tellers*. Illustrated by Trina Schart Hyman. Dutton, 1992 (I:all). A fortune teller's predictions come true.

Applebaum, Diana. *Cocoa Ice*. Illustrated by Holly Meade. Orchard, 1997 (I:5–8 R:4). The book focuses on two girls, one from Santo Domingo and one from Maine.

Arnold, Adoff, ed. *I Am the Darker Brother: An Anthology of Modern Poems by African Americans*, revised edition. Illustrated by Benny Andrews. Simon & Schuster, 1997 (I:10+). This revised edition includes contemporary poets such as Maya Angelou.

Ashabranner, Brent, and Russell Davis. *The Lion's Whiskers: And Other Ethiopian Tales*, revised edition. Illustrated by Helen Siegl. Linnet, 1996 (I:8+). The collection includes sixteen tales.

Bentley, Judith. *Harriet Tubman*. Watts, 1990 (I:10+ R:6). This is a biography of one of the leaders of the Underground Railroad.

Berry, James. *Ajeemah and His Son*. HarperCollins, 1991 (I:10+ R:6). A father and son are taken from Africa and sold into slavery.

Bray, Rosemary L. *Martin Luther King*. Illustrated by Malcah Zeldis. Greenwillow, 1995 (I:7–10 R:4). Folk-art paintings illustrate this biography.

Brown, Kevin. *Malcolm X: His Life and Legacy*. Millbrook, 1995 (I:12+ R:13). This is a biography of the Black Muslim leader.

Bryan, Ashley. *All Night, All Day: A Child's First Book of African-American Spirituals*. Atheneum, 1991 (I:3–8). Words and music accompany the illustrations.

_____ . *Beat the Story-Drum, Pum-Pum*. Atheneum, 1980 (I:6+ R:5). This is a collection of tales.

_____ . *The Cat's Purr*. Atheneum, 1985 (I:6+ R:4). A folktale that reveals why cats purr.

_____ . *The Story of Lightning & Thunder*. Atheneum, 1993 (I:6+ R:5). A Nigerian folktale.

_____ . *Turtle Knows Your Name*. Atheneum, 1989 (I:6+ R:5). This folktale is from the West Indies.

Burns, Khephra and William Miles. *Black Stars in Orbit: NASA's African American Astronauts*. Harcourt Brace, 1995 (I:10+ R:10). The text tells the story of African American astronauts.

Carew, Jan. *Children of the Sun*. Illustrated by Leo and Diane Dillon. Little, Brown, 1980. (I:8+ R:6). Twin boys, the children of the sun, search the world to discover the values they wish to live by.

Clifton, Lucille. *Everett Anderson's Goodbye*. Illustrated by Ann Grifalconi. Holt, Rinehart & Winston, 1983 (I:6–9). Written in poetic form, the story describes a boy's pain after his father's death.

Collier, James, and Christopher Collier. *Jump Ship to Freedom*. Delacorte, 1981 (I:10+ R:7). A slave acquires his freedom and that of his mother.

Cooper, Michael L. *Hell Fighters: African American Soldiers in World War I*. Lodestar, 1997 (I:12+ R:7). The setting is World War I and the mostly African American infantry regiment.

Courlander, Harold. *The Crest and the Hide: And Other African Stories of Heroes, Chiefs, Bards, Hunters, Sorcerers, and Common People*. Illustrated by Monica Vachula. Coward, McCann, 1982 (I:8+ R:5). Twenty tales are from the Ashanti, Swahili, Lega, Tswana, and Yoruba cultures of Africa.

Crews, Donald. *Bigmama's*. Greenwillow, 1991 (I:5–7). Children visit Bigmama in Florida.

_____ . *Shortcut*. Greenwillow, 1992 (I:5–7). The children have a frightening experience when they walk the railroad tracks.

Curry, Barbara K., and James Michael Brodie. *Sweet Words So Brave: The Story of African American Literature*. Illustrated by Jerry Butler. Zino, 1996 (I:10+ R:5). A man tells his granddaughter about the literature of his people.

Day, Nancy Raines. *The Lion's Whiskers: An Ethiopian Folktale*. Illustrated by Ann Grifalconi. Scholastic, 1995 (I:5–8 R:5). A woman discovers how to solve her problems.

Dee, Ruby. *Tower to Heaven*. Illustrated by Jennifer Bent. Holt, 1991 (I:6–9 R:5). The story tells why the god, Onyankopon, lives in the sky.

DeKay, James T. *Meet Martin Luther King, Jr.* Illustrated by Ted Burwell. Random House, 1969 (I:7–12 R:4). This biography stresses the magnitude of Martin Luther King's work and the reasons he fought against injustice.

De Trevino, Elizabeth Borton. *I, Juan de Pareja.* Farrar, Straus & Giroux, 1965 (I:11 R:7). The story is based on the true characters of a seventeenth-century Spanish painter and his African slave.

Dragonwagon, Crescent. *Home Place.* Illustrated by Jerry Pinkney. Macmillan, 1990 (I:6–8 R:4). A family visits an old home site.

Edwards, Pamela Duncan. *Barefoot: Escape on the Underground Railroad.* Illustrated by Henry Cole. HarperCollins, 1997 (I:5–8 R:4). An escaping slave is helped by wild animals.

Ellis, Veronica Freeman. *Afro-Bets First Book About Africa.* Just Us Books, 1990 (I:8–12 R:5). The text includes a natural, social, and political history of Africa.

Everett, Gwen. *John Brown: One Man Against Slavery.* Illustrated by Jacob Lawrence. Rizzoli, 1993 (I:8+ R:5). Sixteen of the artworks created by Lawrence in 1941 are included in this story about John Brown and the raid on Harper's Ferry.

_____ .*Li'l Sis and Uncle Willie: A Story Based on the Life and Paintings of William H. Johnson.* Rizzoli, 1992 (I:all). A fictionalized story is built on the paintings of the artist.

Fairman, Tony, retold by. *Bury My Bones But Keep My Words: African Tales for Retelling.* Illustrated by Meshack Asare. Holt, 1993 (I:8+ R:5). Twelve tales are from various African cultures.

Farmer, Nancy. *A Girl Named Disaster.* Jackson, 1996 (I:10+). A girl leaves her remote village in Mozambique.

Feelings, Muriel. *Jambo Means Hello: Swahili Alphabet Book.* Dial, 1974 (I:all). A beautiful book uses the Swahili alphabet.

_____ . *Moja Means One: Swahili Counting Book.* Illustrated by Tom Feelings. Dial, 1971 (I:all). A beautiful book uses Swahili numbers.

Feelings, Tom. *The Middle Passage: White Ships/Black Cargo.* Dial, 1995 (I:10+). This wordless book provides a historical narrative in pictures.

Ferris, Jeri. *Go Free or Die: A Story of Harriet Tubman.* Carolrhoda, 1988 (I:7+ R:4). The biography describes Tubman's experiences during slavery and the Underground Railroad.

Fields, Julia. *The Green Lion of Zion Street.* Illustrated by Jerry Pinkney, Macmillan, 1988 (I:6–9). Children make up an imaginary story about the stone lion.

Flournoy, Valerie. *The Patchwork Quilt.* Illustrated by Jerry Pinkney. Dial, 1985 (I:5–8 R:4). Constructing a quilt brings a family together.

Fox, Paula. *How Many Miles to Babylon?* Illustrated by Paul Giovanopoulos. White, 1967 (I:8+ R:3). Ten-year-old James discovers who he really is when he is abducted by a gang of boys.

_____ . *Slave Dancer.* Illustrated by Eros Keith. Bradbury, 1973 (I:12+ R:7). In 1840, a fife player experiences the misery of the slave trade.

Gerson, Mary-Joan. *Why the Sky Is Far Away: A Nigerian Folktale.* Illustrated by Carla Golembe. Little, Brown, 1992 (I:4–8 R:5). This is a pourquoi tale from Nigeria.

Gray, Libba Moore. *Little Lil and the Swing-Singing Sax.* Illustrated by Lisa Cohen. Simon & Schuster, 1996 (I:5–9 R:4). Little Lil's uncle is a renowned saxophone player.

Greene, Bette. *Philip Hall Likes Me. I Reckon Maybe.* Illustrated by Charles Lilly. Dial, 1974 (I:10+ R:4). Beth Lambert experiences her first crush.

Greenfield, Eloise. *Nathaniel Talking.* Illustrated by Jan Gilchrist. Black Butterfly Children's Books, 1989 (I:all). A boy's life is revealed through rap and verse.

_____ . *Night on Neighborhood Street.* Illustrated by Jan Spivey Gilchrist. Dial, 1991 (I:5–8 R:4). The text and illustrations depict the activities on a street.

_____ . *Rosa Parks.* Illustrated by Eric Marlow. Crowell, 1973 (I:7–10 R:4). This biography is about the woman who refused to give up her bus seat in Montgomery, Alabama.

_____ . *Sister.* Illustrated by Moneta Barnett. Crowell, 1974 (I:8–12 R:5). Thirteen-year-old Doretha reviews the memories written in her journal.

_____ . *Under the Sunday Tree.* Illustrated by Amos Ferguson. Harper & Row, 1988 (I:all). Poetry is about the Bahamas.

Grifalconi, Ann. *The Village of Round and Square Houses.* Little, Brown, 1986 (I:4–9 R:6). A "why" tale is from Cameroon.

Grimes, Nikki. *Come Sunday.* Illustrated by Michael Bryant. Eerdmans, 1996 (I:4–8). Latasha attends Sunday services.

Guy, Rosa. *Billy the Great.* Illustrated by Caroline Binch. Delacorte, 1992 (I:5–8 R:3). Two boys develop an interracial friendship.

Haley, Gail E. *A Story, a Story.* Atheneum, 1970 (I:6–10 R:6). An African tale tells about a spider man's bargain with Sky God.

Hamilton, Virginia. *Anthony Burns: The Defeat and Triumph of a Fugitive Slave.* Knopf, 1988 (I:10+ R:6). This is the life of the escaped slave, whose trial caused riots in Boston.

_____ . *The Bells of Christmas.* Illustrated by Lambert Davis. Harcourt Brace Jovanovich, 1989 (I:8+ R:5). A prosperous black family experiences Christmas in Ohio in the 1890s.

_____ . *Cousins.* Philomel, 1990 (I:10+ R:5). The text explores emotions and feelings in an extended family.

_____ . *Drylongso.* Illustrated by Jerry Pinkney. Harcourt Brace Jovanovich, 1992 (I:8+ R:4). A family experiencing the drought is helped by an unknown boy.

_____ . Retold by. *Her Stories: African American Folktales, Fairy Tales, and True Tales.* Illustrated by Leo and Diane Dillon. Scholastic, 1995 (I:all R:6). This is a collection of nineteen tales.

_____ . *The House of Dies Drear.* Illustrated by Eros Keith. Macmillan, 1968 (I:11 R:4). A contemporary, suspenseful story tells about a family who is living in a home that was a station on the Underground Railroad.

_____ . *In the Beginning: Creation Stories from Around the World.* Illustrated by Barry Moser. Harcourt Brace Jovanovich, 1988 (I:all R:5). Creation stories come from many cultures.

_____ . *Junius Over Far.* Harper & Row, 1985 (I:10+ R:5). A boy discovers his heritage when he goes to a Caribbean island looking for his grandfather.

_____ . *M. C. Higgins, the Great.* Macmillan, 1974 (I:12+ R:4). M. C. dreams of fleeing from the danger of a strip mining spoil heap, but he decides to stay and build a wall to protect his home.

_____ . *The Magical Adventures of Pretty Pearl.* Harper & Row, 1983 (I:10+ R:5). A god-child disguises herself as a human and helps poor African American people.

_____ . *Many Thousand Gone: African Americans from Slavery to Freedom.* Illustrated by Leo and Diane Dillon. Knopf, 1993 (I:8+ R:5). Short stories tell about people who were involved in fighting for freedom.

Involving Children in Multicultural Literature 659

_____ . *The Mystery of Drear House*. Greenwillow, 1987 (I:11+ R:5). This is a sequel to *The House of Dies Drear.*

_____ . Retold by. *The People Could Fly: American Black Folktales.* Illustrated by Leo and Diane Dillon. Knopf, 1985 (I:9 R:6). A collection of tales is told by or adapted by African Americans.

_____ . *The Planet of Junior Brown*. Macmillan, 1971 (I:12+ R:6). Three outcasts from society create their own world in a secret basement room in a schoolhouse.

_____ . *When Birds Could Talk & Bats Could Sing*. Illustrated by Barry Moser. Scholastic, 1996 (I:all R:5). A collection of African American tales.

_____ . *Zeely*. Illustrated by Symeon Shimin. Macmillan, 1967 (I:8–12 R:4). Geeder is convinced that her tall, stately neighbor is a Watusi queen.

Hansen, Joyce. *I Thought My Soul Would Rise and Fly: The Diary of Patsy, a Freed Girl.* Scholastic, 1997 (I:10+ R:5). The story is set at the time of Reconstruction.

_____ . *Which Way Freedom*. Walker, 1986 (I:10+ R:6). This novel is based on historical accounts of black involvement in the Civil War.

Harris, Joel Chandler. *Jump! The Adventures of Brer Rabbit.* Adapted by Van Dyke Parks. Illustrated by Barry Moser. Harcourt Brace Jovanovich, 1986 (I:all R:4). Five Brer Rabbit stories include "The Comeuppance of Brer Wolf" and "The Moon in the Millpond."

_____ . *Jump Again! More Adventures of Brer Rabbit*. Adapted by Van Dyke Parks. Illustrated by Barry Moser. Harcourt Brace Jovanovich, 1987 (I:all R:4). Five Brer Rabbit stories include "Brer Rabbit, He's a Good Fisherman" and "Brer Rabbit's Courtship."

_____ . *More Tales of Uncle Remus: Further Adventures of Brer Rabbit, His Friends, Enemies, and Others*. Retold by Julius Lester. Dial, 1988 (I:all R:4). This book contains additional tales.

_____ . *The Tales of Uncle Remus: The Adventures of Brer Rabbit.* Retold by Julius Lester. Illustrated by Jerry Pinkney. Dial, 1987 (I:all R:4). This book contains forty-eight Brer Rabbit tales.

Haskins, James. *Bayard Rustin: Behind the Scenes of the Civil Rights Movement*. Hyperion, 1997 (I:10+ R:6). Haskins develops the history of the Civil Rights Movement through one of the leaders.

_____ . *Black Theater in America*. Crowell, 1982 (I:10+ R:7). This book stresses contributions of African Americans to the theater.

_____ . *I Have a Dream: The Life and Words of Martin Luther King, Jr.* Millbrook, 1993 (I:10+ R:7). This biography focuses on the civil rights movement.

_____ . *The Life and Death of Martin Luther King, Jr.* Lothrop, Lee & Shepard, 1977 (I:10+ R:7). This biography covers the life of the civil rights leader.

_____ . *The March on Washington,* HarperCollins, 1993 (I:10+ R:7). The story of the 1963 march and the people who attended.

_____ . *Thurgood Marshall: A Life for Justice*. Holt, 1992 (I:10+ R:7). A biography of the first African American Supreme Court justice.

Havill, Juanita. *Jamaica's Find*. Illustrated by Anne Sibley O'Brien. Houghton Mifflin, 1986 (I:2–6 R:2). A girl discovers how good it feels to return a lost possession.

Hoffman, Mary. *Amazing Grace*. Illustrated by Caroline Binch. Dial, 1991 (I:4–7 R:4). A girl shows that she can be the best Peter Pan.

Hoobler, Dorothy, and Thomas Hoobler. *The African American Family Album*. Oxford University Press, 1995 (I:all). The history of African Americans is developed through photographs.

Hooks, William H. *The Ballad of Belle Dorcus*. Illustrated by Brian Pinkney. Knopf, 1990 (I:8+ R:5). An African American tale about the love between a freeborn woman and a slave.

Hudson, Wade, ed. *Pass It On: African-American Poetry for Children.* Illustrated by Floyd Cooper. Scholastic, 1993 (I:all). The anthology includes poems by poets such as Gwendolyn Brooks, Lucille Clifton, and Langston Hughes.

Hurmence, Belinda. *A Girl Called Boy*. Houghton Mifflin, 1982 (I:10+ R:6). An African American girl goes back in time to 1853 and experiences slavery.

Isadora, Rachel. *At the Crossroads*. Greenwillow, 1991 (I:3–8 R:3). Children wait to welcome their fathers home from working in the South African mines.

Jaquith, Priscilla. *Bo Rabbit Smart for True: Tall Tales from the Gullah*. Illustrated by Ed Young. Philomel, 1995 (I:all R:7). These tales were collected from the Sea Islands.

Johnson, Angela. *The Rolling Store*. Illustrated by Peter Catalanotto. Orchard, 1997 (I:8 R:4). A young girl learns about a peddler's truck.

_____ . *Tell Me a Story, Mama*. Illustrated by David Soman. Watts, 1989 (I:3–8 R:4). This is a picture book in which a mother tells stories about her childhood.

_____ . *Toning the Sweep*. Orchard, 1993 (I:12+ R:6). In 1964, the story develops the history and memories of Grandmama Ola.

Johnson, James Weldon. *Lift Every Voice and Sing*. Illustrated by Elizabeth Catlett. Walker, 1993 (I:all). Linocut prints accompany the song that is often considered the African American national anthem.

Joseph, Lynn. *A Wave in Her Pocket: Stories from Trinidad*. Illustrated by Brian Pinkney. Clarion, 1991 (I:8+ R:5). A great-aunt entertains the children with frightening stories.

Keats, Ezra Jack. *John Henry: An American Legend*. Pantheon, 1965 (I:6–9 R:4). This is a picture storybook of the tall tale about the baby who grew up to be a steel-driving man.

King, Coretta Scott. *My Life with Martin Luther King, Jr.* Holt, 1993 (I:10+ R:5). This is a revised edition of the biography.

Knutson, Barbara, retold by. *How the Guinea Fowl Got Her Spots: A Swahili Tale of Friendship*. Carolrhoda, 1990 (I:4–8 R:4). This Swahili tale is a story of friendship that explains a physical characteristic.

_____ . *Why the Crab Has No Head*. Carolrhoda, 1987 (I:all R:4). This is a "why" tale from Zaire.

Kroll, Virginia. *Masai and I*. Illustrated by Nancy Carpenter. Four Winds, 1992 (I:6–9 R:4). A girl compares her life with that of the Masai.

Langstaff, John. *What a Morning! The Christmas Story in Black Spirituals*. Illustrated by Ashley Bryan. McElderry, 1987 (I:all). Five spirituals focus attention on the Christmas story.

Lasky, Kathryn. *True North*. Scholastic, 1996 (I:12+ R:7). A runaway slave and a white girl join forces.

Lester, Julius. *From Slave Ship to Freedom Road*. Illustrated by Rod Brown. Dial, 1998 (I:10+ R:5). A picture history of slavery to Emancipation.

_____ . *How Many Spots Does a Leopard Have?* Illustrated by David Shannon. Scholastic, 1989 (I:all R:4). Folktales in this collection reflect both African and Jewish traditions.

_____. *John Henry.* Illustrated by Jerry Pinkney. Dial, 1994 (I:all). This is a tall tale from the plantation South.

_____. *The Knee-High Man and Other Tales.* Illustrated by Ralph Pinto. Dial, 1972 (I:all R:4). These six folktales are from the southern United States.

_____. *The Last Tales of Uncle Remus.* Illustrated by Jerry Pinkney. Dial, 1994 (I:all R:4). The text includes thirty-nine selections.

Levine, Ellen. *Freedom's Children: Young Civil Rights Activists Tell Their Own Stories,* Putnam, 1993 (I:10+). This is a collection of the oral histories of African Americans who were teenagers in the 1950s and 1960s.

Lewin, Hugh. *Jafta.* Illustrated by Lisa Kopper. Carolrhoda, 1983 (I:3–7 R:6). A young South African boy is compared to the animals in his environment.

_____. *Jafta and the Wedding.* Illustrated by Lisa Kopper. Carolrhoda, 1983 (I:3–7 R:6). Pictures show a village wedding celebration.

_____. *Jafta's Father.* Illustrated by Lisa Kopper. Carolrhoda, 1983 (I:3–7 R:6). Jafta's father plays with him when he returns to the village.

_____. *Jafta's Mother.* Illustrated by Lisa Kopper. Carolrhoda, 1983 (I:3–7 R:6). Jafta's mother is compared to the South African environment.

Little, Lessie Jones. *Children of Long Ago.* Illustrated by Jan Spivey Gilchrist. Philomel, 1988 (I:all). Poems tell about growing up in the rural South.

Lyons, Mary E. *Letters from a Slave Girl: The Story of Harriet Jacobs.* Scribner's, 1992 (I:10+ R:6). Fictionalized letters tell the story of the slave.

_____, selected by. *Raw Head, Bloody Bones: African-American Tales of the Supernatural.* Scribners, 1991 (I:8+ R:5). This is a collection of fifteen tales.

_____. *Sorrow's Kitchen: The Life and Folklore of Zora Neale Hurston.* Scribner's, 1990 (I:10+ R:6). This is the biography of the first African American author to write a popular book of black folklore.

McCurdy, Michael, edited by. *Escape from Slavery: The Boyhood of Frederick Douglass in His Own Words.* Knopf, 1994 (I:9+). This autobiography presents Douglass's original language.

McDermott, Gerald. *Anansi the Spider: A Tale from the Ashanti.* Holt, Rinehart & Winston, 1972 (I:7–9). This is a colorfully illustrated folktale.

_____. *Zomo the Rabbit: A Trickster Tale from West Africa.* Harcourt Brace Jovanovich, 1992 (I:4–8 R:4). This tale shows the importance of courage, sense, and caution.

McKissack, Patricia. *The Dark-Thirty: Southern Tales of the Supernatural.* Illustrated by Brian Pinkney. Knopf, 1992 (I:8+ R:5). This is a collection of ghost stories.

_____. *Flossie & the Fox.* Illustrated by Rachel Isadora. Dial, 1986 (I:3–8+ R:3). This is a tale of the rural South.

_____. *Jesse Jackson.* Scholastic, 1989 (I:8+ R:5). A biography of the political leader emphasizes his accomplishments.

_____. *Mirandy and Brother Wind.* Illustrated by Jerry Pinkney. Knopf, 1988 (I:4–9 R:5). A girl enters a cakewalk contest.

_____. *Nettie Jo's Friends.* Illustrated by Scott Cook. Knopf, 1989 (I:3–8 R:3). Animal friends help a young girl find a needle so she can make a dress for her doll.

_____, and Frederick McKissack. *The Civil Rights Movement in America from 1865 to the Present,* 2nd ed. Children's Press, 1991 (I:10+ R:6). This is a history of the civil rights movement.

_____, and Frederick McKissack. *A Long Hard Journey: The Story of the Pullman Porter.* Walker, 1989 (I:10+ R:6). This is a history of the porters who formed the first African American-controlled union.

Mathis, Sharon Bell. *The Hundred Penny Box.* Illustrated by Leo and Diane Dillon. Viking, 1975 (I:6–9 R:3). Young Michael loved to hear his elderly aunt tell the story of each penny that stood for her one hundred years.

Medearis, Angela Shelf. *Rum-A-Tum-Tum.* Illustrated by James E. Ransome. Holiday, 1997 (I:4–8). The verses are set in New Orleans in the early 1900s.

Meltzer, Milton. *The Black Americans: A History in Their Own Words, 1619–1983.* Crowell, 1984 (I:10+ R:6). This book provides information for political and social history.

_____. Edited by. *Frederick Douglass: In His Own Words.* Illustrated by Stephen Alcorn. Harcourt Brace, 1995 (I:12+ R:11). This is a collection of Douglass's speeches and writings.

_____. *Langston Hughes: A Biography.* Crowell, 1968 (I:10+ R:6). This is a biography of a writer and poet.

Miller, Douglas. *Frederick Douglass and the Fight for Freedom.* Facts on File, 1988 (I:10+ R:6). The black leader escaped slavery to become a political leader.

Mitchell, Barbara. *Shoes for Everyone: A Story About Jan Matzeliger.* Carolrhoda, 1986 (I:10+ R:6). A biography tells about the man who invented the shoe-lasting machine.

Mollel, Tololwa M. *A Promise to the Sun: A Story of Africa.* Illustrated by Beatriz Vidal. Little, Brown, 1992 (I:4–9 R:4). A "why" tale explains character traits of bats.

Monjo, N. *The Drinking Gourd.* Illustrated by Fred Brenner. Harper & Row, 1970 (I:7–9 R:2). This is an "I Can Read" history book about the Underground Railroad.

Musgrove, Margaret. *Ashanti to Zulu: African Traditions.* Illustrated by Leo and Diane Dillon. Dial, 1976 (I:7–12 R:6). Traditions of twenty-six African peoples are presented in alphabetical order.

Myers, Walter Dean. *Harlem.* Illustrated by Christopher Myers. Scholastic, 1997 (I:8+). This is a poem that presents the author's views about Harlem.

_____. *Malcolm X: By Any Means Necessary.* Scholastic, 1993 (I:10+ R:6). A biography of the African American leader.

_____. *The Mouse Rap.* HarperCollins, 1990 (I:10+ R:5). A contemporary story has a large portion written in rap.

_____. *Now Is Your Time! The African-American Struggle for Freedom.* HarperCollins, 1991 (I:10+ R:6). The author chronicles the lives of numerous people associated with the struggle for freedom.

_____. *Scorpions.* Harper & Row, 1988 (I:11+ R:5). A boy faces problems with a gang.

_____. *Slam!.* Scholastic, 1996 (I:12+ R:5). Basketball helps a boy overcome his problems.

_____. *The Story of Three Kingdoms.* Illustrated by Ashley Bryan. HarperCollins, 1995 (I:7+ R:5). This is a literary folktale.

Naidoo, Beverley. *No Turning Back.* HarperCollins, 1997 (I:10+ R:5). The setting is contemporary Johannesburg, South Africa.

Nelson, Vaunda Micheaux. *Mayfield Crossing.* Illustrated by Leonard Jenkins. Putnam, 1993 (I:8+ R:5). In 1960, the children in a town experience prejudice when they go to a new school.

Palmer, Colin A. *The First Passage: Blacks in the Americas, 1502–1617.* Oxford University Press, 1995 (I:12+ R:10).

This informational book provides a history of African Americans.

Patterson, Lillie. *Frederick Douglass: Freedom Fighter*. Garrard, 1965 (I:6–9 R:3). This is a biography of a great Black American leader.

_____ . *Martin Luther King, Jr. and the Freedom Movement*. Facts on File, 1989 (I:10+ R:6). This book chronicles King's nonviolent struggles against segregation.

Paulsen, Gary. *Nightjohn*. Delacorte, 1993 (I:10+ R:4). A slave teaches children to read even though he is cruelly punished for his actions.

Petry, Ann. *Harriet Tubman: Conductor on the Underground Railroad*. Crowell, 1955 (I:10+ R:6). This is a biography of a woman who led over three hundred slaves to freedom.

Pinkney, Andrea Davis. *Seven Candles for Kwanzaa*. Illustrated by Brian Pinkney. Dial, 1993 (I:5–9 R:4). The book details the preparation for the African American holiday.

Porter, A. P. *Jump at de Sun: The Story of Nora Neale Hurston*. Carolrhoda, 1992 (I:10+ R:5). A biography of the African American writer.

Ringgold, Faith. *Aunt Harriet's Underground Railroad in the Sky*. Crown, 1993 (I:5–9 R:4). This picture book is about a girl who meets Harriet Tubman on a freedom train in the sky.

_____ . *My Dream of Martin Luther King*. Crown, 1995 (I:6–9 R:5). This highly illustrated biography develops King's life through a dream sequence.

_____ . *Tar Beach*. Crown, 1991 (I:4–7 R:4). A girl imagines that she can fly over the city.

Rosales, Melodye, retold by. *'Twas the Night B'fore Christmas: An African American Version*. Scholastic, 1996 (I:5–9). The author presents Clement Moore's poem in an African American context.

Rosen, Michael J. *Elijah's Angel: A Story for Chanukah and Christmas*. Illustrated by Aminah Brenda Lynn Robinson. Harcourt Brace Jovanovich, 1992 (I:7+ R:4). A Jewish boy learns about friendship through the gift of a black wood carver.

Sanfield, Steve. *The Adventures of High John the Conqueror*. Illustrated by John Ward. Watts, 1989 (I:8+ R:4). This text includes a collection of sixteen southern folktales.

San Souci, Robert D. *The Hired Hand*. Illustrated by Jerry Pinkney. Dial, 1997 (I:5). This is an African American folktale.

_____ . *Sukey and the Mermaid*. Illustrated by Brian Pinkney. Four Winds, 1992 (I:5–10 R:5). A folktale that has elements from West Africa, the Caribbean, and the Sea Islands of South Carolina.

_____ . *The Talking Eggs*. Illustrated by Jerry Pinkney. Dial, 1989 (I:all). A folktale from the American South.

Sisulu, Elinor Batezat. *The Day Gogo Went to Vote: South Africa, April 1994*. Little, Brown, 1996 (I:4–8 R:6). A great-great-grandmother explains why she has to vote.

Smalls-Hector, Irene. *Jonathan and His Mommy*. Illustrated by Michael Hays. Little, Brown, 1992 (I:3–8). A boy and his mother take an unusual walk in the neighborhood.

Stanley, Diane, and Peter Vennema. *Shaka: King of the Zulus*. Illustrated by Diane Stanley. Morrow, 1988 (I:6–10 R:6). This is a picture biography.

Steptoe, Javaka, ed. and illustrated by. *In Daddy's Arms I Am Tall: African Americans Celebrating Fathers*. Lee & Low, 1997 (I:all). This is an anthology of poems about fathers.

Steptoe, John. *Creativity*. Illustrated by E. B. Lewis. Clarion, 1997 (I:6+). This is a story about friendship.

_____ . *Daddy Is a Monster . . . Sometimes*. Lippincott, 1980 (I:4–7 R:3). Two children remember the times when their daddy gets angry and takes on his monster image.

_____ . *Mufaro's Beautiful Daughters: An African Tale*. Lothrop, Lee & Shepard, 1987 (I:all R:4). An African folktale has some Cinderella elements.

_____ . *Stevie*. Harper & Row, 1969 (I:3–7 R:3). Robert is unhappy when Stevie plays with his toys and wants his own way.

Stewart, Dianne. *Gift of the Sun: A Tale from South Africa*. Illustrated by Jude Daly. Farrar, Straus & Giroux, 1996 (I:6–9 R:5). This is a variation of the Lazy Jack tale.

Stock, Catherine. *Armien's Fishing Trip*. Morrow, 1990 (I:5–8 R:4). This contemporary story is set in Africa.

Stolz, Mary. *Cezanne Pinto: A Memoir*. Knopf, 1994 (I:12+ R:6). A young slave and an older woman escape slavery on the Underground Railroad.

_____ . *Storm in the Night*. Illustrated by Pat Cummings. Harper & Row, 1988 (I:4–9 R:4). A young boy and his grandfather experience a storm.

Sullivan, Charles, ed. *Children of Promise: African-American Literature and Art for Young People*. Abrams, 1991 (I:10+ R:5). This is an anthology of literature and art.

Taylor, Mildred. *The Gold Cadillac*. Illustrated by Michael Hays. Dial, 1987 (I:8–10 R:3). An African American family experiences racial prejudice when it tries to drive an expensive car into the segregated South.

_____ . *Let the Circle Be Unbroken*. Dial, 1981 (I:10+ R:6). This is a sequel to *Roll of Thunder, Hear My Cry*.

_____ . *Roll of Thunder, Hear My Cry*. Dial, 1976 (I:10+ R:6). A black Mississippi family in 1933 experiences humiliating and frightening situations but retains its pride.

Temple, Frances. *Taste of Salt: A Story of Modern Haiti*. Orchard, 1992 (I:12+ R:6). This story is set in the repressive environment of Haiti.

Thomas, Jane Resh. *Celebration!* Illustrated by Raul Colon. Hyperion, 1997 (I:5–8 R:4). The book celebrates an African American family's Fourth of July picnic.

Towle, Wendy. *The Real McCoy: The Life of an African-American Inventor*. Scholastic, 1993 (I:8+ R:5). This is a biography of the inventor of an automatic oil cup for railroads.

Turner, Glennette Tilley. *Take a Walk in Their Shoes*. Cobblehill Books, 1989 (I:8+ R:4). The text includes short biographies and skits of fourteen black Americans.

Van Laan, Nancy. *With a Whoop and a Holler: A Bushel of Lore from Way Down South*. Illustrated by Scott Cook. Simon & Schuster, 1998 (I:all). A collection of African American folktales.

Walker, Barbara K., retold by. *The Dancing Palm Tree and Other Nigerian Folktales*. Illustrated by Helen Siegl. Texas Tech University Press, 1990 (I:all). This collection of tales is from West Africa.

Walter, Mildred Pitts. *Brother to the Wind*. Illustrated by Diane and Leo Dillon. Lothrop, Lee & Shepard, 1985 (I:all R:3). An African boy wishes to fly.

_____ . *Justin and the Best Biscuits in the World*. Illustrated by Catherine Stock. Lothrop, Lee & Shepard, 1986 (I:7–10 R:5). A young African American boy spends time on his grandfather's ranch.

Ward, Leila. *I Am Eyes, Ni Macho*. Illustrated by Nonny Hogrogian. Greenwillow, 1978 (I:3–7 R:1). An African child wakes to the marvelous sights of her land.

Williams, Karen Lynn. *When Africa Was Home.* Illustrated by Floyd Cooper. Orchard, 1991 (I:4–8 R:4). A family moves back to Africa after they miss their friends.

Williams, Sherley Anne. *Working Cotton.* Illustrated by Carole Byard. Harcourt Brace Jovanovich, 1992 (I:all). This story develops around memories of a migrant family working in the cotton fields of California.

Williams, Vera B. *Cherries and Cherry Pits.* Greenwillow, 1986 (I:3–8 R:3). A girl uses her magic marker to tell stories about people who like cherries.

Wisniewski, David. *Sundiata: Lion King of Mali.* Clarion, 1992 (I:all). This is a highly illustrated legend of an African ruler in the late 1200s.

Yates, Elizabeth. *Amos Fortune, Free Man.* Illustrated by Nora S. Unwin. Dutton, 1950 (I:10+ R:6). An African becomes a slave in Boston.

HISPANIC AMERICAN LITERATURE

Anaya, Rudolfo. *Maya's Children: The Story of La Llorona.* Illustrated by Maria Baca. Hyperion, 1997 (I:5–9 R:4). This is the tale of the crying woman who killed her children and wanders through the night.

Anzaldua, Gloria. *Prietita and the Ghost Woman.* Children's, 1996 (I:5–8 R:5). A girl goes in search of herbs.

Atkin, S. Beth, ed. *Voices from the Fields: Children of Migrant Farmworkers Tell Their Stories.* Little, Brown, 1993 (I:10). The text includes interviews with nine children of migrant farmers.

Beals, Carleton. *Stories Told by the Aztecs: Before the Spaniards Came.* Illustrated by Charles Pickard. Abelard, 1970 (I:10+ R:7). A collection of tales has footnotes and a bibliography.

Behrens, June. *Fiesta!* Photographs by Scott Taylor. Children's Press, 1978 (I:5–8 R:4). This book contains photographs of the Cinco de Mayo fiesta.

Belting, Natalia M. *Moon Was Tired of Walking on Air.* Illustrated by Will Hillenbrand. Houghton Mifflin, 1992 (I:all). This is a collection of traditional tales from the Indians of South America.

Bernardo, Anilu. *Jumping Off to Freedom.* Pinata, 1996 (I:12+ R:6). A father and son escape from Cuba on a raft.

Bertrand, Diane Gonzales. *Sip, Slurp, Soup, Soup/Caldo, Caldo, Caldo.* Illustrated by Alex Pardo DeLanga. Pinata, 1997 (I:4–7). Four children watch as soup is prepared.

Bierhorst, John. *Doctor Coyote: A Native American Aesop's Fables.* Illustrated by Wendy Watson. Macmillan, 1987 (I:all). A fable is from Indians of Mexico.

——, ed. *The Hungry Woman: Myths and Legends of the Aztecs.* Morrow, 1984 (I:12+ R:6). The tales include creation myths and legends about the conquest.

——, ed. *Lightning Inside You and Other Native American Riddles.* Illustrated by Louise Brierley. Morrow, 1992 (I:8+). Riddles from several regions including southern Mexico and western South America.

——, ed. *The Monkey's Haircut and Other Stories Told by the Maya.* Illustrated by Robert Andrew Parker. Morrow, 1986 (I:8+ R:6). This book contains twenty-two tales.

——, *The Mythology of South America.* Morrow, 1988 (I:12+ R:7). This is a good resource for information.

——, trans. *Spirit Child: A Story of the Nativity.* Illustrated by Barbara Cooney. Morrow, 1984 (I:8–12 R:6). Pre-Columbian illustrations accompany an Aztec story.

Blackmore, Vivien. *Why Corn Is Golden: Stories About Plants.* Illustrated by Susana Martinez-Ostos. Little, Brown, 1984 (I:all R:5). This book contains folklore about corn.

Brimner, Larry Dane. *A Migrant Family.* Lerner, 1992 (I:all). The text and photographs describe the life of Mexican American migrant workers in California.

Brown, Tricia. *Hello, Amigos!* Photographs by Fran Ortiz. Holt, Rinehart & Winston, 1986 (I:3–8 R:3). Photographs accompany a boy on his sixth birthday.

Brusca, Maria Cristina. *On the Pampas.* Henry Holt, 1991 (I:6–9 R:5). A nonfiction book provides details of life on the Pampas in Argentina.

Burland, Cottie. *An Aztec Town.* Hutchinson, 1980 (I:all R:5). This is a highly illustrated version of how a town might have appeared.

Cisneros, Sandra. *The House on Mango Street.* Arte Publico, 1983 (I:12+ R:7). A girl records her feelings about the world.

Clark, Ann Nolan. *Secret of the Andes.* Illustrated by Jean Charlot. Viking, 1952, 1980 (I:8+ R:5). A boy learns about the traditions of his Inca ancestors.

Conord, Bruce W. *Cesar Chavez.* Chelsea, 1992 (I:4–6 R:5). A biography of the union leader.

Cozzen, Judy, ed. *Kids Explore America's Hispanic Heritage.* John Muir, 1992 (I:all). This is a report of a school project.

de Gerez, Toni. *My Song Is a Piece of Jade: Poems of Ancient Mexico in English and Spanish.* Illustrated by William Stark. Little, Brown, 1981 (I:all). Ancient Mexican poems are written in English and Spanish.

Delacre, Lulu. *Arroz Con Leche: Popular Songs and Rhymes from Latin America.* Scholastic, 1989 (I:all). This text includes a variety of songs and poems.

dePaola, Tomie. *The Lady of Guadalupe.* Holiday House, 1980 (I:8+ R:6). This is a traditional Mexican tale.

Dorros, Arthur. *Radio Man: A Story in English and Spanish.* HarperCollins, 1993 (I:6–10). This book focuses on migrant farm workers.

Ehlert, Lois. *Cuckoo: A Mexican Folktale.* Translated into Spanish by Gloria de Aragon Andujar. Harcourt Brace, 1997 (I:4–8). This pourquoi tale is written in English and Spanish.

——. *Moon Rope.* Harcourt Brace Jovanovich, 1992 (I:all). This Peruvian tale is about two animals that try to reach the moon.

Ets, Marie Hall, and Aurora Labastida. *Nine Days to Christmas: A Story of Mexico.* Illustrated by Marie Hall Ets. Viking, 1959 (I:5–8 R:3). Ceci is going to have her first Posada with her own piñata.

Fritz, Jean, Katherine Paterson, Patricia McKissack, Fredrick McKissack, Margaret Mahy, and Jamake Highwater. *The World in 1492.* Illustrated by Stefano Vitale. Holt, 1992 (I:8+). The section, "The Americas in 1492," written by Jamake Highwater, includes information about the Aztecs and the Incas.

Galvin, Irene Flum. *The Ancient Maya.* Benchmark, 1996 (I:10+ R:5). This information book presents Mayan art, poetry, and customs.

Garcia, Richard. *My Aunt Otilia's Spirits.* Illustrated by Robin Cherin and Roger Reyes. Children's Press, 1987 (I:5–8 R:2). An aunt from Puerto Rico with magical powers visits her family in the United States.

Gonzalez, Ralfka, and Ana Ruiz. *My First Book of Proverbs.* Children's, 1995 (I:all). A collection of sayings in English and Spanish.

Griego, Margot C. *Tortillitas Para Mama and Other Spanish Nursery Rhymes*. Illustrated by Barbara Cooney. Holt, Rinehart & Winston, 1981 (I:3–7). Nursery rhymes appear in Spanish and English.

Griego y Maestas, José, and Rudolfo A. Anaya. *Cuentos: Tales from the Hispanic Southwest*. Illustrated by Jaime Valdez. Museum of New Mexico, 1980 (I:9+ R:5). This is a collection of tales.

Hall, Lynn. *Danza!* Scribner's, 1981 (I:10+ R:6). A boy and his horse share life on a farm in Puerto Rico.

Herrera, Juan Felipe. *Calling the Doves*. Illustrated by Elly Simmons. Children's, 1995 (I:all). A boy tells about his childhood as a migrant farmworker.

Hinojosa, Francisco, adapted by. *The Old Lady Who Ate People*. Illustrated by Leonel Maciel. Little, Brown, 1984 (I:all R:6). These four frightening folktales are from Mexico.

Jagendorf, M. A., and R. S. Boggs. *The King of the Mountains: A Treasury of Latin American Folk Stories*. Vanguard, 1960 (I:9+ R:6). This is a collection of tales from twenty-six countries.

Jenkins, Lyll Becerra de. *The Honorable Prison*. Lodestar, 1989 (I:10+ R:5). Marta and her family are prisoners of a Latin American country because of the actions of her father.

Kroll, Virginia. *Butterfly Boy*. Illustrated by Gerardo Suzan. Boyds Mills, 1997 (I:5–8 R:4). A boy tries to ensure that red admiral butterflies return for his grandfather's pleasure.

Krumgold, Joseph. *. . . And Now Miguel*. Illustrated by Jean Charlot. Crowell, 1953 (I:10+ R:3). Miguel Chavez is a member of a proud sheep-raising family.

Kurtz, Jane. *Miro in the Kingdom of the Sun*. Illustrated by David Frampton. Houghton Mifflin, 1996 (I:4–7 R:4). This folktale is set in the time of the early Incas.

Lattimore, Deborah. *The Flame of Peace: A Tale of the Aztecs*. Harper & Row, 1987 (I:all R:6). This story is based on Aztec mythology.

Marrin, Albert. *Aztecs and Spaniards: Cortés and the Conquest of Mexico*. Atheneum, 1986 (I:12+ R:7). This book is a history of the Aztecs and tells about the influence of Cortés.

_____ . *Empires Lost and Won: The Spanish Heritage in the Southwest*. Simon & Schuster, 1997 (I:12+ R:7). This history begins with the first stories of cities of gold.

Martinello, Marian L., and Samuel P. Nesmith. *With Domingo Leal in San Antonio 1734*. The University of Texas, Institute of Texas Cultures at San Antonio, 1979 (I:8+ R:4). This book tells the results of research investigating the lives of Spanish settlers who arrived in Texas in the 1730s.

Martinez, Victor. *Parrot in the Oven: Mi Vida*. HarperCollins, 1996 (I:12+ R:6). A Mexican American family struggles against poverty.

Meyer, Carolyn, and Charles Gallenkamp. *The Mystery of the Ancient Maya*. Atheneum, 1985 (I:10 R:8). This book tells about early explorers and discoveries.

Mikaelsen, Ben. *Sparrow Hawk Red*. Hyperion/Little, Brown, 1993 (I:10+ R:6). A thirteen-year-old boy tries to avenge his mother's murder by drug smugglers.

Mohr, Nicholasa. *El Bronx Remembered: A Novella and Stories*. Harper & Row, 1975 (I:10+ R:6). Twelve short stories are set in the inner city.

_____ . *Felita*. Illustrated by Ray Cruz. Dial, 1979 (I:9–12 R:2). Felita is unhappy when her family moves to a new neighborhood.

_____ . *Going Home*. Dial, 1986 (I:10+ R:6). Twelve-year-old Felita spends the summer with relatives in Puerto Rico.

O'Dell, Scott. *The Amethyst Ring*. Houghton Mifflin, 1983 (I:10+ R:6). This is the final story of Julian Escobar.

_____ . *The Captive*. Houghton Mifflin, 1979 (I:10+ R:6). A young Spanish seminarian witnesses the exploitation of the Maya during the 1500s.

_____ . *Carlota*. Houghton Mifflin, 1981 (I:10+ R:6). A high-spirited Spanish American girl fights beside her father during the days of the Mexican War in early California.

_____ . *The Feathered Serpent*. Houghton Mifflin, 1981 (I:10+ R:6). This book is a sequel to *The Captive*.

_____ . *The King's Fifth*. Houghton Mifflin, 1966 (I:10+ R:6). Esteban de Sandoval accompanies Coronado's army in search of the cities of gold.

Politi, Leo. *Song of the Swallows*. Scribner's, 1949 (I:5–8 R:4). Juan lives in Capistrano, California, and excellent illustrations show Spanish architecture.

Rohmer, Harriet, Octavio Chow, and Morris Viduare. *The Invisible Hunters*. Illustrated by Joe Sam. Children's Press, 1987 (I:all R:5). A tale reflects the impact of European traders.

_____ , and Dornminster Wilson. *Mother Scorpion Country*. Illustrated by Virginia Steams. Children's Press, 1987 (I:all R:4). A Central American tale is written in both English and Spanish.

Soto, Gary. *Baseball in April and Other Stories*. Harcourt Brace Jovanovich, 1990 (I:11+ R:6). This is a collection of stories about Mexican-American Youth in California.

_____ . *Neighborhood Odes*. Harcourt Brace Jovanovich, 1992 (I:all). This collection of poems is about a Hispanic neighborhood.

_____ . *Pacific Crossing*. Harcourt Brace Jovanovich, 1992 (I:10+ R:6). In a sequel to *Taking Sides*, boys from the barrio in San Francisco participate in an exchange program to Japan.

_____ . *The Skirt*. Illustrated by Eric Velasquez. Delacorte, 1992 (I:6–8 R:4). A Mexican American girl leaves her folkloric skirt on the school bus and tries to retrieve it.

_____ . *Snapshots from the Wedding*. Illustrated by Stephanie Garcia. Putnam, 1997 (I:5–8 R:4). A wedding is described through the viewpoint of a young Mexican American girl.

_____ . *Taking Sides*. Harcourt Brace Jovanovich, 1991 (I:10+ R:6). A boy faces problems of loyalty as his new basketball team meets the old team from the barrio.

_____ . *Too Many Tamales*. Illustrated by Ed Martinez. Putnam, 1993 (I:6–8 R:4). This family story is set during Christmas Eve.

Stewig, John Warren, retold by. *Princess Florecita and the Iron Shoes: A Spanish Fairy Tale*. Knopf, 1995 (I:9+ R:5). In this Spanish tale, a princess saves a sleeping prince.

Tashlik, Phyllis, ed. *Hispanic, Female and Young: An Anthology*. Pinata, 1994 (I:12+ R:6). This is a collection of interviews and stories by Hispanic authors.

Temple, Frances. *Grab Hands and Run*. Orchard, 1993 (I:10+ R:6). Twelve-year-old Felipe tells about his family's attempts to leave El Salvador after the disappearance of his father.

Villasenor, Victor. *Walking Stars: Stories of Magic and Power*. Arte Publico Press, 1994 (I:10+ R:6). This is a collection of short stories.

Volkmer, Jane Anne, retold by. *Song of Chirimia—A Guatemalan Folktale*. Carolrhoda, 1990 (I:6–10 R:5). A Mayan folktale in

English and Spanish tells how a man tries to win the hand of a Mayan princess.

Winter, Jeanette. *Josefina*. Harcourt Brace, 1996 (I:4–8 R:4). This is a bilingual counting story.

NATIVE AMERICAN LITERATURE

Aliki. *Corn Is Maize: The Gift of the Indians*. Crowell, 1976 (I:6–8 R:2). This is a history of corn, how it grows, and how it was first used.

Ancona, George. *Powwow*. Harcourt Brace Jovanovich, 1993 (I:all). Photographs and text explain the Crow Fair in Montana.

Arnold, Caroline. *The Ancient Cliff Dwellers of Mesa Verde*. Photographs by Richard Hewett. Clarion, 1992 (I:8+ R:6). This nonfiction book is about the Anasazi people.

Baker, Olaf. *Where the Buffaloes Begin*. Illustrated by Stephen Gammell. Warne, 1981 (I:all R:6). A story tells about the lake where the buffaloes were created.

Batherman, Muriel. *Before Columbus*. Houghton Mifflin, 1981 (I:6–9 R:5). Illustrations and text present information about North American inhabitants revealed from archaeological explorations.

Baylor, Byrd. *The Desert Is Theirs*. Illustrated by Peter Parnall. Scribner's, 1975 (I:all). The life of the Papago Indians is captured in illustrations and text.

_____ . *Hawk, I'm Your Brother*. Illustrated by Peter Parnall. Scribner's, 1976 (I:all). Rudy Soto would like to glide through the air like a hawk.

_____ . *Moon Song*. Illustrated by Ronald Himler. Scribner's, 1982 (I:all). Written in poetic style, this Pima Indian tale tells how coyote was born of the moon.

_____ . *The Other Way to Listen*. Illustrated by Peter Parnall. Scribner's 1978 (I:all). If one listens carefully, nature is heard.

_____ . *When Clay Sings*. Illustrated by Tom Bahti. Scribner's, 1972 (I:all). A poetic telling of the ancient way of life is stimulated by designs on prehistoric Indian pottery found in the southwestern desert.

Begay, Shonto. *Ma'ii and Cousin Horned Toad: A Traditional Navajo Story*. Scholastic, 1992 (I:5–8 R:5). In a pourquoi tale, Horned Toad plays tricks on Ma'ii, the coyote, until the coyote promises to leave him alone.

_____ . *Navajo: Visions and Voices Across the Mesa*. Scholastic, 1995 (I:10+). A collection of poems and paintings about the Navajo Indians.

Bierhorst, John. *A Cry from the Earth: Music of the North American Indians*. Four Winds, 1979 (I:all). This is a collection of Indian songs of North America.

_____ . edited by. *The Dancing Fox: Arctic Folktales*. Illustrated by Mary K. Okheena. Morrow, 1997 (I:8+). Bierhorst includes useful notes on the Inuit tales.

_____ , ed. *The Girl Who Married a Ghost*. Four Winds, 1978 (I:10+ R:6). The stories were originally collected by Edward Curtis.

_____ . *The Ring in the Prairie, A Shawnee Legend*. Illustrated by Leo and Diane Dillon. Dial, 1970 (I:all R:6). One of the most skilled Indian hunters discovers a mysterious circle in an opening in the forest.

_____ , ed. *The Sacred Path: Spells, Prayers, and Power Songs of the American Indians*. Morrow, 1983 (I:8+). This is a collection of poems, prayers, and songs.

Bruchac, Joseph. *The Boy Who Lived with the Bears and Other Iroquois Stories*. Illustrated by Murv Jacob. HarperCollins, 1995 (I:8+ R:5). Text includes 6 stories from the Iroquois.

_____ . *Eagle Song*. Illustrated by Dan Andreasen. Dial, 1997 (I:7–10 R:4). A fourth-grade boy moves to Brooklyn from the reservation.

Caduto, Michael J., and Joseph Bruchac. *Keepers of the Animals: Native American Stories and Wildlife Activities for Children*. Illustrated by John Kahionhes Fadden. Fulcrum, 1991 (I:all). The text includes folklore about animals and suggested activities to accompany the tales.

_____ . *Keepers of the Earth: Native American Stories and Environmental Activities for Children*. Illustrated by John Kahionhes Fadden and Carol Wood. Fulcrum, 1989 (I:all). The text includes folklore about the earth and suggested activities to accompany the tales.

Cohlene, Terri. *Turquoise Boy: A Navajo Legend*. Illustrated by Charles Reasoner. Watermill, 1990 (I:5–9 R:4). Folklore reveals how a Navajo boy brought horses to his tribe.

Cohn, Amy L., compiled by. *From Sea to Shining Sea: A Treasury of American Folklore and Folk Songs*. Scholastic, 1993 (I:all). This collection progresses from Native American folklore to folklore of more contemporary times.

Cushing, Frank Hamilton. *Zuni Folk Tales*. University of Arizona Press, 1901, 1986. An adult source contains many tales that may be retold to or read by older students.

Dabcovich, Lydia, retold by. *The Polar Bear Son: An Inuit Tale*. Clarion, 1997 (I:5–8 R:4). A woman adopts a polar bear cub.

DeArmond, Dale, retold by. *The Boy Who Found the Light*. Sierra Club/Little, Brown, 1990 (I:all). A collection of Eskimo folklore.

DeCoteau Orie, Sandra. *Did You Hear Wind Sing Your Name?: An Oneida Song of Spring*. Illustrated by Christopher Canyon. Walker, 1995 (I:4–8). The poetic text depicts the Oneida Indians' view of spring.

dePaola, Tomie. *The Legend of the Bluebonnet*. Putnam, 1983 (I:all R:6). In a Comanche tale, unselfish actions are rewarded.

Dixon, Ann, retold by. *How Raven Brought Light to People*. Illustrated by James Watts. Macmillan, 1993 (I:all R:5). A story about how the trickster brings light from the Sky Chief.

Dorris, Michael. *Morning Girl*. Hyperion, 1992 (I:8+ R:5). This book is set in the Bahamas in 1492.

_____ . *Sees Behind Trees*. Hyperion, 1996 (I:8+ R:5). A partially sighted boy earns his name through his senses.

Duncan, Lois. *The Magic of Spider Woman*. Illustrated by Shonto Begay. Scholastic, 1996 (I:all R:7). A tale from the Navajo Indians.

Ekoomiak, Normee. *Arctic Memories*. Henry Holt, 1990 (I:all). The text is written in both Inuktitut and English.

Esbensen, Barbara Juster, ed. *The Star Maiden*. Illustrated by Helen K. Davie. Little, Brown, 1988 (I:all). A poetic Ojibway tale tells about the creation of water lilies.

Fradin, Dennis Brindell. *Hiawatha: Messenger of Peace*. Macmillan, 1992 (I:10+ R:5). This is a biography of the Native American leader who brought together warring Iroquois tribes in a constitutional relationship.

Freedman, Russell. *Buffalo Hunt*. Holiday House, 1988 (I:8+ R:6). Illustrations and text show the importance of the buffalo to Great Plains Indians.

_____ . *Indian Chiefs*. Holiday House, 1987 (I:10+ R:6). Here are short biographies of six Indian chiefs.

_____ . *An Indian Winter*. Illustrated by Karl Bodmer, Holiday, 1992 (I:8+ R:6). A detailed description of the Mandan and Hidasta tribes.

_____ . *The Life and Death of Crazy Horse*. Photographs by Amos Bad Heart Bull. Holiday, 1996 (I:10+ R:5). The biography includes explanatory notes, chronology of events, and bibliography.

Fritz, Jean. *The Double Life of Pocahontas*. Illustrated by Ed Young. Putnam, 1983 (I:8–10 R:7). A biography of Pocahontas focuses on her involvement with two cultures.

_____ , et al. *The World in 1492*. Illustrated by Stefano Vitale. Holt, 1992 (I:8+). The section "The Americas in 1492" is written by Jamake Highwater and includes Native Americans of North America.

George, Jean Craighead. *The Talking Earth*. Harper & Row, 1983 (I:10+ R:6). An Indian girl tries to discover her heritage.

_____ . *Water Sky*. Harper & Row, 1987 (I:10+ R:6). A boy discovers his Eskimo heritage.

Gleason, Katherine. *Native American Literature*. Chelsea, 1996 (I:10+ R:5). The book presents an introduction to Native American literature and authors.

Goble, Paul. *Beyond the Ridge*. Bradbury; 1989 (I:all R:5). An elderly Indian woman from the Great Plains experiences death and goes to the afterlife.

_____ . *Buffalo Woman*. Bradbury, 1984 (I:all R:6). A bond between animals and humans is developed in a tale from the Great Plains.

_____ . *Death of the Iron Horse*. Bradbury, 1987 (I:8+ R:5). This story is based on an incident in 1867, when a Union Pacific freight train was derailed by Cheyenne Indians.

_____ . *The Dream Wolf*. Bradbury, 1990 (I:all R:6). This tale from the Plains Indians is about how a wolf saves two children.

_____ . *The Gift of the Sacred Dog*. Bradbury, 1980 (I:all R:6). The Sioux tale tells how the horse was given to the people.

_____ . *The Girl Who Loved Wild Horses*. Bradbury, 1978 (I:6–10 R:5). A picture storybook tells about an Indian girl's attachment to horses.

_____ . *Iktomi and the Berries*. Watts, 1989 (I:4–10 R:4). Iktomi is a trickster character from the Lakota Sioux.

_____ . *Iktomi and the Boulder: A Plains Indian Story*. Orchard, 1988 (I:4–10 R:4). This trickster tale is good for choral arrangements.

Goldin, Barbara Diamond, retold by. *Coyote and the Fire Stick: A Pacific Northwest Indian Tale*. Illustrated by Will Hillenbrand. Harcourt Brace, 1996 (I:8+). The trickster brings fire to the people.

_____ . Retold by. *The Girl Who Lived with the Bears*. Illustrated by Andrew Plewes. Harcourt Brace, 1997 (I:8+). This is a tale from the Northwest Coast.

Green, Rayna. *Women in American Indian Society*. Chelsea, 1992 (I:12+ R:7). The text presents the history of Native American women from a time prior to contact with the Europeans to contemporary times.

Hamilton, Virginia. *In the Beginning: Creation Stories from Around the World*. Illustrated by Barry Moser. Harcourt Brace Jovanovich, 1988 (I:all R:5). The creation stories come from many cultures.

Harris, Christie. *The Trouble with Adventurers*. Illustrated by Douglas Tait. Atheneum, 1982 (I:10+ R:6). A collection of stories was drawn from the Northwest Coast tribes.

Highwater, Jamake. *Anpao: An American Indian Odyssey*. Illustrated by Fritz Scholder. Lippincott, 1977 (I:12+ R:5). Anpao journeys across the history of Native American traditional tales in order to search for his destiny.

_____ . *Moonsong Lullaby*. Photographs by Marcia Keegan. Lothrop, Lee & Shepard, 1981 (I:all). Color photographs show the animals and activities as the moon watches.

Hobbs, Will. *Bearstone*. Atheneum, 1989 (I:10+ R:6). A troubled Ute boy is helped by an elderly rancher.

Hoyt-Goldsmith, Diane. *Arctic Hunter*. Photographs by Lawrence Migdale. Holiday, 1992 (I:8+ R:5). A photographic essay follows the life of an Eskimo boy and his family.

Hucko, Bruce. *A Rainbow at Night: The World in Words and Pictures by Navajo Children*. Chronicle, 1997 (I:all). Twenty-three reproductions of paintings by Navajo children are included.

Hudson, Jan. *Sweetgrass*. Philomel, 1989; Tree Frog, 1984 (I:10+ R:4). A Blackfoot girl grows up during the winter of a smallpox epidemic in 1837.

Hunter, Sally M. *Four Seasons of Corn: A Winnebago Tradition*. Photographs by Joe Allen. Lerner, 1997 (I:8+ R:4). The text follows a twelve-year-old boy as he learns about his people's relationship with corn.

Jacobs, Francine. *The Tainos: The People Who Welcomed Columbus*. Illustrated by Patrick Collins, Putnam, 1992 (I:8+ R:5). This is the history of the people who inhabited the Caribbean at the time of Columbus.

Jaffe, Nina. *The Golden Flower*. Illustrated by Enrique O. Sanchez, Simon & Schuster, 1966 (I:all R:5). This Taino tale explains the creation of water and vegetation.

Jassem, Kate. *Sacajawea, Wilderness Guide*. Illustrated by Jan Palmer. Troll Associates, 1979 (I:6–9 R:2). This is an illustrated biography of the Shoshone woman who guided the Lewis and Clark expedition.

Jeffers, Susan. *Brother Eagle, Sister Sky: A Message from Chief Seattle*. Dial, 1991 (I:all). A poetic retelling of the words of Chief Seattle.

Jones, Jennifer Berry. *Heetunka's Harvest: A Tale of the Plains Indians*. Illustrated by Shannon Keegan, Rinehart, 1994 (I:5–9 R:6). A Dakota woman learns her lesson after she is greedy.

Joosse, Barbara M. *Mama, Do You Love Me?* Illustrated by Barbara Lavalle. Chronicle, 1991 (I:3–7). A young child tests her mother's love.

Keegan, Marcia. *Pueblo Boy: Growing Up in Two Worlds*. Cobblehill, 1991 (I:6–10 R:5). A photographic essay depicts the life of a contemporary boy.

Lawlor, Laurie. *Shadow Catcher: The Life and Work of Edward S. Curtis*. Walker, 1994 (I:10+ R:7). This biography is illustrated with reproductions of photographs of Native American life.

Leon, George DeLucenay. *Explorers of the Americas Before Columbus*. This book traces early explorations.

Lewis, Paul Owen. *Storm Boy*. Beyond Words, 1995 (I:7+ R:5). A Native American boy from the Northwest Coast is lost at sea and interacts with masked beings in this literary folktale.

Lipsyte, Robert. *The Brave*. HarperCollins, 1991 (I:12+ R:6). A young Native American man faces many obstacles in his desire to become a boxer.

Littlechild, George. *This Land Is My Land*. Children's, 1993 (I:7+ R:4). A biography is developed through the history of the people.

Luenn, Nancy. *Nessa's Fish*. Atheneum, 1990 (I:4–8 R:4). An Inuit girl and her grandmother go on an ice fishing expedition.

Lyon, George Ella. *Dreamplace*. Orchard, 1993 (I:5–9 R:4). A young girl dreams about the original people who lived on the site of the Anasazies.

McDermott, Gerald. *Raven: A Trickster Tale from the Pacific Northwest.* Harcourt Brace & Jovanovich, 1993 (I:all). This trickster tale tells how light was brought to the people.

Marrin, Albert. *Plains Warrior: Chief Quanah Parker and the Comanches.* Simon & Schuster, 1996 (I:10+ R:6). The biography includes history of the Comanche relationship with the settlers.

Martin, Bill, and John Archambault. *Knots on a Counting Rope.* Holt, Rinehart & Winston, 1987 (I:all). A poetic story is about a blind boy's horse race as told by his grandfather.

Martin, Rafe. *The Boy Who Lived with the Seals.* Putnam, 1993 (I:10+ R:5). This Chinook Indian tale is about a boy who was raised by seals.

Metayer, Maurice, ed. *Tales from the Igloo.* Illustrated by Agnes Nanogak. Hurtig, 1972 (I:all R:5). This is a collection of Copper Eskimo tales.

Miles, Miska. *Annie and the Old One.* Illustrated by Peter Parnall. Little, Brown, 1971 (I:6–8 R:3). Annie's love for her Navaho grandmother causes her to prevent the completion of a rug that she associates with the probable death of her grandmother.

Monroe, Jean Guard, and Ray A. Williamson. *They Dance in the Sky: Native American Star Myths.* Illustrated by Edgar Stewart. Houghton Mifflin, 1987 (I:10+ R:7). This collection of tales is from different peoples.

Morgan, William. *Navajo Coyote Tales.* Ancient City Press, 1988 (I:6+). This collection of tales is for younger readers.

Morrison, Dorothy Nafus. *Chief Sarah: Sarah Winnemucca's Fight for Indian Rights.* Atheneum, 1980 (I:10+ R:6). Sarah was a leader of the Paiute people.

Mowat, Farley. *Lost in the Barrens.* Illustrated by Charles Geer. McClelland & Stewart, 1966, 1984 (I:9+ R:6). A Cree Indian boy and his friend are lost in northern Canada.

Nashone. *Grandmother Stories of the Northwest.* Sierra Oaks, 1988 (I:all). These five stories are from the Northwest.

Norman, Howard, retold by. *The Girl Who Dreamed Only Geese and Other Tales of the Far North.* Illustrated by Leo and Diane Dillon. Harcourt Brace, 1997 (I:9+ R:6). Includes ten tales from Inuit folklore.

Normandin, Christine, ed. *Echoes of the Elders: The Stories and Paintings of Chief Lalooska.* DK, 1997 (I:all). Includes folklore and illustrations from the Kwakiutl people from the Northwest Coast of North America.

O'Dell, Scott. *Black Star, Bright Dawn.* Houghton Mifflin, 1988 (I:8+ R:6). An Eskimo girl enters the Iditarod Trail Sled Dog Race in Alaska.

_____. *Sing Down the Moon.* Houghton Mifflin, 1970 (I:10+ R:6). A young Navaho girl tells of the 1864 forced march of her people.

_____, and Elizabeth Hall. *Thunder Rolling in the Mountains.* Houghton Mifflin, 1992 (I:10+ R:6). This historical novel is told from the point of view of Chief Joseph's daughter.

Oughton, Jerrie. *How the Stars Fell into the Sky: A Navajo Legend.* Illustrated by Lisa Desimini. Houghton Mifflin, 1992 (I:4–8 R:5). Because of Coyote's impatience, First Woman cannot write the laws for the people.

Paulsen, Gary. *Dogsong.* Bradbury, 1988 (I:10+ R:6). An Eskimo boy journeys 1,400 miles by dogsled as he crosses the ice.

Pollock, Penny, retold by. *The Turkey Girl: A Zuni Cinderella Story.* Illustrated by Ed Young. Little, Brown, 1996 (I:5–9 R:6). The original tale is in Frank Hamilton Cushing's *Zuni Folk Tales.*

Prusski, Jeffrey. *Bring Back the Deer.* Illustrated by Neil Waldman. Harcourt Brace Jovanovich, 1988 (I:6+ R:5). A Native American boy discovers the values of respect, wisdom, and patience.

Rosen, Michael, retold by. *Crow and Hawk: A Traditional Pueblo Indian Story.* Illustrated by John Clementson. Harcourt Brace, 1995 (I:5–9 R:5). This is a Pueblo tale.

Roth, Susan. *The Story of Light.* Morrow, 1990 (I:6–10). This is a retelling of a Cherokee myth about the bringing of light.

St. George, Judith. *To See with the Heart: The Life of Sitting Bull.* Putnam, 1996 (I:10+ R:6). This is a biography of the Sioux Chief.

Sewall, Marcia. *People of the Breaking Day.* Atheneum, 1990 (I:8+ R:5). This is a nonfictional description of the Wampanoag nation of southeastern Massachusetts.

Sis, Peter. *A Small Tall Tale from the Far Far North.* Knopf, 1993 (I:6+ R:5). A Czech hero travels to the Arctic in 1893.

Sneve, Virginia Driving Hawk, selected by. *Dancing Teepees: Poems of American Indian Youth.* Illustrated by Stephen Gammell. Holiday House, 1989 (I:all). This is a collection of ancient and contemporary poems.

_____. *High Elk's Treasure.* Illustrated by Oren Lyons. Holiday House, 1972 (I:8–12 R:6). A dream beginning in the autumn of 1876 is renewed in the 1970s when Joe High Elk's family expands the herd of palomino horses.

Speare, Elizabeth George. *The Sign of the Beaver.* Houghton Mifflin, 1983 (I:8–12 R:5). A white boy survives through the help of a Native American friend.

Spencer, Paula Underwood. *Who Speaks for Wolf.* Illustrated by Frank Howell. Tribe of Two Press, 1983 (I:all R:5). This is a Native American learning story.

Steptoe, John. *The Story of Jumping Mouse.* Lothrop, Lee & Shepard, 1984 (I:all R:4). This is a Great Plains Indian legend.

Stevens, Janet. *Coyote Steals the Blanket: A Ute Tale.* Holiday, 1993 (I:all). This trickster tale is from the Southwest.

Swanson, Diane. *Buffalo Sunrise: The Story of a North American Giant.* Little, Brown, 1996 (I:10+ R:9). A section includes a discussion about how the buffalo provided for the Blackfoot families.

Tompert, Ann. *How Rabbit Lost His Tail.* Illustrated by Jacqueline Chwast. Houghton Mifflin, 1997 (I:7+ R:4). This Seneca tale explains how rabbit lost his long tail.

Valgardson, W. D. *Sarah and the People of Sand River.* Illustrated by Ian Wallace. Douglas & McIntyre, 1996 (I:8+ R:4). In a literary folktale a girl is helped by the Cree people.

Van Laan, Nancy, retold by. *Buffalo Dance: A Blackfoot Legend.* Illustrated by Beatriz Vidal. Little, Brown, 1993 (I:7+ R:4). This is a story about respect between humans and animals.

_____, retold by. *Shingebliss: An Ojibwe Legend.* Illustrated by Betsy Bowen. Houghton Mifflin, 1997 (I:7+ R:4). Wisdom and persistence prove to be important values.

Wallas, James. *Kwakiutl Legends.* Recorded by Pamela Whitaker. Hancock House, 1981 (I:all R:4). Tales from British Columbia are told by Chief Wallas of the Quatsino tribe.

Whitaker, Muriel, ed. *Stories from the Canadian North.* Illustrated by Vlasta van Kampen. Hurtig, 1980 (I:12+ R:7). This is a collection of short stories.

White Deer of Autumn. *Ceremony—In the Circle of Life.* Illustrated by Daniel San Souci. Raintree, 1983 (I:all R:5). A nine-year-old boy discovers his ancestors' beliefs.

Yolen, Jane. *Encounter.* Illustrated by David Shannon. Harcourt Brace Jovanovich, 1992 (I:6–10 R:5). This is the hypothetical story of a Taino boy who tells about the landing of Columbus.

Illustration by the National Park Service from *Volcanoes* by Semour Simon, 1988. William
Morrow and Company, Inc.

12 Nonfiction: Biographies and Informational Books

 From Who's-Who to How-To

- Biographies
- Informational Books

 Involving Children in Nonfictional Literature

- Unit Plan: Using Biographies in Creative Dramatizations
- Comparing Attitudes and Checking Facts in Biographies
- Investigating the Qualities of Writers
- Analyzing Literary Elements in Biographies
- Incorporating Literature into the Science Curriculum

From Who's-Who to How-To

uriosity and the desire to make discoveries about the world strongly motivate children to read. Books of nonfiction encourage children to look at the world in new ways, to discover laws of nature and society, and to identify with people different from themselves. Biographer Russell Freedman (1992) develops the importance of and the purposes for nonfiction when he states:

Certainly the basic purpose of nonfiction is to inform, to instruct, hopefully to enlighten. But that's not enough. An effective nonfiction book must animate its subject, infuse it with life. It must create a vivid and believable world that the reader will enter willingly and leave only with reluctance. A good nonfiction book should be a pleasure to read. It should be just as compelling as a good story. After all, there's a story to everything. The task of the nonfiction writer is to find the story—the narrative line—that exists in nearly every subject. (p. 3)

🍃 BIOGRAPHIES

Many children who read well-written biographies feel as if the biographical subjects become personal friends. Often, these children carry with them into adulthood a love of nonfiction that portrays the lives of interesting people with whom they can identify and from whom they can learn. Biography offers children the high adventure and engrossing drama that fiction also supplies, but it also offers the special satisfaction of knowing that the people and events described are "really real."

Writers of biographies have a vast pool of real people from which to choose. There are brave men and women who conquer seas, encounter new continents, and explore space. There are equally brave and intelligent women and men who fight discrimination, change lives through their ministering or inventions, and overcome disabilities in their efforts to achieve. The ways in which writers of children's literature choose to portray these figures, however, change with historical time periods.

Changing Ideas About Biographies for Children

A brief review of biographies for children shows that the authors of biographies have been influenced by social attitudes toward children and attitudes about appropriate content. Children's biographies written in the seventeenth through the nineteenth centuries in Europe and North America were affected by the didactic themes of the Puritan era, the Victorian emphasis on duty to God and parents, the values associated with the American frontier, and the belief that children should be educated in a highly structured environment. In addition, early biographers believed that children's biographies should be tools for religious, political, or social education. Emulation of biographical heroes was considered desirable (Norton, 1984). Consequently, many pre-twentieth century biographies reflected the belief that literature should save children's souls. Jon Stott (1979) concludes that this time produced numerous "biographies of good little children who died early and went to Heaven and of bad little children who died early and went to Hell" (p. 177). For example, in 1671, leading Puritan writer James Janeway published a series of stories about children who died at an early age after leading saintly lives.

In the mid-1800s, the religious zeal of many early Americans was replaced by concern for the nation and the acquisition of the "American dream." Salvation was no longer the primary goal. The supreme achievements were acquisition of power, fame, and wealth. Consequently, biography changed from a religious tool to a political tool.

The early twentieth century brought new insights into child development. The developing science of psychology emphasized the vulnerability of youth and a need for protective legislation. Religious training placed less emphasis on sinfulness and more emphasis on moral development and responsibility toward others. In keeping with these ideas, biographers also protected children from the indiscretions of biographical subjects. Because idealized heroes were still believed to be desirable and necessary, biographers avoided areas concerning sensitive political beliefs and private lives. Taboos imposed by society included infamous people, unsavory or undistinguishing actions, and controversial subjects.

Furthermore, in the early 1900s, as in earlier periods of American history, the contributions of female and nonwhite Americans were either not highly regarded or were considered too controversial. Traditional social patterns kept most women and members of minority groups out of the positions of power and the fame that produced what American society considered the most appropriate subjects of biography. Consequently, few biographies dealt with women, African Americans, Native Americans, and members of other ethnic and racial minorities.

Biographies of most political leaders published through the 1960s continued to present role models for political and social instruction. Omissions and distortions allowed biographers to stress important contributions and to highlight dates of accomplishment. Biographers still did not explore motives. Literary critic Margery Fisher (1976) maintains that biographies for children were controlled by an establishment that exercised a powerful invisible influence. William Epstein (1987) argues, "State-supported American education is more or less a product of middle-class values and aspirations, and biography has almost always been an ally of the dominant structures of authority" (p. 179).

In an effort to increase the ability of children to empathize with political heroes, biographers writing for young readers often focused on the boyhood years of their characters. Still, these biographers tended to glorify the individuals. For example, the titles of several biographies published by Bobbs-Merrill before 1980 indicated the accomplishments that the subjects would achieve: *Thomas Paine: Common Sense Boy* and *John D. Rockefeller: Boy Financier.*

During the late 1960s and the 1970s, traditional social, family, and personal values were changing.

The new openness was reflected in fiction for children. In addition, the previous instructional uses of, and role models in, children's biography were challenged. Some literary critics, educators, and authors of children's biographies maintained that idealizing subjects distorted not only history but also development. According to this argument, if prominent men and women were shown in favorable lights only, children would assume that because they themselves make errors, they could never be great. In an effort to overcome past shortcomings in biographies for children, Marilyn Jurich (1972) advocated a greater variety in the choice of subjects—including great people who were not famous, ordinary people, and antiheroes—as well as a fuller and more honest treatment of all subjects. Biographer Russell Freedman (1988) summarizes the changes when he concludes:

The hero worship of the past has given way to a more realistic approach, which recognizes the warts and weaknesses that humanize the great. And fictionalization has become a naughty word. Many current biographies for children adhere as closely to documented evidence as any scholarly work. And the best of them manage to do so without becoming tedious or abstract or any less exciting than the most imaginative fictionalization. (p. 447)

As with realistic fiction, educators, authors, publishers, and parents today have different opinions about what the content of children's biographies should be. Jean Fritz (1976), a well-known author of historical biographies for young children, says:

Biographies have for the most part lagged behind other types of children's literature, bogged down, for one thing, by didacticism. Famous men and women must be shown in their best colors so children can emulate them. The idea of emulation has been a powerful factor in determining the nature of biography for children; you see the word over and over again in textbooks and courses of study. And I think it has done great harm in distorting history and breeding cynicism; the great men are all gone, the implication is. Because history is old, educators are often guilty of simply repeating it instead of taking a fresh look at it. Because it is complicated, they tend to simplify by watering down material for children, whereas children need more meat rather than less, but selected for their own interests. This, of course, involves original research, a great deal of it, which twenty years ago, I think was rather rare in children's biographies. (p. 125)

Biographies now develop many sides of a person's character—as well as people who are female and nonwhite, like many young readers themselves.

On Writing Biography

JEAN FRITZ, biographer of early American patriots, creates believable characters by admitting their foibles as well as their strengths.

The reason for writing biography for children is the same as for writing biography for adults: to explore human behavior; to come to grips with specific characters interrelating with their specific times. This is not as obvious as it sounds. It was once a commonly held assumption (one that still persists in some quarters) that biographies written for children should portray idealized heroes and heroines, models held up by the adult world to inspire children to attain virtue and, by implication, its concomitant rewards. Furthermore, according to some educators, the motivation of characters should not be examined, only their deeds.

Such an approach, it seems to me, is dull, unrealistic, and unfair. Children look for clues to life. They want the truth, they need the truth, and they deserve it. So I try to present characters honestly with their paradoxes and their complexities, their strengths and their weaknesses. To do this, I involve myself in as much research as I would if I were writing a biography for adults. Contrary to what I call "old-fashioned" biography for children, I do not invent dialogue. I use dialogue only when I can document it. If the text is meaty enough, I do not think that children need facts dressed up in fictional trimmings. Indeed, children welcome hard, specific facts that bring characters to life—not only the important facts but those small vivid details that have a way of lighting up an event or a personality. Had I been present, for instance, to hear Patrick Henry give his famous "liberty or death" speech, I would certainly have been impressed by his dramatic oratory, but I would also have remembered the man in the balcony who became so excited, he spit a wad of tobacco into the audience below. The trivial and the significant generally travel hand in hand and indeed I suspect that most people find that memory of trivial off-the-record detail serves to nail down memory itself. I think of history and biography as *story* and am convinced that the best stories are the true ones.

Readers may discover, through the work of such authors as Jean Fritz, that the heroes of biography were real people who, like other humans, often demonstrated negative qualities. In fact, a biographical subject who is a believable human being may be easier for children to emulate than a subject who is not.

Gertrude B. Herman (1977) relates changing understanding of biography to children's stages of personal development. She maintains that until children are about eight years old, they have difficulty stepping out of their own time and space to explore the lives of real people whom they most likely can never meet. Herman believes that children in the fourth through sixth grades read biographies with increasing understanding and self-identification, as long as the books are about people they are interested in and the authors have written to hold the children's interest. In adolescence, says Herman, children are:

finally ready for causes . . . and for all those fascinating persons who are not necessarily models of perfection, but who are human beings through whose doubts and triumphs, courage or villainy, victories or defeats, young people may try on personalities, life styles, and modes of thought and commitment. It is in investigating, in shifting and winnowing facts and ideas, in empathizing with the deeds and sufferings of others that growth is helped along—intellectual, emotional, and spiritual growth. It is through this integrative function that biography and autobiography, honestly presented with literary and artistic merit, can make important contributions to self-integration and social realization. The testimony of many individuals over many years supports a conviction that young people have much to gain from reading about real human beings in all their complexity, with all their sometimes troubled lives. (p. 88)

As we evaluate current biographies and other nonfiction materials, we should also consider Roger Sutton's (1996) concerns. He maintains that with the awarding of the Newbery Medal to Russell Freedman's *Lincoln: A Photobiography* "we were supposed to get a renaissance" because the award affirmed a groundswell of attention to juvenile nonfiction. However, he is not sure that this has happened. Sutton maintains that "real money has been in series books that are efficient, often eye-catching, and intellectually barren, merely rearranging and/or padding the facts that can be found in any reputable encyclopedia" (p. 665). He is concerned that books of literary quality and books that foster "passion and imagination" are in short supply. As you read biographies and other nonfictional works, try to separate the books that you consider of high quality content from the books that Sutton classifies as merely "Great for Reports!"

Literary Criticism: Evaluating Biographies

Like other literature, biographies should be evaluated according to the criteria for good literature. They should carefully avoid negative stereotypes based on gender, race, ethnicity, and physical ability. With regard to literary elements, characterization is

𝓔 VALUATION CRITERIA

Literary Criticism: Biography

1. Does the biography meet the criteria for good literature?

2. Is the subject of the biography worth reading about?

3. Is the biography factually accurate in relation to characters, plots, and settings?

4. Does the biographer distinguish between fact and judgment and fact and fiction?

5. Does the biographer use primary sources when conducting research for the text? Are these sources included in the bibliographies or other notes to the readers?

6. Does the biographer include photographs and other documents that increase the credibility of the text?

7. If the biographer uses illustrations other than photographs, are the illustrations accurate according to the life and time of the person?

8. Does the writing style appeal to readers?

of primary concern, and authors of biography must place special emphasis on accuracy of detail and use sound research methods. (See the Evaluation Criteria box on this page for additional criteria.)

Characterization. Margaret Fleming and Jo McGinnis (1985) compare the artistry required in the writing of a good biography to the artistry required in the painting of a portrait: The "style and setting only enhance the portrayal of the subject. The development of character is the primary focus" (p. xi). Like other authors, biographers have a responsibility to portray their subjects three-dimensionally. Unlike authors of fiction, biographers are restricted from inventing characters and indicating unsupported thoughts and actions.

Elizabeth Robertson and Jo McGinnis (1985) provide the following guideline for evaluating characterization:

In biography, the writer can only infer from the actions of the subject and other characters what might be going on in the person's head. Look for evidence that the biographer is overstepping the bounds of scholarly writing in this respect. (p. 19)

Robertson and McGinnis recommend that readers analyze the supporting characters in a biography and the influence of these characters on the main character by answering the following questions:

Who are the people who most influenced the life of the subject? How important were these people in the development of the subject's character? Were they positive or negative influences? How are they developed as characters? What differences are there between a fictional development of character and this non-fictional work? How would life for the subject have been different if these influences had not been present? (p. 19)

Another way to analyze the characterization in a biography, according to Robertson and McGinnis, is to examine the biographical subject by analyzing the subject's thoughts about himself or herself as reflected in autobiographies, journals, essays, speeches, and letters. Does the subject perceive himself or herself in a way different from that developed by the biographer? What might account for differences in characterization?

Author Virginia Hamilton (1992) believes that characterization in biography must go beyond the known facts of a life. After the research:

then one proceeds in the same way as with a question. How did this person really move in time and space? Who was he inside, where no one is the wiser about him but himself? Is there any light in there, any way to see? The researcher-novelist must find an opening within the real person of the biography so that the life is in the spotlight in full view, and exists again. (p. 678)

Factual Accuracy. Comparisons between biographies for children and biographies for adults and between biographies and reference books often reveal differences in basic facts. Ann W. Moore (1985) reports:

Errors in contemporary children's biographies fall into one of the following three categories: (1) inaccuracies in numbers, dates, and names, items easily checked in reference books or authorized and/or reputable adult titles; (2) incomplete, unclear, or misleading statements caused by attempts at simplification; and (3) patently false, incorrect information. (p. 34)

Moore emphasizes the need for writers and publishers to improve the accuracy of biographies for children and for reviewers to check the facts against reputable sources. Biographies have a special responsibility to be accurate and authentic in characters and settings. The task is so important and demanding that May Hill Arbuthnot and Dorothy M. Broderick (1969) say that biographers "should be prepared to spend months, and probably longer, in study and research before touching the typewriter" (p. 225). Extensive research should use recent scholarly works and historical materials that indicate what the subjects and others of the time actually said and wrote.

Any search for accuracy should include a wide range of sources. For example, Russell Freedman (1988), author of the 1988 Newbery Medal winner *Lincoln: A Photobiography,* stresses the importance of visiting original sites and studying original materials. Freedman states:

There's something magic about being able to lay your eyes on the real thing—something you can't get from your reading alone. As I sat at my desk in New York City and described Lincoln's arrival in New Salem at the age of twenty-two, I could picture the scene in my mind's eye, because I had walked down those same dusty lanes, where cattle still graze behind split-rail fences and geese flap about underfoot. When I wrote about Lincoln's morning walk from his house to his law office in downtown Springfield, I knew the route because I had walked it myself. (p. 449)

Frank J. Dempsey (1988) verifies Freedman's research in Springfield, Illinois, when he describes Freedman's fervor for on-site research. Other authors often mention research in historical societies, newspaper records, diaries, and letters. Often, they visit actual locations. Even simple biographies for young children must be accurate in the illustrations, as well as in the text, because young children acquire much of their knowledge about a time or a setting from the illustrations rather than from detailed descriptions.

It is helpful if a biographer includes a bibliography. Freedman includes "A Lincoln Sampler" (a listing of quotes from Lincoln's speeches), "In Lincoln's Footsteps" (a listing of historical sites), and "Books About Lincoln" (a listing of additional sources). Both Milton Meltzer's *Benjamin Franklin: The New American* and Virginia Hamilton's *Anthony Burns: The Defeat and Triumph of a Fugitive Slave* also include ex-

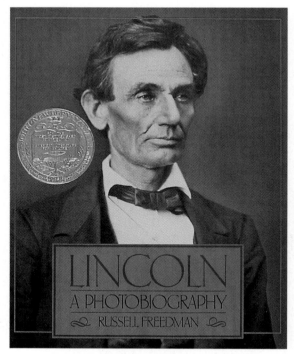

Russell Freedman develops a carefully documented biography in his book. (From Lincoln: A Photobiography *by Russell Freedman, copyright © 1987. Reprinted by permission of Clarion Books, a Houghton Mifflin Company.)*

tensive listings of the primary sources used by the authors.

According to biographer Olivia Coolidge (1974), authors of biographical literature must also distinguish fact from judgment. Coolidge says:

A good biography is also concerned with the effect its hero has on other people, with environment and background, with the nature of . . . achievements, and their value. I find that I examine facts in all these and many other spheres before I form judgments and that it needs great care to do what sounds quite easy, namely to distinguish a fact from a judgment. (p. 146)

Coolidge concludes her concern over fact and judgment by saying:

It simply seems that I need to know everything possible—because knowledge may affect judgment or because I am not yet really certain what I shall use or omit. In other words, I find it necessary to have a habit of worrying about facts, small or large, because my buildings are made up of these bricks, stones, or even pebbles. (p. 148)

In addition to separating fact and judgment, biographers also must contend with separating fact and legend. In her biography, *Calamity Jane: Her Life and Her Legend,* Doris Faber introduces her character by asking "Who Was She?" Then she states:

But was she a real person or just a made-up character in adventure stories? The answer to this question is a little complicated. Yes, there was a real woman nicknamed Calamity Jane, who loved to talk about having lived through many exciting adventures—but much of what she said could not really have happened the way she told it. There also was a writer who somehow got the idea of calling the imaginary heroine of some of his most popular tales Calamity Jane. Then, around a hundred years ago, the actual person and the fictional heroine began merging in the public mind, creating the same kind of legendary figure as Johnny Appleseed, for instance. (p. 1)

Throughout her biography Faber separates fact from legend.

Worthiness of Subject.
The subject of a biography should be worth reading about, just as she or he should be worthy of the meticulous research and time that the author spends in writing. Has the subject made a significant impact on the world—for good or for ill—that children should be aware of? Will children have a better understanding of the complexities of human nature after they have read the biography? Will they discover that history is made up of real people when they read the book? Will they appreciate the contributions of their ancestors or their heritage through the life of the person in the biography?

The subjects of biography and autobiography need not be famous, infamous, or outstanding in a worldly sense in order for their lives to communicate important lessons about people and society. The subjects should be portrayed in believable ways, however. Whether a notable personage or an unsung hero of everyday life, the person upon whom a biographer focuses should have a many-faceted character, just like the people children know. Jean Fritz, for example, has written a series of historical biographies suggesting that leaders of the American Revolution were very human. Fritz portrays Patrick Henry as a practical joker who did not appreciate school in his youth, and Samuel Adams as a man who was not afraid to speak out against the British but who refused to ride a horse.

Whereas Fritz's biographies emphasize the lives of well-known people, John Jakes's *Susanna of the Alamo* develops a story line around unsung heroes. Jakes characterizes a brave woman whose life is spared by Santa Anna, the Mexican general, so that she can take a message to Sam Houston.

Balance Between Fact and Story Line.
Writers of biographies for children must balance the requirement for accuracy with the requirement for a narrative that appeals to children. For example, authors may emphasize humorous facts as they develop plots and characters that present information in story formats. A poor balance between fact and story line may cause problems for young readers. Children have difficulty evaluating differences between fiction and nonfiction. Jean Fritz's (1982) foreword to her own fictionalized autobiography, *Homesick: My Own Story,* clarifies differences between fiction and biography:

Since my childhood feels like a story, I decided to tell it that way, letting the events fall as they would into the shape of a story, lacing them together with fictional bits, adding a piece here and there when memory didn't give me all I needed. I would use conversation freely, for I cannot think of my childhood without hearing voices. So although this book takes place within two years from October 1925 to September 1927, the events are drawn from the entire period of my childhood, but they are all, except in minor details, basically true. The people are real people; the places are dear to me. But most important, the form I have used has given me the freedom to recreate the emotions that I remember so vividly. Strictly speaking, I have to call this book fiction, but it does not feel like fiction to me. It is my story, told as truly as I can tell it. (foreword)

Writers of biographies for older children usually include extensive factual detail. For example, in his note on sources in *Benjamin Franklin: The New American,* Milton Meltzer stipulates that he uses quoted passages from Franklin's own writings. He does, how-

ever, modernize "them as to spelling, capitalization, punctuation, and paragraphing. This, only to make Franklin more easily accessible to today's readers, in preference to preserving the eighteenth-century modes" (p. 280). This type of information allows readers to evaluate the appropriateness of changes.

Biographies in Picture-Book Format.   There are currently numerous biographies written as picture books in which much of the information about the character, the setting, and the times are reflected in the illustrations. The illustrations in many biogra-

---

*I*SSUE   **Children's Biographies: Truth versus Partial Fictionalization in Biographical Writing**

How much of a children's biography, including the dialogue and thoughts of the people, should be actual and verifiable? Is it permissible to create possible dialogues and thoughts? How should the requirements of younger readers influence the writing and illustrating of biographies? These are some of the questions that currently surround biographical writing.

According to Linda Girard,[1] the roles of fact and fiction are important. Girard states:

Critics of children's books have damned a whole generation of biography for its made-up scenes and dialogues and called for a disciplined return from fancy to fact. But does invented dialogue necessarily make bad biography? And should biography return to pure fact? (p. 465)

Girard follows this question with examples from Jean Fritz's biographies. Girard claims that Fritz has brought truth back to biography but "with some stretchers," such as "invented dialogue, indirect discourse, interior monologue, and attribution" (p. 469).

Jean Fritz[2] provides her viewpoints for facts versus fiction by stating:

My facts are my stepping stones, and it seems a very small step to go from Sam Houston's political and emotional stress at the time of the revival meeting to the fact that "his heart welled up and he knew he was ready." . . . Well, I don't make up facts, but at the same time I have no desire to write in a factual style. Nonfiction can be told in a narrative voice and still maintain its integrity. The art of fiction is making up facts; the art of nonfiction is using facts to make up a form. Incidentally, I really do not use quotation marks unless I have a source. (p. 759)

Diane Stanley[3] discusses issues related to writing and illustrating biographies for younger readers. In comparing these biographies to biographies written for older audiences, Stanley states: "Usually the scope is narrower, allowing more room for rich detail, and these books are lavishly illustrated in color. The message they convey is that history is just another fascinating story—as enjoyable to read as a fairy tale" (p. 209).

Stanley uses her own experiences in writing and illustrating *Peter the Great* and *Shaka, King of the Zulus* to highlight her problems and concerns. For example, Stanley discusses the constraints of length, the exclusion of

details inappropriate or boring for younger readers, the need to balance the virtues and vices of the subjects, and the research that allows the illustrations to go beyond the written text.

After reading several biographies for younger and older audiences, identify issues that surround the writing of each type of book. How should the facts be presented in biographical writing? How does the author's style influence the readability of the text? What words and techniques do the biographers use to let the readers know that the dialogue is factual or fictional? (For example, a biographer may use quotations to show that the dialogue is taken from a source or terms such as *perhaps* to let readers know that the text is based on conjecture.) Are these techniques appropriate?

---

[1]Girard, Linda. "The Truth with Some Stretchers." *The Horn Book* (July/August 1988): 464–469.

[2]Fritz, Jean. "Biography: Readability Plus Responsibility." *The Horn Book* (November/December 1988): 759–760.

[3]Stanley, Diane. "Picture Book History." *The New Advocate* 1 (Fall 1988): 209–220.

---

phies written for younger children are especially important according to Katheleen Odean (1996) because the illustrations supplement the spare texts by providing details about the historical era.

When the illustrations provide this type of detail for a person's life, it is very important to critically evaluate the illustrations. Joanna Rudge Long (1997) provides several guidelines that should be considered when evaluating illustrated biographies. For example, the style and visual references should be appropriate for the intended audience. The pictorial motifs should be appropriate for the text. The author and illustrator should provide sources. The attitudes and points of view conveyed by the illustrations should be in harmony with the subject's true spirit. Long believes that illustrated biographies can enhance understandings of a person's life. She states, "An artist's eloquently expressed vision can transform a subject; at best, it can enhance understanding by heightening perceptions, or by presenting a familiar realm in an unexpected light" (p. 48). Long believes that Diane Stanley's *Leonardo da Vinci* and Peter Sis's *Starry Messenger* meet these guidelines for illustrated biographies.

Biographical Subjects

The subjects of biographies and autobiographies for children range from early European explorers and rulers to American space travelers and ordinary people of today. Political leaders rise to eminence in times of need, and social activists speak out against oppression. Great achievers make contributions in science, art, literature, and sports. Common people express uncommon courage in their daily struggle for survival.

Explorers of Earth and Space.   People who question existing boundaries and explore the unknown fascinate children and adults alike, and they are the subjects of numerous biographies. The consequences of the quest of Columbus are familiar to every schoolchild and are portrayed in many biographies. These biographies differ in literary style, focus, amount of detail, and development of character. Consequently, they are good for evaluation and comparison.

Before beginning a discussion of the biographies about early explorers, it is wise to consider some of the concerns generated about these materials in

1992, as numerous biographies and other information literature emerged about the Columbus experience. The National Council for the Social Studies (1992) lists some basic knowledge that critics and educators should consider when they evaluate the sources. First, neither Columbus nor any other of the early explorers discovered a new world. It was a world of people with rich and complex histories. Second, the real America that Columbus encountered in 1492 was different from the pre-contact America often portrayed in texts. It was a world of highly developed and complex civilizations. Third, in 1492, Africa was a part of the social, economic, and political system of the Eastern Hemisphere. Fourth, the encounters of Native Americans, Africans, and Europeans following 1492 are not stories of vigorous white actors confronting passive red and black spectators. All parties borrowed from and influenced the others and were influenced by them. Fifth, as a result of 1492, Native Americans suffered catastrophic mortality rates. Sixth, Columbus's voyages were not just a European phenomenon. They were a facet of Europe's history of interaction with Asia and Africa. Seventh, Spain and Portugal, as well as northwestern Europe, had significant effects on the Americas. As you read various biographies and other informational literature about this time period, also consider how the biographies meet the concerns of the National Council for the Social Studies as well as the criteria for literary standards.

One of the earliest biographical subjects for explorers of earth and space is found in Kathryn Lasky's *The Librarian Who Measured the Earth*. Lasky develops the wonder associated with the Greek geographer, Eratosthenes, who determined the circumference of the earth using techniques such as trying to calculate how long it took camels to get from one city to another, dropping plumb lines, and measuring the angles of shadows. Surprisingly, his measurements accomplished over two thousand years ago are within two hundred miles of those measured with the latest technology. Kevin Hawkes's illustrations develop the ancient setting, the importance of the Alexandria Museum, and Eratosthenes's quest to answer questions about the earth.

Leonard Everett Fisher's *Prince Henry the Navigator* is a heavily illustrated biography written for younger readers. Fisher enhances understanding of Prince Henry and the time period by including a chronology of events that influenced the Iberian

Peninsula and maps that show the various routes of Portuguese explorations.

Although the biography does not include much characterization of Prince Henry, Fisher does emphasize Henry's importance as the founder of the School of Navigation, the first maritime institute in the world for deep-water research. Fisher explains that research at the school improved the circular astrolabe, the triangular quadrant, and the compass. In addition, the explorers associated with the school were required to draw maps, chart currents, and keep daily written logs of their activities at sea. According to Fisher, these activities had not been previously required of sea captains.

The importance of Prince Henry is further emphasized because he developed a new type of vessel, the caravel, which allowed explorers to travel farther and faster. Fisher makes connections with the later Christopher Columbus by explaining that Columbus benefited from Prince Henry's school and his discoveries.

Biographies of Christopher Columbus are found in both highly illustrated versions for young children and carefully documented texts for older readers. Alice Dalgliesh's simple, highly illustrated picture book *The Columbus Story* is characterized by short sentences and repetitive language. For example, Dalgliesh uses the following words to introduce readers to the growing desire of Columbus to go to sea:

Mystery, danger, adventure—what exciting words! Christopher wanted more than ever to be a sailor. The wind that ruffled his red hair seemed to call to him, "Come, come, come!" The waves that lapped the wharves said it over and over. (p. 3, unnumbered)

Dalgliesh focuses on three incidents in Columbus's life: (1) his unsuccessful pleas to the king of Portugal, (2) his successful pleas to the queen of Spain, and (3) his first voyage to America. This simpler version does not develop the problems and disappointments that later plagued Columbus.

Peter Sis's *Follow the Dream* is primarily a picture book that briefly describes the life of Columbus. The strength of the book is the art rather than the text. Compare the text and illustrations in Sis's book with the text and illustrations in David Adler's *Christopher Columbus: Great Explorer*, a book also written for young readers.

Ingri and Edgar Parin D'Aulaire's *Columbus*, written for slightly older children, includes details that

develop a Columbus quite different from the Columbus in the Dalgliesh version. Additional information enables children to visualize an explorer who did not recognize the magnitude of his discovery and who considered himself a failure because he had not reached the Far East. The D'Aulaires say: "Old and tired, Columbus returned to Spain from his fourth and last voyage. While he was searching in vain, the Portuguese had found the seaway to the East by sailing south around Africa. Now Columbus stood in the shadow" (p. 54).

Jean Fritz's *Where Do You Think You're Going, Christopher Columbus?* is written in a light style that appeals to many children. Through use of detailed background information, Fritz creates a lively history inhabited by realistic people. For example, Columbus's sponsor, Queen Isabella of Spain, "was so religious that if she even found Christians who were not sincere Christians, she had them burned at the stake. (Choir boys sang during the burning so Isabella wouldn't have to hear the screams.)" (p. 17). Fritz ends her book with additional historical notes and an index of people and locations discussed in the book.

Biographies of Columbus written for older readers are interesting sources for analysis and comparison. Use Nancy Smiler Levinson's author's note in *Christopher Columbus: Voyager to the Unknown* to introduce a comparative study of biographies about Christopher Columbus that focuses on differences in point of view and facts included in the biographies. In this note, Levinson details some of the uncertainties about Columbus and his voyages:

The reason for these arguments is that much about Columbus's background, life, and journeys is uncertain. Exactly when and where was he born? Who were his ancestors, and how far back can they be traced? Precisely at what time in his life did he decide to sail the uncharted sea? How authentic are the diaries and documents that have been found and translated? There are many other debatable questions as well. Perhaps the most spirited debate centers around the question: Which is the exact island where Columbus landed in the Americas? (p. vii)

Levinson includes additional controversies and concludes her author's note with the following observation:

All of this should remind us that the study of history is not necessarily a matter of definite and factual events with only one point of view. Different viewpoints and new evidence are frequently what make history exciting to scholars. As we celebrate the quincentenary of the discovery of America, the story of Columbus will again come alive for all of us. (p. viii)

You may choose to focus on how authors report some of these uncertainties by reading biographies written for older readers such as Milton Meltzer's *Columbus and the World Around Him*.

Two books that depict Columbus's journals are interesting sources for comparisons and discussions about Columbus. You may compare Peter and Connie Roop's *I, Columbus—My Journal 1492* and Steve Lowe's *Log of Christopher Columbus: The First Voyage: Spring, Summer & Fall, 1492*.

In the fifteenth and sixteenth centuries, astronomers, such as Nicolaus Copernicus and Galileo Galilei, shared and proved the belief of Christopher Columbus that the world is round. Through their explorations of the stars—by means of mathematical equations, naked-eye observations, and the earliest telescopes—such early explorers of space further shook the foundations of European world views. The astronomers discovered that the earth is not only round but also one of numerous planets rotating around the sun and that the sun itself is only one of many astral bodies moving through the universe. In a time when the church insisted that the earth was the stationary center of the one solar system created by God, these beliefs were radical.

In *Starry Messenger: Galileo Galilei,* Peter Sis presents a highly illustrated version of the scientist's life. By reading this biography students discover Galileo's search for truth in a world in which the church considered his findings to be dangerous. Sis adds authenticity to the biography by including Galileo's own writings within the text. The highly detailed illustrations provide the major strength of the biography. As you read the text and view the illustrations, search for the techniques that Sis uses to develop the time period and to add important information about Galileo and the time period.

In *The Remarkable Voyages of Captain Cook,* Rhoda Blumberg uses techniques that make the characters and the settings both interesting and credible. Blumberg introduces the biography of the eighteenth-century explorer with interesting historical background that allows readers to understand the beliefs of the time that influenced history:

There were tales about miserable brutes, ugly giants, and man-eating monsters who lived in the southern part of the globe. There were also stories about kind, beautiful people who dwelled there in luxury on lush, treasure-laden lands. In the eighteenth century, when King George III ruled England, government officials wanted to know the truth about people and places in the "South Seas," a term used to mean "Pacific Ocean." (p. 1)

In addition, Blumberg explains how erroneous theories influence science:

Geographers were positive that a huge continent could be found in the southern waters of the Pacific or Atlantic oceans. They believed that a vast landmass at the bottom of the world anchored our planet and balanced the weight of Europe, Asia, and Africa in the northern hemisphere. It had to be there, or the earth would be so top-heavy it would turn over on itself. (p. 1)

Blumberg continuously separates facts from fiction, provides interesting anecdotes, quotes cultural observations made by Cook, includes detailed maps of the voyages, and provides historical illustrations. Blumberg encourages readers to understand the

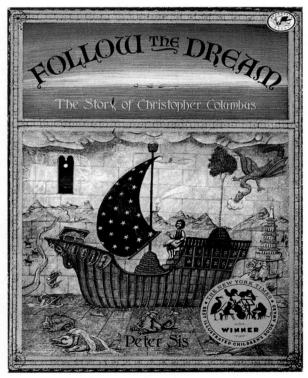

Detailed illustrations provide considerable content in this biography (From Follow the Dream: The Story of Christopher Columbus *by Peter Sis, copyright © 1991, Alfred A. Knopf, Inc. Used by permission of Random House, Inc.)*

impact of Cook's voyages by comparing contemporary exploration: "Captain Cook was embarking upon the eighteenth century's version of a space voyage. Lord Morton speculated that the captain might discover terrestrials who were more highly civilized than Europeans" (p. 1).

The inventions of the Wright Brothers encouraged explorers to open the next great frontier. In *The Wright Brothers: How They Invented the Airplane,* Russell Freedman places readers into the historical context of the time period, provides information about the history of flight, places the inventions of the Wright Brothers into the context of this historical development, supports his text with numerous photographs, and documents his sources.

Amelia Earhart, by Carol Ann Pearce, is the biography of the first woman to fly across the Atlantic Ocean. In showing the early life of Earhart and Earhart's experiences as an aviator, Pearce shows the role of women during early aviation.

Political Leaders and Social Activists. Men and women who have achieved noteworthy political power or who have attempted to bring about social change are common subjects of biography. Often, these public figures are controversial—adored by some, deplored by others. As a result, biographers sometimes create unbalanced portraits of their subjects. Because biographers usually, but not always, choose to write about people they admire, hagiography (literally, "the biography of saints"), rather than objective biography, may result. Even authors who create well-rounded portrayals of political leaders and social activists inevitably express their own perspectives. For example, after reading three books about a certain political leader, one student of children's literature commented that she could have been reading about three different people. Because each author had a specific purpose in writing a biography, characterization of the person, choice of events to discuss, style, and tone created a different bias. If possible, read several biographies about the same person and draw your own conclusions.

Several biographies develop the lives of people who lived in early time periods. Biographies of Cleopatra, born in 69 B.C., are among the most common biographies of people living in the Middle East during this early time. Two biographies may be used for discussions and comparisons. *Cleopa-*

tra by Diane Stanley and Peter Vennema is a highly illustrated biography about the Queen of Egypt. The authors provide an interesting note on ancient sources that might influence how readers approach these biographies: "Everything we know about Cleopatra was written by her enemies. It is not surprising, then, that she was portrayed as a conniving, immoral woman" (unnumbered note). The authors develop a queen who was strong willed, ambitious, and brilliant with a fine education and who also longed to return her country to the glory of its earlier years. The characterization suggests that her strength was her intelligence, courage, and charm. The text includes her relationships first with Caesar and then with Mark Antony. The illustrations, which depict the grandeur of Egypt, look like mosaics. The biography includes a historical atlas of Egypt and Roman Provinces during the accession of Cleopatra, a bibliography, and a pronunciation guide.

Don Nardo's *The Importance of Cleopatra,* a biography written for older readers, also discusses her relationships with the Roman leaders, Julius Caesar and Mark Antony. Nardo's introduction, "Fact Versus Fiction," emphasizes some of the same concerns found in the previous biography although he provides a more in-depth coverage of biased sources. As in the picture book version of the biography, Nardo develops a sympathetic characterization. This biography includes source notes for each chapter. Another interesting feature allows readers to compare the various ways that authors and even films have portrayed Cleopatra. The author uses boxed material that illustrates how other sources treated Cleopatra. For example, there are excerpts from George Bernard Shaw's "Caesar and Cleopatra." The illustrations include photographs from Elizabeth Taylor's film "Cleopatra," statues of principle characters who lived during the time, and paintings that depict the time and people.

Two recent biographies provide brief glimpses on the lives of important women in history and of children who were influenced by the political environment of both famous parents and the government. *HerStory: Women Who Changed the World,* edited by Ruth Ashby and Deborah Gore Ohrn, includes brief biographical histories of important women from prehistory through contemporary times. An introductory discussion compares the roles of women in various cultures such as ancient Egypt, China, and the Middle Ages. Katherine Leiner's *First Children: Growing Up in the White House* provides insights into the lives of the children or grandchildren who were raised in the executive mansion. The author uses a chronological order beginning with the grandchildren of George Washington, who lived with their grandfather in the executive mansion in Philadelphia, 1789–1797, and proceeds to Chelsea Clinton, 1993–   . Leiner focuses on incidents in their lives that would be of interest to juvenile readers. For example, the author includes letters written to Chelsea from children around the country. The book includes an "Afterword" in which the author provides information about the children's lives after they reached adulthood. There is also a chart showing the various presidents' children and the dates of their lives, a bibliography of books categorized by each president, and a list of photographic credits.

The biographer of the following book uses many techniques to make the book an excellent example of biography. Polly Schoyer Brooks develops the characters and settings to capture the people and the times in *Queen Eleanor: Independent Spirit of the Medieval World*. Brooks portrays Eleanor of Aquitaine as she develops from a frivolous, immature girl who acts to satisfy her whims to a mature queen who has a shrewd talent for politics. Brooks uses a variety of techniques to develop colorful characters. Consider, for example, the picture that Brooks paints of Eleanor and her husband, Henry II, through the following comparisons:

Eleanor gradually restored some measure of peace and order to her duchy, using persuasion where Henry had used force. (p. 100)

While Eleanor had become serene, Henry had become more irascible. (p. 126)

From a queen of the troubadours, who had inspired romance and poetry, she became a queen with as much authority as a king. . . . Henry had been admired and feared; Eleanor was admired and loved. (p. 132)

Brooks includes verses composed about Eleanor to describe the attitudes expressed toward the queen and reinforce the mood of medieval chivalry. The following lyrics were written by troubadour Bernard de Ventadour and were included as an integral part of the text:

Lady, I'm yours and yours shall be
Vowed to your service constantly
This is the oath of fealty
I pledged to you this long time past,
As my first joy was all in you,
So shall my last be found there too,
So long as life in me shall last. (p. 107)

Several highly illustrated biographies by Diane Stanley appeal to students in the lower-elementary grades. *Peter the Great* is supported by numerous full-page and half-page illustrations of Russian life in the late 1600s and early 1700s. *Shaka: King of the Zulus* is enhanced by illustrations that provide valuable details about the setting, Zululand in the early 1800s. The illustrations for Diane Stanley and Peter Vennema's *Good Queen Bess: The Story of Elizabeth I of England* encourage readers to visualize the world of the 1500s and the importance of the Elizabethan Age. The illustrations for Fay Stanley's *The Last Princess: The Story of Princess Ka'iulani of Hawai'i* depict the life of the Hawaiian monarch in the late 1800s, before the monarchy was abolished. The illustrations in all four biographies provide background information to help younger readers picture the times, places, and people.

In *The King's Day: Louis XIV of France,* Aliki uses a similar approach to provide background information to young readers. The detailed illustrations depict the social life and customs found in seventeenth- and eighteenth-century France. Aliki's illustrations include explanatory sentences and legends that help clarify the details found in the pictures.

Founding Fathers and Mothers of America. Jean Fritz's stories about Patrick Henry, Samuel Adams, John Hancock, Benjamin Franklin, James Madison, and Sam Houston seem to come alive through Fritz's inclusion of little-known information. Through these books, children discover that heroes, like themselves, have fears, display good and bad characteristics, and are liked by some and disliked by others. For example, Fritz adds humor to *Where Was Patrick Henry on the 29th of May?* by developing the theory that unusual things always seemed to happen to Henry on the date of his birth. She characterizes Henry as not only a great patriot but also a practical joker and a person filled with "passion for fiddling, dancing, and pleasantry."

Similar insights enliven Fritz's biographies of other beloved figures from the Revolutionary War period. Fritz doesn't limit her writing to supporters of American independence from Great Britain, however. In *Traitor: The Case of Benedict Arnold,* Fritz describes a man who wanted to be a success and a hero. Fritz attracts interest in Arnold and prepares the readers for the apparently dramatic changes in a man who chose to support the British by suggesting early in the book the complete reversal of Arnold's popularity. In 1777, following Arnold's successes in the assault on Quebec and in the Saratoga Campaign, George Washington called him "the bravest of the brave." But by 1780, after his plot with John André to betray the American post at West Point, he was regarded as "the veriest villain of centuries past." The incidents that Fritz chooses to include develop many sides of Arnold's character and encourage readers to understand why Arnold joined forces with the British.

In *The Great Little Madison,* Fritz uses jokes that James Madison told on himself and humorous anecdotes to show how Madison overcame his small stature and his weak voice. The early experiences cited by Fritz show why Madison believed in logic, freedom of religion, and the written word.

In *Make Way for Sam Houston,* Fritz uses Houston's belief in destiny to emphasize Houston's interactions with other characters. For example, Houston accepted Andrew Jackson's vision of America because "now he had a picture and words for what he'd call Destiny" (p. 20). Fritz reinforces Houston's belief in destiny by describing Houston's responses each time he saw an eagle, the medicine bird that influenced major decisions in his life.

In *Benjamin Franklin: The New American,* Milton Meltzer carefully introduces readers to the historical background of Franklin. In the following quotation, Meltzer encourages readers to understand the time and place:

It is almost three hundred years since Benjamin Franklin was born in Boston. (The date was January 17, 1706.) It is hard to put yourself back in that time and grasp what it was like. About 12,000 people lived in Boston, and in all the English colonies of North America there were only 250,000. (That's about the same as the population of Rochester, New York, today.) Most of the people were clustered around Boston, the Connecticut and Hudson river valleys. . . . They had little connection with one another. Roads were really paths, and bad weather made them almost impassable. (p. 15)

Meltzer develops a many-sided person by revealing both strengths and weaknesses in Franklin. Meltzer adds credibility to the characterization through numerous quotations drawn from Franklin's writings and speeches.

Meltzer's *George Washington and the Birth of Our Nation* is another carefully researched biography of an American statesman. The text includes maps showing key areas, battles of the Revolutionary War period, and territorial lines. Meltzer's *Thomas Jefferson: The Revolutionary Aristocrat* is an in-depth look at the author of the Declaration of Independence and the third president of the United States. The authenticity of the text is increased by Meltzer's use of historical photographs, list of sources, and maps showing locations discussed in the text. Another viewpoint of the Revolutionary War is found in Jim Murphy's *A Young Patriot: The American Revolution as Experienced by One Boy,* the biography of a fifteen-year-old who enlisted in the army in 1776.

Fiery words and bold actions are not the only forms of patriotism and leadership. Elizabeth Yates's *Amos Fortune, Free Man* depicts a man who advanced freedom. Fortune was an African who was brought to slavery in Boston, learned a trade, and eventually acquired freedom. He represents thousands of unsung heroes of the American Revolution—black and white, male and female. The words on his tombstone, erected in 1801, suggest the fundamental American values that Fortune exemplified: ". . . born free in Africa, a slave in America, he purchased liberty, professed Christianity, lived reputably, and died hopefully" (p. 181).

Leaders of a Growing America. As the United States became more confident of itself as a nation, it began to expand its interests overseas. Rhoda Blumberg's *Commodore Perry in the Land of the Shogun* depicts the attempts of the American naval officer Matthew Perry to open Japanese harbors to American trade in 1853. This book, an excellent choice for multicultural studies, strongly emphasizes the dramatic interactions between Perry and the Japanese. Reproductions of the original drawings that recorded the expedition, Japanese scrolls and handbills, and photographs provide documentation and enhance children's understanding of the setting and Japanese culture.

The best-known biographer of Abraham Lincoln is probably Carl Sandburg. His *Abraham Lincoln: The Prairie Years* was the basis for his biography for children, *Abe Lincoln Grows Up*. Children vicariously share the youth of a great American leader. They discover an impoverished young man of the backwoods who is starved for books, hungry for knowledge, eager to have fun, and ambitious to test himself and his principles in a wider world. Sandburg says:

It seemed that Abe made the books tell him more than they told other people. . . . Abe picked out questions . . . such as "Who has the most right to complain, the Indian or the Negro?" and Abe would talk about it, up one way and down the other, while they were in the cornfield pulling fodder for the winter. (p. 135)

In the 1988 Newbery Medal winner, *Lincoln: A Photobiography,* Russell Freedman uses numerous techniques that students of children's literature should consider. First, Freedman introduces each of the seven chapters with quotations from Lincoln's own writing. For example, Freedman introduces chapter two, "A Backwoods Boy," with this quotation:

It is a great piece of folly to attempt to make anything out of my early life. It can all be condensed into a simple sentence, and that sentence you will find in Gray's Elegy— "the short and simple annals of the poor." That's my life, and that's all you or anyone else can make out of it. (p. 7)

Second, Freedman clearly separates legend from fact. For example, in chapter three, "Law and Politics," Freedman states:

He also fell in love—apparently for the first time in his life. Legend tells us that Lincoln once had a tragic love affair with Ann Rutledge . . . who died at the age of twenty-two. While this story has become part of American folklore, there isn't a shred of evidence that Lincoln ever had a romantic attachment with Ann. Historians believe that they were just good friends. (p. 28)

Third, Freedman supports his text with photographs of various documents of Lincoln's own writing. For example, the text includes a page of Lincoln's autobiographical sketch written in 1859 (p. 6), a page from Lincoln's homemade copybook (p. 13), and a handwritten copy of the Gettysburg Address (p. 103).

Fourth, Freedman includes historical photographs that support the settings and people. There are photographs of battlefields and of Lincoln and his family.

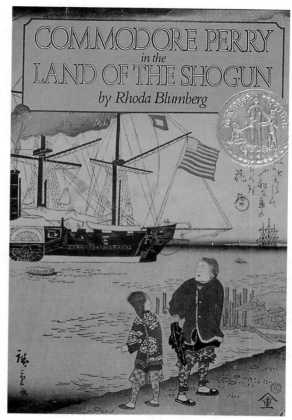

The illustrations reinforce the Japanese setting. (Cover of COMMODORE PERRY IN THE LAND OF THE SHOGUN by Rhoda Blumberg. Lothrop, Lee & Shepard Books, a division of William Morrow & Company, Inc. Cover illustration courtesy of the Library of Congress.)

Fifth, the text includes photographs of authentic posters, newspaper ads, and documents. For example, there is a photograph of the marriage license of Abraham Lincoln and Mary Todd (p. 33), a wanted poster for a runaway slave (p. 44), a victory poster from 1860 (p. 62), and a newspaper cartoon from a Baltimore paper (p. 71). Sixth, Freedman supports the text with references to sources for quotations and major speeches, lists of historical sites, sources for additional books about Lincoln, and lists of acknowledgements and picture credits. You may compare Freedman's biography with Albert Marrin's *Commander in Chief: Abraham Lincoln in the Civil War.*

Cheryl Harness's *Abe Lincoln Goes to Washington: 1837–1867* is a highly illustrated biography of Abraham Lincoln written for younger readers. The text includes interesting details including maps, portraits, and banners.

Biographies of Charles Eastman and Theodore Roosevelt depict people who had great impact on the growth of America. Charles Eastman, the most famous Native American of his time, was a Sioux of the Great Plains, born in 1858. Eastman overcame poverty and racial prejudice to become a physician and a crusader for Native American rights. Peter Anderson's *Charles Eastman: Physician, Reformer, and Native American Leader* looks at the influences that combined to make Eastman a spokesperson for his people, including the forced migration of the Sioux from Minnesota, Eastman's medical education, and Eastman's efforts to provide medical treatment and better living conditions for the Sioux. Eastman worked to restore broken treaties and to encourage Indians and whites to respect Native American culture. Anderson describes Eastman's motives for publishing his first book:

It was Charles's intention to present an accurate picture of the Indian people and their way of life. Too often white people looked upon the Indian people as ignorant and backward. In his writing and lecturing, Charles was quick to correct them, pointing out the many strengths and contributions of America's native people. In addition to their deep respect for nature, Charles wrote about the beauty of their arts and crafts. Indian people, he said, also had developed their own herbal medicines and farming techniques. They knew, as well as anyone, how to live off the land. (p. 90)

Bully for You, Teddy Roosevelt!, by Jean Fritz, is a biography of the twenty-sixth president, who worked especially hard for conservation issues. Fritz's biography includes notes, a bibliography, and an index. It is interesting to compare this biography and the preceding one and to examine the time period through the viewpoints of a Native American man and a president of the United States.

Numerous biographies of escaped slaves develop the importance of freedom and the inhumanity of slavery. Virginia Hamilton's *Anthony Burns: The Defeat and Triumph of a Fugitive Slave* is a narrative history of events surrounding the life of Burns as well as a biography. In the research material, however, there existed no day-to-day calendar of the activities and movements of Burns as an ordinary slave child and youth. The life of Burns became well-documented only after Burns's twentieth year, when Burns was hired out to Richmond, Virginia, and carefully began

to plan his escape. Because of the lack of documentation, Hamilton draws from supporting materials to recreate the early life of Burns.

Hamilton uses an interesting technique to allow readers to understand the early life of Burns. After Burns is captured as a fugitive slave, he goes within himself and remembers his happier childhood days. In the following quotation, Hamilton transfers her character from his unhappy days of imprisonment to his memories: "Anthony was not aware Suttle had gone anywhere, for he had left first and gone deep inside himself, to his childhood. These days seemed endless, perfect. There mornings and waking up were the times he could hardly wait for, he loved them so" (p. 7).

Another excellent book about a nineteenth-century American with a strong social conscience is Anne E. Neimark's *A Deaf Child Listened: Thomas Gallaudet, Pioneer in American Education*. For centuries, children who were deaf had been placed in asylums for the retarded and the insane. Gallaudet, founder of American education specifically for the deaf, helped bring Americans with deafness out of their "silent prison."

In *Mother Jones: Fierce Fighter for Workers' Rights,* Judith Pinkerton Josephson presents the biography of the woman who played a considerable role in organizing labor. The text includes photographs.

Twentieth-Century Leaders in America and Abroad. Biographies written for young children and for older children differ in tone, focus, choice of content, amount of detail, and development of character. Because of the range in intended audiences, biographies about political leaders and social activists in the twentieth century provide opportunities to compare the techniques used by the authors and the content that they include.

First, consider several biographies written for young children: Barbara Cooney's *Eleanor* and Ruth Franchere's *Cesar Chavez*. The books share several features. The readability levels are for the fourth grade, indicating that the books are meant for independent reading. The books contain numerous illustrations, and they emphasize very positive characteristics and situations.

Barbara Cooney's *Eleanor* focuses on Roosevelt as a young girl. Both Cooney's text and illustrations develop characterization that shows her as a lonely and insecure child, especially after her father's death.

The biography has a happy ending as the child realizes that she has special talents. Cooney's illustrations depict the time period and re-create the era of mansions and a wealthy social life.

Ruth Franchere's *Cesar Chavez* looks at the Mexican American political leader's struggles to develop the National Farm Workers Association and to gain political and economic power for Mexican Americans. Franchere arouses sympathy for Chavez's undertakings by showing pictures of the poor living conditions of a migrant farming family and providing details related to Chavez's schooling. Chavez's family moved so often that Chavez attended thirty-six schools while acquiring an eighth-grade education. Franchere's choice of factual content directs readers' attention to Chavez's concerns and values. Franchere relates how Chavez tried to organize classes where Mexican Americans could learn to read and write English. He worked for Mexican American voter registration, and he organized the 1968 grape boycott in order to demand better pay and living conditions for migrant workers.

Next, consider several biographies that have been written for older children. Longer format allows authors to include more details and to develop more information about the historical periods.

Appropriately for an older audience, Russell Freedman's *Franklin Delano Roosevelt* includes many photographs, lists books about Roosevelt, and provides acknowledgments for picture credits. Many of these photographs are from the Franklin D. Roosevelt Library, the Library of Congress, the Bettmann Archive, and the National Archives. The biography includes an in-depth look at Roosevelt's activities during World War II. Consequently, it is a valuable source for authenticating historical fiction about World War II. In *Eleanor Roosevelt: A Life of Discovery*, Freedman realistically portrays Eleanor Roosevelt by drawing heavily on her memoirs. Unlike biographies written for younger readers, Freedman's *Eleanor Roosevelt* includes her reactions when she discovers her husband's love affair. As in Freedman's other biographies, numerous photographs add to the depiction of this political leader's life.

Two biographies written by James Haskins about civil rights leaders encourage readers to understand the historical, political, and social perspectives of the time periods. For example, Haskins's *I Have a Dream: The Life and Words of Martin Luther King, Jr.* not only examines King's life and his achievements but also provides excerpts from his speeches and other communications that shed light on his beliefs and struggles. Haskins's *Thurgood Marshall: A Life for Justice* presents the fight against racism and segregation waged by the first African American Supreme Court justice. The texts include bibliographies of books, articles, other sources, and indexes that encourage older readers to conduct specific research.

John B. Severance's *Gandhi, Great Soul* begins with a chapter that develops the impact of Gandhi's beliefs on other world leaders such as Martin Luther King, Jr. and Nelson Mandela. Severance's biography includes interesting details about his personal life as well as historical events and struggles with the British and various religious groups.

Elizabeth Ferber's *Yasir Arafat: A Life of War and Peace* is the biography of the Palestinian leader. The biographer combines the story of his life with information about the Arab and Israeli conflict. Ferber presents both points of view about the man: a popular leader among displaced Palestinians and a reviled figure in the occupied territories after the Herbron massacre in 1994. Labeled black-and-white photographs accompany the text. There is also a chronology of important dates, source notes for each chapter, a bibliography, and an index.

The importance of memories and friendship is developed in Vedat Dalokay's *Sister Shako and Kolo the Goat: Memories of My Childhood in Turkey*. This book, the winner of the 1995 Mildred Batchelder Honor Award, is a personal remembrance of the former mayor of Ankara, Turkey, in which he lovingly recalls his childhood in rural Turkey and his special friendship with a widow and her remarkable goat, Kolo. The author develops many of the values and beliefs identified in Turkish folklore. For example, the importance of hospitality is shown when the new goat comes into the family unexpectedly and is considered a "Guest of God" because, "If a traveler needs shelter or food, he knocks at the door of any house along the way. The host offers him whatever he needs, because the traveler is considered a guest sent by God. This is a very old Turkish tradition that is still practiced today" (p. 14).

Dalokay develops many of these Turkish values as he remembers Sister Shako's thoughts and advice about subjects such as holy places and death. For example, Sister Shako states her beliefs about death: "Now I am here in this hut, but after death, I shall be in the caterpillar on the black earth, I shall be in the rain seeping into the earth. Blowing winds and rapid rivers will carry me around this world. May death come nicely, smoothly, without pain, without suffering" (p. 58). To clarify understanding, the author includes footnotes that describe various customs and beliefs developed in the story. The cultural is reinforced by the use of regional words, idioms, sayings, and traditions of eastern Turkey.

Achievers and American heroes are always popular subjects for children's biographies. In *The American Hero: The True Story of Charles A. Lindbergh,* Barry Denenberg uses several techniques that stimulate interest in the controversial aviator's life and add a feeling of authenticity. For example, he introduces each of the chapters with quotes from Charles or Anne Lindbergh's own writings. The introduction to the second chapter includes insights into the motivation to learn to fly an airplane: "When I was a child on our Minnesota farm, I spent hours lying on my back . . . hidden from passersby, watching white cumulus clouds drift overhead, staring into the sky. It was a different world up there. You had to be flat on your back, screened in by the grass stalks, to live in it. Those clouds, how far away were they? Nearer than the neighbor's house, untouchable as the moon—unless you had an airplane. How wonderful it would be, I'd thought, if I had an airplane—wings with which I could fly up to the clouds and explore their caves and canyons—wings like the hawk circling above me. Then, I would ride on the wind and be part of the sky . . .—Charles Lindbergh" (p. 19). In addition, photographs showing Lindbergh's experiences, charts, and maps illustrate the biography. The text includes source notes, a bibliography, and an index.

When children do library research, they discover some of the techniques that biographers use. Such investigations may also lead children to outstanding, recently published biographies of other social leaders. (See chapter 11 for a discussion of additional biographies.)

Artists and Authors. Color reproductions of artworks add interest to Leslie Sills's *Inspirations: Stories About Women Artists.* This book includes four biographical sketches of contemporary women artists and artworks for which they are known. Sills's *Visions: Stories About Women Artists* includes additional biographical sketches of women artists and their works.

The series of books "Portraits of Women Artists for Children" includes both brief biographical sketches of the artists and color reproductions of their works. Several of the titles in this series include Robyn Montana Turner's *Frida Kahlo, Mary Cassatt, Georgia O'Keeffe,* and *Rosa Bonheur.* These books also provide much information about art.

In *Leonardo da Vinci,* Diane Stanley introduces readers to the art of the Renaissance artist. Through this biography Stanley presents both da Vinci's accomplishments as a painter and as a scientist. Stanley incorporates miniature reproductions of da Vinci's paintings into her illustrations.

John Duggleby's *Artist in Overalls: The Life of Grant Wood,* the artist of the famous "American Gothic," traces the artist's life from his experiences as a farm boy who uses charcoal to sketch animals on an old cardboard to the emergence of an artist who developed his own style. Duggleby emphasizes the artist's development of self-esteem when he begins to express his feelings about art: " 'I want to reach everyday people, not just the artists and art critics of the world,' he explained. He talked about his years of trying to paint subjects from foreign lands, in other artists' styles, and about how he finally began painting the things he knew best, in the way he felt most comfortable" (p. 49). The biography is illustrated with reproductions of Grant Wood's paintings.

Two additional texts provide both biographical information about artists and introductions to their art. Gary Schwartz's *Rembrandt* and Richard Meryman's *Andrew Wyeth* include information that helps readers understand and interpret their works. Both texts are heavily illustrated with color reproductions of each artist's paintings. Both Schwartz and Meryman are considered leading authorities in art interpretations.

Other current biographies and autobiographies provide insights into the authors and illustrators of children's books. Read about the lives of the authors of *Little Women, The Secret Garden,* and *Charlotte's Web* and then compare the lives of the authors with those of their fictional heroines and heroes.

In *Louisa May: The World and Works of Louisa May Alcott,* Norma Johnston chronicles the life of Louisa May Alcott. Readers will be interested in Johnston's motivation for writing this biography and her point of view. As you read this biography, search for evidence that reflects Johnston's motivation and point of view. For example, Johnston states:

Like generations of readers, I grew up envying the March family everything but their poverty—their closeness, the way they never stayed angry, the way they always, always loved each other. As a young teen, I wept bitterly because I couldn't make my family as picture-perfect as the Marches, and resolved to be, like Louisa, a writer of books for girls. (author's note)

In *Frances Hodgson Burnett: Beyond the Secret Garden,* Angelica Shirley Carpenter and Jean Shirley explore the life of the author of *The Secret Garden* and *Little Lord Fauntleroy.* It is interesting to compare Burnett and Alcott, two successful women authors who wrote during approximately the same time period.

Beverly Gherman's *E. B. White: Some Writer!* chronicles the life of the popular author of *Charlotte's Web, Stuart Little,* and *The Trumpet of the Swan* as well as numerous articles in such journals as *The New Yorker.* Throughout her biography, Gherman relates White's character to scenes from and characters developed in his children's stories. For example, Gherman introduces the book in such a way that readers can visualize a many-sided person:

Whenever E. B. White was asked to accept an award for one of his books, he found an excuse for not attending the ceremony. In 1970, when *Charlotte's Web* won the Claremont Center's Award, he sent them a speech describing how Wilbur fainted with excitement after he won his special prize at the fair. It took a bite from Templeton the rat to revive him. White said he would faint just as Wilbur had if he were forced to stand up before the audience and read his own speech. But he thanked them for liking *Charlotte* and said he felt "very lucky to have gained the ear of children. . . ." (p. 1)

Autobiographies give children insights into the illustrators and authors of children's books. *Bill Peet: An Autobiography* provides information about the artist's experiences as a Disney cartoonist. Peet worked on such films as *Dumbo* and *Fantasia.* This text is heavily illustrated with Peet's drawings. Beverly Cleary's *A Girl from Yamhill: A Memoir* is a chronicle of the early life of the popular realistic fiction author. Numerous photographs should intrigue readers of the "Ramona" series and *Dear Mr. Henshaw.*

Author Sid Fleischman, winner of the Newbery Medal, writes an autobiography of his life in *The Abracadabra Kid: A Writer's Life.* In addition to interesting information about his life, Fleischman intro-

duces each chapter with quotes from his fan letters. The autobiography includes family photographs and illustrations that depict other experiences in his life.

By reading Gary Paulsen's autobiography, *Woodsong,* readers discover that Paulsen learned lessons from nature and from his work with dogs. These lessons are especially meaningful in his fiction, such as *Hatchet* and *Dogsong.* As in his survival stories, Paulsen begins his autobiography with an interest-grabbing introduction:

I understood almost nothing about the woods until it was nearly too late. And that is strange because my ignorance was based on knowledge. Most of my life it seems I've been in the forest or on the sea. Most of my time, sleeping and waking, has been spent outside, in close contact with what we now call the environment. . . . We hunted and killed and though I think now that it is wrong to hunt and kill, at the time I did not think this and I spent virtually all my time hunting. And learned nothing. Perhaps the greatest paradox about understanding "the woods" is that so many who enjoy it, or seem to enjoy it, spend most of their time trying to kill parts of it. (p. 1)

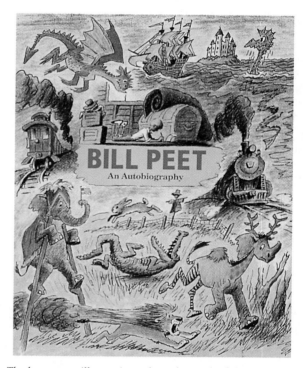

The humorous illustrations show the work of the author. (From Bill Peet: An Autobiography *by Bill Peet, copyright © 1989 by Bill Peet. Reprinted by permission of Houghton Mifflin Company.)*

The rest of Paulsen's autobiography explains how his life changed as a result of running with his dogs in the Minnesota wilderness and entering the Iditarod race across Alaska.

In *War Boy: A Country Childhood,* British author and illustrator Michael Foreman describes his life growing up in England during the 1940s. This is not the normal life of a young boy; it is complicated by bombs, gas masks, and guns. It is also filled, however, with excitement, working together, and new friends. Foreman's detailed illustrations provide background for stories set in World War II. In *After the War Was Over,* Foreman continues illustrating and describing his experiences into his teenage years. Foreman's text and watercolor illustrations present a warm personal account of his post–World War II years in England.

In *Starting from Home: A Writer's Beginnings,* author Milton Meltzer clarifies the problems of writing about his own youth. Meltzer states that the book is a combination of fact and fiction because he has changed some names and circumstances, "not to avoid the truth, but to capture it" and because "this is my life as I see it now. I can't pretend to know exactly how it was when I was five or fifteen. Inevitably the story is colored by what I have become this many years later" (p. 145). In the following quotation, note that Meltzer's introduction encourages readers to join Meltzer's search for identity:

Who was I? No, I don't mean the man who's writing these words down, but the child who was born soon after the twentieth century began. Was he me? The me I am today? Or someone so different in an early photo that I hardly recognize him: small, skinny, wavy brown hair, green eyes, straight nose, pale skin, thin arms and chest encased in a khaki shirt, and an uneasy smile as he looks into my eyes. That's the boy on the outside. Inside was a being no one knew but himself. And often he was not sure who that was. (p. 3)

Whether you read Meltzer's text as autobiography or as fiction, you will receive insights into the life of a prolific author of biographical literature.

Ellen Levine's *Anna Pavlova: Genius of the Dance* is a biography of the ballerina who became one of the most acclaimed dancers in Russia. The author uses excerpts from Pavlova's diary in addition to quotes from her contemporaries to develop a woman who had both a dream and determination. Through her story readers discover some of the history of dance and the training required to be successful. Labeled black-and-white photographs provide background for both Pavlova's career in Russia and across the world. A feeling of her worldwide acclaim is found through the inclusion of illustrations such as a sketch of Pavlova used for a poster announcing the Russian Ballet's 1909 season in Paris. The author includes a glossary of ballet terms, an annotated bibliography, and an index.

The life of Louis Armstrong is developed in picture-book format in Roxane Orgill's *If I Only Had a Horn: Young Louis Armstrong.* The text and Leonard Jenkins's illustrations are set in New Orleans in the early 1900s. As you read the text and analyze the illustrations, notice how both author and illustrator recreate the emotions of jazz.

The author describes and illustrates his life growing up in England. (From War Boy: A Country Childhood *by Michael Foreman. Copyright © 1989 by Michael Foreman. Reprinted by permission of Little, Brown and Company.)*

Selecting, researching, writing, and critically evaluating Holocaust biographies and other literature becomes especially important when we realize that fifty thousand books have been written about the Holocaust in the last fifty years.[1] One of the most important issues discussed in journals, conference presentations, and informational books written about the writing and critical analysis of Holocaust biographies is, How should authors write about the Holocaust?

Hazel Rochman[2] discusses how authors should and should not write about the Holocaust. In a review of Ruth Minsky Sender's *The Holocaust Lady,*[3] Rochman maintains that even though the book is much discussed, it is an example of how authors should not write about the Holocaust. Rochman states, "Sender's suffering as a Holocaust survivor is undeniable. What she has to tell us is of the utmost importance. . . . But, the writing is sentimental and self-centered, full of cliché about horror, pain, and degradation. On almost every page, at least once, her tears glide, glisten, or roll gently down her cheeks, and/or her heart skips a beat; people read her work with quivering hands, their faces distorted with pain" (p. 416).

In contrast, Rochman maintains that the writing in books such as Ida Vos's *Hide and Seek*[4] and Maus Spiegelman's *Maus: A Survivor's Tale*[5] is preferable because the writing represents a controlled style that has greater power.

The style of presentation in *The Diary of a Young Girl: The Definitive Edition*[6] is frequently presented as a role model for Holocaust biographies and autobiographies. In a review of the book, Patricia Hampl[7] states, "The 'Diary,' now 50 years old, remains astonishing and excruciating. It is a work almost sick with terror and tension, even as it performs its miracle of lucidity. . . . All that remains is this diary, evidence of her ferocious appetite for life. It gnaws at us still" (p. 21).

As you read the various biographies set during the Holocaust, try to evaluate the impact of the writing style. For example, Anne Frank's style has been described as positive while Sender's has been described as a tear-stained style. As you read the biographies, consider the following questions: Should the writing style make a difference in Holocaust biographies? What is your viewpoint on the writing style of Holocaust literature? Which of the books are the most effective in their depictions of the time period and of your understanding of the issues surrounding the Holocaust? How would you write a book so that the conflict, the setting, and the characters are understood by your readers?

[1] Lustig, Arnost. "What We Will Never Understand About the Holocaust." Unexpected Encounters with the Holocaust Conference: Texas A&M University, College Station, Texas. April 2, 1997.

[2] Rochman, Hazel. "How Not to Write About the Holocaust." *Booklist* 89 (October 15, 1992): 416.

[3] Sender, Ruth Minsky. *The Holocaust Lady.* New York: Macmillan, 1992.

[4] Vos, Ida. *Hide and Seek.* Boston: Houghton Mifflin, 1991.

[5] Spiegelman, Maus. *Maus: A Survivor's Tale.* New York: Macmillan, 1992.

[6] Frank, Anne. *The Diary of a Young Girl: The Definitive Edition.* New York: Doubleday, 1995.

[7] Hampl, Patricia. "Anne Frank: Diary of a Young Girl: The Definitive Edition." *The New York Times Book Review* (March 5, 1995): 21.

People Who Have Persevered.   Biographies are not always written about famous people or people of great material success. Some excellent biographies and autobiographies portray the courage and perseverance of ordinary people. One such book is David Kherdian's *The Road from Home: The Story of an Armenian Girl.* This story about the author's mother, Vernon Dumehjian, is one of courage, hope, and survival. In 1915, the Turkish government decided to eliminate its Armenian people by deporting them to the Mesopotamian desert or killing them. Vernon spends days in a caravan on the march, days of weakening physical condition, days of not knowing her destination, and days of sadness when family members die from cholera. Days of hope result when Vernon meets kind people who provide her with an education while she waits to return to her home. The security of home does not last long, however, as fighting resumes between Turkey and Greece. When Vernon's aunt is approached by a family whose Armenian American son wants a wife to join him in the United States, Vernon finally finds a way of becoming safe.

Persevering may require the survival of body and soul through such terrible experiences as the

Holocaust. When children of the Holocaust write their autobiographical experiences as adults, they frequently emphasize both the tragedies of their experiences and the hopes for the future that kept them alive during their hiding or internment.

Nelly S. Toll's autobiography, *Behind the Secret Window: A Memoir of a Hidden Childhood During World War Two,* reflects a girl who uses her writing to reveal both the terror of the situation and the possibility for a normal, happy childhood. As you read this quote, try to visualize a frightened girl in hiding who is writing in a diary and also trying to retain a semblance of the happy life that she knew before World War II:

The small black diary was very important to me. Using the logic of a child, I invented my own code that I called my "Esperanto," my universal language and converted such dangerous words as "ghetto" and "Jews" into it. I reasoned that, if the Jestapo ever found my writing, they would not realize that I was Jewish and thus would not destroy it! In the foreword of my diary I wrote, "If I should be killed, at least my pamietnik (memory book) will stay alive so that the whole world can see the terrible things that happened to us."

This journal was my place for recording the frightening reality of my existence during those dark days—unlike the paintings that I created at the same time, which provided me with an escape into a fantasy world. I painted over sixty watercolors, made up cheerful tales about them, and sewed the pictures and stories together into small booklets with white thread; through the magic of art, I became a part of that happy world of illusion. The five-by-seven-inch and seven-by-ten-inch sheets of paper were filled with colorful flowers, blue skies, loving adults, and carefree children busy with normal daily activities. Only symbolically did they reflect my feelings of apprehension about the constant danger surrounding us. (pp. ix–x)

Toll's use of both the descriptions of the terrifying conditions and her inclusion of twenty-nine paintings from this period in her life reveal how she gained insights into her experiences and help readers understand the trauma of living during the Holocaust.

Ana Novac is another author who writes about her own experiences. In *The Beautiful Days of My Youth: My Six Months in Auschwitz and Plaszow,* she tells about finding a pencil stub and recording her experiences in a diary. In *I Have Lived a Thousand Years: Growing Up in the Holocaust,* Livia Bitton-Jackson also describes her experiences when her family is forced into a Jewish ghetto and later sent to Auschwitz. Both of these books are strengthened by the authors' use of personal observations.

Anne Frank's *The Diary of a Young Girl: The Definitive Edition* should be added to the original published version. This latest edition contains about 30 percent more material than was included in the earlier edition. Students of children's literature may compare the two editions as well as other biographies about Anne Frank.

Authors who write biographies about people who have overcome physical disabilities frequently focus on the biographical character's ability to achieve success against considerable odds. In *Out of Darkness: The Story of Louis Braille,* Russell Freedman fo-

A girl remembers happier times through her drawings. (From Behind the Secret Window: A Memoir of a Hidden Childhood During World War Two *by Nelly Toll. Copyright © 1993 by Nelly S. Toll. Reprinted by permission of Dial Books for Young Readers, a division of Penguin Books USA Inc.)*

cuses on Braille's struggle to communicate after he loses his own sight and his additional difficulties in having his system accepted. In *Wilma Unlimited: How Wilma Rudolph Became the World's Fastest Woman,* Kathleen Krull stresses how Rudolph overcame her childhood polio to become at age twenty the first woman to win three gold medals in a single Olympics.

Eloise Greenfield and Lessie Jones Little's *Childtimes: A Three-Generation Memoir* traces a family's experiences. In three parts, an African American grandmother, mother, and daughter tell about growing up in time periods ranging from the late 1800s through the 1940s. Both Greenfield and Little are well-known authors of children's books. This book concludes poignantly:

It's been good, stopping for a while to catch up to the past. It has filled me with both great sadness and great joy. Sadness to look back at suffering, joy to feel the unbreakable threads of strength. Now, it's time for us to look forward again, to see where it is that we're going. Maybe years from now, our descendants will want to stop and tell the story of their time and their place in this procession of children. A childtime is a mighty thing. (p. 175)

The words provide a fitting conclusion to this discussion of biographies written for children. What better purposes are there for sharing biographies with children than allowing them to feel good, to catch up to the past, and to experience the sadness and great joy of other people's lives?

 ## INFORMATIONAL BOOKS

Informational books are available on almost any subject. They are valued by children, teachers, parents, and librarians. This nonfiction, however, requires careful evaluation of the contents.

Values of Informational Books

"I am curious." "It is easier to find the answer from reading than it is to ask my teacher." "I want to learn to take better pictures." "I want to learn about a career I might enjoy." "I like reading the books." These reasons were given to this author by children who were asked why they read informational books. The range of answers also reflects the many values of in-

formational books for children. Nonfiction books provide information about hobbies, experiments, the ways in which things work, the characteristics of plants and animals, and many other phenomena.

Gaining knowledge is a good reason for reading informational books. Many recently published books contain information on timely subjects that children hear about on television or radio or read about in newspapers. For example, children excited by NASA's space explorations can consult Seymour Simon's *Jupiter* and *Saturn* for color photographs and information obtained during NASA's *Pioneer* and *Voyager* space explorations. Sylvia Funston's *The Dinosaur: Question and Answer Book* and Don Lessem's *Dinosaur Worlds* encourage children to expand their knowledge about dinosaurs and fossils and to learn about the current works and discoveries of paleontologists. Janet Mohun's *Drugs, Steroids, and Sports* contains information about various drug scandals in sports. Laurence Pringle's *Saving Our Wildlife* presents endeavors to save vanishing animals. Caroline Arnold's *On the Brink of Extinction: The California Condor* explores scientists' attempts to save the bird from extinction.

Informational books also provide opportunities for children to experience the excitement of new discoveries. For example, Barbara Valenta's *Pop-O-Mania: How to Create Your Own Pop-Ups* provides three-dimensional instructions for creating books using flaps and other pop-up techniques. Step-by-step directions also lead to creative problem solving in Joan Irvine's *How to Make Super Pop-Ups*. Children can make discoveries about art when they read Rosemary Davidson's *Take a Look: An Introduction to the Experience of Art.* They can discover characteristics of the ocean when they follow Simon's directions in *How to Be an Ocean Scientist in Your Own Home.*

Another value of informational books is introduction to the scientific method. Through firsthand experience and reading about the work of scientists, children discover how scientists observe, compare, formulate and test hypotheses, and draw conclusions or withhold them until they uncover more evidence. Children also become familiar with the instruments used by scientists. As children learn about the scientific method, they gain appreciation for the attitudes of the people who use this method. Children discover the importance of careful observation over long periods of time, the need for gathering data from many sources, and the requirement

Color photographs taken during actual space explorations clarify the content of an informational book. (From Jupiter by Seymour Simon. Published by William Morrow & Company, Inc., 1985. Photograph courtesy of NASA.)

that scientists, whatever their field, make no conclusions before all the data have been collected. For example, in Kathryn Lasky's *Dinosaur Dig,* students follow several families as they are guided by paleontologist Keith Rigby on a dig in eastern Montana. In books such as Donna M. Jackson's *The Bone Detectives: How Forensic Anthropologists Solve Crimes and Uncover Mysteries of the Dead,* readers discover the importance of careful research.

Informational books also encourage self-reliance. One enjoyable discovery can motivate children to make further investigations. Parents and educators need to provide books such as David Macaulay's *The Way Things Work* to pique children's interest and then help children explore their environment. A high school student who likes to read informational books emphasizes the satisfaction in following his curiosity into broader and deeper exploration:

I enjoy reading to answer my own curiosity. Fictional books don't have the information that I want. I am more interested in real things. When I was in first grade, astronomy was the first science that interested me; the more I read, the more I learned I didn't know. As I became older I read a lot of books about the stars, space exploration, and theories about the black hole. I discovered that reality is stranger and more exciting than any fiction could be. I could not take fiction and transfer it into the real world; factual books help me learn about the real world.

Informational books can encourage children to develop critical reading and thinking skills. While reading books written on one subject by different authors, children can compare the books to evaluate the objectivity of the authors and determine their qualifications to write about the subject. They can check the copyright dates to see if the information is current. Texts about dinosaurs provide opportunities for developing critical reading and thinking skills. Readers can compare the information presented in Funston's *The Dinosaur Question and Answer Book,* J. Lynett Gillette's *Dinosaur Ghosts: The Mysteries of Coelophysis,* Patricia Lauber's *Living with Dinosaurs,* Don Lessem's *Dinosaur Worlds,* Margery Facklam's *Tracking Dinosaurs in the Gobi* and Helen Roney Sattler's *Stegosaurs: The Solar-Powered Dinosaurs.*

Of course, informational books encourage children to stretch their minds. Chet Raymo (1992), a professor of physics and a science author, stresses:

Creative science depends crucially upon habits of mind that are most readily acquired by children: curiosity; voracious observation; sensitivity to rules and variations within the rules; and fantasy. Children's books that instill these habits of mind sustain science. (p. 561)

When children read Robert McClung's *Lost Wild America: The Story of Our Extinct and Vanishing Wildlife,* Dorothy Hinshaw Patent's *The Whooping Crane: A Comeback Story,* or Michelle Koch's *World Water Watch,* they may discover the perilous balance between animals, the environment, and humans and begin to think of ways in which their generation can conserve animals, plants, and other natural resources. Informational books also inform children about values, beliefs, life-styles, and behaviors different from their own.

Many well-written informational books expand children's vocabularies by introducing new words, including technical terms. Meanings of technical terms are often enriched through photographs or detailed illustrations. For example, in *The Life and Times of the Apple,* Charles Micucci develops the concept of grafting by presenting a series of illustrations that show how a cleft graft joins a scion to a rootstock. Detailed, labeled illustrations show each step in the grafting process.

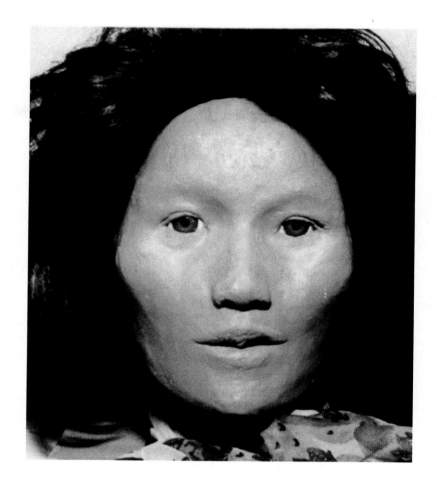

Children discover the importance of careful observation and research in Donna M. Jackson's The Bone Detectives: How Forensic Anthropologists Solve Crimes and Uncover Mysteries of the Dead. *(From* The Bone Detectives: How Forensic Anthropologists Solve Crimes and Uncover Mysteries of the Dead *by Donna M. Jackson, photographs by Charlie Fellenbaum, copyright © 1996. Photo courtesy of the Missouri State Highway Patrol.)*

Remember that one of the greatest values in informational books is *enjoyment*. Children who make new discoveries, become involved in the scientific process, or read because of curiosity are also reading for enjoyment. Enjoyment is often the primary reason children read informational literature. In addition, books such as Sue Macy's *Winning Ways: A Photohistory of American Women in Sports* or Brian Boitano and Suzanne Harper's *Boitano's Edge: Inside the Real World of Figure Skating* may inspire the next generation of athletes.

Evaluating Informational Books

Several science associations concerned with the education of elementary-school children provide valuable guidelines for selecting informational books for children. These guidelines are specifically tailored to

science books but are equally valid for all types of informational books. The guidelines in the Evaluation Box on page 694 are taken from recommendations made by the National Science Teachers Association (1997) and the American Association for the Advancement of Science (Johnston, 1991).

In addition to these criteria, Raymo (1992) emphasizes that good science books should develop "an attitude toward the world—curious, skeptical, undogmatic, forward-looking" (p. 562). Raymo recommends books that convey an "extraordinary adventure story of how the information was obtained, why we understand it to be true, or how it might embellish the landscape of the mind" (p. 561).

Accuracy. Does the author have the scientific qualifications to write a book on the particular subject? Franklyn M. Branley, author of *Saturn: The Spectacular*

Planet and over one hundred other scientific books, has a doctorate, is an astronomer emeritus, and is the former chairman of the American Museum-Hayden Planetarium. Many books, however, provide little or no helpful information by which to evaluate the qualifications of the author.

Are facts and theory clearly distinguished? Children should know if something is a fact or if it is a theory that has not been substantiated. For example, in *Changes in the Wind: Earth's Shifting Climate,* Margery and Howard Facklam examine the changing climate. The Facklams begin their exploration of the subject by discussing several theories, such as the possibility of another ice age or global warming. The Facklams carefully separate fact from theory and opinion. As you read the following excerpt, consider why the authors use such terms as *might, if, could,* and *guess:*

Green plants might even be tapped for energy someday through bioengineering. If a super species of high hydrogen-producing plant could be genetically engineered, it might add to our energy supplies. The EPA closes its report by admitting we can only guess at the results of global warming. (p. 40)

Are significant facts omitted? Authors should present enough significant facts to make the text accurate. Specialized books that give complete histories of certain animals are valuable because they help children understand the evolution of a species, as well as its characteristics and its needs, if any, for protection. To acquire a balanced viewpoint on some topics, readers may require a book with a different focus for comparison. For example, Sneed B. Collard's *Animal Dads* could be used to show that it is not only the mother who protects,

feeds, and teaches the young. Texts that provide historical information should also provide enough facts for readers to understand the concepts. For example, in *Smoke and Ashes: The Story of the Holocaust,* Barbara Rogasky traces the roots of anti-Semitism before presenting the World War II experiences.

Are differing views on controversial subjects presented? Subjects such as ecology and nuclear energy are controversial. For example, in *Nuclear Energy: Troubled Past, Uncertain Future,* Laurence Pringle discusses both sides of the nuclear energy issue even though he presents stronger arguments against nuclear power. A biased author should identify that his or her personal point of view is not necessarily a universally held position. Even the classifications of animals may present differing views. In her book about the history of various animals, *Who Harnessed the Horse? The Story of Animal Domestication,* Margery Facklam identifies various viewpoints when she states: "Scientists are still arguing over the vicuna, which is the smallest of the llamoids and has the softest, most lustrous hair. Some say it is a wild animal. Others say it, too, was domesticated from the guanaco but was allowed to roam wild on purpose" (p. 102).

History texts should present both sides of controversial issues. For example, as you read books such as Leonard A. Stevens's *The Case of Roe v. Wade,* try to decide if or how the author provides both sides of a controversial issue. In this book, the author not only presents history, he also discusses current and possible future ramifications of the decision.

Is the information presented without relying on anthropomorphism? While it is perfectly acceptable for authors of fantasy to write about animals that think, talk, act, and dress like people, authors of informational books should not ascribe human thoughts, motives, or emotions to animals or to plants and other inanimate things (a practice called *anthropomorphism*). Writers of animal information books should describe the animals in terms that can be substantiated through careful observation. For example, in *Batman: Exploring the World of Bats,* Laurence Pringle describes the information about bats discovered by nature photographer Merlin Tuttle as he observed bats and photographed them in numerous locations. In the following example, Pringle describes only behaviors that are observable:

The scientists played recordings of frog calls and lured frog-eating bats into fine-meshed nets, called mist nets, that are used to catch bats in flight. After gently taming the bats, they put them in a large outdoor cage and tested their responses to the recorded calls of different kinds of frogs. Frog-eating bats, they discovered, could distinguish between the calls of edible frogs and poisonous frogs. They avoided the latter. They could also tell the difference between the calls of frogs of edible size and those that were too big to eat. (p. 19)

Is the information as up to date as possible? Because knowledge in some areas is changing rapidly, copyright dates are very important for certain types of informational books. For example, the copyright date is very important in books about technology, such as Gloria Skurzynski's *Almost the Real Thing: Simulation in Your High-Tech World* and *Get the Message: Telecommunications in Your High-Tech World.* What was considered high technology in the 1970s and 1980s may not be high technology in the 1990s. Likewise, books such as Bernard Wolf's *HIV Positive* require the latest information.

Attitudes and values also change. Comparing older factual books with more recent ones is one way to illustrate how attitudes and biases change. No educator or publisher today would condone the untrue and highly offensive descriptions of Native Americans presented in *Carpenter's Geographical Reader, North America* published by Frank G. Carpenter in 1898. For example, the following is Carpenter's depiction of the historical background of Native Americans:

The savage Indians were in former times dangerous and cruel foes. They took delight in killing women and children. They hid behind rocks and bushes to fight. . . . They used tomahawks to brain their victims, and delighted in torturing their captives and in burning them at the stake. (p. 293)

Information about Australian native people is just as biased in Charles Redway Dryer's *Geography, Physical, Economic, and Regional,* published in 1911, while V. M. Hillyer's 1929 text, *A Child's Geography of the World,* says that the most curious animals in Africa are the people. Students of children's literature may not realize how outdated, misinformed, and biased informational books can be until they discover books such as these that influenced the thinking of school children earlier in this century.

Stereotypes. *Does the book violate basic principles against racism and sexism?* As the above examples make clear, informational books, like all books, should be without demeaning racist or sexist stereotypes.

Some contemporary books reflect stereotypes through inclusion or exclusion of certain types of people in certain professions. For example, are people of both sexes and various racial and ethnic groups shown in illustrations of science or science professions? The photographs in Dean R. Snow's *The Archaeology of North America* show both men and women working in the archaeological sites. The illustrations in Joanna Cole's *The Magic School Bus: On the Ocean Floor* show that both boys and girls are interested in scientific subjects. The illustrations in Jackson's *The Bone Detectives: How Forensic Anthropologists Solve Crimes and Uncover Mysteries of the Dead* show that both boys and girls are interested in the subject. In addition, the text includes photographs of both male and female scientists.

Illustrations. *Are the illustrations accurate?* Illustrations should be as accurate as the text and should add to its clarity. Photographs and drawings should be accompanied by explanatory legends keyed directly to the text to allow children to expand their understanding of the principles or terminology presented. Literary critic Barbara Elleman (1992) emphasizes the importance of illustrations when evaluating trends in nonfiction. She states, "When done well, today's visuals are directly connected to the text, are made up of either meticulous, accurately produced drawings or clear, full-color photographs, and have captions that extend the information" (p. 30). David Macaulay's detailed illustrations in *The Way Things Work* are labeled to clarify concepts. *The Incredible Journey of Lewis and Clark,* by Rhoda Blumberg, includes maps showing both the journey west and the return journey east. Key locations are numbered and keyed to dates and pages of discussion within the text. *Money, Money, Money: The Meaning of the Art and Symbols on United States Paper Currency* by Nancy Winslow Parker includes detailed, labeled illustrations showing the symbols on the front and back of United States currency from $1 to $100,000. Detailed illustrations also strengthen the reader's understanding in David Weitzman's *Old Ironsides: Americans Build a Fighting Ship.*

Leonard Everett Fisher (1988), writer and illustrator of nonfictional material, states that illustrations should also create historical mood. Fisher says:

Today what interests me in nonfiction is giving youngsters a visual memory of a fact rather than just the fact. I am trying to present a factual mood. The Tower of London, for instance, is a creepy place, and if I can establish the creepiness of the place so that the youngster gets an unsettled feeling about the tower, then that child is going to have more of an understanding of history than just learning a date. I'm trying to create the emotion of history, the dynamics of history, together with the fact of history. I'm trying to communicate what events in history felt like. These feelings will bring children back to reading information to find out the facts—back to reality! I want to give a sense of history created by the fallible, mortal human beings who made it. (p. 317)

Fisher's illustrations may be found in his texts *The Tower of London, The Great Wall of China,* and *The Wailing Wall.*

Analytical Thinking. *Do children have an opportunity to become involved in solving problems logically?* Many informational books, particularly scientific ones, should encourage children to observe, gather data, experiment, compare, and formulate hypotheses. Informational books should encourage children to withhold judgment until enough data have been gathered or enough facts have been explored. Books that demonstrate scientific facts and principles should encourage children to do more experiments on their own and should stress the value of additional background reading. For example, in *How to Be an Ocean Scientist in Your Own Home,* Seymour Simon develops a series of experiments that proceed from "Let's Find Out" to "Here's What You Will Need" to "Here's What to Do." In addition, Simon includes a bibliography of books about the topics.

Good science writing should also encourage children to become involved with their world. Science writer Patricia Lauber (1992) states that the best science books, like any other literature, "have a point of view. They involve readers by making them care—care about the people, the animals, a town, an idea, and most of all, care how it all comes out. In short, they inspire feeling" (p. 13). This point of view is important when Lauber describes her own aims in writing science books: "Overall, my aims are to help children understand how the earth (or its parts) works

and to try to imbue them with some of my own sense of wonderment, in the hope that they will grow up to be good stewards, who will take care of the earth, not just use (or abuse) it" (p. 14). As children read some of Lauber's books, such as *Volcano: The Eruption and Healing of Mount St. Helens, Flood: Wrestling with the Mississippi,* and *Hurricanes: Earth's Mightiest Storms,* decide if Lauber is able to involve her readers by making them care about the earth.

Organization. *Is the organization logical?* Ideas in informational books should be broken down into easily understood component parts. Authors often use an organization that progresses from the simple to the more complex, or from the familiar to the unfamiliar, or from early to later development. In *Into the Mummy's Tomb: The Real-Life Discovery of Tutankhamun's Treasures,* Nicholas Reeves introduces the topic with a prologue that relates history to more current events. This prologue introduces a mystery in which two secret, locked cupboards in Highclere Castle in England reveal ancient Egyptian treasures that were hidden after the discovery of Tutankhamun's tomb. The text then proceeds in chronological order, beginning with "The Hidden Steps, Cairo, Egypt, 1907" and concluding with "The Tomb's Secrets, Hampshire, England, 1988." Numerous photographs and maps complement this historical progression. Stephen Krensky uses a chronological order to present the history of printing in *Breaking into Print: Before and After the Invention of the Printing Press.*

Are organizational aids included? Reference aids such as a table of contents, an index, a glossary, a bibliography, and a list of suggested readings can encourage children to use organized reference skills. While very young children do not need all of these aids, older children find them helpful. For example, in *Commodore Perry in the Land of the Shogun,* Rhoda Blumberg includes a table of contents, notes, information about the illustrations, a bibliography, an index, and five appendices of additional information about the time period.

Style. *Is the writing style lively and not too difficult for children of a certain age to understand?* Kathryn Lasky's *Sugaring Time* is an excellent example of both stimulating literary style and careful documentation. For example, Lasky describes corn snow, large and granular snow crystals, as follows: "When Jonathan skis it sounds as if he is skimming across the thick frosting of a wedding cake" (p. 7). The maple sap "runs like streams of Christmas tinsel" (p. 19). The environment in the sugarhouse is "like sitting in a maple cloud surrounded by the muffled roar of the fire and the bubbling tumble of boiling sap" (p. 34). The photographs reinforce the language, following the family during all aspects of collecting and processing maple syrup.

Comparisons can help clarify complex ideas or startling facts. For example, in *Shadows of the Night: The Hidden World of the Little Brown Bat,* Barbara Bash compares the weight of a young bat with the weight of a pencil and provides diagrams that compare the structures of human hands and the wings of a bat.

Children's publisher and author of nonfiction, James Cross Giblin (1992) emphasizes the importance of style when writing nonfiction and also presents some of the similarities and differences between writing nonfiction and fiction:

A nonfiction author is telling a story the same as any other author. The only difference is that it's a true story. So there's nothing wrong with using fictional techniques of scene setting and atmosphere building to make factual materials more interesting and involving for the reader. . . . A cautionary note: fictional techniques should never be confused by authors, editors, or book selectors with a distortion of the facts. Anthropomorphizing animals in natural history should be avoided at all costs, and invented dialogue should never be put into the mouths of the figures in biographies; anachronisms and inaccuracies of any type do not belong in nonfiction books. (p. 20)

Authors of credible informational books meet many of these guidelines. Consider in the following sections how authors develop credible books that may stimulate and inform readers.

History and Culture

Informational books about history and culture include books about ancient civilizations as well as more recent ones. The illustrations and photographs in many of the books help children visualize the past.

The Ancient World. Books on archaeology help readers understand the magnitude of history and develop an awareness of how archaeologists help uncover the past. In Kate Duke's *Archaeologists Dig*

for Clues, a highly illustrated book for younger readers, an archaeologist explains the science of archaeology to three children who accompany her on a dig. Lively dialogue, realistic questions, and descriptions of the Archaic Era of six thousand years ago are discussed through such findings as stone knives. Sidebars add information about the content. In *Stone Age Farmers Beside the Sea: Scotland's Prehistoric Village of Skara Brae,* Caroline Arnold focuses on the work of archaeologists to uncover and preserve a prehistoric village inhabited from 3100 to 2500 B.C. Colored photographs, maps, and diagrams add to an understanding of the time period.

John S. Major's *The Silk Route: 7,000 Miles of History* follows the silk route from Chang'an, China, to Byzantium during the Tang Dynasty (A.D. 618–906). A map introduces the text. The remainder of the text and the illustrations focus on the major cities, geography, and obstacles along the route. Stephen Fieser's large, colored illustrations show people, culture, and settings. The book concludes with a section called "A Closer Look" in which the author provides additional background information on topics such as caravan life, invasion routes of inner Asia, and the religions of Central Asia.

Authors who write about the ancient world may develop credible books by citing the latest information gained from their own research or from that of others and by describing details so that readers can visualize an ancient world. Because readers cannot verify facts about the ancient world through their own experiences, authors may include drawings that clarify information or may use photographs of museum objects or archaeological sites.

Ancient Mayan and Aztec civilizations in Central America are the subjects of several books. Carolyn Meyer and Charles Gallenkamp create a hint of mystery and excitement in their introduction to *The Mystery of the Ancient Maya.* Consider the vivid setting, the motivation of the two explorers, and the sense of discovery and anticipation in the following:

Two travelers—one American, one English—struggled through the jungle, hacking away the tangled vines with their machetes. New York City, which they had left that fall of 1839, seemed impossibly far away. Since their arrival in Central America the trip had been grueling. In the past few weeks they had endured hunger and had been thrown into a makeshift prison. They had hung on as their mules picked their way along the edges of cliffs. But now, standing on a river bank in Honduras, they felt hopeful again.

On the opposite shore they could make out a stone wall, perhaps a hundred feet high but nearly hidden by the thick growth of trees. Maybe this was what they had been searching for—the lost city of Copan. (p. 3)

The book proceeds from a history of the early explorers, to revelations about the Mayan civilization, to disclosures about the Mayan people, and to the unanswered questions that are under investigation. Drawings, photographs, and excerpts from early journals add to the sense of time and place.

Archaeological investigations in Europe provide the sources for information in Susan Woodford's *The Parthenon*. Woodford's book, part of the Cambridge History Library, presents a detailed account of the building of the Greek Parthenon. This book follows a chronological order beginning in 490 B.C. and extending through current problems caused by air pollution. Use the labeled drawings, captioned photographs, and detailed descriptions of ancient Greek life and religious practices to expand a study of Greek culture and Greek mythology.

A King's Treasure: The Sutton Ho Ship Burial, by Katherine East, published in association with the British Museum, is based on an archaeological investigation that uncovered the burial site of an Anglo-Saxon king who lived in seventh-century England. East uses information and artifacts discovered at the site to reconstruct that period in history. Nicholas Reeves's *Into the Mummy's Tomb: The Real-Life Discovery of Tutankhamun's Treasures* traces Howard Carter's discovery of the tomb of the king. Rebecca Stefoff's *Finding the Lost Cities* also focuses on Carter's discoveries. Eve Bunting's *I Am the Mummy Heb-Nefert* uses the mummy to retell the story of the life in Egypt. *Mummies & Their Mysteries* by Charlotte Wilcox discusses the process of mummification and introduces readers to mummies found in different parts of the world.

In *Pompeii: Exploring a Roman Ghost Town,* Ron and Nancy Goor use photographs from the archaeological dig to recreate Pompeii before it was destroyed by the eruption of Mt. Vesuvius in A.D. 79. The Goors first introduce the magnitude of the disaster by quoting from a letter that is an eyewitness account about the eruption. Then, the Goors describe the discovery of Pompeii, the probable appearance of the city in A.D. 79, the public and private lives of the people living within the city, and the commercial development of the city. Labeled photographs and drawings clarify the text.

Readers who enjoy traditional literature and historical fiction set in medieval times and adults who would like to help children recreate medieval festivals should find several books rewarding. David Macaulay's *Castle* and *Cathedral: The Story of Its Construction* include detailed drawings to clarify how castles and cathedrals are constructed. Leonard Everett Fisher's *The Tower of London* uses gray illustrations to add a feeling of ominousness to the surroundings. These books should be helpful to librarians, teachers, and other adults who are interested in giving children a feeling for earlier times and cultures.

Authors may trace the history of a common item to show its importance in diverse cultures and across different time periods. Charlotte Yue uses this approach in *Shoes: Their History in Words and Pictures.* The author traces the chronology of shoes from a sandal that was common ten thousand years ago to the styles found today. The author increases reader involvement by asking questions that focus attention on the subject of the text. Drawings of the different shoes from various time periods provide a sense of history and the importance of shoes. James Cross Giblin uses a similar approach in *From Hand to Mouth: Or, How We Invented Knives, Forks, Spoons, and Chopsticks & the Table Manners to Go with Them.* In this text, Giblin also shows that history includes changes in etiquette. Giblin explores the history of table utensils in an often humorous manner.

Informational books may trace the history of important developments that have changed the world such as the printing of books or the changes in medicine. In *Breaking into Print: Before and After the Invention of the Printing Press,* Stephen Krensky uses several techniques that increase understanding and interest. For example, the text follows a chronological order from the days of early parchment and monks creating hand-lettered texts with knife-sharpened quills through the printing press and computerized typesetting. Sidebars provide additional information about the time period; wood engravings add the feeling of historical accuracy; and a time line of the history of printing proceeds from 3500 B.C. through the 1980s. In *Just What the Doctor Ordered: The History of American Medicine,* Brandon Marie Miller begins with descriptions of early Native American ceremonies and herbal remedies and continues through more modern times such as the impact on medical developments that resulted from the Revolutionary War and Civil War.

History also includes religious traditions. Betsy Maestro develops an introduction to various beliefs in *The Story of Religion.* The author begins with a discussion of early polytheistic beliefs and continues into a discussion of other religions such as Taoism, Hinduism, Christianity, and Islam. Giulio Maestro's illustrations relate to the culture of the religion. In *The Passover Journey: A Seder Companion,* Barbara Goldin explains the traditions associated with Passover.

Archaeologist and anthropologist Brian M. Fagan's *The Great Journey: The Peopling of Ancient America* explores in text and photographs the early people who lived in North America. The text is divided into five parts: (1) ideas, (2) ancestry, (3) the crossing, (4) the first Americans, and (5) the great diversity. In addition to photographs, Fagan uses drawings and maps to clarify concepts. Helen Roney Sattler's *Hominids: A Look Back at Our Ancestors* also uses an anthropological approach to look at early hominids and to research the human family. Christopher Santoro's labeled drawings and maps clarify the concepts developed in Sattler's text. Santoro also provides numerous comparative illustrations to help readers. Compare Sattler's text and Joanna Cole's *The Human Body: How We Evolved* as well as Nick Merriman's *Early Humans.*

Just as there are numerous biographies resulting from the circa 1492 studies, there are also many informational books that either trace the early explorations of the New World or depict the period. Books such as Roy Gallant's *Ancient Indians: The First Americans* and George DeLucenay Leon's *Explorers of the Americas Before Columbus* focus on early settlers and explorers. Gallant goes back in time to recreate what may have happened thousands of years ago when the ancestors of Native Americans crossed the bridge linking Siberia to Alaska before the close of the last ice age. In addition to Native Americans, Leon examines the voyages of Eric the Red and Leif Ericsson and explores the discovery of Norse settlements. In a book written for older students, *The Discoverers of America,* Harold Faber includes not only information on the earliest explorers but also information on European politics that influenced the explorations. The book includes important dates related to the discoveries of America, notes on sources, a bibliography, and an index.

In *If You Were There in 1492,* Barbara Brenner presents facts about everyday life during the fifteenth century. Chapters include information about such subjects as food and clothing, education, arts and entertainment, and crime and punishment. John Dyson's *Westward with Columbus* presents a reenactment of the 1492 expedition. The photographs are taken from the 1990 voyage in a replica of the *Nina.* Charlotte and David Yue's *Christopher Columbus: How He Did It* focuses on the knowledge and technology that enabled Columbus to complete his voyage.

Norman Finkelstein's *The Other Fourteen Ninety-Two: Jewish Settlement in the New World* details the history of the Jewish people who were expelled from Spain in 1492. There is information about the Spanish Inquisition, anti-Semitism during the period, and the movement of people and ideas as the Jewish people searched for a location in which to live. The final chapter chronicles the positive Jewish experience in the American colonies. The text includes a bibliography of books and articles and an index.

The World in 1492 by Jean Fritz et al. is an interesting history for readers who are searching for a broader view of the world in 1492. The book includes five chapters, each written by a well-known author (or authors) of children's literature. For example, Jean Fritz writes "Europe in 1492." Additional authors and chapters include Katherine Paterson's "Asia in 1492," Patricia and Frederick McKissack's "Africa in 1492," Margaret Mahy's "Australia and Oceania in 1492," and Jamake Highwater's "The Americas in 1492." Each author includes information about the history, customs, beliefs, and accomplishments of the people. Reproductions of various artworks help readers gain a deeper understanding of the world.

The Modern World. The factual data in informational books about the modern world may be made credible by citing research, quoting authorities, quoting original sources, and providing detailed descriptions of the setting, circumstances, or situations. Photographs also often add authenticity.

You may discover the impact of photographs and illustrations by analyzing books on historical places written for younger students and comparing them with books written for older students. For example, in a book for younger students, *The Great Wall of China,* Leonard Fisher develops a simple text that is extensively illustrated with black-and-white illustrations. The text provides minimal information about

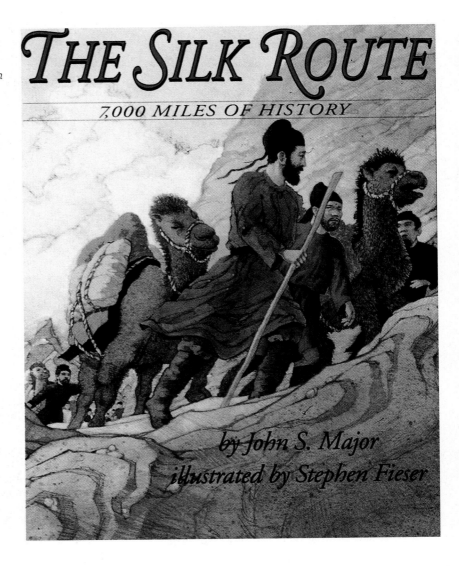

THE SILK ROUTE

7,000 MILES OF HISTORY

by John S. Major

illustrated by Stephen Fieser

the reasons for building the wall and the actual construction of the wall. The illustrations are labeled with Chinese characters that are translated on the final page. Likewise, Karla Kuskin's *Jerusalem, Shining Still* is a highly illustrated book that tells the history of Jerusalem as a storyteller might reveal the battles, the people, and the rebuilding. In both books, illustrations, rather than photographs and drawings, and emphasis on sequence of actions and plot, rather than exact historical dates, present the impression of a story rather than a history. In *The Golden City: Jerusalem's 3,000 Years,* a book for older readers, Neil Waldman focuses on the history of this sacred city and includes information about the early con-

flicts. To add an additional feeling of historical change, Waldman's watercolor illustrations are labeled with both time and place. The author also includes Biblical text. Even though he includes the historic conflicts, he concludes his book on a positive note: "Just as in centuries past, thousands of people from faraway places come to visit Jerusalem each year. They are drawn by the splendor of the place, the magnificent domed mosques and the narrow alleyways, the delicate carvings and the massive ramparts, the ancient shrines and modern museums. But hidden beneath all these visible things is the mysterious feeling that, as you pass through the city gates, you are actually drifting back past the days of

The Great Fire, *by Jim Murphy tells, in story and pictures about the Chicago fire of 1871. (Dust jacket from* THE GREAT FIRE *by Jim Murphy. Copyright © 1995 by Jim Murphy. Reprinted by permission of Scholastic, Inc.)*

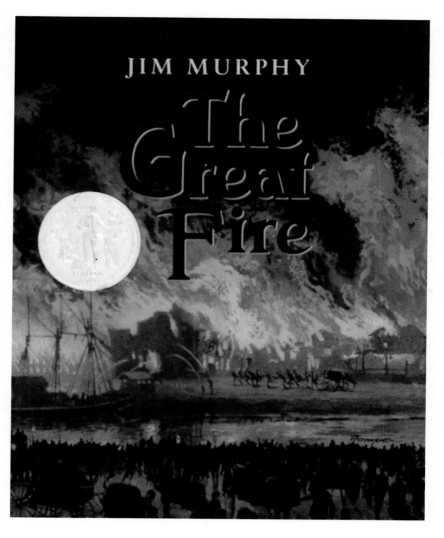

fabled knights and prophets, to the time when a young boy slew a giant with a slingshot" (unnumbered). In *Talking Walls,* a book for readers in the middle-elementary grades, Margy Burns Knight presents a history of some of the most famous walls in the world, including the Great Wall of China, the Vietnam Veterans Memorial, and the Berlin Wall.

Jim Murphy's *The Great Fire* presents details associated with the Chicago fire of 1871. In addition to being selected a 1996 Newbery Honor Award winner, the book received starred reviews in *Booklist, Horn Book,* and *School Library Journal.* Consequently, this book provides an excellent source for applying the evaluation criteria for information liter-

ature. For example, under accuracy of facts, students of children's literature will discover that Murphy provides a bibliography and sources for accounts that are presented in the book, and he uses carefully selected documents and personal accounts to provide the details associated with the fire. The author frequently distinguishes between fact and theory, or in this case facts and rumors. For example, when Murphy reports the common belief that the fire department had given up because they could do nothing, Murphy states, "That wasn't exactly accurate. Much of the fire department was still at work, even though they knew the fire was completely out of control. Engines and men had scattered as the fire advanced and were now operating on their own, essentially trying to save individual buildings here and there. Chief Marshall Williams, for instance, had jumped aboard a passing engine and was now at one of the remaining bridge crossings, hosing it down" (p. 67). The author also separates facts from rumors in the concluding chapter, "Myth and Reality," in which he discusses questions such as "Did Mrs. O'Leary's cow cause the fire?" and "Was the drunken fire department to blame for the spread of the fire?"

The book is illustrated with reproductions of drawings that originated at the time of the event. Each drawing is labeled and includes its source and date of origin. For example, the drawing on page 44 shows fire ravaging the Crosby Opera House and identifies the source as *Harper's Weekly,* October 28, 1871.

The history of the early postal service is developed in Steven Kroll's *Pony Express!.* Kroll attracts the readers' attention by beginning the book with a help wanted ad:

> Wanted.
> YOUNG SKINNY WIRY FELLOWS
> not over eighteen. Must be expert riders willing
> to risk death daily. Orphans preferred. WAGES $25
> perweek. Apply, Central Overland Express,
> Alta Bldg., Montgomery St. (unnumbered)

Kroll then places the need for the pony express in its historical context by discussing the Gold Rush in California and the need to get mail from New York to California in less than the six months required for a ship to travel around Cape Horn. Kroll highlights the development of the overland routes including stagecoach travel and the impact of additional gold discoveries in Colorado and Nevada. The major part of the text then describes the pony express beginning with the first ride on April 3–April 13, 1860. Dan Andreasen's illustrations place the text into its historical context. The book concludes with an author's note that discusses the mail service through modern time. The text includes a map of the Pony Express Route, a Mini Photo Museum that traces the mail service from clipper ships to bar code sorters in a modern post office, a bibliography, and an index.

In Roxie Munro's almost wordless *The Inside-Outside Book of Washington, D.C.,* large, detailed illustrations provide a great deal of factual information. The only text provided in the book introduces each series of illustrations. Detailed illustrations include the Library of Congress, the Supreme Court of the United States, the National Air and Space Museum, the East Room of the White House, and the Senate Wing of the United States Capitol.

Nancy Winslow Parker's *Money, Money, Money: The Meaning of the Art and Symbols on United States Paper Currency* is both an informative text about the meaning of each of the figures or symbols on various paper currencies and a history that provides historical information about the people or symbols pictured on the bills. Parker introduces the subject with an enlarged fifty-dollar bill in which she identifies each of the symbols on the portrait. In the remainder of the book she provides information about the Secretary of the Treasury, the people whose portraits are on the bills, the seal of the United States, the White House, Independence Hall, engraving and printing, counterfeiters, the Federal Reserve System, and architectural capitals. To add clarity to the text, each of the illustrations are labeled.

The presidency and the White House provide interesting subjects for authors of informational books. Alice Provensen's *The Buck Stops Here: The Presidents of the United States* is a pictorial representation of the presidents and the major happenings during each time period. This heavily illustrated book contains excellent information for readers at all levels. The book also contains interesting background information for children reading stories set in various time periods. Suzanne Hilton's *A Capital City: 1790–1814* is a history of the District of Columbia. Sources such as pamphlets, advertisements, and letters add details that bring the history to life. In *Full Steam Ahead: The Race to Build a Transcontinental Railroad,* Blumberg focuses on the signing of the Pacific Railroad Act of 1862 and the forces that influenced the building of the railroad.

Many informational books about the modern world help children understand the varied people on the earth, including their struggles and achievements and their impact on history. Students may make interesting comparisons between books related to the writing of the Constitution and the people of that time. Jean Fritz's *Shh! We're Writing the Constitution* is for younger children. Fritz writes about the constitutional leaders in the lighter, often humorous style found in her biographies.

Doris and Harold Faber's *We the People: The Story of the United States Constitution Since 1787* is a comprehensive text written for older students. The Fabers begin with the delegation meeting and con-

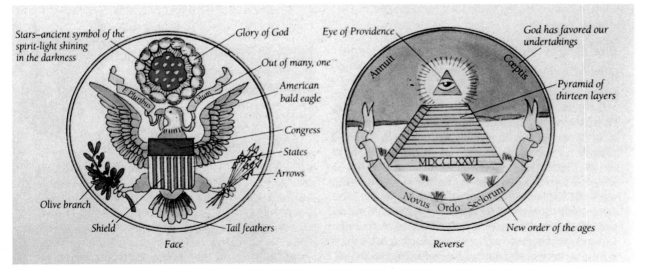

Face

- Stars—ancient symbol of the spirit-light shining in the darkness
- Glory of God
- Out of many, one
- American bald eagle
- Congress
- States
- Arrows
- Olive branch
- Shield
- Tail feathers
- E Pluribus Unum

Reverse

- Eye of Providence
- God has favored our undertakings
- Annuit
- Coeptis
- Pyramid of thirteen layers
- MDCCLXXVI
- Novus Ordo Seclorum
- New order of the ages

Detailed, labeled illustrations enhance understanding of currency. (From MONEY, MONEY, MONEY: The Meaning of the Art and Symbols on United States Paper Currency, copyright © 1995 by Nancy Winslow Parker. HarperCollins Children's Books, a division of HarperCollins Publishers. Used by permission of HarperCollins Publishers.)

clude with the most recent changes in the Constitution. Compare the description of the debate over the Randolph proposal cited in Fritz's text with the same debate over the Randolph proposal described on pages 23–34 in the Fabers' text. Consider the differences in style and information, and discuss how those differences relate to the age levels of the children for which the books were written. *The Birth of a Nation: The Early Years of the United States,* also by the Fabers, extends beyond the days of the Constitutional Convention. Milton Meltzer's *The American Revolutionaries: A History in Their Own Words, 1750–1800* is an excellent source for the original writings of the people who fought in the Revolutionary War or designed the Constitution. The text includes actual letters, diaries, journals, and speeches. In *Who Were the Founding Fathers? Two Hundred Years of Reinventing American History,* Steven H. Jaffe considers how various groups have interpreted the words of the founding fathers.

Several current books explore the history of the United States at war. In *A Nation Torn: The Story of How the Civil War Began,* Delia Ray explores the causes of the Civil War. This book includes a map of the United States that designates free states and slave states, a glossary, a bibliography, and an index. In *The Long Road to Gettysburg,* Jim Murphy describes the events of the 1863 battle through the perspec-

tives of two soldiers who took part in the battle. One is a nineteen-year-old Confederate soldier and the other is a seventeen-year-old Union soldier.

Rhoda Blumberg presents two excellent histories of explorations in more modern times. *Commodore Perry in the Land of the Shogun* follows Commodore Perry as he opens Japan to world trade in the 1850s. The illustrations, which are reproductions of works of William Heine or Eliphalet Brown, Jr. (the official artists on Perry's expedition), add authenticity. *The Incredible Journey of Lewis and Clark* chronicles the 1803–1806 explorations of the Lewis and Clark expedition. Labeled maps and illustrations follow the quest for a water passage to the Pacific Ocean. Extensive notes, sources of illustrations, a bibliography, and an index add to the usefulness and scholarly feeling of the text.

In 1845, Sir John Franklin, two ships, and the crews sailed the Arctic waters in search of the Northwest Passage. The ships and crews disappeared. In *Buried in Ice: The Mystery of a Lost Arctic Expedition,* Owen Beattie and John Geiger document the search for the missing ships. Photographs and drawings heighten the interest in the book.

Robert D. Ballard describes an even more recent exploration in *Exploring the Titanic.* Photographs from the 1912 *Titanic* are used extensively to show what the boat and interior rooms looked like before the "unsinkable" boat sank. Color photographs and text then document the finding of the *Titanic* in 1985 and subsequent exploration of the ship. A glossary of terms and a time line add to the text.

Quality information books should separate facts and theories and present differing views on controversial subjects. Lou Eschle's *The Curse of Tutankhamen* discusses the conflicting theories associated with the deaths in 1922 following the opening of King Tut's tomb. The text includes an introduction which discusses the Carter-Carnarvon expedition and how science investigated the curse. Conflicting theories are presented in an interesting style. For example, "Some say Howard Carter's crew uncovered a tablet with another curse: 'Death comes on wings to he who enters the tomb of a pharaoh.' The tablet, however, if it ever existed, has disappeared. No evidence of it remains" (p. 26). When presenting another theory, the author states, "The ancient priests may have been able to preserve the poisons from these deadly desert beasts (cobra and scorpion) in a form that would kill or stricken grave robbers" (p. 33). In order to encourage reader speculation, the author asks, "Is it possible that poisonous substances placed inside Tutankhamen's tomb were responsible for some of the deaths?" (p. 34).

Norman Finkelstein's *Sounds in the Air: The Golden Age of Radio* is a history of radio programs in the 1930s and 1940s. Finkelstein uses quotes from the programs to depict the subject vividly.

Highly emotional periods in history are difficult to present objectively. Seymour Rossel, however, approaches *The Holocaust* with a historian's detachment. He traces Adolf Hitler's rise to power; describes the harassment, internment, and extermination of many Jewish people; and discusses the Nuremberg trials of the Nazis. Rossel effectively quotes from original sources, such as diaries and letters, to allow readers to draw their own conclusions.

Barbara Rogasky's *Smoke and Ashes: The Story of the Holocaust* begins with the history of anti-Semitism and proceeds to the 1933–1945 experience. This text shows life in the camps and explores such questions as, Why and how did it happen? Didn't anyone try to stop the Holocaust? Photographs add to the feeling of tragedy. Milton Meltzer's *Rescue: The Story of How Gentiles Saved Jews in the Holocaust* develops another side of the Holocaust and shows that many people risked their lives to help the Jewish people.

Books that describe or depict nuclear war also vary depending on the intended audiences and the messages to be related. Compare the highly visual and personalized descriptions in Toshi Maruki's *Hiroshima No Pika (The Flash of Hiroshima)* with Carl B. Feldbaum and Ronald J. Bee's historical and scientific descriptions in *Looking the Tiger in the Eye: Confronting the Nuclear Threat*. Using a picture-storybook format, Maruki relates the experiences of seven-year-old Mii on August 6, 1945, as the child and her mother pass by fire, death, and destruction. Maruki, who actively campaigns for nuclear disarmament and world peace, concludes her book on a hopeful note: "It can't happen again if no one drops the bomb" (p. 43, unnumbered). Feldbaum and Bee's text includes the history of nuclear weapons and discusses decisions made by political, scientific, and military officials.

History is made up of people who immigrate to a new country as developed in Dorothy and Thomas Hoobler's *The Jewish American Family Album*. According to the authors, about 2.5 million Jewish immigrants arrived in the United States between 1880 and 1924. This nonfictional book provides descriptions of families as they leave Europe, arrive in America, begin new lives, and become part of American life. Photographs and first-hand descriptions add to the authenticity of the book. It is interesting to compare these experiences with those described in historical fiction. Many of the Jewish immigrants express desires for education and freedom. These desires mirror the conflicts, settings, and themes found in many historical fiction books written about this same time period. There are many excerpts from this book that may be used for comparisons and for authentication of historical fiction.

Nature

Effective informational books about nature encourage children to understand their own bodies, observe nature, explore the life cycles of animals, consider the impact of endangered species, experiment with plants, understand the balance of the smallest ecosystem, and explore the earth's geology. In order to create effective and credible books, authors must blend fact into narrative. The authors must gain these facts about animals from observation and research. Close-up photography is especially effective in clarifying information and stimulating interest.

Two writers of history informational books, Dorothy and Thomas Hoobler,[1] explore some of the issues associated with history books for children. They begin their article with the following concern:

Studies show that children in the United States have little knowledge of history. . . . Certainly one of the most important reasons is that the subject is just not taught in the lower grades. This lack of knowledge has its effect on the reading students choose outside the classroom. Children who have no background in this area are unlikely to read it for recreation. . . . A look at the children's section of a bookstore will show little more than a few biographies, and many of these are about current sports figures and celebrities. (p. 37)

The Hooblers then suggest several additional reasons why few history books are written for children. For example, they argue that publishers are not interested in publishing children's books about periods before World War II. In addition, discussion of issues associated with conflicts in history may make the books controversial.

The Hooblers summarize their own experiences with the mixed reviews of *Vietnam: Why We Fought: An Illustrated History.* They state: "Unfortunately, we found that after almost 20 years, the controversy over the conflict is still very much alive. Our approach offended some people, although many publications praised our book" (p. 38). After read-

ing this article, discuss some of the following issues:

1. How pervasive is the lack of historical understanding in children in the elementary and middle grades? If there is a lack of understanding, how does this lack influence the history books read by children?

2. What should the publisher's role be in publishing and promoting books about history before World War II?

3. Should authors write controversial history books for children? Why or why not?

[1] Hoobler, Dorothy, and Thomas Hoobler. "Writing History for Children." *School Library Journal* 38 (January 1992):37–38.

For example, photographs may illustrate what happens inside an egg or a nest or follow the life cycle of an animal or a plant. Labeled diagrams may clarify text descriptions. Maps may show natural habitats of animals, migration patterns of birds, or locations of earthquakes. If authors present new vocabulary or concepts, they should define the terms, illustrate them with diagrams or photographs, and proceed from known to unknown information. Clearly developed activities that encourage children to observe and experiment can make a book even more useful. A bibliography, an index, and a list of additional readings are helpful, too.

The Human Body. Informational books about the human body are especially interesting to readers who are curious about their own bodies and how they function. Books for children about the human body range from overviews to detailed discussions of one aspect of the body, such as the brain or the eyes. Some books also discuss body-related issues, such as the right to live or to die, genetic engineering, and human origins.

Two books on the human body illustrate the importance of labeled diagrams when studying anatomy. Jonathan Miller's *The Human Body* is a fascinating, twelve-page pop-up book. Each two-page spread, along with tabs that simulate functions, explains some part of the human body. Body parts are labeled with numbers and then explained in the captions for the pop-up illustrations. Ruth and Bertel Bruun clarify their longer text, *The Human Body,* with diagrams and drawings that show the interiors of various body regions and the relationships of these regions to each other.

Stephen Parker and John Bavosi's *Life Before Birth: The Story of the First Nine Months* is a straightforward discussion of the facts related to the fertilization of the egg, the development and growth of the fetus, and the birth of the baby. The book, which is enhanced with color illustrations adapted from a slide program at the British Museum, concludes with a photograph of a newborn baby. Joanna Cole's *How You Were Born* is a revision of her earlier book. Through text and illustrations the author describes the process of conception and birth.

A series of books provides a history of various drugs and discusses their effects on the brain and the body, treatments for addicts, and ways to resist peer pressure. David Friedman's *Focus on Drugs and the Brain* discusses the brain and how drugs influence it. Friedman distinguishes differences between drugs used for medicine and drugs used for harmful purposes. These books emphasize specific drugs and provide clear warnings about their harmful influences: Catherine O'Neill's *Focus on Alcohol,* Robert Perry's *Focus on Nicotine and Caffeine,* Laurence Pringle's *Drinking: A Risky Business,* Jeffrey Shulman's *Focus on Cocaine and Crack,* and Paula Klevan Zeller's *Focus on Marijuana.*

Texts on the AIDS virus are available for both younger and older readers. In Rosmarie Hausherr's *Children and the AIDS Virus,* the text and illustrations look at ways in which children may or may not get the disease. Hausherr's text is written for two levels of readers. The large print is to be read to or by younger children. The smaller print provides additional information for older children. Bernard Wolf's *HIV Positive* is a photo-essay written for readers in the middle grades. He focuses on a mother with AIDS and her two young children. The author emphasizes the emotional and social impact of the illness. In another book written for older readers, *100 Questions and Answers About AIDS: A Guide for Young People,* Michael Thomas Ford uses a question and answer format to answer common questions about topics such as methods of transmission, diagnosis, treatment, and prevention. The text includes detailed diagrams on subjects related to the prevention of AIDS. The text includes interviews with AIDS patients and listings of support groups.

The world of forensics is explored in Donna M. Jackson's *The Bone Detectives: How Forensic Anthropologists Solve Crimes and Uncover Mysteries of the Dead.* The text discusses several cases in which forensic anthropology was used to solve crimes. The text includes labeled photographs. Several of the photographs clarify size by a measurement device. For example, one photograph is labeled, "Back at the police station, detectives organize and photograph evidence collected at the scene. A yardstick or ruler is usually included in such photographs to indicate scale" (p. 13). The text includes information on how sex, race, and age can be determined; how markings on bones can establish cause of death; and how a clay reconstructed face can help solve crimes.

Animals. Authors who write effectively about prehistoric animals or about modern-day reptiles and amphibians, birds, land invertebrates (earthworms), insects, and mammals must present their facts clearly, and they must not give their animals human qualities and emotions. Because books about animals are popular with many different age groups, authors must consider the readers' backgrounds when they develop new concepts.

Dinosaurs. With scientists as detectives and fossils as clues, twentieth-century children can experience the thrill of investigating the earth's prehuman past. Children who learn about dinosaurs in books, study about them in museums, search for fossilized footprints or bones, and make dinosaur models often become enthusiastic amateur paleontologists. Books depicting excavation sites, such as Caroline Arnold's *Dinosaur Mountain: Graveyard of the Past,* Margery Facklam's *Tracking Dinosaurs in the Gobi* and Kathryn Lasky's *Dinosaur Dig,* present the work of paleontologists and show the careful work that has provided answers about dinosaurs. Books on dinosaurs range from highly illustrated texts for younger children, such as Russell Freedman's *Dinosaurs and Their Young* and Gail Gibbons's *Dinosaurs,* to texts for older children that provide extensive scientific details, such as Helen Roney Sattler's *Dinosaurs of North America.* Freedman's book explores the significance of a 1978 discovery that raised questions about how these animals raised their young. Drawings of both dinosaurs and excavation sites clarify the text. In contrast, Sattler's book is arranged by geologic time periods. It describes the characteristics and habitats of more than eighty types of dinosaurs. Further readings and an index add to the usefulness.

The authors of two new books about ancient dinosaurs develop their content through a question-and-answer approach. In *New Questions and Answers About Dinosaurs,* Seymour Simon asks and answers twenty-two questions about dinosaurs. These questions range from "What are dinosaurs?" to "Why did the dinosaurs become extinct?" and "What are some new discoveries about dinosaurs?" A helpful index includes a pronunciation guide.

In *The Dinosaur Question and Answer Book,* Sylvia Funston includes questions and answers to more than one hundred questions asked by students. The questions resulted when readers of two children's magazines were asked to submit one question each about dinosaurs. More than 11,000 questions were received. The book then repeats the most frequently asked questions and answers them. The scientists working on the Dinosaur Project, which is composed of a team of Chinese and Canadian scientists, answer such questions as, What was it like working in the Gobi Desert and the Arctic? and How can you tell whether each dinosaur ate plants or meat? The answers separate fact from theory, especially in relation to the destruction of the dinosaurs. For example, when answering the question, Did something from space destroy the dinosaurs?, the text states:

Today, more scientists than ever are ready to think so. Why? A few years ago, a thin layer of a mineral called iridium was discovered all over the world. Iridium is normally found in much greater concentrations in meteorites and heads of comets than on Earth. This iridium layer was deposited on Earth in the Cretaceous period, 65 million years ago—exactly when the dinosaurs died out. Furthermore, it's full of shocked quartz, which is only produced in colossal explosions. (p. 50)

In answer to the next question, Did volcanoes cause the death of the dinosaurs?, the text states:

According to one interesting theory, volcanoes may have caused the dinosaurs' extinction. If enough volcanoes were spewing lava and ash into the air at the same time, they would have the same effect as the impact of a giant meteor. All of the resulting dust, chemicals, gas and ash would cause significant changes in the Earth's climate. (p. 50)

The book includes a glossary, a list of dinosaur terms, and an index as well.

The large illustrations and text in Patricia Lauber's *Living with Dinosaurs* take readers back into a time seventy-five million years ago when dinosaurs lived in prehistoric Montana. The book concludes with information about how fossils are formed and discovered. This book also includes an index and pronunciation guide. Lauber's *How Dinosaurs Came to Be* provides a highly interesting and factual account of the emergence of dinosaurs, explains how they evolved from the amphibians and reptiles, and discusses the appearance of mammals. Douglas Henderson's illustrations depict what dinosaurs might have looked like in their natural habitats.

Eleven varieties of stegosaurs are described in Helen Roney Sattler's *Stegosaurs: The Solar-Powered Dinosaurs.* Sattler discusses current theories about

their eggs and the plates along their spines. A reading list and a location map add to the text. J. Lynett Gillette also focuses on one type of dinosaur in *Dinosaur Ghosts: The Mystery of Coelophysis.* The author attracts readers' attention by introducing the subject by showing the remains of three hundred dinosaurs who died very rapidly. The author explores various theories about their extinction.

William Mannetti's *Dinosaurs in Your Backyard* challenges some previous theories about dinosaurs and provides new interpretations suggesting that birds are feathered dinosaurs, dinosaurs may have been warm blooded, and some dinosaurs previously believed to be water inhabitants spent most of the time on land. Mannetti, however, implies that the theories he presents are accepted by all authorities, and he does not refer to opposing viewpoints or discuss how others have interpreted the same evidence.

Patricia Lauber makes comparisons and uses contrasts to clarify points in her *Dinosaurs Walked Here and Other Stories Fossils Tell.* For example, Lauber compares photographs of a 315-million-year-old amphibian and a bullfrog to highlight similarities. She also compares photographs of fossils of the oldest known bird and the skeleton of a barn owl. To illustrate contrasts among animals, Lauber compares photographs showing the teeth of a duckbill, which are meant to grind plants, and the teeth of a tyrannosaurus rex, which are suited for tearing flesh. In *The News About Dinosaurs,* Lauber presents past beliefs as well as newer information, which often refutes earlier beliefs.

Descriptions of both prehistoric and contemporary animals are included in *Giants of Land, Sea & Air: Past & Present,* by David Peters. This Sierra Club book describes over seventy large animals. All of the illustrations are drawn to the same scale (1 inch = 22 ½ inches). Some of the pages are foldouts so that readers may compare the sizes of dinosaurs, such as the brachiosaurus and apatosaurus, and those of contemporary mammals, such as the sperm whale and the blue whale. In *Dinosaur Worlds,* Don Lessem also provides contrasts between prehistoric and contemporary times. For example, he shows that some of the desert locations where dinosaur bones are found today were jungles in prehistoric times. Lessem connects dinosaurs to their geographical location by discussing the environment in which they lived.

Illustrations and text present old and new information about dinosaurs. (From The News About Dinosaurs *by Patricia Lauber, copyright © 1989 by Patricia Lauber. Reprinted by permission of Bradbury Press.)*

Insects, Spiders, Snakes, and Turtles. Books for younger children frequently present nature in familiar environments. Bianca Lavies's *Tree Trunk Traffic* presents the various spiders, insects, and other animals that are found in a maple tree during spring and summer. Color photographs add to the visual appeal of the book and encourage readers to search for inhabitants in the tree and to explore trees in their own neighborhoods. Lavies's *Compost Critters* explores life in a compost pile. Margery Facklam's *Creepy, Crawly Caterpillars* presents details about thirteen different types of caterpillars. There is a close up of each of the caterpillars that provides information about its habitat. A band on the lower part of each double-page spread pictures the life cycle from eggs to caterpillar to cocoon to moth. The text includes a glossary of terms. Sandra Markle's *Creepy, Crawly Baby Bugs* provides colored close-up photographs of various insects. Molly McLaughlin's *Dragonflies* follows the life cycle of these insects. Photographs of dragonflies resting on hands indicate sizes. Other photographs are magnified to reveal physical characteristics. Lavies's text and illustrations in *Backyard Hunter: The Praying Mantis* follow the life cycle of this interesting insect.

Three books about butterflies provide both basic facts about and beautiful illustrations of monarch butterflies. Bianca Lavies's *Monarch Butterflies: Mysterious Travelers* is a photo essay that includes full-page photographs of the developmental stages of the butterfly. Lavies then focuses on the winter home of the butterfly, in the Sierra Madre mountains of Mexico. The text includes information about the home of the butterfly and other facts related to their survival. Kathryn Lasky's *Monarchs* takes readers through the life cycle of the monarch, discusses sites related to the monarch, and tells about people who are interested in the welfare of the monarch. Laurence Pringle's *An Extraordinary Life: The Story of a Monarch Butterfly* follows the often perilous route of the butterfly as it migrates from New England to Mexico. The illustrations and captions provide details about various aspects of the life cycle of the monarch. The text includes maps and diagrams that clarify information. There is also a list of further reading and an index.

Authors of informational books may entice children by presenting challenges or comparisons. In *Someone Saw a Spider: Spider Facts and Folktales,* Shirley Climo compares factual information and spider folklore from various cultures.

Frank Staub's *Sea Turtles* stimulates reader involvement by asking readers to be word detectives as they search for words in the text and try to identify meaning. A glossary is included to help readers verify the meanings. Labeled, colored photographs also clarify the meanings. Another way that the author clarifies meaning is by comparing characteristics of the turtles with known objects. For example, "Leatherbacks are the biggest reptiles alive today. They can grow as big as a bathtub" (p. 13). Brenda Z. Guiberson's *Into the Sea* follows the life cycle of a sea turtle. The author concludes the book with a discussion on ways people are trying to protect sea turtles.

Mammals. *Sierra Club Book of Great Mammals* is an introduction to the world of mammals. The heavily illustrated text begins with a general discussion about mammals and explores such topics as "What is a mammal?," "Three groups of mammals," "Mammal beginnings," "Where mammals live," and "Mammals in danger." The book then focuses on specific mammals, such as kangaroos, orangutans, bears, and whales. This book includes a glossary, a listing of classifications of mammals, and an index. *The Sierra Club*

Book of Small Mammals is a companion book. This book provides an introduction to the world of such small mammals as monkeys, rabbits, and hyraxes.

Several books on animals are especially appropriate for young readers because the subjects are familiar. Joanna Cole's *A Cat's Body* explores characteristic cat behaviors, such as pouncing, reacting to moving objects, and purring. The text and photographs may encourage children to observe their own pets. In *My Puppy Is Born,* Cole presents the birth of miniature dachshund puppies. Jerome Wexler's photographs show the pregnant dog going into her box, the emergence of the first puppy, born inside a sac, and the mother tearing the sac and licking the puppy. The book follows the growth of the puppies during their first eight weeks, as they are unable to see or hear, as they nurse, and then as they open their eyes and take their first steps.

Illustrated books about familiar animals help younger children develop their observational and descriptive abilities. Such books include David McPhail's *Farm Morning,* which accompanies a young girl and her father as they take care of the barnyard animals; zoologist Dorothy Hinshaw Patent's *Appaloosa Horses;* and Tana Hoban's *A Children's Zoo.*

Millicent Selsam and Joyce Hunt have written several books designed for young children. Both *A First Look at Animals with Horns* and *A First Look at Seals, Sea Lions, and Walruses* answer simple questions and encourage readers to observe physical characteristics. In *A First Look at Animals with Horns,* Selsam and Hunt differentiate between goats and sheep by stating, "The horns of sheep sweep down and around" (p. 18), while "the horns of goats sweep up and straight back" (p. 19). Illustrations accompany the text and show these characteristics of sheep and goats. In *Keep Looking!,* Selsam and Hunt encourage readers to search for animals in the yard of a country house.

In another book for young children, *Young Lions,* by Toshi Yoshida, the text and illustrations follow three young lions as they move across the African plain. The illustrations show other animals that live in Africa, including water buffaloes, rhinoceroses, and zebras. A more in-depth view of the rhinoceros is found in Sally M. Walker's *Rhinos.* Gerry Ellis's photographs clarify understanding by showing similarities and differences among various types of rhinos. A map shows locations of the animals. As in many books about similar subjects, Walker concludes her text by emphasizing how humans have caused the loss of rhinos through hunting for sport and poaching for horns.

Diane Swanson's *Buffalo Sunrise: The Story of a North American Giant* traces the history, characteristics, and future of the bison. Swanson concludes her discussion with a section on the preservation of the buffalo. Swanson uses vivid comparisons to illustrate the rapid demise of the buffalo. For example, she states that in the nineteenth century "people reported herds that blackened the plains as far as the eye could see . . . herds so huge they measured 2 miles (3 kilometers) across and 25 miles (40 kilometers) deep. In those days, about 60 million buffaloes roamed North America. . . . But the numbers fell fast and far. By 1830, they had dropped to 40 million; just 60 years later there were only about 1,000 buffaloes left—including those in zoos" (p. 45). Swanson then chronicles the efforts to protect the buffalo until in 1994 there are about 200,000 buffaloes in North America.

Polar Bear Cubs, by Downs Matthews, includes characteristics of polar bears and adventures typical of cubs. In this book, two cubs explore their arctic home. The color photographs capture the feeling of the far northern landscape as well as provide insight into the lives of animals in the arctic.

In a book for older readers, *Who Harnessed the Horse? The Story of Animal Domestication,* Margery Facklam traces the domestication of such animals as horses, cats, dogs, and cows. Hope Ryden's *Your Cat's Wild Cousins* describes the behavior and physical traits of eighteen species of cats, such as the Canada lynx. Ryden's text and illustrations encourage observation and comparison.

Wild mammals, their contributions, and their survival are topics common in informational books. Authors may describe the contributions of animals, argue for their protection by means of responsible population control, and use statistics to develop points on survival and to demonstrate their plight. In *Whales, Giants of the Deep,* Dorothy Hinshaw Patent concludes her discussion of whales with a history of whaling and the consequences of an unregulated industry. While Patent states the arguments against a moratorium on whaling presented by Japan, Norway, and the former USSR, she concludes with a strong statement in favor of the moratorium:

While the whaling nations argue that some whale species are not diminishing and will not become extinct even with continued whaling, conservationists believe that without a ban on commercial whaling, whales will disappear from the Earth. Unfortunately, all nations that kill whales do not belong to the IWC. So even if Norway, Japan, and the U.S.S.R. decide to abide by the IWC moratorium, some whaling may continue. We can only hope that it is not enough to further endanger these magnificent animals. (p. 82)

The history of the whaling industry is presented in Catherine Gourley's *Hunting Neptune's Giants: True Stories of American Whaling*. The materials in the book came from sources such as stories preserved in maritime libraries, letters, diaries, and ships' logs. Each chapter is introduced with quotes selected to entice the interest of the reader. For example, the chapter, "The Loss of the Arctic Fleet," is introduced with these thoughts by Clara Wheldon: "Through all this month I have been very comfortable; though very cold, and the ship has been covered with ice; the fog congealed to the rigging, and every rope encased in an icy tube . . . The men have looked very solemn, having neither danced nor sung. They can have no fire, and it's a mystery to me how they keep from freezing" (p. 51). The book is illustrated with paintings, lithographs, and drawings from this early time period. There is a list of sources, further information, places to visit and call, and an index.

Other excellent books about wild animals and protection of species include Dorothy Hinshaw Patent's *Back to the Wild*, Laurence Pringle's *Saving Our Wildlife*, and Nicholas and Theodore Nirgiotis's *No More Dodos: How Zoos Help Endangered Wildlife*. Bruce McMillan's *Going on a Whale Watch* is a highly illustrated text that uses both photographs of whales and illustrations to show the major physical features of several types of whales. The book shows the happy experiences that are possible when children are allowed to observe whales in their natural environment. In *Sharks: Challengers of the Deep*, Mary M. Cerullo presents information about a mammal that is usually greatly feared. Cerullo, however, discusses the shark's benefits to people and warns that all creatures are important.

Eric S. Grace's *Seals* is an excellent introduction to seals, sea lions, and walruses. The photographs and charts clarify the text. For example, one drawing illustrates the ancestry of the pinniped. Another two-page illustration shows the differences between true seals and eared seals. Maps show the range of the northern fur seals and the routes of harp seal migration. The color photographs add even more information.

Depending upon their purposes and points of view, authors approach monkeys, apes, and chimpanzees quite differently. For example, Jane Goodall's *The Chimpanzee Family Book* explores chimpanzees in their natural habitat in the Gombe Natural Park, Tanzania. In this text, the natural environment seems to be the only appropriate one. The settings for Paul Hermann Burgel and Manfred Hartwig's *Gorillas* vary from the freedom of the Virunga Park in central Africa to the confines of zoos. The full-color photographs allow readers to glimpse the habitat of this endangered species. The differences between the photographs taken in the natural environment and in a zoo should generate interesting discussions about the future of this mammal.

Birds. The topics of informational books about birds range from common barnyard fowl to exotic tropical birds. In these books, the authors use various techniques to create interest for young children and to present new concepts to older children.

In *A First Look at Bird Nests*, a book written for young readers, Millicent Selsam and Joyce Hunt describe the nests of common American birds and tell how the nests are built. Selsam and Hunt stimulate observation by asking questions and providing puzzles. The answers to the questions are located in the accompanying illustrations. In *About Birds: A Guide for Children*, Cathryn Sill uses large illustrations and minimal text to appeal to young children. The author's afterword provides additional information about each illustration. In *Spoonbill Swamp*, Brenda Z. Guiberson focuses on one day in the lives of two animals that live in the swamp: spoonbills and alligators. The text and illustrations proceed back and forth between the lives of the two swamp creatures. Young readers will understand that both creatures live in the swamp and are dependent upon the swamp for survival. An endnote by Guiberson provides information about dangers to the animals and their environment.

In a book for younger readers, Barbara Juster Esbensen focuses on specific birds and their habitats. In *Tiger with Wings: The Great Horned Owl*, Esbensen and Mary Barrett Brown present insights into the life and habitat of horned owls. A combination of illustration and text allows vivid comparisons. For example, Esbensen describes the horned owl as:

The great horned owl is such a fierce hunter that it is often compared to a tiger. Like the tiger, the great horned

The photographs follow a day in the life of Jane Goodall, the British naturalist. (From The Chimpanzee Family Book *by Jane Goodall, copyright © 1989 by the Jane Goodall Institute for Wildlife Research, Education and Conservation. Photos copyright © 1989 by Michael Neugebauer. Reprinted by permission of Picture Book Studio.)*

The **Chimpanzee Family Book** Jane Goodall

owl hunts in the dark, and it kills instantly. Its stripes let it blend with the forest patterns of dim light and shadow. Its two-inch feather tufts look like a tiger's ears, and it has a face like an angry cat. It is a tiger with wings—a tiger that can fly almost unseen through the darkness. (p. 2, unnumbered)

Brown's two-page illustration shows an owl flying through the woods as a transparent tiger follows behind.

Think Like an Eagle: At Work with a Wildlife Photographer, a book for older readers, depicts both animal behavior and the requirements to be a wildlife photographer. In this book, Kathryn Lasky uses many effective writing techniques to appeal to older readers. For example, Lasky introduces the book with a language style that encourages readers to visualize the setting and the life of the wildlife photographer:

He follows a silver thread of moonlight through the forest. The tangled shadows of bare-branched trees spread across the snowy ground. . . . Now Jack crosses a stream that feeds into the reservoir. The water slides like a black satin ribbon under snow bridges and curls around billowing white banks. . . . Jack is wrapped in the silence of the forest when suddenly from somewhere behind him, deep in the heart of the woods, comes the flat hooo hoooo of the great horned owl. Hooo hoooo. The call thrums through the forest. (p. 5)

Such vivid language is found throughout the text. Lasky also makes comparisons that readers understand, such as the following comparison of time spent watching animals with time spent watching television:

But the most important part of the blind is the rectangular window slot. This slot is Jack's window on the world. He has spent as much time peering through it as many people spend in front of a television. He can't switch the channel. He can't change the scene. He must wait for the real-life action to happen in front of this small rectangle. It does. (p. 8)

Later, Lasky contrasts hunting and photography. Finally, she encourages critical thinking by suggesting to readers that an animal photographer must become a student of animal behavior and think like the animal, whether the animal is an eagle, a great egret, a beaver, or a deer. This concept provides interesting discussions when readers consider, What would a photographer of _____ need to know about the animal's behavior?

Powerful flying birds and exotic water birds have interested a number of eminent researchers, writers, and photographers. Because the birds and their environments may be new to young readers, many books for young children present most of their information through photographs. For example, in Caroline Arnold's *Saving the Peregrine Falcon,* the large photographs alone are sufficient to show scientists raising the endangered birds in captivity, encouraging them to identify with falcons rather than with humans, and releasing them into the environment.

Authors of nonfiction informational books frequently focus on endangered species. Dorothy Hinshaw Patent's *The Whooping Crane: A Comeback Story* explores attempts to save this bird, which was almost extinct. Peter and Connie Roop's *Seasons of the Cranes* begins in the spring and follows whooping cranes as they mate in northern Canada, raise their young, and migrate to their winter home in Texas. The Roops provide a map to let young readers follow the flyway of the cranes. The Roops also use the familiar to help clarify the unfamiliar. For example, when they describe the crane eggs, they say, "The two eggs, twice as long as chicken eggs, lie side by side in the shallow bowl of bulrushes" (p. 6). In *Operation Siberian Crane: The Story Behind the International Effort to Save an Amazing Bird,* Judi Friedman examines efforts to save this endangered bird through the International Crane Foundation, established by two Americans in 1972.

In *The Book of Eagles,* Helen Roney Sattler looks at several kinds of eagles and dangers to eagles. Numerous illustrations, by Jean Day Zallinger, help readers understand the characteristics of the birds. Maps show specific locations of eagles throughout the world. Sattler also relates unknown content to known and emphasizes cause-and-effect relationships. She says, for example:

An eagle's wing and tail feathers are incredibly strong. They are made of keratin, the same material as human fingernails. . . . The wings are flatter on the bottom than on the top, like the wings of an aircraft. Small feathers called coverts grow along the forward edges of the wings, making them thicker in front. This causes the air to flow faster over the top, providing lift. (p. 11)

Readers may observe and compare three quite different habitats for birds by reading books by Barbara Bash, Joanne Ryder, and Mary Barrett Brown. Bash's *Urban Roosts: Where Birds Nest in the City* uses illustrations and text to disclose how birds adjust in this harsh environment. The illustrations, which show birds nesting on street lights, in traffic lights, and on buildings, should encourage observation by children who live in cities. San Francisco gardens are the settings for Ryder's *Dancers in the Garden.* Ryder's lyrical text is accompanied by Judith Lopez's watercolors, which enhance the delicate nature of the hummingbird. Brown's *Wings Along the Waterway* provides a short descriptive chapter on each of twenty-one types of birds that live in the wetlands of America. Brown's numerous color illustrations detail the environments. These three books encourage readers to understand that birds live in many different locations. All of the locations and the birds that live in them, however, are influenced by people.

Plants. Informational books about plants should develop clear details in logical order, include diagrams and photographs that illustrate terminology, and encourage children to become involved in learning. In *Cotton,* by Millicent E. Selsam, a dime next to the first two leaves of a cotton seedling clarifies the size, close-up photographs effectively illustrate the stages in plant development, and labeled photographs and drawings clarify the terminology.

Close-up photographs provide an excellent introduction to an unusual plant that takes four years to bloom in Jerome Wexler's *Jack-in-the-Pulpit.* Wexler also increases readers' interests by asking questions that draw their attention to the photographs.

The natural world of plants and the environment are depicted by Thomas Locker. Locker's *Sky Tree: Seeing Science Through Art* follows the sequence of the seasons through paintings of the same tree. The book concludes with a section, "Connecting Art and Science in Sky Tree" in which the author asks questions such as, "This is the same tree in the same place. What makes this painting different?" (unnumbered). The author then discusses the painting.

Desert Giant: The World of the Saguaro Cactus, by Barbara Bash, is part of the Tree Tales series of Sierra Club Books. This book is written for young readers. It emphasizes that the cactus provides food and shelter for desert inhabitants. Large illustrations show the interior as well as the exterior of the cactus. Labeled drawings clarify flower fertilization and detail seed interiors.

Detailed, labeled photographs and illustrations enhance books on plants. In *Roses Red, Violets Blue: Why Flowers Have Colors,* Sylvia Johnson explores the reasons for the variety of colors of flowers. Labeled color photographs by Yuko Sato clarify the text. The text also describes how readers can conduct an experiment with anthocyanin pigments. Photographs show readers how to conduct each step in the experiment.

Milton Meltzer uses a historical perspective in *The Amazing Potato.* In this book, Meltzer traces the history of the potato from the time of the Incas and the conquistadors through its current influences in the world marketplace. Katya Arnold and Sam Swope also relate history to plants in *Katya's Book of Mushrooms.* They discuss the history and origin of mushrooms as well as provide basic facts about the types of scientific labels. Although they promote the hunting of mushrooms, they also caution readers about the dangers of poisonous varieties.

Charles Micucci's *The Life and Times of the Apple* is another book that combines information about the plant and its history. Detailed, labeled drawings show a cross-section of an apple and illustrate such concepts as cross-fertilization of apples, grafting,

parts of an apple flower, pollination, growth, and harvesting. The text then discusses uses for apples, leading apple-growing states and countries, and apple varieties. The author provides a time line to show the history of the apple from 2,500,000 B.C. through the 1600s. An illustrated map of the United States shows the impact of the apple on America, from the first grafting of domestic apples in Virginia in 1647, to the legend of Johnny Appleseed, to the Franciscan priests who planted orchards in New Mexico and other Spanish territories, and to pioneers who brought apples west in covered wagons. *The Life and Times of the Apple* provides lessons in geography and history as well as plant science. Micucci uses a similar approach in *The Life and Times of the Peanut.* Marjorie Priceman's *How to Make an Apple Pie and See the World* is another entertaining book that also presents information on food origins.

Geology and Geography. Geology and geography books encourage readers to develop insights into changes in the earth, to understand the consequences of natural and human-produced disasters, and to understand the importance of developing

An illustrated time line helps readers understand the history of the apple. (From The Life and Times of the Apple *by Charles Micucci. Copyright © 1992 by Charles Micucci. Reprinted by permission of the publisher, Orchard Books, New York.)*

cultural awareness. Kathryn Lasky's *Surtsey: The Newest Place on Earth* provides glimpses of what earlier land creations might have been like. Christopher G. Knight's photographs depict the birth of this island in the North Atlantic south of Iceland. Lasky's text provides a literary connection, with quotations from Snorri Sturluson's *Prose Edda* to enrich the prose.

Because children often see the results of earthquakes and various other disasters on television, geology may be a subject that interests them, especially if they live in portions of the world that have earthquakes or have experienced other disasters. Seymour Simon's *Earthquakes* has vivid photographs that show the consequences of earthquakes in various parts of North America. Books about earthquakes provide interesting background information for children who also read Laurence Yep's novel *Dragonwings,* which describes the great San Francisco earthquake of 1906. The photographs in Terry Carr's *Spill! The Story of the Exxon Valdez* vividly illustrate the environmental consequences of the oil spill and show the possible magnitude of human-produced disasters.

Since the eruption of Mount St. Helens, several books emphasizing volcanic activity in North America have appeared. In *The Mount St. Helens Disaster: What We've Learned,* Thomas and Virginia Aylesworth discuss the chronological order of the seismic events that led up to the eruption. The Aylesworths enrich the text with eyewitness accounts, photographs, diagrams, and maps. Patricia Lauber's *Volcano: The Eruption and Healing of Mount St. Helens* is an excellent photographic essay of the eruption and of the changes since the eruption. Photographs showing minute changes in time are effective, as are photographs of specific settings taken before and after the eruption. Seymour Simon's *Volcanoes* is a source for studying volcanic eruptions in other parts of the world.

Storms and other natural disasters are popular subjects for informational books. In *Hurricanes: Earth's Mightiest Storms,* Patricia Lauber discusses the weather conditions that create the storms and technological developments that allow meteorologists to track the storms. Colored photographs, maps, and lists of further readings help clarify the subject. In *Flood: Wrestling with the Mississippi,* Lauber presents the history of the river, highlights the 1927 and 1993 floods, and discusses ways that

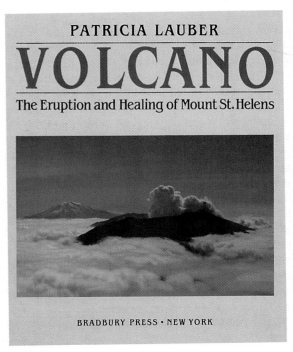

Color photographs show important sequences in the Mount St. Helens eruption. (From Volcano: The Eruption and Healing of Mount St. Helens *by Patricia Lauber, copyright* © 1986. Reprinted by permission of Bradbury Press.)

people have tried to control the river. Colored photographs provide dramatic examples of various types of storms including hurricanes and tornadoes in Stephen Kramer's *Eye of the Storm: Chasing Storms with Warren Faidley.* In *Lightning,* Seymour Simon provides a vivid introduction to lightning through colored photographs, statistics about lightning, and explanatory information. In *Storm on the Desert,* Carolyn Lesser focuses on storms in the Sonoran Desert in Arizona. Ted Rand's illustrations depict the drama of nature.

Humor provides strong interest in Joanna Cole's *The Magic School Bus: Inside the Earth* and *The Magic School Bus: On the Ocean Floor.* Dialogue between children is presented in cartoon-type bubbles, while information is presented in both conventional text and examples of reports written by a school class. Magic and learning occur when the teacher drives a bus full of children into the earth, where they learn about rocks and the structure of the earth. In the second book, the school bus and Miss Frizzle's class take a trip in which they make discoveries about the ocean and the animals and plants that live there. Librarians and teachers who work with children indicate that many children enjoy the various books in Cole's "The Magic School Bus" series and that after reading the books, the children are frequently stimulated to make additional discoveries about the subject matter.

Books on cultural geography frequently focus on such questions as, How did the people who live here get here? How did they decide where to settle and how to make a living? How have they influenced their environment (land and climate) and how has it affected them? A major focus of cultural geography is the fit between culture and environment. Two books by Jim Brandenburg present the natural history of various locations on the continent. In *Sand and Fog: Adventures in Southern Africa,* the text and photographs focus on the Namib desert in southwestern Africa. The author provides information on the desert, the contrasts, and the animal life. *An American Safari: Adventures on the North American Prairie* provides a photographic essay of the prairie lands that extend from Texas into Canada. Labeled photographs provide visual images of scenes such as prairie dogs, bison, and rattlesnakes. Brandenburg urges readers to pay attention to the fragile nature of the environment and to conserve the prairie ecology. He includes addresses for prairie preserves. Interactions among people and geography are developed in both Rebecca L. Johnson's *Braving the Frozen Frontier: Women Working in Antarctica* and Will Steger and Jon Bowermaster's *Over the Top of the World: Explorer Will Steger's Trek Across the Arctic.*

Large colored photographs present the geography and inhabitants of various types of wetlands in Molly Cone's *Squishy, Misty, Damp & Muddy: The In-Between World of Wetlands.* In addition to the characteristics of wetlands, Cone discusses the ecological purposes of wetlands as they purify dirty water by filtering pollutants. Cone concludes her book by pleading for the preservation of the wetlands.

The undersea world of the marine biologist is presented in Diane Swanson's *Safari Beneath the Sea: The Wonder World of the North Pacific Coast.* The large colored photographs by the Royal British Columbia Museum present a beautiful world of creatures such as jellyfish, mud crabs, sea stars, and sea anemone. This book won the Orbis Pictus Award for Outstanding Nonfiction for Children. Consequently, students of children's literature might analyze the book to decide what features it has that make it an award-winning text.

Many current books develop the thesis that the earth must be protected if it is to survive. Sally Lodge (1992) states:

In virtually every format, for youngsters on all reading levels, publishers are releasing books emphasizing the importance of preserving the earth's natural resources and cleaning up our planet. A glance at a sampling of these recent and forthcoming titles, and conversations with some of the individuals busy creating, publishing, and selling them, underscore the fact that the greening of the earth is no longer perceived as a natural, annual occurrence. The emphasis is now on the much more complex, urgent, perennial issue of returning our earth to its original green state. (p. 22)

Books on ecology and conservation frequently introduce the importance of and the beauty associated with the subject and then present a plea to readers to help solve the problem. In *Everglades,* Jean Craighead George introduces the subject through a Native American storyteller who is taking five children through the Everglades and telling them a story about the environment. He begins, "First there was sunshine on a blue-green sea. It was the Age of the Seashells. The seashells formed a rock called limestone on the sea bottom. Over the eons the sea lowered, and the rock became land. The long Florida peninsula took shape in warm, sunny waters" (unnumbered). The storyteller continues by including a description of the thousands of birds and animals that inhabited the area. After the storyteller is almost finished with his story, George allows readers to ponder the changes in the Everglades as the children question the storyteller: "Where are the clouds of egrets?" and "Where are the quantities of alligators?" The storyteller now tells the children why the numbers have diminished. George ends the ecology tale on a hopeful note in which the children grow up, run the earth, and return the Everglades to its former glory. The children have learned their lesson as George concludes, " 'That's a much better story,' said the children. 'Now pole us home quickly so we can grow up' " (unnumbered).

Books on protecting the planet range from humorous approaches that use cartoon-like drawings, such as Laurie Krasny Brown and Marc Brown's *Dinosaurs to the Rescue! A Guide to Protecting Our Planet,* to environmental protection books for slightly older readers, such as Vicki

Cartoon-type bubbles and reports add to the information in this book about oceans. (From The Magic School Bus: On the Ocean Floor *by Joanna Cole, illustrated by Bruce Degen. Text copyright © 1992 by Joanne Cole. Illustrations copyright © 1992 by Bruce Degen. Reprinted by permission of Scholastic Inc. The Magic School Bus is a registered trademark of Scholastic, Inc.)*

McVey's *The Sierra Club Kid's Guide to Planet Care & Repair,* to in-depth analysis of the problems for older readers, such as Barry Commoner's *Making Peace with the Planet.* McVey, who has a Ph.D. in cultural geography, writes frequently on this topic. Her book includes games, projects, and practical ideas that her readers may use. Commoner, the director of the Center for the Biology of Natural Systems, is a frequent writer on the science of survival.

Other books on the earth and the need for environmental changes highlight actual projects that have resulted in change. One example is Molly Cone's *Come Back, Salmon.* The text and photographs by Sidnee Wheelwright follow the actions of a group of students in Everett, Washington, who cleaned up a stream, stocked the stream with salmon, and watched carefully to see if their efforts to improve the fish habitat succeeded. When reading this book, many children become personally involved in the students' efforts and are ready to try a similar project in their own neighborhoods. Most children understand the underlying message of the book: We can and must make a difference if we want the planet to improve.

Discoveries and How Things Work

Some informational books answer children's questions about discoveries of the past and present or provide explanations of how machines work. Authors may clarify their texts through step-by-step directions, carefully labeled diagrams, photographs that illustrate concepts, and content that proceeds from the simple to the complex or from the known to the unknown.

Discoveries. Books about discoveries may describe the basic principles of past discoveries or the latest space or computer technology. Some books combine information about discoveries with experiments designed to help children understand and duplicate earlier experiments. One such book is Seymour Simon's *How to Be an Ocean Scientist in Your Own Home.* Simon first asks a question, such as How can you make fresh water from seawater? Next, he presents information in a "Let's Find Out" section. Then, he tells students "Here's What You Will Need" and provides detailed directions in "Here's What to Do."

Patrick Moore's series of beginning astronomy books designed for children in the lower elementary grades present basic information about comets, planets, stars, and the moon. The text and illustrations are presented to clarify understandings for young readers or listeners. For example, in *Comets and Shooting Stars* the author introduces the subject "What makes a shooting star?" and the friction in meteors this way: "If you pump up a bicycle tire, you will find that the pump gets hot, because the air inside is being squashed; this sets up friction, and this causes heat. A meteor moving into the upper air sets up so much heat by friction against the air that it catches fire, and burns away" (p. 11). Photographs of a child pointing a flashlight at a ball held by another child show how the planets are illuminated by the sun in *The Planets*. In *The Stars,* illustrations compare the size of the sun with Vega and Spica and show diagrams of the Great Bear or Big Dipper. In *The Sun and Moon,* the illustrations show the various phases of an eclipse.

Informational books about space and space travel should reflect current knowledge. Copyright dates may, therefore, be a very important consideration when selecting these books. Franklyn M. Branley, former chairman of the Hayden Planetarium in New York City, emphasizes the expanding nature of knowledge about space in *Saturn: The Spectacular Planet* by pointing out that the *Pioneer* and *Voyager* space probes have provided more knowledge than had previously been gathered during the more than three hundred years since Galileo first saw the planet in a telescope.

Patricia Lauber's *Journey to the Planets* contains large black-and-white NASA photographs of Earth and the other planets. These photographs clarify an interesting discussion of the search for intelligent life on other planets and the constructions that may indicate intelligent life, even from millions of miles out in space. Seymour Simon has written several readable books that, through words and photographs, take young readers into the far reaches of space and explain comets and planets. Simon's *The Long View into Space, Saturn, Jupiter,* and *Galaxies* provide information in a simple and illuminating way. For example, in *The Long View into Space,* Simon explains why space distances between earth and the planets are not measured in miles by saying that to measure in miles would be like "trying to measure the distance between New York and London in inches" (p. 4, unnumbered).

Questions related to the universe are explored in Heather Couper and Nigel Henbest's *The Space Atlas:* *A Pictorial Atlas of Our Universe.* Compare the coverage of the planets in this text with that in Seymour Simon's *Jupiter* and *Saturn.* Couper and Henbest's book is a highly illustrated overview of the planets, moon, and other bodies of the solar system. The text also includes star maps. An index helps readers find information. In *Before the Sun Dies: The Story of Evolution,* Roy Gallant compares the known and unknown to help readers understand the galaxies. This book includes numerous labeled drawings, a glossary of terms, a list of further readings, and an index.

A humorous and very visual introduction to the solar system is provided in Joanna Cole's *The Magic School Bus: Lost in the Solar System.* The facts about the solar system are introduced when Ms. Frizzle and her class enter the magic school bus, find themselves in outer space, and explore the planets in the solar system. Information about the solar system also is provided in reports written by the students in the class. Many of these reports use a question-and-answer format, such as What is the solar system?, What makes night and day?, Why are spaceships launched with rockets?, What is gravity?, and Why is it so hot on Venus? This book includes a planet chart and a mobile of the solar system. As with the other books in "The Magic School Bus" series, you may use this book to suggest various projects.

How Things Work. Several informational books appeal to children's curiosity about how common home appliances and bigger machines actually work. These books usually contain detailed diagrams or photographs that accompany two or three pages of descriptive text about each item. While the readability and interest levels are usually considered upper-elementary and above, many younger children ask questions about how percolators, dishwashers, or Thermos bottles work. Therefore, parents may find these books helpful when answering the questions of young children. (One mother said that her six-year-old son's favorite book was one containing diagrams of machines at work.)

David Macaulay's *The Way Things Work* includes over three hundred pages of detailed diagrams of almost every conceivable instrument. The text is arranged in four sections, including "The Mechanics of Movement," "Harnessing the Elements," "Working with Waves," and "Electricity & Automation."

This topic is debated in two journal articles in the *School Library Journal.* In May 1991, Marsha Broadway and Malia Howland[1] published results of their research in "Science Books for Young People: Who Writes Them?" These researchers analyzed the qualifications of authors of children's science books reviewed over a five-year period in the journal *Science Books and Films,* published by the American Association for the Advancement of Science. Broadway and Howland found that 43 percent of the authors had degrees in English, journalism, or the humanities, and 37 percent of the authors had degrees in science-related fields. Only 12 percent of the respondents had science-related primary occupations. In addition, 19 percent of the authors indicated that they selected topics on the basis of their own experience and expertise. After analyzing the results of the returned questionnaires, Broadway and Howland conclude:

The findings suggest an insufficient concern about the qualifications and authority of those who write science and technology books for children and adolescents. Perhaps too many publishers and authors may believe that writing ability and interest qualify authors to write science books for children, regardless of credentials in a particular subject. (p. 37)

These researchers then provide several guidelines that they believe should be used for the authors of science books:

1. Ideally, the authors of science books for children and adolescents would be experts in their fields.
2. Another useful step in increasing the quality of informational books is to help make those who work with young people—and the young people themselves—more aware of the authors writing informational books and their credentials.
3. Publishers should recruit authors who are knowledgeable about specific topics and who have appropriate credentials and experience. (p. 38)

In the October 1992 issue of *School Library Journal,*[2] nonfiction author Gloria Skurzynski, who is an experienced writer but not a scientist, challenges Broadway and Howland's conclusions. Skurzynski argues that experienced writers are better at creating science books than are scientists, because experienced writers, even though they are not experienced in that specific scientific field know how to bring the subject to life. Whether they write fiction or nonfiction, they're storytellers. They've learned all the ways to hook young readers. In contrast, books written by experts tend to be bogged down in the very weight of their expertise. (p. 46)

Further, Skurzynski believes:

Since experienced writers are generally not sci-tech savants, they'll be curious about the same aspects of a subject as the audience. They'll want to know what readers want to know. Experts are so familiar with their own spheres of knowledge that they rarely have a clue as to what fascinates, or bewilders, general readers. (p. 46)

Skurzynski also defends a technique used by many writers of nonfictional works, blending fact and fiction within the book. She states:

I'm willing to sugarcoat hardcore information with every sweetener in the storyteller's bag of tricks, provided the coating doesn't obscure the facts. My job is twofold: to attract young readers to the book, and to make sure the information in it is absolutely correct. (p. 46)

After reading these two articles, debate the following issues:

1. Should there be any requirements about who writes children's informational books that have scientific contents?
2. What should be the qualifications of writers of nonfictional books for children?
3. What role does fiction have in nonfictional books written for children?

---

[1]Broadway, Marsha D., and Malia Howland. "Science Books for Young People: Who Writes Them?" *School Library Journal* 37 (May 1991): 35–38.

[2]Skurzynski, Gloria. "Blended Books." *School Library Journal* 38 (October 1992): 46–47.

The book includes a glossary of technical terms and an index. The humorous analogies used throughout the text appeal to many readers. Ronnie Krauss's *Take a Look, It's in a Book: How Television Is Made at Reading Rainbow* follows the process of producing the children's television show.

Cars and How They Go, by Joanna Cole, explains how the pistons, crankshaft, drive shaft, and axles work interdependently to motorize a car. Gail Gibbons's illustrations and Cole's text clarify a subject that otherwise might be too complex for many elementary children.

Chronological order is an important concept in many books that explain how things work. Byron Barton's *Airport,* an excellent picture book for young children, answers many questions about airports and airline travel, following passengers from arrival at the airport to boarding the plane.

Hobbies, Crafts, and How-To Books

One of the main reasons that older elementary-school children give for reading is learning more about their hobbies and interests. Children told one educator who asked them how teachers could improve enjoyment of reading that teachers should ask them about their hobbies and help them find books about them. Informational books cover almost every hobby and craft. The more useful books contain clearly written directions, provide guidelines for choosing equipment or other materials, or give interesting background information.

Books on hobbies, crafts, and how-to-projects are important for expanding children's interests. Developing art appreciation is a goal found in several new information books. For example, a series of four books written by Colleen Carroll focuses on different subjects in art including animals, people, elements, and weather. In each of the books Carroll discusses the art in a way that stimulates the imagination and the senses. The books in this series include *How Artists See Animals: Mammal Fish Bird Reptile; How Artists See People: Boy Girl Man Woman; How Artists See the Elements: Earth Air Fire Water;* and *How Artists See the Weather: Sun Rain Wind Snow.* Joy Richardson's *Looking at Pictures: An Introduction to Art for Young People* uses art from the National Gallery in London to show children how they can observe and appreciate paintings. Lucy Micklethwait's *A Child's Book of Play in Art* encourages children not only to look at art but to create their own works of art. Peggy Thomson and Barbara Moore's *The Nine-Ton Cat: Behind the Scenes at an Art Museum* takes readers behind the scenes at the National Gallery in Washington, D.C. This book may increase interest in visiting a museum or even in exploring careers associated with art and museums.

Creative Arts.   Clear, detailed drawings that illustrate the points made in the text are important in informational books. Jim Arnosky's *Drawing from Nature* not only provides directions for drawing water,

land forms, plants, and animals but also stimulates interest in carefully observing nature and increases understanding of science concepts. The step-by-step pencil sketches illustrate techniques that let artists accurately interpret nature. A careful reading and viewing of this text may encourage children to answer Arnosky's invitation:

Drawing from nature is discovering the upside down scene through a water drop. It is noticing how much of a fox is tail. Drawing from nature is learning how a tree grows and a flower blooms. It is sketching in the mountains and breathing air bears breathe. . . . I invite you to sharpen your pencils, your eyesight, and your sense of wonder. Turn to a fresh leaf in your drawing pad and come outdoors. (foreword)

Detailed directions and illustrations are important in books that show how to make various objects. Joan Irvine's *How to Make Super Pop-Ups* includes explicit, step-by-step directions and drawings to help readers measure, fold, cut, draw, or connect various parts to each project. Barbara Valenta's *Pop-O-Mania: How to Create Your Own Pop-Ups* also provides clear directions for projects.

Step-by-step instructions for eleven art projects designed to be completed by young children are found in Denis Roche's *Loo-Loo, Boo, and Art You Can Do.* In addition to directions for such art projects as making potato prints, the author provides helpful hints that make cleaning up easier.

How-to-books should have clear directions for projects that can be accomplished by readers. Diane Rhoades's *Garden Crafts for Kids: 50 Great Reasons to Get Your Hands Dirty* includes detailed step-by-step directions for various outdoor projects. For example, chapter four, "Starting Your Garden," includes a list of needed materials, instructions that are numbered in the appropriate sequence, photographs that show children completing the various tasks, lists of plants that are grown from seeds and those that are set from transplants, and tips to make the activity successful. The section concludes with an experiment in which readers can try planting according to a moon planting calendar.

Marion Dane Bauer, a Newbery Medal author, provides guidance for young writers in her *What's Your Story? A Young Person's Guide to Writing Fiction.* The content covers such important subjects as developing a story plan, choosing your best idea, developing strong characters, focusing your story, developing the plot, choosing a point of view, and polishing the story. Bauer relates many of the subjects to her own writing. This book also provides guidelines for readers to use when they are evaluating literature.

Rachel Isadora, a professional dancer, focuses on her daughter's training in *Lili at Ballet*. The illustrations and the text show various aspects of ballet classes. Captioned drawings clarify the text and provide practical information for readers who may themselves become future ballet professionals. For music lovers, Anne Gatti's *The Magic Flute* includes a CD of the opera that is coded to each page of the book.

Children who read frontier stories and survival stories may be interested in discovering more about the foods eaten by the characters. Barbara M. Walker's *The Little House Cookbook: Frontier Foods from Laura Ingalls Wilder's Classic Stories* presents frontier foods that Wilder wrote about in her "Little House" stories. Walker searched for authentic recipes by reading the writings of Wilder and her daughter Rose, pioneer diaries, and local recipe collections. Her hope in sharing this collection is that children will rediscover basic connections between the foods on the table and the grains in the field and the cows in the pasture, as well as between people in the past and today. Walker uses liberal excerpts from the "Little House" books and the original Garth Williams illustrations in discussing the foods and their preparation.

Many books encourage children to consider new hobbies or to learn more about existing ones.

SUGGESTED ACTIVITIES

for Adult Understanding of Biographies and Informational Books

- In order to provide accurate information and differentiate fact from opinion, biographers must research many sources. Select a writer of biographies for children and identify the sources that the writer used in researching for a book. Do you believe that these sources were sufficient? Why or why not?

- Choose someone who has had several biographies written about him or her. Read several interpretations of that person's life. Compare the biographies in terms of content, accuracy of information, sources of references indicated by the author, balance of facts with story line for young readers, intended audience for the biography, and author's style.

- Select a well-known author who has written several biographies for older children, such as Milton Meltzer, and another biographer who has written several biographies for younger children, such as Jean Fritz. What techniques does each author use in order to write a biography that will appeal to a specific age group?

- Select a content area, such as science or social studies, that is taught in an elementary- or middle-school grade. From the curriculum, identify names of men and women who are discussed in that content area. Develop an annotated bibliography of literature on a subject, such as biology, to stimulate interest in the subject and provide additional information about the contributors.

- Select the work of an outstanding author of informational books for children, such as Millicent E. Selsam, Seymour Simon, or Laurence Pringle. Evaluate the books according to the criteria listed in this chapter. Share with the class the characteristics of the books that make them highly recommended.

- Analyze several books that received a starred review or Selectors' Choices in a list such as "Outstanding Science Trade Books for Children" (*Science and Children,* March 1997). For example, you might critically evaluate Donna M. Jackson's *The Bone Detectives: How Forensic Anthropologists Solve Crimes and Uncover Mysteries of the Dead,* Jerry Booth's *You Animal!,* Barbara Juster Esbensen's *Echoes for the Eye: Poems to Celebrate Patterns in Nature,* Karen Pandell's *Animal Action ABC,* Debbie S. Miller's *Flight of the Golden Plover: The Amazing Migration Between Hawaii and Alaska,* Deborah Heiligman's *From Caterpillar to Butterfly,* Gail Jarrow and Paul Sherman's *The Naked Mole-Rat Mystery: Scientific Sleuths at Work,* and Pat Schories's *Over Under in the Garden: An Alphabet Book.* Why do you believe the panel of judges selected these books as excellent examples of books that meet scientific guidelines?

- Select several informational books that include many illustrations. Evaluate the illustrations according to the value of the explanatory legends presented next to the illustrations, the accuracy of the illustrations, and the possibility that the illustrations will stimulate children's interest in the subject.

- Choose several informational books that encourage logical problem solving. Share the books with a peer group and present rationales for your belief that these books will encourage logical problem solving.

- Search the elementary social studies or science curriculum for a given grade level. With a peer group, develop an annotated bibliography of informational books that will reinforce the curriculum and stimulate the acquisition of additional information.

- ■ A middle school teacher has invited several parents to come to class and describe their careers. Use the database to find books that will be appropriate for a Career Awareness Week display. Print your list.

- ■ Develop a list of biographies of inventors suitable for a primary class. Print your list.

- ■ Develop as complete a list as possible of books to support a fourth grade unit on explorers and explorations. Organize your list so that it will be the most useful to your students as they prepare to work in small groups that will focus on an individual explorer. Reorganize your list to accommodate small groups that will focus on explorations during a specific historical time frame. Compare the process you used to develop each list with another member of the class. Write down how your processes were similar and how they were different.

Involving Children in Nonfictional Literature

 hildren often find biographies and other informational books more exciting than textbooks. The lively dialogues, the confrontations between people and ideas, and the joys and sorrows in many biographies are natural sources for creative dramatizations and discussions. Thus, you can use biographies to help children understand people of the past and present. With informational books, you also can help children acquire abilities related to the content areas, such as using the parts of a book, locating sources of information, understanding science vocabulary, reading for meaning, evaluating science literature, and applying learning to practical problems.

UNIT PLAN: USING BIOGRAPHIES IN CREATIVE DRAMATIZATIONS

The biographies of significant people of the past and present are filled with lively dialogue, confrontations, and the joys connected with discovery. Consequently, biographies provide many opportunities for children to dramatize the momentous experiences in people's lives. Children can create "You Are There" dramas based on scenes of historical significance. They can also create imaginary conversations between two people from the past or present or from different time periods who had some common traits but were never able to communicate because of time or distance. The following ideas are only samples of the creative dramatizations that can result from using biographies in the classroom.

Jean Fritz's stories of Revolutionary War heroes, with their humorous and human portrayals, are excellent sources for dramatizations. For example, you can read *Where Was Patrick Henry on the 29th of May?* and ask children how Patrick Henry acted and how they would act if they were Patrick Henry. Then read the story a second time, letting the children dramatize it.

There is another way to approach this dramatization. After the children listen to or read the book, have them identify and discuss scenes that they would like to depict and then act out each one. Children have identified the following scenes as being of special interest in Patrick Henry's life:

1. Going fishing with a pole over his shoulder.
2. Going hunting for deer or opossum, with a rifle in his hands, accompanied by a dog at his heels.
3. Walking barefoot through the woods, and then lying down while listening to the rippling of a creek or the singing of birds and imitating their songs.
4. Listening to rain on the roof, his father's fox horn, and the music of flutes and fiddles.
5. Teaching himself to play the flute while he is recovering from a broken collarbone.
6. Listening to his Uncle Langloo Winston making speeches.
7. Waiting for the school day to end.
8. Playing practical jokes on his friends, including upsetting a canoe.
9. Trying to be a storekeeper without success.
10. Attempting to be a tobacco farmer.
11. Attending court and discovering that he likes to watch and listen to lawyers.
12. Beginning his law practice and not finding many clients.
13. Defending his first big case in court and winning.
14. Arguing against taxation without representation as a member of Virginia's House of Burgesses.
15. Delivering his "give me liberty or give me death" speech at St. John's Church.
16. Governing Virginia.

17. Hearing the news that the Continental army has defeated the English troops at Saratoga, New York.
18. Speaking against the enactment of the Constitution of the United States and for individual and states' rights after the war is over.
19. Retiring on his estate in western Virginia.

These scenes may also be developed into a sequence game that involves careful observation by all players, who must interpret what someone else is doing and, according to directions written on their cue cards, stand and perform the next action at the correct time. (Players must be able to read to do this activity.) Develop cue cards for scenes from Patrick Henry's life. The first cue card would look approximately like this:

You begin the game.
Pretend that you are a young, barefoot Patrick Henry happily going fishing with a pole over your shoulder.
When you are finished, sit down in your seat.

The second card would read:

Cue: Someone pretends to be a young Patrick Henry going fishing with a pole over his shoulder.
You are a young Patrick Henry happily going hunting for deer or opossum, with a rifle in your hands and accompanied by a dog running at your heels.
When you are finished, sit down in your seat.

Place the rest of the scenes, written in a similar manner, on cards. It is helpful if the cue and the directions for the dramatization are written in different colors. Mix the cards and distribute them randomly. There should be at least one cue card for each player, but you may add more scenes if a whole class is taking part in the activity. If there are fewer players, you can reduce the number of scenes or give each player more than one cue card. Ask the children to pay close attention and wait for each player to complete the dramatization.

It is helpful if you have a master cue sheet with all of the cues in correct order so that you can help if someone misinterprets a scene, the children seem uncertain, or the group loses its direction. To involve as many children as possible, you may divide large groups into three small groups. Have each small group dramatize a set of identical cue cards independently. Let a child act as leader of each group and follow the master sheet.

Incidents in the lives of other Fritz heroes—described in *Why Don't You Get a Horse, Sam Adams?, The Great Little Madison, What's the Big Idea, Ben Franklin?,* and *Bully for You, Teddy Roosevelt!*—also make enjoyable dramas.

When appropriate, encourage children to pantomime scenes. Children can pantomime the actions of writers and storytellers as in *Jump at de Sun: The Story of Zora Neale Hurston,* by A. P. Porter; the actions of actors, as in *An Actor's Life for Me!,* by Lillian Gish as told to Selma Lanes; and the actions of singers as in *Beverly Sills,* by Bridget Paolucci.

"You Are There" Dramatizations

Biographies allow children to experience some very exciting moments in history through the emotions, words, and contributions of the people who created those moments. Consequently, reenactments of those scenes can allow children to experience the excitement and realize that history is made up of real people and actual incidents.

A group of seventh graders chose to return in time to Rome in 1632, during the cruel days of the Inquisition. Their "You Are There" drama, based on Sidney Rosen's *Galileo and the Magic Numbers,* began after Galileo had published his *A Dialogue on the Two Great Systems of the World* and was facing an angry Pope Urban. Have children perform the following dramatization.

1. To the audience, an announcer says: "You are there; the year is 1632; Galileo is facing an angry Pope Urban. The Pope's face is reddened in anger, his eyes are flashing venom. He is pounding his fists on the arms of the papal throne. Shouting, he declares:"

That scoundrel! That ingrate! We try to befriend him. And how does he repay us? By doing all this behind our back! Well this time he has gone too far! Let him take care! It is out of our hands now. This is a matter for the Holy Office! (p. 192)

"With these words, the slow process of the Inquisition begins. Galileo's enemies are winning, and he is to be charged with heresy."
2. The announcer, the action, and the dialogue go back to Florence. Galileo waits anxiously with his health failing, his fever returning, and his eyesight failing.

3. In October, the Inquisitor of Florence appears at Galileo's door with a summons. Galileo has thirty days in which to appear before the Holy Office in Rome.

4. On April 12, 1633, Galileo is summoned to the Inquisition chambers, where he is exhaustively questioned and threatened with torture for many days. He finally signs a document confessing his wrongdoing; he then feels shame and guilt for his weakness.

5. On June 21, Galileo discovers that signing the document is not sufficient; he is to be tried for heresy before ten cardinals who will be his judges. A bent, graying Galileo is in front of the men dressed in red cloaks and hats, sitting about a great semicircular table. The questioning begins. The judges ask Galileo whether he does, indeed, believe that the earth moves about the sun. Silence hangs over the hall as the judges await Galileo's response.

6. On June 22, 1633, Galileo is dressed in the shirt of penitence, awaiting the verdict of the Inquisition. A hush falls over the hall. Galileo, kneeling before the cardinals, listens to the long document of charges read against him. At last, he hears the words that crush all hope:

But in order that your terrible error may not go altogether unpunished, and that you may be an example and a warning to others to abstain from such opinions, we decree that your book, *A Dialogue on the Two Great Systems of the World,* be banned publicly; also, we condemn you to the formal prison of this Holy Office for an indefinite period convenient to our pleasure. So we, the subscribing and presiding cardinals pronounce! (p. 202)

Galileo and the Magic Numbers contains vivid settings and characters and enough dialogue that children can develop a realistic "You Are There" drama. With the help of an announcer, the actors can develop the dialogue as they proceed, or they can choose some actual dialogue from the book. The seventh-grade group chose a combination of these two approaches.

You can create a "You Are There" episode around Christopher Columbus's meeting with Queen Isabella, his exploration of America, and his return to the Spanish court. Also, you can create a "You Are There" episode around Benjamin Franklin's testifying before the English Parliament. In *Benjamin Franklin: The New American,* a biography of Benjamin Franklin,

Milton Meltzer describes the setting in which 174 questions are asked and answered. Have students research questions and answers concerning the Stamp Act. Another possibility is to have students recreate exciting moments from Virginia Hamilton's *Anthony Burns: The Defeat and Triumph of a Fugitive Slave,* in which the Boston Vigilance Committee defended the rights of Anthony Burns, a fugitive slave. There are numerous possibilities for developing vivid scenes after reading Russell Freedman's *Franklin Delano Roosevelt* or *Eleanor Roosevelt: A Life of Discovery.*

Imaginary Conversations Between People of Two Time Periods

Children enjoy contemplating what historic personalities might say to each other if they had the opportunity to meet. Because this is impossible except through imagination, children can be motivated to read biographies in order to enter into such conversations. For example, an exciting conversation could result if Theodore Roosevelt (Jean Fritz's *Bully for You, Teddy Roosevelt!*) met with a panel of loggers from the Northwest and with the administration in Washington, D.C. as the group tries to develop policies about logging and the endangering of the owl (use newspaper, journal, or television reports).

Other historical biographical characters might have stimulating conversations if they could meet with world figures of the 1990s. What views would emerge if Patrick Henry could share his opinions on states' rights and the rights of individuals with the current president of the United States? What would be Amelia Earhart's or the Wright Brothers' response to space travel and exploration? What questions would they ask of a contemporary astronaut? What role would they want if they could be involved in the space program? When children read in order to role-play a character's actions, express a character's feelings, or state dialogue that a character might express, they interact with the character on a human level and often read until they feel empathy with that character and the historic time period.

 ## COMPARING ATTITUDES AND CHECKING FACTS IN BIOGRAPHIES

Elizabeth Robertson and Jo McGinnis (1985) recommend that students compare the tone and attitude of a biographer as reflected in a biography about a specific person with the tone and attitude expressed by the biographical subject in his or her own writing. Ann W. Moore (1985) recommends that reviewers check the accuracy of facts in juvenile biographies by referring to reputable adult titles and other reference books.

Biographies about Eleanor Roosevelt are excellent sources for comparisons in the classroom. There are numerous children's biographies, including one written by Elliott Roosevelt, reputable adult biographies, and autobiographies written by Eleanor Roosevelt herself. The following books are sources for such comparisons. Biographies for children include Russell Freedman's *Eleanor Roosevelt: A Life of Discovery,* Jane Goodsell's *Eleanor Roosevelt,* and Sharon Whitney's *Eleanor Roosevelt.* A biography for children written by Eleanor Roosevelt's son is Elliott Roosevelt's *Eleanor Roosevelt, with Love.* Barbara Cooney's *Eleanor* is an illustrated biography for younger readers. Biographies for adults include Joseph P. Lash's *Eleanor and Franklin* and *Eleanor: The Years Alone,* Elliott Roosevelt and James Brough's *An Untold Story: The Roosevelts of Hyde Park* and *Mother R: Eleanor Roosevelt's Untold Story,* and Lorena Hickok's *Eleanor Roosevelt: Reluctant First Lady.* Autobiographies include Eleanor Roosevelt's *The Autobiography of Eleanor Roosevelt, On My Own, This I Remember, This Is My Story, Tomorrow Is Now,* and *You Learn by Living.*

Other good subjects for comparisons include Christopher Columbus, Abraham Lincoln, Franklin D. Roosevelt, Martin Luther King, Jr., and Benjamin Franklin. All of these biographical subjects have been chosen by numerous authors.

 ## INVESTIGATING THE QUALITIES OF WRITERS

What are the qualities that characterize successful writers of children's literature? Is there any way for students to discover these qualities? Are these qualities important in the lives of school children? Patricia J. Cianciolo (1985) believes that the words of authors as expressed in their autobiographies, journals, and interviews are excellent for discovering the abilities, attitudes, and character traits of competent writers. Cianciolo analyzed the comments about writing expressed by children's authors Rosemary Sutcliff,

Donald Hall, Katherine Paterson, M. E. Kerr, Mollie Hunter, Lois Duncan, Alan Garner, Julia Cunningham, Vera and Bill Cleaver, and Barbara Wersba.

You may have students read some of the sources identified by Cianciolo and read other autobiographies by children's authors, such as Beverly Cleary's *A Girl from Yamhill: A Memoir,* Sid Fleischman's *The Abracadabra Kid: A Writer's Life,* Milton Meltzer's *Starting from Home: A Writer's Beginnings,* and Bill Peet's *Bill Peet: An Autobiography.* Have the students search for comments that reflect the authors' attitudes about writing. They may find some of the same important abilities, attitudes, and character traits as did Cianciolo.

1. A good writer must be a good reader.
2. A good writer cares intensely about language and is sensitive to it.
3. A good writer is well educated.
4. A good writer is an alert observer.
5. A good writer is a storyteller and enjoys stories told by others.
6. A good writer is a compulsive writer.

After identifying these characteristics of a good writer, lead a discussion in which the students identify the importance of each quality and discuss how the students might use these qualities to improve their own writing and reading.

In a related activity, encourage students to read autobiographies or biographies about an author and then to read other literary works by the same author. Have the students analyze whether or not there are relationships between the biography and the literary works. Why does an author write about certain subjects? Does the literary work develop the style, the character, the emotions, and the beliefs of the writer? Examples for this activity include Beverly Cleary's *A Girl from Yamhill: A Memoir* and Cleary's various books about Ramona and Henry Huggins or *Dear Mr. Henshaw;* Milton Meltzer's *Starting from Home: A Writer's Beginnings* and any of Meltzer's biographies and informational books; Bill Peet's *Bill Peet: An Autobiography* and any of Peet's humorous fictional books, such as *No Such Thing;* Gary Paulsen's autobiography *Woodsong* and Paulsen's survival literature, such as *Hatchet* and *Dogsong;* Norma Johnston's biography *Louisa May: The World and Works of Louisa May Alcott* and Alcott's fictional *Little Women;* and Angelica Shirley Carpenter and Jean Shirley's biography

Frances Hodgson Burnett: Beyond the Secret Garden and Hodgson's fictional *The Secret Garden* and *Little Lord Fauntleroy.*

A related activity is discovering some of the principles of writing biography that students can use in their own writing. An author of adult biographies, Steve Weinberg (1993), provides guidelines for writing biographies that can be adapted by adults who work with children who would also like to write biographies. Weinberg provides the following ten principles you can discuss, adapt, and use as students develop their own biographies:

1. A life should be told in chronological order because actions become clearer when viewed as the outgrowth of previous actions.
2. Biographers should always use primary sources and check the authenticity of their details.
3. In order to explain the life of a person, biographers should provide the context of the times.
4. Biographers should not let hindsight intrude on the chronological order of their stories.
5. Biographers should have sympathy or empathy for their subjects, trying to see the world through the subjects' eyes.
6. Biographers should practice psychological analysis of subjects sparingly because authors cannot really know the thoughts of subjects whom they have rarely or never met.
7. Biographers should try to understand the complexity of subjects' lives and of the people who influenced them.
8. Biographers should be honest with readers when trying to fill in undocumented gaps in a person's life.
9. Biographers should be selective when choosing from the masses of material that may be available.
10. Biographers should consider style as seriously as they do content in providing readers with the feel for the facts.

Emphasizing the importance of developing the feel in biography, Weinberg concludes:

Some of the writing techniques used to create that "feel" are borrowed from fiction. Biographies and novels are concerned with birth, death, love, hate, and moral dilemmas galore. The techniques used in each genre might include scene-by-scene construction based on immersion in geographic setting, physical description of the key individuals, dialogue, imagery, symbolism, irony, contrast, and shifting points of view among various characters. (p. 25)

Use Weinberg's guidelines to evaluate previously published biographies or to help students make major decisions when they are writing their own biographies.

 ## ANALYZING LITERARY ELEMENTS IN BIOGRAPHIES

In addition to evaluating the accuracy of characterization in biographies by comparing the characterizations in biographies written by different authors, have students analyze and evaluate plot, setting, and theme in biographies. For example, to analyze plot in biographies, have students identify the pattern of action, locate examples of specific types of conflict developed in a biography, analyze why the biographer emphasizes those types of conflict, consider why and how the conflicts relate to the biographer's purpose in writing, and locate examples of ways in which the biographer develops the readers' interest. To evaluate setting in biographies, have students identify the various settings, identify the ways in which the biographer informs readers about the important details related to the time period; analyze how much influence the setting has on the plot and characters; find specific locations mentioned in the biography and locate these places on a map, in geography texts, or in other nonfictional sources; evaluate the authenticity of settings by comparing the various nonfictional sources; check the accuracy of dates and happenings in other nonfictional sources; draw a setting as if it were a backdrop for a stage production; and evaluate whether or not there is enough information about setting to complete a drawing. To evaluate theme in biography, have the students find the primary, or main, theme in a biography and several secondary themes. Have the students consider how these themes are integrated into the biography, analyze whether or not the title of the biography reflects the theme, search for evidence of the biographical subject's ability to triumph over obstacles, identify and compare the themes developed in several biographies written about the same person, and compare the themes in biographies written for younger children and those written for young adults.

Are we living in the midst of a paradigm shift that is moving from a print-based culture to one based on virtual images? Have we progressed from books to television to computers? Is "in print" being replaced by "on line"? If we are shifting, will the shift continue? This is a huge question. We will cover it in two issues. First, is there evidence of a paradigm shift, and, if so, will it continue? Second, what are the positive and negative effects of using technology in relation to literature?

Two editorials in *The New York Times* highlight the question of a possible or future paradigm shift. Richard C. Hsu and William E. Mitchel[1] argue that printed books provide superior technology. They hypothesize about what would have happened if books in print and books on computer had been marketed simultaneously. They compare the two according to topics such as cost, durability, portability, and editorial quality and conclude that books are superior. They state, "print, for all its recent challenges, remains for many applications, a superior technology" (p. 12).

In contrast, Jack McGarvey[2] argues that his students are the "Generation of Multimedia" and describes the role of computers and software programs that he believes will eventually change education. As seen in these articles, one viewpoint does not imagine a world without books, while the other sees a world influenced by the computer screen.

As you consider the possibility of a paradigm shift, you may find it interesting to think about possible future roles for technology. Paul Hilts[3] introduces an article in which he interviews publishing executives with this belief: "On the eve of a new millennium, publishing faces what has been described as the greatest change since Gutenberg" (p. 125). The various interviews discuss such areas as decreasing the time from finished manuscript to bound books and replacing CDs with Web sites and the Internet. One interviewee is so emphatic about the paradigm shift that he states, "In the future, the act of printing words on paper will be as common as writing in stone is today" (p. 128).

Before you discuss the possible changes resulting from technology, consider a quote by educator Neil Postman in an interview with Renee Olson[4]: "I do make the claim that the god of technology has invaded the minds of many educators. Most educators, when they talk about reforming education, put their hopes on technology. I do believe that it is a mistake, a distraction. I'm old enough to remember when people thought that 16mm film was the panacea. I also remember when they thought 8mm film would do it, when they thought structured teacher-proof textbooks would do it. Now, of course, it's computers. In America, we're always looking for a technological fix. I think that while computers will play a role in the future of education as libraries will, I don't think that there's any substitute for the interaction of teacher and student face-to-face" (p. 20).

Which of these viewpoints expresses your own beliefs? What is your viewpoint on the current and future use of technology? Are we in a paradigm shift? If we are, will it continue? In your own life, what is the role of technology?

[1] Hsu, Richard C., and William E. Mitchel. "Books Have Endured for a Reason . . ." *The New York Times,* Sunday, May 25, 1997: Section 3, p. 12.

[2] McGarvey, Jack. ". . . But Computers Are Clearly the Future." *The New York Times,* Sunday, May 25, 1997: Section 3, p. 12.

[3] Hilts, Paul. "The Road Ahead: Publishing Visionaries Look at the Change That Digital Technology Might Bring." *Publishers Weekly* 244 (July 1997): 125–128.

[4] Olson, Renee. "When It Comes to Technology . . . The Postman Always Thinks Twice." *School Library Journal* 42 (May 1996): 19–22.

INCORPORATING LITERATURE INTO THE SCIENCE CURRICULUM

James Rutherford (1991), the Chief Education Officer of the American Association for the Advancement of Science, argues that trade books rather than textbooks should be a primary source of science materials in the early grades. He states:

I would say that the elementary school classroom, in the earliest grades, should not have science textbooks. They are too ordered, too assertive by their nature, too given to explanations. . . . Furthermore, textbooks are rarely very relevant to the real neighborhoods where the children go to school. . . . Nevertheless, despite this ban on textbooks in the early grades, books should be an essential part of science learning. What that means is that once we rule out the conventional textbook, we have to think very carefully and more creatively about the role that books really should play. (p. 27)

When recommending the types of books that should be used in the early grades Rutherford states, "The kind I am recommending are those which are adventurous, in which the story is built around finding things out, and which emphasize the excitement of discovery" (p. 29). Rutherford concludes: "elementary classroom books should promote the legitimacy of imaginative thinking, just as much as they promote activity. It is just this combination of action, thought, and imagination that makes science so powerful" (p. 30).

Lazer Goldberg (1991) reinforces Rutherford's beliefs about the quality of trade books in the science curriculum. He believes that good science books should foster questions and critical thinking because "critical thinking is at the heart of science" (p. 34).

Science author Laurence Pringle (1991) also argues the benefits of trade books over textbooks in the science curriculum. He states:

It is the process of science, and how scientists think, that needs more attention in children's books. Textbooks do a lot of telling and defining; they're often curiosity-killers. They usually fail to convey a sense of excitement in scientific research. (p. 52)

Pringle also believes that good trade books should foster critical thinking and reasoning. Pringle warns, however, that science trade books must be chosen with the same scrutiny used in choosing textbooks. Poorly written trade books can also kill curiosity and restrict critical thinking and reasoning.

Several values of informational books relate to the science curriculum. Interesting books—such as those by Seymour Simon, Millicent Selsam, and Laurence Pringle—allow children to experience the excitement of discovery. Through books such as Simon's *How to Be an Ocean Scientist in Your Own Home,* children can observe, experiment, compare, formulate hypotheses, test hypotheses, draw conclusions, and evaluate their evidence. Children can become directly involved in the scientific method. Through the experiments and information found in many informational books, children can learn about the world of nature. Because many informational books that deal with science subjects have greater depth of coverage than do science textbooks, such informational books are valuable for extending knowledge and understanding.

Communication abilities, such as graphing, illustrating, recording, and reporting, are especially important to science. Authors of science information books frequently use these communication abilities when writing. Consequently, children are introduced to reading and interpreting graphs and can present their own ideas and findings in graphic form. Children need many opportunities to interpret data and to make predictions from them. Such experiences help children become actively involved in reading and discovery.

However, the nature of science materials—with their heavy concentration of facts and details, new scientific principles, and new technical vocabulary—may cause reading problems for children who are accustomed to the narrative writing style.

Use excellent informational materials on science-related topics to encourage children to develop their abilities to read science-related materials and to understand science-related concepts. This text considers abilities that relate to both literature and the content areas: using the parts of the book, locating sources of information, using science vocabulary, reading for meaning, evaluating science materials, and applying data from reading to practical problems. The specific books mentioned are only examples of the numerous books that you can use in the classroom. You may wish to add other informational books.

Using the Parts of a Book

Science informational books reinforce the ability to use parts of a book because many books contain a table of contents, a glossary, a bibliography of further readings, and an index. Children can use the table of contents in conjunction with an index to locate specific content. For example:

1. Find the chapter describing fossils and the geological record in Roy A. Gallant's *Before the Sun Dies: The Story of Evolution* (chapter 7, p. 61).
2. Find the chapter on "Gentle, Intelligent, and Endangered" in Laurence Pringle's *Batman: Exploring the World of Bats* (chapter 3, p. 18).
3. Find the chapter on "People and Whales" in Dorothy Hinshaw Patent's *Whales: Giants of the Deep* (chapter 5, p. 73).
4. Find the chapter describing how the potato may save people from hunger in Milton Meltzer's *The*

Amazing Potato (chapter 6, "The Answer to World Hunger?," p. 66).

5. Find the chapter describing damage caused by mudflows in Patricia Lauber's *Volcano: The Eruption and Healing of Mount St. Helens* (chapter 2, pp. 15–17).

Laurence Pringle's books usually have a glossary of technical terms, an index, and a list of further readings that can provide additional information about a subject. Use these books to reinforce the importance of each part of the book, the kind of information that is available, and locational aids. Books that include lists of further reading and biographical sources, such as Rhoda Blumberg's *Commodore Perry in the Land of the Shogun* and Jim Murphy's *The Great Fire,* provide opportunities for students to locate additional subjects.

Locating Sources of Information

You can use the lists of references at the back of many informational books to show children how to use a library filing system for more information. For

---

ISSUE   What Are the Positive and Negative Effects of Using Technology in Relation to Literature?

Although in the previous issue on paradigm shifts there were viewpoints that praised and criticized the future of technology, there are also positions that discuss positive and negative effects of technology in relation to literature and libraries. What do you believe are the advantages and disadvantages of technology? It is apparent that the issue is important. Reports of funding for schools indicate that federal funding for technology has increased 450 percent in 1997.[1] Responses to technology range from the 25,000 schools in the United States that use and endorse computerized reading management programs to a warning by a school district in which parents are asked to "Discourage Heavy Use of Television and Electronic Media."[2]

Responses to issues about using technology in relation to literature and research indicate that most people are in favor of teaching children to use technology. They are concerned, however, with the quality of the technology and the applications being used. A review of current viewpoints on technology printed in journals indicates that authors, especially librarians, are concerned with the quality and evaluation of various technological approaches related to literature and library use. For example, Betty Carter[3] provides a skeptical evaluation of computerized reading management programs such as Accelerated Reader and Electronic Bookshelf, programs that she believes do not teach a love of reading. She maintains that schools must teach children to evaluate and synthesize information whether it is within books, video frames, or CD-ROMs. She states, "Schools can use their money for many different materials and their staff time in many different ways. They can teach children to read for points or for pleasure; to record finite answers to questions on a computer or explore the Internet. Teachers and librarians can manage motivational systems or they can promote books and reading; they can award prizes to students who recall factual information or design instruction that helps children seek answers to their own questions" (p. 25).

The quality of Web sites is another area of concern expressed in the journals. Ann K. Symons[4] maintains, "The amount of useless content on the Web boggles the imagination . . . it's obvious that you would never select more than one percent of what's on the Web for your print collection" (p. 22). Consequently, Symons suggests the development of criteria that emphasizes purpose, depth of content, navigation, accuracy, accessibility, design, style, and performance.

What do you believe are the positive and negative effects of using technology with literature and with libraries? What criteria would you develop to assure that the techniques are effective? How is technology being used effectively in libraries and schools in your areas? What weaknesses, if any, do you observe?

---

[1] "Federal Technology Funding for Schools Jumps 450 Percent." *School Library Journal* 42 (November 1996): 14.

[2] Routman, Regie. *Literacy at the Crossroads: Crucial Talk About Reading, Writing, and Other Teaching Dilemmas.* Portsmouth, N.H.: Heineman, 1996, 189.

[3] Carter, Betty. "Hold the Applause! Do Accelerated Reader & Electronic Bookshelf Send the Right Message?" *School Library Journal* 42 (October 1996): 22–25.

[4] Symons, Ann K. "Sizing Up Sites: How to Judge What You Find on the Web." *School Library Journal* 43 (April 1997): 22–25.

example, Milton Meltzer's *The Amazing Potato* includes a bibliography of thirty-two additional books and journals that provide information related to the potato. Laurence Pringle's *Batman: Exploring the World of Bats* includes twelve additional sources—newspapers, books, and journals. Charlotte and David Yue's *Christopher Columbus: How He Did It* includes twenty-two additional books that provide further information. Helping children learn how to make their own additional discoveries about a subject fosters important scientific goals.

Using Science Vocabulary

The glossary in many informational books is also a source of information about the meaning of technical terminology found in the book. Authors such as Caroline Arnold in *Saving the Peregrine Falcon* and Sally Walker in *Glaciers: Ice on the Move* and *Rhinos* use boldface type to identify terms that are defined in the glossary. Authors of informational books for children often present the meaning of new words through their context in the text. You should specifically point out this technique to children to help them understand the meanings of words. In *Almost the Real Thing: Simulation in Your High-Tech World,* Gloria Skurzynski presents meaning in both the text and a glossary. For example, in the text, she states: "Simulations are imitations of things that exist in the real world. Almost anything can be simulated—in images, in solid models you can touch, in sound, in motion, or in elements that you can feel, like the wind" (p. 7). In the glossary, she provides additional information for *simulation:* "an imitation that represents a real object, like an airplane's cockpit; or represents a force, like the wind; or an abstract idea, such as nuclear winter" (p. 63).

Authors also clarify the meanings of technical terminology through photographs, diagrams, and charts. Even books written for young children often use labeled drawings to clarify meanings of technical terminology. Millicent Selsam and Joyce Hunt's books for young children, including *A First Look at Caterpillars, A First Look at Animals with Horns,* and *A First Look at Seals, Sea Lions, and Walruses,* discuss specific characteristics that are easy to observe in illustrations. Selsam and Hunt use technical terms frequently and ask children to use their knowledge to answer questions. In *Creepy, Crawly Caterpillars,* Margery Facklam's terms are reinforced by Paul

Facklam's illustrations that include labeled details in the lower portion of the page. For example, on a page showing the monarch caterpillar, the lower illustrations show the changes from egg to butterfly.

Reading for Meaning

A major reason that many students give for reading informational science books is to acquire facts; therefore, comprehending the meaning is important. Unlike writings that stress make-believe, informational science books are based on accuracy. Children often need encouragement to note main ideas and supporting details and to see organization. Reading methods books usually include several chapters on these comprehension abilities, but a few approaches considered here allow content area teachers and parents to reinforce and encourage the abilities through informational books.

Noting Main Ideas. Because many informational books written for children have a main idea as a topic sentence at the beginning of a paragraph, many teachers have children read a paragraph and then visualize the author's organization of the material according to the main idea and important details. (This technique may also help children evaluate whether the author uses a logical organization and help them use similar structures in their own nonfiction writing.) A typical paragraph may follow this organization (Norton, 1997):

Main Idea

Supporting Detail
Supporting Detail
Supporting Detail
Supporting Detail

Seymour Simon's writing tends to follow this structure. Use this diagram with material from *New Questions and Answers About Dinosaurs* to help children identify the main idea and supporting details and to evaluate whether or not the organization is logical. On page 4 of Simon's book are two paragraphs that answer the question, "What are dinosaurs?" Arrange the paragraph in the following way:

Main idea: Answer the question, What are dinosaurs?

Supporting details:

A group of reptiles that appeared about 225 million years ago.

Dinosaurs lived during the Mesozoic era, sometimes called the Age of Reptiles.

Dinosaurs died about 65 million years ago, long before there were humans.

There were hundreds of different kinds and sizes of dinosaurs.

Some dinosaurs were meat-eaters and some were plant-eaters.

Dinosaurs were spread across the world.

Dinosaurs lived for 160 million years.

Have children discuss whether or not Simon developed his main idea and answered the question with sufficient supporting details. The remainder of Simon's book uses a similar approach. Each two-page spread answers a question using one or two short paragraphs. The text includes such questions as Were all ancient reptiles dinosaurs?, How else are new dinosaurs discovered?, How are dinosaurs named?, and Were dinosaurs cold-blooded or warm-blooded? If children do not receive sufficient answers to any of their questions, encourage them to expand their knowledge through further reading and investigations.

Noting Supporting Details.　When noting main ideas, children should learn to identify supporting details in diagrams and questions. In informational science books, size, color, number, location, and texture are also supporting details. Have the children listen to or read a description from an informational science book and draw a picture that shows the important details. The following descriptions are examples of sources that you can use:

1. The description of the process associated with grafting found on pages 8–9 in Charles Micucci's *The Life and Times of the Apple.*
2. The description of lightning found in Stephen Kramer's *Lightning* (various sections of this book).

Seeing an Author's Organization.　A logical organization of information is often critical in the science content areas. Use books that emphasize the life cycles of plants and animals, the correct steps to use in following an experiment, or a chain of events to help children increase their ability to note scientific organization and to evaluate an author's ability to organize logically. Also use books that organize content according to subject. For example, discuss why David Macaulay chose the following organizational plan for the relationships among the objects pictured in *The Way Things Work:* (1) the mechanics of movement, (2) harnessing the elements, (3) working with waves, and (4) electricity and automation.

To organize content according to geographic area, on a large world map mark in different colors the six areas identified in Joyce Pope's *Kenneth Lilly's Animals: A Portfolio of Paintings.* Have students list the characteristics of the areas, the animals in each area, and the characteristics of the animals. The areas are (1) hot forests, (2) cool forests, (3) seas and rivers, (4) grasslands, (5) deserts, and (6) mountains. Have the students search through geography texts to identify additional characteristics of these areas. Ask the students to consider why Pope's organization seems logical. Have them compare the effectiveness of Pope's organization with the effectiveness of organization in other texts in the library that use maps to identify locations of animals. Another book that encourages students to analyze author's organization through a map is John S. Major's *The Silk Route: 7,000 Miles of History.* The text follows the ancient route from Chang'an to Byzantium.

Evaluating Science Materials

Evaluation requires critical thinking. Critical reading and thinking go beyond factual comprehension; they require weighing the validity of facts, identifying the problem, making judgments, interpreting implied ideas, distinguishing fact from opinion, drawing conclusions, determining the adequacy of a source of information, and suspending judgment until all of the facts have been accumulated. For example, have students develop questions to ask when evaluating science materials. For this activity, have them consider the evaluation criteria used by the book review journal *Appraisal: Science Books for Young People* and develop questions around the following guidelines recommended by Diane Holzheimer (1991) for that journal. First, accuracy is extremely important. Consequently, materials should be completely correct and as up to date as possible. Second, the organization should be logical for the book. Third, the writing should be clear and logical. Fourth, writers should use language with precision and grace and should encourage readers to participate in the subject. Fifth, the illustrations should aid understanding and be appealing. Sixth, if the book includes activities and experiments, the instructions should be clear. Seventh, the book should exemplify scientific attitudes, stimulate imagination, and encourage readers to examine firsthand the wonders of the world.

In addition to developing questions that allow the students to evaluate the text, develop questions that allow students to consider authors' qualifications. For example, help students develop the following list of questions about the authors:

1. *Why did the author write this book?* Was it to present information? Was it to promote a point of view? Was it to advertise? Was it to propagandize? Was it to entertain?
2. *How competent is the author to write an article on this topic for this purpose?* What is the author's background? What is the author's reputation? Does the author have any vested interests in this topic? What is the author's professional position?

To help children critically evaluate authors of informational books (this list and activity are excellent for all informational books, not just those related to science), provide access to many books by different authors and biographical information about the authors. One teacher of upper-elementary students divided a class into five research groups according to a category of interest that each group chose to investigate. The categories included botany, birds, earth and geology, land mammals, and insects. (You may use the list of authors and books in the Children's Literature at the end of this chapter to help you and your students identify books and topics.)

Next, the students found as many books as possible on these categories in the library, including each author's most recent publications on the subject. The students read the information about the author on the dust jacket or elsewhere in the book and searched for biographical data and magazine or journal articles written by the author. Then, the students evaluated the author's background and read and reread the books, searching for each author's point of view and purpose for writing the book.

After the students had carefully read the books, they evaluated the content of the materials according to the criteria developed earlier.

The children also read background information in science textbooks, encyclopedias, and magazines or journals. They checked the copyright dates of the materials; scrutinized the photographs, graphs, charts, and diagrams; and evaluated whether or not the author differentiated fact from opinion. If the students found more than one viewpoint on the subject, they tried to discover if the author presented both.

Finally, the groups presented their information on the authors and their books to the rest of the class. The students learned how to critically evaluate informational books and authors. They also learned much about the content area and the procedures that writers of informational books should use when they research their subjects.

Several authors of informational science books develop themes related to endangered species and ecology. Books with these themes can provide stimulating sources for topics of debate and independent research. Have students use the criteria for evaluating authors and content that were given earlier in this section. In addition, have students test the validity of an argument presented in written materials. For example, have them strip the argument of any excess words or sentences; identify all of the premises upon which an author's conclusion rests; determine whether the author is referring to all of a group, some of a group, or none of a group; and determine whether the conclusion logically follows from the premises.

Then, have students independently evaluate whether the author's conclusion is logical and supported by facts. Also, have them enter into debates, choosing different sides of an issue, researching outside sources, and developing contrasting viewpoints. For example, use Helen Roney Sattler's *The Book of Eagles* to help students form a debate about the plight of eagles and the role of humans in this plight. After reading Sattler's chapter five, "Humans: Friends or Foes?" have students debate whether humans are doing more to help or to harm eagles. Have the students do additional research related to the issue. Ask: Should farmers be allowed to use certain poisons to kill insects and weeds even though the poisons cause the eggs of eagles to be too thin to hatch? Should stricter pollution standards be made into law because eagles die from eating polluted animals and fish?

Have the students choose sides in these issues, complete additional research, and present their positions in debate format. They may include the following points that show humans as friends of eagles:

1. Scientists are attempting to restore nesting populations to former nesting areas. Scientists are raising eaglets in captivity and then releasing them into natural habitats.
2. Millions of acres of land have been set aside as sanctuaries for eagles.
3. The government grants special licenses to people who care for sick or injured eagles in their homes.
4. Money is being donated for research to help scientists learn more about eagles.
5. Scientists are banding eaglets to track the maturing birds and to help them discover information about the eagles.

The following points show humans as foes to eagles:

1. Humans have moved into wilderness areas that were the natural habitats of eagles, cut trees, cleared land, and destroyed the habitats. Most eagles will not nest or hunt in areas occupied by humans.
2. Contaminated food kills eagles because farmers use poisons to kill insects and weeds. The insecticides cause the eggshells to become so thin that the eggs break in the nest.
3. Factories use chemicals that pollute the air and water. Eagles die after they eat animals and fish that have been poisoned.
4. Sheep farmers have shot thousands of eagles because the farmers believed that eagles killed lambs.
5. Sportsmen have killed eagles because the eagles occasionally killed game birds.
6. Accidents kill eagles when they land on power lines and are electrocuted.

Some animals are not endangered because people hunt or poison them. Instead, pollution or land development has endangered their survival. Books on this subject can spark debates whether the interests of people are in opposition to the interests of animals and whether the protective measures designed for animals also protect humans. You also may use Caroline Arnold's *Saving the Peregrine Falcon* and Nicholas and Theodore Nirgiotis's *No More Dodos: How Zoos Help Endangered Wildlife* for this purpose.

Other books about animals that have been endangered include Dorothy Hinshaw Patent's *Whales:*
Giants of the Deep,* Judi Friedman's *Operation Siberian Crane: The Story Behind the International Effort to Save an Amazing Bird,* Dorothy Hinshaw Patent's *Where the Bald Eagles Gather,* and Brenda Z. Guiberson's *Into the Sea.*

Applying Data from Reading to Practical Problems

After children critically evaluate the subjects of water, land, and air pollution discussed in informational books, they may be interested in evaluating the extent of pollution in their own environment. An informational book that can spark this kind of critical evaluation through experimentation and observation is Betty Miles's *Save the Earth! An Ecology Handbook for Kids.* Projects that appeal to third and fourth graders include planning a new town to make the best possible use of land, recording air pollution by placing several cards covered with a thin layer of petroleum jelly outside in different locations and noting after twenty-four hours the pollution that has collected on the cards, and tracking water pollution in their own neighborhood, town, or city.

This last project reinforces observation, critical evaluation, and graphic interpretation abilities. A fourth-grade class identified various waterways in their town. Then, they walked beside several creeks, a lake, a river, and a pond, making notes about the pollution that they found. When the students returned to school, they drew a large map of the waterways and used their notes to mark on the map any pollution found. Next, they filled in the type of building or human activity that was near the pollution so that they could more closely evaluate the possible causes of the pollution. When the students discovered a definite problem, they took pictures of the evidence, wrote letters to the newspaper, made "clean up the waterways" posters, and asked people to make pledges to clean up their waterways.

After students develop their own ecology projects, have the students read about another school in which students decided to tackle problems in their own neighborhood. Have students read Molly Cone's *Come Back, Salmon* and compare what they accomplished with the experiences of the elementary students in Everett, Washington.

Deciding whether information about animals is fact or fantasy is another way for children to apply data from reading to a practical problem. Develop discussions that encourage the children to observe and analyze differences in behavior of real animals, behavior of real animals depicted in informational books, and behavior of the same animals depicted in folktales and modern fantasy. For example, bring a cat or kitten into the classroom for observational purposes. Have the children observe the eating, sleeping, and moving of the cat. Also, have them observe the cat's appearance. Then, have the children compare their observations with the presentation of cats in an informational book such as *A Cat's Body* by Joanna Cole. Finally, have the children consider the behavior of cats in a folktale such as Charles Perrault's *Puss in Boots* and a fantasy such as Ursula K. LeGuin's *Catwings*. Finally, have the children discuss the differences in behavior and identify different purposes for writing and reading these types of literature.

 ## SUGGESTED ACTIVITIES

for Involving Children in Biographies and Informational Books

- Prepare a sequencing game that identifies both the cues and the directions for a dramatic activity. Share the game with a group of children.

- Select a biographical incident that you believe would make an excellent "You Are There" creative dramatization. Identify the introductory scene and circumstances, the consecutive scenes to use, the characters to involve, and the questions to ask children while they discuss and develop the drama.

- Select several biographies written about the same person. Plan a discussion that encourages children to consider the strengths and weaknesses of each biography.

- Identify the parts of a book that are necessary if children are to use informational materials effectively at a particular grade level. Choose a specific part of a book, such as the table of contents, index, glossary, or bibliography of further readings, and select several informational books to encourage the development and use of this aid. Prepare an activity that increases children's understanding of that part of the book.

- Visit a public library or school library. What reference aids are available to assist children in finding nonfiction materials? Ask librarians how they help children find information.

- Choose several books by authors who have effectively presented the meanings of new technical terminology through text or photographs, diagrams, and charts. Share the books with a peer group and suggest how you would use the books with children.

- Search through a science or social studies curriculum to identify the graphic aids that children at a particular grade level are expected to use, understand, or develop themselves. Develop an annotated bibliography of informational books that include accurate, clear graphic aids. Include page numbers for each aid that you identify.

- Choose a reading-for-meaning requirement for science-related materials. Use a science-related book not discussed in this chapter, develop a lesson to encourage children to find the main idea of a selection, to identify supporting details, or to note the author's organization.

- Select an informational book that encourages children to perform an experiment in order to understand a scientific principle. Perform the experiment as directed. Are the directions clear? Should they be modified or clarified for use with children? Make any necessary modifications, and encourage a child to perform the experiment. Follow each step of the experiment and discuss the scientific principle with the child.

- Develop a lesson that encourages children to critically evaluate what they read, including the author's purpose for writing the book, the author's competence, and the adequacy and accuracy of the content.

- With older students try one of the activities developed in Larry R. Johannessen's *Teaching the Literature of the Vietnam War* (1992). Develop a lesson around another time in history such as World War I or World War II.

CHILDREN'S LITERATURE

BIOGRAPHIES

Adler, David. *Christopher Columbus: Great Explorer.* Illustrated by Lyle Miller. Holiday House, 1991 (I:6–10 R:4). This is a brief biography of Columbus.

Aliki. *The King's Day: Louis XIV of France.* Crowell, 1989 (I:8+ R:6). This is a highly illustrated depiction of life and customs in seventeenth- and eighteenth-century France.

Anderson, William. *Pioneer Girl.* Illustrated by Dan Andreson. HarperCollins, 1998 (I:7+ R:4). This is a picture-book biography of Laura Ingalls Wilder.

Ashby, Ruth, and Deborah Gore Ohrn, eds. *HerStory: Women Who Changed the World.* Viking, 1995 (I:9+ R:6). The text provides a history through short biographies of women.

Bains, Rae. *Harriet Tubman: The Road to Freedom*. Illustrated by Larry Johnson. Troll, 1982 (I:8–12 R:4). This is an illustrated version of Tubman's experiences with the Underground Railroad.

Bitton-Jackson, Livia. *I Have Lived a Thousand Years: Growing Up in the Holocaust*. Simon & Schuster, 1997 (I:12+ R:6). A girl tells about living in a Jewish ghetto and in Auschwitz.

Blumberg, Rhoda. *Commodore Perry in the Land of the Shogun*. Lothrop, Lee & Shepard, 1985 (I:10+ R:6). In 1853, Perry leads an expedition to open trade with Japan.

———. *The Remarkable Voyages of Captain Cook*. Bradbury, 1991 (I:9+ R:6). This is an account of the discovery of Australia and Hawaii.

Bode, Janet. *Beating the Odds*. Watts, 1991 (I:12+ R:6). This text focuses on teenagers who have battled against unexpected circumstances.

Brewster, Hugh. *Anastasia's Album*. Hyperion, 1996 (I:10+ R:6). This book about the Russian Czar's youngest daughter is illustrated with photographs from the family's albums.

Brooks, Polly Schoyer. *Queen Eleanor: Independent Spirit of the Medieval World*. Lippincott, 1983 (I:10+ R:8). This is a biography of the twelfth-century queen.

Carpenter, Angelica Shirley, and Jean Shirley. *Frances Hodgson Burnett: Beyond the Secret Garden*. Lerner, 1990 (I:8+ R:5). This is a biography about the author of *The Secret Garden*.

Christopher, Matt. *In the Huddle with . . . Steve Young*. Little, Brown, 1996 (I:9+ R:5). This is a biography of the quarterback of the San Francisco 49ers.

Cleary, Beverly. *A Girl from Yamhill: A Memoir*. Morrow, 1988 (I:8+ R:5). This popular author tells of her early life through high school.

Cooney, Barbara. *Eleanor*. Viking, 1996 (I:5–9 R:4). This is a heavily illustrated biography of Eleanor Roosevelt as a young girl.

Dalgliesh, Alice. *The Columbus Story*. Illustrated by Leo Politi. Scribner's Sons, 1955 (I:5–8 R:3). A picture book provides a version of Columbus's first voyage to America.

Dalokay, Vedat. *Sister Shako and Kolo the Goat: Memories of My Childhood in Turkey*. Translated by Guner Ener. Lothrop, Lee & Shepard, 1994 (I:10+ R:5). The former mayor of Ankara recalls memories of childhood.

D'Aulaire, Ingri, and Edgar Parin D'Aulaire. *Abraham Lincoln*. Doubleday, 1939, 1957 (I:8–11 R:5). This is a book for young children.

———. *Benjamin Franklin*. Doubleday, 1950 (I:8–12 R:6). This is a colorfully illustrated biography.

———. *Columbus*. Doubleday, 1955 (I:7–10 R:5). This is a colorfully illustrated biography.

Denenberg, Barry. *An American Hero: The True Story of Charles A. Lindbergh*. Scholastic, 1996 (I:12+ R:8). A biography of the aviator.

Duggleby, John. *Artist in Overalls: The Life of Grant Wood*. Chronicle, 1995 (I:8+ R:8). This is a biography of the artist whose most famous painting is "American Gothic."

I = Interest by Age Range.

R = Readability by Grade Level.

Faber, Doris. *Calamity Jane: Her Life and Her Legend*. Houghton Mifflin, 1992 (I:8+ R:4). This is a biography of the Wild West heroine.

Ferber, Elizabeth. *Yasir Arafat: A Life of War and Peace*. Millbrook, 1995 (I:12+ R:12). This biography develops the life of the emerging Palestinian leader.

Fisher, Leonard Everett. *Prince Henry the Navigator*. Macmillan, 1990 (I:7–10 R:5). This is an illustrated biography of the Portuguese prince whose school of navigation expanded understanding of the seas.

Fleischman, Sid. *The Abracadabra Kid: A Writer's Life*. Greenwillow, 1996 (I:10+ R:6). An autobiography of the author.

Foreman, Michael. *After the War Was Over*. Arcade, 1996 (I:all). This is an illustrated autobiography of Foreman's experiences after World War II.

———. *War Boy: A Country Childhood*. Arcade, 1990 (I:all). The author focuses on his experiences growing up in England during World War II.

Franchere, Ruth. *Cesar Chavez*. Illustrated by Earl Thollander. Crowell, 1970 (I:7–9 R:4). This is an illustrated biography of Chavez's struggles to improve the pay and living conditions of migrant workers.

Frank, Anne. *The Diary of a Young Girl: The Definitive Edition*. Edited by Otto H. Frank and Mirjam Pressler. Translated by Susan Massotty. Doubleday, 1995 (I:12+ R:8). This autobiography includes material not included in the earlier diary.

Freedman, Russell. *Eleanor Roosevelt: A Life of Discovery*. Clarion, 1993 (I:8+ R:5). This is a detailed biography about this political leader.

———. *Franklin Delano Roosevelt*. Clarion, 1990 (I:8+ R:5). Numerous photographs accompany the text.

———. *Lincoln: A Photobiography*. Clarion, 1987 (I:8+ R:6). This is a carefully documented biography of Abraham Lincoln.

———. *Out of Darkness: The Story of Louis Braille*. Illustrated by Kate Kiesler. Clarion, 1997 (I:8+ R:5). The book chronicles Braille's life and his development of the alphabet for the blind.

———. *The Wright Brothers: How They Invented the Airplane*. Holiday House, 1991 (I:all). Photographs help document the life and accomplishments of the Wright Brothers.

Fritz, Jean. *Bully for You, Teddy Roosevelt!* Illustrated by Mike Wimmer. Putnam, 1991 (I:8+ R:5). This is a biography of the president who lived between 1858 and 1919.

———. *The Great Little Madison*. Putnam, 1989 (I:9+ R:6). This biography traces the life of the fourth president of the United States.

———. *Make Way for Sam Houston*. Illustrated by Elise Primavera. Putnam, 1986 (I:9 R:6). This is the biography of a nineteenth-century hero.

———. *Stonewall*. Illustrated by Stephen Gammell. Putnam, 1979 (I:10+ R:6). This is a biography of a famous Civil War general, Thomas Jackson.

———. *Traitor: The Case of Benedict Arnold*. Putnam, 1981 (I:8+ R:5). This is the life of the man who chose the British cause in the Revolutionary War.

———. *What's the Big Idea, Ben Franklin?* Illustrated by Margot Tomes. Coward, McCann, 1978 (I:7–10 R:5). This is a biography of the inventor, ambassador, and coauthor of the Declaration of Independence.

_____. *Where Do You Think You're Going, Christopher Columbus?* Illustrated by Margot Tomes. Putnam, 1980 (I:7–12 R:5). Fritz's style creates a believable background for the four voyages of Columbus.

_____. *Where Was Patrick Henry on the 29th of May?* Illustrated by Margot Tomes. Coward, McCann, 1975 (I:7–10 R:5). This is a humorous telling of incidents in Patrick Henry's youth and political career.

_____. *Why Don't You Get a Horse, Sam Adams?* Illustrated by Trina Schart Hyman. Coward, McCann, 1974 (I:7–10 R:5). This is a humorous story about Samuel Adams, his refusal to ride a horse, and his final decision to ride.

Gherman, Beverly. *E. B. White: Some Writer!* Atheneum, 1992 (I:10+ R:5). The biographer develops the life of the author of *Charlotte's Web*.

Gish, Lillian, as told to Selma Lanes. *An Actor's Life for Me!* Illustrated by Patricia Lincoln. Viking, 1987 (I:8+ R:6). This is a biography of Gish's childhood years.

Gold, Alison Leslie. *Memories of Anne Frank: Reflections of a Childhood Friend.* Scholastic, 1997 (I:8+ R:6). This biography is told through the viewpoint of Hannah Goslar, Anne Frank's friend.

Goodsell, Jane. *Eleanor Roosevelt.* Illustrated by Wendell Minor. Crowell, 1970 (I:7–10 R:2). This book tells of Eleanor's life as a shy child, as well as her years in the White House and her work after her husband's death.

Greenfield, Eloise, and Lessie Jones Little. *Childtimes: A Three-Generation Memoir.* Crowell, 1979 (I:10+ R:5). Three African American women tell about their childhood.

Gross, Ruth Belov. *True Stories About Abraham Lincoln.* Illustrated by Jill Kastner. Lothrop, Lee & Shepard, 1990 (I:7–10 R:4). This book includes a series of short stories that emphasize aspects of Lincoln's life, especially his early years.

Hamilton, Virginia. *Anthony Burns: The Defeat and Triumph of a Fugitive Slave.* Knopf, 1988 (I:10+ R:6). This is the story of the escaped slave whose trial caused riots in Boston.

Harness, Cheryl. *Abe Lincoln Goes to Washington: 1837–1865.* National Geographic, 1997 (I:5–9 R:4). This heavily illustrated book presents facts about Lincoln's family life and career.

Haskins, James. *I Have a Dream: The Life and Words of Martin Luther King, Jr.* Millbrook, 1993 (I:10+ R:6). This biography examines King's life and achievements.

_____. *Spike Lee: By Any Means Necessary.* Walker, 1997 (I:12+ R:6). The biography includes a bibliography, photographs, and notes.

_____. *Thurgood Marshall: A Life for Justice.* Holt, 1992 (I:10+ R:6). This is a biography of the first African American Supreme Court justice.

Hodges, Margaret. *Making a Difference: The Story of an American Family.* Scribner's Sons, 1989 (I:12+ R:6). This is the biography of Mary Sherwood, 1864–1963.

Hyman, Trina Schart. *Self-Portrait: Trina Schart Hyman.* Addison-Wesley, 1981 (I:9–12 R:5). This is the autobiography of an artist.

Jakes, John. *Susanna of the Alamo.* Illustrated by Paul Bacon. Harcourt Brace Jovanovich, 1986 (I:7–12 R:6). A survivor of the Alamo retells the story of the battle.

Johnson, Rebecca L. *Braving the Frozen Frontier: Women Working in Antarctica.* Lerner, 1997 (I:9+ R:6). The text focuses on the women scientists who work in Antarctica.

Johnston, Norma. *Louisa May: The World and Works of Louisa May Alcott.* Four Winds, 1991 (I:10+ R:6). This is a biography of the author of *Little Women*.

Josephson, Judith Pinkerton. *Mother Jones: Fierce Fighter for Workers' Rights.* Lerner, 1997 (I:10+ R:6). This is a biography of a labor organizer.

Kent, Zachary. *Christopher Columbus: Expeditions to the New World.* Children's Press, 1991 (I:10+ R:6). Numerous illustrations add to the life and times of Columbus.

Kherdian, David. *The Road from Home: The Story of an Armenian Girl.* Greenwillow, 1979 (I:12+ R:6). In 1915, an Armenian girl experiences the horrors of the Turkish persecution of Christian minorities.

Krull, Kathleen. *Lives of the Musicians: Good Times, Bad Times (And What the Neighbors Thought).* Harcourt Brace Jovanovich, 1993 (I:9+ R:5). This book includes biographical sketches about famous musicians.

Kunhardt, Edith. *Honest Abe.* Illustrated by Malcah Zeldis. Greenwillow, 1993 (I:5–8 R:4). This is a highly illustrated biography of the former president.

Lasker, Joe. *The Great Alexander the Great.* Viking, 1983 (I:6–9 R:6). This is a highly illustrated version of the life of the conqueror.

Lasky, Kathryn. *The Librarian Who Measured the Earth.* Illustrated by Kevin Hawkes. Little, Brown, 1994 (I:8+ R:6). This is a heavily illustrated biography.

Leiner, Katherine. *First Children: Growing Up in the White House.* Illustrated by Katie Keller. Tambourine, 1996 (I:10+ R:9). The author uses a chronological order to develop the lives of presidential children from Washington to Clinton.

Lester, Helen. *Author: A True Story.* Houghton Mifflin, 1997 (I:all). The author tells about her experiences writing children's books.

Levine, Ellen. *Anna Pavlova: Genius of the Dance.* Scholastic, 1995 (I:12+ R:9). A biography of the Russian ballerina.

Levison, Nancy Smiler. *Christopher Columbus: Voyager to the Unknown.* Lodestar, 1990 (I:9+ R:5). Author's notes, a chronology of events, articles of capitulation, a letter of introduction, a listing of crews, suggested readings, and an index add to the biography.

Lipman, Jean, and Margaret Aspinwall. *Alexander Calder and His Magical Mobiles.* Hudson Hills, 1981 (I:9+ R:6). This book begins with the artist's early work and illustrates his work in wood, bronze, wire, and mobiles.

Lowe, Steve, ed. *Log of Christopher Columbus: The First Voyage: Spring, Summer & Fall, 1492.* Illustrated by Robert Sabuda. Philomel, 1992 (I:all). This book provides a day-by-day commentary on Columbus's voyage.

Macy, Sue. *Winning Ways: A Photohistory of American Women in Sports.* Holt, 1996 (I:12+ R:7). This is a history of outstanding women in sports.

Marrin, Albert. *Commander In Chief: Abraham Lincoln and the Civil War.* (I:10+ R:7). The author includes direct quotations and period photographs.

_____. *Hitler.* Viking, 1987 (I:10+ R:7). This biography emphasizes Hitler's rise to power, his victories, and his final defeat.

_____. *Stalin: Russia's Man of Steel.* Viking, 1988 (I:10+ R:7). This biography emphasizes how Stalin shaped Russia.

Meltzer, Milton. *Andrew Jackson and His America.* Watts, 1993 (I:10+ R:6). This biography includes source notes as well as suggestions for additional topics to research.

———. *Benjamin Franklin: The New American.* Watts, 1988 (I:10+ R:6). This is a carefully documented biography of an American statesman.

———. *Columbus and the World Around Him.* Watts, 1990 (I:10+ R:6). A list of sources and index add to the depiction of Columbus and his voyages.

———. *Dorothea Lange, Life Through the Camera.* Viking, 1985 (I:10+ R:5). Lange's photographs increase understanding of the photographer.

———. *George Washington and the Birth of Our Nation.* Watts, 1986 (I:10+ R:6). A comprehensive biography tells of Washington from his birth through his leadership years and his death.

———. *Starting from Home: A Writer's Beginnings.* Viking Kestrel, 1988 (I:10+ R:5). This book tells the early life experiences of the biographical author.

———. *Thomas Jefferson: The Revolutionary Aristocrat.* Watts, 1991 (I:10+ R:6). This is a biography of the president who lived between 1734 and 1826.

Meryman, Richard. *Andrew Wyeth.* Abrams, 1991 (I:10+ R:6). This biography of the artist is heavily illustrated with reproductions of his paintings.

Miller, Douglas. *Frederick Douglass and the Fight for Freedom.* Facts on File, 1988 (I:10+ R:6). This book tells the life of the black leader who escaped slavery to become a political leader.

Murphy, Jim. *A Young Patriot: The American Revolution as Experienced by One Boy.* Clarion, 1996 (I:10+ R:6). The author tells about the war through the eyes of a boy who enlisted in 1776.

Myers, Elizabeth. *John D. Rockefeller: Boy Financier.* Bobbs-Merrill, 1973 (I:8+ R:5). This text covers the early life of a financial giant.

———. *Thomas Paine: Common Sense Boy.* Bobbs-Merrill, 1976 (I:8+ R:5). This text covers the early life of a political hero.

Nardo, Don. *The Importance of Cleopatra.* Lucent, 1994 (I:12+ R:8). This biography discusses the life of the ruler of Egypt.

Neimark, Anne E. *A Deaf Child Listened: Thomas Gallaudet, Pioneer in American Education.* Morrow, 1983 (I:10+ R:7). This book traces the life of the founder of American education for the deaf.

Novac, Ana. *The Beautiful Days of My Youth: My Six Months in Auschwitz and Plaszow.* Translated by George L. Newman. Holt, 1997 (I:12+). This is a memoir of survival.

Orgill, Roxane. *If I Only Had a Horn: Young Louis Armstrong.* Illustrated by Leonard Jenkins. Houghton Mifflin, 1997 (I:4–8 R:4). This is a highly illustrated biography of the jazz musician.

Paolucci, Bridget. *Beverly Sills.* Chelsea House, 1990 (I:12+ R:7). This biography tells about the life of the opera singer.

Pasachoff, Naomi. *Alexander Graham Bell: Making Connections.* Oxford University Press, 1996 (I:10+ R:6). The emphasis in this biography is on Bell's work as an inventor and an educator.

Patterson, Lillie. *Frederick Douglass: Freedom Fighter.* Garrard, 1965 (I:6–9 R:3). This is the biography of a great African American leader.

———. *Martin Luther King, Jr. and the Freedom Movement.* Facts on File, 1989 (I:10+ R:6). This book tells of King's nonviolent struggles against segregation.

Paulsen, Gary. *Woodsong.* Bradbury, 1990 (I:10+ R:6). This autobiography explores the author's life in the wilderness.

Pearce, Carol Ann. *Amelia Earhart.* Facts on File, 1988 (I:8+ R:5). This book tells about the first woman pilot to fly across the Atlantic Ocean.

Peet, Bill. *Bill Peet: An Autobiography.* Houghton Mifflin, 1989 (I:all R:5). This text is highlighted with numerous drawings by Peet.

Porter, A. P. *Jump at de Sun: The Story of Zora Neale Hurston.* Carolrhoda, 1992 (I:8+ R:5). This is a biography of the African American writer and storyteller.

Provensen, Alice, and Martin Provensen. *The Glorious Flight Across the Channel with Louis Bleriot, July 25, 1909.* Viking, 1983 (I:all R:4). This is a highly illustrated account of the first flight across the English Channel.

Quackenbush, Robert. *Mark Twain? What Kind of a Name Is That? A Story of Samuel Langhorne Clemens.* Prentice-Hall, 1984 (I:7–10 R:5). Humorous illustrations appeal to younger readers.

Reiss, Johanna. *The Upstairs Room.* Crowell, 1972 (I:11 R:4). This is the story of a Jewish girl's experience in hiding from the Nazis.

Roop, Peter, and Connie Roop, eds. *I, Columbus—My Journal 1492.* Illustrated by Peter Hanson. Walker, 1900 (I:all). This book is edited from a journal of Columbus.

Roosevelt, Elliott. *Eleanor Roosevelt, with Love.* Dutton, 1984 (I:10+ R:7). Eleanor's life is told from the viewpoint of her son.

Rosen, Sidney. *Galileo and the Magic Numbers.* Illustrated by Harie Stein. Little, Brown, 1958 (I:10+ R:6). This story tells about the astronomer and mathematician who invented the first telescope.

Sandburg, Carl. *Abe Lincoln Grows Up.* Illustrated by James Daugherty. Harcourt Brace Jovanovich, 1926, 1928, 1954 (I:10+ R:6). This book tells about the first nineteen years of Lincoln's life.

———. *Abraham Lincoln: The Prairie Years.* Harcourt Brace Jovanovich, 1926 (I:12+ R:7). This biography covers a portion of Lincoln's life.

Schwartz, Gary. *Rembrandt.* Abrams, 1992 (I:10+ R:6). This biography of the artist is heavily illustrated with reproductions of his paintings.

Scott, John Anthony, and Robert Alan Scott. *John Brown of Harper's Ferry.* Facts on File, 1988 (I:10+ R:6). This book tells about an abolitionist.

Severance, John B. *Gandhi, Great Soul.* Clarion, 1997 (I:10+ R:6). In addition to his life, the author discusses Gandhi's impact on other leaders.

Sills, Leslie. *Inspirations: Stories About Women Artists.* Whitman, 1989 (I:8+ R:5). This book includes biographical sketches of four artists.

———. *Visions: Stories About Women Artists.* Whitman, 1993 (I:8+ R:5). This book includes biographical sketches and examples of the works of Mary Cassatt, Betye Saar, Leonore Carrington, and Mary Frank.

Sim, Dorrith M. *In My Pocket.* Illustrated by Gerald Fitzgerald. Harcourt Brace, 1997 (I:5–8 R:4). The author tells the story of her own experiences when she left Germany in 1939.

Sis, Peter. *Follow the Dream.* Knopf, 1991 (I:5–9 R:4). This heavily illustrated biography is for younger readers.

———. *Starry Messenger: Galileo Galilei.* Farrar, Straus & Giroux, 1996 (I:all). This heavily illustrated book includes considerable information in the illustrations.

Smith, Barry. *The First Voyage of Christopher Columbus.* Viking, 1992 (I:6–8 R:4). A sailor describes the voyage of Columbus.

Sofer, Barbara. *Shalom, Haver: Goodbye, Friend.* Kar-Ben, 1996 (I:7–9 R:5). This is a testimonial to Israeli prime minister Yitzhak Rabin.

Stanley, Diane. *Leonardo da Vinci.* Morrow, 1996 (I:all). A heavily illustrated biography of the artist.

_____ . *Peter the Great*. Four Winds, 1986 (I:8+ R:7). This is a highly illustrated biography of the emperor of Russia who lived from 1672 to 1725.

_____ , and Peter Vennema. *Cleopatra*. Illustrated by Diane Stanley. Morrow, 1994 (I:all). The illustrations in this picture biography have the quality of mosaic designs.

_____ , and Peter Vennema. *Good Queen Bess: The Story of Elizabeth I of England*. Four Winds, 1990 (I:7–10 R:5). This biography is about the queen who lived between 1533 and 1603.

_____ , and Peter Vennema. *Shaka: King of the Zulus*. Illustrated by Diane Stanley. Morrow, 1988 (I:8+ R:5). This is a biography of a Zulu chief who lived from 1787 to 1828.

Stanley, Fay. *The Last Princess: The Story of Princess Ka'iulani of Hawai'i*. Illustrated by Diane Stanley. Four Winds, 1991 (I:7–10 R:6). This is a biography of the princess who lived from 1875 to 1899.

Szabo, Corinne. *Sky Pioneer: A Photobiography of Amelia Earhart*. National Geographic, 1997 (I:8–12 R:5). There are numerous captioned black-and-white photographs in the text.

Toll, Nelly S. *Behind the Secret Window: A Memoir of a Hidden Childhood During World War Two*. Dial, 1993 (I:all R:5). This autobiography includes both experiences during the Holocaust and drawings completed during that time.

Turner, Robyn Montana. *Portraits of Women Artists for Children: Frida Kahlo*. Little, Brown, 1993 (I:8+ R:5). This book develops the life and work of the Mexican painter who lived from 1907 to 1954.

_____ . *Portraits of Women Artists for Children: Georgia O'Keeffe*. Little, Brown, 1991 (I:8+ R:5). This book develops the life and work of the painter who lived from 1887 to 1986.

_____ . *Portraits of Women Artists for Children: Mary Cassatt*. Little, Brown, 1992 (I:8+ R:5). This book develops the life and work of the painter who lived from 1844 to 1926.

_____ . *Portraits of Women Artists for Children: Rosa Bonheur*. Little, Brown, 1991 (I:8+ R:5). This book develops the life and work of the French painter who lived between 1822 and 1899.

Ventura, Piero. Based on text by Gian Paolo Ceserani. *Christopher Columbus*. Random House, 1978 (I:all R:6). This is a picture biography of Columbus.

West, Delno C., and Jean M. West. *Christopher Columbus: The Great Adventure and How We Know about It*. Atheneum, 1991 (I:10+ R:6). Boxes within the text ask and respond to many of the questions about Columbus.

Whitney, Sharon. *Eleanor Roosevelt*. Watts, 1982 (I:10+ R:5). This book follows the life of Roosevelt from childhood through work with the United Nations.

Yates, Elizabeth. *Amos Fortune, Free Man*. Illustrated by Nora S. Unwin. Dutton, 1950 (I:10+ R:6). A man is captured by slave traders in Africa and brought to Boston.

INFORMATIONAL BOOKS

Anderson, Joan. *Cowboys: Roundup on an American Ranch*. Photographs by George Ancona. Scholastic, 1996 (I:8+ R:8). A photographic essay of cowboys in New Mexico.

Appelbaum, Diana. *Giants in the Land*. Illustrated by Michael McCurdy. Houghton Mifflin, 1993 (I:6–9 R:4). This is an account of the cutting of white pines in eighteenth-century New England to use as masts of British warships.

Arnold, Caroline. *Dinosaur Mountain: Graveyard of the Past*. Photographs by Richard Hewett. Clarion, 1989 (I:8–12 R:6). Text and photographs depict excavations at Dinosaur National Monument in Utah.

_____ . *On the Brink of Extinction: The California Condor*. Photographs by Michael Wallace. Harcourt, 1993 (I:9+ R:5). This book records the mission of trying to preserve an endangered species.

_____ . *Saving the Peregrine Falcon*. Photographs by Richard R. Hewett. Carolrhoda, 1985 (I:8–12 R:7). This book describes various ways that people are trying to save the falcon from extinction.

_____ . *Stone Age Farmers Beside the Sea: Scotland's Prehistoric Village of Skara Brae*. Photographs by Arthur P. Arnold. Clarion, 1997 (I:8–12 R:6). This prehistoric village was inhabited from 3100 to 2500 b.c.

Arnold, Katya, and Sam Swope. *Katya's Book of Mushrooms*. Illustrated by Katya Arnold. Holt, 1997 (I:6–10 R:5). This is a field guide to mushroom hunting.

Arnosky, Jim. *Drawing Life in Motion*. Lothrop, Lee & Shepard, 1984 (I:all R:6). This book provides directions for drawing action in nature.

_____ . *Drawing from Nature*. Lothrop, Lee & Shepard, 1982 (I:all R:6). This book provides directions for drawing water, land, plants, and animals.

_____ . *Freshwater Fish and Fishing*. Four Winds, 1982 (I:8–12 R:5). This book provides information about trout, perch, and pike and how to catch them.

Arthur, Alex. *Shell*. Knopf, 1989 (I:9+ R:6). A highly illustrated reference book examines different types of shells.

Ash, Russell. *Incredible Comparisons*. DK, 1996 (I:10+ R:5). The author makes comparisons for such areas as speed and weight.

Ashabranner, Brent. *To Seek a Better World: The Haitian Minority in America*. Photographs by Paul Conklin. Cobblehill, 1997 (I:10+ R:6). The author provides a history of Haitian Americans.

Aylesworth, Thomas G., and Virginia Aylesworth. *The Mount St. Helens Disaster: What We've Learned*. Watts, 1983 (I:10+ R:6). This book tells about the environmental effects resulting from the volcanic eruption.

Ballard, Robert D. *Exploring the Titanic*. Scholastic, 1988 (I:8+ R:5). This book tells of the history of the ship and its discovery in the ocean.

Bartoletti, Susan Campbell. *Growing Up in Coal Country*. Houghton Mifflin, 1996 (I:10+ R:5). The text includes photographs of children working in the coal mines about one hundred years ago.

Barton, Byron. *Airport*. Crowell, 1982 (I:3–8). Large illustrations follow passengers as they get ready to board a plane.

Bash, Barbara. *Desert Giant: The World of the Saguaro Cactus*. Sierra Club/Little Brown, 1989 (I:5–9 R:4). The text and illustrations are about the life cycle of the saguaro cactus.

_____ . *Shadows of Night: The Hidden World of the Little Brown Bat*. Sierra Club, 1993 (I:5–9 R:4). Illustrations and text depict the life of the bat.

_____ . *Urban Roosts: Where Birds Nest in the City*. Little, Brown, 1990 (I:4–9 R:5). This book explores birds that live in the cities.

Bauer, Marion Dane. *What's Your Story? A Young Person's Guide to Writing Fiction.* Clarion, 1992 (I:10+ R:5). The author provides guidelines for writing various literary elements.

Beattie, Owen, and John Geiger. *Buried in Ice: The Mystery of a Lost Arctic Expedition.* Scholastic, 1992 (I:9+ R:4). This book explores the tragedy of the ships lost as they tried to discover the Northwest Passage.

Berger, Melvin. *Germs Make Me Sick!* Illustrated by Marylin Hafner. Crowell, 1985 (I:5–8 R:6). This book tells how viruses affect people.

Bergman, Thomas. *Finding a Common Language: Children Living with Deafness.* Gareth Stevens, 1989 (I:7–12 R:5). This book introduces readers to people who are deaf.

Birdseye, Debbie Holsclaw and Tom Birdseye. *What I Believe: Kids Talk about Faith.* Photographs by Robert Crum. Holiday, 1996 (I:8+ R:4). Hindu, Christian, Buddhist, Muslim, and Jewish students tell about their faith.

Bishop, Nic. *The Secrets of Animal Flight.* Illustrated by Amy Bartlett Wright. Houghton Mifflin, 1997 (I:8+ R:4). The author explores the mechanics of birds' flight.

Bitton-Jackson, Livia. *I Have Lived a Thousand Years: Growing Up in the Holocaust.* Simon & Schuster, 1997 (I:12+ R:6). The author describes Auschwitz and other experiences associated with being Jewish in Hungary.

Blumberg, Rhoda. *Commodore Perry in the Land of the Shogun.* Lothrop, Lee & Shepard, 1985 (I:9+ R:6). The illustrations depicting Japanese life in the nineteenth century add authenticity.

_____. *Full Steam Ahead: The Race to Build a Transcontinental Railroad.* National Geographic, 1996 (I:9+ R:6). Photographs and maps help tell the story of the railroad.

_____. *The Great American Gold Rush.* Bradbury, 1989 (I:9+ R:6). The text covers the California Gold Rush from 1848 to 1852.

_____. *The Incredible Journey of Lewis and Clark.* Lothrop, Lee & Shepard, 1987 (I:9+ R:6). Maps showing the journey clarify the text.

Boitano, Brian and Harper, Suzanne. *Boitano's Edge: Inside the Real World of Figure Skating.* Simon & Schuster, 1997 (I:8+ R:4). Skating information and personal anecdotes present an interesting text.

Booth, Jerry. *You Animal!* Illustrated by Nancy King. Harcourt Brace, 1996 (I:8+ R:4). The text includes a variety of activities.

Brandenburg, Jim. *An American Safari: Adventures on the North American Prairie.* Walker, 1995 (I:8+ R:5). Photographs and text present the ecology of the prairie.

_____. *Sand and Fog: Adventures in Southern Africa.* Walker, 1994 (I:10+ R:5). The focus for this photographic essay is Namibia in southwest Africa.

Branley, Franklyn M. *Saturn: The Spectacular Planet.* Illustrated by Leonard Kessler. Harper & Row, 1983 (I:9+ R:6). This book uses information from the *Pioneer* and *Voyager* space explorations.

Brenner, Barbara. *If You Were There in 1492.* Macmillan, 1991 (I:8+ R:5). This book describes fifteenth-century Europe.

Brown, Laurie Krasny, and Marc Brown. *Dinosaurs to the Rescue! A Guide to Protecting Our Planet.* Little, Brown, 1992 (I:5–8 R:4). Humorous cartoon figures provide environmental guidelines.

Brown, Mary Barrett. *Wings Along the Waterway.* Orchard, 1992 (I:10+ R:6). Illustrations and text explore the birds living in wetlands across the United States.

Bruun, Ruth Dowling, and Bertel Bruun. *The Human Body.* Illustrated by Patricia J. Wynne. Random, 1982 (I:9+ R:6). This book provides an overview of the body systems.

Bunting, Eve. *I Am the Mummy Heb-Nefert.* Illustrated by David Christiana. Harcourt Brace, 1997 (I:all). This picture book provides considerable information about life in early Egypt.

Burandt, Harriet and Shelly Dale. *Tales from the Homeplace: Adventures of a Texas Farm Girl.* Holt, 1997 (I:9+ R:5). The author tells about growing up on a cotton farm in the Depression.

Burgel, Paul Hermann, and Manfred Hartwig. *Gorillas.* Carolrhoda, 1992 (I:8+ R:5). Photographs show the life of gorillas in the rainforests.

Carr, Terry. *Spill! The Story of the Exxon Valdez.* Watts, 1991 (I:8+ R:6). Photographs show the destruction in Alaska's Prince William Sound.

Carrick, Carol. *Whaling Days.* Illustrated by David Frampton. Clarion, 1993 (I:8+ R:4). This is a history of Yankee whalers.

Carrick, Donald. *Milk.* Greenwillow, 1985 (I:4–8). Large illustrations trace milk from a dairy farm to a grocery store.

Carroll, Colleen. *How Artists See Animals: Mammal Fish Bird Reptile.* Abbeville, 1996 (I:all). Paintings of animals are discussed.

_____. *How Artists See the Elements: Earth Air Fire Water.* Abbeville, 1996 (I:all). The author discusses paintings of the elements.

_____. *How Artists See People: Boy Girl Man Woman.* Abbeville, 1996 (I:all). The author uses paintings of people to discuss art.

Cerullo, Mary M. *The Octopus: Phantom of the Sea.* Photographs by Jeffery L. Rotman. Cobblehill, 1997 (I:9+ R:5). Photographs help inform readers about this intelligent sea animal.

_____. *Sharks: Challengers of the Deep.* Photographs by Jeffrey L. Rotman. Cobblehill, 1993 (I:9+ R:5). This book describes the physical characteristics of the shark.

Clifford, Nick. *Incredible Earth.* DK, 1996 (I:10+ R:6). Diagrams and drawings explain the earth's structure.

Climo, Shirley. *Someone Saw a Spider: Spider Facts and Folktales.* Illustrated by Dirk Zimmer. Crowell, 1985 (I:10+ R:6). The author retells spider folktales and discusses facts about spiders.

Cole, Joanna. *A Bird's Body.* Photographs by Jerome Wexler. Morrow, 1983 (I:8–12 R:4). Photographs and diagrams show the anatomy of birds.

_____. *Cars and How They Go.* Illustrated by Gail Gibbons. Harper & Row, 1983 (I:6–10 R:4). This is a simplified explanation of how parts of the car function.

_____. *A Cat's Body.* Photographs by Jerome Wexler. Morrow, 1982 (I:6–12 R:4). Photographs and text show how a cat responds physically in different moods and activities.

_____. *Cuts, Breaks, Bruises and Burns: How Your Body Heals.* Illustrated by True Kelley. Crowell, 1985 (I:8–10 R:4). This book tells how the body heals various injuries.

_____. *A Horse's Body.* Photographs by Jerome Wexler. Morrow, 1981 (I:2–6 R:5). The text explains the horse's anatomy.

_____. *How You Were Born.* Photographs by Margaret Miller. Morrow, 1993 (I:4–8 R:4). This is a book about birth for young children.

_____ . *The Human Body: How We Evolved.* Illustrated by Walter Gaffney-Kessell and Juan Carolos Barberis. Morrow, 1987 (I:10+ R:5). This book traces the development of humans from prehistoric ancestors.

_____ . *An Insect's Body.* Photographs by Jerome Wexler and Raymond A. Mendez. Morrow, 1984 (I:8–12 R:4). The anatomy of a cricket is explained in text and photographs.

_____ . *The Magic School Bus: Inside the Earth.* Illustrated by Bruce Degen. Scholastic, 1987 (I:6–8 R:4). This book provides a humorous approach to the study of the earth.

_____ . *The Magic School Bus: Lost in the Solar System.* Illustrated by Bruce Degen. Scholastic, 1990 (I:6–8 R:4). This is a humorous approach to the study of the planets and the solar system.

_____ . *The Magic School Bus: On the Ocean Floor.* Illustrated by Bruce Degen. Scholastic, 1992 (I:6–8 R:4). This is a humorous approach to the study of oceans and marine animals.

_____ . *My Puppy Is Born.* Photographs by Jerome Wexler. Morrow, 1991 (I:7–9 R:2). The text and photographs follow puppies from their birth through their first eight weeks of life.

Collard, Sneed B. *Animal Dads.* Illustrated by Steve Jenkins. Houghton Mifflin, 1997 (I:5–8 R:4). Cut-paper collages illustrate various fish, birds, and mammals.

Colman, Penny. *Corpses, Coffins, and Crypts; A History of Burial.* Holt, 1997 (I:10+ R:6). The author describes rituals and ceremonies.

Commoner, Barry. *Making Peace with the Planet.* Pantheon, 1990 (I:12+ R:7). The author discusses various influences on nature.

Cone, Molly. *Come Back, Salmon.* Photographs by Sidnee Wheelwright. Sierra Club, 1992 (I:8+ R:5). A group of elementary-school children improve the fish habitat in Washington state.

_____ . *Squishy, Misty, Damp & Muddy: The In-Between World of Wetlands.* Sierra Club, 1996 (I:all R:7). The author describes the wetlands and their purposes.

Couper, Heather, and Nigel Henbest. *The Space Atlas: A Pictorial Atlas of Our Universe.* Harcourt Brace Jovanovich, 1992 (I:8+ R:5). Using a large-book format, the authors provide numerous details about space.

Cowan, Paul. *A Torah Is Written.* Photographs by Rachel Cowan. Jewish Publication Society, 1986 (I:all R:5). This book describes the process for creating handwritten Torah scrolls.

Cummins, Julie. *The Inside-Outside Book of Libraries.* Illustrated by Roxie Munroe. Dutton, 1996 (I:6–9 R:4). The text explores thirteen different libraries.

Davidson, Rosemary. *Take a Look: An Introduction to the Experience of Art.* Viking, 1994 (I:10+ R:6). Develops an introduction to art appreciation and purposes for art.

dePaola, Tomie. *The Popcorn Book.* Holiday House, 1978 (I:3–8 R:5). The illustrations and story present facts about popcorn.

Duke, Kate. *Archaeologists Dig for Clues.* HarperCollins, 1997 (I:6–9 R:5). The text includes sidebars that add additional information.

Dyson, John. *Westward with Columbus.* Photographs by Peter Christopher. Scholastic, 1991 (I:10+ R:5). The photographs are taken from a replica of the *Nina*.

East, Katherine. *A King's Treasure: The Sutton Hoo Ship Burial.* Illustrated by Dinah Cohen. Kestrel, 1982 (I:9+ R:8). The text and illustrations describe the excavation of the burial ground of a seventh-century king.

Englander, Roger. *Opera, What's All the Screaming About?* Walker, 1983 (I:10+ R:7). This is a listener's guide to opera.

Esbensen, Barbara Juster. *Echoes for the Eye: Poems to Celebrate Patterns in Nature.* Illustrated by Helen K. Davie. Harper-Collins, 1996 (I:all). The poems celebrate patterns in nature.

_____ . *Tiger with Wings: The Great Horned Owl.* Illustrated by Mary Barrett Brown. Orchard, 1991 (I:5–9 R:4). Illustrations and text depict the life of the great horned owl and how it is influenced by interactions with people.

Eschle, Lou. *The Curse of Tutankhamen.* Lucent, 1994 (I:9+ R:7). This book discusses the conflicting theories about the deaths associated with the 1922 opening of King Tut's tomb.

Faber, Doris, and Harold Faber. *The Birth of a Nation: The Early Years of the United States.* Scribner's Sons, 1989 (I:10+ R:7). This book covers major events in early United States history.

_____ . *We the People: The Story of the United States Constitution Since 1787.* Scribner's Sons, 1987 (I:10+ R:7). This book discusses the writing of the Constitution and subsequent changes in the Constitution.

Faber, Harold. *The Discoverers of America.* Scribner's Sons, 1992 (I:10+ R:7). In a comprehensive text, the author chronicles the discoverers of America.

Facklam, Margery. *Creepy, Crawly Caterpillars.* Little, Brown, 1996 (I:4–9 R:7). This book describes thirteen different types of caterpillars.

_____ . *Tracking Dinosaurs in the Gobi.* 21st Century, 1997 (I:10+ R:6). This is the story of the American expedition in the 1920s.

_____ . *Who Harnessed the Horse? The Story of Animal Domestication.* Illustrated by Steven Parton. Little, Brown, 1992 (I:10+ R:5). This book details the ways in which humans and animals have worked together.

_____ , and Howard Facklam. *Changes in the Wind: Earth's Shifting Climate.* Harcourt Brace Jovanovich, 1986 (I:10+ R:7). This book, which includes a glossary, a bibliography, and an index, discusses changes in climate.

Fagan, Brian M. *The Great Journey: The Peopling of Ancient America.* Thames & Hudson, 1987 (I:10+ R:7). This book tells the history of early people in North America.

Falk, John H., et. al. *Bubble Monster: And Other Science Fun.* Illustrated by Charles C. Somerville. Chicago Review, 1996 (I:4–8). The text includes directions for science activities for adults to use with children.

Feldbaum, Carl B., and Ronald J. Bee. *Looking the Tiger in the Eye: Confronting the Nuclear Threat.* Harper & Row, 1988 (I:12+ R:7). This book tells the history of nuclear weapons.

Finkelstein, Norman. *The Other Fourteen Ninety-Two: Jewish Settlement in the New World.* Scribner's Sons, 1989 (I:10+ R:6). This book describes the history of the Jewish people as a consequence of the expulsion from Spain in 1492.

_____ . *Sounds in the Air: The Golden Age of Radio.* Scribner's Sons, 1993 (I:10+ R:6). This is a history of radio programs in the 1930s and 1940s.

Fischer-Nagel, Heiderose, and Andraes Fischer-Nagel. *Life of the Honey Bee.* Carolrhoda, 1986 (I:6–10 R:6). Close-up photographs show various stages in the life cycle of the honey bee.

Fisher, Leonard Everett. *The Alamo.* Holiday House, 1987 (I:8+ R:7). This is a history of the fort in San Antonio, Texas.

_____ . *The Great Wall of China.* Macmillan, 1986 (I:all R:6). This is a highly illustrated history of the Great Wall.

———. *The Tower of London*. Macmillan, 1987 (I:all R:6). This is a highly illustrated history of the tower.

———. *The Wailing Wall*. Macmillan, 1989 (I:all R:6). This is a highly illustrated history of the Wailing Wall in Jerusalem.

Fleisher, Paul. *Life Cycles of a Dozen Diverse Creatures*. Millbrook, 1996 (I:9+ R:6). The text discusses the life cycles of twelve animals.

Ford, Michael Thomas. *100 Questions and Answers About AIDS: A Guide for Young People*. New Discovery Books, 1992 (I:10+ R:7). The emphasis of the book is on AIDS prevention.

Freedman, Russell. *Dinosaurs and Their Young*. Illustrated by Leslie Morrill. Holiday House, 1983 (I:6–9 R:4). This is a picture-book version of discoveries about the duck-billed dinosaurs.

Friedman, David. *Focus on Drugs and the Brain*. Illustrated by David Neuhaus. 21st Century Books, 1990 (I:10+ R:6). The author discusses how drugs affect the brain.

Friedman, Judi. *Operation Siberian Crane: The Story Behind the International Effort to Save an Amazing Bird*. Macmillan, 1992 (I:10+ R:5). The author chronicles the efforts of the International Crane Foundation.

Fritz, Jean. *Shh! We're Writing the Constitution*. Illustrated by Tomie dePaola. Putnam, 1987 (I:7–10 R:5). This is a description of the Constitutional Convention of 1787.

———, et al. *The World in 1492*. Illustrated by Stefano Vitale. Holt, 1992 (I:8+). This book includes sections written by different authors.

Funston, Sylvia. *The Dinosaur Question and Answer Book*. Little, Brown, 1992 (I:all). Findings from the Dinosaur Project are used to answer questions.

Gallant, Roy A. *Ancient Indians: The First Americans*. Enslow, 1989 (I:10+ R:6). This book discusses the early Indian cultures.

———. *Before the Sun Dies: The Story of Evolution*. Macmillan, 1989 (I:10+ R:6). This text presents theories and scientific thinking about the earth.

Gatti, Anne, retold by. *The Magic Flute*. Illustrated by Peter Malone. Chronicle, 1997 (I:8+). An enclosed CD of the opera is coded to each page in the book.

George, Jean Craighead. *Everglades*. Illustrated by Wendell Minor. HarperCollins, 1995 (I:7+ R:5). This story about ecology presents the history of the Everglades.

George, William T. *Box Turtle at Long Pond*. Illustrated by Lindsay Barrett George. Greenwillow, 1989 (I:3–8 R:3). An illustrated book introduces turtles to young children.

Gibbons, Gail. *Beacons of Light: Lighthouses*. Morrow, 1990 (I:7–9 R:4). The illustrations and text present the history of lighthouses.

———. *Dinosaurs*. Holiday House, 1987 (I:4–8 R:3). This is a highly illustrated and simplified text.

Giblin, James Cross. *From Hand to Mouth: Or, How We Invented Knives, Forks, Spoons, and Chopsticks & the Table Manners to Go with Them*. Crowell, 1987 (I:8+ R:6). This is a history of table etiquette.

Gillette, J. Lynett. *Dinosaur Ghosts: The Mystery of Coelophysis*. Illustrated by Douglas Henderson. Dial, 1997 (I:9+ R:6). The author examines ways that scientists try to answer the mysteries of the death of the dinosaurs.

Goldin, Barbara. *The Passover Journey: A Seder Companion*. Illustrated by Neil Waldman. Viking, 1994 (I:all). The text details the traditions of Passover.

Goodall, Jane. *The Chimpanzee Family Book*. Photographs by Michael Neugebauer. Picture Book Studio, 1989 (I:8+ R:5). This book tells about the chimpanzees of Gombe National Park.

Goor, Ron, and Nancy Goor. *Pompeii: Exploring a Roman Ghost Town*. Crowell, 1986 (I:10+ R:7). Photographs enhance a text describing Pompeii as it might have been in A.D. 79.

Gourley, Catherine. *Hunting Neptune's Giants: True Stories of American Whaling*. Millbrook, 1995 (I:10+ R:8). The author tells numerous stories about whaling.

Grace, Eric S. *Seals*. Photographs by Fred Bruemmer. Sierra Club/Little, Brown, 1991 (I:8+ R:6). This book provides details about seals, sea lions, and walruses.

Graff, Nancy Price. *The Strength of the Hills: A Portrait of a Family Farm*. Photographs by Richard Howard. Little, Brown, 1989 (I:all R:5). The author documents the work of a Vermont farm family.

Granfield, Linda. *Circus: An Album*. DK, 1998 (I:8+ R:6). The text traces the history of the circus.

———. *In Flanders Fields: The Story of the Poem by John McCrae*. Doubleday, 1996 (I:9+ R:6). The text discusses this World War I poem.

Greene, Carol. *Police Officers Protect People*. Child's World, 1996 (I:4–7 R:4). Color photographs help tell the story of police officers.

Guiberson, Brenda Z. *Into the Sea*. Illustrated by Alix Berenzy. Holt, 1996 (I:5–8 R:4). The author explores the life of the sea turtle.

———. *Spoonbill Swamp*. Illustrated by Megan Lloyd. Holt, 1992 (I:4–7 R:4). This highly illustrated book is about the residents of the swamp: a spoonbill and an alligator.

Haldane, Suzanne. *Helping Hands: How Monkeys Assist People Who Are Disabled*. Dutton, 1991 (I:8+ R:5). The author develops a photo essay about a quadriplegic and a capuchin monkey.

Hausherr, Rosmarie. *Children and the AIDS Virus*. Clarion, 1989 (I:7+ R:4). This text includes two levels of information, with large print for younger children and smaller print for older children and adults.

———. *My First Kitten*. Four Winds, 1985 (I:6–9 R:3). This book is about selecting and caring for a kitten.

Hearne, Betsy. *Seven Brave Women*. Illustrated by Bethanne Andersen. Greenwillow, 1997 (I:5–8 R:5). Hearne writes about members of her family who lived during different time periods.

Heiligman, Deborah. *From Caterpillar to Butterfly*. Illustrated by Bari Weissman. HarperCollins, 1996 (I:5–8 R:4). Text includes a guide to butterflies.

Heinz, Brian J. *The Wolves*. Illustrated by Bernie Fauchs. Dial, 1996 (I:5–8 R:5). The text and illustrations follow the natural world of the wolf.

Hilton, Suzanne. *A Capital City: 1790–1814*. Atheneum, 1992 (I:10+ R:7). Photographs illustrate this history of Washington, D.C.

Hirst, Robin, and Sally Hirst. *My Place in Space*. Illustrated by Roland Harvey and Joe Levine. Orchard, 1990 (I:5–8 R:5). Detailed drawings provide a humorous introduction to astronomy.

Hoban, Tana. *A Children's Zoo*. Greenwillow, 1985 (I:2–6). Each photograph is accompanied by a list of three words that describe the animal.

Hoobler, Dorothy, and Thomas Hoobler. *The Jewish American Family Album*. Oxford, 1995 (I:all R:10). The book focuses on the lives of many Jewish immigrants.

———. *Vietnam: Why We Fought: An Illustrated History*. Knopf, 1990 (I:12+ R:5). This is a history of the Vietnam conflict.

Irvine, Joan. *How to Make Super Pop-Ups*. Illustrated by Linda Hendry. Morrow, 1992 (I:8+ R:4). Detailed directions encourage readers to make objects such as masks and pop-up pictures.

Isadora, Rachel. *Lili at Ballet*. Putnam, 1993 (I:4–8 R:5). The text and illustrations follow a young girl's experience.

Jackson, Donna M. *The Bone Detectives: How Forensic Anthropologists Solve Crimes and Uncover Mysteries of the Dead*. Photographs by Charlie Fellenbaum. Little, Brown, 1996 (I:10+ R:9). The text discusses forensic cases that were used to solve crimes.

Jacobs, Francine. *Follow That Trash! All About Recycling*. Illustrated by Mavis Smith. Grosset & Dunlap, 1996 (I:5 R:4). The text stresses ecology.

Jaffe, Steven H. *Who Were the Founding Fathers? Two Hundred Years of Reinventing American History*. Holt, 1996 (I:12+ R:7). This history presents various ways that diverse groups have interpreted the words of the founding fathers.

Jarrow, Gail, and Paul Sherman. *The Naked Mole-Rat Mystery: Scientific Sleuths at Work*. Lerner, 1996 (I:9+ R:6). The text discusses how scientists investigated the naked mole rat.

Johnson, Neil. *All in a Day's Work: Twelve Americans Talk About Their Jobs*. Little, Brown, 1989 (I:10+ R:6). This book includes first-person reports about jobs and job satisfaction.

Johnson, Rebecca L. *Braving the Frozen Frontier: Women Working in Antarctica*. Lerner, 1997 (I:9+ R:6). The text focuses on the women scientists who work in Antarctica.

Johnson, Sylvia. *Roses Red, Violets Blue: Why Flowers Have Colors*. Photographs by Yuko Sato. Lerner, 1991 (I:10+ R:5). Color photographs enhance this book on flowers.

Johnston, Ginny, and Judy Cutchins. *Scaly Babies: Reptiles Growing Up*. Morrow, 1988 (I:7+ R:5). Photographs and text cover baby snakes, lizards, crocodilians, and turtles.

King, Casey, and Linda Barrett Osborne. *Kids Talk About the Civil Rights Movement with the People Who Made It Happen*. Knopf, 1997 (I:9+). Fourth graders developed the interviews.

King-Smith, Dick. *I Love Guinea Pigs*. Illustrated by Anita Jeram. Candlewick, 1995 (I:4–8 R:4). The history and care of guinea pigs are presented in text and illustrations.

Knight, Margy Burns. *Talking Walls*. Illustrated by Anne Sibley O'Brien. Tilbury House, 1992 (I:8+ R:5). The illustrations and text present some of the great walls found in the world.

Koch, Michelle. *World Water Watch*. Greenwillow, 1993 (I:4–8 R:4). This picture book asks readers to help save the oceans.

Kovack, Deborah and Madin, Kate. *Beneath Blue Waters: Meetings with Remarkable Deep-Sea Creatures*. Viking, 1996 (I:10+ R:6). This photographic essay explores the deep sea with oceanographers.

Kramer, Stephen. *Eye of the Storm: Chasing Storms with Warren Faidley*. Putnam, 1997 (I:9+ R:5). Color photographs illustrate different types of storms.

———. *Lightning*. Photographs by Warren Faidley. Carolrhoda, 1992 (I:8+ R:6). The author discusses many aspects of lightning.

Krauss, Ronnie. *Take a Look, It's in a Book: How Television Is Made at Reading Rainbow*. Walker, 1997 (I:all R:5). The book discusses the making of the children's show.

Krensky, Steven B. *Breaking into Print: Before and After Invention of the Printing Press*. Little, Brown, 1996 (I:8+ R:5). The text provides a history of printing.

Kroll, Steven. *Pony Express!* Illustrated by Dan Andreasen. Scholastic, 1996 (I:10+ R:9). Presents the history of the pony express.

Kuklin, Susan. *Fighting Back: What Some People Are Doing About AIDS*. Putnam, 1989 (I:12+ R:6). This book includes reactions of people who have AIDS.

Kuskin, Karla. *Jerusalem, Shining Still*. Illustrated by David Frampton. Harper & Row, 1987 (I:8+ R:5). Three thousand years of history is told in simple storytelling style.

Lasky, Kathryn. *Dinosaur Dig*. Photographs by Christopher Knight. Morrow, 1990 (I:9+ R:5). Several families are guided on a dig by a paleontologist.

———. *Monarchs*. Photographs by Christopher Knight. Harcourt Brace Jovanovich, 1993 (I:all). This book tells the life and migration cycle of the monarch butterfly.

———. *The Most Beautiful Roof in the World: Exploring the Rainforest Canopy*. Photographs by Christopher G. Knight. Harcourt Brace, 1997 (I:9+ R:6). The setting for the text is Belize.

———. *Sugaring Time*. Photographs by Christopher Knight. Macmillan, 1983 (I:all R:6). Photographs show and text describes collecting and processing maple sap.

———. *Think Like an Eagle: At Work with a Wildlife Photographer*. Photographs by Christopher G. Knight and Jack Swedberg. Little, Brown, 1992 (I:8+ R:6). The text and photographs follow a photographer.

Lauber, Patricia. *Dinosaurs Walked Here and Other Stories Fossils Tell*. Bradbury, 1987 (I:all R:6). This book presents information on how fossils reveal characteristics of the prehistoric world.

———. *Flood: Wrestling with the Mississippi*. National Geographic, 1996 (I:8+ R:6). The author discusses the 1927 and 1993 floods.

———. *How Dinosaurs Came to Be*. Illustrated by Douglas Henderson. Simon & Schuster, 1996 (I:6–10 R:4). The author explores the emergence of dinosaurs.

———. *Hurricanes: Earth's Mightiest Storms*. Scholastic, 1996 (I:9+ R:6). Text focuses on weather conditions related to hurricanes.

———. *Journey to the Planets*. Crown, 1982 (I:8–12 R:4). Photographs and text highlight the prominent features of each planet in our solar system.

———. *Living with Dinosaurs*. Illustrated by Douglas Henderson. Bradbury, 1991 (I:8+ R:6). The illustrations and text recreate life in North America seventy-five million years ago.

———. *The News About Dinosaurs*. Bradbury, 1989 (I:8+ R:6). This book presents new findings about dinosaurs.

———. *Snakes Are Hunters*. Illustrated by Holly Keller. Crowell, 1988 (I:4–8 R:3). This is an introductory book on snakes.

———. *Volcano: The Eruption and Healing of Mount St. Helens*. Bradbury, 1986 (I:all). Photographs and text follow progress of the eruption.

Lavies, Bianca. *Backyard Hunter: The Praying Mantis*. Dutton, 1990 (I:5–9 R:4). The life cycle is presented in text and illustrations.

_____ . *Compost Critters*. Dutton, 1993 (I:8–10 R:4). Photographs show the creatures living in a compost pile.

_____ . *A Gathering of Garter Snakes*. Dutton, 1993 (I:9–12 R:5). A photo essay presents the red-sided garter snakes of Manitoba, Canada.

_____ . *Lily Pad Pond*. Dutton, 1989 (I:5–9 R:3). Photographs follow tadpoles and other pondlife.

_____ . *Monarch Butterflies: Mysterious Travelers*. Dutton, 1992 (I:8+ R:5). Photographs show the home of the monarch in Mexico.

_____ . *Tree Trunk Traffic*. Dutton, 1989 (I:5–9 R:3). Wildlife live in an old maple tree.

Lawlor, Laurie. *Where Will This Shoe Take You?: A Walk Through the History of Footwear*. Walker, 1996 (I:10+ R:5). The author invites readers to imagine that they were wearing a particular shoe.

Lens, Sidney. *Vietnam: A War on Two Fronts*. Lodestar, 1990 (I:12+ R:6). This is a history of the involvement in the Vietnam War.

Leon, George DeLucenay. *Explorers of the Americas Before Columbus*. Watts, 1990 (I:8+ R:6). This book examines early explorers such as Eric the Red.

Lerner, Carol. *Dumb Cane and Daffodils: Poisonous Plants in the House and Garden*. Morrow, 1990 (I:10+ R:5). Detailed drawings add to the discussion about poisonous plants.

Lessem, Don. *Bigger Than T. Rex*. Illustrated by Robert F. Walters. Crown, 1997 (I:9+ R:5). The text explores facts about Gigantosaurus.

_____ . *Dinosaur Worlds*. Boyd Mills, 1996 (I:10+ R:6). The text integrates dinosaurs into their environments.

Lesser, Carolyn. *Storm on the Desert*. Illustrated by Ted Rand. Harcourt Brace, 1997 (I:all). The location is the Sonoran Desert in Arizona.

Levine, Ellen. *The Tree That Would Not Die*. Illustrated by Ted Rand. Scholastic, 1995 (I:6–9 R:4). The text and illustrations cover the four hundred years of an oak tree that was poisoned in 1989 and then saved by a massive effort.

Lewin, Ted. *Tiger Trek*. Macmillan, 1990 (I:10+ R:6). The illustrations take readers on a safari in the Indian jungle.

Locker, Thomas. *Sky Tree: Seeing Science Through Art*. HarperCollins, 1995 (I:6–8 R:5). The text includes a sequence of seasons.

McClung, Robert. *Lost Wild America: The Story of Our Extinct and Vanishing Wildlife*. Illustrated by Bob Hines. Linnet, 1993 (I:12+ R:7). Text presents a history of wildlife conservation.

McDonald, Megan. *Is This a House for Hermit Crab?* Illustrated by S. D. Schindler. Orchard, 1990 (I:3–6). This picture book follows a crab as it looks for a new home.

McLaughlin, Molly. *Dragonflies*. Walker, 1989 (I:7–12 R:5). The text and photographs show the life cycle of dragonflies.

McMillan, Bruce. *Going on a Whale Watch*. Scholastic, 1992 (I:3–8). Photographs and illustrations develop concepts related to whales.

McPhail, David. *Farm Morning*. Harcourt Brace Jovanovich, 1985 (I:2–5). A young girl and her father explore the barnyard.

McVey, Vicki. *The Sierra Club Kid's Guide to Planet Care & Repair*. Illustrated by Martha Weston. Sierra Club, 1993 (I:8+ R:5). This book provides background and activities that may be accomplished by children.

Macaulay, David. *Cathedral: The Story of Its Construction*. Houghton Mifflin, 1973 (I:all R:5). Detailed drawings show construction of a cathedral.

_____ . *Mill*. Houghton Mifflin, 1983 (I:9+ R:5). This book discusses the mills of nineteenth-century New England.

_____ . *Ship*. Houghton Mifflin, 1993 (I:10+ R:5). This book describes the recovery of artifacts from a ship that sank over five hundred years ago.

_____ . *The Way Things Work*. Houghton Mifflin, 1988 (I:all R:6). Humorous analogies add to detailed drawings.

Macy, Sue. *A Whole New Ball Game: The Story of the All-American Girls Professional Baseball League*. Holt, 1993 (I:10+ R:5). This book provides details about the history of the league.

_____ . *Winning Ways: A Photohistory of American Women in Sports*. Henry Holt, 1996 (I:10+ R:7). This is a history of women's sports.

Maestro, Betsy. *The Story of Money*. Illustrated by Giulio Maestro. Clarion, 1993 (I:8+ R:4). The author traces the development of trade.

_____ . *The Story of Religion*. Illustrated by Giulio Maestro. Clarion, 1996 (I:8+ R:6). This is an introduction to a study of religion.

Major, John S. *The Silk Route: 7,000 Miles of History*. Illustrated by Stephen Fieser. HarperCollins, 1995 (I:8+ R:6). Discusses the history of the route between China and Byzantium.

Mann, Elizabeth. *The Brooklyn Bridge*. Illustrated by Alan Witschonke. Mikaya, 1996 (I:9+ R:5). The text presents step-by-step descriptions of the construction of the bridge.

_____ . *The Great Pyramid*. Illustrated by Laura Lo Turco. Mikaya, 1996 (I:9+ R:5). The text focuses on the construction.

Mannetti, William. *Dinosaurs in Your Backyard*. Atheneum, 1982 (I:9+ R:6). This book discusses some new theories about dinosaurs.

Markle, Sandra. *Creepy, Crawly Baby Bugs*. Walker, 1996 (I:7–9 R:4). Photographs show insect babies.

Marrin, Albert. *Aztecs and Spaniards: Cortez and the Conquest of Mexico*. Atheneum, 1986 (I:12+ R:7). This history of the Aztecs tells the influences of Cortez.

Maruki, Toshi. *Hiroshima No Pika*. Lothrop, Lee & Shepard, 1982 (I:8–12 R:4). A powerfully illustrated picture book shows the aftereffects of the first atomic bomb.

Matthews, Downs. *Polar Bear Cubs*. Photographs by Dan Guravich. Simon & Schuster, 1989 (I:5–10 R:5). The photographs and text follow polar bear cubs as they explore their arctic homes.

Maynard, Caitlin, and Thane Maynard. *Rain Forests & Reefs: A Kid's-Eye View of the Tropics*. Photographs by Stan Rullman. Watts, 1996 (I:9+ R:5). The text follows teenagers as they hike through the rain forest.

Meltzer, Milton. *The Amazing Potato*. HarperCollins, 1992 (I:8+ R:6). This book presents the history of the potato.

_____ , ed. *The American Revolutionaries: A History in Their Own Words, 1750–1800*. Crowell, 1987 (I:10+). This is a collection of letters, diaries, interviews, and speeches.

_____ . *Rescue: The Story of How Gentiles Saved Jews in the Holocaust*. Harper & Row, 1988 (I:10+ R:7). Non-Jewish individuals helped Jewish people during World War II.

_____ . *Voices from the Civil War*. Crowell, 1989 (I:10+). Excerpts from speeches, diaries, and letters form this collection.

Merriman, Nick. *Early Humans*. Knopf, 1989 (I:all R:5). The text and photographs present a history of humans.

Meyer, Carolyn, and Charles Gallenkamp. *The Mystery of the Ancient Maya.* Atheneum, 1985 (I:10+ R:8). This book tells about early explorers and discoveries.

Micklethwait, Lucy. *A Child's Book of Play in Art.* Dorling Kindersley, 1996 (I:4–9 R:5). Provides discussions about how adults can interact with children using art.

Micucci, Charles. *The Life and Times of the Apple.* Orchard, 1992 (I:all). Illustrations and text provide both information about the apple as a plant and the history of the apple.

———. *The Life and Times of the Peanut.* Houghton Mifflin, 1997 (I:5–9 R:4). The text describes how peanuts grow and how they are produced.

Miles, Betty. *Save the Earth! An Ecology Handbook for Kids.* Illustrated by Claire A. Nivola. Knopf, 1974 (I:8+ R:5). Activities are designed to help children explore their environment.

Miller, Brandon Marie. *Just What the Doctor Ordered: The History of American Medicine.* Lerner, 1997 (I:10+ R:6). The text begins with early uses of plants and herbs and continues through contemporary medicine.

Miller, Debbie S. *Disappearing Lake: Nature's Magic in Denali National Park.* Illustrated by John Van Zyle. Walker, 1997 (I:all). Text and illustrations describe the life cycle of a seasonal lake.

———. *Flight of the Golden Plover: The Amazing Migration Between Hawaii and Alaska.* Illustrated by Daniel Van Zyle. Alaska Northwest, 1996 (I:8+ R:5). This migration covers three thousand miles.

Miller, Jonathan. *The Human Body.* Viking, 1983 (I:9+). A pop-up book illustrates the human body.

Miller, Margaret. *Who Uses This?* Greenwillow, 1990 (I:2–5). Readers must turn the page to check if they have identified the correct user of a tool.

Mohun, Janet. *Drugs, Steroids, and Sports.* Watts, 1988 (I:12+ R:6). This book explores abuse of drugs in sports.

Moore, Patrick. *Comets and Shooting Stars.* Illustrated by Paul Doherty. Copper Beech, 1995 (I:6–9 R:6). Describes the composition and orbits of comets.

———. *The Planets.* Illustrated by Paul Doherty. Copper Beech, 1995 (I:6–9 R:6). The text discusses the sizes and makeup of the planets.

———. *The Stars.* Illustrated by Paul Doherty. Copper Beech, 1995 (I:6–9 R:6). Text examines types, birth, and death of stars.

———. *The Sun and Moon.* Illustrated by Paul Doherty. Copper Beech, 1995 (I:6–9 R:5). The text focuses on explanations of how eclipses occur.

Moses, Amy. *Doctors Help People.* Child's World, 1996 (I:5–7). Doctors are shown treating children.

Munro, Roxie. *The Inside-Outside Book of Washington, D.C.* Dutton, 1987 (I:all). Illustrations in an almost wordless book show major structures in our capital.

Murphy, Jim. *The Great Fire.* Scholastic, 1995 (I:10+ R:7). The illustrations and text cover the Chicago fire of 1871.

———. *The Long Road to Gettysburg.* Clarion, 1992 (I:10+ R:5). The battle is developed from the points of view of a Confederate soldier and a Union soldier.

Nirgiotis, Nicholas and Theodore Nirgiotis. *No More Dodos: How Zoos Help Endangered Wildlife.* Lerner, 1996 (I:10+ R:6). The text discusses organizations that help endangered animals.

O'Connor, Karen. *Homeless Children.* Lucent Books, 1989 (I:10+ R:6). Photographs and text focus on the urban homeless.

O'Neill, Catherine. *Focus on Alcohol.* Illustrated by David Neuhaus. 21st Century Books, 1990 (I:10+ R:6). The author discusses how alcohol affects the body.

Pandell, Karen. *Animal Action ABC.* Photographs by Art Wolfe and Nancy Sheehan. Dutton, 1996 (I:all). Photography and poetry highlight animal actions.

Parker, Nancy Winslow. *Money, Money, Money: The Meaning of the Art and Symbols on United States Paper Currency.* HarperCollins, 1995 (I:9+ R:6). The author discusses the meaning of the art and symbols on currency.

Parker, Steve. *Mammal.* Knopf, 1989 (I:8–12 R:7). This heavily illustrated reference book examines the world of mammals.

Parker, Stephen, and John Bavosi. *Life Before Birth: The Story of the First Nine Months.* Cambridge, 1979 (I:9+ R:6). Illustrations are from a British Museum program.

Pascoe, Elaine. *The Right to Vote.* Millbrook, 1997 (I:8+ R:4). The text discusses various court cases.

Patent, Dorothy Hinshaw. *Appaloosa Horses.* Photographs by William Munoz. Holiday House, 1988 (I:5–8 R:5). This book explores the origins and characteristics of Appaloosas.

———. *Back to the Wild.* Illustrated by William Munoz. Harcourt Brace, 1997 (I:9+ R:6). The author describes programs for conserving endangered animals.

———. *Biodiversity.* Photographs by William Munoz. Clarion, 1996 (I:9+ R:6). The author discusses topics such as DNA and natural selection.

———. *Prairies.* Photographs by William Munoz. Holiday, 1996 (I:8+ R:6). Colored photographs add to the discussion of the prairies.

———. *The Whooping Crane: A Comeback Story.* Photographs by William Munoz. Clarion, 1988 (I:8+ R:6). This book discusses attempts to save the whooping crane.

Perry, Robert. *Focus on Nicotine and Caffeine.* Illustrated by David Neuhaus. 21st Century Books, 1990 (I:10+ R:5). The author focuses on how nicotine and caffeine affect the body.

Peters, David. *Giants of Land, Sea & Air: Past & Present.* Knopf/Sierra Club, 1986 (I:10+ R:10). An illustrated resource describes some of the largest animals.

Pope, Joyce. *Kenneth Lilly's Animals: A Portfolio of Paintings.* Illustrated by Kenneth Lilly. Lothrop, Lee & Shepard, 1988 (I:all R:7). Animals are divided according to geographic regions.

Priceman, Marjorie. *How to Make an Apple Pie and See the World.* Knopf, 1994 (I:5–8). The text presents information on food origins.

Pringle, Laurence. *Batman: Exploring the World of Bats.* Photographs by Merlin Tuttle. Scribner's Sons, 1991 (I:8+ R:5). Photographs and text develop important details about bats.

———. *Death Is Natural.* Four Winds, 1977 (I:9–12 R:6). Death in nature is an essential part of life.

———. *Drinking: A Risky Business.* Morrow, 1997 (I:10+ R:6). The text includes a history of the temperance movement.

———. *An Extraordinary Life: The Story of a Monarch Butterfly.* Illustrated by Bob Marstall. Orchard, 1997 (I:8+ R:6). The text covers the life of the butterfly and its migratory route.

———. *Living in a Risky World.* Morrow, 1989 (I:12+ R:7). People experience difficulties when evaluating risks.

———. *Nuclear Energy: Troubled Past, Uncertain Future.* Macmillan, 1989 (I:10+ R:6). This book provides a history and discusses issues related to nuclear energy.

_____ . *Saving Our Wildlife.* Enslow, 1990 (I:10+ R:6). The author describes how people are attempting to save wildlife.

Provensen, Alice. *The Buck Stops Here: The Presidents of the United States.* HarperCollins, 1990 (I:all). This is a picture history of the presidents.

_____ and Martin. *Leonardo da Vinci.* Viking, 1984 (I:all). A movable book presents the concepts.

Ray, Delia. *A Nation Torn: The Story of How the Civil War Began.* Lodestar, 1990 (I:10+ R:6). This book discusses causes of the Civil War.

Reeves, Nicholas. *Into the Mummy's Tomb: The Real-Life Discovery of Tutankhamun's Treasures.* Scholastic, 1992 (I:8+ R:5). This book traces Howard Carter's discovery of the tomb.

Reid, Barbara. *Playing with Plasticine.* Morrow, 1989 (I:8+ R:5). This book gives directions for making plasticine sculptures.

Reynolds, Jan. *Sahara Vanishing Cultures.* Harcourt Brace Jovanovich, 1991 (I:8+ R:4). Large color photographs add to the understanding of this nomadic culture.

Rhoades, Diane. *Garden Crafts for Kids: 50 Great Reasons to Get Your Hands Dirty.* Sterling, 1995 (I:9+ R:8). Directions for projects associated with all phases of planning and planting a garden.

Richardson, Joy. *Looking at Pictures: An Introduction to Art for Young People.* Illustrated by Charlotte Voake. Abrams, 1997 (I:10+). The works discussed are from the National Gallery in London.

Roche, Denis. *Loo-Loo, Boo, and Art You Can Do.* Houghton Mifflin, 1996 (I:4–9). Text includes directions for eleven art projects.

Rogasky, Barbara. *Smoke and Ashes: The Story of the Holocaust.* Holiday House, 1988 (I:10+ R:6). This is a history of the 1933–1945 Holocaust.

Roop, Peter, and Connie Roop. *Seasons of the Cranes.* Walker, 1989 (I:8+ R:5). Progressing from spring through winter, this book describes the life of the whooping crane.

Rossel, Seymour. *The Holocaust.* Watts, 1981 (I:9+ R:6). This book examines Germany in the 1930s, Hitler's dictatorship, and the Nuremberg trials.

Ryden, Hope. *Your Cat's Wild Cousins.* Lodestar, 1992 (I:8+ R:4). The author describes the behavior and physical traits of eighteen species.

Ryder, Joan. *Dancers in the Garden.* Illustrated by Judith Lopez. Sierra Club, 1992 (I:all). The text and illustrations are based on observations of hummingbirds in various San Francisco gardens.

St. George, Judith. *Panama Canal: Gateway to the World.* Putnam, 1989 (I:12+ R:7). This book tells about the building and operating of the canal.

Sattler, Helen Roney. *The Book of Eagles.* Illustrated by Jean Day Zallinger. Lothrop, Lee & Shepard, 1989 (I:8+ R:6). This book presents the behavior and life cycle of eagles.

_____ . *Dinosaurs of North America.* Illustrated by Anthony Rao. Lothrop, Lee & Shepard, 1981 (I:9+ R:6). In addition to discussions about various dinosaurs, the book includes theories about their extinction.

_____ . *The Earliest Americans.* Illustrated by Jean Day Zallinger. Clarion, 1993 (I:10+ R:6). The author chronicles the arrival of humankind in North America.

_____ . *Hominids: A Look Back at Our Ancestors.* Illustrated by Christopher Santoro. Lothrop, Lee & Shepard, 1988 (I:10+ R:6). This is a history of early hominids.

_____ . *Stegosaurs: The Solar-Powered Dinosaurs.* Illustrated by Turi MacCombie. Lothrop, Lee & Shepard, 1992 (I:all R:6). The author provides details about eleven varieties of stegosaurs.

Sayre, April Pulley. *Put on Some Antlers and Walk Like a Moose: How Scientists Find, Follow, and Study Wild Animals.* 21st Century, 1997 (I:10+ R:5). This text discusses the work of field scientists.

Schmitt, Lois. *Smart Spending: A Young Consumer's Guide.* Scribner's Sons, 1989 (I:12+ R:6). This book explores such topics as comparison shopping.

Schories, Pat. *Over Under in the Garden: An Alphabet Book.* Farrar, 1996 (I:5–8). This ABC book illustrates plants and animals found in the garden.

Selsam, Millicent E. *Cotton.* Photographs by Jerome Wexler. Morrow, 1982 (I:7–10 R:5). This book tells the history, stages in development, and uses of cotton.

_____ . *How to Be a Nature Detective.* Illustrated by Ezra Jack Keats. Harper & Row, 1958, 1963 (I:5–8 R:4). This book encourages children to identify animals by observing their tracks.

_____ . *Mushrooms.* Photographs by Jerome Wexler. Morrow, 1986 (I:7–10 R:6). This book tells the history and life cycle of the common edible mushroom.

_____ , and Joyce Hunt. *A First Look at Animals with Horns.* Illustrated by Harriet Springer. Walker, 1989 (I:5–8 R:3). This book discusses characteristics of animals with horns.

_____ . *A First Look at Animals That Eat Other Animals.* Illustrated by Harriet Springer. Walker, 1990 (I:5–8 R:3). This introductory book defines carnivores and discusses animal groups.

_____ . *A First Look at Caterpillars.* Illustrated by Harriett Springer. Walker, 1987 (I:5–8 R:3). This book tells the life cycle and habits of the caterpillar.

_____ . *A First Look at Seals, Sea Lions, and Walruses.* Illustrated by Harriett Springer. Walker, 1988 (I:5–8 R:3). This book tells characteristics of the animals.

_____ . *Keep Looking!* Illustrated by Normand Chartier. Macmillan, 1989 (I:3–7 R:3). This book encourages readers to find animals in a winter setting.

Shahan, Sherry. *Dashing Through the Snow: The Story of the Jr. Iditarod.* Millbrook, 1997 (I:8+ R:5). Colored photographs add to the description of the race.

Shemie, Bonnie. *Houses of Snow, Skin, and Bones.* Tundra, 1989 (I:7–12 R:5). Drawings and text present construction of igloos, sod houses, and tents.

Shulman, Jeffrey. *Focus on Cocaine and Crack.* Illustrated by David Neuhaus. 21st Century Books, 1990 (I:10+ R:6). The author discusses how cocaine and crack affect the body.

Sierra Club. *Sierra Club Book of Great Mammals.* Sierra Club, 1992 (I:8+ R:5). The text and illustrations cover a wide variety of mammals.

_____ . *The Sierra Club Book of Small Mammals.* Sierra Club, 1993 (I:8+ R:5). Photographs and text introduce many smaller mammals.

Sill, Cathryn. *About Birds: A Guide for Children.* Illustrated by John Sill. Peachtree, 1991 (I:3–8). Large colorful illustrations and minimal text introduce various types of birds.

Simon, Seymour. *Earthquakes.* Morrow, 1991 (I:8+ R:6). Text and colored photographs examine the phenomenon of earthquakes.

_____ . *Galaxies.* Morrow, 1988 (I:5–8 R:5). This book examines the Milky Way and other galaxies.

_____. *How to Be an Ocean Scientist in Your Own Home.* Illustrated by David A. Carter. Lippincott, 1988 (I:8+ R:5). This book describes twenty-four experiments.

_____. *Jupiter.* Morrow, 1985 (I:5–8 R:5). Color photographs from NASA reveal knowledge.

_____. *Lightning.* Morrow, 1997 (I:8+ R:6). Colored photographs add to the discussion of lightning.

_____. *Little Giants.* Illustrated by Pamela Carroll. Morrow, 1983 (I:7–12 R:4). Animals that are giants are compared to others of their kind.

_____. *New Questions and Answers About Dinosaurs.* Illustrated by Jennifer Dewey. Morrow, 1990 (I:7+ R:5). Twenty-two questions about dinosaurs are asked and answered.

_____. *Poisonous Snakes.* Illustrated by William R. Downey. Four Winds, 1981 (I:7–10 R:5). This book discusses the important role of poisonous snakes, where they live, and their behavior.

_____. *Saturn.* Morrow, 1985 (I:5–8 R:5). Color photographs from NASA add to the information.

_____. *Soap Bubble Magic.* Illustrated by Stella Ormai. Lothrop, Lee & Shepard, 1985 (I:6–9 R:3). This book encourages observation of and experimentation with soap bubbles.

_____. *Storms.* Morrow, 1989 (I:8–12 R:5). This book tells about tornadoes, lightning, and storm clouds.

_____. *Volcanoes.* Morrow, 1988 (I:8–12 R:5). Full-page photographs show dramatic volcanoes.

Skurzynski, Gloria. *Almost the Real Thing: Simulation in Your High-Tech World.* Bradbury, 1991 (I:10+ R:5). This book describes how scientists simulate events.

_____. *Get the Message: Telecommunications in Your High-Tech World.* Bradbury, 1993 (I:10+ R:5). The author explores principles of telecommunication.

_____. *Waves: The Electromagnetic Universe.* National Geographic, 1996 (I:8+ R:6). Discusses physical characteristics of electromagnetic waves.

Smith, Roland. *Inside the Zoo Nursery.* Photographs by William Munoz. Dutton, 1993 (I:10+ R:5). Color photographs of baby animals enhance the text.

Snow, Dean R. *Archaeology of North America.* Chelsea House, 1989 (I:10+ R:5). This book discusses the origins of North American Indians.

Staub, Frank. *Sea Turtles.* Lerner, 1995 (I:7+ R:5). Presents the life cycles of five types of sea turtles.

Stefoff, Rebecca. *Finding the Lost Cities.* Oxford, 1997 (I:8+ R:5). The text emphasizes Carter's discoveries.

Steger, Will, and Jon Bowermaster. *Over the Top of the World: Explorer Will Steger's Trek Across the Arctic.* Scholastic, 1997 (I:9+ R:6). This is a photo-journalistic presentation of the trip.

Stevens, Leonard A. *The Case of Roe v. Wade.* Putnam, 1996 (I:12+ R:7). The author discusses the abortion issue.

Swanson, Diane. *Buffalo Sunrise: The Story of a North American Giant.* Little, Brown, 1996 (I:10+ R:8). The book traces the history and characteristics of the bison.

_____. *Safari Beneath the Sea: The Wonder World of the North Pacific Coast.* Photographs by the Royal British Columbia Museum. Sierra Club, 1994 (I:all). Marine biology from the Northwest Coast is discussed.

Tanaka, Shelley, and Hugh Brewster, eds. *Anastasia's Album.* Hyperion, 1996 (I:10+ R:6). The text includes photographs from the family albums of the Romanovs.

Thomson, Peggy, and Barbara Moore. *The Nine-Ton Cat: Behind the Scenes at an Art Museum.* Houghton Mifflin, 1997 (I:9+ R:6). Discusses the National Gallery in Washington, D.C.

Valenta, Barbara. *Pop-O-Mania: How to Create Your Own Pop-Ups.* Dial, 1997 (I:all). The text includes instructions.

Van Loon, Hendrik Willem. *The Story of Mankind.* Liveright, 1921, 1984 (I:9+ R:5). This historical information book was the first Newbery Medal winner.

Waldman, Neil. *The Golden City: Jerusalem's 3,000 Years.* Atheneum, 1995 (I:8–12 R:10). This illustrated book traces the history of Jerusalem from BCE through the Six Day War in 1967.

Walker, Barbara M. *The Little House Cookbook: Frontier Foods from Laura Ingalls Wilder's Classic Stories.* Illustrated by Garth Williams. Harper & Row, 1979 (I:8–12 R:7). This book provides authentic pioneer recipes.

Walker, Sally. *Glaciers: Ice on the Move.* Carolrhoda, 1990 (I:9+ R:5). Photographs help clarify the concepts.

_____. *Rhinos.* Photographs by Gerry Ellis. Carolrhoda, 1996 (I:8+ R:5). Colored photographs add to the discussion of rhinos.

Wallace, Karen. *Imagine You Are a Crocodile.* Holt, 1997 (I:3–6). children are asked to imagine life as a crocodile.

Warren, James A. *Cold War: The American Crusade Against World Communism, 1945–1991.* Lothrop, Lee & Shepard, 1996 (I:12+ R:7). The author chronicles the history of the cold war.

_____. *Portrait of a Tragedy: America and the Vietnam War.* Lothrop, Lee & Shepard, 1990 (I:12+ R:6). This is a history of the Vietnam conflict.

Weitzman, David. *Old Ironsides: Americans Build a Fighting Ship.* Houghton, Mifflin, 1997 (I:9+ R:6). This story chronicles the building of the war ship, the *Constitution.*

Wexler, Jerome. *Jack-in-the-Pulpit.* Dutton, 1993 (I:6–12 R:5). Close-up photographs provide details.

Wilcox, Charlotte. *Mummies & Their Mysteries.* Carolrhoda, 1993 (I:8–12 R:5). This book introduces readers to mummies found in different parts of the world.

_____. *Trash!* Photographs by Jerry Bushey. Carolrhoda, 1988 (I:8–12 R:5). This book is about trash collecting and recycling.

Wilkinson, Philip. *Super Structures.* DK, 1996 (I:10+ R:5). The author discusses such constructions as skyscrapers and the Chunnel.

Wolf, Bernard. *HIV Positive.* Dutton, 1997 (I:8+ R:6). The author focuses on a young woman with AIDS and her two children.

Woodford, Susan. *The Parthenon.* Cambridge/Lerner, 1983 (I:10+ R:7). Drawings, photographs, and text describe the design, building, and destruction of the Parthenon.

Yoshida, Toshi. *Young Lions.* Philomel, 1989 (I:3–9 R:4). This book is about lion cubs on an African plain.

Yue, Charlotte. *Shoes: Their History in Words and Pictures.* Illustrated by David Yue. Houghton Mifflin, 1997 (I:8+ R:6). The author traces the history of shoes.

_____, and David Yue. *Christopher Columbus: How He Did It.* Houghton Mifflin, 1992 (I:9+ R:5). This book discusses the knowledge and technology that allowed Columbus to complete his voyage.

Zeinert, Karen. *The Salem Witchcraft Trials.* Watts, 1989 (I:12+ R:7). This book is about events at Salem, Massachusetts, in 1692.

Zeller, Paula Klevan. *Focus on Marijuana.* Illustrated by David Neuhaus. 21st Century Books, 1990 (I:10+ R:6). The author discusses how marijuana affects the body.

References

Adams, Karen I. "The 'Born Again' Phenomenon and Children's Books." *Children's Literature Association Quarterly* 14 (Spring 1989): 5–9.

Aiken, Joan. "Interpreting the Past." *Children's Literature in Education* 16 (Summer 1985): 67–83.

Alderson, Brian. "Children Who Live in Boxes." *The New York Times Book Review* (November 14, 1993a): 17.

_____. *Ezra Jack Keats: Artist and Picture-Book Maker.* Gretna, Louisiana: Pelican, 1994.

_____. "Maurice Before Max: The Yonder Side of the See-Saw." *The Horn Book* (May/June 1993b): 291–295.

_____. *Sing a Song of Sixpence.* New York: Cambridge University Press, 1986.

_____, ed. and trans. *Three Centuries of Children's Books in Europe.* Cleveland, Oh.: World, 1959.

Aoki, M. Elaine. "Are You Chinese? Are You Japanese? Or Are You Just a Mixed-Up Kid?—Using Asian American Children's Literature." *The Reading Teacher* 34 (January 1981): 382–385.

Applebee, Arthur S. "Children and Stories: Learning the Rules of the Game." *Language Arts* 56 (September 1979).

Apseloff, Marilyn Fain. "Abandonment: The New Realism of the Eighties." *Children's Literature in Education* 23 (December 1992): 101–106.

_____. "New Trends in Children's Books from Europe and Japan." *School Library Journal* 32 (November 1985): 30–32.

Arbuthnot, May Hill, and Dorothy M. Broderick. *Time for Biography.* Glenview, Ill.: Scott, Foresman, 1969.

Ashe, Rosalind, and Lisa Tuttle. *Children's Literary Houses: Famous Dwellings in Children's Fiction.* New York: Facts on File, 1984.

Ashton, John. *Chap-Books of the Eighteenth Century.* London: Chatto & Windus, 1882.

Association of Women Psychologists. "Statement of Resolutions and Motions." Miami, Fla.: American Psychological Association Convention, September 1970.

Atwood, Ann. *Haiku: The Mood of Earth.* New York: Scribner's Sons, 1971.

Au, Kathryn H. *Literacy Instruction in Multicultural Settings.* Orlando: Harcourt Brace Jovanovich, 1993.

Avery, Gillian. "Beginnings of Children's Reading to c. 1700." In *Children's Literature: An Illustrated History,* edited by Peter Hunt. Oxford: Oxford University Press, 1995, 1–25.

Avi. "The Child in Children's Literature." *The Horn Book* 69 (January/February 1993): 40–50.

Babbitt, Natalie. "Read This, It's Good For You." *The New York Times Book Review.* (May 18, 1997): 23–24.

Bader, Barbara. " 'They Shall Not Wither': John Biehorst's Quiet Crusade for Native American Literature." *The Horn Book* 73 (May/June 1997): 268–281.

Bagley, Ayers. *An Invitation to Wisdom and Schooling.* Society of Professors of Education Monograph Series, 1985.

Baker, Gwendolyn C. "The Role of the School in Transmitting the Culture of All Learners in a Free and Democratic Society." *Educational Leadership* 36 (November 1978): 134–138.

Ballinger, Franchot. "A Matter of Emphasis: Teaching the 'Literature' in Native American Literature Courses." *American Indian Culture and Research Journal* 8 (1984): 1–12.

Banfield, Beryle. "Racism in Children's Books: An Afro-American Perspective." In *The Black American in Books for Children: Readings in Racism,* edited by Donnarae MacCann and Gloria Woodard. Metuchen, N.J.: Scarecrow, 1985.

Barclay, Donald A. "Interpreted Well Enough: Two Illustrators' Visions of *Adventures of Huckleberry Finn.*" *The Horn Book* 68 (May/June 1992): 311–319.

Barnes, B. "Using Children's Literature in the Early Anthropology Curriculum." *Social Education* (January 1991): 17–18.

Barr, Rebecca, and Marilyn W. Sadow. "Influence of Basal Programs on Fourth-Grade Reading Instruction." *Reading Research Quarterly* 24 (Winter 1989): 44–71.

Barrett, Thomas C. "Taxonomy of Reading Comprehension." In *Reading 360 Monograph.* Lexington, Mass.: Ginn, 1972.

Barsam, Richard. *A Peaceable Kingdom: The Shaker Abecedarius.* New York: Viking, 1978.

Bartel, Nettie. "Assessing and Remediating Problems in Language Development." In *Teaching Children with Learning and Behavior Problems,* edited by Donald Hammill and Nettie Bartel. Boston: Allyn & Bacon, 1990.

Bascom, William. "The Forms of Folklore: Prose Narratives." *Journal of American Folklore* 78 (January/March 1965): 3–20.

Bauermeister, Erica, and Holly Smith. *Let's Hear It for the Girls.* New York: Penguin, 1997.

Baylor, Byrd. *And It Is Still That Way.* New York: Scribner's Sons, 1976.

Beckham, Stephen Dow. In *Echoes of the Elders: The Stories and Paintings of Chief Lelooska* by Christine Normandin. New York: DK, 1977, 4–5.

Bedard, Michael. *Emily.* New York: Delacorte, 1992.

Behn, Harry. *Chrysalis, Concerning Children and Poetry.* New York: Harcourt Brace Jovanovich, 1968.

Bernstein, Joanne E. "Bibliotherapy: How Books Can Help Young Children Cope." In *Children's Literature: Resource for the Classroom,* edited by Masha Kabakow Rudman. Norwood, Mass.: Christopher Gordon, 1989.

_____ . *Books to Help Children Cope with Separation and Loss,* 2nd ed. New York: Bowker, 1983.

Bettelheim, Bruno. *The Uses of Enchantment: The Meaning and Importance of Fairy Tales.* New York: Knopf, 1976.

Bierhorst, John. "Children's Books." *New York Times Book Review* (May 23, 1993).

_____ . *The Mythology of North America.* New York: Morrow, 1985.

_____ , ed. *The Red Swan: Myths and Tales of the American Indians.* New York: Farrar, Straus & Giroux, 1976.

Bingham, Jane, and Grayce Scholt. *Fifteen Centuries of Children's Literature: An Annotated Chronology of British and American Works in Historical Context.* Westport, Conn.: Greenwood, 1980.

_____ . "The Great Glass Slipper Search: Using Folk Tales with Older Children." *Elementary English* 51 (October 1974): 990–998.

Bitzer, Lucy. "The Art of Picture Books: Beautiful Treasures of Bookmaking." *Top-of-the-News* 38 (Spring 1992): 226–232.

Blatt, Gloria Toby. "Violence in Children's Literature: A Content Analysis of a Select Sampling of Children's Literature and a Study of Children's Responses to Literary Episodes Depicting Violence." East Lansing, Mich.: Michigan State University, 1972. University Microfilm No. 72-29, 931.

Blenz-Clucas, Beth. "History's Forgotten Heroes: Women on the Frontier." *School Library Journal* 39 (March 1993): 118–123.

Bloom, Benjamin. *Taxonomy of Educational Objectives.* New York: Longman, 1956.

Blos, Joan W. "Newbery Medal Acceptance." *The Horn Book* 56 (August 1980): 369–377.

Blough, Glenn O. "The Author and the Science Book." *Library Trends* 22 (April 1974): 419–424.

Bond, Nancy. "Conflict in Children's Fiction." *The Horn Book* 60 (June 1984): 297–306.

Book Review Subcommittee of the National Council for the Social Studies—Children's Book Council Joint Committee. "Notable 1991 Children's Trade Books in the Field of Social Studies." *Social Education* 56 (April/May 1992): 253–264.

Booss, Claire. *Scandinavian Folk & Fairy Tales.* New York: Avenel Books, 1984.

Booth, David. "Imaginary Gardens with Real Toads: Reading and Drama in Education." *Theory into Practice* 24 (1985): 193–198.

Borgman, Harry. *Art and Illustration Techniques.* New York: Watson-Guptill, 1979.

Borusch, Barbara. Personal correspondence with author, December 1, 1980.

Boulanger, Susan. "Language, Imagination, Vision: Art Books for Children." *The Horn Book* 72 (May/June 1996): 295–304.

Braga, Laurie, and Joseph Braga. *Learning and Growing: A Guide to Child Development.* Englewood Cliffs, N.J.: Prentice-Hall, 1975.

Braine, Martin. "The Ontogeny of English Phrase Structure: The First Phase." In *Readings in Language Development,* edited by Lois Bloom. New York: John Wiley, 1978.

Bridge, Ethel Brooks. "Using Children's Choices of and Reactions to Poetry as Determinants in Enriching Literary Experience in the Middle Grades." Philadelphia: Temple University, 1966. University Microfilm No. 67-6246.

Briggs, Katharine. *Dictionary of British Folk-Tales.* 4 volumes. London: Routledge & Kegan Paul, 1970–1971.

Briggs, Nancy E., and Joseph A. Wagner. *Children's Literature Through Storytelling and Drama.* Dubuque, Iowa: Brown, 1979.

Brink, Carol Ryrie. *Caddie Woodlawn.* Illustrated by Trina Schart Hyman. New York: Macmillan, 1935, 1973.

Broderick, Dorothy May. *The Image of the Black in Popular and Recommended American Juvenile Fiction, 1827–1967.* New York: Columbia University, 1971. University Microfilm No. 71-4090.

Broudy, H. S. "Arts Education As Artistic Perception." In G. W. Hardiman and T. Zernich (Eds.), *Foundations for Curriculum Development and Evaluation in Art Education.* Champaign, Ill.: Stipes, 1981, 9–17.

_____ , "How Basic Is Aesthetic Education? or Is It the Fourth R?" *Language Arts* 54 (September 1977): 631–637.

Brown, Roger. *A First Language/The Early Stages.* Cambridge, Mass.: Harvard Univ. Press, 1973.

Browne, C. A. *The Story of Our National Ballads.* Edited by Willard Heaps. New York: Crowell, 1960.

Bryan, Ashley. *The Dancing Granny and Other African Stories.* New York: Caedmon, 1985.

Buckley, Marilyn Hanf. "Focus on Research: We Listen a Book a Day: We Speak a Book a Week: Learning from Walter Loban." *Language Arts* 69 (December 1992): 622–626.

Bulzone, Marisa. "Children's Book Illustration: Is This the New Golden Age?" *Communication Arts* 34 (January/February 1993): 94–106.

Burke, Eileen M. *Early Childhood Literature: For Love of Child and Book.* Boston: Allyn & Bacon, 1986.

Burton, Hester. "The Writing of Historical Novels." In *Children and Literature: Views and Reviews,* edited by Virginia Haviland. Glenview, Ill.: Scott, Foresman, 1973, 299–304.

Butler, Dorothy. "From Books to Buttons: Reflections from the Thirties to the Eighties." *The Arbuthnot Lectures: 1980–1989.* Chicago: American Library Association, 1990.

Byars, Betsy. Interview conducted by Ilene Cooper. "The Booklist Interview." *Booklist* 89 (January 15, 1993): 906–907.

Byler, Mary Gloyne. "American Indian Authors for Young Readers." In *Cultural Conformity in Books for Children,* edited by Donnarae MacCann and Gloria Woodard. Metuchen, N.J.: Scarecrow, 1977.

Cadogan, Mary, and Patricia Craig. *You're a Brick, Angela! A New Look at Girls' Fiction from 1839 to 1975.* London: Gollancz, 1976.

Caduto, Michael J., and Joseph Bruchac. *Keepers of the Animals: Native American Stories and Wildlife Activities for Children.* Golden, Colo.: Fulcrum, 1991.

_____ . *Keepers of the Earth: Native American Stories and Environmental Activities for Children.* Golden, Colo.: Fulcrum, 1989.

Cafakum, Leslie. "Alphabet Books Grow Up!" *Book Links* 2 (May 1993): 41–45.

Cai, Mingshui. "A Balanced View of Acculturation: Comments on Laurence Yep's Three Novels." *Children's Literature in Education* 23 (June 1992): 107–118.

_____. "Folks, Friends and Foes: Relationships Between Humans and Animals in Some Eastern and Western Folktales." *Children's Literature in Education* 24 (1993): 73–83.

Campbell, Joseph. *The Power of Myth.* New York: Doubleday, 1988.

_____. *Transformations of Myth Through Time.* New York: Harper & Row, 1990.

Carlson, Julia Ann. *A Comparison of the Treatment of the Negro in Children's Literature in the Periods 1929–1938 and 1959–1968.* Storrs, Conn.: University of Connecticut, 1969. University Microfilm No. 70-1245.

Carlson, Ruth Kearney. "World Understanding Through the Folktale." In *Folklore and Folk Tales Around the World,* edited by Ruth Kearney Carlson. Newark, Del.: International Reading Association, 1972.

Carmichael, Carolyn Wilson. "A Study of Selected Social Values as Reflected in Contemporary Realistic Fiction for Children," East Lansing, Mich.: Michigan State University, 1971, University Microfilm No. 71-31.

Caroff, Susan, and Elizabeth Moje. "A Conversation with David Wiesner: 1992 Caldecott Medal Winner." *The Reading Teacher* 46 (December 1992/January 1993): 284–289.

Carpenter, Frank G. *Carpenter's Geographical Reader, North America.* New York: American Book, 1898.

Carter, Betty. "Hold the Applause! Do Accelerated Reader & Electronic Bookshelf Send the Right Message?" *School Library Journal* 42 (October 1996): 22–25.

Carvajal, Doreen. "In Kids' Pop Culture, Fear Rules." *The New York Times* (Sunday, June 1, 1997): E. 5.

Cavendish, Richard, ed. *Legends of the World.* New York: Schocken Books, 1982.

Chall, Jeanne S., and Emily W. Marston. "The Reluctant Reader: Suggestions from Research and Practice." *Catholic Library World* 47 (February 1976): 274–275.

Chapman, Raymond. *The Victorian Debate: English Literature and Society 1832–1901.* New York: Basic Books, 1968.

Charpenel, Mauricio. "Literature About Mexican American Children." College Station, Tex.: Texas A&M University, Children's Literature Conference, 1980.

Cheatham, Bertha M. "News of '85: SLJ's Annual Roundup." *School Library Journal* 32 (December 1985): 19–27.

"Children's Choices for 1992." *The Reading Teacher* 46 (October 1992): 127–141.

"Children's Choices for 1993: A Project of the International Reading Association and the Children's Book Council." *The Reading Teacher* 47 (October 1993): 127–141.

Children's Literature Association. *Touchstones: A List of Distinguished Children's Books.* Lafayette, Ind.: Purdue University; Children's Literature Association, 1985.

Cianciolo, Patricia J. "A Look at the Illustrations in Children's Favorite Picture Books." In *Children's Choices: Teaching with Books Children Like,* edited by Nancy Roser and Margaret Frith. Newark, Del.: International Reading Association, 1983.

_____. *Picture Books for Children,* 3rd ed. Chicago: American Library Association, 1990.

_____. "Reading Literature, and Writing from Writers' Perspectives." *English Journal* 74 (December 1985): 65–69.

Cirker, Blanche. *The Book of Kells: Selected Plates in Full Color.* New York: Dover, 1982.

Clark, Anne. "Books in the Classroom: Poetry." *The Horn Book* 68 (September/October 1992): 624–627.

Clark, Leonard. "Poetry for the Youngest." In *Horn Book Reflections,* edited by Elinor Whitney Field. Boston: Horn Book, 1969.

Clay, Marie M. "Child Development." In *Handbook of Research on Teaching the English Language Arts,* edited by James Flood, Julie M. Jensen, Diane Lapp, and James R. Squire. Upper Saddle River, N.J.: Merrill/Prentice Hall, 1991, 40–45.

Coe, Michael. *The Maya,* 3d ed. New York: Thames & Hudson, 1984.

_____, Dean Snow, and Elizabeth Benson. *Atlas of Ancient America.* New York: Facts on File, 1986.

Cohen, Caron Lee. "The Quest in Children's Literature." *School Library Journal* 31 (August 1985): 28–29.

Commire, Anne. *Something About the Author: Facts and Pictures About Contemporary Authors and Illustrators of Books for Young People.* Detroit: Gale, 1971.

Committee on Geographic Education. *Guidelines for Geographic Education: Elementary and Secondary Schools.* Washington, D.C.: National Council for Geographic Education and the Association of American Geographers, 1983.

Connell, Christopher. "Middle-Class Housewife Writes High-Class Children's Tales." Bryan-College Station *Eagle* (March 28, 1984): 1F.

Cook, Elizabeth. *The Ordinary and the Fabulous: An Introduction to Myths, Legends, and Fairy Tales,* 2d ed. Cambridge: University Press, 1976.

Coolidge, Olivia E. *Legends of the North.* Boston: Houghton Mifflin, 1951.

_____. "My Struggle with Facts." *Wilson Library Bulletin* 49 (October 1974): 146–151.

Cooper, Ilene. "The African American Experience in Picture Books." *Booklist* 88 (February 1, 1992): 1036–1037.

Council on Interracial Books for Children. "Chicano Culture in Children's Literature: Stereotypes, Distortions and Omissions." In *Cultural Conformity in Books for Children,* edited by Donnarae MacCann and Gloria Woodard. Metuchen, N.J.: Scarecrow, 1977a.

_____. "Criteria for Analyzing Books on Asian Americans." In *Cultural Conformity in Books for Children,* edited by Donnarae MacCann and Gloria Woodard. Metuchen, N.J.: Scarecrow, 1977b.

Courlander, Harold. *A Treasury of African Folklore.* New York: Crown, 1975.

Cowen, John E. "Conversations with Poet Jose Garcia Villa on Teaching Poetry to Children." In *Teaching Reading Through the Arts,* edited by John E. Cowen. Newark, Del.: International Reading Association, 1983, 78–87.

Crane, Walter. *The Decorative Illustration of Books Old and New.* London: Bracken, 1984.

Crossley-Holland, Kevin. *The Faber Book of Northern Legends.* Boston: Faber & Faber, 1983.

Crowley, Daniel. Foreword to *"On Another Day . . ." Tales Told Among the Nkundo of Zaire,* collected by Mabel Ross and Barbara Walker. Hamden, Conn.: Archon, 1979.

Cullinan, Beatrice, Marilyn C. Scalo, and Virginia Schroeder. *Three Voices: An Invitation to Poetry Across the Curriculum.* York, Me.: Stenhouse, 1995.

Cummins, Julie. "Taste Trends: A Cookie Lover's Assortment of Picture Book Art." *School Library Journal* 42 (September 1996): 118–123.

"Curriculum Connectors: Family Secrets." *School Library Journal* 43 (March 1997): 112–113.

Cushing, Frank Hamilton. *Zuni Folktales.* Tucson: University of Arizona Press, 1986.

Danoff, Michael. Quoted in *The Art of Nancy Ekholm Burkert,* edited by David Larkin. New York: Harper & Row, 1977.

Darton, F. J. Harvey. *Children's Books in England: Five Centuries of Social Life.* New York: Cambridge University Press, 1932, 1966.

Davis, Joann. "Trade News: Sendak on Sendak." As told to Jean F. Mercier. *Publishers Weekly* (April 10, 1981): 45–46.

Day-Lewis, Cecil. *Poetry for You.* New York: Oxford, 1947.

DelFattore, Joan. *What Johnny Shouldn't Read: Textbook Censorship in America.* New Haven: Yale University Press, 1992.

Dempsey, Frank J. "Russell Freedman." *The Horn Book* (July/August 1988): 452–456.

De Wit, Dorothy. *Children's Faces Looking Up: Program Building for the Storyteller.* Chicago: American Library Association, 1979.

Diakiw, J. "Children's Literature and Global Education: Understanding the Developing World." *The Reading Teacher* 43 (1990): 296–300.

Dole, J., G. Duffy, L. Roehler, and P. D. Pearson. "Moving from the Old to the New: Research on Reading Comprehension Instruction." *Review of Educational Research* 61 (1991): 239–264.

Donelson, Ken. "Almost 13 Years of Book Protests—Now What?" *School Library Journal* 31 (March 1985): 93–98.

Dorris, Michael. "Native American Literature in an Ethnohistorical Context." *College English* 41 (October 1979): 147–162.

_____ . "On *Morning Girl.*" Press Release by Hyperion Books, 1992.

Dressel, Janice Hartwick. "Abstraction in Illustration: Is It Appropriate for Children?" *Children's Literature in Education* 15 (Summer 1984): 103–112.

Dryer, Charles Redway. *Geography, Physical, Economic, and Regional.* New York: American Books, 1911.

Duffy, Gerald G. "Crucial Elements in the Teaching of Poetry Writing." In *The Language Arts in the Middle School,* edited by Martha L. King, Robert Emans, and Patricia J. Cianciolo. Urbana, Ill.: National Council of Teachers of English, 1973.

Dundes, Alan. "Interpreting Little Red Riding Hood Psychoanalytically." In *The Brothers Grimm and Folktale,* edited by James M. McGlathey. Urbana: University of Illinois Press, 1988, 16–51.

Dunning, Stephen, and William Stafford. *Getting the Knack: 20 Poetry Writing Exercises.* Urbana: National Council of Teachers of English, 1992.

Early, Margaret. "What Ever Happened To . . . ?" *The Reading Teacher* 46 (December 1992/January 1993): 302–308.

Eccleshare, Julie. "Children's Books: Letter From London." *Publishers Weekly* 244 (August 18, 1997): 25.

Egoff, Sheila. "The Problem Novel." In *Only Connect: Readings on Children's Literature,* edited by Sheila Egoff, G. T. Stubbs, and L. F. Ashley. Toronto: Oxford University Press, 1980.

_____ . *Worlds Within: Children's Fantasy from the Middle Ages to Today.* Chicago: American Library Association, 1988.

Eichenberg, Fritz. "Bell, Book and Candle." In *The Arbuthnot Lectures: 1980–1989.* Chicago: American Library Association, 1990, 51–66.

Elleman, Barbara. "The Nonfiction Scene: What's Happening." In *Using Nonfiction Trade Books in the Elementary Classroom,* edited by Evelyn Freedman and Diane Person. Urbana, Ill.: National Council of Teachers of English, 1992, 26–33.

English Journal Forum. "When Minority Becomes Majority." *English Journal* 79 (January 1990): 15.

Epstein, William H. "Introducing Biography." *Children's Literature Association Quarterly* 12 (Winter, 1987): 177–179.

Erisman, Fred Raymond. "There Was a Child Went Forth: A Study of St. Nicholas Magazine and Selected Children's Authors, 1890–1915," Minneapolis: University of Minnesota, 1966, University Microfilm No. 66–12.

Ernest, Edward. *The Kate Greenaway Treasury.* Cleveland, Oh.: World, 1967.

Esmonde, Margaret P. "Children's Science Fiction." In *The First Steps: Best of the Early ChLA Quarterly.* Compiled by Patricia Dooley. Lafayette, Ind.: Purdue University; Children's Literature Association, 1984.

Evans, Dilys. "An Extraordinary Vision: Picture Books of the Nineties." *The Horn Book* 68 (November/December 1992): 759–763.

Faulkner, William J. *The Days When the Animals Talked.* Illustrated by Troy Howell. Chicago: Follett, 1977.

Favat, F. André. *Child and Tale: The Origins of Interest.* Urbana, Ill.: National Council of Teachers of English, 1977.

"Federal Technology Funding for Schools Jumps 450 Percent." *School Library Journal* 42 (November 1996): 14.

Feitelson, D., B. Kita, and Z. Goldstein. "Effects of Listening to Series Stories on First Graders' Comprehension and Use of Language." *Research in the Teaching of English* 20 (1986): 339–355.

Feldman, Edmund Burke. *Varieties of Visual Experience.* New York: Abrams, 1972.

Feldstein, Barbara. "Selection as a Means of Diffusing Censorship." In *Children's Literature: Resource for the Classroom,* edited by Masha Kabakow Rudman. Norwood, Mass.: Christopher Gordon, 1993, 147–167.

Fillmore, Lily Wong. "Educating Citizens for a Multicultural 21st Century." *Multicultural Education* 1 (Summer 1993): 10–12, 37.

Fisher, Carol, and Margaret Natarella. "Young Children's Preferences in Poetry: A National Survey of First, Second, and Third Graders." *Research in the Teaching of English* 16 (December 1982): 339–354.

Fisher, Leonard Everett. "The Artist at Work: Creating Nonfiction." *The Horn Book* (May/June 1988): 315–323.

Fisher, Margery. "Life Course or Screaming Farce?" *Children's Literature in Education* 7 (Autumn 1976): 108–115.

Fleming, Margaret, and Jo McGinnis, eds. *Portraits: Biography and Autobiography in the Secondary School.* Urbana, Ill.: National Council of Teachers of English, 1985.

Flender, Mary G. "Charting Book Discussions: A Method of Presenting Literature in the Elementary Grades." *Children's Literature in Education* 16 (Summer 1985): 84–92.

Fohr, Samuel Denis. *Cinderella's Gold Slipper: Spiritual Symbolism in the Grimms' Tales.* Wheaton, Ill.: Quest Books, 1991.

Ford, Paul Leicester. *The New-England Primer.* New York: Columbia University, Teachers College, 1962.

Forman, Jack. "Young Adult Books: Politics—The Last Taboo." *The Horn Book* 61 (July/August 1985): 469–471.

Fowke, Edith, and Joe Glazer. *Songs of Work and Protest.* New York: Dover, 1973.

Fox, Dan. *Go In and Out the Window: An Illustrated Songbook for Young People.* New York: The Metropolitan Museum of Art and H. Holt, 1987.

Fraser, James H., ed. *Society and Children's Literature.* Boston: Godine, 1978.

Frasher, Ramona. "A Feminist Look at Literature for Children: Ten Years Later." In *Sex Stereotypes and Reading: Research and Strategies,* edited by E. Marcia Sheridan. Newark, N.J.: International Reading Association, 1982.

Freedman, Russell. "Fact or Fiction?" In *Using Nonfiction Trade Books in the Elementary Classroom,* edited by Evelyn Freeman and Diane Person. Urbana, Ill.: National Council of Teachers of English, 1992, 2–10.

———. "Newbery Medal Acceptance." *The Horn Book* (July/August 1988): 444–451.

Friedan, Betty. "My Quest for the Fountain of Age." *Time* 142 (September 6, 1993): 61–64.

Fritz, Jean. *Homesick: My Own Story.* New York: Putnam, 1982.

———. "Making It Real." *Children's Literature in Education* 22 (Autumn 1976): 125–127.

Frobenius, Leo, and Douglas Fox. *African Genesis.* Berkeley, Calif.: Turtle Island for the Netzahualcoyal Historical Society, 1983.

Fry, Edward. "Fry's Readability Graph: Clarifications, Validity, and Extension." *Journal of Reading* 21 (December 1977): 249.

Frye, Northrop, Sheridan Baker, and George Perkins. *The Harper Handbook to Literature.* New York: Harper & Row, 1985.

Furnivall, Frederick J., ed. *Caxton's Book of Curtesye.* London: Oxford University Press, 1868.

Gage, N. L., and David C. Berliner. *Educational Psychology.* Chicago: Rand McNally, 1979.

Galda, Lee. "Accent on Art." *The Reading Teacher* 44 (February 1991): 406–414.

———. "Readers, Texts and Contexts: A Response-Based View of Literature in the Classroom." *The New Advocate* 1 (Spring, 1988): 92–102.

Garfield, Leon. "Historical Fiction for Our Global Times." *The Horn Book* (November/December 1988): 736–742.

Garrett, Jeffrey. "Far-Away Wisdom: Three Nominees for the 1992 Andersen Prize." *The Reading Teacher* 46 (December 1992/January 1993): 310–314.

Gay, Carol. "Children's Literature and the Bicentennial." *Language Arts* 53 (January 1976): 11–16.

Geller, Linda Gibson. *Wordplay and Language Learning for Children.* Urbana, Ill.: National Council of Teachers of English, 1985.

Gensler, Kinereth, and Nina Nyhart. *The Poetry Connection: An Anthology of Contemporary Poems with Ideas to Stimulate Children's Writing.* New York: Teachers & Writers, 1978.

GEO News Handbook. (November 11–17, 1990): 7.

George, Jean Craighead. "Science Is Stories." In *Vital Connections: Children, Science, and Books,* edited by Wendy Saul and Sybille A. Jagusch. Washington: Library of Congress, 1991, 67–70.

Gerke, Pamela. *Multicultural Plays for Children, Volume II, Grades 4–6.* New Hampshire: Smith & Kraus, 1996.

Gibbons, Euell. *Stalking the Wild Asparagus.* New York: McKay, 1962, 1970.

Giblin, James Cross. "The Rise and Fall and Rise of Juvenile Nonfiction, 1961–1988." In *Using Nonfiction Trade Books in the Elementary Classroom,* edited by Evelyn Freedman and Diane Person. Urbana, Ill.: National Council of Teachers of English, 1992, 17–25.

Gibson, Louis Rauch, and Laura M. Zaidman. "Death in Children's Literature: Taboo or Not Taboo?" *Children's Literature Association Quarterly* 16 (Winter 1992): 232–234.

Gillespie, Margaret C. *Literature for Children: History and Trends.* Dubuque, Iowa: Brown, 1970.

Gillin, Richard. "Romantic Echoes in the Willow." *Children's Literature* 16 (1988): 169–174.

Gillmor, Frances. *The King Danced in the Marketplace.* Salt Lake City: University of Utah Press, 1977.

Glazer, Joan. *Literature for Young Children.* Upper Saddle River, N.J.: Merrill/Prentice Hall, 1991.

Glazer, Tom. *A New Treasury of Folk Songs.* New York: Bantam Books, 1961.

Gleason, Katherine. *Native American Literature.* New York: Chelsea, 1996.

Goble, Paul. *Notes by Goble About the Illustrations for* The Girl Who Loved Wild Horses. New York: Bradbury Press, 1978.

Godden, Rumer. "Shining Popocatapetl: Poetry for Children." *The Horn Book* (May/June 1988): 305–314.

Goldberg, Lazer. "Gaps and Emphases." In *Vital Connections: Children, Science, and Books,* edited by Wendy Saul and Sybille A. Jagusch. Washington: Library of Congress, 1991, 31–41.

Good, Carter. *Dictionary of Education.* New York: McGraw-Hill, 1973.

Gordon, Christine J. "Modeling Inference Awareness Across the Curriculum." *Journal of Reading* 28 (February 1985): 444–447.

Gosa, Cheryl. "Moral Development in Current Fiction for Children and Young Adults." *Language Arts* 54 (May 1977): 529–536.

Gough, John. "Experiencing a Sequence of Poem: Ted Hughes's *Season Songs.*" *Children's Literature Association Quarterly* 13 (Winter 1988): 191–194.

———. "Poems in a Context: Breaking the Anthology Trap." *Children's Literature in Education* 15 (Winter 1984): 204–210.

Granstrom, Jane, and Anita Silvey. "A Call for Help: Exploring the Black Experience in Children's Books." In *Cultural Conformity in Books for Children,* edited by Donnarae MacCann and Gloria Woodard. Metuchen, N.J.: Scarecrow, 1977.

Graves, Donald. *Writing: Teachers and Children at Work.* Exeter, N.H.: Heinemann, 1988.

Greaney, Vincent. "Factors Related to Amount and Type of Leisure Time Reading." *Reading Research Quarterly* 15 (1980): 337–357.

Green, Roland J. "Modern Science Fiction and Fantasy: A Frame of Reference." *Illinois School Journal* 57 (Fall 1977): 45–53.

Greenfield, Eloise. "Writing for Children—A Joy and a Responsibility." In *The Black American in Books for Children: Readings in Racism,* edited by Donnarae MacCann and Gloria Woodard. Metuchen, N.J.: Scarecrow, 1985.

Greenway, William, and Betty Greenway. "Meeting the Muse: Teaching Contemporary Poetry by Teaching Poetry Writing." *Children's Literature Association Quarterly* 15 (1990): 138–142.

Griego y Maestas, Jose, and Rudolfo A. Anaya. *Cuentos: Tales from the Hispanic Southwest.* Santa Fe: Museum of New Mexico, 1980.

Griffiths, Antony, ed. *Landmarks in Print Collecting.* London: British Museum, 1996.

Groff, Patrick. "Where Are We Going with Poetry for Children?" In *Horn Book Reflections,* edited by Elinor Whitney Field. Boston: Horn Book, 1969.

Gross, John. "Pop-Up Books: The Magical Art of Making Movable Pictures over the Years." *The New York Times* (Sunday, January 17, 1988): 33H.

Haight, Anne Lyon. *Banned Books: 387 B.C. to 1978 A.D.* New York: R. R. Bowker, 1978.

Haining, Peter. *Movable Books: An Illustrated History.* London: New English Library Limited, 1979.

Haley, Gail E. "From the Ananse Stories to the Jack Tales: My Work with Folktales." *Children's Literature Association Quarterly* 11 (Fall 1986): 118–121.

Hall, Ann E. "Contemporary Realism in American Children's Books." *Choice* (November 1977): 1171–1178.

Hall, Edwin S., Jr. *The Eskimo Storyteller: Folktales from Noatak, Alaska.* Knoxville: The University of Tennessee Press, 1976.

Hamilton, Martha, and Mitch Weiss. "Children as Storytellers: Teaching the Basic Tools." *School Library Journal* 39 (April 1993): 30–33.

———. *Children Tell Stories: A Teaching Guide.* Katonah, N.Y.: Richard C. Owen, 1990.

Hamilton, Virginia. *The People Could Fly: American Black Folktales.* New York: Knopf, 1985.

———. "Planting Seeds." *The Horn Book* 68 (November/December 1992): 674–680.

Hampl, Patricia. "A Review of *The Diary of a Young Girl: Anne Frank, the Definitive Edition.*" *The New York Times Book Review* (March 5, 1995): 21.

Hanson, W. D., and M. O. Eisenbise. *Human Behavior and American Indians.* Rockville, Md.: National Institute of Mental Health, 1983. ERIC Document Reproduction Service, ED 231–589.

Harris, Violet. "Multiethnic Children's Literature." In *Exploring Literature in the Classroom: Content and Methods,* edited by K. D. Wood and A. Moss. Norwood, Mass.: Christopher-Gordon, 1992, 169–201.

Harrison, Barbara. "Howl Like the Wolves." *Children's Literature* 15 (1987): 67–90.

Harvey, Karen D., Lisa D. Harjo, and Jane K. Jackson. *Teaching About Native Americans.* Washington, D.C.: National Council for the Social Studies, 1990.

Haugaard, Erik. "When Does the Past Become History?" In *The Child and the Family: Selected Papers from International Conference of the Children's Literature Association,* edited by Susan R. Gannon and Ruth Anne Thompson. New York: Pace University, 1988, 5–11.

Haviland, Virginia. *Children and Literature: View and Reviews.* Glenview, Ill.: Scott, Foresman, 1973.

———. *North American Legends.* New York: Collins, 1979.

Hawley, John C. "The Water-Babies as Catechetical Paradigm." *Children's Literature Association Quarterly* 14 (Spring 1989): 19–21.

Hayden, Carla D., ed. *Venture into Cultures: A Resource Book of Multicultural Materials and Programs.* Chicago: American Library Association, 1992.

Hayden, Gretchen Purtell. "A Descriptive Study of the Treatment of Personal Development in Selected Children's Fiction Books Awarded the Newbery Medal." Detroit: Wayne State University, 1969, University Microfilm No. 70-19, 060.

Hearn, Michael Patrick. Preface to *Histories or Tales of Past Times,* by Charles Perrault. New York: Garland, 1977.

Hearne, Betsy. *Beauty and the Beast: Visions and Revisions of an Old Tale.* Chicago: University of Chicago Press, 1989.

———. "Booking the Brothers Grimm: Art, Adaptations, and Economics." In *The Brothers Grimm and Folktale,* edited by James M. McGlathery. Urbana, Ill.: University of Illinois Press, 1988, 220–233.

———. "Cite the Source: Reducing Cultural Chaos in Picture Books, Part One." *School Library Journal* 39 (July 1993a): 22–27.

———. "Contemporary Issues—Child Abuse." *Booklist* 81 (May 1, 1985): 1261–1262.

———. "Patterns of Sound, Sight, and Story: From Literature to Literacy." *The Lion and the Unicorn* 16 (June 1992): 17–42.

———. "Picture Books: More Than a Story." *Booklist* 30 (December 1, 1983): 577–578.

———. "Respect the Source: Reducing Cultural Chaos in Picture Books, Part Two." *School Library Journal* 39 (August 1993b): 33–37.

Heins, Paul. "Coming to Terms with Criticism." In *Crosscurrents of Criticism: Horn Book Essays 1968–1977.* Boston: The Horn Book, 1978a, 82–87.

———. "Out on a Limb with the Critics: Some Random Thoughts on the Present State of the Criticism of Children's Literature." In *Crosscurrents of Criticism: Horn Book Essays 1968–1977.* Boston: The Horn Book, 1978b, 72–81.

———. "A Second Look: The Adventures of Pinocchio." *The Horn Book* (April 1982): 200–204.

Hendrick, Joanne. *The Whole Child,* 4th ed. Upper Saddle River, N.J.: Merrill/Prentice Hall, 1992.

Henke, James T. "Dicey, Odysseus, and Hansel and Gretel: The Lost Children of Voigt's *Homecoming.*" *Children's Literature in Education* 16 (Spring 1985): 45–52.

Hepler, Susan Ingrid. "Profile, Tomie de Paola: A Gift to Children." *Language Arts* 56 (March 1979): 269–301.

Herb, Steve. "Building Blocks for Literacy: What Current Research Shows." *School Library Journal* 43 (July 1997): 23.

Herbst, Laura. "That's One Good Indian: Unacceptable Images in Children's Novels." In *Cultural Conformity in Books for Children,* edited by Donnarae MacCann and Gloria Woodard. Metuchen, N.J.: Scarecrow, 1977.

Herman, Gertrude B. " 'Footprints on the Sands of Time': Biography for Children." *Children's Literature in Education* 9 (Summer 1977): 85–94.

Hewett, Gloria J., and Jean C. Rush. "Finding Buried Treasures: Aesthetic Scanning with Children." *Art Education* 40 (January 1987): 41–43.

Hillocks, George. *Research on Written Composition: New Directions for Teaching.* Urbana, Ill.: National Conference on Research in English, 1986.

Hillyer, V. M. *A Child's Geography of the World.* Illustrated by Mary Sherwood Wright Jones. New York: Century, 1929.

Hilts, Paul. "The Road Ahead: Publishing Visionaries Look at the Change That Digital Technology Might Bring." *Publishers Weekly* 244 (July 1997): 125–128.

Hockwald, Lambeth. "Little Book, Big Controversy." *Publishers Weekly*, 243 (July 29, 1996): 32–33.

Holzheimer, Diane. "Appraisal: A Book Review Journal." In *Vital Connections: Children, Science, and Books*, edited by Wendy Saul and Sybille A. Jagusch. Washington: Library of Congress, 1991, 91–96.

Homze, Alma Cross. "Interpersonal Relationships in Children's Literature from 1920 to 1960." University Park, Pa.: Pennsylvania State University, 1963. University Microfilm No. 64-5366.

Hopkins, Dianne McAfee. "Put It in Writing: What You Should Know About Challenges to School Library Materials." *School Library Journal* 39 (January 1993): 26–30.

Hopkins, Lee Bennett. *Pass the Poetry, Please!* New York: Harper & Row, 1987.

"The Horn Book Guide to Children's and Young Adult Books." *The Horn Book* 4 (Spring 1993): 18–51.

Houghton Mifflin Company. *Eliminating Stereotypes, School Division Guidelines.* Boston: Houghton Mifflin, 1981.

Houston, James. "A Primitive View of the World." In *The Arbuthnot Lectures, 1980–1989.* Chicago: American Library Association, 1990, 99–111.

Hsu, Richard C., and William E. Mitchell. "Books Have Endured for a Reason . . ." *The New York Times* 3 (Sunday, May 25, 1997): 12.

Huck, Charlotte S., Susan Hepler, and Janet Hickman. *Children's Literature in the Elementary School.* Madison, Wis.: Brown & Benchmark, 1997.

Hunt, Peter, ed. *Children's Literature: An Illustrated History.* New York: Oxford University Press, 1995.

———. "Dialogue and Dialectic: Language and Class in *The Wind in the Willows.*" *Children's Literature* 16 (1988): 159–168.

Hürlimann, Bettina. "Fortunate Moments in Children's Books." In *The Arbuthnot Lectures, 1970–1979*, compiled by Zena Sutherland. Chicago: American Library Association, 1980, 61–80.

Huus, Helen. "Teaching Literature at the Elementary School Level." *The Reading Teacher* 26 (May 1973): 795–801.

Iskander, Sylvia Patterson. " 'Goody Two-Shoes' and *The Vicar of Wakefield.*" *Children's Literature Association Quarterly* 13 (Winter 1988): 165–168.

Jacobs, Melville. *The Content and Style of an Oral Literature: Clackamas Chinook Myths and Tales.* Chicago: University of Chicago Press, 1959.

Jaffe, Nina. "Reflections on the Work of Harold Courlander." *School Library Journal* 42 (September 1996): 132–133.

James, Grace. *Green Willow and Other Japanese Fairy Tales.* New York: Avenel, 1987.

Janson, H. W., and Anthony F. Janson. *History of Art for Young People*, 5th ed. New York: Abrams, 1995.

Jerome, Judson. *Poetry: Premeditated Art.* Boston: Houghton Mifflin, 1968.

Johannessen, Larry R. *Teaching the Literature of the Vietnam War.* Urbana, Ill.: National Council of Teachers of English, 1992.

Johnston, Kathleen S. "Choosing Books." In *Vital Connections: Children, Science, and Books*, edited by Wendy Saul and Sybille A. Jagusch. Washington, D.C.: Library of Congress, 1991, 97–103.

Jones, Leigh Ann. "Better Libraries Through Censorship." *School Library Journal* 42 (October 1996): 54.

Jorgensen, Karin. "Making the Reading, Writing, Social Studies Connection." *Social Studies and the Young Learner* 2 (March/April 1990): 20–22.

Judson, Hallowell. "What Is in a Picture?" *Children's Literature in Education* 20 (March 1989): 59–68.

Jurich, Marilyn. "What's Left Out of Biography for Children?" *Children's Literature: The Great Excluded* 1 (1972): 143–151.

Kaminski, Winfred. "War and Peace in Recent German Children's Literature." *Children's Literature* 15 (1987): 55–66.

Karl, Jean E. "What Sells—What's Good?" *The Horn Book* 63 (July/August 1987): 505–508.

Kean, John M., and Carl Personke. *The Language Arts: Teaching and Learning in the Elementary School.* New York: St. Martin, 1976.

Keith, Harold. *The Obstinate Land.* New York: Crowell, 1977.

Kelly, Robert Gordon. "Mother Was a Lady: Self and Society in Selected American Children's Periodicals, 1865–1890," Iowa City, Iowa: University of Iowa, 1970, University Microfilm No. 71-5770.

———. "Social Factors Shaping Some Nineteenth-Century Children's Periodical Fiction." In *Society and Children's Literature*, edited by James H. Fraser. Boston: Godine, 1978.

Kennemer, Phyllis K. "Reviews of Fiction Books: How They Differ." *Top of the News* 40 (Summer 1984): 419–421.

Kherdian, David. *Feathers and Tails: Animal Fables from Around the World.* New York: Philomel, 1992.

Killheffer, Robert K. J. "Fantasy Charts New Realms." *Publishers Weekly* 244 (June 16, 1997): 34–40.

Kimmel, Mary, and Elizabeth Segel. *For Reading Out Loud.* New York: Dell, 1983.

Kingsbury, Mary. "Perspectives on Criticism." *The Horn Book* 60 (February 1984): 17–23.

Kingsley, Mary. *West African Studies*, 3rd ed. New York: Barnes & Noble, 1964.

Kiska, Paula. "Slavic Wonder Tales: An Overview." *Children's Literature Association Quarterly* 11 (Fall 1986): 123–128.

Knorr, Susan M., and Margaret Knorr. *Books on the Move: A Read-About-It Go-There Guide to America's Best Family Destinations.* Minneapolis: Free Spirit, 1993.

Kobus, Doni Kwolek. "Multicultural/Global Education: An Educational Agenda for the Rights of the Child." *Social Education* 56 (April/May 1992): 224–227.

Koch, Kenneth. *Wishes, Lies, and Dreams.* New York: Vintage Books/Chelsea House, 1970.

Kohlberg, Lawrence. *Essays on Moral Development: The Philosophy of Moral Development.* New York: Harper & Row, 1981.

Kukla, Kaile. "David Booth: Drama as a Way of Knowing." *Language Arts* 64 (January 1987): 73–78.

Kun-yu, Bu. "Between Two Cultures." *Social Education* 52 (September 1988): 378–383.

Kuo, Louise, and Yuan-hsi Kuo. *Chinese Folk Tales.* Millbrae, Calif.: Celestial Arts, 1976.

Kutiper, Karen Sue. "A Survey of the Adolescent Poetry Preferences of Seventh, Eighth, and Ninth Graders." University of Houston: Ed.D. Dissertation, 1985. DAI 47:451–452A.

Lacy, Lyn Ellen. *Art and Design in Children's Picture Books: An Analysis of Caldecott Award-Winning Illustrations.* Chicago: American Library Association, 1986.

Laliberté, Norman, and Alex Mogelon. *The Reinhold Book of Art Ideas.* New York: Van Nostrand Reinhold, 1976.

Lamb, Charles, and Mary Lamb. *Tales from Shakespeare.* New York: Children's Classics, 1986.

Lamme, Linda Leonard. "Reading Aloud to Young Children." *Language Arts* 53 (November/December 1976): 886–888.

_____, and Frances Kane. "Children, Books, and Collage." *Language Arts* 53 (November/December 1976): 902–905.

Lanes, Selma. *The Art of Maurice Sendak.* New York: Abradale Press, 1980.

Larrick, Nancy. *Let's Do a Poem.* New York: Delacorte Press, 1991.

Lasky, Kathryn. *Beyond the Divide.* New York: Macmillan, 1983.

Latimer, Bettye I. *Starting Out Right: Choosing Books About Black People for Young Children.* Madison, Wis.: Wisconsin Department of Public Instruction, 1972, Bulletin No. 2314.

_____. "Telegraphing Messages to Children About Minorities." *The Reading Teacher* 30 (November 1976): 151–156.

Lauber, Patricia. "The Evolution of a Science Writer." In *Using Nonfiction Trade Books in the Elementary Classroom,* edited by Evelyn Freedman and Diane Person. Urbana, Ill.: National Council of Teachers of English, 1992, 11–16.

_____. "The Heart of the Matter." In *Vital Connections: Children, Science, and Books,* edited by Wendy Saul and Sybille A. Jagusch. Washington, D.C.: Library of Congress, 1991, 45–50.

Laws, Frederick. "Randolph Caldecott." In *Only Connect: Readings on Children's Literature,* edited by Sheila Egoff, G. T. Stubbs, and L. F. Ashley. 2nd ed. Toronto: Oxford University Press, 1980.

Leeson, Robert. *Children's Books and Class Society.* London: Writers & Readers, 1977.

Lehr, Susan, ed. *Battling Dragons: Issues and Controversy in Children's Literature.* Portsmouth, N.H.: Heinemann, 1995.

Lenaghan, R. T., ed. *Caxton's Aesop.* Cambridge, Mass.: Harvard University Press, 1967.

Lenz, Liza. "Crossroads of Literacy and Orality: Reading Poetry Aloud. *Language Arts* 69 (December 1992): 597–603.

Le Pere, Jean. "For Every Occasion: Poetry in the Reading Program." Albuquerque, N.M.: Eighth Southwest Regional Conference, International Reading Association, 1980.

Lepman-Logan, Claudia. "Books in the Classroom: Moral Choices in Literature." *The Horn Book* (January/February 1989): 108–111.

Leroi-Gourhan, Andre. *Treasures of Prehistoric Art.* New York: Abrams.

Lewis, Naomi. "Introduction." In Peter Christen Asbjörnsen and Jorgen Moe's *East O' the Sun and West O' the Moon.* Cambridge, Mass.: Candlewick, 1991.

Lewis, Rena, and Donald Doorlag. *Teaching Special Students in the Mainstream.* 2nd ed. Upper Saddle River, N.J.: Merrill/Prentice Hall, 1987.

Lindauer, Shelley L. Knudsen. "Wordless Books: An Approach to Visual Literacy." *Children's Literature in Education* 19 (1988): 136–142.

Linder, Enid, and Leslie Linder. *The Art of Beatrix Potter.* London: Frederick Warne, 1980.

Lipkis, Rita. "Books in the Classroom: Young Hands on Old Books." *The Horn Book* 69 (January/February 1993): 115–118.

Livingston, Myra Cohn. "Not the Rose . . ." In *Horn Book Reflections,* edited by Elinor Whitney Field. Boston: Horn Book, 1969.

_____. *Poems of Lewis Carroll.* New York: Crowell, 1973.

_____. *Poetry-Making: Ways to Begin Writing Poetry.* New York: HarperCollins, 1991.

Loban, Walter. *Language Development: Kindergarten Through Grade Twelve.* Urbana, Ill.: National Council of Teachers of English, 1976.

Lobsenz, Norman. "News from the Home Front." *Family Weekly* (August 2, 1981): 9.

Locke, John. "Some Thoughts Concerning Education." In *English Philosophers,* edited by Charles W. Eliot. New York: Villier, 1910.

Lodge, Sally, compiled by. "Children's Books for Fall." *Publishers Weekly* 243 (July 22, 1996): 158–205.

_____. "Rolling Out the Green Carpet: Environmental Books for Kids." *Publishers Weekly* 239 (March 2, 1992): 22–25.

_____. "Spanish-Language Publishing for Kids in the U.S. Picks Up Speed." *Publishers Weekly* Special Supplement (August 25, 1997): 548–549.

Lofaro, Michael A. *The Tall Tales of Davy Crockett: The Second Nashville Series of Crockett Almanacs, 1839–1841.* Knoxville: University of Tennessee Press, 1987.

Long, Joanna Rudge. "Eloquent Visions: Perspectives In Picture Book Biography." *School Library Journal* 43 (April 1997): 48–49.

Lonsdale, Bernard J., and Helen K. Macintosh. *Children Experience Literature.* New York: Random House, 1973.

Lottman, Herbert R. "In the Studio with Satomi Ichikawa." *Publishers Weekly* 240 (June 7, 1993): 19.

Lowell, Amy. *Poetry and Poets.* New York: Biblo, 1971.

Lukens, Rebecca J. *A Critical Handbook of Children's Literature.* Glenview, Ill.: Scott, Foresman, 1990.

Lunstrum, John P., and Bob L. Taylor. *Teaching Reading in the Social Studies.* Newark, Del.: International Reading Association, 1978.

Lustig, Arnost. "What We Will Never Understand About the Holocaust." Unexpected Encounters With the Holocaust Conference: Texas A&M University, College Station, Texas, April 2, 1997.

Lystad, Mary. *From Dr. Mather to Dr. Seuss: Two Hundred Years of American Books for Children.* Boston: G. K. Hall, 1980.

McCall, Cecelia. "A Historical Quest for Literacy." *Interracial Books for Children Bulletin* 19 (1989): 3–5.

MacCann, Donnarae, and Olga Richard. *The Child's First Books: A Critical Study of Pictures and Texts.* New York: Wilson, 1973.

MacLeod, Anne Scott. *American Childhood.* Athens: University of Georgia Press 1994.

_____. "Children's Literature in America from the Puritan Beginnings to 1870." In *Children's Literature: An Illustrated History,* edited by Peter Hunt. Oxford: Oxford University Press, 1995, 102–129.

McClenathan, Day Ann K. "Realism in Books for Young People. Some Thoughts on Management of Controversy." In *Developing Active Readers: Ideas for Parents, Teachers, and Librarians,* edited by Dianne L. Monson and Day Ann K. McClenathan. Newark, Del.: International Reading Association, 1979.

McCord, David. *One at a Time: Collected Poems for the Young.* Boston: Little, Brown, 1977.

McCord, Sue. *The Storybook Journey: Pathways to Literacy Through Story and Play.* Upper Saddle River, N.J.: Merrill/Prentice Hall, 1995.

McCulloch, Lou J. *An Introduction to Children's Literature: Children's Books of the 19th Century.* Des Moines, Iowa: Wallace-Honestead, 1979.

McDermott, Beverly Brodsky. *The Golem.* Philadelphia: Lippincott, 1976.

MacDonald, Robert. "Signs from the Imperial Quarter: Illustrations in *Chums,* 1892–1914." *Children's Literature* 16 (1988): 31–55.

McElderry, Margaret. "The Best Times, the Worst Times, Children's Book Publishing 1917–1974." *The Horn Book* (October 1974): 85–94.

McGarvey, Jack. ". . . But Computers Are Clearly the Future." *The New York Times* (Sunday, May 25, 1997): 12.

McGrath, Robin. "Words Melt Away Like Hills in Fog: Putting Inuit Legends Into Print." *Children's Literature Association Quarterly* 13 (Spring 1988): 9–12.

McGuire, Sandra. "Promoting Positive Attitudes Toward Aging." *Childhood Education* 69 (Summer 1993): 204–210.

McIntyre, Barbara M. *Creative Drama in the Elementary School.* Itasca, Ill.: Peacock, 1974.

McKay, Gwendda. "Poetry and the Young Child." *English in Australia* (June 1986): 52–58.

Madsen, Jane M., and Elaine B. Wickersham. "A Look at Young Children's Realistic Fiction." *The Reading Teacher* 34 (December 1980): 273–279.

Maguire, Jack. "Sounds and Sensibilities: Storytelling as an Educational Process." *Children's Literature Association Quarterly* 13 (Spring, 1988): 6–9.

Maher, Susan Naramore. "Encountering Others: The Meeting of Cultures in Scott O'Dell's *Island of the Blue Dolphins* and *Sing Down the Moon.*" *Children's Literature in Education* 23 (1992): 215–227.

_____. "Recasting Crusoe: Frederick Marryat, R. M. Ballantyne and the Nineteenth-Century Robinsonade." *Children's Literature Association Quarterly* 13 (Winter 1988): 169–175.

Manguel, Alberto. *A History of Reading.* New York: Viking, 1996.

_____, and Gianni Guadalupi. *The Dictionary of Imaginary Places.* Illustrated by Graham Greenfield and James Cook. New York: Macmillan, 1980.

Marantz, Sylvia S. *Picture Books for Looking and Learning: Awakening Visual Perceptions Through the Art of Children's Books.* Phoenix: Oryx Press, 1992.

Marcus, Leonard S. "Awakened by the Moon." *Publishers Weekly* 238 (July 26, 1991): 16–20.

Marshall, Cynthia. "Allegory, Orthodoxy, Ambivalence: MacDonald's *The Day Boy and the Night Girl.*" *Children's Literature* 16 (1988): 57–75.

Martin, Sue Anne Gillespi. "The Caldecott Medal Award Books, 1938–1968: Their Literary and Oral Characteristics as They Relate to Storytelling." Detroit, Mich.: Wayne State University, 1969. University Microfilm No. 72-16, 219.

Martinez, Miriam, and Nancy Roser. "Children's Responses to Literature." In *Handbook of Research on Teaching the English Language Arts,* edited by James Flood, Julie M. Jensen, Diane Lapp, and James R. Squire. New York: Macmillan, 1991, 643–654.

Maryles, Daisy. "Behind the Bestsellers." *Publishers Weekly* 243 (July 22, 1996): 141.

Maughan, Shannon. "Dealing the Straight Dope." *Publishers Weekly* 239 (April 13, 1992): 23.

Maxim, George. *The Very Young: Guiding Children from Infancy Through the Early Years.* Upper Saddle River, N.J.: Merrill/Prentice Hall, 1993.

Meigs, Cornelia, Elizabeth Nesbitt, Anne Thaxter Eaton, and Ruth Hill. *A Critical History of Children's Literature: A Survey of Children's Books in English.* New York: Macmillan, 1969.

Mendelson, Michael. "*The Wind in the Willows* and the Plotting of Contrast." *Children's Literature* 16 (1988): 125–144.

Mendoza, Alicia. "Reading to Children: Their Preferences." *The Reading Teacher* 38 (February 1985): 522–527.

Merriam, Eve. *Rainbow Writing.* New York: Atheneum, 1976.

Merrick, Brian. "With a Straight Eye: An Interview with Charles Causley." *Children's Literature in Education* 19 (Winter 1988): 123–135.

Metcalf, Eva-Maria, and Michael J. Meyer. "Society, Child Abuse, and Children's Literature." *Children's Literature Association Quarterly.* 17 (Fall 1992): 2–3.

Miller, Peggy J. "Peter Rabbit and Mr. McGregor Reconciled, Charlotte Lives: Preschoolers Recreate the Classics." *The Horn Book* 73 (May/June 1997): 282–283.

Miller, Winifred. "Dragons—Fact or Fantasy?" *Elementary English* 52 (April 1975): 582–585.

Milne, A. A. *The Christopher Robin Story Book.* New York: Dutton, 1966.

Mittelstadt, Michelle. "Texas High on Watchdog Group's Censorship List." Associated Press. Bryan, College Station, Tex.: *The Eagle* (Thursday, September 2, 1993): A9.

Monson, Dianne, and Sam Sebesta. "Reading Preferences." In *Handbook of Research on Teaching the English Language Arts,* edited by James Flood, Julie M. Jensen, Diane Lapp, and James R. Squire. New York: Macmillan, 1991, 664–673.

Moore, Ann W. "A Question of Accuracy: Errors in Children's Biographies." *School Library Journal* 31 (February 1985): 34–35.

Moore, Eva. *The Fairy Tale Life of Hans Christian Andersen.* Illustrated by Trina Schart Hyman. New York: Scholastic, 1969.

Moore, Lilian. "A Second Look: The Poetry of Lillian Morrison." *The Horn Book* 69 (May/June 1993): 303–306.

_____. "A Second Look: Small Poems." *The Horn Book* (July/August 1988): 470–473.

Morache, Jette. "Use of Quotes in Teaching Literature." *English Journal* 76 (October 1987): 61–63.

Morgan, Betty M. *An Investigation of Children's Books Containing Characters from Selected Minority Groups Based on Specified Criteria.* Carbondale, Ill.: Southern Illinois University, 1973. University Microfilm No. 74-6232.

Moritz, Charles. *Current Biography Yearbook.* New York: Wilson, 1968.

Morrison, Lillian. *The Sidewalk Racer and Other Poems of Sport and Motion.* New York: Lothrop, Lee & Shepard, 1977.

Morrow, Lesley Mandel. "Promoting Voluntary Reading." In *Handbook of Research on Teaching the English Language Arts,* edited by James Flood, Diane Lapp, and James R. Squire. New York: Macmillan, 1991, 681–690.

Morse, Samuel French. "Speaking of the Imagination." In *Horn Book Reflections,* edited by Elinor Whitney Field. Boston: Horn Book, 1969.

Muir, Percy. *English Children's Books, 1600 to 1900.* New York: Praeger, 1954.

Musleah, Rahel. "Rediscovering the Jewish Folktale." *Publishers Weekly* 239 (September 21, 1992): 42–43.

Mussen, Paul Henry, John Janeway Conger, and Jerome Kagan. *Child Development and Personality.* New York: Harper & Row, 1989.

National Council for the Social Studies. "The Columbian Quincentenary: An Educational Opportunity." *Social Education* 56 (April/May 1992): 248–249.

National Science Teachers Association. "Criteria for Selection—Outstanding Science Trade Books for Children." *Science and Children* 34 (March 1997): 23.

Natov, Roni. "Internal and External Journeys: The Child Hero in *The Zabajaba Jungle* and *Linnea in Monet's Garden*." *Children's Literature In Education* 20 (June 1989): 91–101.

Nelson, Mary Ann. *A Comparative Anthology of Children's Literature.* New York: Holt, Rinehart & Winston, 1972.

Nesbit, E., retold by. *Beautiful Stories from Shakespeare.* New York: Weathervane. Facsimile of 1907 edition.

Neufeld, John. "Preaching to the Unconverted." *School Library Journal* 42 (July 1996): 36.

Newcomb, Franc J. *Navajo Folk Tales.* Santa Fe: Museum of Navajo Ceremonial Art, 1967, xvi.

Nikola-Lisa, W. "Scribbles, Scrawls, and Scratches: Graphic Play as Subtext in the Picture Books of Ezra Jack Keats." *Children's Literature in Education* 22 (December 1991): 247–155.

Nilsen, Aileen Pace. "Women in Children's Literature." *College English* 32 (May 1971): 918–926.

_____ , and Kenneth L. Donelson. *Literature for Today's Young Adults,* 4th ed. New York: HarperCollins, 1993.

Nitschke, August. "The Importance of Fairy Tales in German Families Before the Grimms." In *The Brothers Grimm and Folktale,* edited by James M. McGlathery. Urbana, Ill.: University of Illinois Press, 1988, 164–177.

Noble, Judith Ann. "The Home, the Church, and the School as Portrayed in American Realistic Fiction for Children 1965–1969." East Lansing, Mich.: Michigan State University, 1971. University Microfilm No. 31-271.

Noble, William. *Bookbanning in America: Who Bans Books?—and Why.* Middlebury, Vt.: Eriksson, 1990.

Nodelman, Perry. "How Children Respond to Art." *School Library Journal* 31 (December 1984a): 40–41.

_____ . "Some Presumptuous Generalizations About Fantasy." In *The First Steps: Best of the Early ChLA Quarterly.* Compiled by Patricia Dooley. Purdue University; Children's Literature Association, 1984b, 15–16.

_____ . "Which Children? Some Audiences for Children's Books." *The Horn Book* 63 (January/February 1987): 35–40.

_____ . *Words About Pictures.* Athens: University of Georgia Press, 1988.

Noel, Ruth S. *The Mythology of Middle Earth.* Boston: Houghton Mifflin, 1977.

Norton, Donna E. "Centuries of Biographies for Childhood." *Vitae Scholasticae* 3 (Spring 1984): 113–129.

_____ . *The Effective Teaching of Language Arts,* 5th ed. Upper Saddle River, N.J.: Merrill/Prentice Hall, 1997.

_____ . "The Expansion and Evaluation of a Multiethnic Reading/Language Arts Program Designed for 5th, 6th, 7th, and 8th Grade Children." Meadows Foundation Grant, No. 55614, A Three Year Longitudinal Study. Texas A&M University, 1984–1987.

_____ . "Folklore and the Language Arts." In *Language Arts Instruction and the Beginning Teacher,* edited by Dale Johnson and Carl Personke. Englewood Cliffs, N.J.: Prentice-Hall, 1987a.

_____ . "Genres in Children's Literature: Identifying, Analyzing, and Appreciating." In *Children's Literature: Resource for the Classroom,* edited by Masha Kabakow Rudman. Norwood, Mass.: Christopher-Gordon, 1993, 75–94.

_____ . *The Impact of Literature-Based Reading.* Upper Saddle River, N.J.: Merrill/Prentice Hall, 1992.

_____ . "The Intrusion of an Alien Culture: The Impact and Reactions as Seen Through Biographies and Autobiographies of Native Americans." *Vitae Scholasticae* 6 (Spring 1987): 59–75.

_____ . "Moral Stages of Children's Biographical Literature: 1800s–1900s." *Vitae Scholasticae* (Fall 1986).

_____ . "Teaching Multicultural Literature in the Reading Program." *The Reading Teacher* 44 (September 1990): 28–40.

_____ . "A Three-Year Study Developing and Evaluating Children's Literature Units in Children's Literature Courses." Paper presented at the College Reading Association, National Conference, Baltimore, Md., October, 1980.

_____ . *Through the Eyes of a Child: An Introduction to Children's Literature,* 3rd ed. Upper Saddle River, N.J.: Merrill/Prentice Hall, 1991.

_____ . "A Web of Interest." *Language Arts* 54 (November 1977): 928–932.

_____ , and James F. McNamara. *An Evaluation of the Multicultural Reading/Language Arts Program for Elementary and Junior High School Students.* College Station, Tex.: Texas A&M University, 1988.

_____ , and Saundra E. Norton. *Language Arts Activities for Children,* 4th ed. Up-

per Saddle River, N.J.: Merrill/Prentice Hall, 1999.

Noss, Philip A. "Description in Gbaya Literary Art." In *African Folklore,* edited by Richard Dorse. Bloomington, Ind.: Indiana University Press, 1972.

"Notable Children's Trade Books in the Field of Social Studies." *Social Education* (April/May 1992): 253–264.

Odean, Katheleen. "Adventures and Accomplishments: Picture-Book Biographies of Women." *School Library Journal* 42 (December 1996): 664–665.

Olson, Renee. "When It Comes To Technology . . . The Postman Always Thinks Twice." *School Library Journal* 42 (May 1996): 19–22.

Opler, Morris Edward. *Myths and Tales of the Jicarilla Apache Indians.* Memoirs 31. New York: American Folklore Society, 1938.

Parsons, Elsie Clews. *Folktales of Andros Island, Bahamas.* New York: American Folklore Society, 1918.

Paulin, Mary Ann. *Creative Uses of Children's Literature.* Hamden, Conn.: Library Professional Pubs., 1985.

Peck, Richard. "The Great Library-Shelf Witch Hunt." *Booklist* 88 (January 1, 1992): 816–817.

Pellowski, Anne. *The Family Story-Telling Handbook.* New York: Macmillan, 1987.

_____ . *Hidden Stories in Plants.* New York: Macmillan, 1990.

_____ . *The World of Storytelling.* New York: Bowker, 1977.

Perrine, Laurence. *Literature: Structure, Sound, and Sense,* 4th ed. San Diego: Harcourt Brace Jovanovich, 1983.

Phelan, Carolyn. "Talking with Mem Fox." *Book Links* 2 (May 1993): 29–32.

Phelps, Ruth M. "A Comparison of Newbery Award Winners in the First and Last Decade of the Award (1922–31 and 1976–85). Miami University, 1985, DAI 47: 453A.

Piaget, Jean, and B. Inhelder. *The Psychology of the Child.* New York: Basic Books, 1969.

Piper, David. "Language Growth in the Multiethnic Classroom." *Language Arts* 63 (January 1986): 23–36.

Polking, Kirk, ed. *Writing A to Z.* Cincinnati, Oh.: Writer's Digest Books, 1990.

Poole, Roger. "The Books Teachers Use." *Children's Literature in Education* 17 (Fall 1986): 159–180.

Preble, Duane. *Art Forms.* New York: Harper & Row, 1978.

Pringle, Laurence. "The Thinking Gap." In *Vital Connections: Children, Science, and Books,* edited by Wendy Saul and Sybille A. Jagusch. Washington: Library of Congress, 1991, 51–56.

———. *Wild Foods: A Beginner's Guide to Identifying, Harvesting and Preparing Safe and Tasty Plants from the Outdoors.* Illustrated by Paul Breeden. New York: Four Winds, 1978.

Probst, Robert. "Response to Literature." In *Handbook of Research on Teaching the English Language Arts,* edited by James Flood, Julie M. Jensen, Diane Lapp, and James R. Squire. New York: Macmillan, 1991, 633–655.

———. "Teaching the Reading of Literature." In *Content Area Reading and Learning: Instructional Strategies,* edited by Diane Lapp, James Flood, and N. Farnan. Englewood Cliffs, N.J.: Prentice Hall, 1989, 179–186.

Proett, Jackie, and Kent Gill. *The Writing Process in Action: A Handbook for Teachers.* Urbana, Ill.: National Council of Teachers of English, 1986.

Propp, Vladimir. *Morphology of the Folktale.* Translated by Laurence Scott. Austin, Tex.: University of Texas, 1968.

"Publishers Weekly: Children's Bestsellers." *Publishers Weekly* 244 (July 21, 1997): 177.

Purves, Alan C. "The School Subject Literature." In *Handbook of Research on Teaching the English Language Arts,* edited by James Flood, Julie M. Jensen, Diane Lapp, and James R. Squire. New York: Macmillan, 1991, 674–680.

———, and Dianne L. Monson. *Experiencing Children's Literature.* Glenview, Ill.: Scott, Foresman, 1984.

Quammen, David. "The Look of the Wild: How Styles of Illustration Have Changed the Way We Look at Animals." *The New York Times Book Review* (November 7, 1993): 12.

Quayle, Eric. *The Collector's Book of Children's Books.* New York: Clarkson N. Potter, 1971.

Rauch, Alan. "A World of Faith on a Foundation of Science: Science and Religion in British Children's Literature: 1761–1878." *Children's Literature Association Quarterly* 14 (Spring 1989): 13–19.

Raugust, Karen. "Sports Leagues Target Young Fans With Books." *Publishers Weekly* 244 (August 18, 1997): 34–35.

Raymo, Chet. "Dr. Seuss and Dr. Einstein: Children's Books and Scientific Imagination." *The Horn Book* 68 (September/October 1992): 560–567.

Reed, Susan Nugent. "Career Idea: Meet the Poet at His Craft." In *Using Literature and Poetry Affectively,* edited by Jon E. Shapiro. Newark, Del.: International Reading Association, 1979.

Rees, David. "The Virtues of Improbability: Joan Aiken." *Children's Literature in Education* 19 (Spring 1988): 42–54.

Rees-Williams, Gladys, and Brian Rees-Williams, eds. *What I Cannot Tell My Mother Is Not Fit for Me to Know.* New York: Oxford University Press, 1981.

Reichard, Gladys A. *An Analysis of Coeur d'Alene Indian Myths.* Philadelphia: American Folklore Society, 1974.

Reiss, Johanna. *The Upstairs Room.* New York: Crowell, 1972.

Rice, Daniel. "Vision and Culture: The Role of Museums in Visual Literacy." *The Journal of Museum Education* 13 (1988): 13–17.

Roback, Diane, and Cindi Di Marzo. "Children's Book Survey: Consumer Awareness." *Publishers Weekly* 244 (June 16, 1997): 28–31.

Roback, Diane, and Shannon Maughan, eds. "Fall 1996 Children's Books: The Road Ahead." *Publishers Weekly* 243 (July 22, 1996): 151–153.

Robertson, Elizabeth, and Jo McGinnis. "Biography as Art: A Formal Approach." In *Portraits: Biography and Autobiography in the Secondary School,* edited by Margaret Fleming and Jo McGinnis. Urbana, Ill.: National Council of Teachers of English, 1985.

Rochman, Hazel. "The African American Journey: From Slavery to Freedom." *Booklist* 89 (February 15, 1993): 1052–1053.

———. *Against Borders: Promoting Books for a Multicultural World.* Chicago: American Library Association, 1992a.

———. "The Booklist Interview: Maurice Sendak." *Booklist* 88 (June 15, 1992b): 1848–1849.

———. "The Booklist Interview: Virginia Hamilton." *Booklist* 88 (February 1, 1992c): 1020–1021.

———. "Booktalking: Going Global." *The Horn Book* (January-February 1989): 30–35.

———. "How Not to Write About the Holocaust." *Booklist* 89 (October 15, 1992): 416.

———. "Loose Canon." *Booklist* 92 (September 1, 1996): 114–115.

———. "Young Adult Books: Childhood Terror." *The Horn Book* 61 (September/October 1985): 598–602.

Roehler, Laura, and Gerald G. Duffy. "Direct Explanation of Comprehension Processes." In *Comprehension Instruction,* edited by Gerald G. Duffy, Laura R. Roehler, and Jana Mason. New York: Longman, 1984, 265–280.

Roller, Cathy. "Classroom Interaction Patterns: Reflections of a Stratified Society." *Language Arts* 66 (September 1989): 492–500.

Root, Shelton L. "The New Realism—Some Personal Reflections." *Language Arts* 54 (January 1977): 19–24.

Rosenberg, Liz. "Has Poetry for Kids Become a Child's Garden of Rubbish?" *The New York Times Book Review* (November 10, 1991): 55.

Rosenblatt, Louise. "Language, Literature, and Values." In *Language, Schooling, and Society,* edited by S. N. Tchudi. Upper Montclair, N.J.: Boyton/Cook, 1985, 64–80.

———. "Literary Theory." In *Handbook of Research on Teaching the English Language Arts,* edited by James Flood, Julie M. Jensen, Diane Lapp, and James R. Squire. Upper Saddle River, N.J.: Merrill/Prentice Hall, 1991, 57–62.

———. *The Reader, the Text, and the Literary Work.* Carbondale, Ill.: Southern Illinois Press, 1978.

Ross, A. C., and D. Brave Eagle. *Value Orientation—A Strategy for Removing Barriers.* Denver, Colo.: Coalition of Indian Controlled School Boards, 1975. ERIC Document Reproduction, ED 125–811.

Ross, Elinor P. "Comparison of Folk Tale Variants." *Language Arts* 56 (April 1979): 422–426.

Ross, Jan. "Small Is Tall—Children and Self-Esteem." *Book Links* 2 (January 1993): 53–59.

Ross, Mabel, and Barbara Walker. *"On Another Day . . ." Tales Told Among the Nkundo of Zaire.* Hamden, Conn.: Archon, 1979.

Ross, Ramon R. *Storyteller,* 2d ed. Upper Saddle River, N.J.: Merrill/Prentice Hall, 1980.

Routman, Regle. *Literacy At the Crossroads: Crucial Talk About Reading, Writing, and Other Teaching Dilemmas.* Portsmouth, N.H.: Heineman, 1996.

Ruddell, Robert. "A Whole Language and Literature Perspective: Creating a Meaning-Making Instructional Environment." *Language Arts* 69 (December 1992): 612–619.

Rudman, Masha Kabakow. "Children's Literature in the Reading Program." In *Children's Literature: Resource for the Classroom,* edited by Masha Kabakow Rudman. Norwood, Mass.: Christopher-Gordon, 1993a, 171–199.

_____ . *Children's Literature: An Issues Approach,* 2d ed. New York: Longman, 1984.

_____ . "People Behind the Books: Illustrators." In *Children's Literature: Resource for the Classroom,* edited by Masha Kabakow Rudman. Norwood, Mass.: Christopher-Gordon, 1993b, 19–41.

_____ , and Anna Markus Pearce. *For Love of Reading: A Parent's Guide to Encouraging Young Readers from Infancy Through Age 5.* Mount Vernon, N.Y.: Consumers Union, 1988.

Rutherford, James. "Vital Connections: Children, Books, and Science." In *Vital Connections: Children, Books, and Science,* edited by Wendy Saul and Sybille A. Jagusch. Washington D.C.: Library of Congress, 1991, 21–30.

Sacks, David. "Breathing New Life Into Ancient Greece and Rome." *School Library Journal,* 42 (November 1996): 38–39.

Sagan, Carl. *Cosmos.* Public Broadcasting System, October 26, 1980.

Sage, Mary. "A Study of the Handicapped in Children's Literature." In *Children's Literature, Selected Essays and Bibliographies,* edited by Anne S. MacLeod. College Park, Md.: University of Maryland College of Library and Informational Services, 1977.

Sale, Roger. *Fairy Tales and After: From Snow White to E. B. White.* Cambridge, Mass.: Harvard University Press, 1978.

Sam Houston Area Reading Conference, Sam Houston State University, February 1981.

Sandburg, Carl. *The American Songbag.* New York: Harcourt Brace Jovanovich, 1927.

San Diego Museum of Art. *Dr. Seuss from Then to Now.* New York: Random House, 1986.

Sarafino, Edward P., and James W. Armstrong. *Child and Adolescent Development.* Glenview, Ill.: Scott, Foresman, 1986.

Saturday Review 48 (September 11, 1965), 63–65, 84–85.

Saul, Wendy. "Introduction." In *Vital Connections: Children, Science, and Books,* edited by Wendy Saul and Sybille A. Jagusch. Washington D.C.: Library of Congress, 1991, 3–18.

Schamel, Wynell Burroughs, and Jean West. "The Fight for Equal Rights: A Recruiting Poster for Black Soldiers in the Civil War." *Social Education* 56 (February 1992): 118–120.

Schoenherr, John. "Caldecott Medal Acceptance." *The Horn Book* 64 (July/August 1988): 457–459.

Schwarcz, Joseph. *Ways of the Illustrator: Visual Communication in Children's Literature.* Chicago: American Library Association, 1982.

Schwartz, Alvin. *And the Green Grass Grew All Around.* New York: HarperCollins, 1992.

Sealey, D. Bruce. "Measuring the Multicultural Quotient of a School." *TESL Canada Journal/Revue TESL Du Canada* 1 (March 1984): 21–28.

Sears, Roebuck and Co., Consumers Guide: 1900. Reprint. Northfield, Ill.: DBI Books, 1970.

Sebesta, Sam. "Choosing Poetry." In *Children's Choices,* edited by Nancy Roser and Margaret Frith. Newark, Del.: International Reading Association, 1983.

_____ . "What Do Young People Think About the Literature They Read?" *Reading Newsletter,* no. 8. Rockleigh, N.J.: Allyn & Bacon, 1979.

Seeger, Ruth Crawford. *American Folksongs for Children—In Home, School, and Nursery School.* New York: Doubleday, 1948.

Seki, Keigo, ed. *Folktales of Japan.* Translated by Robert J. Adams. Chicago: University of Chicago, 1963, xv.

Sendak, Maurice. *Posters by Maurice Sendak.* New York: Harmony Books, 1986.

Sender, Ruth Minsky. *The Holocaust Lady.* New York: Macmillan, 1992.

Sewell, Helen. *A Book of Myths, Selections from Bulfinch's Age of Fable.* New York: Macmillan, 1942, 1962.

Shaffer, David R. *Developmental Psychology: Childhood and Adolescence,* 2nd ed. Pacific Grove, Calif.: Brooks/Cole, 1989.

Shannon, George. "Once and Forever a Platypus: Child Reader to Writing Adult." *Children's Literature Association Quarterly* 13 (Fall 1988): 122–124.

_____ . "Sharing Honey from the Hive." *Children's Literature Association Quarterly* 11 (Fall, 1986): 115–118.

Shapiro, Jon E., ed. *Using Literature and Poetry Affectively.* Newark, Del.: International Reading Association, 1979.

Shaw, Jean Duncan. "An Historical Survey of Themes Recurrent in Selected Children's Books Published in America Since 1850," Philadelphia: Temple University, 1966, University Microfilm No. 67-11, 437.

Shulevitz, Uri. *Writing with Pictures: How to Write and Illustrate Children's Books.* New York: Watson-Guptill, 1985.

Sibley, Brian. *The Land of Narnia.* New York: Harper & Row, 1989.

Sidney, Sir Philip. *An Apologie for Poetrie.* London: 1595.

Sierra, Judy. *Multicultural Folktales for the Feltboard and Readers' Theater.* Phoenix: Oryx, 1996.

Siks, Geraldine. *Drama with Children.* New York: Harper & Row, 1983.

Silvey, Anita. "The Goats." *The Horn Book* (January/February 1988): 23.

Simmons, John S. *Censorship: A Threat to Reading, Learning, Thinking.* Newark, Del.: International Reading Association, 1994.

Sipe, Lawrence R. "In Their Own Words: Author's Views on Issues in Historical Fiction." *The New Advocate* 10 (Summer 1997): 243–258.

Sis, Peter. "The Artist At Work." *The Horn Book* 68 (November/December 1992): 681–687.

Smith, Amanda. "The Lively Art of Leo Lionni." *Publishers Weekly* 238 (April 5, 1991): 118–119.

Smith, Lane. "The Artist at Work." *The Horn Book* 69 (January/February 1993): 64–70.

Spang, A. "Counseling the Indian." *Journal of American Indian Education* 5 (1965): 10–15.

St. Clair, Jean. "Recreating Black Life in Children's Literature." *Interracial Books for Children Bulletin* 19 (1989): 7–11.

Stacks, John F. "Aftershocks of the 'Me' Decade." *Time* (August 3, 1981): 18.

Stander, Bella. "Spring Titles for Kids Highlight Heroes and Their Times." *Publishers Weekly* 239 (December 14, 1992): 28–29.

Stanley, Diane. "Is That Book Politically Correct? Truth and Trends in Historical Literature For Young People. A Writer Speaks . . ." *Journal of Youth Services in Libraries* 7 (Winter 1994): 172–175.

Stark, Myra. *Florence Nightingale.* New York: Feminist Press, 1979.

Steele, Mary Q. "Realism, Truth, and Honesty." *The Horn Book* 46 (February 1971): 17–27.

Sterck, Kenneth. "Landscape and Figures in the Poetry of De la Mare." *Children's Literature in Education* 19 (Spring 1988): 17–31.

Stewig, John Warren. "The Emperor's New Clothes." *Book Links* 2 (May 1993): 35–38.

_____ . "A Literary and Linguistic Analysis of Scott O'Dell's *The Captive.*" *Children's Literature Association Quarterly* 14 (Fall, 1989): 135–138.

_____ . *Reading Pictures: Exploring Illustrations with Children.* New Berlin, Wis.: Jenson, 1988.

Stokstad, Marilyn. *Art History: Volume One.* New York: Abrams, 1995.

_____ . *Art History: Volume Two.* New York: Abrams, 1995.

Storey, Denise C. "Fifth Graders Meet Elderly Book Characters." *Language Arts* 56 (April 1979): 408–412.

Stott, Jon C. "Biographies of Sports Heroes and the American Dream." *Children's Literature in Education* 10 (Winter 1979): 174–185.

_____ . "Native Tales and Traditions in Books for Children." *The American Indian Quarterly* 16 (Summer 1992): 373–380.

Strickland, Dorothy S. "Prompting Language and Concept Development." In *Literature and Young Children,* edited by Bernice Cullinan. Urbana, Ill.: National Conference of Teachers of English, 1977.

Sutherland, Zena. *Children and Books,* 9th ed. New York: Longman, 1997.

_____ , and Betsy Hearne. "In Search of the Perfect Picture Book Definition." In *Jump over the Moon: Selected Professional Readings,* edited by Pamela Barron and Jennifer Burley. New York: Holt, Rinehart & Winston, 1984.

_____ , and Myra Cohn Livingston. *The Scott, Foresman Anthology of Children's Literature.* Glenview, Ill.: Scott, Foresman, 1984.

Sutton, Roger. "Where's That Renaissance?" *The Horn Book* 72 (November/December 1996): 664–665.

Swanton, Susan. "Minds Alive: What and Why Gifted Students Read for Pleasure." *School Library Journal* 30 (March 1984): 99–102.

Symons, Ann K. "Sizing Up Sites: How to Judge What You Find on the Web." *School Library Journal* 43 (April 1997): 22–25.

Taggart, James. " 'Hansel and Gretel' in Spain and Mexico." *Journal of American Folklore* 99 (1986): 435–460.

Tanner, Fran. *Creative Communication: Projects in Acting, Speaking, Oral Reading.* Pocatello, Idaho: Clark, 1979.

Temple, Frances. *Taste of Salt: A Story of Modern Haiti.* New York: Orchard, 1992.

Terry, Ann. *Children's Poetry Preferences: A National Survey of the Upper Elementary Grades.* Urbana, Ill.: National Council of Teachers of English, 1974.

Thomas, Joyce. "The Tales of the Brothers Grimm: In the Black Forest." In *Touchstones: Reflections on the Best in Children's Literature,* edited by Perry Nodelman. West Lafayette, Ind.: Children's Literature Association, 1987, 104–117.

Thompson, Stith. *The Folktale.* Berkeley: University of California Press, 1977.

Thurman, Judith. *Flashlight and Other Poems.* New York: Atheneum, 1976.

Tolkien, J. R. R. *Fellowship of the Ring.* Boston: Houghton Mifflin, 1965.

Totten, Herman L., Carolyn Garner, and Risa W. Brown. *Culturally Diverse Library Collections for Youth.* New York: Neal-Schuman, 1996.

Townsend, John Rowe. *Written for Children: An Outline of English-Language Children's Literature.* New York: Lippincott, 1975.

Trafzer, Clifford E. "The Word Is Sacred to the Child: American Indians and Children's Literature." *The American Indian Quarterly* 16 (Summer 1992): 381–396.

Travers, P. T. *About the Sleeping Beauty.* Illustrated by Charles Keeping. New York: McGraw-Hill, 1975.

Trease, Geoffrey. "The Historical Story: Is It Relevant Today?" *The Horn Book* (February 1977): 21–28.

Trelease, Jim. *The New Read-Aloud Handbook.* New York: Viking, 1989.

Tremearne, A. J. *Hausa Superstitions and Customs: An Introduction to the Folklore and the Folk.* London: Frank Cass, 1970.

Tuer, Andrew W. *Stories from Forgotten Children's Books.* London: Leadenhall Press, 1898; Bracken Books, 1986.

Tunnell, Michael O. "Alexander's Chronicles of Prydain: Twenty Years Later." *School Library Journal* 34 (April 1988): 27–31.

_____ . "Books in the Classroom." *The Horn Book* 63 (July/August 1987): 509–511.

_____ , and James S. Jacobs. "Using 'Real' Books: Research Findings on Literature Based Reading Instruction." *The Reading Teacher* 42 (March 1989): 470–477.

Tway, Eileen. "Dimensions of Multicultural Literature for Children." In *Children's Literature: Resource for the Classroom,* edited by Masha Kabakow Rudman. Needham Heights, Mass.: Christopher-Gordon, 1989, 109–138.

Unsworth, Robert. "Welcome Home . . . I Think." *School Library Journal* 35 (May 1988): 48–49.

Vallone, Lynne. "The Crisis of Education: Eighteenth-Century Adolescent Fiction for Girls." *Children's Literature Association Quarterly* 14 (Summer 1988): 63–67.

Vasilakis, Nancy. "Young Adult Books: An Eighties Perspective." *The Horn Book* 61 (November/December 1985): 768–769.

Vrooman, Diana. "Characterization Techniques in *Sarah, Plain and Tall.*" College Station: Texas A&M University, 1989.

Walker, Barbara. *The Dancing Palm Tree and Other Nigerian Folktales.* Illustrated by Helen Siegl. Lubbock: Texas Tech University Press, 1990.

Walmsley, S. A., and T. P. Walp. *Teaching Literature in Elementary School: A Report on the Elementary School Antecedents of Secondary School Literature Instruction.* Report Series 1.3 Albany, N.Y.: Center for the Teaching and Learning of Literature. University at Albany, State University of New York (ERIC No. ED 315 754), 1989.

Ward, Nel, and Patrick Jones. "Homelessness in America." *Booklist* 89 (October 1, 1992): 340–341.

Weaver, Warren. *Alice in Many Tongues.* Madison, Wis.: University of Wisconsin, 1964.

Weinberg, Steve. "Biography: Telling the Untold Story." *The Writer* (February 1993): 23–25.

Werner, Craig, and Frank P. Riga. "The Persistence of Religion in Children's Literature." *Children's Literature Association Quarterly* 14 (Spring, 1989): 2–3.

West, Mark I. *Trust Your Children: Voices Against Censorship in Children's Literature.* New York: Neal-Schuman, 1988.

Western, Linda. "A Comparative Study of Literature Through Folk Tale Variants." *Language Arts* 57 (April 1980): 395–402.

Weston, Annette H. "Robert Lawson: Author and Illustrator." *Elementary English* 47 (January 1970): 74–84.

Whalen-Levitt, Peggy. "Making Picture Books Real: Reflections on a Child's-Eye View." In *The First Steps: Best of the Early ChLA Quarterly,* compiled by Patricia Dooley. Lafayette, Ind.: Purdue University, Children's Literature Association, 1984.

Whitehead, Jane. "'This Is Not What I Wrote!': The Americanization of British Children's Books—Part I." *The Horn Book* (November/December 1996): 687–693.

_____ . "'This Is Not What I Wrote!': The Americanization of British Children's Books—Part II." *The Horn Book* (January/February 1997): 27–34.

Wigginton, Eliot. *The Foxfire Book.* New York: Doubleday, 1972.

Wilkin, Binnie Tate. *Survival Themes in Fiction for Children and Young People.* Metuchen, N.J.: Scarecrow, 1978.

Winkler, Karen J. "Academe and Children's Literature: Will They Live Happily Ever After?" *Chronicle of Higher Education* (June 15, 1981).

Wintle, Justin, and Emma Fisher. *The Pied Pipers: Interviews with the Influential Creators of Children's Literature.* New York: Paddington, 1974.

Wisniewski, David. *Sundiata: Lion King of Mali.* New York: Clarion, 1992.

Wolkstein, Diane. "Twenty-Five Years of Storytelling: The Spirit of the Art." *The Horn Book* 68 (November/December 1992): 702–708.

Worth, Valerie. "Capturing Objects in Words." *The Horn Book* 68 (September/October 1992): 568–569.

Worthy, M. Jo, and Janet W. Bloodgood. "Enchancing Reading Instruction Through Cinderella Tales." *The Reading Teacher* 46 (December 1992/January 1993): 290–301.

Wright, Jone P., and Elizabeth G. Allen. "Sixth-Graders Ride with Paul Revere." *Language Arts* 53 (January 1976): 46–50.

Wrightson, Patricia. "Stones into Pools." In *The Arbuthnot Lectures: 1980–1989.* Chicago: American Library Association, 1990, 67–77.

Wyndham, Robert. *Tales the People Tell in China.* New York: Messner, 1971.

Yates, Elizabeth. *We, the People.* Illustrated by Nora Unwin. Hanover, N.H.: Regional Center for Educational Training, 1974.

Yep, Laurence. *The Rainbow People.* New York: Harper & Row, 1989.

Yolen, Jane. "Magic Mirrors: Society Reflected in the Glass of Fantasy." *Children's Literature Association Quarterly* 11 (Summer 1986): 88–90.

_____ . "Past Time: The Writing of the Picture Book *Encounter.*" *The New Advocate* (September 1992): 234–239.

_____ . "Taking Time: On How Things Have Changed in the Last Thirty-Five Years of Children's Publishing." *The New Advocate* 10 (Fall 1997): 285–291.

Young, Beverly. "The Young Female Protagonist in Juvenile Fiction: Three Decades of Evolution." Washington State University, 1985, DAI 46: 3276A.

APPENDIX A

Book Awards

Awards for outstanding children's books are presented yearly by organizations, publishers, and other interested groups. These awards have multiplied since the instigation of the Newbery Award in 1922. The following lists include the books, authors, and illustrators who have received the Caldecott Medal and honor awards, the Newbery Medal and honor awards, the Children's Book Award, the Hans Christian Andersen International Medal, or the Laura Ingalls Wilder Medal. Following this list are examples of additional awards presented in the United States, Canada, and the United Kingdom. Complete lists of book award winners, including United States, British Commonwealth, and international awards, are found in *Children's Books: Awards and Prizes,* compiled and edited by the Children's Book Council. An annotated bibliography of Newbery and Caldecott books is available in *Newbery and Caldecott Medal and Honor Books,* compiled by Linda Kauffman Peterson and Marilyn Leathers Solt.

CALDECOTT MEDAL AND HONOR AWARDS

The Caldecott awards, named after a British illustrator of children's books, Randolph Caldecott, are granted by the Children's Services Division of the American Library Association. The medal and honor awards are presented annually to the illustrators of the most distinguished picture books published in the United States. The first Caldecott Medal and honor awards were presented in 1938.

1938 *Animals of the Bible* by Helen Dean Fish, ill. by Dorothy P. Lathrop, Stokes

Honor Books: *Seven Simeon: A Russian Tale* by Boris Artzybasheff, Viking; *Four and Twenty Blackbirds: Nursery Rhymes of Yesterday Recalled for Children of Today* by Helen Dean Fish, ill. by Robert Lawson, Stokes

1939 *Mei Li* by Thomas Handforth, Doubleday

Honor Books: *The Forest Pool* by Laura Adams Armer, Longmans; *Wee Gillis* by Munro Leaf, ill. by Robert Lawson, Viking; *Snow White and the Seven Dwarfs* by Wanda Gág, Coward; *Barkis* by Clare Newberry, Harper; *Andy and the Lion: A Tale of Kindness Remembered or the Power of Gratitude* by James Daugherty, Viking

1940 *Abraham Lincoln* by Ingri and Edgar Parin d'Aulaire, Doubleday

Honor Books: *Cock-a-Doodle Doo: The Story of a Little Red Rooster* by Berta and Elmer Hader, Macmillan; *Madeline* by Ludwig Bemelmans, Simon & Schuster; *The Ageless Story,* by Lauren Ford, Dodd

1941 *They Were Strong and Good* by Robert Lawson, Viking

Honor Book: *April's Kittens* by Clare Newberry, Harper

1942 *Make Way for Ducklings* by Robert McCloskey, Viking

Honor Books: *An American ABC* by Maud and Miska Petersham, Macmillan; *In My Mother's House* by Ann Nolan Clark, ill. by Velino Herrera, Viking; *Paddle-to-the-Sea* by Holling C. Holling, Houghton; *Nothing at All* by Wanda Gág, Coward

1943 *The Little House* by Virginia Lee Burton, Houghton

Honor Books: *Dash and Dart* by Mary and Conrad Buff, Viking; *Marshmallow* by Clare Newberry, Harper

1944 *Many Moons* by James Thurber, ill. by Louis Slobodkin, Harcourt Brace Jovanovich

Honor Books: *Small Rain: Verses from the Bible* selected by Jessie Orton Jones, ill. by Elizabeth Orton Jones, Viking; *Pierre Pigeon* by Lee Kingman, ill. by Arnold E. Bare, Houghton; *The Mighty Hunter* by Berta and Elmer Hader, Macmillan; *A Child's Good Night Book* by Margaret Wise Brown, ill. by Jean Charlot, W. R. Scott; *Good Luck Horse* by Chih-Yi-Chan, ill. by Plato Chan, Whittlesey

1945 *Prayer for a Child* by Rachel Field, ill. by Elizabeth Orton Jones, Macmillan

Honor Books: *Mother Goose: Seventy-Seven Verses with Pictures* ill. by Tasha Tudor, Walck; *In the Forest* by Marie Hall Ets, Viking; *Yonie Wondernose* by Marguerite de Angeli, Doubleday; *The Christmas Anna Angel* by Ruth Sawyer, ill. by Kate Seredy, Viking

1946 *The Rooster Crows . . .* ill. by Maud and Miska Petersham, Macmillan

Honor Books: *Little Lost Lamb* by Golden MacDonald, ill. by Leonard Weisgard, Doubleday; *Sing Mother Goose* by Opal Wheeler, ill. by Marjorie Torrey, Dutton; *My Mother Is the Most Beautiful Woman in the World* by Becky Reyher, ill. by Ruth Gannett, Lothrop; *You Can Write Chinese* by Kurt Wiese, Viking

1947 *The Little Island* by Golden MacDonald, ill. by Leonard Weisgard, Doubleday

Honor Books: *Rain Drop Splash* by Alvin Tresselt, ill. by Leonard Weisgard, Lothrop; *Boats on the River* by Marjorie Flack, ill. by Jay Hyde Barnum, Viking; *Timothy Turtle* by Al Graham, ill. by Tony Palazzo, Viking; *Pedro, the Angel of Olvera Street* by Leo Politi, Scribner's; *Sing in Praise: A Collection of the Best Loved Hymns* by Opan Wheeler, ill. by Marjorie Torrey, Dutton

1948 *White Snow, Bright Snow* by Alvin Tresselt, ill. by Roger Duvoisin, Lothrop

Honor Books: *Stone Soup: An Old Tale* by Marcia Brown, Scribner's; *McElligot's*

Pool by Dr. Seuss, Random; *Bambino the Clown* by George Schreiber, Viking; *Roger and the Fox* by Lavinia Davis, ill. by Hildegard Woodward, Doubleday; *Song of Robin Hood* ed. by Anne Malcolmson, ill. by Virginia Lee Burton, Houghton

1949 *The Big Snow* by Berta and Elmer Hader, Macmillan

Honor Books: *Blueberries for Sal* by Robert McCloskey, Viking; *All Around the Town* by Phyllis McGinley, ill. by Helen Stone, Lippincott; *Juanita* by Leo Politi, Scribner's; *Fish in the Air* by Kurt Wiese, Viking

1950 *Song of the Swallows* by Leo Politi, Scribner's

Honor Books: *America's Ethan Allen* by Stewart Holbrook, ill. by Lynd Ward, Houghton; *The Wild Birthday Cake* by Lavinia Davis, ill. by Hildegrad Woodward, Doubleday; *The Happy Day* by Ruth Krauss, ill. by Marc Simont, Harper; *Bartholomew and the Oobleck* by Dr. Seuss, Random; *Henry Fisherman* by Marcia Brown, Scribner's

1951 *The Egg Tree* by Katherine Milhous, Scribner's

Honor Books: *Dick Whittington and His Cat* by Marcia Brown, Scribner's; *The Two Reds* by William Lipkind, ill. by Nicholas Mordvinoff, Harcourt Brace Jovanovich; *If I Ran the Zoo* by Dr. Seuss, Random; *The Most Wonderful Doll in the World* by Phyllis McGinley, ill. by Helen Stone, Lippincott; *T-Bone, the Baby Sitter* by Clare Newberry, Harper

1952 *Finders Keepers* by William Lipkind, ill. by Nicholas Mordvinoff, Harcourt Brace Jovanovich

Honor Books: *Mr. T. W. Anthony Wood: The Story of a Cat and a Dog and Mouse* by Marie Hall Ets. Viking; *Skipper John's Cook* by Marcia Brown, Scribner's; *All Falling Down* by Gene Zion, ill. by Margaret Bloy Graham, Harper: *Bear Party* by William Pène du Bois, Viking; *Feather Mountain* by Elizabeth Olds, Houghton

1953 *The Biggest Bear* by Lynd Ward, Houghton

Honor Books: *Puss in Boots* by Charles Perrault, ill. and tr. by Marcia Brown, Scribner's; *One Morning in Maine* by Robert McCloskey, Viking; *Ape in a Cape: An Alphabet of Odd Animals* by Fritz Eichenberg, Harcourt Brace Jovanovich; *The Storm Book* by Charlotte

Zolotow, ill. by Margaret Bloy Graham, Harper; *Five Little Monkeys* by Juliet Kepes, Houghton

1954 *Madeline's Rescue* by Ludwig Bemelmans, Viking

Honor Books: *Journey Cake, Ho!* by Ruth Sawyer, ill. by Robert McCloskey, Viking; *When Will the World Be Mine?* by Miriam Schlein, ill. by Jean Charlot, W. R. Scott; *The Steadfast Tin Soldier* by Hans Christian Andersen, ill. by Marcia Brown, Scribner's; *A Very Special House* by Ruth Krauss, ill. by Maurice Sendak, Harper; *Green Eyes* by A. Birnbaum, Capitol

1955 *Cinderella, or the Little Glass Slipper* by Charles Perrault, tr. and ill. by Marcia Brown, Scribner's

Honor Books: *Book of Nursery and Mother Goose Rhymes,* ill. by Marguerite de Angeli, Doubleday; *Wheel on the Chimney* by Margaret Wise Brown, ill. by Tibor Gergely, Lippincott; *The Thanksgiving Story* by Alice Dalgliesh, ill. by Helen Sewell, Scribner's

1956 *Frog Went A-Courtin'* ed. by John Langstaff, ill. by Feodor Rojankovsky, Harcourt Brace Jovanovich

Honor Books: *Play with Me* by Marie Hall Ets, Viking: *Crow Boy* by Taro Yashima, Viking

1957 *A Tree Is Nice* by Janice May Udry, ill. by Marc Simont, Harper

Honor Books: *Mr. Penny's Race Horse* by Marie Hall Ets, Viking; *1 Is One* by Tasha Tudor, Walck; *Anatole* by Eve Titus, ill. by Paul Galdone, McGraw; *Gillespie and the Guards* by Benjamin Elkin, ill. by James Daugherty, Viking; *Lion* by William Pène du Bois, Viking

1958 *Time of Wonder* by Robert McCloskey, Viking

Honor Books: *Fly High, Fly Low* by Don Freeman, Viking; *Anatole and the Cat* by Eve Titus, ill. by Paul Galdone, McGraw

1959 *Chanticleer and the Fox* adapted from Chaucer and ill. by Barbara Cooney, Crowell

Honor Books: *The House That Jack Built: A Picture Book in Two Languages* by Antonio Frasconi, Harcourt Brace Jovanovich; *What Do You Say, Dear?* by Sesyle Joslin, ill. by Maurice Sendak, W. R. Scott; *Umbrella* by Taro Yashima, Viking

1960 *Nine Days to Christmas* by Marie Hall Ets, and Aurora Labastida, ill. by Marie Hall Ets. Viking

Honor Books: *Houses from the Sea* by Alice E. Goudey, ill. by Adrienne Adams, Scribner's; *The Moon Jumpers* by Janice May Udry, ill. by Maurice Sendak, Harper

1961 *Baboushka and the Three Kings* by Ruth Robbins, ill. by Nicolas Sidjakov, Parnassus

Honor Book: *Inch by Inch* by Leo Lionni, Obolensky

1962 *Once a Mouse . . .* by Marcia Brown, Scribner's

Honor Books: *The Fox Went Out on a Chilly Night: An Old Song* by Peter Spier, Doubleday; *Little Bear's Visit* by Else Holmelund Minarik, ill. by Maurice Sendak, Harper; *The Day We Saw the Sun Come Up* by Alice E. Goudey, ill. by Adrienne Adams, Scribner's

1963 *The Snowy Day* by Ezra Jack Keats, Viking

Honor Books: *The Sun Is a Golden Earring* by Natalia M. Belting, ill. by Bernarda Bryson, Holt; *Mr. Rabbit and the Lovely Present* by Charlotte Zolotow, ill. by Maurice Sendak, Harper

1964 *Where the Wild Things Are* by Maurice Sendak, Harper

Honor Books: *Swimmy* by Leo Lionni, Pantheon; *All in the Morning Early* by Sorche Nic Leodhas, ill. by Evaline Ness, Holt; *Mother Goose and Nursery Rhymes* ill. by Philip Reed, Atheneum

1965 *May I Bring a Friend?* by Beatrice Schenk de Regniers, ill. by Beni Montresor, Atheneum

Honor Books: *Rain Makes Applesauce* by Julian Scheer, ill. by Marvin Bileck, Holiday; *The Wave* by Margaret Hodges, ill. by Blair Lent, Houghton; *A Pocketful of Cricket* by Rebecca Caudill, ill. by Evaline Ness, Holt

1966 *Always Room for One More* by Sorche Nic Leodhas, ill. by Nonny Hogrogian, Holt

Honor Books: *Hide and Seek Fog* by Alvin Tresselt, ill. by Roger Duvoisin, Lothrop; *Just Me* by Marie Hall Ets, Viking; *Tom Tit Tot* by Evaline Ness, Scribner's

1967 *Sam, Bangs & Moonshine* by Evaline Ness, Holt

Honor Book: *One Wide River to Cross* by Barbara Emberley, ill. by Ed Emberley, Prentice

1968 *Drummer Hoff* by Barbara Emberley, ill. by Ed Emberley, Prentice

Honor Books: *Frederick* by Leo Lionni, Pantheon; *Seashore Story* by Taro

Yashima, Viking; *The Emperor and the Kite* by Jane Yolen, ill. by Ed Young, World

1969 *The Fool of the World and the Flying Ship* by Arthur Ransome, ill. by Uri Shulevitz, Farrar

Honor Book: *Why the Sun and the Moon Live in the Sky: An African Folktale* by Elphinstone Dayrell, ill. by Blair Lent, Houghton

1970 *Sylvester and the Magic Pebble* by William Steig, Windmill

Honor Books: *Goggles!* by Ezra Jack Keats, Macmillan; *Alexander and the Wind-Up Mouse* by Leo Lionni, Pantheon; *Pop Corn and Ma Goodness* by Edna Mitchell Preston, ill. by Robert Andrew Parker, Viking; *Thy Friend, Obadiah* by Brinton Turkle, Viking; *The Judge: An Untrue Tale* by Harve Zemach, ill. by Margot Zemach, Farrar

1971 *A Story—A Story: An African Tale* by Gail E. Haley, Atheneum

Honor Books: *The Angry Moon* by William Sleator, ill. by Blair Lent, Atlantic-Little; *Frog and Toad Are Friends* by Arnold Lobel, Harper; *In the Night Kitchen* by Maurice Sendak, Harper

1972 *One Fine Day* by Nonny Hogrogian, Macmillan

Honor Books: *If All the Seas Were One Sea* by Janina Domanska, Macmillan; *Moja Means One: Swahili Counting Book* by Muriel Feelings, ill. by Tom Feelings, Dial; *Hildilid's Night* by Cheli Duran Ryan, ill. by Arnold Lobel, Macmillan

1973 *The Funny Little Woman* retold by Arlene Mosel, ill. by Blair Lent, Dutton

Honor Books: *Anansi the Spider: A Tale from the Ashanti* adapted and ill. by Gerald McDermott, Holt; *Hosie's Alphabet* by Hosea Tobias and Lisa Baskin, ill. by Leonard Baskin, Viking; *Snow White and the Seven Dwarfs* translated by Randall Jarrell, ill. by Nancy Ekholm Burkert, Farrar; *When Clay Sings* by Byrd Baylor, ill. by Tom Bahti, Scribner's

1974 *Duffy and the Devil* by Harve Zemach, ill. by Margot Zemach, Farrar

Honor Books: *Three Jovial Huntsmen* by Susan Jeffers, Bradbury; *Cathedral: The Story of Its Construction* by David Macaulay, Houghton

1975 *Arrow to the Sun* adapted and ill. by Gerald McDermott, Viking

Honor Book: *Jambo Means Hello: A Swahili Alphabet Book* by Muriel Feelings, ill. by Tom Feelings, Dial

1976 *Why Mosquitoes Buzz in People's Ears* retold by Verna Aardema, ill. by Leo and Dian Dillon, Dial

Honor Books: *The Desert Is Theirs* by Byrd Baylor, ill. by Peter Parnall, Scribner's; *Strega Nona* retold and ill. by Tomie de Paola, Prentice

1977 *Ashanti to Zulu: African Traditions* by Margaret Musgrove, ill. by Leo and Diane Dillon, Dial

Honor Books: *The Amazing Bone* by William Steig, Farrar; *The Contest* retold and ill. by Nony Hogrogian, Greenwillow; *Fish for Supper* by M. B. Goffstein, Dial; *The Golem: A Jewish Legend* by Beverly Brodsky McDermott, Lippincott; *Hawk, I'm Your Brother* by Byrd Baylor, ill. by Peter Parnall, Scribner's

1978 *Noah's Ark* by Peter Spier, Doubleday

Honor Books: *Castle* by David Macaulay, Houghton; *It Could Always Be Worse* retold and ill. by Margot Zemach, Farrar

1979 *The Girl Who Loved Wild Horses* by Paul Goble, Bradbury

Honor Books: *Freight Train* by Donald Crews, Greenwillow; *The Way to Start a Day* by Byrd Baylor, ill. by Peter Parnall, Scribner's

1980 *Ox-Cart Man* by Donald Hall, ill. by Barbara Cooney, Viking

Honor Books: *Ben's Trumpet* by Rachel Isadora, Greenwillow; *The Treasure* by Uri Shulevitz, Farrar; *The Garden of Abdul Gasazi* by Chris Van Allsburg, Houghton

1981 *Fables* by Arnold Lobel, Harper

Honor Books: *The Bremen-Town Musicians* by Ilse Plume, Doubleday; *The Grey Lady and the Strawberry Snatcher* by Molly Bang, Four Winds; *Mice Twice* by Joseph Low, Atheneum; *Truck* by Donald Crews, Greenwillow

1982 *Jumanji* by Christ Van Allsburg, Houghton

Honor Books: *A Visit to William Blake's Inn: Poems for Innocent and Experienced Travelers* by Nancy Willard, ill. by Alice and Martin Provensen, Harcourt Brace Jovanovich; *Where the Buffaloes Begin* by Olaf Baker, ill. by Stephen Gammell, Warner; *On Market Street* by Arnold Lobel, ill. by Anita Lobel, Greenwillow; *Outside Over There* by Maurice Sendak, Harper

1983 *Shadow* by Blaise Cendrars, ill. by Marcia Brown, Scribner's

Honor Books: *When I Was Young in the Mountains* by Cynthia Rylant, ill. by Diane Goode, Dutton; *Chair for My Mother* by Vera B. Williams, Morrow

1984 *The Glorious Flight: Across the Channel with Louis Bleriot* by Alice and Martin Provensen, Viking

Honor Books: *Ten, Nine, Eight* by Molly Bang, Greenwillow; *Little Red Riding Hood* retold and ill. by Trina Schart Hyman, Holiday House

1985 *St. George and the Dragon* retold by Margaret Hodges, ill. by Trina Schart Hyman, Little, Brown

Honor Books: *Hansel and Gretel* retold by Rika Lesser, ill. by Paul O. Zelinsky, Dodd; *Have You Seen My Duckling?* by Nancy Tafuri, Greenwillow; *The Story of Jumping Mouse* by John Steptoe, Lothrop

1986 *The Polar Express* by Chris Van Allsburg, Houghton

Honor Books: *King Bidgood's in the Bathtub* by Audrey Wood, ill. by Don Wood, Harcourt; *The Relatives Came* by Cynthia Rylant, ill. by Stephen Gammell, Bradbury

1987 *Hey, Al* by Arthur Yorinks, ill. by Richard Egielski, Farrar, Straus & Giroux

Honor Books: *Alphabatics* by Suse MacDonald, Bradbury; *Rumpelstiltskin* retold and ill. by Paul O. Zelinsky; *The Village of Round and Square Houses* by Ann Grifalconi, Little, Brown

1988 *Owl Moon* by Jane Yolen, ill. by John Schoenherr, Philomel

Honor Book: *Mufaro's Beautiful Daughters: An African Tale* by John Steptoe, Lothrop, Lee & Shepard

1989 *Song and Dance Man* by Karen Ackerman, ill. by Stephen Gammell

Honor Books: *The Boy of the Three-Year Nap* by Dianne Snyder, ill. by Allen Say, Houghton Mifflin; *Free Fall* by David Wiesner, Lothrop, Lee & Shepard; *Goldilocks* retold and ill. by James Marshall, Dial; *Mirandy and Brother Wind* by Patricia C. McKissack, ill. by Jerry Pinkney, Knopf

1990 *Lon Po Po: A Red-Riding Hood Story from China* translated and ill. by Ed Young, Philomel

Honor Books: *Bill Peet: An Autobiography* by Bill Peet, Houghton Mifflin; *Color Zoo* by Lois Ehlert, Lippincott; *Hershel and the Hanukkah Goblins* by Eric Kimmel, ill. by Trina Schart Hyman, Holiday House; *The Talking Egg* by Robert D. SanSouci, ill. by Jerry Pinkney, Dial

1991 *Black and White* by David Macaulay, Houghton Mifflin

Honor Books: *More, More, More Said the Baby* by Vera Williams, Greenwillow; *Puss in Boots* by Charles Perrault, ill. by Fred Marcellino, Farrar Straus & Giroux

1992 *Tuesday* by David Wiesner, Clarion

Honor Book: *Tar Beach* by Faith Ringgold, Crown

1993 *Mirette on the High Wire* by Emily Arnold McCully, Putnam's

Honor Books: *Seven Blind Mice* by Ed Young, Philomel; *Stinky Cheese Man and Other Fairly Stupid Tales* by Jon Scieszka, ill. by Lane Smith, Viking; *Working Cotton* by Sherely Anne Williams, ill. by Carole Byard, Harcourt Brace

1994 *Grandfather's Journey* by Allen Say, Houghton Mifflin

Honor Books: *Owen* by Kevin Henkes, Greenwillow; *Peppe, the Lamplighter* by Elisa Bartone, Lothrop, Lee & Shepard; *Raven* by Gerald McDermott, Harcourt Brace; *In the Small, Small Pond* by Denise Fleming, Holt; *Yo! Yes?* by Chris Raschka, Orchard

1995 *Smoky Night* by Eve Bunting, ill. by David Diaz, Harcourt Brace

Honor Books: *John Henry* by Julius Lester, ill. by Jerry Pinkney, Dial; *Swamp Angel* by Anne Issacs, ill. by Paul O. Zelinsky, Dutton; *Time Flies* by Eric Rohmann, Crown

1996 *Officer Buckle and Gloria* by Peggy Rathman, Putnam

Honor Books: *Alphabet City* by Stephen T. Johnson, Viking; *The Faithful Friend* by Robert D. San Souci, ill. by Brian Pinkney, Simon & Schuster; *Tops and Bottoms* by Janet Stevens, Harcourt Brace; *Zin! Zin! Zin! A Violin* by Lloyd Moss, ill. by Marjorie Priceman, Simon & Schuster

1997 *Golem* by David Wisniewski, Clarion

Honor Books: *Hush! A Thai Lullaby* by Minfong Ho, ill. by Holly Meade, Orchard; *The Paperboy* by Dav Pilkey, Orchard; *Starry Messenger* by Peter Sis, Farrar, Straus & Giroux

1998 *Rapunzel* by Brothers Grimm, Illustrated by Paul O. Zelinsky, Dutton

Honor Books: *The Gardener* by Sarah Steward, ill. by David Small, Farrar, Straus & Giroux; *Harlem* by Walter Dean Myers, ill. by Christopher Myers, Scholastic; *There Was an Old Woman Who Swallowed a Fly* by Simms Taback, Viking

THE NEWBERY MEDAL AND HONOR AWARDS

The Newbery award, named after the first English publisher of books for children, John Newbery, is granted by the Children's Services Division of the American Library Association. The medal and honor awards are presented annually for the most distinguished contributions to children's literature published in the United States. The first Newbery Medal and honor awards were presented in 1922.

1922 *The Story of Mankind* by Hendrik Willem van Loon, Liveright

Honor Books: *The Great Quest* by Charles Hawes, Little; *Cedric the Forester* by Bernard Marshall, Appleton; *The Old Tobacco Shop: A True Account of What Befell a Little Boy in Search of Adventure* by William Bowen, Macmillan; *The Golden Fleece and the Heroes Who Lived before Achilles* by Padriac Colum, Macmillan; *Windy Hill* by Cornelia Meigs, Macmillan

1923 *The Voyages of Doctor Dolittle* by Hugh Lofting, Lippincott

Honor Books: No record

1924 *The Dark Frigate* by Charles Hawes, Atlantic/Little

Honor Books: No record

1925 *Tales from Silver Lands* by Charles Finger, Doubleday

Honor Books: *Nicholas: A Manhattan Christmas Story* by Anne Carroll Moore, Putnam; *Dream Coach* by Anne Parrish, Macmillan

1926 *Shen of the Sea* by Arthur Bowie Chrisman, Dutton

Honor Book: *Voyagers: Being Legends and Romances of Atlantic Discovery* by Padraic Colum, Macmillan

1927 *Smoky, the Cowhorse* by Will James, Scribner's

Honor Books: No record

1928 *Gayneck, The Story of a Pigeon* by Dhan Gopal Mukerji, Dutton

Honor Books: *The Wonder Smith and His Son: A Tale from the Golden Childhood of the World* by Ella Young, Longmans; *Downright Dencey* by Caroline Snedeker, Doubleday

1929 *The Trumpeter of Krakow* by Eric P. Kelly, Macmillan

Honor Books: *Pigtail of Ah Lee Ben Loo* by John Bennett, Longmans; *Millions of Cats* by Wanda Gág, Coward; *The Boy Who Was* by Grace Hallock, Dutton; *Clearing Weather* by Cornelia Meigs,

Little; *Runaway Papoose* by Grace Moon, Doubleday; *Tod of the Fens* by Elinor Whitney, Macmillan

1930 *Hitty, Her First Hundred Years* by Rachel Field, Macmillan

Honor Books: *Daughter of the Seine: The Life of Madame Roland* by Jeanette Eaton, Harper; *Pran of Albania* by Elizabeth Miller, Doubleday; *Jumping-off Place* by Marian Hurd McNeely, Longmans; *Tangle-coated Horse and Other Tales: Episodes from the Fionn Saga* by Ella Young, Longmans; *Vaino: A Boy of New England* by Julia Davis Adams, Dutton; *Little Blacknose* by Hildegarde Swift, Harcourt Brace Jovanovich

1931 *The Cat Who Went to Heaven* by Elizabeth Coatsworth, Macmillan

Honor Books: *Floating Island* by Anne Parrish, Harper; *The Dark Star of Itza: The Story of a Pagan Princess* by Alida Malkus, Harcourt Brace Jovanovich; *Queer Person* by Ralph Hubbard, Doubleday; *Mountains Are Free* by Julia Davis Adams, Dutton; *Spice and the Devil's Cave* by Agnes Hewes, Knopf; *Meggy Macintosh* by Elizabeth Janet Gray, Doubleday; *Garram the Hunter: A Boy of the Hill Tribes* by Herbert Best, Doubleday; *Ood-Le-Uk the Wanderer* by Alice Lide and Margaret Johansen, Little

1932 *Waterless Mountain* by Laura Adams Armer, Longmans

Honor Books: *The Fairy Circus* by Dorothy P. Lathrop, Macmillan; *Calico Bush* by Rachel Field, Macmillan; *Boy of the South Seas* by Eunice Tietjens, Coward; *Out of the Flame* by Eloise Lownsbery, Longmans; *Jane's Island* by Marjorie Allee, Houghton; *Truce of the Wolf and Other Tales of Old Italy* by Mary Gould Davis, Harcourt Brace Jovanovich

1933 *Young Fu of the Upper Yangtze* by Elizabeth Foreman Lewis, Winston

Honor Books: *Swift Rivers* by Cornelia Meigs, Little; *The Railroad to Freedom: A Story of the Civil War* by Hildegarde Swift, Harcourt Brace Jovanovich; *Children of the Soil: A Story of Scandinavia* by Nora Burglon, Doubleday

1934 *Invincible Louisa: The Story of the Author of 'Little Women'* by Cornelia Meigs, Little

Honor Books: *The Forgotten Daughter* by Caroline Snedeker, Doubleday; *Swords of Steel* by Elsie Singmaster, Houghton; *ABC Bunny* by Wanda Gág, Coward;

Winged Girl of Knossos by Erik Berry, Appleton; *New Land* by Sarah Schmidt, McBride; *Big Tree of Bunlahy: Stories of My Own Countryside* by Padraic Colum, Macmillan; *Glory of the Seas* by Agnes Hewes, Knopf; *Apprentice of Florence* by Ann Kyle, Houghton

1935 *Dobry* by Monica Shannon, Viking

Honor Books: *Pageant of Chinese History* by Elizabeth Seeger, Longmans; *Davy Crockett* by Constance Rourke, Harcourt Brace Jovanovich; *Day on Skates: The Story of a Dutch Picnic* by Hilda Van Stockum, Harper

1936 *Caddie Woodlawn* by Carol Ryrie Brink, Macmillan

Honor Books: *Honk, the Moose* by Phil Stong, Dodd; *The Good Master* by Kate Seredy, Viking; *Young Walter Scott* by Elizabeth Janet Gray, Viking; *All Sail Set: A Romance of the Flying Cloud* by Armstrong Sperry, Winston

1937 *Roller Skates* by Ruth Sawyer, Viking

Honor Books: *Phoebe Fairchild: Her Book* by Lois Lenski, Stokes; *Whistler's Van* by Idwal Jones, Viking; *Golden Basket* by Ludwig Bemelmans, Viking; *Winterbound* by Margery Bianco, Viking; *Audubon* by Constance Rourke, Harcourt Brace Jovanovich; *The Codfish Musket* by Agnes Hewes, Doubleday

1938 *The White Stag* by Kate Seredy, Viking

Honor Books: *Pecos Bill* by James Cloyd Bowman, Little; *Bright Island* by Mabel Robinson, Random; *On the Banks of Plum Creek* by Laura Ingalls Wilder, Harper

1939 *Thimble Summer* by Elizabeth Enright, Rinehart

Honor Books: *Nino* by Valenti Angelo, Viking; *Mr. Popper's Penguins* by Richard and Florence Atwater, Little; *"Hello the Boat!"* by Phyllis Crawford, Holt; *Leader by Destiny: George Washington, Man and Patriot* by Jeanette Eaton, Harcourt Brace Jovanovich; *Penn* by Elizabeth Janet Gray, Viking

1940 *Daniel Boone* by James Daugherty, Viking

Honor Books: *The Singing Tree* by Kate Seredy, Viking; *Runner of the Mountain Tops: The Life of Louis Agassiz* by Mabel Robinson, Random; *By the Shores of Silver Lake* by Laura Ingalls Wilder, Harper; *Boy with a Pack* by Stephen W. Meader, Harcourt Brace Jovanovich

1941 *Call It Courage* by Armstrong Sperry, Macmillan

Honor Books: *Blue Willow* by Doris Gates, Viking; *Young Mac of Fort Vancouver* by Mary Jane Carr, Crowell; *The Long Winter* by Laura Ingalls Wilder, Harper; *Nansen* by Anna Gertrude Hall, Viking

1942 *The Matchlock Gun* by Walter D. Edmonds, Dodd

Honor Books: *Little Town on the Prairie* by Laura Ingalls Wilder, Harper; *George Washington's World* by Genevieve Foster, Scribner's; *Indian Captive: The Story of Mary Jemison* by Lois Lenski, Lippincott; *Down Ryton Water* by Eva Roe Gaggin, Viking

1943 *Adam of the Road* by Elizabeth Janet Gray, Viking

Honor Book: *The Middle Moffat* by Eleanor Estes, Harcourt Brace Jovanovich; *Have You Seen Tom Thumb?* by Mabel Leigh Hunt, Lippincott

1944 *Johnny Tremain* by Esther Forbes, Houghton

Honor Books: *The Happy Golden Years* by Laura Ingalls Wilder, Harper; *Fog Magic* by Julia Sauer, Viking; *Rufus M.* by Eleanor Estes, Harcourt Brace Jovanovich; *Mountain Born* by Elizabeth Yates, Coward

1945 *Rabbit Hill* by Robert Lawson, Viking

Honor Books: *The Hundred Dresses* by Eleanor Estes, Harcourt Brace Jovanovich; *The Silver Pencil* by Alice Dalgliesh, Scribner's; *Abraham Lincoln's World* by Genevieve Foster, Scribner's; *Lone Journey: The Life of Roger Williams* by Jeanette Eaton, Harcourt Brace Jovanovich

1946 *Strawberry Girl* by Lois Lenski, Lippincott

Honor Books: *Justin Morgan Had a Horse* by Marguerite Henry, Rand; *The Moved-Outers* by Florence Crannell Means, Houghton; *Bhimsa, the Dancing Bear* by Christine Weston, Scribner's; *New Found World* by Katherine Shippen, Viking

1947 *Miss Hickory* by Carolyn Sherwin Bailey, Viking

Honor Books: *Wonderful Year* by Nancy Barnes, Messner; *Big Tree* by Mary and Conrad Buff, Viking; *The Heavenly Tenants* by William Maxwell, Harper; *The Avion My Uncle Flew* by Cyrus Fisher, Appleton; *The Hidden Treasure of Glaston* by Eleanore Jewett, Viking

1948 *The Twenty-One Balloons* by William Pène du Bois, Viking

Honor Books: *Pancakes-Paris* by Claire Huchet Bishop, Viking; *Li Lun, Lad of Courage* by Carolyn Treffinger, Abind-

gon; *The Quaint and Curious Quest of Johnny Longfoot, The Shoe-King's Son* by Catherine Besterman, Bobbs; *The Cow-tail Switch, and Other West African Stories* by Harold Courlander, Holt; *Misty of Chincoteague* by Marguerite Henry, Rand

1949 *King of the Wind* by Marguerite Henry, Rand

Honor Books: *Seabird* by Holling C. Holling, Houghton; *Daughter of the Mountains* by Louise Rankin, Viking; *My Father's Dragon* by Ruth S. Gannett, Random; *Story of the Negro* by Arna Bontemps, Knopf

1950 *The Door in the Wall* by Marguerite de Angeli, Doubleday

Honor Books: *Tree of Freedom* by Rebecca Caudill, Viking; *The Blue Cat of Castle Town* by Catherine Coblentz, Longmans; *Kildee House* by Rutherford Montgomery, Doubleday; *George Washington* by Genevieve Foster, Scribner's; *Song of the Pines: A Story of Norwegian Lumbering in Wisconsin* by Walter and Marion Havighurst, Winston

1951 *Amos Fortune, Free Man* by Elizabeth Yates, Aladdin

Honor Books: *Better Known as Johnny Appleseed* by Mabel Leigh Hunt, Lippincott; *Ghandi, Fighter Without a Sword* by Jeanette Eaton, Morrow; *Abraham Lincoln, Friend of the People* by Clara Ingram Judson, Follett; *The Story of Appleby Capple* by Anne Parish, Harper

1952 *Ginger Pye* by Eleanor Estes, Harcourt Brace Jovanovich

Honor Books: *Americans Before Columbus* by Elizabeth Baity, Viking; *Minn of the Mississippi* by Holling C. Holling, Houghton; *The Defender* of Nicholas Kalashnikoff, Scribner's; *The Light at Tern Rock* by Julia Sauer, Viking; *The Apple and the Arrow* by Mary and Conrad Buff, Houghton

1953 *Secret of the Andes* by Ann Nolan Clark, Viking

Honor Books: *Charlotte's Web* by E. B. White, Harper; *Moccasin Trail* by Eloise McGraw, Coward; *Red Sails to Capri* by Ann Weil, Viking; *The Bears on Hemlock Mountain* by Alice Dalgliesh, Scribner's; *Birthdays of Freedom,* Vol. 1, by Genevieve Foster, Scribner's

1954 *. . . and now Miguel* by Joseph Krumgold, Crowell

Honor Books: *All Alone* by Claire Huchet Bishop, Viking; *Shadrach* by Meindert DeJong, Harper; *Hurry Home Candy* by

Meindert DeJong, Harper; *Theodore Roosevelt, Fighting Patriot* by Clara Ingram Judson, Follett; *Magic Maize* by Mary and Conrad Buff, Houghton

1955 *The Wheel on the School* by Meindert DeJong, Harper

Honor Books: *The Courage of Sarah Noble* by Alice Dalgliesh, Scribner's; *Banner in the Sky* by James Ullman, Lippincott

1956 *Carry on, Mr. Bowditch* by Jean Lee Latham, Houghton

Honor Books: *The Secret River* by Marjorie Kinnan Rawlings, Scribner's; *The Golden Name Day* by Jennie Linquist, Harper; *Men, Microscopes, and Living Things* by Katherine Shippen, Viking

1957 *Miracles on Maple Hill* by Virginia Sorensen, Harcourt Brace Jovanovich

Honor Books: *Old Yeller* by Fred Gipson, Harper; *The House of Sixty Fathers* by Meindert DeJong, Harper; *Mr. Justice Holmes* by Clara Ingram Judson, Follett; *The Corn Grows Ripe* by Dorothy Rhoads, Viking; *Black Fox of Lorne* by Marguerite de Angeli, Doubleday

1958 *Rifles for Watie* by Harold Keith, Crowell

Honor Books: *The Horsecatcher* by Mari Sandoz, Westminster; *Goneaway Lake* by Elizabeth Enright, Harcourt Brace Jovanovich; *The Great Wheel* by Robert Lawson, Viking; *Tom Paine, Freedom's Apostle* by Leo Gurko, Crowell

1959 *The Witch of Blackbird Pond* by Elizabeth George Speare, Houghton

Honor Books: *The Family Under the Bridge* by Natalie Savage Carlson, Harper; *Along Came a Dog* by Meindert DeJong, Harper; *Chucaro: Wild Pony of the Pampa* by Francis Kalnay, Harcourt Brace Jovanovich; *The Perilous Road* by William O. Steele, Harcourt Brace Jovanovich

1960 *Onion John* by Joseph Krumgold, Crowell

Honor Books: *My Side of the Mountain* by Jean George, Dutton; *America Is Born* by Gerald W. Johnson, Morrow; *The Gammage Cup* by Carol Kendall, Harcourt Brace Jovanovich

1961 *Island of the Blue Dolphins* by Scott O'Dell, Houghton

Honor Books: *America Moves Forward* by Gerald W. Johnson, Morrow; *Old Ramon* by Jack Schaefer, Houghton; *The Cricket in Times Square* by George Selden, Farrar

1962 *The Bronze Bow* by Elizabeth George Speare, Houghton

Honor Books: *Frontier Living* by Edwin Tunis, World; *The Golden Goblet* by Eloise McCraw, Coward; *Belling the Tiger* by Mary Stolz, Harper

1963 *A Wrinkle in Time* by Madeleine L'Engle, Farrar

Honor Books: *Thistle and Thyme: Tales and Legends from Scotland* by Sorche Nic Leodhas, Holt; *Men of Athens* by Olivia Coolidge, Houghton

1964 *It's Like This, Cat* by Emily Cheney Neville, Harper

Honor Books: *Rascal* by Sterling North, Dutton; *The Loner* by Ester Wier, McKay

1965 *Shadow of a Bull* by Maia Wojciechowska, Atheneum

Honor Book: *Across Five Aprils* by Irene Hunt, Follett

1966 *I, Juan de Pareja* by Elizabeth Borten de Treviño, Farrar

Honor Books: *The Black Cauldron* by Lloyd Alexander, Holt; *The Animal Family* by Randall Jarrell, Pantheon; *The Noonday Friends* by Mary Stolz, Harper

1967 *Up a Road Slowly* by Irene Hunt, Follet

Honor Books: *The King's Fifth* by Scott O'Dell, Houghton; *Zlateh the Goat and Other Stories* by Isaac Bashevis Singer, Harper; *The Jazz Man* by Mary H. Weik, Atheneum

1968 *From the Mixed-Up Files of Mrs. Basil E. Frankweiler* by E. L. Konigsburg, Atheneum

Honor Books: *Jennifer, Hecate, Macbeth, William McKinley, and Me, Elizabeth* by E. L. Konigsburg, Atheneum; *The Black Pearl* by Scott O'Dell, Houghton; *The Fearsome Inn* by Isaac Bashevis Singer, Scribner's; *The Egypt Game* by Zilpha Keatley Snyder, Atheneum

1969 *The High King* by Lloyd Alexander, Holt

Honor Books: *To Be a Slave* by Julius Lester, Dial; *When Shlemiel Went to Warsaw and Other Stories* by Isaac Bashevis Singer, Farrar

1970 *Sounder* by William H. Armstrong, Harper

Honor Books: *Our Eddie* by Sulamith Ish-Kishor, Pantheon; *The Many Ways of Seeing: An Introduction to the Pleasures of Art* by Janet Gaylord Moore, World; *Journey Outside* by Mary Q. Steele, Viking

1971 *Summer of the Swans* by Betsy Byars, Viking

Honor Books: *Kneeknock Rise* by Natalie Babbitt, Farrar; *Enchantress from the Stars* by Sylvia Louise Engdahl, Atheneum; *Sing Down the Moon* by Scott O'Dell, Houghton

1972 *Mrs. Frisby and the Rats of NIMH* by Robert C. O'Brien, Atheneum

Honor Books: *Incident at Hawk's Hill* by Allan W. Eckert, Little; *The Planet of Junior Brown* by Virginia Hamilton, Macmillan; *The Tombs of Atuan* by Ursula K. Le Guin, Atheneum; *Annie and the Old One* by Miska Miles, Atlantic-Little; *The Headless Cupid* by Zilpha Keatley Sunder, Atheneum

1973 *Julie of the Wolves* by Jean Craighead George, Harper

Honor Books: *Frog and Toad Together* by Arnold Lobel, Harper; *The Upstairs Room* by Johanna Reiss, Crowell; *The Witches of Worm* by Zilpha Keatley Snyder, Atheneum

1974 *The Slave Dancer* by Paula Fox, Bradbury

Honor Book: *The Dark Is Rising* by Susan Cooper, Atheneum

1975 *M C. Higgins, the Great* by Virginia Hamilton, Macmillan

Honor Books: *Figgs & Phantoms* by Ellen Raskin, Dutton; *My Brother Sam Is Dead* by James Lincoln Collier & Christopher Collier, Four Winds; *The Perilous Gard* by Elizabeth Marie Pope, Houghton; *Philip Hall Likes Me. I Reckon Maybe* by Bette Greene, Dial

1976 *The Grey King* by Susan Cooper, Atheneum

Honor Books: *The Hundred Penny Box* by Sharon Bell Mathis, Viking; *Dragonwings* by Laurence Yep, Harper

1977 *Roll of Thunder, Hear My Cry* by Mildred D. Taylor, Dial

Honor Books: *Abel's Island* by William Steig, Farrar; *A String in the Harp* by Nancy Bond, Atheneum

1978 *Bridge to Terabithia* by Katherine Paterson, Crowell

Honor Books: *Ramona and Her Father* by Beverly Cleary, Morrow; *Anpao: An American Indian Odyssey* by Jamake Highwater, Lippincott

1979 *The Westing Game* by Ellen Raskin, Dutton

Honor Book: *The Great Gilly Hopkins* by Katherine Paterson, Crowell

1980 *A Gathering of Days: A New England Girl's Journal 1830–32* by Joan Blos, Scribner's

Honor Book: *The Road from Home: The Story of an Armenian Girl* by David Kherdian, Greenwillow

1981 *Jacob Have I Loved* by Katherine Paterson, Crowell

Honor Books: *The Fledgling* by Jane Langton, Harper; *A Ring of Endless Light* by Madeleine L'Engle, Farrar

1982 *A Visit to William Blake's Inn: Poems for Innocent and Experienced Travelers* by Nancy Willard, Harcourt Brace Jovanovich

Honor Books: *Ramona Quimby, Age 8* by Beverly Cleary, Morrow; *Upon the Head of the Goat: A Childhood in Hungary, 1939–1944* by Aranka Siegal, Farrar

1983 *Dicey's Song* by Cynthia Voigt, Atheneum

Honor Books: *Blue Sword* by Robin McKinley, Morrow; *Dr. DeSoto* by William Steig, Farrar; *Graven Images* by Paul Fleischman, Harper; *Homesick: My Own Story* by Jean Fritz, Putnam's; *Sweet Whisper, Brother Rush,* by Virginia Hamilton, Philomel.

1984 *Dear Mr. Henshaw* by Beverly Cleary, Morrow

Honor Books: *The Sign of the Beaver* by Elizabeth George Speare, Houghton; *A Solitary Blue* by Cynthia Voigt, Atheneum; *The Wish Giver* by Bill Brittain, Harper

1985 *The Hero and the Crown* by Robin McKinley, Greenwillow

Honor Books: *Like Jake and Me* by Mavis Jukes, Knopf; *The Moves Make the Man* by Bruce Brooks, Harper; *One-Eyed Cat* by Paula Fox, Bradbury

1986 *Sarah, Plain and Tall* by Patricia MacLachlan, Harper

Honor Books: *Commodore Perry in the Land of the Shogun* by Rhoda Blumberg, Lothrop; *Dogsong* by Gary Paulsen, Bradbury

1987 *The Whipping Boy* by Sid Fleischman, Greenwillow

Honor Books: *A Fine White Dust* by Cynthia Rylant, Bradbury; *On My Honor* by Marion Dane Bauer *Volcano: The Eruption and Healing of Mount St. Helens* by Patricia Lauber, Bradbury

1988 *Lincoln: A Photobiography* by Russell Freedom, Clarion

Honor Books: *After the Rain* by Norma Fox Mazer, Morrow; *Hatchet* by Gary Paulsen, Bradbury

1989 *Joyful Noise: Poems for Two Voices* by Paul Fleischman, Harper

Honor Books: *In the Beginning: Creation Stories from Around the World* by Virginia Hamilton, Harcourt; *Scorpions* by Walter Dean Myers, Harper & Row

1990 *Number the Stars* by Lois Lowry, Houghton Mifflin

Honor Books: *After of the Elves* by Janet Taylor Lisle, Orchard; *Shabanu, Daughter of the Wind,* by Susan Fisher Staples, Knopf; *The Winter Room* by Gary Paulsen, Orchard

1991 *Maniac Magee* by Jerry Spinelli, Little, Brown

Honor Book: *The True Confessions of Charlotte Doyle* by Avi, Orchard

1992 *Shiloh* by Phyllis Reynolds Naylor, Atheneum

Honor Books: *Nothing But the Truth* by Avi, Orchard; *The Wright Brothers: How They Invented the Airplane* by Russell Freedman, Holiday

1993 *Missing May* by Cynthia Rylant, Orchard

Honor Books: *The Dark-Thirty: Southern Tales of the Supernatural* by Patricia McKissack, Knopf; *Somewhere in the Darkness* by Walter Dean Myers, Scholastic; *What Hearts* by Bruce Brooks, HarperCollins

1994 *The Giver* by Lois Lowry, Houghton Mifflin

Honor Books: *Crazy Lady* by Jane Leslie Conly, HarperCollins; *Dragon's Gate* by Laurence Yep, HarperCollins; *Eleanor Roosevelt: A Life of Discovery* by Russell Freedman, Clarion

1995 *Walk Two Moons* by Sharon Creech, HarperCollins

Honor Books: *Catherine, Called Birdy* by Karen Cushman, Clarion; *The Ear, the Eye, and the Arm* by Nancy Farmer, Jackson/Orchard

1996 *The Midwife's Apprentice* by Karen Cushman, Clarion

Honor Books: *The Great Fire* by Jim Murphy, Scholastic; *The Watson's Go to Birmingham—1963* by Christopher Paul Curtis, Delacorte; *What Jamie Saw* by Carolyn Coman, Front Street; *Yolonda's Genius* by Carol Fenner, McElderry/Simon & Schuster

1997 *The View from Saturday* by E. L. Konigsburg, Atheneum

Honor Books: *Belle Prater's Boy* by Ruth White, Farrar, Straus & Giroux; *A Girl Named Disaster* by Nancy Farmer, Jackson/Orchard; *Moorchild* by Eloise McGraw, McElderry/Simon & Schuster; *The Thief* by Megan Whalen Turner, Greenwillow/Morrow

1998 *Out of the Dust* by Karen Hesse, Scholastic.

Honor Books: *Ella Enchanted* by Gail Carson Levine, Harper Collins; *Lily's Crossing* by Patricia Reilly Giff, Delacort; *Ringer* by Jerry Spinelli, HarperCollins.

CHILDREN'S BOOK AWARD

The Children's Book Award is presented annually by the International Reading Association to a children's author whose work shows unusual promise. The award was established in 1975.

1975 *Transport 7-41-R* by T. Degens, Viking

1976 *Dragonwings* by Laurence Yep, Harper

1977 *A String in the Harp* by Nancy Bond, Atheneum

1978 *A Summer to Die* by Lois Lowry, Houghton

1979 *Reserved for Mark Anthony Crowder* by Alison Smith, Dutton

1980 *Words by Heart* by Ouida Sebestyen, Little

1981 *My Own Private Sky* by Delores Beckman, Dutton

1982 *Good Night, Mr. Tom* by Michelle Magorian, Harper

1983 *The Darkangel* by Meredith Ann Pierce, Atlantic/Little

1984 *Ratha's Creature* by Clare Bell, Atheneum

1985 *Badger on the Barge* by Janni Howker, Greenwillow

1986 *Prairie Songs* by Pam Conrad, Harper

1987 *The Line Up Book* by Marisa Russo (picture book), Greenwillow; *After the Dancing Days* by Marisa Russo (older readers), Harper

1988 *The Third-Story Cat* by Leslie Baker (picture book), Little; *Ruby in the Smoke* by Philip Pullman (older readers), Knopf

1989 *Rechenka's Eggs* by Patricia Polacco (picture book), Philomel; *Probably Still Nick Swanson* by Virginia Euwer Wolff (older readers), H. Holt

1990 *No Star Nights* by Anna Egan Smucker and Steve Johnson (picture book), Knopf; *Children of the River* by Linda Crew (older readers), Delacorte

1991 *Is This a House for Hermit Crab?* by Megan McDonald and S. D. Schindler (picture book), Orchard; *Under the Hawthorn Tree* by Marita Conlon-McKenna (older readers), Holiday

1992 *Ten Little Rabbits* by Virginia Grossman and Sylvia Long (picture book), Chronicle; *Rescue Josh McGuire* by Ben Mikaelsen (older readers), Hyperion

1993 *Old Turtle* by Douglas Wood and Cheng-Khee Chee (picture book), Pfeiffer-Hamilton; *Letters from Rifka* by Karen Hesse (older readers), Henry Holt

1994 *Sweet Clara and the Freedom Quilt* by Deborah Hopkinson and James Ransome (picture book), Knopf; *Behind the Secret Window: A Memoir of a Hidden Childhood During World War Two* by Nancy Toll (older readers) Dial

1995 *The Ledgerbook of Thomas Blue Eagle* by Gay Mattaei and Jewel Grutman, ill. by Adam Cvijanovic (younger), Thomasson-Grant; *Spite Fences* by Trudy Krisher (older), Bantam Books; *Stranded at Plimoth Plantation 1626* by Gary Bowen (informational), HarperCollins

1996–1997 *More Than Anything Else* by Marie Bradby, ill. by Chris K. Soentpiet (younger), Orchard Books; *The King's Shadow* by Elizabeth Alder (older), Farrar, Straus & Giroux; *The Case of the Mummified Pigs and Other Mysteries in Nature* by Susan E. Quinlan (informational), Boyds Mill Press

HANS CHRISTIAN ANDERSEN INTERNATIONAL MEDAL

This international award was established in 1956 by the International Board on Books for Young People. It is presented every two years to a living author and a living artist whose total works have made an outstanding contribution to children's literature. A committee of five members, each from a different country, judges the selections.

1956 Eleanor Farjeon (Great Britain)
1958 Astrid Lindgren (Sweden)
1960 Erich Kästner (Germany)
1962 Meindert DeJong (United States)
1964 René Guillot (France)
1966 Author: Tove Jansson (Finland); Illustrator: Alois Carigiet (Switzerland)
1968 Authors: James Krüss (Germany); Jose Maria Sanchez-Silva (Spain); Illustrator: Jiri Trnka (Czechoslovakia)
1970 Author: Gianni Rodari (Italy); Illustrator: Maurice Sendak (United States)
1972 Author: Scott O'Dell (United States); Illustrator: Ib Spang Olsen (Denmark)
1974 Author: Maria Gripe (Sweden); Illustrator: Farshid Mesghali (Iran)
1976 Author: Cecil Bodker (Denmark); Illustrator: Tatjana Mawrina (Union of Soviet Socialist Republics)
1978 Author: Paula Fox (United States); Illustrator: Svend Otto S. (Denmark)
1980 Author: Bohumil Riha (Czechoslovakia); Illustrator: Suekichi Akaba (Japan)
1982 Author: Lygia Bojunga Nunes (Brazil); Illustrator: Zbigniew Rychlicki (Poland)

1984 Author: Christine Nostlinger (Austria); Illustrator: Mitsumasa Anno (Japan)
1986 Author: Patricia Wrightson (Australia); Illustrator: Robert Ingpen (Australia)
1988 Author: Annie M. G. Schmidt (Netherlands); Illustrator: Dusan Kallay (Czechoslovakia)
1990 Author: Tormod Haugen (Norway); Illustrator: Lisbeth Zwerger (Austria)
1992 Author: Virginia Hamilton (United States); Illustrator: Kveta Pacovoska
1994 Author: Michio Mado (Japan); Illustrator: Jorg Muller (Switzerland)
1996 Author: Uri Orlev (Israel); Illustrator: Klaus Ensikat (Germany)

LAURA INGALLS WILDER MEDAL

The Laura Ingalls Wilder award, named after the author of the "Little House" series, is presented every five years by the American Library Association, Children's Book Division, to an author or illustrator whose books have made a lasting contribution to children's literature. Since 1983, it has been given every three years. The award was established in 1954 and is restricted to books published in the United States.

1954 Laura Ingalls Wilder
1960 Clara Ingram Judson
1965 Ruth Sawyer
1970 E. B. White
1975 Beverly Cleary
1980 Theodor Geisel (Dr. Seuss)
1983 Maurice Sendak
1986 Jean Fritz
1989 Elizabeth George Speare
1992 Marsha Brown
1995 Virginia Hamilton
1998 Russell Freedman

MILDRED L. BATCHELDER AWARD

The Batchelder award is presented each year by the American Library Association, Children's Services Division, Chicago. The award is given to the publisher of the most outstanding book originally issued in a foreign language. The award was established in 1968.

1968 *The Little Man* by Erich Kastner, translated from German by James Kirkup, Knopf
1969 *Don't Take Teddy* by Babbis Friis-Baastad, translated from Norwegian by Lise Somme McKinnon, Scribner
1970 *Wildcat Under Glass* by Aliki Zei, translated from Greek by Edward Fenton, Holt

1971 *In the Land of Ur: The Discovery of Ancient Mesopotamia* by Hans Baumann, translated from German by Stella Humphries, Pantheon
1972 *Friedrich* by Hans Peter Richter, translated from German by Edite Kroll, Holt
1973 *Pulga* by S. R. Van Iterson, translated from Dutch by Alexander and Alison Gode, Morrow
1974 *Petros' War* by Aliki Zei, translated from Greek by Edward Fenton, Dutton
1975 *An Old Tale Carved in Stone* by Aleksander Mikhailovich Linevski, translated from Russian by Maria Poluskin, Crown
1976 *The Cat and Mouse Who Share a House* by Ruth Hurlimann, translated from German by Anthea Bell, Walck
1977 *The Leopard* by Cecil Bodker, translated from Danish by Gunnar Poulsen, Atheneum
1978 *Konrad* by Christine Nostlinger, translated from German by Anthea Bell, Watts
1979 *Rabbit Island* by Jorg Steiner, translated from German by Jorg Muller, Harcourt Brace
1980 *The Sound of Dragons' Feet* by Aliki Zei, translated from Greek by Edward Fenton, Dutton
1981 *The Winter When Time Was Frozen* by Els Pelgrom, translated from Dutch by Maryka and Raphael Rudnik, Morrow
1982 *Battle Horse* by Harry Kullman, translated from Swedish by George Blecher and Lone Thygesen-Belcher, Bradbury
1983 *Hiroshima No Pika* by Toshi Maruki, Lothrop, Lee & Shepard
1984 *Ronia the Robber's Daughter* by Astrid Lindgren, translated from Swedish by Patricia Crampton, Viking
1985 *The Island on Bird Street* by Uri Orlev, translated from Hebrew by Hillel Halkin, Houghton Mifflin
1986 *Rose Blanche* by Christophe Gallaz and Roberto Innocenti, translated from French by Martha Coventry and Richard Graglia, Creative Education
1987 *No Hero for the Kaiser* by Rudolf Frank, translated from German by Patricia Crampton, Lothrop, Lee, & Shepard
1988 *If You Didn't Have Me* by Ulf Nilsson, translated from Swedish by George Blecher and Lone Thygesen-Blecher, McElderry
1989 *Crutches* by Peter Hartling, translated from German by Elizabeth D. Crawford, Lothrop, Lee, & Shepard

1990 *Buster's World* by Bjarne Reuter, translated from Danish by Anthea Bell, Dutton

1991 *A Handful of Stars* by Rafik Schami, translated from German by Rika Lesser, Dutton

1992 *The Man from the Other Side* by Uri Orlev, translated from Hebrew by Hillel Halkin, Houghton Mifflin

1993 (No Award)

1994 *The Apprentice* by Pilar Molina Llorente, illustrated by Juan Ramon Alonso, translated from Spanish by Robin Longshaw, Farrar, Straus & Giroux

1995 *The Boys from St. Petri* by Bjarne Reuter, translated from Danish by Anthea Bell, Dutton

1996 *The Lady with the Hat* by Uri Orlev, translated from Hebrew by Hillel Halkin, Houghton Mifflin

1997 *The Friends* by Kazumi Yumoto, translated from Japanese by Cathy Hirano, Farrar, Straus & Giroux

1998 *The Robber and Me* by Joseph Holub, translated by Elizabeth D. Crawford

EXAMPLES OF ADDITIONAL BOOK AWARDS FOR CHILDREN'S LITERATURE

Amelia Frances Howard-Gibbon Medal, Canadian Library Association, is awarded annually to a Canadian illustrator for outstanding illustrations in a children's book published in Canada. First presented in 1971.

Boston Globe/Horn Book Awards, Boston Globe, Boston, Mass., are awarded annually, since 1967, to an author of fiction, an author of nonfiction, and an illustrator.

The Canadian Library Awards, Canadian Library Association, are given annually to a children's book of literary merit written by a Canadian citizen and to a book of literary merit published in French. First presented in 1947 (Canadian citizen) and 1954 (French publication).

The Carnegie Medal, British Library Association, is awarded annually, since 1936, to an outstanding book first published in the United Kingdom.

Charles and Bertie G. Schwartz Award, National Jewish Welfare Board, New York, is awarded annually to a book that combines literary merit with an affirmative expression of Jewish thought. Established in 1952.

CIBC Award for Unpublished Writers, Council on Interracial Books for Children, New York, awards the United States writer from a racial minority whose manuscript best challenges stereotypes, supplies role models, and portrays distinctive aspects of a culture. Given for the first time in 1969.

Coretta Scott King Award is made to one black author and one black illustrator for outstandingly inspirational contributions to children's literature. The award was first given in 1970.

Jane Addams Children's Book Award, Jane Addams Peace Association and the Women's International League for Peace and Freedom, New York, is given annually, since 1953, to honor the book that most effectively promotes peace, world community, and social justice.

The Kate Greenaway Medal, British Library Association, is awarded each year to the most distinguished work in illustration first published in the United Kingdom. Established in 1956.

National Book Awards, Association of American Publishers, New York, are given annually to United States authors whose books have contributed most significantly to human awareness, national culture, and the spirit of excellence. Established in 1969 (Children's Literature Division).

William Allen White Children's Book Award, William Allen White Library, Kansas State Teachers College, Emporia, Kansas, is given annually, since 1953, to an outstanding children's book selected by Kansas children.

Abingdon Press
Div. of United Methodist Publishing House
201 Eighth Ave. S.
Nashville, Tenn. 37203-3957

Accent Books
Division of Accent Publications
4050 Lee Vance View
Colorado Springs, Colo. 80918

Addison-Wesley Publishing Co., Inc.
One Jacob Way
Reading, Mass. 01867

Arte Publico Press
University of Houston
4800 Calhoun
Houston, Tex. 77204-2090

Associated Features, Inc.
Box 1762, Murray Hill Station
New York, N.Y. 10156

Atheneum Publishers
Subs. of Simon & Schuster
1230 Avenue of the Americas
New York, N.Y. 10020

Avon Books
Div. of The Hearst Corp.
1350 Avenue of the Americas
New York, N.Y. 10019

Baha'i Publishing Trust
415 Linden Ave.
Wilmette, Ill. 60091

Ball-Stick-Bird Publications, Inc.
Box 592
Stony Brook, N.Y. 11790

Bantam Books, Inc.
Div. of Bantam Doubleday Dell Publishing
1540 Broadway
New York, N.Y. 10036

Barron's Educational Series Inc.
250 Wireless Blvd.
Hauppauge, N.Y. 11788

Peter Bedrick Books Inc.
2112 Broadway, Ste. 318
New York, N.Y. 10023

Bellerophon Books
122 Helena
Santa Barbara, Calif. 93101

Berkley Publishing Group
Subs. of The Putnam Berkley Group Inc.
200 Madison Ave.
New York, N.Y. 10016

Broadman & Holman Publishers
Div. of Southern Baptist Convention
Sunday School Board
127 Ninth Ave. N.
Nashville, Tenn. 37234

Brunner/Mazel Publishing
Subs. of Taylor & Francis
1900 Frost Rd., Suite 101
Bristol, Penn. 19007

Carolrhoda Books, Inc.
Div. of The Learner Publishing Group
241 First Ave. N.
Minneapolis, Minn. 55401

Chelsea House Publishers
Div. of Main Line Book Co.
1974 Sproul Rd., Suite 400
Broomall, Penn. 19008

Children's Book Press
246 First St., Suite 101
San Francisco, Calif. 94105

Children's Press
A Grolier Company
90 Sherman Tpke
Dansbury, Conn. 06816

The Child's World Inc.
P.O. Box 326
Chanhassen, Minn. 55317-0326

China Books & Periodicals, Inc.
2929 24th St.
San Francisco, Calif. 94110

Cinco Puntos Press
2709 Louisville
El Paso, Tex. 79930

Clarion Books
Div. of Houghton Mifflin Co.
215 Park Ave. S.
New York, N.Y. 10003

Cobblesmith
Patterson's Wheeltrack
Freeport, Me. 04032

Crabtree Publishing Co.
350 Fifth Ave.
Suite 3308
New York, N.Y. 10118

Dell Publishing
Subs. of Bantam Doubleday Dell Publishing Group, Inc.
1540 Broadway
New York, N.Y. 10036

Deseret Book Co.
40 E. South Temple
Salt Lake City, Utah 84130

Dial Books for Young Readers
Division of Penguin USA
375 Hudson St.
New York, N.Y. 10014–3657

Dillon Press, Inc.
Imprint of Simon & Schuster Education Groups
299 Jefferson Rd.
Parsippany, N.J. 07054-0480

Doubleday
Div. of Bantam Doubleday Dell Publishing Group, Inc.
1540 Broadway
New York, N.Y. 10036

Dufour Editions, Inc.
P.O. Box 7
Chester Springs, Pa. 19425-0007

Dutton
Imprint of Penguin USA
375 Hudson St.
New York, N.Y. 10014

Eakin Press
Div. of Sunbelt Media Inc.
P.O. Drawer 90159
Austin, Tex. 78709-0159

Enslow Publishers Inc.
Box 699
44 Fadem Rd.
Springfield, N.J. 07081

M. Evans & Co., Inc.
216 E. 49th St.
New York, N.Y. 10017

Faber & Faber, Inc.
Subs. of Faber & Faber Ltd.
53 Shore Rd.
Winchester, Mass. 01890

Farrar, Straus & Giroux Inc.
19 Union Sq. W.
New York, N.Y. 10003

The Feminist Press at The City University
of New York
311 E. 94th St.
New York, N.Y. 10128

Ferguson Publishing Co.
200 W. Madison St.
Third Floor
Chicago, Ill. 60606

Friendship Press
Subs. of National Council of the Churches
of Christ U.S.A.
475 Riverside Dr.
New York, N.Y. 10115

Galison Books
Subs. of GMG Publishing
36 W. 44th St.
New York, N.Y. 10036

Gareth Stevens, Inc.
1555 N. River Center Dr.
Suite 201
Milwaukee, Wis. 53212

Garrett Educational Corp.
Box 1588
130 E. 13th S.
Ada, Okla. 74820

Gessler Publishing Co., Inc.
10 E. Church Ave.
Roanoke, Vir. 24011

The C. R. Gibson Co.
Subs. of Thomas Nelson Inc.
32 Knight St.
Norwalk, Conn. 06856

David R. Godine Publisher Inc.
9 Lewis St.
Lincoln, Mass. 01773

Golden Books Family
Entertainment
888 Seventh Ave.
New York, N.Y. 10106

Good Books
Subs. of Good Enterprises, Inc.
Box 419, Main St.
Intercourse, Pa. 17534

Graphic Arts Center Publishing Co.
Box 10306
3019 N.W. Yeon Ave.
Portland, Ore. 97296-0306

Greenwillow Books
Div. of William Morrow & Co. Inc.
1350 Avenue of the Americas
New York, N.Y. 10019

Grey Castle Press
Pocket Knife Sq.
Lakeville, Conn. 06039

Grosset & Dunlap Publishers
Div. of The Putnam & Grosset
Group
200 Madison Ave.
New York, N.Y. 10016

Harcourt Brace Children's Books
Imprint of Harcourt Brace & Co.
525 B St. Suite 1900
San Diego, Calif. 92101–4495

Harmony Books
Div. of Crown Publishers Inc.
201 E. 50th St.
New York, N.Y. 10022

Harper & Row Publishers, Inc.
10 E. 53rd St.
New York, N.Y. 10022

Harrison House Publishers
2448 E. 81 St., Suite 5600
Tulsa, Okla. 74137-4256

Hebrew Publishing Co.
Box 157
Rockway Beach, N.Y. 11693

Heian International, Inc.
1815 W. 205 St., Suite 205
Torrance, Calif. 90501

Heyday Books
Box 9145
Berkeley, Calif. 94709

Hill & Wang
Div. of Farrar, Straus & Giroux, Inc.
19 Union Sq. W.
New York, N.Y. 10003

Holiday House, Inc.
425 Madison Ave.
New York, N.Y. 10017

Henry Holt & Co. Inc.
115 W. 18th St.
New York, N.Y. 10011

Holt, Rinehart & Winston
Subs. of Harcourt Brace & Co.
1120 S. Capital of Texas Hwy.
Austin, Tex. 78746

Houghton Mifflin Co.
222 Berkeley St.
Boston, Mass. 02116

Hunter House, Inc., Publishers
Box 2914
Alameda, Calif. 94501-0914

Huntington House Publishers
104 Row 2, Suite A-1 & A-2
Lafayette, La. 70508

Ideals Publications Inc.
535 Metroplex Dr., Suite 250
Nashville, Tenn. 37211

Jalmar Press
Subs. of B L Winch & Associates
24426 S. Main St., Suite 702
Carson, Calif. 90745

Jewish Publication Society
1930 Chestnut Street
Philadelphia, Pa. 19103-4599

Kane/Miller Book Publishers
Box 310529
Brooklyn, N.Y. 11231-0529

Kar-Ben Copies, Inc.
6800 Tildenwood Lane
Rockville, Md. 20852

Alfred A. Knopf, Inc.
Subs. of Random House, Inc.
201 E. 50th St.
New York, N.Y. 10022

KTAV Publishing House, Inc.
Box 6249
900 Jefferson St.
Hoboken, N.J. 07030

Lerner Publications Co.
Div. of The Lerner Publishing Group
241 First Ave. N.
Minneapolis, Minn. 55401

Liguori Publications
One Liguori Dr.
Liguori, Mo. 63057-9999

Lion Books Publisher
Div. of Sayre Publishing Inc.
210 Nelson Rd., Suite B
Scarsdale, N.Y. 10583

Lippincott-Raven Publishers
Subs. of Wolters Kluwer
227 E. Washington Sq.
Philadelphia, Pa. 19106

Little, Brown and Company Inc.
Div. of Time Warner Trade Publishing
3 Center Plaza
Boston, Mass. 02108

Lothrop, Lee & Shepard Books
Div. of William Morrow & Co., Inc.
1350 Ave. of the Americas
New York, N.Y. 10019

McGraw-Hill Companies
1221 Avenue of the Americas
New York, N.Y. 10020

Macmillan Books for Young Readers
Imprint of Simon & Schuster
    Children's Division
1230 Avenue of the Americas
New York, N.Y. 10020

Macmillan Children's Book Group
Division of Macmillan Publishing Co.
866 Third Ave. 25th Floor
New York, N.Y. 10022

Mage Publishers, Inc.
1032 29th St. N.W.
Washington, D.C. 20007

Marshall Cavendish Corp.
Member of Times Publishing Group
99 White Plains Rd.
Tarrytown, N.Y. 10591-9001

Meadowbrook Press, Inc.
5451 Smetana Dr.
Minnetonka, Minn. 55343

Meriwether Publishing Ltd/Contemporary
    Drama Service
885 Elkton Dr.
Colorado Springs, Colo. 80907-3557

Mesorah Publications Ltd.
4401 Second Ave.
Brooklyn, N.Y. 11232

Microsoft Press
Div. of Microsoft Corp.
One Microsoft Way
Redmond, Wash. 98052-6399

Middle Atlantic Press
10 Twosome Dr.
Moorestown, N.J. 08057

Modern Publishing
Div. of Unisystems, Inc.
155 E. 55th St.
New York, N.Y. 10022

Joshua Morris Publishing
Subs. of Reader's Digest Assoc.
355 Riverside Ave.
Westport, Conn. 06880-4810

Morrow Junior Books
Imprint of William Morrow & Co., Inc.
1350 Ave. of the Americas
New York, N.Y. 10019

William Morrow & Co., Inc.
Subs. of the Hearst Corp.
1350 Avenue of the Americas
New York, N.Y. 10019

National Geographic Society
1145 17th St. N.W.
Washington, D.C. 20036

Thomas Nelson, Inc.
Nelson Place at Elm Hill Pike
Nashville, Tenn. 37214

Oxford University Press, Inc.
198 Madison Ave.
New York, N.Y. 10016-4314

Pantheon Books/Schocken Books
Div. of Random House
201 E. 50th St.
New York, N.Y. 10022

Paraclete Press
Div. of Creative Joys Inc.
P. O. Box 1568
Orleans, Mass. 02653

Pauline Books and Media
50 S. St. Paul's Ave.
Boston, Mass. 02130

Pelican Publishing Co., Inc.
Box 3110
Gretna, La. 70054-3110

Penguin USA
375 Hudson St.
New York, N.Y. 10014

Pittenbruach Press
Box 553
15 Walnut St.
Northampton, Mass. 01061

Playmore Inc. Publishers
230 Fifth Ave. Rm 711
New York, N.Y. 10001-7704

Pleasant Co. Publications
Subs of Pleasant Co.
Box 998
Middleton, Wis. 53562-0998

Prentice-Hall, Inc.
A Division of Simon & Schuster
One Lake St.
Upper Saddle River, N.J. 07458

Price Stern Sloan, Inc.
Div. of Putnam Group
11835 Olympic Blvd.
5th floor
Los Angeles, Calif. 90064

The Putnam Berkley Group, Inc.
Subs of MCA Inc.
200 Madison Ave.
New York, N.Y. 10016

Random House, Inc.
201 E. 50th St.
New York, N.Y. 10022

Santillana USA Publishing Co., Inc.
2105 NW 86 Ave.
Miami, Fla. 33122

Scholastic, Inc.
555 Broadway
New York, N.Y. 10012

Charles Scribner's Sons Books for Young
    Readers
Imprint of Simon & Schuster
1230 Avenue of the Americas
New York, N.Y. 10020

The Shoe String Press, Inc.
Box 657
2 Linsley St.
North Haven, Conn. 06473

Simon & Schuster
1230 Avenue of the Americas
New York, N.Y. 10020

Stemmer House Publishers, Inc.
2627 Caves Rd.
Owings Mills, Md. 21117

Troll Communications LLC
100 Corporate Dr.
Mahwah, N.J. 07430

Tundra Books of Northern New York
Div. of McClelland & Stewart
Box 1030
Plattsburgh, N.Y. 12901

Charles E. Tuttle Co., Inc.
153 Milk St., 5th Floor
Boston, Mass. 02109

Twenty-First Century Books
Div. of Henry Holt & Co., Inc.
115 W. 18th St.
New York, N.Y. 10011

UAHC Press
Div. of Union of American Hebrew
    Congregations
838 Fifth Ave.
New York, N.Y. 10021-7064

Viking Penguin
Imprint of Penguin USA
375 Hudson St.
New York, N.Y. 10014

Volcano Press, Inc.
Box 270
Volcano, Calif. 95689-0270

Walker & Co.
Div. of Walker Publishing Co., Inc.
435 Hudson St.
New York, N.Y. 10014

Frederick Warne & Co., Inc.
Imprint of Penguin USA
375 Hudson St.
New York, N.Y. 10014

Warner Books, Inc.
Subs. of Time, Inc.
1271 Avenue of the Americas
New York, N.Y. 10020

The Westminster/John Knox Press
Div. of Presbyterian Publishing Co.
100 Witherspoon St.
Louisville, Ky. 40202-1396

Albert Whitman & Co.
6340 Oakton St.
Morton Grove, Ill. 60053-2723

World Book, Inc.
A Scott Fetzer Co.
525 W. Monroe, 20th Floor
Chicago, Ill. 60661

Young Discovery Library
217 Main St.
Ossining, N.Y. 10562-4704

Zondervan Publishing House
Div. of HarperCollins Publishers Inc.
5300 Patterson Ave. S.E.
Grand Rapids, Mich. 49530

Author, Illustrator, Title Index

Subject Index

Abstract art, 179–180
Accessibility, 133–134
Acrylics, 173
Activities, suggested, 50–51
  contemporary realistic fiction,
    500, 512
  evaluation criteria, 140
  historical fiction, 559–560, 572–573
  history of children's literature, 106
  illustrations, 180, 181, 190–191,
    204, 262
  literary elements, 154
  modern fantasy, 385, 399
  multicultural literature, 631, 656
  nonfiction, 720–721, 734
  picture books, 247–248, 262
  poetry, 436–437, 449
  traditional literature, 326, 341
Adoption, 30
Adventure stories, early, 68–69, 80–81
Aesthetic responses, 46, 47, 48. *See also*
    Art appreciation
  and abstract art, 180
  aesthetic scanning, 192–195
  questioning strategies for, 152–154
Aesthetic scanning, 192–195
Africa, books about. *See also* African
    folktales
  informational books, 227, 228–229
  picture storybooks, 48, 215–216,
    246, 597
  science fiction, 384
African American folktales, 310–312,
    592–594
  illustrations, 184, 594
  unit study, 638–639
African American literature, 585–586,
    592–603. *See also* African American
    unit study; Slavery, books about
  annotated bibliography, 658–662
  characterization in, 122–123
  contemporary realistic fiction,
    598–601, 641–642
  folktales, 184, 310–312, 592–594,
    638–639

historical fiction, 398, 554–555,
  641
illustrations, 184, 201, 594
nonfiction, 601–603, 639–641
picture storybooks, 595–597
plot in, 118–120
poetry, 433, 641
stereotypes in, 21, 83, 230, 554, 582,
  587, 595, 631
African American unit study, 634–642
  African American folktales, 638–639
  African folktales, 634–638
  contemporary realistic fiction,
    641–642
  historical fiction, 641
  nonfiction, 639–641
  poetry, 641
African folktales, 309, 586–592
  and cognitive development, 22–23
  cross-cultural comparison, 286–287
  illustrations, 165, 174–175, 184
  literary elements in, 113, 151,
    240, 290
  unit study, 634–638
Allegory, 358–361, 387
Alliteration, 216, 374, 414–415
Alphabet books, 222–227
  animal themes, 224–225
  annotated bibliography, 264–265
  and cognitive development, 19
  early, 223–224
  illustrations, 167, 175
  suggested activities, 248, 262
Amelia Frances Howard-Gibbon Medal,
  A-8–9
American Revolution, books about,
  541–542, 682
Angelico, Fra, 182
Anger, 29–30, 33
Animals, books about. *See also* Fables
  in alphabet books, 224–225
  in contemporary realistic fiction, 458,
    459, 493–495, 500
  in folktales, 114–115, 281, 291, 293,
    298, 308, 310–311

informational books, 169, 210, 224,
  694–695, 706–712, 733–734
in modern fantasy, 367–372, 385, 458,
  459
and personality development, 24, 28,
  29
in picture storybooks, 238, 243–245
and plot, 114
in poetry, 434–435
Annotated bibliographies. *See also* Book
    lists
  African American literature, 658–662
  alphabet books, 264–265
  Asian American literature, 657–658
  Asian folktales, 341–342
  biographies, 734–738
  British folktales, 342–343
  concept books, 266–267
  contemporary realistic fiction,
    512–519
  counting books, 265–266
  easy-to-read books, 267–268
  evaluation criteria, 154–158
  fables, 347
  French folktales, 343
  German folktales, 343–344
  Hispanic American literature, 662–664
  historical fiction, 573–576
  illustrations, 204–211
  informational books, 738–746
  Jewish folktales, 344–345
  legends, 348
  modern fantasy, 399–405
  multicultural literature, 657–667
  myths, 347–348
  Native American literature, 664–667
  Norwegian folktales, 345
  nursery rhymes, 262–263
  picture books, 262–275
  picture storybooks, 268–275
  poetry, 449–455
  Russian folktales, 345
  toy books, 263–264
  traditional literature, 341–348
  wordless picture books, 267

Islam, 322
Italian folktales, 289

Jane Addams Children's Book Award, A-9
Japanese American internment, 558–559
Japanese folktales, 172, 293, 307–308.
    See also Asian folktales
Jealousy, 28–29, 480–481
Jewish folktales, 304–306, 336
    annotated bibliography, 344–345
    characterization in, 289
    cross-cultural comparison, 286–287
    humor in, 242, 243
    illustrations, 179, 180, 181
    writing activities, 260
Jewish legends, 325–326
Jones, Mother, 684
Joseph, Chief, 617
Journals, 49, 111–112, 215–216, 247

Kaimshibai, 654–655
Kate Greenaway Medal, 75, 198, A-9
King, Martin Luther, Jr., 601–602, 685
Korean folktales, 309

Language. See Language development;
    Style
Language development, 5–13
    books for, 6–9
    elementary-age children, 8–9, 11–13
    and informational books, 692
    preschool children, 5, 6–11
    suggested activities, 50
Language experience approach, 254–255
Lap reading. See Reading aloud
Laura Ingalls Wilder Medal, A-8
Legends, 278, 322–326
    annotated bibliography, 348
    characteristics of, 280
    defined, 282
    dumbing down, 362
    illustrations, 169, 171, 174, 199–200
    and modern fantasy, 388
Limericks, 411, 421, 437, 447–448
Lincoln, Abraham, 683–684
Lindbergh, Charles, 686
Line, 162–164, 172
Line arrangement for choral speaking,
    442–443
Literal recognition, 510
Literary criticism, 111. See also Evaluation
    criteria
Literary elements, 113–132. See also
    Characterization; Plot; Point of view;
    Setting; Style; Theme
    in biographies, 673–674, 726
    in contemporary realistic fiction,
        469–474
    in historical fiction, 523–529
    in modern fantasy, 353–355

suggested activities, 154
    webbing, 152, 153
Literary folktales, 62, 72–73, 184,
    356–358, 621
Literature program objectives, 110
Little people, 376–378
Logicomathematical ability, 18, 19
Louis XIV (King of France), 681
Lullabies, 10, 417, 432
Lyric poetry, 419

Madison, James, 682
Magic and wonder tales, 281. See also
    Folktales
Main ideas, 730–731
Maori folklore, 322
Maya, books about
    folktales, 177, 178
    historical fiction, 522, 524, 537–538,
        652
    informational books, 624–625, 652,
        697–698
Medieval Europe
    books about, 152, 153, 524, 529,
        534–536
    family life, 86–87
    storytelling, 64, 278, 420
Messages. See Didactic literature
Metaphors, 130, 417, 437
Middle Ages. See Medieval Europe
Middle Eastern folklore, 322
Mildred L. Batchelder Award, A-8
Modeling techniques, 144–146
Modern fantasy, 352–405
    and allegory, 358–361
    animals in, 367–372, 385, 458,
        459
    annotated bibliography, 399–405
    art activities, 389–391
    children's preferences, 387
    vs. contemporary realistic fiction,
        458, 459
    early precursors, 79–80
    evaluation criteria, 352–355
    humor in, 374–375
    illustrations, 363, 364, 365, 366, 367,
        368, 384, 388–389
    and literary folktales, 356–358
    little people in, 376–378
    mythical elements in, 131, 361–366,
        384, 388
    picture books, 387
    plot in, 353, 397, 398
    point of view in, 132, 355, 367, 371,
        372, 385
    science fiction, 81, 125–126, 380–384
    setting in, 125–126, 127, 147,
        354–355, 386, 389, 398, 399
    spirits in, 378–379
    strange worlds in, 375–376

style in, 131, 353–354, 362, 364, 370,
        374, 376, 397, 399
    suggested activities, 385, 399
    time warps in, 379–380
    toys in, 372–374
    unit studies, 397–399
    webbing, 391–393, 399
Mongol folktales, 309
Montage, 390
Mood
    and color, 165–166
    informational books, 696
    in mysteries, 496
    in poetry, 432–434
    and setting, 123–124, 146–147,
        527
    and shape, 167–168
    and storytelling, 328
Moral development, 41–44, 45
Mosaics, 390–391
Mother Goose rhymes. See Nursery
    rhymes
Motifs, 291–293
Motivation, 47–48
    and wordless picture books, 254–255
    for writing poetry, 445–446
Movable books, 198. See also Toy books
Movement activities. See Creative
    dramatization
Multicultural literature, 580–585. See also
    specific cultural groups
    annotated bibliography, 657–667
    author background, 627
    cultural diffusion, 283
    defined, 580–581
    evaluation criteria, 584–585
    nursery rhymes, 219–220
    past portrayals, 581–584
    and personality development, 25, 31
    and social development, 32, 37, 40
    study sequence overview, 633–634
    suggested activities, 631, 656
    universality in, 655–656
    values of, 4, 113, 581
Murals, 389–390
Music, 10, 446, 570–572
Mysteries, 495–497
Myths, 316–322
    annotated bibliography, 347–348
    authenticity, 285
    characteristics of, 280
    creative dramatization, 339
    defined, 282
    vs. folktales, 317
    and legends, 323, 324
    and modern fantasy, 131, 361–366,
        384, 388
    and Native American poetry, 612
    and oral tradition, 64
    values of, 282–283

Credits

About the Author

Following the completion of her doctorate at the University of Wisconsin, Madison, Donna E. Norton joined the College of Education faculty at Texas A&M University where she teaches courses in children's literature, language arts, and reading. Dr. Norton is the recipient of the Texas A&M Faculty Distinguished Achievement Award in Teaching. This award is given "in recognition and appreciation of ability, personality, and methods which have resulted in distinguished achievements in the teaching and the inspiration of students." She is also the recipient of the 1992 Virginia Hamilton Essay Award, which is presented by the Virginia Hamilton Conference Advisory Board at Kent State University. This annual award recognizes an article that "makes a significant contribution to the professional literature concerning multicultural literary experiences for youth." Dr. Norton is listed in *Who's Who of American Women, Who's Who in America*, and *Who's Who in the World*.

Dr. Norton is the author of three books in addition to this volume: *The Effective Teaching of Language Arts, 5th ed., Language Arts Activities for Children, 4th ed.,* and *The Impact of Literature-Based Reading*. She is on the editorial board of several journals and is a frequent contributor to journals and presenter at professional conferences. The focus of her current research is multicultural literature, literature-based reading programs, and the literature and writing connection. The multicultural research includes a longitudinal study of multicultural literature in classroom settings. This research is supported by grants from the Meadows Foundation. She currently has grants from the King Foundation and the GTE Foundation to develop institutes in children's literature and literacy. In conjunction with research in comparative education, she developed graduate courses that enable students to study children's literature and reading instruction in England and Scotland.

Prior to her college teaching experience, Dr. Norton was an elementary teacher in River Falls, Wisconsin and in Madison, Wisconsin. She was a Language Arts/Reading Consultant for federally funded kindergarten through adult basic education programs. In this capacity she developed, provided in-service instruction, and evaluated kindergarten programs, summer reading and library programs, remedial reading programs, learning disability programs for middle school children, elementary and secondary literature programs for the gifted, and diagnostic and intervention programs for reading-disabled adults. Dr. Norton's continuing concern for literature programs results in frequent consultations with educators from various disciplines, librarians, and school administrators and teachers.

Dr. Norton will present her most recent research, *Plot Structures and Archetypes in Recent Award-Winning Books*, at the invitational Conference on Children's Literature at Providence University in Taiwan. Dr. Norton has received a grant for bilingual education for doctoral students, which ties literature into bilingual programs.

Saundra Norton is completing doctoral studies at the University of South Carolina where she is a lecturer of literature in the English department. She completed her masters degree at Texas A&M University where she majored in literature with an emphasis in children's literature. Under the sponsorship of a Jordon Fellowship she studied language, culture, and folklore at the Goethe Institute in Germany. Her current research interests include biography, textual bibliography, and women's studies. She is a frequent participant at both national and international conferences. Her paper presented at the 15th International Ezra Pound Conference in Italy was presented the Bates Award for the best essay written by a graduate student at the University of South Carolina. Saundra is taking French studies at the Institute de Français. She has been accepted at the Paris Writer's Workshop in Paris, France.

The *Through the Eyes of a Child* children's literature database allows you to:

- Find books quickly in a database of over 2600 titles
- List books by title, author, reading level, and/or other information
- Trim a list to browse as much or as little of this information as you want
- View a complete record of information for any book on a list
- Search for specific key words (such as names, titles, topics, etc.)
- Print a summary or complete record of all of the books in a list
- Annotate books of interest with your own User Comments
- Add your own books to the database

Menus and buttons allow you to proceed with just a few mouse clicks or keystrokes. All of the frequently used commands have shortcut keys that are displayed in the menus for easy reference. On-line Help guides you through the more complex commands. And an Undo command allows you to undo your most recent action.